mA

CAMPING
FRANCE 2013

Selection 2013

2,400 selected camping sites including:

)80 with chalets, bungalows and mobile homes

1,370 with campervan facilities

*D*ear Reader,

The Michelin Camping Guide is perfect for all those who love the great outdoors and enjoy spending their leisure time in a tent, caravan, campervan, chalet or mobile home. We have selected the best campsites in France with our usual care, listing those with the best facilities in the most pleasant surroundings.

Using the traditional Michelin classification method, this guide provides you with an easy, speedy reference for assessing the category of each site: 1 to 5 tents ▲▲▲▲ *(see pages 8–9).*

The guide is updated each year, so consult the latest edition for the most up-to-date information and pricing.

Here are a few tips on how to use the guide

→ *To select a campsite*

The guide covers all 22 regions of France – see the map and list of regions on pages 4–5. Each region has been colour-coded so that you can find your way around the guide easily: the band at the top of the page matches the colour used in the map. Once you have selected a region, turn to the detailed map at the start of that region's section. It shows all the localities that have at least one campsite. The localities with campsites and their descriptions are listed alphabetically within each region section.

→ *To find a specific place or locality*

Refer to the index on page 886, where all the places are listed in alphabetical order.

→ *To make a selection based on specific criteria*

See the list of campsites on pages 868–885 for an at-a-glance summary of the main type of facilities available at each site, region by region.

→ *For a detailed description of each individual site*

The essential information and brief description given for each site are supplemented by symbols, which provide a wealth of additional information and detail. See pages 10–13 for the key to the symbols used in both the campsite entries and the maps.

→ *Glossary of French terms*

For a list of useful words, turn to the Glossary on page 14 for a translation of common terms.

→ *Descriptions of the sites start on page 17*

For more information on visiting particular towns or regions, consult the relevant regional Michelin Green Guide. We also recommend you use the appropriate Michelin regional map to locate your selected campsite, to calculate distances and to work out the best route.

→ *To get the most out of this Camping Guide, read pages 6–13 carefully.*

FINGAL COUNTY LIBRARIES	
FCL00000430174	
Bertrams	08/04/2013
914.4	£11.99
MA	

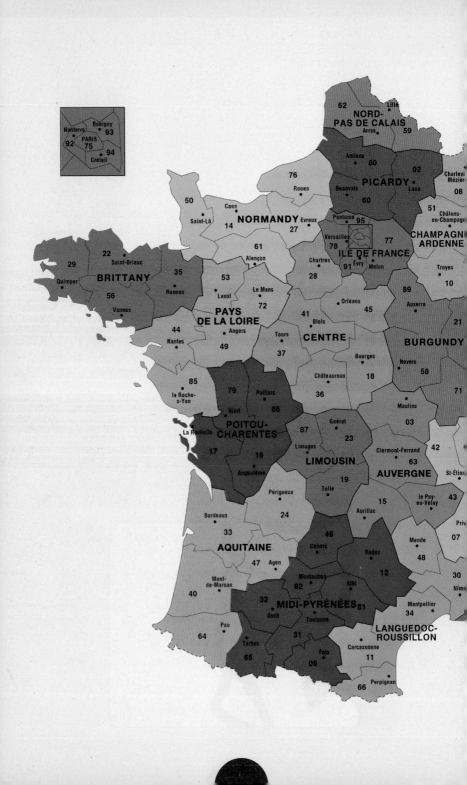

We welcome your feedback on our listed campsites.

Please email us at:
campingfrance@tp.michelin.com

Many thanks in advance!

Practical information for each location with
cross reference to Michelin maps

Michelin classification of selected sites

Services and leisure facilities available

Brief description of the site and its capacity

Peak season rates

Rental options and rates

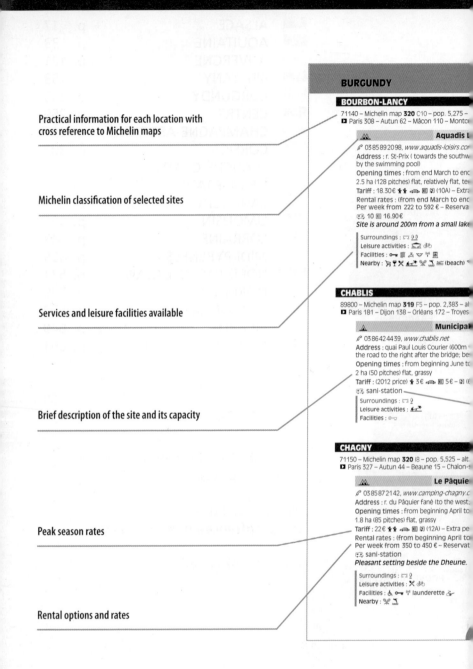

BURGUNDY

BOURBON-LANCY
71140 – Michelin map **320** C10 – pop. 5,275 –
▶ Paris 308 – Autun 62 – Mâcon 110 – Montce

Aquadis L
℘ 03 85 89 20 98, www.aquadis-loisirs.com
Address : r. St-Prix (towards the southw
by the swimming pool)
Opening times : from end March to end
2.5 ha (128 pitches) flat, relatively flat, te
Tariff : 18.30€ ♣♣ ⇌ 🖫 🕸 (10A) – Extra
Rental rates : (from end March to end
Per week from 222 to 592 € – Reserva
🕸 10 🖫 16.90€
Site is around 200m from a small lake

Surroundings : 🖵 ᵠᵠ
Leisure activities : 🖼 ♻️
Facilities : ⊶ ▦ ♨ ▽ ⍦ 🖽
Nearby : 🖢 🍴 ✕ ⟷ ✻ ⅃ ≋ (beach) ◂

CHABLIS
89800 – Michelin map **319** F5 – pop. 2,383 – al
▶ Paris 181 – Dijon 138 – Orléans 172 – Troyes

Municipal
℘ 03 86 42 44 39, www.chablis.net
Address : quai Paul Louis Courier (600m
the road to the right after the bridge; be
Opening times : from beginning June to
2 ha (50 pitches) flat, grassy
Tariff : (2012 price) ⍦ 3€ ⇌ 🖫 5€ – 🕸 (
🕸 sani-station
Surroundings : 🖵 ᵠ
Leisure activities : ⟷
Facilities : ⊶

CHAGNY
71150 – Michelin map **320** I8 – pop. 5,525 – alt.
▶ Paris 327 – Autun 44 – Beaune 15 – Chalon-s

Le Pâquie
℘ 03 85 87 21 42, www.camping-chagny.c
Address : r. du Pâquier fanè (to the west;
Opening times : from beginning April to
1.8 ha (85 pitches) flat, grassy
Tariff : 22€ ♣♣ ⇌ 🖫 🕸 (12A) – Extra pe
Rental rates : (from beginning April to
Per week from 350 to 450 € – Reservat
🕸 sani-station
Pleasant setting beside the Dheune.

Surroundings : 🖵 ᵠ
Leisure activities : ✕ ♻️
Facilities : ♿ ⊶ ⍦ launderette ⟋
Nearby : ✻ ⅃

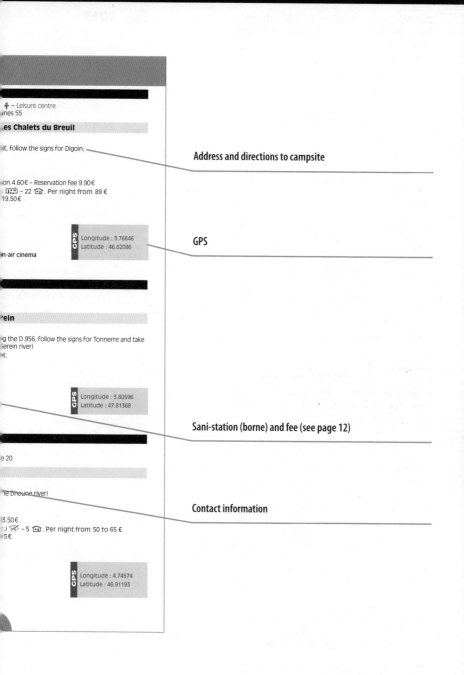

✠ – Leisure centre
...ines 55

...es Chalets du Breuil

...it, follow the signs for Digoin;

...on 4.60€ – Reservation fee 9.90€
[...] – 22 🏠. Per night from 89 €
...19.50€

GPS Longitude : 3.76646
Latitude : 46.62086

...n-air cinema

...ein

...g the D 956, follow the signs for Tonnerre and take
...Serein river)
...t.

GPS Longitude : 3.80596
Latitude : 47.81368

...e 20

...ne Dheune river)

...3.50€
...:.) ⚡ – 5 🏠. Per night from 50 to 65 €
...5€

GPS Longitude : 4.74574
Latitude : 46.91193

Address and directions to campsite

GPS

Sani-station (borne) and fee (see page 12)

Contact information

For key to the symbols, see pages 10–13

The Michelin Camping Guide selection lists the best sites in each 'comfort' category:

Extremely comfortable, equipped to a very high standard	
Very comfortable, equipped to a high standard	
Comfortable and well equipped	
Reasonably comfortable	
Satisfactory	

Exceptional campsites in each category are awarded an additional rating:

Particularly pleasant setting, good quality and range of services available

How the selection works:

• Campsites are ranked according to their location, facilities, etc., and are awarded a number of tent symbols – see above.

• In order for the guide to remain wholly objective, the selection is made on an entirely independent basis. There is no charge for being selected for the guide.

• The Michelin classification (⚠️...⚠️) is totally independent of the official star classification system awarded by the local prefecture or other official organisation.

• All the practical information and classifications are revised and updated annually in order for the information to be as reliable and up to date as possible. Some information or pricing may have changed since the guide went to press. We recommend you check the price list online in advance or at the entrance to the campsite and enquire about possible restrictions.

• Our inspectors make regular visits to campsites; our readers' comments are also a valuable source of information, and regular follow-up visits are undertaken.

18 camping sites have been classified ⚠️ / ⚠️ and 93 ⚠️ / ⚠️ in 2013. This selection can be found above right and on page 9.

⚠️ 2013

BERNY-RIVIÈRE	La Croix du Vieux Pont
CANET-PLAGE	Yelloh! Village Le Brasilia
CARNAC	Les Castels La Grande Métairie
DOL-DE-BRETAGNE	Les Castels Domaine des Ormes
PIERREFITTE-SUR-SAULDRE	Les Alicourts

⚠️ 2013

AGAY	Esterel Caravaning
ARGELÈS-SUR-MER	La Sirène et l'Hippocampe
BADEN	Mané Guernehué
BÉNODET	Sunêlia
BISCARROSSE	Club Airotel Domaine de la Rive
LABENNE-OCÉAN	Yelloh! Village le Sylvamar
LECTOURE	Yelloh! Village Le Lac des 3 Vallées
MESSANGES	Club Airotel Le Vieux Port
ROQUEBRUNE-SUR-ARGENS	Domaine de la Bergerie
SÉRIGNAN-PLAGE	Yelloh! Village Le Sérignan Plage
ST-AVIT-DE-VIALARD	Les Castels St-Avit Loisirs
ST-BREVIN-LES-PINS	Sunêlia Le Fief
VALRAS-PLAGE	Domaine de La Yole

You can look up a particular village or town in the index on page 886.

⛰ 2013

BÉNODET	Le Letty
BIRON	FranceLoc Le Moulinal
CANET-DE-SALARS	Les Castels Le Caussanel
CARANTEC	Yelloh! Village Les Mouettes
DIENNE	Le Domaine de Dienné
GHISONACCIA	Arinella-Bianca
GRANVILLE	Les Castels Le Château de Lez-Eaux
GRIMAUD	Les Prairies de la Mer
HOURTIN-PLAGE	Club Airotel La Côte d'Argent
LACANAU-OCÉAN	Yelloh! Village Les Grands Pins
LONGEVILLE-SUR-MER	MS Vacances Les Brunelles
MONTCLAR	Yelloh! Village Domaine d'Arnauteille
MUROL	Sunêlia La Ribeyre
NOYAL-MUZILLAC	Moulin de Cadillac
PERROS-GUIREC	Yelloh! Village Le Ranolien
PYLA-SUR-MER	Yelloh! Village Panorama du Pyla
QUIMPER	Les Castels L'Orangerie de Lanniron
RAMATUELLE	Le Kon Tiki
SARLAT-LA-CANÉDA	La Palombière
SOMMIÈRES	Les Castels Le Domaine de Massereau
ST-CAST-LE-GUILDO	Les Castels Le Château de la Galinée
ST-CRÉPIN-ET-CARLUCET	Les Peneyrals
ST-JULIEN-DES-LANDES	Les Castels La Garangeoire
ST-JUST-LUZAC	Les Castels Sequoia Parc
ST-LÉON-SUR-VÉZÈRE	Le Paradis
VALLON-PONT-D'ARC	Les Castels L'Ardéchois
VIAS-PLAGE	Yelloh! Village Club Farret

⛰ 2013

AIGUES-MORTES	Yelloh! Village La Petite Camargue
ARGELÈS-GAZOST	Sunêlia Les Trois Vallées
ARGELÈS-SUR-MER	Le Front de Mer
ARGELÈS-SUR-MER	Le Soleil
ARZANO	Les Castels Ty Nadan
AVRILLÉ	FranceLoc Le Domaine Des Forges
BELVÈS	FranceLoc Les Hauts de Ratebout
BIDART	Les Castels Le Ruisseau des Pyrénées
BIDART	Yelloh! Village Ilbarritz
BISCARROSSE	Mayotte Vacances
BONIFACIO	Pertamina Village – U-Farniente
CARNAC-PLAGE	Les Menhirs
CASTELLANE	Les Castels Le Domaine du Verdon
CHAMBON-SUR-LAC	Le Pré Bas
CHASSIERS	Les Ranchisses
COL-ST-JEAN	Yelloh! Village L'Étoile des Neiges
CONTIS-PLAGE	Yelloh! Village Lous Seurrots
CORCIEUX	Yelloh! Village en Voges Domaine des Bans
DOUCIER	Domaine de Chalain

FOUESNANT	Sunêlia L'Atlantique
FRÉJUS	La Baume - la Palmeraie
GHISONACCIA	Homair Vacances Marina d'Erba Rossa
GIEN	Les Bois du Bardelet
GIGNY-SUR-SAÔNE	Domaine de l'Épervière
ÎLE DE RÉ	Sunêlia Interlude
ÎLE DE RÉ	L'Océan
ÎLE D'OLÉRON	Camping-Club Verébleu
ÎLE D'OLÉRON	Club Airotel Les Gros Joncs
LA FAVIÈRE	Le Camp du Domaine
LA PALMYRE	Village Siblu Bonne Anse Plage
LA TRANCHE-SUR-MER	Vagues-Océanes Les Blancs Chênes
LACANAU-OCÉAN	Club Airotel de l'Océan
LARNAS	FranceLoc Le Domaine d'Imbours
LES MATHES	La Pinède
LIT-ET-MIXE	Village Center Les Vignes
MARIGNY	Les Castels La Pergola
MARSEILLAN-PLAGE	Les Méditerranées-Beach Club Nouvelle Floride
MÉZOS	Club Airotel Le Village Tropical Sen Yan
MIMIZAN-PLAGE	Club Airotel Marina-Landes
ONZAIN	Siblu Le Domaine de Dugny
PORNIC	Club Airotel La Boutinardière
PORTIRAGNES-PLAGE	Les Sablons
RAMATUELLE	Yelloh! Village les Tournels
RONCE-LES-BAINS	Village Siblu La Pignade
RUOMS	Domaine de Chaussy
SAMPZON	Yelloh! Village Soleil Vivarais
SARLAT-LA-CANÉDA	Les Castels Le Moulin du Roch
SÉRIGNAN-PLAGE	Yelloh! Village Aloha
SOUSTONS	Village Vacances Framissima Nature
ST-ALBAN-AURIOLLES	Sunêlia Le Ranc Davaine
ST-AYGULF	L'Étoile d'Argens
ST-CYPRIEN-PLAGE	Cala Gogo
STE-CATHERINE-DE-FIERBOIS	Les Castels Parc de Fierbois
ST-HILAIRE-DE-RIEZ	Les Biches
ST-JEAN-DE-MONTS	Les Amiaux
ST-JEAN-DE-MONTS	Le Bois Joly
ST-RAPHAËL	Les Castels Douce Quiétude
TALMONT-ST-HILAIRE	Yelloh! Village Le Littoral
TORREILLES-PLAGE	Sunêlia Les Tropiques
TORREILLES-PLAGE	Mar I Sol
VARENNES-SUR-LOIRE	Les Castels Domaine de la Brèche
VIAS-PLAGE	Sunêlia Domaine de la Dragonnière
VIELLE-SAINT-GIRONS	Sunêlia Le Col Vert
VINSOBRES	Franceloc Le Sagittaire
VITRAC	Domaine Soleil Plage
VOGÜÉ	Domaine du Cros d'Auzon

CAMPING SITES

Michelin classification

𝖠𝖠𝖠𝖠 𝖠𝖠𝖠𝖠	Extremely comfortable, equipped to a very high standard
𝖠𝖠𝖠 𝖠𝖠𝖠	Very comfortable, equipped to a high standard
𝖠𝖠𝖠 𝖠𝖠𝖠	Comfortable and well equipped
𝖠𝖠 𝖠𝖠	Reasonably comfortable
𝖠 𝖠	Satisfactory

• **Campsites are ranked according to their location, facilities, etc., within each category and are awarded a number of tent symbols – see page 8.**

• **The Michelin classification (𝖠𝖠𝖠𝖠 ... 𝖠) is totally independent of the official star classification system awarded by the local prefecture or other official organisation.**

Opening times

permanent	Site open all year round

Special features

❄	Winter caravan sites: these sites are specially equipped for a winter holiday in the mountains. Facilities generally include central heating, electricity and drying rooms for clothes and equipment
👥	Child-friendly sites, including washing facilities for young children, playgrounds and activities monitored by professionals

Exceptional in its category

𝖠𝖠𝖠𝖠 ... 𝖠	Particularly pleasant setting, quality and range of services available
🦢 🦢	Tranquil, isolated site – Quiet site, particularly at night
≪ ≪	Exceptional view – Interesting or panoramic view

General information

ℰ	Telephone
Access	Direction from nearest listed locality: north, south, east, west
�	24-hour security: a warden usually lives on site and is contactable during reception hours, although this does not mean round-the-clock surveillance outside normal hours
☐⟳	Day security only
🐕	No dogs (if dogs permitted, a current vaccination certificate is required)
℗	Cars must be parked away from pitches
℞	Reservations not accepted
⊘	Credit cards not accepted
✓	Chèques-vacances (French holiday vouchers) not accepted
cc	Camping Cheques accepted

Site information

3 ha	Area available in hectares (1ha = 2.47 acres)
60 ha/3 ha for camping	Total area of the property/ total area available for camping
90 pitches	Number of pitches
⬭	Marked-off pitches
♀ ♀♀ ♀♀♀	Shade: fair amount of shade to well shaded
⚠	Waterside location with swimming area

Facilities

▥	Heating facilities
♿	Facilities for the disabled
👶	Baby changing facilities
⌁	Running water
⚄ ⚇	Each bay is equipped with water/drainage

Services

🚐	Services for campervans
sani-station 4€	Type of service points and rates (see page 12)
3 ▣ 15.50€	Number of pitches equipped for campervans/ daily rate per pitch
🌙	Special FFCC price for campervan at site (Fédération Française de Camping et Caravaning)
🔲	Washing machines, laundry
🛒 🍽	Supermarket – Grocery
🍴	Takeaway meals
(ı)	Internet or Wifi point

Sports and leisure facilities

🍸	Bar (serving alcohol)
✗	Eating places (restaurant, snack bar, etc.)
🏠	Common room or games room
🎭	Miscellaneous activities (sports, culture, leisure)
👫	Children's club
🏋	Exercise room or gym
⎉s	Sauna
🛝	Playground
🚲	Cycle hire
✗ ▨	Tennis courts: open-air/ indoor
⛳ m	Minigolf
▨ ▨	Swimming pool: indoor/ open-air
🏊	Bathing allowed (or supervised bathing)
🛝	Waterslide
🐟	Fishing
🚣	Canoeing
⚓	Sailing (school or centre)
⚓	Mooring pontoon (river mooring)
🐎	Pony trekking or riding

• **The majority of outdoor leisure facilities are only open in season and during peak periods; opening times are not necessarily the same as those of the site and some facilities are only available during the summer season.**

Nearby	The guide only features facilities that are within the vicinity of the campsite

Charges in euros

Daily charge:

🧍 5€	per person
🚗 2€	per vehicle
▣ 7.50€	per pitch (tent/caravan)
⚡ 2.50€ (4A)	for electricity (calculated by number of ampere units)

Inclusive rates:

25€ 🧍🧍🚗	pitch for 2 people
▣ ⚡ (10A)	including vehicle and electricity

• **The prices listed were supplied by the campsite owners in 2012 (if prices were not available, those from the previous year are given). The fees should be regarded as basic charges and may fluctuate with inflation.**

• **Listings shown in light type (i.e. not bold) indicate that not all revised charges have been provided by the owners.**

• **Additional charges may apply for some facilities (e.g., swimming pool, tennis courts), as well as for long stays.**

• **Special rates may apply for children – ask owner for details.**

Rentals

12	Number of mobile homes
20	Number of chalets
6	Number of rooms to rent
Per night 30–50€	Minimum/maximum rate per night
Per week 300–1,000€	Minimum/maximum rate per week

LOCALITY INFORMATION

23700	Postcode
343 B8	Michelin map reference
Rennes 47	Distance in kilometres
1,050 pop.	Population
alt. 675	Altitude (in metres)
♨	Spa
1,200/1,900m	Altitude (in metres) of resort/highest point reached by lifts
2	Number of cable cars
14	Number of ski and chairlifts
	Cross-country skiing
	Maritime services

• Should you have grounds for complaint during your stay at a campsite about your reservation, the prices, standards of hygiene or facilities available, we recommend that you first try to resolve the problem with the proprietor or with the person responsible.

• If you are unable to resolve the disagreement, and if you are sure that you are within your rights, you could take the matter up with the relevant prefecture of the department.

• We welcome all suggestions and comments, whether in criticism or praise, relating to the campsites recommended in our guide. However, we must stress that we have neither the facilities nor the authority to deal with complaints between campers and proprietors.

A sani-station, known in French as a 'borne', can be one of several proprietary commercial makes or a local, home-made 'artisanale' device. In return for a payment of a few euros or using a 'jeton', a pre-paid token, you receive fresh water, mains electricity and access to rubbish bins, plus grey and black waste disposal.

borne	sani-station
borne artisanale	local sani-station
borne eurorelais, flot bleu, raclet, Urbaco	different types of commercial sani-station
borne autre	other type of sani-station

KEY TO THE MICHELIN AND REGIONAL MAPS

Roads

	Motorway
	Dual carriageway with motorway characteristics
❶ ❷	Interchanges: complete, limited access
	Major road
	Secondary road
	Other/minor road
	One-way road – Toll
	Cycle track (or cart track/footpath)
	Gradient (increases in the direction of the arrow) 5 to 9%; 9 to 13%; 13% +
	Pass – Ferry – Drawbridge or swing bridge
	Railway, station
	Steam railway
③	Load limit (given when less than 5 tonnes)
	Headroom (given when less than 3 metres)

Sights of interest

	Church, chapel
	Castle, château
	Lighthouse – Megalithic monument – Cave
	Ruins – Miscellaneous sights
	Viewpoint indicator, panoramic view – Viewpoint

Landmarks

	Towns with a plan in the Michelin Guide
	Tourist Information Centre – General Post Office
	Church, chapel
	Castle, château
	Ruins – Monument or building – Water tower
	Hospital – Factory or power station
	Fort – Dam
	Lighthouse
	Wayside cross – Cemetery
	Airport – Airfield – Gliding airfield
	Stadium – Golf course – Racecourse
	Equestrian centre – Zoo
	Skating rink
	Cable car, chairlift
	Forest, wood
	Outdoor or indoor swimming pool
	Bathing spot
	Leisure centre/park – Sailing – Tennis courts
	Shopping centre
	Locality with campsite
	Locality with campsite and rental option
Moyaux	Locality with at least one pleasant campsite
Vannes	Locality with campsite and campervan area
	Motorway service area for campervans

accès difficile	difficult access	église	church
accès direct à	direct access to…	embouteillage	traffic jam
accidenté	uneven, hilly	emplacement (empl.)	pitch
adhésion	membership	entrée	way in, entrance
aire (de repos)	rest area	entrée fleurie	attractive floral entrance/reception area
après-midi	afternoon		
arrêt	stop (traffic instruction)	essence	petrol, gas
		étang	lake, pool
Ascension	Feast of the Ascension	été	summer
assurance obligatoire	insurance cover compulsory	falaise	cliff
		famille	family
août	August	fermé	closed
automne	autumn	feu rouge	traffic lights
avenue (av.)	avenue	février (fév.)	February
avril	April	forêt	forest
baie	bay	garage	parking
bain	bath	garage pour caravans	covered parking for caravans
base de loisirs	leisure and activity park/centre		
		garderie (d'enfants)	(children's) crèche
bois, boisé	wood, wooded	gare routière	bus/coach station
bord	shore, riverbank	gare (S.N.C.F.)	railway station
au bord de la mer	by the sea	à gauche	on/to the left
borne	sani-station (see page 12)	gazole	diesel
		goudronné	surfaced road
boucher	butcher	GPL	LPG
boulanger	baker	gratuit	free, no charge
boulevard (bd.)	boulevard.	gravier	gravel
au bourg	in town/in the village	gravillons	fine gravel
		hammam	Turkish-style steam bath with plunge pools
cadre agréable	attractive setting		
cadre sauvage	natural setting		
carrefour	crossroads	herbeux	grassy
cases réfrigérées	refrigerated food storage facilities	hiver	winter
		hors saison	out of season
cedez le passage	give way (on roads)		
centre équestre	equestrian centre	île, îlot	island
chambre d'hôte	guesthouse, B&B	incliné	sloping
château	castle	indispensable	essential
chemin	path	interdit	forbidden, prohibited
conseillé	advised	intersection	junction
cotisation obligatoire	membership charge obligatory	janvier (janv.)	January
		jeudi	Thursday
croisement difficile	difficult access	jour	day
en cours d'aménagement	rebuilding work in progress	juillet (juil.)	July
		juin	June
crêperie	pancake restaurant/ stall	lac	lake
		lande	heath/moorland
décembre (déc.)	December	licence obligatoire	camping licence/ international camping carnet compulsory
déjeuner	lunch		
derrière	behind		
dimanche	Sunday		
dîner	dinner	au lieu-dit	in the small locality of/at the place known as
douche	shower		
à droite	on/to the right		

lundi	Monday
mai	May
mairie	town hall
marché	market
mardi	Tuesday
mars	March
matin	morning
mer	sea
mercredi	Wednesday
mineurs non accompagnés non admis	under 18s must be accompanied by an adult
montagne	mountain
Noël	Christmas
non clos	open site (landscape)
novembre (nov.)	November
nuit	night
à la nuitée	per night, on a nightly basis
octobre (oct.)	October
ouvert	open
ouverture prévue	opening scheduled
en panne	broken down
Pâques	Easter
parcours de santé	fitness trail
passage non admis	no touring pitches
péage	toll
pelouse	lawn
pente	sloping/slope
Pentecôte	Whitsun
personne (pers.)	person
petit-déjeuner	breakfast
pierreux	stony
piéton	pedestrian
pinède	pine trees, pine wood
place (pl.)	square
places limitées pour le passage	limited number of touring pitches
plage	beach
plan d'eau	stretch of water, artificial lake
plat	flat
pneu	tyre
pont	bridge
port	port, harbour
prairie	grassland, lawn
pré	meadow
près de	near
presqu'île	peninsula
prévu	projected
printemps	spring
en priorité	as a priority

priorité à droite	priority to right (give way to traffic from right, traffic joining roundabouts has priority, traffic on minor roads has right-of-way onto major roads, sign: black cross inside red triangle)
à proximité	nearby
quartier	quarter, district, area
Rameaux	Palm Sunday
réservé	reserved, booked
rive droite, gauche	right, left bank
rivière	river
rocailleux	stony, rocky, rugged
rocheux	rocky
rond-point	roundabout
route (rte)	road
rue (r.)	street
ruisseau	stream
sablonneux	sandy
saison (tourist)	tourist season
samedi	Saturday
avec sanitaires	with sanitary facilities
schéma	local map
semaine	week
à la semaine	per week, on a weekly basis
septembre (sept.)	September
soir	evening
sortie	way out, exit
sous-bois	undergrowth
(face) à la station	(opposite) at the filling station
supplémentaire (suppl.)	extra
en terrasses	terraced
toboggan aquatique	water slide
torrent	torrent (river/stream)
Toussaint	All Saints' Day (1 Nov)
tout compris	all inclusive
tout droit	straight ahead
unleaded	sans plomb
vacances scolaires	school holidays
vallonné	undulating
vendredi	Friday
verger	fruit trees, orchard
vers	in the direction of/ towards
Voie Verte	green trail
voir	see

YOU ALREADY KNOW THE GREEN GUIDE,
NOW FIND OUT ABOUT THE MICHELIN GROUP

MALAHIDE LIBRARY
PH: 8704430

MICHELIN
A better way forward

René Mattes / hemis.fr

Alsace is perhaps the most romantic of France's regions, a place of fairy-tale castles, gentle vine-clad hills and picturesque villages perched on rocky outcrops or nestling in lush, green valleys. From Colmar's 'Little Venice' with its flower-decked balconies, famous storks (the region's iconic emblem) and wonderful Unterlinden Museum, to the spectacular lights and tempting delights of Strasbourg's Christmas market, via the atmospheric half-timbered houses, reflected in the meandering River Ill, Alsace radiates an inviting warmth that even the winter temperatures cannot chill. The region is known for its wonderful scenery, traditional cuisine, local produce and excellent wine. Head to a brasserie and enjoy a regional beer in a lively atmosphere or relax in a local *winstub* (wine lounge), tucking into a steaming dish of *choucroute* (sauerkraut with smoked pork) and a generous slice of *Kugelhopf* cake, all washed down with a glass of fruity Sylvaner or Riesling. Alsace has something for everyone.

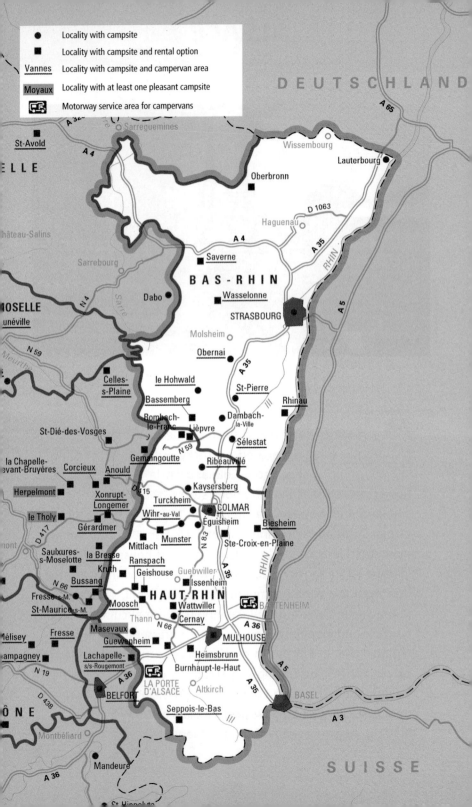

BASSEMBERG

67220 – Michelin map **315** H7 – pop. 268 – alt. 280
▶ Paris 432 – Barr 21 – St-Dié 35 – Sélestat 19

Campéole Le Giessen

✆ 03 88 58 98 14, *www.camping-vosges.net*
Address : rte de Villé (take northeastern exit on the D 39; beside the Giessen river)
4 ha (79 pitches) flat, grassy
Rentals : ♿ (1 mobile home) – 50 🚐 – 20 🏠 – 10 tent bungalows.
🚏 sani-station
Pretty site near a water park.

Surroundings : ⟨ 🖾
Leisure activities : 🍷 ⊙daytime 🚣 🚲
Facilities : ♿ ⊶ ⊞ 🛁 ☂ ⚐ 🍴 🔲
Nearby : 🍴 🖾 🔲 ⚒ 🏊

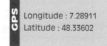
Longitude : 7.28911
Latitude : 48.33602

This guide is updated regularly, so buy your new copy every year!

BIESHEIM

68600 – Michelin map **315** J8 – pop. 2,398 – alt. 189
▶ Paris 520 – Strasbourg 85 – Freiburg-im-Breisgau 37 – Basel 68

Village Center L'Ile du Rhin

✆ 03 89 72 57 95, *www.village-center.fr*
Address : touristic area of Île du Rhin (5km east along the N 415, follow the signs for Fribourg)
Opening times : from beginning April to end Sept.
3 ha (220 pitches) flat and relatively flat, grassy
Tariff : (2012 Price) 20€ 🏕🏕 🚐 🔲 ⚡ (10A) – Extra per person 5€
Rental rates : (2012 price) (from beginning April to end Sept.) – 14 🚐.
Per night from 34 to 77 € – Per week from 608 to 668 €
🚏 sani-station 5€
Pleasant site and setting between the Rhine and the Canal d'Alsace on the Franco-German border.

Surroundings : ♀
Leisure activities : ✕ 🖾 ⊙daytime 🚲
Facilities : ♿ ⊶ 🆔 ☂ ⚐ 🍴 launderette 🍽 ☂
Nearby : 🔲 ⚒ 🏊 🐟 water skiing, marina

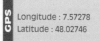
Longitude : 7.57278
Latitude : 48.02746

BURNHAUPT-LE-HAUT

68520 – Michelin map **315** G10 – pop. 1,596 – alt. 300
▶ Paris 454 – Altkirch 16 – Belfort 32 – Mulhouse 17

Les Castors

✆ 03 89 48 78 58, *www.camping-les-castors.fr*
Address : 4 rte de Guewenheim (2.5km northwest along the D 466)
Opening times : from beginning April to end Oct.
2.5 ha (135 pitches) flat, grassy
Tariff : (2012 Price) 17.50€ 🏕🏕 🚐 🔲 ⚡ (10A) – Extra per person 4.20€
Rental rates : (from beginning April to end Oct.) – 3 🚐. Per night from 40 to 60 €
Per week from 300 to 650 € – Reservation fee 15€
Rural setting beside a river and a lake. Extensive green spaces.

Surroundings : ♀
Leisure activities : 🍷 ✕ 🚣 🐟
Facilities : ♿ ⊶ 🆔 ☂ 🍴 launderette

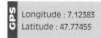
Longitude : 7.12383
Latitude : 47.77455

CERNAY

68700 – Michelin map **315** H10 – pop. 11,288 – alt. 275
▶ Paris 461 – Altkirch 26 – Belfort 39 – Colmar 37

▲ Les Cigognes

📞 03 89 75 56 97, www.camping-les-cigognes.com
Address : 16 r. René Guibert (take the exit following signs for Belfort then take a right turn after the bridge; beside the Thur river)
3.5 ha (138 pitches) flat, grassy
🚐 sani-station
Pretty, green pitches within the town.

Surroundings : ♀
Leisure activities : 🛋
Facilities : ⅙ ☞ �󰀄 ♨ 🗏
Nearby : ✕ 🖾 🗒 (open-air in season)

GPS
Longitude : 7.16876
Latitude : 47.80519

*Using the traditional Michelin classification method, the guide provides
you with an easy, speedy reference for assessing the category of each site:
1 to 5 tents (see page 10).*

COLMAR

68000 – Michelin map **315** I8 – pop. 67,214 – alt. 194
▶ Paris 450 – Basel 68 – Freiburg 51 – Nancy 140

⛰ L'Ill

📞 03 89 41 15 94, www.campingdelill.com
Address : situated 2km east along the N 415, follow the signs for Fribourg; beside the Ill river
Opening times : from mid March to beginning Jan.
2.2 ha (150 pitches) flat, terrace, grassy
Tariff : (2012 Price) 18.20€ ✝✝ ⭰ 🗉 (⅍) (10A) – Extra per person 3.50€
🚐 sani-station 6.20€
Shaded site on the peaceful banks of the Ill river.

Surroundings : ♀♀
Leisure activities : ⏣ ✕ 🛋 ⚄ ⤳
Facilities : ⅙ ☞ ⓜ ⓣ 🗏 ⚄ ⛴

GPS
Longitude : 7.38676
Latitude : 48.07838

DAMBACH-LA-VILLE

67650 – Michelin map **315** I7 – pop. 1,946 – alt. 210
▶ Paris 443 – Barr 17 – Obernai 24 – Saverne 61

▲ L'Ours

📞 03 88 92 46 09, alavignette@orange.fr
Address : 2 r. du stade (1.2km east along the D 210, follow the signs for Ebersheim and take road to the left)
1.8 ha (120 pitches) flat, grassy
A shaded setting in the countryside, with an attractive view of the mountain.

Surroundings : ≤ ♀
Facilities : ⅙ ☞ ♨ 🗏
Nearby : ⚄ ✕ 🖾

GPS
Longitude : 7.44324
Latitude : 48.32274

ÉGUISHEIM

68420 – Michelin map **315** H8 – pop. 1,622 – alt. 210
▶ Paris 452 – Belfort 68 – Colmar 7 – Gérardmer 52

Des Trois Châteaux

✆ 03 89 23 19 39, *www.eguisheimcamping.fr*
Address : 10 r. du Bassin (to the west)
Opening times : from end March to end Dec.
2 ha (133 pitches) flat and relatively flat, grassy
Tariff : (2012 Price) 16.40 € ♦♦ ⇔ ▣ ⚡ (6A) – Extra per person 4 € – Reservation fee 6 €
Rental rates : (2012 price) (from end March to end Dec.) – 14 ▦. Per night from 43 to 90 €
Per week from 290 to 630 € – Reservation fee 6 €
Sanitary facilities are a little jaded, but pleasant location near a vineyard and the very beautiful village of Eguisheim.

Surroundings : ☜ ⋚ ♀
Facilities : ♿ ⚬ ☂ ▨

GPS
Longitude : 7.29909
Latitude : 48.04274

GEISHOUSE

68690 – Michelin map **315** G9 – pop. 484 – alt. 730
▶ Paris 467 – Belfort 53 – Bussang 23 – Colmar 55

Au Relais du Grand Ballon

✆ 03 89 82 30 47, *www.aurelaisdugrandballon.com* – limited spaces for one-night stay
Address : 17 Grand-Rue (southern exit)
Opening times : permanent
0.3 ha (24 pitches) flat, grassy
Tariff : 19.85 € ♦♦ ⇔ ▣ ⚡ (10A) – Extra per person 4.60 €
Rental rates : (permanent) – 4 ⌂. Per night from 52 € – Per week from 325 to 435 €
A small but pretty site out in the mountains. Family atmosphere with a very busy restaurant.

Surroundings : ☜ ☐ ♀
Leisure activities : ♟ ✗ ☒ ⚓
Facilities : ♿ ⚬ ▥ ☂ launderette

GPS
Longitude : 7.05852
Latitude : 47.88056

GUEWENHEIM

68116 – Michelin map **315** G10 – pop. 1,256 – alt. 323
▶ Paris 458 – Altkirch 23 – Belfort 36 – Mulhouse 21

La Doller

✆ 03 89 82 56 90, *www.campingdoller.com*
Address : r. du Cdt Charpy (located 1km north along the D 34, follow the signs for Thann and take the road to the right; beside the Doller river)
Opening times : from beginning April to end Oct.
0.8 ha (40 pitches) flat, grassy
Tariff : 15.40 € ♦♦ ⇔ ▣ ⚡ (6A) – Extra per person 4 €
Rental rates : (2012 price) (permanent) – 6 ▦. Per night from 45 to 75 € – Per week from 300 to 550 €
▦ sani-station 2 € – 5 ▣ 13.50 € – 8 €
Family atmosphere in a green setting surrounded by flowers. Lovely dining room.

Surroundings : ☜ ♀
Leisure activities : ♟ ☒ ⚓ ⚒ ⌇
Facilities : ♿ ⚬ ▥ ☂ ⚴ ⌇ ☂ ▨
Nearby : ⚘ ⌇

GPS
Longitude : 7.09827
Latitude : 47.75597

ALSACE

HEIMSBRUNN

68990 – Michelin map **315** H10 – pop. 1,453 – alt. 280
▶ Paris 456 – Altkirch 14 – Basel 50 – Belfort 34

Parc la Chaumière

𝒫 0389819343, *www.camping-lachaumiere.com* – limited spaces for one-night stay
Address : 62 r. de Galfingue (take the southern exit along the D 19, follow the signs for Altkirch)
Opening times : permanent
1 ha (53 pitches) flat, grassy, fine gravel
Tariff : 13.50€ ⚫⚫ ⟷ ▣ (🔌) (10A) – Extra per person 3.50€
Rental rates : (permanent) – 4 ▥. Per night from 15 to 35 € – Per week from 100 to 490 €
⟲ sani-station 4€ – 6 ▣ 10.50€ – ⟲9€
Convivial and family-orientated site in a pleasant setting among trees.

Surroundings : ⟋ ⟑ ♀
Leisure activities : ⚡⟶ ⟰ (small swimming pool)
Facilities : ⟿ ⫿⫿⫿ ⫽ ⟰

GPS
Longitude : 7.22477
Latitude : 47.72242

LE HOHWALD

67140 – Michelin map **315** H6 – pop. 496 – alt. 570 – Winter sports : 600/1,100 m⟋ 1 ⚞
▶ Paris 430 – Lunéville 89 – Molsheim 33 – St-Dié 46

Municipal

𝒫 0388083090, *lecamping.herrenhaus@orange.fr* – alt. 615
Address : 28 r. du Herrenhaus (take the western exit along the D 425, follow the signs for Villé)
Opening times : permanent
2 ha (100 pitches) very uneven, terraced, grassy, fine gravel
Tariff : (2012 Price) ⚫ 3.70€ ⟷ 1.80€ ▣ 2.20€ – (🔌) (6A) 4.20€
⟲ 10 ▣ 9€ – ⟲9€
Pleasant setting in the mountains among pines, spruces and beech trees.

Surroundings : ♀
Leisure activities : ⟐ ⚡⟶ sports trail
Facilities : ⟿ ⫿⫿⫿ ⟰

GPS
Longitude : 7.32328
Latitude : 48.4063

ISSENHEIM

68500 – Michelin map **315** H9 – pop. 3,418 – alt. 245
▶ Paris 487 – Strasbourg 98 – Colmar 24 – Mulhouse 22

Le Florival

𝒫 0389742047, *www.camping-leflorival.com*
Address : rte de Soultz (2.5km southeast along the D 430, follow the signs for Mulhouse and take D 5 to the left, follow the signs for Issenheim)
Opening times : from mid April to mid Oct.
3.5 ha (73 pitches) flat, stony, grassy
Tariff : (2012 Price) ⚫ 3.80€ ⟷ ▣ 7.20€ – (🔌) (6A) 3.80€
Rental rates : (2012 price) (from mid April to mid Oct.) ⚿ (2 chalets) ⟰ (from mid-Apr to mid-Oct) – 20 ⟰. Per night from 50 to 88 € – Per week from 262 to 568 €
A pleasant setting at the edge of the woods. Swimming facilities with an Olympic-size pool nearby.

Surroundings : ⟜ ⟑
Leisure activities : ⟐ ⚡⟶
Facilities : ⚿ ⟿ ⫿⫿⫿ ⟰ ⫽ launderette
Nearby : ⟰ ⟰ ⟰

GPS
Longitude : 7.23879
Latitude : 47.90014

KAYSERSBERG

68240 – Michelin map **315** H8 – pop. 2,721 – alt. 242
▶ Paris 438 – Colmar 12 – Gérardmer 46 – Guebwiller 35

 Municipal

ℰ 0389471447, *www.camping-kaysersberg.fr* ✖ (Jul–Aug)
Address : r. des Acacias (take northwestern exit along the N 415, follow the signs for St-Dié and take a right turn)
Opening times : from beginning April to end Sept.
1.6 ha (115 pitches) flat, grassy
Tariff : 👤 4.25€ 🚗 2.55€ 🔲 3.20€ – 🔌 (13A) 4.30€
🚽 sani-station
Charming site beside the La Weiss river.

Surroundings : ≤ ♀
Leisure activities : 🎦 🚣 ✖
Facilities : ⌒ 👃 🚿 🚗 🚰 launderette

GPS Longitude : 7.25404
Latitude : 48.14887

*We have selected the best campsites in France with our usual care,
listing those with the best facilities in the most pleasant surroundings.*

KRUTH

68820 – Michelin map **315** F9 – pop. 1,029 – alt. 498
▶ Paris 453 – Colmar 63 – Épinal 68 – Gérardmer 31

 Le Schlossberg

ℰ 0389822676, *www.schlossberg.fr*
Address : rue du Bourbaach (2.3km northwest along the D 13b, follow the signs for La Bresse and take turning to the left; beside the Bourbach)
Opening times : from end March to beginning Oct.
5.2 ha (200 pitches) relatively flat, terrace, grassy
Tariff : (2012 Price) 👤 4.50€ 🚗 1.10€ 🔲 4.20€ – 🔌 (6A) 3€ – Reservation fee 10€
Rental rates : (2012 price) (permanent) – 9 🏠. Per night from 45 to 58 €
Per week from 275 to 580€ – Reservation fee 10€
In a pleasant location in the heart of the Parc des Ballons, close to the Magnificent Lac de Kruth. Cycle path at the entrance.

Surroundings : 🐟 ≤ ♀
Leisure activities : 🍴 🚣
Facilities : 👤 ⌒ 🏢 👃 🚰 launderette

GPS Longitude : 6.9546
Latitude : 47.94535

LAUTERBOURG

67630 – Michelin map **315** N3 – pop. 2,266 – alt. 115
▶ Paris 519 – Haguenau 40 – Karlsruhe 22 – Strasbourg 63

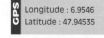 **Municipal des Mouettes**

ℰ 0388546860, *camping-lauterbourg@wanadoo.fr* – limited spaces for one-night stay ✖
Address : located 1.5km southwest along the D 3 and take road to the left, 100m from a small lake (direct access)
2.7 ha (136 pitches) flat, grassy
Large expanses of grass beside a large leisure and activity park.

Leisure activities : 🍴 ✖
Facilities : 👤 ⌒ 🏢 🚰 📷
Nearby : 🚣 🏊 🎣 ⚓

GPS Longitude : 8.1654
Latitude : 48.9708

LIEPVRE

68660 – Michelin map **315** H7 – pop. 1,751 – alt. 272
▶ Paris 428 – Colmar 35 – Ribeauvillé 27 – St-Dié-des-Vosges 31

Haut-Koenigsbourg

☏ 0389584320, *www.liepvre.fr/camping*
Address : rte de La Vancelle (900m east along the C 1 follow the signs for la Vancelle)
Opening times : from mid March to mid Oct.
1 ha (56 pitches) flat and relatively flat, grassy
Tariff : 15.70€ ☗☗ ⇌ 回 ⑭ (8A) – Extra per person 4€
Rental rates : (from mid March to mid Oct.) ⌇ – 6 ⌂. Per night from 60 to 80 €
Per week from 320 to 575 €

Entrance marked by a centuries-old sequoia; an oasis of absolute peace in the middle of the countryside.

Surroundings : ⅏ ≼ ♌
Leisure activities : 🎱 🏊
Facilities : ♿ ⛽ 🚿 🚰 🚽

Longitude : 7.2903
Latitude : 48.27303

MASEVAUX

68290 – Michelin map **315** F10 – pop. 3,278 – alt. 425
▶ Paris 440 – Altkirch 32 – Belfort 24 – Colmar 57

Le Masevaux

☏ 0389824229, *www.camping-masevaux.com*
Address : 3 r. du Stade (beside the Doller river)
Opening times : from mid March to end Oct.
3.5 ha (133 pitches) flat, grassy
Tariff : 18€ ☗☗ ⇌ 回 ⑭ (6A) – Extra per person 4.70€

Pleasant, wooded setting with lots of flowers. Several trails start at the site.

Surroundings : ♌♌
Leisure activities : 🍷 🎱 🏊 ⚓
Facilities : ♿ ⛽ 🚿 🚰 launderette
Nearby : 🛒 🍴 🏊 🎿

Longitude : 6.99093
Latitude : 47.77833

Some information or pricing may have changed since the guide went to press.
We recommend you check the price list online in advance or at the entrance to
the campsite and enquire about possible restrictions.

MITTLACH

68380 – Michelin map **315** G8 – pop. 323 – alt. 550
▶ Paris 467 – Colmar 28 – Gérardmer 42 – Guebwiller 44

Municipal Langenwasen

☏ 0389776377, *www.mittlach.fr* – alt. 620
Address : chemin du Camping (3km southwest; beside a stream)
3 ha (77 pitches) relatively flat, flat, terrace, grassy, gravelled
Rentals : 1 studio.
Wooded site at the bottom of a peaceful valley.

Surroundings : ⅏ ≼ ⌑ ♌
Leisure activities : 🎱 🏊
Facilities : ⛽ 🚽

Longitude : 7.01867
Latitude : 47.98289

MOOSCH

68690 – Michelin map **315** G9 – pop. 1,764 – alt. 390
▶ Paris 463 – Colmar 51 – Gérardmer 42 – Mulhouse 28

▲ La Mine d'Argent

℘ 0389823066, *www.camping-la-mine-argent.com* – limited spaces for one-night stay
Address : r. de la Mine d'Argent (located 1.5km southwest along the r. de la Mairie; beside a stream)
Opening times : from mid April to mid Oct.
2 ha (75 pitches) relatively flat, flat, terraced, grassy
Tariff : 15.80€ ✦✦ ⟹ 🔲 [∮] (10A) – Extra per person 3.95€
Rental rates : (from mid April to mid Oct.) – 4 🛏. Per night from 30 to 69 €
Per week from 220 to 400 € – Reservation fee 20€
🚰 sani-station
On a lush, green, hilly site among the mountains.

Surroundings : ⚲ ≼ ♀
Leisure activities : 🎦 🏊
Facilities : ⟲ launderette

GPS Longitude : 7.03054
Latitude : 47.85102

MULHOUSE

68100 – Michelin map **315** I10 – pop. 111,156 – alt. 240
▶ Paris 465 – Basel 34 – Belfort 43 – Besançon 130

⚠ L'Ill

℘ 0389062066, *www.camping-de-lill.com*
Address : 1 r. Pierre de Coubertin (to the southwest, along the A 36, take the exit for Dornach)
Opening times : from beginning April to mid Oct.
5 ha (193 pitches) flat, grassy
Tariff : 19.45€ ✦✦ ⟹ 🔲 [∮] (10A) – Extra per person 5.15€ – Reservation fee 5€
Rental rates : (from beginning April to mid Oct.) ⚲ – 8 🛏 – 15 chalets (without sanitary facilities). Per night 85€ – Per week 550€ – Reservation fee 15€
🚰 sani-station 5€ – 11 🔲 16€
Wooded setting beside a river and along Euro cycle route 6.

Surroundings : ♀♀
Leisure activities : 🎦 🏊
Facilities : 🚻 ⟲ 🏛 ♈ 🔲 🧺
Nearby : 🐎 ☒ skating rink, mountain biking, skateboarding

GPS Longitude : 7.32283
Latitude : 47.73424

MUNSTER

68140 – Michelin map **315** G8 – pop. 4,889 – alt. 400
▶ Paris 458 – Colmar 19 – Gérardmer 34 – Guebwiller 40

▲ Village Center Le Parc de la Fecht

℘ 0825002030, *www.village-center.fr*
Address : rte de Gunsbach (located 1km east along the D 10, follow the signs for Turckheim)
Opening times : from end April to end Sept.
4 ha (192 pitches) flat, grassy
Tariff : (2012 Price) 17€ ✦✦ ⟹ 🔲 [∮] (6A) – Extra per person 4€
Rental rates : (2012 price) (from end April to end Sept.) – 12 🛏. Per night from 25 to 82 €
Per week from 506 to 709 €
🚰 sani-station 4€
Wooded site beside the Fecht river, but the sanitary facilities are a little jaded.

Surroundings : ♀♀
Leisure activities : 🎦 🌀 🏊 🚲
Facilities : ⟲ ☒ ♈ 🔲
Nearby : ☒

GPS Longitude : 7.15102
Latitude : 48.04316

OBERBRONN

67110 – Michelin map **315** J3 – pop. 1,543 – alt. 260
▶ Paris 460 – Bitche 25 – Haguenau 24 – Saverne 36

L'Oasis

℘ 0388097196, *www.oasis-alsace.com*

Address : 3 r. du Frohret (located 1.5km south along the D 28, follow the signs for Ingwiller and take the road to the left)

Opening times : from beginning April to end Oct.

2.5 ha (139 pitches) flat and relatively flat, grassy, stony

Tariff : 20.90€ ♥♥ ⇔ 🔲 🛱 (6A) – Extra per person 4.60€ – Reservation fee 10€

Rental rates : (from beginning April to end Oct.) – 28 🏠. Per night from 87 to 98 €

Per week from 339 to 679 € – Reservation fee 15€

🚽 sani-station 4.65€ – 7 🔲 16€

On the edge of a forest with a magnificent view over the mountain and the village of Oberbronn.

Surroundings : ⤵ ≤
Leisure activities : ♥ ✕ 🏠 🚣 ✂ ⚓ sports trail, spa therapy centre
Facilities : ♿ ⚲ ⏣ 🚿 ♨ 🔲 🚰
Nearby : 🎿

Longitude : 7.60347
Latitude : 48.9286

OBERNAI

67210 – Michelin map **315** I6 – pop. 10,803 – alt. 185
▶ Paris 488 – Colmar 50 – Erstein 15 – Molsheim 12

Municipal le Vallon de l'Ehn

℘ 0388953848, *www.obernai.fr*

Address : 1 r. de Berlin (take the western exit along the D 426, follow the signs for Ottrott, for caravans, recommended route via the bypass (rocade) south of the town)

3 ha (150 pitches) flat, relatively flat, grassy

🚽 sani-station

Restful site with a pretty view of Mont Saint Odile.

Surroundings : ≤ ♨
Leisure activities : 🏠 🚣 🎿
Facilities : ♿ ⚲ ⏣ ♨ 🚰 ⚐ 🚿 launderette
Nearby : ✂ 🏓 ⚓ 🐎

Longitude : 7.46715
Latitude : 48.46505

RANSPACH

68470 – Michelin map **315** G9 – pop. 852 – alt. 430
▶ Paris 459 – Belfort 54 – Bussang 15 – Gérardmer 38

Flower Les Bouleaux

℘ 0389826470, *www.alsace-camping.com*

Address : 8 r. des Bouleaux (south of the town along the N 66)

Opening times : permanent

1.75 ha (75 pitches) flat, grassy

Tariff : 23.50€ ♥♥ ⇔ 🔲 🛱 (6A) – Extra per person 5€ – Reservation fee 10€

Rental rates : (permanent) ♿ (2 chalets) – 25 🏠. Per night from 46 to 99 €

Per week from 230 to 693 € – Reservation fee 10€

🚽 sani-station 3.50€ – 3 🔲 23.50€

Extensive and attractive green spaces in the shade of birch trees, but sanitary facilities are a little old.

Surroundings : ≤ ♨
Leisure activities : ♥ ✕ 🏠 🚣 🚲 🎿 🎿
Facilities : ♿ ⚲ 🚿 🚰 launderette

Longitude : 7.01037
Latitude : 47.88085

RHINAU

67860 – Michelin map **315** K7 – pop. 2,698 – alt. 158
▶ Paris 525 – Marckolsheim 26 – Molsheim 38 – Obernai 28

Ferme des Tuileries

℘ 0388746045, *www.fermedestuileries.com* – ℞ ✍

Address : 1 r. des Tuileries (take the northwestern exit, follow the signs for Benfeld)
Opening times : from beginning April to end Sept.
4 ha (150 pitches) flat, grassy
Tariff : 🜨 4€ ⇌ 🗉 4€ – 🔌 (6A) 3.20€
Rental rates : (from beginning April to end Dec.) ✍ – 5 🏠. Per night from 50 to 85 €
Per week from 350 to 600 €
🚮 sani-station 2€
Well-equipped site scattered with fruit trees, next to a magnificent lake.

Surroundings : ⌗ ♀
Leisure activities : ✗ 🍽 ᵭᵒ 🖈 ᵭᵒ ✂ ₘ ⅃ ≌ (lake) ⛵ ⤳
Facilities : ⚬━ 🚿 ⊿ launderette ⤳

GPS Longitude : 7.6986
Latitude : 48.32224

To visit a town or region, use the MICHELIN Green Guides.

RIBEAUVILLÉ

68150 – Michelin map **315** H7 – pop. 4,798 – alt. 240
▶ Paris 439 – Colmar 16 – Gérardmer 56 – Mulhouse 60

Municipal Pierre-de-Coubertin

℘ 0389736671, *www.camping-alsace.com/-camping-pierre-de-coubertin-ribeauville-.h* – ℞
Address : 23 r. de Landau (take the eastern exit along the D 106 then take the turning to the left)
Opening times : from mid March to mid Nov.
3.5 ha (208 pitches) flat, grassy
Tariff : 🜨 5€ ⇌ 🗉 4€ – 🔌 (16A) 3.60€
🚮 sani-station – 18 🗉
Pretty view of the mountain, vineyards and château.

Surroundings : ⌗ ≼ ♀
Leisure activities : 🍽 ᵭᵒ ✂
Facilities : ⚽ ⚬━ 🚿 ⊿ ⚲ ↻ ᵛ 🗉 🖥
Nearby : 🔲 ⅃ ⤳

GPS Longitude : 7.336
Latitude : 48.195

ROMBACH-LE-FRANC

68660 – Michelin map **315** H7 – pop. 877 – alt. 290
▶ Paris 431 – Colmar 38 – Ribeauvillé 30 – St-Dié 34

Municipal les Bouleaux

℘ 0389584156, *www.valdargent.com/camping-rombach-les-bouleaux.htm* – access difficult for caravans
Address : rte de la Hingrie (located 1.5km to the northwest)
Opening times : from mid April to mid Oct.
1.3 ha (38 pitches) open site, flat and relatively flat, grassy
Tariff : 🜨 2.50€ ⇌ 1.85€ 🗉 1.85€ – 🔌 (13A) 2.40€
Rental rates : (permanent) ✍ – 5 🏠. Per week from 265 to 395 €
In a valley surrounded by pines and crossed by a stream.

Surroundings : ⌗ ♀
Leisure activities : 🍽 ᵭᵒ
Facilities : ⚽ ⚬⇌ 🖵 🚿 launderette

GPS Longitude : 7.2402
Latitude : 48.2877

ST-PIERRE

67140 – Michelin map **315** I6 – pop. 589 – alt. 179
▶ Paris 498 – Barr 4 – Erstein 21 – Obernai 12

Les Reflets de St-Pierre

☎ 0389586431, *reflets@calixo.net*
Address : 14 r. de l'Eglise (in the town, behind the church; beside the Muttlbach river)
0.6 ha (47 pitches) flat, grassy
sani-station
Peaceful site beside a watercourse.

Surroundings : ⌸
Leisure activities : ✂
Nearby : 🏇

GPS Longitude : 7.47472
Latitude : 48.38254

*The classification (1 to 5 tents, **black** or **red**) that we award to selected sites in this guide is our own system. It should not be confused with the classification (1 to 5 stars) of official organisations.*

STE-CROIX-EN-PLAINE

68127 – Michelin map **315** I8 – pop. 2,661 – alt. 192
▶ Paris 471 – Belfort 78 – Colmar 10 – Freiburg-im-Breisgau 49

Clair Vacances

☎ 0389492728, *www.clairvacances.com*
Address : rte de Herrlisheim (On the D1)
Opening times : from beginning April to mid Oct.
4 ha (145 pitches) flat, grassy
Tariff : 25€ 🚻 🚐 🖹 [₺] (16A) – Extra per person 7.50€ – Reservation fee 10€
Rental rates : (from mid April to mid Oct.) – 12 🚎. Per night from 55 to 130 €
Per week from 290 to 795 € – Reservation fee 10€
Attractive trees and shrubs, peaceful site with plenty of charm.

Surroundings : ⌸
Leisure activities : 🏓 🏇 ⍐
Facilities : ♿ ⚷ ⌷ ⌷ 🍴 launderette

GPS Longitude : 7.35289
Latitude : 48.01454

SAVERNE

67700 – Michelin map **315** I4 – pop. 12,046 – alt. 200
▶ Paris 450 – Lunéville 88 – St-Avold 89 – Sarreguemines 65

Seasonova Les Portes d'Alsace

☎ 0388913565, *www.vacances-seasonova.com*
Address : 40 r. du Père Libermann (1.3km southwest along the D 171)
2.1 ha (180 pitches) relatively flat, flat, grassy
Rental rates : 4 🚎.
sani-station – 16 🖹
A little bit of countryside in an urban environment; peaceful and well appointed.

Surroundings : ⩽ ♀
Leisure activities : 🏓 🏇
Facilities : ♿ ⚷ ⌷ ⌁ launderette
Nearby : ✂ 🐎

GPS Longitude : 7.35539
Latitude : 48.73095

SÉLESTAT

67600 – Michelin map **315** I7 – pop. 19,332 – alt. 170
▶ Paris 441 – Colmar 24 – Gérardmer 65 – St-Dié 44

⚠ Municipal les Cigognes

☎ 0389920398, *www.selestat-tourisme.com ou http://camping-selestat.monsite-orang*
Address : 1 r. de la 1ère Division France Libre
Opening times : from beginning April to end Dec.
0.7 ha (48 pitches) flat, grassy
Tariff : (2012 Price) 16.95€ ⚏⚏ ⚏ 回 (6A) – Extra per person 4.30€
🚽 sani-station 5.40€
Charming site 5min from the town centre.

Surroundings : ♀
Leisure activities : 🏊
Facilities : ⚏ 🏛 ⚏ 🚿
Nearby : ✂ 🎣 🏊

GPS
Longitude : 7.44828
Latitude : 48.25444

SEPPOIS-LE-BAS

68580 – Michelin map **315** H11 – pop. 1,164 – alt. 390
▶ Paris 454 – Altkirch 13 – Basel 42 – Belfort 38

⚠ Village Center Les Lupins

☎ 0389256537, *www.village-center.com*
Address : 1 r. de la gare (take the northeastern exit along the D 17 2, follow the signs for Altkirch)
Opening times : from beginning April to end Sept.
3.5 ha (158 pitches) flat, terrace, grassy
Tariff : 17€ ⚏⚏ ⚏ 回 (6A) – Extra per person 4€ – Reservation fee 5€
Rental rates : (from beginning April to end Sept.) 🅿 – 1 ⛺ – 10 🏠.
Per night from 28 to 99 € – Per week from 189 to 699 € – Reservation fee 30€
🚽 5 回 17€ – 🔌12€
A leafy, green setting on the site of an old station; the site is long and narrow.

Surroundings : 🌲 ♀
Leisure activities : 🎬 🎯 🏊 🏊
Facilities : ♿ ⚏ 🏛 🚿 ⚏ launderette
Nearby : ✗

GPS
Longitude : 7.17893
Latitude : 47.53956

STRASBOURG

67000 – Michelin map **315** K5 – pop. 271,708 – alt. 143
▶ Paris 488 – Stuttgart 160 – Baden-Baden 63 – Karlsruhe 87

⚠ Aquadis Loisirs La Montagne Verte

☎ 0388302546, *www.aquadis-loisirs.com*
Address : 2 r. Robert Forrer
Opening times : permanent
2.5 ha (183 pitches) flat, grassy
Tariff : 19.40€ ⚏⚏ ⚏ 回 (10A) – Extra per person 4.65€ – Reservation fee 9.50€
Urban site but quiet and with good shade.

Surroundings : ♀
Leisure activities : 🍷 ✗ 🎬 🚲
Facilities : ♿ ⚏ 🚿 ⚏ launderette
Nearby : 🏊

GPS
Longitude : 7.71441
Latitude : 48.57537

TURCKHEIM

68230 – Michelin map **315** H8 – pop. 3,747 – alt. 225
▶ Paris 471 – Colmar 7 – Gérardmer 47 – Munster 14

Les Cigognes

📞 03 89 27 02 00, *www.camping-turckheim.com*
Address : quai de la gare (to the west of the town, behind the stadium – access via the road between the level crossing and the bridge)
2.5 ha (117 pitches) flat, grassy
sani-station
Beside a small canal and near the Fecht river.

Surroundings :
Leisure activities :
Facilities : & o— 🎱 🛎 launderette
Nearby : ✗

GPS Longitude : 7.27144
Latitude : 48.08463

WASSELONNE

67310 – Michelin map **315** I5 – pop. 5,562 – alt. 220
▶ Paris 464 – Haguenau 42 – Molsheim 15 – Saverne 15

Municipal

📞 03 88 87 00 08, *www.camping-wasselonne.com/*
Address : r. des Sapins (located 1km west along the D 224, follow the signs for Wangenbourg)
Opening times : from mid April to mid Oct.
1.5 ha (100 pitches) terraced, grassy
Tariff : (2012 Price) 15.90€ ✶✶ ⊕ 🅴 (10A) – Extra per person 4€
Rental rates : (2012 price) (from beginning March to end Oct.) & (1 chalet) – 12 🏠.
Per night from 50 to 77 € – Per week from 310 to 470 €
sani-station 2€ – 10 🅴 15.90€ – 🐟 15.90€
Pretty green spaces within the grounds of a leisure centre.

Surroundings :
Leisure activities :
Facilities : o— 🅴 🛎 launderette
Nearby : ✗ ✗

GPS Longitude : 7.44869
Latitude : 48.63691

WATTWILLER

68700 – Michelin map **315** H10 – pop. 1,734 – alt. 356
▶ Paris 478 – Strasbourg 116 – Freiburg-im-Breisgau 81 – Basel 56

Les Sources ♣♣

📞 03 89 75 44 94, *www.campinglessources.com*
Address : rte des Crêtes
Opening times : from beginning April to end Sept.
15 ha (200 pitches) terraced, stony, gravelled
Tariff : 31€ ✶✶ ⊕ 🅴 (6A) – Extra per person 7€
Rental rates : (from beginning April to end Oct.) – 80 🛏 – 20 🏠. Per night from 35 to 120 €
Per week from 210 to 840 € – Reservation fee 10€
sani-station 3€ – 5 🅴 14€ – 🐟 17€
Pleasant, wooded site, but infrastructure and sanitary facilities are getting old.

Surroundings :
Leisure activities : 🍷 ✗ 🏠 daytime 🎿 ✗ 🎱
Facilities : & o— 🛎 launderette 🚰
Nearby : 🐎

GPS Longitude : 7.16736
Latitude : 47.83675

WIHR-AU-VAL

68230 – Michelin map **315** H8 – pop. 1,237 – alt. 330
▶ Paris 463 – Colmar 14 – Gérardmer 38 – Guebwiller 35

⚠ La Route Verte

📞 03 89 71 10 10, *www.camping-routeverte.com*

Address : 13 r. de la Gare (take the southern exit along the D 43, follow the signs for Soultzbach-les-Bains)

1.2 ha (55 pitches) relatively flat, flat, grassy

🚐 sani-station – 5 ▣

Small but lovely family-orientated site in the heart of a charming village surrounded by vineyards.

Surroundings : 🦢 ♀
Leisure activities : 🏊
Facilities : ♿ ⚷ 🖥
Nearby : ♟ ✗

Longitude : 7.20513
Latitude : 48.05159

© Hachette Tourisme / Renaud / Rosebud

AQUITAINE

Romain Cintrat / hemis.fr

Welcome to Aquitaine, home to prehistoric remains, fortified towns and a mosaic of landscapes, as distinctive and welcoming as the hospitality and humour of its locals. A quick stop to buy *confit d'oie* (confit of goose) could lead to an invitation to look around the farm! Aquitaine has dense forests, imposing mountains and sweeping beaches; it is home to picturesque villages, bustling cities, large estates and imposing châteaux. No stay would be complete without visiting at least one of the renowned vineyards of Bordeaux. Then head to the 'Silver Coast', with its many surfers, rugby fans and bullfighters, all raised on *gâteau Basque*, a cake made with almond flour, and *piment d'Espelette*, a rather spicy pepper. This rugged, sunlit land between the Pyrenees and the Atlantic remains fiercely proud of its identity. Spend a little time in a sleepy Basque village and you will soon see proudly displayed the region's traditional colours of red, white and green.

AGEN

47000 – Michelin map **336** F4 – pop. 33,920 – alt. 50
▶ Paris 662 – Auch 74 – Bordeaux 141 – Pau 159

⚠ Le Moulin de Mellet

℘ 0553875089, *www.camping-moulin-mellet.com*
Address : loacated at St Hilaire de Lusignan, rte de Prayssas (head 8km northwest along the D 813 and take a right turn along the D 107)
5 ha/3.5 ha for camping (48 pitches) flat, grassy, stream, small lake
Rentals : ⚒ – 2 ⌕ – 2 ⌂.
⌕ 2 ▣

Surroundings : ♧♧
Leisure activities : ⌂ ⚓ ⤬ ⤓ ↝
Facilities : ⚹ ⊶ ⌂ ⑂ ▣

GPS Longitude : 0.54188
Latitude : 44.2436

For more information on visiting particular towns or regions, consult the relevant regional MICHELIN Green Guide. We also recommend you use the appropriate Michelin regional map to locate your selected campsite, to calculate distances and to work out the best route.

AINHOA

64250 – Michelin map **342** C3 – pop. 672 – alt. 130
▶ Paris 791 – Bayonne 28 – Biarritz 29 – Cambo-les-Bains 11

⚠ Xokoan

℘ 0559299026, *etchartenea@orange.fr*
Address : Dancharia quartier, south of the town (head 2.5km southwest then take the left turn before the customs post; beside a stream (border with Spain)
Opening times : permanent
0.6 ha (30 pitches) flat, relatively flat, grassy
Tariff : 17.50€ ⚹⚹ ⇔ ▣ ⑂ (10A) – Extra per person 5.50€
Rental rates : (permanent) – 2 ⌕ – 6 ⊨. Per night from 90 € – Per week from 360 to 420 €
⌕ sani-station 6€ – 6 ▣ 14.50€

Surroundings : ⩗ ♧♧
Leisure activities : ♈ ✗ ⌂
Facilities : ⚹ ⊶ ⚏ ⑂ launderette ⚲
Nearby : ⌸

GPS Longitude : -1.50369
Latitude : 43.29139

⚠ Aire Naturelle Harazpy

℘ 0559298938
Address : Gastelu-Gaïna quartier (to the northwest of the town, behind the church)
Opening times : from beginning April to end Sept.
1 ha (25 pitches) relatively flat, terrace, grassy
Tariff : 14.50€ ⚹⚹ ⇔ ▣ ⑂ (10A) – Extra per person 5.50€
⌕ sani-station 6€ – 10 ▣ 14.50€

Surroundings : ⩗ ⪌♧
Leisure activities : ⌂
Facilities : ⚹ ⊶ ⊟ launderette

GPS Longitude : -1.50172
Latitude : 43.3089

AIRE-SUR-L'ADOUR

40800 – Michelin map **335** J12 – pop. 6,275 – alt. 80
▶ Paris 722 – Auch 84 – Condom 68 – Dax 77

▲   Les Ombrages de l'Adour

℘ 05 58 71 75 10, *www.camping-adour-landes.com*
Address : r. des Graviers (located near the bridge, behind the arenas; beside the Adour river)
Opening times : from mid April to end Oct.
2 ha (100 pitches) flat, grassy
Tariff : (2012 price) 17.60€ ⁂ ⚏ ▣ ⅃ (10A) – Extra per person 3.80€
Rental rates : (2012 price) (from mid April to end Oct.) – 8 ⟐ – 2 tent bungalows.
Per night from 40 to 64 € – Per week from 195 to 385 €
⟐ sani-station – 10 ▣ 10.50€
Near the town centre.

Surroundings : ⋟ ⍨
Leisure activities : ⚓ ⚑
Facilities : ⊙ ⚐ launderette
Nearby : ⚓

Longitude : -0.25793
Latitude : 43.70257

ALLAS-LES-MINES

24220 – Michelin map **329** H6 – pop. 204 – alt. 85
▶ Paris 564 – Bordeaux 193 – Périgueux 61 – Cahors 83

⋀⋀   Domaine Le Cro-Magnon ⚏

℘ 05 53 29 13 70, *www.domaine-cro-magnon.com*
Address : at Le Raisse (access strongly recommended via Berbiguières on the D 50)
Opening times : from beginning May to mid Sept.
22 ha/6 ha for camping (160 pitches) flat, stony, grassy
Tariff : 30.90€ ⁂ ⚏ ▣ ⅃ (6A) – Extra per person 7.50€ – Reservation fee 19€
Rental rates : (from beginning May to mid Sept.) – 11 ⟐ – 22 ⟐.
Per night from 67 to 79 € Per week from 271 to 997 € – Reservation fee 25€
A natural wooded setting.

Surroundings : ⋟ ⟐ ⍨
Leisure activities : ⛊ ✕ ⚑ ⟐ ⚓ ⚲ ⚲ ⚑ ▣ ⚓ ⚓ multi-sports ground
Facilities : ⚒ ⊙ ⚑ ⚐ launderette ⚓ ⚓

Longitude : 1.06241
Latitude : 44.83621

ALLES-SUR-DORDOGNE

24480 – Michelin map **329** G6 – pop. 344 – alt. 70
▶ Paris 534 – Bergerac 36 – Le Bugue 12 – Les Eyzies-de-Tayac 22

⋀   Port de Limeuil

℘ 05 53 63 29 76, *www.leportdelimeuil.com*
Address : 3km northeast on the D 51e, near the bridge at Limeuil, where the Dordogne and the Vézère rivers meet
Opening times : from beginning May to end Sept.
7 ha/4 ha for camping (90 pitches) flat, grassy, sandy
Tariff : (2012 price) 31.30€ ⁂ ⚏ ▣ ⅃ (6A) – Extra per person 7€ – Reservation fee 13€
Rental rates : (2012 price) (from beginning May to end Sept.) – 13 ⟐ – 1 gîte.
Per night from 25 to 141 € – Per week from 175 to 990 € – Reservation fee 13€
⟐ sani-station – 9 ▣ 27.50€

Surroundings : ⋟ ⍨ ⚑
Leisure activities : ⛊ ⟐ ⚓ ⚲ ⚲ ⚓ ⚓
Facilities : ⚒ ⊙ ⚑ ⚓ ⚐ launderette ⚓ ⚓
Nearby : ✕ ⚓

Longitude : 0.88599
Latitude : 44.87969

ANGLET

64600 – Michelin map **342** C2 – pop. 37,661 – alt. 20
▶ Paris 773 – Bordeaux 187 – Pamplona 108 – Donostia-San Sebastián 51

 Le Parme

℘ 05 59 23 03 00, *www.campingdeparme.com*
Address : 2 allée Etchecopar
Opening times : from beginning April to beginning Nov.
3.5 ha (187 pitches) terraced, flat and relatively flat
Tariff : (2012 price) 36 € ♦♦ ⇌ ▤ ⚡ (10A) – Extra per person 6.50 € – Reservation fee 20 €
Rental rates : (2012 price) (permanent) – 53 ⬚ – 14 ⌂. Per night from 52 to 129 €
Per week from 364 to 903 € – Reservation fee 20 €

Surroundings : ⌧ ♤♤
Leisure activities : ♟ ✕ 🎮 ⛳ ✠ 🏄 🚲 ⛵ multi-sports ground
Facilities : ♿ ☛ ⌲ ⚑ launderette ⚏ ⚒

GPS
Longitude : -1.53238
Latitude : 43.4643

The information in the guide may have changed since going to press.

ANGOISSE

24270 – Michelin map **329** H3 – pop. 610 – alt. 345
▶ Paris 445 – Bordeaux 180 – Périgueux 51 – Limoges 53

 Rouffiac en Périgord

℘ 05 53 52 68 79, *www.semitour-locations-perigord.com* – traditional camp. spaces also available
Address : at the Roufflac leisure centre (4km southeast along the D 80, follow the signs for Payzac, 150m from a small lake (direct access)
Opening times : from end April to mid Sept.
54 ha/6 ha for camping (40 pitches) relatively flat, flat, grassy
Tariff : (2012 price) ♦ 5.20 € ⇌ ▤ 8 € ⚡ (16A)
Rental rates : (2012 price) (permanent) – 3 ⬚ – 22 ⌂. Per night from 75 to 140 €
Per week from 140 to 650 €
Organised cultural and sporting holidays based around the sailing centre.

Surroundings : ⋚ ⌧ ♤♤
Leisure activities : ♟ 🎮
Facilities : ♿ ☛ ㏄ ⚑ 📷
Nearby : 🚲 ⛷ 🏊 (beach) 🛶 🏇 forest trail, paintballing, climbing wall

GPS
Longitude : 1.16648
Latitude : 45.41449

ANTONNE-ET-TRIGONANT

24420 – Michelin map **329** F4 – pop. 1,203 – alt. 106
▶ Paris 484 – Bordeaux 139 – Périgueux 10 – Limoges 91

 Au Fil de l'Eau

℘ 05 53 06 17 88, *www.campingaufildeleau.com*
Address : in Antonne, 6 allées des Platanes (take the northeastern exit and follow the signs for Escoire to the right; beside the island, on the D 6)
Opening times : from mid April to mid Oct.
1.5 ha (50 pitches) open site, flat, grassy
Tariff : (2012 price) 17.50 € ♦♦ ⇌ ▤ ⚡ (6A) – Extra per person 4 €
Rental rates : (2012 price) (from mid April to mid Oct.) – 7 ⬚ – 4 tent bungalows.
Per night from 50 to 80 € – Per week from 200 to 550 €

Surroundings : ♤♤
Leisure activities : ✠ 🎣 🏊
Facilities : ♿ ☛ ⌲ ⚑ 📷

GPS
Longitude : 0.83754
Latitude : 45.213

ARAMITS

64570 – Michelin map **342** H4 – pop. 677 – alt. 293
▶ Paris 829 – Mauléon-Licharre 27 – Oloron-Ste-Marie 15 – Pau 49

Barétous-Pyrénées

℘ 0559341221, *www.camping-pyrenees.com*
Address : Ripaude quartier (take the western exit along the D 918, follow the signs for Mauléon-Licharre; beside the Vert de Barlanes (river)
Opening times : from mid Feb. to end Oct.
2 ha (61 pitches) flat, grassy
Tariff : (2012 price) 26.70€ ♥♥ ⇔ 圁 (6) (10A) – Extra per person 5.90€ – Reservation fee 13.50€
Rental rates : (2012 price) (from mid Dec. to end Oct.) ⑤ (chalet) – 10 ⟦.⟧ – 11 ☖ – 3 tent bungalows. Per night from 31 to 97 € – Per week from 220 to 680 € – Reservation fee 16.50€
Very comfortable wooden chalets (hotel service available on request).

Surroundings : ⚘ ⊏⊐ ♀♀
Leisure activities : ♀ ✕ ▭ ⊜ jacuzzi ⚒ ♨ ⟰
Facilities : ⑤ ⊶ ⟦cc⟧ ⟦⟧ ⟦⟧ launderette ⟰

Longitude : -0.73243
Latitude : 43.12135

There are several different types of sani-station ('borne' in French) – sanitation points providing fresh water and disposal points for grey water. See page 12 for further details.

ARES

33740 – Michelin map **335** E6 – pop. 5,548 – alt. 6
▶ Paris 627 – Arcachon 47 – Bordeaux 48

Les Goëlands

℘ 0556825564, *www.goelands.com*
Address : 64 av. de la Libération (1.7km southeast, near lakes and 500m from the quayside)
10 ha/6 ha for camping (400 pitches) flat, sandy
Rentals : 20 ⟦.⟧.

Surroundings : ⚘ ⊏⊐ ♀♀
Leisure activities : ♀ ✕ ⊝ ⚒ ⚒ ♨ ⟰ multi-sports ground
Facilities : ⑤ ⊶ ⟰ launderette ⟰ ⟰
Nearby : ≈ (lake) ⚘ ◊

Longitude : -1.11979
Latitude : 44.75747

Village Vacances Les Rives de St-Brice
(rental of maisonettes only)

℘ 0557269931, *www.nemea.fr*
Address : 61 r. Jean Briaud (1.7km southeast, near lakes and 450m from the quayside)
4 ha sandy
Rentals : ⑤ ℗ – 110 ☖.

Surroundings : ⚘ ♀♀
Leisure activities : ▭ ⚒ ♨ ⟰ ⟰
Facilities : ⊶ ⟰ ⟰ launderette ⟰
Nearby : ♀ ✕ ◊

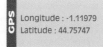
Longitude : -1.11899
Latitude : 44.75735

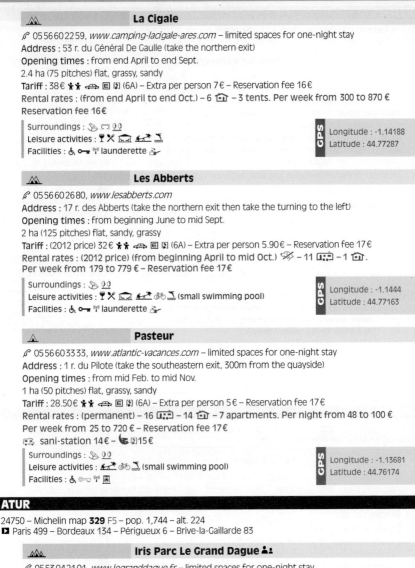

La Cigale

℘ 05 56 60 22 59, *www.camping-lacigale-ares.com* – limited spaces for one-night stay
Address : 53 r. du Général De Gaulle (take the northern exit)
Opening times : from end April to end Sept.
2.4 ha (75 pitches) flat, grassy, sandy
Tariff : 38 € ♦♦ ⇔ 🗐 ⑭ (6A) – Extra per person 7 € – Reservation fee 16 €
Rental rates : (from end April to end Oct.) – 6 🏠 – 3 tents. Per week from 300 to 870 €
Reservation fee 16 €

Surroundings : ⊗ 🗆 ⥀⥀
Leisure activities : 🍸✗ 🖼 ⛵ 🛶
Facilities : 🚿 ⊶ 🚰 launderette 🛒

GPS Longitude : -1.14188
Latitude : 44.77287

Les Abberts

℘ 05 56 60 26 80, *www.lesabberts.com*
Address : 17 r. des Abberts (take the northern exit then take the turning to the left)
Opening times : from beginning June to mid Sept.
2 ha (125 pitches) flat, sandy, grassy
Tariff : (2012 price) 32 € ♦♦ ⇔ 🗐 ⑭ (6A) – Extra per person 5.90 € – Reservation fee 17 €
Rental rates : (2012 price) (from beginning April to mid Oct.) ⌇ – 11 🚐 – 1 🏠.
Per week from 179 to 779 € – Reservation fee 17 €

Surroundings : ⊗ ⥀⥀
Leisure activities : 🍸✗ 🖼 ⛵ 🚲 🛶 (small swimming pool)
Facilities : 🚿 ⊶ 🚰 launderette 🛒

GPS Longitude : -1.1444
Latitude : 44.77163

Pasteur

℘ 05 56 60 33 33, *www.atlantic-vacances.com* – limited spaces for one-night stay
Address : 1 r. du Pilote (take the southeastern exit, 300m from the quayside)
Opening times : from mid Feb. to mid Nov.
1 ha (50 pitches) flat, grassy, sandy
Tariff : 28.50 € ♦♦ ⇔ 🗐 ⑭ (6A) – Extra per person 5 € – Reservation fee 17 €
Rental rates : (permanent) – 16 🚐 – 14 🏠 – 7 apartments. Per night from 48 to 100 €
Per week from 25 to 720 € – Reservation fee 17 €
🚏 sani-station 14 € – 🚰⑭15 €

Surroundings : ⊗ ⥀⥀
Leisure activities : ⛵ 🚲 🛶 (small swimming pool)
Facilities : 🚿 ⊶ 🚰 🖼

GPS Longitude : -1.13681
Latitude : 44.76174

ATUR

24750 – Michelin map **329** F5 – pop. 1,744 – alt. 224
▶ Paris 499 – Bordeaux 134 – Périgueux 6 – Brive-la-Gaillarde 83

Iris Parc Le Grand Dague 🏊

℘ 05 53 04 21 01, *www.legranddague.fr* – limited spaces for one-night stay
Address : rte du Grand Dague (3km southeast following signs for St-Laurent-sur-Manoire – if on southern diversion coming from Brive or Limoges, take the road towards Bergerac and then the road to the right)
Opening times : from beginning May to end Sept.
22 ha/12 ha for camping (382 pitches) terraced, flat, grassy
Tariff : (2012 price) 35 € ♦♦ ⇔ 🗐 ⑭ (10A) – Extra per person 7.50 € – Reservation fee 20 €
Rental rates : (2012 price) (from beginning May to end Sept.) 🚿 ⌇ Ⓟ – 260 🚐 – 80 tents.
Per night from 2 to 47 € – Per week from 154 to 973 € – Reservation fee 20 €
Well-equipped indoor children's play area.

Surroundings : ⊗ 🗆 ⥀⥀
Leisure activities : 🍸✗ 🖼 🎱 🏌 ⛵ 🎯 🛶 🏊 paintballing
Facilities : 🚿 ⊶ 🆒 🍽 ⛱ 🚰 launderette 🛁 🛒

GPS Longitude : 0.77656
Latitude : 45.14816

AUREILHAN

40200 – Michelin map **335** D9 – pop. 935 – alt. 10
▶ Paris 689 – Bordeaux 103 – Mont-de-Marsan 79 – La Teste 59

Village Center Aurilandes ♣♣

℘ 0825002030, *www.village-center.fr*
Address : located 1km to the northeast, near the lake
Opening times : from mid April to mid Sept.
6 ha (440 pitches) flat, sandy, grassy
Tariff : (2012 price) 25€ ♦♦ ⇔ 🔲 ⚡ (16A) – Extra per person 6€
Rental rates : (2012 price) (permanent) – 50 📠 – 30 mobile homes (without sanitary facilities). Per night from 22 to 86 € – Per week from 154 to 890 €

Surroundings : 🔋 🎿⚘
Leisure activities : 🎭 ⓖ 🕺 🎣 🛶 jacuzzi 🚣 🚲 🎱 🏹 multi-sports ground
Facilities : ♿ ⚘ ⓒ🛁🍽 launderette 🚰🛒
Nearby : 🐎 ⚓

GPS Longitude : -1.20314
Latitude : 44.22306

We value your opinion and welcome your feedback.
Do email us at campingfrance@tp.michelin.com

AZUR

40140 – Michelin map **335** D12 – pop. 575 – alt. 9
▶ Paris 730 – Bayonne 54 – Dax 25 – Mimizan 79

FranceLoc La Paillotte ♣♣

℘ 0558481212, *www.paillotte.com* 🚫
Address : 66 rte des Campings (located 1.5km southwest; beside the Lac de Soustons)
Opening times : from beginning May to end Sept.
7 ha (310 pitches) flat, sandy, grassy
Tariff : (2012 price) 39€ ♦♦ ⇔ 🔲 ⚡ (10A) – Extra per person 7.50€ – Reservation fee 22€
Rental rates : (2012 price) (from beginning May to end Sept.) 🚫 – 205 📠 – 50 🏠.
Per night from 51 to 191 € – Per week from 182 to 1,337 € – Reservation fee 22€
Exotically decorated, attractive chalet village and a large water park beside the lake.

Surroundings : 🔋 ❮ 🛏 🎿⚘
Leisure activities : 🍴✗ 🎭 ⓖ 🕺 🚣 🔳 🎱 🏹 pedalos 🚴
Facilities : ♿ ⚘ 🛁🛒🍽 launderette 🚰🛒
Nearby : 🚲🎾 ⛸ 🚣 pedalos

GPS Longitude : -1.30875
Latitude : 43.78731

Azur Rivage

℘ 0558483072, *www.campingazurivage.com*
Address : 720 rte des Campings (situated 2km to the south, 100m from the lake at Soustons)
Opening times : from mid June to mid Sept.
6.5 ha (250 pitches) flat, sandy, stony, grassy
Tariff : (2012 price) 31.50€ ♦♦ ⇔ 🔲 ⚡ (16A) – Extra per person 7.10€ – Reservation fee 17€
Rental rates : (2012 price) (from beginning April to mid Sept.) 🚫 – 60 📠.
Per night from 38 to 75 € – Per week from 266 to 995 € – Reservation fee 17€
🚉 sani-station

Surroundings : 🔋 🎿
Leisure activities : 🚣 🎱 🏹 multi-sports ground
Facilities : ♿ ⚘ (Jul-Aug) 🛁🛒🍽 🖥 🚰🛒 refrigerated food storage
Nearby : 🚲🎾 ⛸ 🛶 pedalos

GPS Longitude : -1.23047
Latitude : 43.78477

41

BADEFOLS-SUR-DORDOGNE

24150 – Michelin map **329** F6 – pop. 211 – alt. 42
▶ Paris 542 – Bergerac 27 – Périgueux 54 – Sarlat-la-Canéda 47

⋀⋀⋀⋀ Club Airotel Les Bö Bains

℘ 05 53 73 52 52, *www.bo-bains.com* – limited spaces for one-night stay
Address : rte de Bergerac (take the western exit, along the D 29; beside the Dordogne)
Opening times : from beginning April to end Sept.
5 ha (97 pitches) terraced, flat, grassy
Tariff : 13 € ♣ ♣ ⇌ 🔲 (10A) – Extra per person 3 €
Rental rates : (from beginning April to end Sept.) ⅃ – 49 ⎕⚏ – 35 🏠.
Per night from 45 to 145 € Per week from 25 to 1,000 €

Surroundings : ← ⊏⊐ ♤♤	
Leisure activities : 🍴 ✗ 🖼 ⊙evening ⸚⸚ 🏓 ⚡ ᖴᖮ ᒧ ⚐ ≈	**GPS** Longitude : 0.78541
Facilities : ⅃ ⊶ ⚆ ᗺ ᵗᵗ launderette 🚿	Latitude : 44.84155
Nearby : ✗	

*The Michelin classification (⋀⋀⋀⋀ … ⋀) is totally independent of the
official star classification system awarded by the local prefecture or
other official organisation.*

LA BASTIDE-CLAIRENCE

64240 – Michelin map **342** E4 – pop. 984 – alt. 50
▶ Paris 767 – Bayonne 26 – Hasparren 9 – Peyrehorade 29

⋀⋀⋀ Village Vacances Les Collines Iduki
(rental of apartments and maisonettes only)

℘ 05 59 70 20 81, *www.location-vacances-paysbasque.com*
Address : at Pont de Port
Opening times : permanent
2.5 ha terraced
Rental rates : ⅃ (1 apartment) – 6 🏠 – 30 apartments. Per night from 64 to 184 €
Per week from 89 to 1,901 €
Pretty Basque buildings.

Surroundings : ⊛ ← ♤♤	
Leisure activities : ✗ 🖼 ⚡ ᒧ	**GPS** Longitude : -1.25742
Facilities : ⅃ ⊶ ⓟ ᵗᵗ launderette	Latitude : 43.43324
Nearby : ✗	

⋀ Village Vacances Les Chalets de Pierretoun
(rental of chalets only)

℘ 05 59 29 68 88, *www.chalets-de-pierretoun.com*
Address : at Pessarou (located 7km southeast along the D 123)
Opening times : from beginning May to end Sept.
5 ha terraced, extremely uneven
Rental rates : (2012 price) – 16 🏠. Per night from 145 to 220 € – Per week from 500 to 920 €
Choose the renovated chalets if possible.

Surroundings : ⊛ ← ♤♤	
Leisure activities : 🖼 ᒧ donkey rides	**GPS** Longitude : -1.20944
Facilities : ⊶ ⛏ 🆑 ᵗᵗ 🔲 🚿	Latitude : 43.4108

BAUDREIX

64800 – Michelin map **342** K3 – pop. 537 – alt. 245 – Leisure centre
▶ Paris 791 – Argelès-Gazost 39 – Lourdes 26 – Oloron-Ste-Marie 48

Les Ôkiri

📞 05 59 92 97 73, *www.lesokiri.com* ✂ (Jul–Aug)
Address : av. du Lac (At the leisure and activity park)
Opening times : from beginning April to end Sept.
20 ha/2 ha for camping (60 pitches) flat, grassy
Tariff : 26.27 € ♥ ♥ 🚗 🔲 (½) (10A) – Extra per person 7.10 € – Reservation fee 10 €
Rental rates : (permanent) ✂ 🅿 – 10 🚐 – 24 🏠 – 5 tent bungalows.
Per night from 50 to 92 € Per week from 295 to 705 € – Reservation fee 10 €

Surroundings : 🏊 ⌷ ♡♡ ⛰
Leisure activities : 🍹 ✗ 🛶 🚴 ≋ (beach) ⛱ 🎣 pedalos, climbing wall,
fitness trail, cable wakeboarding 🛥
Facilities : 👩‍🦽 ⊶ (Jul–Aug) 📷 🍴 launderette 🚿

GPS Longitude : -0.26124
Latitude : 43.20439

BEAUVILLE

47470 – Michelin map **336** H4 – pop. 584 – alt. 208
▶ Paris 641 – Agen 26 – Moissac 32 – Montaigu-de-Quercy 16

Les 2 Lacs

📞 05 53 95 45 41, *www.les2lacs.info*
Address : at Vallon de Gerbal (900m southeast along the D 122, follow the signs for Bourg de Visa)
Opening times : from beginning April to end Oct.
22 ha/2.5 ha for camping (80 pitches) open site, flat, terrace, grassy
Tariff : ♥ 5 € 🚗 🔲 9 € – (½) (6A) 2.80 €
Rental rates : (from beginning April to end Oct.) – 3 🚐 – 7 tent bungalows.
Per night from 25 to 70 € – Per week from 160 to 630 €

Snack-bar terrace beside lake.

Surroundings : 🏊 ⌷ ♡♡
Leisure activities : 🍹 ✗ 🛶 ✂ ≋ 🎣 boats for hire 🛥
Facilities : 👩‍🦽 ⊶ 🍴 launderette

GPS Longitude : 0.88819
Latitude : 44.27142

This guide is updated regularly, so buy your new copy every year!

BÉLUS

40300 – Michelin map **335** E13 – pop. 605 – alt. 135
▶ Paris 749 – Bayonne 37 – Dax 18 – Orthez 36

La Comtesse

📞 05 58 57 69 07, *www.campinglacomtesse.com*
Address : at Claquin (2.5km northwest along the D 75 and take turning to the right)
Opening times : permanent
6 ha (115 pitches) flat, grassy
Tariff : (2012 price) ♥ 3.20 € 🚗 1.50 € 🔲 5.20 € – (½) (10A) 3.10 € – Reservation fee 10 €
Rental rates : (2012 price) (permanent) – 26 🚐 – 2 tent bungalows.
Per week from 180 to 725 € – Reservation fee 10 €

A pleasant grove of poplar trees beside a lake.

Surroundings : 🏊 ⌷ ♡♡
Leisure activities : 🍹 ✗ 🏠 ⛹ ✂ 🎿 ⛱ 🎣
Facilities : 👩‍🦽 ⊶ 🛖 🍴 launderette 🚿

GPS Longitude : -1.13075
Latitude : 43.60364

43

BELVÈS

24170 – Michelin map **329** H7 – pop. 1,432 – alt. 175
▶ Paris 553 – Bergerac 52 – Le Bugue 24 – Les Eyzies-de-Tayac 25

FranceLoc Les Hauts de Ratebout ♣♨

✆ 05 53 29 02 10, *www.camping-hauts-ratebout.fr* ✇

Address : at Ste-Foy-de-Belves: Ratebout (7km southeast along the D 710, follow the signs for Fumel, D 54 and take turning to the left)

Opening times : from end April to mid Sept.

12 ha/6 ha for camping (200 pitches) terraced, flat and relatively flat, grassy

Tariff : (2012 price) 42 € ♣♣ ⇌ 🔲 (½) (10A) – Extra per person 5 € – Reservation fee 27 €

Rental rates : (2012 price) (from end April to mid Sept.) ✇ – 4 caravans – 153 🛏 – 8 tents – 5 gîtes. Per night from 39 to 158 € c Per week from 154 to 1,176 € – Reservation fee 27 €

A pretty, renovated Périgord farmhouse with a very good children's play area.

Surroundings : 🏞 ≤ ♨♨
Leisure activities : ♈ ✕ 🎬 🎲 ⛹ 🏊 ✇ ♫ 🎿 🎱 ♨
Facilities : ♿ ⊶ 🏕 🍽 🚿 ♒ ☂ launderette 🚮 🔧

| | Longitude : 1.04529 |
| GPS | Latitude : 44.74151 |

RCN Le Moulin de la Pique ♣♨

✆ 05 53 29 01 15, *www.rcn.fr*

Address : at Moulin de la Pique (3km southeast along the D 710, follow the signs for Fumel; near the Nauze river, a lake and a milllake)

Opening times : from mid April to end Sept.

15 ha/6 ha for camping (200 pitches) terrace, flat, grassy

Tariff : 49 € ♣♣ ⇌ 🔲 (½) (6A) – Extra per person 5.50 € – Reservation fee 19.50 €

Rental rates : (from mid April to end Sept.) – 51 🛏 – 3 apartments. Per night 167 €

Per week 1,169 € – Reservation fee 19.50 €

🚮 sani-station 16 €

Based near a pretty 18th-century mill and its outbuildings.

Surroundings : 🏕 ♨♨
Leisure activities : ♈ ✕ 🎬 🎲 ⛹ 🏊 🚲 ✇ ♫ 🎱 ♨ 🎣
Facilities : ♿ ⊶ 🏧 🏕 🍽 🚿 ☂ launderette 🔧

| | Longitude : 1.01371 |
| GPS | Latitude : 44.7305 |

Flower Les Nauves ♣♨

✆ 05 53 29 12 64, *www.lesnauves.com*

Address : at Le Bos Rouge (4.5km southwest along the D 53, follow the signs for Monpazier and turn left following the signs for Larzac)

Opening times : from beginning April to end Sept.

40 ha/5 ha for camping (100 pitches) sloping, relatively flat, grassy

Tariff : 15.50 € ♣♣ ⇌ 🔲 (½) (10A) – Extra per person 3 € – Reservation fee 15 €

Rental rates : (from beginning April to beginning Nov.) – 30 🛏 – 3 🏠 – 3 tent bungalows. Per night from 30 to 113 € – Per week from 210 to 791 € – Reservation fee 15 €

🚮 ⛽ (½) 14 €

Surroundings : 🏞 🏕 ♨♨
Leisure activities : ♈ ✕ 🎬 ⛹ 🏊 🎱
Facilities : ♿ ⊶ 🚿 ☂ 🔲 🔧
Nearby : 🏇

| | Longitude : 0.98184 |
| GPS | Latitude : 44.75497 |

Some information or pricing may have changed since the guide went to press. We recommend you check the price list online in advance or at the entrance to the campsite and enquire about possible restrictions.

BEYNAC-ET-CAZENAC

24220 – Michelin map **329** H6 – pop. 522 – alt. 75
▶ Paris 537 – Bergerac 62 – Brive-la-Gaillade 63 – Fumel 60

⚠ Le Capeyrou

⌀ 05 53 29 54 95, *www.campinglecapeyrou.com* – **FR**
Address : rte de Sarlat (take the eastern exit, along the D 57; beside the Dordogne river)
Opening times : from end April to end Sept.
4.5 ha (120 pitches) flat, grassy
Tariff : (2012 price) ✝ 6.20€ ⇌ 回 9.90€ – (4) (10A) 4.20€
Rental rates : (2012 price) (from end April to end Sept.) – 2 tents.
Per night from 35 to 55€ – Per week from 195 to 650 € – Reservation fee 10€
🚐 sani-station 6€

Surroundings : ≤ Château de Beynac 👭
Leisure activities : ⛲ 🏛 🏊 🎣 ≈ 🐾
Facilities : ⅋ ⚬ 🔖 ⑤ ⚐ 🗘 ⁞ launderette
Nearby : 🛒 ✕ 🏇 🎾

GPS
Longitude : 1.14843
Latitude : 44.83828

BIARRITZ

64200 – Michelin map **342** C4 – pop. 25,397 – alt. 19
▶ Paris 772 – Bayonne 9 – Bordeaux 190 – Pau 122

⚠ Club Airotel Biarritz-Camping

⌀ 05 59 23 00 12, *www.biarritz.camping.fr*
Address : 28 r. Harcet
Opening times : from beginning April to end Sept.
3 ha (190 pitches) terraced, sloping, flat, grassy
Tariff : (2012 price) 36€ ✝✝ ⇌ 回 (4) (10A) – Extra per person 6€ – Reservation fee 15€
Rental rates : (2012 price) (from beginning April to end Sept.) 📺 – 72 🛏 – 14 tent
bungalows. Per night from 45 to 70 € – Per week from 300 to 865 € – Reservation fee 15€
300m from the Maritime Museum and 700m from the beach.

Surroundings : 👭
Leisure activities : ⛲ ✕ jacuzzi 🏊 🏊
Facilities : ⅋ ⚬ ⑤ ⁞ launderette 🖥 🗘
Nearby : 🏇

GPS
Longitude : -1.56685
Latitude : 43.46199

BIAS

40170 – Michelin map **335** D10 – pop. 736 – alt. 41
▶ Paris 706 – Castets 33 – Mimizan 7 – Morcenx 30

⚠ Municipal Le Tatiou

⌀ 05 58 09 04 76, *www.campingletatiou.com*
Address : rte de Lespecier (situated 2km west)
Opening times : from beginning April to end Sept.
10 ha (501 pitches) flat, sandy, grassy
Tariff : (2012 price) ✝ 5.50€ ⇌ 回 6.10€ – (4) (10A) 5.50€ – Reservation fee 20€
Rental rates : (2012 price) (from beginning April to end Sept.) – 152 🛏.
Per week from 400 to 650 € – Reservation fee 20€

Surroundings : 🌊 👭
Leisure activities : ⛲ ✕ 🏛 🏊 🚲 🎾 ⛵ 🏊
Facilities : ⅋ ⚬ 🔖 ⑤ ⁞ launderette 🖥 🗘 refrigerated food
storage

GPS
Longitude : -1.24029
Latitude : 44.14531

BIDART

64210 – Michelin map **342** C2 – pop. 6,117 – alt. 40
▶ Paris 783 – Bordeaux 196 – Pau 119 – Bayonne 13

Les Castels Le Ruisseau des Pyrénées ♣♣
(rental of mobile homes, chalets and tent bungalows only)

𝒫 0559419450, *www.camping-le-ruisseau.fr* – traditional camp. spaces also available
Address : r. Burruntz (situated 2km east; beside the Ouhabia river and a stream – in two separate areas)
Opening times : from end April to end Sept.
15 ha/7 ha for camping (440 pitches) terraced, flat, grassy
Rental rates : 150 🚐 – 7 🏠 – 4 tent bungalows. Per night from 40 to 180 €
Per week from 80 to 1,290 €
🚽 sani-station
Pretty water parks. Ample pitches for owner-occupiers and tour operators.

Surroundings : 🏕 ♨♨
Leisure activities : 🍷 ✗ 🎱 ⊙ ☆☆ 🎣 ⊜s jacuzzi 🏊 ⮳ ⛳ 🎾 ᵐ 🔲 🛝
🏊 🎣 fitness trail
Facilities : ♿ ⊶ 🅒♨ ᵗᵗ launderette 🗑 ⟿
Nearby : 🐎 🚴

Longitude : -1.56835
Latitude : 43.43704

Yelloh! Village Ilbarritz ♣♣

𝒫 0559230029, *www.camping-ilbarritz.com*
Address : av. de Biarritz (situated 2km to the north)
Opening times : from mid March to mid Nov.
6 ha (400 pitches) terraced, relatively flat, grassy, sandy
Tariff : 45€ 🏕🏕 ⮰ 🅔 💧 (10A) – Extra per person 9€
Rental rates : (from mid March to mid Nov.) – 115 🚐 – 58 🏠. Per week from 310 to 1,465 €
Beautiful and spacious entrance with pretty buildings in the Basque style.

Surroundings : 🏕 ♨♨
Leisure activities : 🍷 ✗ 🎱 ⊙ ☆☆ jacuzzi 🏊 🔲 🛝 🏊 surfing
multi-sports ground
Facilities : ♿ ⊶ ♨ ᵗᵗ launderette 🗑 ⟿ refrigerated food storage
Nearby : ᵐ disco

Longitude : -1.57374
Latitude : 43.45315

Sunêlia Berrua ♣♣

𝒫 0559549666, *www.berrua.com*
Address : r. Berrua (500m east, follow the signs for Arbonne)
Opening times : from end March to end Sept.
5 ha (270 pitches) relatively flat, terraced, grassy
Tariff : 43.50€ 🏕🏕 ⮰ 🅔 💧 (6A) – Extra per person 7.60€ – Reservation fee 35€
Rental rates : (from end March to end Sept.) – 144 🚐 – 10 🏠 – 2 tent bungalows.
Per night from 42 to 121 € – Per week from 290 to 1,505 € – Reservation fee 35€
🚽 sani-station
Well-maintained site, with lots of flowers and some very luxurious rental options.

Surroundings : 🏕 ♨♨
Leisure activities : 🍷 ✗ 🎱 ⊙ ☆☆ hammam 🏊 ⮳ 🎾 🔲 🛝
multi-sports ground
Facilities : ♿ ⊶ 🅒♨ ᵗᵗ launderette 🗑 ⟿
Nearby : surfing

Longitude : -1.58176
Latitude : 43.43824

Club Airotel Oyam

𝒫 0559549161, *www.camping-oyam.com*

Address : Chemin Oyhamburua (located 1km east along the follow the signs for Arbonne then take the turning to the right)

Opening times : from mid April to end Sept.

7 ha (350 pitches) flat and relatively flat, terrace, grassy

Tariff : (2012 price) 37.50€ ♣♣ ⇌ 🔲 ᚹ (6A) – Extra per person 6.50€ – Reservation fee 20€

Rental rates : (2012 price) (from mid April to end Sept.) – 84 🏠 – 18 🏠 – 14 apartments – 3 teepees – 8 tent bungalows – 30 tents. Per night from 41 to 59 € – Per week from 203 to 868 € – Reservation fee 20€

🚉 sani-station 10€ – 11 🔲 20€

Surroundings : 🏕 ⚲⚲
Leisure activities : 🍴 ✗ 🏠 🏃 🛶 ⊥ multi-sports ground
Facilities : & ⊶ 🛁 ᵞ launderette ♨

Longitude : -1.58278
Latitude : 43.43501

Ur-Onea

𝒫 0559265361, *www.uronea.com*

Address : r. de la Chapelle (300m east, 500m from the beach)

Opening times : from mid April to end Sept.

5 ha (280 pitches) relatively flat, terraced, grassy, sandy

Tariff : 34.50€ ♣♣ ⇌ 🔲 ᚹ (10A) – Extra per person 7€ – Reservation fee 27€

Rental rates : (from end March to end Sept.) ⚡ – 51 🏠 – 5 🏠.

Per night from 35 to 115 € – Per week from 45 to 805 € – Reservation fee 37€

Surroundings : ⚲⚲
Leisure activities : 🍴 ✗ 🏠 🛶 ⊥
Facilities : & ⊙ 🏕 🚿 ᵞ launderette ♨ refrigerated food storage

Longitude : -1.59035
Latitude : 43.43416

Pavillon Royal

𝒫 0559230054, *www.pavillon-royal.com* ⚡

Address : av. du Prince de Galles (situated 2km to the north; beside the beach)

Opening times : from mid May to end Sept.

5 ha (303 pitches) flat, terraced, sandy

Tariff : 56€ ♣♣ ⇌ 🔲 ᚹ (5A) – Extra per person 13€ – Reservation fee 25€

Rental rates : (from mid May to end Sept.) ⚡ – 3 🏠. Per week from 473 to 1,085 €
Reservation fee 25€

Secluded location near a golf course, château and the ocean.

Surroundings : 🏞 ≼ 🏕 ⚲ ⚠
Leisure activities : 🍴 ✗ 🏠 🏌 🛶 ⊥ beauty treatments, massages, surfing
Facilities : & ⊶ 🅿 🛁 🏕 🚿 ᵞ launderette 🍺 ♨
Nearby : 🎵 disco

Longitude : -1.57642
Latitude : 43.45469

Flower Harrobia

𝒫 0559265471, *www.harrobia.fr*

Address : Maurice Pierre quartier (1.2km to the south, 400m from the beach)

Opening times : from beginning March to end Nov.

3 ha (200 pitches) terraced, grassy

Tariff : (2012 price) 38€ ♣♣ ⇌ 🔲 ᚹ (10A) – Extra per person 7.50€ – Reservation fee 25€

Rental rates : (2012 price) (from beginning March to end Nov.) – 135 🏠 – 2 🏠 – 5 apartments. Per night from 49 to 135 – Per week from 196 to 950 – Reservation fee 25€

🚉 sani-station

Surroundings : 🏕 ⚲⚲
Leisure activities : 🍴 🏠 🛶 ⊥
Facilities : & ⊶ 🛁 ᵞ 🔲

Longitude : -1.59903
Latitude : 43.42773

BIGANOS

33380 – Michelin map **335** F7 – pop. 9,464 – alt. 16
▶ Paris 629 – Andernos-les-Bains 15 – Arcachon 27 – Bordeaux 47

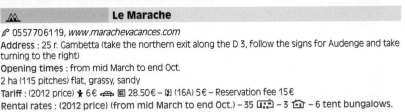

Le Marache

✆ 05 57 70 61 19, *www.marachevacances.com*
Address : 25 r. Gambetta (take the northern exit along the D 3, follow the signs for Audenge and take turning to the right)
Opening times : from mid March to end Oct.
2 ha (115 pitches) flat, grassy, sandy
Tariff : (2012 price) ♣ 6€ ⇔ 📧 28.50€ – ⚡ (16A) 5€ – Reservation fee 15€
Rental rates : (2012 price) (from mid March to end Oct.) – 35 🚐 – 3 🏠 – 6 tent bungalows.
Per week from 180 to 805 € – Reservation fee 20€
🚰 sani-station 6€

Surroundings : 🛞 ᴑᴑ
Leisure activities : 🍷 ✗ 🎱 ⤴ multi-sports ground
Facilities : 🚿 ⚱ 🍴 📧 ⤴

GPS Longitude : -0.97943
Latitude : 44.65081

*The prices listed were supplied by the campsite owners in 2012
(if prices were not available, those from the previous year are given).
The fees should be regarded as basic charges and may fluctuate
with inflation.*

BIRON

24540 – Michelin map **329** G8 – pop. 182 – alt. 200
▶ Paris 583 – Beaumont 25 – Bergerac 46 – Fumel 20

FranceLoc Le Moulinal 👥

✆ 05 53 40 84 60, *www.campings-franceloc.fr* – limited spaces for one-night stay
Address : at Étang du Moulinal (4km to the south, follow the signs for Lacapelle-Biron then continue 2km following signs for Villeréal to the right)
Opening times : from beginning April to mid Sept.
10 ha/5 ha for camping (300 pitches) terraced, flat, grassy
Tariff : (2012 price) 19€ ♣♣ ⇔ 📧 ⚡ (10A) – Extra per person 7€ – Reservation fee 27€
Rental rates : (2012 price) (from beginning April to mid Sept.) – 260 🚐 – 10 🏠.
Per night from 44 to 107 € – Per week from 175 to 1,358 € – Reservation fee 27€
Pleasant location beside a lake; lush foliage.

Surroundings : 🛞 ← 🛞 ᴑᴑ
Leisure activities : 🍷 ✗ 🎱 ⚱ ⚶ ⛵ 🚴 ✗ ♁ 🏊 ⤴ ⛱ (beach) ⛷
🏄 🛶 multi-sports ground, entertainment room
Facilities : 🚿 ⚱ 🍴 ⚶ 🛁 launderette 🛞 ⤴

GPS Longitude : 0.87116
Latitude : 44.60031

Village Vacances Castelwood
(rental of chalets) only)

✆ 05 53 57 96 08, *www.castelwood.fr*
Address : at Bois du Château-Les Fargues (located 1km south along the D 53, follow the signs for Lacapelle-Biron)
1 ha terraced, relatively flat, wood
Rentals : 🚿 (1 chalet) – 15 🏠.
Luxury chalets nestling in the Périgord pourpre (purple) forest.

Surroundings : 🛞 🌳
Leisure activities : ⤴
Facilities : ⚱ 🍴 📧

GPS Longitude : 0.87701
Latitude : 44.62495

BISCARROSSE

40600 – Michelin map **335** E8 – pop. 12,163 – alt. 22
▶ Paris 656 – Arcachon 40 – Bayonne 128 – Bordeaux 74

Club Airotel Domaine de la Rive ♣♣

℘ 0558781233, *www.larive.fr*

Address : rte de Bordeaux (8km northeast along the D 652, follow the signs for Sanguinet, then continue 2.2km along the turning to the left, beside the Étang de Cazaux (lake)
Opening times : from beginning April to beginning Sept.
15 ha (800 pitches) flat, sandy, grassy
Tariff : 51€ ♣♣ ⇔ ▣ 🅷 (10A) – Extra per person 10€ – Reservation fee 30€
Rental rates : (from beginning April to beginning Sept.) ♿ 🚿 – 310 🚐 – 34 🏠.
Per night from 71 to 299 € – Per week from 527 to 2,123 € – Reservation fee 30€
🚰 sani-station
Pretty swimming area, partially covered.

Surroundings : 🏊 ⛵ 🎣 ⛲
Leisure activities : 🍴 ✗ 🎠 ⛳ 🏕 🏌 🛶 hammam, jacuzzi ⛵ 🚴 🏓
🏊 📺 🎿 ⛵ (beach) ⛷ 🏹 🚣 water skiing, multi-sports ground, spa therapy centre, entertainment room, skate park
Facilities : 🚿 ⚡ 🆑 🚿 🚰 🚐 🍴 launderette 🛒 🥖 refrigerated food storage

GPS
Longitude : -1.1299
Latitude : 44.46022

Mayotte Vacances ♣♣

℘ 0558780000, *www.mayottevacances.com*

Address : 368 chemin des Roseaux (6km north following signs for Sanguinet then turn left at Goubern and continue for 2.5km; 150m from the Étang de Cazaux (lake, direct access)
Opening times : from beginning April to end Sept.
15 ha (709 pitches) flat, sandy, grassy
Tariff : 50€ ♣♣ ⇔ ▣ 🅷 (16A) – Extra per person 9€ – Reservation fee 30€
Rental rates : (from beginning April to end Sept.) – 256 🚐. Per night from 46 to 107 €
Per week from 322 to 2,009 € – Reservation fee 30€

Surroundings : 🏊 🚗 🎣 ⛲
Leisure activities : 🍴 ✗ 🎠 ⛳ 🏕 🏌 🛶 hammam, jacuzzi ⛵ 🚴 🏓
📺 🎿 ⛷ 🏹 🚣 fitness trail, kite-surfing, multi-sports ground, spa therapy centre, entertainment room
Facilities : 🚿 ⚡ 🚿 🚰 🚐 🍴 launderette 🛒 🥖 refrigerated food storage

GPS
Longitude : -1.1538
Latitude : 44.43488

Les Écureuils ♣♣

℘ 0558098000, *www.ecureuils.fr* – limited spaces for one-night stay
Address : 646 chemin de Navarrosse (4.2km north following signs for Sanguinet and turn left towards Navarrosse; 400m from the Étang de Cazaux (lake)
Opening times : from beginning April to end Sept.
6 ha (183 pitches) flat, grassy, sandy
Tariff : (2012 price) 47€ ♣♣ ⇔ ▣ 🅷 (10A) – Extra per person 8€ – Reservation fee 32€
Rental rates : (2012 price) (from beginning April to end Sept.) 🚿 – 3 🚐 – 2 🏠.
Per week from 350 to 950 € – Reservation fee 32€
🚰 sani-station 3€
Pretty shrubs and flowers.

Surroundings : 🚗 🎣
Leisure activities : 🍴 ✗ 🎠 🏕 jacuzzi ⛵ 🚴 🏓 🏌 🎿 ⛵ (beach) 🎯
Facilities : 🚿 ⚡ 🚿 🍴 launderette 🚿 🥖
Nearby : 🛒 🚣 🚣

GPS
Longitude : -1.16765
Latitude : 44.42947

Bimbo

☎ 05 58 09 82 33, *www.campingbimbo.fr* – limited spaces for one-night stay

Address : 176 chemin de Bimbo (3.5km north following signs for Sanguinet and turn left towards Navarrosse)

Opening times : from beginning April to end Sept.

6 ha (177 pitches) flat, sandy, grassy

Tariff : 43.50€ ✦✦ ⇔ ▣ ⒢ (6A) – Extra per person 8.50€ – Reservation fee 25€

Rental rates : (from end March to mid Nov.) – 32 ⟨...⟩ – 12 ⌂ – 5 tent bungalows.
Per night from 35 to 94 € – Per week from 182 to 1,235 € – Reservation fee 25€

Surroundings : ⟨...⟩
Leisure activities : ⟨...⟩ multi-sports ground
Facilities : ⟨...⟩ launderette ⟨...⟩ refrigerated food storage
Nearby : ⟨...⟩

GPS Longitude : -1.16137
Latitude : 44.42588

Village Vacances La Fontaine de Nava
(rental of mobile homes only)

☎ 05 58 09 83 11, *www.lesfontainesdenava.com*

Address : chemin de Bimbo, at Navarrosse (3.5km north following signs for Sanguinet then follow the signs for Navarrosse)

12 ha/7 ha for camping flat, sandy, grassy

Rentals : ⟨...⟩ – 35 ⟨...⟩.

Surroundings : ⟨...⟩
Leisure activities : ⟨...⟩ multi-sports ground
Facilities : ⟨...⟩

GPS Longitude : -1.16763
Latitude : 44.39439

Campéole de Navarrosse ♠♣

☎ 05 58 09 84 32, *www.camping-navarrose.com*

Address : 712 chemin de Navarrosse (5km to the north, follow the signs for Sanguinet and turn left towards Navarrosse; beside the Étang de Cazaux (lake)

Opening times : from mid April to mid Sept.

9 ha (500 pitches) flat, sandy, grassy

Tariff : (2012 price) 31.60€ ✦✦ ⇔ ▣ ⒢ (10A) – Extra per person 9.40€ – Reservation fee 25€

Rental rates : (2012 price) (from mid April to mid Sept.) ⟨...⟩ (1 mobile home) – 46 ⟨...⟩ – 11 ⌂ – 139 tent bungalows. Per night from 30 to 74 € – Per week from 280 to 1,211 € Reservation fee 25€

⟨...⟩ sani-station 4€ – ⟨...⟩ 12€

Surroundings : ⟨...⟩
Leisure activities : ⟨...⟩ multi-sports ground
Facilities : ⟨...⟩ launderette ⟨...⟩
Nearby : ⟨...⟩

GPS Longitude : -1.16765
Latitude : 44.42822

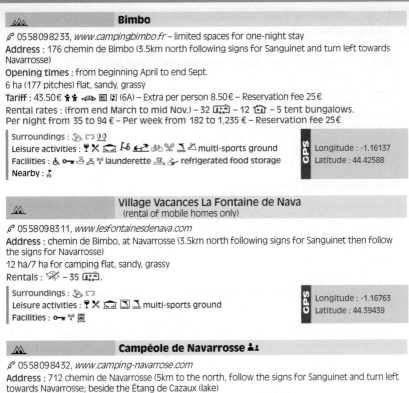

Michelin classification:

🔺🔺🔺🔺 *Extremely comfortable, equipped to a very high standard*
🔺🔺🔺 *Very comfortable, equipped to a high standard*
🔺🔺 *Comfortable and well equipped*
🔺 *Reasonably comfortable*
🔺 *Satisfactory*

BISCARROSSE-PLAGE

40600 – Michelin map **335** E8
▶ Paris 669 – Bordeaux 91 – Mont-de-Marsan 100

Campéole le Vivier

☎ 0558782576, *www.camping-biscarosse.info*
Address : 681 r. du Tit (north of the resort, 700m from the beach)
Opening times : from end April to mid Sept.
17 ha (830 pitches) flat, undulating, sandy, grassy
Tariff : (2012 price) 33.30€ ♣ ♣ ⬠ 🔲 (♨) (10A) – Extra per person 10€ – Reservation fee 25€
Rental rates : (permanent) ♿ (1 mobile home) – 74 🚐 – 20 🏠 – 186 tent bungalows.
Per night from 32 to 154 € – Per week from 490 to 1,078 € – Reservation fee 25€

> **Surroundings :** 🗐 🗐
> **Leisure activities :** ♟ 🎱 🎲 🏃 🏊 🚴 🎯 ⛷ multi-sports ground, entertainment room
> **Facilities :** ♿ ☛ 🎪 launderette 🔧 refrigerated food storage
> **Nearby :** 🛶

> **GPS**
> Longitude : -1.24056
> Latitude : 44.45938

Routes nationales are main roads and their identifying numbers begin with N or RN. Routes départementales are generally quieter roads and begin with D or DN.

BLASIMON

33540 – Michelin map **335** K6 – pop. 866 – alt. 80
▶ Paris 607 – Bordeaux 47 – Mérignac 63 – Pessac 60

Le Lac

☎ 0556715962, *www.entredeuxmers.com*
Address : Domaine départemental Volny Favory (at the leisure and activity park)
50 ha/0.5 (39 pitches) flat, grassy

> **Surroundings :** 🗑 🗐 🗐
> **Leisure activities :** 🎱
> **Facilities :** ♿ ☛ 🎪
> **At the leisure/activities centre :** ✗ 🔧 🏃 ⛷ 🌊 (beach) 🎣

> **GPS**
> Longitude : -0.08757
> Latitude : 44.75541

BLAYE

33390 – Michelin map **335** H4 – pop. 4,882 – alt. 7
▶ Paris 546 – Bordeaux 49 – Jonzac 52 – Libourne 45

Municipal de la Citadelle

☎ 0557420020, *www.blaye.fr*
Address : in the citadel itself on the banks of the Garonne
Opening times : from beginning May to end Aug.
1 ha (47 pitches) flat, relatively flat, terraced, grassy
Tariff : (2012 price) ♣ 5.80€ ⬠ 🔲 – (♨) (15A) 2.60€

Great setting within the citadel walls, but very poor sanitary facilities.

> **Surroundings :** 🗑 ⩤ 🗐 🗐
> **Facilities :** ☛

> **GPS**
> Longitude : -0.66634
> Latitude : 45.12943

BORDEAUX

33000 – Michelin map **335** H5 – pop. 236,725 – alt. 4
▶ Paris 572 – Mont-de-Marsan 138 – Bayonne 191 – Arcachon 72

International de Bordeaux Lac

℘ 05 57 87 70 60, *www.camping-bordeaux.com*
Address : at Bordeaux Lac (commune de Bruges, bd Jacques Chaban-Delmas (from the bypass (rocade), take exit 5 Parc des Expositions (Exhibition Centre)
Opening times : permanent
13 ha/6 ha for camping (193 pitches) flat, grassy
Tariff : 19€ ✶✶ ⇦ 🔲 🅷 (10A) – Extra per person 5€
Rental rates : (permanent) ⅊ – 136 🛏 – 9 🏠 . Per night from 39 to 220 €
Per week from 73 to 1,540 €
🚮 sani-station – 15 🔲 19€
Based around several small but pretty lakes.

Surroundings : 🏞🏞
Leisure activities : ✗ 🛶 🚴 🎣 🛶
Facilities : ⅊ ⟞ ▥ 🚿 ⛺ ♨ 🍴 launderette 🅿 🛒
Nearby : 🏊 💧

GPS Longitude : -0.5827
Latitude : 44.89759

BRANTÔME

24310 – Michelin map **329** E3 – pop. 2,140 – alt. 104
▶ Paris 470 – Angoulême 58 – Limoges 83 – Nontron 23

Brantôme Peyrelevade

℘ 05 53 05 75 24, *www.camping-dordogne.net*
Address : av. André Maurois (located 1km east along the D 78; beside the Dronne river)
Opening times : from beginning May to end Sept.
5 ha (170 pitches) flat, grassy
Tariff : (2012 price) 23€ ✶✶ ⇦ 🔲 🅷 (10A) – Extra per person 4.50€ – Reservation fee 10€
Rental rates : (2012 price) (from beginning May to end Sept.) – 15 🛏 .
Per night from 30 to 40 € Per week from €250 to 714 € – Reservation fee 10€
🚮 sani-station – 10 🔲 14€

Surroundings : 🛥 🛏 🏞🏞
Leisure activities : ✗ 🚴 🎾 🛶 ≋ (beach) 🎣
Facilities : ⅊ ⟞ ▥ ⛺ 🍴 launderette

GPS Longitude : 0.66043
Latitude : 45.36107

LE BUGUE

24260 – Michelin map **329** G6 – pop. 2,800 – alt. 62
▶ Paris 522 – Bergerac 47 – Brive-la-Gaillarde 72 – Cahors 86

Vagues-Océanes La Linotte ♣♦

℘ 08 20 15 00 40, *www.vagues-oceanes.com*
Address : rte de Rouffignac (3.5km northeast along the D 710 following the signs for Périgueux and turn right onto D 32)
Opening times : from beginning April to mid Sept.
13 ha/2.5 ha for camping (120 pitches) terraced, relatively flat, flat, grassy
Tariff : (2012 price) 33€ ✶✶ ⇦ 🔲 🅷 (6A) – Extra per person 6.70€ – Reservation fee 26€
Rental rates : (2012 price) (from beginning April to mid Sept.) – 2 caravans – 99 🛏 – 7 🏠 .
Per night from 31 to 161 € – Per week from €217 to 1,127€ – Reservation fee 26€

Surroundings : 🛥 ⟜ 🛏 🎠
Leisure activities : 🍴 🏠 🏋 jacuzzi 🚴 🛶 🏊 multi-sports ground
Facilities : ⅊ ⟞ ⛺ 🍴 launderette 🛒

GPS Longitude : 0.93659
Latitude : 44.93386

Les Trois Caupain

℘ 05 53 07 24 60, *www.camping-des-trois-caupain.com*
Address : allée Paul-Jean Souriau
Opening times : from beginning April to end Oct.
4 ha (160 pitches) flat, grassy
Tariff : 22.90€ ♦ ♦ ⇐ 回 (4) (16A) – Extra per person 5.20€ – Reservation fee 5€
Rental rates : (from beginning April to end Oct.) – 36 ⟨⟩. Per night from 35 to 55 €
Per week from 159 to 680 € – Reservation fee 12€
⟨⟩ sani-station 9.90€ – ⟨⟩ (4)12.70€

Surroundings : ⟨⟩ ♨
Leisure activities : ✗ ♨ ➴ multi-sports ground
Facilities : ⟨⟩ ⟨⟩ ⟨⟩ ♨ ⟨⟩ ⟨⟩ launderette ⟨⟩
Nearby : ⟨⟩ large aquarium

Longitude : 0.93178
Latitude : 44.90916

LE BUISSON-DE-CADOUIN

24480 – Michelin map **329** G6 – pop. 2,143 – alt. 63
▶ Paris 532 – Bergerac 38 – Périgueux 52 – Sarlat-la-Canéda 36

Domaine defromengal ♣♣

℘ 05 53 63 11 55, *www.domaine-fromengal.com*
Address : at La Combe de Cussac (6.5km southwest along the D 29, follow the signs for Lalinde, turn left onto the D 2, follow the signs for Cadouin and take the road to the right)
Opening times : from beginning April to end Oct.
22 ha/3 ha for camping (90 pitches) terraced, grassy, adjacent wood
Tariff : (2012 price) 33.50€ ♦ ♦ ⇐ 回 (4) (10A) – Extra per person 8.50€ – Reservation fee 19€
Rental rates : (2012 price) (from beginning April to end Oct.) – 26 ⟨⟩ – 21 ⟨⟩ – 4 tent bungalows. Per night from 35 to 140 € – Per week from 45 to 980 € – Reservation fee 19€

Surroundings : ⟨⟩ ⟨⟩ ♨
Leisure activities : ✗ ⟨⟩ ⟨⟩ ⟨⟩ ♨ ✗ ♨ ♨
Facilities : ⟨⟩ ⟨⟩ ⟨⟩ ⟨⟩ ♨ ⟨⟩ ⟨⟩ launderette ⟨⟩ ⟨⟩

Longitude : 0.86006
Latitude : 44.82292

This guide is not intended as a list of all the camping sites in France; its aim is to provide a selection of the best sites in each category.

BUNUS

64120 – Michelin map **342** F3 – pop. 147 – alt. 186
▶ Paris 820 – Bayonne 61 – Hasparren 38 – Mauléon-Licharre 22

Inxauseta

℘ 05 59 37 81 49, *www.inxauseta.fr*
Address : in the town, near the church
Opening times : from end June to mid Sept.
0.8 ha (40 pitches) relatively flat, terraced, grassy
Tariff : (2012 price) ♦ 4€ ⇐ 回 4€ – (4) (5A) 2.60€

Pleasant games/recreation rooms in an old renovated Basque house.

Surroundings : ⟨⟩ ⟨⟩ ♨
Leisure activities : ⟨⟩
Facilities : ⟨⟩ ⟨⟩ ⟨⟩

Longitude : -1.06794
Latitude : 43.20974

CAMBO-LES-BAINS

64250 – Michelin map **342** D2 – pop. 6,466 – alt. 67 – ⚕ (end Feb-mid-Dec)
▶ Paris 783 – Bayonne 20 – Biarritz 21 – Pau 115

⚠ Bixta Eder

📞 05.59.29.94.23, *www.campingbixtaeder.com*
Address : 52 av. d'Espagne (1.3km southwest along the D 918, follow the signs for St-Jean-de-Luz)
Opening times : from mid April to mid Oct.
1 ha (90 pitches) sloping, flat, grassy, gravelled
Tariff : 19.50€ ⚁⚁ ⇔ 🅳 🅼 (10A) – Extra per person 3.50€ – Reservation fee 15€
Rental rates : (from mid March to beginning Nov.) – 19 🚐 – 3 🏠. Per night from 32 to 45€
Per week from 203 to 620 € – Reservation fee 15€

Surroundings : 🖼 ♨♨
Leisure activities : 🎦
Facilities : ⚿ ☞ (Jun-Sept) ♨ ▮ launderette 🔲
Nearby : ✕ 🏊

GPS
Longitude : -1.41448
Latitude : 43.35567

CAMPAGNE

24260 – Michelin map **329** G6 – pop. 367 – alt. 60
▶ Paris 542 – Bergerac 51 – Belvès 19 – Les Eyzies-de-Tayac 7

⚠ Le Val de la Marquise ♣↔

📞 05 53 54 74 10, *www.levaldelamarquise.com*
Address : at Le Moulin (500m east along the D 35, follow the signs for St-Cyprien)
Opening times : from beginning April to end Sept.
4 ha (104 pitches) terraced, flat, grassy, lake
Tariff : 23.80€ ⚁⚁ ⇔ 🅳 🅼 (15A) – Extra per person 5.50€
Rental rates : (from beginning April to end Sept.) ✂ – 16 🚐 – 8 🏠.
Per night from 34 to 117 € – Per week from 238 to 819 € – Reservation fee 20€
🚐 sani-station 11.30€

Surroundings : 🖼 ♨♨
Leisure activities : ✕ 🎦 🏃 ⚓ 🏊 🎣
Facilities : ⚿ ☞ ▮ ♨ ▮ launderette 🔲

GPS
Longitude : 0.9743
Latitude : 44.90637

CARSAC-AILLAC

24200 – Michelin map **329** I6 – pop. 1,479 – alt. 80
▶ Paris 536 – Brive-la-Gaillarde 59 – Gourdon 18 – Sarlat-la-Canéda 9

⚠ Le Plein Air des Bories

📞 05 53 28 15 67, *www.camping-desbories.com*
Address : at Les Bories (1.3km south along the D 703, follow the signs for Vitrac and take road to the left; beside the Dordogne river)
Opening times : from mid April to end Sept.
3.5 ha (110 pitches) flat, grassy, sandy
Tariff : (2012 price) ⚁ 6.50€ ⇔ 🅳 8.90€ – 🅼 (6A) 3.50€ – Reservation fee 15€
Rental rates : (2012 price) (from mid April to end Sept.) – 33 🚐 – 8 tent bungalows.
Per night from 25 to 60€ – Per week from 160 to 720 € – Reservation fee 15€

Surroundings : 🦢 🖼 ♨♨
Leisure activities : 🎦 ⚓ 🔲 (open-air in season) 🎣 🚣
Facilities : ⚿ ☞ ♨ ▮ 🔲

GPS
Longitude : 1.2684
Latitude : 44.83299

Le Rocher de la Cave

℘ 05 53 28 14 26, *www.rocherdelacave.com*
Address : at La Pommarède (1.7km south along the D 703, follow the signs for Vitrac and take road to the left; beside the Dordogne)
Opening times : from beginning May to end Sept.
5 ha (150 pitches) flat, grassy
Tariff : (2012 price) ♣ 5.70€ ⬅ 🅴 7.40€ – 🚽 (16A) 3.40€
Rental rates : (2012 price) (from beginning May to end Sept.) – 23 🛖 – 14 tent bungalows.
Per night from 28 to 97 € – Per week from 200 to 680 €

Surroundings : 🏞 ♨
Leisure activities : 🍽 🏊 🛶 ⚓ 🎣
Facilities : ♿ ⚬ 🚿 ᵀ launderette 🚗

Longitude : 1.26719
Latitude : 44.82977

CASTELJALOUX

47700 – Michelin map **336** C4 – pop. 4,773 – alt. 52 – Leisure centre
▶ Paris 674 – Agen 55 – Langon 55 – Marmande 23

Village Vacances Castel Chalets
(rental of chalets only)

℘ 05 53 93 07 45, *www.castel-chalets.com*
Address : rte de Mont de Marsan, at the Lac de Clarens (2.5km southwest along the D 933, follow the signs for Mont-de-Marsan)
Opening times : permanent
4 ha flat, sandy
Rental rates : ♿ (1 chalet) – 25 🏠. Per week from 75 to 680 €
🚐 sani-station 15€ – 20 🅴 15€
Small chalet village beside the lake, opposite the very well-equipped leisure and activity park.

Surroundings : 🏞 ≤ ♨ ⛰
Leisure activities : 🎦 🏊
Facilities : ⚬ 🏧 ᵀ
Nearby : 🍽 ✕ 🚲 ✂ ⛷ 🐎 forest trail, paintballing

Longitude : 0.0725
Latitude : 44.29278

Fire safety doesn't stop when you leave your accommodation.
Always take care and consider the fire risks.

CASTELMORON-SUR-LOT

47260 – Michelin map **336** E3 – pop. 1,755 – alt. 49
▶ Paris 600 – Agen 33 – Bergerac 63 – Marmande 35

Village Vacances Port-Lalande
(rental of chalets only)

℘ 04 68 37 65 65, *www.grandbleu.fr*
Address : located 1.5km southeast
Opening times : from beginning March to beginning Nov.
4 ha flat, grassy
Rental rates : ♿ (1 chalet) 🅿 – 60 🏠. Per night from 65 to 85 € – Per week from 196 to 917 €
Beside the Lot river and a marina.

Surroundings : 🏞 ≤ ♀
Leisure activities : 🎦 🏋 ♨ hammam 🏊 spa therapy centre
Facilities : 🏧 launderette
Nearby : ⚓

Longitude : 0.50661
Latitude : 44.38803

CASTELNAUD-LA-CHAPELLE

24250 – Michelin map **329** H7 – pop. 477 – alt. 140
▶ Paris 539 – Le Bugue 29 – Les Eyzies-de-Tayac 27 – Gourdon 25

Flower Lou Castel

📞 0553298924, *www.loucastel.com*

Address : at Prente Garde (take the southern exit along the D 57 then continue 3.4km along the road to the château, for caravans, access is strongly recommended via Pont-de-Cause and the D 50, follow the signs for Veyrines-de-Domme)

Opening times : from mid April to beginning Sept.

5.5 ha/2.5 ha for camping (110 pitches) flat, grassy, stony, adjacent wood

Tariff : 33€ ♥♥ ⇔ 🗐 🖟 (10A) – Extra per person 6€ – Reservation fee 18€

Rental rates : (from beginning April to mid Sept.) 🏚 – 2 caravans – 50 🖽 – 20 🏠 – 11 tent bungalows – 3 tents – 5 gîtes. Per night from 28 to 140 € – Per week from 160 to 994 €

Reservation fee 18€

In a pleasant setting among oak trees.

Surroundings : 🐟 🗔 ⛰
Leisure activities : 🎮 ⛵ 🏊 ⛷ multi-sports ground
Facilities : ♿ ⊶ 🚿 🔥 ⚐ ⚊ launderette

GPS Longitude : 1.13182
Latitude : 44.79746

Maisonneuve

📞 0553295129, *www.campingmaisonneuve.com*

Address : chemin de Maisonneuve (located 1km southeast along the D 57 and take road to the left; beside the Céou river)

Opening times : from beginning April to end Oct.

6 ha/3 ha for camping (140 pitches) open site, flat, grassy

Tariff : (2012 price) 20.40€ ♥♥ ⇔ 🗐 🖟 (10A) – Extra per person 5.15€ – Reservation fee 15€

Rental rates : (from beginning April to end Oct.) 🏚 – 10 🖽 – 2 tents – 1 gîte.
Per night from 44 to 70 € – Per week from 250 to 820 € – Reservation fee 15€

🚐 sani-station

Based around an old renovated farmhouse and surrounded by flowers.

Surroundings : ⟨ 🗔 ⚊
Leisure activities : ⛹ ✕ 🎮 ⛵ ⛰ 🏊 🚣 🎣
Facilities : ♿ ⊶ 🚿 ⚐ launderette 🐴

GPS Longitude : 1.15822
Latitude : 44.80482

The guide is updated each year, so consult the latest edition for the most up-to-date information and pricing.

CASTELS

24220 – Michelin map **329** H6 – pop. 647 – alt. 50
▶ Paris 551 – Bordeaux 181 – Montauban 145 – Brive-la-Gaillarde 73

Village Vacances La Noyeraie
(rental of chalets) only)

📞 0553312443, *www.chaletlanoyeraie.fr*

Address : at Le Grelat (located 1km southeast along the D 703, follow the signs for Sarlat)

Opening times : permanent

1.5 ha flat, grassy

Rental rates : 🏚 🅿 – 18 🏠. Per week from 20 to 870 € – Reservation fee 15€

Surroundings : ⚊
Leisure activities : 🎮 ⛵ 🏊
Facilities : ⊶ 🗭 🎬 launderette

GPS Longitude : 1.08071
Latitude : 44.85004

CASTETS

40260 – Michelin map **335** E11 – pop. 1,945 – alt. 48
▶ Paris 710 – Dax 21 – Mimizan 40 – Mont-de-Marsan 61

Municipal Le Galan

℘ 05 58 89 43 52, *www.camping-legalan.com*
Address : 73 rue du Stade (located 1km east along the D 42, follow the signs for Taller and take turning to the right)
4 ha (181 pitches) flat, relatively flat, sandy, grassy
Rentals : 8 📺 – 5 🏠 – 3 tent bungalows – 1 cabin.
🚐 sani-station
Pilgrims on their way to Santiago di Compostella can stay in a small wooden chalet

Surroundings : 🔲 🗘🗘
Leisure activities : 🎮 ⚓️ ⤴
Facilities : ♿ ⌇ ⚐ 🚿 ᵞ launderette
Nearby : ⚜ fitness trail

GPS Longitude : -1.13754
Latitude : 43.88059

To make the best possible use of this guide,
please read pages 2–15 carefully.

CASTILLON LA BATAILLE

33350 – Michelin map **335** K5 – pop. 3,203 – alt. 17
▶ Paris 549 – Bergerac 46 – Libourne 18 – Montpon-Ménestérol 27

Municipal La Pelouse

℘ 05 57 40 04 22, *www.castillonlabataille.fr*
Address : 2 prom. Dubourdieu (east of the town; beside the Dordogne river)
Opening times : from mid May to mid Oct.
0.5 ha (38 pitches) flat, grassy
Tariff : 13€ � ⚑ 📧 🗘 (15A) – Extra per person 4€

Surroundings : 🏞 🗘🗘
Leisure activities : 🎣
Facilities : ♿ ⌇ 🚽 🆒 ᵞ 📷

GPS Longitude : -0.03569
Latitude : 44.85337

CÉNAC-ET-ST-JULIEN

24250 – Michelin map **329** I7 – pop. 1,218 – alt. 70
▶ Paris 537 – Le Bugue 34 – Gourdon 20 – Sarlat-la-Canéda 12

Le Pech de Caumont

℘ 05 53 28 21 63, *www.pech-de-caumont.com*
Address : situated 2km to the south
Opening times : from beginning April to end Sept.
2.2 ha (100 pitches) terraced, relatively flat, grassy
Tariff : (2012 price) ✦ 5.20€ ⚑ 📧 7€ – 🗘 (10A) 3.50€ – Reservation fee 12.50€
Rental rates : (2012 price) (from beginning April to end Sept.) ⚒ – 20 📺 – 6 🏠.
Per night from 32 to 90 € – Per week from 208 to 635 € – Reservation fee 12.50€
🚐 10 📧 17.40€
Looking out over the Dordogne valley, opposite the village of Domme.

Surroundings : 🏞 ⩤ 🔲 🗘🗘
Leisure activities : 🍽 🏠 ⚓️ ⤴
Facilities : ♿ 🚽 🚿 ᵞ 📷 ⤶

GPS Longitude : 1.20908
Latitude : 44.78654

LA CHAPELLE-AUBAREIL

24290 – Michelin map **329** I5 – pop. 471 – alt. 230
▶ Paris 515 – Brive-la-Gaillarde 40 – Les Eyzies-de-Tayac 21 – Montignac 9

La Fage

☎ 0553507650, *www.camping-lafage.com*
Address : at La Fage (1.2km northwest following signs for St-Amand-de-Coly, head towards D 704 and take road to the left)
Opening times : from mid April to mid Oct.
5 ha (60 pitches) terraced, relatively flat, grassy
Tariff : 28€ ♣♣ ⚌ 🔲 🔌 (10A) – Extra per person 6€ – Reservation fee 10€
Rental rates : (from mid April to mid Oct.) – 17 🚐 – 3 🏠 – 3 tents. Per night from 24 to 65 €
Per week from 170 to 790 € – Reservation fee 10€
🚐 5 🔲 28€

Surroundings : 🏊 🗀 ♨️
Leisure activities : ✗ 🎬 ⛵ 🛶
Facilities : ♿ ⚷ 🆑🍴 🚿 ⟲ 🚰 launderette 🛒

GPS
Longitude : 1.1882
Latitude : 45.01745

COLY

24120 – Michelin map **329** I5 – pop. 226 – alt. 113 – Leisure centre
▶ Paris 504 – Brive-la-Gaillarde 29 – Lanouaille 45 – Périgueux 53

Village Vacances Goelia Les Cottages du Lac
(rental of chalets only)

☎ 0553509442, *www.vacances-lascaux-dordogne.com*
Address : at La Prade (situated 2km southeast along the D 62, follow the signs for la Cassagne; beside a small lake)
18 ha flat, grassy, lakes
Rentals : ♿ (1 chalet) – 73 🏠.

Some chalets have terraces looking out onto the water.

Surroundings : 🏊 ⟨ ♀
Leisure activities : ⛵ 🚲 🎿 🛶 ⚓ fitness trail ⚿ multi-sports ground
Facilities : ⌾ 🚰 🏛 launderette

GPS
Longitude : 1.27945
Latitude : 45.07271

CONTIS-PLAGE

40170 – Michelin map **335** D10
▶ Paris 714 – Bayonne 87 – Castets 32 – Dax 52

Yelloh! Village Lous Seurrots ♣♣

☎ 0558428582, *www.lous-seurrots.com*
Address : 606 av. de l'Océan (take the southeastern exit along the D 41, near the Courant de Contis (small river), 700m from the beach)
Opening times : from mid April to end Sept.
14 ha (610 pitches) flat, undulating, sloping, sandy, grassy
Tariff : 46€ ♣♣ ⚌ 🔲 🔌 (16A) – Extra per person 8€ – Reservation fee 20€
Rental rates : (from mid April to end Sept.) ♿ (1 chalet) – 180 🚐 – 114 🏠 – 27 tent bungalows – 3 gîtes. Per night from 35 to 209 € – Per week from 45 to 1,463 €
Reservation fee 20€

Surroundings : 🗀 ♨️
Leisure activities : 🍴 ✗ 🎬 🎭 (open-air theatre) 🏃 ⛵ 🚲 🎿 🛶 multi-sports ground
Facilities : ♿ ⚷ 🏛 🚿 🚰 launderette ⟲ 🛒 refrigerated food storage
Nearby : 🏇 ♨ surfing

GPS
Longitude : -1.31685
Latitude : 44.08878

COURBIAC

47370 – Michelin map **336** I3 – pop. 110 – alt. 145
▶ Paris 623 – Bordeaux 172 – Agen 46 – Montauban 59

Le Pouchou

℘ 05 53 40 72 68, *www.camping-le-pouchou.com*
Address : head 1.8km west following signs for Tournon-d'Agenais, take road to the left
Opening times : from beginning March to end Nov.
15 ha/2 ha for camping (30 pitches) open site, relatively flat, grassy
Tariff : 18.65€ ★★ ⇌ 🔲 🔌 (10A) – Extra per person 4.60€
Rental rates : (from beginning March to end Nov.) ⅙ (1 chalet) – 1 🔲 – 7 🏠.
Per night from 53 to 96 € – Per week from 41 to 630 €
🔲 sani-station 5€ – 3 🔲 5€ – 🚐 13€
Pleasant setting among undulating hills, set around a small lake.

Surroundings : ⛱ ≤ ♨
Leisure activities : ⛵ 🏠 🚲🛶 🎣 walking trails
Facilities : ⅙ ⌇ ♨ 🛏 🍴 launderette

GPS Longitude : 1.02293
Latitude : 44.37854

COUX-ET-BIGAROQUE

24220 – Michelin map **329** G7 – pop. 993 – alt. 85
▶ Paris 548 – Bergerac 44 – Le Bugue 14 – Les Eyzies-de-Tayac 17

Les Valades

℘ 05 53 29 14 27, *http://www.lesvalades.com*
Address : at Les Valades (4km northwest along the D 703, follow the signs for Les Eyzies then take left turning)
Opening times : from mid June to mid Sept.
11 ha (85 pitches) terraced, grassy, undulating, small lake, natural setting among trees and bushes
Tariff : 28€ ★★ ⇌ 🔲 🔌 (10A) – Extra per person 6.50€
Rental rates : (from mid April to end Sept.) ⅙ (1 chalet) – 6 🔲 – 19 🏠.
Per week from 250 to 800 €

Surroundings : ⛱ ≤ ⊏ ♨♨
Leisure activities : ✕ 🏠 🏊 🛶 ≊ (beach) 🎣 ⚲
Facilities : ⅙ ⌇ 🛏 ♨ – 10 individual sanitary facilities (🚿⬇🚽 wc) 🛏 ⚡ 🍴 launderette 🐾

GPS Longitude : 0.96367
Latitude : 44.8599

COUZE-ET-ST-FRONT

24150 – Michelin map **329** F7 – pop. 775 – alt. 45
▶ Paris 544 – Bergerac 21 – Lalinde 4 – Mussidan 46

Les Moulins

℘ 06 89 85 76 24, *www.campingdesmoulins.com* – limited spaces for one-night stay
Address : at Les Maury Bas (take the southeastern exit along the D 660, follow the signs for Beaumont and take a right turn, near the sports field; beside the Couze river)
Opening times : from beginning April to end Oct.
2.5 ha (50 pitches) relatively flat, flat, grassy
Tariff : 29€ ★★ ⇌ 🔲 🔌 (10A) – Extra per person 8€ – Reservation fee 10€
Rental rates : (from beginning April to end Oct.) – 10 🔲. Per night from 50 to 75 €
Per week from 220 to 520 €– Reservation fee 10€
🔲 sani-station 12€ – 8 🔲 12€ – 🚐 🔌12€
Green setting perched on a rocky spur opposite the village.

Surroundings : ≤ ⊏ ♨♨
Leisure activities : ⛵ 🏠 🏀 🏊 🎿 🛶 🎣
Facilities : ⅙ ⌇ 🍴 launderette

GPS Longitude : 0.70448
Latitude : 44.82646

DAGLAN

24250 – Michelin map **329** I7 – pop. 555 – alt. 101
▶ Paris 547 – Cahors 48 – Fumel 40 – Gourdon 18

ᗰ Club Airotel Le Moulin de Paulhiac ♠♠

℘ 0553282088, *www.moulin-de-paulhiac.com*
Address : rte de St-Cybranet (4km northwest along the D 57; beside the Céou river)
5 ha (150 pitches) flat, grassy
Rentals : 13 ⬛ – 2 tents .

Surroundings : ⌇ ⊏ ♈
Leisure activities : ♈ ✕ ⛝ ⛾ ⚓ ▦ (open-air in season) ≋ ⛰ ⚲
Facilities : ♿ �o━ ⛺ ⛩ ⬚ ⫶ launderette ⬚ ⚲

Longitude : 1.17654
Latitude : 44.76772

ᗰ La Peyrugue

℘ 0553284026, *www.peyrugue.com*
Address : at La Peyrugue (located 1.5km north along the D 57, follow the signs for St-Cybranet, 150m from the Céou river)
Opening times : from beginning April to end Sept.
5 ha/2.5 ha for camping (85 pitches) terrace, open site, relatively flat to hilly, grassy, stony
Tariff : 30€ ♣♣ ⇎ ▣ ⬚ (10A) – Extra per person 7.50€ – Reservation fee 10€
Rental rates : (from beginning April to end Sept.) ♿ (2 chalets) – 5 ⬛ – 10 ⌂ .
Per night from 40 to 115 € – Per week from 80 to 805 € – Reservation fee 10€

Surroundings : ⌇ ♈
Leisure activities : ♈ ⛝ ⚓ ⚲
Facilities : ♿ o━ ⛺ ⫶ launderette ⚲

Longitude : 1.18798
Latitude : 44.75267

Do not confuse:
⛺ *to* ᗰᗰᗰ : *MICHELIN classification*
with
★ *to* ★★★★★ : *official classification*

DAX

40100 – Michelin map **335** E12 – pop. 21,003 – alt. 12 – ♨
▶ Paris 727 – Bayonne 54 – Biarritz 61 – Bordeaux 144

ᗰᗰᗰ Les Chênes ♠♠

℘ 0558900553, *www.camping-les-chenes.fr*
Address : allée du Bois de Boulogne (1.8km west of the town centre, in the Bois de Boulogne, 200m from the Adour river)
Opening times : from mid March to mid Nov.
5 ha (230 pitches) flat, grassy, sandy, fine gravel
Tariff : (2012 price) 18.30€ ♣♣ ⇎ ▣ ⬚ (10A) – Extra per person 6€ – Reservation fee 7.50€
Rental rates : (2012 price) (from mid March to mid Nov.) – 34 ⬛ – 20 ⌂ .
Per night from 53 to 79 € – Per week from 366 to 558 € – Reservation fee 7.50€
▦ sani-station 6€ – ⬚ ⬚18.30€
Pleasant oak wood near a lake.

Surroundings : ⌇ ⊏ ♈
Leisure activities : ⛝ ⛩ ⚓ ⛾ ⛴
Facilities : ♿ o━ ▥ ⛺ ⛩ ⫶ launderette ⬚
Nearby : ♈ ✕ ⚲ ⛐

Longitude : -1.07174
Latitude : 43.71138

Le Bascat

℘ 05 58 56 16 68, www.campinglebascat.com
Address : r. de Jouandin (2.8km west from the town centre through the Bois de Boulogne, access from the Vieux Pont (left bank) and the avenue running along the banks of the Adour)
Opening times : from beginning March to mid Nov.
3.5 ha (160 pitches) flat, terraced, gravelled, grassy
Tariff : 17.70€ ★ ★ ⇌ ▣ ⚡ (6A) – Extra per person 4.20€ – Reservation fee 5€
Rental rates : (from mid March to mid Nov.) – 38 ⬛. Per night from 35 to 50 €
Per week from 212 to 330 € – Reservation fee 5€
⬛ sani-station – 12 ▣ 16.30€ – 🔋 11€

Surroundings : 🌿 ♨
Leisure activities : ▱
Facilities : ⚑ ⊶ ⫘ ⌂ ⊻ ¶ launderette ⏚

GPS Longitude : -1.07043
Latitude : 43.70617

DOMME

24250 – Michelin map **329** I7 – pop. 989 – alt. 250
▶ Paris 538 – Cahors 51 – Fumel 50 – Gourdon 20

Village Vacances Les Ventoulines
(rental of chalets only)

℘ 05 53 28 36 29, www.gites-dordogne-sarlat.fr
Address : at Les Ventoulines (3.6km to the southeast)
Opening times : from mid March to mid Nov.
3 ha open site, terraced, grassy
Rental rates : ⓟ – 18 ⬛. Per night from 73 to 89 € – Per week from 364 to 930 €

Surroundings : 🌿 ♨
Leisure activities : ▱ ⚒ 🏊
Facilities : ⚑ ⊶ ⫘ ¶ launderette

GPS Longitude : 1.22588
Latitude : 44.84048

Perpetuum ♣

℘ 05 53 28 35 18, www.campingleperpetuum.com.
Address : head 2km south along the D 50 and take road to the right; beside the Dordogne river
Opening times : from beginning May to mid Oct.
4.5 ha (120 pitches) flat, grassy
Tariff : ★ 6.90€ ⇌ 2.50€ ▣ 6.90€ – ⚡ (10A) 4€ – Reservation fee 12€
Rental rates : (from beginning May to end Sept.) ⚒ – 30 ⬛. Per night from 60 to 110 €
Per week from 250 to 750 € – Reservation fee 12€
⬛ sani-station 12€ – 🔋⚡12€

Surroundings : 🌿 ♨
Leisure activities : ✗ ▱ ⚐ ⚒ 🏊 ⌇ ⚓ multi-sports ground,
entertainment room
Facilities : ⚑ ⊶ ⌂ ¶ launderette ⏚

GPS Longitude : 1.22065
Latitude : 44.81542

Village Vacances de la Combe
(rental of chalets only)

℘ 05 53 29 77 42, www.sarlat-gites-dordogne.com
Address : at Le Pradal (located 1.5km southeast)
Opening times : permanent
2 ha flat, terraced, grassy
Rental rates : ⚑ (1 chalet) ⓟ – 12 ⬛. Per week from 330 to 730 € – Reservation fee 16€
⬛ sani-station 8€

Surroundings : 🌿 ♨
Leisure activities : ▱ 🏊
Facilities : ⊶ ⌂ ⫘ ¶ ▣

GPS Longitude : 1.22243
Latitude : 44.8161

Le Bosquet

℘ 0553283739, *www.lebosquet.com*

Address : at La Rivière (900m south of Vitrac-Port, along the D 46)

Opening times : from beginning April to end Sept.

1.5 ha (60 pitches) open site, flat, grassy

Tariff : 19€ ✝✝ ⇔ 🖩 ⚡ (10A) – Extra per person 5€ – Reservation fee 8€

Rental rates : (from beginning April to end Sept.) – 21 🚐. Per night from 34 to 50 €

Per week from 10 to 650 € – Reservation fee 8€

🚐 sani-station 9€ – 🚐9€

Surroundings : 🦌 ◁ 🛏 ♡♡
Leisure activities : ✗ 🛏 ⚓ 🏊
Facilities : ᨔ ⊶ 🛁 🚿 🖼 🚲

GPS Longitude : 1.22555 Latitude : 44.82185

Le Moulin de Caudon

℘ 0553310369, *www.campingdordogne.com*

Address : at Caudon (6km northeast along the D 46e and the D 50, follow the signs for Groléjac; near the Dordogne – recommended route for caravans via Vitrac-Port)

Opening times : permanent

2 ha (60 pitches) flat, grassy

Tariff : (2012 price) ✝ 3.50€ ⇔ 3.50€ 🖩 2.80€ – ⚡ (10A) 2.80€

Rental rates : (2012 price) (from beginning June to mid Sept.) 🏕 – 4 🚐.

Per night from 30 to 75 € – Per week from 200 to 500 €

Surroundings : 🛏 ♡♡
Leisure activities : 🛏 ⚓
Facilities : ᨔ ⊶ (season) 🚿🛁 🖼
Nearby : 🏊

GPS Longitude : 1.24466 Latitude : 44.82061

EYMET

24500 – Michelin map **329** D8 – pop. 2,563 – alt. 54
▶ Paris 560 – Bergerac 24 – Castillonnès 19 – Duras 22

Le Château

℘ 0553238028, *www.eymetcamping.com*

Address : r. de la Sole (behind the château; beside the Dropt river)

Opening times : from end April to end Sept.

1.5 ha (66 pitches) flat, grassy, adjacent public garden

Tariff : 15€ ✝✝ ⇔ 🖩 ⚡ (10A) – Extra per person 4€

Pleasant location near the river, the municipal park and the town ramparts.

Surroundings : 🦌 🛏 ♡♡
Leisure activities : 🚲 🎣 ⚓
Facilities : ᨔ ⊶ 🚐 📷 🚿 🖼

GPS Longitude : 0.39584 Latitude : 44.66925

For more information on visiting particular towns or regions, consult the relevant regional MICHELIN Green Guide. We also recommend you use the appropriate Michelin regional map to locate your selected campsite, to calculate distances and to work out the best route.

LES EYZIES-DE-TAYAC

24620 – Michelin map **329** H6 – pop. 839 – alt. 70
▶ Paris 536 – Brive-la-Gaillarde 62 – Fumel 62 – Lalinde 35

Vacances Directes Le Mas ▲:
(rental of mobile homes and chalets only)

℘ 0825 133 400, www.campinglemas.com
Address : 7 km east along the D 47 follow the signs for Sarlat-la-Canéda then continue 2.5km following signs for Sireuil to the left
Opening times : from beginning May to mid Sept.
5 ha terraced, grassy
Rental rates : (2012 price) – 109 ⬛ – 6 ⬛. Per night from 33 to 115 €
Per week from 231 to 805 € – Reservation fee 20€

Surroundings : ⬛ ⬛ ⬛
Leisure activities : ▮ ✗ (farm-inn) ⬛ ⬛ ⬛ ⬛ ⬛
Facilities : ⬛ ⬛ ⬛ ⬛ launderette ⬛ ⬛

Longitude : 1.0849
Latitude : 44.93675

La Rivière

℘ 05 53 06 97 14, www.lariviereleseyzies.com
Address : 3 rte du Sorcier (located 1km northwest along the D 47, follow the signs for Périgueux and take the turning to the left after the bridge, 200m from the Vézère)
Opening times : from beginning April to end Oct.
7 ha/3 ha for camping (120 pitches) flat, grassy
Tariff : (2012 price) ▮ 6.40€ ⬛ ⬛ 9.80€ – ⬛ (10A) 4.50€ – Reservation fee 4€
Rental rates : (2012 price) (from beginning April to end Oct.) – 13 ⬛ – 6 ⬛ – 1 tent.
Per night from 35 to 95 € – Per week from 160 to 865 € – Reservation fee 4€
⬛ sani-station 5€ – ⬛ ⬛15€

Surroundings : ⬛ ⬛
Leisure activities : ▮ ✗ ⬛ ⬛ ⬛
Facilities : ⬛ ⬛ ⬛ ⬛ ⬛ ⬛ ⬛ launderette ⬛

Longitude : 1.00582
Latitude : 44.93732

La Ferme du Pelou

℘ 05 53 06 98 17, www.lafermedupelou.com
Address : at Le Pelou (4km northeast along the D 706, follow the signs for Montignac then take the turning to the right)
Opening times : from mid March to mid Nov.
1 ha (65 pitches) relatively flat, flat, grassy
Tariff : 14.65€ ▮ ▮ ⬛ ⬛ ⬛ (10A) – Extra per person 3.95€
Rental rates : (from mid March to mid Nov.) – 2 ⬛. Per night from 44 to 70 €
Per week from 310 to 490 €
⬛ sani-station – 5 ⬛ 12.20€
Farm campsite.

Surroundings : ⬛ ⬛ ⬛
Leisure activities : ⬛ ⬛
Facilities : ⬛ ⬛ ⬛ launderette
Nearby : ⬛

Longitude : 1.04472
Latitude : 44.95527

FUMEL

47500 – Michelin map **336** H3 – pop. 5,186 – alt. 70
▶ Paris 594 – Agen 55 – Bergerac 64 – Cahors 48

Village Vacances Domaine de Guillalmes

(rental of chalets only)

☎ 0553710199, *www.domainedeguillalmes.com*
Address : 3km east along the D 911, follow the signs for Cahors, at Condat exit follow right turn for 1km; beside the Lot river
Opening times : from beginning March to mid Nov.
3 ha flat, grassy
Rental rates : ♿ (1 chalet) – 2 🚐 – 18 🏠. Per night from 60 to 80 €
Per week from 300 to 660 € – Reservation fee 10€
🚉 8 ▣ 14€

Surroundings : 🏊 ♒♒
Leisure activities : ▼ ✗ 🛶 🚴 🎿 🛶 🛶 ⚙
Facilities : ⚬🔄 🅿 📅 🏢 ♒ 🔲 🔆

GPS Longitude : 1.00955
Latitude : 44.48343

Les Catalpas

☎ 0553711199, *www.les-catalpas.com*
Address : at La Tour, chemin de la plaine de Condat (situated 2km east along the D 911, follow the signs for Cahors; at the Condat exit, follow the road to the right for 1.2km; beside the Lot river)
Opening times : from beginning March to mid Nov.
2 ha (80 pitches) flat, grassy, hard surface areas
Tariff : 19€ 🚻 🚻 🚐 ▣ 🔌 (10A) – Extra per person 5€
Rental rates : (2012 price) (permanent) – 3 🚐 – 3 🏠 – 1 gîte. Per night from 40 to 65 €
Per week from 50 to 550 €
🚉 5 ▣ 13€

Surroundings : 🏊 ♒♒
Leisure activities : 🎿
Facilities : ⚬🔄 🔲 🏢 🔆

In order for the guide to remain wholly objective, the selection is made on an entirely independent basis. There is no charge for being selected for the guide.

GABARRET

40310 – Michelin map **335** L11 – pop. 1,270 – alt. 153
▶ Paris 715 – Agen 66 – Auch 76 – Bordeaux 140

Parc Municipal Touristique la Chêneraie

☎ 0558449262, *la-cheneraie@orange.fr*
Address : take the eastern exit along the D 35, follow the signs for Castelnau-d'Auzan and take the road to the right
Opening times : from beginning March to end Oct.
0.7 ha (36 pitches) relatively flat, flat, grassy, sandy
Tariff : (2012 price) 11€ 🚻 🚻 🚐 ▣ 🔌 (10A) – Extra per person 2.77€
Rental rates : (2012 price) (permanent) – 4 🚐 – 10 gîtes. Per night from 48 to 56 €
Per week from 162 to 294 €

Surroundings : 🏊 🚃 ♒♒
Leisure activities : 🛶 🚴
Facilities : ♿ ⚬🔄 📅 🔲 🏢 🔆
Nearby : 🎣 🎿

GPS Longitude : 0.01622
Latitude : 43.98361

GRADIGNAN

33170 – Michelin map **335** H6 – pop. 23,386 – alt. 26
▶ Paris 592 – Bordeaux 9 – Lyon 550 – Nantes 336

⚠ Beausoleil

ℰ 05 56 89 17 66, *www.camping-gradignan.com*
Address : 371 cours du Général de Gaulle (on the bypass (rocade), take exit 16 for Gradignan)
Opening times : permanent
0.5 ha (31 pitches) relatively flat, flat, grassy, fine gravel
Tariff : 20€ ♦♦ ⟺ 🖃 ⑼ (10A) – Extra per person 3.50€
Rental rates : (permanent) ⚡ – 3 🛏. Per week from 250 to 400 €
Shuttle bus for the tram to Bordeaux.

Surroundings : 🖵 ᪲
Facilities : ♿ ⊶ ⌁ 🎪 ⚲ ↝ ᵀ launderette

GPS Longitude : -0.6278
Latitude : 44.75573

*Using the traditional Michelin classification method, the guide provides
you with an easy, speedy reference for assessing the category of each site:
1 to 5 tents (see page 10).*

GROLÉJAC

24250 – Michelin map **329** I7 – pop. 654 – alt. 67
▶ Paris 537 – Gourdon 14 – Périgueux 80 – Sarlat-la-Canéda 13

ᘰ Les Granges ♣♦

ℰ 05 53 28 11 15, *www.lesgranges-fr.com* – limited spaces for one-night stay
Address : in the village
Opening times : from beginning April to end Sept.
6 ha (188 pitches) flat, sloping, terraced, grassy
Tariff : 29.50€ ♦♦ ⟺ 🖃 ⑼ (6A) – Extra per person 7.50€ – Reservation fee 30€
Rental rates : (from end April to beginning Sept.) – 49 🛏 – 17 🏠. Per night from 42 to 110 €
Per week from 299 to 722 € – Reservation fee 30€

Surroundings : ⌖ 🖵 ᪲
Leisure activities : ᵀ ✕ 🎬 ⑨evening 🏓 🏋 ⚙ₘ 🎱 ⚲
Facilities : ♿ ⊶ ⌁ ⚲ ↝ ᵀ launderette ⚲
Nearby : ⚓

GPS Longitude : 1.29117
Latitude : 44.81579

⚠ Le Lac de Groléjac

ℰ 05 53 59 48 70, *www.camping-dulac-dordogne.com*
Address : at Le Roc Percé (situated 2km south along the D 704, D 50, follow the signs for Domme
and turn left, following signs for Nabirat)
Opening times : from mid April to mid Sept.
2 ha (92 pitches) open site, flat, grassy
Tariff : 17.10€ ♦♦ ⟺ 🖃 ⑼ (10A) – Extra per person 3.90€ – Reservation fee 15€
Rental rates : (from mid April to mid Sept.) – 13 🛏 – 9 tent bungalows.
Per week from 210 to 680 €– Reservation fee 15€
🖂 sani-station – ⚱ 10.50€

Surroundings : ⌖ ⟜ 🖵 ᪲ ⚠
Leisure activities : 🏋 pedalos, boats for hire ⚲
Facilities : ♿ ⊶ (Jul-Aug) ⚲ ⚲ ᵀ 🖼
Nearby : ⚓

GPS Longitude : 1.29441
Latitude : 44.802

HAGETMAU

40700 – Michelin map **335** H13 – pop. 4,539 – alt. 96
▶ Paris 737 – Aire-sur-l'Adour 34 – Dax 45 – Mont-de-Marsan 29

Municipal de la Cité Verte

☎ 05 58 79 79 79, *www.laciteverte.com*
Address : chemin des Loussets (to the south along the av. du Dr-Édouard-Castera, near some arenas and the swimming pool; beside a river)
Opening times : from beginning June to end Sept.
0.4 ha (24 pitches) flat, grassy
Tariff : (2012 price) 🛉 ⇌ 🔳 22.50€ 🔌 (16A)
🚰 sani-station – 10 🔳
Close to municipal sports buildings and leisure facillities.

Surroundings : 🐌 ⌁ 🎯
Leisure activities : ✗ 🎬 ⚓ 🎣
Facilities : ⚏ 🅿 🚿 – 24 individual sanitary facilities (🚿⚐🚻 WC) 🔥 🔧
Nearby : 🎾 📺 🏊 sports trail

GPS Longitude : -0.59215
Latitude : 43.65233

We value your opinion and welcome your feedback.
Do email us at campingfrance@tp.michelin.com

HAUTEFORT

24390 – Michelin map **329** H4 – pop. 1,086 – alt. 160
▶ Paris 466 – Bordeaux 190 – Périgueux 60 – Brive-la-Gaillarde 57

Village Vacances Les Sources
(rental of chalets only)

☎ 05 53 51 96 56, *www.dordogne-gite.fr*
Address : at La Génèbre (2.6km south along the D 704 and the D 62E4)
30 ha/5 ha for camping undulating
Rentals : 🅿 – 12 🏠 – 3 gîtes.

Surroundings : 🐌 ⩤ Château de Hautefort
Leisure activities : 🎏 🎬 ⚓ 🏊 paintballing, quad biking
Facilities : ⚐ ⚏ 🏚 🎪 launderette

GPS Longitude : 1.12641
Latitude : 45.25085

HENDAYE

64700 – Michelin map **342** B4 – pop. 14,412 – alt. 30
▶ Paris 799 – Biarritz 31 – Pau 143 – St-Jean-de-Luz 12

Club Airotel Ametza

☎ 05 59 20 07 05, *www.camping-ametza.com*
Address : bd de l'Empereur (located 1km east)
Opening times : from beginning May to end Sept.
4.5 ha (280 pitches) terraced, flat and relatively flat, grassy
Tariff : 37€ 🛉🛉 ⇌ 🔳 🔌 (6A) – Extra per person 7.30€ – Reservation fee 15€
Rental rates : (from mid April to end Sept.) ⚐ (1 mobile home) 🏊 – 27 🏚 – 3 🏠.
Per night from 70 to 110 € – Per week from 330 to 1,080 € – Reservation fee 15€
🚰 3 🔳 31€

Surroundings : 🎯
Leisure activities : 🎏 ✗ 🎬 🚴 ⚓ 🎾 🏊
Facilities : ⚐ ⚏ 🎪 launderette 🏊 🔧

GPS Longitude : -1.75578
Latitude : 43.37285

Eskualduna

℘ 0559200464, *www.camping-eskualduna.fr*
Address : rte de la Corniche (situated 2km east, rte da la Corniche; beside a stream)
Opening times : from beginning May to end Sept.
10 ha (330 pitches) undulating, terraced, sloping, grassy
Tariff : ♥ 6€ ⇔ 4€ 🔲 6€ – 🔋 (10A) 6€ – Reservation fee 20€
Rental rates : (from mid April to end Oct.) – 75 🚐 – 11 🏠. Per night from 60 to 85€
Per week from 190 to 1,500€ – Reservation fee 20€
🚽 sani-station 12€
Free shuttle service to the beach. Choose pitches away from the road in preference.

Surroundings : 🞰🞰
Leisure activities : 🍸✗ 🎏 🖎🕴🛝 🛶 ⅃
Facilities : ⚬ ⚱ ⚗ 🍴 launderette 🔌 🚿 refrigerators

GPS
Longitude : -1.73925
Latitude : 43.37555

Dorrondeguy

℘ 0559202616, *www.camping-dorrondeguy.com*
Address : r. de la Glacière
Opening times : from beginning April to end Oct.
4 ha (120 pitches) terrace, flat and relatively flat
Tariff : (2012 price) 30€ ♥♥ ⇔ 🔲 🔋 (6A) – Extra per person 6€ – Reservation fee 15€
Rental rates : (2012 price) (from beginning April to end Oct.) ♿ ✂ 🅿 – 27 🚐 – 11 🏠 –
4 tent bungalows. Per night from 35 to 125 € – Per week from 40 to 1,030 €
Reservation fee 20€

Surroundings : 🖌 ▱ 🞰🞰
Leisure activities : 🍸 🎏 🛝 ⅃ Basque pelota walled court
Facilities : ♿ ⚬ ⚗ 🍴 launderette 🚿

GPS
Longitude : -1.74727
Latitude : 43.36867

HOURTIN
33990 – Michelin map **335** E3 – pop. 3,001 – alt. 18
▶ Paris 638 – Andernos-les-Bains 55 – Bordeaux 65 – Lesparre-Médoc 17

La Rotonde – Le Village Western ♣♣

℘ 0556091060, *www.village-western.com*
Address : chemin de Bécassine (head 1.5km west along the av. du Lac and take road to the left,
500m from the lake (direct access)
Opening times : from mid April to end Sept.
17 ha/11 ha for camping (300 pitches) flat, grassy, sandy
Tariff : (2012 price) 35.70€ ♥♥ ⇔ 🔲 🔋 (10A) – Extra per person 8.60€
Rental rates : (2012 price) (from mid April to end Sept.) – 82 🚐 – 10 🏠 – 12 teepees –
10 tent bungalows. Per night from 30 to 97€ – Per week from 10 to 1,260€
🚽 sani-station 2€ – 🚐12€
Original Wild West décor, based around the riding centre.

Surroundings : 🖌 🞰
Leisure activities : 🍸✗ 🎏 🖎evening 🕴🛝 🚲 ⅃ ⚲ 🐎
Facilities : ♿ ⚬ 🔲⚗ ⚱ ⚗ 🍴 launderette 🔌 🚿
Nearby : ✂ 🖼

GPS
Longitude : -1.07468
Latitude : 45.17935

*Some information or pricing may have changed since the guide went to press.
We recommend you check the price list online in advance or at the entrance to
the campsite and enquire about possible restrictions.*

Les Ourmes ▲⁑

📞 0556091276, *www.lesourmes.com*
Address : 90 av. du Lac (located 1.5km west)
Opening times : from beginning May to mid Sept.
7 ha (300 pitches) flat, grassy, sandy
Tariff : 34€ 🛉🛉 🚐 🔲 🚿 (10A) – Extra per person 6€ – Reservation fee 16€
Rental rates : (from beginning May to mid Sept.) 🏠 – 37 🚐. Per night from 30 to 85 €
Per week from 180 to 755 € – Reservation fee 16€

Surroundings : 🏊 ♨♨
Leisure activities : 🍸 ✗ 🎬 🎮evening 🏸 🏊 🛶
Facilities : 🔥 ⛽ (Jul–Aug) ☕ 🍴 launderette 🔲 🚿
Nearby : 🎿 🖾 🏇 🎣

GPS Longitude : -1.07584
Latitude : 45.18204

Aires Naturelles l'Acacia et le Lac

📞 0556738080, *www.campinglacacia.com*
Address : rte de Carcans (7km southwest along the D 3 and take the road to the right)
Opening times : from mid June to end Sept.
5 ha/2 ha for camping (50 pitches) flat, grassy, sandy, adjacent pine trees
Tariff : 20.20€ 🛉🛉 🚐 🔲 🚿 (9A) – Extra per person 6€
Rental rates : (from mid June to mid Sept.) 🏠 – 2 tent bungalows. Per week from 90 to 380 €

Surroundings : 🏊 ♨♨
Leisure activities : 🏊 🚲
Facilities : ⛽ 🍴launderette

GPS Longitude : -1.06361
Latitude : 45.13561

HOURTIN-PLAGE

33990 – Michelin map **335** D3
▶ Paris 556 – Andernos-les-Bains 66 – Bordeaux 76 – Lesparre-Médoc 26

Club Airotel La Côte d'Argent ▲⁑

📞 0556091025, *www.cca33.com*
Address : 500m from the beach
Opening times : from mid May to mid Sept.
20 ha (870 pitches) undulating, terraced, flat, sandy
Tariff : 43€ 🛉🛉 🚐 🔲 🚿 (10A) – Extra per person 9€ – Reservation fee 35€
Rental rates : (from mid May to mid Sept.) 🏠 – 252 🚐 – 12 🛏. Per night from 51 to 250 €
Per week from 04 to 1 750 – Reservation fee 35€
🚐 sani-station

Surroundings : 🏊 ♨♨
Leisure activities : 🍸 ✗ 🎬 🎮 🏸 🎿 🏊 🚲 🎿 🖾 🛶 🏊 🏇 multi-sports ground
Facilities : 🔥 ⛽ 🖾 ☕ 🍴 launderette 🛒 🚚 refrigerated food storage

GPS Longitude : -1.16446
Latitude : 45.22259

LA HUME

33470 – Michelin map **335** E7
▶ Paris 645 – Bordeaux 59 – Mérignac 62 – Pessac 56

Verdalle

📞 0556661262, *www.campingdeverdalle.com*
Address : 2 allée de l'Infante (continue north along the av. de la Plage and take the road to the right; beside the Bassin d'Arcachon, direct access to the beach)
1.5 ha (108 pitches) flat, sandy, stony
Rentals : 6 tent bungalows.
🚐 sani-station

Surroundings : 🏊 ⛰ 🚐 ♨♨
Facilities : 🔥 ⛽ 🍴 🔲
Nearby : 🛶

GPS Longitude : -1.11099
Latitude : 44.64397

ITXASSOU

64250 – Michelin map **342** D3 – pop. 2,031 – alt. 39
▶ Paris 787 – Bayonne 24 – Biarritz 25 – Cambo-les-Bains 5

Hiriberria

☎ 0559299809, *www.hiriberria.com*
Address : located 1km northwest along the D 918, follow the signs for Cambo-les-Bains and take the road to the right
Opening times : permanent
4 ha (228 pitches) terrace, relatively flat, flat, grassy, fine gravel
Tariff : 👤 7€ 🚗 🅴 7€ – 🔌 (10A) 4€
Rental rates : (from beginning March to end Nov.) – 14 🚐 – 19 🏠.
Per night from 55 to 100€ **Per week** from 245 to 655€
🚱 sani-station 3.50€
Small but pretty chalet village.

Surroundings : ← ⌂ 🎯
Leisure activities : 🔲 🏊 🔳 (open-air in season)
Facilities : 👤 🚿 🏢 🍽 🧺 launderette

GPS
Longitude : -1.40137
Latitude : 43.33887

LABENNE-OCÉAN

40530 – Michelin map **335** C13
▶ Paris 763 – Bordeaux 185 – Mont-de-Marsan 98 – Pau 129

Yelloh! Village le Sylvamar 👥

☎ 0559457516, *www.sylvamar.fr*
Address : av. de l'Océan (continue along the D 126, follow the signs for the beach, near Le Boudigau)
Opening times : from end March to beginning Nov.
25 ha (750 pitches) flat, sandy, grassy
Tariff : 50€ 👥 🚗 🅴 🔌 (10A) – Extra per person 9€
Rental rates : (from end March to end Oct.) 👤 (chalets) 🛏 – 220 🚐 – 60 🏠 – 1 cabin in the trees. **Per night** from 39 to 280 € – **Per week** from 73 to 1,960 €
Large water park with indoor paddling pool and play area and a range of luxury rental options.

Surroundings : 🌿 ⌂ 🎯
Leisure activities : 🍴 ✕ 🔲 🎭 (open-air theatre) 🏓 🎣 🛁 hammam, jacuzzi 🏊 🚴 🎾 🔳 🏊 🏐 multi-sports ground, spa therapy centre
Facilities : 👤 🚿 🍽 🧺 launderette 🍴 refrigerated food storage
Nearby : 🏇 🦌 wildlife park

GPS
Longitude : -1.45687
Latitude : 43.59532

Côte d'Argent 👥

☎ 0559454202, *www.camping-cotedargent.com*
Address : 60 av. de l'Océan (along the D 126, follow the signs for the beach)
Opening times : from mid March to end Oct.
4 ha (215 pitches) flat, grassy, sandy
Tariff : 38.10€ 👥 🚗 🅴 🔌 (6A) – Extra per person 5.80€ – Reservation fee 25€
Rental rates : (from mid March to end Oct.) – 22 🚐 – 34 🏠 – 3 apartments – 12 tent bungalows. **Per night** from 40 to 68 € – **Per week** from 199 to 930 € – Reservation fee 25€
🚱 sani-station 3.50€

Surroundings : ⌂ 🎯
Leisure activities : 🍴 ✕ 🎭 daytime 🏓 🏊 🚴 🏇 🏐 multi-sports ground
Facilities : 👤 🚿 🆑 🏢 🍽 🧺 launderette 🍴
Nearby : 🍴 🎾

GPS
Longitude : -1.45687
Latitude : 43.59532

Municipal Les Pins Bleus

C 0559454113, *www.lespinsbleus.com*

Address : av. de l'Océan (along the D 126 follow the signs for the beach; beside the Boudigau river)

Opening times : from beginning April to end Oct.

6.5 ha (120 pitches) flat, sandy, grassy

Tariff : (2012 price) 18.70€ ♣♣ ⇔ ▣ ⚡ (16A) – Extra per person 3.50€ – Reservation fee 17.50€

Rental rates : (2012 price) (from beginning April to end Oct.) ♿ (1 chalet) – 3 ⬜ – 22 ⬜ – 4 tent bungalows. Per night from 31 to 88 € – Per week from 17 to 610 € – Reservation fee 17.50€

⬜ sani-station 4€ – 14 ▣ 9€ – ⬛⚡11€

Surroundings : ⚲⚲
Leisure activities : ✗ ⚓
Facilities : ⊶ ⚐ refrigerated food storage

GPS Longitude : -1.45687
Latitude : 43.60229

LACANAU

33680 – Michelin map **335** E5 – pop. 4,412 – alt. 17
▶ Paris 625 – Bordeaux 47 – Mérignac 45 – Pessac 51

Talaris Vacances ♣♣

C 0556030415, *www.talaris-vacances.fr*

Address : at La Moutchic (5km west along the D 6, follow the signs for Lacanau-Océan)

Opening times : from beginning April to end Sept.

10 ha (336 pitches) flat, grassy, small lake

Tariff : (2012 price) 41.50€ ♣♣ ⇔ ▣ ⚡ (10A) – Extra per person 8.50€ – Reservation fee 25€

Rental rates : (2012 price) (from beginning April to end Sept.) – 120 ⬜ – 5 ⬜ – 23 tent bungalows – 8 tents. Per night from 26 to 191€ – Per week from 182 to 1,337€ Reservation fee 25€

⬜ sani-station

A pleasant, wooded site.

Surroundings : ⚲ ⚲⚲
Leisure activities : ⚑ ✗ ⬜ ⚲ ⚓ ⚒ ⚲ ⚲ ⚲ ⚲ ⚲ multi-sports ground
Facilities : ♿ ⊶ ⚲ ⚐ launderette ⚲ ⚲

GPS Longitude : -1.11236
Latitude : 45.008

Le Tedey ♣♣

C 0556030015, *www.le-tedey.com* ⚲ (Jul–Aug)

Address : at the Moutchic, rte de Longarisse (3km south and take road to the left)

Opening times : from end April to mid Sept.

14 ha (700 pitches) flat, sandy, adjacent wooded dunes

Tariff : (2012 price) 30€ ♣♣ ⇔ ▣ ⚡ (10A) – Extra per person 6€ – Reservation fee 20€

Rental rates : (from end April to mid Sept.) ⚲ – 38 ⬜. Per week from 330 to 750€ Reservation fee 20€

⬜ sani-station

Pleasant site beside the Lac de Lacanau, shaded by pine trees, but with poor sanitary facilities.

Surroundings : ⚲ ⬜ ⚲⚲ ⚲
Leisure activities : ⚑ ⚲ ⚓ ⚒ ⚲ ⚲ ⚲ ⚓
Facilities : ♿ ⊶ ⚲ ⚐ launderette ⚲ ⚲

GPS Longitude : -1.13652
Latitude : 44.9875

This guide is not intended as a list of all the camping sites in France; its aim is to provide a selection of the best sites in each category.

Villages Vacances Le Gîte Autrement
(rental of chalets only)

📞 05 57 17 22 47, *www.gite-autrement.com*
Address : at Narsot (2.5km northeast along the D 104E4 follow the signs for Brach)
Opening times : permanent
1 ha flat, grassy, sandy
Rental rates : ✂ – 9 🏠. Per night from 56 to 61€ – Per week from 300 to 730€
Reservation fee 10€

Surroundings : ♨
Leisure activities : ⚓ 🚴 🏊 (open-air in season)
Facilities : ⚡ 🏕 ✗ 🍴 ☕

GPS
Longitude : -1.04908
Latitude : 44.98457

The Michelin classification (🔺🔺🔺 ... 🔺) is totally independent of the official star classification system awarded by the local prefecture or other official organisation.

LACANAU-OCÉAN

33680 – Michelin map **335** D4 – pop. 3,142
▶ Paris 636 – Andernos-les-Bains 38 – Arcachon 87 – Bordeaux 63

Yelloh! Village Les Grands Pins ♣♣

📞 05 56 03 20 77, *www.lesgrandspins.com*
Address : Plage Nord (north of the resort, 500m from the beach – direct access)
Opening times : from end April to end Sept.
11 ha (570 pitches) terraced, undulating, sandy
Tariff : 50€ ♀♀ 🚐 🔲 🔌 (10A) – Extra per person 9€
Rental rates : (from end April to end Sept.) – 218 🏠. Per night from 35 to 252 €
Per week from 45 to 1,764 €
🚽 sani-station 1€
No vehicle access to one part of the site.

Surroundings : 🐟 🚤 ♨
Leisure activities : 🍴 ✗ 🎣 🎱 🎯 🎿 ⚓ 🚴 🎾 🏊 ⛲ fitness trail, multi-sports ground, spa therapy centre hammam, jacuzzi
Facilities : ♿ ⚡ 🅿 ⛺ ☕ launderette 🛒 ❄ refrigerated food storage

GPS
Longitude : -1.19517
Latitude : 45.01088

Club Airotel de l'Océan ♣♣

📞 05 56 03 24 45, *www.airotel-ocean.com*
Address : 24 r. du Repos (Plage Nord (North Beach)
Opening times : from beginning April to end Sept.
9 ha (550 pitches) flat, terraced, undulating, sandy
Tariff : (2012 price) 47.60€ ♀♀ 🚐 🔲 🔌 (16A) – Extra per person 9.10€ – Reservation fee 28€
Rental rates : (2012 price) (from beginning April to end Sept.) ✂ – 250 🏠.
Per night from 37 to 160 € – Per week from 11 to 1,115 € – Reservation fee 28€
🚽 20 🔲 47.60€

Surroundings : ♨
Leisure activities : 🍴 ✗ 🎱 🎯 🎿 ⚓ 🚴 🎾 🏊 ⛲ disco, surfing
Facilities : ♿ ⚡ ⛺ ☕ launderette 🛒 ❄ refrigerated food storage

GPS
Longitude : -1.1928
Latitude : 45.00868

AQUITAINE

LAMONZIE-MONTASTRUC

24520 – Michelin map **329** E6 – pop. 632 – alt. 50
▶ Paris 587 – Bordeaux 131 – Périgueux 46 – Agen 103

L'Escapade ♣♣

🎧 0553572379, *www.campinglescapade.com*
Address : at Les Roussilloux (follow the signs for St-Alvère)
Opening times : from mid June to beginning Sept.
4.5 ha (85 pitches) terraced, flat, grassy, undulating
Tariff : 30€ ♦♦ ⊞ ▣ (♿) (10A) – Extra per person 7.60€ – Reservation fee 26€
Rental rates : (from beginning April to mid Sept.) 🚹 – 60 ⛺ – 20 🏠.
Per night from 56 to 118€ – **Per week** from 392 to 826 € – Reservation fee 26€

Surroundings : 🌿 ⌂ ≀
Leisure activities : ♈ ✗ 🏠 ⚕ 🔥 hammam, jacuzzi ⚐ 🚴 ⛓ ☒ ⟰
🛷 donkey rides, multi-sports ground
Facilities : 🚹 ⊶ 🛁 ♈ launderette ⚒

Longitude : 0.60793
Latitude : 44.88636

LANOUAILLE

24270 – Michelin map **329** H3 – pop. 989 – alt. 209 – Leisure centre
▶ Paris 446 – Brantôme 47 – Limoges 55 – Périgueux 46

Village Vacances Le Moulin de la Jarousse
(rental of chalets, yurts, cabins in the trees, gîtes only)

🎧 0553523791, *www.location-en-dordogne.com*
Address : at Payzac, at La Jarousse (continue 9km northeast along the D 704 to l'Hépital, then take right turn along the D 80)
Opening times : permanent
8 ha terraced, lake, forest
Rental rates : 🚹 (1 gîte) – 8 🏠 – 8 yurts – 8 cabins in the trees – 1 tent – 11 gîtes.
Per night 185€ – **Per week** from 300 to 1,295€
Natural wooded setting overlooking the lake.

Surroundings : 🌿 ⪕ ♨
Leisure activities : ⚐ 🚴 ☒ (open-air in season) 🛷 ⚲ pedalos,
farm or petting farm, quad biking ⚒
Facilities : ⊶ 🅿 ⟰ ⧉ ♈ ▣

Longitude : 1.18411
Latitude : 45.43694

LARRAU

64560 – Michelin map **342** G4 – pop. 204 – alt. 636
▶ Paris 840 – Bordeaux 254 – Pamplona 110 – Donostia-San Sebastián 142

Village Vacances Les Chalets d'Iraty
(rental of chalets only)

🎧 0559285129, *www.chalets-iraty.com* – alt. 1 327
Address : at the col de Bagargui (14km west along the D 19, follow the signs for St-Jean-Pied-de-Port)
Opening times : permanent
2 000 ha/4 ha for camping undulating, grassy
Rental rates : (2012 price) 🅿 – 40 🏠. **Per week** from 275 to 325€
Site spread out in the Forêt d'Iraty, between the Col de Bagargui and the Col Hegui Xouri.

Surroundings : 🌿 ♨
Leisure activities : 🚴 ⚒
Facilities : ⊶ ⧉ ♈ ▣
Nearby : ⚐ ♈ ✗ ⚒ ⚲ 🐎 cross-country skiing

Longitude : -1.03532
Latitude : 43.03638

LARUNS

64440 – Michelin map **342** J5 – pop. 1,326 – alt. 523
▶ Paris 811 – Argelès-Gazost 49 – Lourdes 51 – Oloron-Ste-Marie 34

Les Gaves

✆ 0559053237, *www.campingdesgaves.com* – limited spaces for one-night stay
Address : Pon quartier (located 1.5km southeast of Larun, follow the signs for Le Col d'Aubisque and take the road to the left; beside the Gave d'Ossau (river)
Opening times : permanent
2.4 ha (101 pitches) flat, grassy, gravelled
Tariff : 26.90€ 🏕🏕 ⇔ 🔲 (½) (10A) – Extra per person 4.80€ – Reservation fee 17€
Rental rates : (permanent) 🅿 – 20 ⏢ – 5 🏠 – 5 apartments – 1 gîte.
Per night from 36 to 97 € **Per week from** 252 to 679 € – Reservation fee 20€
🚐 sani-station – 5 🔲 11€ – 🛒11€

Surroundings : ❄ 🐾 ⟨ ▭ 🎱
Leisure activities : 🍽 🏛 🏊
Facilities : ⌾ 🏢 🧺 🤟 🌳 launderette

GPS Longitude : -0.41772
Latitude : 42.98306

LÈGE-CAP-FERRET

33950 – Michelin map **335** E6 – pop. 7,527 – alt. 9
▶ Paris 629 – Arcachon 65 – Belin-Beliet 56 – Bordeaux 50

🔺

La Prairie

✆ 0556600975, *www.campinglaprairie.com*
Address : 93 av. du Médoc (located 1km northeast along the D 3, follow the signs for Le Porge)
Opening times : from beginning March to end Oct.
2.5 ha (118 pitches) flat, grassy, sandy
Tariff : 20€ 🏕🏕 ⇔ 🔲 (½) (10A) – Extra per person 3.80€
Rental rates : (from beginning April to end Sept.) – 16 ⏢ – 3 tent bungalows.
Per night from 7 to 60 € – **Per week from** 160 to 636 €
🚐 sani-station – 20 🔲 9€ – 🛒9€

Surroundings : ▭ 🎱
Leisure activities : 🏛 🏊 🌊
Facilities : ♿ ⌾ 🧺 🤟 🖼

GPS Longitude : -1.13375
Latitude : 44.80271

LÉON

40550 – Michelin map **335** D11 – pop. 1,830 – alt. 9
▶ Paris 724 – Castets 14 – Dax 30 – Mimizan 42

Yelloh! Village Punta Lago 👥

✆ 0558492440, *www.camping-puntalago.com*
Address : 1395 av. du Lac (located 1.5km northwest along the D 142, opposite the municipal stadium, 200m from the lake)
Opening times : from beginning April to end Sept.
5.5 ha (300 pitches) flat, grassy, sandy
Tariff : 45€ 🏕🏕 ⇔ 🔲 (½) (10A) – Extra per person 7€
Rental rates : (from beginning April to end Sept.) – 85 ⏢. **Per night from** 39 to 202 €
Per week from 73 to 1,414 €

Surroundings : 🐾 ▭ 🎱
Leisure activities : 🍽 🏛 🎮 🏊 🛶 🏊 🔲 🌊 multi-sports ground
Facilities : ♿ ⌾ 🔥 🧺 🤟 🌳 launderette 🐾
Nearby : 🏊 ✗

GPS Longitude : -1.31342
Latitude : 43.88382

LESCUN

64490 – Michelin map **342** I5 – pop. 178 – alt. 900
▶ Paris 846 – Lourdes 89 – Oloron-Ste-Marie 37 – Pau 70

Le Lauzart

☎ 05 59 34 51 77, *camping-lescun.com*
Address : located 1.5km southwest along the D 340
1 ha (50 pitches) flat and relatively flat, terraced, stony, grassy, rocks
Magnificent mountain site, although the sanitary facilities are a little jaded.

Surroundings : 🌳 ≤ 🏔
Facilities : ♿ 🚮 ▥ 🛁 🖼

 Longitude : -0.64217
Latitude : 42.92761

LIMEUIL

24510 – Michelin map **329** G6 – pop. 328 – alt. 65
▶ Paris 528 – Bergerac 43 – Brive-la-Gaillarde 78 – Périgueux 48

La Ferme des Poutiroux

☎ 05 53 63 31 62, *www.poutiroux.com*
Address : take the northwestern exit along the D 31, follow the signs for Trémolat then continue 1km along the road for Paunat to the right
Opening times : from beginning April to end Sept.
2.5 ha (45 pitches) terraced, flat and relatively flat, grassy
Tariff : 👤 5.30€ 🚗 ▣ 5.90€ – 🔋 (6A) 4€ – Reservation fee 13€
Rental rates : (permanent) ♿ – 20 🚐. Per night from 26 to 38 € – Per week from 170 to 610 € Reservation fee 13€
🚐 sani-station 3€ – 4 ▣ 12€

Surroundings : 🌳 ≤ 🏔
Leisure activities : 🖼 🚣 🏊
Facilities : ♿ 🚮 🛒 🛁 🍴 launderette

Longitude : 0.87946
Latitude : 44.89332

There are several different types of sani-station ('borne' in French) – sanitation points providing fresh water and disposal points for grey water.
See page 12 for further details.

LINXE

40260 – Michelin map **335** D11 – pop. 1,236 – alt. 33
▶ Paris 712 – Castets 10 – Dax 31 – Mimizan 37

FranceLoc Domaine Lila

☎ 05 58 43 96 25, *www.franceloc.fr*
Address : 190, rte de Mixe (located 1.5km northwest along the D 42, follow the signs for St-Girons and take D 397, turning to the right)
2 ha (100 pitches) flat, sandy, fine gravel
Rentals : 50 🚐.
Natural swimming pool.

Surroundings : 🏔
Leisure activities : 🖼 🏓 🚴 🚣 🏊 ⛷
Facilities : ♿ 🚮 🛁 launderette

Longitude : -1.25758
Latitude : 43.93185

LIT-ET-MIXE

40170 – Michelin map **335** D10 – pop. 1,497 – alt. 13
▶ Paris 710 – Castets 21 – Dax 42 – Mimizan 22

Village Center Les Vignes ♠♣

(rental of mobile homes, chalets and tent bungalows only)

℘ 05 58 42 85 60, *www.village-center.fr*

Address : 2.7km southwest along the D 652 and take the D 88, to the right, follow the signs for Le Cap de l'Homy

Opening times : from beginning April to end Sept.

15 ha (495 pitches) flat, sandy

Rental rates : 2012 price) ⅙ (2 mobile homes) – 330 🚐 – 60 🏠 – 19 tent bungalows.
Per night from 32 to 161 € – Per week from 24 to 1,099 € – Reservation fee 30€

Leisure activities : ♈ ✗ 🎱 ⑨ (big top staging activities and shows) 👫 🚴 ⚅ ♒ 🎱 ⚄ ⚃ cinema, multi-sports ground
Facilities : ⅙ ⚊ 🏧♨⚑ launderette 🗑 ⚒

GPS Longitude : -1.28275
Latitude : 44.02401

Municipal du Cap de l'Homy

℘ 05 58 42 83 47, *www.camping-cap.com* ✍

Address : at Cap-de-l'Homy, 600 av. de l'Océan (8km west along the D 652 and take D 88 to the right; 300m from the beach (direct access)

Opening times : from beginning May to end Sept.

10 ha (474 pitches) flat, undulating, sandy

Tariff : (2012 price) 27.10 € ♈♈ 🚐 ▣ ⑨ (6A) – Extra per person 6.10€ – Reservation fee 30€

Rental rates : (2012 price) (from beginning May to mid Sept.) ✍ – 15 tent bungalows.
Per week from 16 to 622 € – Reservation fee 30€

🚐 sani-station 5.80€ – 36 ▣ 15.80€

Sheltered by a pleasant pine wood.

Surroundings : 🌿 ♒
Leisure activities : 🎱 🚴
Facilities : ⅙ ⚊ 🏧♨⚑ launderette, refrigerated food storage
Nearby : ⚘ ♈ ✗ ⚒ surfing

GPS Longitude : -1.33435
Latitude : 44.03712

The pitches of many campsites are marked out with low hedges of attractive bushes and shrubs.

MARCILLAC-ST-QUENTIN

24200 – Michelin map **329** I6 – pop. 791 – alt. 235
▶ Paris 522 – Brive-la-Gaillarde 48 – Les Eyzies-de-Tayac 18 – Montignac 21

Les Tailladis

℘ 05 53 59 10 95, *www.tailladis.com*

Address : at Les Tailladis (situated 2km to the north, near the D 48; beside the Beune river and a lake)

Opening times : from mid March to end Oct.

25 ha/8 ha for camping (90 pitches) flat, terraced, sloping, grassy, stony

Tariff : 23.90€ ♈♈ 🚐 ▣ ⑨ (10A) – Extra per person 6.25€ – Reservation fee 10€

Rental rates : (from mid March to end Oct.) – 3 🚐 – 4 🏠 – 3 tents. Per night 60€
Per week from 380 to 700 € – Reservation fee 10€

🚐 sani-station

Surroundings : 🌿 ⚀ ♒
Leisure activities : ♈ ✗ ⚄ ⚘
Facilities : ⅙ ⚊ ▥ ♨⚑ launderette ⚘ ⚒

GPS Longitude : 1.18789
Latitude : 44.97465

MAULÉON-LICHARRE

64130 – Michelin map **342** G5 – pop. 3,205 – alt. 140
▶ Paris 802 – Oloron-Ste-Marie 31 – Orthez 39 – Pau 60

Uhaitza – Le Saison

℘ 0559281879, *www.camping-uhaitza.com*
Address : located 1.5km south along the D 918, follow the signs for Tardets-Sorholus; beside the Saison river
Opening times : from beginning April to mid Oct.
1 ha (50 pitches) flat, grassy
Tariff : (2012 price) 🚶 5.73€ 🚗 2.95€ 📧 5.49€ – 🔌 (10A) 4.98€ – Reservation fee 10€
Rental rates : (2012 price) (from beginning March to end Nov.) 🏠 (From end Jun to end Aug) – 2 🚐 – 5 🏠. Per week 599€ – Reservation fee 10€
🚰 sani-station 5.10€

Surroundings : 🌳 🗆 ♤♤	
Leisure activities : 🍴 🏛 ⚓ 🏊 🎣	**Longitude** : -0.8972
Facilities : & ☕🛒🏕 🚿 ☆ 🚾 🍴 launderette	**Latitude** : 43.20789

Aire Naturelle La Ferme Landran

℘ 0559281955, *www.gites64.com/la-ferme-landran*
Address : at Ordiarp, Larréguy (4.5km southwest along the D 918, follow the signs for St-Jean-Pied-de-Port then continue 1.5km along the road for Lambarre to the right)
Opening times : from mid April to end Sept.
1 ha (25 pitches) sloping, terraced, grassy
Tariff : 13.50€ 🚶🚶 🚗 📧 🔌 (6A) – Extra per person 3€
Rental rates : (2012 price) (permanent) – 2 🏠 – 1 gîte. Per night from 50 €
Per week from 240 to 350 €
🚰 sani-station 3€
Farm campsite.

Surroundings : 🌳 ≤ ♀	
Leisure activities : 🏛 ⚓	**Longitude** : -0.93933
Facilities : & ☕🛒🏕 📷	**Latitude** : 43.20185

Using the traditional Michelin classification method, the guide provides you with an easy, speedy reference for assessing the category of each site: 1 to 5 tents (see page 10).

MÉNESPLET

24700 – Michelin map **329** B5 – pop. 1,646 – alt. 43
▶ Paris 532 – Bergerac 44 – Bordeaux 69 – Libourne 35

Camp'Gîte

℘ 0553818439, *www.campgite.com* – 🅟
Address : at Les Loges (3.8km southwest of the town, following signs for Laser)
Opening times : permanent
1 ha (29 pitches) flat, grassy
Tariff : (2012 price) 13€ 🚶🚶 🚗 📧 🔌 (16A) – Extra per person 3€
🚰 4 📧 10€

Surroundings : 🌳 🗆 ♀	
Leisure activities : 🏛	**Longitude** : 0.0717
Facilities : & 🛒🏕🚿 🍴 launderette	**Latitude** : 44.9987

MESSANGES

40660 – Michelin map **335** C12 – pop. 986 – alt. 8
▶ Paris 734 – Bayonne 45 – Castets 24 – Dax 33

Club Airotel Le Vieux Port ▲▲

0825 70 40 40, www.levieuxport.com

Address : rte de la Plage Sud (2.5km southwest along the D 652, follow the signs for Vieux-Boucau-les-Bains then continue 800m along the road to the right; 500m from the beach, direct access)
Opening times : from end March to end Sept.
40 ha/30 ha for camping (1546 pitches) undulating, flat, sandy, grassy
Tariff : 64 € ♣♣ ⇔ 🔲 🔣 (8A) – Extra per person 9.50 € – Reservation fee 40 €
Rental rates : (from end March to end Sept.) ♿ (1 mobile home) 🛖 – 420 🚐 – 75 🏚.
Per night from 76 to 160 € – Per week from 84 to 1,120 € – Reservation fee 40 €
🔁 sani-station
Spacious landscaped water park with plenty of shops and services at the entrance.

Surroundings : 〰〰 Leisure activities : ♟ ✗ 🎱 🎦 (cinema/theatre) 🤸 ⛵ hammam, jacuzzi 🏊 🚲 ✂ ♨ 🎯 🎱 ⛷ 🐎 multi-sports ground, spa therapy centre Facilities : ♿ ⚡ 🔲 ⛺ 🚿 🚰 🍴 launderette 🛒 🛒 refrigerated food storage	**GPS** Longitude : -1.39995 Latitude : 43.79773

Village Vacances Club Airotel Lou Pignada ▲▲
(rental of caravans, mobile homes and chalets only)

0825 70 40 40, www.loupignada.com

Address : rte d'Azur (situated 2km south along the D 652 then continue 500m down road to the left)
Opening times : from end March to end Sept.
8 ha (430 pitches) flat, sandy
Rental rates : ♿ (1 mobile home) 🛖 – 115 🚐 – 50 🏚. Per night from 66 to 145 €
Per week from 44 to 1,015 € – Reservation fee 40 €
🔁 sani-station

Surroundings : 🛏 〰〰 Leisure activities : ♟ ✗ 🎦 🤸 🎯 ⛵ 🏊 🚲 ✂ 🎱 ⛷ multi-sports ground Facilities : ♿ ⚡ 🔲 🍴 launderette ⚡ 🛒 refrigerated food storage Nearby : 🛒	**GPS** Longitude : -1.38245 Latitude : 43.79747

La Côte

0558 48 94 94, www.campinglacote.com

Address : chemin de la Côte (2.3km southwest along the D 652, follow the signs for Vieux-Boucau-les-Bains and take the road to the right)
Opening times : from beginning April to end Sept.
3.5 ha (143 pitches) flat, grassy, sandy
Tariff : 29.20 € ♣♣ ⇔ 🔲 🔣 (10A) – Extra per person 6 € – Reservation fee 18 €
Rental rates : (from beginning April to end Sept.) 🛖 – 11 🚐 – 1 gîte.
Per night from 50 to 70 € – Per week from 50 to 750 € – Reservation fee 20 €
🔁 sani-station

Surroundings : 🌳 〰〰 Leisure activities : 🎱 jacuzzi 🏊 🎱 Facilities : ♿ ⚡ ⛺ 🚿 🚰 🍴 launderette, refrigerated food storage Nearby : 🛒	**GPS** Longitude : -1.39171 Latitude : 43.80035

Les Acacias

℘ 0558480178, *www.lesacacias.com*

Address : rte d'Azur, Delest quartier (situated 2km south along the D 652, follow the signs for Vieux-Boucau-les-Bains then continue 1km along the turning to the left)

Opening times : from end March to end Oct.

1.7 ha (128 pitches) flat, grassy, sandy

Tariff : 23.20€ ♥♥ ⟲ ▤ ⦿ (10A) – Extra per person 4.60€ – Reservation fee 15€

Rental rates : (from end March to mid Oct.) – 11 ⟨⟩. Per night from 50 to 65 €
Per week from 240 to 670 € – Reservation fee 15€

Surroundings : 🐾 ⚘
Leisure activities : ⛺ ⛵
Facilities : ⛐ ⊶ ⛺ ⚲ ⚙ ⚑ launderette
Nearby : ⛴

Longitude : -1.37567
Latitude : 43.79757

MÉZOS

40170 – Michelin map **335** E10 – pop. 866 – alt. 23
▶ Paris 700 – Bordeaux 118 – Castets 24 – Mimizan 16

Club Airotel Le Village Tropical Sen Yan ♠♠

℘ 0558426005, *www.sen-yan.com*

Address : av. de la Gare (located 1km east, follow the signs for Le Cout)

Opening times : from beginning June to mid Sept.

8 ha (310 pitches) flat, sandy

Tariff : 43€ ♥♥ ⟲ ▤ ⦿ (8A) – Extra per person 8.10€ – Reservation fee 26€

Rental rates : (2012 price) (from beginning May to mid Sept.) ⚑ – 180 ⟨⟩ – 41 ⌂ .
Per night from 62 to 173 € – Per week from 434 to 1,211 € – Reservation fee 26€

Pretty complex with swimming pools, palm trees, plantations and a small ecological lake.

Surroundings : 🐾 ⛲ ⚘⚘
Leisure activities : ♟ ✗ ⛺ ⚲ ⚶ 🎣 ⛵ ⚑ ⚙ ✂ ⛲ ⛱ ⚓ (lake)
⚑ multi-sports ground
Facilities : ⛐ ⊶ ⛺ ⚲ ⚙ ⚑ launderette ⛱ ⚑

Longitude : -1.15657
Latitude : 44.07164

The classification (1 to 5 tents, black or red) that we award to selected sites in this guide is our own system. It should not be confused with the classification (1 to 5 stars) of official organisations.

MIALET

24450 – Michelin map **329** G2 – pop. 665 – alt. 320
▶ Paris 436 – Limoges 49 – Nontron 23 – Périgueux 51

Village Vacances L'Étang de Vivale
(rental of chalets only)

℘ 0553526605, *www.vivaledordogne.com*

Address : 32 av. de Nontron (700m west along the D 79; beside the lake)

Opening times : from end March to beginning Nov.

30 ha flat, slightly undulating

Rental rates : 20 ⌂ . Per night from 70 to 110 € – Per week from 400 to 770 €

Surroundings : 🐾 ⛲ ⚘
Leisure activities : ♟ ⛺ ⚑ ⚙ ⛱ ⚓ boats for hire ⚑
Facilities : ⛐ ⊶ ⓟ ⚑ ▣

Longitude : 0.89788
Latitude : 45.54793

MIMIZAN

40200 – Michelin map **335** D9 – pop. 7,000 – alt. 13
▶ Paris 692 – Arcachon 67 – Bayonne 109 – Bordeaux 109

Municipal du Lac

𝒫 05 58 09 01 21, *www.mimizan-camping.com*

Address : av. de Woolsack (situated 2km north along the D 87, follow the signs for Gastes; beside the Lac d'Aureilhan)

Opening times : from end April to beginning Sept.

8 ha (466 pitches) flat, sandy, grassy

Tariff : (2012 price) ⚹ 7.65€ 🚗 2.25€ 🔲 9.95€ – 🔌 (6A) 2€ – Reservation fee 20€

Rental rates : (2012 price) (from end April to beginning Sept.) – 19 tent bungalows.
Per night from 24 to 44 €– Per week from 162 to 505 € – Reservation fee 20€

🚿 sani-station 2€ – 21 🔲 12.50€

Surroundings : ♀
Leisure activities : ✗ 🏊
Facilities : ♿ � 🛁 🗃 🚰 🛒
Nearby : 🎣 🚣 🦆 pedalos

GPS Longitude : -1.2299
Latitude : 44.21968

MIMIZAN-PLAGE

40200 – Michelin map **335** D9
▶ Paris 706 – Bordeaux 128 – Mont-de-Marsan 84

Club Airotel Marina-Landes ♟⚹

𝒫 05 58 09 12 66, *www.marinalandes.com*

Address : 8, r. Marina (500m from La Plage du Sud (beach)

Opening times : from beginning May to mid Sept.

9 ha (536 pitches) flat, sandy

Tariff : (2012 price) 52€ ⚹⚹ 🚗 🔲 🔌 (10A) – Extra per person 10€ – Reservation fee 35€

Rental rates : (2012 price) (from beginning May to mid Sept.) – 100 🛖 – 6 🏠 – 24 studios – 7 teepees – 10 tent bungalows. Per night from 30 to 174 € – Per week from 207 to 1,220 € Reservation fee 35€

🚿 sani-station 2€

Surroundings : ▭ ♀♀
Leisure activities : 🍸 ✗ 🎮 🎣 🏓 🏖 🏊 🚴 ✂ ♪ 🔲 🏊 ⛷
multi-sports ground, entertainment room
Facilities : ♿ � ▦ 🛁 🍴 launderette 🚰 🛒
Nearby : 🏇

GPS Longitude : -1.2909
Latitude : 44.2043

Municipal de la Plage ♟⚹

𝒫 05 58 09 00 32, *www.mimizan-camping.com*

Address : bd de l'Atlantique (northern quartier)

Opening times : from beginning May to mid Sept.

16 ha (608 pitches) flat, sandy, undulating, grassy

Tariff : (2012 price) 22.35€ ⚹⚹ 🚗 🔲 🔌 (10A) – Extra per person 9.25€ – Reservation fee 20€

Rental rates : (2012 price) (from beginning May to mid Sept.) 🅿 – 32 🛖 – 15 🏠.
Per week from 185 to 745 € – Reservation fee 20€

🚿 sani-station 1.50€ – 18 🔲 10.35€

Welcomes surfer groups.

Surroundings : ▭
Leisure activities : ✗ 🏓 🏊 climbing wall, multi-sports ground
Facilities : ♿ � 🛁 🍴 launderette 🚰 🛒 refrigerated food storage

GPS Longitude : -1.28384
Latitude : 44.21719

MOLIETS-PLAGE

40660 – Michelin map **335** C11
▶ Paris 716 – Bordeaux 156 – Mont-de-Marsan 89 – Bayonne 67

Le Saint-Martin

☎ 0558485230, *www.camping-saint-martin.fr*
Address : av. de l'Océan (on the D 117, direct access to the beach)
Opening times : from end March to beginning Nov.
18 ha (660 pitches) undulating, flat and relatively flat, sandy
Tariff : (2012 price) 43.90€ ♥♥ ⇎ 🅴 🔌 (10A) – Extra per person 8.50€ – Reservation fee 35€
Rental rates : (2012 price) (from end March to beginning Nov.) – 227 🏠 – 6 tents.
Per night from 88 to 310€ – Per week from 205 to 1,480 € – Reservation fee 35€
🚮 sani-station 18.80€ – 45 🅴 54.40€

Surroundings : 🖙 ♀
Leisure activities : ♈ ✗ 🎦 ◈ ⛵ multi-sports ground
Facilities : ⅙ ⚬– 🛁 ⚘ ⛟ ⛾ launderette ⛗ refrigerated food storage
Nearby : ⛙ 🚲

GPS Longitude : -1.38731
Latitude : 43.85259

MONPAZIER

24540 – Michelin map **329** G7 – pop. 522 – alt. 180
▶ Paris 575 – Bergerac 47 – Fumel 26 – Périgueux 75

Le Moulin de David ♣♦

☎ 0553226525, *www.moulindedavid.com*
Address : 3km southwest along the D 2, follow the signs for Villeréal and take road to the left;
beside a stream
Opening times : from beginning April to end Sept.
16 ha/4 ha for camping (160 pitches) flat, terrace, grassy
Tariff : (2012 price) 24€ ♥♥ ⇎ 🅴 🔌 (10A) – Extra per person 5€ – Reservation fee 15€
Rental rates : (2012 price) (from beginning April to end Sept.) – 56 🚐 – 2 tent bungalows –
4 tents. Per night from 24 to 42 € – Per week from 168 to 903 € – Reservation fee 15€

Surroundings : 🌳 🖙 ♀♀
Leisure activities : ♈ ✗ 🎦 ◈ 🎯 ⛷ 🏊 ≊ (lake) 🏄
Facilities : ⅙ ⚬– 🛁 ⚘ ⛟ ⛾ launderette ◲ ⛗

GPS Longitude : 0.87873
Latitude : 44.65979

MONTIGNAC

24290 – Michelin map **329** H5 – pop. 2,851 – alt. 77
▶ Paris 513 – Brive-la-Gaillarde 39 – Périgueux 54 – Sarlat-la-Canéda 25

Le Moulin du Bleufond

☎ 0553518395, *www.bleufond.com*
Address : av. Aristide Briand (500m south along the D 65 follow the signs for Sergeac; near the
Vézère river)
Opening times : from beginning April to end Sept.
1.3 ha (84 pitches) flat, grassy
Tariff : ♀ 7.20€ ⇎ 🅴 8.60€ – 🔌 (10A) 4.90€
Rental rates : (from beginning April to end Sept.) – 17 🚐. Per night from 60 to 120 €
Per week from 230 to 700 €
🚮 🛒 10€
Pretty pitches near an old mill.

Surroundings : 🌳 🖙 ♀♀
Leisure activities : ✗ 🎦 ≊ jacuzzi ⛷ 🏊
Facilities : ⅙ ⚬– ▥ 🛁 ⚘ ⛾ launderette ⛗
Nearby : ✂ ⛷

GPS Longitude : 1.15864
Latitude : 45.05989

MONTORY

64470 – Michelin map **342** H4 – pop. 330 – alt. 350
▶ Paris 827 – Bordeaux 241 – Pamplona 121 – Pau 56

Village Vacances Les Chalets de Soule
(rental of mobile homes only)

⌀ 05 59 28 53 28, *www.leschaletsdesoule.com*
Address : Cazenave quartier
Opening times : permanent
2 ha flat, grassy
Rental rates : (2012 price) **P** – 11 ⊡. Per night from 63 to 76 € – Per week from 305 to 490 €

Surroundings :
Leisure activities :
Facilities :
Nearby : ✗ quad biking

Longitude : -0.81399
Latitude : 43.09458

MONTPON-MÉNESTÉROL

24700 – Michelin map **329** B5 – pop. 5,535 – alt. 93
▶ Paris 532 – Bergerac 40 – Bordeaux 75 – Libourne 43

La Cigaline

⌀ 05 53 80 22 16, *www.lacigaline.fr*
Address : take the northern exit along the D 708, follow the signs for Ribérac and take the turning to the left before the bridge
Opening times : from beginning April to end Oct.
2 ha (120 pitches) flat, grassy
Tariff : (2012 price) 14.90€ ♦♦ ⟾ 🔲 ⚡ (10A) – Extra per person 3.50€
Rental rates : (2012 price) (from beginning April to end Oct.) ⚒ – 4 ⊡.
Per night from 40 to 75 € – Per week from 395 to 495 € – Reservation fee 30€
⟾ ⚡15.90€
Beside the Isle river.

Surroundings :
Leisure activities :
Facilities :
Nearby :

Longitude : 0.15839
Latitude : 45.01217

NAVARRENX

64190 – Michelin map **342** H3 – pop. 1,104 – alt. 125
▶ Paris 787 – Oloron-Ste-Marie 23 – Orthez 22 – Pau 43

Beau Rivage

⌀ 05 59 66 10 00, *www.beaucamping.com*
Address : allée des Marronniers (to the west of the town, neare the Gave d'Oloron (river) and the village ramparts)
Opening times : from end March to mid Oct.
2.5 ha (67 pitches) terraced, flat, grassy, fine gravel
Tariff : 26.40€ ♦♦ ⟾ 🔲 ⚡ (10A) – Extra per person 5.30€
Rental rates : (from end March to mid Oct.) ⚡ (1 chalet) – 10 ⌂. Per week from 90 to 690 €
⟾ sani-station
Near the Gave d'Oloron (river) and the village ramparts.

Surroundings :
Leisure activities :
Facilities : launderette
Nearby :

Longitude : -0.76121
Latitude : 43.32003

NONTRON

24300 – Michelin map **329** E2 – pop. 3,421 – alt. 260
▶ Paris 464 – Bordeaux 175 – Périgueux 49 – Angoulême 47

Camping De Nontron

⌖ 05 53 56 02 04, *www.campingdenontron.com*
Address : at St-Martial-de-Valette (located 1km south on the D 675, follow the signs for Périgueux)
Opening times : from beginning Jan. to mid Dec.
2 ha (70 pitches) flat, grassy, beside river
Tariff : 16.50€ ⚹⚹ ⇔ 🅴 (10A) – Extra per person 4.30€
Rental rates : (from beginning Jan. to mid Dec.) – 2 🛖 – 1 ⛏ – 7 studios.
Per week from 215 to 475 €
🚽 sani-station
Beside a large indoor water park.

Surroundings : ⌕ ♨♨
Leisure activities : 🎮 🎣
Facilities : ♿ ⛽ 🗄 🛁 🍴 📦 ♨
Nearby : ♨ hammam jacuzzi 🎣 ⛷

GPS
Longitude : 0.65807
Latitude : 45.51951

OLORON-STE-MARIE

64400 – Michelin map **342** I5 – pop. 11,029 – alt. 224
▶ Paris 809 – Bayonne 105 – Dax 83 – Lourdes 58

Le Stade

⌖ 05 59 39 11 26, *www.camping-du-stade.com*
Address : chemin de la Gravette (4.5km to the south, towards Saragosse)
Opening times : from beginning May to end Sept.
5 ha (170 pitches) flat, grassy
Tariff : 12€ ⚹⚹ ⇔ 🅴 (6A) – Extra per person 4€
Rental rates : (permanent) – 1 🛖 – 10 🏠. Per week from 285 to 530 €
Free admission to the nearby water park during July and August.

Surroundings : 🏞 ⌕ ♨♨
Leisure activities : 🎮 🏊
Facilities : ♿ ⛽ 🗄 🗄 ⛴ 📦
Nearby : 🏊 ✕ ✂ 🎣 🎿 ⛷

GPS
Longitude : -0.62386
Latitude : 43.17848

ONDRES

40440 – Michelin map **335** C13 – pop. 4,479 – alt. 37
▶ Paris 761 – Bayonne 8 – Biarritz 15 – Dax 48

Du Lac

⌖ 05 59 45 28 45, *www.camping-du-lac.fr*
Address : 518 r. de Janin (2.2km north along the N 10 then take the D 26, follow the signs for Ondres-Plage then head towards Le Turc, road to the right; near a lake)
Opening times : from mid March to end Oct.
3 ha (115 pitches) flat, terrace, grassy, sandy
Tariff : (2012 price) 40€ ⚹⚹ ⇔ 🅴 (10A) – Extra per person 7€ – Reservation fee 20€
Rental rates : (2012 price) (from mid March to end Oct.) – 1 caravan – 26 🛖 – 3 🏠 – 7 tent bungalows. Per night from 29 to 165 € – Per week from 203 to 1,435 € – Reservation fee 20€
🚽 sani-station 17€

Surroundings : 🏞 ⌕ ♨♨
Leisure activities : 🍴 ✕ 🎮 ♨ hammam 🏊 🚲 🎿
Facilities : ♿ ⛽ 🗄 🛁 🍴 launderette ♨
Nearby : 🎣

GPS
Longitude : -1.45249
Latitude : 43.56499

PARCOUL

24410 – Michelin map **329** B4 – pop. 363 – alt. 70
▶ Paris 503 – Bergerac 69 – Blaye 72 – Bordeaux 75

Le Paradou

℘ 05 53 91 42 78, *www.leparadou24.fr*
Address : at the Vaures leisure centre (situated 2km southwest along the D 674, follow the signs for La Roche-Chalais)
Opening times : permanent
20 ha/4 ha for camping (100 pitches) flat, grassy, stony
Tariff : (2012 price) ⚲ 5.30€ ⬛ 13€ (10A) – Reservation fee 11€
Rental rates : (2012 price) (permanent) ♿ (1 chalet) – 64 🚐 – 4 🏠.
Per night from 35 to 70 € – Per week from 180 to 710 € – Reservation fee 11€
🔲 ⬛10.50€
Surroundings : ▭ 🎋
Leisure activities : 🛶 🚣 ✂ 🎣 ⛵ (lake) ⛷ 🎣
Facilities : ♿ ⚡ 🚿 ⚐ launderette, refrigerators
Nearby : 🍴 ✕ 🚲 pedalos

GPS Longitude : 0.02578
Latitude : 45.19038

In order for the guide to remain wholly objective, the selection is made on an entirely independent basis. There is no charge for being selected for the guide.

PARENTIS-EN-BORN

40160 – Michelin map **335** E8 – pop. 5,187 – alt. 32
▶ Paris 658 – Arcachon 43 – Bordeaux 76 – Mimizan 25

L'Arbre d'Or

℘ 05 58 78 41 56, *www.arbre-dor.com*
Address : 75 rte du lac (located 1.5km west along the D 43)
Opening times : from beginning April to end Oct.
4 ha (200 pitches) open site, flat, sandy, grassy
Tariff : 27.60€ ⚲⚲ ⬛ (10A) – Extra per person 6.30€
Rental rates : (from beginning April to end Oct.) – 13 🚐 – 3 🏠 – 2 tent bungalows.
Per week from 200 to 1,030 €
🔲 ⬛14€
Surroundings : ♀
Leisure activities : 🍴 ✕ 🛶 🏃 🚣 🎣 ⛷ multi-sports ground
Facilities : ♿ ⚡ 🍴 launderette 🚲 refrigerators

GPS Longitude : -1.09232
Latitude : 44.34615

Municipal Pipiou ♦♦

℘ 05 58 78 57 25, *www.campingpipiou.parentis.com/*
Address : rte des Campings (2.5km west along the D 43 and take the turning to the right, 100m from the lake)
Opening times : from mid Feb. to mid Nov.
6 ha (324 pitches) flat, sandy
Tariff : (2012 price) 23.50€ ⚲⚲ ⬛ (10A) – Extra per person 5€ – Reservation fee 20€
Rental rates : (2012 price) (from mid Feb. to mid Nov.) – 20 🚐. Per night from 39 to 49
Per week from 145 to 710 – Reservation fee 20€
Surroundings : 🌳 ▭
Leisure activities : 🍴 ✕ 🏃 🚣 🎡
Facilities : ♿ ⚡ 🍴 ⚐ 🚿 ⚡ launderette 🚲 🚲
Nearby : 🏖 ⛵ (beach) 🎣 ♦

GPS Longitude : -1.10135
Latitude : 44.3457

PAUILLAC

33250 – Michelin map **335** G3 – pop. 5,135 – alt. 20
▶ Paris 625 – Arcachon 113 – Blaye 16 – Bordeaux 54

Municipal Les Gabarreys

𝒫 05 56 59 10 03, www.pauillac-medoc.com
Address : rte de la Rivière (located 1km to the south, near the Gironde river)
Opening times : from beginning April to mid Oct.
1.6 ha (59 pitches) flat, grassy, fine gravel
Tariff : (2012 price) 20.50 € ♟ ♟ ⛺ 🔲 ⚡ (6A) – Extra per person 4.50 € – Reservation fee 11 €
Rental rates : (2012 price) (from beginning April to mid Oct.) ♿ (1 mobile home) – 7 🚍.
Per night from 42 to 94 € – Per week from 241 to 566 € – Reservation fee 11 €
🚐 sani-station 4.50 € – ⚡ ⚡16 €
Outside jacuzzi, with panoramic view of the Gironde.

Surroundings : 🌳 🗏 ♨♨
Leisure activities : 🎱 ≋ jacuzzi ⛵ ⚓
Facilities : ♿ ⚙ ⓦ launderette

GPS Longitude : -0.74226
Latitude : 45.18517

PETIT-PALAIS-ET-CORNEMPS

33570 – Michelin map **335** K5 – pop. 676 – alt. 35
▶ Paris 532 – Bergerac 51 – Castillon-la-Bataille 18 – Libourne 20

Flower Le Pressoir

𝒫 05 57 69 73 25, www.campinglepressoir.com
Address : 29 Queyrai (1.7km northwest along the D 21, follow the signs for St-Médard-de-Guizières and take road to the left)
Opening times : permanent
2 ha (100 pitches) relatively flat, flat, grassy
Tariff : 25.50 € ♟ ♟ ⛺ 🔲 ⚡ (10A) – Extra per person 7 € – Reservation fee 15 €
Rental rates : (permanent) – 35 🚍 – 8 tent bungalows. Per night from 32 to 64 €
Per week from 160 to 791 € – Reservation fee 15 €
🚐 ⚡14 €
Surroundings : 🌳 ≼ 🗏 ♨♨
Leisure activities : 🍽 ✗ ≋ ⛵ 🚲 ♨
Facilities : ♿ ⚙ ⚗ ⓦ launderette

GPS Longitude : -0.06301
Latitude : 44.99693

PEYRIGNAC

24210 – Michelin map **329** I5 – pop. 514 – alt. 200
▶ Paris 508 – Brive-la-Gaillarde 33 – Juillac 33 – Périgueux 44

La Garenne

𝒫 05 53 50 57 73, www.lagarennedordogne.com
Address : at Le Combal (800m north of the village, near the stadium)
Opening times : permanent
4 ha/1.5 (70 pitches) flat, relatively flat, grassy
Tariff : 20.60 € ♟ ♟ ⛺ 🔲 ⚡ (10A) – Extra per person 4.80 € – Reservation fee 3.50 €
Rental rates : (permanent) – 25 🚍 – 10 🏠 – 2 tent bungalows – 1 tent.
Per night from 42 to 66 € Per week from 185 to 745 € – Reservation fee 11 €
🚐 4 🔲 17.40 € – ⚡ ⚡15.60 €
Surroundings : 🌳 ♨♨♨
Leisure activities : 🎱 ≋ hammam, jacuzzi ⛵ ♨
Facilities : ♿ ⚙ ⚏ 🅿 ♨ ⚗ ⓦ 🖼 ⚒
Nearby : ✗ 🖼

GPS Longitude : 1.1837
Latitude : 45.16175

PEYRILLAC-ET-MILLAC

24370 – Michelin map **329** J6 – pop. 213 – alt. 88
▶ Paris 521 – Brive-la-Gaillarde 45 – Gourdon 23 – Sarlat-la-Canéda 22

Au P'tit Bonheur

⌖ 05 53 29 77 93, www.camping-auptitbonheur.com
Address : at Combe de Lafon (2.5km north along the follow the signs for Le Bouscandier)
Opening times : from beginning April to end Sept.
2.8 ha (113 pitches) terraced, sloping, grassy, stony
Tariff : (2012 price) 21.30 € ♥♥ ⇔ 🗐 (10A) – Extra per person 5.30 € – Reservation fee 16 €
Rental rates : (2012 price) (from beginning April to end Sept.) – 29 🚐 – 8 🏠 – 3 tent
bungalows – 6 tents. Per night from 5 to 105 – Per week from 28 to 718 – Reservation fee 16 €
🚐 sani-station

Surroundings : 🏊 ⌷ ⭕⭕
Leisure activities : ♀ ✕ 🖾 😑 jacuzzi ⚡⚞ ♂️ 🏊
Facilities : ♿ ⊶ 🛁 ⅄ ⸯ 🖼 ⅃

Longitude : 1.40356
Latitude : 44.93214

Some campsites benefit from proximity to a municipal leisure centre.

PISSOS

40410 – Michelin map **335** G9 – pop. 1,315 – alt. 46
▶ Paris 657 – Arcachon 72 – Biscarrosse 34 – Bordeaux 75

Municipal de l'Arriu

⌖ 05 58 08 90 38, www.pissos.fr – ℝ
Address : 525 Chemin de l'Arriu (1.2km east along the D 43, follow the signs for Sore and take the
road to the right, after the swimming pool)
Opening times : from beginning July to mid Sept.
3 ha (74 pitches) flat, sandy
Tariff : (2012 price) ♥ 3.20 € ⇔ 🗐 5.10 € – (12A) 2.10 €
Rental rates : (2012 price) (from beginning July to mid Sept.) – 3 tent bungalows.
Per week from 61

Surroundings : 🏊 ⭕⭕
Facilities : ♿ ⅄ ⅄ ⅄
Nearby : 🖼 🖾 ♂️ ✕ 🏊 ⅄

Longitude : -0.77047
Latitude : 44.3027

PLAZAC

24580 – Michelin map **329** H5 – pop. 725 – alt. 110
▶ Paris 527 – Bergerac 65 – Brive-la-Gaillarde 53 – Périgueux 40

Le Lac ⚐⚐

⌖ 05 53 50 75 86, www.campinglelac-dordogne.com
Address : at the lake (800m southeast along the D 45, follow the signs for Thonac)
Opening times : from beginning May to end Sept.
7 ha/2.5 ha for camping (130 pitches) flat and relatively flat, terraced, grassy
Tariff : (2012 price) ♥ 5.70 € ⇔ 🗐 5.70 € – (10A) 3.60 € – Reservation fee 12 €
Rental rates : (2012 price) (from beginning May to end Sept.) ♿ (1 mobile home) – 40 🚐 –
4 🏠. Per night from 34 to 80 € – Per week from 35 to 720 € – Reservation fee 12 €
🚐 3 🗐 20.70 €
Beside the lake, in the shade of walnut and Holm oak trees.

Surroundings : 🏊 ⌷ ⭕⭕ ⛰
Leisure activities : ♀ ✕ 🖾 ⚞⚞ ⚡⚞ ✕ 🏊 🏊 ⸙ multi-sports ground
Facilities : ♿ ⊶ 🛁 ⅄ ⅄ ⸯ launderette ⅃

Longitude : 1.14794
Latitude : 45.03125

AQUITAINE

PONT-DU-CASSE

47480 – Michelin map **336** G4 – pop. 4,305 – alt. 67
▶ Paris 658 – Bordeaux 147 – Toulouse 122 – Montauban 96

Village Vacances de Loisirs Darel
(rental of chalets only)

✆ 05 53 67 96 41, *accueil@ville-pontducasse.fr*
Address : at Darel (7km northeast along the D 656, follow the signs for Cahors and take a right turn towards St-Ferréol)
Opening times : permanent
34 ha/2 ha for camping undulating
Rental rates : (2012 price) **P** – 15 ⌂. Per night from 53 € – Per week from 175 to 359 €
Reservation fee 27 €
A pleasant location surrounded by trees, near a large riding centre.

Surroundings :
Leisure activities :
Facilities :

Longitude : 0.68536
Latitude : 44.21698

LE PORGE

33680 – Michelin map **335** E5 – pop. 2,428 – alt. 8
▶ Paris 624 – Andernos-les-Bains 18 – Bordeaux 47 – Lacanau-Océan 21

Municipal la Grigne ♣⁏

✆ 05 56 26 54 88, *www.camping-leporge.fr*
Address : 35 av. de l'Océan (9.5km west along the D 107, 1km from Le Porge-Océan)
Opening times : from beginning April to end Sept.
30 ha (700 pitches) undulating, flat, sandy
Tariff : (2012 price) 22 € ♦♦ ⇔ 回 ⅜ (10A) – Extra per person 2.70 € – Reservation fee 18 €
Rental rates : (2012 price) (from beginning April to end Sept.) ⅜ – 24 ⌂ – 10 tents.
Per week from 305 to 645 € – Reservation fee 18 €

Surroundings :
Leisure activities :
Facilities : launderette
Nearby : forest trail, surfing

Longitude : -1.20314
Latitude : 44.89363

PYLA-SUR-MER

33115 – Michelin map **335** D7
▶ Paris 648 – Arcachon 8 – Biscarrosse 34 – Bordeaux 66

Yelloh! Village Panorama du Pyla ♣⁏

✆ 05 56 22 10 44, *www.camping-panorama.com*
Address : rte de Biscarrosse (7km south along the D 218)
Opening times : from mid April to end Sept.
15 ha/10 ha for camping (450 pitches) undulating, terraced, flat, sandy
Tariff : 44 € ♦♦ ⇔ 回 ⅜ (10A) – Extra per person 8 €
Rental rates : (from mid April to end Sept.) – 80 ⌂ – 10 ⌂ – 15 tent bungalows.
Per night from 30 to 159 € – Per week from 210 to 1,113 €
sani-station
Access to the beach via a pedestrian path and steep steps.

Surroundings :
Leisure activities : hang-gliding, paragliding, skate park
Facilities : launderette refrigerated food storage

Longitude : -1.22502
Latitude : 44.57738

FranceLoc Domaine Le Petit Nice ▲▴

℘ 05 56 22 74 03, *www.petitnice.com*
Address : rte de Biscarrosse (at the foot of the Dune du Pyla)
Opening times : from beginning April to mid Sept.
5 ha (209 pitches) terraced, flat, sandy, extremely uneven
Tariff : (2012 price) 39€ ♦♦ ⇔ 🄴 🄵 (8A) – Extra per person 7€ – Reservation fee 30€
Rental rates : (2012 price) (from beginning April to mid Sept.) – 4 caravans – 90 🄲🄼 – 10 tents.
Per night from 44 to 161 € – Per week from 175 to 1,302 € – Reservation fee 30€
🄲🄻 sani-station

Surroundings : ⌕ ⪡ Banc d'Arguin National Park 🌳🌳
Leisure activities : ▾ ✕ 🄲🄳 🄴 ⅋ ⚓ ⛵ 🄹 ⚒ multi-sports ground
Facilities : ⚹ ⟊ 🄼 🄷 ⁇ launderette 🄻, ⚘ refrigerated food storage
Nearby : paragliding

GPS Longitude : -1.22043
Latitude : 44.57274

Village Center La Forêt

℘ 05 56 22 73 28, *www.village-center.fr*
Address : 3 km at the south via the D 218, rte Biscarrosse (at the foot of the Dune du Pyla)
Opening times : from beginning April to end Sept.
8 ha (460 pitches) undulating, flat and relatively flat, sandy
Tariff : 36€ ♦♦ ⇔ 🄴 🄵 (15A) – Extra per person 8€ – Reservation fee 10€
Rental rates : (from beginning April to end Sept.) ⚹ (2 mobile homes) – 96 🄲🄼 – 12 🄷.
Per night from 5 to 145 € – Per week from 175 to 1,019 € – Reservation fee 10€
🄲🄻 sani-station

Surroundings : 🌳🌳
Leisure activities : ✕ multi-sports ground
Facilities : ⚹ ⟊ 🄲🄷 ⁇

GPS Longitude : -1.20857
Latitude : 44.58542

There are several different types of sani-station
('borne' in French) – sanitation points providing
fresh water and disposal points for grey water.
See page 12 for further details.

RAUZAN

33420 – Michelin map **335** K6 – pop. 1,148 – alt. 69
▶ Paris 596 – Bergerac 57 – Bordeaux 39 – Langon 35

Le Vieux Château

℘ 05 57 84 15 38, *www.camping-levieuxchateau.com*
Address : take the northern exit follow the signs for St-Jean-de-Blaignac and take road to the left
(1.2km)
2.5 ha (74 pitches) open site, flat, relatively flat, grassy
Rentals : 8 🄲🄼 – 4 🄷 – 2 tent bungalows.
🄲🄻 sani-station – 1 🄴
At the foot of a ruined 12th-century fortress, with a pedestrian path to the village.

Surroundings : ⌕ 🌳🌳
Leisure activities : ▾ ✕ 🄲🄳 🄹
Facilities : ⚹ ⟊ ⁇ 🄰

GPS Longitude : -0.12715
Latitude : 44.78213

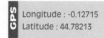

RIVIÈRE-SAAS-ET-GOURBY

40180 – Michelin map **335** E12 – pop. 1,168 – alt. 50
▶ Paris 742 – Bordeaux 156 – Mont-de-Marsan 68 – Bayonne 44

⚠ Lou Bascou

℘ 05 58 97 57 29, *http://www.campingloubascou.fr* – limited spaces for one-night stay
Address : 250 rte de Houssat (to the northeast of the town)
Opening times : from mid April to mid Oct.
1 ha (41 pitches) flat, grassy
Tariff : 22 € ♦♦ ⇦ 回 ⬚ (16A) – Extra per person 9 €
Rental rates : (permanent) – 12 ⌂. Per night from 54 to 138 € – Per week from 273 to 693 €
🚐 sani-station 13 – 15 € 回 13 €

Surroundings : 🐾 ⊏ ⬚⬚
Leisure activities : 🖵 entertainment room
Facilities : ⅋ ⊶ ⬚ launderette
Nearby : 🏊 ✗

GPS | Longitude : -1.14971
| Latitude : 43.68203

LA ROCHE-CHALAIS

24490 – Michelin map **329** B5 – pop. 2,857 – alt. 60
▶ Paris 510 – Bergerac 62 – Blaye 67 – Bordeaux 68

⚠ Municipal de Gerbes

℘ 05 53 91 40 65, *www.larochechalais.com*
Address : at Les Gerbes (located 1km west; beside the river)
Opening times : from mid April to end Sept.
3 ha (100 pitches) flat, terrace, grassy, small adjacent wood
Tariff : (2012 price) 12.68 € ♦♦ ⇦ 回 ⬚ (10A) – Extra per person 2.50 €
Rental rates : (2012 price) (from mid April to end Sept.) – 4 ⬚⬚ – 1 gîte.
Per night from 25 to 53 € Per week from 161 to 321 €
🚐 sani-station – 16 回 11.68 € – 🔥⬚ 9 €

Surroundings : 🐾 ⊏ ⬚⬚
Leisure activities : 🖵 ⛹ 🛶 ✈
Facilities : ⅋ ⊶ 🛒 ⒸⒸ ⬚ 🔲

GPS | Longitude : -0.00207
| Latitude : 45.14888

To visit a town or region, use the MICHELIN Green Guides.

LA ROQUE-GAGEAC

24250 – Michelin map **329** I7 – pop. 416 – alt. 85
▶ Paris 535 – Brive-la-Gaillarde 71 – Cahors 53 – Fumel 52

⛰ Le Beau Rivage ⚎

℘ 05 53 28 32 05, *www.beaurivagedordogne.com*
Address : at Le Gaillardou (4km east on the D 46; beside the Dordogne river)
Opening times : from end April to beginning Sept.
8 ha (199 pitches) flat, terraced, grassy, sandy
Tariff : 27.35 € ♦♦ ⇦ 回 ⬚ (6A) – Extra per person 5.50 € – Reservation fee 20 €
Rental rates : (from end April to beginning Sept.) – 44 ⬚⬚. Per week from 202 to 888 €
Reservation fee 20 €

Surroundings : ⬚⬚ ⛰
Leisure activities : ▼ ✗ 🖵 ⊙ evening 🏃 🛶 ✗ 🏊 ✈
Facilities : ⅋ ⊶ ⬚ 🛒 ⬚ ⬚ launderette 🏊 ⬚
Nearby : 🚲

GPS | Longitude : 1.21422
| Latitude : 44.81587

ROUFFIGNAC

24580 – Michelin map **329** G5 – pop. 1,552 – alt. 300
▶ Paris 531 – Bergerac 58 – Brive-la-Gaillarde 57 – Périgueux 32

La Ferme Offrerie

🖀 05 53 35 33 26, *www.camping-ferme-offrerie.com*
Address : at Le Grand Boisset (situated 2km south along the D 32, follow the signs for Les Grottes de Rouffignac and take a right turn)
Opening times : from beginning May to end Sept.
3.5 ha (48 pitches) flat, relatively flat, terraced, grassy
Tariff : (2012 price) ✚ 5.60€ ⬅ 🗐 7.30€ – (⚡) (10A) 3.60€ – Reservation fee 10€
Rental rates : (2012 price) (from beginning May to end Sept.) – 19 – 10 tent bungalows.
Per night from 5 to 45 – Per week from 150 to 715 € – Reservation fee 10€
🚐 sani-station 4€ – 1 🗐 11€ – 🛥11€

Surroundings : 🖅 ⌑ 🞉
Leisure activities : ✗ 🖅 ⚓ m 🛝
Facilities : ⚊ 🛁 ♺ 🗐 🔧
GPS Longitude : 0.97109
Latitude : 45.02775

La Nouvelle Croze

🖀 05 53 05 38 90, *www.lanouvellecroze.com*
Address : 2.5km southeast along the D 31, follow the signs for Fleurac and take the road to the right
Opening times : from beginning April to beginning Nov.
1.3 ha (40 pitches) flat, grassy
Tariff : (2012 price) 22€ ✚✚ ⬅ 🗐 (⚡) (16A) – Extra per person 5.50€
Rental rates : (2012 price) (from beginning April to beginning Nov.) – 19 – 4 🛏 – 1 gîte.
Per night from 8 to 121 € – Per week from 200 to 850 €

Surroundings : 🖅 🞉
Leisure activities : 🍷 ✗ 🖅 ⚓ 🛝
Facilities : ♿ ⚊ 🛁 ♺ 🗐
GPS Longitude : 0.99783
Latitude : 45.02412

Bleu Soleil

🖀 05 53 05 48 30, *www.camping-bleusoleil.com*
Address : at Domaine Touvent (located 1.5km north along the D 31, follow the signs for Thenon and take turning to the right)
Opening times : from beginning April to end Sept.
41 ha/7 ha for camping (110 pitches) terraced, relatively flat, flat, grassy
Tariff : (2012 price) ✚ 5.90€ ⬅ 🗐 10.20€ – (⚡) (10A) 3.70€
Rental rates : (2012 price) (from beginning April to end Sept.) – 21 🏠.
Per night from 31 to 47 € Per week from 378 to 728 €

Surroundings : 🖅 ≤ 🞉
Leisure activities : 🍷 ✗ 🖅 ⚓ 🛝 multi-sports ground
Facilities : ♿ ⚊ 🛁 ♺ 🗐 refrigerated food storage
GPS Longitude : 0.98586
Latitude : 45.05507

Do not confuse:
🛆 *to* 🛆🛆🛆 *: MICHELIN classification*
with
★ *to* ★★★★★ *: official classification*

SABRES

40630 – Michelin map **335** C10 – pop. 1,200 – alt. 78
▶ Paris 676 – Arcachon 92 – Bayonne 111 – Bordeaux 94

⚠ Le Domaine de Peyricat

☎ 05 58 07 51 88, *www.vtf-vacances.com*
Address : take the southern exit along the D 327, follow the signs for Luglon
Opening times : from mid June to mid Sept.
20 ha/2 ha for camping (69 pitches) flat, sandy, grassy
Tariff : (2012 price) 22.30€ ♦♦ ⟵ 🅴 (5A) – Extra per person 2.50€
Rental rates : (2012 price) (from mid April to end Oct.) ⚡ – 4 🚐 – 8 🏠.
Per night from 32 to 58 € – Per week from 275 to 675 €
🚽 sani-station
Lots of activities at the adjacent Holiday Village.

Surroundings : ▭
Facilities : ♿ ⊙⟶ 🍴
At Village Vacances : launderette 🍴 ✗ 🍳 🏊 ⇌ ✂ 🏊

GPS Longitude : -0.74235
Latitude : 44.144

ST-AMAND-DE-COLY

24290 – Michelin map **329** I5 – pop. 382 – alt. 180
▶ Paris 515 – Bordeaux 188 – Périgueux 58 – Cahors 104

⚠ Yelloh! Village Lascaux Vacances ♣♣

☎ 05 53 50 81 57, *www.campinglascauxvacances.com*
Address : at Les Malénies (located 1km south along the D 64, follow the signs for St-Geniès)
Opening times : from mid May to mid Sept.
12 ha (150 pitches) terraced, flat, stony, very uneven
Tariff : 33€ ♦♦ ⟵ 🅴 (10A) – Extra per person 7€
Rental rates : (from mid May to mid Sept.) – 90 🚐 – 10 🏠. Per night from 45 to 135 €
Per week from 315 to 945 €
🚽 sani-station – 30 🅴 17€ – 🔌 (4)21€

Surroundings : 🏊 ▭ ▨
Leisure activities : 🍴 ✗ 🏊 ⚡ 🚴 🏇 🎣 🏊 ⛴ multi-sports ground
Facilities : ♿ ⊙⟶ 🏊 ✗ 🍴 launderette ⇲

GPS Longitude : 1.24191
Latitude : 45.05461

ST-ANTOINE-D'AUBEROCHE

24330 – Michelin map **329** C5 – pop. 145 – alt. 152
▶ Paris 491 – Brive-la-Gaillarde 96 – Limoges 105 – Périgueux 24

⚠ La Pélonie

☎ 05 53 07 55 78, *www.lapelonie.com*
Address : at La Pélonie (1.8km southwest towards Milhac-Gare -from Fossemagne, continue 6 km along the RN 89 and take the road to the right)
Opening times : from mid April to mid Oct.
5 ha (60 pitches) open site, flat, grassy
Tariff : ♦ 5.70€ ⟵ 🅴 6.90€ – (4) (10A) 3.80€ – Reservation fee 10€
Rental rates : (from mid April to mid Oct.) – 25 🚐. Per week from 490 to 660 €
Reservation fee 10€
🚽 sani-station 14€ – 4 🅴 14€

Surroundings : 🏊 ▭ ▨
Leisure activities : 🍴 ✗ 🍳 ⚡ 🏊 ⛴
Facilities : ♿ ⊙⟶ 🏛 🏊 🍴 launderette ⇲

GPS Longitude : 0.92845
Latitude : 45.13135

ST-ANTOINE-DE-BREUILH

24230 – Michelin map **329** B6 – pop. 2,073 – alt. 18
▶ Paris 555 – Bergerac 30 – Duras 28 – Libourne 34

La Rivière Fleurie

℘ 05 53 24 82 80, *www.la-riviere-fleurie.com*
Address : at St-Aulaye-de-Breuilh, 180 r. Théophile-Cart (3km southwest, 100m from the Dordogne river)
Opening times : from mid April to mid Sept.
2.5 ha (60 pitches) flat, grassy
Tariff : (2012 price) 24.90€ ✚✚ ⇔ ▣ (10A) – Extra per person 5.80€ – Reservation fee 18€
Rental rates : (2012 price) (from mid April to mid Sept.) – 21 ⊞ – 5 tent bungalows – 4 gîtes.
Per night from 50 to 68 € – Per week from 50 to 660 € – Reservation fee 18€

Surroundings : ⌀ ☐ ⌀⌀
Leisure activities : ♟ ✕ ⌂ ⇆ ⌿
Facilities : ♿ ⚬⚬ ▣♨ ♜ launderette ⌿
Nearby : ✖

Longitude : 0.12235
Latitude : 44.82879

ST-AULAYE

24410 – Michelin map **329** B4 – pop. 1,360 – alt. 61
▶ Paris 504 – Bergerac 56 – Blaye 79 – Bordeaux 81

Municipal de la Plage

℘ 05 53 90 62 20, *www.saint-aulaye.com*
Address : Les Ponts (take the northern exit along the D 38, follow the signs for Aubeterre; beside the Dronne river)
Opening times : from mid June to mid Sept.
1 ha (70 pitches) flat, grassy
Tariff : 11€ ✚✚ ⇔ ▣ (10A) – Extra per person 2€
Rental rates : (from beginning June to mid Sept.) – 11 ⊞ – 14 ⌂.
Per week from 120 to 390 € – Reservation fee 30€
⊞ sani-station 3€

Surroundings : ☐ ⌀⌀
Leisure activities : ⌂ ⇆ ⚙ ✖ ♜ ⌿ ⌀ ⚘
Facilities : ♿ ⚬⚬ ⌿ ▣⌿ ♜ launderette
Nearby : ✕ ⌿ ≊ (beach)

Longitude : 0.13274
Latitude : 45.20786

ST-AVIT-DE-VIALARD

24260 – Michelin map **329** G6 – pop. 145 – alt. 210
▶ Paris 520 – Bergerac 39 – Le Bugue 7 – Les Eyzies-de-Tayac 17

Les Castels St-Avit Loisirs ♠♠

℘ 05 53 02 64 00, *www.saint-avit-loisirs.com* – limited spaces for one-night stay
Address : at Malefon (1.8km to the northwest)
Opening times : from end March to mid Sept.
55 ha/15 ha for camping (400 pitches) undulating, flat, grassy, natural setting among trees and bushes
Tariff : ♦ 11€ ⇔ 6€ ▣ 15.80€ – (6A) 6€ – Reservation fee 19€
Rental rates : (from end March to mid Sept.) – 7 ⊞ – 35 ⌂ – 30 ▭ – 15 studios –
15 apartments. Per night from 88 to 103 € – Per week from 343 to 1,211 €
Reservation fee 25€

Spacious, hilly site with trees and an attractive swimming area.

Surroundings : ⌀ ☐ ⌀⌀
Leisure activities : ♟ ✕ ⌂ ⚙ ⣏ ♫ jacuzzi ⇆ ⚙ ✖ ♜ ▣ ⌿ ⌀
quad biking, guided tours, multi-sports ground, entertainment room
Facilities : ♿ ⚬⚬ ⌿ ⌿ ♜ launderette ⣿ ⌿

Longitude : 0.84971
Latitude : 44.95174

ST-CRÉPIN-ET-CARLUCET

24590 – Michelin map **329** I6 – pop. 493 – alt. 262
▶ Paris 514 – Brive-la-Gaillarde 40 – Les Eyzies-de-Tayac 29 – Montignac 21

Les Peneyrals ▲▴

℘ 05 53 28 85 71, *www.peneyrals.com*
Address : at St Crépin (located 1km south along the D 56, follow the signs for Proissans)
Opening times : from beginning May to mid Sept.
12 ha/8 ha for camping (250 pitches) terraced, grassy, stony, very uneven, lake
Tariff : (2012 price) ♦ 9.10€ 🚐 🔲 13.10€ – (≵) (10A) 4.10€ – Reservation fee 18€
Rental rates : (2012 price) (from beginning May to mid Sept.) ⚹ (1 chalet) – 38 ⏣ – 27 ⌂.
Per week from 870 to 1 060 € – Reservation fee 30€
🚾 sani-station
Hilly setting with pitches among trees or beside a lake.

Surroundings : 🔋 🖿 🞈
Leisure activities : ♈ ✕ 🕋 ⌕ 🏋 🛶 ⛑ ✂ 🕍 🔲 🔱 △ 🞈
Facilities : ⚹ ⚲ �🕌 🚿 ⅋ launderette ⚏ 🞈

GPS	Longitude : 1.27267
	Latitude : 44.95785

Village Vacances Les Gîtes de Combas
(rental of gîtes only)

℘ 05 53 28 64 00, *www.perigordgites.com*
Address : at Les Combas (situated 2km south along the D 56, follow the signs for Proissans)
Opening times : permanent
4 ha undulating, grassy
Rental rates : ⚹ (1 gîte) ℗ – 22 gîtes. Per week from 310 to 1,150 €
Some of the old farm buildings made of local stone have been turned into gîtes.

Surroundings : 🔋 🞈
Leisure activities : ♈ 🕋 🛶 ✂ 🔲 🔱
Facilities : ⚲ 🕌 ⅋ 🞈 🞈

GPS	Longitude : 1.27718
	Latitude : 44.94871

*Some information or pricing may have changed since the guide went to press.
We recommend you check the price list online in advance or at the entrance to
the campsite and enquire about possible restrictions.*

ST-CYBRANET

24250 – Michelin map **329** I7 – pop. 376 – alt. 78
▶ Paris 542 – Cahors 51 – Les Eyzies-de-Tayac 29 – Gourdon 21

Bel Ombrage

℘ 05 53 28 34 14, *www.belombrage.com*
Address : via the D 50 (800m to the northwest; beside the Céou river)
Opening times : from beginning June to beginning Sept.
6 ha (180 pitches) flat, grassy
Tariff : ♦ 5.70€ 🚐 🔲 7.30€ – (≵) (10A) 4€

Surroundings : 🔋 🖿 🞈 ⛰
Leisure activities : 🕋 🛶 🔱
Facilities : ⚹ ⚲ ⅋ launderette
Nearby : ✕

GPS	Longitude : 1.16244
	Latitude : 44.79082

ST-ÉMILION

33330 – Michelin map **335** K5 – pop. 2,005 – alt. 30
▶ Paris 584 – Bergerac 58 – Bordeaux 40 – Langon 49

⋏⋏⋏ Yelloh! Saint-Émilion ♣♣

𝒫 05 57 24 75 80, *www.camping-saint-emilion.com*
Address : rte de Montagne (3km north along the D 122, follow the signs for Lussac and take turning to the right – caravans and camper vans are not permitted to pass through St-Émilion)
Opening times : from end April to end Sept.
4.5 ha (160 pitches) flat, grassy
Tariff : 39 € ♦♦ ⇔ 🄴 🄗 (10A) – Extra per person 8 €
Rental rates : (from end April to end Sept.) – 47 ⟦⟧. Per night from 39 to 181 €
Per week from 73 to 1,267 €
🚻 sani-station – 20 🄴 39 €
Free shuttle bus to St Émilion.

Surroundings : ⋐ ⟐ 🙂
Leisure activities : ✗ 🎦 ⋔ ⛵ 🚲 ⛾ 🎣 🛝 ⛰ ⌇ pedalos,
fitness trail 🏊
Facilities : ♿ ⊶ ⛺ 🚰 launderette ⛲ 🚿

GPS Longitude : -0.14241
Latitude : 44.91675

Michelin classification:

⋏⋏⋏⋏ *Extremely comfortable, equipped to a very high standard*
⋏⋏⋏ *Very comfortable, equipped to a high standard*
⋏⋏⋏ *Comfortable and well equipped*
⋏⋏ *Reasonably comfortable*
⋏ *Satisfactory*

ST-ÉTIENNE-DE-BAIGORRY

64430 – Michelin map **342** D3 – pop. 1,618 – alt. 163
▶ Paris 820 – Bordeaux 241 – Pau 160 – Pamplona 69

⋏ Municipal l'Irouleguy

𝒫 05 59 37 43 96, *comstetiennebaigorry@wanadoo.fr*
Address : Borciriette quartier (take the northeastern exit along the D 15, follow the signs for St-Jean-Pied-de-Port and take road to the left in front of the swimming pool and behind the Irouléguy wine co-operative; beside the Nive river)
Opening times : from beginning March to end Oct.
1.5 ha (67 pitches) flat, grassy
Tariff : 13 € ♦♦ ⇔ 🄴 🄗 (5A) – Extra per person 3.50 €
Green setting extending along the river.

Surroundings : ≤ 🙂
Leisure activities : ⛵
Facilities : ♿ ⊶ 🚿 🚰 🖼
Nearby : 🛒 🍽 ✗ ⛵ 🛝

GPS Longitude : -1.33551
Latitude : 43.18386

ST-GENIÈS

24590 – Michelin map **329** I6 – pop. 941 – alt. 232
▶ Paris 515 – Brive-la-Gaillarde 41 – Les Eyzies-de-Tayac 29 – Montignac 13

Club Airotel La Bouquerie ⚑

📞 05 53 28 98 22, *www.labouquerie.com* – limited spaces for one-night stay
Address : located 1.5km northwest along the D 704, follow the signs for Montignac and take the road to the right
Opening times : from beginning April to beginning Sept.
8 ha/4 ha for camping (183 pitches) flat, relatively flat, terraced, grassy, stony, lake
Tariff : (2012 price) 👤 8€ 🚗 🔲 12.70€ – 🔌 (10A) 3.90€ – Reservation fee 20€
Rental rates : (2012 price) (from beginning April to beginning Sept.) ♿ (1 mobile home) – 96 🏕 – 45 🏠. Per week from 240 to 1,100 € – Reservation fee 30€
🚱 sani-station – 6 🔲 12.70€
Pretty, shady pitches among oak trees.

Surroundings : 🛶 🚡 ♨
Leisure activities : 🍴 ✗ 🎦 🎮 🏃 🛝 ⛹ 🎯 🔲 🏊 ⛱ 🎣 paintballing, multi-sports ground
Facilities : ♿ ⚡ 🚿 ⛽ 🍴 launderette 🛒 🚰
Nearby : 🏇

GPS
Longitude : 1.24594
Latitude : 44.99892

ST-GIRONS-PLAGE

40560 – Michelin map **335** C11
▶ Paris 728 – Bordeaux 142 – Mont-de-Marsan 79 – Bayonne 73

Eurosol ⚑

📞 05 58 47 90 14, *www.camping-eurosol.com*
Address : rte de la Plage (350m from the beach)
Opening times : from mid May to mid Sept.
33 ha/18 ha for camping (510 pitches) undulating, flat, sloping, sandy, grassy
Tariff : 37€ 👤👤 🚗 🔲 🔌 (10A) – Extra per person 6€ – Reservation fee 25€
Rental rates : (from mid May to mid Sept.) ♨ 🅿 – 144 🏕 – 16 🏠.
Per night from 92 to 156 € – Per week from 322 to 1,092€ – Reservation fee 25€
🚱 sani-station 19€ – 10 🔲 19€

Surroundings : 🛶 ♨
Leisure activities : 🍴 ✗ 🎦 🎮 🏃 ⛹ 🚲 🎯 🔲 🏊 multi-sports ground
Facilities : ♿ ⚡ ⛽ 🍴 launderette 🛒 🚰
Nearby : 🏇

GPS
Longitude : -1.35162
Latitude : 43.95158

Campéole les Tourterelles ⚑

📞 05 58 47 93 12, *www.camping-tourterelles.com*
Address : rte de la plage (5.2km west along the D 42, 300m from the ocean (direct access)
Opening times : from beginning May to end Sept.
18 ha (822 pitches) undulating, flat, sloping, sandy
Tariff : (2012 price) 33.30€ 👤👤 🚗 🔲 🔌 (10A) – Extra per person 10€ – Reservation fee 25€
Rental rates : (2012 price) (from beginning May to end Sept.) ♿ (2 mobile homes) – 134 🏕 – 20 🏠 – 115 tent bungalows. Per night from 5 to 175 € – Per week from 175 to 1,225 € Reservation fee 25€
🚱 sani-station 2€ – 49 🔲 9.30€
Welcomes groups of surfers.

Surroundings : ♨
Leisure activities : 🎮 🏃 ⛹ 🚲 🏊 multi-sports ground
Facilities : ♿ ⚡ ⛽ 🍴 launderette 🚰 refrigerated food storage

GPS
Longitude : -1.35691
Latitude : 43.95439

ST-JEAN-DE-LUZ

64500 – Michelin map **342** C4 – pop. 13,742 – alt. 3
▶ Paris 785 – Bayonne 24 – Biarritz 18 – Pau 129

Club Airotel Itsas Mendi

𝒫 05 59 26 56 50, *www.itsas-mendi.com*
Address : Acotz quartier, chemin Duhartia (5km to the northeast, 500m from the beach)
Opening times : from end March to beginning Nov.
8.5 ha (472 pitches) terraced, sloping, grassy
Tariff : (2012 price) 18.50€ ♀♀ ⇔ 🗉 (2) (10A) – Extra per person 4.10€ – Reservation fee 10€
Rental rates : (2012 price) (from end March to beginning Nov.) – 130 �🚐.
Per night from 7 to 148 € – Per week from 189 to 1,036 € – Reservation fee 10€
🚏 sani-station
Attractive swimming area.

Surroundings : ♤♤
Leisure activities : ♀ ✕ ⊕ ⚲ jacuzzi ⚑ ⚜ ⌇ ⚊ surfing
Facilities : ♿ ⊶ ⌨ 🍴 launderette ⚏ ⚄ refrigerated food storage

GPS
Longitude : -1.61726
Latitude : 43.41347

Atlantica

𝒫 05 59 47 72 44, *www.campingatlantica.com*
Address : Acotz quartier, chemin Miquélénia (5km to the northeast, 500m from the beach)
3.5 ha (200 pitches) flat, terraced, grassy
Rentals : ⚶ – 95 ⚐ – 6 🏠.
🚏 sani-station

Surroundings : ⌂ ♤♤
Leisure activities : ♀ ✕ ⚘ ⚬ jacuzzi ⚑ ⌇ ⚊ multi-sports ground
Facilities : ♿ ⊶ ⚏ ⚄ ⚲ ☐ ⚄ refrigerated food storage

GPS
Longitude : -1.61688
Latitude : 43.41525

Inter-Plages

𝒫 05 59 26 56 94, *www.campinginterplages.com*
Address : Acotz quartier, 305 rte des Plages (5km to the northeast, 150m from the beach (direct access)
2.5 ha (100 pitches) flat, sloping, grassy
Rentals : ⚶ – 23 ⚐ – 5 🏠.
Attractive location looking out over the ocean.

Surroundings : ⚲ ≤ ⌂ ♤♤
Leisure activities : ⚘ ⚑ ⚬ ⌇
Facilities : ♿ ⊶ ⚑ ⚏ ⚄ ⚲ ☐
Nearby : ⚏ ♀ ✕ ⚄ ⌇ surfing

GPS
Longitude : -1.62667
Latitude : 43.41527

La Ferme Erromardie

𝒫 05 59 26 34 26, *www.camping-erromardie.com*
Address : 40 chemin Erromardie (1.8km to the northeast, near the beach)
Opening times : ??????
2 ha (176 pitches) flat, grassy
Tariff : 30€ ♀♀ ⇔ 🗉 (2) (16A) – Extra per person 6€ – Reservation fee 18€
Rental rates : (from mid March to end Sept.) – 41 ⚐. Per night from 35 to 53 €
Per week from 230 to 850 € – Reservation fee 18€
🚏 sani-station

Surroundings : ⚲ ⌂ ♤♤
Leisure activities : ♀ ✕ ⚘ ⚑
Facilities : ♿ ⊶ ⚏ 🍴 launderette ⚏ ⚄

GPS
Longitude : -1.64202
Latitude : 43.40564

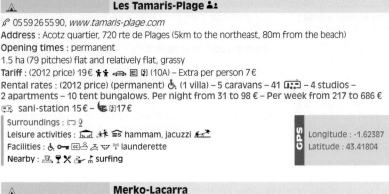

Les Tamaris-Plage ▲⚐

📞 0559265590, *www.tamaris-plage.com*
Address : Acotz quartier, 720 rte de Plages (5km to the northeast, 80m from the beach)
Opening times : permanent
1.5 ha (79 pitches) flat and relatively flat, grassy
Tariff : (2012 price) 19€ �; ⚏ 回 (④ (10A) – Extra per person 7€
Rental rates : (2012 price) (permanent) ⚕ (1 villa) – 5 caravans – 41 ⬛ – 4 studios –
2 apartments – 10 tent bungalows. Per night from 31 to 98 € – Per week from 217 to 686 €
⬛ sani-station 15€ – ⬛ (④17€

Surroundings : ⬛ ♀
Leisure activities : ⬛ ⚣ ⛱ hammam, jacuzzi ⚓
Facilities : ⚕ ⚲ ⬛ ⚶ ⚶ launderette
Nearby : ⬛ ♈ ✕ ⚶ surfing

GPS Longitude : -1.62387
Latitude : 43.41804

Merko-Lacarra

📞 0559265676, *www.merkolacarra.com*
Address : Acotz quartier, 820 rte des Plages (5km to the northeast, 150m from the beach d'Acotz)
Opening times : from end March to beginning Oct.
2 ha (123 pitches) terraced, sloping, flat, grassy
Tariff : 33€ �; ⚏ 回 (④ (16A) – Extra per person 7€ – Reservation fee 16€
Rental rates : (from end March to beginning Oct.) ⚓ – 27 ⬛. Per night from 40 to 81 €
Per week from 80 to 777 € – Reservation fee 27.50€
⬛ sani-station 6€

Leisure activities : ⬛ ⚓
Facilities : ⚕ ⚲ ⚶ launderette
Nearby : ⬛ ♈ ✕ ⚶ surfing

GPS Longitude : -1.62366
Latitude : 43.41855

ST-JEAN-PIED-DE-PORT

64220 – Michelin map **342** E4 – pop. 1,477 – alt. 159
▶ Paris 817 – Bayonne 54 – Biarritz 55 – Dax 105

Narbaïtz

📞 0559371013, *www.camping-narbaitz.com*
Address : at Ascarat (2.5km northwest along the D 918, follow the signs for Bayonne and take the
turning to the left; 50m from the Nive river and beside a stream)
Opening times : from beginning April to mid Sept.
2.5 ha (133 pitches) flat and relatively flat, grassy
Tariff : (2012 price) 36.50€ �; ⚏ 回 (④ (10A)
Extra per person 6€ – Reservation fee 18€
Rental rates : (2012 price) (permanent) ⚓ – 12 ⬛ – 3 ⬛ – 3 gîtes.
Per night from 60 to 70 € – Per week from 90 to 730 € – Reservation fee 18€
⬛ sani-station

Surroundings : ⚶ of the 'Irouléguy' vineyard ♀♀
Leisure activities : ⬛ ⚣ ⚘
Facilities : ⚕ ⚲ ⬛ ⚶ ⚶ launderette ⚶
Nearby : ⚓

GPS Longitude : -1.25911
Latitude : 43.17835

Fire safety doesn't stop when you leave your accommodation.
Always take care and consider the fire risks.

Europ'Camping

℘ 0559371278, *www.europ-camping.com*

Address : at Ascarat (situated 2km northwest along the D 918, follow the signs for Bayonne and take road to the left)

Opening times : from beginning April to end Sept.

2 ha (110 pitches) relatively flat, flat, grassy

Tariff : (2012 price) 33€ ♣♣ ⟚ 🔲 🐾 (10A) – Extra per person 6€ – Reservation fee 22€

Rental rates : (2012 price) (from beginning April to end Sept.) 🚐 (from beg Apr to beg Sept) – 41 🚐. Per night from 60 to 80 € – Per week from 60 to 720 € – Reservation fee 22€

Surroundings : ⟚ ⋜ the 'Irouléguy' vineyard ♤♤
Leisure activities : ♟ ✕ 🎯 ⟐ 🏊
Facilities : ♿ ⚊ 🏕 ⚐ 🍴 launderette ⟿
Nearby : 🦐

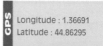
Longitude : -1.25398
Latitude : 43.17279

ST-JULIEN-DE-LAMPON

24370 – Michelin map **329** J6 – pop. 613 – alt. 120
▶ Paris 528 – Brive-la-Gaillarde 51 – Gourdon 17 – Sarlat-la-Canéda 17

⚠ **Le Mondou**

℘ 0553297037, *www.camping-dordogne.info*

Address : at Le Colombier (located 1km east along the D 50, follow the signs for Mareuil and take the road to the right)

1.2 ha (60 pitches) relatively flat, stony, grassy

Rentals : 🚐 – 4 🚐 – 8 tents.

Surroundings : ⟚ ⊏ ♤♤
Leisure activities : 🎯 🚣 🏊
Facilities : ♿ ⚊ 🏕 🍴 📷 ⟿
Nearby : launderette

Longitude : 1.36691
Latitude : 44.86295

These symbols are used for a campsite that is exceptional in its category:
⚠⚠⚠ ...⚠ *Particularly pleasant setting, quality and range of services available*
⟚ ⟚ *Tranquil, isolated site – quiet site, particularly at night*
⋜⋜ *Exceptional view – interesting or panoramic view*

ST-JULIEN-EN-BORN

40170 – Michelin map **335** D10 – pop. 1,450 – alt. 22
▶ Paris 706 – Castets 23 – Dax 43 – Mimizan 18

⚠ **Municipal la Lette Fleurie**

℘ 0558427409, *www.camping-municipal-plage.com*

Address : at La Lette, rte de l'Océan (4km northwest along the D 41, follow the signs for Contis-Plage)

Opening times : from beginning April to end Sept.

8.5 ha (457 pitches) undulating, flat, sandy

Tariff : (2012 price) ♣ 5.43€ ⟚ 🔲 6.29€ – 🐾 (10A) 4.56€ – Reservation fee 15€

Surroundings : ⟚ ♤♤
Leisure activities : ♟ ✕ 🎯 🚣 🎿 🏊
Facilities : ♿ ⚊ 🔲 🏕 🍴 launderette 🗄 ⟿ refrigerated food storage

Longitude : -1.26173
Latitude : 44.08139

ST-JUSTIN

40240 – Michelin map **335** J11 – pop. 922 – alt. 90
▶ Paris 694 – Barbotan-les-Thermes 19 – Captieux 41 – Labrit 31

Le Pin

⌂ 05 58 44 88 91, *www.campinglepin.com*
Address : rte de Roquefort (2.3km north on the D 626; beside a small lake)
Opening times : from beginning April to end Oct.
3 ha (80 pitches) flat, grassy, sandy
Tariff : 22 € ♥♥ ⇔ ▣ [♫] (10A) – Extra per person 5.50 € – Reservation fee 15 €
Rental rates : (from beginning April to end Oct.) – 6 ⛺ – 8 🏠. Per night from 50 to 75 €
Per week from 350 to 525 € – Reservation fee 15 €

Surroundings : ♤♤
Leisure activities : ❢✕ ♨ ⛵ ⚒ ⊶
Facilities : ⚅ ⚬━ ♨ ♈ launderette ⚄

Longitude : -0.23468
Latitude : 44.00188

*The guide covers all 22 regions of France – see the map
and list of regions on pages 4–5.*

ST-LAURENT-MEDOC

33112 – Michelin map **335** G4 – pop. 4,054 – alt. 6
▶ Paris 603 – Bordeaux 45 – Mérignac 41 – Pessac 48

Le Paradis

⌂ 05 56 59 42 15, *www.leparadis-medoc.com*
Address : at Fourthon (2.5km north along the D 1215, follow the signs for Lesparre)
3 ha (70 pitches) flat, grassy
Rentals : 29 ⛺ – 4 🏠 – 3 tent bungalows.

Surroundings : ▭ ♤♤
Leisure activities : ▧ ⚐
Facilities : ⚅ ⚬━ ♈

Longitude : -0.83995
Latitude : 45.17495

ST-LÉON-SUR-VÉZÈRE

24290 – Michelin map **329** H5 – pop. 428 – alt. 70
▶ Paris 523 – Brive-la-Gaillarde 48 – Les Eyzies-de-Tayac 16 – Montignac 10

Le Paradis ♣♦

⌂ 05 53 50 72 64, *www.le-paradis.fr*
Address : at La Rebeyrolle (4km southwest along the D 706, follow the signs for Les Eyzies-de-Tayac; beside the Vézère)
Opening times : from beginning April to end Oct.
7 ha (200 pitches) flat, grassy
Tariff : (2012 price) 32.60 € ♥♥ ⇔ ▣ [♫] (10A) – Extra per person 7.90 € – Reservation fee 20 €
Rental rates : (2012 price) (from beginning April to end Oct.) – 42 ⛺ – 3 tents.
Per night from 43 to 136 € – Per week from 301 to 949 € – Reservation fee 20 €
⛽ sani-station 2 €
Upmarket facilities based around an old renovated farmhouse.

Surroundings : ⚘ ▭ ♤♤
Leisure activities : ❢✕ ▦ ⚐ ♣ ♨ ⚲ ⚒ ❀ multi-sports ground
Facilities : ⚅ ⚬━ ▣⊞ ⚆ ⚄ ♝ ♈ launderette ⚄ ⚄

Longitude : 1.0712
Latitude : 45.00161

ST-MARTIAL-DE-NABIRAT

24250 – Michelin map **329** I7 – pop. 666 – alt. 175
▶ Paris 546 – Cahors 42 – Fumel 45 – Gourdon 11

Calmésympa

℘ 05 53 28 43 15, *www.http:camping-calmesympa.jimdo.com*
Address : at Lagrèze (2.2km northwest along the D 46, follow the signs for Domme and take road to the left)
2.7 ha (50 pitches) terraced, relatively flat, grassy
Rentals : 8 ⊡ – 7 gîtes.
In the shade of some 500-year-old chestnut trees.

Surroundings : ⌂ 🞉🞉
Leisure activities : 🏊
Facilities : 🚿 ⊶ 🜊 🖼

GPS Longitude : 1.23951
Latitude : 44.75444

ST-MARTIN-DE-SEIGNANX

40390 – Michelin map **335** C13 – pop. 4,724 – alt. 57
▶ Paris 766 – Bayonne 11 – Capbreton 15 – Dax 42

Lou P'tit Poun ▲⊥

℘ 05 59 56 55 79, *www.louptitpoun.com*
Address : 110 av. du Quartier Neuf (4.7km southwest along the N 117, follow the signs for Bayonne and take road to the left)
Opening times : from beginning June to mid Sept.
6.5 ha (168 pitches) flat and relatively flat, terraced, grassy
Tariff : 35.10€ ✶✶ ⇔ 🅔 🛙 (10A) – Extra per person 8.10€ – Reservation fee 30€
Rental rates : (from beginning June to mid Sept.) ⬙ – 2 ⊡ – 16 🏠.
Per week from 235 to 819 € Reservation fee 30€
🚏 sani-station 7€ – 🚿 🛙15.10€

Surroundings : ⌂ 🞉🞉
Leisure activities : 🏛 🏸 🚣 🏊
Facilities : 🚿 ⊶ 🜊 🜊 🜊 🜊 🖼 🜊

GPS Longitude : -1.41195
Latitude : 43.52437

A chambre d'hôte is a guesthouse or B & B-style accommodation.

ST-PAUL-LES-DAX

40990 – Michelin map **335** E12 – pop. 12,343 – alt. 21
▶ Paris 731 – Bordeaux 152 – Mont-de-Marsan 53 – Pau 89

Les Pins du Soleil ▲⊥

℘ 05 58 91 37 91, *www.pinsoleil.com*
Address : rte des Minières (5.8km northwest along the N 124, follow the signs for Bayonne and take the turning to the left along the D 459)
Opening times : from beginning April to end Oct.
6 ha (145 pitches) flat and relatively flat, grassy, sandy
Tariff : 20.50€ ✶✶ ⇔ 🅔 🛙 (10A) – Extra per person 6€ – Reservation fee 10€
Rental rates : (from beginning April to end Oct.) 🚿 (1 chalet) – 45 ⊡ – 10 🏠 – 4 tent bungalows. Per night from 39 to 101 € – Per week from 270 to 709 € – Reservation fee 17€
🚏 sani-station

Surroundings : ⌂ 🞉🞉
Leisure activities : 🍽 ✗ 🏛 🏸 jacuzzi 🚣 🏊
Facilities : 🚿 ⊶ 🜊 🜊 🜊 🜊 🜊 launderette 🜊

GPS Longitude : -1.09373
Latitude : 43.72029

L'Étang d'Ardy

📞 05 58 97 57 74, *www.camping-ardy.com*

Address : allée d'Ardy (5.5km northwest along the N 124, follow the signs for Bayonne then take road to the left before the access road, continuing for 1.7km; beside a lake)

Opening times : from beginning April to mid Oct.

5 ha/3 ha for camping (102 pitches) flat, grassy, sandy

Tariff : 21.30€ ⚦⚦ ⇔ 🔲 🚰 (10A) – Extra per person 6 €

Rental rates : (from beginning April to end Oct.) – 21 🏚 – 5 🏠. Per night from 62 to 100 €
Per week from 245 to 630 €

Surroundings : 🌊 🛏 〰️
Leisure activities : 🎣 🚣
Facilities : ♿ 🚿 – 56 individual sanitary facilities (🚿⛲ wc) 🪑 ⚰ ⚚ launderette

Longitude : -1.12256
Latitude : 43.72643

Abesses

📞 05 58 91 65 34, *www.thermes-dax.com*

Address : allée du Château (7.5km northwest following signs for Bayonne, D 16 to the right and take the Chemin d'Abesse)

4 ha (198 pitches) flat, grassy, sandy, small lake

Rentals : 16 🏚.

🚉 sani-station

Minimum stay 20 nights.

Surroundings : 🌊 🛏 〰️
Leisure activities : 🏛 🚣
Facilities : ♿ 🚿 ⬚ 🪑 ⚚ launderette

Longitude : -1.09715
Latitude : 43.74216

ST-PÉE-SUR-NIVELLE

64310 – Michelin map **342** C4 – pop. 5,550 – alt. 30
▶ Paris 785 – Bayonne 22 – Biarritz 17 – Cambo-les-Bains 17

Goyetchea

📞 05 59 54 19 59, *www.camping-goyetchea.com*

Address : Ibarron quartier (1.8km north along the D 855, follow the signs for Ahetze and take a right turn)

Opening times : from beginning June to mid Sept.

3 ha (140 pitches) flat and relatively flat, grassy

Tariff : 27€ ⚦⚦ ⇔ 🔲 🚰 (2A) – Extra per person 5.50€ – Reservation fee 13€

Rental rates : (from end April to mid Sept.) 🏕 – 2 'gypsy' caravans – 34 🏚.
Per night from 50 to 60 € – Per week from 30 to 780 – Reservation fee 13€

Surroundings : 🌊 ⩤ 〰️
Leisure activities : ✗ 🏛 ⚓ 🚣
Facilities : ♿ 🚿 🛁 ⚚ launderette 🛒 refrigerators

Longitude : -1.56683
Latitude : 43.36275

Key to rentals symbols:

12 🏚   *Number of mobile homes*
20 🏠   *Number of chalets*
6 🛏   *Number of rooms to rent*
Per night   *Minimum/maximum rate per night*
30–50€
Per week   *Minimum/maximum rate per week*
300–1,000€

L'Ibarron

☏ 0559541043, *www.camping-ibarron.com*

Address : Ibarron quartier (2km, take the western exit, on the D 918, follow the signs for St-Jean-de-Luz, near the Nivelle river)

Opening times : from end April to end Sept.

2.9 ha (142 pitches) flat, grassy

Tariff : (2012 price) 16.95€ ✶✶ ⇔ ▣ ⓖ (6A) – Extra per person 3.35€ – Reservation fee 10€

Rental rates : (2012 price) (from end April to end Sept.) ⌇ – 23 ⌷⌷. Per night from 49 to 92 € Per week from 30 to 640 € – Reservation fee 10€

⛽ sani-station 5€ – 20 ▣ 13.60€

Surroundings : ◌◌
Leisure activities : ☷ ⚓ ⌇
Facilities : ⚹ ⟲ ⓣ launderette
Nearby : ⛟ ☂✗ ⚬ ⚲

GPS Longitude : -1.5749
Latitude : 43.3576

24700 – Michelin map **329** C6 – pop. 432 – alt. 80
▶ Paris 542 – Bergerac 33 – Libourne 46 – Montpon-Ménestérol 10

Les Cottages en Périgord
(rental of chalets only)

☏ 0553805946, *www.cottagesenperigord.com*

Address : at Les Pommiers (continue north following signs for Montpon-Ménestérol along the D 708)

Opening times : from mid Jan. to mid Dec.

7 ha/1 ha for camping, flat, small lake, adjacent wood

Rental rates : ⚹ (1 chalet) – 3 caravans – 8 ⌂. Per night 100€ – Per week from 250 to 650€ Reservation fee 10€

Surroundings : ⌇ ◌◌
Leisure activities : ☷ ⚏s jacuzzi ⌇ ⚌
Facilities : ⟲ ⤳ ⒸⒸ⽥ ⓣ ▣

GPS Longitude : 0.16333
Latitude : 44.96024

Routes nationales are main roads and their identifying numbers begin with N or RN. Routes départementales are generally quieter roads and begin with D or DN.

24470 – Michelin map **329** F2 – pop. 864 – alt. 370
▶ Paris 443 – Brive-la-Gaillarde 105 – Châlus 23 – Limoges 57

Kawan Village Château Le Verdoyer ♣♣

☏ 0553569464, *www.verdoyer.fr*

Address : 2.5km northwest along the D 79, follow the signs for Nontron and take D 96, follow the signs for Abjat-sur-Bandiat; near lakes

15 ha/5 ha for camping (170 pitches) terraced, relatively flat, grassy, stony, lakes

Rentals : 2 'gypsy' caravans – 20 ⌷⌷ – 10 ⌂ – 5 ⍯ – 2 tent bungalows.

⛽ sani-station

Surroundings : ⌇ ⊏ ◌◌
Leisure activities : ☂✗ ☷ ⚶ ⚓ ⚲ ⚌ ⌇ ⚏ ⚌ ⚲
Facilities : ⚹ ⟲ ⚖ ⚟ ⤳ launderette ⚌ ⚖ refrigerated food storage
Nearby : ⚌ (beach)

GPS Longitude : 0.79595
Latitude : 45.55133

ST-VINCENT-DE-COSSE

24220 – Michelin map **329** H6 – pop. 374 – alt. 80
▶ Paris 540 – Bergerac 61 – Brive-la-Gaillarde 65 – Fumel 58

Le Tiradou

☎ 05 53 30 30 73, *www.camping-le-tiradou.com*
Address : at Larrit (500m southwest of the village; beside a stream)
Opening times : from beginning May to mid Oct.
2 ha (60 pitches) flat, grassy
Tariff : (2012 price) ♠ 4.50€ ⬚ 🔲 6€ – 🔋 (10A) 3.30€ – Reservation fee 10€
Rental rates : (2012 price) (from beginning May to mid Oct.) 🏠 – 17 🔲 – 5 🏠 – 4 ⛺.
Per night from 70 to 100 € – Per week from 200 to 555 € – Reservation fee 15€

Surroundings : ▭ 💧💧
Leisure activities : ✗ 🎦 jacuzzi ⛵ 🏊
Facilities : ⚐ ☛ 🛁 🍴 launderette 🛒

GPS
Longitude : 1.11268
Latitude : 44.83747

Gîtes range from small maisonettes to old farmhouses with several bedrooms.

STE-EULALIE-EN-BORN

40200 – Michelin map **335** D9 – pop. 1,116 – alt. 26
▶ Paris 673 – Arcachon 58 – Biscarrosse 98 – Mimizan 11

Les Bruyères

☎ 05 58 09 73 36, *www.camping-les-bruyeres.com*
Address : 719 rte de Laffont (2.5km north along the D 652)
Opening times : from beginning May to end Sept.
3 ha (177 pitches) flat, sandy, grassy
Tariff : 28.90€ ♠♠ ⬚ 🔲 🔋 (10A) – Extra per person 7.90€ – Reservation fee 16€
Rental rates : (from beginning May to end Sept.) – 22 🔲 – 1 🏠. Per night from 38 to 70 €
Per week from 66 to 800 € – Reservation fee 16€
Local home-made produce to taste and buy.

Surroundings : 🌿 ▭ 💧💧
Leisure activities : 🍸 ✗ 🎦 🎣 🏊
Facilities : ⚐ ☛ 🛁 🚿 🍴 launderette 🛒 🛒

GPS
Longitude : -1.17949
Latitude : 44.29387

STE-FOY-LA-GRANDE

33220 – Michelin map **335** M5 – pop. 2,544 – alt. 10
▶ Paris 555 – Bordeaux 71 – Langon 59 – Marmande 53

La Bastide

☎ 05 57 46 13 84, *www.camping-bastide.com* 🏠
Address : at Pineuilh, allée du Camping (take northeastern exit along the D 130; beside the Dordogne river)
Opening times : from beginning April to end Oct.
1.2 ha (38 pitches) flat, grassy
Tariff : 23.50€ ♠♠ ⬚ 🔲 🔋 (10A) – Extra per person 5.50€ – Reservation fee 10€
Rental rates : (from beginning April to end Oct.) 🏠 – 10 🔲. Per night from 90 to 135 €
Per week from 20 to 695 € – Reservation fee 15€
🚐 3 🔲 23.60€

Surroundings : 🌿 💧💧
Leisure activities : 🎦 ⛵ 🏊
Facilities : ⚐ ☛ 🍴 launderette
Nearby : 🎣

GPS
Longitude : 0.22462
Latitude : 44.84403

SALIES-DE-BÉARN

64270 – Michelin map **342** G4 – pop. 4,886 – alt. 50 – ⚲
▶ Paris 762 – Bayonne 60 – Dax 36 – Orthez 17

⚠ Municipal de Mosqueros

ℰ 05 59 38 12 94, *www.tourisme-bearn-gaves.com*
Address : av. Al Cartero (take the western exit along the D 17, follow the signs for Bayonne, at the outdoor activity centre)
0.7 ha (60 pitches) terraced, grassy, gravelled
Rentals : 2 🏕.
🚐 sani-station – 16 ▣

Surroundings : 🌳 ♨
Leisure activities : 🛶
Facilities : ₲ ⚏ 🛁 ⚡ launderette
Nearby : 🎿 ⛵

GPS Longitude : -0.93814
Latitude : 43.47643

SALIGNAC-EYVIGUES

24590 – Michelin map **329** I6 – pop. 1,141 – alt. 297
▶ Paris 509 – Brive-la-Gaillarde 34 – Cahors 84 – Périgueux 70

⚠⚠ Flower Le Temps de Vivre

ℰ 05 53 28 93 21, *www.temps-de-vivre.com*
Address : located 1.5km south along the D 61 and take the road to the right
Opening times : from end April to end Sept.
4.5 ha (50 pitches) terraced, grassy, adjacent wood
Tariff : 26.90€ ✹ ✹ 🚗 ▣ 🔌 (10A) – Extra per person 5€ – Reservation fee 10€
Rental rates : (from beginning April to end Sept.) – 18 🏕 – 4 tent bungalows.
Per night from 32 to 102 € – Per week from 160 to 714 € – Reservation fee 15€
🚐 5 ▣ 11.50€ – 🚐 🔌11.50€

Surroundings : 🌳 🏕 ♨
Leisure activities : 🍹 🛶 🚣 ⛵
Facilities : ₲ ⚏ 🛁 ⚐ launderette 🐾

GPS Longitude : 1.32817
Latitude : 44.96355

In order for the guide to remain wholly objective, the selection of campsites is made on an entirely independent basis.

SALLES

33770 – Michelin map **335** F7 – pop. 6,044 – alt. 23
▶ Paris 632 – Arcachon 36 – Belin-Béliet 11 – Biscarrosse 122

⚠⚠ Le Park du Val de l'Eyre ⚑⚑

ℰ 05 56 88 47 03, *www.valdeleyre.com*
Address : 8 rte du Minoy (take the southwestern exit along the D 108e , follow the signs for Lugos; beside the Eyre river and a lake –from the A 63, take exit 21)
Opening times : from beginning March to mid Nov.
13 ha/4 ha for camping (150 pitches) relatively flat, flat, grassy, sandy
Tariff : (2012 price) ✹ 9€ 🚗 ▣ 17€ 🔌 (16A) – Reservation fee 20€
Rental rates : (2012 price) (from beginning March to mid Nov.) – 48 🏕 – 4 🏠.
Per week from 253 to 790 € – Reservation fee 20€
🚐 sani-station

Surroundings : 🌳 ♨
Leisure activities : 🍹 🍴 🛶 🏊 🚣 🏛 ⛵ 🏄 🎣
Facilities : ₲ ⚏ 🚿 🛁 🛀 ⚐ launderette 🐾
Nearby : 🛒

GPS Longitude : -0.87399
Latitude : 44.54606

SALLES

47150 – Michelin map **336** H2 – pop. 314 – alt. 120
▶ Paris 588 – Agen 59 – Fumel 12 – Monflanquin 11

Des Bastides

℘ 0553408309, *www.campingdesbastides.com*
Address : Terre Rouge (located 1km to the northeast, follow the signs for Fumel, at junction of D 150 and D 162)
Opening times : from beginning April to end Oct.
6 ha (96 pitches) terraced, grassy
Tariff : 33€ ✶✶ ⇔ ▣ 🔌 (6A) – Extra per person 5.50€ – Reservation fee 18€
Rental rates : (from beginning April to end Oct.) ⅙ – 12 ▦ – 5 🏠 – 1 yurt – 2 tent bungalows – 4 tents. Per night from 38 to 142 €– Per week from 266 to 994 €
Reservation fee 18€

Surroundings : ▭ ♤♤
Leisure activities : ▾ ✗ jacuzzi ⬳ ♻ ⟰ ⩙ multi-sports ground
Facilities : ⅙ ⊶ ▥ ♨ – 2 individual sanitary facilities (⋔⇌⊔ wc) ¶ launderette ⨺

GPS Longitude : 0.88161
Latitude : 44.55263

SANGUINET

40460 – Michelin map **335** E8 – pop. 3,133 – alt. 24
▶ Paris 643 – Arcachon 27 – Belin-Béliet 26 – Biscarrosse 120

Lou Broustaricq ♣♣

℘ 0558827482, *www.lou-broustaricq.com* – limited spaces for one-night stay ⅙
Address : 2315 rte Langeot (2.8km northwest following signs for Bordeaux, 300m from the Étang de Cazaux (lake)
Opening times : from beginning April to end Oct.
18.8 ha (570 pitches) flat, sandy
Tariff : (2012 price) 36€ ✶✶ ⇔ ▣ 🔌 (16A) – Extra per person 7€ – Reservation fee 25€
Rental rates : (2012 price) (from beginning April to end Oct.) ⅙ – 156 ▦.
Per night from 36 to 142 € – Per week from 52 to 994 € – Reservation fee 25€

Surroundings : ⊛ ▭ ♤♤
Leisure activities : ▾ ✗ ▦ ⒢ ⥉ jacuzzi ⬳ ♻ ✗ ⫪ ▣ ⟰ ⩙ entertainment room
Facilities : ⅙ ⊶ ▥ ♨ ¶ launderette ⬱ ⨺
Nearby : ⚓ ⬥

GPS Longitude : -1.0789
Latitude : 44.50006

SARE

64310 – Michelin map **342** C5 – pop. 2,434 – alt. 70
▶ Paris 794 – Biarritz 26 – Cambo-les-Bains 19 – Pau 138

La Petite Rhune

℘ 0559542397, *www.lapetiterhune.com* – limited spaces for one-night stay
Address : Lehenbiscaye quartier (situated 2km south along the road connecting D 406 and D 306)
Opening times : from mid June to mid Sept.
1.5 ha (56 pitches) terraced, relatively flat, sloping, grassy
Tariff : (2012 price) 25.80€ ✶✶ ⇔ ▣ 🔌 (10A) – Extra per person 5.50€ – Reservation fee 10€
Rental rates : (2012 price) (permanent) ⅙ (Jul-Aug) – 15 🏠 – 5 gîtes.
Per night from 60 to 70 € – Per week from 30 to 670 – Reservation fee 10€

Surroundings : ⊛ ⋜ ♤♤
Leisure activities : ▦ ⬳ ✗ ⟰ (small swimming pool), multi-sports ground
Facilities : ⅙ ⊶ ⍋♨ ¶ launderette
Nearby : ▾ ✗

GPS Longitude : -1.58771
Latitude : 43.30198

SARLAT-LA-CANÉDA

24200 – Michelin map **329** I6 – pop. 9,541 – alt. 145
▶ Paris 526 – Bergerac 74 – Brive-la-Gaillarde 52 – Cahors 60

La Palombière ♣♨

🕿 05 53 59 42 34, *www.lapalombiere.fr* – limited spaces for one-night stay
Address : at Ste Nathalène, at Galmier (9km northeast on the D 43 and take the turning to the left)
Opening times : from end April to mid Sept.
8.5 ha/4 ha for camping (177 pitches) relatively flat, terraced, stony, grassy
Tariff : ☆ 8.40€ 🚗 回 12.20€ – 🔌 (10A) 3€ – Reservation fee 25€
Rental rates : (from end April to mid Sept.) – 51 🏚 – 10 🏠. Per night from 42 to 132 €
Per week from 300 to 925 € – Reservation fee 25€

Surroundings : 🏖 🗟 🞯
Leisure activities : 🍴 ✕ 🞯 🖈 🏊 🚴 🎯 🔭 🛶 🏊
Facilities : 🛁 🚰 🗄 🖛 "🍴 launderette 🗑 🚻

Longitude : 1.29157
Latitude : 44.90639

Les Castels Le Moulin du Roch ♣♨

🕿 05 53 59 20 27, *www.moulin-du-roch.com* ✻
Address : at St-André d'Allas, via the D 47 (10km to the northwest, follow the signs for Les Eyzies; beside a stream)
Opening times : from beginning May to mid Sept.
8 ha (200 pitches) terraced, relatively flat, flat, grassy, small lake
Tariff : 37€ ☆☆ 🚗 回 🔌 (6A) – Extra per person 9.50€ – Reservation fee 12€
Rental rates : (from beginning May to mid Sept.) ✻ – 55 🏚 – 6 🏠 – 17 chalets
(without sanitary facilities). Per night from 40 to 100 €– Per week from 495 to 1,350 €
Reservation fee 12€

Based around an old Périgord windmill.

Surroundings : 🗟 🞯
Leisure activities : 🍴 ✕ 🖾 🞯 🖈 🚴 🔭 🛶 🞰
Facilities : 🛁 🚰 🖳 🗄 🖛 "🍴 launderette 🗑 🚻

Longitude : 1.11481
Latitude : 44.90843

La Châtaigneraie ♣♨

🕿 05 53 59 03 61, *www.camping-lachataigneraie24.com*
Address : at Prats de Carlux, at La Garrigue Basse (10km east along the D 47 at take turning to the right)
Opening times : from end April to mid Sept.
9 ha (140 pitches) terraced, flat, grassy, sandy
Tariff : 32.50€ ☆☆ 🚗 回 🔌 (10A) – Extra per person 8.10€ – Reservation fee 20€
Rental rates : (from end April to mid Sept.) ✻ (Jul–Aug) – 60 🏚 – 11 🏠 – 3 gîtes – 7 mobile homes (without sanitary facilities). Per night from 31 to 170 € – Per week from 220 to 1,190 €
Reservation fee 20€

Pretty water park and play area surrounded by low walls made of local stone.

Surroundings : 🏖 🗟 🞯
Leisure activities : 🍴 ✕ 🖾 🖈 🚴 🔭 🛶 🏊 sports trail, mountain biking
Facilities : 🛁 🚰 🗄 🖛 "🍴 launderette 🗑 🚻

Longitude : 1.29871
Latitude : 44.90056

The Michelin classification (△△△ ... △) is totally independent of the official star classification system awarded by the local prefecture or other official organisation.

Les Grottes de Roffy ♠♣

☎ 0553591561, *www.roffy.fr*
Address : at Ste-Nathalène, in locality of Roffy (8km east, along the D 47)
Opening times : from mid April to mid Sept.
5 ha (165 pitches) open site, terraced, flat, grassy
Tariff : (2012 price) 16.50€ ♦♦ ⇔ 🅴 (8A) – Extra per person 5.40€ – Reservation fee 18€
Rental rates : (2012 price) (from beginning March to mid Sept.) – 28 🛏.
Per night from 54 to 120 € – Per week from 390 to 950 € – Reservation fee 18€

Surroundings : ⤳ ⟨ ⌑ ♧♧
Leisure activities : ♟ ✗ 🎱 ⟲ 🚴 ⛵ ✳ ⚓
Facilities : ♿ ⛟ ⌂ ⌸ ⟲ 🍴 launderette ⚏ ⛽

GPS Longitude : 1.28211
Latitude : 44.90417

Domaine de Loisirs le Montant ♠♣

☎ 0553591850, *www.camping-sarlat.com*
Address : at Négrelat (situated 2km southwest along the D 57, follow the signs for Bergerac then continue 2.3km along the road to the right)
Opening times : from beginning April to end Sept.
70 ha/8 ha for camping (135 pitches) terraced, undulating, flat, grassy, very uneven
Tariff : (2012 price) ♦ 7.50€ ⇔ 🅴 14.90€ – (4) (10A) 4.50€ – Reservation fee 20€
Rental rates : (2012 price) (from beginning April to end Sept.) – 16 🛏 – 14 ⌂ – 2 gîtes.
Per week from 300 to 949 € – Reservation fee 25€
Range of luxury rental options in a natural wooded and hilly setting.

Surroundings : ⤳ ⟨ ⌑ ♧♧
Leisure activities : ♟ ✗ 🎱 ⚐ evening 🚴 jacuzzi 🚣 🚵 ⛳ 🎱 ⛱ ⚓ multi-sports ground
Facilities : ♿ ⛟ 🔊 ⌂ ⌸ ⟲ 🍴 launderette ⛽

GPS Longitude : 1.18903
Latitude : 44.86573

Domaine Des Chênes Verts ♠♣

☎ 0553592107, *www.chenes-verts.com* – limited spaces for one-night stay
Address : rte de Sarlat et Souillac (8.5km southeast)
8 ha (143 pitches) flat, relatively flat, terraced, grassy
Rentals : 72 🛏 – 31 ⌂.
🛢 sani-station – 4 🅴

Surroundings : ⤳ ⌑ ♧♧
Leisure activities : ♟ ✗ 🎱 🚴 🚣 🚵 ⛱ ⚓
Facilities : ♿ ⛟ ⌂ 🍴 launderette ⚏ ⛽

GPS Longitude : 1.2972
Latitude : 44.86321

La Ferme de Villeneuve ♠♣

☎ 0553303090, *www.fermedevilleneuve.com*
Address : at St-André-d'Allas, in locality of Villeneuve (8km northwest along the D 47, follow the signs for Les Eyzies-de-Tayac and take turning to the left)
Opening times : from beginning April to end Oct.
20 ha/2.5 ha for camping (100 pitches) terraced, relatively flat, flat, grassy, natural setting among trees and bushes, lake
Tariff : ♦ 6.30€ ⇔ 🅴 6.95€ – (4) (10A) 3.80€ – Reservation fee 9€
Rental rates : (from beginning April to end Oct.) 🚐 – 2 caravans – 11 🛏 – 4 teepees – 5 tent bungalows – 2 tents. Per night from 39 to 90 € – Per week from 90 to 665 €
Reservation fee 9€
🛢 sani-station 2€ – 4 🅴 12€
Farm campsite.

Surroundings : ⤳ ⟨ ⌑ ♧♧
Leisure activities : ♟ ✗ 🚴 🚣 🚵 ⚓
Facilities : ♿ ⛟ ⌂ 🍴 launderette ⛽
Nearby : cinema/activity centre

GPS Longitude : 1.14051
Latitude : 44.90438

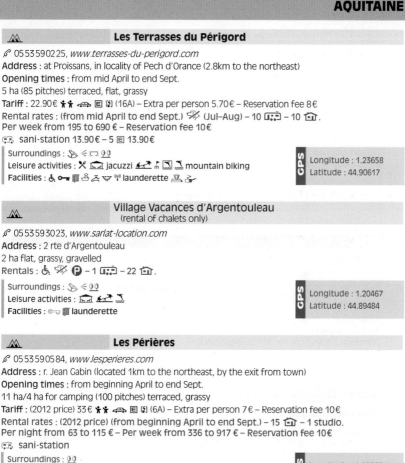

Les Terrasses du Périgord

𝄢 0553590225, *www.terrasses-du-perigord.com*
Address : at Proissans, in locality of Pech d'Orance (2.8km to the northeast)
Opening times : from mid April to end Sept.
5 ha (85 pitches) terraced, flat, grassy
Tariff : 22.90€ ♦♦ ⇔ 🔲 ⒝ (16A) – Extra per person 5.70€ – Reservation fee 8€
Rental rates : (from mid April to end Sept.) ⅋ (Jul–Aug) – 10 🔲 – 10 🏠.
Per week from 195 to 690 € – Reservation fee 10€
🚐 sani-station 13.90€ – 5 🔲 13.90€

Surroundings : ⅘ ≤ ⌂ 𝄞
Leisure activities : ✕ 🔲 jacuzzi ⬈ 🔸 🔲 ⅃ mountain biking
Facilities : ᖼ ⊶ ◫ 🔸 ⤴ ⤸ ╹ launderette ⤲ ᖰ

GPS Longitude : 1.23658
Latitude : 44.90617

Village Vacances d'Argentouleau
(rental of chalets only)

𝄢 0553593023, *www.sarlat-location.com*
Address : 2 rte d'Argentouleau
2 ha flat, grassy, gravelled
Rentals : ᖼ ⅋ ⓟ – 1 🔲 – 22 🏠.

Surroundings : ⅘ ≤ 𝄞
Leisure activities : 🔲 ⬈
Facilities : ⊶ ◫ launderette

GPS Longitude : 1.20467
Latitude : 44.89484

Les Périères

𝄢 0553590584, *www.lesperieres.com*
Address : r. Jean Gabin (located 1km to the northeast, by the exit from town)
Opening times : from beginning April to end Sept.
11 ha/4 ha for camping (100 pitches) terraced, grassy
Tariff : (2012 price) 33€ ♦♦ ⇔ 🔲 ⒝ (6A) – Extra per person 7€ – Reservation fee 10€
Rental rates : (2012 price) (from beginning April to end Sept.) – 15 🏠 – 1 studio.
Per night from 63 to 115 € – Per week from 336 to 917 € – Reservation fee 10€
🚐 sani-station

Surroundings : 𝄞
Leisure activities : ╹ 🔲 ⬆ ⬈ ⅋ 🔲 ⅃ sports trail
Facilities : ᖼ ⊶ ◫ ⤴ ⤸ ╹ launderette

GPS Longitude : 1.22767
Latitude : 44.89357

Les Charmes

𝄢 0553310289, *www.campinglescharmesdordogne.com*
Address : at St-André-d'Allas, in locality of Malartigue Haut (10km west along the D 25, follow the signs for Le Bugue and take road to the right)
Opening times : from beginning April to mid Oct.
5.5 ha/1.8 (100 pitches) flat and relatively flat, terraced, grassy
Tariff : (2012 price) 22.60€ ♦♦ ⇔ 🔲 ⒝ (6A) – Extra per person 5.70€ – Reservation fee 9€
Rental rates : (2012 price) (from beginning April to mid Oct.) – 6 🔲 – 5 🏠 – 9 tent bungalows. Per night from 35 to 70 € – Per week from 160 to 770 €– Reservation fee 9€

Surroundings : ⅘ ⌂ 𝄟
Leisure activities : ╹ ⬈ 🔲 ⅃ ⬩ multi-sports ground
Facilities : ᖼ ⊶ ╹ 🔲 ᖰ

GPS Longitude : 1.11365
Latitude : 44.89412

*This guide is not intended as a list of all the camping sites in France;
its aim is to provide a selection of the best sites in each category.*

Les Acacias

⌂ 0553310850, *www.acacias.fr*
Address : Bourg de la Canéda, r. Louis de Champagne (6km southeast along the D 704 and take a right turn at the Leclerc hypermarket)
Opening times : from beginning April to end Sept.
4 ha (122 pitches) flat, relatively flat, terraced, grassy
Tariff : 21.50€ ★ ★ ⇔ 国 ⚡ (10A) – Extra per person 5.40€ – Reservation fee 10€
Rental rates : (from beginning April to end Sept.) ⌗ – 20 ⟦⟧. Per night from 41 to 63 €
Per week from 40 to 690 € – Reservation fee 10€
⟨⟩ sani-station 4€
Bus shuttle service to Sarlat.

Surroundings : ≼ ⊏ ♁♁
Leisure activities : ♟ ⚐ ⊛ ⤓ multi-sports ground
Facilities : ⚭ ⊶ ⫿ ♒ ⚲ ♟ launderette ⚘

GPS Longitude : 1.23699
Latitude : 44.85711

SAUBION

40230 – Michelin map **335** C12 – pop. 1,323 – alt. 17
▶ Paris 747 – Bordeaux 169 – Mont-de-Marsan 79 – Pau 106

Club Airotel La Pomme de Pin

⌂ 0558770071, *www.camping-lapommedepin.com*
Address : 825 rte de Seignosse (situated 2km southeast along the D 652 and take D 337, follow the signs for Saubion)
Opening times : from end March to end Sept.
5 ha (252 pitches) flat, grassy, sandy
Tariff : 32€ ★ ★ ⇔ 国 ⚡ (6A) – Extra per person 6.20€ – Reservation fee 20€
Rental rates : (from end March to end Sept.) – 45 ⟦⟧ – 24 tent bungalows.
Per night from 36 to 59 € – Per week from 24 to 889 € – Reservation fee 20€
⟨⟩ sani-station
Indoor swimming area.

Surroundings : ⊏ ♁♁
Leisure activities : ♟ ✕ ⊡ ⊙jacuzzi ⚐ ▣ (open-air in season)
Facilities : ⚭ ⊶ ♒ ♟ launderette ▨, ⚘ refrigerated food storage

GPS Longitude : -1.35563
Latitude : 43.67608

A 'quartier' is a district or area of a town or village.

SAUVETERRE-LA-LÉMANCE

47500 – Michelin map **336** I2 – pop. 587 – alt. 100
▶ Paris 572 – Agen 68 – Fumel 14 – Monflanquin 27

Flower Le Moulin du Périé

⌂ 0553406726, *www.camping-moulin-perie.com*
Address : at Moulin du Périé (3km east following signs for Loubejac; beside a stream)
Opening times : from mid May to mid Sept.
4 ha (125 pitches) flat, grassy
Tariff : (2012 price) 32.55€ ★ ★ ⇔ 国 ⚡ (10A) – Extra per person 7.60€ – Reservation fee 20€
Rental rates : (2012 price) (from mid May to mid Sept.) ⌗ – 14 ⟦⟧ – 4 ⌂ – 12 tent bungalows. Per night from 35 to 128 € – Per week from 245 to 896 € – Reservation fee 35€
⟨⟩ sani-station

Surroundings : ⊚ ⊏ ♁♁
Leisure activities : ♟ ✕ ⊡ ⚐ ⊛ ⤓ ≋
Facilities : ⚭ ⊶ ▦♒ launderette ⚘

GPS Longitude : 1.04743
Latitude : 44.5898

SEIGNOSSE OCEAN

40510 – Michelin map **335** C12
▶ Paris 763 – Bordeaux 184 – Mont-de-Marsan 89 – Pau 115

Village Camping Océliances ▲▲

⌗ 05 58 43 30 30, *www.oceliances.com*
Address : av. des Tucs (along the D 79e, 500m from the beach at Les Bourdaines)
Opening times : from beginning April to mid Nov.
13 ha (432 pitches) flat, undulating, sandy
Tariff : (2012 price) 33.50€ ♛♛ ⛬ 🅴 (½) (6A) – Extra per person 4€ – Reservation fee 20€
Rental rates : (2012 price) (from beginning April to mid Nov.) ⚑ – 75 🚐 – 20 🏠 – 18 tent
bungalows. Per night from 80 to 161 €– Per week from 225 to 800 € – Reservation fee 20€
🚐 18 🅴 21.10€

Surroundings : 🌳🌳
Leisure activities : 🍹 ✕ 🎬 🎯🏃 🛝 🎣🦆 ♨ surfing, multi-sports ground
Facilities : ♿ ⛲ 🚿 🛁 ✀ 🍴 launderette 🔌 🗄 refrigerated food
storage

GPS Longitude : -1.43039
Latitude : 43.69358

*The prices listed were supplied by the campsite owners in 2012
(if prices were not available, those from the previous year are given).
The fees should be regarded as basic charges and may fluctuate
with inflation.*

SIORAC-EN-PÉRIGORD

24170 – Michelin map **329** G7 – pop. 1,015 – alt. 77
▶ Paris 548 – Bergerac 45 – Cahors 68 – Périgueux 60

Le Port

⌗ 05 53 31 63 81, *www.campingduport.net*
Address : to the northeast of the town, access via the D 25, follow the signs for Buisson-Cussac and
take the road in front of Carrefour supermarket; beside the Dordogne and the Nauze rivers
Opening times : from beginning April to end Oct.
2.5 ha (83 pitches) flat, grassy
Tariff : ♛ 4.25€ ⛬ 🅴 3.50€ – (½) (10A) 3€
Rental rates : (from beginning April to end Oct.) – 10 🚐 – 2 teepees.
Per night from 2 to 40 € – Per week from 150 to 465 €

Surroundings : 🌿 🌳🌳
Leisure activities : 🎬 🛝 ≋ 🎣
Facilities : ♿ ⚡ (mid-Jul–mid-Aug) 🚿
Nearby : 🛒 🍹 ✕ ✂

GPS Longitude : 0.98755
Latitude : 44.82472

SORDE-L'ABBAYE

40300 – Michelin map **335** E13 – pop. 646 – alt. 17
▶ Paris 758 – Bayonne 47 – Dax 27 – Oloron-Ste-Marie 63

Municipal la Galupe

⌗ 05 58 73 18 13, *mairie.sordelabbaye@wanadoo.fr*
Address : 242 chemin du Camping (1.3km west along the D 29, follow the signs for Peyrehorade,
D 123 to the left and take the road before the bridge; near the Gave d'Oloron (river)
0.6 ha (28 pitches) flat, grassy, stony

Surroundings : 🏞 🌿 🌳
Facilities : ♿

GPS Longitude : -1.0561
Latitude : 43.52983

SOULAC-SUR-MER

33780 – Michelin map **335** E1 – pop. 2,711 – alt. 7
▶ Paris 515 – Bordeaux 99 – Lesparre-Médoc 31 – Royan 12

Les Lacs ♣♠

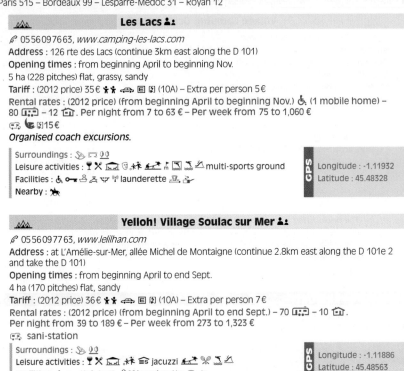

🖉 0556097663, *www.camping-les-lacs.com*
Address : 126 rte des Lacs (continue 3km east along the D 101)
Opening times : from beginning April to beginning Nov.
5 ha (228 pitches) flat, grassy, sandy
Tariff : (2012 price) 35€ ♣♣ ⇔ 回 (Ḥ) (10A) – Extra per person 5€
Rental rates : (2012 price) (from beginning April to beginning Nov.) ঔ (1 mobile home) –
80 ᐵᐵᐵ – 12 ᐵᐵ. Per night from 7 to 63 € – Per week from 75 to 1,060 €
ᐵᐵ ᐵᐵ (Ḥ)15€
Organised coach excursions.

Surroundings : ᐵᐵ ᐵᐵ ᐵᐵ
Leisure activities : ♟ ✗ 🏠 (Ⓨ)♣♣ ♣♣ ♣ 🔲 🗻 ⚿ multi-sports ground
Facilities : ঔ ⚲ ♣♣ 🏠 ᐵᐵ ᐵᐵ ♟ launderette 🏊 ᐵᐵ
Nearby : ᐵᐵ

Longitude : -1.11932
Latitude : 45.48328

Yelloh! Village Soulac sur Mer ♣♠

🖉 0556097763, *www.lelilhan.com*
Address : at L'Amélie-sur-Mer, allée Michel de Montaigne (continue 2.8km east along the D 101e 2
and take the D 101)
Opening times : from beginning April to end Sept.
4 ha (170 pitches) flat, sandy
Tariff : (2012 price) 36€ ♣♣ ⇔ 回 (Ḥ) (10A) – Extra per person 7€
Rental rates : (2012 price) (from beginning April to end Sept.) – 70 ᐵᐵᐵ – 10 ᐵᐵ.
Per night from 39 to 189 € – Per week from 273 to 1,323 €
ᐵᐵ sani-station

Surroundings : ᐵᐵ ᐵᐵ
Leisure activities : ♟ ✗ 🏠 ♣♣ 🗝 jacuzzi ♣♣ ♞ 🗻 ⚿
Facilities : ঔ ⚲ (Jul–Aug) ᐵᐵ ♟ launderette 🏊 ᐵᐵ

Longitude : -1.11886
Latitude : 45.48563

L'Océan

🖉 0556097610, *www.perso.wanadoo.fr/camping.ocean*
Address : 62 allée de la Négade (take the eastern exit along the D 101e 2 and take the D 101,
300m from the beach)
Opening times : from beginning June to mid Sept.
6 ha (300 pitches) gravelled, sandy, flat, grassy
Tariff : (2012 price) ♣ 5.10€ ⇔ 回 13.40€ – (Ḥ) (10A) 4.10€ – Reservation fee 15€
Natural wooded setting.

Surroundings : ᐵᐵ ᐵᐵ
Leisure activities : ♟ 🏠 ᐵᐵ ♞
Facilities : ঔ ⚲ ᐵᐵ ♟ launderette 🏊 ᐵᐵ

Longitude : -1.14533
Latitude : 45.48043

*For more information on visiting particular towns or regions, consult the
relevant regional MICHELIN Green Guide. We also recommend you use
the appropriate Michelin regional map to locate your selected campsite,
to calculate distances and to work out the best route.*

SOUSTONS

40140 – Michelin map **335** D12 – pop. 7,240 – alt. 9
▶ Paris 732 – Biarritz 53 – Castets 23 – Dax 29

Village Vacances Sunêlia Le Framissima Nature
(rental of mobile homes, chalets and tent lodges only)

℘ 05 58 77 70 00, *www.camping-nature-soustons.fr*
Address : at Nicot-les-Pins, 63 av. Port d'Albret (follow the signs for Les Lacs)
Opening times : from mid April to end Sept.
14 ha (250 pitches) flat, sandy
Rental rates : ⅙ (1 mobile home) ⚡ Ⓟ – 200 ▭ – 12 ⌂ – 37 tents.
Per night from 42 to 80 € Per week from 45 to 1,540 €

Organised excursions – natural swimming pool – plenty of activities for children and teenagers.

Surroundings : 🐚 ♉
Leisure activities : ♈ ✗ 🎬 ⏏ (open-air theatre) ♈ ⚐ ⚏ hammam, jacuzzi ⚏ ⚲ ⚮ ☲ multi-sports ground, spa therapy centre, entertainment room
Facilities : ◦⚊ ⚐ launderette ⚏ ⚋

GPS Longitude : -1.35999
Latitude : 43.75593

L'Airial

℘ 05 58 41 12 48, *www.camping-airial.com*
Address : 67 av. de Port d'Albret (situated 2km west along the D 652, follow the signs for Vieux-Boucau-les-Bains, 200m from the Étang de Soustons)
13 ha (440 pitches) flat, undulating, sandy
Rentals : ⅙ (2 mobile homes) ⚡ – 58 ▭ – 28 ⌂.

Surroundings : ♉
Leisure activities : ♈ ✗ 🎬 ⏏ daytime ♈ ⚲ ⚮ ♬ ▤ ☲ multi-sports ground
Facilities : ⅙ ◦⚊ ⚐ ⚐ launderette ⚏ ⚋ refrigerated food storage

GPS Longitude : -1.35195
Latitude : 43.75433

Village Vacances Le Dunéa
(rental of chalets only)

℘ 05 58 48 00 59, *www.club-dunea.com*
Address : at Souston-Plage, port d'Albret sud, 1 square de l'Herté (200m from the lake)
Opening times : from beginning April to mid Oct.
0.5 ha flat, undulating, sandy
Rental rates : ⚡ – 20 ⌂. Per night from 90 to 100 € – Per week from 50 to 1,150 €

Surroundings : 🐚 ♉
Leisure activities : 🎬 ☲
Facilities : ◦⚊ Ⓟ ⚐ ▣
Nearby : ⚮ ♞

GPS Longitude : -1.40065
Latitude : 43.7731

LE TEICH

33470 – Michelin map **335** E7 – pop. 6,485 – alt. 5
▶ Paris 633 – Arcachon 20 – Belin-Béliet 34 – Bordeaux 50

Ker Helen ♣♣

℘ 05 56 66 03 79, *www.kerhelen.com*
Address : 119 av. de la Côte d'Argent (situated 2km west along the D 650, follow the signs for Gujan-Mestras)
4 ha (170 pitches) flat, grassy
Rentals : ⅙ (1 chalet) – 45 ▭ – 10 ⌂ – 12 tent bungalows.
⚒ sani-station – 7 ▣

Surroundings : ▭ ♉
Leisure activities : ♈ ✗ ⏏ evening ♈ ⚏ ⚲ ☲
Facilities : ⅙ ◦⚊ ⚐ ⚏ ⚲ launderette ⚋

GPS Longitude : -1.04284
Latitude : 44.63975

TERRASSON-LAVILLEDIEU

24120 – Michelin map **329** I5 – pop. 6,222 – alt. 90
▶ Paris 497 – Brive-la-Gaillarde 22 – Juillac 28 – Périgueux 53

La Salvinie

℘ 05 53 50 06 11, *www.camping-salvinie.com*

Address : at Bouillac Sud (take the southern exit along the D 63, follow the signs for Chavagnac then continue 3.4km, following signs for Condat;on the right after the bridge)

Opening times : from beginning April to end Oct.

2.5 ha (70 pitches) flat, grassy

Tariff : ♠ 5€ ⇔ 国 5.80€ – 🔌 (6A) 3.80€

Rental rates : (from beginning April to end Oct.) – 9 🏠. Per night from 50 to 90 €
Per week from 40 to 580

🚐 sani-station 11€ – 20 国 11€ – ⚡🔌14€

Surroundings : ≼ ⊏⊐ ⵕⵕ
Leisure activities : 🎬 🛶 ⚒
Facilities : ⅙ ⊶ ⥮ launderette

GPS
Longitude : 1.26216
Latitude : 45.12069

Village Vacances le Clos du Moulin
(rental of chalets only)

℘ 05 53 51 68 95, *www.leclosdumoulin.com*

Address : at Le Moulin de Bouch (6km west of Terrasson-Lavilledieu along the N 89, follow the signs for St-Lazare and take the D 62 following signs for Coly; beside the river)

Opening times : from beginning March to end Nov.

1 ha flat, grassy

Rental rates : 🅿 – 14 🏠 – 14 gîtes. Per night from 60 to 100 €– Per week from 280 to 950 €
Reservation fee 16€

Surroundings : ⵕ
Leisure activities : 🍷 🚴 ⚒
Facilities : ⅙ ⊶ ⯐ ⥮ 🔲

GPS
Longitude : 1.26337
Latitude : 45.10288

The prices listed were supplied by the campsite owners in 2012
(if prices were not available, those from the previous year are given).
The fees should be regarded as basic charges and may fluctuate
with inflation.

LA TESTE-DE-BUCH

33260 – Michelin map **335** E7 – pop. 24,597 – alt. 5
▶ Paris 642 – Andernos-les-Bains 35 – Arcachon 5 – Belin-Béliet 44

Village Vacances FranceLoc La Pinèda ♣♣
(rental of mobile homes only)

℘ 05 56 22 23 24, *www.campinglapinede.net*

Address : rte de Cazaux (11km south along the D 112; beside the Les Landes canal – 2.5km from Cazaux)

5 ha (200 pitches) flat, sandy, grassy

Rentals : ⅙ (1 mobile home) – 200 🏠.

Surroundings : 🌊 ⊏⊐ ⵕⵕ
Leisure activities : 🍷 ✗ 🎬 🗺 ⛹ 🛶 🚴 🖼 ⚒ ⚓
Facilities : ⅙ ⊶ 🍳 ⥮ launderette 🛶
Nearby : ⚓ water skiing

GPS
Longitude : -1.15055
Latitude : 44.55516

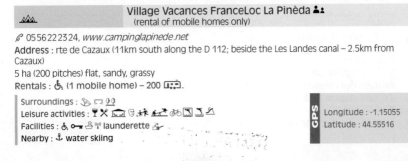

THENON

24210 – Michelin map **329** H5 – pop. 1,283 – alt. 194
▶ Paris 515 – Brive-la-Gaillarde 41 – Excideuil 36 – Les Eyzies-de-Tayac 33

Le Verdoyant

✆ 05 53 05 20 78, *www.campingleverdoyant.fr*
Address : rte de Montignac-Lascaux (4km southeast along the D 67, near two lakes)
Opening times : from end Feb. to end Sept.
9 ha/3 ha for camping (67 pitches) open site, terraced, flat, grassy
Tariff : 17.90€ ✱✱ ⇔ 🗐 (10A) – Extra per person 4.60€
Rental rates : (from end March to end Sept.) – 12 🖼 – 2 🏠. Per night from 48 to 126 €
Per week from 20 to 730
🚐 sani-station – 5 🗐 12.10€

Surroundings : ⩽ ♡♡
Leisure activities : ⍨ ✕ 🏊 🔨
Facilities : & ⊶ ⌘ 🏖 ⁋ launderette 🐾

GPS Longitude : 1.09102
Latitude : 45.11901

To make the best possible use of this guide,
please read pages 2–15 carefully.

THIVIERS

24800 – Michelin map **329** G3 – pop. 3,121 – alt. 273
▶ Paris 449 – Brive-la-Gaillarde 81 – Limoges 62 – Nontron 33

Le Repaire

✆ 06 84 77 61 78, *www.camping-le-repaire.fr*
Address : situated 2km southeast along the D 707, follow the signs for Lanouaille and take the road to the right
10 ha/4.5 ha for camping (100 pitches) flat, relatively flat, terrace, grassy, adjacent wood
Rentals : 🅿 – 10 🏠 – 2 yurts.
Attractive pitches around a small lake.

Surroundings : ⌑ ♡
Leisure activities : 🖼 ⇌s jacuzzi 🏊 🔨 fitness trail
Facilities : & ⊶ ⁋ 🔲
Nearby : ✕ 🏊 (beach)

GPS Longitude : 0.9321
Latitude : 45.41305

TOCANE-ST-APRE

24350 – Michelin map **329** D4 – pop. 1,679 – alt. 95
▶ Paris 498 – Brantôme 24 – Mussidan 33 – Périgueux 25

Municipal le Pré Sec

✆ 05 53 90 40 60, *www.campingdupresec.com*
Address : north of the town along the D 103, follow the signs for Montagrier, near the stadium; beside the Dronne river
Opening times : from beginning May to end Sept.
1.8 ha (80 pitches) open site, flat, grassy
Tariff : ✱ 1.95€ ⇔ 🗐 4.45€ – 🔌 (15A) 1.80€
Rental rates : (permanent) – 14 🏠. Per night from 27 to 40 € – Per week from 245 to 380 €
🚐 sani-station 2€ – 🛒

Surroundings : 🏊 ⌑ ♡♡
Leisure activities : 🖼 🛶 ✕ 🏊 (beach) 🔨 🛹 skate park
Facilities : & ⊶ 🗑 🏖 ⁋ 🔲

GPS Longitude : 0.49685
Latitude : 45.25649

MALAHIDE LIBRARY
PH: 8704430

TRENTELS

47140 – Michelin map **336** H3 – pop. 821 – alt. 50
▶ Paris 607 – Agen 42 – Bergerac 72 – Cahors 60

Village Vacances Municipal de Lustrac
(rental of chalets only)

℘ 05 53 70 77 22, *mairie.trentels@wanadoo.fr* – traditional camp. spaces also available
Address : at Lustrac (2.5km northeast along the D 911, follow the signs for Fumel and take the road to the right, towards Lustrac; beside the Lot river)
Opening times : permanent
0.5 ha flat, grassy
Rental rates : &. – 7 🏠. Per night from 45 to 90 € – Per week from 200 to 440 €

Surroundings : 🐾 🗂 ♨
Leisure activities : 🎪
Facilities : 🚮 cc ⛲ launderette
Nearby : 🍴

GPS Longitude : 0.88316
Latitude : 44.4335

Fire safety doesn't stop when you leave your accommodation.
Always take care and consider the fire risks.

TURSAC

24620 – Michelin map **329** H6 – pop. 319 – alt. 75
▶ Paris 536 – Bordeaux 172 – Périgueux 48 – Brive-la-Gaillarde 57

Le Vézère Périgord

℘ 05 53 06 96 31, *www.levezereperigord.com*
Address : 800m northeast along the D 706, follow the signs for Montignac and take the road to the right
Opening times : from mid April to end Oct.
3.5 ha (103 pitches) terraced, relatively flat, grassy, stony
Tariff : 23.60 € ⛺⛺ 🚗 🔲 ⚡ (10A) – Extra per person 4.75 €
Rental rates : (from mid April to end Oct.) – 25 🏠 – 3 tent bungalows – 2 tents.
Per night from 31 to 103 € – Per week from 217 to 720 €
🚽 sani-station

Surroundings : 🐾 🗂 ♨♨♨
Leisure activities : 🍴 ✗ 🎪 jacuzzi 🏊 🚲 🍴 🏓
Facilities : &. ⚓ cc ⛲ ⛲ launderette 🚿

GPS Longitude : 1.04637
Latitude : 44.97599

URDOS

64490 – Michelin map **342** I7 – pop. 69 – alt. 780
▶ Paris 850 – Jaca 38 – Oloron-Ste-Marie 41 – Pau 75

Municipal Le Gave d'Aspe

℘ 05 59 34 88 26, *www.campingaspe.com*
Address : r. du Moulin de la Tourette (located 1.5km northwest along the N 134 and take the road in front of the old station; beside the Gave d'Aspe (river)
1.5 ha (80 pitches) open site, flat and relatively flat, terrace, grassy, stony
Rentals : 🚐 – 2 🏠.
🚽 sani-station – 5 🔲

Surroundings : 🐾 ≤ ♨
Leisure activities : 🎪 🏊 🎣
Facilities : &. ⚓ ⛲ launderette

GPS Longitude : -0.55642
Latitude : 42.87719

[MALAHIDE LIBRA...
PH. 8704430

URRUGNE

64122 – Michelin map **342** B4 – pop. 8,427 – alt. 34
▶ Paris 791 – Bayonne 29 – Biarritz 23 – Hendaye 8

Sunêlia Col d'Ibardin ▲±

𝄞 05 59 54 31 21, *www.col-ibardin.com*
Address : rte d'Olhette (4km south along the D 4, follow the signs for Ascain and Le Col d'Ibardin; beside a stream)
Opening times : from beginning April to end Sept.
8 ha (150 pitches) undulating, terraced, relatively flat, flat, grassy
Tariff : 35€ ♣♣ ⇦ 🔲 (₤) (10A) – Extra per person 7€ – Reservation fee 30€
Rental rates : (from end March to mid Nov.) ♿ (1 mobile home) ⌇ – 55 ⟦⟧ – 31 ⌂ –
6 tents. Per night from 45 to 130 € – Per week from 315 to 910 € – Reservation fee 30€
🛒 2 🔲 16€ – 🔋 (₤)25€
In the middle of an oak forest; pitches beside a stream.

Surroundings : 🦫 ⊏ 𝄯
Leisure activities : ♈ ✗ 🎱 ⛷ ⛵ ⛵ ⛳ multi-sports ground
Facilities : ♿ ⊶ ⛺ ⚗ ⛄ ♈ launderette ☰ ⟿

GPS
Longitude : -1.68461
Latitude : 43.33405

Larrouleta

𝄞 05 59 47 37 84, *www.larrouleta.com*
Address : Socoa quartier, 210 rte de Socoa (3km to the south)
Opening times : permanent
5 ha (263 pitches) flat, grassy
Tariff : (2012 price) 25.50€ ♣♣ ⇦ 🔲 (₤) (5A) – Extra per person 7.75€
🛒 sani-station
Very pleasant site set around a small lake (swimming possible).

Surroundings : ⚐⚐
Leisure activities : ♈ ✗ 🎱 ⛵ ⛵ ▣ (open-air in season) ≅ (beach) ⌇ pedalos
Facilities : ♿ ⊶ ▥ ⛺ ⚗ ⛄ ♈ launderette ☰ ⟿

GPS
Longitude : -1.6859
Latitude : 43.37036

The information in the guide may have changed since going to press.

URT

64240 – Michelin map **342** E4 – pop. 2,183 – alt. 41
▶ Paris 757 – Bayonne 17 – Biarritz 24 – Cambo-les-Bains 28

Etche Zahar

𝄞 05 59 56 27 36, *www.etche-zahar.fr*
Address : allée de Mesplès (located 1km west along the D 257, towards Urcuit and take the turning to the left)
Opening times : from beginning March to mid Nov.
1.5 ha (43 pitches) open site, flat and relatively flat, grassy
Tariff : ♣ 4.40€ ⇦ 3€ 🔲 12€ – (₤) (10A) 3.70€ – Reservation fee 13€
Rental rates : (from beginning March to mid Nov.) ♿ (2 chalets) – 8 ⟦⟧ – 9 ⌂ –
5 tent bungalows – 4 tents. Per night from 26 to 69 €– Per week from 182 to 665 €
Reservation fee 13€
🛒 2 🔲 23€

Surroundings : 🦫 ⊏ ⚐
Leisure activities : 🎱 ⛵ 🎠 ⛳
Facilities : ♿ ⊶ ♈ launderette ⟿
Nearby : 🍴

GPS
Longitude : -1.2961
Latitude : 43.4925

VENDAYS-MONTALIVET

33930 – Michelin map **335** E2 – pop. 2,288 – alt. 9
▶ Paris 535 – Bordeaux 82 – Lesparre-Médoc 14 – Soulac-sur-Mer 21

La Chesnays

℘ 0556417274, *www.camping-montalivet.com*
Address : 8 rte de Soulac, at Mayan
Opening times : from end April to end Sept.
1.5 ha (59 pitches) flat, grassy
Tariff : (2012 price) 24.50€ ♛♛ ⟺ 🗐 ⧫ (10A) – Extra per person 5€ – Reservation fee 14€
Rental rates : (2012 price) (from end April to end Sept.) ⤢ – 4 ⟐ – 3 🏠 – 4 tent bungalows. Per night from 36 to 61 € – Per week from 40 to 730 € – Reservation fee 14€

Surroundings : ⌑ 🙾
Facilities : ♿ ⚷ ⛺ ⑂

GPS
Longitude : -1.08262
Latitude : 45.37602

Le Mérin

℘ 0556417864, *www.campinglemerin.com*
Address : 7 rte du Mérin (3.7km northwest along the D 102, follow the signs for Montalivet and take road to the left)
Opening times : from beginning April to end Oct.
3.5 ha (165 pitches) flat, grassy, sandy
Tariff : ♛ 3.50€ ⟺ 🗐 5.60€ – ⧫ (10A) 3.40€
Rental rates : (from beginning April to end Oct.) ⤢ – 6 ⟐ – 3 🏠. Per night from 45 to 62 € – Per week from 10 to 440 €

Surroundings : ⧖ ⌑ 🙾
Leisure activities : ⛵
Facilities : ⚷ ⧈ 🖼

GPS
Longitude : -1.09932
Latitude : 45.36703

In order for the guide to remain wholly objective, the selection is made on an entirely independent basis. There is no charge for being selected for the guide.

VENSAC

33590 – Michelin map **335** E2 – pop. 854 – alt. 5
▶ Paris 528 – Bordeaux 82 – Lesparre-Médoc 14 – Soulac-sur-Mer 18

Les Acacias

℘ 0556095881, *www.les-acacias-du-medoc.fr*
Address : 44 rte de St-Vivien (located 1.5km northeast along the N 215, follow the signs for Verdon-sur-Mer and take the road to the right)
Opening times : from beginning April to end Oct.
3.5 ha (175 pitches) flat, grassy, sandy
Tariff : (2012 price) 27.50€ ♛♛ ⟺ 🗐 ⧫ (10A) – Extra per person 5€ – Reservation fee 15€
Rental rates : (2012 price) (from beginning April to end Oct.) – 57 ⟐. Per night from 40 to 155 € Per week from 335 to 940 € – Reservation fee 15€

Surroundings : ⌑ 🙾
Leisure activities : ✗ 🖵 ⏾evening ⛵ ⛷ 🛶
Facilities : ♿ ⚷ ⛺ ⛫ ⑂ launderette ⟿

GPS
Longitude : -1.03252
Latitude : 45.40887

LE-VERDON-SUR-MER

33123 – Michelin map **335** E2 – pop. 1,334 – alt. 3
▶ Paris 514 – Bordeaux 100 – La Rochelle 80

Sunêlia La Pointe du Médoc ▲▲

✆ 05 56 73 39 99, *www.camping-lapointedumedoc.com*
Address : rte de la Pointe de Grave (on the D 1215)
6.5 ha (260 pitches) terraced, flat, sandy
Rentals : ♿ (1 mobile home) – 123 ⛺ – 31 🏠.

Surroundings : ⚲
Leisure activities : 🍴 ✗ 🎬 🎮 🏃 ⛵ 🚲 🎣 🏊 ⛲ multi-sports ground, entertainment room
Facilities : ♿ ⛽ 🛁 🚿 🚰 🍴 launderette 🏖 🚿

GPS Longitude : -1.07965
Latitude : 45.54557

A 'quartier' is a district or area of a town or village.

VÉZAC

24220 – Michelin map **329** I6 – pop. 617 – alt. 90
▶ Paris 535 – Bergerac 65 – Brive-la-Gaillarde 60 – Fumel 53

Les Deux Vallées

✆ 05 53 29 53 55, *www.campingles2vallees.com*
Address : at La Gare (to the west, behind the old station; beside a little lake)
Opening times : from mid Feb. to mid Nov.
2.5 ha (100 pitches) flat, grassy
Tariff : (2012 price) 🚹 6.90€ 🚗 ▣ 8.90€ – 🔌 (10A) 3.90€ – Reservation fee 15€
Rental rates : (2012 price) (from mid March to mid Oct.) – 18 ⛺ – 10 tent bungalows – 2 gîtes. Per night 59€ – Per week from 145 to 865 € – Reservation fee 15€
🚐 4 ▣
An uninterrupted view of the Château de Beynac from some pitches.

Surroundings : 🌲 ≤ 🏕 ⚲
Leisure activities : 🍴 ✗ 🎬 ⛵ 🚲 🎣 🏊 🎣
Facilities : ♿ ⛽ 🚿 🛁 🍴 launderette 🚿 refrigerators

GPS Longitude : 1.15844
Latitude : 44.83542

VIELLE-SAINT-GIRONS

40560 – Michelin map **335** D11 – pop. 1,160 – alt. 27
▶ Paris 719 – Castets 16 – Dax 37 – Mimizan 32

Sunêlia Le Col Vert ▲▲

✆ 08 90 71 00 01, *www.colvert.com*
Address : 1548 rte de l'Étang (5.5km south along the D 652; beside the Étang de Léon)
Opening times : from mid April to end Sept.
24 ha (800 pitches) flat, sandy, grassy
Tariff : 44.90€ 🚹🚹 🚗 ▣ 🔌 (6A) – Extra per person 7.10€ – Reservation fee 30€
Rental rates : (from mid April to end Sept.) ♿ (1 mobile home) – 315 ⛺ – 34 🏠 – 38 tent bungalows. Per night from 5 to 197 € – Per week from 175 to 1,379 € – Reservation fee 33.50€
🚐 sani-station – 25 ▣ 12€ – 🚐 🔌17€
Free shuttle service to St-Girons-Plage (beach).

Surroundings : ⚲⚲ ⛰
Leisure activities : 🍴 ✗ 🎬 🎮 🏃 💆 ♨ hammam, jacuzzi ⛵ 🚲 ✂ 🏊 ⛲ 🎯 🎣 multi-sports ground
Facilities : ♿ ⛽ 🛁 – 6 individual sanitary facilities (🚿🛁🚽 wc) 🚿 🚰 🍴 launderette 🏖 🚿 refrigerated food storage
Nearby : 🎣 🐴 ⛵ boats for hire

GPS Longitude : -1.30946
Latitude : 43.90416

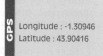

117

L'Océane

📞 05 58 42 94 37, *www.camping-oceane.fr* – limited spaces for one-night stay – 🏠
Address : rte des Lacs (located 1km to the north)
Opening times : from mid June to mid Sept.
3 ha (99 pitches) flat, sandy, grassy
Tariff : 28.50 € ♣♣ ⇔ 🔲 (₪ (16A) – Extra per person 10 €
Rental rates : (from beginning May to end Sept.) – 58 🚐 – 1 apartment.
Per night from 33 to 105 € – Per week from 200 to 735 € – Reservation fee 25 €

An attractive setting among pine trees.

Surroundings : 🌳
Leisure activities : 🍴 ✕ 🏛 ⚓ 🚲 ⛴
Facilities : ☕ (Jul–Aug) 🚰 launderette 🚿

GPS Longitude : -1.30611
Latitude : 43.92278

VIEUX-BOUCAU-LES-BAINS

40480 – Michelin map **335** C12 – pop. 1,577 – alt. 5
▶ Paris 740 – Bayonne 41 – Biarritz 48 – Castets 28

Municipal les Sablères

📞 05 58 48 12 29, *www.camping-les-sableres.com*
Address : bd du Marensin (to the northwest, 250m from the beach (direct access)
Opening times : from beginning April to mid Oct.
11 ha (517 pitches) undulating, sandy, grassy
Tariff : (2012 price) 24 € ♣♣ ⇔ 🔲 (₪ (10A) – Extra per person 5 € – Reservation fee 20 €
Rental rates : (2012 price) (from beginning April to mid Oct.) – 7 🚐 – 11 🏠 – 3 tent bungalows. Per night from 37 to 54 € – Per week from 185 to 770 € – Reservation fee 20 €
🚐 sani-station

Surroundings : ♀
Leisure activities : ⚓ multi-sports ground
Facilities : ♿ ☕ ♨ 🚿 ☝ 🚰 launderette, refrigerated food storage
Nearby : 🏊 🍴 ✕ 🎾

GPS Longitude : -1.40596
Latitude : 43.79326

---

*The classification (1 to 5 tents, **black** or red) that we award to selected sites in this guide is our own system. It should not be confused with the classification (1 to 5 stars) of official organisations.*

VIEUX-MAREUIL

24340 – Michelin map **329** E3 – pop. 329 – alt. 129
▶ Paris 499 – Bordeaux 166 – Périgueux 43 – Angoulême 43

L'Étang Bleu

📞 05 53 60 92 70, *www.letangbleu.com*
Address : situated 2km north along the D 93, follow the signs for St-Sulpice-de-Mareuil
Opening times : from beginning April to mid Oct.
10 ha/6 ha for camping (167 pitches) flat, grassy, adjacent wood, lake
Tariff : 23 € ♣♣ ⇔ 🔲 (₪ (10A) – Extra per person 5.50 € – Reservation fee 25 €
Rental rates : (from beginning April to mid Oct.) – 3 🚐. Per night from 35 to 80 €
Per week from 20 to 665 € – Reservation fee 25 €

Surroundings : 🏞 🚤 ♀
Leisure activities : 🍴 ✕ 🏛 ⚓ ⛴ 🎣
Facilities : ♿ ☕ 🚰 launderette 🚿

GPS Longitude : 0.50855
Latitude : 45.44617

VILLERÉAL

47210 – Michelin map **336** G2 – pop. 1,286 – alt. 103
▶ Paris 566 – Agen 61 – Bergerac 35 – Cahors 76

⚏⚏⚏ Yelloh! Village Le Château de Fonrives ▲⚲

📞 05 53 36 63 38, *www.campingchateaufonrives.com*
Address : rte d'Issigeac, at Rives (2.2km northwest along the D 207 and take the turning to the left, by the château)
Opening times : from mid April to end Sept.
20 ha/10 ha for camping (370 pitches) flat, relatively flat, terrace, grassy, stony
Tariff : 38€ 👫 ⌖ 🔌 (10A) – Extra per person 8€
Rental rates : (from mid April to end Sept.) – 124 🛖 – 38 🏠. Per night from 42 to 220 €
Per week from 94 to 1,540 €
🚐 sani-station – 5 🔲 18€

Surroundings : 🌳 🗑 ⚲⚲
Leisure activities : 🍴 ✗ 🎪 ⛳ 🏃 🎠 ⛵ jacuzzi 🏊 🚲 ✂ ♨ 🎱 ⛷ 🏌 🎣 sports trail
Facilities : ♿ 🚿 ♨ ⚗ 🚽 🍴 launderette 🚮 🚏
GPS Longitude : 0.7314 Latitude : 44.65739

⚠ Fontaine du Roc

📞 05 53 36 08 16, *www.fontaineduroc.com*
Address : at Dévillac (7.5km southeast along the D 255 and take the turning to the left)
Opening times : from beginning April to end Sept.
2 ha (60 pitches) flat, grassy
Tariff : 👤 6€ ⌖ 🔲 8€ – 🔌 (10A) 4.50€
Rental rates : (from beginning April to end Sept.) – 3 🛖 – 3 🏠. Per night from 75 to 120 €
Per week from 350 to 665 €
🚐 sani-station – 🚐 11€

Surroundings : 🌳 ⚲⚲
Leisure activities : 🎪 ⛵ jacuzzi 🏊 ⛷
Facilities : ♿ 🚿 ⚗ 🍴 launderette
GPS Longitude : 0.8187 Latitude : 44.61414

This guide is not intended as a list of all the camping sites in France; its aim is to provide a selection of the best sites in each category.

VITRAC

24200 – Michelin map **329** I7 – pop. 870 – alt. 150
▶ Paris 541 – Brive-la-Gaillarde 64 – Cahors 54 – Gourdon 23

⚏⚏⚏ Domaine Soleil Plage ▲⚲

📞 05 53 28 33 33, *www.soleilplage.fr*
Address : at Caudon (beside the Dordogne river)
Opening times : from mid April to end Sept.
8 ha/5 ha for camping (199 pitches) flat, grassy
Tariff : (2012 price) 36.60€ 👫 ⌖ 🔲 🔌 (16A) – Extra per person 7.70€ – Reservation fee 39€
Rental rates : (2012 price) (from mid April to end Sept.) 🅿 – 79 🛖 – 27 🏠.
Per night from 46 to 108 € – Per week from 300 to 1,230 € – Reservation fee 39€
🚐 sani-station 3€ – 10 🔲 21€
Small, pretty, good-quality chalet village.

Surroundings : 🌳 ⚓ 🗑 ⚲⚲
Leisure activities : 🍴 ✗ 🎪 ⛳ 🏃 🏊 ✂ ♨ ⛷ 🏊 (beach) 🏂 🎣 multi-sports ground
Facilities : ♿ 🚿 📶 ♨ ⚗ 🚽 🍴 launderette 🚮 🚏
GPS Longitude : 1.25374 Latitude : 44.82387

La Bouysse de Caudon

0553283305, *www.labouysse.com*

Address : at Caudon (2.5km east, near the Dordogne river)

Opening times : from mid April to end Sept.

6 ha/3 ha for camping (160 pitches) flat, grassy, walnut trees

Tariff : (2012 price) 6.20€ 8€ – (10A) 4.50€ – Reservation fee 20€

Rental rates : (2012 price) (from mid April to mid Sept.) – 4 – 9 – 6 gîtes. Per week from 50 to 740 €

sani-station 3€

Surroundings :

Leisure activities : (beach)

Facilities : launderette refrigerators

GPS
Longitude : 1.25063
Latitude : 44.82357

AUVERGNE

Gérard Labriet / Photononstop

Shhh! Don't wake the volcanoes. They are the giant sleeping beauties of the Auvergne, a stunning region at the heart of France. Dormant for several millennia, they form a natural barrier that keeps them secure from any encroachment by man. If you listen very carefully, you may just make out a distant rumble from Vulcania, the interactive and educational European Park of Volcanism, where you can learn all you could possibly want to know about volcanoes. The region's domes and peaks, sculpted by volcanic fire, are the source of countless mountain springs that cascade down the steep slopes into brooks, rivers and crystal-clear lakes. Renowned for the therapeutic qualities of its waters, the Auvergne has long played host to well-heeled visitors at its elegant spa resorts, but many find it simply impossible to follow doctor's orders when faced with the tempting aroma of an Auvergne country stew, a savoury *Pounti* cake or a full-bodied Cantal cheese!

ABREST

03200 – Michelin map **326** H6 – pop. 2,696 – alt. 290 – Leisure centre
▶ Paris 361 – Clermont-Ferrand 70 – Moulins 63 – Montluçon 94

La Croix St-Martin

📞 0470326774, *www.camping-vichy.com*
Address : 99 av. des Graviers (to the north, near the Allier river)
Opening times : from beginning April to mid Oct.
3 ha (100 pitches) flat, grassy
Tariff : (2012 price) ♦ 5€ ⊞ 6€ – (10A) 3.30€
Rental rates : (2012 price) (from beginning April to mid Oct.) – 16 ⬜.
Per night from 39 to 66 € – Per week from 330 to 510 €
🚐 sani-station 5€

Surroundings : ρ
Leisure activities : ⊿
Facilities : ⅏ ⟳ ⁿ launderette
Nearby : ⊱ ※ 🚣 ⬛ ⟍, casino

Longitude : 3.44012
Latitude : 46.10819

To visit a town or region, use the MICHELIN Green Guides.

ALLEYRAS

43580 – Michelin map **331** E4 – pop. 173 – alt. 779
▶ Paris 549 – Brioude 71 – Langogne 43 – Le Puy-en-Velay 32

Municipal Au Fil de l'Eau

📞 0471575686, *camping-municipal.alleyras.fr* – alt. 660
Address : Le Pont-d'Alleyras (2.5km to the northwest, direct access to the Allier river)
Opening times : from mid April to mid Oct.
0.9 ha (60 pitches) flat and relatively flat, terrace, grassy
Tariff : (2012 price) 12.20€ ♦♦ ⊞ (6A) – Extra per person 4.20€
🚐 sani-station 3€

Surroundings : ⊗ ⊰
Leisure activities : ⟿
Facilities : ⅏ (Jul–Aug) launderette
Nearby : ⟐ ※ ⟍

Longitude : 3.67005
Latitude : 44.91786

AMBERT

63600 – Michelin map **326** J9 – pop. 6,962 – alt. 535
▶ Paris 438 – Brioude 63 – Clermont-Ferrand 77 – Montbrison 47

Municipal Les Trois Chênes

📞 0473823468, *www.camping-ambert.com*
Address : rte du Puy (located 1.5km south along the D 906, follow the signs for La Chaise-Dieu; near the Dore river)
Opening times : from end April to end Sept.
3 ha (120 pitches) flat, grassy
Tariff : 19.95€ ♦♦ ⊞ (10A) – Extra per person 4.60€
Rental rates : (permanent) – 18 ⬜. Per week from 265 to 690 €
🚐 sani-station 2€ – ⬛ 11€
in a pleasant, leafy setting.

Surroundings : ⊰ ⊟ ρρ
Leisure activities : ⬛ ⬛ ⟿
Facilities : ⅏ ⟳ ⟐ ⟐ ⟳ ⁿ launderette
At the river : ⊱ ⟐ ✕ ⟐ ⟿ 🚣 ⟿ ⟍ fitness trail

Longitude : 3.7291
Latitude : 45.53953

AUVERGNE

ARNAC

15150 – Michelin map **330** B4 – pop. 148 – alt. 620
▶ Paris 541 – Argentat 38 – Aurillac 35 – Mauriac 36

Village Vacances La Gineste
(rental of mobile homes and chalets only)

℘ 04 71 62 91 90, *www.village-vacances-cantal.com*

Address : at La Gineste (3km northwest along the D 61, follow the signs for Pleaux then continue 1.2km along the road to the right)

Opening times : permanent

3 ha terraced, grassy

Rental rates : (2012 price) Ⓟ – 40 🚐 – 40 🏠 . Per night from 50 to 75 €
Per week from 385 to 600 € – Reservation fee 13 €

🚽 sani-station 2 € – 2 🔲

Pleasant location on a spit of land in the Lac de Enchanet.

Surroundings : 🏞 ⪡ 🗐 🎣
Leisure activities : 🍸 ✖ 🎦 🎯 🏄 ※ 🛶 🏖 (beach) 🎣 🐎
Facilities : 🔧 🚿 🔲 🔁 ♿
Nearby : watersports centre

GPS Longitude : 2.2121
Latitude : 45.08285

ARPAJON-SUR-CÈRE

15130 – Michelin map **330** C5 – pop. 6,009 – alt. 613
▶ Paris 559 – Argentat 56 – Aurillac 5 – Maurs 44

La Cère

℘ 04 71 64 55 07, *www.camping.caba.fr*

Address : south of the town, access via the D 920, opposite the Esso service station; beside the river

Opening times : from beginning June to end Sept.

2 ha (106 pitches) flat, grassy

Tariff : (2012 price) 15 € ✝✝ 🚐 🔲 ⚡ (10A) – Extra per person 6 €

Rental rates : (2012 price) (from beginning April to end Oct.) – 10 🚐 .
Per night from 36 to 68 € – Per week from 252 to 476 €

A wooded setting and a well-kept site.

Surroundings : 🗐 🎣
Leisure activities : 🎦 🏄 🛶
Facilities : ♿ 🚿 🔲
Nearby : 🍴 ※ 🎯

GPS Longitude : 2.46246
Latitude : 44.89858

AURILLAC

15000 – Michelin map **330** C5 – pop. 28,207 – alt. 610
▶ Paris 557 – Brive-la-Gaillarde 98 – Clermont-Ferrand 158 – Montauban 174

Municipal l'Ombrade

℘ 04 71 48 28 87, *www.camping.caba.fr*

Address : head 1km north along the D 17 and take r. du Gué-Bouliaga to the right; on both sides of the Jordanne

Opening times : from mid June to mid Sept.

7.5 ha (200 pitches) flat, terraced, grassy

Tariff : (2012 price) 13.60 € ✝✝ 🚐 🔲 ⚡ (10A) – Extra per person 6 €

🚽 sani-station – 25 🔲 15.60 €

Surroundings : 🎣
Leisure activities : 🎦
Facilities : ♿ 🚿 🔁 🚽 🔲
Nearby : 🍴

GPS Longitude : 2.4559
Latitude : 44.93562

AYDAT

63970 – Michelin map **326** E9 – pop. 2,122 – alt. 850
▶ Paris 438 – La Bourboule 33 – Clermont-Ferrand 21 – Issoire 38

🏔 Lac d'Aydat

☎ 04 73 79 38 09, *www.camping-lac-aydat.com*

Address : beside the lake, Foret du Lot (head 2km northeast along the D 90 and take the road to the right; near the lake)

Opening times : from beginning April to end Sept.

7 ha (150 pitches) very uneven, terraced, flat, grassy, stony

Tariff : 25€ ♦♦ ⇌ 🔲 ⚡ (15A) – Extra per person 5€ – Reservation fee 20€

Rental rates : (permanent) – 50 🚐 – 14 🏠. Per week from 280 to 735 €
Reservation fee 20€

🚱 sani-station 25€

Situated among pine trees.

Surroundings : 🎋🎋
Leisure activities : ▼ ✗ 🎦 ⊙ 🏊
Facilities : ♿ ⌂ 🏢 ♨ ⛲ launderette
Nearby : 🚣 🎿 🚡 🚴 🏄 (beach) 🎣 ⚓ 🐎 forest trail

GPS Longitude : 2.98907 | Latitude : 45.66903

BAGNOLS

63810 – Michelin map **326** C9 – pop. 496 – alt. 862
▶ Paris 483 – Bort-les-Orgues 19 – La Bourboule 23 – Bourg-Lastic 38

🏔 Municipal la Thialle

☎ 04 73 22 28 00, *www.bagnols63.fr*

Address : rte de St-Donat (take southeastern exit along the D 25; beside the Thialle river)

Opening times : from beginning April to beginning Nov.

2.8 ha (70 pitches) flat, grassy, fine gravel

Tariff : ♦ 4€ ⇌ 2.10€ 🔲 2.10€ – ⚡ (3A) 3€

Rental rates : (permanent) – 8 🏠. Per night from 50 to 59 € – Per week from 237 to 546 €

🚱 sani-station

Surroundings : ♀
Leisure activities : 🎦 🏊 ⛺ 🏊 (small swimming pool) 🎣
Facilities : ♿ ⌂ (season) 🎿 🏢 launderette
Nearby : 🏊 ▼ ✗

GPS Longitude : 2.63466 | Latitude : 45.49758

BILLOM

63160 – Michelin map **326** H8 – pop. 4,637 – alt. 340
▶ Paris 437 – Clermont-Ferrand 28 – Cunlhat 30 – Issoire 31

🏔 Municipal le Colombier

☎ 04 73 68 91 50, *www.billom.fr*

Address : r. Carnot (To the northeast of the town, follow the signs for Lezoux)

Opening times : from mid June to mid Sept.

1 ha (40 pitches) flat and relatively flat, grassy

Tariff : (2012 price) ♦ 2.80€ ⇌ 1.60€ 🔲 2.30€ – ⚡ (10A) 3€

Rental rates : (permanent) – 12 🏠. Per night from 70 € – Per week from 340 to 390 €

Surroundings : 🏞 ♀
Leisure activities : 🎦 🏊
Facilities : ♿ ⌂ 🎿 ⛲ 🖼
Nearby : 🚴 ✗ 🎦 🎿 🏊 🐎

GPS Longitude : 3.3459 | Latitude : 45.72839

LA BOURBOULE

63150 – Michelin map **326** D9 – pop. 1,961 – alt. 880 – ♨ (beg Feb to end Oct)
▶ Paris 469 – Aubusson 82 – Clermont-Ferrand 50 – Mauriac 71

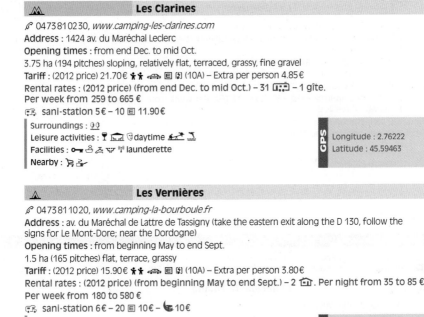

⛰ Les Clarines

✆ 0473810230, *www.camping-les-clarines.com*
Address : 1424 av. du Maréchal Leclerc
Opening times : from end Dec. to mid Oct.
3.75 ha (194 pitches) sloping, relatively flat, terraced, grassy, fine gravel
Tariff : (2012 price) 21.70€ ✚✚ ⇔ 🔲 (½) (10A) – Extra per person 4.85€
Rental rates : (2012 price) (from end Dec. to mid Oct.) – 31 🚐 – 1 gîte.
Per week from 259 to 665 €
🚐 sani-station 5€ – 10 🔲 11.90€

Surroundings : 🞡🞡
Leisure activities : 🍷 🖼 🕓daytime 🏖 🏊
Facilities : 🚿 ♨ 🛁 ☁ ⁛ launderette
Nearby : 🛒 🚴

Longitude : 2.76222
Latitude : 45.59463

⛰ Les Vernières

✆ 0473811020, *www.camping-la-bourboule.fr*
Address : av. du Maréchal de Lattre de Tassigny (take the eastern exit along the D 130, follow the signs for Le Mont-Dore; near the Dordogne)
Opening times : from beginning May to end Sept.
1.5 ha (165 pitches) flat, terrace, grassy
Tariff : (2012 price) 15.90€ ✚✚ ⇔ 🔲 (½) (10A) – Extra per person 3.80€
Rental rates : (2012 price) (from beginning May to end Sept.) – 2 🏠. Per night from 35 to 85 €
Per week from 180 to 580 €
🚐 sani-station 6€ – 20 🔲 10€ – 🚐 10€

Surroundings : ⇐ ☁ 🞡
Leisure activities : 🍷 ✗ 🖼 🏖 🎣
Facilities : 🚿 🚿 ⁛ 🖼 🚴
Nearby : 🛒 🍴 🎱 🏊

Longitude : 2.75285
Latitude : 45.58943

This guide is updated regularly, so buy your new copy every year!

BRAIZE

03360 – Michelin map **326** C2 – pop. 290 – alt. 240
▶ Paris 297 – Dun-sur-Auron 30 – Cérilly 16 – Culan 35

⛰ Le Champ de la Chapelle

✆ 0470061545, *www.champdelachapelle.com*
Address : Champ de la Chapelle (5.7km south along the D 28, follow the signs for Meaulnes and turn left onto D 978a, follow the signs for Tronçais then continue 1km along the gravel road to the left)
Opening times : from mid April to mid Oct.
5.6 ha (80 pitches) flat and relatively flat, hilly/uneven, grassy
Tariff : 19€ ✚✚ ⇔ 🔲 (½) (10A) – Extra per person 3.25€
Rental rates : (from mid April to mid Oct.) 🞰 – 2 🚐. Per night from 50 to 65 €
Per week from 320 to 400 €
An attractive location in the woods.

Surroundings : 🗻 🞡🞡
Leisure activities : 🏖 🎿 (beach)
Facilities : 🚿 🚿 🛁 ⁛ 🖼
At the Étang de St-Bonnet : 🍷 ✗ 🍴 🎣 💧 watersports centre

Longitude : 2.65558
Latitude : 46.64304

CEAUX-D'ALLEGRE

43270 – Michelin map **331** E2 – pop. 453 – alt. 905
▶ Paris 523 – Allègre 5 – La Chaise-Dieu 21 – Craponne-sur-Arzon 23

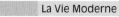

La Vie Moderne

℘ 0471007966, *www.laviemoderne.com*
Address : Langlade (located 1km northeast along the D 134, follow the signs for Bellevue-la-Montagne and take road to the left; beside the Borne river and near a lake)
0.5 ha (35 pitches) flat, grassy, stony
Rentals : 6 yurts.

Surroundings :	Longitude : 3.74832
Facilities :	Latitude : 45.18907
Nearby :	

*Using the traditional Michelin classification method, the guide provides
you with an easy, speedy reference for assessing the category of each site:
1 to 5 tents (see page 10).*

CEYRAT

63122 – Michelin map **326** F8 – pop. 5,371 – alt. 560
▶ Paris 423 – Clermont-Ferrand 6 – Issoire 36 – Le Mont-Dore 42

Le Chanset

℘ 0473613073, *www.campingdeceyrat63.com* – alt. 600
Address : r. du Camping (av. J.-B.-Marrou)
Opening times : permanent
5 ha (140) flat, sloping, grassy
Tariff : (2012 price) 20.70€ ★ ★ ⇔ 🅴 🔌 (10A) – Extra per person 3.80€
Rental rates : (2012 price) (permanent) – 20 ⨎ – 14 🏠 – 1 tent. Per night from 49 to 80 €
Per week from 161 to 657 €
🚉 sani-station

Surroundings : ⚲
Leisure activities : 🍽 ✕ 🎦 ⌂ 🏊
Facilities : 🛁 🏠 🍴 launderette 🔥 🅰

Longitude : 3.06196
Latitude : 45.73852

LA CHAISE-DIEU

43160 – Michelin map **331** E2 – pop. 730 – alt. 1,080
▶ Paris 503 – Ambert 29 – Brioude 35 – Issoire 59

Municipal les Prades

℘ 0471000788, *andre.brivadis@orange.fr*
Address : situated 2km northeast along the D 906, follow the signs for Ambert, near the small lake at La Tour (direct access)
3 ha (100 pitches) relatively flat, grassy
Rental rates : 10 🏠.
🚉 sani-station

Surroundings : ⚲⚲
Leisure activities : 🛶
Facilities : 🛁 ⌒ 🔲
Nearby : ✕ 🚿 🐎

Longitude : 3.70496
Latitude : 45.33321

CHAMBON-SUR-LAC

63790 – Michelin map **326** E9 – pop. 352 – alt. 885 – Winter sports : 1,150/1,760 m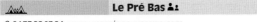9
▶ Paris 456 – Clermont-Ferrand 37 – Condat 39 – Issoire 32

Le Pré Bas ▲

℘ 0473886304, *www.campingauvergne.com*
Address : near the lake (direct access)
Opening times : from mid April to mid Sept.
3.8 ha (180 pitches) flat and relatively flat, grassy
Tariff : (2012 price) 29.90€ ♀♀ ⬛ (6A) – Extra per person 6.70€ – Reservation fee 17€
Rental rates : (2012 price) (from mid April to mid Sept.) – 106 🛒 – 1 gîte.
Per night from 47 to 77 € – Per week from 282 to 977 € – Reservation fee 17€
sani-station – 30 ⬛ 17.70€
Beautiful flowers and shrubs and a large, partially covered water park.

Surroundings : ≤ 🗆 ♀
Leisure activities : ♈ ✕ 🔲 ⚇ 🕺 ⛓ jacuzzi ⬛ 🔲 🏊 ⚐ family
centre, multi-sports ground, spa therapy centre
Facilities : ৬ ⚷ ⛺ ⴹ **launderette** ৯
Nearby : ⛱ ≌ ⚓ ⚐ ⛷ quad biking

Longitude : 2.91427
Latitude : 45.57516

Les Bombes

℘ 0473886403, *www.camping-les-bombes.com*
Address : ch. de Pétary (east of Chambon-sur-Lac, head towards Murol and take a right turn; beside
the Couze de Chambon river)
Opening times : from beginning May to mid Sept.
5 ha (150 pitches) flat, grassy
Tariff : ♀ 5€ ⬛ ⬛ 14€ – (16A) 4.60€ – Reservation fee 12€
Rental rates : (from beginning May to mid Sept.) – 2 caravans – 15 🛒 – 3 tents.
Per night from 40 to 65 € – Per week from 180 to 660 € – Reservation fee 12€
sani-station 3€ – 30 ⬛ 7€

Surroundings : 🕸 ≤ Vallée de Chaudefour ♀
Leisure activities : ♈ ✕ 🔲 ⬛ ⚲ 🏊 ⚓
Facilities : ৬ ⚷ ⛺ ⴹ **launderette** ৯
At the lake : ⛱ ≌ (beach) ⚐ ⛷

Longitude : 2.90188
Latitude : 45.56994

Serrette

℘ 0473886767, *www.campingdeserrette.com* – alt. 1,000
Address : Serrette (2.5km west along the D 996, follow the signs for Le Mont-Dore and take D 636
(to the left) follow the signs for Chambon des Neiges)
Opening times : from beginning May to mid Sept.
2 ha (75 pitches) terraced, sloping, grassy, stony
Tariff : (2012 price) ♀ 4.90€ ⬛ ⬛ 8.30€ – (6A) 4.80€ – Reservation fee 12€
Rental rates : (2012 price) (from beginning May to mid Sept.) – 8 🛒 – 3 🏠 – 6 tent
bungalows. Per night from 30 to 60 € – Per week from 170 to 720 € – Reservation fee 12€
A lovely view over the lake and the surrounding area.

Surroundings : 🕸 ≤ Lac Chambon and mountains ♀
Leisure activities : ♈ 🔲 🔲 (open-air in season)
Facilities : ৬ ⚷ ⴹ ⬛
At the lake : ⚒ ⛱ ≌ (beach) ⛷

Longitude : 2.89105
Latitude : 45.57099

*The guide covers all 22 regions of France – see the map
and list of regions on pages 4–5.*

LE CHAMBON-SUR-LIGNON

43400 – Michelin map **331** H3 – pop. 2,690 – alt. 967
▶ Paris 573 – Annonay 48 – Lamastre 32 – Le Puy-en-Velay 45

⚠ Les Hirondelles

✆ 0471597384, *www.campingleshirondelles.fr* – alt. 1,000
Address : rte de la Suchère (located 1km south along the D 151 and turn left onto D 7)
1 ha (45 pitches) flat, terraced, grassy
Tariff : (2012 price) 17.95€ ♣♣ ⇔ ▣ ⚡ (6A) – Extra per person 4.20€
Rental rates : (2012 price) (from mid April to end Oct.) ⚡ – 3 🏠. Per week from 230 to 460 €
🚐 sani-station 10€
Pleasant setting overlooking the village.

Surroundings : ⛰ ⩽ ⌂ ♨
Leisure activities : ♟ 🎦 🏋
Facilities : ♿ �o━ 🛁 ⚀ ▣ 🚿
At the river : 🎣 ✗ 🎦 ≅ 🐎 sports trail

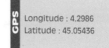

GPS
Longitude : 4.2986
Latitude : 45.05436

⚠ Le Lignon

✆ 0471597286, *www.campingdulignon.eu* – alt. 1,000
Address : rte du Stade (take the southwestern exit along the D 15, follow the signs for Mazet-sur-Voy and take a right turn before the bridge, near the river)
Opening times : from beginning May to end Sept.
2 ha (130 pitches) flat, grassy
Tariff : (2012 price) 12€ ♣♣ ⇔ ▣ ⚡ (10A) – Extra per person 5€
Rental rates : (2012 price) (from beginning May to end Sept.) ⚡ – 1 🚚. Per night from 30 €
Per week from 300 to 400 €
🚐 3 ▣ 12€

Surroundings : ♨
Leisure activities : 🎦 🏋 🚲
Facilities : ♿ o━ 🍽 ⚀ ♛ ▣
At the river : 🎣 ✗ 🎦 ≅ 🐎 sports trail, forest trail

GPS
Longitude : 4.29686
Latitude : 45.05944

The information in the guide may have changed since going to press.

CHAMPAGNAC-LE-VIEUX

43440 – Michelin map **331** D1 – pop. 234 – alt. 880
▶ Paris 486 – Brioude 16 – La Chaise-Dieu 25 – Clermont-Ferrand 76

⚠ Le Chanterelle

✆ 0471763400, *www.champagnac.com*
Address : Le Prat Barrat (1.4km north along the D 5, follow the signs for Auzon, and take the road to the right)
Opening times : from mid April to mid Oct.
4 ha (90 pitches) terraced, grassy, fine gravel
Tariff : ♣ 3.90€ ⇔ 2.60€ ▣ 6€ – ⚡ (10A) 3.60€
Rental rates : (2012 price) (from mid April to mid Oct.) – 4 🚚 – 20 🏠 – 10 tent bungalows.
Per night from 38 to 71 €– Per week from 228 to 784 € – Reservation fee 15€
A lush, green site near a small lake.

Surroundings : ⛰ ⌂ ♨♨
Leisure activities : 🎋 🏋 🚲
Facilities : ♿ o━ 🍽 ⚁ ⚐ ♛ launderette
Nearby : 🎦 ✗ ≅ (beach) 🐎 fitness trail

GPS
Longitude : 3.50575
Latitude : 45.3657

AUVERGNE

CHAMPS-SUR-TARENTAINE

15270 – Michelin map **330** D2 – pop. 1,035 – alt. 450
▶ Paris 500 – Aurillac 90 – Clermont-Ferrand 82 – Condat 24

Les Chalets de l'Eau Verte
(rental of chalets only)

℘ 04 71 78 78 78, *www.auvergne-chalets.fr*
Address : Le Jagounet
Opening times : permanent
8 ha relatively flat, flat, grassy
Rental rates : 🅿 – 10 🏠. Per night from €39 to 95 – Per week from 273 to 798 €
Reservation fee 10€

2-night minimum stay in low season.

Surroundings : 🐾
Leisure activities : 🎮
Facilities : 🍴 📱
Nearby : ✕ 🏊 ◗ 🏇

GPS Longitude : 2.63853
Latitude : 45.40595

*There are several different types of sani-station
('borne' in French) – sanitation points providing
fresh water and disposal points for grey water.
See page 12 for further details.*

CHÂTELGUYON

63140 – Michelin map **326** F7 – pop. 6,223 – alt. 430 – ⚑ (beg May to end Sept)
▶ Paris 411 – Aubusson 93 – Clermont-Ferrand 21 – Gannat 31

Clos de Balanède ♣♣

℘ 04 73 86 02 47, *www.balanede.com*
Address : rte de la Piscine (take southeastern exit along the D 985, follow the signs for Riom)
4 ha (285 pitches) flat and relatively flat, grassy
Rentals : 2 caravans – 40 🛖 – 2 🏠 – 4 teepees.
🚐 20 📧

Surroundings : 🌳🌳
Leisure activities : 🍷 ✕ 🎮 🎣 👫 🏊 ♨🏋 ⛱
Facilities : ♿ ⚡ 🚿 🚾 🧺 🍴 launderette 🐾

GPS Longitude : 3.07732
Latitude : 45.91491

La Croze ♠

℘ 04 73 86 08 27, *www.campingcroze.com*
Address : at St-Hippolyte, rte de Mozac (located 1km southeast along the D 227, follow the signs for Riom)
Opening times : from beginning April to end Oct.
3.7 ha (100 pitches) flat, relatively flat, terraced
Tariff : 🚶 3.10€ 🚗 1.80€ 📧 3.50€ – ⚡ (10A) 3.10€
Rental rates : (from beginning April to end Oct.) ♿ (1 chalet) – 17 🛖 – 9 🏠.
Per night from 40 to 68 € – Per week from 300 to 530 €

Surroundings : 🐾♨
Leisure activities : ✕ 🏊 ⛱
Facilities : ♿ 🚿 🚾 🍴 launderette

GPS Longitude : 3.06083
Latitude : 45.90589

CHAUDES-AIGUES

15110 – Michelin map **330** G5 – pop. 940 – alt. 750 – 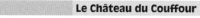 (end Apr to end Oct)
▶ Paris 538 – Aurillac 94 – Entraygues-sur-Truyère 62 – Espalion 54

Le Château du Couffour

⌂ 0471235708, *www.camping-chaudes-aigues.fr* – alt. 900
Address : at the stadium (situated 2km south along the D 921, follow the signs for Laguiole then take the road to the right)
Opening times : from beginning May to end Oct.
2.5 ha (170 pitches) flat, relatively flat, terrace, grassy
Tariff : 14€ ★ ★ ⇔ 🅔 ⑷ (10A) – Extra per person 3.50€
🏕 sani-station 2.50€ – 🛁⑷14€

Surroundings : 🌿 ⩽ ♨
Leisure activities : 🎮 🏓 ✂
Facilities : 🔧 ⛱ 🚻 🍴 🅿
Nearby : 🚴 🏊 ⛏ climbing, casino

GPS
Longitude : 3.00071
Latitude : 44.8449

COULEUVRE

03320 – Michelin map **326** E2 – pop. 584 – alt. 267
▶ Paris 289 – Bourbon-l'Archambault 18 – Cérilly 10 – Cosne-d'Allier 27

Municipal la Font St-Julien

⌂ 0470661045, *www.couleuvre-troncais.fr*
Address : at La Font St-Julien (take the southwestern exit along the D 3, follow the signs for Cérilly and take a right turn)
2 ha (50 pitches) relatively flat, grassy
Beside a lake.

Surroundings : 🌿 ♨
Leisure activities : 🏓 ✂ ⛏ 🎣 wildlife park
Facilities : 🅿

GPS
Longitude : 2.90457
Latitude : 46.67173

Some information or pricing may have changed since the guide went to press.
We recommend you check the price list online in advance or at the entrance
to the campsite and enquire about possible restrictions.

COURNON-D'AUVERGNE

63800 – Michelin map **326** G8 – pop. 19 494 – alt. 380 – Leisure centre
▶ Paris 422 – Clermont-Ferrand 12 – Issoire 31 – Le Mont-Dore 54

Municipal le Pré des Laveuses

⌂ 0473848130, *www.cournon-auvergne.fr/camping*
Address : head 1.5km east via road to Billom and take the beach road to the left
5 ha (150 pitches) flat, grassy, stony, gravelled
Rentals : 12 🛖 – 18 🏠 – 12 tent bungalows.
🏕 sani-station – 10 🅔
By a small landscaped lake and the Allier river.

Surroundings : ♨♨ ⛰
Leisure activities : 🍴 ✕ 🎮 🏓 ⛏
Facilities : 🔧 ⛱ 🚿 🍴 launderette
Nearby : 🛒 🏊 ⛵ 🎣

GPS
Longitude : 3.22271
Latitude : 45.74029

COURPIÈRE

63120 – Michelin map **326** I8 – pop. 4,514 – alt. 320
▶ Paris 399 – Ambert 40 – Clermont-Ferrand 50 – Issoire 53

Municipal les Taillades

☎ 04 73 53 01 21, *www.ville-courpiere.fr*
Address : Les Taillades (take the southern exit along the D 906, follow the signs for Ambert, take the D 7 to the left, follow the signs for Aubusson-d'Auvergne and take the road to the right; by the swimming pool and near a stream)
0.5 ha (40 pitches) flat, grassy
Rentals : 3 ⛺.

Surroundings : 🌳 🗔
Leisure activities : 🏕 ⛴
Facilities : ⚕ ⛏ 🖥
Nearby : 🛒 🚲 🎾 🐴

| | Longitude : 3.5487 |
| GPS | Latitude : 45.75354 |

A 'quartier' is a district or area of a town or village.

DOMPIERRE-SUR-BESBRE

03290 – Michelin map **326** J3 – pop. 3,184 – alt. 234
▶ Paris 324 – Bourbon-Lancy 19 – Decize 46 – Digoin 27

Municipal Les Bords de Bresbe

☎ 04 70 34 55 57, *camping@mairie-dsb.fr*
Address : La Madeleine (take the southeastern exit along the N 79, follow the signs for Digoin; near the Besbre river and not far from a lake)
Opening times : from mid May to mid Sept.
2 ha (70 pitches) flat, grassy
Tariff : (2012 price) 🧍 2.50€ ⛟ 🅿 2€ – 🔌 (10A) 2.30€
🚱 sani-station 2€
Pretty shrubs and flowers.

Surroundings : 🌳 🗔 🌿
Leisure activities : 🚣 🚲 🎾
Facilities : ⛏ 🍴 🔲 🚿 🖥
Nearby : 🛒 ⛴ wildlife park, amusement park

| | Longitude : 3.68289 |
| GPS | Latitude : 46.51373 |

GANNAT

03800 – Michelin map **326** G6 – pop. 5,853 – alt. 345
▶ Paris 383 – Clermont-Ferrand 49 – Montluçon 78 – Moulins 58

Municipal Le Mont Libre

☎ 04 70 90 12 16, *www.camping-gannat.fr*
Address : 10 rte de la Batisse (located 1km south along the N 9 and take turning to the right)
Opening times : from beginning April to end Oct.
1.5 ha (70 pitches) terraced, grassy
Tariff : 11.10€ 🧍🧍 ⛟ 🅿 🔌 (10A) – Extra per person 2.60€
Rental rates : (from beginning April to end Oct.) – 13 ⛺. Per week from 233 to 498 €
🚱 sani-station 4€ – 6 🅿 11.10€ – 🚐 🔌 11.10€

Surroundings : ⛰ 🗔 🌿
Leisure activities : 🏊 🚣 ⛴ (small swimming pool)
Facilities : ⚕ ⛏ 🚾 🖥
Nearby : 🛒 🎾 🔲 🔲

| | Longitude : 3.19403 |
| GPS | Latitude : 46.0916 |

ISLE-ET-BARDAIS

03360 – Michelin map **326** D2 – pop. 275 – alt. 285
▶ Paris 280 – Bourges 60 – Cérilly 9 – Montluçon 52

Les Écossais

✆ 0470666257, *www.campingstroncais.com*
Address : located 1km south via road to Les Chamignoux
Opening times : from beginning April to end Sept.
2 ha (70 pitches) flat, relatively flat, grassy
Tariff : (2012 price) ♦ 2.85€ – ⇔ 1.34€ 🅴 2.40€ – ⚡ (10A) 3.25€ – Reservation fee 15€
Rental rates : (2012 price) (from beginning April to end Sept.) – 2 🛏 – 7 gîtes.
Per night from 48 to 63 € – Per week from 222 to 450 € – Reservation fee 15€
Beside the Étang de Pirot (lake) and at the edge of theTroncáis forest.

Surroundings : 🐟 🗺 ♨
Leisure activities : ♟ 🏠 ✕ ♫ ≋ (beach)
Facilities : ⌕ ♦ launderette
Nearby : 🚴 🎣

GPS
Longitude : 2.78814
Latitude : 46.68278

ISSOIRE

63500 – Michelin map **326** G9 – pop. 13,949 – alt. 400
▶ Paris 446 – Aurillac 121 – Clermont-Ferrand 36 – Le Puy-en-Velay 94

Château La Grange Fort

✆ 0473710243, *www.lagrangefort.eu*
Address : 4km southeast along the D 996, follow the signs for la Chaise-Dieu then take a right turn, 3km along the D 34, follow the signs for Auzat-sur-Allier,from the A 75, take exit 13 towards Parentignat
Opening times : from mid April to end Oct.
23 ha/4 ha for camping (120 pitches) flat, relatively flat, grassy
Tariff : 26.75€ ♦♦ ⇔ 🅴 ⚡ (6A) – Extra per person 6€ – Reservation fee 25€
Rental rates : (permanent) ✕ (from mid-Apr to end Sept) – 16 🛏 – 9 🏠 – 5 🛏 –
3 apartments – 5 tent bungalows – 1 gîte. Per night from €51 to 110
Per week from 215 to 1 050 – Reservation fee 25€
🚐 sani-station – 12 🅴 18€
In the grounds of a picturesque medieval château overlooking the Allier river.

Surroundings : 🐟 < 🗺 ♨
Leisure activities : ♟ ✕ 🏠 ≋ jacuzzi 🚴 🚲 ✕ 🔲 🏊
Facilities : ♿ ⌕ 🅿 🏢 🚿 ♦ launderette 🧺

GPS
Longitude : 3.28501
Latitude : 45.50859

Municipal du Mas

✆ 0473890359, *www.camping-issoire.com*
Address : r. du Dr Bienfait (2.5km east along the D 9, follow the signs for Orbeil and take a right turn, 50m from a lake and 300m from the Allier river;from A 75 take exit 12)
Opening times : from beginning April to beginning Nov.
3 ha (138 pitches) flat, grassy
Tariff : (2012 price) 18.85€ ♦♦ ⇔ 🅴 ⚡ (10A) – Extra per person 5.27€
Rental rates :(2012 price) (from beginning April to beginning Nov.) – 4 🛏 – 6 🏠 – 3 tent bungalows. Per night from 33 to 78 € – Per week from 210 to 500 €
🚐 sani-station 3€ – 6 🅴 18.85€

Surroundings : 🐟 ♨
Leisure activities : 🏠 ⏰daytime 🚴 ♫
Facilities : ⌕ 🅾 🏢 🚿 🧺 ♦ launderette
Nearby : 🛒 ✕ 🚲 ✕ 🎣 bowling

GPS
Longitude : 3.27397
Latitude : 45.55108

LACAPELLE-DEL-FRAISSE

15120 – Michelin map **330** C6 – pop. 306 – alt. 830
▶ Paris 624 – Clermont-Ferrand 174 – Aurillac 23 – Rodez 74

△ **Village Vacances Les Chalets du Veinazes**
(rental of chalets only)

𝒞 0471625690, *www.cantal-chalets.com*
Address : at La Case (situated 2km southeast along the D 20)
2.5 ha flat, grassy
Rentals : ⚏ – 13 🏠.

Surroundings : ⌂ ⩽
Leisure activities : ⛊
Nearby : ⛾ ✗

GPS Longitude : 2.46271
Latitude : 44.76068

The Michelin classification (△△△... △) is totally independent of the official star classification system awarded by the local prefecture or other official organisation.

LANOBRE

15270 – Michelin map **330** D2 – pop. 1,400 – alt. 650
▶ Paris 493 – Bort-les-Orgues 7 – La Bourboule 33 – Condat 30

🕭 **Les Ch'tis de la Siauve**

𝒞 0471403185, *www.camping-chtis-15.com* – alt. 660
Address : r. du Camping (3km southwest along the D 922, follow the signs for Bort-les-Orgues and take turning to the right, 200m from the lake (direct access)
8 ha (220 pitches) terraced, grassy
Rentals : 17 ⛻ – 19 🏠.

Surroundings : ⌂ ⩽ ⌂ ♀
Leisure activities : ⛾ ✗ 🎲 ⊙daytime ⛵ ⊶
Facilities : ♿ ⊶ 🚿 ⛟ ⛿
Nearby : ⚐ ⛊ ≈ (beach), watersports centre

GPS Longitude : 2.50407
Latitude : 45.4306

LAPALISSE

03120 – Michelin map **326** I5 – pop. 3,162 – alt. 280
▶ Paris 346 – Digoin 45 – Mâcon 122 – Moulins 50

△ **Camping Communautaire**

𝒞 0470992631, *www.lapalisse-tourisme.com*
Address : r. des Vignes (take the southeastern exit along the N 7; beside the Besbre river, pedestrian path linking campsite to town centre)
Opening times : from beginning April to end Sept.
0.8 ha (66 pitches) flat, grassy
Tariff : ⚲ 2.40€ ⇔ 1.80€ ▣ 1.85€ – [≴] (16A) 2.40€
Rental rates : (from beginning April to end Sept.) – 2 ⛻ – 6 🏠. Per night from 30 to 60 €
Per week from €150 to 370

Surroundings : ♀
Leisure activities : ⛵ ⚐ ⌁ fitness trail
Facilities : ♿ ⊶ 🚿 ⛟ ⛿

GPS Longitude : 3.6395
Latitude : 46.2433

LAPEYROUSE

63700 – Michelin map **326** E5 – pop. 561 – alt. 510
▶ Paris 350 – Clermont-Ferrand 74 – Commentry 15 – Montmarault 14

Municipal les Marins

0473523706, www.63lapeyrouse.free.fr
Address : Étang de La Loge (lake) (situated 2km southeast along the D 998, follow the signs for Echassières and turn right onto D 100, follow the signs for Durmignat)
Opening times : permanent
2 ha (68 pitches) flat, grassy
Tariff : (2012 price) 16€ � 囯 ⱷ (10A) – Extra per person 4€
Rental rates : (2012 price) (permanent) – 6 ⌂. Per week from 230 to 460 €
Ornamental trees and shrubs surround the pitches. Near a small lake.

Surroundings :
Leisure activities : (beach)
Facilities :
Nearby :

GPS Longitude : 2.8837
Latitude : 46.22125

LAVOÛTE-SUR-LOIRE

43800 – Michelin map **331** F3 – pop. 725 – alt. 561
▶ Paris 540 – La Chaise-Dieu 37 – Craponne-sur-Arzon 28 – Le Puy-en-Velay 13

Municipal les Longes

0471081879, www.cc/emblavez.fr
Address : at Les Longes (located 1km east along the D 7, follow the signs for Rosières then continue 400m along the turning to the left; near the Loire river (direct access)
Opening times : from beginning May to mid Sept.
1 ha (57) flat, grassy
Tariff : (2012 price) 15.50€ � 囯 ⱷ (6A) – Extra per person 3€

Surroundings :
Leisure activities :
Facilities :
Nearby :

GPS Longitude : 3.92196
Latitude : 45.12495

Routes nationales are main roads and their identifying numbers begin with N or RN. Routes départementales are generally quieter roads and begin with D or DN.

MASSIAC

15500 – Michelin map **330** H3 – pop. 1,841 – alt. 534
▶ Paris 484 – Aurillac 84 – Brioude 23 – Issoire 38

L'Allagnon

0471230393, www.campingallagnon.com
Address : 800m west along the N 122, follow the signs for Murat; beside the river
2.5 ha (90 pitches) flat, grassy
Rentals : 2 ▥ – 1 tent.
▤ sani-station

Surroundings :
Leisure activities :
Facilities :
Nearby :

GPS Longitude : 3.19222
Latitude : 45.24863

MAURIAC

15200 – Michelin map **330** B3 – pop. 3,854 – alt. 722
▶ Paris 490 – Aurillac 53 – Le Mont-Dore 77 – Riom-ès-Montagnes 37

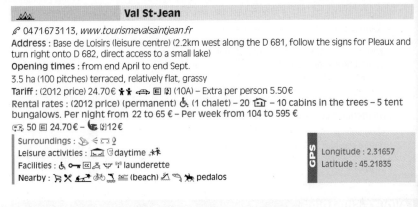

Val St-Jean

📞 0471673113, *www.tourismevalsaintjean.fr*
Address : Base de Loisirs (leisure centre) (2.2km west along the D 681, follow the signs for Pleaux and turn right onto D 682, direct access to a small lake)
Opening times : from end April to end Sept.
3.5 ha (100 pitches) terraced, relatively flat, grassy
Tariff : (2012 price) 24.70€ ⚤ 🚐 ▣ (10A) – Extra per person 5.50€
Rental rates : (2012 price) (permanent) (1 chalet) – 20 🏠 – 10 cabins in the trees – 5 tent bungalows. Per night from 22 to 65 € – Per week from 104 to 595 €
🚐 50 ▣ 24.70€ – 🔌12€

Surroundings : ≤ 🛢
Leisure activities : daytime ✦✦
Facilities : ▣ launderette
Nearby : 🍴✗ 🚴 ≋ (beach) 🐎 pedalos

Longitude : 2.31657
Latitude : 45.21835

Some campsites benefit from proximity to a municipal leisure centre.

MAURS

15600 – Michelin map **330** B6 – pop. 2,213 – alt. 290
▶ Paris 568 – Aurillac 43 – Entraygues-sur-Truyère 50 – Figeac 22

Municipal le Vert

📞 0471490415, *www.ville-maurs.fr*
Address : av. du stade (800m southeast along the D 663, follow the signs for Décazeville; beside the Rance)
1.2 ha (58 pitches) flat, grassy
Rentals : 4 🏠.

Surroundings : 🛢
Leisure activities : ✦✦ ✗ 🏊
Facilities : 🚿 ▣
Nearby : 🍴🚴🐎

Longitude : 2.2064
Latitude : 44.70507

LE MAYET-DE-MONTAGNE

03250 – Michelin map **326** J6 – pop. 1,555 – alt. 535
▶ Paris 369 – Clermont-Ferrand 81 – Lapalisse 23 – Moulins 73

Municipal du Lac

📞 0470597052, *www.lemayetdemontagne.planet-allier.com*
Address : chemin de Fumouse (1.2km south along the D 7, follow the signs for Laprugne)
Opening times : from mid March to end Oct.
1 ha (50 pitches) relatively flat, flat, grassy
Tariff : (2012 price) ✦ 1.90€ 🚐 ▣ 2.10€ – (10A) 1.90€
Rental rates : (2012 price) (from mid April to mid Oct.) – 1 🚐. Per night 50€
Per week 280€
Near the Lac des Moines.

Surroundings : 🛢
Leisure activities : ✦✦ ✗
Facilities : 🚿 (Jul–Aug) ▣
Nearby : 🏊

Longitude : 3.66854
Latitude : 46.06104

MONISTROL-D'ALLIER

43580 – Michelin map **331** D4 – pop. 219 – alt. 590
▶ Paris 535 – Brioude 58 – Langogne 56 – Le Puy-en-Velay 28

Municipal le Vivier

📞 04 71 57 24 14, www.monistroldallier.com
Address : to the south, near the Allier river (direct access)
Opening times : from beginning April to mid Sept.
1 ha (48 pitches) flat, grassy, stony
Tariff : (2012 price) 14.40€ ✶✶ ⇌ 🔲 🔌 (6A) – Extra per person 3.20€

Surroundings : ≤ ♀
Leisure activities : 🏞
Facilities : ⅄ ☍ ⌐
Nearby : ✗ 🚣 ☇ 🏊 ⚓ 🎣 rafting and canyoning

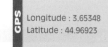
Longitude : 3.65348
Latitude : 44.96923

LE MONT-DORE

63240 – Michelin map **326** D9 – pop. 1,391 – alt. 1,050 – ⛲ (beg May-end Oct) – Winter sports : 1,050/
1,850 m ⛷ 2 ⛷ 18 ⛷
▶ Paris 462 – Aubusson 87 – Clermont-Ferrand 43 – Issoire 49

Municipal l'Esquiladou

📞 04 73 65 23 74, www.mairie-mont-dore.fr – alt. 1,010
Address : at Queureuilh, rte des Cascades (head along the D 996, following signs for Murat-le-Quaire
and take turning to the right)
Opening times : from mid April to end Oct.
1.8 ha (100 pitches) terraced, fine gravel
Tariff : ✶ 3.80€ ⇌ 🔲 3.90€ – 🔌 (16A) 4€
Rental rates : (from end Dec. to end Oct.) – 17 🛖. Per night from 48 to 90 €
Per week from 270 to 530 €
🚐 sani-station
In the mountains, very green with woods and forests.

Surroundings : 🌲 ≤ ⌂
Leisure activities : 🏞 jacuzzi 🚣 🔲
Facilities : ⅄ ☍ ▥ ⌁ launderette
Nearby : ☇ 🎣 🐎

Longitude : 2.80162
Latitude : 45.58706

MURAT-LE-QUAIRE

63150 – Michelin map **326** D9 – pop. 476 – alt. 1,050
▶ Paris 478 – Clermont-Ferrand 45 – Aurillac 120 – Cournon d'Auvergne 60

Le Panoramique

📞 04 73 81 18 79, www.campingpanoramique.fr/ – alt. 1,000
Address : 1.4km east along the D 219, follow the signs for Le Mont-Dore and take road to the left
Opening times : from mid May to end Sept.
3 ha (85 pitches) terraced, grassy
Tariff : ✶ ⇌ 🔲 17.30€ – 🔌 (10A) 6.60€
Rental rates : (from mid Dec. to end Oct.) – 5 🛖. Per week from 395 to 735 €
🚐 sani-station 3.50€ – 🚐 17.30€
Attractive, elevated location.

Surroundings : 🌲 ≤ Les Monts Dore and Dordogne valley
Leisure activities : ⛾ ✗ 🏞 🚣 🔲
Facilities : ⅄ ☍ ⌐ ▥ 🍴 ☌ ⌁ 🖥

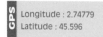
Longitude : 2.74779
Latitude : 45.596

Municipal les Couderts

☎ 0473655481, *www.camping-couderts.e-monsite.com/* – alt. 1,040
Address : Les Couderts (take the northern exit; beside a stream)
Opening times : from beginning April to mid Oct.
1.7 ha (58 pitches) flat, relatively flat, terraced, grassy
Tariff : (2012 price) 12.20€ ★★ ⇌ 圓 ⚡ (10A) – Extra per person 3€
Rental rates : (2012 price) (permanent) – 1 ⊡ – 5 ⌂. Per night 80€ – Per week 515€

Surroundings : ⌇ ⋞ ⊡ ♀
Leisure activities : ⛵
Facilities : ⚐ ⌸ 🖭 ⛺ ♔ launderette

GPS
Longitude : 2.73511
Latitude : 45.59937

MUROL

63790 – Michelin map **326** E9 – pop. 546 – alt. 830
▶ Paris 456 – Besse-en-Chandesse 10 – Clermont-Ferrand 37 – Condat 37

Sunêlia La Ribeyre ▲

☎ 0473886429, *www.laribeyre.com*
Address : at Jassat (1.2km to the south, follow the signs for Jassat; beside a stream)
Opening times : from beginning May to mid Sept.
10 ha (460 pitches) flat, grassy, lake
Tariff : 40.25€ ★★ ⇌ 圓 ⚡ (10A) – Extra per person 7.70€ – Reservation fee 30€
Rental rates : (from beginning May to mid Sept.) ⚐ ⚟ – 141 ⊡. Per night from 34 to 197 €
Per week from 238 to 1,379 € – Reservation fee 30€
Excellent water park.

Surroundings : ⌇ ⋞ ♀♀
Leisure activities : ♔ ✗ ⛵ ⊙ ⋇ jacuzzi ⛵ ✂ ⊡ ⊒ ≋ (lake) ⌇
Facilities : ⚐ ⊶ ⛺ ⌅ ⊸ ♔ launderette ⚒ ⊱
Nearby : ⚲

GPS
Longitude : 2.93719
Latitude : 45.56232

Le Repos du Baladin

☎ 0473886193, *www.camping-auvergne-france.com*
Address : at Groire (located 1.5km east along the D 146, follow the signs for St-Diéry)
Opening times : from mid April to mid Sept.
1.6 ha (88 pitches) flat and relatively flat, terrace, grassy
Tariff : 23.30€ ★★ ⇌ 圓 ⚡ (10A) – Extra per person 4.90€ – Reservation fee 13€
Rental rates : (from mid April to mid Sept.) – 21 ⊡. Per night from 43 to 59 €
Per week from 225 to 680 – Reservation fee 13€

Surroundings : ⋞ ⊡ ♀♀
Leisure activities : ♔ ✗ ⛵ ⊜s ⛵ ⊒
Facilities : ⚐ ⊶ ⛺ ♔ 圓 ⊱

GPS
Longitude : 2.95728
Latitude : 45.57379

These symbols are used for a campsite that is exceptional in its category:
△△△...△ *Particularly pleasant setting, quality and range of services available*
⌇ *Tranquil, isolated site – quiet site, particularly at night*
⋞⋞ *Exceptional view – interesting or panoramic view*

NÉBOUZAT

63210 – Michelin map **326** E8 – pop. 774 – alt. 860
▶ Paris 434 – La Bourboule 34 – Clermont-Ferrand 20 – Pontgibaud 19

Les Dômes

📞 0473871406, *www.les-domes.com* – alt. 815
Address : Les Quatre Routes de Nébouzat (along the D 216, follow the signs for Rochefort-Montagne)
Opening times : from end April to mid Sept.
1 ha (65 pitches) flat, grassy
Tariff : 23.40€ ✦✦ ⇔ 🖩 🚿 (16A) – Extra per person 6.90€ – Reservation fee 10€
Rental rates : (from end April to mid Sept.) – 8 🛖 – 5 🏠 – 5 tent bungalows.
Per night from 49 to 76 € – Per week from 237 to 671 € – Reservation fee 10€
🚐 5 🖩 18.70€ – 🔌15€
Entrance surrounded by flowers, well-kept, green setting.

Surroundings : ≤ ⌢
Leisure activities : 🎱 🔲 (open-air in season)
Facilities : 🚿 ⌂ 🚾 🍴 🖨
Nearby : 🍸 ✕ ⛴ 🦆 🐎

GPS **Longitude** : 2.89028
Latitude : 45.72538

NÉRIS-LES-BAINS

03310 – Michelin map **326** C5 – pop. 2,705 – alt. 364
▶ Paris 336 – Clermont-Ferrand 86 – Montluçon 9 – Moulins 73

Municipal du Lac

📞 0470032470, *www.ville-neris-les-bains.fr*
Address : av. Marx Dormoy (to the southwest along the D 155, follow the signs for Villebret; beside the river)
Opening times : from end March to beginning Nov.
3.5 ha (135 pitches) flat and relatively flat, terrace, grassy, fine gravel
Tariff : (2012 price) 15.37€ ✦✦ ⇔ 🖩 🚿 (10A) – Extra per person 4€
Rental rates : (2012 price) (permanent) – 21 🏠 – 7 apartments. Per week from 230 to 550 €
🚐 sani-station – 6 🖩 7€
Pleasant location near an old station and a lake.

Surroundings : 🌿 ⌂ ⌢
Leisure activities : 🍸 ✕ 🎱 🏃 🛝 🔍
Facilities : 🚿 🚾 ⌂ 🍴 🖨
Nearby : 🚴 🎾 🖼 🛝 🔲 fitness trail

GPS **Longitude** : 2.65174
Latitude : 46.28702

NEUSSARGUES-MOISSAC

15170 – Michelin map **330** F4 – pop. 959 – alt. 834
▶ Paris 509 – Aurillac 58 – Brioude 49 – Issoire 64

Municipal de la Prade

📞 0471205021, *www.neussargues-moissac.fr*
Address : rte de Murat (take the western exit along the D 304, follow the signs for Murat; beside the Alagnon river)
1 ha (32 pitches) terraced, flat, grassy, fine gravel, small wood
Tariff : 11.10€ ✦✦ ⇔ 🖩 🚿 (6A) – Extra per person 1.95€
Rental rates : (permanent) 🅿 – 6 🛖 – 6 🏠. Per week from 234 to 494 €

Surroundings : 🌿 ≤ ⌂ ⌢⌢
Leisure activities : 🎱 🛝 🔍
Facilities : 🚿 🚾 ⌂ 🍴 🖨

GPS **Longitude** : 2.96695
Latitude : 45.12923

NEUVÉGLISE

15260 – Michelin map **330** F5 – pop. 1,130 – alt. 938
▶ Paris 528 – Aurillac 78 – Entraygues-sur-Truyère 70 – Espalion 66

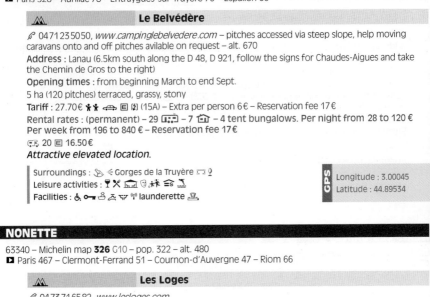

△ Le Belvédère

☎ 0471235050, *www.campinglebelvedere.com* – pitches accessed via steep slope, help moving caravans onto and off pitches avilable on request – alt. 670
Address : Lanau (6.5km south along the D 48, D 921, follow the signs for Chaudes-Aigues and take the Chemin de Gros to the right)
Opening times : from beginning March to end Sept.
5 ha (120 pitches) terraced, grassy, stony
Tariff : 27.70€ ♛♛ ⇌ 🅴 (½) (15A) – Extra per person 6€ – Reservation fee 17€
Rental rates : (permanent) – 29 🏕 – 7 🏠 – 4 tent bungalows. Per night from 28 to 120 € Per week from 196 to 840 € – Reservation fee 17€
🚐 20 🅴 16.50€
Attractive elevated location.

Surroundings : ⅗ ≤ Gorges de la Truyère 🖙 ⚲
Leisure activities : ⛳ ✗ 🎱 ⊝ ☇ 🏖 🏊
Facilities : ⚹ ⟞ 🖇 ⚶ ♨ ⚹ launderette 🏧

GPS Longitude : 3.00045 Latitude : 44.89534

NONETTE

63340 – Michelin map **326** G10 – pop. 322 – alt. 480
▶ Paris 467 – Clermont-Ferrand 51 – Cournon-d'Auvergne 47 – Riom 66

△ Les Loges

☎ 0473716582, *www.lesloges.com*
Address : situated 2km south along the D 722, follow the signs for Le Breuil-sur-Couze then continue 1km along the road near the bridge; beside the Allier river
Opening times : from beginning April to mid Sept.
4 ha (126 pitches) flat, grassy
Tariff : 20.90€ ♛♛ ⇌ 🅴 (½) (6A) – Extra per person 4.80€ – Reservation fee 6€
Rental rates : (from beginning April to mid Sept.) – 25 🏕. Per night from 70 to 80 € Per week from 490 to 560 € – Reservation fee 6€

Surroundings : ⅗ 🖙 ⚲
Leisure activities : ⛳ ✗ ⚡ 🏊 ⚞ ⤸
Facilities : ⚹ ⟞ 🖇 ⚹ 🖼 🏧

GPS Longitude : 3.27158 Latitude : 45.47367

ORCET

63670 – Michelin map **326** G8 – pop. 2,729 – alt. 400
▶ Paris 424 – Billom 16 – Clermont-Ferrand 14 – Issoire 25

△ Clos Auroy

☎ 0473842697, *www.camping-le-clos-auroy.com*
Address : 15 r. de la Narse (200m south of the town, near the Auzon river)
Opening times : permanent
3 ha (91 pitches) flat, terraced, grassy
Tariff : (2012 price) ♛ 6€ ⇌ 🅴 13.20€ – (½) (10A) 5€
Rental rates : (2012 price) (from beginning April to end Oct.) ⌀ – 8 🏕.
Per night from 65 to 75 € – Per week from 275 to 750 € – Reservation fee 20€
🚐 sani-station 3.50€
Attractive shrubs and bushes border the pitches.

Surroundings : 🖙
Leisure activities : ✗ 🎱 ⊝ daytime ⌗ jacuzzi ⚡ 🏊
Facilities : ⚹ ⟞ ▥ ⚶ ⚹ ♨ launderette
Nearby : ✗

GPS Longitude : 3.16912 Latitude : 45.70029

ORLÉAT

63190 – Michelin map **326** H7 – pop. 2,010 – alt. 380
▶ Paris 440 – Clermont-Ferrand 34 – Roanne 76 – Vichy 38

Le Pont-Astier

℘ 0473536440, *www.camping-lepont-astier.fr*
Address : Base de loisirs (leisure centre) (5km east along the D 85, D 224 and take road to the left; beside the Dore river)
Opening times : permanent
2 ha (90 pitches) flat, grassy
Tariff : (2012 price) 16.50€ ⚹⚹ ⮞ 🔲 ⚡ (16A) – Extra per person 5€
Rental rates : (2012 price) (permanent) – 6 🚐. Per night from 60 €
Per week from 260 to 390 €
🚐 30 🔲 13€

Surroundings : ⬍ ⌣
Leisure activities : 🍷 ✕ ⚤ ⚲ ⚼ ⚱
Facilities : ♿ ⚷ 🔲 ⚐ 🔳
Nearby : ⚓

GPS
Longitude : 3.47664
Latitude : 45.86813

PAULHAGUET

43230 – Michelin map **331** D2 – pop. 959 – alt. 562
▶ Paris 495 – Brioude 18 – La Chaise-Dieu 24 – Langeac 15

La Fridière

℘ 0471766554, *www.campingfr.nl*
Address : 6 rte d'Esfacy (located to the southeast along the D 4; beside the Senouire river)
Opening times : from beginning April to end Sept.
3 ha (45 pitches) flat, grassy
Tariff : (2012 price) 17.30€ ⚹⚹ ⮞ 🔲 ⚡ (16A) – Extra per person 3.50€
🚐 sani-station

Surroundings : ⚲ ⌣
Leisure activities : 🍷 🏠 ⚤ ⚓
Facilities : ♿ ⚷ ⚐ ⚑ ⚇ ⚘ ⚐ 🔳

GPS
Longitude : 3.52
Latitude : 45.199

PERS

15290 – Michelin map **330** B5 – pop. 303 – alt. 570
▶ Paris 547 – Argentat 45 – Aurillac 25 – Maurs 24

Le Viaduc

℘ 0471647008, *www.camping-cantal.com*
Address : Le Ribeyrès (5km northeast along the D 32 and take the D 61; beside the lake at St-Etienne-Cantalès)
Opening times : from end April to mid Oct.
1 ha (65 pitches) terraced, grassy, fine gravel
Tariff : 18.80€ ⚹⚹ ⮞ 🔲 ⚡ (10A) – Extra per person 4.80€ – Reservation fee 12€
Rental rates : (2012 price) (from end April to mid Oct.) – 8 🚐 – 1 🏠.
Per night from 70 to 90 € – Per week from 280 to 545 € – Reservation fee 12€
🚐 sani-station 6€
Pleasant location.

Surroundings : ⚲ ⬍ ⌣ ⚲
Leisure activities : 🍷 🏠 ⚤ ⚱ ⚓ ⚑ ⚘ ⚰
Facilities : ♿ ⚷ ⚐ launderette ⚲
Nearby : watersports centre

GPS
Longitude : 2.2556
Latitude : 44.90602

PIERREFITTE-SUR-LOIRE

03470 – Michelin map **326** J3 – pop. 518 – alt. 228
▶ Paris 324 – Bourbon-Lancy 20 – Lapalisse 50 – Moulins 42

Municipal le Vernay

✆ 04 70 47 02 49, *www.pierrefitte03.fr*
Address : Le Vernay (take the northwestern exit along the N 79, follow the signs for Dompierre, left onto D 295, follow the signs for Saligny-sur-Roudon then continue 900m along the road to the right after the bridge, 200m from the canal)
2 ha (35 pitches) flat, grassy
Rentals : 12 .
sani-station
Near a small lake.

Surroundings : ≤ ⌑
Facilities : 点 ⚬━ ▥ ▨
Nearby : ♀ ✗ ⬌ ⬚ ≌ (beach) ⬚ fitness trail

GPS
Longitude : 3.80334
Latitude : 46.51734

PLEAUX

15700 – Michelin map **330** B4 – pop. 1,609 – alt. 641
▶ Paris 534 – Argentat 29 – Aurillac 46 – Égletons 44

Municipal de Longayroux

✆ 04 71 40 48 30, *www.mairie.wanadoo.fr/pleaux/* – crossing difficult for 6km – limited spaces for one-night stay
Address : at Longayroux (15km south along the D 6, follow the signs for St-Christophe-les-Gorges; beside the Lac d'Enchanet)
Opening times : from beginning April to mid Oct.
0.6 ha (48 pitches) relatively flat, grassy, fine gravel
Tariff : (2012 price) 14.70€ ✝✝ ⇔ 回 ⑭ (5A) – Extra per person 3.20€
Rental rates : (2012 price) (from beginning April to mid Oct.) – 9 tent bungalows.
Per week from 150 to 200 €

In a pleasant location.

Surroundings : ⬚ ≤ ⌑ ⍾
Leisure activities : ♀ ⬌ ≌ (beach) ⬚
Facilities : 点 (Jul–Aug) ⬚ ▨

GPS
Longitude : 2.22753
Latitude : 45.0813

PONTGIBAUD

63230 – Michelin map **326** E8 – pop. 745 – alt. 735
▶ Paris 432 – Aubusson 68 – Clermont-Ferrand 23 – Le Mont-Dore 37

Municipal de la Palle

✆ 04 73 88 96 99, *campongibaud.free.fr*
Address : rte de la Miouze (500m southwest along the D 986, follow the signs for Rochefort-Montagne; beside the Sioule river)
Opening times : from mid April to end Sept.
4.5 ha (85 pitches) flat, grassy
Tariff : (2012 price) 16.50€ ✝✝ ⇔ 回 ⑭ (16A) – Extra per person 4.65€
Rental rates : (2012 price) (from mid April to end Sept.) 点 (1 chalet) – 6 ⬚ – 2 ⬚.
Per night from 60 € – Per week from 250 to 470 €
sani-station 2.50€

Surroundings : ⌑
Leisure activities : ⬚ ⬌ ⬚
Facilities : 点 ⚬━ ⬚⬚ ⬚ launderette
Nearby : ♀ ✗

GPS
Longitude : 2.84516
Latitude : 45.82982

LE PUY-EN-VELAY

43000 – Michelin map **331** F3 – pop. 18,810 – alt. 629
▶ Paris 539 – Aurillac 168 – Clermont-Ferrand 129 – Lyon 134

Bouthezard

📞 0471095509
Address : at Aiguilhe (to the northwest; beside the Borme river)
1 ha (80 pitches) flat, grassy

Surroundings : 〇〇
Leisure activities : 🎦
Facilities : ♿ ⊶ ▥ 🍴 🖼
Nearby : ✂ 🎣 🏊

Longitude : 3.88105
Latitude : 45.05051

PUY-GUILLAUME

63290 – Michelin map **326** H7 – pop. 2,631 – alt. 285
▶ Paris 374 – Clermont-Ferrand 53 – Lezoux 27 – Riom 35

Municipal de la Dore

📞 0473947851, *www.puy-guillaume.com* – ℞ ✂
Address : 86 r. Joseph-Claussat (take the western exit along the D 63, follow the signs for Randan and take a right turn before the bridge, near the river)
Opening times : from mid June to beginning Sept.
3 ha (100 pitches) flat, grassy
Tariff : (2012 price) 👤 3.85 € 🚗 🅴 4.50 € – 🔌 (0A) 3.85 €

Surroundings : 〇
Leisure activities : 🎦 🛝 🏊 🎣
Facilities : ♿ ⊶ ◨ 🖼
Nearby : 🍺 ✕ ✂ fitness trail

Longitude : 3.46623
Latitude : 45.96223

Some information or pricing may have changed since the guide went to press.
We recommend you check the price list online in advance or at the entrance
to the campsite and enquire about possible restrictions.

ROYAT

63130 – Michelin map **326** F8 – pop. 4,431 – alt. 450 – ⚕ (end Mar to end Oct)
▶ Paris 423 – Aubusson 89 – La Bourboule 47 – Clermont-Ferrand 5

Indigo Royat ♣

📞 0473359705, *www.camping-indigo.com*
Address : rte de Gravenoire (situated 2km southeast along the D 941c, follow the signs for Le Mont-Dore and take a right turn D 5, follow the signs for Charade)
Opening times : from end March to beginning Nov.
7 ha (200 pitches) terraced, relatively flat, gravelled, grassy
Tariff : (2012 price) 29.10 € 👤👤 🚗 🅴 🔌 (10A) – Extra per person 5.90 € – Reservation fee 20 €
Rental rates : (2012 price) (from end March to beginning Nov.) – 31 🚐 – 6 🏠 – 9 tents.
Per night from 46 to 124 € – Per week from 241 to 868 € – Reservation fee 20 €
🚰 sani-station 7 €
Pleasantly leafy setting offering plenty of shade.

Surroundings : 🌳 〇
Leisure activities : 🍺 ✕ 🎦 🎲 🧒 🛝 🚲 ✂ 🏊
Facilities : ♿ ⊶ 🆑 ▥ 🛝 🖼

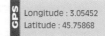
Longitude : 3.05452
Latitude : 45.75868

SAIGNES

15240 – Michelin map **330** C2 – pop. 892 – alt. 480
▶ Paris 483 – Aurillac 78 – Clermont-Ferrand 91 – Mauriac 26

⚠ Municipal Bellevue

ℰ 0471406840, *www.saignes-mairie.fr*
Address : take the northwestern exit, by the stadium
Opening times : from beginning July to end Aug.
1 ha (42 pitches) flat, grassy
Tariff : (2012 price) ✶ 2.20€ ⇔ 1.15€ 🔲 1.35€ – ⚡ (16A) 2.40€
Rental rates : (2012 price) (from beginning July to end Aug.) – 3 ⟦⟧. Per night from 40 to 50 €
Per week from 250 to 310 €

Surroundings : ⇐ ▱ ♀
Leisure activities : 🖼 ⚓
Facilities : ⅙ ⊙ 🗶 🔊
Nearby : ✄ 🛷

GPS Longitude : 2.47416
Latitude : 45.33678

To visit a town or region, use the MICHELIN Green Guides.

ST-AMANT-ROCHE-SAVINE

63890 – Michelin map **326** I9 – pop. 539 – alt. 950
▶ Paris 474 – Ambert 12 – La Chaise-Dieu 39 – Clermont-Ferrand 65

⚠ Municipal Saviloisirs

ℰ 0473957360, *www.saviloisirs.com*
Address : 7 pl. de la Liberté (east of the town)
Opening times : from beginning May to end Oct.
1.3 ha (19 pitches) terraced, grassy
Tariff : ✶ 3.45€ ⇔ 3.60€ 🔲 2.25€ ⚡ (16A)
Rental rates : (permanent) – 30 🏠. Per night from 67 to 95 € – Per week from 253 to 408 €
⟦⟧ sani-station – ⚡ ⚡ 12€

Surroundings : ⇐ ▱
Leisure activities : 🖼 ⚕ ⚓
Facilities : ⅙ ▥ ⊿ ⇝ ⍾ launderette
Nearby : ⚏ ♟ ✗ ✄

GPS Longitude : 3.63389
Latitude : 45.64347

ST-BONNET-TRONÇAIS

03360 – Michelin map **326** D3 – pop. 751 – alt. 224
▶ Paris 301 – Bourges 57 – Cérilly 12 – Montluçon 44

⚠ Centre de Tourisme de Champ Fossé

ℰ 0470061130, *www.campingtroncais.com*
Address : pl. du Champ de Foire (700m southwest)
Opening times : from beginning April to end Sept.
3 ha (110 pitches) relatively flat, grassy
Tariff : (2012 price) ✶ 4.37€ ⇔ 1.24€ 🔲 4.37€ – ⚡ (10A) 3.40€ – Reservation fee 15€
Rental rates : (2012 price) (from beginning April to end Sept.) – 12 ⟦⟧ – 10 gîtes.
Per night from 57 to 119 € – Per week from 195 to 518 € – Reservation fee 15€
Attractive location beside the Étang de St-Bonnet (lake).

Surroundings : ⚲ ⇐ ♀
Leisure activities : ♟ 🖼 🐎 ⚒
Facilities : ⊙ ⍾ launderette
Nearby : ⚓ 🚲 ✗ ⚏ 🛶 (beach) ⛷ ⚓ pedalos

GPS Longitude : 2.68841
Latitude : 46.65687

ST-DIDIER-EN-VELAY

43140 – Michelin map **331** H2 – pop. 3,313 – alt. 830
▶ Paris 538 – Annonay 49 – Monistrol-sur-Loire 11 – Le Puy-en-Velay 58

La Fressange

⌖ 0471662528, www.saint-didier.com/camping
Address : 800m southeast along the D 45, follow the signs for St-Romain-Lachalm and take the turning to the left; beside a stream
Opening times : from end April to end Sept.
1.5 ha (104 pitches) sloping, relatively flat, terraced, grassy
Tariff : (2012 price) 17.10€ ✝✝ ⇌ 圓 ⬦ (15A) – Extra per person 4.70€
Rental rates : (2012 price) (from beginning April to end Oct.) – 11 ⌂. Per night from 45 €
Per week from 180 to 480 €

Leisure activities : ⤢ ♨
Facilities : ⅌ ⟞ ⬦ ▣
Nearby : ✕ ⏚ sports trail

GPS Longitude : 4.28302
Latitude : 45.30119

ST-ÉLOY-LES-MINES

63700 – Michelin map **326** E6 – pop. 3,703 – alt. 490
▶ Paris 358 – Clermont-Ferrand 64 – Guéret 86 – Montluçon 31

Municipal la Poule d'Eau

⌖ 0473854547, selm.maire@wanadoo.fr – ♯
Address : r. de la Poule d'Eau (southern exit from the N 144, signs for Clermont, then right turn, 1.3km on the D110, rte de Pionsat)
Opening times : from mid June to mid Sept.
1.8 ha (50 pitches) relatively flat, grassy
Tariff : (2012 price) ✝ 6.50€ ⇌ 圓 – ⬦ (6A) 3€
⟐ 4 圓 6.60€
Green setting beside two lakes.

Surroundings : ⟜ ⬚ ⚲ ⛰
Leisure activities : ⤢ ⬱
Facilities : ⅌ ⟞⬚
Nearby : ⟐ ♈ ✕ ✕ ▨ ▣ ≈ (beach) fitness trail

GPS Longitude : 2.83057
Latitude : 46.15064

To make the best possible use of this guide,
please read pages 2–15 carefully.

ST-FLOUR

15100 – Michelin map **330** G4 – pop. 6,689 – alt. 783
▶ Paris 513 – Aurillac 70 – Issoire 67 – Millau 132

International Roche-Murat

⌖ 0471604363, www.camping-saint-flour.com
Address : rte de Clermont-Ferrand (4.7km northeast along the D 921, N 9 and before the A 75 motorway junction, take the road to the left, at the roundabout – from the A 75, take exit 28)
3 ha (119 pitches) terraced, grassy, pine trees nearby
Rentals : ⅌ (1 chalet) – 11 ⌂.
⟐ sani-station

Surroundings : ⟜ ⬚
Leisure activities : ▤ ⤢
Facilities : ⅌ ⟞ ▥ ⬚ ⥺ launderette

GPS Longitude : 3.10792
Latitude : 45.05056

AUVERGNE

ST-GERMAIN-L'HERM

63630 – Michelin map **326** I10 – pop. 508 – alt. 1,050
▶ Paris 476 – Ambert 27 – Brioude 33 – Clermont-Ferrand 66

St-Éloy

℘ 04 73 72 05 13, www.camping-le-saint-eloy.fr
Address : rte de la Chaise-Dieu (take the southeastern exit, on the D 999)
Opening times : from beginning May to end Sept.
3 ha (63 pitches) flat, terraced, undulating, grassy
Tariff : 18.50€ ✦✦ ⇔ 国 (½) (10A) – Extra per person 4.50€
Rental rates : (permanent) – 13 🏠. Per night from 120 to 155 € – Per week from 220 to 700 €
🚐 10 国 15€ – 🔌(½)18.50€

Surroundings : ≤
Leisure activities : ✗ 🏞 ⚓ 🚴 ⤢
Facilities : 🕭 ⚓ ⌂ ᵗ 🔲
Nearby : 🏊 🍽 ⚓

GPS Longitude : 3.54781
Latitude : 45.45653

ST-GÉRONS

15150 – Michelin map **330** B5 – pop. 209 – alt. 526
▶ Paris 538 – Argentat 35 – Aurillac 24 – Maurs 33

Les Rives du Lac

℘ 06 25 34 62 89, www.lesrivesdulac.fr
Address : 8.5km southeast along the follow the signs for Espinet; 300m from the lake at St-Étienne-Cantalès
Opening times : from mid March to mid Nov.
3 ha (105 pitches) relatively flat, grassy, wood
Tariff : 19€ ✦✦ ⇔ 国 (½) (10A) – Extra per person 5€ – Reservation fee 10€
Rental rates : (from mid March to mid Nov.) – 22 🚐. Per night from 50 to 70 €.
Per week from 200 to 550 € – Reservation fee 16€
🚐 sani-station 2€ – 🔌11€
In a pleasant setting.

Surroundings : 🏞 🚩 🎡
Leisure activities : 🍷 ⚓ 🏊 ⤢
Facilities : 🕭 ⚓ ⌂ ᵗ launderette 🏊
Nearby : ✗ 🍽 ⚓ (beach) 🎣

GPS Longitude : 2.23057
Latitude : 44.93523

ST-GERVAIS-D'AUVERGNE

63390 – Michelin map **326** D6 – pop. 1,304 – alt. 725 – Leisure centre
▶ Paris 377 – Aubusson 72 – Clermont-Ferrand 55 – Gannat 41

Municipal de l'Étang Philippe

℘ 04 73 85 74 84, www.ville-stgervais-auvergne.fr
Address : Mazières (take the northern exit along the D 987, follow the signs for St-Éloy-les-Mines; near a small lake)
Opening times : from beginning April to end Sept.
3 ha (130 pitches) flat and relatively flat, grassy
Tariff : (2012 price) 10€ ✦✦ ⇔ 国 (½) (10A) – Extra per person 1.50€ – Reservation fee 20€
Rental rates : (2012 price) (permanent) – 6 🏠. Per week from 225 to 390 €
🚐 sani-station 2€

Surroundings : 🚩 ♨ ⚠
Leisure activities : 🏞
Facilities : 🕭 ⚓ ⌂ ᵗ 🔲
Nearby : 🏇 ⚓ 🍽 🏊 (beach) 🎣 🐎

GPS Longitude : 2.81804
Latitude : 46.03688

ST-JUST

15320 – Michelin map **330** H5 – pop. 206 – alt. 950
▶ Paris 531 – Chaudes-Aigues 29 – Ruynes-en-Margeride 22 – St-Chély-d'Apcher 16

⚠ Municipal

☎ 0471737048, *www.saintjust.com*
Address : in the village (southeast; beside a stream – follow A 75: take exit 31 or 32)
Opening times : from beginning April to end Sept.
2 ha (60 pitches) flat and relatively flat, terrace, grassy
Tariff : 12€ ♥♥ ⇔ 🔲 (4) (10A) – Extra per person 2.10€
Rental rates : (permanent) – 7 🛖 – 5 🏠 – 7 gîtes. Per night from 59 to 127 €
Per week from 195 to 423 €
🚽 sani-station 2€ – 6 🔲 9.80€ – 🚿 (4)9.50€

Surroundings : 🌳 ♀
Leisure activities : 🎮 🎥evening 🚲
Facilities : ⚡ 🚿 🚰 launderette
Nearby : 🏊 🍸 🍴 🐎 🎿 🚣

GPS Longitude : 3.20938
Latitude : 44.88993

*In order for the guide to remain wholly objective, the selection of
campsites is made on an entirely independent basis.*

ST-MAMET-LA-SALVETAT

15220 – Michelin map **330** B5 – pop. 1,494 – alt. 680
▶ Paris 555 – Argentat 53 – Aurillac 20 – Maurs 24

⚠ Municipal

☎ 0471647521, *campingstmamet15@hotmail.fr*
Address : chemin du Stade (head east, access via the D 20, follow the signs for Montsalvy)
0.8 ha (30 pitches) relatively flat, grassy
Rentals : 3 🛖 – 7 🏠.

Surroundings : 🌳 🚐
Leisure activities : 🎮 🏇
Facilities : ♿ ⚡ 🚰 🔲
Nearby : 🎿 🚣 🏊

GPS Longitude : 2.30958
Latitude : 44.85407

ST-MARTIN-VALMEROUX

15140 – Michelin map **330** C4 – pop. 856 – alt. 646
▶ Paris 510 – Aurillac 33 – Mauriac 21 – Murat 53

⚠ Municipal Le Moulin du Teinturier

☎ 0471694312, *lemoulinduteinturier@orange.fr*
Address : 9 r. de Montjoly (take the western exit, on the D 37, follow the signs for Ste-Eulalie-Nozières; beside the Maronne)
Opening times : from mid June to mid Sept.
3 ha (100 pitches) flat, grassy
Tariff : (2012 price) 16€ ♥♥ ⇔ 🔲 (4) (10A) – Extra per person 3.40€ – Reservation fee 30€
Rental rates : (2012 price) (from mid April to mid Nov.) – 20 🏠. Per night from 33 to 73 €
Per week from 233 to 507 €
🚽 sani-station 2€ – 8 🔲 6€

Surroundings : ⋜ 🚐
Leisure activities : 🎮 🏇 🎣
Facilities : ♿ ⚡ 🚿 🚰 🍴 🚰 🔲
Nearby : 🎿 🏛 🚣

GPS Longitude : 2.42336
Latitude : 45.11619

ST-NECTAIRE

63710 – Michelin map **326** E9 – pop. 732 – alt. 700 – (mid-Apr to mid Oct)
▶ Paris 453 – Clermont-Ferrand 43 – Issoire 27 – Le Mont-Dore 24

⚠ Le Viginet

☎ 0473885380, *www.camping-viginet.com*
Address : take southeastern exit along the D 996 then continue 600m along the road to the left (opposite the Ford garage)
Opening times : from beginning April to end Sept.
2 ha (61 pitches) flat, relatively flat, sloping, grassy, stony
Tariff : (2012 price) 24€ ♣♣ ⇌ ▣ ☕ (10A) – Extra per person 4.80€ – Reservation fee 7€
Rental rates : (2012 price) (permanent) – 12 ☷ – 14 ☖. Per night from 120 to 160 €
Per week from 270 to 795 € – Reservation fee 7€
☷ 2 ▣ 24€
Lovely views of surrounding countryside.

Surroundings : ⌖ ⋖ ⌑ ⚲
Leisure activities : ☷ ⛵ ⊼
Facilities : ⚐ �o—ᵀ ↑↑ ▣
Nearby : ✕ ♠ fitness trail

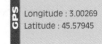 **GPS** Longitude : 3.00269
Latitude : 45.57945

⚠ La Clé des Champs

☎ 0473885233, *www.campingcledeschamps.com*
Address : take southeastern exit along the D 996 and take the D 642, follow the signs for Les Granges; beside a stream and 200m from the Couze de Chambon (river)
Opening times : from beginning April to end Sept.
1 ha (84 pitches) flat, relatively flat, terraced, grassy
Tariff : (2012 price) 24.10€ ♣♣ ⇌ ▣ ☕ (6A) – Extra per person 5€ – Reservation fee 16€
Rental rates : (2012 price) (from beginning April to end Sept.) – 18 ☷ – 9 ☖.
Per night from 33 to 90 € – Per week from 180 to 840 €
☷ sani-station 4€ – 3 ▣ 19.60€

Surroundings : ⌑ ⚲
Leisure activities : ☕ ✕ ☷ ⛵ ⊼ ⤳
Facilities : ⚐ o—ᵀ ⇌ ↑↑ ▣ ⤵

GPS Longitude : 2.99934
Latitude : 45.57602

Gîtes range from small maisonettes to old farmhouses with several bedrooms.

ST-PAULIEN

43350 – Michelin map **331** E3 – pop. 2,398 – alt. 795
▶ Paris 529 – La Chaise-Dieu 28 – Craponne-sur-Arzon 25 – Le Puy-en-Velay 14

⚠ La Rochelambert

☎ 0471005402, *www.camping-rochelambert.com*
Address : rte de Lanthenas (head 2.7km southwest along the D 13, follow the signs for Allègre and turn left onto D 25, follow the signs for Loudes; near the Borne river (direct access)
Opening times : from beginning April to end Sept.
3 ha (100 pitches) flat, grassy, terraced
Tariff : (2012 price) 21.40€ ♣♣ ⇌ ▣ ☕ (16A) – Extra per person 4.70€ – Reservation fee 7€
Rental rates : (2012 price) (from beginning April to end Sept.) – 2 caravans – 12 ☖.
Per night from 58 to 85 € – Per week from 230 to 589 € – Reservation fee 7€
☷ sani-station 3€ – ⬤ 11€

Surroundings : ⌑
Leisure activities : ☕ ✕ ⛵ ✕ ⊼
Facilities : ⚐ o—⟍ ↑↑ launderette

GPS Longitude : 3.81192
Latitude : 45.13547

ST-POURÇAIN-SUR-SIOULE

03500 – Michelin map **326** G5 – pop. 5,030 – alt. 234

▶ Paris 325 – Montluçon 66 – Moulins 33 – Riom 61

△ **L'Ile de la Ronde**

𝒫 04 70 45 45 43, www.campingiledelaronde.fr

Address : quai de la Ronde

1.5 ha (50 pitches) flat, grassy

🚉 sani-station

In a public park, beside the Sioule river.

Surroundings : 🗂 ⚲
Leisure activities : 🏊 🚲 ⚓
Facilities : & ⊶ 🖼
Nearby : 🏪 ✗ 🎣 🚉

GPS Longitude : 3.29265
Latitude : 46.30605

ST-RÉMY-SUR-DUROLLE

63550 – Michelin map **326** I7 – pop. 1,847 – alt. 620

▶ Paris 395 – Chabreloche 13 – Clermont-Ferrand 55 – Thiers 7

⚠ **Révéa Les Chanterelles**

𝒫 04 73 94 31 71, www.revea-camping.fr

Address : 3km northeast along the D 201 and take the road to the right – take A 72: exit 3

Opening times : from end April to mid Sept.

5 ha (150 pitches) sloping, terraced, grassy

Tariff : 20.20€ ✶✶ ⚌ 🗐 🗓 (10A) – Extra per person 4.10€ – Reservation fee 10€

Rental rates : (from end April to mid Sept.) – 8 🏠. Per night from 65 to 80 €

Per week from 225 to 550 € – Reservation fee 25€

🚉 2 🗐 16.60€

Pleasant location in the highlands near a small lake.

Surroundings : ⩽ ⚲
Leisure activities : 🏠 🏊
Facilities : & ⊶ 🆑 🖼
At the lake : 🏪 🏖 ⛱ ✗ ✗ 🖼 ⚓ 🎣 🛶 (beach) ⛵ ⚓ squash

GPS Longitude : 3.59918
Latitude : 45.90308

STE-SIGOLÈNE

43600 – Michelin map **331** H2 – pop. 5,900 – alt. 808

▶ Paris 551 – Annonay 50 – Monistrol-sur-Loire 8 – Montfaucon-en-Velay 14

⚠ **Kawan Village de Vaubarlet** ♣♦

𝒫 04 71 66 64 95, www.vaubarlet.com – alt. 600

Address : head 6km southwest along the D 43, follow the signs for Grazac

Opening times : from beginning May to end Sept.

15 ha/3 ha for camping (131 pitches) flat, grassy

Tariff : 25€ ✶✶ ⚌ 🗐 🗓 (16A) – Extra per person 4€ – Reservation fee 15€

Rental rates : (from beginning May to end Sept.) & (2 chalets) – 18 🚐 – 5 🏠 –

8 tent bungalows – 4 tents. Per night from 35 to 95 € – Per week from 245 to 665 €

Reservation fee 30€

🚉 sani-station

In a green valley crossed by the Dunière river.

Surroundings : 🌿 ⩽
Leisure activities : ✗ ✗ 🖼 ⚲daytime 🏫 🏊 🚲 🛶
Facilities : & ⊶ 🆑 🖲 🕯 launderette 🚿

GPS Longitude : 4.21254
Latitude : 45.21634

SAUGUES

43170 – Michelin map **331** D4 – pop. 1,873 – alt. 960
▶ Paris 529 – Brioude 51 – Mende 72 – Le Puy-en-Velay 43

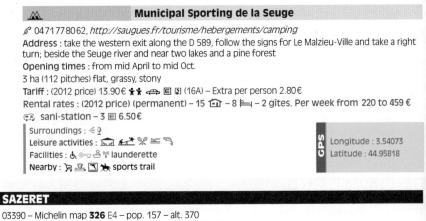

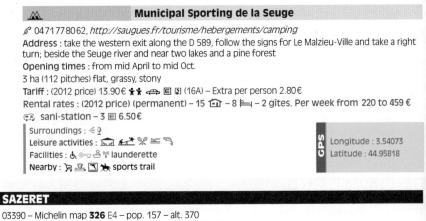 Municipal Sporting de la Seuge

✆ 0471778062, *http://saugues.fr/tourisme/hebergements/camping*
Address : take the western exit along the D 589, follow the signs for Le Malzieu-Ville and take a right turn; beside the Seuge river and near two lakes and a pine forest
Opening times : from mid April to mid Oct.
3 ha (112 pitches) flat, grassy, stony
Tariff : (2012 price) 13.90€ ♂♂ ⇌ 🔲 🔌 (16A) – Extra per person 2.80€
Rental rates : (2012 price) (permanent) – 15 🏠 – 8 🛏 – 2 gîtes. Per week from 220 to 459 €
🚐 sani-station – 3 🔲 6.50€

Surroundings : ⩽ 🌳
Leisure activities : 🏛 ⚽ ❀ ⛷ 🎣
Facilities : ♿ 🚿 🛁 🍽 launderette
Nearby : 🐎 ⛵ 🏊 🎠 sports trail

GPS Longitude : 3.54073
Latitude : 44.95818

SAZERET

03390 – Michelin map **326** E4 – pop. 157 – alt. 370
▶ Paris 348 – Gannat 44 – Montluçon 34 – Montmarault 4

La Petite Valette

✆ 0470076457, *www.valette.nl* – access difficult in some places (track)
Address : 5.5km to the northeast, access via rte Les Deux-Chaises parallel to the N 79 and Chemin des Prugnes on the left -from the A 71, take exit 11.
Opening times : from mid March to end Sept.
4 ha (55 pitches) flat
Tariff : 24.95€ ♂♂ ⇌ 🔲 🔌 (6A) – Extra per person 5.25€ – Reservation fee 15.90€
Rental rates : (from end April to end Sept.) ⚞ – 8 🚐 – 2 🏠. Per night from 70 to 80 €
Per week from 250 to 595 € – Reservation fee 15.90€
🚐 2 🔲 24.95€
Site based around an old farm; attractive flowers and shrubs.

Surroundings : 🌿 🗨 🌳
Leisure activities : ✗ 🚴 ⛷ 🎣
Facilities : ♿ 🚰 🚽 🍽 🍴 🔲
Nearby : ❀ 🐎

GPS Longitude : 2.99231
Latitude : 46.3596

SINGLES

63690 – Michelin map **326** C9 – pop. 170 – alt. 737
▶ Paris 484 – Bort-les-Orgues 27 – La Bourboule 23 – Bourg-Lastic 20

Le Moulin de Serre ♟

✆ 0473211606, *www.moulindeserre.com*
Address : 1.7km south of the Guinguette, along the D 73, follow the signs for Bort-les-Orgues; beside the Burande river
Opening times : from mid April to mid Sept.
7 ha/2.6 ha for camping (90 pitches) flat, grassy
Tariff : (2012 price) 23.45€ ♂♂ ⇌ 🔲 🔌 (10A) – Extra per person 4.45€ – Reservation fee 15€
Rental rates : (2012 price) (from mid April to mid Sept.) – 23 🚐 – 12 tent bungalows.
Per night 56€ – Per week from 161 to 686 € – Reservation fee 15€
🚐 sani-station 4€ – 4 🔲 5€
A green setting in a small valley.

Surroundings : 🌿 ⩽ 🗨 🌳
Leisure activities : 🍴 ✗ 🏛 🎮 🤾 ⚽ 🚴 ❀ ⛷ 🎣 🛶
Facilities : ♿ 🚰 🍽 🛁 🍴 launderette 🐕

GPS Longitude : 2.54235
Latitude : 45.54357

TAUVES

63690 – Michelin map **326** C9 – pop. 768 – alt. 820
▶ Paris 474 – Bort-les-Orgues 27 – La Bourboule 13 – Bourg-Lastic 29

 Les Aurandeix

📞 0473211406, *www.camping-les-aurandeix.fr*
Address : at the Stade (east of the village)
Opening times : from mid April to end Sept.
2 ha (50 pitches) flat, terraced, sloping, grassy
Tariff : (2012 price) 20€ 🏕🏕 ⛟ 🔲 (2) (10A) – Extra per person 4.55€ – Reservation fee 10€
Rental rates : (2012 price) (from mid April to end Sept.) – 13 🚐. Per night 99€
Per week 549€ – Reservation fee 19€
🚐 sani-station 5€

Surroundings : 🔲 ♀
Leisure activities : 🎮 🏋 🏊 ⛵
Facilities : ♿ ⛟ 🛁 🍴 launderette
Nearby : 🎿 🔲 🏊 fitness trail, at the lake at La Tour d'Auvergne

Longitude : 2.62473
Latitude : 45.56101

TREIGNAT

03380 – Michelin map **326** B4 – pop. 443 – alt. 450
▶ Paris 342 – Boussac 11 – Culan 27 – Gouzon 25

Municipal de l'Étang d'Herculat

📞 0470070389, *mairie-treignat@pays-allier.com*
Address : 2.3km to the northeast, access via the road to the left, after the church
Opening times : from beginning April to mid Sept.
1.6 ha (35 pitches) sloping, relatively flat, flat, grassy
Tariff : (2012 price) 🏕 5.60€ ⛟ 🔲 – (2) (10A) 1.70€

A pleasant location beside the lake.

Surroundings : 🌳 🔲 ⛰
Leisure activities : 🎮 🏋 🎣
Facilities : ♿ ⛟ (Jul–Aug) 🔲 ⛲

Longitude : 2.3673
Latitude : 46.35611

Do not confuse:
🔺 *to* 🔺🔺🔺 *: MICHELIN classification*
with
★ *to* ★★★★★ *: official classification*

VALLON-EN-SULLY

03190 – Michelin map **326** C3 – pop. 1,693 – alt. 192
▶ Paris 313 – La Châtre 55 – Cosne-d'Allier 23 – Montluçon 25

Municipal les Soupirs

📞 0630659258, *mondocher.com*
Address : head 1km southeast along the D 11, near the Cher river and the Canal du Berry, take the road to the right
2 ha (50 pitches) flat, grassy, lake

Surroundings : 🌳 ♀
Leisure activities : 🎿 🎣
Facilities : ⛟
Nearby : 🍷 ✕ 🏋 🏊

Longitude : 2.61437
Latitude : 46.53032

VIC-SUR-CÈRE

15800 – Michelin map **330** D5 – pop. 1,988 – alt. 678
▶ Paris 549 – Aurillac 19 – Murat 29

⋀⋀⋀ La Pommeraie

℘ 04 71 47 54 18, *www.camping-la-pommeraie.com* – alt. 750
Address : at Daïsses (2.5km southeast along the D 54, D 154 and take the road to the right)
Opening times : from beginning May to beginning Sept.
2.8 ha (100 pitches) terraced, grassy, stony
Tariff : 34€ ♀♀ ⇐ 回 (½) (10A) – Extra per person 6.50€ – Reservation fee 18€
Rental rates : (2012 price) (from beginning May to end May) – 40 ⟨⟩ – 3 tent bungalows.
Per night from 41 to 125 € – Per week from 200 to 875 € – Reservation fee 18€
An attractive elevated location.

Surroundings : ⊱ ≼ mountain peaks, Vallée de la Cère and small town
of Vic-sur-Cère ⊂⊃ ♀
Leisure activities : ▼ ✗ ⌂ ⊚ evening ⚗ ⅍ ▧ ⅃ ⚁ walking trails
Facilities : ᕧ ⦿ ⫲ ⭗ ⅍ ⌇ ◷ launderette ⛲ ⿻

GPS Longitude : 2.63307
Latitude : 44.9711

VIVEROLS

63840 – Michelin map **326** K10 – pop. 396 – alt. 860
▶ Paris 463 – Ambert 25 – Clermont-Ferrand 103 – Montbrison 38

⋀ Municipal le Pradoux

℘ 04 73 95 34 31, *viverols@wanadoo.fr* – limited spaces for one-night stay
Address : Le Ruisseau (to the southwest of the village along the D 111, follow the signs for
Medeyrolles, near the Ligonne river)
Opening times : from beginning April to end Oct.
1.2 ha (49 pitches) flat, grassy
Tariff : (2012 price) ♀ 1.70€ ⇐ 1.70€ 回 1.70€ – (½) (6A) 3€
⊡ sani-station 2€ – 5 回

Leisure activities : ⌂ ⚌
Facilities : ᕧ ⭗ ⅍ ◷
Nearby : ⅍ ⟿

GPS Longitude : 3.88224
Latitude : 45.43159

VOREY

43800 – Michelin map **331** F2 – pop. 1,428 – alt. 540
▶ Paris 544 – Ambert 53 – Craponne-sur-Arzon 18 – Le Puy en Velay 23

⋀⋀⋀ Les Moulettes

℘ 04 71 03 70 48, *www.camping-les-moulettes.fr*
Address : Chemin de Félines (to the west of the town centre; beside the Arzon river)
Opening times : from beginning May to mid Sept.
1.3 ha (45 pitches) flat, grassy
Tariff : (2012 price) ♀ 5€ ⇐ 回 7€ – (½) (10A) 3.20€
Rental rates : (2012 price) (from beginning April to mid Oct.) – 6 ⟨⟩ – 6 ⛺.
Per week from 240 to 560 €
⊡ sani-station 3€ – 5 回 2€

Surroundings : ⊂⊃ ⚌
Leisure activities : ▼ ✗ ⌂ ⚌ ⅃ ⚁
Facilities : ᕧ ⦿ ⭗ ⅍ ◷ ⌇ ◷
Nearby : ⅍ ⟿

GPS Longitude : 3.90363
Latitude : 45.18637

BRITTANY

Tristan Deschamps / Photononstop

Brittany, or Breizh, as it is known to those lucky enough to live there, is a region of harsh granite coastlines, mysterious dolmens and menhirs, enchanted forests and pretty ports, dotted with colourful fishing boats. Its charm lies in its sea breeze, seafood and sea-faring history; in its varied landscapes, extensive coastline and delightful islands; in its gastronomy, music and traditional festivals. Its inhabitants were born – or so they claim – with a drop of salt water in their blood. Proud of the language handed down from their Celtic ancestors, today's Bretons nurture their identity with lively celebrations of folklore and customs. Naturally, such devotion to culture demands plenty of delicious and wholesome nourishment: sweet and savoury pancakes, thick slices of butter cake and mugs of cold cider. However, Brittany's gastronomic reputation doesn't end there and gourmets can feast on the oysters, lobster and crab for which it is famous. A visit to Brittany is a jigsaw of wonderful experiences.

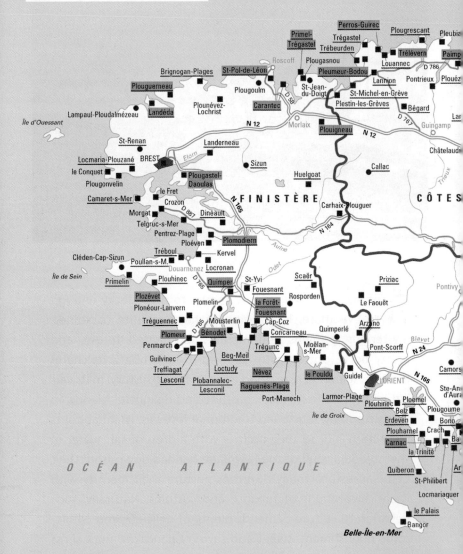

MANCHE

●	Locality with campsite
■	Locality with campsite and rental option
Vannes	Locality with campsite and campervan area
Moyaux	Locality with at least one pleasant campsite
🚐	Motorway service area for campervans

Île d'Ouessant

Île de Sein

Île de Groix

Belle-Île-en-Mer

OCÉAN ATLANTIQUE

FINISTÈRE

CÔTES

Primel-Trégastel
Perros-Guirec
Trégastel
Trébeurden
Plougrescant
Pleubia
Trélévern
Paimp
Louannec
Pontrieux
Plouéz
Roscoff
Plougasnou
St-Pol-de-Léon
Pleumeur-Bodou
Lannion
Brignogan-Plages
St-Jean-du-Doigt
St-Michel-en-Grève
Bégard
Plouguerneau
Plougoulm
Carantec
Plestin-les-Grèves
D 787
Lampaul-Ploudalmézeau
Landéda
Plounévez-Lochrist
Morlaix
Guingamp
Lar
St-Renan
Landerneau
Plouigneau
Châteaud
N 12
Locmaria-Plouzané
BREST
Sizun
Callac
le Conquet
Elorn
Huelgoat
Plougonvelin
Plougastel-Daoulas
le Fret
Crozon
Camaret-s-Mer
Morgat
Dinéault
Telgruc-s-Mer
Carhaix-Plouguer
Pentrez-Plage
N 165
N 164
Ploéven
Plomodiern
Aulne
Tréboul
Kervel
Cléden-Cap-Sizun
Poullan-s-M.
Douarnenez
Locronan
Odet
Primelin
Plouhinec
Quimper
St-Yvi
Scaër
Priziac
Pontivy
Plozévet
Fouesnant
Rosporden
Le Faouët
Plomelin
Plonéour-Lanvern
la Forêt-Fouesnant
Mousterlin
Arzano
Tréguennec
Bénodet
Cap-Coz
Quimperlé
Plomeur
Concarneau
Pont-Scorff
Penmarch
Trégunc
Moëlan-s-Mer
Blavet
N 24
Guilvinec
Beg-Meil
Camors
Treffiagat
Loctudy
Névez
le Pouldu
Guidel
Lesconil
Plobannalec-Lesconil
Raguenès-Plage
LORIENT
N 165
Ste-An
d'Aura
Port-Manech
Larmor-Plage
Plouhinec
Ploemel
Plougoume
Bono
Belz
Erdeven
Bono
Ba
Plouharnel
Crach
Carnac
la Trinité
Quiberon
Ar
St-Philibert
Locmariaquer
le Palais
Bangor

BRITTANY

AMBON

56190 – Michelin map **308** P9 – pop. 1,676 – alt. 30
▶ Paris 465 – Muzillac 7 – Redon 42 – La Roche-Bernard 22

Le Bédume ▲▲

📞 02 97 41 68 13, *www.bedume.com*
Address : 40 r. du Bédume (6km southeast; at Betahon-Plage)
Opening times : from beginning April to end Oct.
5 ha (200 pitches) flat, grassy
Tariff : (2012 price) 22€ ♦♦ ⇔ 🔲 (∮) (6A) – Extra per person 5€ – Reservation fee 10€
Rental rates : (2012 price) (from beginning April to end Oct.) – 20 🚐.
Per night from 76 to 117 € – Per week from 194 to 880 € – Reservation fee 10€

Surroundings : 🔲 🏔
Leisure activities : 🎏 🏠 🎣 🚶 ⛵ 🏊 ⛱ multi-sports ground
Facilities : ♿ ⛽ 🚿 🍴 launderette 🔧

GPS Longitude : -2.50828
Latitude : 47.52484

D'Arvor

📞 02 97 41 16 69, *www.campingdarvor.com* – limited spaces for one-night stay
Address : located 1.5km west along the D 20, follow the signs for Sarzeau and take the turning to the left, follow the signs for Brouel
Opening times : from beginning April to end Oct.
4 ha (140 pitches) flat, grassy, lake
Tariff : ♦ 5.50€ ⇔ 🔲 9.50€ – (∮) (6A) 3.60€ – Reservation fee 6€

Surroundings : 🎣
Leisure activities : 🎏 🍴 🏠 🎣 🚶 ⛵ 🚲 🔲 🏊 ⛱ 🎣
Facilities : ♿ ⛽ 🍴 launderette

GPS Longitude : -2.57221
Latitude : 47.55654

We value your opinion and welcome your feedback.
Do email us at campingfrance@tp.michelin.com

ARRADON

56610 – Michelin map **308** O9 – pop. 5,301 – alt. 40
▶ Paris 467 – Auray 18 – Lorient 62 – Quiberon 49

Penboch ▲▲

📞 02 97 44 71 29, *www.camping-penboch.fr*
Address : 9 chemin de Penboch (situated 2km southeast following signs for Roguedas, 200m from the beach)
Opening times : from beginning April to end Sept.
4 ha (175 pitches) flat and relatively flat, grassy
Tariff : 34.80€ ♦♦ ⇔ 🔲 (∮) (10A) – Extra per person 6.20€
Rental rates : (2012 price) (from beginning April to end Sept.) – 40 🚐 – 3 🏠.
Per night from 40 to 170 € – Per week from 230 to 1,190 € – Reservation fee 20€
🚐 sani-station 4€ – 🚐 (∮)14€
Leafy location offering pleasant shade.

Surroundings : 🌿 🔲 🎣
Leisure activities : 🎏 🏠 🚶 jacuzzi ⛵ ⛺ 🔲 🏊 ⛱ multi-sports ground
Facilities : ♿ ⛽ 🛁 🚿 – 4 individual sanitary facilities (🚿 wc) 🚿 🍴 launderette 🔧 refrigerators
Nearby : 🏖 🎣

GPS Longitude : -2.80085
Latitude : 47.62217

L'Allée

℘ 0297440198, *www.camping-allee.com*
Address : located 1.5km west, follow the signs for Le Moustoir and take the turning to the left
Opening times : from beginning April to mid Oct.
3 ha (148 pitches) flat and relatively flat, grassy
Tariff : (2012 price) ✦ 4.95€ ⬢ 9.20€ – (10A) 4.60€ – Reservation fee 20€
Rental rates : (2012 price) (permanent) – 28 ⬡ – 6 ⬡ – 2 gîtes. Per night from 90 to 110€
Per week from 190 to 690€ – Reservation fee 20€
sani-station

Surroundings :
Leisure activities :
Facilities : (Jul-Aug) launderette
Nearby :

GPS
Longitude : -2.84025
Latitude : 47.62109

ARZANO

29300 – Michelin map **308** K7 – pop. 1,403 – alt. 91
▶ Paris 508 – Carhaix-Plouguer 54 – Châteaulin 82 – Concarneau 40

Les Castels Ty Nadan ▲▴

℘ 0298717547, *www.tynadan-vacances.fr*
Address : at Locunolé, rte d'Arzano (3km west; beside the Ellé river)
Opening times : from end April to beginning Sept.
20.5 ha/5 ha for camping (325 pitches) flat and relatively flat, grassy
Tariff : 46€ ✦✦ ⬢ (10A) – Extra per person 8.80€ – Reservation fee 25€
Rental rates : (from end April to beginning Sept.) – 80 ⬡ – 9 ⬡ – 2 apartments – 6 tents –
1 gîte. Per night from 54 to 119€ – Per week from 324 to 833€ – Reservation fee 30€
sani-station 30€
Partially indoor water park with good sporting activities and lesiure facillities.

Surroundings :
Leisure activities : jacuzzi (beach)
climbing wall, forest trail, quad biking entertainment room
Facilities : launderette

GPS
Longitude : -3.47461
Latitude : 47.90476

To visit a town or region, use the MICHELIN Green Guides.

ARZON

56640 – Michelin map **308** N9 – pop. 2,132 – alt. 9
▶ Paris 487 – Auray 52 – Lorient 94 – Quiberon 81

Municipal le Tindio

℘ 0297537559, *www.camping-arzon.fr*
Address : 2 r. du Bilouris, at Kermers (800m to the northeast)
Opening times : from beginning April to beginning Nov.
5 ha (220 pitches) flat and relatively flat, grassy
Tariff : (2012 price) ✦ 4.10€ ⬢ 4.10€ – (10A) 3.25€
Rental rates : (2012 price) (from beginning April to beginning Nov.) (3 chalets) – 18 ⬡.
Per week from 260 to 680€
sani-station 2€ – 19 ⬢ 10€ – 10€
Beside the sea.

Surroundings :
Leisure activities : multi-sports ground
Facilities : launderette

GPS
Longitude : -2.8828
Latitude : 47.55562

BADEN

56870 – Michelin map **308** N9 – pop. 4,077 – alt. 28
▶ Paris 473 – Auray 9 – Lorient 52 – Quiberon 40

Mané Guernehué ♠♣

02 97 57 02 06, www.camping-baden.com
Address : 52 r. Mané Er Groëz (located 1km southwest, follow the signs for Mériadec and take a right turn)
Opening times : from beginning April to beginning Nov.
18 ha/8 ha for camping (377 pitches) undulating, terraced, flat and relatively flat, grassy, lake, natural setting among trees and bushes
Tariff : (2012 price) 43.90€ ♦♦ ⇔ 回 (10A) – Extra per person 7.90€ – Reservation fee 20€
Rental rates : (from beginning April to beginning Nov.) ♿ – 4 caravans – 142 ▦ – 18 ⌂ – 1 studio – 4 tents – 6 gîtes. Per night from 35 to 199 € – Per week from 245 to 1,393 € Reservation fee 20€
sani-station 6€ – ⛟ 15€
Attractive indoor spa area and riding centre with ponies and horses.

Surroundings :
Leisure activities : ♥ ✗ ▦ ⛲ ♨ ⛷ hammam jacuzzi ⛵ ⚙ zip wiring, forest trail, multi-sports ground, spa therapy centre, water park, entertainment room
Facilities : ♿ ⊶ ⌨ 🍴 launderette
Nearby : ✗

GPS Longitude : -2.92531
Latitude : 47.61418

BÉGARD

22140 – Michelin map **309** C3 – pop. 4,652 – alt. 142
▶ Paris 499 – Rennes 147 – St-Brieuc 51 – Quimper 132

Donant

02 96 45 46 46, www.camping-donant-bretagne.com
Address : at Gwénézhan
Opening times : from beginning April to end Sept.
3 ha (91 pitches) terraced, flat, grassy
Tariff : (2012 price) ♦ 3.15€ ⇔ 1.90€ 回 3.15€ – (10A) 2.80€
Rental rates : (permanent) ♿ (1 chalet) – 15 ⌂. Per night from 100 € Per week from 225 to 467 €
sani-station 3.50€ – ⛟ 10.90€

Surroundings :
Leisure activities : ▦ ⛲ entertainment room
Facilities : ♿ ⊶ (Jul–Aug) 🍴 launderette
Nearby : ♥ ▦ ⛷ leisure park

GPS Longitude : -3.2837
Latitude : 48.61807

BEG-MEIL

29170 – Michelin map **308** H7
▶ Paris 562 – Rennes 211 – Quimper 23 – Brest 95

La Piscine

02 98 56 56 06, www.campingdelapiscine.com
Address : 51 Hent Kerleya (4km to the northwest)
Opening times : from mid April to mid Sept.
3.8 ha (185 pitches) flat, grassy, small lake
Tariff : 35.60€ ♦♦ ⇔ 回 (10A) – Extra per person 7.20€ – Reservation fee 20€
Rental rates : (from mid April to mid Sept.) – 35 ▦ – 4 ⌂. Per week from 220 to 890€ Reservation fee 20€
sani-station 4€

Surroundings :
Leisure activities : ▦ hammam jacuzzi ⛷ mountain biking
Facilities : ♿ ⊶ 🍴 launderette

GPS Longitude : -4.01579
Latitude : 47.86672

La Roche Percée
(rental of mobile homes only)

℘ 02 98 94 94 15, *www.camping-larochepercee.com*

Address : 30 Hent Kerveltrec (located 1.5km north along the D 45, follow the signs for Fouesnant, 500m from the beach at Kerveltrec)

Opening times : from end March to end Sept.

2 ha flat and relatively flat, grassy

Rental rates : 60 ⬚. Per night from 40 to 90€ – Per week from 290 to 860€
Reservation fee 16€

Surroundings : 🌿 ☐
Leisure activities : ♈ 🚲 🏊 ☐ 🛝
Facilities : ⚊ 🚿 launderette
Nearby : ✗ 🎾 🐎

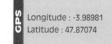

Longitude : -3.98981
Latitude : 47.87074

Le Kervastard

℘ 02 98 94 91 52, *www.campinglekervastard.com*

Address : chemin de Kervastard (150m from the town)

Opening times : from beginning April to end Sept.

2 ha (128 pitches) flat, grassy

Tariff : 28.50€ 🚶🚶 ⬛ 🔲 (10A) – Extra per person 5.90€ – Reservation fee 15€
Rental rates : (2012 price) (from beginning April to end Sept.) – 20 ⬚.
Per night from 40 to 90 € – Per week from 224 to 620€ – Reservation fee 15€
🔲 sani-station 3€ – 🔵 10€

Surroundings : ☐ 〽
Leisure activities : 🖼 🛝
Facilities : ♿ ⚊ 🚿 launderette
Nearby : 🛝 ✗

Longitude : -3.98825
Latitude : 47.86015

BELLE-ÎLE

56360 – Michelin map **308** – pop. 2,457 – alt. 7
Reservation required in summer for motor vehicles and campervans for the 45-min trip on the Quiberon (Port Maria) to Le Palais ferry. www.compagnie-oceane.fr *℘* 08 20 056 156

Bangor 56360 – Michelin map **308** L11 – pop. 926 – alt. 45
▶ Paris 513 – Rennes 162 – Vannes 53

Municipal de Bangor

℘ 02 97 31 89 75, *camping.bangor@orange.fr*

Address : to the west of the town

0.8 ha (75 pitches) sloping, relatively flat, grassy

Rentals : 6 ⬚ – 16 🛏.

Surroundings : 🌿 ☐
Leisure activities : 🛝
Facilities : ♿ ⚊
Nearby : 🎾 🐎

Longitude : -3.19103
Latitude : 47.31453

Key to rentals symbols:

12 ⬚	*Number of mobile homes*	
20 🏠	*Number of chalets*	
6 🛏	*Number of rooms to rent*	
Per night 30–50€	*Minimum/maximum rate per night*	
Per week 300–1,000€	*Minimum/maximum rate per week*	

Le Palais 56360 – Michelin map **308** M10 – pop. 2,545 – alt. 7
▶ Paris 508 – Rennes 157 – Vannes 48

Bordenéo

℘ 02 97 31 88 96, *www.bordeneo.com*
Address : 1.7km northwest following signs for Port Fouquet, 500m from the sea
Opening times : from beginning April to end Sept.
5.5 ha (202 pitches) flat, grassy
Tariff : ♣ 7.10€ ⇌ 2.60€ ▣ 11€ – ⌀ (5A) 3.50€ – Reservation fee 15€
Rental rates : (permanent) – 54 ⛺ – 12 ⌂. Per night from 70 to 100 €
Per week from 280 to 820 € – Reservation fee 15€
⛽ sani-station
Attractive flowers and shrubs.

Surroundings : ⬚ ⛲ ♨
Leisure activities : ♟ ⛏ ⊞evening ⚴ ⛷ ✂ ⚒ ⚄
Facilities : ⅙ ⟜ ⛺ ⚐ launderette ⚏
Nearby : ⛏ ⛴ scuba diving

GPS
Longitude : -3.16711
Latitude : 47.35532

L'Océan

℘ 02 97 31 83 86, *www.camping-ocean-belle-ile.com*
Address : at Rosboscer (to the southwest of the town, 500m from the port)
Opening times : from beginning April to end Oct.
2.8 ha (125 pitches) flat and relatively flat, grassy
Tariff : (2012 price) ♣ 5.30€ ⇌ ▣ 8.50€ – ⌀ (10A) 3.85€ – Reservation fee 5€
Rental rates : (2012 price) (from beginning April to end Oct.) ⅙ – 26 ⛺ – 26 ⌂.
Per night from 45 to 75 € – Per week from 252 to 602 € – Reservation fee 10€

Surroundings : ⬚ ⛲ ♨
Leisure activities : ♟ ✕ ⚴ ⚒
Facilities : ⅙ ⟜ ⛺ ⚐ ⚐ ♔ launderette ⚏
Nearby : ⛏ ⛴ scuba diving

GPS
Longitude : -3.13996
Latitude : 47.53473

The Michelin classification (⋀⋀⋀ … ⋀) is totally independent of the official star classification system awarded by the local prefecture or other official organisation.

BELZ

56550 – Michelin map **308** L8 – pop. 3,476 – alt. 12
▶ Paris 494 – Rennes 143 – Vannes 34 – Lorient 25

Le Moulin des Oies

℘ 02 97 55 53 26, *www.lemoulindesoies.com*
Address : 21 r. de la Côte
Opening times : from beginning April to end Sept.
1.9 ha (90 pitches) flat, grassy
Tariff : 19.70€ ♣♣ ⇌ ▣ ⌀ (6A) – Extra per person 5.10€ – Reservation fee 12€
Rental rates : (from beginning April to end Sept.) – 18 ⛺. Per night from 53 to 75€
Per week from 236 to 633€ – Reservation fee 12€
⛽ sani-station
Beside the Ria d'Étel river.

Surroundings : ⬚ ⛲ ♨
Leisure activities : ⛲ ⚴ ⊠ (seawater pool), multi-sports ground
Facilities : ⅙ ⟜ ▣ ♔ launderette

GPS
Longitude : -3.17603
Latitude : 47.68045

BÉNODET

29950 – Michelin map **308** G7 – pop. 3,271
 Paris 563 – Concarneau 19 – Fouesnant 8 – Pont-l'Abbé 13

Sunêlia L'Escale St-Gilles ♣♣

☎ 02 98 57 05 37, *www.stgilles.fr* – limited spaces for one-night stay ✂ (Jul–Aug)
Address : Corniche de la mer (located at La Pointe St-Gilles (headland)
Opening times : from mid April to end Sept.
11 ha/7 ha for camping (480 pitches) flat, grassy
Tariff : 42€ ♣♣ ⇌ 回 🅷 (10A) – Extra per person 8€ – Reservation fee 35€
Rental rates : (from mid April to end Sept.) ✂ – 150 🛏 – 2 tent bungalows.
Per night from 35 to 119€ – Per week from 89 to 483€ – Reservation fee 35€

Attractive location opposite the ocean, near the beach. Option for full and half-board stays.

Surroundings : 🐟 ⛱ ♧♧
Leisure activities : ♈ ✗ 🎱 🎣 🏊 🎿 🚡 hammam, jacuzzi 🏄 🚲 ✗
🎳 🎿 ⛸ spa therapy centre, water park, entertainment room
Facilities : 🚿 ⛽ 🏕 🗑 🗑 ♨ 🍴 launderette 🔌 🚐
Nearby : 🛶 🐎

GPS Longitude : -4.09669
Latitude : 47.86325

Le Letty ♣♣

☎ 02 98 57 04 69, *www.campingduletty.com*
Address : impasse de Creisanguer
Opening times : from mid June to beginning Sept.
10 ha (493 pitches) flat, grassy
Tariff : 39.50€ ♣♣ ⇌ 回 🅷 (10A) – Extra per person 9€ – Reservation fee 12€
Rental rates : (from mid June to beginning Sept.) ✂ – 6 tent bungalows.
Per week from 425 to 700€ – Reservation fee 12€
🚽 sani-station

Attractive location close to the beach with plenty of places for tents and caravans.

Surroundings : 🐟 ♧♧ ⛰
Leisure activities : ♈ 🎱 🎣 🏊 🎿 🏊 hammam, jacuzzi 🏄 ✗ 🎳 🎿
🔱 ⛸ library ✿ entertainment room
Facilities : 🚿 ⛽ 🗑 ♨ 🍴 launderette 🔌 🚐
Nearby : 🎣 🧗 🛶, squash

GPS Longitude : -4.08995
Latitude : 47.86537

Le Poulquer

☎ 02 98 57 04 19, *www.campingdupoulquer.com*
Address : 23 r. du Poulquer (150m from the sea)
Opening times : from beginning May to end Sept.
3 ha (215 pitches) flat and relatively flat, grassy
Tariff : ♣ 6.50€ ⇌ 3€ 回 7€ – 🅷 (10A) 4.80€ – Reservation fee 20€
Rental rates : (from beginning May to end Sept.) ✂ – 30 🛏. Per night from 60 to 80 €
Per week from 250 to 800€ – Reservation fee 20€

Green setting with plenty of shade.

Surroundings : ⛱ ♧♧
Leisure activities : ✗ 🎱 🏄 🎿 ⛸ entertainment room
Facilities : 🚿 ⛽ 🍴 launderette
Nearby : ✗ 🎣 🧗 🛶

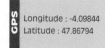

GPS Longitude : -4.09844
Latitude : 47.86794

BINIC

22520 – Michelin map **309** F3 – pop. 3,602 – alt. 35
▶ Paris 463 – Guingamp 37 – Lannion 69 – Paimpol 31

⚠ Le Panoramic

✆ 02 96 73 60 43, *www.lepanoramic.net*
Address : r. Gasselin 1km to south)
Opening times : from end March to end Sept.
4 ha (150 pitches) terrace, relatively flat, flat, grassy
Tariff : (2012 price) 27.10€ ⚷⚷ ⇦ 🔲 (10A) – Extra per person 6.15€
Rental rates : (from end March to end Sept.) – 1 caravan – 40 🚐 – 8 🏠.
Per night from 50 to 120 € – Per week from 250 to 840 € – Reservation fee 10€

Surroundings : 🛏 🞅🞅
Leisure activities : 🍴✗ 🖼 🏊 🔲 (open-air in season)
Facilities : 🚻 ⛲ 🗻🚿 launderette

GPS Longitude : -2.82304
Latitude : 48.59098

⚠ Municipal des Fauvettes

✆ 02 96 73 60 83, *www.ville-binic.fr*
Address : r. des Fauvettes
1 ha (83 pitches) terraced, flat and relatively flat, grassy
Rentals : 🏠 – 6 🚐.
🚐 sani-station – 5 🔲
Rentals reserved for the Gendarmerie (police) during July and August (beach patrol).

Surroundings : 🐚 ≼ of the Baie de St-Brieuc 🞅
Leisure activities : 🏊
Facilities : 🚻 ⛲ 🚿 🖼

GPS Longitude : -2.82122
Latitude : 48.60635

*The prices listed were supplied by the campsite owners in 2012
(if prices were not available, those from the previous year are given).
The fees should be regarded as basic charges and may fluctuate
with inflation.*

BONO

56400 – Michelin map **308** N9 – pop. 2,198 – alt. 10
▶ Paris 475 – Auray 6 – Lorient 49 – Quiberon 37

⚠ Parc-Lann

✆ 02 97 57 93 93, *www.campingduparclann.fr*
Address : r. Thiers (1.2km northeast along the D 101e, follow the signs for Plougoumelen)
Opening times : from mid April to end Sept.
2 ha (60 pitches) flat, grassy
Tariff : ⚷ 4.50€ ⇦ 🔲 5.60€ – (6A) 3€
Rental rates : (permanent) – 5 'gypsy' caravans – 2 🏠 – 1 gîte. Per night from 50 to 110€
Per week from 250 to 750€
🚐 6 🔲 14.70€

Surroundings : 🐚 🛏 🞅🞅
Leisure activities : 🖼 🏊
Facilities : 🚻 ⛲ (Jul–Aug) 🗑🚿 launderette
Nearby : ✗

GPS Longitude : -2.93746
Latitude : 47.64411

BREST

29200 – Michelin map **308** E4 – pop. 141,315 – alt. 35
▶ Paris 596 – Lorient 133 – Quimper 72 – Rennes 246

Le Goulet ▲▲

☎ 02 98 45 86 84, www.campingdugoulet.com
Address : chemin de Lanhouarnec (6km west along the D 789, follow the signs for Le Conquet then take the left turning rte de Ste-Anne-du-Portzic, 500m from the sea)
4.5 ha (155 pitches) terraced, grassy, gravelled
Rentals : ⌂ – 33 ⊡.

Surroundings : ⌂ ⊡ ♀
Leisure activities : ♀ ✗ ⊡ ⅍ ⚔ ⅏ ⚐ entertainment room
Facilities : & ⊶ ⫸ ⌂ ⌂ ⚐ launderette

GPS Longitude : -4.54032
Latitude : 48.36544

This guide is not intended as a list of all the camping sites in France; its aim is to provide a selection of the best sites in each category.

BRIGNOGAN-PLAGES

29890 – Michelin map **308** F3 – pop. 848 – alt. 17
▶ Paris 585 – Brest 41 – Carhaix-Plouguer 83 – Landerneau 27

La Côte des Légendes

☎ 02 98 83 41 65, www.campingcotedeslegendes.com
Address : r. Douar ar Pont (situated 2km to the northwest)
Opening times : from beginning April to mid Nov.
3.5 ha (150 pitches) flat, grassy, sandy
Tariff : (2012 price) 18.50€ ♣♣ ⇔ 国 (₴) (10A) – Extra per person 4.45€
Rental rates : (2012 price) (from beginning April to mid Nov.) – 11 ⊡ – 3 ⌂ – 4 tent bungalows. Per night from 40 to 90 € – Per week from 225 to 629 €
⊡ sani-station 2.70€ – 4 国 6.80€
Beside La Plage Des Crapauds (beach).

Surroundings : ⌂ ⊡ ♀ ⚐
Leisure activities : ⊡ ⚔
Facilities : & ⊶ (Jul–Aug) ⌂ ⅌ 国
Nearby : ♦

GPS Longitude : -4.32928
Latitude : 48.67284

CALLAC

22160 – Michelin map **309** B4 – pop. 2,359 – alt. 172
▶ Paris 510 – Carhaix-Plouguer 22 – Guingamp 28 – Morlaix 41

Municipal Verte Vallée

☎ 02 96 45 58 50, commune@mairie-callac.fr
Address : pl. Jean Auffret (take the western exit along the D 28, follow the signs for Morlaix and turn left onto av. Ernest-Renan; 50m from a small lake)
Opening times : from mid June to mid Sept.
1 ha (60 pitches) relatively flat, flat, grassy, lake
Tariff : (2012 price) ♣ 2.60€ ⇔ 1.30€ 国 2€ – (₴) (32A) 2€
⊡ sani-station 2€ – 8 国
Surroundings : ⌂ ⊡ ♀♀
Leisure activities : ✗ ♠ ⚐
Facilities : & ⊶ (Jul–Aug) ⅌

GPS Longitude : -3.43765
Latitude : 48.40174

CAMARET-SUR-MER

29570 – Michelin map **308** D5 – pop. 2,576 – alt. 4
▶ Paris 597 – Brest 4 – Châteaulin 45 – Crozon 11

Le Grand Large

℘ 02 98 27 91 41, *www.campinglegrandlarge.com*
Address : at Lambézen (3km northeast along the D 355 and take turning to the right; 400m from the beach)
Opening times : from beginning April to end Sept.
2.8 ha (123 pitches) flat and relatively flat, grassy
Tariff : 27.30€ ♣ ♣ ⬅ 回 ⚡ (10A) – Extra per person 4.90€ – Reservation fee 16€
Rental rates : (from beginning April to end Sept.) – 27 🚐 – 3 🏠. Per night from 40 to 93 €
Per week from 245 to 750 € – Reservation fee 16€
🚽 sani-station
Surroundings : 🏞 ⬅ 🗔
Leisure activities : 🍴 🎱 ⛵ ⛰ 🏊 ⛷
Facilities : ♿ o⟶ 回⟨⟩ ⛲ 🚿 ⚙ launderette 🏊 🐎

GPS Longitude : -4.56472 Latitude : 48.28083

CAMORS

56330 – Michelin map **308** M7 – pop. 2,788 – alt. 113
▶ Paris 472 – Auray 24 – Lorient 39 – Pontivy 31

Municipal du Petit Bois

℘ 02 97 39 18 36, *www.camors56.com*
Address : r. des Mésanges (located 1km west along the D 189, follow the signs for Lambel-Camors)
1 ha (30 pitches) terraced, flat, grassy
🚽 sani-station
Near lakes and a national forest.

Surroundings : 🏞 ⚲
Facilities : ♿ ⛲ 🚿 🚽 🔲
Nearby : ⛲ 🎣 sports trail

GPS Longitude : -3.01304 Latitude : 47.84613

We have selected the best campsites in France with our usual care,
listing those with the best facilities in the most pleasant surroundings.

CANCALE

35260 – Michelin map **309** K2 – pop. 5,374 – alt. 50
▶ Paris 398 – Avranches 61 – Dinan 35 – Fougères 73

Le Bois Pastel

℘ 02 99 89 66 10, *www.campingboispastel.fr*
Address : 13 r. de la Corgnais (7km northwest along the D 201 coast road and take the turning to the left)
Opening times : from beginning April to end Sept.
5.2 ha (250 pitches) flat, grassy
Tariff : ♣ 4.70€ ⬅ 2€ 回 11€ – ⚡ (6A) 4€ – Reservation fee 15€
Rental rates : (permanent) – 19 🚐 – 6 tent bungalows. Per week from 220 to 660€
Reservation fee 15€
🚽 sani-station 4.50€
Surroundings : 🏞 ⚲⚲
Leisure activities : 🍴 ⛲ 🔲 (open-air in season)
Facilities : ♿ o⟶ ⚙ launderette 🏊 🐎

GPS Longitude : -1.86861 Latitude : 48.68875

CAP-COZ

29170 – Michelin map **308** H7
▶ Paris 558 – Rennes 207 – Quimper 22 – Brest 93

Pen an Cap

☏ 02 98 56 09 23, www.penancap.com – **R**
Address : 27 rte du Port Cap Coz (north of the resort; 300m from the beach)
Opening times : from beginning May to mid Sept.
1.3 ha (100 pitches) relatively flat, grassy, fruit trees
Tariff : (2012 price) 19.20€ ♣♣ ⟺ ▣ ⚡ (10A) – Extra per person 4.60€
Rental rates : (from beginning May to mid Sept.) – 9 ⟤. Per night from 55 to 60€
Per week from 560€

Surroundings : 🌲 ♉♉
Leisure activities : 🎣 ⚡ 🏊
Facilities : ⊶ 🗑 launderette
Nearby : 🍴 🛶

GPS Longitude : -3.98915
Latitude : 47.89132

CARANTEC

29660 – Michelin map **308** H2 – pop. 3,249 – alt. 37
▶ Paris 552 – Brest 71 – Lannion 53 – Morlaix 14

Yelloh! Village Les Mouettes ♣♣

☏ 02 98 67 02 46, www.les-mouettes.com – limited spaces for one-night stay
Address : 50 rte de la Grande Grève (located 1.5km southwest following the signs for St-Pol-de-Léon and take right turn.)
Opening times : from mid April to mid Sept.
14 ha (434 pitches) flat, terraced, grassy, lake
Tariff : 47€ ♣♣ ⟺ ▣ ⚡ (10A) – Extra per person 9€
Rental rates : (from mid April to mid Sept.) ♿ ⓟ – 315 ⟤ – 34 ⌂.
Per night from 39 to 219 € – Per week from 250 to 1,533 €
⟤ sani-station
Landscaped water park with giant waterchutes and upmarket rental options.

Surroundings : 🌲 ⟟ ♉
Leisure activities : 🍴 ✕ 🎣 ☷ 🏃 ≋ jacuzzi ⚡ 🚲 🍴 ♣ 🔲 🏊 ⚡
library, spa therapy centre, entertainment room
Facilities : ♿ ⊶ 🛁 🗑 ⟲ ⚡ launderette 🗑 🗑

GPS Longitude : -3.92802
Latitude : 48.65922

CARHAIX-PLOUGUER

29270 – Michelin map **308** J5 – pop. 7,717 – alt. 138
▶ Paris 506 – Brest 86 – Concarneau 66 – Guingamp 49

Municipal de la Vallée de l'Hyères

☏ 02 98 99 10 58, www.ville-carhaix.com
Address : rte de Kerniguez (head 2.3km west towards Morlaix and take turning in front of the police station; beside the Hyères river)
1 ha (62 pitches) flat, grassy
Rentals : 3 ⟤.
Decorative trees and shrubs, near some lakes.

Surroundings : 🌲 ♉♉
Leisure activities : 🍴
Facilities : ⊶ launderette
Nearby : 🏇 fitness trail, forest trail

GPS Longitude : -3.60202
Latitude : 48.27758

CARNAC

56340 – Michelin map **308** M9 – pop. 4,362 – alt. 16
▶ Paris 490 – Auray 13 – Lorient 49 – Quiberon 19

Les Castels La Grande Métairie ▲▪

℘ 02 97 52 24 01, *www.lagrandemetairie.com* – limited spaces for one-night stay
Address : rte de Kerlescan (2.5km to the northeast)
Opening times : from end March to beginning Sept.
15 ha/11 ha for camping (575 pitches) flat and relatively flat, grassy
Tariff : (2012 price) ♣ 8€ ⇐ 🚗 📧 26€ – (½) (10A) 2€
Rental rates : (2012 price) (from end March to beginning Sept.) ♿ – 8 caravans – 177 🏠 –
2 cabins in the trees. Per night from 70 to 300€ – Per week from 245 to 1,660€
🚰 sani-station 6€
Site beside the Étang de Kerloquet (lake) with a range of very comfortable rental options.

Surroundings : 🏕 ♧♧
Leisure activities : ♥ ✗ 🎦 ⑨ (open-air theatre) 🏓 jacuzzi ⚓ 🚲
❄ 🎿 🏊 🏖 disco (14-18 years), zip wiring, forest trail, scuba diving,
mountain biking, skate park
Facilities : ♿ ⊶ 🏢 🖙 🚿 🐟 🍴 launderette 🚮 🐾

GPS
Longitude : -3.05975
Latitude : 47.59647

Kawan Village Le Moustoir ▲▪

℘ 02 97 52 16 18, *www.lemoustoir.com*
Address : 71 rte du Moustoir (situated 3km to the northeast)
Opening times : from mid April to mid Sept.
5 ha (165 pitches) flat and relatively flat, grassy
Tariff : (2012 price) ♣ 5.50€ ⇐ 🚗 📧 20€ – (½) (10A) 5.50€
Rental rates : (2012 price) (from mid April to mid Sept.) – 80 🏠 – 20 🏠 – 4 ⊨.
Per night from 45 to 120€ – Per week from 210 to 900€
🚰 sani-station
Surroundings : 🏕 ♧♧
Leisure activities : ♥ ✗ 🎦 ⑨ 🏓 ⚓ ❄ 🎿 🏊 🏖 zip wiring
Facilities : ♿ ⊶ 🏢 🚿 🐟 🍴 launderette 🚮 🐾

GPS
Longitude : -3.06689
Latitude : 47.60829

Moulin de Kermaux ▲▪

℘ 02 97 52 15 90, *www.camping-moulinkermaux.com*
Address : rte de Kerlescan (2.5km to the northeast)
Opening times : from mid April to mid Sept.
3 ha (150 pitches) flat and relatively flat, grassy
Tariff : ♣ 5.30€ ⇐ 🚗 📧 22.50€ (½) (15A) – Reservation fee 18€
Rental rates : (from mid April to mid Sept.) ♿ – 70 🏠 – 3 tent bungalows. Per night 160€
Per week from 210 to 800€ – Reservation fee 20€

Surroundings : 🐟 🏕 ♧
Leisure activities : ♥ ✗ 🎦 ⑨ 🏓 ☲ jacuzzi ⚓ ❄ 🏊 (open-air in
season) 🏖 multi-sports ground
Facilities : ♿ ⊶ 🚿 🍴 launderette 🐾
Nearby : 🐎

GPS
Longitude : -3.06523
Latitude : 47.59512

*Using the traditional Michelin classification method, the guide provides
you with an easy, speedy reference for assessing the category of each site:
1 to 5 tents (see page 10).*

Flower Le Lac

✆ 02 97 55 78 78, *www.lelac-carnac.com*

Address : Passage du Lac (6.3km to the northeast; beside the lake)
Opening times : from beginning April to end Oct.
2.5 ha (140 pitches) terraced, flat, grassy
Tariff : (2012 price) 👤 5.20€ 🚗 📱 12€ – ⚡ (4A) 5€
Rental rates : (2012 price) (from beginning April to end Sept.) – 3 caravans – 22 🚐 – 2 🛏 – 2 tent bungalows. Per night from 45 to 85 € – Per week from 196 to 595 €
🚰 sani-station

Surroundings :
Leisure activities : multi-sports ground
Facilities : launderette
Nearby :

GPS	Longitude : -3.02912
	Latitude : 47.61117

Kérabus

✆ 02 97 52 24 90, *www.camping-kerabus.com*

Address : 13 allée des Alouettes (situated 2km to the northeast)
Opening times : from beginning May to mid Sept.
1.4 ha (86 pitches) flat, grassy
Tariff : 👤 5€ 🚗 📱 8.80€ – ⚡ (6A) 3.45€
Rental rates : (from beginning April to end Sept.) – 7 🚐. Per night from 44 to 147 €
Per week from 202 to 650 €
🚰 sani-station 3.50€ – ⚡10€

Surroundings :
Leisure activities : multi-sports ground
Facilities : launderette

GPS	Longitude : -3.07648
	Latitude : 47.59641

Les Bruyères

✆ 02 97 52 30 57, *www.camping-lesbruyeres.com*

Address : at Kérogile (3km to the north)
Opening times : from beginning April to end Sept.
2 ha (115 pitches) flat, grassy
Tariff : 26.20€ 👤👤 📱 ⚡ (10A) – Extra per person 6€ – Reservation fee 10€
Rental rates : (from beginning April to end Sept.) – 26 🚐. Per night from 28 to 119 €
Per week from 196 to 833 € – Reservation fee 20€
🚰 sani-station

Surroundings :
Leisure activities : (open-air in season)
Facilities :
Nearby : bowling

GPS	Longitude : -3.08884
	Latitude : 47.60437

L'Étang

✆ 02 97 52 14 06, *www.camping-etang.fr*

Address : at Kerlann (head 2km north along the D 119 towards Auray then take left turning, 50m from a lake)
2.5 ha (165 pitches) flat, grassy
Rentals : 9 🚐 – (with/without sanitary facilities).

Surroundings :
Leisure activities : multi-sports ground
Facilities : launderette
Nearby :

GPS	Longitude : -3.08137
	Latitude : 47.60107

Vacances Directes Le Domaine de Kermario
(rental of mobile homes and gîtes only)

☏ 0825 13 34 00, *www.campingkermario.com*

Address : 1 chemin de Kerluir (situated 2km to the northeast)

Opening times : from mid April to end Sept.

4 ha flat, lake

Rental rates : (2012 price) ℗ – 123 🚐 – 9 gîtes. Per night from 31 to 105€
Per week from 217 to 735 € – Reservation fee 20€

Furnished gîtes in an old farmhouse that has been beautifully restored.

Surroundings : ☜ 🎿
Leisure activities : ✕ 🎣 🕹 👫 🚵 🎠 ⚓ entertainment room
Facilities : ⛽ 🍴 launderette 🚿

GPS Longitude : -3.06636
Latitude : 47.59521

CARNAC-PLAGE

56340 – Michelin map **308** M9
▶ Paris 494 – Rennes 143 – Vannes 34

Les Menhirs ♨♨

☏ 02 97 52 94 67, *www.lesmenhirs.com* – limited spaces for one-night stay

Address : allée Saint Michel

Opening times : from mid April to end Sept.

6 ha (360 pitches) flat, grassy

Tariff : 🚶 8.30€ 🚗 ▣ 30.45€ – ⚡ (10A) 4.30€ – Reservation fee 20€

Rental rates : (from mid April to end Sept.) ♿ (1 mobile home) ⚡ – 61 🚐 – 1 🏠 –
2 cabins. Per night from 85 to 141€ – Per week from 392 to 999€ – Reservation fee 20€

🚾 sani-station

400m from the beach and the town centre.

Surroundings : ☜ 🏛 🎣
Leisure activities : 🏓 🏟 🕹 👫 🎿 ♨ jacuzzi 🚵 ✂ 🎬 ⚓ 🎯
multi-sports ground, spa therapy centre, entertainment room
Facilities : ♿ ⛽ 🚿 🍴 launderette 🍽 🚿
Nearby : 🛒 🚴

GPS Longitude : -3.06979
Latitude : 47.57683

Les Druides

☏ 02 97 52 08 18, *www.camping-les-druides.com*

Address : 55 ch. de Beaumer (To the east, in part of town called Beaumer, 500m from the beach)

Opening times : from mid April to beginning Sept.

2.5 ha (110 pitches) flat and relatively flat, grassy

Tariff : 38.10€ 🚶🚶 🚗 ▣ ⚡ (10A) – Extra per person 6.80€ – Reservation fee 20€

Rental rates : (from beginning April to beginning Sept.) ⚡ – 15 🚐 – 3 apartments.
Per week from 265 to 770€ – Reservation fee 20€

🚾 sani-station

Surroundings : 🎿
Leisure activities : 🏟 🚵 ⚓ multi-sports ground
Facilities : ♿ ⛽ 🚿 🍴 launderette
Nearby : 🛒

GPS Longitude : -3.05689
Latitude : 47.58012

Do not confuse:
⛺ to ⛺⛺⛺⛺⛺ : MICHELIN classification
with
★ to ★★★★★ : official classification

Le Men-Du

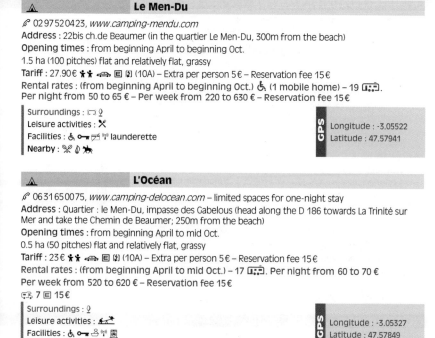

℘ 02 97 52 04 23, www.camping-mendu.com
Address : 22bis ch.de Beaumer (in the quartier Le Men-Du, 300m from the beach)
Opening times : from beginning April to beginning Oct.
1.5 ha (100 pitches) flat and relatively flat, grassy
Tariff : 27.90€ ♣♣ ⇔ 回 ⊕ (10A) – Extra per person 5€ – Reservation fee 15€
Rental rates : (from beginning April to beginning Oct.) ⅙ (1 mobile home) – 19 ⌷⍰.
Per night from 50 to 65 € – Per week from 220 to 630 € – Reservation fee 15€

Surroundings : ⌷ ℚ
Leisure activities : ✕
Facilities : ⅙ ⊶ ⊠ ♈ launderette
Nearby : ※ ◊ ☃

GPS Longitude : -3.05522
Latitude : 47.57941

L'Océan

℘ 06 31 65 00 75, www.camping-delocean.com – limited spaces for one-night stay
Address : Quartier : le Men-Du, impasse des Gabelous (head along the D 186 towards La Trinité sur Mer and take the Chemin de Beaumer; 250m from the beach)
Opening times : from beginning April to mid Oct.
0.5 ha (50 pitches) flat and relatively flat, grassy
Tariff : 23€ ♣♣ ⇔ 回 ⊕ (10A) – Extra per person 5€ – Reservation fee 15€
Rental rates : (from beginning April to mid Oct.) – 17 ⌷⍰. Per night from 60 to 70 €
Per week from 520 to 620 € – Reservation fee 15€
⌷⍰ 7 回 15€

Surroundings : ℚ
Leisure activities : ♐
Facilities : ⅙ ⊶ ♈ 回
Nearby : ⌷ ※ ◊ ☃

GPS Longitude : -3.05327
Latitude : 47.57849

Some information or pricing may have changed since the guide went to press.
We recommend you check the price list online in advance or at the entrance
to the campsite and enquire about possible restrictions.

CAUREL

22530 – Michelin map **309** D5 – pop. 381 – alt. 188
▶ Paris 461 – Carhaix-Plouguer 45 – Guingamp 48 – Loudéac 24

Nautic International

℘ 02 96 28 57 94, www.campingnautic.fr
Address : rte de Beau Rivage (situated 2km southwest along the D 111; beside the lake at Guerlédan)
Opening times : from mid May to mid Sept.
3.6 ha (100 pitches) terraced, flat and relatively flat, grassy, very uneven
Tariff : 28.90€ ♣♣ ⇔ 回 ⊕ (10A) – Extra per person 6€ – Reservation fee 22.90€
Rental rates : (from mid May to mid Sept.) – 5 ⌷⍰. Per week from 280 to 610 €
Reservation fee 22.90€

Leafy, woodland setting.

Surroundings : ⌷ ℚ ℚ △
Leisure activities : ⌷ ♐ ※ ⍠ ⌇
Facilities : ⅙ ⊶ △ ⊌ launderette ⊠
Nearby : ♈ ✕ ⚓ water skiing

GPS Longitude : -3.04847
Latitude : 48.2069

LA CHAPELLE-AUX-FILTZMEENS

35190 – Michelin map **309** L4 – pop. 726 – alt. 40
▶ Paris 388 – Rennes 39 – Saint-Malo 42 – Fougères 83

Le Domaine du Logis

℘ 02 99 45 25 45, *www.domainedulogis.com*
Address : at Le Logis (located 1.5km west on the D 13, follow the signs for St-Domineuc)
Opening times : from beginning April to beginning Nov.
20 ha/6 ha for camping (180 pitches) flat, grassy
Tariff : 30€ ♦♦ ⟺ 🗐 🌢 (16A) – Extra per person 5.50€
Rental rates : (from beginning April to beginning Nov.) – 20 🛏. Per night from 65 to 80€
Per week from 300 to 780€ – Reservation fee 10€
🚐 🛒 🌢20€

Surroundings : 🛏 ♀
Leisure activities : ♟ ✕ 🖼 🏋 🎣 🏊 ♒ 🎿 mountain biking
Facilities : ♿ ⟜ 🖾 🚿 launderette 🛒
Nearby : ⟋

GPS Longitude : -1.83566
Latitude : 48.38306

In order for the guide to remain wholly objective, the selection of campsites is made on an entirely independent basis.

CHÂTEAUGIRON

35410 – Michelin map **309** M6 – pop. 6,450 – alt. 45
▶ Paris 336 – Angers 114 – Châteaubriant 45 – Fougères 56

Les Grands Bosquets

℘ 02 99 37 89 02, *www.tourisme-payschateaugiron.fr*
Address : rte d'Ossé (take the eastern exit along the D 34)
Opening times : from end April to beginning Sept.
0.6 ha (33 pitches) flat, grassy
Tariff : 60€ ♦♦ ⟺ 🗐 🌢 (0A) – Extra per person 2€
Beside a small lake.

Surroundings : ♀♀
Leisure activities : 🏖 (beach) ⟋
Facilities : 🗑
Nearby : 🎣 ✕

GPS Longitude : -1.49734
Latitude : 48.04983

CHÂTELAUDREN

22170 – Michelin map **309** E3 – pop. 1,047 – alt. 105
▶ Paris 469 – Guingamp 17 – Lannion 49 – St-Brieuc 18

Municipal de l'Étang

℘ 02 96 74 10 38, *www.chatelaudren.fr* – ℞
Address : r. de la Gare (in the town; beside a large, beautiful lake)
Opening times : from beginning May to end Sept.
0.2 ha (17 pitches) open site, flat, grassy
Tariff : (2012 price) ♦ 2.90€ ⟺ 1€ 🗐 4.10€ – 🌢 (10A) 2.90€

Surroundings : 🛏 ♀
Leisure activities : ⟋
Facilities : 🗑
Nearby : 🎣

GPS Longitude : -2.9709
Latitude : 48.53883

CHÂTILLON-EN-VENDELAIS

35210 – Michelin map **309** O5 – pop. 1,698 – alt. 133
▶ Paris 311 – Fougères 17 – Rennes 49 – Vitré 13

▲ Municipal du Lac

📞 02 99 76 06 32, *www.chatillon-en-vendelais.fr*
Address : rte de Parce, at l'Épine (500m north along the D 108; beside the Étang de Châtillon)
Opening times : from beginning May to end Sept.
0.6 ha (61 pitches) relatively flat, grassy
Tariff : ♦ 2.56 € ⇌ 1.24 € 回 1.92 € – 劇 (6A) 3.51 €
Rental rates : (permanent) – 1 🏠. Per night from 43 € – Per week from 215 €
🚏 sani-station – 5 回 – 💧劇12 €
Pleasant location and green setting.

Surroundings : 🌄 ≤ 🗔 ♨ ⛰
Leisure activities : 🎣
Facilities : 📶 Ⅲ
Nearby : 🍷 ✗ ⛵ pedalos

GPS Longitude : -1.18026
Latitude : 48.22909

CLÉDEN-CAP-SIZUN

29770 – Michelin map **308** D6 – pop. 1,003 – alt. 30
▶ Paris 608 – Audierne 11 – Douarnenez 27 – Quimper 46

▲ La Baie

📞 02 98 70 64 28– ⛩
Address : at Lescleden (2.5km west)
Opening times : permanent
0.4 ha (27 pitches) relatively flat, terrace, grassy
Tariff : ♦ 3.40 € ⇌ 2.20 € 回 3.50 € – 劇 (8A) 2.50 €

Surroundings : 🌄 ≤
Leisure activities : 🍷 ✗
Facilities : ⊶ 📶 🔧

GPS Longitude : -4.68312
Latitude : 48.04842

CONCARNEAU

29900 – Michelin map **308** H7 – pop. 19,352 – alt. 4
▶ Paris 546 – Brest 96 – Lorient 49 – Quimper 22

⚠ Les Sables Blancs ♠♦

📞 02 98 97 16 44, *www.camping-lessablesblancs.com*
Address : r. des Fleurs (100m from the beach)
Opening times : from beginning April to end Oct.
3 ha (149 pitches) terraced, relatively flat, flat, grassy
Tariff : (2012 price) 29 € ♦♦ ⇌ 回 劇 (13A) – Extra per person 7 €
Rental rates : (2012 price) (from beginning April to end Oct.) – 31 🚐 – 2 🏠.
Per night from 90 to 130 € – Per week from 220 to 760 €
🚏 sani-station
Some pitches with a sea view.

Surroundings : 🌄 🗔 ♨
Leisure activities : 🍷 ✗ 🎮 🏃 ⛹ ⛷
Facilities : ♿ ⊶ 🔥 launderette 🔧
Nearby : 🎐

GPS Longitude : -3.92836
Latitude : 47.88203

Les Prés Verts

ℰ 02 98 97 09 74, *www.presverts.com*
Address : Kernous-Plage BP 612 (3km northwest along the coast road and take left turn; 250m from the beach (direct access)
3 ha (150 pitches) relatively flat, sloping, flat, grassy
Rentals : 4 ⛺ – 6 🏠.
🚰 sani-station
Some pitches with a sea view.

Surroundings : 🏞
Leisure activities : 🎱 🏊 ⓜ 🛶
Facilities : ⚟ 🍴 launderette
Nearby : 🛒

GPS
Longitude : -3.93333
Latitude : 47.88333

LE CONQUET

29217 – Michelin map **308** C4 – pop. 2,635 – alt. 30
▶ Paris 619 – Brest 24 – Brignogan-Plages 59 – St-Pol-de-Léon 85

Les Blancs Sablons

ℰ 02 98 36 07 91, *www.les-blancs-sablons.com*
Address : at Le Théven (5km northeast along the D 67 and take D 28, follow the signs for the beach at Les Blancs Sablons, 400m from the beach – passenger walkway to town)
Opening times : from mid March to mid Nov.
12 ha (360 pitches) flat, grassy, sandy
Tariff : (2012 price) 15.50€ ✶✶ 🚐 ▣ 🔌 (16A) – Extra per person 4.50€
Rental rates : (2012 price) (permanent) – 8 ⛺ – 3 🏠. Per night from 65 to 90 €
Per week from 270 to 670€
In a lovely wild and natural setting, near the beach.

Surroundings : 🏞 🚤
Leisure activities : 🍷 🍴 🎯 🛶
Facilities : ♿ ⚟ launderette

GPS
Longitude : -4.76071
Latitude : 48.36687

There are several different types of sani-station ('borne' in French) – sanitation points providing fresh water and disposal points for grey water. See page 12 for further details.

CRACH

56950 – Michelin map **308** M9 – pop. 3,276 – alt. 35
▶ Paris 482 – Auray 6 – Lorient 46 – Quiberon 29

Le Fort Espagnol

ℰ 02 97 55 14 88, *www.fort-espagnol.com*
Address : rte du Fort Espagnol (800m east, follow the signs for La Rivière d'Auray)
5 ha (190 pitches) relatively flat, flat, grassy
Rentals : 1 caravan – 16 ⛺ – 4 🏠 – 10 tent bungalows – 2 tents.

Surroundings : 🏞 🚤 ♨
Leisure activities : 🍷 🍴 🎱 🏊 🛶 ⛳
Facilities : ♿ ⚟ 🎨 launderette 🚿
Nearby : 🛒 🍴 ⛵

GPS
Longitude : -2.98988
Latitude : 47.61539

CROZON

29160 – Michelin map **308** E5 – pop. 7,697 – alt. 85
▶ Paris 587 – Brest 60 – Châteaulin 35 – Douarnenez 40

Les Pins

📞 06 60 54 40 09, *www.camping-crozon-lespins.com*
Address : rte de Dinan (situated 2km southwest along the D 308 follow the signs for La Pointe de Dinan (headland)
Opening times : from mid May to mid Sept.
4 ha (155 pitches) open site, flat, sloping, grassy, sandy
Tariff : ☆ 4.60€ ⟺ 🔲 9€ – 🔌 (10A) 3.50€
Rental rates : (from mid March to mid Nov.) ♿ – 11 🛏 – 13 🏠. Per night from 60 to 87 €
Per week from 420 to 609 €

Surroundings : 🗠🗠
Leisure activities : ⟿ 🔳 (small swimming pool)
Facilities : ♿ ⟿ 🗑 🛁 ♍
Nearby : forest trail

Longitude : -4.51462
Latitude : 48.24153

DINÉAULT

29150 – Michelin map **308** G5 – pop. 1,739 – alt. 160
▶ Paris 560 – Rennes 208 – Quimper 36 – Brest 54

Ty Provost

📞 02 98 86 29 23, *www.typrovost.com*
Address : 4km southeast along the C 1, follow the signs for Châteaulin and take road to the left
Opening times : from beginning June to mid Sept.
1.2 ha (44 pitches) terraced, flat and relatively flat, grassy
Tariff : 16€ ☆☆ ⟺ 🔲 🔌 (10A) – Extra per person 4€
Rental rates : (permanent) ♿ (2 chalets) – 5 🛏 – 7 🏠 – 1 studio – 1 gîte.
Per night from 49 to 69 € – Per week from 297 to 454 €
🚽 sani-station – 4 🔲 12€
Pleasant site and setting.

Surroundings : ⩽ 🗠
Leisure activities : 🍷 🛶 ⟿
Facilities : ♿ ⟿ 🛁 ♍ launderette

Longitude : -4.12421
Latitude : 48.20706

DOL-DE-BRETAGNE

35120 – Michelin map **309** L3 – pop. 5,163 – alt. 20
▶ Paris 378 – Alençon 154 – Dinan 26 – Fougères 54

Les Castels Domaine des Ormes

📞 02 99 73 53 00, *www.lesormes.com* – limited spaces for one-night stay
Address : at Épiniac (7.5km south along the D 795, follow the signs for Combourg then take the road to the left)
Opening times : from end April to beginning Sept.
200 ha/40 ha for camping (750 pitches) relatively flat, flat, grassy, forest
Tariff : (2012 price) 58.90€ ☆☆ ⟺ 🔲 🔌 (16A) – Extra per person 7.80€ – Reservation fee 20€
Rental rates : (2012 price) (permanent) – 81 🛏 – 38 🏠 – 45 🛏 – 11 studios – 25 apartments – 30 cabins in the trees – 4 gîtes. Per night from 75 to 290€ – Per week from 390 to 2,030€
Reservation fee 20€
🚽 sani-station
In the grounds of a 16th-century château, with wide spaces and plenty of activities including a partially covered water park.

Surroundings : 🌳 ⩽ 🗠🗠
Leisure activities : 🍷 ✕ 🛶 🎣 🕴 🛝 ⛱ ⟿ 🚲 ✂ ♒ 🔳 🏊 ⛸ 🏹
🏇 disco, climbing wall, forest trail, golf course & driving range,
multi-sports ground, water park, entertainment room
Facilities : ♿ ⟿ ♍ launderette 🗑 🛒

Longitude : -1.72722
Latitude : 48.49139

Le Vieux Chêne

ℰ 0299480955, *www.camping-vieuxchene.fr*
Address : rte de Pontorson (5km east, along the N 176, follow the signs for Pontorson, east of Baguer-Pican on the D 57 – Recommended route via the diversion, take exit Dol-de-Bretagne-Est and take D 80, D 576)
Opening times : from mid May to mid Sept.
4 ha/2 ha for camping (199 pitches) relatively flat, flat, grassy
Tariff : 30.60€ ✚ ✚ ⇔ 🔲 (½) (10A) – Extra per person 5.25€
Rental rates : (from mid April to mid Sept.) – 18 🛖 – 18 🏠. Per week from 259 to 765€
🚐 sani-station 5€ – 2 🔲 30.60€
A pleasant location near some lakes.

Surroundings : 🐾 ⌑ 🎿
Leisure activities : ♟ ✕ 🎱 ⛵ ✂ ♞ 🏊 🎿 🐎
Facilities : ♿ ⌂ ▥ 🚿 ⌬ ⌦ 🍴 launderette 🧺 🔧

Longitude : -1.68361
Latitude : 48.54945

For more information on visiting particular towns or regions, consult the relevant regional MICHELIN Green Guide. We also recommend you use the appropriate Michelin regional map to locate your selected campsite, to calculate distances and to work out the best route.

ERDEVEN

56410 – Michelin map **308** M9 – pop. 3,402 – alt. 18
▶ Paris 492 – Auray 15 – Carnac 10 – Lorient 28

La Croëz-Villieu

ℰ 0297559043, *www.la-croez-villieu.com* – limited spaces for one-night stay
Address : at Kernogan, rte de Kerhillio (located 1km southwest along the beach road at Kerhillio)
Opening times : from beginning May to end Sept.
3 ha (158 pitches) flat, grassy
Tariff : (2012 price) 29.70€ ✚ ✚ ⇔ 🔲 (½) (6A) – Extra per person 6.60€
Rental rates : (2012 price) (from beginning April to mid Oct.) – 26 🛖.
Per night from 115 to 220€ – Per week from 255 to 770€
Partially covered water park.

Surroundings : 🐾 ⌑ 🎿
Leisure activities : 🛁 hammam, jacuzzi 🔲 🏊 🎿
Facilities : ⌂ 🚿 ⌬ 🍴 launderette
Nearby : 🐎

Longitude : -3.15838
Latitude : 47.63199

L' Idéal

ℰ 0297556766, *www.camping-l-ideal.com* – limited spaces for one-night stay
Address : rte de la plage
Opening times : from beginning April to end Sept.
0.6 ha (30 pitches) flat, grassy
Tariff : (2012 price) 35€ ✚ ✚ ⇔ 🔲 (½) (20A) – Extra per person 5.30€ – Reservation fee 20€
Rental rates : (2012 price) (from beginning April to end Sept.) – 27 🛖 – 3 🏠 – 4 apartments.
Per night from 37 to 117 € – Per week from 260 to 819 € – Reservation fee 20€
🚐 2 🔲 35€

Surroundings : 🐾 🎿
Leisure activities : 🛁 🔲
Facilities : ♿ ⌂ 🍴 launderette

Longitude : -3.16317
Latitude : 47.62115

ERQUY

22430 – Michelin map **309** H3 – pop. 3,802 – alt. 12
▶ Paris 451 – Dinan 46 – Dinard 39 – Lamballe 21

Le Vieux Moulin ▲▲

🖉 02 96 72 34 23, *www.camping-vieux-moulin.com*
Address : 14 r. des Moulins (situated 2km east)
Opening times : from mid April to beginning Sept.
2.5 ha (173 pitches) flat, grassy
Tariff : 39€ ♦♦ ⇔ 🔲 ⛽ (10A) – Extra per person 7€ – Reservation fee 13€
Rental rates : (from mid April to beginning Sept.) – 72 🔲. Per night from 47 to 143 €
Per week from 329 to 1,001 €
🚽 sani-station 5€
Well-kept, green setting.

Surroundings : ⌐ 🌿🌿
Leisure activities : 🍷 ✕ 🏠 🚴 🛶 ⛵ 🔲 🏊 🎣 multi-sports ground
Facilities : ᵬ ⊶ 🛁 🔥 ⚐ 🍴 launderette 🚿 🛒
Nearby : 🏌 🎯 ⛴

GPS
Longitude : -2.44249
Latitude : 48.63828

Yelloh! Village Les Pins ▲▲

🖉 02 96 72 31 12, *www.yellohvillage.fr/camping/les_pins.com*
Address : at Le Guen, r. des Moulins (located 1km to the north, on the corner of r. des Moulins and r. Léon Hamonet)
10 ha (488 pitches) relatively flat, flat, grassy
Rentals : ᵬ – 136 🔲 – 6 🏠 – 11 tent bungalows.

Surroundings : 🏖 ⌐ 🌿🌿
Leisure activities : 🍷 ✕ 🏠 🎮 🚴 🛶 ⛴ hammam, jacuzzi 🛶 🏌 🔲
🏊 🎣 spa centre
Facilities : ᵬ ⊶ 🛁 🍴 launderette 🚿 🛒
Nearby : ⛴

GPS
Longitude : -2.45573
Latitude : 48.63802

Bellevue ▲▲

🖉 02 96 72 33 04, *http://www.campingbellevue.fr*
Address : rte de la Libération (5.5km southwest)
Opening times : from mid April to mid Sept.
3.5 ha (160 pitches) flat, grassy
Tariff : 22.50€ ♦♦ ⇔ 🔲 ⛽ (10A) – Extra per person 5.40€
Rental rates : (from mid April to mid Sept.) – 20 🔲 – 4 tents. Per night from 45 to 102€
Per week from 270 to 720€
🚽 sani-station – 10 🔲 16.50€ – 🚐14€
Entrance surrounded by flowers, pitches surrounded by trees and shrubs.

Surroundings : ⌐ 🌿🌿
Leisure activities : 🍷 🏠 🚴 🛶 ⛴ 🔲 (open-air in season),
multi-sports ground
Facilities : ᵬ ⊶ 🛁 🍴 launderette 🛒
Nearby : 🚿

GPS
Longitude : -2.48486
Latitude : 48.59377

---

*The classification (1 to 5 tents, **black or red**) that we award to selected sites
in this guide is our own system. It should not be confused with the
classification (1 to 5 stars) of official organisations.*

St-Pabu

📞 0296722465, www.saintpabu.com
Address : at St-Pabu (at the beach at Saint-Pabu, 4km southwest)
Opening times : from beginning April to mid Oct.
5.5 ha (409 pitches) terraced, flat, grassy
Tariff : 26.25€ ♦♦ ⇌ 🔳 ⚡ (10A) – Extra per person 5.90€ – Reservation fee 20€
Rental rates : (from beginning April to mid Oct.) – 37 🚐. Per night from 65 to 101€
Per week from 275 to 705€ – Reservation fee 20€
🚾 sani-station 6€
By the Baie d'Erquy.

Surroundings : 🏖 ← 🏕 ⛰
Leisure activities : 🍷 🏓 🏇
Facilities : ♿ ⚡ 🏠 🍴 launderette 🧺
Nearby : 🤿 scuba diving, sand yachting

GPS Longitude : -2.49459
Latitude : 48.60878

Les Roches

📞 0296723290, www.camping-les-roches.com
Address : r. Pierre Vergos (3km southwest)
Opening times : from beginning April to end Sept.
3 ha (160 pitches) flat, terraced, grassy
Tariff : ♦ 3.90€ ⇌ 2.90€ 🔳 5.80€ – ⚡ (10A) 3.70€ – Reservation fee 8€
Rental rates : (from beginning April to end Sept.) – 18 🚐. Per night from 44 to 59€
Per week from 250 to 640€ – Reservation fee 8€
🚾 sani-station
Near the beach and Caroual Village.

Surroundings : 🏖 🌊
Leisure activities : 🏓 🏇 ⛰
Facilities : ♿ ⚡ 🏠 🍴 launderette 🧺

GPS Longitude : -2.4769
Latitude : 48.6094

Des Hautes Grées

📞 0296723478, www.camping-hautes-grees.com
Address : 123 r. St Michel, at Les Hopitaux (3.5km to the northeast, 400m from the St-Michel beach)
3 ha (177 pitches) flat, grassy
Rentals : 30 🚐.
🚾 sani-station

Surroundings : 🏖 🏕
Leisure activities : 🏓 🎣 ⛵ 🏇 🏊
Facilities : ♿ ⚡ 🏠 🍴 launderette

GPS Longitude : -2.42491
Latitude : 48.64254

Michelin classification:
🏔🏔🏔🏔 *Extremely comfortable, equipped to a very high standard*
🏔🏔🏔 *Very comfortable, equipped to a high standard*
🏔🏔 *Comfortable and well equipped*
🏔 *Reasonably comfortable*
⛰ *Satisfactory*

ÉTABLES-SUR-MER

22680 – Michelin map **309** E3 – pop. 3,091 – alt. 65
▶ Paris 467 – Guingamp 31 – Lannion 56 – St-Brieuc 19

L'Abri-Côtier

℘ 02 96 70 61 57, *www.camping-abricotier.fr*
Address : 12 r. De Robien (located 1km north following signs for St-Quay-Portrieux and take the turning to the left)
Opening times : from beginning May to mid Sept.
2 ha (140 pitches) flat and relatively flat, grassy
Tariff : 22.50€ ✝✝ ⇔ 🗐 (10A) – Extra per person 5€
Rental rates : (2012 price) (from beginning May to mid Sept.) – 14 🚐 – 5 tent bungalows. Per night 70€ – Per week from 230 to 610 €

Surroundings : ☜
Leisure activities : 🍷 jacuzzi ⊿
Facilities : ⅙ ⌑ 🏢 🛁 ⚁ ☞ ⛾ launderette ⚎ ⚄
Nearby : ℀ 🏌 🐴

GPS Longitude : -2.83529
Latitude : 48.6354

LE FAOUËT

56320 – Michelin map **308** J6 – pop. 2,893 – alt. 68
▶ Paris 516 – Carhaix-Plouguer 35 – Lorient 40 – Pontivy 47

Municipal Beg er Roch

℘ 02 97 23 15 11, *camping.lefaouet@wanadoo.fr*
Address : rte de Lorient (situated 2km southeast along the D 769, follow the signs for Lorient)
Opening times : from mid March to end Sept.
3 ha (65 pitches) flat, grassy
Tariff : (2012 price) ✝ 4€ ⇔ 2.35€ 🗐 3.55€ – (10A) 3€ – Reservation fee 9€
Rental rates : (2012 price) (from mid March to end Sept.) – 8 🚐. Per night from 56 to 60 € Per week from 216 to 423 € – Reservation fee 15€

Pleasant setting beside the Ellé river.

Surroundings : ♀
Leisure activities : 🎣 🏌 ⟋
Facilities : ⅙ ⌑ 🏢 ⚁ launderette

GPS Longitude : -3.46973
Latitude : 48.01794

FEINS

35440 – Michelin map **309** M5 – pop. 798 – alt. 104
▶ Paris 369 – Avranches 55 – Fougères 44 – Rennes 30

Municipal La Bijouterie

℘ 02 99 69 63 23, *www.pays-aubigne.fr/camping*
Address : at the Domaine de Boulet (situated 2km northeast along the D 91, follow the signs for Marcillé-Raoul and take road to the left)
Opening times : from beginning April to end Oct.
1.5 ha (62 pitches) flat, grassy
Tariff : (2012 price) 10€ ✝✝ ⇔ 🗐 (10A) – Extra per person 3.50€
Rental rates : (2012 price) (from beginning April to end Oct.) – 6 🏠. Per night from 42 to 57€ Per week from 191 to 760€

A pleasant location beside the lake.

Surroundings : ☜ ⟨ ▭ ♀ ⚠
Leisure activities : 🎣 🏄 ⟋
Facilities : ⅙ ⌑ (Jul–Aug) ⚁ ☞ ⛾ launderette, refrigerated food storage
Nearby : ℀ 🐴 🐴 watersports centre

GPS Longitude : -1.63863
Latitude : 48.33845

LA FORÊT-FOUESNANT

29940 – Michelin map **308** H7 – pop. 3,299 – alt. 19
▶ Paris 553 – Rennes 202 – Quimper 18 – Brest 94

Kerleven

🖉 02 98 56 98 83, *www.campingdekerleven.com*
Address : at at Kerleven, 11 rte de Port La Forêt, (situated 2km southeast, 200m from the beach)
Opening times : from mid April to end Sept.
4 ha (235 pitches) terraced, flat, grassy
Tariff : (2012 price) 🛉 7.50€ ⚎ 🔲 13€ – 🔌 (10A) 4.60€ – Reservation fee 9€
Rental rates : (2012 price) (from mid April to end Sept.) – 37 ⛽. Per night from 50 to 65€
Per week from 240 to 790€ – Reservation fee 9€
🚐 sani-station 2€

Surroundings : 🏕 🟊🟊
Leisure activities : ✗ 🎬 🕄evening 🎣 🔲 ⟙ 🏊
Facilities : ♿ ⚏🚿 🚰 launderette 🖳 🚿
Nearby : 🎣

GPS Longitude : -3.96788
Latitude : 47.89807

Club Airotel Kérantérec

🖉 02 98 56 98 11, *www.camping-keranterec.com*
Address : at Kerleven (2.8km southeast)
Opening times : from mid April to end Sept.
6.5 ha (265 pitches) relatively flat, terraced, flat, grassy, very uneven
Tariff : 16€ 🛉🛉 ⚎ 🔲 🔌 (10A) – Extra per person 8.50€ – Reservation fee 30€
Rental rates : (from mid April to end Sept.) – 52 ⛽. Per night from 60 to 100€
Per week from 220 to 900€ – Reservation fee 30€
🚐 sani-station 4€
Based around an old renovated farmhouse beside the ocean.

Surroundings : 🚣 🏕 🎣 ⛰
Leisure activities : ✗ 🎬 🕄 ✗ 🔲 ⟙ 🏊entertainment room
Facilities : ♿ ⚏🚿 🚿 🚽 🚰 launderette

GPS Longitude : -3.95538
Latitude : 47.89903

Les Saules

🖉 02 98 56 98 57, *www.camping-les-saules.com*
Address : at Kerléven, 54 rte de la Plage (2.5km southeast; beside the beach at Kerléven (direct access)
Opening times : from beginning May to mid Sept.
4 ha (242 pitches) relatively flat, flat, grassy
Tariff : (2012 price) 31.30€ 🛉🛉 ⚎ 🔲 🔌 (6A) – Extra per person 6.65€ – Reservation fee 18€
Rental rates : (from beginning April to end Sept.) ♿ (1 mobile home) – 39 ⛽.
Per night from 90 to 190 € – Per week from 199 to 899 € – Reservation fee 18€
Dvided into 2 separate campsites.

Surroundings : 🏕 🎣 ⛰
Leisure activities : 🍽 ✗ 🎬 ⟙ 🏊
Facilities : ⚏🚿 🚿 🚰 launderette 🖳
Nearby : 🎣

GPS Longitude : -3.9611
Latitude : 47.899

*Routes nationales are main roads and their identifying numbers
begin with N or RN. Routes départementales are generally quieter
roads and begin with D or DN.*

⛰ Manoir de Penn ar Ster

☏ 02 98 56 97 75, *www.camping-pennarster.com*

Address : 2 ch. de Penn-Ar-Ster (take the northeastern exit, follow the signs for Quimper and take the turning to the left)

Opening times : from beginning March to beginning Nov.

3 ha (105 pitches) terraced, flat, grassy

Tariff : 28€ ✶✶ ⇔ 🆖 🚿 (10A) – Extra per person 7€ – Reservation fee 15€

Rental rates : (from beginning March to beginning Nov.) ♿ – 8 🚐 – 2 🏠 .
Per night from 43 to 92 € – Per week from 250 to 650 € – Reservation fee 15€

🚚 sani-station 5€ – 5 🆖 10€

Pretty stone manor house with adjacent garden.

Surroundings : 🦌 🚂 ♨♨
Leisure activities : 🎮 ✗ 🔥
Facilities : ♿ ⚓ 🎱 🎿 🗑 ✂ ♈ launderette

GPS Longitude : -3.97977
Latitude : 47.91215

⛰ FranceLoc Domaine du St-Laurent

☏ 02 98 56 97 65, *www.campings-franceloc.fr*

Address : at Kerleven (3km southeast, 500m from the large beach at Kerleven)

Opening times : from beginning April to end Sept.

5.4 ha (230 pitches) terraced, flat, grassy

Tariff : (2012 price) 29€ ✶✶ ⇔ 🆖 🚿 (10A) – Extra per person 7€ – Reservation fee 27€

Rental rates : (2012 price) (from beginning April to end Sept.) ♿ (1 mobile home) – 185 🚐 .
Per night from 33 to 75 € – Per week from 133 to 1,155 € – Reservation fee 27€

Some pitches have a view of the sea and the Glénan islands.

Surroundings : 🦌 🚂 ♨♨ ⛰
Leisure activities : 🍷 🎯 ⚡️ 🛶 ⛷ 🚴 ✗ 🔥 🎱 🏊 🏄 🎣 multi-sports ground
Facilities : ♿ ⚓ 🎿 ♈ launderette 🛒
Nearby : 🎣

GPS Longitude : -3.9547
Latitude : 47.89623

The pitches of many campsites are marked out with low hedges of attractive bushes and shrubs.

FOUESNANT

29170 – Michelin map **308** G7 – pop. 9,356 – alt. 30
▶ Paris 555 – Carhaix-Plouguer 69 – Concarneau 11 – Quimper 16

⛰ Sunêlia L'Atlantique ⚑⚑

☏ 02 98 56 14 44, *www.latlantique.fr* – limited spaces for one-night stay ❄

Address : 4.5km to the south, towards La Chapelle de Kerbader, 400m from the beach (direct access)

Opening times : from end April to beginning Sept.

10 ha (432 pitches) flat, grassy

Tariff : 41€ ✶✶ ⇔ 🆖 🚿 (6A) – Extra per person 8€ – Reservation fee 35€

Rental rates : (from end April to beginning Sept.) ♿ ❄ – 166 🚐 – 2 yurts – 10 tents.
Per night from 29 to 186€ – Per week from 203 to 1,302€ – Reservation fee 35€

🚚 sani-station 41€ – 🛒 🚿 15€

Pretty swimming area and spa.

Surroundings : 🦌 🚂 ♨♨
Leisure activities : 🍷 🎮 🎯 ⚡️ 🦶 ♨ hammam, jacuzzi 🛶 🚴 ✗ 🔥 🎱 🏊 🏄 spa therapy centre, entertainment room
Facilities : ♿ ⚓ 📺 🎿 🗑 ♈ launderette 🏊 🛒

GPS Longitude : -4.01854
Latitude : 47.85487

FOUGÈRES

35300 – Michelin map **309** O4 – pop. 19,820 – alt. 115
▶ Paris 326 – Caen 148 – Le Mans 132 – Nantes 158

▲ Municipal de Paron

🐾 02 99 99 40 81, *campingmunicipal35@orange.fr*
Address : rte de la Chapelle-Janson (located 1.5km east along the D 17, access recommended via the eastern bypass (rocade)
Opening times : from beginning May to mid Sept.
2.5 ha (90 pitches) flat, relatively flat, grassy
Tariff : (2012 price) 🛉 3.35€ 🚐 2.55€ 🔲 5.60€ – 🔌 (10A) 4.10€
🚉 sani-station – 14 🔲 5.60€
Pleasant setting among trees.

Surroundings : 🏞 ☐ ♨♨
Leisure activities : ⚓
Facilities : ☐ 🔳 launderette
Nearby : 🐴 ✗ 🗺 ♞ 🐎

GPS Longitude : -1.18193
Latitude : 48.35371

A chambre d'hôte is a guesthouse or B & B-style accommodation.

LE FRET

29160 – Michelin map **308** D5
▶ Paris 591 – Rennes 239 – Quimper 56 – Brest 10

▲ Gwel Kaër

🐾 02 98 27 61 06, *www.camping-gwel-kaer.com*
Address : 40 r. de Pen-An-Ero (take the southeastern exit along the D 55, follow the signs for Crozon; beside the sea)
Opening times : from beginning April to end Sept.
2.2 ha (98 pitches) terraced, flat and relatively flat, grassy
Tariff : 🛉 4.25€ 🚐 2.25€ 🔲 4.10€ – 🔌 (6A) 3.30€
Rental rates : (from beginning April to end Sept.) ⚡ – 7 🏚. Per night from 40 to 65 €
Per week from 290 to 515 €

Surroundings : 🏞 ⬍ ♨ ⛰
Leisure activities : ⚓
Facilities : 🚻 ☐ (from mid-Jun to mid-Sept) ♨ ♨ 🔳

GPS Longitude : -4.50237
Latitude : 48.28132

LE GUERNO

56190 – Michelin map **308** Q9 – pop. 818 – alt. 60
▶ Paris 460 – Muzillac 8 – Redon 30 – La Roche-Bernard 17

▲ Municipal de Borg-Néhué

🐾 02 97 42 94 76, *www.leguerno.fr*
Address : r. du Borg Nehué (500m northwest following signs for Noyal-Muzillac)
Opening times : from beginning April to end Oct.
1.4 ha (50 pitches) flat, grassy
Tariff : (2012 price) 11.10€ 🛉🛉 🚐 🔲 🔌 (10A) – Extra per person 2.80€
Rental rates : (2012 price) (permanent) – 9 🏚. Per night from 82 to 94 €
Per week from 143 to 417 €
🚉 sani-station

Surroundings : 🏞 ☐ ♨♨
Leisure activities : ⚓
Facilities : 🚻 ☐ 🏠 ♨ 🔳
Nearby : ✗

GPS Longitude : -2.41557
Latitude : 47.58251

GUIDEL

56520 – Michelin map **308** K8 – pop. 10,174 – alt. 38
▶ Paris 511 – Nantes 178 – Quimper 60 – Rennes 162

Les Jardins de Kergal

℘ 02 97 05 98 18, *www.camping-lorient.com*

Address : rte des Plages (3km southwest along the D 306, follow the signs for Guidel-Plages and take road to the left)

Opening times : from beginning April to end Sept.

5 ha (153 pitches) flat, grassy

Tariff : (2012 price) 31 € ♣♣ ⚌ ▣ ⟨⟩ (10A) – Extra per person 4 €

Rental rates : (2012 price) (from beginning April to mid Nov.) – 78 ⟨⟩ – 41 ⟨⟩.
Per night from 50 to 270 € – Per week from 200 to 830 € – Reservation fee 20 €

Pleasant wooded site.

Surroundings : ⚬ ⟨⟩
Leisure activities : ⟨⟩ ⟨⟩ ⟨⟩ ⟨⟩ ⟨⟩ ⟨⟩ ⟨⟩ multi-sports ground
Facilities : ⟨⟩ ⟨⟩ ⟨⟩ ⟨⟩ launderette
Nearby : ⟨⟩ ⟨⟩ sports trail

GPS Longitude : -3.50734
Latitude : 47.77464

GUILVINEC

29730 – Michelin map **308** F8 – pop. 2,945 – alt. 5
▶ Paris 584 – Douarnenez 44 – Pont-l'Abbé 10 – Quimper 30

Yelloh! Village La Plage ♣♣

℘ 02 98 58 61 90, *www.villagelaplage.com*

Address : rte des Fusillés de Poulguen (situated 2km west, follow the signs for La pointe de Penmarc'h (headland), 100m from the beach (direct access)

Opening times : from mid April to mid Sept.

14 ha (410 pitches) flat, grassy, sandy

Tariff : 44 € ♣♣ ⚌ ▣ ⟨⟩ (10A) – Extra per person 8 €

Rental rates : (from mid April to mid Sept.) – 210 ⟨⟩ – 4 ⟨⟩. Per night from 39 to 189 €
Per week from 273 to 1,323 €

Surroundings : ⟨⟩
Leisure activities : ⟨⟩ ⟨⟩ ⟨⟩ ⟨⟩ ⟨⟩ ⟨⟩ ⟨⟩ ⟨⟩ ⟨⟩ ⟨⟩
pedal go-carts, multi-sports ground
Facilities : ⟨⟩ ⟨⟩ ⟨⟩ ⟨⟩ launderette ⟨⟩
Nearby : ⟨⟩

GPS Longitude : -4.31194
Latitude : 47.8035

HUELGOAT

29690 – Michelin map **308** I4 – pop. 1,604 – alt. 149
▶ Paris 523 – Brest 66 – Carhaix-Plouguer 18 – Châteaulin 36

La Rivière d'Argent

℘ 02 98 99 72 50, *www.larivieredargent.com*

Address : at La Coudraie (3.4km east along the D 769a, follow the signs for Locmaria-Berrien and take the road to the right)

Opening times : from beginning March to mid Oct.

5 ha (90 pitches) flat, grassy

Tariff : ♣ 4.80 € ⚌ 2 € ▣ 6.20 € – ⟨⟩ (10A) 4.30 €

Rental rates : (2012 price) (from beginning March to mid Oct.) – 12 ⟨⟩ – 1 teepee – 1 tent.
Per night from 25 to 70 € – Per week from 140 to 610 € – Reservation fee 15 €
⟨⟩ sani-station 3 €

Attractive location beside a river on the edge of a forest.

Surroundings : ⚬ ⟨⟩ ⟨⟩
Leisure activities : ⟨⟩ ⟨⟩ ⟨⟩ ⟨⟩
Facilities : ⟨⟩ ⟨⟩ ⟨⟩ ⟨⟩ ⟨⟩ ⟨⟩ ⟨⟩

GPS Longitude : -3.71681
Latitude : 48.36428

Municipal du Lac

⌂

℘ 0298997880, *mairie.huelgoat@wanadoo.fr*

Address : at Le Fao (800m west following signs for Brest; beside a river and a lake)

1 ha (85 pitches) flat, grassy

🚻 sani-station – 10 🗉

Surroundings : 🖵 ♀		Longitude : -3.75561
Leisure activities : 🦞		Latitude : 48.36358
Facilities : 🕭 ⊶ ⩜ ⨡		
Nearby : ✼ ⟁		

ÎLE-AUX-MOINES

56780 – Michelin map **308** N9 – pop. 601 – alt. 16
▶ Paris 483 – Rennes 132 – Vannes 15 – Lorient 59

Municipal du Vieux Moulin

⌂

℘ 0297263068, *www.mairie-ileauxmoines.fr* ✻

Address : at Le Vieux Moulin (take southeastern exit from town, follow the signs for La Pointe de Brouel (headland)

Opening times : from mid April to end Sept.

1 ha (44 pitches) flat and relatively flat, grassy

Tariff : (2012 price) ✦ 7 € ⇔ ⧅ (0A)

Rental rates : (2012 price) (from mid April to end Sept.) ✻ – 3 tents. Per night from 45 to 87 €
Per week from 150 to 210 € – Reservation fee 5 €

Site with no electricity supply reserved for tents.

Surroundings : 🦫		Longitude : -2.84514
Leisure activities : 🏊		Latitude : 47.59292
Facilities : ⊶		
Nearby : 🖼		

The Michelin classification (🛆🛆🛆 ... 🛆) is totally independent of the official star classification system awarded by the local prefecture or other official organisation.

JOSSELIN

56120 – Michelin map **308** P7 – pop. 2,533 – alt. 58
▶ Paris 428 – Dinan 86 – Lorient 76 – Pontivy 35

Le Bas de la Lande

⌂

℘ 0297222220, *domainedekerelly@orange.fr*

Address : situated 2km west along the D 778 and take the D 724, follow the signs for Guégon to the left, 50m from the Oust river, take the western exit Guégon along the dual carriageway

2 ha (60 pitches) flat, relatively flat, terraced, grassy, adjacent pine trees

Rentals : 8 🚐.

🚻 sani-station

Surroundings : 🖵 ♀		Longitude : -2.57352
Leisure activities : ⍦ 🖼 🏊		Latitude : 47.95239
Facilities : 🕭 ⊶ ⛺ ¶ launderette		
Nearby : 🏇 🦞		

JUGON-LES-LACS

22270 – Michelin map **309** I4 – pop. 1,683 – alt. 29
▶ Paris 417 – Lamballe 22 – Plancoët 16 – St-Brieuc 59

Au Bocage du Lac

☏ 02 96 31 60 16, *www.camping-location-bretagne.com*
Address : r. du Bocage (located 1km southeast along the D 52, follow the signs for Mégrit)
Opening times : from mid April to mid Sept.
4 ha (180 pitches) flat and relatively flat, grassy
Tariff : 27.60€ ♣♣ ⇔ 回 ⚡ (10A) – Extra per person 5.95€ – Reservation fee 17€
Rental rates : (from mid April to end Sept.) – 6 📷 – 30 🏠 – 6 tent bungalows – 3 gîtes.
Per night from 56 to 165€ – Per week from 277 to 799€ – Reservation fee 17€
📷 sani-station 2.50€ – 2 回 5€ – 🔋 ⚡15.60€
Beside the large Étang de Jugon (lake).

Surroundings : ▭ 𝚚
Leisure activities : 🍷 🏠 🎯 ⛵ 🎣 🏊 ⛵ 🏹 wildlife park
Facilities : ♿ ⚿ 🚿 🍴 launderette
Nearby : 🚴 🎿 🎣

Longitude : -2.31663
Latitude : 48.40165

This guide is updated regularly, so buy your new copy every year!

KERVEL

29550 – Michelin map **308** F6
▶ Paris 586 – Rennes 234 – Quimper 24 – Brest 67

FranceLoc Domaine de Kervel ♣♣

☏ 02 98 92 51 54, *www.franceloc.fr*
Address : at Kervel
Opening times : from beginning April to mid Sept.
7 ha (300 pitches) flat, grassy
Tariff : (2012 price) 33€ ♣♣ ⇔ 回 ⚡ (10A) – Extra per person 7€ – Reservation fee 27€
Rental rates : (2012 price) (from beginning April to mid Sept.) ♿ – 147 📷.
Per night from 37 to 137€ – Per week from 147 to 952€ – Reservation fee 27€

Surroundings : 𝚚𝚚
Leisure activities : 🍷 🏠 🎯 🏃 ⛵ 🚴 🎿 🎣 🏊 🏊 ⛵ multi-sports ground
Facilities : ♿ ⚿ 🚿 🧺 🍴 launderette 🏠 🛒

Longitude : -4.26737
Latitude : 48.11617

KERVOYAL

56750 – Michelin map **308** P9
▶ Paris 471 – Rennes 124 – Vannes 30 – Lorient 87

Oasis

☏ 02 97 41 10 52, *www.campingloasis.com*
Address : r. Port Lestre (100m from the beach)
Opening times : from beginning April to end Sept.
3 ha (150 pitches) flat, grassy
Tariff : (2012 price) 21.40€ ♣♣ ⇔ 回 ⚡ (6A) – Extra per person 3.50€
Rental rates : (2012 price) (from mid April to end Sept.) – 11 📷. Per week from 215 to 595€
Reservation fee 15€
📷 sani-station 7€

Surroundings : 🏖 𝚚𝚚
Leisure activities : ⛵
Facilities : ⚿ 🍴 launderette

Longitude : -2.55013
Latitude : 47.51897

LAMPAUL-PLOUDALMEZEAU

29830 – Michelin map **308** D3 – pop. 753 – alt. 24
▶ Paris 613 – Brest 27 – Brignogan-Plages 36 – Ploudalmézeau 4

Municipal des Dunes

& 02 98 48 14 29, *lampaul-ploudalmezeau.mairie@wanadoo.fr*
Address : at Le Vourc'h (700m north of the town, beside the sports field and 100m from the beach (direct access)
Opening times : from mid June to mid Sept.
1.5 ha (150 pitches) open site, flat, sandy, grassy, dunes
Tariff : (2012 price) ♦ 4.50€ ⇔ 🔲 – 🔋 (10A) 2.50€

Surroundings : 🐾
Leisure activities : 🔲
Facilities : ♿ ⚬ (Jul–Aug) 🚮 launderette

GPS Longitude : -4.65639
Latitude : 48.56785

Some campsites benefit from proximity to a municipal leisure centre.

LANDÉDA

29870 – Michelin map **308** D3 – pop. 3,620 – alt. 52
▶ Paris 604 – Brest 28 – Brignogan-Plages 25 – Ploudalmézeau 17

Les Abers ▲▲

& 02 98 04 93 35, *www.camping-des-abers.com*
Address : 51 Toull Tréaz (2.5km to the northwest; by the dunes at Ste-Marguerite)
Opening times : from end April to end Sept.
4.5 ha (180 pitches) terraced, flat, sandy, grassy, dunes
Tariff : 20€ ♦♦ ⇔ 🔲 🔋 (10A) – Extra per person 4€
Rental rates : (from end April to end Sept.) – 22 🛏 – 1 studio – 1 apartment. Per week from 280 to 630 €
🚐 sani-station
Pleasant location close to the beach; information and map table on site.

Surroundings : 🐾 ≤ ⛰
Leisure activities : 🔲 🎨 🏌 ⚽ 🚴
Facilities : ♿ ⚬ 🛁 🍴 launderette 🏪
Nearby : 🍷 ✕

GPS Longitude : -4.60306
Latitude : 48.59306

LANLOUP

22580 – Michelin map **309** E2 – pop. 272 – alt. 58
▶ Paris 484 – Guingamp 29 – Lannion 44 – St-Brieuc 36

Le Neptune

& 02 96 22 33 35, *www.leneptune.com*
Opening times : from beginning April to mid Oct.
2 ha (84 pitches) flat, relatively flat, grassy
Tariff : (2012 price) ♦ 5.50€ ⇔ 🔲 10€ – 🔋 (10A) 4€ – Reservation fee 7€
Rental rates : (2012 price) (from beginning April to mid Oct.) 🌾 – 12 🛏 – 10 🏠.
Per night from 50 to 120 € – Per week from 229 to 729 € – Reservation fee 7€
🚐 sani-station 8€
Set among attractive trees.

Surroundings : 🌳 ♟
Leisure activities : 🍷 🔲 ⚽ 🚴 🎯 🔳 (open-air in season)
Facilities : ♿ ⚬ 🔲🛁 🍴 launderette 🏪
Nearby : 🍴

GPS Longitude : -2.96704
Latitude : 48.71372

LANNION

22300 – Michelin map **309** B2 – pop. 19,847 – alt. 12
▶ Paris 516 – Brest 96 – Morlaix 42 – St-Brieuc 65

Les Plages de Beg-Léguer

✆ 02 96 47 25 00, *www.campingdesplages.com*
Address : rte de la Côte (6km west following signs for Trébeurden and take the turning to the left, 500m from the beach)
Opening times : from mid April to mid Nov.
5 ha (240 pitches) relatively flat, flat, grassy
Tariff : (2012 price) 🧍 7.50€ 🚗 ▣ 8.50€ – 🔌 (6A) 3.60€
Rental rates : (2012 price) (from mid April to mid Nov.) Ⓟ – 40 🚐 – 7 🏠 – 6 tent bungalows. Per night from 33 to 106€ – Per week from 231 to 742€
🚰 sani-station

Surroundings : 🌿 🗔 ♨
Leisure activities : 🍴✗ 🖼 🏋 🚲 🍴 ⬜ 🏊 ⛷ multi-sports ground
Facilities : ♿ 🔑 🛁 🍴 launderette 🚿

GPS Longitude : -3.545
Latitude : 48.73834

Municipal des 2 Rives

✆ 02 96 46 31 40, *www.ville-lannion.fr*
Address : r. du Moulin du Duc (situated 2km southeast along the D 767, follow the signs for Guingamp and take the turning to the right after the Leclerc commercial centre)
Opening times : permanent
2.3 ha (116 pitches) flat, grassy
Tariff : (2012 price) 🧍 2.80€ 🚗 1.70€ ▣ 2.85€ – 🔌 (10A) 2.55€
Rental rates : (2012 price) (permanent) ♿ (1 chalet) – 14 🏠 – 8 tent bungalows. Per night from 37 to 68€ – Per week from 218 to 454€

Attractive trees and shrubs. Set on both banks of the Léguer river.

Surroundings : 🌿 ♨
Leisure activities : 🍴 🏋 🚣
Facilities : ♿ 🛁 🚿 ⇄ 🍴 launderette
Nearby : 🚶 walking trails

GPS Longitude : -3.44584
Latitude : 48.72293

*The classification (1 to 5 tents, **black** or **red**) that we award to selected sites in this guide is our own system. It should not be confused with the classification (1 to 5 stars) of official organisations.*

LANTIC

22410 – Michelin map **309** E3 – pop. 1,483 – alt. 50
▶ Paris 466 – Brest 139 – Lorient 133 – Rennes 116

Les Étangs

✆ 02 96 71 95 47, *www.campinglesetangs.com*
Address : r. des Terres Neuvas (situated 2km east along the D 4, follow the signs for Binic, near two lakes)
1.5 ha (110 pitches) terrace, relatively flat, flat, grassy
Rentals : 10 🚐 – 2 tent bungalows.
🚰 sani-station

Surroundings : 🌿 ♨
Leisure activities : 🖼 🏋 🏊
Facilities : ♿ 🔑 🛁 🍴 📺
Nearby : 🚣

GPS Longitude : -2.86254
Latitude : 48.6068

LARMOR-PLAGE

56260 – Michelin map **308** K8 – pop. 8,423 – alt. 4 – Leisure centre
▶ Paris 510 – Lorient 7 – Quimper 74 – Vannes 66

⚠ La Fontaine

☎ 02 97 33 71 28, *www.campingdelafontaine.fr*
Address : at Kerdeff, r. de Quéhello (to the west of the resort, 300m from the D 152 (recommended route)
Opening times : permanent
4 ha (130 pitches) flat, relatively flat, grassy
Tariff : (2012 price) 20.93€ ♣♣ ⟷ 回 ⑤ (16A) – Extra per person 4.82€ – Reservation fee 14.20€
Rental rates : (2012 price) (permanent) – 11 ▦ – 1 studio. Per week from 250 to 528 €
▦ sani-station 5.98€ – 5 回 10.29€ – ⚑ ⑤ 11.36€

Surroundings : ⟋ ▭ ♫♫ Leisure activities : ▱ ⛹ Facilities : ⅙ ☞ ▥ ⚎ ↯ launderette

GPS Longitude : -3.39212
Latitude : 47.70912

These symbols are used for a campsite that is exceptional in its category:
⛰⛰⛰…⛰ *Particularly pleasant setting, quality and range of services available*
⟋⟋ *Tranquil, isolated site – quiet site, particularly at night*
≼ ≼ *Exceptional view – interesting or panoramic view*

LESCONIL

29740 – Michelin map **308** F8
▶ Paris 581 – Douarnenez 41 – Guilvinec 6 – Loctudy 7

⚠ La Grande Plage

☎ 02 98 87 88 27, *www.campinggrandeplage.com*
Address : 71 r. Paul Langevin (located 1km west, follow the signs for Guilvinec, 300m from the beach (direct access)
Opening times : from mid April to end Sept.
2.5 ha (120 pitches) flat, relatively flat, grassy
Tariff : (2012 price) ♣ 5€ ⟷ 2.70€ 回 7.40€ – ⑤ (10A) 5.25€
Rental rates : (2012 price) (from mid April to end Sept.) ⚌ – 20 ▦ – 5 tent bungalows.
Per night from 40 to 99 € – Per week from 250 to 812 €
▦ sani-station 2€

Surroundings : ▭ ♫♫ Leisure activities : ▱ ⛵ Facilities : ⅙ ☞ ⚎ ᵞ launderette

GPS Longitude : -4.22897
Latitude : 47.79804

⚠ Les Dunes

☎ 02 98 87 81 78, *www.camping-lesdunes-29.com*
Address : 67 r. Paul-Langevin (located 1km west, follow the signs for Guilvinec; 150m from the beach (direct access)
2.8 ha (120 pitches) flat, grassy
Rentals : 4 ▦.

Surroundings : ▭ ♀ Leisure activities : ▱ ⛵ Facilities : ⅙ ☞ ⚎ ᵞ launderette

GPS Longitude : -4.22856
Latitude : 47.79716

▲ Keralouet

𝒫 02 98 82 23 05, *www.campingkeralouet.com*
Address : 11 r. Eric Tabarly (located 1km east on the Loctudy road)
Opening times : from beginning April to end Sept.
1 ha (64 pitches) flat, grassy
Tariff : (2012 price) 19.45€ ♥♥ ⇔ ▣ ⚡ (8A) – Extra per person 4.20€
Rental rates : (2012 price) (from beginning April to end Sept.) ♿ (2 chalets) – 6 🛏 – 12 🏠 –
4 tent bungalows. Per night from 35 to 60€ – Per week from 185 to 635€

A well-kept, pleasant campsite.

Surroundings : ⚬⚬
Leisure activities : ⛵ ⅃
Facilities : ♿ � ☖ ⁛ 🖥
Nearby : ◊

GPS
Longitude : -4.20595
Latitude : 47.80424

LOCMARIA-PLOUZANÉ

29280 – Michelin map **308** D4 – pop. 4,837 – alt. 65
▶ Paris 610 – Brest 15 – Brignogan-Plages 50 – Ploudalmézeau 23

▲ Municipal de Portez

𝒫 02 98 48 49 85, *camping-portez@locmaria-plouzane.fr*
Address : at Portez (3.5km southwest along the D 789 and follow the signs for the beach at Trégana;
200m from the beach)
2 ha (110 pitches) open site, terraced, flat, grassy
Rentals : 4 🛏.
🚿 sani-station – 9 ▣

Surroundings : ⤬ ⟨ ▭ ⚬
Leisure activities : 🎠 ⛵
Facilities : ♿ � ☖ ⁛ launderette
Nearby : ♟ ✕

GPS
Longitude : -4.66344
Latitude : 48.3582

*Using the traditional Michelin classification method, the guide provides
you with an easy, speedy reference for assessing the category of each site:
1 to 5 tents (see page 10).*

LOCMARIAQUER

56740 – Michelin map **308** N9 – pop. 1,692 – alt. 5
▶ Paris 488 – Auray 13 – Quiberon 31 – La Trinité-sur-Mer 10

⛰ Lann-Brick

𝒫 02 97 57 32 79, *www.camping-lannbrick.com*
Address : at Lann Brick – rte de Kérinis (2.5km northwest following signs for Kérinis, 200m from the
beach)
Opening times : from beginning April to mid Oct.
1.2 ha (98 pitches) flat, grassy
Tariff : (2012 price) ♥ ⇔ ▣ 19.80€ – ⚡ (10A) 4.70€
Rental rates : (2012 price) (from beginning April to mid Oct.) – 20 🛏 – 3 tent bungalows.
Per week from 220 to 698 € – Reservation fee 15€

Surroundings : ▭ ⚬
Leisure activities : ♟ 🎠 ⛵ ⚵ ⅃ spa therapy centre
Facilities : ♿ ⌐ ☖ ⁛ launderette
Nearby : ✕ ♒ ◊

GPS
Longitude : -2.97436
Latitude : 47.57838

LOCRONAN

29180 – Michelin map **308** F6 – pop. 798 – alt. 105
▶ Paris 580 – Rennes 229 – Quimper 17

Le Locronan

☎ 02 98 91 87 76, *www.camping-locronan.fr*
Address : r. de la Troménie
Opening times : from mid April to mid Nov.
2.6 ha (103 pitches) terraced, flat, grassy, very uneven
Tariff : (2012 price) ✚ 5.40€ ⟶ 1.70€ 🔲 6.20€ – ⚡ (10A) 4.20€ – Reservation fee 5€
Rental rates : (2012 price) (from mid April to mid Nov.) – 17 ▥ – 2 tent bungalows.
Per week from 215 to 760 € – Reservation fee 15€
▥ sani-station

Surroundings : 🏊 ⬭ 〇〇
Leisure activities : ⟵➤ 🖾
Facilities : ♿ ⊙⟶🎣 ¶ launderette

GPS Longitude : -4.19918
Latitude : 48.09582

LOCTUDY

29750 – Michelin map **308** F8 – pop. 4,207 – alt. 8
▶ Paris 578 – Bénodet 18 – Concarneau 35 – Pont-l'Abbé 6

Les Hortensias

☎ 02 98 87 46 64, *www.camping-loctudy.com*
Address : 38 r. des Tulipes (3km southwest following signs for Larvor, 500m from the beach at Lodonnec)
Opening times : from beginning April to end Sept.
1.5 ha (100 pitches) flat, grassy
Tariff : 23€ ✚✚ ⟶ 🔲 ⚡ (10A) – Extra per person 4.50€
Rental rates : (from beginning April to end Sept.) – 1 'gypsy' caravan – 20 ▥.
Per night from 50 to 100 € – Per week from 220 to 725 €
▥ sani-station 5€ – 🚐 11€

Surroundings : 〇〇
Leisure activities : ⟵➤ ⋔ 🛝
Facilities : ♿ ⊙⟶ ¶ launderette
Nearby : ⍓ ✕

GPS Longitude : -4.1823
Latitude : 47.81259

LOUANNEC

22700 – Michelin map **309** B2 – pop. 2,946 – alt. 53
▶ Paris 527 – Rennes 175 – St-Brieuc 77 – Lannion 10

Municipal Ernest Renan

☎ 02 96 23 11 78, *www.camping-louannec.fr*
Address : located 1km west; beside the sea
Opening times : from end April to end Sept.
4 ha (265 pitches) flat, grassy
Tariff : (2012 price) 17.40€ ✚✚ ⟶ 🔲 ⚡ (16A) – Extra per person 3.60€
Rental rates : (2012 price) (from beginning April to end Sept.) – 8 ▥.
Per night from 52 to 87€ – Per week from 260 to 603€
▥ sani-station 4.15€ – 13 🔲 9.90€

Surroundings : ⇐ ⚠
Leisure activities : ⍓ 🎬 〇daytime ⟵➤ 🛝 ◊
Facilities : ♿ ⊙⟶ 🎣 ▽ ¶ launderette ▦ 🚿
Nearby : 🐎

GPS Longitude : -3.42723
Latitude : 48.79666

MARCILLÉ-ROBERT

35240 – Michelin map **309** N7 – pop. 929 – alt. 65
▶ Paris 333 – Bain-de-Bretagne 33 – Châteaubriant 30 – La Guerche-de-Bretagne 11

⚠ Municipal de l'Étang

𝒫 06 02 08 60 22, *camping.marcillerobert@yahoo.fr*
Address : r. des Bas Gasts (take the southern exit along the D 32, follow the signs for Arbrissel)
Opening times : permanent
0.5 ha (22 pitches) terraced, flat, grassy
Tariff : 10.40€ ⚄ ⚄ ⚄ 🔲 🛁 (10A) – Extra per person 2.95€
Rental rates : (permanent) – 1 🏠. Per night from 23 to 35€ – Per week from 250€
Pleasant setting looking out over a lake.

Surroundings : ≤ ⊏ 🔟	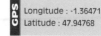 Longitude : -1.36471
Facilities : 🔶 ⊐	Latitude : 47.94768
Nearby : 🏊 ✗ 🎣 pedalos	

MARTIGNÉ-FERCHAUD

35640 – Michelin map **309** O8 – pop. 2,650 – alt. 90
▶ Paris 340 – Bain-de-Bretagne 31 – Châteaubriant 15 – La Guerche-de-Bretagne 16

⚠ Municipal du Bois Feuillet

𝒫 02 99 47 84 38, *www.ville-martigne-ferchaud.fr*
Address : at Étang de la Forge (to the northwest of the town)
1.7 ha (50 pitches) terraced, flat, grassy
🚐 sani-station

Surroundings : ≤ ⊏ 🔟	Longitude : -1.31599
Leisure activities : 🎴	Latitude : 47.83385
Facilities : 🔶 ⊙ 🔏 ⚙ 🔲	
Nearby : 🏊 ✗ 🏖 (beach) 🎣 💧 pedalos	

> *To make the best possible use of this guide,*
> *please read pages 2–15 carefully.*

MATIGNON

22550 – Michelin map **309** I3 – pop. 1,647 – alt. 70
▶ Paris 425 – Dinan 30 – Dinard 23 – Lamballe 23

⚠ Le Vallon aux Merlettes

𝒫 02 96 41 11 61, *www.camping-matignon.com*
Address : 43 r. du Dr-Jobert (to the southwest along the D 13, follow the signs for Lamballe, by the stadium)
Opening times : from beginning May to end Sept.
3 ha (100 pitches) relatively flat, flat, grassy
Tariff : ⚄ 3.80€ ⚄ 🔲 5.70€ – 🛁 (8A) 3.30€
Rental rates : (from beginning April to end Sept.) – 5 🛖. Per night from 40 to 50€
Per week from 205 to 455€ – Reservation fee 10€
🚐 sani-station 2€ – 3 🔲 12€

Surroundings : 🌳 🍃	Longitude : -2.29607
Leisure activities : 🎴 ✗ 🎯	Latitude : 48.59168
Facilities : 🔶 ⊙ 🔏 ⚙ launderette	
Nearby : 🛒	

MERDRIGNAC

22230 – Michelin map **309** H5 – pop. 2,916 – alt. 140
▶ Paris 411 – Dinan 47 – Josselin 33 – Lamballe 40

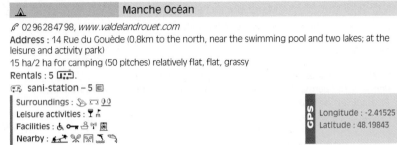

⚠ Manche Océan

℘ 02 96 28 47 98, *www.valdelandrouet.com*
Address : 14 Rue du Gouède (0.8km to the north, near the swimming pool and two lakes; at the leisure and activity park)
15 ha/2 ha for camping (50 pitches) relatively flat, flat, grassy
Rentals : 5 🛖.
🚐 sani-station – 5 🅴

Surroundings : 🌿 🛒 ♨️
Leisure activities : ⛱ ♒
Facilities : ♿ ⚡ 🛁 🚽 🖼
Nearby : 🚣 ✂ 🎣 ⛵

GPS
Longitude : -2.41525
Latitude : 48.19843

MEUCON

56890 – Michelin map **308** O8 – pop. 2,131 – alt. 80
▶ Paris 467 – Rennes 116 – Vannes 8 – Lorient 62

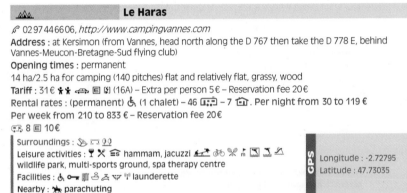

⛰ Le Haras

℘ 02 97 44 66 06, *http://www.campingvannes.com*
Address : at Kersimon (from Vannes, head north along the D 767 then take the D 778 E, behind Vannes-Meucon-Bretagne-Sud flying club)
Opening times : permanent
14 ha/2.5 ha for camping (140 pitches) flat and relatively flat, grassy, wood
Tariff : 31€ ✶✶ 🚗 🅴 💧 (16A) – Extra per person 5€ – Reservation fee 20€
Rental rates : (permanent) ♿ (1 chalet) – 46 🛖 – 7 🏠. Per night from 30 to 119 €
Per week from 210 to 833 € – Reservation fee 20€
🚐 8 🅴 10€

Surroundings : 🌿 🛒 ♨️
Leisure activities : ⛱ ✗ ♨️ hammam, jacuzzi 🚣 🚴 ✂ ♒ 🖼 🎣 ⛷
wildlife park, multi-sports ground, spa therapy centre
Facilities : ♿ ⚡ 🚿 🛁 🚽 💧 launderette
Nearby : 🪂 parachuting

GPS
Longitude : -2.72795
Latitude : 47.73035

MOËLAN-SUR-MER

29350 – Michelin map **308** J8 – pop. 6,956 – alt. 58
▶ Paris 523 – Carhaix-Plouguer 66 – Concarneau 27 – Lorient 27

⚠ L'Île Percée

℘ 02 98 71 16 25, *www.camping-ile-percee.fr*
Address : plage de Trenez (5.8km west along the D 116, follow the signs for Kerfany-les-Pins, then continue 1.7km along the turning to the left)
Opening times : from beginning April to mid Sept.
1 ha (65 pitches) flat, grassy
Tariff : (2012 price) 20.10€ ✶✶ 🚗 🅴 💧 (10A) – Extra per person 4.20€ – Reservation fee 8€
Rental rates : (2012 price) (from beginning April to mid Sept.) – 4 🛖.
Per night from 45 to 80€ – Per week from 290 to 600 – Reservation fee 58€

Pleasant, natural site looking out over the ocean.

Surroundings : 🌿 ≤ ♀ ⛰
Leisure activities : 🪁
Facilities : ♿ ⚡ 🚿 🛁 💧
Nearby : ✗ 🪂 walking trails

GPS
Longitude : -3.70241
Latitude : 47.78872

MORGAT

29160 – Michelin map **308** E5 – pop. 7,535
▶ Paris 590 – Rennes 238 – Quimper 55 – Brest 15

⚠ Les Bruyères

✆ 0298261487, *www.camping-bruyeres-crozon.com*
Address : at Le Bouis (located 1.5km along the D 255, follow the signs for Le Cap de la Chèvre and take road to the right)
4 ha (130 pitches) flat and relatively flat, grassy
Rentals : ⚞ – 17 ⬚.

Natural setting with access to Morgat via a pedestrian path.

Surroundings : 🌳 ♀
Leisure activities : 🛶
Facilities : ⚍ ⌂ ⁋ launderette

GPS Longitude : -4.53183
Latitude : 48.22293

> *There are several different types of sani-station ('borne' in French) – sanitation points providing fresh water and disposal points for grey water. See page 12 for further details.*

MOUSTERLIN

29170 – Michelin map **308** G7
▶ Paris 563 – Rennes 212 – Quimper 22 – Brest 94

⚠ FranceLoc Le Grand Large

✆ 0298560406, *www.campings-franceloc.fr* – limited spaces for one-night stay
Address : 48 rte du Grand Large (near the beach)
Opening times : from beginning April to beginning Sept.
5.8 ha (287 pitches) flat, grassy
Tariff : (2012 price) 29€ ✶✶ ⇌ 🔲 ⚡ (10A) – Extra per person 7€ – Reservation fee 27€
Rental rates : (2012 price) (from beginning April to beginning Sept.) ⅃ – 220 ⬚.
Per night from 33 to 151 € – Per week from 133 to 1,050 € – Reservation fee 27€

Surroundings : 🌳 ♀
Leisure activities : 🖾 ⑬ ⬷ ⚲ ⚞ 🔲 (open-air in season) ⚑ multi-sports ground
Facilities : ⅃ ⚍ ⌂ ⚑ ⚟ ⁋ launderette ⚏ ⚟
Nearby : ✗

GPS Longitude : -4.0367
Latitude : 47.84809

⚠ Kost-Ar-Moor

✆ 0298560416, *www.camping-fouesnant.com*
Address : 17 rte du Grand Large (500m from the beach)
Opening times : from beginning May to mid Sept.
3.5 ha (177 pitches) flat, grassy
Tariff : 27.50€ ✶✶ ⇌ 🔲 ⚡ (10A) – Extra per person 5.30€ – Reservation fee 15€
Rental rates : (from mid April to mid Sept.) – 20 ⬚ – 5 apartments. Per night from 50 to 60 € Per week from 220 to 714 € – Reservation fee 15€

Surroundings : 🌳 ♀♀
Leisure activities : 🖾 🛶 ⬷ ⚞
Facilities : ⅃ ⚍ ⌂ ⁋ launderette
Nearby : ◗

GPS Longitude : -4.03421
Latitude : 47.85106

NAIZIN

56500 – Michelin map **308** O7 – pop. 1,695 – alt. 106
▶ Paris 454 – Ploërmel 40 – Pontivy 16 – Rennes 106

Municipal de Coetdan

✆ 02 97 27 43 27, *naizin.fr* – ℝ
Address : r. des Peupliers (600m east along the D 17 and take D 203 towards Réguiny)
Opening times : from beginning May to end Sept.
0.7 ha (28 pitches) flat and relatively flat, grassy
Tariff : (2012 price) ✝ 3€ ⇌ 2€ ▣ 2€ – 🔌 (9A) 3€
Pleasant setting near a small lake.

Surroundings : ⌂ 🌳🌳
Leisure activities : 🎣
Facilities : ♿ 🚿
Nearby : 🚣 🏃 fitness trail, farm or petting farm

GPS Longitude : -2.82616
Latitude : 47.99336

NÉVEZ

29920 – Michelin map **308** I8 – pop. 2,718 – alt. 40
▶ Paris 541 – Concarneau 14 – Pont-Aven 8 – Quimper 40

Les Chaumières

✆ 02 98 06 73 06, *camping-des-chaumieres.com*
Address : 24 Hameau de Kerascoët (head 3km south along the D 77 towards Port Manec'h then take the turning to the right)
Opening times : from mid May to mid Sept.
3 ha (110 pitches) flat, grassy
Tariff : 21.30€ ✝✝ ⇌ ▣ 🔌 (10A) – Extra per person 5€
Rental rates : (from beginning April to end Sept.) – 6 🚐 – 2 tents. Per night 50€
Per week from 180 to 580€ – Reservation fee 10€
🚽 sani-station 5€

Surroundings : 🏖 ⌂ ♨
Facilities : ♿ ☎ (Jul–Aug) 🍴 launderette
Nearby : ▼ ✗

GPS Longitude : -3.77433
Latitude : 47.79598

NOYAL-MUZILLAC

56190 – Michelin map **308** Q9 – pop. 2,410 – alt. 52
▶ Paris 468 – Rennes 108 – Vannes 31 – Lorient 88

Moulin de Cadillac

✆ 02 97 67 03 47, *www.camping-moulin-cadillac.com*
Address : 4.5km northwest following signs for Berric
Opening times : from mid April to mid Sept.
7 ha (192 pitches) flat, grassy, lake, adjacent wood
Tariff : (2012 price) ✝ 6.20€ ⇌ ▣ 12.50€ – 🔌 (10A) 3.80€ – Reservation fee 10€
Rental rates : (2012 price) (from mid April to mid Sept.) – 55 🚐 – 10 🏠 – 4 tent bungalows.
Per week from 250 to 700€ – Reservation fee 10€
🚽 sani-station – 5 ▣ 25€
Pleasant setting based around an indoor water park; beside the Kervily river.

Surroundings : 🏖 ⌂ ♨
Leisure activities : ▼ 🎲 🛶 🚣 🎿 🏃 🖥 🏊 ⛵ 🎣 wildlife park, multi-sports ground, entertainment room
Facilities : ♿ ☎ 🚿 🍴 launderette

GPS Longitude : -2.50199
Latitude : 47.61412

PAIMPOL

22500 – Michelin map **309** D2 – pop. 7,828 – alt. 15
▶ Paris 494 – Guingamp 29 – Lannion 33 – St-Brieuc 46

△ Municipal de Cruckin-Kérity

☏ 02 96 20 78 47, *www.camping-paimpol.com*
Address : at Kérity (head 2km southeast along the D 786, follow the signs for St-Quay-Portrieux, next to the stadium, 100m from the beach at Cruckin)
Opening times : from beginning April to end Sept.
2 ha (130 pitches) flat, grassy
Tariff : 20.45€ ♣♣ ⇌ 🖥 ⚡ (10A) – Extra per person 4€ – Reservation fee 20€
Rental rates : (from beginning April to end Sept.) – 5 tent bungalows.
Per week from 220 to 360€ – Reservation fee 20€
🚮 sani-station 12.50€ – 10 🖥 12.50€

Surroundings : 🐚 ⌗ ♀
Leisure activities : 🎱 ⚓
Facilities : ♿ ⚌ 🚿 🚰 launderette
Nearby : ✗ 🔓 fitness trail

GPS Longitude : -3.02224
Latitude : 48.76972

PAIMPONT

35380 – Michelin map **309** I6 – pop. 1,641 – alt. 159
▶ Paris 390 – Dinan 60 – Ploërmel 26 – Redon 47

△ Municipal Paimpont Brocéliande

☏ 02 99 07 89 16, *www.camping-paimpont-broceliande.com* – ℞
Address : 2 r. du Chevalier Lancelot du Lac (take the northern exit along the D 773, near the lake)
Opening times : from beginning April to end Sept.
1.5 ha (90 pitches) flat, grassy
Tariff : (2012 price) 14.80€ ♣♣ ⇌ 🖥 ⚡ (5A) – Extra per person 3.50€
Rental rates : (2012 price) (permanent) ♿ (1 chalet) – 6 🏠. Per week from 200 to 490 €
🚮 sani-station – 10 🖥 8.30€

Surroundings : ⌗
Leisure activities : 🎱 ⚓
Facilities : ♿ ⚌ (Jul-Aug) 🚰 launderette
Nearby : 🍴

GPS Longitude : -2.17248
Latitude : 48.02404

PÉNESTIN

56760 – Michelin map **308** Q10 – pop. 1,867 – alt. 20
▶ Paris 458 – La Baule 29 – Nantes 84 – La Roche-Bernard 18

⋀⋀ Le Cénic ♣♣

☏ 02 99 90 45 65, *www.lecenic.com*
Address : rte de La Roche-Bernard (located 1.5km east along the D 34; beside a lake)
Opening times : from mid April to mid Sept.
5.5 ha (310 pitches) flat and relatively flat, grassy
Tariff : 32€ ♣♣ ⇌ 🖥 ⚡ (6A) – Extra per person 6€ – Reservation fee 15€
Rental rates : (from end April to mid Sept.) – 50 🚐 – 10 🏠. Per night from 85 to 115 €
Per week from 260 to 760 € – Reservation fee 15€
🚮 sani-station 3€
Partially open-air water park.

Surroundings : ⌗ ♀♀
Leisure activities : 🍸 🎱 🎮 🏓 ≋ hammam ⚓ 🎣 🔓 🎰 🏊 ⛱ 🌊
entertainment room
Facilities : ♿ ⚌ 🚿 🚰 launderette

GPS Longitude : -2.45547
Latitude : 47.47889

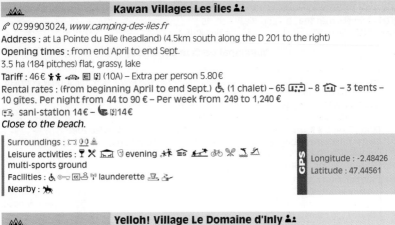

Kawan Villages Les Îles ♠♠

☎ 02 99 90 30 24, *www.camping-des-iles.fr*
Address : at La Pointe du Bile (headland) (4.5km south along the D 201 to the right)
Opening times : from end April to end Sept.
3.5 ha (184 pitches) flat, grassy, lake
Tariff : 46€ ♦♦ ⇔ 🔲 (10A) – Extra per person 5.80€
Rental rates : (from beginning April to end Sept.) ♿ (1 chalet) – 65 🛏 – 8 🏠 – 3 tents –
10 gîtes. Per night from 44 to 90 € – Per week from 249 to 1,240 €
🚐 sani-station 14€ – 🔋14€
Close to the beach.

Surroundings : 🏕 ♤♤ ⚠ **Leisure activities** : 🍷 🍴 🔲 evening 🏃 🛶 🚣 🚴 ✂ 🏊 🏄 multi-sports ground **Facilities** : ♿ ⚡ 🚿 🛁 🍴 launderette 🔲 🏃 **Nearby** : 🐎	**Longitude** : -2.48426 **Latitude** : 47.44561

Yelloh! Village Le Domaine d'Inly ♠♠

☎ 02 99 90 35 09, *www.camping-inly.com* – limited spaces for one-night stay
Address : rte de Couarne (situated 2km southeast along the D 201 and take turning to the left)
Opening times : from mid May to mid Sept.
30 ha/12 ha for camping (500 pitches) flat, grassy, stony
Tariff : 42€ ♦♦ ⇔ 🔲 (10A) – Extra per person 7€
Rental rates : (from mid April to mid Sept.) – 100 🛏 – 4 🏠. Per night from 39 to 189€
Per week from 224 to 1,323€

Surroundings : 🏊 🏕 ♤♤ **Leisure activities** : 🍷 🍴 🔲 🏃 🛶 🚴 ✂ 🔲 🏊 🚣 🏄 pedalos 🛟 **Facilities** : ⚡ 🛁 🚿 🍴 launderette 🔲 🏃	**Longitude** : -2.46694 **Latitude** : 47.47138

Les Parcs

☎ 02 99 90 30 59, *www.camping-lesparcs.com*
Address : rte de la Roche-Bernard (500m east along the D 34)
Opening times : from beginning April to end Sept.
3 ha (100 pitches) flat, sloping, grassy
Tariff : (2012 price) 23.60€ ♦♦ ⇔ 🔲 (6A) – Extra per person 5.30€ – Reservation fee 15€
Rental rates : (2012 price) (from beginning April to end Sept.) – 20 🛏.
Per week from 180 to 600€ – Reservation fee 15€

Surroundings : 🏕 ♤♤ **Leisure activities** : 🍷 🔲 (open-air in season) **Facilities** : ♿ ⚡ 🛁 🍴 launderette **Nearby** : 🛒	**Longitude** : -2.46583 **Latitude** : 47.48166

PENMARCH

29760 – Michelin map **308** E8 – pop. 5,749 – alt. 7
▶ Paris 585 – Audierne 40 – Douarnenez 45 – Pont-l'Abbé 12

Municipal de Toul ar Ster

☎ 02 98 58 86 88, *mairie@penmarch.fr*
Address : 110 r. Edmond Michelet (1.4km southeast following signs for Guilvinec along the coast and take turning to the right, 100m from the beach (direct access)
3 ha (202 pitches) flat, grassy, sandy

Surroundings : 🏊 **Leisure activities** : 🔲 **Facilities** : ♿ ⚡ 🛁 🍴 launderette **Nearby** : 🛶	**Longitude** : -4.33726 **Latitude** : 47.81246

PENTREZ-PLAGE

29550 – Michelin map **308** F5
▶ Paris 566 – Brest 55 – Châteaulin 18 – Crozon 18

Homair Vacances Le Ker'Ys – Les Tamaris ▲▲

📞 0820 201 207, *www.homair.com/camping_domaine_de_ker_ys.html* – limited spaces for one-night stay

Address : chemin des Dunes (opposite the beach)
3 ha (190 pitches) flat and relatively flat, grassy
Rentals : 120.

Surroundings :
Leisure activities : daytime
Facilities : launderette
Nearby :

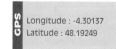

Longitude : -4.30137
Latitude : 48.19249

Do not confuse:
▲ *to* ▲▲▲ *: MICHELIN classification*
with
★ *to* ★★★★★ *: official classification*

PERROS-GUIREC

22700 – Michelin map **309** B2 – pop. 7,375 – alt. 60
▶ Paris 527 – Lannion 12 – St-Brieuc 76 – Tréguier 19

Yelloh! Village Le Ranolien ▲▲

📞 02 96 91 65 65, *www.leranolien.fr*
Address : at Ploumanac'h, bd du Sémaphore (located 1km southeast along the D 788, 200m from the sea)
Opening times : from mid April to mid Sept.
15 ha (525 pitches) flat and relatively flat, grassy, rocks, very uneven
Tariff : 44€ ★★ (10A) – Extra per person 9€
Rental rates : (from mid April to mid Sept.) – 5 'gypsy' caravans – 330.
Per night from 78 to 273 €
Per week from 684 to 1,596 €
sani-station – 8 14€ – 14€
Very pleasant spa centre (open all year round).

Surroundings :
Leisure activities : hammam, jacuzzi disco, multi-sports ground, spa therapy centre, entertainment room
Facilities : launderette

Longitude : -3.4747
Latitude : 48.82677

Claire Fontaine ▲

📞 02 96 23 03 55, *www.camping-claire-fontaine.com*
Address : r. de Toul al Lann (2.6km southwest along the r. des Frères- Mantrier, follow the signs for Pleumeur-Bodou and take turning to the right)
3 ha (180 pitches) relatively flat, flat, grassy
Rentals : 2 – 6 – 1 gîte.
sani-station
Pleasant setting based around an old renovated farmhouse of great character.

Surroundings :
Leisure activities :
Facilities : launderette

Longitude : -3.46538
Latitude : 48.80598

LE PERTRE

35370 – Michelin map **309** P6 – pop. 1,434 – alt. 174
▶ Paris 303 – Châteaubriant 55 – Laval 25 – Redon 116

Municipal le Chardonneret

✆ 06 79 50 41 77, www.lepertre.fr – ⚑ ⚒

Address : r. du Chardonneret (take the southwestern exit along the D 43, follow the signs for Brielles and take turning to the right)

Opening times : from beginning April to mid Oct.

1 ha (31 pitches) relatively flat, flat, grassy

Tariff : (2012 price) ⚹ 2.90€ ⇔ ▣ 1.95€ – ⚡ (16A) 3.70€

Rental rates : (2012 price) (from beginning April to mid Oct.) ⚒ – 2 ▣.
Per week from 190 to 341 €

Near a small lake.

Surroundings : ⚲ ⌂ ♨♨
Facilities : ⚹ ⊐ ▥
Nearby : ⚡ ⚒ ▧ ⚑ ⚓ (beach) ⚲

GPS Longitude : -1.03943
Latitude : 48.03286

PLANCOËT

22130 – Michelin map **309** I3 – pop. 3,079 – alt. 41
▶ Paris 417 – Dinan 17 – Dinard 20 – St-Brieuc 46

Municipal Les Vergers

✆ 02 96 84 03 42, mairie-plancoet@wanadoo.fr

Address : r. du Verger (Continue towards southeastern exit, follow the signs for Dinan, behind the fire station; beside the Arguenon river and a small lake)

Opening times : from beginning July to end Aug.

1.2 ha (100 pitches) flat, grassy

Tariff : (2012 price) ⚹ 2.50€ ⇔ 1.20€ ▣ 2.50€ – ⚡ (10A) 2.30€

Surroundings : ≼ the village of Plancoët ⌂ ♀
Leisure activities : ⚲
Facilities : ⚹ ⚏ (Jul–Aug), launderette
Nearby : ⚡

GPS Longitude : -2.23366
Latitude : 48.52041

Routes nationales are main roads and their identifying numbers begin with N or RN. Routes départmentales are generally quieter roads and begin with D or DN.

PLANGUENOUAL

22400 – Michelin map **309** G3 – pop. 1,919 – alt. 76
▶ Paris 440 – Guingamp 52 – Lannion 84 – St-Brieuc 19

Municipal

✆ 02 96 32 71 93, www.planguenoual.fr

Address :at Le Val (2.5km northwest along the D 59)

1.5 ha (64 pitches) terraced, flat, grassy

Surroundings : ⚲ ≼ ⌂ ♀
Facilities : ⚏ ▣

GPS Longitude : -2.59757
Latitude : 48.54702

PLÉNEUF-VAL-ANDRÉ

22370 – Michelin map **309** G3 – pop. 3,942 – alt. 52
▶ Paris 446 – Dinan 43 – Erquy 9 – Lamballe 16

Campéole Les Monts Colleux

📞 02 96 72 95 10, *www.camping-montscolleux.com*
Address : 26 r. Jean Lebrun
Opening times : from beginning April to end Sept.
5 ha/200 ha for camping terrace, flat, grassy
Tariff : (2012 price) 23.10€ ✶✶ 🚐 🅴 🄻 (10A) – Extra per person 6.70€ – Reservation fee 25€
Rental rates : (2012 price) (from beginning April to end Sept.) ♿ (1 mobile home) – 46 🛖 –
23 🏠. Per night from 37 to 101€ – Per week from 483 to 784€ – Reservation fee 25€
🚐 sani-station
Surroundings : 🌳 ≤
Facilities : ⚷ 🛏 🍴 launderette 🧺

Longitude : -2.5508
Latitude : 48.5898

*The guide covers all 22 regions of France – see the map
and list of regions on pages 4–5.*

PLESTIN-LES-GRÈVES

22310 – Michelin map **309** A3 – pop. 3,644 – alt. 45
▶ Paris 528 – Brest 79 – Guingamp 46 – Lannion 18

Municipal St-Efflam

📞 02 96 35 62 15, *www.camping-municipal-bretagne.com*
Address : at St-Efflam, pl. de Lan-Carré (3.5km to the northeast, follow the signs for St-Michel-en-Grève; 200m from the sea)
Opening times : from beginning April to end Sept.
4 ha (190 pitches) terraced, relatively flat, flat, grassy
Tariff : (2012 price) 17.58€ ✶✶ 🚐 🅴 🄻 (10A) – Extra per person 3.50€
Rental rates : (2012 price) (from beginning April to end Sept.) ♿ (1 mobile home) – 10 🛖 –
8 🏠. Per night from 40 to 71 € – Per week from 200 to 405 €
🚐 sani-station 3€ – 10 🅴 12.20€
Surroundings : ≤ ♨
Leisure activities : 🍸 🎡 ⛵ 🔲
Facilities : ♿ 🚰 (Jul-Aug) 🛏 🍴 launderette
Nearby : ✗ ♨

Longitude : -3.60108
Latitude : 48.66834

Aire Naturelle Ker-Rolland

📞 02 96 35 08 37, *www.camping-ker-rolland.com*
Address : at Ker Rolland (2.2km southwest along the D 786, follow the signs for Morlaix and take the turning to the left, following signs for Plouégat-Guérand)
Opening times : from mid June to beginning Sept.
1.6 ha (22 pitches) flat, grassy
Tariff : 11.60€ ✶✶ 🚐 🅴 🄻 (8A) – Extra per person 2.80€
Rental rates : (permanent) – 4 🛖. Per night from 35 to 53 € – Per week from 200 to 370 €
Reservation fee 50€
Farm campsite (market garden).

Surroundings : 🌳
Leisure activities : 🎡
Facilities : ♿ 🚰 🧺 ✍ 🍴 🅿

Longitude : -3.64337
Latitude : 48.64338

PLEUBIAN

22610 – Michelin map **309** D1 – pop. 2,577 – alt. 48
▶ Paris 506 – Lannion 31 – Paimpol 13 – St-Brieuc 58

Port la Chaîne

℘ 02 96 22 92 38, *www.portlachaine.com*
Address : situated 2km north along the D 20, follow the signs for Larmor-Pleubian and take turning to the left
Opening times : from beginning April to end Sept.
4.9 ha (200 pitches) terraced, relatively flat, flat, grassy
Tariff : 27.10€ 🛉🛉 ⇔ 🗉 🔊 (16A) – Extra per person 6.50€
Rental rates : (from beginning April to end Sept.) – 42 🚐 – 3 tent bungalows.
Per night from 36 to 119 € – Per week from 226 to 833 € – Reservation fee 15€
Plenty of shade provided by centuries-old maritime pines; beside the sea.

Surroundings : 🦢 ♨️ 🛖
Leisure activities : 🍷 🎬 🛥️ 🖼️ 🎴
Facilities : 🕎 ⚿ 🖏 🛁 🗑️ 🍴 launderette

GPS Longitude : -3.13284
Latitude : 48.85545

PLEUMEUR-BODOU

22560 – Michelin map **309** A2 – pop. 4,039 – alt. 94
▶ Paris 523 – Lannion 8 – Perros-Guirec 10 – St-Brieuc 72

Le Port

℘ 02 96 23 87 79, *www.camping-du-port-22.com*
Address : 3 ch. des Douaniers (6km to the north, to the south of Trégastel-Plage)
Opening times : from beginning April to mid Oct.
2 ha (80 pitches) open site, flat and relatively flat, grassy, rocks
Tariff : 20.50€ 🛉🛉 ⇔ 🗉 🔊 (15A) – Extra per person 5.50€ – Reservation fee 15€
Rental rates : (from beginning April to mid Oct.) – 30 🚐 – 6 🏠 – 2 tent bungalows – 4 tents.
Per night from 35 to 60€ – Per week from 150 to 600€ – Reservation fee 15€
🚐 sani-station 10€
Beside the sea; some pitches are virtually 'on top of the water'.

Surroundings : 🦢 ⬌ 🛖
Leisure activities : 🍷 🗙 🛥️ 🚲 ⛵
Facilities : 🕎 ⚿ 🖏 🛁 🍴 launderette

GPS Longitude : -3.54278
Latitude : 48.81029

To visit a town or region, use the MICHELIN Green Guides.

PLÉVEN

22130 – Michelin map **309** I4 – pop. 587 – alt. 80
▶ Paris 431 – Dinan 24 – Dinard 28 – St-Brieuc 38

Municipal

℘ 02 96 84 46 71, *www.pleven.fr*
Address : in the village (in the park belonging to the town hall)
Opening times : from beginning April to mid Nov.
1 ha (40 pitches) flat and relatively flat, grassy
Tariff : 8.50€ 🛉🛉 ⇔ 🗉 🔊 (10A) – Extra per person 1.70€

Surroundings : ♨️
Facilities : 🕎 ⚿ 🚐 🍴
Nearby : 🧺 🎾

GPS Longitude : -2.31911
Latitude : 48.48914

PLOBANNALEC-LESCONIL

29740 – Michelin map **308** F8 – pop. 3,326 – alt. 16
▶ Paris 578 – Audierne 38 – Douarnenez 38 – Pont-l'Abbé 6

Yelloh! Village L'Océan Breton ▲▴

☎ 02 98 82 23 89, *www.camping-bretagne-oceanbreton.fr* – limited spaces for one-night stay
Address : rte de Plobannalec, at Le Manoir de Kerlut (1.6km south along the D 102, follow the signs for Lesconil and take the road to the left)
Opening times : from mid April to mid Sept.
12 ha/8 ha for camping (240 pitches) flat, grassy
Tariff : 44€ ✱✱ ⇦ 🗉 (10A) – Extra per person 8€
Rental rates : (from mid April to mid Sept.) – 180 🛏 – 14 🏠. Per night from 39 to 199€
Per week from 231 to 1,288€
🚮 sani-station 5€ – 10 🗉 18€ – 🛥 18€
Access to the beach via free shuttle service.

Surroundings : 🗭 ♨
Leisure activities : ☂ 🏠 ⊕ ⚓ 🎣 ≋ ⚒ 🎠 ✗ 🖾 ⚏ △ ⚐ forest trail
Facilities : ♿ ⌐ 🖵 ⚲ launderette 🍴 🛒

GPS
Longitude : -4.22574
Latitude : 47.81167

Fire safety doesn't stop when you leave your accommodation.
Always take care and consider the fire risks.

PLOEMEL

56400 – Michelin map **308** M9 – pop. 2,508 – alt. 46
▶ Paris 485 – Auray 8 – Lorient 34 – Quiberon 23

Municipal St-Laurent

☎ 02 97 56 85 90, *www.campingdesaintlaurent.com*
Address : at Kergonvo (2.5km to the northwest, follow the signs for Belz, near D 22 junction, take D 186)
Opening times : from beginning April to end Oct.
3 ha (90 pitches) flat and relatively flat, grassy
Tariff : 20.90€ ✱✱ ⇦ 🗉 (10A) – Extra per person 5€ – Reservation fee 10€
Rental rates : (from beginning April to end Oct.) – 23 🛏 – 2 tent bungalows.
Per night from 90 to 155 € – Per week from 205 to 755 € – Reservation fee 10€
🚮 sani-station 5€

Surroundings : 🗭 ♨♨
Leisure activities : ✗ ⚓ 🖾
Facilities : ⌐ 🖵 ⚲ 🛒

GPS
Longitude : -3.10013
Latitude : 47.66369

Kergo

☎ 02 97 56 80 66, *www.campingkergo.com*
Address : situated 2km southeast along the D 186, follow the signs for La Trinité-sur-Mer and take the turning on the left
Opening times : from beginning May to end Sept.
2.5 ha (135 pitches) relatively flat, flat, grassy
Tariff : 18€ ✱✱ ⇦ 🗉 (10A) – Extra per person 4€
Rental rates : (from beginning April to beginning Nov.) – 12 🛏. Per night from 35 to 75 €
Per week from 225 to 560 € – Reservation fee 10€
🚮 sani-station 6€ – 🛥 13€

Surroundings : 🐾 ♨
Leisure activities : 🖾 ≋ jacuzzi 🎠
Facilities : ♿ ⌐ 🖵 ⚲

GPS
Longitude : -3.05362
Latitude : 47.64403

PLOÉVEN

29550 – Michelin map **308** F6 – pop. 505 – alt. 60
◗ Paris 585 – Brest 64 – Châteaulin 15 – Crozon 25

La Mer

℘ 02 98 81 29 19, *www.campingdelamer29.fr*
Address :at Ty Anquer Plage (3km southwest, 300m from the beach)
Opening times : from beginning June to end Sept.
1 ha (54 pitches) flat, grassy
Tariff : ★ 4.20€ ⇔ 2.50€ ▣ 4.20€ – ⟨∄⟩ (10A) 4.30€
Rental rates : (from beginning June to mid Sept.) – 1 ⌷⟐ – 6 tent bungalows.
Per night from 70 to 90 € – Per week from 180 to 500 €

Surroundings : ♀
Facilities : ⚍ ⤳ ⁙ ▣

GPS Longitude : -4.26796
Latitude : 48.14806

The Michelin classification (△△△△ … △) is totally independent of the official star classification system awarded by the local prefecture or other official organisation.

PLOMEUR

29120 – Michelin map **308** F7 – pop. 3,634 – alt. 33
◗ Paris 579 – Douarnenez 39 – Pont-l'Abbé 6 – Quimper 26

Aire Naturelle Kéraluic

℘ 02 98 82 10 22, *www.keraluic.fr*
Address : at Keraluic (4.3km northeast along the D 57, follow the signs for Plonéour-Lanvern)
Opening times : from beginning May to end Oct.
1 ha (25 pitches) flat, grassy
Tariff : 18.90€ ★★ ⇔ ▣ ⟨∄⟩ (6A) – Extra per person 4.50€
Rental rates : (permanent) ⬥⬥ – 2 ⊨ – 3 studios – 1 apartment – 2 tents.
Per week from 395 to 495€
Old farmhouse buildings that have been attractively renovated.

Surroundings : ⬥ ♀
Leisure activities : ▦ ⤳
Facilities : ⚹ ⚍ ♨ ⁙ ▣

GPS Longitude : -4.26624
Latitude : 47.86148

Lanven

℘ 02 98 82 00 75, *www.campinglanven.com*
Address : at La Chapelle de Beuzec (3.5km northwest along the D 57, follow the signs for Plonéour-Lanvern then take the road to the left)
Opening times : from beginning April to end Sept.
3.7 ha (159 pitches) flat, grassy
Tariff : (2012 price) ★ 3.95€ ⇔ ▣ 5.80€ – ⟨∄⟩ (10A) 3€
Rental rates : (2012 price) (from beginning April to end Sept.) – 6 ⌷⟐.
Per night from 45 to 60€ – Per week from 200 to 530€
Summer camps are held here.

Surroundings : ⬥ ⊏⊐ ♀
Leisure activities : ⛨ ✗ ⤳
Facilities : ⚍ ⁙ launderette

GPS Longitude : -4.30663
Latitude : 47.8505

PLOMODIERN

29550 – Michelin map **308** F5 – pop. 2,182 – alt. 60
▶ Paris 559 – Brest 60 – Châteaulin 12 – Crozon 25

L'Iroise

☎ 02 98 81 52 72, *www.camping-iroise.fr*
Address : Plage de Pors-Ar-Vag (5km southwest, 100m from the beach)
Opening times : from beginning April to end Sept.
2.5 ha (132 pitches) terraced, flat and relatively flat, grassy
Tariff : ♣ 5.60€ ⇦ 🔳 10€ – ⚡ (10A) 4.90€ – Reservation fee 16€
Rental rates : (permanent) – 2 caravans – 16 🚐 – 16 🏠. Per night from 56 to 89€
Per week from 250 to 820€ – Reservation fee 16€
🚽 sani-station

Surroundings : 🌊 ≤ Baie de Douarnenez ♀
Leisure activities : 🍸 🔲 jacuzzi ⚡ 🎣 🖼 ⛷
Facilities : 🕭 ⚿ 🏠 ⚐ 🚻 launderette 🐎
Nearby : ✗ watersports centre

GPS Longitude : -4.29397
Latitude : 48.17006

PLONÉOUR-LANVERN

29720 – Michelin map **308** F7 – pop. 5,725 – alt. 71
▶ Paris 578 – Douarnenez 25 – Guilvinec 14 – Plouhinec 21

Municipal de Mariano

☎ 02 98 87 74 80, *www.ploneour-lanvern.fr*
Address : Impasse du Plateau (to the north along the D 57)
1 ha (59 pitches) flat, grassy
Rentals : 3 🏠.

Surroundings : 🌊 🚐 ♀♀
Leisure activities : 🔲 ⚡ ✂ ❀
Facilities : 🕭 ⚿ launderette

GPS Longitude : -4.2839
Latitude : 47.90645

This guide is updated regularly, so buy your new copy every year!

PLOUÉZEC

22470 – Michelin map **309** E2 – pop. 3,368 – alt. 100
▶ Paris 489 – Guingamp 28 – Lannion 39 – Paimpol 6

Domaine du Launay

☎ 02 96 20 63 15, *www.domaine-du-launay.com*
Address : 11 rte de Toul Veign (3.1km southwest along the D 77, follow the signs for Yvias and take turning to the right)
Opening times : from beginning April to end Oct.
4 ha (90 pitches) terraced, grassy
Tariff : 15€ ♣♣ ⇦ 🔳 ⚡ (16A) – Extra per person 4.50€ – Reservation fee 10€
Rental rates : (from beginning April to end Oct.) – 10 🚐. Per night from 70 €
Per week from 250 to 800 €– Reservation fee 10€
🚽 sani-station 3€ – 10 🔳 12€ – 🚐 ⚡12€
Decorative trees and shrubs.

Surroundings : 🌊 ≤ 🚐 ♀
Leisure activities : 🍸 🔲 ⚡ 🚲 🎣 ⛷ entertainment room
Facilities : 🕭 ⚿ 🚻 launderette
Nearby : ✂ ◊ 🐎

GPS Longitude : -3.00286
Latitude : 48.73523

Le Cap Horn Cap des Îles

℡ 02 96 20 64 28, *www.lecaphorn.com*
Address : r. de Port Lazo (2.3km northeast along the D 77, direct access to the beach)
Opening times : from beginning April to end Sept.
4 ha (149 pitches) terraced, relatively flat, grassy, stony
Tariff : 26€ ✶✶ 🚐 🔲 🔌 (18A) – Extra per person 3.50€ – Reservation fee 12€
Rental rates : (from beginning April to end Sept.) – 31 🛖. Per night from 33 to 99 €
Per week from 235 to 700 € – Reservation fee 12€
🚐 sani-station 11€ – 6 🔲 17€ – 🛶 11€
Overlooking the Anse de Paimpol (cove) and the Ile de Bréhat.

Surroundings : 🌿 ⛰ 🏞	
Leisure activities : 🍴 🎱 🚣 🚲 🔲 🏊	**GPS** Longitude : -2.96311
Facilities : ♿ ⊶ 🌳 🍴 launderette 🔲	Latitude : 48.76
Nearby : 🎿 🔨 🌊 🐎	

PLOUGASNOU

29630 – Michelin map **308** I2 – pop. 3,268 – alt. 55
▶ Paris 545 – Brest 76 – Guingamp 62 – Lannion 34

Flower Domaine de Mesqueau

℡ 02 98 67 37 45, *www.camping-bretagne-mer.com*
Address : 870 rte de Mesqueau (3.5km south along the D 46, follow the signs for Morlaix then continue 800m along the turning to the left, 100m from a small lake (direct access)
Opening times : from end March to end Sept.
7.5 ha (100 pitches) flat, grassy
Tariff : 32€ ✶✶ 🚐 🔲 🔌 (6A) – Extra per person 4€ – Reservation fee 12€
Rental rates : (from end March to end Sept.) 🅿 – 30 🛖 – 5 tent bungalows.
Per night from 20 to 113€ – Per week from 140 to 791€ – Reservation fee 12€

Surroundings : 🌿 ♨	
Leisure activities : 🎱 🚣 🎿 🏊 multi-sports ground	**GPS** Longitude : -3.78101
Facilities : ♿ ⊶ 🌳 🍴 🔲	Latitude : 48.66462
Nearby : ✖ 🚣 🎣	

PLOUGASTEL-DAOULAS

29470 – Michelin map **308** E4 – pop. 13,304 – alt. 113
▶ Paris 596 – Brest 12 – Morlaix 60 – Quimper 64

St-Jean 👥

℡ 02 98 40 32 90, *www.campingsaintjean.com*
Address : at Saint-Jean (4.6km northeast along the D 29 et N 165, take the exit for the Leclerc commercial centre)
Opening times : from mid April to end Sept.
203 ha (125 pitches) terraced, flat and relatively flat, grassy, gravelled
Tariff : (2012 price) ✶ 5.10€ 🚐 🔲 15.30€ – 🔌 (10A) 3.10€ – Reservation fee 15€
Rental rates : (2012 price) (from mid April to end Sept.) – 44 🛖. Per night from 46 to 72€
Per week from 224 to 714€ – Reservation fee 15€
Pleasant location and setting beside the estuary of the Elorn river.

Surroundings : 🌿 🏞 ♨ 🏔	
Leisure activities : 🍴 ✖ 🎱 🎦 evening 🎿 🚣 🚲 🔲 🏊	**GPS** Longitude : -4.35334
multi-sports ground	Latitude : 48.40122
Facilities : ♿ ⊶ 🔲 🌳 🍴 launderette 🚐	

PLOUGONVELIN

29217 – Michelin map **308** C4 – pop. 3,693 – alt. 44
▶ Paris 616 – Brest 21 – Brignogan-Plages 56 – Quimper 95

Les Terrasses de Bertheaume
(rental of mobile homes only)

℘ 02 98 48 32 37, *www.camping-brest.com* – traditional camp. spaces also available
Address : rte de Perzel
Opening times : permanent
2 ha terraced, grassy
Rental rates : 36 ⸬. Per night from 38 to 100€ – Per week from 167 to 620€

Surroundings : ⸬ ≼
Leisure activities : ⸬ ⸬ ⸬ (small swimming pool)
Facilities : ⸬ ⸬ launderette
Nearby : scuba diving

GPS Longitude : -4.70303
Latitude : 48.33989

PLOUGOULM

29250 – Michelin map **308** G3 – pop. 1,805 – alt. 60
▶ Paris 560 – Brest 58 – Brignogan-Plages 27 – Morlaix 24

Municipal du Bois de la Palud

℘ 02 98 29 81 82, *www.plougoulm.fr*
Address : Creach ar Feunteun (900m west of the D 10-D 69 junction (Criossant de Plougoulm), following signs for Plouescat and take the road to the right)
0.7 ha (34 pitches) terraced, relatively flat, grassy

Surroundings : ⸬ ≼ ⸬ ⸬
Facilities : ⸬ ⸬ ⸬
Nearby :

GPS Longitude : -4.05323
Latitude : 48.67236

PLOUGOUMELEN

56400 – Michelin map **308** N9 – pop. 2,378 – alt. 27
▶ Paris 471 – Auray 10 – Lorient 51 – Quiberon 39

La Fontaine du Hallate

℘ 06 16 30 08 33, *www.camping-en-morbihan.fr*
Address : 8 ch. de Poul Fetan (3.2km southeast towards Ploeren and follow the signs for Baden to the right; at Hallate)
Opening times : from beginning April to end Oct.
3 ha (94 pitches) relatively flat, flat, grassy, lake
Tariff : 19.35€ ⸬⸬ ⸬ ⸬ ⸬ (6A) – Extra per person 2.88€
Rental rates : (from beginning April to end Oct.) – 12 ⸬ – 1 yurt. Per night from 60 to 70 € Per week from 195 to 599 €

Surroundings : ⸬ ≼ ⸬ ⸬
Leisure activities : ⸬
Facilities : ⸬ ⸬ ⸬ ⸬ ⸬ launderette

GPS Longitude : -2.8989
Latitude : 47.6432

Municipal Kergouguec

℘ 02 97 57 88 74, *www.plougoumelen.fr/*
Address : r. Notre-Dame-de-Bequerel (500m south of the town, following signs for Baden, by the stadium)
1.5 ha (80 pitches) flat, grassy

Surroundings : ⸬⸬
Leisure activities : ⸬
Facilities : ⸬ ⸬

GPS Longitude : -2.92446
Latitude : 47.64881

PLOUGRESCANT

22820 – Michelin map **309** C1 – pop. 1,347 – alt. 53
▶ Paris 516 – Lannion 26 – Perros-Guirec 23 – St-Brieuc 68

Le Gouffre

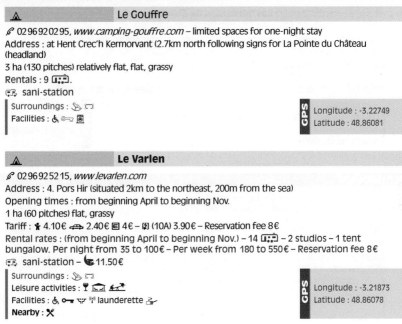

✆ 02 96 92 02 95, *www.camping-gouffre.com* – limited spaces for one-night stay
Address : at Hent Crec'h Kermorvant (2.7km north following signs for La Pointe du Château (headland)
3 ha (130 pitches) relatively flat, flat, grassy
Rentals : 9 ⛺.
sani-station

Surroundings :
Facilities :

Longitude : -3.22749
Latitude : 48.86081

Le Varlen

✆ 02 96 92 52 15, *www.levarlen.com*
Address : 4. Pors Hir (situated 2km to the northeast, 200m from the sea)
Opening times : from beginning April to beginning Nov.
1 ha (60 pitches) flat, grassy
Tariff : ♦ 4.10€ 2.40€ 4€ – (10A) 3.90€ – Reservation fee 8€
Rental rates : (from beginning April to beginning Nov.) – 14 ⛺ – 2 studios – 1 tent bungalow. Per night from 35 to 100€ – Per week from 180 to 550€ – Reservation fee 8€
sani-station – 11.50€

Surroundings :
Leisure activities :
Facilities : launderette
Nearby : ✕

Longitude : -3.21873
Latitude : 48.86078

This guide is not intended as a list of all the camping sites in France;
its aim is to provide a selection of the best sites in each category.

PLOUGUERNEAU

29880 – Michelin map **308** D3 – pop. 6,411 – alt. 60
▶ Paris 604 – Brest 27 – Landerneau 33 – Morlaix 68

La Grève Blanche

✆ 02 98 04 70 35, *www.campinggreveblanche.com*
Address : at St-Michel (4km north along the D 32, follow the signs for Le Mont-St-Michel and take the turning to the left; beside beach)
Opening times : from end March to mid Oct.
2.5 ha (100 pitches) flat and relatively flat, grassy, sandy, rocks
Tariff : (2012 price) ♦ 3.40€ 1.70€ 3.40€ – (10A) 2.90€
Rental rates : (2012 price) (permanent) – 2 caravans – 2 ⛺. Per night from 125€
Per week from 290 to 530€
sani-station 4€ – 9€
Natural setting near rocks and overlooking the beach.

Surroundings :
Leisure activities :
Facilities :

Longitude : -4.523
Latitude : 48.6305

Du Vougot

℘ 0298256151, *www.campingplageduvougot.com*

Address : rte de Prat Ledan (7.4km northeast along the D 13 and the D 10, follow the signs for Guisseny, then take the D 52; along the bank of the Vougot, 250m from the sea)

Opening times : from beginning April to end Oct.

2.5 ha (55 pitches) flat, sandy, grassy

Tariff : 19.80€ ♥♥ ⇔ 回 ⓰ (10A) – Extra per person 4.50€

Rental rates : (from beginning April to end Oct.) – 16 ⓵⁞ – 1 tent. Per night from 48 to 77 €
Per week from 190 to 585 €

🚽 sani-station 4€ – 🔋8€

Surroundings : 🌿 ⌂ ♀
Leisure activities : ⛵
Facilities : ⚬⇥ ¶ launderette
Nearby : watersports centre

GPS Longitude : -4.45
Latitude : 48.63132

PLOUHA

22580 – Michelin map **309** E2 – pop. 4,582 – alt. 96
▶ Paris 479 – Guingamp 24 – Lannion 49 – St-Brieuc 31

Les Castels Le Domaine de Keravel

℘ 0296224913, *www.keravel.com*

Address :at La Trinité (situated 2km to the northeast, near the chapel)

Opening times : from beginning June to mid Sept.

5 ha/2 ha for camping (116 pitches) terraced, relatively flat, grassy

Tariff : (2012 price) 44.50€ ♥♥ ⇔ 回 ⓰ (16A) – Extra per person 7.40€ – Reservation fee 5€

Rental rates : (2012 price) (permanent) – 6 ⓵⁞ – 4 apartments – 3 gîtes.
Per night from 55 to 90 € – Per week from 310 to 880 € – Reservation fee 5€

🚽 sani-station – 20 回 26.70€

In the pleasant grounds of a manor house.

Surroundings : 🌿 ⌂ ♀♀
Leisure activities : 🎬 ⛵ ✳ 🏊
Facilities : ♿ ⚬⇥ 🛁 ⚲ ⇝ ¶ launderette
Nearby : 🛒 ♞

GPS Longitude : -2.9092
Latitude : 48.68936

Gîtes range from small maisonettes to old farmhouses with several bedrooms.

PLOUHARNEL

56340 – Michelin map **308** M9 – pop. 2,000 – alt. 21
▶ Paris 490 – Auray 13 – Lorient 33 – Quiberon 15

Kersily

℘ 0297523965, *www.camping-kersily.com*

Address : at Ste-Barbe (2.5km northwest on the D 781, follow the signs for Lorient and take the rte de Ste-Barbe on the left)

Opening times : from beginning April to end Oct.

2.5 ha (120 pitches) relatively flat, flat, grassy

Tariff : (2012 price) ♥ 5.40€⇔ 回 8.90€ – ⓰ (10A) 3.90€ – Reservation fee 10€

Rental rates : (2012 price) (from beginning April to end Oct.) – 24 ⓵⁞.
Per night from 50 to 70€ – Per week from 200 to 490 € – Reservation fee 10€

🚽 sani-station 2€

Surroundings : 🌿 ♀♀
Leisure activities : ✗ 🎬 ☕evening ⛵ ✳ 🏊 ⚲ entertainment room
Facilities : ♿ ⚬⇥ 🛁 ⚲ ⇝ ¶ launderette

GPS Longitude : -3.1316
Latitude : 47.61107

⛺ Les Goélands

📞 02 97 52 31 92, *www.camping-lesgoelands.com*
Address : at Kergonan (located 1.5km east along the D 781, follow the signs for Carnac then continue 500m along the turning to the left)
1.6 ha (80 pitches) flat, grassy
Rentals : 🚐 – 3 🏠.
🚮 sani-station

Surroundings : 🏖 ⛲
Leisure activities : 🏄 ⛴
Facilities : ⚡ 🚿 🔥
Nearby : 🍴

GPS	Longitude : -3.09657 Latitude : 47.59461

PLOUHINEC

29780 – Michelin map **308** E6 – pop. 4,217 – alt. 101
▶ Paris 594 – Audierne 5 – Douarnenez 18 – Pont-l'Abbé 27

⛺ Kersiny-Plage

📞 02 98 70 82 44, *www.kersinyplage.com*
Address : 1 r. Nominoé (take the western exit along the D 784, follow the signs for Audierne then continue 1km south following signs for Kersiny, 100m from the beach (direct access)
Opening times : from mid May to mid Sept.
2 ha (70 pitches) terraced, relatively flat, grassy
Tariff : (2012 price) 16.20€ ⛺⛺ 🚐 🔲 🅿 (16A) – Extra per person 4.50€ – Reservation fee 10€
Rental rates : (2012 price) (from beginning April to mid Sept.) 🚐 – 4 🏠 – 3 🏠.
Per week from 300 to 530€ – Reservation fee 10€
🚮 sani-station
Attractive location.

Surroundings : 🏖 ≤ sea 🚐
Facilities : ⚡ 🚿 🔥 🔥
Nearby : 🍴

GPS	Longitude : -4.50819 Latitude : 48.00719

In order for the guide to remain wholly objective, the selection is made on an entirely independent basis. There is no charge for being selected for the guide.

PLOUHINEC

56680 – Michelin map **308** L8 – pop. 4,922 – alt. 10
▶ Paris 503 – Auray 22 – Lorient 18 – Quiberon 30

⛰ Moténo

📞 02 97 36 76 63, *www.camping-le-moteno.com*
Address : r. du Passage d'Étel (4.5km southeast along the D 781 and take a right turn, follow the signs for Le Magouër)
Opening times : from end April to end Sept.
4 ha (230 pitches) flat, grassy
Tariff : (2012 price) 34€ ⛺⛺ 🚐 🔲 🅿 (10A) – Extra per person 6.50€ – Reservation fee 25€
Rental rates : (from end April to end Sept.) – 90 🏠 – 22 🏠. Per night from 60 to 105 €
Per week from 616 to 1,001 € – Reservation fee 25€
🚮 sani-station

Surroundings : 🚐 ⛲
Leisure activities : ❌ 🎮 daytime 🏸 ⛲ jacuzzi 🚴 🏊 ⛴ ⛳
multi-sports ground, entertainment room
Facilities : ♿ ⚡ 🚿 🔥 launderette 🏪 🚐

GPS	Longitude : -3.22127 Latitude : 47.66492

PLOUIGNEAU

29610 – Michelin map **308** I3 – pop. 4,685 – alt. 156
▶ Paris 526 – Brest 72 – Carhaix-Plouguer 43 – Guingamp 44

Aire Naturelle la Ferme de Croas Men

℘ 02 98 79 11 50, *http://ferme-de-croasmen.com*
Address : at Croas Men (2.5km northwest along the D 712 and the D 64, follow the signs for Lanmeur then continue 4.7km following signs for Lanleya to the left, then follow the signs for Garlan)
Opening times : from beginning April to end Oct.
1 ha (25 pitches) flat, grassy, fruit trees
Tariff : (2012 price) ★ 3.20€ ⚓ 回 6€ – (½) (6A) 3.20€
Rental rates : (2012 price) (permanent) – 2 caravans – 3 🚐 – 3 🏠 – 2 tents.
Per night from 60 to 90 € – Per week from 350 to 480 €
🚉 sani-station 15.40€
Working educational farm; museum of farming tools.

Surroundings : 🏞 ♀
Leisure activities : 🎞 🚣
Facilities : ♿ ⊶ ☂ launderette
Nearby : 🐎

Longitude : -3.73792
Latitude : 48.60465

PLOUNÉVEZ-LOCHRIST

29430 – Michelin map **308** F3 – pop. 2,398 – alt. 70
▶ Paris 576 – Brest 41 – Landerneau 24 – Landivisiau 22

Municipal Odé-Vras

℘ 02 98 61 65 17, *www.plounevez-lochrist.fr* – ℞
Address : at Ode Vras (4.5km to the north, along the D 10, 300m from the Baie de Kernic (direct access)
Opening times : from beginning June to beginning Sept.
3 ha (135 pitches) flat, sandy, grassy
Tariff : (2012 price) ★ 2.70€ ⚓ 1€ 回 1.30€ – (½) (6A) 2.35€
Rental rates : (2012 price) (from beginning June to beginning Sept.) – 1 🚐.
Per week from 255 to 330€

Surroundings : 🌳 ♀
Leisure activities : 🎞 🚣
Facilities : ⊶ ☂ 🅖 launderette

Longitude : -4.23942
Latitude : 48.64564

PLOZÉVET

29710 – Michelin map **308** E7 – pop. 2,988 – alt. 70
▶ Paris 588 – Audierne 11 – Douarnenez 19 – Pont-l'Abbé 22

La Corniche

℘ 02 98 91 33 94, *www.campinglacorniche.com*
Address : ch. de la Corniche (take the southern exit along the coast road)
Opening times : from end March to end Sept.
2 ha (120 pitches) flat, grassy
Tariff : 23.30€ ★★ ⚓ 回 (½) (10A) – Extra per person 4.80€ – Reservation fee 10€
Rental rates : (from end March to end Sept.) – 12 🚐 – 9 🏠 – 4 tent bungalows.
Per night from 38 to 62€ – Per week from 200 to 695€ – Reservation fee 10€
🚉 sani-station 4€

Surroundings : 🏞
Leisure activities : 🍴 🎞 🚣 🏊
Facilities : ♿ ⊶ 🅖 ☂ ♨ 🍴 launderette

Longitude : -4.4287
Latitude : 47.98237

PLURIEN

22240 – Michelin map **309** H3 – pop. 1,396 – alt. 48
▶ Paris 436 – Dinard 34 – Lamballe 25 – Plancoët 23

⚠ Municipal la Saline

✆ 02 96 72 17 40, *commune.plurien@orange.fr*
Address : r. du Lac, at Sables d'or-Les Pins (1.2km northwest along the D 34, follow the signs for Sables-d'Or-les-Pins; 500m from the sea)
3 ha (150 pitches) terraced, flat, grassy

Surroundings : ⩽ ⚲
Leisure activities : 🏊🎯
Facilities : ⚹ ⛟ launderette

Longitude : -2.41396
Latitude : 48.63281

> *For more information on visiting particular towns or regions, consult the relevant regional MICHELIN Green Guide. We also recommend you use the appropriate Michelin regional map to locate your selected campsite, to calculate distances and to work out the best route.*

PONTRIEUX

22260 – Michelin map **309** D2 – pop. 1,053 – alt. 13
▶ Paris 491 – Guingamp 18 – Lannion 27 – Morlaix 67

⚠ Traou-Mélédern

✆ 02 96 95 69 27, *www.camping-pontrieux.com*
Address : 400m south of the town; beside the Trieux river
Opening times : permanent
1 ha (50 pitches) relatively flat, flat, grassy
Tariff : (2012 price) ⚹ 3.80€ ⇔ 🅿 5€ – 🔌 (7A) 3€
Rental rates : (2012 price) (permanent) – 1 🛖 – 2 gîtes. Per night from 50 €
Per week from 260 to 360 €

Surroundings : ⌁ ⚲⚲
Leisure activities : 🏊🎯
Facilities : ⚹ ⛟ (from mid-Jun to mid-Sept) 🔧 🍴 📷
Nearby : marina

Longitude : -3.16355
Latitude : 48.6951

PONT-SCORFF

56620 – Michelin map **308** K8 – pop. 3,167 – alt. 42
▶ Paris 509 – Auray 47 – Lorient 11 – Quiberon 56

⚠ Ty Nénez

✆ 02 97 32 51 16, *www.lorient-camping.com*
Address : rte de Lorient (1.8km southwest along the D 6)
Opening times : permanent
2.5 ha (93 pitches) flat, relatively flat, grassy
Tariff : ⚹ 4.50€ ⇔ 🅿 7€ – 🔌 (8A) 3€
Rental rates : (permanent) – 12 🛖 – 2 tents. Per night from 37 to 99 €
Per week from 259 to 693 €
🔧 sani-station 2€ – 7 🅿 10.30€ – 🚐 8€

Surroundings : ⌁ ⚲
Leisure activities : 🍴 🏊🎯
Facilities : ⚹ ⛟ 🏧 ⛩ 🍴 launderette

Longitude : -3.40664
Latitude : 47.82081

PORDIC

22590 – Michelin map **309** F3 – pop. 5,923 – alt. 97
▶ Paris 459 – Guingamp 33 – Lannion 65 – St-Brieuc 11

Les Madières

℘ 02 96 79 02 48, *www.campinglesmadieres.com et www.camping-lesmadieres.com*
Address : at Le Vat the Madec (situated 2km northeast following signs for Binic and take a right turn)
Opening times : from beginning April to end Oct.
1.6 ha (93 pitches) relatively flat, flat, grassy
Tariff : 🕴 5.50€ 🚐 🗉 7.50€ – 🔌 (10A) 4.50€
Rental rates : (2012 price) (from beginning April to end Oct.) – 9 ⛺.
Per night from 70 to 90 € – Per week from 310 to 580 € – Reservation fee 10€
🚐 4 🗉 14€
A pleasant, leafy setting, with good shade. Some pitches with a view of the sea and the port at St-Quay-Portrieux.

Surroundings : 🌳 ⌂ ♤♤
Leisure activities : 🍸 ✕ 🏊
Facilities : ♿ ⊶ ▥ ᵀ launderette

GPS
Longitude : -2.80475
Latitude : 48.58266

Le Roc de l'Hervieu

℘ 02 96 79 30 12, *www.campinglerocdelhervieu.fr* – limited spaces for one-night stay
Address : 19 r. d'Estienne d'Orves (3km northeast following signs for La Pointe de Pordic (headland) and take the road to the right)
Opening times : from beginning May to end Sept.
2.5 ha (166 pitches) flat, grassy
Tariff : 🕴 4.50€ 🚐 3.80€ 🗉 4.50€ – 🔌 (10A) 3.80€ – Reservation fee 30€
Rental rates : (from mid April to end Sept.) – 20 ⛺. Per night from 40 to 60€
Per week from 300 to 500€
🚐 sani-station 3€

Surroundings : 🌳 ⌂
Leisure activities : 🎣 🏇
Facilities : ♿ ⊶ ᵀ 🖫

GPS
Longitude : -2.7811
Latitude : 48.58188

Some campsites benefit from proximity to a municipal leisure centre.

PORT-MANECH

29920 – Michelin map **308** I8
▶ Paris 545 – Carhaix-Plouguer 73 – Concarneau 18 – Pont-Aven 12

St-Nicolas

℘ 02 98 06 89 75, *www.campinglesaintnicolas.com*
Address : at Port-Manech (north of the town, 200m from the beach)
Opening times : from end April to mid Sept.
3 ha (180 pitches) flat, sloping, terraced, grassy
Tariff : (2012 price) 27€ 🕴🕴 🚐 🗉 🔌 (10A) – Extra per person 6€ – Reservation fee 7€
Rental rates : (2012 price) (from end March to mid Sept.) ⌸ – 13 ⛺.
Per night from 30 to 115€ – Per week from 210 to 806€ – Reservation fee 7€
Pretty shrubs and flowers.

Surroundings : ⌂ ♤♤
Leisure activities : 🎣 🏓 🏊 ⛷
Facilities : ♿ ⊶ ᵀ launderette
Nearby : 🍸 ⌑

GPS
Longitude : -3.74541
Latitude : 47.80512

LE POULDU

29360 – Michelin map **308** J8
▶ Paris 521 – Concarneau 37 – Lorient 25 – Moëlan-sur-Mer 10

Les Embruns

✆ 02 98 39 91 07, www.camping-les-embruns.com
Address : r. du Philosophe Alain (in the town, 350m from the beach)
Opening times : from mid April to mid Sept.
5.5 ha (180 pitches) flat and relatively flat, grassy, sandy, fruit trees
Tariff : 33 € ♣ ♣ ⇔ 回 ⑭ (16A) – Extra per person 6.50 € – Reservation fee 20 €
Rental rates : (from mid April to mid Sept.) – 35 ⛺. Per night from 50 to 130 €
Per week from 250 to 900 € – Reservation fee 20 €
⛽ sani-station 5 € – 14 回 15 € – ⛺ ⑭14 €
Pretty shrubs and flowers.

> **Surroundings** : ⌑ ♀♀
> **Leisure activities** : � daytime ⌘ hammam 🚣 🚴 ⛏ 🖼
> (open-air in season) ⛷ wildlife park
> **Facilities** : ♿ ⚡ ▥ ♨ 🚿 🚰 🍴 launderette
> **Nearby** : ⚓ ✕ 🎣 🍽 🍷

GPS Longitude : -3.54696 Latitude : 47.76947

Keranquernat

✆ 02 98 39 92 32, www.camping.keranquernat.com
Address : Keranquernat (at the roundabout, take northeastern exit)
Opening times : from end April to beginning Sept.
1.5 ha (100 pitches) flat and relatively flat, grassy
Tariff : ♣ 4 € ⇔ 回 8.50 € – ⑭ (10A) 4 €
Rental rates : (from end April to beginning Sept.) ⛺ – 10 ⛺. Per night 85 € – Per week 490 €
⛽ sani-station
Pleasant setting shaded by apple trees and surrounded by flowers.

> **Surroundings** : ⛰ ⌑ ♀♀
> **Leisure activities** : ♫ ⌘ ♨
> **Facilities** : ♿ ⚡ (Jul–Aug) 🚿 ♨ 🍴 launderette
> **Nearby** : ⚓ ✕ 🍽 🍷

GPS Longitude : -3.54332 Latitude : 47.7727

Locouarn

✆ 02 98 39 91 79, www.camping-locouarn.com
Address : situated 2km north along the D 49, follow the signs for Quimperlé
Opening times : from beginning June to mid Sept.
2.5 ha (100 pitches) relatively flat, flat, grassy, open site
Tariff : 16.30 € ♣ ♣ ⇔ 回 ⑭ (10A) – Extra per person 3.30 €
Rental rates : (from end April to mid Sept.) – 15 ⛺. Per night from 80 to 100 €
Per week from 160 to 490 € – Reservation fee 5 €

> **Surroundings** : ♀
> **Leisure activities** : ♨
> **Facilities** : ♿ ⚡ 🚿 ♨ 🚰 🍴 launderette
> **Nearby** : ⚓ ♈ ✕ 🐎

GPS Longitude : -3.54793 Latitude : 47.7855

We value your opinion and welcome your feedback.
Do email us at campingfrance@tp.michelin.com

Les Grands Sables

℘ 02 98 39 94 43, www.camping-lesgrandssables.com

Address : 22 r. Philosophe Alain (in the town, 200m from the beach)
Opening times : from beginning April to mid Sept.
2.4 ha (133 pitches) flat and relatively flat, terrace, grassy, sandy
Tariff : 19.40€ ♣ ♣ ⊖ 🗉 🕸 (4A) – Extra per person 4.75€ – Reservation fee 9€
Rental rates : (permanent) – 17 🚐. Per night from 43 to 61€ – Per week from 203 to 580€
Reservation fee 9€

In a leafy location with plenty of shade and a view of the pretty chapel of Notre-Dame-de-la-Paix.

Surroundings : ♀
Facilities : o━ 🗗 🖰 🏺 launderette
Nearby : 🏖 ✕ 🍴 ◊

GPS Longitude : -3.54716
Latitude : 47.7683

Croas An Ter

℘ 02 98 39 94 19, www.campingcroasanter.com

Address : at Quelvez (located 1.5km north along the D49, follow the signs for Quimperlé)
Opening times : from beginning May to mid Sept.
3.5 ha (90 pitches) flat, sloping, grassy
Tariff : 15.70€ ♣ ♣ ⊖ 🗉 🕸 (6A) – Extra per person 3.60€
Rental rates : (permanent) – 2 🚐 – 1 tent. Per week from 355 to 475€

Surroundings : 🏞 🗁 ♀♀
Leisure activities : ✕
Facilities : ♿ o━ 🗗 🖰 🏺

GPS Longitude : -3.54104
Latitude : 47.78515

Key to rentals symbols:
12 🚐 **Number of mobile homes**
20 🏠 **Number of chalets**
6 🛏 **Number of rooms to rent**
Per night **Minimum/maximum rate per night**
30–50€
Per week **Minimum/maximum rate per week**
300–1,000€

POULLAN-SUR-MER

29100 – Michelin map **308** E6 – pop. 1,499 – alt. 79
▶ Paris 596 – Rennes 244 – Quimper 30 – Brest 80

Flower le Pil Koad ♣♣

℘ 02 98 74 26 39, www.camping-douarnenez.com

Address : 30 r. Luc Robert (600m east of the town along the D7)
Opening times : from mid April to mid Sept.
5.7 ha (190 pitches) flat, grassy
Tariff : 32€ ♣ ♣ ⊖ 🗉 🕸 (10A) – Extra per person 5.50€
Rental rates : (from mid April to mid Sept.) – 73 🚐 – 20 🏠 – 7 tents.
Per night from 40 to 139€ – Per week from 196 to 973€
🚐 sani-station 2€ – 🔋 🕸 12€

Surroundings : 🏞 🗁 ♀♀
Leisure activities : 🍴 ✕ 🎦 🎲 evening 🎯 🏋 🚲 ✂ ♪ 🎱 🏊 🏓 🎣
multi-sports ground
Facilities : ♿ o━ 🖰 🛁 ✐ 🏺 launderette 🏖 🔥

GPS Longitude : -4.40634
Latitude : 48.08162

PRIMEL-TRÉGASTEL

29630 – Michelin map **308** I2
▶ Paris 554 – Rennes 198 – Quimper 105 – Brest 79

▲ Municipal de la Mer

⌀ 02 98 72 37 06, *www.mairie-plougasnou.fr*
Address : 15 rte de Karreg An Ty (4km north along the D 46)
Opening times : from beginning June to end Sept.
1 ha (63 pitches) flat and relatively flat, terrace, grassy
Tariff : (2012 price) ♦ 3.70€ ⇌ 1.25€ 圓 6.80€ (½) (10A)
Rental rates : (2012 price) (from beginning June to end Sept.) – 2 tent bungalows.
Per week from 250 to 350 €
⛽ sani-station
Excellent location beside the sea.

Surroundings : ⅋ ≤ Île de Batz and Roscoff ⛰
Leisure activities : 🖥 ⛵
Facilities : ♿ ☕ (Jul–Aug) ⚑ launderette
Nearby : ♥ ✕

GPS Longitude : -3.81527
Latitude : 48.71477

A chambre d'hôte is a guesthouse or B & B-style accommodation.

PRIMELIN

29770 – Michelin map **308** D6 – pop. 742 – alt. 78
▶ Paris 605 – Audierne 7 – Douarnenez 28 – Quimper 44

⛰ Municipal de Kermalero

⌀ 02 98 74 84 75, *www.mairie-primelin.fr*
Address : rte de l'Océan (take the western exit towards the port)
Opening times : from beginning March to end Oct.
1 ha (75 pitches) flat and relatively flat, grassy
Tariff : (2012 price) 15€ ♦♦ ⇌ 圓 (½) (6A) – Extra per person 3.50€ – Reservation fee 10€
⛽ sani-station 2€ – 6 圓 3€

Surroundings : ⅋ ≤ ⌂
Leisure activities : 🖥 ⛵
Facilities : ♿ ☕ (Jul–Aug) ⚏ ⚒ ⚑ launderette
Nearby : ✕

GPS Longitude : -4.61067
Latitude : 48.02544

PRIZIAC

56320 – Michelin map **308** K6 – pop. 1,046 – alt. 163
▶ Paris 498 – Concarneau 55 – Lorient 42 – Pontivy 39

▲ Municipal Bel Air

⌀ 02 97 34 63 55, *priziac.com*
Address : at l'Etang du Bel Air (500m north along the D 109 and take the turning to the left)
1.5 ha (60 pitches) flat, grassy
Rentals : 4 🏠.
⛽ sani-station
Green setting and plenty of shade, near a small lake.

Surroundings : ⅋ ♨ ⛰
Leisure activities : 🖥
Facilities : ♿ launderette
Nearby : ♥ ⛵ ✕ ≈ (beach) ⚓ ⚓ watersports centre

GPS Longitude : -3.41418
Latitude : 48.06155

QUIBERON

56170 – Michelin map **308** M10 – pop. 5,027 – alt. 10
▶ Paris 505 – Auray 28 – Concarneau 98 – Lorient 47

Flower Le Bois d'Amour ♣♨

✆ 0297501352, *www.quiberon-camping.com*
Address : r. Saint-Clément (located 1.5km southeast, 300m from the sea and sea spa centre)
4.6 ha (272 pitches) flat, sandy, grassy
Rentals : 190 ⛺.

Surroundings : ▭ ♀
Leisure activities : ♟ ✗ 🏛 🎱 🚶 🏊 🚴 🎿
Facilities : ♿ ⚷ ☂ ♨ launderette 🚿

Nearby : ✂ ♨ ⚘ 🐎

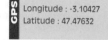
Longitude : -3.10427
Latitude : 47.47632

Do.Mi.Si.La.Mi. ♣♨

✆ 0297502252, *www.domisilami.com*
Address : at St-Julien, 31 r. de la Vierge (600m to the north, 100m from the beach)
4.4 ha (350 pitches) relatively flat, flat, grassy
Rentals : ⚡ – 70 ⛺.
🚐 6 ▣

Free shuttle service to Quiberon.

Surroundings : ▭ ♀
Leisure activities : ♟ ✗ 🏛 🚶 🏊 🚴 multi-sports ground
Facilities : ♿ ⚷ ☂ ♨ ♨ launderette ♨ 🚿

Longitude : -3.12045
Latitude : 47.49937

Les Joncs du Roch

✆ 0297502437, *www.lesjoncsduroch.com*
Address : r. de l'Aérodrome (situated 2km southeast, 500m from the sea)
Opening times : from end March to end Sept.
2.3 ha (163 pitches) flat, grassy
Tariff : (2012 price) 23.80€ ♦♦ ⚡ ▣ (💧) (10A) – Extra per person 5€
Rental rates : (2012 price) (from end March to end Sept.) ⚡ – 20 ⛺ – 2 tent bungalows.
Per night from 20 to 117€ – Per week from 180 to 705€

Surroundings : ▭ ♀
Leisure activities : 🏛 🏊 multi-sports ground, entertainment room
Facilities : ♿ ⚷ ☂ ♨ ♨ launderette

Nearby : ✂ ♨ ⚘ 🐎

Longitude : -3.10098
Latitude : 47.47946

Beauséjour

✆ 0297304493, *www.campingbeausejour.com*
Address : bd du Parco (800m to the north, 50m from the beach)
Opening times : from mid April to end Sept.
2.4 ha (160 pitches) relatively flat, flat, grassy, sandy
Tariff : ♦ 4€ ⚡ ▣ 15€ – (💧) (10A) 5.20€
Rental rates : (from mid April to end Sept.) – 15 ⛺. Per night from 60 to 100€
Per week from 310 to 690 – Reservation fee 18€
🚐 sani-station 4€

Leisure activities : 🏛 🏊
Facilities : ♿ ⚷ (Jul–Aug) ☂ ♨ ♨ launderette

Nearby : 🛒 ♟ ✗ 🚿

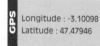
Longitude : -3.12027
Latitude : 47.5003

QUIMPER

29000 – Michelin map **308** G7 – pop. 63,387 – alt. 41 – Leisure centre
▶ Paris 564 – Brest 73 – Lorient 67 – Rennes 215

Les Castels L'Orangerie de Lanniron ♣♨

✆ 02 98 90 62 02, www.lanniron.com
Address : allée de Lanniron (3km south along the ring road (périphérique), then take the exit towards Bénodet and a right turn; near the leisure centre at Creac'h Gwen)
Opening times : from mid May to mid Sept.
38 ha/6.5 ha for camping (235 pitches) flat, grassy
Tariff : 42.60€ ♣♣ ⇦ 回 [∮] (10A) – Extra per person 8.20€ – Reservation fee 20€
Rental rates : (permanent) ⚡ – 32 ⬚ – 11 studios – 1 apartment – 6 gîtes.
Per night from 79 to 139 €– Per week from 441 to 1,148€ – Reservation fee 20€
⬚ sani-station 4.50€
In the magnificent park and grounds of a 15th-century manor house; beside the Odet river.

Surroundings : ▭ ♋♋
Leisure activities : ♈ ✗ ▱ ⊕ ♣ jacuzzi ⬲ ♠ ♈ ♒ ⬔ ⬳ ⬱
Facilities : ♿ ⊶ ♨ ⬔ ⬛ ♈ launderette ⬚ ♨

GPS Longitude : -4.10338
Latitude : 47.97923

QUIMPERLÉ

29300 – Michelin map **308** J7 – pop. 11,384 – alt. 30
▶ Paris 517 – Carhaix-Plouguer 57 – Concarneau 32 – Pontivy 76

Municipal de Kerbertrand

✆ 02 98 39 31 30, www.quimperle-tourisme.com
Address : r. du Camping (located 1.5km west along the D 783, follow the signs for Concarneau and take the road to the right, after the stadium, opposite the Leclerc commercial centre)
Opening times : from beginning June to mid Sept.
1 ha (40 pitches) flat, grassy
Tariff : (2012 price) ♣ 2.85€ ⇦ 1.20€ 回 2.20€ – [∮] (10A) 1.85€

Surroundings : ⬱ ♋♋
Leisure activities : ▱ ⬲
Facilities : ⊶ ⬚
Nearby : ⬱ ✗ ▨ ⬛

GPS Longitude : -3.57044
Latitude : 47.872

To visit a town or region, use the MICHELIN Green Guides.

RAGUENÈS-PLAGE

29920 – Michelin map **308** I8
▶ Paris 545 – Carhaix-Plouguer 73 – Concarneau 17 – Pont-Aven 12

Les Deux Fontaines ♣♨

✆ 02 98 06 81 91, www.les2fontaines.com
Address : at Feunten Vihan (1.3km north following signs for Névez and Trémorvezen)
9 ha (270 pitches) flat, grassy
Rentals : 35 ⬚ – 11 ⬚.
⬚ sani-station
Partially open-air water park.

Surroundings : ⬱ ▭ ♋♋
Leisure activities : ♈ ✗ ▱ ⬲ ♣ ⬲ ⬲ ✗ ⬛ ♒ ⬔ pool scuba diving
Facilities : ♿ ⊶ ♨ ⬔ ⬛ ♈ launderette ⬚ ♨

GPS Longitude : -3.79129
Latitude : 47.7992

Club Airotel Le Raguenès-Plage

📞 02 98 06 80 69, *www.camping-le-raguenes-plage.com*
Address : 19 r. des Îles (400m from the beach, direct access)
Opening times : from end March to end Sept.
6 ha (287 pitches) flat, grassy
Tariff : 36.80€ ♥♥ � 🖲 🖩 (6A) – Extra per person 6€
Rental rates : (from end March to end Sept.) – 60 🚐. Per night from 36 to 119€
Per week from 252 to 830€
🚏 sani-station 16.50€ – 10 🖲 16.50€ – 🛥16.50€

> Surroundings : ♀♀
> Leisure activities : ✗ 🎱 🎆evening ✦✦ 🎣 ⛵ ⚓ ⚲
> Facilities : ♿ ⊶🏠🚿 ♨ 🍴 launderette 🖲 🛆

Longitude : -3.80085
Latitude : 47.79373

Le Vieux Verger – Ty Noul

📞 02 98 06 86 08, *www.campingduvieuxverger.com*
Address : 20 Kéroren (take the northern exit, follow the signs for Névez)
Opening times : from mid April to mid Sept.
2.5 ha (110 pitches) flat, grassy
Tariff : 22.50€ ♥♥ � 🖲 🖩 (10A) – Extra per person 5€ – Reservation fee 10€
Rental rates : (from mid April to mid Sept.) 🏚 – 10 🚐 – 1 apartment.
Per week from 185 to 660€ – Reservation fee 10€
In two separate sections with a small but attractive water park.

> Surroundings : ♀
> Leisure activities : 🏊 🚲 ⚓ ⚲
> Facilities : ♿ ⊶ 🍴

Longitude : -3.79777
Latitude : 47.79663

L'Océan

📞 02 98 06 87 13, *www.camping-ocean.fr*
Address : 15 Imp. des Mouettes, at Kéroren (take the northern exit, follow the signs for Névez and take a right turn, 350m from the beach (direct access)
Opening times : from mid May to mid Sept.
2.2 ha (150 pitches) flat, grassy, sandy
Tariff : 27.40€ ♥♥ � 🖲 🖩 (10A) – Extra per person 6€
Rental rates : (from mid May to mid Sept.) 🏚 – 8 🚐. Per week from 320 to 580€
🚏 sani-station

> Surroundings : 🌊 ⬅ 🏖 ♀
> Leisure activities : 🎱 🏊 🖼 (open-air in season)
> Facilities : ♿ ⊶🏠 🍴 launderette
> Nearby : ✹ ♨

Longitude : -3.79789
Latitude : 47.79471

Michelin classification:

🏔🏔🏔🏔 *Extremely comfortable, equipped to a very high standard*
🏔🏔🏔 *Very comfortable, equipped to a high standard*
🏔🏔 *Comfortable and well equipped*
🏔 *Reasonably comfortable*
⛰ *Satisfactory*

RENNES

35000 – Michelin map **309** L6 – pop. 206,604 – alt. 40
▶ Paris 349 – Angers 129 – Brest 246 – Caen 185

Municipal des Gayeulles

☎ 02 99 36 91 22, *www.camping-rennes.com*
Address : r. Maurice-Audin (take the northeastern exit towards the N 12, follow the signs for Fougères then take the av. des Gayeulles near a small lake)
Opening times : permanent
3 ha (179 pitches) flat, grassy
Tariff : (2012 price) � 4€ ⟷ 1.70€ ▣ 5.80€ – 🔌 (16A) 4€
🚐 sani-station 2€
In the middle of the Parc de Gayeulles, an immense wooded park.

Surroundings : ⌖ ⌑ ♨
Leisure activities : ⛵⛷
Facilities : ♿ ⛽ (Jul–Aug) cc ▦ ⛺ ⚏ ⛾ launderette
Nearby : ⛹ ✗ ▩ ♨ ⛳ (open-air in season) skating rink, wildlife park

GPS Longitude : -1.64772
Latitude : 48.13455

LA ROCHE-BERNARD

56130 – Michelin map **308** R9 – pop. 757 – alt. 38
▶ Paris 444 – Nantes 70 – Ploërmel 55 – Redon 28

Municipal le Pâtis

☎ 02 99 90 60 13, *www.camping-larochebernard.com*
Address : 3 ch. du Pâtis (to the west of the town towards the marina)
Opening times : from mid March to mid Oct.
1 ha (58 pitches) flat, grassy
Tariff : (2012 price) 20.65€ � � ⟷ ▣ 🔌 (6A) – Extra per person 4€
Rental rates : (2012 price) (from mid March to mid Oct.) – 2 🛏. Per night from 84 to 178 €
Per week from 231 to 641 €
🚐 sani-station 2€ – 18 ▣ 10.65€
Beside the Vilaine river, opposite the port.

Surroundings : ⌑ ♨
Leisure activities : ▦ ⚵
Facilities : ♿ ⛽ (Jul–Aug) ▦ ⛺ launderette
Nearby : ⛷ ⚓

GPS Longitude : -2.30523
Latitude : 47.51923

ROCHEFORT-EN-TERRE

56220 – Michelin map **308** Q8 – pop. 662 – alt. 40
▶ Paris 431 – Ploërmel 34 – Redon 26 – Rennes 82

Le Moulin Neuf

☎ 02 97 43 37 52, *www.campingaugredesvents.com*
Address : located 1km southwest along the D 774, follow the signs for Péaule and take the road to the right; 500m from a small lake
Opening times : from beginning April to end Sept.
2.5 ha (60 pitches) sloping, flat, grassy
Tariff : (2012 price) 24.30€ � � ⟷ ▣ 🔌 (10A) – Extra per person 5.50€
Rental rates : (2012 price) (from beginning April to end Sept.) – 5 🛏 – 2 tents.
Per night from 55 to 95 € – Per week from 280 to 625 €

Surroundings : ⌖
Leisure activities : ⛷ ✗ ⛳ (open-air in season)
Facilities : ♿ ⛽ ⛺ ⛾ launderette
Nearby : ✗ ≈ (beach) ⚓

GPS Longitude : -2.34736
Latitude : 47.69587

ROHAN

56580 – Michelin map **308** O6 – pop. 1,637 – alt. 55
▶ Paris 451 – Lorient 72 – Pontivy 17 – Quimperlé 86

⚠ **Municipal le Val d'Oust**

☎ 02 97 51 57 58, *rohan.fr*
Address : r. de St-Gouvry (take the northwestern exit)
Opening times : from mid May to mid Sept.
1 ha (45 pitches) flat, grassy
Tariff : (2012 price) ⚬ 3.30€ ⊞ 1.45€ ▣ 1.80€ – ⚡ (15A) 3.20€
⛺ 15 ▣
Beside the Nantes-Brest canal and near a small lake.

Surroundings : <u>♤♤</u>
Leisure activities : ⚓⛵ ✎
Facilities : ⚬ ⊟ ▣
Nearby : ▾ ✗ ✗ ≊ (beach) ⚓ sports trail

Longitude : -2.7548
Latitude : 48.07077

The pitches of many campsites are marked out with low hedges of attractive bushes and shrubs.

ROSPORDEN

29140 – Michelin map **308** I7 – pop. 7,126 – alt. 125
▶ Paris 544 – Carhaix-Plouguer 51 – Châteaulin 50 – Concarneau 15

⚠ **Municipal Roz-an-Duc**

☎ 02 98 59 90 27, *www.rosporden.fr*
Address : r. de Coray (located 1km north along the D 36, follow the signs for Châteauneuf-du-Faou and take a right turn; by the swimming pool, 100m from a lake)
Opening times : from end June to beginning Sept.
1 ha (49 pitches) open site, terraced, flat, grassy
Tariff : ⚬ 2.65€ ⊞ 1.45€ ▣ 2.55€ – ⚡ (10A) 2.60€
Pleasant wooded setting beside the Aven river.

Surroundings : ⚘ ⊡ <u>♤♤</u>
Facilities : ⚬ ⟲ ⊟ launderette
Nearby : ⛏ ✗ ▦ ◰ ✎ sports trail

Longitude : -3.82645
Latitude : 47.9666

ROZ-SUR-COUESNON

35610 – Michelin map **309** M3 – pop. 1,034 – alt. 65
▶ Paris 365 – Rennes 82 – Caen 134 – St-Lô 99

⚠ **Les Couesnons**

☎ 02 99 80 26 86, *www.lescouesnons.com*
Address : l'Hopital (situated 2km southeast on the D 797)
Opening times : from end March to beginning Nov.
1 ha (57 pitches) flat, grassy
Tariff : (2012 price) 19€ ⚬⚬ ⊞ ▣ ⚡ (10A) – Extra per person 5€
Rental rates : (2012 price) (from end March to beginning Nov.) – 8 ⛺ – 1 tent.
Per night from 30 to 120€ – Per week from 270 to 620€

Surroundings : ⊡ <u>♤♤</u>
Leisure activities : ✗ ▱
Facilities : ⚬ ⟲ ▥ ⚘ ⚲

Longitude : -1.60904
Latitude : 48.59597

ST-BRIAC-SUR-MER

35800 – Michelin map **309** J3 – pop. 1,955 – alt. 30
▶ Paris 411 – Dinan 24 – Dol-de-Bretagne 34 – Lamballe 41

Émeraude

📞 02 99 88 34 55, *www.campingemeraude.com*
Address : 7 ch. de la Souris
Opening times : from mid April to mid Sept.
3.2 ha (194 pitches) relatively flat, flat, grassy
Tariff : (2012 price) ⚕ 6.60€ 回 15.30€ – (4) (6A) 4€ – Reservation fee 16€
Rental rates : (2012 price) (from mid April to mid Sept.) ♿ – 63 🚐 – 14 🏠.
Per night from 61 to 102 € – Per week from 256 to 714€ – Reservation fee 16€
🚰 sani-station 2.50€
Attractive swimming area.

Surroundings : 🏊 🖼 ♨
Leisure activities : 🍸 ✕ 🎱 🛶 🚴 🎣 🎿 ⛵ entertainment room
Facilities : ♿ 🔑 🚿 ♨ 🍴 launderette 🐾

GPS
Longitude : -2.13012
Latitude : 48.62735

The information in the guide may have changed since going to press.

ST-CAST-LE-GUILDO

22380 – Michelin map **309** I3 – pop. 3,500 – alt. 52
▶ Paris 427 – Avranches 91 – Dinan 32 – St-Brieuc 50

Les Castels Le Château de la Galinée ♣♦

📞 02 96 41 10 56, *www.chateaudegalinee.com*
Address : r. de Galinée (7km to the south, access via the D 786, near the crossroads with the road to St-Cast-le-Guildo)
Opening times : from beginning May to beginning Sept.
14 ha (272 pitches) flat, grassy
Tariff : ⚕ 6.90€ 🚙 4.10€ 回 19.80€ – (4) (10A) 5.30€ – Reservation fee 20€
Rental rates : (from mid April to beginning Sept.) 🏕 – 2 caravans – 40 🚐 – 5 🏠 – 6 tent bungalows. Per night from 38 to 165€ – Per week from 266 to 1,155 € – Reservation fee 20€
🚰 sani-station 19.80€

Surroundings : 🏊 🖼 ♨♨
Leisure activities : 🍸 🎱 🎯 🚴 🛝 🛶 ✂ 🎣 🖼 🎿 ⛵ 🎏 multi-sports ground, entertainment room
Facilities : ♿ 🔑 🖼 ▥ 🚿 – 4 individual sanitary facilities (🚽 wc) 🚿 launderette 🐾

GPS
Longitude : -2.25725
Latitude : 48.58403

Le Châtelet ♣♦

📞 02 96 41 96 33, *www.lechatelet.com* – limited spaces for one-night stay
Address : r. des Nouettes (located 1km west, 250m from the beach (direct access)
Opening times : from mid April to mid Sept.
9 ha/3.9 ha for camping (216 pitches) terraced, flat, grassy, very uneven, small lake
Tariff : ⚕ 7.42€ 🚙 回 22€ – (4) (8A) 6€ – Reservation fee 23€
Rental rates : (from mid April to mid Sept.) – 59 🚐 – 6 tents. Per night from 48 to 95 €
Per week from 335 to 950 € – Reservation fee 23€
🚰 sani-station
Site overlooking the Baie de la Frênaye.

Surroundings : 🏊 ⛰ 🖼 ♨
Leisure activities : 🍸 🎱 🎯 🚴 🛶 🖼 (open-air in season) 🎏
Facilities : ♿ 🔑 ♨ 🚿 launderette 🐾
Nearby : 🍴 ✕ 🚴

GPS
Longitude : -2.26959
Latitude : 48.63773

Vert-Bleu Les Mielles
(rental of mobile homes only)

✆ 02 96 41 87 60, *www.campings-vert-bleu.com* – open from mid-Mar to beg Jan for campervans
Address : bd de la Vieux-Ville (take the southern exit along the D 19, follow the signs for St-Malo, right next to the stadium and 200m from the beach)
Opening times :from mid March to mid Nov.
3.5 ha (160 pitches) flat, grassy
Rentals : 50 🚐.
🚽 sani-station

Surroundings : 🏕 🎋
Leisure activities : 🎦 🚣 🏊
Facilities : ♿ ⛟ 🚮 ✂ 🔥 🍴 launderette
Nearby : 🍽 🎣 ♨

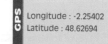
GPS Longitude : -2.25402
Latitude : 48.62694

ST-COULOMB

35350 – Michelin map **309** K2 – pop. 2,454 – alt. 35
▶ Paris 398 – Cancale 6 – Dinard 18 – Dol-de-Bretagne 21

Le Tannée

✆ 02 99 89 41 20, *www.campingdetannee.com* – limited spaces for one-night stay
Address : at Saint-Méloir
Opening times : from beginning April to end Sept.
0.6 ha (30 pitches) flat and relatively flat
Tariff : 19.90€ 👫 🚗 🔲 📶 (10A) – Extra per person 3.60€ – Reservation fee 15€
Rental rates : (from beginning April to end Sept.) – 11 🚐. Per week from 255 to 670€
Reservation fee 15€

Surroundings : 🌳 ≤ 🏕
Leisure activities : 🚲 🎣 (open-air in season)
Facilities : ♿ ⛟ 🚮 🔥 🍴 launderette

GPS Longitude : -1.889
Latitude : 48.68655

Du Guesclin

✆ 02 99 89 03 24, *www.camping-duguesclin.com* – limited spaces for one-night stay
Address : r. de Tannée (2.5km northeast along the D 355, follow the signs for Cancale and take turning to the left)
Opening times : from beginning April to end Oct.
0.9 ha (43 pitches) relatively flat, flat, grassy
Tariff : 20€ 👫 🚗 🔲 📶 (10A) – Extra per person 4.50€
Rental rates : (from beginning April to end Oct.) – 16 🚐. Per night from 50 to 90€
Per week from 245 to 620€ – Reservation fee 15€

Surroundings : 🌳 ≤ 🏕 🎋
Leisure activities : 🎦 🚣 🚲
Facilities : ♿ ⛟ 🚮 🔥 ♨ 🍴 🍴

GPS Longitude : -1.89027
Latitude : 48.68628

There are several different types of sani-station ('borne' in French) – sanitation points providing fresh water and disposal points for grey water. See page 12 for further details.

ST-GILDAS-DE-RHUYS

56730 – Michelin map **308** N9 – pop. 1,647 – alt. 10
▶ Paris 483 – Arzon 9 – Auray 48 – Sarzeau 7

Le Menhir ▲▲

🖉 02 97 45 22 88, www.camping-bretagnesud.com
Address : rte de Port-Crouesty (3.5km north – recommended route via the D 780, follow the signs for Port-Navalo)
5 ha/3 ha for camping (180 pitches) relatively flat, flat, grassy
Rentals : ⌖ – 48 ▥.
🔄 sani-station

Surroundings : ☐ ♤♤
Leisure activities : ▼ ▦ ▟ ☆ % ♪ ⴷ ⴵ
Facilities : ♿ ⌐ ⵣ ⵥ ⵀ ⵟ launderette ⵙ ⵕ

GPS Longitude : -2.84781
Latitude : 47.52874

Goh'Velin

🖉 02 97 45 21 67, www.camping-gohvelin.fr
Address : 89 r. Guernevé (located 1.5km to the north, 300m from the beach)
Opening times : from beginning April to end Sept.
1 ha (93 pitches) flat, grassy
Tariff : 26.50€ ✹✹ ⇔ ▣ ⑭ (16A) – Extra per person 5.50€ – Reservation fee 12€
Rental rates : (from beginning April to end Sept.) ⌖ – 18 ▥. Per night from 50 to 75€
Per week from 240 to 720€ – Reservation fee 12€

Surroundings : ☐ ♤
Leisure activities : ▦ ⵣ ⴷ
Facilities : ⌐ ⵟ ▤
Nearby : ♪ ⵠ

GPS Longitude : -2.84515
Latitude : 47.51204

These symbols are used for a campsite that is exceptional in its category:
▲▲▲...▲ *Particularly pleasant setting, quality and range of services available*
⫷⫸ *Tranquil, isolated site – quiet site, particularly at night*
⪡⪡ *Exceptional view – interesting or panoramic view*

ST-JEAN-DU-DOIGT

29630 – Michelin map **308** I2 – pop. 623 – alt. 15
▶ Paris 544 – Brest 77 – Guingamp 61 – Lannion 33

Municipal du Pont Ar Gler

🖉 02 98 67 32 15, st-jean-du-doigt-mairie@wanadoo.fr
Address : at Pont ar Gler (in the town)
Opening times : from end June to end Aug.
1 ha (34 pitches) terraced, flat, grassy
Tariff : (2012 price) ✹ 3.15€ ⇔ 1.65€ ▣ 2.95€ – ⑭ (6A) 2.70€

Surroundings : ⵣ ☐ ♤
Leisure activities : ▦ ⵣ
Facilities : ♿ ⌐ ⵥ ⵀ ▤

GPS Longitude : -3.77487
Latitude : 48.69405

ST-JOUAN-DES-GUÉRETS

35430 – Michelin map **309** K3 – pop. 2,699 – alt. 31
▶ Paris 396 – Rennes 63 – St-Helier 10 – St-Brieuc 85

Le P'tit Bois ▲♨

℘ 02 99 21 14 30, *www.ptitbois.com*
Address : at La Chalandouze (access via the N 137)
Opening times : from mid April to mid Sept.
6 ha (274 pitches) flat, grassy
Tariff : ♦ 5€ ➡ 🅴 8.60€ – 🔋 (10A) 5€ – Reservation fee 10€
Rental rates : (from mid April to mid Sept.) – 158 🛏 – 4 apartments.
Per night from 40 to 146€ – Per week from 280 to 1,022€ – Reservation fee 10€
🚐 sani-station 7€
A pleasant rural site.

Surroundings : 🗔 ♌
Leisure activities : 🍹 🏠 ♒ 🏃 hammam, jacuzzi ⚿ 🚲 ✂ ⛰ 🖼 ⛴
🏊 multi-sports ground, entertainment room
Facilities : ♿ ⊶ 🖏 🗜 ♒ 🍴 launderette 🗜 🍴

GPS
Longitude : -1.9869
Latitude : 48.60966

ST-LUNAIRE

35800 – Michelin map **309** J3 – pop. 2,309 – alt. 20
▶ Paris 410 – Rennes 76 – St-Helier 16 – St-Brieuc 83

La Touesse

℘ 02 99 46 61 13, *www.campinglatouesse.com*
Address : 171 r. Ville Géhan (situated 2km east along the D 786, follow the signs for Dinard; 400m from the beach)
Opening times : from beginning April to end Sept.
2.5 ha (141 pitches) flat, grassy
Tariff : (2012 price) ♦ 5.50€ ➡ 3.10€ 🅴 7.90€ – 🔋 (10A) 3.70€ – Reservation fee 16€
Rental rates : (2012 price) (from beginning April to end Sept.) – 50 🛏 – 3 studios
– 11 apartments – 1 gîte. Per night from 50 to 100€ – Per week from 210 to 686€
– Reservation fee 16€
🚐 sani-station 6€

Surroundings : ♌♌
Leisure activities : 🍹 ✕ 🏠 ♒s ⚿
Facilities : ♿ ⊶ ▥ 🖏 🗜 ♒ 🍴 launderette 🗜 🍴
Nearby : 🏇

GPS
Longitude : -2.08425
Latitude : 48.63086

ST-MALO

35400 – Michelin map **309** J3 – pop. 47,045 – alt. 5
▶ Paris 404 – Alençon 180 – Avranches 68 – Dinan 32

Domaine de la Ville Huchet ▲♨

℘ 02 99 81 11 83, *www.lavillehuchet.com*
Address : rte de la Passagère, at Quelmer (5km south along the D 301, follow the signs for Dinard and take turning for La Grassinais to the left in front of the Mercedes showroom)
Opening times : from beginning April to end Sept.
6 ha (198 pitches) flat, grassy
Tariff : 35.70€ ♦♦ ➡ 🅴 🔋 (6A) – Extra per person 6.80€ – Reservation fee 18€
Rental rates : (from beginning April to end Sept.) ♿ (1 mobile home) – 72 🛏 – 13 🏠
– 3 apartments. Per night from 35 to 136€ – Per week from 245 to 952€ – Reservation fee 18€
🚐 sani-station 5€
Pleasant site near a small but pretty château.

Surroundings : 🗔 ♌♌
Leisure activities : 🍹 ✕ 🏠 🏃 ⚿ 🚲 ⛰ 🖼 ⛴ 🏊 multi-sports ground
Facilities : ♿ ⊶ 🖏 🍴 launderette 🗜 🍴

GPS
Longitude : -1.98704
Latitude : 48.61545

ST-MARCAN

35120 – Michelin map **309** M3 – pop. 455 – alt. 60
▶ Paris 370 – Dinan 42 – Dol-de-Bretagne 14 – Le Mont-St-Michel 17

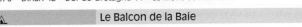

Le Balcon de la Baie

✆ 02 99 80 22 95, *www.lebalcondelabaie.com*
Address :at Le Verger (500m southeast along the D 89, follow the signs for Pleine-Fougères and turn left after the cemetery)
2.8 ha (66 pitches) flat, grassy
Rentals : 12 🚐.

Surroundings : ⛱ ≤ Baie du Mont-St-Michel ⛺ ♧♧
Leisure activities : 🎦 ⚷ ⤳
Facilities : ♿ ⊶ ♨ launderette

Longitude : -1.62929
Latitude : 48.58942

The classification (1 to 5 tents, black or red) that we award to selected sites in this guide is our own system. It should not be confused with the classification (1 to 5 stars) of official organisations.

ST-MICHEL-EN-GRÈVE

22300 – Michelin map **309** A2 – pop. 480 – alt. 12
▶ Paris 526 – Guingamp 43 – Lannion 11 – Morlaix 31

Les Capucines

✆ 02 96 35 72 28, *www.lescapucines.fr*
Address : ancienne Voie Romaine, at Kervourdon (located 1.5km north following signs for Lannion and take road to the left)
Opening times : from end March to end Sept.
4 ha (100 pitches) relatively flat, flat, grassy
Tariff : 27€ ✶✶ ⤳ 🖪 ⚡ (7A) – Extra per person 5.50€ – Reservation fee 15€
Rental rates : (from end March to end Sept.) ♿ (1 chalet) – 11 🚐 – 5 🏠.
Per night from 50 to 100€ – Per week from 230 to 530€ – Reservation fee 15€
⛽ sani-station – 🚐 14.50€

Surroundings : ⛱ ⛺ ♧
Leisure activities : 🍴 🎦 ⚷ 🚲 ♠ 🏊 (open-air in season), multi-sports ground
Facilities : ♿ ⊶ ♨ ⚷ ⚐ ⛲ launderette ♨

Longitude : -3.55694
Latitude : 48.69278

ST-PÈRE

35430 – Michelin map **309** K3 – pop. 2,289 – alt. 50
▶ Paris 392 – Cancale 14 – Dinard 15 – Dol-de-Bretagne 16

Bel Évent

✆ 02 99 58 83 79, *www.camping-bel-event.com*
Address : at Bellevent (located 1.5km southeast along the D 74, follow the signs for Châteauneuf and take the road to the right)
2.5 ha (115 pitches) flat, grassy
Rentals : 17 🚐 – 1 🏠.
⛽ sani-station

Surroundings : ⛺ ♧
Leisure activities : 🍴 🎦 ⚷ ♠ 🏊 multi-sports ground
Facilities : ♿ ⊶ ♨ ⛲ launderette

Longitude : -1.91838
Latitude : 48.57347

ST-PHILIBERT

56470 – Michelin map **308** N9 – pop. 1,520 – alt. 15
▶ Paris 486 – Auray 11 – Locmariaquer 7 – Quiberon 27

Les Palmiers

✆ 02 97 55 01 17, *www.campinglespalmiers.com*
Address : at Kernivilit (situated 2km west, 500m from the river at Crach (sea)
Opening times : from beginning April to mid Oct.
3 ha (115 pitches) flat, relatively flat, grassy
Tariff : 23.50€ ♣♣ ⟷ 🔲 (10A) – Extra per person 5.50€ – Reservation fee 16.50€
Based around an old renovated farmhouse.

Surroundings : ♀
Leisure activities : ♀ ✗ 🏠 ⚽ 🚴 ♨ △ entertainment room
Facilities : ♿ ⚬ 🚿 ♈ launderette
Nearby : ✗

GPS Longitude : -3.01504
Latitude : 47.58831

Le Chat Noir

✆ 02 97 55 04 90, *www.campinglechatnoir.com*
Address : rte de la Trinité sur Mer (located 1km to the north)
1.7 ha (98 pitches) flat and relatively flat, grassy
Rentals : 31 .

Surroundings : 🏕 ♀♀
Leisure activities : 🏠 ⚽ ♨ △
Facilities : ♿ ⚬ 🚿 ♈ launderette
Nearby : 🛒 ✗ ◊

GPS Longitude : -2.99778
Latitude : 47.59591

*The prices listed were supplied by the campsite owners in 2012
(if prices were not available, those from the previous year are given).
The fees should be regarded as basic charges and may fluctuate
with inflation.*

ST-POL-DE-LÉON

29250 – Michelin map **308** H2 – pop. 7,043 – alt. 60
▶ Paris 557 – Brest 62 – Brignogan-Plages 31 – Morlaix 21

Ar Kleguer ♣♣

✆ 02 98 69 18 81, *www.camping-ar-kleguer.com*
Address : Plage Ste-Anne (beach) (east of the town)
Opening times : from beginning April to end Sept.
5 ha (173 pitches) flat and relatively flat, undulating, grassy, rocks
Tariff : (2012 price) 27.20€ ♣♣ ⟷ 🔲 (10A) – Extra per person 5.90€ – Reservation fee 18€
Rental rates : (2012 price) (from beginning April to end Sept.) – 45 – 5 🏠 – 3 gîtes.
Per night from 48 to 100€ – Per week from 270 to 760€ – Reservation fee 18€
🚐 sani-station
A pleasant and spacious natural park with lovely scenery.

Surroundings : 🏞 ⟷ 🏕 ♀ ⛰
Leisure activities : ♀ 🏠 🎮 ⚽ ✗ ♨ △ multi-sports ground
Facilities : ♿ ⚬ (Jul-Aug) 🏪 🚿 ♈ launderette

GPS Longitude : -3.9677
Latitude : 48.6907

Le Trologot

📞 02 98 69 06 26, *www.camping-trologot.com*

Address : at Grève du Man (To the east, follow the signs for Îlot St-Anne; near the beach)
Opening times : from beginning May to end Sept.
2 ha (100 pitches) flat, grassy
Tariff : (2012 price) 👤 4.80€ �foodcar 2.10€ 📧 6.75€ – 🔌 (10A) 3.60€ – Reservation fee 10€
Rental rates : (2012 price) (from mid April to end Sept.) – 15 🚐. Per night from 42 to 70€
Per week from 255 to 645€ – Reservation fee 15€
🚽 sani-station – 8 📧 13.60€ – 🛒 11€

Surroundings : ▱ ♀
Leisure activities : 👤 ⚓ ⛷
Facilities : ♿ o━ 📺 🎣 launderette

GPS
Longitude : -3.9698
Latitude : 48.6935

ST-RENAN

29290 – Michelin map **308** D4 – pop. 7,468 – alt. 50
▶ Paris 605 – Brest 14 – Brignogan-Plages 43 – Ploudalmézeau 14

Municipal de Lokournan

📞 02 98 84 37 67, *www.saint-renan.com*

Address : rte de l'Aber (take northwestern exit along the D 27 and take the road to the right; near the stadium)
0.8 ha (30 pitches) sandy, flat, grassy
🚽 sani-station
Near a small lake.

Surroundings : 🏞 ▱ ♀♀
Leisure activities : 🎳
Facilities : ♿
Nearby : 🖼

GPS
Longitude : -4.62929
Latitude : 48.43991

Some information or pricing may have changed since the guide went to press.
We recommend you check the price list online in advance or at the entrance
to the campsite and enquire about possible restrictions.

ST-SAMSON-SUR-RANCE

22100 – Michelin map **309** J4 – pop. 1,514 – alt. 64
▶ Paris 401 – Rennes 57 – St-Brieuc 64 – St-Helier 34

Municipal Beauséjour

📞 02 96 39 53 27, *www.beausejour-camping.com* ✖

Address : at La Hisse (3km east, along the D 57 and take the D 12 to the right, 200m from the port – access via steep slope)
Opening times : from mid May to end Sept.
3 ha (120 pitches) flat, grassy
Tariff : 👤 4.50€ �foodcar 📧 5.50€ – 🔌 (10A) 3.45€
Rental rates : (permanent) ✖ – 6 🚐 – 12 ⌂ – 3 gîtes. Per night from 45 to 80€
Per week from 215 to 510€
🚽 sani-station 3€ – 🛒 10.50€
Pretty gîtes in local stone.

Surroundings : 🏞
Leisure activities : 🎳 ⛷
Facilities : ♿ o━ 📺🎣 launderette
Nearby : 👤 🏇 🎣

GPS
Longitude : -2.00889
Latitude : 48.48889

ST-YVI

29140 – Michelin map **308** H7 – pop. 2,755 – alt. 105
▶ Paris 563 – Rennes 212 – Quimper 17 – Vannes 119

Village Center Le Bois de Pleuven

⌀ 0825002030, *www.village-center.fr*
Opening times : from end April to end Sept.
17 ha/10 ha for camping (280 pitches) flat, grassy
Tariff : (2012 price) 23€ ♦♦ ⇔ 🗉 🖗 (12A) – Extra per person 5€ – Reservation fee 10€
Rental rates : (2012 price) (from end April to end Sept.) – 35 �📰 – 15 tent bungalows.
Per night from 25 to 43€ – Per week from 354 to 790€ – Reservation fee 30€

Natural, woodland setting among trees and bushes.

Surroundings : 🐾 ⌐ ⁂
Leisure activities : ⚹ ⌁ 🖾 ⤳ ⟋
Facilities : ⟐ ⟲ ⛺

GPS Longitude : -3.97056
Latitude : 47.95028

For more information on visiting particular towns or regions, consult the relevant regional MICHELIN Green Guide. We also recommend you use the appropriate Michelin regional map to locate your selected campsite, to calculate distances and to work out the best route.

STE-ANNE-D'AURAY

56400 – Michelin map **308** N8 – pop. 2,347 – alt. 42
▶ Paris 475 – Auray 7 – Hennebont 33 – Locminé 27

Municipal du Motten

⌀ 0297576027, *contact@sainte-anne-auray.com*
Address : allée des Pins (located 1km southwest along the D 17, follow the signs for Auray and take r. du Parc to the right)
1.5 ha (115 pitches) flat, grassy

Surroundings : ⚬⚬
Leisure activities : 🖾 ⚶⚶ ⚹
Facilities : ⟐ ⊙⌐
Nearby : 🖾

GPS Longitude : -2.96251
Latitude : 47.69831

SARZEAU

56370 – Michelin map **308** O9 – pop. 7,659 – alt. 30
▶ Paris 478 – Nantes 111 – Redon 62 – Vannes 23

FranceLoc Domaine An Trest ♠♠

⌀ 0297417960, *www.an-trest.com*
Address : 1 ch. du Treste (2.5km to the south, follow the signs for Le Roaligen)
Opening times : from mid April to mid Sept.
5 ha (225 pitches) flat, grassy, terrace
Tariff : 35€ ♦♦ ⇔ 🗉 🖗 (10A) – Extra per person 5€ – Reservation fee 11€
Rental rates : (from mid April to mid Sept.) ⟐ (1 mobile home) – 120 �📰.
Per night from 33 to 103€ – Per week from 133 to 1,022 € – Reservation fee 27€

Surroundings : ⚬
Leisure activities : 🍷✗ 🖾 ⚇ ⚶⚶ ⚶⚶ 🚲⌁ 🖾 ⤳ ⟋
Facilities : ⟐ ⟲ ⛺ ⚏ launderette
Nearby : ⚏ 🐎

GPS Longitude : -2.77208
Latitude : 47.50612

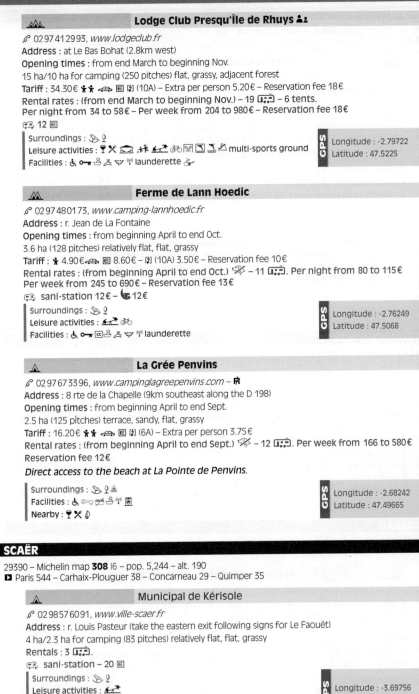

Lodge Club Presqu'île de Rhuys 🔺🔺

☎ 02 97 41 29 93, www.lodgeclub.fr

Address : at Le Bas Bohat (2.8km west)

Opening times : from end March to beginning Nov.

15 ha/10 ha for camping (250 pitches) flat, grassy, adjacent forest

Tariff : 34.30€ 🔺🔺 ⛺ 🔲 🔣 (10A) – Extra per person 5.20€ – Reservation fee 18€

Rental rates : (from end March to beginning Nov.) – 19 🔳 – 6 tents.

Per night from 34 to 58€ – Per week from 204 to 980€ – Reservation fee 18€

🔳 12 🔲

Surroundings : 🌊 ⛲

Leisure activities : 🍸 ✕ 🏠 🏃 🚣 🚴 🎯 🔲 🏊 ⛷ multi-sports ground

Facilities : 🦽 ⚡ 🚿 🏕 🚰 🍴 launderette 🐕

GPS Longitude : -2.79722 / Latitude : 47.5225

Ferme de Lann Hoedic

☎ 02 97 48 01 73, www.camping-lannhoedic.fr

Address : r. Jean de La Fontaine

Opening times : from beginning April to end Oct.

3.6 ha (128 pitches) relatively flat, flat, grassy

Tariff : 🔺 4.90€ ⛺ 🔲 8.60€ – 🔣 (10A) 3.50€ – Reservation fee 10€

Rental rates : (from beginning April to end Oct.) 🔲 – 11 🔳. Per night from 80 to 115€

Per week from 245 to 690€ – Reservation fee 13€

🔳 sani-station 12€ – 🚐 12€

Surroundings : 🌊 ⛲

Leisure activities : 🚣 🚴

Facilities : 🦽 ⚡ 🔲 🚿 🏕 🚰 🍴 launderette

GPS Longitude : -2.76249 / Latitude : 47.5068

La Grée Penvins

☎ 02 97 67 33 96, www.campinglagreepenvins.com – ℝ

Address : 8 rte de la Chapelle (9km southeast along the D 198)

Opening times : from beginning April to end Sept.

2.5 ha (125 pitches) terrace, sandy, flat, grassy

Tariff : 16.20€ 🔺🔺 ⛺ 🔲 🔣 (6A) – Extra per person 3.75€

Rental rates : (from beginning April to end Sept.) 🔲 – 12 🔳. Per week from 166 to 580€

Reservation fee 12€

Direct access to the beach at La Pointe de Penvins.

Surroundings : 🌊 ⛲ 🏖

Facilities : 🦽 ⚡ 🔲 🚿 🍴 📺

Nearby : 🍸 ✕ ⛲

GPS Longitude : -2.68242 / Latitude : 47.49665

SCAËR

29390 – Michelin map **308** I6 – pop. 5,244 – alt. 190

▶ Paris 544 – Carhaix-Plouguer 38 – Concarneau 29 – Quimper 35

Municipal de Kérisole

☎ 02 98 57 60 91, www.ville-scaer.fr

Address : r. Louis Pasteur (take the eastern exit following signs for Le Faouët)

4 ha/2.3 ha for camping (83 pitches) relatively flat, flat, grassy

Rentals : 3 🔳.

🔳 sani-station – 20 🔲

Surroundings : 🌊 ⛲

Leisure activities : 🚣

Facilities : 🦽 ⚡ launderette

Nearby : ✕ 🏊 fitness trail

GPS Longitude : -3.69756 / Latitude : 48.0278

SÉRENT

56460 – Michelin map **308** P8 – pop. 2,985 – alt. 80
▶ Paris 432 – Josselin 17 – Locminé 31 – Ploërmel 19

▲ Municipal du Pont Salmon

℘ 02 97 75 91 98, *www.serent.fr*
Address : 29 r. du Gal De Gaulle (in the town, follow the signs for Ploërmel)
1 ha (30 pitches) flat, grassy
Rentals : ⅋ (1 chalet) – 4 ⌂.
Free use of the municipal swimming pool

Surroundings : ○○
Leisure activities : ◂⭢
Facilities : ⊶ ▥ launderette
Nearby : ✗ ⤢

GPS Longitude : -2.50191
Latitude : 47.82506

*Fire safety doesn't stop when you leave your accommodation.
Always take care and consider the fire risks.*

SIZUN

29450 – Michelin map **308** G4 – pop. 2,221 – alt. 112
▶ Paris 572 – Brest 37 – Carhaix-Plouguer 44 – Châteaulin 36

▲ Municipal du Gollen

℘ 02 98 24 11 43, *www.mairie-sizun.fr* – ℞
Address : at Le Gollen (located 1km south along the D 30, follow the signs for St-Cadou and take the turning to the left; beside the Elorn river)
Opening times : from mid April to end Sept.
0.6 ha (30 pitches) open site, flat, grassy
Tariff : (2012 price) ★ 3€ ⇔ 2€ ▣ 2.50€ – ⚡ (10A) 2.50€
▧ sani-station 2€

Surroundings : ◌ ○
Leisure activities : ◝
Facilities : ⅋ ⊟ ⛱
Nearby : ✗ ⤢

GPS Longitude : -4.07659
Latitude : 48.4

SULNIAC

56250 – Michelin map **308** P8 – pop. 3,133 – alt. 125
▶ Paris 457 – Rennes 106 – Vannes 21 – Nantes 112

▲▲▲ Village Vacances La Lande du Moulin
(rental of chalets, gîtes and mobile homes only)

℘ 02 97 53 29 39, *www.la-lande-du-moulin.com*
Address : at le Nounène (located 1.5km east along the D 104 and follow the signs for Theix)
Opening times : from beginning April to beginning Nov.
12 ha terraced, lake
Rental rates : ⅋ (3 chalets) – 2 ⛺ – 50 ⌂ – 17 gîtes. Per night from 90 to 160€
Per week from 310 to 870 €
▧ 3 ▣ 15€
Option for full or half-board accommodation.

Surroundings : ◌ ○
Leisure activities : ▼ ✗ ▭ ☺ ⟜ ⅃ ⭢ ☮ ✗ ▢ ⤢ △ ◝
Facilities : ⊶ ▥ ☂ launderette ⌂

GPS Longitude : -2.56557
Latitude : 47.66686

TADEN

22100 – Michelin map **309** J4 – pop. 2,340 – alt. 46
▶ Paris 404 – Rennes 71 – St-Brieuc 64 – St-Helier 34

Municipal de la Hallerais

℘ 02 96 39 15 93, *http://www.camping-lahallerais.com*
Address : 4 r. de la Robardais (to the southwest of the town)
Opening times : from mid March to mid Nov.
7 ha (225 pitches) terraced, sloping, flat, grassy
Tariff : ✶ 3.96€ ▱ 🔲 12.42€ (10A)
Rental rates : (from mid March to mid Nov.) – 8 🛏 – 11 ⛺. Per night from 61 to 135€
Per week from 172 to 463€
sani-station – 17 🔲 21.34€

Surroundings : 🐟 ☂ ♨♨
Leisure activities : ♈ ✗ 🎦 🚣 🎣 ⛰ 🏊 multi-sports ground
Facilities : 🔧 ☕ 🍽 🚿 ♨ 🚽 launderette 🚰 🖙
Nearby : 🎿 🐎 🛶

GPS Longitude : -2.0232
Latitude : 48.47181

TAUPONT

56800 – Michelin map **308** Q7 – pop. 2,140 – alt. 81
▶ Paris 422 – Josselin 16 – Ploërmel 5 – Rohan 37

La Vallée du Ninian

℘ 02 97 93 53 01, *www.camping-ninian.fr*
Address : at Ville Bonne, le Rocher (take the northern exit along the D 8, follow the signs for la Trinité-Phoët, then continue 2.5km along the turning to the left, direct access to the river)
Opening times : from beginning April to end Sept.
2.7 ha (100 pitches) flat, grassy, fruit trees
Tariff : (2012 price) ✶ 4.50€ ▱ 🔲 6.50€ – (10A) 4.60€
Rental rates : (2012 price) (from beginning April to end Sept.) – 10 🛏 – 2 tent bungalows – 3 tents. Per night from 32 to 67€ – Per week from 155 to 610€ – Reservation fee 10€
sani-station

Evening events organised, centred around the bread oven or the apple press.

Surroundings : 🐟 ☂ ♨♨
Leisure activities : ♈ 🎦 🚣 🏊 🐎
Facilities : 🔧 ☕ 🚿 ♨ 🚽 launderette 🚰

GPS Longitude : -2.47
Latitude : 47.96928

TELGRUC-SUR-MER

29560 – Michelin map **308** E5 – pop. 2,088 – alt. 90
▶ Paris 572 – Châteaulin 25 – Douarnenez 29 – Quimper 39

Armorique

℘ 02 98 27 77 33, *www.campingarmorique.com*
Address : 112 rue de la Plage (1.2km southwest following signs for Trez-Bellec-Plage)
Opening times : from beginning April to end Sept.
2.5 ha (100 pitches) terraced, relatively flat, flat, grassy
Tariff : (2012 price) ✶ 5€ ▱ 🔲 9€ – (10A) 3.70€ – Reservation fee 16€
Rental rates : (2012 price) (permanent) – 25 🛏 – 4 ⛺. Per night from 45 to 55€
Per week from 240 to 710€ – Reservation fee 16€

Surroundings : 🐟 ≤ ☂ ♨
Leisure activities : ♈ ✗ 🎦 🚣 🏊 🏖
Facilities : 🔧 ☕ 🚿 ♨ launderette 🖙

GPS Longitude : -4.37085
Latitude : 48.22531

THEIX

56450 – Michelin map **308** P9 – pop. 6,765 – alt. 5
▶ Paris 464 – Ploërmel 51 – Redon 58 – La Roche-Bernard 33

Rhuys

𝄐 02 97 54 14 77, *http://campingderhuys.free.fr*
Address : r. Dugay Trouin, at Le Poteau Rouge (3.5km to the northwest, along the N 165; if coming from Vannes, take exit Sarzeau exit)
Opening times : from beginning April to end Oct.
2 ha (66 pitches) relatively flat, grassy
Tariff : (2012 price) 🚶 4.50€ 🚗 🅿 4.70€ – 🔌 (10A) 3.30€
Rental rates : (2012 price) (from beginning April to mid Oct.) – 6 🚐 – 2 🏠.
Per night from 35 to 100€ – Per week from 175 to 620€ – Reservation fee 15€
🚐 sani-station – 🔋 11€

Surroundings : 🍃
Leisure activities : 🏊 (small swimming pool)
Facilities : 🔧 🛒 🚿 🚰 🍴 🍽
Nearby : 🛒 🍷 ✕ 🖼

Longitude : -2.69413
Latitude : 47.64108

To visit a town or region, use the MICHELIN Green Guides.

TINTÉNIAC

35190 – Michelin map **309** K5 – pop. 3,304 – alt. 40
▶ Paris 377 – Avranches 70 – Dinan 28 – Dol-de-Bretagne 30

Les Peupliers

𝄐 02 99 45 49 75, *www.les-peupliers-camping.fr*
Address : at the Domaine de la Besnelais (situated 2km southeast along the old road to Rennes; near lakes, along the N 137, take the exit for Tinténiac Sud)
Opening times : from beginning April to end Sept.
4 ha (100 pitches) flat, grassy
Tariff : (2012 price) 22.30€ 🚶🚶 🚗 🅿 🔌 (6A) – Extra per person 5.50€
Rental rates : (2012 price) (from beginning April to end Oct.) – 6 🚐 – 2 🏠 – 1 gîte.
Per night from 35 to 100€ – Per week from 245 to 700€
🚐 sani-station – 4 🅿 17.60€ – 🔋 10.50€

Surroundings : 🏞 🍃
Leisure activities : 🍷 🖼 🏊 🚲 🎯 🏊 🎣
Facilities : 🔧 🛒 🚿 🚰 🍴 launderette

Longitude : -1.82167
Latitude : 48.30917

LE TOUR-DU-PARC

56370 – Michelin map **308** P9 – pop. 1,105
▶ Paris 476 – La Baule 62 – Redon 57 – St-Nazaire 81

Le Cadran Solaire

𝄐 02 97 67 30 40, *www.campingcadransolaire.fr*
Address : r. De Banastère (situated 2km south along the D 324, follow the signs for Sarzeau)
Opening times : from beginning April to end Oct.
2 ha (115 pitches) flat, grassy
Tariff : 🚶 4.60€ 🚗 🅿 9.50€ – 🔌 (12A) 3.50€ – Reservation fee 10€
Rental rates : (from beginning April to end Oct.) 🚫 – 10 🚐. Per night from 40 to 60€
Per week from 200 to 600€ – Reservation fee 10€

Surroundings : 🏞 🍃🍃
Leisure activities : 🖼 🏊 🎯
Facilities : 🔧 🛒 🚿 🍴 launderette

Longitude : -2.65748
Latitude : 47.5208

TRÉBEURDEN

22560 – Michelin map **309** A2 – pop. 3,714 – alt. 81
▶ Paris 525 – Lannion 10 – Perros-Guirec 14 – St-Brieuc 74

⚠ L'Espérance

☎ 07 86 17 48 08, *www.camping-esperance.com*
Address : r. de Kéralégan (5km northwest along the D 788, follow the signs for Trégastel; near the sea)
1 ha (70 pitches) open site, flat, grassy
Rentals : 6 ▣.
🚻 sani-station

Surroundings : ≤ ▭ ♨
Leisure activities : ▾ ▨
Facilities : ⅍ ☞ launderette

GPS Longitude : -3.55743
Latitude : 48.79096

Do not confuse:
⚠ *to* ⚠⚠⚠ *: MICHELIN classification*
with
★ *to* ★★★★★ *: official classification*

TRÉBOUL

29100 – Michelin map **308** E6
▶ Paris 591 – Rennes 239 – Quimper 29 – Brest 75

⚠ Kerleyou

☎ 02 98 74 13 03, *www.camping-kerleyou.com*
Address : 15 ch. de Kerleyou (located 1km to the west)
Opening times : from mid April to mid Sept.
3.5 ha (100 pitches) relatively flat, flat, grassy
Tariff : (2012 price) 22.68€ ✦✦ ⇦ ▣ ⒧ (10A) – Extra per person 4.45€ – Reservation fee 12€
Rental rates : (2012 price) (from mid April to mid Sept.) – 39 ▣ – 4 ☖.
Per night from 39 to 71€ – Per week from 201 to 731€ – Reservation fee 15€

Surroundings : ⟋ ▭ ♨
Leisure activities : ▾ ▨ ⇄ ⟰
Facilities : ⅍ ☞ ⚐ launderette ☞

GPS Longitude : -4.36198
Latitude : 48.09842

⚠ Trézulien

☎ 02 98 74 12 30, *www.camping-trezulien.com*
Address : 14 rte de Trezulien (via the r. Frédéric-Le-Guyader)
Opening times : from beginning April to end Sept.
5 ha (199 pitches) terraced, relatively flat, flat, grassy, uneven
Tariff : 20.30€ ✦✦ ⇦ ▣ ⒧ (10A) – Extra per person 4.30€ – Reservation fee 10€
Rental rates : (from beginning April to end Sept.) – 12 ▣ – 4 ☖ – 1 gîte.
Per night from 42 to 75€ – Per week from 160 to 660€ – Reservation fee 13€
🚻 sani-station 9€

Surroundings : ⟋ ≤ ⒬
Leisure activities : ▾ ▨ ⇄ ⟰ ◹
Facilities : ⅍ ☞ (season) ⚐ launderette

GPS Longitude : -4.34931
Latitude : 48.09311

TREFFIAGAT

29730 – Michelin map **308** F8 – pop. 2,343 – alt. 20
▶ Paris 582 – Audierne 39 – Douarnenez 41 – Pont-l'Abbé 8

Les Ormes

℘ 0298582127, *www.campingdesormes.fr.gd*

Address : at Kerlay (situated 2km to the south, follow the signs for Lesconil and take the turning to the right 400m from the beach (direct access)

Opening times : from beginning May to end Sept.

2 ha (76 pitches) flat, grassy

Tariff : (2012 price) ★ 3.95€ ⇌ 2.45€ 🔲 4.10€ – (7) (6A) 3.40€ – Reservation fee 6.25€

Rental rates : (2012 price) (from beginning April to end Sept.) ⌦ – 2 🏠 – 1 🛏.
Per week from 350 to 450 € – Reservation fee 6.25€

🚐 sani-station

Surroundings : ⟁ ⌂ ₪
Leisure activities : ⚓
Facilities : ⚬⊶ ✂ launderette
Nearby : ◊

Longitude : -4.25518
Latitude : 47.79666

TRÉGASTEL

22730 – Michelin map **309** B2 – pop. 2,435 – alt. 58
▶ Paris 526 – Lannion 11 – Perros-Guirec 9 – St-Brieuc 75

Tourony-Camping

℘ 0296238661, *www.camping-tourony.com*

Address : 105 r. de Poul Palud (1.8km east along the D 788, follow the signs for Perros-Guirec; 500m from the beach)

Opening times : from beginning April to end Sept.

2 ha (100 pitches) flat, grassy

Tariff : 22€ ★★ ⇌ 🔲 (7) (10A) – Extra per person 5.40€

Rental rates : (from beginning April to end Sept.) – 17 🛖 – 2 🏠. Per night from 46 to 72 €
Per week from 225 to 580 €

🚐 sani-station – 10 🔲 10.40€

Opposite the marina.

Surroundings : ₪
Leisure activities : ⚑ ✕ ⚓
Facilities : ♿ ⌂⊶ ⊗ ⚲ ⚇ ⚐ launderette
Nearby : ⇝ ⚒ ⚹

Longitude : -3.49131
Latitude : 48.82565

TRÉGUENNEC

29720 – Michelin map **308** F7 – pop. 348 – alt. 31
▶ Paris 582 – Audierne 27 – Douarnenez 27 – Pont-l'Abbé 11

Kerlaz

℘ 0298877679, *www.kerlaz.com*

Address : rte de la mer (in the village, along the D 156)

Opening times : from beginning April to end Sept.

1.25 ha (80 pitches) flat, grassy

Tariff : (2012 price) ★ 4€ ⇌ 2.25€ 🔲 5.50€ – (7) (10A) 3.65€ – Reservation fee 10€

Rental rates : (2012 price) (from beginning April to end Sept.) – 11 🛖 – 5 🏠.
Per night from 61 to 71€ – Per week from 249 to 624 € – Reservation fee 10€

🚐 sani-station 7.75€

Surroundings : ₪
Leisure activities : ⚑ ⚓ ⚲ 🎱 (open-air in season)
Facilities : ♿ ⊶ (Jul–Aug) launderette
Nearby : ⚖ ✕ 🐎

Longitude : -4.32848
Latitude : 47.89457

TRÉGUNC

29910 – Michelin map **308** H7 – pop. 6,785 – alt. 45
▶ Paris 543 – Concarneau 7 – Pont-Aven 9 – Quimper 29

Le Pendruc

℘ 02 98 97 66 28, *www.domainedependruc.com* – limited spaces for one-night stay
Address : at Roz Penanguer (2.8km southwest, follow the signs for Pendruc and take the turning to the left)
Opening times : from beginning April to end Sept.
6 ha (200 pitches) flat, grassy
Tariff : (2012 price) 🛉 5 € 🚗 2.50 € 🔲 8 € – (🚐) (6A) 4 € – Reservation fee 10 €
Rental rates : (2012 price) (from mid April to end Sept.) 🛏 – 43 🚐.
Per week from 180 to 790 € – Reservation fee 20 €
🚐 sani-station – 4 🔲 15 €

Surroundings : 🎣 🖾 ♀
Leisure activities : ✗ 🖾 🏕 🏊 🚴 🖾 🎿 multi-sports ground
Facilities : 🚰 launderette 🦽
Nearby : 🎣

GPS
Longitude : -3.88093
Latitude : 47.84086

La Pommeraie

℘ 02 98 50 02 73, *www.campingdelapomeraie.com*
Address : at Kerdalidec (6km south along the D 1, follow the signs for La Pointe de Trévignon (headland) and take the turning to the left following signs for St-Philibert)
7 ha (198 pitches) flat, grassy
Rental rates : – 34 🚐.

Surroundings : 🖾 ♀
Leisure activities : 🖾 🏕 🚴 🎿 multi-sports ground, entertainment room
Facilities : ♿ 🚰 🍳 🚿 🍴 launderette 🦽

GPS
Longitude : -3.83698
Latitude : 47.80786

Routes nationales are main roads and their identifying numbers begin with N or RN. Routes départementales are generally quieter roads and begin with D or DN.

TRÉLÉVERN

22660 – Michelin map **309** B2 – pop. 1,390 – alt. 76
▶ Paris 524 – Lannion 13 – Perros-Guirec 9 – St-Brieuc 73

RNC Port-l'Épine

℘ 02 96 23 71 94, *www.rcn.fr*
Address : 10 Venelle de Pors Garo (1.5km northwest then take a road to the left; at Port-l'Épine)
Opening times : from mid April to mid Sept.
3 ha (160 pitches) terrace, relatively flat, flat, grassy
Tariff : 36.50 € 🛉🛉 🚗 🔲 (🚐) (6A) – Extra per person 5 € – Reservation fee 19.50 €
Rental rates : (from mid April to mid Sept.) – 32 🚐 – 15 🏠. Per night from 30 to 135 €
Per week from 215 to 950 € – Reservation fee 19.50 €

Surroundings : 🎣 ⩽ Baie de Perros-Guirec 🖾 ♀ ⛰
Leisure activities : 🍴 ✗ 🏊 🚴 🎿
Facilities : ♿ 🚰 🍳 🚿 🍴 launderette 🦽

GPS
Longitude : -3.38594
Latitude : 48.8128

232

LA TRINITÉ-SUR-MER

56470 – Michelin map **308** M9 – pop. 1,622 – alt. 20
▶ Paris 488 – Auray 13 – Carnac 4 – Lorient 52

La Plage ▲:

☎ 02 97 55 73 28, *www.camping-plage.com*
Address : plage de Kervillen (located 1km to the south, direct access to the beach)
Opening times : from beginning May to mid Sept.
3 ha (200 pitches) relatively flat, sandy, flat, grassy**Tariff** : 43.30€ ♦♦ ⇌ 国 [≀] (10A) –
Extra per person 4.30€ – Reservation fee 15€
Rental rates : (from beginning May to mid Sept.) – 32 ⊡ – 6 tent bungalows.
Per week from 215 to 870 € – Reservation fee 15€
⊞ sani-station 3€ – ⊜[≀]14€

Surroundings : ⊡ ℓ ⛰
Leisure activities : ⊡ ⊕ ⋆⋆ jacuzzi ⬳ ♦⬥ ℥ ⊿ ⛾
Facilities : ♿ ⊶ ⊕ ⌲ ⚲ ⍾ launderette
Nearby : ⊿ ♟ ✕ ⊱ ℥ ♪

GPS
Longitude : -3.02869
Latitude : 47.57562

Kervilor

☎ 02 97 55 76 75, *www.camping-kervilor.com*
Address : rte du Latz (1.6km to the north)
Opening times : from end March to mid Sept.
5 ha (230 pitches) relatively flat, flat, grassy
Tariff : (2012 price) 33.60€ ♦♦ ⇌ 国 [≀] (10A) – Extra per person 5.55€ – Reservation fee 18€
Rental rates : (2012 price) (from end March to mid Sept.) – 68 ⊡. Per night from 108 to 190 €
Per week from 270 to 947 € – Reservation fee 18€

Surroundings : ℥ ⊡ ℓℓ
Leisure activities : ♟ ⊡ ♬ jacuzzi ⬳ ♦⬥ ℥ ♪ ⊡ ⊿ ⛾ multi-sports
ground
Facilities : ♿ ⊶ ⍾ launderette ⊿ ⊱ refrigerators

GPS
Longitude : -3.03588
Latitude : 47.60168

La Baie ▲:

☎ 02 97 55 73 42, *www.campingdelabaie.com* – limited spaces for one-night stay
Address : plage de Kervillen (located 1.5km to the south, 100m from the beach)
Opening times : from beginning May to mid Sept.
2.2 ha (170 pitches) flat, grassy, sandy
Tariff : (2012 price) ♦ 8€ ⇌ 国 26.90€ – [≀] (10A) 3.50€ – Reservation fee 22€
Rental rates : (2012 price) (from beginning May to mid Sept.) – 40 ⊡.
Per night from 36 to 130 € – Per week from 252 to 910 € – Reservation fee 22€

Surroundings : ℥ ⊡ ℓ
Leisure activities : ⊡ ⊕ ⋆⋆ ⬳ ♦⬥ ⊿ ⛾
Facilities : ♿ ⊶ ⊕ ⌲ ⚲ ⍾ launderette
Nearby : ⊿ ♟ ✕ ⊱ ℥ ♪

GPS
Longitude : -3.02789
Latitude : 47.57375

Key to rentals symbols:

12  **Number of mobile homes**

20 ⌂ **Number of chalets**

6 ⊨ **Number of rooms to rent**

Per night **Minimum/maximum rate per night**
30–50€

Per week **Minimum/maximum rate per week**
300–1,000€

APV Park-Plijadur ♣♦

℘ 02 97 55 72 05, www.camping-apv.com
Address : 94 rte de Carnac (1.3km northwest on the D 781)
Opening times : from beginning April to end Sept.
5 ha (198 pitches) sandy, flat, grassy, lake**Tariff :** (2012 price) 25.20€ ♣♣ ⇔ ▣ ⑭ (10A) –
Extra per person 7.10€ – Reservation fee 27€
Rental rates : (2012 price) (from beginning April to end Sept.) – 55 ▥ – 2 apartments.
Per night from 57 to 80 € – Per week from 200 to 990 € – Reservation fee 27€
⊞ sani-station 14.50€
Choose pitches away from the road in preference.

Surroundings : ▭ 〇〇
Leisure activities : ▽ ▨ ▨ 木 ⅙ ⊆ hammam, jacuzzi ♨ ▥ ▣ ▨
▨ ◁
Facilities : ♿ ⊶ ⌂ ♈ launderette ▨

GPS Longitude : -3.04394
Latitude : 47.60464

56000 – Michelin map **308** 09 – pop. 52,683 – alt. 20
▶ Paris 459 – Quimper 122 – Rennes 110 – St-Brieuc 107

Flower Le Conleau

℘ 02 97 63 13 88, www.vannes-camping.com
Address : at la Pointe de Conleau (to the south, towards the Parc du Golfe (leisure park) along the av. du Maréchal Juin)
Opening times : from beginning April to end Sept.
5 ha (260 pitches) terraced, relatively flat, grassy
Tariff : 24.50€ ♣♣ ⇔ ▣ ⑭ (10A) – Extra per person 4.50€ – Reservation fee 15€
Rental rates : (from beginning April to end Sept.) – 41 ▥ – 15 tents.
Per night from 42 to 103 € – Per week from 210 to 721 € – Reservation fee 15€
⊞ sani-station 5.50€ – 34 ▣ 12€
Pleasant location opposite the Golfe du Morbihan (gulf).

Surroundings : ≤ 〇〇
Leisure activities : ▽ ▨ ▨ 木 ♨ ◷
Facilities : ♿ ⊶ ⌂ ♈ launderette, refrigerated food storage
Nearby : ⊨

GPS Longitude : -2.77994
Latitude : 47.63326

BURGUNDY

Hervé Lenain / hemis.fr

A visit to Burgundy takes you back in time to an era when the influence of the mighty Burgundian dukes rivalled that of the kings of France. Stately castles and imposing abbeys still bear witness to a past golden age of ostentation and power. It is hard now to reproach the dukes too much for a flamboyance that has today made Dijon a world-renowned city of art, endowed with an exceptional architectural heritage. And who would dispute their claim to be the lords of the best wines in Christendom when wine lovers still flock to the region in search of the finest cellars and vintages? A dedication to time-honoured traditions remains at the heart of the region's cuisine, from the pungent *Époisses* cheese to delicious gingerbread dripping with honey. After indulging in such gourmet delights, what could be better than a barge trip down the region's canals and rivers to relax in peace amid gloriously unspoilt countryside?

ANCY-LE-FRANC

89160 – Michelin map **319** H5 – pop. 1,007 – alt. 180
▶ Paris 215 – Auxerre 54 – Châtillon-sur-Seine 38 – Montbard 27

⚠ Municipal

℘ 03 86 75 13 21, www.cc-ancylefranc.net
Address : take the southern exit along the D 905, follow the signs for Montbard, opposite the château; beside a stream and near a lake
0.5 ha (30 pitches) flat, grassy
🚐 sani-station

Surroundings : 0̲0̲	
Facilities : &	**GPS** Longitude : 4.16484
Nearby : ✗	Latitude : 47.77354

In order for the guide to remain wholly objective, the selection is made on an entirely independent basis. There is no charge for being selected for the guide.

ANDRYES

89480 – Michelin map **319** D6 – pop. 471 – alt. 162
▶ Paris 204 – Auxerre 39 – Avallon 44 – Clamecy 10

⚠ Au Bois Joli

℘ 03 86 81 70 48, www.campingauboisjoli.fr
Address : rte de Villeprenoy (800m southwest)
Opening times : from beginning April to end Oct.
5 ha (100 pitches) sloping, terraced, grassy, stony
Tariff : 27.65€ ✦✦ ⇔ 🗐 (10A) – Extra per person 6€ – Reservation fee 8.50€
Rental rates : (from beginning April to end Oct.) ✗ – 4 🛖 – 2 tents.
Per night from 69 to 89 € – Per week from 290 to 654 € – Reservation fee 8.50€
Wooded site.

Surroundings : 🌳 0̲0̲	
Leisure activities : 🖼 ⚽ 🚲 ⛱ quad biking	**GPS** Longitude : 3.47969
Facilities : & ⛽ 🏧 ⚒	Latitude : 47.51655
Nearby : ✗	

ARNAY-LE-DUC

21230 – Michelin map **320** G7 – pop. 1,674 – alt. 375
▶ Paris 285 – Autun 28 – Beaune 36 – Chagny 38

⚠ L'Étang de Fouché

℘ 03 80 90 02 23, www.campingfouche.com
Address : r. du 8 mai 1945 (700m east along the D 17c, follow the signs for Longecourt)
Opening times : from beginning April to mid Oct.
8 ha (209 pitches) flat, relatively flat, grassy
Tariff : (2012 price) 22.70€ ✦✦ ⇔ 🗐 (10A) – Extra per person 6.70€ – Reservation fee 15€
Rental rates : (2012 price) (from beginning April to mid Oct.) – 19 🛖 – 19 🏠 – 6 tent bungalows. Per night from 33 to 114 € – Per week from 231 to 798 € – Reservation fee 30€
Pleasant location beside a lake.

Surroundings : 🌳 ⪡ �	
Leisure activities : ▼ ✗ 🖼 daytime 🤸 ⚽ 🚲 🎣	**GPS** Longitude : 4.49802
Facilities : & ⛽ 🏧 ⚒ launderette 🏊	Latitude : 47.13414
Nearby : ✗ 🏖 (beach) 🚣	

ASQUINS

89450 – Michelin map **319** F7 – pop. 324 – alt. 146
▶ Paris 219 – Dijon 123 – Auxerre 49 – Avallon 17

Municipal le Patis

𝄐 03 86 33 30 80, *mairie.asquins@wanadoo.fr*
Address : rte de Givry (500 m, after the bridge on the left)
1 ha (33 pitches) flat, grassy

Surroundings : ♀
Leisure activities : 🎱 🛶
Facilities : ♿ ▥ 🛁 📷
Nearby : ⚓

GPS
Longitude : 3.75899
Latitude : 47.48293

AUTUN

71400 – Michelin map **320** F8 – pop. 14,496 – alt. 326
▶ Paris 287 – Auxerre 128 – Avallon 78 – Chalon-sur-Saône 51

Aquadis Loisirs La Porte d'Arroux

𝄐 03 85 52 10 82, *www.aquadis-loisirs.com*
Address : Les Chaumottes (take the northern exit along the D 980, follow the signs for Saulieu, Arroux suburb; beside the Ternin river)
Opening times : from end March to end Oct.
2.8 ha (104 pitches) flat, grassy
Tariff : 16€ ✿✿ 🚗 ▣ 🔌 (16A) – Extra per person 3.40€ – Reservation fee 9.90€
Rental rates : (from end March to end Oct.) – 2 🏠. Per night from 62 €
Per week from 157 to 499 € – Reservation fee 19.50€
🚐 sani-station 5.20€ – 4 ▣ 16€ – 🚐 11€
Pretty, shady pitches beside the Ternin river.

Surroundings : ▭ ♀♀
Leisure activities : 🍴 ✕ 🎱 🛶 🚲 ⚓ ⚲ ☈
Facilities : ♿ ⚷ 🆑 ▥ 📷 ⚒

GPS
Longitude : 4.29358
Latitude : 46.96447

The classification (1 to 5 tents, black or red) that we award to selected sites in this guide is our own system. It should not be confused with the classification (1 to 5 stars) of official organisations.

AUXERRE

89000 – Michelin map **319** E5 – pop. 36,702 – alt. 130
▶ Paris 166 – Bourges 144 – Chalon-sur-Saône 176 – Chaumont 143

Municipal

𝄐 03 86 52 11 15, *camping.mairie@auxerre.com*
Address : 8 rte de Vaux (to the southeast of the town, near the stadium, 150m from the Yonne river)
Opening times : from mid April to mid Sept.
4.5 ha (220 pitches) flat, grassy
Tariff : ✿ 3.80€ 🚗 ▣ 3.30€ – 🔌 (6A) 3.10€
🚐 sani-station 2.80€

Surroundings : ♀♀
Leisure activities : 🎱 🛶 ☈
Facilities : ♿ ⚷ ▥ 🛁 launderette ⚲
Nearby : ✂ ▨ 🖼 ⛷

GPS
Longitude : 3.58703
Latitude : 47.7865

AVALLON

89200 – Michelin map **319** G7 – pop. 7,252 – alt. 250
▶ Paris 220 – Dijon 106 – Auxerre 55 – Autun 80

⚠ Municipal Sous Roches

✆ 0386341039, *www.ville-avallon.fr*
Address : rte de Méluzien
Opening times : from beginning April to mid Oct.
2.7 ha (402 pitches) terraced, flat, grassy
Tariff : (2012 price) 17.20€ ♀♀ 🚐 🗐 🔌 (10A) – Extra per person 3.60€
Rental rates : (2012 price) (from beginning March to beginning Nov.) 🚫 – 4 🏠.
Per night from 65 to 90 € – Per week from 250 to 590 €
🚽 sani-station 5€

Surroundings : 🏞
Leisure activities : 🎬 🏊 🎣
Facilities : ♿ ⚡ 🖳 🚰 launderette

GPS Longitude : 3.91293
Latitude : 47.47993

For more information on visiting particular towns or regions, consult the relevant regional MICHELIN Green Guide. We also recommend you use the appropriate Michelin regional map to locate your selected campsite, to calculate distances and to work out the best route.

BEAUNE

21200 – Michelin map **320** I7 – pop. 22,516 – alt. 220
▶ Paris 308 – Autun 49 – Auxerre 149 – Chalon-sur-Saône 29

🏔 Municipal les Cent Vignes

✆ 0380220391, *campinglescentvignes@mairie-beaune.fr*
Address : take the northern exit along the r. du Faubourg-St-Nicolas and take D 18 to the left
Opening times : from mid March to end Oct.
2 ha (116 pitches) flat, grassy, fine gravel
Tariff : (2012 price) 17.90€ ♀♀ 🚐 🗐 🔌 (10A) – Extra per person 4.50€

Pitches well marked out with hedges; attractive entrance with flowers.

Surroundings : 🔲 ♀
Leisure activities : ♀ ✗ 🎬 🏊 multi-sports ground
Facilities : ♿ ⚡ 🏢 ⚗ 🚰 launderette

GPS Longitude : 4.8386
Latitude : 47.03285

BLIGNY-SUR-OUCHE

21360 – Michelin map **320** I7 – pop. 863 – alt. 360
▶ Paris 295 – Dijon 63 – Chalon-sur-Saône 48 – Le Creusot 62

⚠ Les Isles

✆ 0380200064, *www.camping-des-isles.fr*
Address : 2 allée de la Gare
1.2 ha (70 pitches) flat, grassy
🚽 sani-station – 6 🗐

Surroundings : ♀♀
Facilities : ♿ ⚡ 🚰 launderette
Nearby : ✗

GPS Longitude : 4.66019
Latitude : 47.10864

BOURBON-LANCY

71140 – Michelin map **320** C10 – pop. 5,275 – alt. 240 – ⚓ – Leisure centre
▶ Paris 308 – Autun 62 – Mâcon 110 – Montceau-les-Mines 55

 Aquadis Loisirs Les Chalets du Breuil

𝒞 0385892098, *www.aquadis-loisirs.com*
Address : r. St-Prix (towards the southwestern exit, follow the signs for Digoin; by the swimming pool)
Opening times : from end March to end Oct.
2.5 ha (128 pitches) flat, relatively flat, terraced
Tariff : 18.30€ ♦♦ ⇌ 🔲 🔌 (10A) – Extra per person 4.60€ – Reservation fee 9.90€
Rental rates : (from end March to end Oct.) – 4 🛏 – 22 🏠. Per night from 89 €
Per week from 222 to 592 € – Reservation fee 19.50€
🚐 10 🔲 16.90€
Site is around 200m from a small lake.

Surroundings : 🔲 🌳
Leisure activities : 🎣 🚲
Facilities : 🚿 🎱 ⛱ ✂ 🐟 🍽
Nearby : 🍴 🍷 ✕ 🏊 🎿 🛶 ≈ (beach) 🎣 🐎 open-air cinema

GPS Longitude : 3.76646
Latitude : 46.62086

CHABLIS

89800 – Michelin map **319** F5 – pop. 2,383 – alt. 135
▶ Paris 181 – Dijon 138 – Orléans 172 – Troyes 76

▲ **Municipal du Serein**

𝒞 0386424439, *www.chablis.net*
Address : quai Paul Louis Courier (600m west along the D 956, follow the signs for Tonnerre and take the road to the right after the bridge; beside the Serein river)
Opening times : from beginning June to mid Sept.
2 ha (50 pitches) flat, grassy
Tariff : (2012 price) ♦ 3€ ⇌ 🔲 5€ – 🔌 (6A) 2€
🚐 sani-station
Surroundings : 🔲 🌳
Leisure activities : 🏊
Facilities : 🚿

GPS Longitude : 3.80596
Latitude : 47.81368

CHAGNY

71150 – Michelin map **320** I8 – pop. 5,525 – alt. 215
▶ Paris 327 – Autun 44 – Beaune 15 – Chalon-sur-Saône 20

 Le Pâquier Fané

𝒞 0385872142, *www.camping-chagny.com*
Address : r. du Pâquier fané (to the west; beside the Dheune river)
Opening times : from beginning April to end Oct.
1.8 ha (85 pitches) flat, grassy
Tariff : 22€ ♦♦ ⇌ 🔲 🔌 (12A) – Extra per person 3.50€
Rental rates : (from beginning April to end Oct.) 🚐 – 5 🏠. Per night from 50 to 65 €
Per week from 350 to 450 € – Reservation fee 15€
🚐 sani-station
Pleasant setting beside the Dheune.

Surroundings : 🔲 🌳
Leisure activities : ✕ 🚲
Facilities : ♿ 🚿 🍽 launderette ✂
Nearby : 🎿 🛶

GPS Longitude : 4.74574
Latitude : 46.91193

CHAMBILLY

71110 – Michelin map **320** E12 – pop. 523 – alt. 249
▶ Paris 363 – Chauffailles 28 – Digoin 27 – Dompierre-sur-Besbre 55

⚠ La Motte aux Merles

℘ 03 85 25 37 67, *campingpicard@yahoo.fr*
Address : rte de la Palisse (5km southwest along the D 990 and take road to the left)
Opening times : from beginning April to end Oct.
1 ha (25 pitches) flat, relatively flat, grassy
Tariff : ♀ 2.95 € ⇔ 回 4 € – ⓖ (10A) 2.40 €
Rental rates : (from beginning April to end Oct.) – 2 🏠. Per night 31 € – Per week 217 €
🚐 sani-station – 3 回 12.30 €

Surroundings : ⅋ ≤
Leisure activities : ♣ ♂ 🚣 (small swimming pool)
Facilities : & ☛ 🚿 ʷ 🖫

GPS	Longitude : 3.95755
	Latitude : 46.26443

LA CHARITÉ-SUR-LOIRE

58400 – Michelin map **319** B8 – pop. 5,203 – alt. 170
▶ Paris 212 – Bourges 51 – Clamecy 54 – Cosne-sur-Loire 30

⚠ Municipal la Saulaie

℘ 03 86 70 00 83, *www.lacharitesurloire-tourisme.com*
Address : quai de La Saulaie (southwestern exit)
Opening times : from mid April to end Sept.
1.7 ha (100 pitches) flat, grassy
Tariff : (2012 price) ♀ 6.20 € ⇔ 回 – ⓖ (16A) 3.20 €
Rental rates : (2012 price) (from mid April to end Sept.) – 2 caravans.
Per night from 75 to 105 € – Per week from 405 to 660 €
On the Île de la Saulaie, near the beach.

Surroundings : ♀
Leisure activities : 🎱 🚣 ﹏
Facilities : & ☛ 🖭 🛁 🛒 ʷ
Nearby : 🍴 🎣

GPS	Longitude : 3.00927
	Latitude : 47.17879

CHAROLLES

71120 – Michelin map **320** F11 – pop. 2,807 – alt. 279
▶ Paris 374 – Autun 80 – Chalon-sur-Saône 67 – Mâcon 55

⚠ Municipal

℘ 03 85 24 04 90, *http://www.ville-charolles.fr/*
Address : rte de Viry (take the northeastern exit, follow the signs for Mâcon and turn left onto D 33)
Opening times : from beginning April to beginning Oct.
1 ha (60 pitches) flat, grassy, fine gravel
Tariff : (2012 price) ♀ 2.50 € ⇔ 2 € 回 4.20 € – ⓖ (16A) 2.50 €
Rental rates : (2012 price) (from beginning April to beginning Oct.) 🚫 – 4 🚐.
Per week from 220 to 360 €
🚐 sani-station 3 € – 10 回 3 €
Pleasant setting beside the Arconce river.

Surroundings : 🗺 ♀
Leisure activities : 🏃
Facilities : & ☛ 🛁 🛒 ʷ 🖫
Nearby : 🎱 🚣 ﹏

GPS	Longitude : 4.28209
	Latitude : 46.43959

CHÂTEAU-CHINON

58120 – Michelin map **319** G9 – pop. 2,137 – alt. 510
▶ Paris 281 – Autun 39 – Avallon 60 – Clamecy 65

Municipal du Perthuy d'Oiseau

✆ 03 86 85 08 17, *mairiechateauchinonville@wanadoo.fr*
Address : r. du Perthuy d'Oiseau (take the southern exit along the D 27, follow the signs for Luzy and take a right turn)
Opening times : from beginning May to end Sept.
1.8 ha (50 pitches) relatively flat to hilly, grassy
Tariff : (2012 price) ♦ 2€ 🚐 2.50€ 🔲 1.50€ – ⚡ (10A) 2.50€
sani-station
At the edge of a forest.

Surroundings :
Leisure activities :
Facilities :

GPS Longitude : 3.92613
Latitude : 47.05518

Using the traditional Michelin classification method, the guide provides you with an easy, speedy reference for assessing the category of each site: 1 to 5 tents (see page 10).

CHÂTILLON-SUR-SEINE

21400 – Michelin map **320** H2 – pop. 5,613 – alt. 219
▶ Paris 233 – Auxerre 85 – Avallon 75 – Chaumont 60

Municipal Louis-Rigoly

✆ 03 80 91 03 05, *www.mairie-chatillon-sur-seine.fr*
Address : esplanade St-Vorles (follow the signs for Langres)
0.8 ha (54 pitches) relatively flat, flat, grassy, hard surface areas
Rentals : 2 .
sani-station
On the shaded slopes of the town.

Surroundings :
Facilities :
Nearby :

GPS Longitude : 4.56969
Latitude : 47.87051

CHAUFFAILLES

71170 – Michelin map **320** G12 – pop. 3,939 – alt. 405
▶ Paris 404 – Charolles 32 – Lyon 77 – Mâcon 64

Municipal les Feuilles

✆ 03 85 26 48 12, *www.chauffailles.com*
Address : to the southwest along the r. du Chatillon
4 ha (75 pitches) flat and relatively flat, grassy, fine gravel
Rentals : 16 tent bungalows.
sani-station
Green setting beside the Botoret river.

Surroundings :
Leisure activities :
Facilities :
Nearby :

GPS Longitude : 4.33817
Latitude : 46.20004

CLAMECY

58500 – Michelin map **319** E7 – pop. 4,238 – alt. 144
▶ Paris 208 – Auxerre 42 – Avallon 38 – Bourges 105

Le Pont Picot

℘ 03 86 27 05 97, *clamecycamping@orange.fr*
Address : r. de Chevroches (to the south; beside the Yonne and the Nivernais canal, recommended route via Beaugy)
Opening times : from beginning April to end Sept.
1 ha (90 pitches) flat, grassy
Tariff : (2012 price) 14.50€ ✦✦ ⇌ 回 (6A) – Extra per person 3€
Rental rates : (2012 price) (from beginning April to end Sept.) – 5 ⛺.
Per night from 40 to 60 € – Per week from 250 to 300 € – Reservation fee 90€
Pleasant location on a small island.

Surroundings : 🐟 ♀
Leisure activities : 🎣
Facilities : ♿ ⟞ ⚑ launderette

GPS Longitude : 3.52784
Latitude : 47.45203

CLUNY

71250 – Michelin map **320** H11 – pop. 4,624 – alt. 248
▶ Paris 384 – Chalon-sur-Saône 49 – Charolles 43 – Mâcon 25

Municipal St-Vital

℘ 03 85 59 08 34, *www.cluny-camping.blogspot.com*
Address : 30 r. des Griottons (take the eastern exit along the D 15, follow the signs for Azé)
Opening times : from end April to mid Oct.
3 ha (174 pitches) flat, grassy, relatively flat
Tariff : (2012 price) 17.85€ ✦✦ ⇌ 回 (6A) – Extra per person 4.25€
Rental rates : (2012 price) (from end April to mid Oct.) 🏕 – 2 🏠. Per night from 60 to 65 €
Per week from 300 to 370 €

Surroundings : ≤
Facilities : ⟞ ▥ ⚑ 📷
Nearby : ✂ ▨ ⏃ 🐎

GPS Longitude : 4.66778
Latitude : 46.43088

CORMATIN

71460 – Michelin map **320** I10 – pop. 544 – alt. 212
▶ Paris 371 – Chalon-sur-Saône 37 – Mâcon 36 – Montceau-les-Mines 41

Le Hameau des Champs

℘ 03 85 50 76 71, *www.le-hameau-des-champs.com*
Address : take the northern exit along the D 981, follow the signs for Chalon-sur-Saône
Opening times : from beginning April to end Sept.
5.2 ha (60 pitches) flat, grassy
Tariff : (2012 price) ✦ 3.80€ ⇌ 回 5.80€ – (13A) 3.25€
Rental rates : (2012 price) (permanent) – 10 🏠. Per night from 64 to 87 €
Per week from 355 to 498 €
🚐 sani-station 3€ – 🚰 14€
Site is 150m from a small lake and the Givry-Cluny Voie Verte (Green Trail).

Surroundings : 🐟
Leisure activities : 🍸 ✕ ⛴ 🚲
Facilities : ♿ ⟞ 🅰 ⚑ 📷
Nearby : 🎣

GPS Longitude : 4.68391
Latitude : 46.54868

COUCHES

71490 – Michelin map **320** H8 – pop. 1,493 – alt. 320
▶ Paris 328 – Autun 26 – Beaune 31 – Le Creusot 16

Municipal la Gabrelle

📞 03 85 45 59 49, *campinglagabrelle@free.fr*
Address : 1.7km northwest along the D 978, follow the signs for Autun, near a small lake
1 ha (50 pitches) terraced, grassy
🚐 sani-station

Surroundings : 🖵
Leisure activities : 🍴 ✗ 🏛 ⚓
Facilities : ✇ ⊶ 🖼

Longitude : 4.5588
Latitude : 46.87586

> *The Michelin classification (△△△△ ... △) is totally independent of the*
> *official star classification system awarded by the local prefecture or*
> *other official organisation.*

CRÊCHES-SUR-SAÔNE

71680 – Michelin map **320** I12 – pop. 2,838 – alt. 180
▶ Paris 398 – Bourg-en-Bresse 45 – Mâcon 9 – Villefranche-sur-Saône 30

△ Municipal Port d'Arciat

📞 03 85 37 11 83, *http://pagesperso-orange.fr/campingduportdarciat/*
Address : rte du Port d'Arciat (located 1.5km east along the D 31, follow the signs for Pont de Veyle)
Opening times : from mid May to mid Sept.
5 ha (160 pitches) flat, grassy
Tariff : (2012 price) 15.30€ ⚹⚹ ⟺ 🗉 🔌 (5A) – Extra per person 4€
Beside the Saône river and near a small lake, direct access.

Surroundings : ♀
Leisure activities : ⚓ ⌣
Facilities : ✇ ⊶ ⸮ 🖼
Nearby : 🍴 ✗ ☂ ≃ ⚑

Longitude : 4.80581
Latitude : 46.24037

CRUX-LA-VILLE

58330 – Michelin map **319** E9 – pop. 410 – alt. 319
▶ Paris 248 – Autun 85 – Avallon 138 – La Charité-sur-Loire 45

⚠ Aquadis Loisirs Le Merle

📞 03 86 58 38 42, *www.aquadis-loisirs.com*
Address : at Le Merle (4.5km southwest along the D 34, follow the signs for St-Saulge and turn right onto D 181, follow the signs for Ste-Marie; beside the lake)
Opening times : from end March to end Oct.
2.6 ha (100 pitches) flat, relatively flat, grassy
Tariff : 17.20€ ⚹⚹ ⟺ 🗉 🔌 (16A) – Extra per person 4.70€ – Reservation fee 9.90€
Rental rates : (from end March to end Oct.) – 11 🛏 – 5 🏠. Per night from 62 to 68 €
Per week from 173 to 599 € – Reservation fee 19.50€
🚐 4 🗉 17.20€

Surroundings : 🏞 ♤♤ △
Leisure activities : ✗ 🏛 ⚓ 🚲 ⌣
Facilities : ✇ ⊶ 💳 ⸮ 🖼
Nearby : pedalos

Longitude : 3.52478
Latitude : 47.1624

DIGOIN

71160 – Michelin map **320** D11 – pop. 8,460 – alt. 232
▶ Paris 337 – Autun 69 – Charolles 26 – Moulins 57

⚠ La Chevrette

ℰ 03 85 53 11 49, *www.lachevrette.com*

Address : r. de la Chevrette (take the western exit towards Moulins, towards the municipal swimming pool; near the Loire river)

Opening times : from mid March to mid Oct.

1.6 ha (100 pitches) flat, terrace, grassy, fine gravel

Tariff : 16.90€ ✶✶ ⇔ 🔲 🚰 (10A) – Extra per person 3.70€

Rental rates : (from mid March to mid Oct.) ⚡ – 2 🛖 – 2 🏠. Per night from 48 to 76 € Per week from 45 to 73 €

🚉 sani-station

Surroundings : 🔲 ♀
Leisure activities : ✗ 🛤 🚲 🏊 (small swimming pool)
Facilities : 🔥 ⚤ ▥ 🚿 🗑 🍴 launderette
Nearby : 🔥 🎣

GPS Longitude : 3.96768
Latitude : 46.47983

DOMPIERRE-LES-ORMES

71520 – Michelin map **320** G11 – pop. 922 – alt. 480
▶ Paris 405 – Chauffailles 28 – Cluny 23 – Mâcon 35

⚠⚠ Le Village des Meuniers

ℰ 03 85 50 36 60, *www.villagedesmeuniers.com*

Address : take the northwestern exit along the D 41, follow the signs for La Clayette and take the road to the right, near the stadium

Opening times : from mid March to end Oct.

3 ha (113 pitches) terraced, flat and relatively flat

Tariff : ✶ 7.50€ ⇔ 🔲 11€ – 🚰 (15A) 4.50€ – Reservation fee 6€

Rental rates : (permanent) – 16 🛖 – 8 🏠 – 2 tent bungalows – 3 gîtes. Per night from 40 to 120 € – Per week from 280 to 840 € – Reservation fee 15€

🚉 sani-station 6€ – 2 🔲 28€ – 🚐 13.50€

Elevated panoramic location.

Surroundings : 🌿 ≤ 🔲
Leisure activities : ♀ ✗ 🛤 🎲 evening ⚽ 🔥 🏊 ⛷
Facilities : 🔥 ⚤ 🚿 🗑 🍴 🚻
Nearby : ✗

GPS Longitude : 4.47468
Latitude : 46.36393

ÉPINAC

71360 – Michelin map **320** H8 – pop. 2,357 – alt. 340
▶ Paris 304 – Arnay-le-Duc 20 – Autun 19 – Chagny 29

⚠ Municipal le Pont Vert

ℰ 03 85 82 00 26, *www.campingdupontvert.com*

Address : take the southern exit along the D 43 and take the road to the right; beside the Drée river

Opening times : from beginning April to end Oct.

2.9 ha (71 pitches) flat, grassy

Tariff : (2012 price) 17€ ✶✶ ⇔ 🔲 🚰 (10A) – Extra per person 2.90€

Rental rates : (2012 price) (from beginning April to end Oct.) – 1 🛖. Per night 58€ Per week 405€ – Reservation fee 10€

🚉 sani-station 2€ – 2 🔲 – 🚐 11€

Surroundings : 🌿 🔲 ♀
Leisure activities : 🛤
Facilities : 🔥 ⚤ 🍴 🚻
Nearby : ♀ ✗ ⚽ 🔥 🎣

GPS Longitude : 4.50617
Latitude : 46.98577

GIGNY-SUR-SAÔNE

71240 – Michelin map **320** J10 – pop. 522 – alt. 178
▶ Paris 355 – Chalon-sur-Saône 29 – Le Creusot 51 – Louhans 30

Les Castels Château de l'Épervière ▲▲

℘ 03 85 94 16 90, *www.domaine-eperviere.com* – limited spaces for one-night stay
Address : r. du Château (located 1km to the south; at Épervière)
Opening times : from end March to end Sept.
7 ha (100 pitches) flat, grassy, fine gravel
Tariff : ♀ 8.90 € – ⛺ 🅿 14.50 € – 🔌 (10A) 5.60 € – Reservation fee 10 €
Rental rates : (from end March to end Sept.) 🏕 – 5 🚐 – 3 🏡 – 3 gîtes.
Per week from 419 to 869 € – Reservation fee 20 €
🚰 sani-station – 30 🅿 14.50 €
Pleasant wooded park beside a lake.

Surroundings : 🏊 🚲 ♨♨
Leisure activities : ▼ ✕ 🎦 ⚹ 🚦 jacuzzi 🏊 🚴 🖼 🎿 ≈ (pool) 🎣
paddling pool
Facilities : 🚻 ⚲ 🛀 ♒ 🔥 🖥 🎣
Nearby : ✂

GPS Longitude : 4.94386
Latitude : 46.65446

To visit a town or region, use the MICHELIN Green Guides.

GIMOUILLE

58470 – Michelin map **319** B10 – pop. 479 – alt. 210
▶ Paris 257 – Dijon 195 – Nevers 11 – Bourges 59

Village Vacances Domaine du Grand Bois
(rental of chalets only)

℘ 03 86 21 09 21, *www.grand-bois.com*
Address : rte de Fertôt
Opening times : from beginning April to beginning Jan.
15 ha undulating, grassy
Rental rates : (2012 price) 🚻 (5 chalets) 🅿 – 65 🏡. Per night 245 € – Per week 1,316 €
Reservation fee 10 €

Surroundings : 🏊
Leisure activities : ▼ 🎦 🎸 🏊 🚴 ✂ 🖼 🎿 🎣 🐎 adventure park 🎯
Facilities : 🚻 ♒ ♒ launderette 🖥
Nearby : ✕

GPS Longitude : 3.09923
Latitude : 46.92812

GUEUGNON

71130 – Michelin map **320** E10 – pop. 7,638 – alt. 243
▶ Paris 335 – Autun 53 – Bourbon-Lancy 27 – Digoin 16

Municipal de Chazey

℘ 03 85 85 23 11, *www.ccpaysgueugnon.fr*
Address : zone de Chazey (4km south along the D 994, follow the signs for Digoin and take the road
to the right)
1 ha (20 pitches) flat, grassy
Rentals : 3 🏡.
Near a small canal and two lakes.

Surroundings : 🏊 🚲
Leisure activities : 🎦 🏊
Facilities : 🚻 ⚲ 🛀 🖥
Nearby : ⛲ ≈ (beach) 🎣

GPS Longitude : 4.05386
Latitude : 46.57077

L'ISLE-SUR-SEREIN

89440 – Michelin map **319** H6 – pop. 747 – alt. 190
▶ Paris 209 – Auxerre 50 – Avallon 17 – Montbard 36

Municipal le Parc du Château

℘ 03 86 33 93 50, *www.campingl'islesurserein*
Address : rte d'Avallon (800m south along the D 86; by the stadium, 150m from the Serein river)
1 ha (40 pitches) flat, grassy
Rentals : 4 🏠.
sani-station – 2 🔲

Surroundings : 🌳
Facilities : ⚬ ▥ 🛝 🚰
Nearby : 🏊 🎾 sports trail

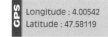

Longitude : 4.00542
Latitude : 47.58119

ISSY-L'EVÊQUE

71760 – Michelin map **320** D9 – pop. 842 – alt. 310
▶ Paris 325 – Bourbon-Lancy 25 – Gueugnon 17 – Luzy 12

Flower L'Etang Neuf

℘ 03 85 24 96 05, *www.atouvert.com*
Address : r. de l'Étang (located 1km west along the D 42, follow the signs for Grury and take the road to the right)
Opening times : from beginning May to end Sept.
6 ha/3 ha for camping (71 pitches) flat, relatively flat, grassy, fine gravel
Tariff : (2012 price) 21.70€ ✿✿ 🚗 🔲 💧 (10A) – Extra per person 3.20€
Rental rates : (2012 price) (from beginning May to end Sept.) – 2 🏠 – 6 🏠.
Per week from 310 to 450 €
sani-station 2.50€
Pleasant location beside a lake and a wood.

Surroundings : 🌳 ← 🏕
Leisure activities : 🍽 🎰 🏊 🛶
Facilities : ♿ ⚬ 🛝 ☑ 🚰 📷
Nearby : 🏊 🚣 🎣 🐎

Longitude : 3.9602
Latitude : 46.7078

LAIVES

71240 – Michelin map **320** J10 – pop. 997 – alt. 198
▶ Paris 355 – Chalon-sur-Saône 20 – Mâcon 48 – Montceau-les-Mines 49

Les Lacs de Laives – la Héronnière

℘ 03 85 44 98 85, *www.camping-laheronniere.com*
Address : rte de la Ferté (4.2km north along the D 18, follow the signs for Buxy and take right turn)
Opening times : from beginning April to mid Oct.
1.5 ha (80 pitches) flat, grassy
Tariff : (2012 price) 27.90€ ✿✿ 🚗 🔲 💧 (15A) – Extra per person 5.90€ – Reservation fee 10€
Rental rates : (from beginning April to mid Oct.) – 2 🏠. Per night from 57 to 73 €
Per week from 399 to 511 € – Reservation fee 10 €
sani-station 5€ – 5 🔲 27€
Close to the lakes at Laives.

Surroundings : 🌳 🏕 🌳
Leisure activities : 🚲 🛶
Facilities : ♿ ⚬ 🚰 📷
Nearby : 🍽 ✕ 🚣

Longitude : 4.83426
Latitude : 46.67448

LIGNY-LE-CHÂTEL

89144 – Michelin map **319** F4 – pop. 1,334 – alt. 130
▶ Paris 178 – Auxerre 22 – Sens 60 – Tonnerre 28

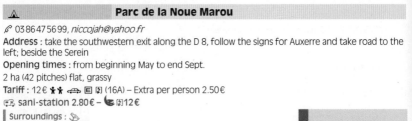

△ Parc de la Noue Marou

⌀ 03 86 47 56 99, *niccojah@yahoo.fr*
Address : take the southwestern exit along the D 8, follow the signs for Auxerre and take road to the left; beside the Serein
Opening times : from beginning May to end Sept.
2 ha (42 pitches) flat, grassy
Tariff : 12€ ♦♦ ⇔ 🗐 🔌 (16A) – Extra per person 2.50€
🚐 sani-station 2.80€ – 🧺 🔌 12€

Surroundings : 🍃
Leisure activities : 🎣
Facilities : 🔥 ⚬━ ☑ 💧 🔲
Nearby : 🏇 🍴 🏊

GPS | Longitude : 3.75274
Latitude : 47.89597

LOUHANS

71500 – Michelin map **320** L10 – pop. 6,451 – alt. 179
▶ Paris 373 – Bourg-en-Bresse 61 – Chalon-sur-Saône 38 – Dijon 85

△ Municipal

⌀ 03 85 75 19 02, *www.louhans-chateaurenaud.fr*
Address : at La Chapellerie (located 1km southwest along the D 971, follow the signs for Tournus and take the D 12, following signs for Romenay, turn left after the stadium)
Opening times : from beginning April to end Sept.
1 ha (60 pitches) flat, grassy, fine gravel
Tariff : (2012 price) ♦ 2€ ⇔ 2€ 🗐 2€ – 🔌 (20A) 3.70€
Rental rates : (2012 price) (from beginning April to end Sept.) – 2 . Per night from 70 € Per week from 280 to 380 €
🚐 sani-station – 26 🗐 5€
Green setting beside a river.

Surroundings : 🔭 ♧♧
Facilities : 🔥 (Jul–Aug) ⇄ 💧
Nearby : 🍴 🛶 🎣

GPS | Longitude : 5.21714
Latitude : 46.62436

LUZY

58170 – Michelin map **319** G11 – pop. 2,018 – alt. 275
▶ Paris 314 – Autun 34 – Château-Chinon 39 – Moulins 62

⋀⋀ Club Airotel Château de Chigy ♣

⌀ 03 86 30 10 80, *www.chateaudechigy.com.fr*
Address : 4km southwest along the D 973, follow the signs for Bourbon-Lancy then take the road to the left
Opening times : from end April to end Sept.
70 ha/15 ha for camping (200 pitches) flat, relatively flat, terraced, grassy
Tariff : (2012 price) 28.50€ ♦♦ ⇔ 🗐 🔌 (6A) – Extra per person 7.10€
Rental rates : (2012 price) (from beginning April to mid Nov.) – 6 🚐 – 29 🏠 – 3 apartments – 5 tents – 6 gîtes. Per night from 20 to 115 € – Per week from 140 to 805 €
Spacious site in the grounds of a château, with meadows, woods and lakes.

Surroundings : 🍃 ≼
Leisure activities : 🍷 🍴 🎦 🗂 🏃 🏇 ⛳ 🔲 🛶 🏊 🎣 multi-sports ground
Facilities : 🔥 ⚬━ 🧺 🔲 🚿

GPS | Longitude : 3.94445
Latitude : 46.75716

MARCENAY

21330 – Michelin map **320** G2 – pop. 115 – alt. 220
▶ Paris 232 – Auxerre 72 – Chaumont 73 – Dijon 89

Les Grèbes du Lac

☎ 03 80 81 61 72, www.campingmarcenaylac.com
Address : 800m north of the village
Opening times : permanent
2.4 ha (90 pitches) flat, grassy
Tariff : 21.20€ ✦✦ ⇌ 🅴 [½] (10A) – Extra per person 4€
Rental rates : (permanent) ⚹ – 5 🚐. Per night from 45 to 65 € – Per week from 252 to 392 €
🚐 sani-station 3€ – 7 🅴 14€ – 🔌 [½]11€
Pleasant location near a lake.

Surroundings : 🐟 🗗 ⛰
Leisure activities : 🍸 🎣
Facilities : ♿ �o-┳ ▥ ⚖ 🕈 🖻 ⚲
Nearby : ✕ ⌢ ≊ (beach)

Longitude : 4.40554
Latitude : 47.87095

MATOUR

71520 – Michelin map **320** G12 – pop. 1,095 – alt. 500
▶ Paris 405 – Chauffailles 22 – Cluny 24 – Mâcon 36

Le Paluet

☎ 03 85 59 70 92, www.matour.com
Address : 2 r. de la Piscine (located to the west; follow the signs for la Clayette and take a left turn)
Opening times : from beginning May to end Sept.
3 ha (75 pitches) flat and relatively flat, terraced, grassy, fine gravel
Tariff : 19.30€ ✦✦ ⇌ 🅴 [½] (10A) – Extra per person 4.90€ – Reservation fee 12€
Rental rates : (from mid March to mid Nov.) – 10 🏠 – 4 tent bungalows – 2 tents – 2 gîtes.
Per night from 30 to 92 € – Per week from 150 to 644 € – Reservation fee 25€
🚐 6 🅴
Beside a lake and near a leisure centre.

Surroundings : 🐟 🗗 ♀
Leisure activities : 🎣 🛶 🚲 ✂ ⌢ ⚖ ⚖ ⚲ multi-sports ground
Facilities : ♿ o-┳ (season) 🆑 ⌇ 🕈 launderette

Longitude : 4.48232
Latitude : 46.30677

MEURSAULT

21190 – Michelin map **320** I8 – pop. 1,542 – alt. 243
▶ Paris 326 – Dijon 56 – Chalon-sur-Saône 28 – Le Creusot 40

La Grappe d'Or

☎ 03 80 21 22 48, www.camping-meursault.com
Address : 2 rte de Volnay
Opening times : from beginning April to mid Oct.
4.5 ha (170 pitches) terraced, flat and relatively flat, grassy, fine gravel
Tariff : (2012 price) 22€ ✦✦ ⇌ 🅴 [½] (10A) – Extra per person 3.80€ – Reservation fee 10€
Rental rates : (2012 price) (from end April to beginning Oct.) ⚹ – 20 🚐 – 1 gîte.
Per night from 45 to 70 € – Per week from 315 to 490 € – Reservation fee 15€
🚐 sani-station 4€

Surroundings : ⋚ ♀
Leisure activities : ✕ 🛶 🚲 ✂ ⚖ ⚖
Facilities : o-┳ 🆑 🕈 ⚖ ⚲

Longitude : 4.76987
Latitude : 46.98655

MIGENNES

89400 – Michelin map **319** E4 – pop. 7,360 – alt. 87
▶ Paris 162 – Dijon 169 – Auxerre 22 – Sens 46

⚠ Les Confluents

✆ 03 86 80 94 55, *www.les-confluents.com*
Address : allée Léo Lagrange (near the stadium)
1.5 ha (63 pitches) flat, grassy
Rentals : 12 ⬚.
⬚ sani-station

Surroundings : ⬚ ♀
Leisure activities : ✕ 🎦 🚣 🚲 ⛷
Facilities : ⚬⬚ ▥ ♨ ⬚ ⬚ ⬚ ⬚
Nearby : ✂ ⬚ watersports centre

GPS Longitude : 3.5095 Latitude : 47.95613

This guide is updated regularly, so buy your new copy every year!

MONTBARD

21500 – Michelin map **320** G4 – pop. 5,527 – alt. 221
▶ Paris 240 – Autun 87 – Auxerre 81 – Dijon 81

⚠ Municipal

✆ 03 80 92 69 50, *www.montbard.com*
Address : r. Michel Servet (along the D 980 diversion northwest of the town, near the swimming complex)
Opening times : from beginning March to end Oct.
2.5 ha (80 pitches) flat, grassy, fine gravel
Tariff : (2012 price) 20.90€ ⚥ ⬚ 🔲 (16A) – Extra per person 5.10€
Rental rates : (2012 price) (from beginning March to mid Oct.) – 2 ⬚ – 20 ⬚.
Per night from 30 to 80 € – Per week from 255 to 505 €
⬚ sani-station 3.10€ – 4 🔲 2€
Attractive trees and shrubs surrounding pitches.

Surroundings : ≼ ⬚ ♀
Leisure activities : 🎦 ⬚ daytime 🚣 multi-sports ground
Facilities : ♿ ⚬⬚ ▥ ⬚ ⬚ ⬚ ⬚
Nearby : ⬚ hammam ⬚ ⬚ ⬚

GPS Longitude : 4.33129 Latitude : 47.63111

MONTIGNY-EN-MORVAN

58120 – Michelin map **319** G9 – pop. 319 – alt. 350
▶ Paris 269 – Château-Chinon 13 – Corbigny 26 – Nevers 64

⚠ Municipal du Lac

✆ 03 86 84 71 77, *montigny-en-morvan.fr* – ⬚
Address : Continue 2.3km northeast along the D 944, D 303 towards the dam at Pannecière-Chaumard and take the road to the right.
Opening times : permanent
2 ha (59 pitches) undulating, flat, grassy, stony
Tariff : (2012 price) ⚥ 2.50€ ⬚ 1.70€ 🔲 2€ – ⬚ (20A) 1.90€
Pleasant location near a lake.

Surroundings : ⬚ ♀
Leisure activities : 🚣 ⬚
Facilities : ♿ ⬚
Nearby : ⬚

GPS Longitude : 3.8735 Latitude : 47.15573

NOLAY

21340 – Michelin map **320** H8 – pop. 1,510 – alt. 299
▶ Paris 316 – Autun 30 – Beaune 20 – Chalon-sur-Saône 34

La Bruyère

℘ 0380218759, *www.bourgogne-sante-services.com*
Address : r. de Moulin Larché (1.2km west along the D 973, follow the signs for Autun and take road to the left)
Opening times : permanent
1.2 ha (22 pitches) flat, terraced, grassy
Tariff : (2012 price) 10.50€ ✦✦ ⇔ 国 (4) (10A) – Extra per person 2.30€
Rental rates : (2012 price) (permanent) – 3 ⌂. Per week from 249 to 332 €
⊞ sani-station 5€ – 3 国 10.50€

Surroundings : ⌗ ≤
Leisure activities : ⌂
Facilities : ♿ ☞ ▥ ⚑ launderette

GPS Longitude : 4.62202
Latitude : 46.95055

PALINGES

71430 – Michelin map **320** F10 – pop. 1,512 – alt. 274
▶ Paris 352 – Charolles 16 – Lapalisse 70 – Lyon 136

Le Lac

℘ 0385881449, *www.campingdulac.eu*
Address : at Lac du Fourneau (located 1km northeast along the D 128, rte de Génelard)
Opening times : from beginning April to end Oct.
1.5 ha (44 pitches) terraced, relatively flat, grassy
Tariff : 22€ ✦✦ ⇔ 国 (4) (10A) – Extra per person 3.80€
Rental rates : (from beginning April to end Oct.) – 6 ⌂. Per night from 45 to 170 €
Per week from 270 to 700 €
⊞ sani-station 1€
Near a small lake.

Surroundings : ⌗
Leisure activities : ⌂ ⚓ ☝
Facilities : ♿ ☞ ⬚ ⍾ ⚑ ▣ refrigerators
Nearby : ✗ ☰ (beach) ⌇

GPS Longitude : 4.22521
Latitude : 46.56106

PRÉMERY

58700 – Michelin map **319** C8 – pop. 2,031 – alt. 237
▶ Paris 231 – La Charité-sur-Loire 28 – Château-Chinon 57 – Clamecy 41

Municipal

℘ 0386379942, *mairie-premery@wanadoo.fr*
Address : ch. des Prés de la Ville (take the northeastern exit along the D 977, follow the signs for Clamecy and take the road to the right)
Opening times : permanent
1.6 ha (46 pitches) flat and relatively flat, grassy, fine gravel
Tariff : (2012 price) 8€ ✦✦ ⇔ 国 (4) (60A) – Extra per person 3.25€
Rental rates : (2012 price) (permanent) – 10 ⌂. Per night from 40 to 46 €
Per week from 220 to 316 €
⊞ sani-station 9.30€
Near the Nièvre river and a small lake.

Leisure activities : ⌇
Facilities : ♿ ☞ (Jul–Aug) ⅽⅽ ⍾ ⚑ ▣
Nearby : ⚓ ✗ ☰

GPS Longitude : 3.33683
Latitude : 47.1781

ST-GERMAIN-DU-BOIS

71330 – Michelin map **320** L9 – pop. 1,935 – alt. 210
▶ Paris 367 – Chalon-sur-Saône 33 – Dole 58 – Lons-le-Saunier 29

⚠ Municipal de l'Étang Titard

℘ 03 85 72 06 15, *st-germaindubois.fr*
Address : rte de Louhans (take the southern exit along the D 13)
Opening times : from mid May to beginning Sept.
1 ha (40 pitches) flat, terrace, relatively flat, grassy
Tariff : (2012 price) 🧍 2.30€ 🚗 1.50€ 🔲 1.20€ – ⚡ (16A) 2.50€
Rental rates : (2012 price) (permanent) 🛖 – 5 🏠. Per night from 42 to 60 €
Per week from 294 to 420 €

Near a lake.

Surroundings : ♀
Leisure activities : 🖼
Facilities : ⚴ 🚿 🆑 ⛲ 🔳
Nearby : 🎾 🖼 🚣 🎣 sports trail

GPS
Longitude : 5.24617
Latitude : 46.74635

These symbols are used for a campsite that is exceptional in its category:
🔺🔺🔺 ...🔺 *Particularly pleasant setting, quality and range of services available*
🦢🦢 *Tranquil, isolated site – quiet site, particularly at night*
≤≤ *Exceptional view – interesting or panoramic view*

ST-HONORÉ-LES-BAINS

58360 – Michelin map **319** G10 – pop. 841 – alt. 300 – ♨ (2 Apr-13 oct)
▶ Paris 303 – Château-Chinon 28 – Luzy 22 – Moulins 69

🔺 Camping et Gîtes des Bains 👥

℘ 03 86 30 73 44, *www.campinglesbains.com*
Address : 15 av. Jean Mermoz (take the western exit, follow the signs for Vandenesse)
4.5 ha (130 pitches) flat, grassy
Rentals : 4 🚐 – 19 🏠 – 1 🛏 – 1 studio – 2 apartments.
🚽 sani-station – 5 🔲

Surroundings : 🔲 ♀
Leisure activities : 🍴 🍽 🚴 ⛹ 🎣 🚣 ⛵ 🐎
Facilities : ⚴ 🔑 ⛺ ⚐ launderette 🚿

GPS
Longitude : 3.82832
Latitude : 46.90684

⚠ Municipal Plateau du Gué

℘ 03 86 30 76 00, *http://st-honore-les-bains.com/*
Address : 13 r. Eugène-Collin (in the town, 150m from the post office)
Opening times : from beginning April to end Oct.
1.2 ha (73 pitches) flat and relatively flat, grassy
Tariff : (2012 price) 🧍 2.50€ 🚗 1.80€ 🔲 1.80€ – ⚡ (10A) 2.90€
🚽 sani-station 2€ – 10 🔲 1.80€

Surroundings : ♀
Leisure activities : 🖼 🚴
Facilities : ⚴ 🚿 🔳 🔳

GPS
Longitude : 3.83918
Latitude : 46.90376

ST-LÉGER-DE-FOUGERET

58120 – Michelin map **319** G9 – pop. 289 – alt. 500
▶ Paris 308 – Dijon 122 – Nevers 65 – Le Creusot 69

L'Etang de la Fougeraie

𝒫 03 86 85 11 85, *www.campingfougeraie.com* ⚒
Address : at Hameau de champs (2.4km southeast along the D 157, follow the signs for Onlay)
Opening times : from beginning April to end Sept.
7 ha (60 pitches) flat, undulating, terraced, grassy
Tariff : 18€ ♦♦ ⇌ 🔲 ⓗ (10A) – Extra per person 5.50€ – Reservation fee 7.50€
Rental rates : (permanent) – 5 🏠 – 3 tents. Per night from 40 to 95 €
Per week from 280 to 495 € – Reservation fee 15€
🔳 sani-station – 🔋11€
Rural setting around a lake.

Surroundings : 🦆 ≤
Leisure activities : ⵟ ✕ 🚲 ☈ 🎣
Facilities : ⅙ ⊶ ☖ ♚ launderette 🍴 refrigerators

Longitude : 3.90492
Latitude : 47.00616

ST-PÉREUSE

58110 – Michelin map **319** F9 – pop. 280 – alt. 355
▶ Paris 289 – Autun 54 – Château-Chinon 15 – Clamecy 57

Le Manoir de Bezolle

𝒫 03 86 84 42 55, *www.camping-bezolle.com*
Address : to the southeast along the D 11, 300m from the D 978, follow the signs for Château-Chinon
Opening times : permanent
8 ha/5 ha for camping (140 pitches) terraced, flat and relatively flat, grassy, small lakes
Tariff : 28.44€ ♦♦ ⇌ 🔲 ⓗ (10A) – Extra per person 5.50€ – Reservation fee 5€
Rental rates : (from beginning April to end Oct.) – 2 caravans – 4 🚐 – 12 🏠 – 4 tents.
Per night from 35 to 103 € – Per week from 245 to 845 € – Reservation fee 5€
🔳 sani-station – 🔋ⓗ17.44€
In the grounds of the manor house.

Surroundings : 🦆 ≤ 🌳
Leisure activities : ⵟ ✕ 🎏 🏊 🎣 🎠
Facilities : ⅙ ⊶ 🖥 ♨ ☖ ☈ ⚐ ♚ launderette 🏊 🍴

Longitude : 3.8158
Latitude : 47.05732

ST-POINT

71520 – Michelin map **320** H11 – pop. 341 – alt. 335
▶ Paris 396 – Beaune 90 – Cluny 14 – Mâcon 26

Lac de St-Point-Lamartine

𝒫 03 85 50 52 31, *www.campingsaintpoint.com*
Address : take the southern exit along the D 22, follow the signs for Tramayes; beside a lake
Opening times : from beginning April to end Oct.
3 ha (102 pitches) flat and relatively flat, terraced, grassy
Tariff : 16€ ♦♦ ⇌ 🔲 ⓗ (13A) – Extra per person 3€
Rental rates : (from beginning April to end Oct.) – 3 🚐 – 11 🏠. Per night from 35 to 60 €
Per week from 175 to 380 €
🔳 sani-station – 🔋ⓗ10€
Surroundings : 🦆 ≤ 🏞
Leisure activities : 🎏 🏊 🚲 🎣
Facilities : ⅙ ⊶ ☖ ♚ 📷
Nearby : ⵟ ✕ ☈ 🎣 pedalos

Longitude : 4.61175
Latitude : 46.33703

ST-SAUVEUR-EN-PUISAYE

89520 – Michelin map **319** C6 – pop. 946 – alt. 259
▶ Paris 174 – Dijon 184 – Moulins 146 – Tours 242

Parc des Joumiers

℘ 03 86 45 66 28, *www.camping-motel-joumiers.com*
Address : 2.3km northwest along the D 7 and take the road to the right
Opening times : from end March to mid Oct.
21 ha/7 ha for camping (100 pitches) flat and relatively flat, grassy, lake
Tariff : ♦ 3.80€ 🚗 3€ ▣ 4.50€ – 🔌 (10A) 4€
Rental rates : (from beginning April to mid Oct.) – 14 🚃 – 3 🏠 – 10 ⊨.
Per night from 55 to 149 € – Per week from 319 to 781 €
🚽 sani-station 5€
Beside a lake.

Surroundings : 🐚 ⊡ ⛰
Leisure activities : ✗ 🛶 🛷 🤿
Facilities : ♿ ⊶ 🗄 🏕 🚰 ⬧ 🔲
Nearby : pedalos

GPS Longitude : 3.19357
Latitude : 47.63082

Some campsites benefit from proximity to a municipal leisure centre.

SALORNAY-SUR-GUYE

71250 – Michelin map **320** H10 – pop. 826 – alt. 210
▶ Paris 377 – Chalon-sur-Saône 51 – Cluny 12 – Paray-le-Monial 44

Municipal de la Clochette

℘ 03 85 59 90 11, *mairie.salornay@wanadoo.fr*
Address : pl. de la Clochette (in the village, access via the road in front of the post office)
Opening times : from mid May to beginning Sept.
1 ha (60 pitches) flat, terrace, grassy
Tariff : ♦ 3.50€ 🚗 ▣ 3€ – 🔌 (10A) 3€ – Reservation fee 5€
🚽 sani-station 5€
Beside La Gande (river).

Surroundings : ⊡ ♀
Leisure activities : 🤿
Facilities : ♿ 🚻 🔲
Nearby : 🍴

GPS Longitude : 4.59907
Latitude : 46.51659

SANTENAY

21590 – Michelin map **320** I8 – pop. 827 – alt. 225
▶ Paris 330 – Autun 39 – Beaune 18 – Chalon-sur-Saône 25

Les Sources

℘ 03 80 20 66 55, *www.campingsantenay.com*
Address : av. des Sources (head 1km southwest following signs for Cheilly-les-Maranges, near the spa centre)
3.1 ha (150 pitches) flat and relatively flat, grassy
Rentals : 🏕 – 2 🚃.

Surroundings : ≤ ♀
Leisure activities : ✗ 🛶 👟ₘ
Facilities : ♿ ⊶ 🚻 🔲 ⬧ 🧺
Nearby : 🍴 🛷

GPS Longitude : 4.6857
Latitude : 46.90716

SAULIEU

21210 – Michelin map **320** F6 – pop. 2,574 – alt. 535
▶ Paris 248 – Autun 40 – Avallon 39 – Beaune 65

⚠ Aquadis Loisirs Saulieu

℘ 0380641619, *www.aquadis-loisirs.com*
Address : located 1km northwest along the N 6, follow the signs for Paris; near a lake
Opening times : from beginning March to beginning Nov.
8 ha (157 pitches) flat and relatively flat, grassy
Rental rates : (from beginning March to beginning Nov.) – 4 ⟮⟯ – 6 ⟮⟯ – 20 tent bungalows.
Per night from 26 to 85 € – Per week from 111 to 626 €
🚐 sani-station

Leisure activities : 🎣 🛶 🚲 ✂ ♨ ⅃
Facilities : ♿ ⊶ 🚿 ⊠ 🔲 ▥ 🛁 ☇ ⚟ 🖼

GPS Longitude : 4.22373
Latitude : 47.28934

SAVIGNY-LÈS-BEAUNE

21420 – Michelin map **320** I7 – pop. 1,371 – alt. 237
▶ Paris 314 – Dijon 39 – Mâcon 93 – Lons-le-Saunier 109

⚠ Les Premiers Prés

℘ 0380261506, *www.camping-savigny-les-beaune.fr*
Address : rte de Bouilland (located 1km northwest along the D 2)
1.5 ha (90 pitches) flat and relatively flat, grassy
🚐 sani-station
Green setting beside a stream.

Surroundings : ⊙⊙
Leisure activities : 🛶
Facilities : ♿ ⊶ ⚟

GPS Longitude : 4.82192
Latitude : 47.06246

*The Michelin classification (⚠⚠⚠... ⚠) is totally independent of the
official star classification system awarded by the local prefecture or
other official organisation.*

LES SETTONS

58230 – Michelin map **319** H8 – Leisure centre
▶ Paris 259 – Autun 41 – Avallon 44 – Château-Chinon 25

⚠ Les Mésanges

℘ 0386845577, *www.campinglesmesanges.fr*
Address : rive gauche, L'Huis-Gaumont (4km south along the D193, D 520, follow the signs for
Planchez and turn left towards Chevigny, 200m from the lake)
Opening times : from mid May to mid Sept.
5 ha (100 pitches) relatively flat, terraced, grassy, lake
Tariff : (2012 price) 19.90€ ✶✶ ⊖ ▣ ⌂ (16A) – Extra per person 5€
🚐 sani-station – ⛽11€
Pleasant location beside a lake.

Surroundings : ⊜ ⊡ ⊙
Leisure activities : 🛶 ⊷
Facilities : ♿ ⊶ 🛁 ☇ ⚟ ⅃ launderette
Nearby : ≋

GPS Longitude : 4.05385
Latitude : 47.18077

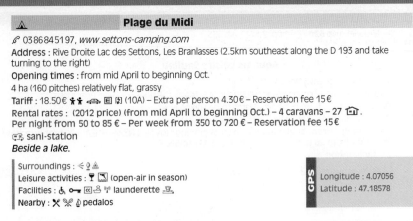

⛺ Plage du Midi

✆ 0386845197, *www.settons-camping.com*

Address : Rive Droite Lac des Settons, Les Branlasses (2.5km southeast along the D 193 and take turning to the right)

Opening times : from mid April to beginning Oct.

4 ha (160 pitches) relatively flat, grassy

Tariff : 18.50€ 👥 🚗 ▣ ⚡ (10A) – Extra per person 4.30€ – Reservation fee 15€

Rental rates : (2012 price) (from mid April to beginning Oct.) – 4 caravans – 27 🏠.
Per night from 50 to 85 € – Per week from 350 to 720 € – Reservation fee 15€

🚐 sani-station

Beside a lake.

Surroundings : ⋞ ♀ ⛵
Leisure activities : 🍸 ▨ (open-air in season)
Facilities : ♿ 🔑 ▣ ♨ 📶 launderette ⛱
Nearby : ✕ ✂ ⛵ pedalos

GPS Longitude : 4.07056
Latitude : 47.18578

⛺ La Plage des Settons

✆ 0386845199, *www.camping-chalets-settons.com*

Address : Rive Gauche-Lac des Settons (300m south of the dam)

Opening times : from beginning April to end Sept.

2.6 ha (68 pitches) terraced, fine gravel, grassy

Tariff : 18€ 👥 🚗 ▣ ⚡ (10A) – Extra per person 5.50€

Rental rates : (2012 price) (from beginning March to end Nov.) – 20 🏠.
Per night from 115 to 180 € – Per week from 360 to 700 €

🚐 sani-station – 40 ▣ 18€ – 🌙 ⚡11€

Pleasant pitches on terraces, opposite the lake.

Surroundings : ♨ ⋞ ▭
Leisure activities : 🏠 ⛹
Facilities : ♿ 🔑 ♨ 📶 ▣
Nearby : 🍸 ✕ ⛹

GPS Longitude : 4.06132
Latitude : 47.18958

We value your opinion and welcome your feedback.
Do email us at campingfrance@tp.michelin.com

TONNERRE

89700 – Michelin map **319** G4 – pop. 5,246 – alt. 156
▶ Paris 199 – Auxerre 38 – Montbard 45 – Troyes 60

⛺ Municipal de la Cascade

✆ 0386551544, *www.revea-camping.fr*

Address : av. Aristide-Briand (take the northern exit along the D 905, follow the signs for Troyes and take D 944, towards the town centre; beside the Yonne canal)

Opening times : from mid April to end Sept.

3 ha (115 pitches) flat, grassy

Tariff : 13.60€ 👥 🚗 ▣ ⚡ (10A) – Extra per person 3.60€ – Reservation fee 10€

Rental rates : (from mid April to end Sept.) – 6 🏠. Per night from 60 to 70 €
Per week from 190 to 460 € – Reservation fee 25€

🚐 4 ▣ 13.60€

Surroundings : ♀
Leisure activities : ✕ 🏠 🚲
Facilities : ♿ 🔑 ▣ ▥ 📶 ▣
Nearby : ≋ ⚓

GPS Longitude : 3.98415
Latitude : 47.8603

TOURNUS

71700 – Michelin map **320** J10 – pop. 5,884 – alt. 193
▶ Paris 360 – Bourg-en-Bresse 70 – Chalon-sur-Saône 28 – Lons-le-Saunier 58

Camping de Tournus

℘ 03 85 51 16 58, www.camping-tournus.com
Address : 14 r. des Canes (located 1km north of the town; take the r. St-Laurent opposite the station. situated right next to the swimming pool and 150m from the Saône (direct access)
Opening times : from end March to end Sept.
2 ha (90 pitches) flat, grassy
Tariff : ✛ 5.90€ 🚗 🅴 9.30€ – 🔌 (10A) 4.70€ – Reservation fee 5€
🚐 sani-station – 25 🅴 9.30€

Leisure activities : 🎱
Facilities : 🛁 ⚲ 🖂 🛗 🚰 🔥
Nearby : 🍽 🎣 🛶

GPS Longitude : 4.90932
Latitude : 46.57375

We have selected the best campsites in France with our usual care, listing those with the best facilities in the most pleasant surroundings.

VANDENESSE-EN-AUXOIS

21320 – Michelin map **320** H6 – pop. 279 – alt. 360
▶ Paris 275 – Arnay-le-Duc 16 – Autun 42 – Châteauneuf 3

Sunêlia Le Lac de Panthier ▲▲

℘ 03 80 49 21 94, www.lac-de-panthier.com
Address : situated 2.5km northeast along the D 977bis; follow the road to Commarin and take turning to the left; near the lake
Opening times : from beginning April to beginning Oct.
5.2 ha (207 pitches) terraced, flat and relatively flat, grassy
Tariff : 28€ ✛✛ 🚗 🅴 🔌 (6A) – Extra per person 7€ – Reservation fee 15€
Rental rates : (from beginning April to beginning Oct.) – 45 🛖 – 14 🏠.
Per night from 42 to 147 € – Per week from 294 to 1,029 € – Reservation fee 15€

Surroundings : 🏞 ⛰ 🏕 ♨ ⛰
Leisure activities : 🍽 🍴 🎱 🏃 🎣 ⛵ 🚤 🚲 🏊 🛶 ⛷ 🎣
Facilities : 🛁 ⚲ 🖂 🛗 🚰 🔥 🚮 🚿
Nearby : 🏊 🎣

GPS Longitude : 4.62507
Latitude : 47.24935

VARZY

58210 – Michelin map **319** D7 – pop. 1,329 – alt. 249
▶ Paris 224 – La Charité-sur-Loire 37 – Clamecy 17 – Cosne-sur-Loire 43

Municipal du Moulin Naudin

℘ 03 86 29 43 12, mairievarzy@wanadoo.fr
Address : rte de Corvol (located 1.5km north along the D 977)
Opening times : from mid May to end Sept.
3 ha (50 pitches) flat, relatively flat, terraced, grassy
Tariff : (2012 price) 12€ ✛✛ 🚗 🅴 🔌 (5A) – Extra per person 2.90€
Near a small lake.

Surroundings : 🏕 ♨
Leisure activities : 🎣
Facilities : 🛁 🚮 🚿 🚰 🔥
Nearby : 🍽 🏊

GPS Longitude : 3.38312
Latitude : 47.3722

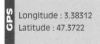

VENAREY-LES-LAUMES

21150 – Michelin map **320** G4 – pop. 2,981 – alt. 235
▶ Paris 259 – Avallon 54 – Dijon 66 – Montbard 15

 Municipal Alésia

📞 03 80 96 07 76, *www.venareyleslaumes.fr*

Address : take the western exit along the D 954, follow the signs for Semur-en-Auxois and take a right turn before the bridge; beside the Brenne river and near a small lake

Opening times : from beginning April to mid Oct.

1.5 ha (67 pitches) flat, grassy, fine gravel

Tariff : 🛉 3.50€ 🚐 1€ 🔲 3.80€ – 🔌 (16A) 3€

Rental rates : (permanent) – 5 🏠 – 1 🛏. Per night from 50 to 70 €
Per week from 270 to 395 €

🚐 sani-station 2€ – 🚐 🔌 11.70€

Surroundings : 🏕 ♨
Leisure activities : 🎦 🏕 🎣
Facilities : 🚿 ⚲ cc ♨ ⛱ ♨ 🔲
Nearby : 🍴 🏖 (beach)

Longitude : 4.45151
Latitude : 47.54425

VERMENTON

89270 – Michelin map **319** F6 – pop. 1,183 – alt. 125
▶ Paris 190 – Auxerre 24 – Avallon 28 – Vézelay 28

Municipal les Coullemières

📞 03 86 81 53 02, *www.camping.vermenton.com*

Address : at Les Coullemières (to the southwest of the town, behind the station)

1 ha (50 pitches) flat, grassy

Rentals : 6 🏠.

🚐 5 🔲

Pleasant setting near La Cure (river).

Surroundings : ♨ ⛰
Leisure activities : 🎦 🏕 🚴 🍴
Facilities : 🚿 ⚲ ♨ 🚰 🔲 🚿
Nearby : 🏖 (beach) sports trail

Longitude : 3.73123
Latitude : 47.65843

VIGNOLES

21200 – Michelin map **320** J7 – pop. 810 – alt. 202
▶ Paris 317 – Dijon 40 – Chalon-sur-Saône 34 – Le Creusot 51

Les Bouleaux

📞 03 80 22 26 88, *camping-les-bouleaux@hotmail.fr*

Address : 11 r. Jaune (located at Chevignerot; beside a stream)

Opening times : permanent

1.6 ha (46 pitches) flat, grassy

Tariff : 🛉 4€ 🚐 2.10€ 🔲 3.60€ – 🔌 (6A) 3.80€

Surroundings : 🏕 ♨♨
Leisure activities : 🎦
Facilities : 🚿 ⚲ 🚰 ✉ ♨ 🔲
Nearby : 🐴 🐎

Longitude : 4.88298
Latitude : 47.02668

Philippe Body / hemis.fr

Sleeping Beauty is said to slumber still within the thick stone walls of one of the Loire's fairy-tale castles. Does she await that kiss in Chambord, Azay-le-Rideau, Chenonceau, or perhaps one of the many other wonderful châteaux that lie in wait for you? To list all the Centre's architectural wonders set in the most glorious of gardens would take far too long, but visitors can appreciate some of the Loire's treasures during a season of spectacular *son et lumière* (sound and light) shows. The landscape of the region has inspired a host of writers, from Pierre de Ronsard, the 16th-century 'Prince of Poets', to Balzac and Georges Sand. All succumbed to the charm and beauty of this valley of kings, with its untamed river and atmospheric woodlands. In order to savour the region's twin talents for storytelling and culinary arts to the full, enjoy a delicious chicken stew before listening to your host's tales of werewolves and other local legends!

AUBIGNY-SUR-NÈRE

18700 – Michelin map **323** K2 – pop. 5,879 – alt. 180
▶ Paris 180 – Bourges 48 – Cosne-sur-Loire 41 – Gien 30

Flower Les Étangs

✆ 02 48 58 02 37, www.camping-aubigny.com
Address : rte de Oizon (1.4km east along the D 923, near a lake (direct access)
Opening times : from beginning April to end Oct.
3 ha (100 pitches) flat, grassy
Tariff : 21€ ✹✹ ⇔ 回 ☖ (6A) – Extra per person 4€
Rental rates : (permanent) – 1 caravan – 8 ⌂ – 6 ⌂ – 2 tent bungalows.
Per night from 33 to 117 € – Per week from 165 to 702 € – Reservation fee 15€

Surroundings : ♋
Leisure activities : 🎦 ⚓
Facilities : ♿ ⚮ 🚿 ⛟ 🚰 🖼
Nearby : ✂ 🖼 🎣

GPS Longitude : 2.46101
Latitude : 47.48574

AZAY-LE-RIDEAU

37190 – Michelin map **317** L5 – pop. 3,418 – alt. 51
▶ Paris 265 – Châtellerault 61 – Chinon 21 – Loches 58

Municipal le Sabot

✆ 02 47 45 42 72, www.azaylerideau.fr ✁
Address : r. du Stade (take the eastern exit along the D 84, follow the signs for Artannes and take turning to the right)
Opening times : from beginning April to end Oct.
6 ha (256 pitches) flat, grassy
Tariff : (2012 price) 12.50€ ✹✹ ⇔ 回 ☖ (10A) – Extra per person 3.70€
🚐 sani-station 3€
Pleasant location near the château and the Indre river.

Surroundings : 🌿
Leisure activities : 🎦 ⚓ 🚲 🎣
Facilities : ♿ ⚮ 🚿 🚰 launderette
Nearby : ✂ 🏊 🛶

GPS Longitude : 0.46963
Latitude : 47.25863

BALLAN-MIRÉ

37510 – Michelin map **317** M4 – pop. 8,152 – alt. 88
▶ Paris 251 – Azay-le-Rideau 17 – Langeais 20 – Montbazon 13

La Mignardière

✆ 02 47 73 31 00, www.mignardiere.com
Address : 22 av. des Aubépines (2.5km northeast of the town, not far from the small lake at Joué-Ballan)
Opening times : from beginning April to mid Sept.
2.5 ha (177 pitches) flat, grassy, small adjacent wood
Tariff : 27.50€ ✹✹ ⇔ 回 ☖ (10A) – Extra per person 5.80€ – Reservation fee 5€
Rental rates : (from beginning April to mid Sept.) – 4 'gypsy' caravans – 15 ⌂ – 23 ⌂.
Per night from 35 to 80 € – Per week from 245 to 763 € – Reservation fee 10€
🚐 sani-station 4€

Surroundings : 🌿
Leisure activities : ⚓ 🚲 ✂ 🖼 🛶
Facilities : ♿ ⚮ 🚿 🚰 ⛟ 🚰 🖼 ⛲
Nearby : 🍴 ✗ 🐎 🏊

GPS Longitude : 0.63402
Latitude : 47.35524

BARAIZE

36270 – Michelin map **323** F8 – pop. 313 – alt. 240
▶ Paris 318 – Orléans 192 – Châteauroux 47 – Guéret 86

Municipal Montcocu

⌂

℘ 0254253428, *syndicat.laceguzon@wanadoo.fr* – for caravans – from the 'Montcocu' locality, 12% gradient for 1km

Address : at Montcocu (4.8km southeast along the D 913, follow the signs for Éguzon and take D 72, take left turn for Pont-de-Piles)

Opening times : from beginning April to end Oct.

1 ha (26 pitches) terraced, grassy

Tariff : ♦ 2.20€ ⇔ 🗉 2.70€ – ⚡ (8A) 3.10€

Rental rates : (from beginning April to end Oct.) ⚡ – 4 🏠 – 5 tent bungalows.
Per night 11€ – Per week from 138 to 433 €

Pleasant location and setting in the Creuse valley.

| Surroundings : ⚘ 🗔 ♀ ⛰ |
| Leisure activities : 🍴 🎣 ⛵ |
| Facilities : ⚿ ☌ 🗒 cc ⊪ |

Longitude : 1.60023
Latitude : 46.47159

This guide is not intended as a list of all the camping sites in France; its aim is to provide a selection of the best sites in each category.

LA BAZOCHE-GOUET

28330 – Michelin map **311** B7 – pop. 1,314 – alt. 185
▶ Paris 146 – Brou 18 – Chartres 61 – Châteaudun 33

Municipal la Rivière

⌂

℘ 0237493649, *commune-bazoche-gouet-28330@wanadoo.fr*

Address : located 1.5km southwest along the D 927, follow the signs for la Chapelle-Guillaume and take road to the left

Opening times : from beginning April to end Sept.

1.8 ha (30 pitches) flat, grassy

Tariff : (2012 price) 6.50€ ♦♦ ⇔ 🗉 ⚡ (10A) – Extra per person 2.90€

Beside the Yerre river and close to some lakes.

| Leisure activities : 🏊 🚲 🎣 |
| Facilities : ⚿ 🗒 📷 |
| Nearby : 🍴 |

Longitude : 0.9689
Latitude : 48.129

BEAULIEU-SUR-LOIRE

45630 – Michelin map **318** N6 – pop. 1,779 – alt. 156
▶ Paris 170 – Aubigny-sur-Nère 36 – Briare 15 – Gien 27

Municipal Touristique du Canal

⌂

℘ 0238353216, *www.beaulieu-sur-loire.fr*

Address : take the eastern exit along the D 926, near the canal (stopping place)

Opening times : from beginning May to beginning Nov.

0.6 ha (37 pitches) flat, grassy

Tariff : (2012 price) ♦ 2.60€ ⇔ 🗉 1.40€ – ⚡ (10A) 3.20€

🗒 sani-station

| Surroundings : 🗔 ♀ |
| Facilities : ⚿ 🗒 cc ⚿ |
| Nearby : 🍴 🎣 ⚓ |

Longitude : 2.8176
Latitude : 47.5435

LE BLANC

36300 – Michelin map **323** C7 – pop. 6,946 – alt. 85
▶ Paris 326 – Bellac 62 – Châteauroux 61 – Châtellerault 52

 l'Isle d'Avant

⌀ 02 54 37 88 22, *www.tourisme-leblanc.fr* – ℞

Address : 60 av. Pierre Mendès-France (situated 2km east on N 151, follow the signs for Châteauroux; beside the Creuse river)

Opening times : from beginning April to mid Oct.

1 ha (75 pitches) flat, grassy

Tariff : (2012 price) 11€ � ✥ 🔲 🅗 (8A) – Extra per person 2.50€

Rental rates : (2012 price) (from beginning April to mid Oct.) – 1 🔳.
Per night from 40 to 45 € – Per week from 275 to 300 €

🚰 sani-station 2€ – 10 🔲 11€

Surroundings : 🔲 🟤🟤
Leisure activities : 🖼 🏹
Facilities : 🚰 (Jul–Aug) 🛒 🔌 launderette
Nearby : 🍴 🛝

GPS
Longitude : 1.09178
Latitude : 46.63189

BONNEVAL

28800 – Michelin map **311** E6 – pop. 4,565 – alt. 128
▶ Paris 117 – Ablis 61 – Chartres 31 – Châteaudun 14

Le Bois Chièvre

⌀ 02 37 47 54 01, *www.camping-bonneval-28.fr*

Address : rte de Vouvray (located 1.5km south following signs for Conie and take turning to the right; beside the Loir river)

Opening times : from beginning April to end Oct.

4.5 ha/2.5 ha for camping (104 pitches) relatively flat, flat, grassy, gravelled, adjacent wood

Tariff : 15.85€ � ✥ 🔲 🅗 (6A) – Extra per person 4.20€

Rental rates : (from beginning April to end Oct.) – 3 🔳 – 1 studio. Per night 75€
Per week 395€

🚰 sani-station – 1 🔲 15.85€ – 🍵 🅗 11€

Pleasant site among oak trees, overlooking the Loir river.

Surroundings : 🦌 🔲 🟤🟤
Leisure activities : 🖼 🔥 🎣 🏹
Facilities : 🚻 🚰 🍴 🛀 🔌 🔲 🛒
Nearby : 🍴 🖼

GPS
Longitude : 1.3864
Latitude : 48.1708

BOURGES

18000 – Michelin map **323** K4 – pop. 66,786 – alt. 153
▶ Paris 244 – Châteauroux 65 – Dijon 254 – Nevers 69

Municipal Robinson

⌀ 02 48 20 16 85, *www.ville.bourges.fr* – ℞

Address : 26 bd de l'Industrie (head towards the southern exit along the N 144, follow the signs for Montluçon and take the turning to the left, near the Lac d'Auron, take exit A 71 and follow the signs for Bourges Centre)

Opening times : from mid March to mid Nov.

2.2 ha (116 pitches) flat and relatively flat, grassy, gravelled

Tariff : 🚹 4.30€ ✥ 5.50€ 🔲 5.50€ – 🅗 (16A) 8.40€

Surroundings : 🔲 🟤
Leisure activities : 🔥 🎣
Facilities : 🚻 🚰 🍴 🛀 🔌 🔲
Nearby : 🍴 🖼 🛝 🏊 🐎 🐟

GPS
Longitude : 2.39488
Latitude : 47.07232

BOURGUEIL

37140 – Michelin map **317** J5 – pop. 3,924 – alt. 42
▶ Paris 281 – Angers 81 – Chinon 16 – Saumur 23

Municipal Parc Capitaine

✆ 02 47 97 85 62, *www.bourgueil.fr*
Address : 31 av. du Gal de Gaulle (1.5 km south along the D 749, follow the signs for Chinon)
Opening times : from mid May to mid Sept.
2 ha (80 pitches) flat, grassy
Tariff : (2012 price) 13.35 € 🕴🕴 ⇔ 🗐 🛛 (7A) – Extra per person 2.20 €
🚏 1 🗐 13.35 €
Leafy, green setting offering plenty of shade, near a small lake.

Surroundings : ⌇ ⓠ
Leisure activities : 🛖 ⤳
Facilities : 🚾 ☞ 🚽 🖻
Nearby : 🍵 🍸 🚤 ✗ 🖾 🗖 ⪼ 🏂

GPS Longitude : 0.16684
Latitude : 47.27381

BRACIEUX

41250 – Michelin map **318** G6 – pop. 1,256 – alt. 70
▶ Paris 185 – Blois 19 – Montrichard 39 – Orléans 64

Indigo Les Châteaux

✆ 02 54 46 41 84, *www.camping-indigo.com*
Address : 11 r. Roger-Brun (take the northern exit, follow the signs for Blois; beside the Beuvron river)
Opening times : from end March to beginning Nov.
8 ha (350 pitches) flat, grassy
Tariff : (2012 price) 27.90 € 🕴🕴 ⇔ 🗐 🛛 (10A) – Extra per person 5.80 € – Reservation fee 20 €
Rental rates : (2012 price) (from end March to beginning Nov.) 🚾 (1 chalet) – 6 caravans – 14 🛏 – 10 🏚 – 20 tents. Per night from 40 to 112 € – Per week from 196 to 784 € – Reservation fee 20 €
🚏 sani-station 7 €
Wooded setting with a variety of tree species.

Surroundings : 🖾 ⓠ
Leisure activities : 🖾 🚤 ✗ 🛶
Facilities : 🚾 ☞ launderette

GPS Longitude : 1.53821
Latitude : 47.55117

To visit a town or region, use the MICHELIN Green Guides.

BRIARE

45250 – Michelin map **318** N6 – pop. 5,688 – alt. 135
▶ Paris 160 – Orléans 85 – Gien 11 – Montargis 50

Le Martinet

✆ 02 38 31 24 50, *campinglemartinet.fr*
Address : at Val Martinet (located 1km north via town centre, near the Loire river and the canal)
4.5 ha (160 pitches) flat, grassy
Rentals : 🛏 – 3 tent bungalows.
🚏 sani-station – 40 🗐

Surroundings : 🖾 ⓠ
Leisure activities : 🛖
Facilities : 🚾 ☞ 🎼 🛆 ⚐ 🚽 🖻
Nearby : 🛶 ⤳

GPS Longitude : 2.72441
Latitude : 47.64226

CENTRE

BUZANÇAIS

36500 – Michelin map **323** E5 – pop. 4,501 – alt. 111
▶ Paris 286 – Le Blanc 47 – Châteauroux 25 – Châtellerault 78

Aquadis Loisirs La Tête Noire

℘ 0254841727, www.aquadis-loisirs.com
Address : to the northwest along the r. des Ponts; beside the Indre river, near the stadium
Opening times : from end April to end Sept.
2.5 ha (134 pitches) flat, grassy
Tariff : ♀ 3.60€ ⚘ 2.10€ 🔲 3.60€ – (ⱡ) (10A) 3.60€ – Reservation fee 9.90€
Rental rates : (from end April to end Sept.) – 4 🚐. Per night from 36 to 52 €
Per week from 195 to 255 € – Reservation fee 19.50€
🚐 sani-station 11€ – 5 🔲 3.60€ – 🍷11€

Surroundings : 🌊 ♤♤
Leisure activities : 🎦 ⛹ ⤳
Facilities : ♿ ⊶ ♨ ™ 🔲
Nearby : ✗ ⚓ skateboarding

GPS Longitude : 1.41805
Latitude : 46.89285

CANDÉ-SUR-BEUVRON

41120 – Michelin map **318** E7 – pop. 1,462 – alt. 70
▶ Paris 199 – Blois 15 – Chaumont-sur-Loire 7 – Montrichard 21

La Grande Tortue

℘ 0254441520, www.la-grande-tortue.com
Address : 3, rte de Pontlevoy (500m south along the D 751, follow the signs for Chaumont-sur-Loire and take the turning to the left, follow the signs for La Pieuse, not far from the Beuvron)
Opening times : from beginning April to end Sept.
5 ha (208 pitches) relatively flat, flat, grassy, sandy
Tariff : 34€ ♀♀ ⚘ 🔲 (ⱡ) (10A) – Extra per person 10€ – Reservation fee 12€
Rental rates : (from beginning March to beginning Nov.) – 28 🚐 – 8 🏠.
Per night from 50 to 120 € – Per week from 260 to 840 € – Reservation fee 12€
🚐 sani-station

Surroundings : 🌊 ⊏ ♤♤
Leisure activities : ♈ ✗ 🎦 ⛹ 🔲 (open-air in season)
Facilities : ♿ ⊶ ⓒ ⟰ ⚡ ™ 🔲 ⚐

GPS Longitude : 1.2583
Latitude : 47.48992

CHAILLAC

36310 – Michelin map **323** D8 – pop. 1,136 – alt. 180
▶ Paris 333 – Argenton-sur-Creuse 35 – Le Blanc 34 – Magnac-Laval 34

△ Municipal les Vieux Chênes

℘ 0254256139, chaillac36.fr
Address : allée des Vieux Chênes (to the southwest of the town, by the sports field; near a small lake and 500m from the Étang de Rochegaudon)
Opening times : permanent
2 ha (40 pitches) relatively flat to hilly, grassy
Tariff : (2012 price) ♀ 2€ ⚘ 3.15€ 🔲 2.50€ – (ⱡ) (20A) 3.15€
Rental rates : (2012 price) (permanent) – 3 🏠. Per night from 40 to 63 €
Per week from 203 to 315 €

Green, well-kept site with lots of flowers,

Surroundings : ⊏ ♀
Leisure activities : ⛹ ⤳ fitness trail
Facilities : ⊶ 🗑 ⬛ ⟰ 🔲
Nearby : ✗ ⚓ ⚓ pedalos

GPS Longitude : 1.29539
Latitude : 46.43224

CHARTRES

28000 – Michelin map **311** E5 – pop. 39,122 – alt. 142
▶ Paris 92 – Orléans 84 – Dreux 38 – Rambouillet 45

Les Bords de l'Eure

📞 0237287943, *www.auxbordsdeleure.com*
Address : 9 r. de Launay
Opening times : from beginning March to mid Nov.
4 ha (110 pitches) flat, grassy
Tariff : ★ 4.60€ ⇌ ▣ 4€ – ⚡ (6A) 3.40€
Rental rates : (from mid March to mid Nov.) – 2 caravans – 1 🛏. Per night from 30 to 65 €
Per week from 200 to 350 €
🚽 sani-station 3.50€
Pleasant wooded setting near the river.

Surroundings : 🌳🌳
Leisure activities : 🎬 ⚓ ᵐ pedalos
Facilities : 🚹 ⚡ 🏢 🛁 ☂ 🚰 🔲
Nearby : 🎾 🎣 sports trail

Longitude : 1.4951
Latitude : 48.43265

CHÂTEAUMEILLANT

18370 – Michelin map **323** J7 – pop. 2,082 – alt. 247
▶ Paris 313 – Aubusson 79 – Bourges 66 – La Châtre 19

Municipal l'Étang Merlin

📞 0248613138, *http://ot.chateaumeillant.free.fr*
Address : rte de Vicq (located 1km northwest along the D 70, follow the signs for Beddes and take
D 80 to the left)
Opening times : from beginning May to end Sept.
1.5 ha (30 pitches) flat, grassy
Tariff : (2012 price) ★ 2.70€ ⇌ 3.20€ ▣ 3.20€ – ⚡ (5A) 2.20€
Rental rates : (2012 price) (from beginning May to end Sept.) 🚹 – 2 🛏 – 6 🏠.
Per night from 32 to 48 € – Per week from 215 to 287 €

Chalets pleasantly located beside the lake.

Surroundings : 🏞🌳
Leisure activities : 🎬 ⚓ 🚲 🎣
Facilities : 🚹 ⚡ 🍴 🛁 ☂ 🚰 🔲
Nearby : 🎾 ⛵

Longitude : 2.19034
Latitude : 46.56818

CHÂTEAUROUX

36000 – Michelin map **323** G6 – pop. 46,386 – alt. 155
▶ Paris 265 – Blois 101 – Bourges 65 – Châtellerault 98

Aquadis Loisirs Le Rochat Belle-Isle

📞 0254089629, *www.aquadis-loisirs.com*
Address : 17 av. du Parc de Loisirs (continue north along the av. de Paris and take turning to the left;
beside the Indre river and 100m from a small lake)
Opening times : from end March to end Oct.
4 ha (205 pitches) flat, grassy, fine gravel
Tariff : 19.20€ ★★ ⇌ ▣ ⚡ (10A) – Extra per person 4.20€ – Reservation fee 9.90€
Rental rates : (from end March to end Oct.) – 6 🛏. Per night from 68 €
Per week from 204 to 521 € – Reservation fee 19.50€
🚽 sani-station 11€ – 10 ▣ 19.20€ – 🚐 11€
Free bus service nearby to the town centre.

Surroundings : 🏞🌳🌳
Leisure activities : 🎬 ⚓
Facilities : 🚹 ⚡ ♿ 🛁 ☂ 🚰 🚰 launderette
Nearby : 🍖 🍷 ✖ 🎬 🏊 ⛵ 🎣 bowling, fitness trail

Longitude : 1.69472
Latitude : 46.8236

CHÂTILLON-COLIGNY

45230 – Michelin map **318** O5 – pop. 1,962 – alt. 130
▶ Paris 140 – Auxerre 70 – Gien 26 – Joigny 48

⚠ Municipal de la Lancière

✆ 06.16.09.30.26, *lalanciere@wanadoo.fr* – limited spaces for one-night stay
Address : rte de la Lancière (south of the town, near the Loing river and the Briare canal)
Opening times : from beginning April to end Sept.
1.9 ha (55 pitches) flat, grassy
Tariff : (2012 price) 🧍 2€ 🚗 1.30€ 🔲 1.70€ – 🔌 (6A) 3.10€

Surroundings : 🗒 ⑨⑨
Leisure activities : 🏊 🛝 (small swimming pool)
Facilities : 🚿 🚽 launderette, refrigerated food storage
Nearby : ⚓

GPS Longitude : 2.84394
Latitude : 47.81816

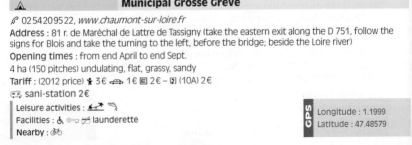

There are several different types of sani-station
('borne' in French) – sanitation points providing
fresh water and disposal points for grey water.
See page 12 for further details.

LA CHÂTRE

36400 – Michelin map **323** H7 – pop. 4,477 – alt. 210
▶ Paris 298 – Bourges 69 – Châteauroux 37 – Guéret 53

⚠ Intercommunal le Val Vert

✆ 02 54 48 32 42, *s.administratif@cc-lachatre-stesevere.fr*
Address : at Vavres (take the southeastern exit along the D 943, follow the signs for Montluçon then continue 2km along the D 83a, follow the signs for Briante to the right)
2 ha (77 pitches) terraced, flat, grassy
On a very green, rural site, near the Indre river.

Surroundings : 🌿 🗒
Facilities : ♿ 🚿 🚽 🔧
Nearby : 🎣 🐎

GPS Longitude : 1.99618
Latitude : 46.56748

CHAUMONT-SUR-LOIRE

41150 – Michelin map **318** E7 – pop. 1,037 – alt. 69
▶ Paris 201 – Amboise 21 – Blois 18 – Contres 24

⚠ Municipal Grosse Grève

✆ 02 54 20 95 22, *www.chaumont-sur-loire.fr*
Address : 81 r. de Maréchal de Lattre de Tassigny (take the eastern exit along the D 751, follow the signs for Blois and take the turning to the left, before the bridge; beside the Loire river)
Opening times : from end April to end Sept.
4 ha (150 pitches) undulating, flat, grassy, sandy
Tariff : (2012 price) 🧍 3€ 🚗 1€ 🔲 2€ – 🔌 (10A) 2€
🚾 sani-station 2€

Leisure activities : 🏊 🎣
Facilities : ♿ 🚿 🚽 launderette
Nearby : 🚲

GPS Longitude : 1.1999
Latitude : 47.48579

CHÉMERY

41700 – Michelin map **318** F7 – pop. 940 – alt. 90
▷ Paris 213 – Blois 32 – Montrichard 29 – Romorantin-Lanthenay 29

△ Municipal le Gué

℘ 02 54 23 97 40, *www.camping-le-gue.com*
Address : rte de Couddes (to the west of the village; beside a stream)
Opening times : permanent
1.2 ha (50 pitches) flat, grassy
Tariff : 16.90€ ✴✴ ⇔ 🗉 🛢 (10A) – Extra per person 2.60€
Rental rates : (permanent) – 2 🛖. Per night from 20 to 199 – Per week from 99 to 590 €
🚽 sani-station 3.50€ – 🛢 9.80€

Surroundings : 🐾 ♀
Leisure activities : 🏊
Facilities : ⚊ 📷 🖼
Nearby : 🎣

GPS Longitude : 1.47388
Latitude : 47.34562

CHEMILLÉ-SUR-INDROIS

37460 – Michelin map **317** P6 – pop. 221 – alt. 97
▷ Paris 244 – Châtillon-sur-Indre 25 – Loches 16 – Montrichard 27

△ Les Coteaux du Lac

℘ 02 47 92 77 83, *www.lescoteauxdulac.com*
Address : at base de loisirs (leisure centre) (to the southwest of the town)
Opening times : from end March to mid Oct.
1 ha (72 pitches) relatively flat, flat, grassy
Tariff : 25€ ✴✴ ⇔ 🗉 🛢 (16A) – Extra per person 5.90€ – Reservation fee 16€
Rental rates : (permanent) – 29 🛖 – 4 tent bungalows. Per night from 55 to 141 €
Per week from 195 to 987 € – Reservation fee 16€
🚽 sani-station – 4 🗉 13.40€ – 🛢 11€
Attractive location near a small lake.

Surroundings : ≤
Facilities : ⚊ 🚰
Nearby : 🍴 ✕ 🚣 🎿 🏊 🚤 🎣 pedalos

GPS Longitude : 1.15889
Latitude : 47.15772

This guide is updated regularly, so buy your new copy every year!

CHEVERNY

41700 – Michelin map **318** F7 – pop. 939 – alt. 110
▷ Paris 194 – Blois 14 – Châteauroux 88 – Orléans 73

△ Les Saules ♟♟

℘ 02 54 79 90 01, *www.camping-cheverny.com*
Address : rte de Contres (3km southeast along the D 102)
Opening times : from beginning April to mid Sept.
8 ha (164 pitches) flat, grassy
Tariff : 31.50€ ✴✴ ⇔ 🗉 🛢 (10A) – Extra per person 4.50€
Rental rates : (from beginning April to mid Sept.) ⛺ – 11 🛖 – 4 tent bungalows.
Per night from 40 to 125 € – Per week from 245 to 630 €
🚽 sani-station – 🛢 14€

Surroundings : ♀♀
Leisure activities : 🍴 ✕ 📺 ⛹ 🚣 🚴 🎯 🏊 🎣 sports trail
Facilities : ♿ ⚊ 📷 🚰 launderette 🏊 🚿

GPS Longitude : 1.45184
Latitude : 47.47871

CHINON

37500 – Michelin map **317** K6 – pop. 7,986 – alt. 40
▶ Paris 285 – Châtellerault 51 – Poitiers 80 – Saumur 29

Intercommunal de l'Île Auger

℘ 02 47 93 08 35, *www.camping-chinon.com*
Address : quai Danton
Opening times : from beginning April to end Oct.
4.5 ha (277 pitches) flat, grassy
Tariff : (2012 price) 13.50€ ✶✶ ⇔ 🗐 ⌷ (12A) – Extra per person 2.50€
Rental rates : (2012 price) (from beginning May to end Sept.) 🗶 – 4 tent bungalows.
Per night from 35 to 40 € – Per week from 210 to 240 €
⊑ sani-station 4.50€
Pleasant location opposite the château and beside the Vienne river.

Surroundings : ⩽ town and Château de Chinon ♀
Leisure activities : 🏊 🎣
Facilities : ⅙ ⊶ (summer) 🛁 🚻 🗐
Nearby : ✗ 🖵 🏊

GPS Longitude : 0.23654
Latitude : 47.16379

Some campsites benefit from proximity to a municipal leisure centre.

CLOYES-SUR-LE-LOIR

28220 – Michelin map **311** D8 – pop. 2,692 – alt. 97
▶ Paris 143 – Blois 54 – Chartres 57 – Châteaudun 13

Parc de Loisirs – Le Val Fleuri

℘ 02 37 98 50 53, *www.val-fleuri.fr* – limited spaces for one-night stay
Address : rte de Montigny (take the northern exit along the N 10, follow the signs for Chartres then turn left onto D 23)
Opening times : from mid March to mid Nov.
5 ha (196 pitches) flat, grassy
Tariff : (2012 price) 26.40€ ✶✶ ⇔ 🗐 ⌷ (6A) – Extra per person 6.20€ – Reservation fee 16€
Rental rates : (2012 price) (from mid March to mid Nov.) – 10 ⌷. Per week from 295 to 707 €
Reservation fee 22€
Pleasant location beside the Loir river.

Surroundings : ⊏ ♀
Leisure activities : 🍽 ✗ 🖵 🏊 🚲 ⅿ 🏊 ◿ 🎣 pedalos 🏄
Facilities : ⅙ ⊶ 🛁 🚽 🚻 launderette 🖵 🛒
Nearby : ✗ ♨

GPS Longitude : 1.2333
Latitude : 48.0024

COULLONS

45720 – Michelin map **318** L6 – pop. 2,424 – alt. 166
▶ Paris 165 – Aubigny-sur-Nère 18 – Gien 16 – Orléans 60

Municipal Plancherotte

℘ 02 38 29 20 42, *www.coullons.fr*
Address : rte de la Brosse (located 1km west along the D 51, follow the signs for Cerdon and take turning to the left, 50m from a small lake (direct access)
1.9 ha (80 pitches) flat, grassy
Pitches attractively marked out.

Surroundings : 🏞 ⊏ ♀
Facilities : ⅙ ⊶ 🛁 🚽 🚻
Nearby : 🏊 ✗ 🎣 🚵 mountain biking

GPS Longitude : 2.48458
Latitude : 47.62311

COURVILLE-SUR-EURE

28190 – Michelin map **311** D5 – pop. 2,776 – alt. 170
▶ Paris 111 – Bonneval 47 – Chartres 20 – Dreux 37

Municipal les Bords de l'Eure

📞 02 37 23 76 38, www.courville-sur-eure.fr
Address : r. Thiers (take the southern exit along the D 114)
1.5 ha (56 pitches) flat, grassy
🚰 sani-station – 10 ▣
Wooded setting on the banks of the river.

Surroundings : 🗔 ♀
Leisure activities : 🎣
Facilities : ♿ ☍ 🖼
Nearby : 🚴 ⛏

GPS Longitude : 1.2414
Latitude : 48.4462

DESCARTES

37160 – Michelin map **317** N7 – pop. 3,817 – alt. 50
▶ Paris 292 – Châteauroux 94 – Châtellerault 24 – Chinon 51

Municipal la Grosse Motte

📞 02 47 59 85 90, www.ville-descartes.fr
Address : allée Léo Lagrange (take the southern exit along the D 750, follow the signs for Le Blanc and take road to the right; beside the Creuse river)
Opening times : from beginning May to end Sept.
1 ha (50 pitches) flat, undulating, grassy
Tariff : (2012 price) 9.20€ ✦✦ ⇔ ▣ ⚡ (15A) – Extra per person 2.40€
Rental rates : (2012 price) (permanent) ⌘ – 8 🏠. Per week from 250 to 370 €
🚰 7 ▣ 9.20€
Shady park next to a leisure centre and the municipal gardens.

Surroundings : 🌳 🗔 ♀♀
Leisure activities : 🎣
Facilities : ☍ 🛁 ⚑
Nearby : 🚴 ✂ ⛏ 🛶 ⛷

GPS Longitude : 0.69715
Latitude : 46.96961

ÉGUZON

36270 – Michelin map **323** F8 – pop. 1,362 – alt. 243 – Leisure centre
▶ Paris 319 – Argenton-sur-Creuse 20 – La Châtre 47 – Guéret 50

Municipal du Lac Les Nugiras

📞 02 54 47 45 22, www.campingmunicipal-eguzon.com
Address : rte de Messant (3km southeast along the D 36, follow the signs for the Lac de Chambon then continue 500m along the turning to the right; 450m from the lake)
Opening times : permanent
4 ha (180 pitches) terraced, relatively flat, flat, grassy, stony
Tariff : (2012 price) 12.20€ ✦✦ ⇔ ▣ ⚡ (10A) – Extra per person 3.20€
Rental rates : (2012 price) (permanent) – 7 🏠 – 5 tent bungalows. Per night from 32 to 123 €
Per week from 140 to 443 €
🚰 sani-station 4.87€ – 15 ▣ 9.13€

Surroundings : ≤ ♀
Leisure activities : ♟ 🛶
Facilities : ♿ ☍ 🗑 🛁 ⚑ ⚑ 🖼 🔧
Nearby : 🚴 🏖 (beach) ⛷ 🎣 ♦ water skiing, climbing

GPS Longitude : 1.604
Latitude : 46.433

FONTAINE-SIMON

28240 – Michelin map **311** C4 – pop. 870 – alt. 200
▶ Paris 117 – Chartres 40 – Dreux 40 – Évreux 66

⚠ Du Perche

☎ 02 37 81 88 11, *www.campingduperche.com*
Address : r. de la Ferrière (1.2km north following signs for Senonches and take turning to the left)
5 ha (115 pitches) flat, grassy
Rentals : 🛖 – 2 🚐 – 2 🏠.
🚾 sani-station – 7 ▣
Beside the Eure river and a small lake.

Leisure activities : 🏊 🎣 **Facilities** : 🚻 ⚡ 🧺 🚿 🔥 **Nearby** : 🍴 🏊 ♨ 🎿	**GPS** Longitude : 1.0194 Latitude : 48.5132

In order for the guide to remain wholly objective, the selection is made on an entirely independent basis. There is no charge for being selected for the guide.

GARGILESSE-DAMPIERRE

36190 – Michelin map **323** F7 – pop. 326 – alt. 220
▶ Paris 310 – Châteauroux 45 – Guéret 59 – Poitiers 113

⚠ La Chaumerette

☎ 02 54 47 84 22, *www.gargilesse.fr*
Address : at Le Moulin (1.4km southwest along the D 39, follow the signs for Argenton-sur-Creuse and take the road to the left leading to the Barrage de La Roche au Moine (dam)
2.6 ha (72 pitches) flat, grassy, stony
Rentals : 🛖 – 8 🏠.
Picturesque setting, part of the site is on an island in the Creuse river.

Surroundings : 🌳 🎣 **Leisure activities** : 🍸 🍴 🎣 **Facilities** : 🚻 ⚡	**GPS** Longitude : 1.58346 Latitude : 46.5077

GIEN

45500 – Michelin map **318** M5 – pop. 15,161 – alt. 162
▶ Paris 149 – Auxerre 85 – Bourges 77 – Cosne-sur-Loire 46

⚠ Les Bois du Bardelet ♨

☎ 02 38 67 47 39, *www.bardelet.com*
Address : at Le Petit Bardelet, rte de Bourges (5km southwest along the D 940 et 2km along the turning to the left – recommended route for vehicles coming from Gien, take the D 53, follow the signs for Poilly-lez-Gien and take first turning to the right)
Opening times : from mid April to end Sept.
15 ha/8 ha for camping (260 pitches) flat, grassy, lake
Tariff : 27.40€ 🚶🚶 🚐 ▣ ⚡ (10A) – Extra per person 7€ – Reservation fee 9€
Rental rates : (from mid April to end Sept.) 🅿 – 33 🚐 – 45 🏠. Per night from 56 to 152 €
Per week from 392 to 1,064 € – Reservation fee 9€
🚾 sani-station – 25 ▣ 25.60€ – 🚐 ⚡12€

Surroundings : 🌳 🎣 **Leisure activities** : 🍸 🍴 🎲 🏓 💆 ♨ jacuzzi 🏊 🚲 🎿 🏸 🏊 🛝 🎣 🐎 **Facilities** : 🚻 ⚡ 📶 🚿 🛁 – 4 individual sanitary facilities (🚿 wc) 🧺 🚿 launderette 🧺 🛒	**GPS** Longitude : 2.61619 Latitude : 47.64116

LA GUERCHE-SUR-L'AUBOIS

18150 – Michelin map **323** N5 – pop. 3,395 – alt. 184

▶ Paris 242 – Bourges 48 – La Charité-sur-Loire 31 – Nevers 22

⚠ **Municipal le Robinson**

℘ 02 48 74 18 86, *www.laguerche-aubois.fr*

Address : 2 r. de Couvache (1.4km southeast along the D 200, follow the signs for Apremont then take a right turn, 600m along the D 218 and take road to the left)

Opening times : from beginning May to end Sept.

1.5 ha (33 pitches) relatively flat, flat, grassy

Tariff : ✦ 2.60€ ⬅ 2.10€ 回 2.60€ – ⑭ (6A) 3.60€

Rental rates : (from beginning May to end Sept.) – 4 🛖 – 2 🏠. Per night from 48 to 60 €
Per week from 310 to 405 €

Pleasant location beside a small lake.

Surroundings : ⌂ ⑨
Leisure activities : 🎦 ♏ ⚲
Facilities : ⚐ ⚑ 🔲
Nearby : ⛾ 🛶 ⚓ pedalos

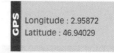

GPS Longitude : 2.95872
Latitude : 46.94029

L'ÎLE-BOUCHARD

37220 – Michelin map **317** L6 – pop. 1,754 – alt. 41

▶ Paris 284 – Châteauroux 118 – Châtellerault 49 – Chinon 16

⚠ **Les Bords de Vienne**

℘ 02 47 95 23 59, *http://www.campingbordsdevienne.com*

Address : 4 allée du camping (near the St-Gilles quartier, upstream of the bridge over the Vienne, near the river)

Opening times : from beginning March to end Oct.

1 ha (90 pitches) flat, grassy

Tariff : 21€ ✦✦ ⬅ 回 ⑭ (16A) – Extra per person 5€

Rental rates : (permanent) – 4 🛖 – 1 gîte. Per night from 60 to 74 €
Per week from 223 to 510 € – Reservation fee 20€

🚐 sani-station 2€

Surroundings : ⑨⑨
Leisure activities : 🛶 ⚲
Facilities : ⚐ ⚷ ⚑ 🔲
Nearby : 🐎 ✗ 🏊

GPS Longitude : 0.42833
Latitude : 47.12139

ISDES

45620 – Michelin map **318** K5 – pop. 612 – alt. 152

▶ Paris 174 – Bourges 75 – Gien 35 – Orléans 40

⚠ **Municipal les Prés Bas**

℘ 06 78 43 46 28, *www.isdes.fr*

Address : take the northeastern exit along the D 59, near a lake

Opening times : from beginning April to end Oct.

0.5 ha (20 pitches) flat, grassy

Tariff : (2012 price) ✦ 2.50€ ⬅ 1.20€ 回 4.50€ ⑭ (15A)

Surroundings : ⌂
Leisure activities : ⚲
Facilities : ⚐ 🗑 ⚱ ⚒
Nearby : 🛶

GPS Longitude : 2.2565
Latitude : 47.6744

JARS

18260 – Michelin map **323** M2 – pop. 483 – alt. 285
▶ Paris 188 – Aubigny-sur-Nère 24 – Bourges 47 – Cosne-sur-Loire 21

La Balance

✆ 02 48 58 74 50
Address : Le Noyer, at Les Vèves (800m southwest along the D 74 and take the road to the right)
0.9 ha (25 pitches) relatively flat, flat, grassy
Near a lake.

Surroundings : ♀
Facilities : ⌂
Nearby : ♈ ✗ ♪ ⇒ ⤳

Longitude : 2.68009
Latitude : 47.38894

The information in the guide may have changed since going to press.

LORRIS

45260 – Michelin map **318** M4 – pop. 2,941 – alt. 126
▶ Paris 132 – Gien 27 – Montargis 23 – Orléans 55

L'Étang des Bois

✆ 02 38 92 32 00, *www.canal-orleans.fr*
Address : 6km west along the D 88, follow the signs for Châteauneuf-sur-Loire, near the lake at Les Bois
Opening times : from beginning April to end Sept.
3 ha (150 pitches) flat, fine gravel
Tariff : (2012 price) ♀ 3.40€ ⇔ 🗐 5.70€ – ⑵ (10A) 4.50€
Rental rates : (2012 price) (from beginning April to end Sept.) – 2 🚐.
Per night from 50 to 65 € – Per week from 300 to 400 €
Wooded setting in a pleasant location.

Surroundings : ⌂ ♀♀
Leisure activities : 🎣 ♪
Facilities : ⚲ ⌿ ⌂ ⚲ 🖥
Nearby : ✗ 🏊 ⇒ (beach) ⤳ 🐎

Longitude : 2.44454
Latitude : 47.87393

LUÇAY-LE-MÂLE

36360 – Michelin map **323** E4 – pop. 1,496 – alt. 160
▶ Paris 240 – Le Blanc 73 – Blois 60 – Châteauroux 43

Municipal la Foulquetière

✆ 02 54 40 43 31, *www.lucaylemale.fr*
Address : at La Foulquetière (3.8km southwest along the D 960, follow the signs for Loches, D 13, follow the signs for Ecueillé to the left and take the road to the right)
Opening times : from beginning April to mid Oct.
1.5 ha (30 pitches) flat and relatively flat, grassy
Tariff : 8€ ♀♀ ⇔ 🗐 ⑵ (6A) – Extra per person 2€
Rental rates : (permanent) – 3 🏠 – 2 gîtes. Per night 86€ – Per week 322€
🚐 sani-station 3€
Site is 80m from a small lake that is very popular with anglers.

Surroundings : ⌂ ♀
Leisure activities : ⇙
Facilities : ⚲ ⌿ ⌂ ⦀ ⌂ 🖥
Nearby : ♈ ✗ ⇒ ✗ ♪ ⇒ (beach) ⤳ pedalos

Longitude : 1.40417
Latitude : 47.1109

LUNERY

18400 – Michelin map **323** J5 – pop. 1,449 – alt. 150
▶ Paris 256 – Bourges 23 – Châteauroux 51 – Issoudun 28

⚠   Intercommunal de Lunery

℘ 02 48 68 07 38, www.cc-fercher.fr – ℞
Address : 6 r. de l'Abreuvoir (in the town, near the church)
Opening times : from mid April to mid Sept.
0.5 ha (37 pitches) flat, grassy
Tariff : (2012 price) ⚹ 4€ 🚐 ▣ 6€ – 🔌 (10A) 2€

Based near the ruins of an old windmill by the Cher river.

Surroundings : ⌑ ♀
Leisure activities : 🎦 ⚓
Facilities : ♿ ⚡ 🚿
Nearby : ♟ ✗ ※

Longitude : 2.27038
Latitude : 46.93658

MARCILLY-SUR-VIENNE

37800 – Michelin map **317** M6 – pop. 559 – alt. 60
▶ Paris 280 – Azay-le-Rideau 32 – Chinon 30 – Châtellerault 29

⚠   Intercommunal la Croix de la Motte

℘ 02 47 65 20 38, www.cc-saintemauredetouraine.fr
Address : 1.2km north along the D 18, follow the signs for L'Ile-Bouchard and take turning to the right
1.5 ha (61 pitches) flat, grassy
Rentals : ⚒ – 2 � – 1 tent.
🚽 sani-station
Pleasant, shaded surroundings near the Vienne river.

Surroundings : 🏞 ⌑ ♀
Leisure activities : ⚓ ⚒
Facilities : ♿ ⚡ ⛺ 🔲

Longitude : 0.54337
Latitude : 47.05075

The classification (1 to 5 tents, black or red) that we award to selected sites in this guide is our own system. It should not be confused with the classification (1 to 5 stars) of official organisations.

MENNETOU-SUR-CHER

41320 – Michelin map **318** I8 – pop. 878 – alt. 100
▶ Paris 209 – Bourges 56 – Romorantin-Lanthenay 18 – Selles-sur-Cher 27

⚠   Municipal Val Rose

℘ 02 54 98 11 02, mairie.mennetou@wanadoo.fr
Address : r. de Val Rose (south of the town, to the right after the bridge over the canal, 100m from the Cher river)
Opening times : from mid May to mid Sept.
0.8 ha (50 pitches) flat, grassy
Tariff : (2012 price) ⚹ 2€ 🚐 ▣ 2.50€ – 🔌 (4A) 2€
🚽 sani-station 2€ – 10 ▣

Surroundings : ⌑ ♀
Leisure activities : ⚓
Facilities : ♿ ⚡ 🚿
Nearby : ※ ⛷ ⚒ ♦

Longitude : 1.86173
Latitude : 47.26937

MESLAND

41150 – Michelin map **318** D6 – pop. 547 – alt. 79
▶ Paris 205 – Amboise 19 – Blois 23 – Château-Renault 20

Yelloh! Village Le Parc du Val de Loire ⚑⚐

℘ 02 54 70 27 18, *www.parcduvaldeloire.com*
Address : 155 rte de Fleuray (located 1.5km west)
Opening times : from beginning April to end Sept.
15 ha (300 pitches) relatively flat, flat, grassy
Tariff : 35€ ♛♛ ⏢ ▣ (½) (10A) – Extra per person 8€
Rental rates : (from beginning April to end Sept.) ◰ – 145 – 15 ⌂.
Per night from 39 to 116 € – Per week from 273 to 812 €
⛽ 150 ▣ 18€
Wooded setting opposite a vineyard.

Surroundings : ⬚ ⊟ ♨♨
Leisure activities : ♟ ✗ ⬚ ⁂ ⬳ ⚲ ✂ ⌐ ▣ ⍑ ◿
Facilities : ₺ ⊶ ⬚⬧ ⌂ ⥏ ⍦ ▣ ⊒ ⦚

GPS Longitude : 1.10477
Latitude : 47.51001

MONTARGIS

45200 – Michelin map **318** N4 – pop. 15,020 – alt. 95
▶ Paris 109 – Auxerre 252 – Nemours 36 – Nevers 126

Municipal de la Forêt

℘ 02 38 98 00 20, *campings.agglo.montargoise@wanadoo.fr*
Address : 38 av. Louis-Maurice Chautemps (take the northern exit along the D 943 and continue 1km along the D 815, follow the signs for Paucourt)
Opening times : from beginning Feb. to end Nov.
5.5 ha (100 pitches) stony, sandy, flat, grassy
Tariff : (2012 price) ♛ 3€ ⏢ 2.30€ ▣ 3€ – (½) (10A) 7€
⛽ sani-station – 20 ▣ 5.70€ – ⛟ 11€

Surroundings : ♨♨
Leisure activities : ⬚ ⁂
Facilities : ₺ ⊶ ▥ ⥏ ⍦ ⍦
Nearby : ✂ ⍑

GPS Longitude : 2.75102
Latitude : 48.00827

A 'quartier' is a district or area of a town or village.

MONTBAZON

37250 – Michelin map **317** N5 – pop. 3,904 – alt. 59
▶ Paris 247 – Châtellerault 59 – Chinon 41 – Loches 33

La Grange Rouge

℘ 02 47 26 06 43, *www.camping-montbazon.com*
Address : rte de Tours, RD 910 (after the bridge over the Indre; behind the tourist office and near the stadium)
2 ha (108 pitches) flat, grassy
Rentals : 15 .
Pleasant location beside a river and not far from the town centre.

Surroundings : ♨♨
Leisure activities : ✗ ⬚ ⍑
Facilities : ₺ ⊶ ⬧ ⍦ ▣
Nearby : ✂ ⬚ ⌐ sports trail

GPS Longitude : 0.7159
Latitude : 47.29049

MONTLOUIS-SUR-LOIRE

37270 – Michelin map **317** N4 – pop. 10,448 – alt. 60
▶ Paris 235 – Amboise 14 – Blois 49 – Château-Renault 32

Aquadis Loisirs Les Peupliers

☎ 02 47 50 81 90, www.aquadis-loisirs.com
Address : located 1.5km west along the D 751, follow the signs for Tours, 100m from the Loire river
Opening times : from end April to end Oct.
6 ha (252 pitches) flat, grassy
Tariff : 16.80€ ✚✚ 🚐 ▣ ⑭ (10A) – Extra per person 3.75€ – Reservation fee 9.90€
Rental rates : (from end April to end Oct.) – 11 🚖. Per night from 84 to 94 €
Per week from 204 to 518 € – Reservation fee 19.50€
🛒 sani-station 11€ – 18 ▣ 16.80€ – 🔋 11€
Pleasant wooded site.

Surroundings : 🗔 🍃
Leisure activities : ♟ 🖼 ⚔
Facilities : ♿ ⛟ 🆑🍴 🙌 🔲 ⚗
Nearby : ✂ ⛴ 🎣

GPS Longitude : 0.81144
Latitude : 47.39437

MONTOIRE-SUR-LE-LOIR

41800 – Michelin map **318** C5 – pop. 4,081 – alt. 65
▶ Paris 186 – Blois 52 – Château-Renault 21 – La Flèche 81

Municipal les Reclusages

☎ 02 54 85 02 53, www.mairie-montoire.fr
Address : at Les Reclusages (southwestern exit, follow the signs for Tours and follow the signs for Lavardin to the left after the bridge)
Opening times : from beginning May to end Sept.
2 ha (133 pitches) flat, grassy
Tariff : (2012 price) ✚ 3.60€ 🚐 ▣ 1.95€ – ⑭ (10A) 3.75€
Rental rates : (2012 price) (from beginning May to end Sept.) – 4 🚖.
Per week from 205 to 330 €
Beside the Loir river.

Surroundings : 🍃
Leisure activities : ♟ 🎣
Facilities : ♿ ⛟ 🙌 🔲
Nearby : ⚔ ₘ 🖼 ⛴

GPS Longitude : 0.86289
Latitude : 47.74788

MORÉE

41160 – Michelin map **318** E4 – pop. 1,117 – alt. 96
▶ Paris 154 – Blois 42 – Châteaudun 24 – Orléans 58

Municipal de la Varenne

☎ 02 54 89 15 15, mairie-de-moree@wanadoo.fr
Address : to the west of the town; beside a small lake, recommended route via the D 19, follow the signs for St-Hilaire-la-Gravelle and take road to the left
0.8 ha (43 pitches) flat, grassy
Rentals : 2 'gypsy' caravans – 1 🚖.
🛒 sani-station – 8 ▣

Surroundings : 🏖
Leisure activities : 🏖 (beach) 🎣
Facilities : ♿ ⛟ 🍴 🙌
Nearby : ⚔

GPS Longitude : 1.23424
Latitude : 47.9031

MUIDES-SUR-LOIRE

41500 – Michelin map **318** G5 – pop. 1,350 – alt. 82
▶ Paris 169 – Beaugency 17 – Blois 20 – Chambord 9

Château des Marais ▲▲

℘ 02 54 87 05 42, *www.chateau-des-marais.com*

Address : 27 r. de Chambord (to the southeast along the D 103, follow the signs for Crouy-sur-Cosson – for caravans, access via the D 112 and take D 103 to the right)

Opening times : from beginning May to mid Sept.

8 ha (299 pitches) flat, grassy

Tariff : 40€ ★ ★ ⇔ 🗉 ⒃ (10A) – Extra per person 8€ – Reservation fee 15€

Rental rates : (from mid April to mid Sept.) 🚿 – 21 🚐 – 20 🏠 – 1 cabin in the trees.
Per night from 66 to 177 € – Per week from 462 to 1,239 € – Reservation fee 15€

🚾 sani-station 6€ – 4 🗉 26€ – 🚐 26€

In the pleasantly wooded grounds of a 17th-century château.

Surroundings : 🐾 🏕 ♧♧
Leisure activities : 🍴 ✕ 🎦 ⑨ evening 🏃 ⛵ hammam 🚣 🚲 ⅏ 🏇
🎮 🏊 ⛰ 🎣
Facilities : 🚻 🔗 🗑 ♨ 🧴 🚰 ⛲ launderette 🛒 🚿

GPS Longitude : 1.52897
Latitude : 47.66585

Municipal Bellevue

℘ 02 54 87 01 56, *mairie.muides@wanadoo.fr* – ⛔

Address : av. de la Loire (north of the town along the D 112, follow the signs for Mer and take the turning to the left before the bridge; near the Loire river)

2.5 ha (100 pitches) flat, grassy, sandy

🚾 sani-station

Facilities : 🚻 🔗 ⛲ 🖼
Nearby : 🚣 ⅏

GPS Longitude : 1.52607
Latitude : 47.67178

*Routes nationales are main roads and their identifying numbers
begin with N or RN. Routes départementales are generally quieter
roads and begin with D or DN.*

NEUNG-SUR-BEUVRON

41210 – Michelin map **318** H6 – pop. 1,223 – alt. 102
▶ Paris 183 – Beaugency 33 – Blois 39 – Lamotte-Beuvron 20

Municipal de la Varenne

℘ 02 54 83 68 52, *www.neung-sur-beuvron.fr*

Address : 34 r. de Veillas (located 1km to the northeast, access via the turning to the left of the church; near the Beuvron river)

Opening times : from beginning April to mid Oct.

4 ha (73 pitches) relatively flat, flat, grassy, sandy

Tariff : (2012 price) 11.80€ ★ ★ ⇔ 🗉 ⒃ (10A) – Extra per person 2.70€

Rental rates : (2012 price) (from mid Oct. to end Oct.) – 4 🚐. Per night from 57 €
Per week from 237 to 412 € – Reservation fee 70€

🚾 sani-station – 🚐 ⒃ 11.80€

Pleasant wooded site.

Surroundings : 🐾 🏕 ♧♧
Leisure activities : 🎦 ⅏ 🎣
Facilities : 🚻 🔗 ⛲ 🖼

GPS Longitude : 1.81507
Latitude : 47.53849

NEUVY-ST-SÉPULCHRE

36230 – Michelin map **323** G7 – pop. 1,690 – alt. 186
▶ Paris 295 – Argenton-sur-Creuse 24 – Châteauroux 29 – La Châtre 16

Municipal les Frênes

℘ 02 54 30 82 51, *www.campingdeneuvy.new.fr* – **R**
Address : rte de l'Augère (take the western exit along the D 927, follow the signs for Argenton-sur-Creuse then continue 600m along the turning to the left and take the road to the right, 100m from a lake and the Bouzanne river)
Opening times : from mid June to mid Sept.
1 ha (35 pitches) flat, grassy
Tariff : (2012 price) 11.50€ ★ ★ ⟲ 回 [½] (9A) – Extra per person 2€
Rental rates : (2012 price) (permanent) ⌗ – 2 🏠. Per night from 90 €
Per week from 240 to 270 €

Surroundings : ⧠ ▱ ♀
Leisure activities : ⚤ ⚓
Facilities : ⊶ ⚲ ⚐ ⚑ launderette
Nearby : ▼ ✕ ⚲ ⚲

GPS Longitude : 1.7828
Latitude : 46.5903

Gîtes range from small maisonettes to old farmhouses with several bedrooms.

NOGENT-LE-ROTROU

28400 – Michelin map **311** A6 – pop. 11,121 – alt. 116
▶ Paris 146 – Alençon 65 – Chartres 54 – Châteaudun 55

Municipal des Viennes

℘ 02 37 52 80 51, *www.ville-nogent-le-rotrou.fr*
Address : r. des Viennes (north of the town along the av. des Prés (D 103)
0.5 ha (30 pitches) flat, grassy
Beside the Huisne river.

Surroundings : ▱ ♀
Leisure activities : ⚤
Facilities : ⊶ ⚲ ⚐
Nearby : ⇝ ✕ ▦ ⚲

GPS Longitude : 0.8159
Latitude : 48.3249

NOUAN-LE-FUZELIER

41600 – Michelin map **318** J6 – pop. 2,439 – alt. 113
▶ Paris 177 – Blois 59 – Cosne-sur-Loire 74 – Gien 56

La Grande Sologne

℘ 02 54 88 70 22, *www.campingrandesologne.com*
Address : r. des Peupliers (take the southern exit along the D 2020, then the road to the left opposite the station)
Opening times : from beginning April to mid Oct.
10 ha/4 ha for camping (180 pitches) flat, grassy
Tariff : (2012 price) ★ 5.70€ ⟲ 回 8.10€ – [½] (10A) 3€
Rental rates : (2012 price) (from beginning April to mid Oct.) – 7 ⌂ – 4 tents.
Per night from 30 to 75 € – Per week from 175 to 660 €
⟲ sani-station
In a wooded setting beside a lake.

Surroundings : ♀♀
Leisure activities : ✕ ⌂ ⚤ ⚲ ⚲ ⚲
Facilities : ⚅ ⊶ ⚐ ⚑ 回 ⚖
Nearby : ▼ ✕ ⚓

GPS Longitude : 2.03631
Latitude : 47.53337

OLIVET

45160 – Michelin map **318** I4 – pop. 19,806 – alt. 100
▶ Paris 137 – Orléans 4 – Blois 70 – Chartres 78

Municipal

℘ 0238635394, *www.camping-olivet.org*
Address : r. du Pont Bouchet (situated 2km southeast along the D 14, follow the signs for St-Cyr-en-Val)
Opening times : from beginning April to mid Oct.
1 ha (46 pitches) flat, grassy
Tariff : (2012 price) 20.80€ ★★ ⇐ 🗐 🕸 (16A) – Extra per person 4.30€
🚰 sani-station 5.20€ – 6 🗐 17.50€
Pleasant location where the Loiret and Dhuy rivers meet.

Surroundings : 🗔 ΩΩ
Leisure activities : 🎣
Facilities : ᴕ ⌕ 🎽 ᴂ ⩔ 🕈 🖼
Nearby : 🏄 🛶

GPS Longitude : 1.92543
Latitude : 47.85601

ONZAIN

41150 – Michelin map **318** E6 – pop. 3,449 – alt. 69
▶ Paris 201 – Amboise 21 – Blois 19 – Château-Renault 24

Siblu Le Domaine de Dugny
(rental of mobile homes only)

℘ 0254207066, *www.domaine-de-dugny.fr*
Opening times : from beginning April to end Sept.
12 ha relatively flat, grassy, stony
Rental rates : (2012 price) 🏠 – 320 🚐. Per night from 40 to 180 €
Per week from 280 to 1,260 € – Reservation fee 15€
Numerous owner-occupied mobile homes.

Surroundings : 🏞 🗔 ΩΩ
Leisure activities : 🍴 ✗ 🎦 🗐 ⫛ jacuzzi ⭆ 🚲 ✗ 🎣 🖾 🛶 ⛵ 🎣
pedalos, multi-sports ground, entertainment room
Facilities : ᴕ ⌕ 🎽 ᴂ ⩔ 🕈 launderette 🍽 🚿
Nearby : 🐎

GPS Longitude : 1.18735
Latitude : 47.52602

PIERREFITTE-SUR-SAULDRE

41300 – Michelin map **318** J6 – pop. 848 – alt. 125
▶ Paris 185 – Aubigny-sur-Nère 23 – Blois 73 – Bourges 55

Les Alicourts ♠♠

℘ 0254886334, *www.lesalicourts.com*
Address : at the Domaine des Alicourts (6km northeast along the D 126 and take the D 126b; beside a small lake)
Opening times : from end April to beginning Sept.
21 ha/10 ha for camping (420 pitches) terraced, flat, grassy, sandy
Tariff : (2012 price) 56€ ★★ ⇐ 🗐 🕸 (6A) – Extra per person 12€
Rental rates : (from end April to beginning Sept.) ᴕ (3 chalets) 🏠 – 170 🚐 – 112 🏠 –
8 cabins in the trees. Per night from 60 to 280 € – Per week from 420 to 1,960 €
🚰 sani-station
Indoor swimming pool open to all, mornings only.

Surroundings : 🏞 🗔 ΩΩ
Leisure activities : 🍴 ✗ 🎦 🗐 ⫛ 🏋 ♨ hammam jacuzzi ⭆ 🚲 ✗
🎣 🛶 ≊ (beach) 🛶 🎣 pedalos, mountain biking 🧖 spa therapy centre,
entertainment room, skate park
Facilities : ᴕ ⌕ 🏖 ᴂ ⩔ 🕈 launderette 🍽 🚿

GPS Longitude : 2.191
Latitude : 47.54482

PREUILLY-SUR-CLAISE

37290 – Michelin map **317** O7 – pop. 1,075 – alt. 80
▶ Paris 299 – Le Blanc 31 – Châteauroux 64 – Châtellerault 35

⚠ Municipal

📞 02 47 94 50 04, www.preuillysurclaise.fr ✂

Address : to the southwest of the town; near the swimming pool, the Claise river and a small lake
Opening times : from beginning June to end Sept.
0.7 ha (37 pitches) flat, grassy
Tariff : 👤 2.50€ ⛐ 📧 3€ – 🔌 (6A) 4€
Rental rates : (from mid April to end Oct.) ✂ – 2 🚐. Per night from 50 to 60 €
Per week from 200 to 250 €
🚮 sani-station
Green setting in the middle of a leisure centre.

Surroundings : 🏞 ♀ Leisure activities : 🎣 Facilities : ⊙ 🛁 ♈ 🖻 Nearby : 🏇 ✂ 🛖 🏊 sports trail	**GPS** Longitude : 0.92618 Latitude : 46.85305

RILLÉ

37340 – Michelin map **317** K4 – pop. 300 – alt. 82
▶ Paris 282 – Orléans 158 – Tours 47 – Nantes 160

⚠ Huttopia Rillé

📞 02 47 24 62 97, www.huttopia.com

Address : at the Lac de Rillé (situated 2km to the east along the D49)
Opening times : from mid April to beginning Nov.
5 ha (120 pitches) flat, grassy
Tariff : (2012 price) 33.20€ 👤👤 ⛐ 📧 🔌 (10A) – Extra per person 7.60€ – Reservation fee 20€
Rental rates : (2012 price) (from mid April to beginning Nov.) – 10 'gypsy' caravans – 22 🚐 –
10 tents. Per night from 61 to 156 € – Per week from 320 to 1,092 € – Reservation fee 20€

Surroundings : ♀♀ Leisure activities : ✗ Facilities : 🔥 ⊙ 🅿 ♨	**GPS** Longitude : 0.33278 Latitude : 47.44584

ROMORANTIN-LANTHENAY

41200 – Michelin map **318** H7 – pop. 17,092 – alt. 93
▶ Paris 202 – Blois 42 – Bourges 74 – Châteauroux 72

⚠ Tournefeuille

📞 02 54 95 37 08, www.camping-romorantin.com

Address : 32 r. des Lices (take the eastern exit, follow the signs for Salbris and then Long-Eaton;
beside the Sauldre river)
Opening times : from beginning April to end Sept.
1.5 ha (103 pitches) flat, grassy
Tariff : 👤 7.75€ ⛐ – 🔌 (10A) 4.20€ – Reservation fee 5€
Rental rates : (permanent) – 6 🚐. Per night from 52 to 69 € – Per week from 340 to 495 €
Reservation fee 5€
🚮 sani-station – 3 📧 10.80€ – 🚐 15.50€

Surroundings : 🏞 ♀ Leisure activities : ✗ 🛶 🏇 🚲 Facilities : 🔥 ⊙ 🏛 🛁 ♿ ♈ 🖻 Nearby : 🛒 ✂ 🎣 🏊	**GPS** Longitude : 1.75586 Latitude : 47.35503

ROSNAY

36300 – Michelin map **323** D6 – pop. 615 – alt. 112
▶ Paris 307 – Argenton-sur-Creuse 31 – Le Blanc 16 – Châteauroux 44

△ Municipal

🕿 02 54 37 80 17, *rosnay-mairie@wanadoo.fr*
Address : rte de St-Michel-en-Brenne (500m north along the D 44)
Opening times : from mid Feb. to mid Nov.
2 ha (36 pitches) flat, grassy
Tariff : (2012 price) 🕴 2€ 🚗 2€ 🅴 2.50€ – (✷) (6A) 2€
🚃 sani-station – 15 🅴 2.50€
Pleasant complex adjacent to a lake.

Surroundings : 🏞 ♨
Leisure activities : ✂ ⚓
Facilities : 🚿 ⛺ ♨ 🔲

GPS Longitude : 1.21172
Latitude : 46.70645

Do not confuse:
△ *to* 🛆🛆🛆 *: MICHELIN classification*
with
★ *to* ★★★★★ *: official classification*

ST-AMAND-MONTROND

18200 – Michelin map **323** L6 – pop. 10,952 – alt. 160
▶ Paris 282 – Bourges 52 – Châteauroux 65 – Montluçon 56

△ Municipal de la Roche

🕿 02 48 96 09 36, *www.entreprisefrery.com*
Address : ch. de La Roche (take the southwestern exit along the D 2144, follow the signs for Montluçon, take the Chemin de la Roche to the right before the canal; near the Cher river)
Opening times : from beginning April to end Sept.
4 ha (120 pitches) flat and relatively flat, grassy
Tariff : 🕴 3.30€ 🚗 🅴 4.50€ – (✷) (6A) 3.10€
Rental rates : (from beginning April to end Sept.) – 3 tent bungalows. Per night from 58 €
Per week from 190 to 310 €

Surroundings : 🏞 ♨
Leisure activities : 🛖 ⚓ ✂
Facilities : ♿ ⚡ 🔲 📷 🔲
Nearby : 🏊

GPS Longitude : 2.49108
Latitude : 46.71816

ST-AVERTIN

37550 – Michelin map **317** N4 – pop. 13,946 – alt. 49
▶ Paris 245 – Orléans 121 – Tours 7 – Blois 70

△ Les Rives du Cher

🕿 02 47 27 27 60, *www.camping-lesrivesducher.com*
Address : 61 r. de Rochepinard (to the north along the left bank of the Cher river)
2 ha (90 pitches) flat, grassy
Rentals : 4 🛖.
🚃 sani-station – 20 🅴
Near a small lake.

Surroundings : ▭ ♨
Facilities : ♿ ⚡ 🔲 ♨ launderette
Nearby : ⚓ ✂ 🔲 ⚓ ♨

GPS Longitude : 0.72296
Latitude : 47.37064

ST-PÈRE-SUR-LOIRE

45600 – Michelin map **318** L5 – pop. 1,056 – alt. 115
▶ Paris 147 – Aubigny-sur-Nère 38 – Châteauneuf-sur-Loire 40 – Gien 25

Hortus-Le Jardin de Sully

℘ 02 38 36 35 94, *www.hortus-sully.com*
Address : 1 rte de St-Benoit (to the west along the D 60, follow the signs for Châteauneuf-sur-Loire; near the river)
Opening times : from beginning April to mid Nov.
2.7 ha (80 pitches) flat, grassy, stony, gravelled
Tariff : 17€ ✦✦ ⇌ ▣ ⒣ (10A) – Extra per person 4€ – Reservation fee 5€
Rental rates : (from beginning April to mid Nov.) – 14 ⛺ – 6 🏠. Per night from 40 to 85 €
Per week from 280 to 735 € – Reservation fee 10€
🚐 sani-station 2€ – ⛽11€

Leisure activities : 🎱 🏹
Facilities : ᕦ ⟶ ⫾ ⟱ ⵣ 🚰 launderette
Nearby : ✗ ⛴

Longitude : 2.36229
Latitude : 47.7718

ST-PLANTAIRE

36190 – Michelin map **323** G8 – pop. 549 – alt. 300
▶ Paris 339 – Orléans 214 – Châteauroux 68 – Limoges 95

Municipal de Fougères

℘ 02 54 47 20 01, *www.www.saint-plantaire.fr*
Address : 19 plage de Fougères
Opening times : from beginning April to end Oct.
4.5 ha (150 pitches) flat, grassy, terraced, relatively flat, stony
Tariff : 11€ ✦✦ ⇌ ▣ ⒣ (10A) – Extra per person 4€
Rental rates : (from beginning March to end Dec.) – 4 ⛺ – 15 🏠 – 4 tent bungalows.
Per night from 38 to 108 € – Per week from 142 to 572 €
Pleasant location beside the Lac de Chambon.

Surroundings : ≤ ⌇
Leisure activities : 🎱 🏹 ✗ 🎯 ⚊ ⚓ ⌇
Facilities : ᕦ ⟶ 🚰 launderette 🚰
Nearby : ✗ ⛴ pedalos

Longitude : 1.61952
Latitude : 46.42756

ST-SATUR

18300 – Michelin map **323** N2 – pop. 1,627 – alt. 155
▶ Paris 194 – Aubigny-sur-Nère 42 – Bourges 50 – Cosne-sur-Loire 12

Flower Les Portes de Sancerre

℘ 02 48 72 10 88, *www.camping-cher-sancerre.com*
Address : quai de Loire (located 1km east along the D 2)
Opening times : from beginning April to end Sept.
1 ha (85 pitches) flat, grassy
Tariff : 21.50€ ✦✦ ⇌ ▣ ⒣ (10A) – Extra per person 4€ – Reservation fee 15€
Rental rates : (from beginning April to end Sept.) – 16 ⛺ – 3 tent bungalows.
Per night from 41 to 100 € – Per week from 205 to 600 € – Reservation fee 15€
🚐 sani-station – 4 ▣ 11.90€ – ⛽13.95€
Near the Loire river (direct access).

Surroundings : ⌇ ⌇
Leisure activities : 🎱 ✗
Facilities : ᕦ ⟶ ⵣ 🚰 🖼
Nearby : 🚴 🖼 ⛴ ⚊ ⌇

Longitude : 2.86671
Latitude : 47.34251

STE-CATHERINE-DE-FIERBOIS

37800 – Michelin map **317** M6 – pop. 657 – alt. 114
▶ Paris 263 – Azay-le-Rideau 25 – Chinon 37 – Ligueil 19

Les Castels Parc de Fierbois ♣♣

📞 02 47 65 43 35, www.fierbois.fr
Address : 1.2km to the south
Opening times : from beginning May to beginning Sept.
30 ha/12 ha for camping (420 pitches) terraced, flat, grassy
Tariff : 49 € ♦♦ ⇔ ▣ ⦗⦘ (6A) – Extra per person 9 €
Rental rates : (from beginning May to beginning Sept.) – 130 ▥ – 34 ⌂ – 8 apartments –
8 cabins in the trees. Per night from 47 to 145 € – Per week from 329 to 1,015 €
▥ sani-station – 🍽 14 €
Pleasant and spacious site with woods, lake and a water park.

Surroundings : ▭ ⏣ ⛰
Leisure activities : ♟ ✗ ▱ ⊙ ✦ ⌕ ⚓ 🚲 ✂ ♁ ▣ ⊒ ≋ (beach)
🏊 🚣
Facilities : ⅙ ⚬⊸ ♨ 🛁 ⚐ ⸮ launderette ⚑ ⚘ refrigerated food storage
Nearby : adventure park

GPS Longitude : 0.6549
Latitude : 47.1486

STE-MAURE-DE-TOURAINE

37800 – Michelin map **317** M6 – pop. 4,072 – alt. 85
▶ Paris 273 – Le Blanc 71 – Châtellerault 39 – Chinon 32

Municipal de Marans

📞 02 47 65 44 93, camping@sainte-maure-de-touraine.fr – ℝ
Address : r. de Toizelet (located 1.5km southeast along the D 760, follow the signs for Loches, and
take the turning to the left; 150m from a small lake)
Opening times : from end April to beginning Sept.
1 ha (66 pitches) relatively flat, flat, grassy
Tariff : (2012 price) 11.30 € ♦♦ ⇔ ▣ ⦗⦘ (16A) – Extra per person 2.95 €
▥ sani-station
Leisure activities : ✂ sports trail
Facilities : ⅙ ⚬⊸ ⇝ 🛁 ⸮
Nearby : ⊒ ⚓

GPS Longitude : 0.6252
Latitude : 47.10509

SALBRIS

41300 – Michelin map **318** J7 – pop. 5,682 – alt. 104
▶ Paris 187 – Aubigny-sur-Nère 32 – Blois 65 – Lamotte-Beuvron 21

Le Sologne

📞 02 54 97 06 38, http://www.campingdesologne.fr
Address : 8 allée de la Sauldre (take northeastern exit along the D 55, follow the signs for Pierrefitte-
sur-Sauldre; beside a lake and near the Sauldre river)
Opening times : from beginning April to end Sept.
2 ha (81 pitches) flat, grassy
Tariff : 18.50 € ♦♦ ⇔ ▣ ⦗⦘ (10A) – Extra per person 4.50 €
Rental rates : (from beginning April to end Sept.) ✂ – 5 ▥ – 1 ⌂ .
Per night from 55 to 90 € – Per week from 225 to 497
▥ sani-station
Surroundings : ▭ ♀
Leisure activities : ▱ ⚓
Facilities : ⅙ ⚬⊸ 🛁 ⸮ ⸮ ▦
Nearby : 🛒 ✂ ▨ ▣ ⊒

GPS Longitude : 2.05522
Latitude : 47.43026

SAVIGNY-EN-VÉRON

37420 – Michelin map **317** J5 – pop. 1,447 – alt. 40
▶ Paris 292 – Chinon 9 – Langeais 27 – Saumur 20

Municipal la Fritillaire

📞 02 47 58 03 79, *www.aquadis-loisirs.com*
Address : r. Basse (to the west of the town centre; 100m from a lake)
2.5 ha (100 pitches) flat, grassy
Rentals : 1 🏠 – 5 tent bungalows.

Surroundings : 🐾 🗔
Leisure activities : 🎣🛶
Facilities : ♿ ⊙ 🔳 ♨ 🚿 🛁 📶 🗄
Nearby : 🛒 ✖ 🗔 ⛵ 🎣 🐎

Longitude : 0.13937
Latitude : 47.20039

SAVONNIÈRES

37510 – Michelin map **317** M4 – pop. 3,041 – alt. 47
▶ Paris 263 – Orléans 139 – Tours 17 – Blois 88

Confluence

📞 02 47 50 00 25, *tourisme-en-confluence.com*
Address : rte du Bray (take the northern exit from the town; beside Cher)
flat, grassy
Beside the Cher river and a cycle path.

Surroundings : 🗔 ⚲
Leisure activities : ✖
Facilities : ♿ ⊙ 🛁 🚿
Nearby : ✖

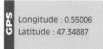
Longitude : 0.55006
Latitude : 47.34887

> *The Michelin classification (⛺... ⛺) is totally independent of the official star classification system awarded by the local prefecture or other official organisation.*

SENONCHES

28250 – Michelin map **311** C4 – pop. 3,186 – alt. 223
▶ Paris 115 – Chartres 38 – Dreux 38 – Mortagne-au-Perche 42

Huttopia Senonches ♨♨

📞 02 37 37 81 40, *www.huttopia.com*
Address : Etang de Badouleau
Opening times : from mid April to beginning Nov.
10.5 ha (126 pitches) undulating, flat, grassy
Tariff : (2012 price) 30.60€ ✦✦ 🚗 🔲 🔌 (10A) – Extra per person 6.40€ – Reservation fee 20€
Rental rates : (2012 price) (from mid April to beginning Nov.) 🅿 – 10 🏠 – 10 tents.
Per night from 62 to 156 € – Per week from 325 to 1,092 € – Reservation fee 20€
🛁 sani-station 7€
Beside the lake and on the edge of the national forest at Senonches.

Surroundings : ⚲⚲ ⛰
Leisure activities : 🗔 🌞 daytime 🏓 🎣🛶 ⛵ 🎣
Facilities : ⊙ 🅿 🔳 ♨ launderette 🖊
Nearby : 🛒 ✖ ✖ 🐎

Longitude : 1.0435
Latitude : 48.553

SONZAY

37360 – Michelin map **317** L3 – pop. 1,298 – alt. 94
▶ Paris 257 – Château-la-Vallière 39 – Langeais 26 – Tours 25

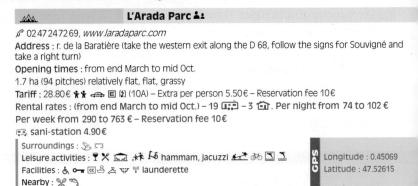

L'Arada Parc ♣≗

☎ 02 47 24 72 69, *www.laradaparc.com*
Address : r. de la Baratière (take the western exit along the D 68, follow the signs for Souvigné and take a right turn)
Opening times : from end March to mid Oct.
1.7 ha (94 pitches) relatively flat, flat, grassy
Tariff : 28.80€ ♣♣ ⇌ 🔲 💧 (10A) – Extra per person 5.50€ – Reservation fee 10€
Rental rates : (from end March to mid Oct.) – 19 🚐 – 3 🏠. Per night from 74 to 102 €
Per week from 290 to 763 € – Reservation fee 10€
🚐 sani-station 4.90€

Surroundings : 🌿 🗔
Leisure activities : ♈ ✗ 🛶 🏇 ⌂ hammam, jacuzzi 🏊 🚲 🖫 ⟱
Facilities : ⅙ ⟋ 📺 ⌂ 🚿 ⟺ ℉ launderette
Nearby : 🎾 🎣

GPS
Longitude : 0.45069
Latitude : 47.52615

SUÈVRES

41500 – Michelin map **318** F5 – pop. 1,481 – alt. 83
▶ Paris 170 – Beaugency 18 – Blois 15 – Chambord 16

Les Castels Le Château de la Grenouillère ♣≗

☎ 02 54 87 80 37, *www.camping-loire.com* ⚘
Address : 3km northeast on the D 2152
Opening times : from end April to mid Sept.
11 ha (250 pitches) flat, grassy
Tariff : 33€ ♣♣ ⇌ 🔲 💧 (10A) – Extra per person 8€ – Reservation fee 15€
Rental rates : (permanent) ⚘ – 40 🚐 – 27 🏠. Per night from 45 to 141 €
Per week from 300 to 990 € – Reservation fee 15€

Wooded park and a pleasant orchard.

Surroundings : 🗔 𝕲
Leisure activities : ♈ ✗ 🛶 ⊙ 🏇 jacuzzi 🏊 🚲 🎾 🖫 ⟱ ⟰
Facilities : ⅙ ⟋ ⌂ 🚿 ⟺ ℉ launderette 🖳 ⛽

We value your opinion and welcome your feedback.
Do email us at campingfrance@tp.michelin.com

THORÉ-LA-ROCHETTE

41100 – Michelin map **318** C5 – pop. 899 – alt. 75
▶ Paris 176 – Blois 42 – Château-Renault 25 – La Ferté-Bernard 58

Intercommunal la Bonne Aventure

☎ 02 54 72 00 59, *www.vendome.eu*
Address : rte de la Cunaille (head 1.7km north along the D 82, follow the signs for Lunay and take turning to the right; near the stadium; beside the Loir)
2 ha (60 pitches) flat, grassy

Surroundings : 🌿 𝕲
Leisure activities : 🛶 🏊 🚲 🎾 🎣
Facilities : ⅙ ⟋ 🖨
Nearby : 🏊

GPS
Longitude : 0.95855
Latitude : 47.80504

VALENÇAY

36600 – Michelin map **323** F4 – pop. 2,617 – alt. 140
◨ Paris 233 – Blois 59 – Bourges 73 – Châteauroux 42

Municipal les Chênes

✆ 02 54 00 03 92, *commune@mairie-valencay.fr*
Address : located 1km west on the D 960, follow the signs for Luçay-le-Mâle
Opening times : from beginning May to mid Sept.
5 ha (50 pitches) relatively flat, flat, grassy
Tariff : (2012 price) ♣ 3.80€ ⇔ 🔲 4.40€ – [⚡] (10A) 4.50€
🚽 sani-station 4€
Pleasant, green site beside a lake.

Surroundings : ⊏⊐ 🔾🔾
Leisure activities : 🏊⤴ 🛶 🎣
Facilities : ⚹ ⌓ 🔲

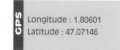
Longitude : 1.55542
Latitude : 47.15808

To make the best possible use of this guide,
please read pages 2–15 carefully.

VATAN

36150 – Michelin map **323** G4 – pop. 2,059 – alt. 140
◨ Paris 235 – Blois 78 – Bourges 50 – Châteauroux 31

⚹ Municipal

✆ 02 54 49 91 37, *www.vatan-en-berry.com*
Address : r. du Collège (take the western exit along the D 2, follow the signs for Guilly and take the turning to the left)
Opening times : from mid April to mid Sept.
2.4 ha (55 pitches) flat, grassy, stony
Tariff : 9€ ♣♣ ⇔ 🔲 [⚡] (16A) – Extra per person 4.50€
Rental rates : (from beginning April to end Sept.) – 3 🏠. Per week from 200 to 250 €
🚽 sani-station 5€
Beside a charming lake.

Surroundings : ⊏⊐ 🔾🔾
Leisure activities : 🏊⤴ 🏊
Facilities : ⚹ 🗑 🛀 ⚗ 🔲
Nearby : 🎾 🛶

Longitude : 1.80601
Latitude : 47.07146

VEIGNÉ

37250 – Michelin map **317** N5 – pop. 6,055 – alt. 58
◨ Paris 252 – Orléans 128 – Tours 16 – Joué-lès-Tours 11

⚹ La Plage

✆ 02 47 26 23 00, *www.touraine-vacance.com*
Address : rte de Tours (take the northern exit along the D 50)
2 ha (120 pitches) flat, grassy
Rentals : 15 tent bungalows.
🚽 sani-station

Surroundings : 🔾
Leisure activities : 🍷 ✗ 🎱 🚣 🎠 🎣 🛶 🎣
Facilities : ⚹ ⌓ 🛀 🍽 launderette

Longitude : 0.73464
Latitude : 47.28929

LA VILLE-AUX-DAMES

37700 – Michelin map **317** N4 – pop. 4,889 – alt. 50
▶ Paris 244 – Orléans 120 – Tours 7 – Blois 53

Les Acacias

𝒫 02 47 44 08 16, *www.camplvad.com*
Address : r. Berthe Morisot (to the northeast of the town, near the D 751)
Opening times : permanent
2.6 ha (90 pitches) flat, grassy
Tariff : 19€ ♦♦ ⇌ 🔲 (10A) – Extra per person 3.50€
Rental rates : (permanent) – 6 ⬜ – 4 ⌂. Per night from 60 to 90 €
Per week from 290 to 540 €
🚐 sani-station 6€

Surroundings :
Leisure activities : ✕ ⛵
Facilities : & ⚲ ▥ ⚐ launderette
Nearby : �ⓍⓍ fitness trail

GPS Longitude : 0.7772
Latitude : 47.40224

VILLIERS-LE-MORHIER

28130 – Michelin map **311** F4 – pop. 1 338 – alt. 99
▶ Paris 83 – Orléans 108 – Chartres 24 – Versailles 61

Les Ilots de St-Val

𝒫 02 37 82 71 30, *www.campinglesilotsdestval.com* – limited spaces for one-night stay
Address : At Le Haut Bourray (4.5km northwest along the D 983, follow the signs for Nogent-le-Roi then continue 1km along the D 1013, follow the signs for Neron to the left)
Opening times : from beginning Feb. to mid Dec.
10 ha/6 ha for camping (153 pitches) sloping, flat, grassy, stony
Tariff : ♦ 5.40€ ⇌ 2€ 🔲 5.40€ – 🔌 (10A) 6.60€
Rental rates : (from beginning Feb. to mid Dec.) ⚲ – 14 ⬜ – 4 ⌂.
Per night from 160 to 300 € – Per week from 240 to 485 €
🚐 sani-station 5€

Surroundings : ⚲
Leisure activities : ▣ ⛵ ⚲
Facilities : & ⚲ ▥ ⚲ ⚐ ▣
Nearby : ⛷ 🐎

GPS Longitude : 1.5476
Latitude : 48.6089

Fire safety doesn't stop when you leave your accommodation.
Always take care and consider the fire risks.

VITRY-AUX-LOGES

45530 – Michelin map **318** K4 – pop. 1,826 – alt. 120
▶ Paris 111 – Bellegarde 17 – Châteauneuf-sur-Loire 11 – Malesherbes 48

Étang de la Vallée

𝒫 02 38 92 32 00, *www.canal.orleans.monsite.wanadoo.fr*
Address : at base de loisirs (leisure centre) (3.3km to the northwest, 100m from the lake)
3.7 ha (180 pitches) flat, grassy
🚐 10 🔲
Pleasant wooded setting near a leisure and activity park.

Surroundings : ▭ ⚲
Leisure activities : ⛵ ▵
Facilities : & ⚲ ⚲ ⚲ ▣
Nearby : ♥✕ ⚍ (beach) ⚲ pedalos

GPS Longitude : 2.28162
Latitude : 47.95868

VOUVRAY

37210 – Michelin map **317** N4 – pop. 3,076 – alt. 55
▶ Paris 240 – Amboise 18 – Château-Renault 25 – Chenonceaux 30

⚠ Municipal Le Bec de Cisse

℘ 0247526881, *www.tourismevouvrey-valdeloire.com*
Address : south of the town; beside the Cisse river
2 ha (33 pitches) flat, grassy
📶 8 ▣

Surroundings : ▱ ♀
Facilities : ৬ ⌐ ᗑ ⚲ ▣
Nearby : ✗ ⤲ ⩰ ⚲ Rochecorbon leisure park

GPS Longitude : 0.79623
Latitude : 47.40871

von Dachsberg/Sime/Photononstop

Gérard Labriet / Photononstop

It's easy to spot visitors heading to the Champagne-Ardenne region by the sparkle in their eyes and the look of pure anticipation and delight on their faces as they gaze out at endless vineyards. They are already imagining themselves sipping the famous delicacy that was once known as 'devil's wine' before a monk discovered the secret of its divine bubbles. As those lucky enough to taste the delights of Champagne continue their voyage, they will see the beautiful cathedral of Reims rise up ahead. They will drink in the sight of the delightful half-timbered houses of Troyes and savour the taste of *andouillettes* (chitterling sausages). Visitors can then explore the Ardennes forest by bike or by walking along its hiking trails. This ancient woodland paradise, bordered by the gentle river Meuse, has other delights as well: watch the graceful flight of the crane over a lake as smooth as glass, or succumb to the temptation of a plate of local wild boar.

AIX-EN-OTHE

10160 – Michelin map **313** CA – pop. 2,417 – alt. 149
▶ Paris 144 – Châlons-en-Champagne 116 – Troyes 33 – Auxerre 66

⚠ Municipal de la Nosle

℘ 06 76 83 76 96, *www.village-campagne-center.fr*
Address : r. Joseph Anglade
3 ha (90 pitches) flat, grassy
Rentals : 10 ⛺ – 25 🏠 – 65 🚐.
🚽 sani-station – 10 🔲

Surroundings : ♀
Facilities : ⛶ ⊶ ⚊ ⁿⁱ
Nearby : 🍽 🍷 ✗ 📷 🐾

| GPS | Longitude : 3.73727 |
| --- | Latitude : 48.21842 |

ANDELOT

52700 – Michelin map **313** L4 – pop. 919 – alt. 286
▶ Paris 287 – Bologne 14 – Chaumont 23 – Joinville 33

⚠ Municipal du Moulin

℘ 03 25 03 39 29, *www.camping-andelot.com*
Address : r. Gué (located 1km north along the D 147, follow the signs for Vignes-la-Côte; beside the Rognon river)
1.9 ha (56 pitches) flat, grassy
Rentals : 4 ⛺.

Pleasant setting beside river.

Surroundings : ⊡ ♀
Leisure activities : 📷 🚣 ⚓
Facilities : ⛶ ⊶ launderette

| GPS | Longitude : 5.29893 |
| --- | Latitude : 48.25219 |

*For more information on visiting particular towns or regions, consult the
relevant regional MICHELIN Green Guide. We also recommend you use
the appropriate Michelin regional map to locate your selected campsite,
to calculate distances and to work out the best route.*

BANNES

52360 – Michelin map **313** M6 – pop. 401 – alt. 388
▶ Paris 291 – Chaumont 35 – Dijon 86 – Langres 9

⚠ Hautoreille

℘ 03 25 84 83 40, *www.campinghautoreille.com*
Address : 6 r. du Boutonnier (take the southwestern exit along the D 74, follow the signs for Langres then continue 700m along the road to the left)
Opening times : from beginning Jan. to end Nov.
3.5 ha (100 pitches) flat, relatively flat, grassy
Tariff : 19.40€ ✦✦ 🚐 🔲 🔌 (10A) – Extra per person 5€

Surroundings : 🦌 ♀♀
Leisure activities : 🍷 ✗ 📷
Facilities : ⛶ ⊶ ⑂ ⛺ ⁿⁱ 🔲

| GPS | Longitude : 5.39519 |
| --- | Latitude : 47.89508 |

BOURBONNE-LES-BAINS

52400 – Michelin map **313** O6 – pop. 2,255 – alt. 290 – ♨ (beg Mar to end Nov)
▶ Paris 313 – Chaumont 55 – Dijon 124 – Langres 39

⚠ Le Montmorency

℘ 03 25 90 08 64, *www.camping-montmorency.com*
Address : r. du Stade (take the western exit following signs for Chaumont and take turning to the right; 100m from the stadium)
2 ha (74 pitches) relatively flat, grassy, fine gravel
Rentals : 11 🚐.
🚐 sani-station – 5 🔳

Surroundings : 🌳 ⇚ ▭ 𝟬𝟬
Facilities : o━ ▥ 🚿 ⚐ ⚑ launderette
Nearby : 🍴 🔲 (open-air in season)

GPS Longitude : 5.74027
Latitude : 47.95742

BOURG-STE-MARIE

52150 – Michelin map **313** N4 – pop. 94 – alt. 329
▶ Paris 330 – Châlons-en-Champagne 153 – Chaumont 50 – Metz 142

⚠ Les Hirondelles

℘ 03 10 20 61 64, *www.camping-les-hirondelles.eu*
Address : at Romain-sur-Meuse, r. du Moulin de Dona (located 1.5km to the south, along the D 74, follow the signs for Montigny-le-Roi)
Opening times : permanent
4.6 ha (54 pitches) flat, grassy, fine gravel
Tariff : ♥ 4€ ⇙ 🔳 5€ – ⚡ (10A) 3.50€
Rental rates : (permanent) – 7 🏠 – 1 gîte. Per night from 35 to 85 €
Per week from 210 to 380 €
🚐 15 🔳 16.50€ – 🚐 ⚡14€

Surroundings : 🌳 ⇚ ▭ ⚲
Leisure activities : 🎮 🚣 🚲
Facilities : ♿ o━ ▥ 🚿 🚿 ⚐ ⚑ launderette

GPS Longitude : 5.55533
Latitude : 48.17234

In order for the guide to remain wholly objective, the selection of campsites is made on an entirely independent basis.

BRAUCOURT

52290 – Michelin map **313** I2
▶ Paris 220 – Bar-sur-Aube 39 – Brienne-le-Château 29 – Châlons-en-Champagne 69

⚠ Flower La Presqu'île de Champaubert ▲▲

℘ 03 25 04 13 20, *www.lescampingsduder.com*
Address : 3km northwest along the D 153
Opening times : permanent
3.6 ha (200 pitches) flat, grassy, fine gravel
Tariff : 36€ ♥♥ ⇙ 🔳 ⚡ (10A) – Extra per person 7€
Rental rates : (permanent) – 62 🚐. Per week from 300 to 800 €
🚐 20 🔳 12€
Pleasant location beside Lac du Der-Chantecoq.

Surroundings : 🌳 ⇚ ▭ 𝟬𝟬 ⛰
Leisure activities : 🍴 ✕ 🎮 ⚙ 🎯 🚣 🍴 🎣
Facilities : ♿ o━ 🚿 launderette
Nearby : ⛵ ⚓ pedalos

GPS Longitude : 4.562
Latitude : 48.55413

BUZANCY

08240 – Michelin map **306** L6 – pop. 372 – alt. 176
▶ Paris 228 – Châlons-en-Champagne 86 – Charleville-Mézières 58 – Metz 130

⚠ La Samaritaine

℘ 03 24 30 08 88, *www.campinglasamaritaine.com*
Address : 3 r. des Étangs (1.4km southwest along the road to the right near the leisure and activity park)
2 ha (110 pitches) flat, grassy, stony
Rentals : 10 ⬜ – 9 ⬜.
🚐 sani-station – 3 ▣

Surroundings : ♨ ▭ ♀
Leisure activities : ▭
Facilities : � ⚬▬ ♨ ♨ ☂ 🔖
Nearby : ≊ (lake)

GPS
Longitude : 4.9402
Latitude : 49.42365

CHÂLONS-EN-CHAMPAGNE

51000 – Michelin map **306** I9 – pop. 46,236 – alt. 83
▶ Paris 188 – Charleville-Mézières 101 – Metz 157 – Nancy 162

⚠ **Aquadis Loisirs Châlons en Champagne**

℘ 03 26 68 38 00, *www.aquadis-loisirs.fr*
Address : r. de Plaisance (take the southeastern exit along the N 44, follow the signs for Vitry-le François and take D 60, following signs for Sarry)
Opening times : from beginning March to beginning Nov.
3.5 ha (148 pitches) flat, grassy, gravelled
Tariff : ☗ 5.25€ ⇔ 3.45€ ▣ 5.25€ – ⚡ (10A) 3.90€ – Reservation fee 9.90€
Rental rates : (from beginning March to beginning Nov.) – 8 ⬜. Per night from 70 €
Per week from 159 to 508 € – Reservation fee 19.50€
🚐 sani-station 14€ – 28 ▣ 5.25€ – ⚡14€
Flowers around entrance and pleasant setting beside a lake.

Surroundings : ▭ ♀♀
Leisure activities : ✗ ▭ ☀ ✻ ♣ ⤳
Facilities : ⅲ ⚬▬ ▣ ⫿ ♨ ☂ ☞ ☝ launderette

GPS
Longitude : 4.38309
Latitude : 48.98582

We value your opinion and welcome your feedback.
Do email us at campingfrance@tp.michelin.com

CHARLEVILLE-MÉZIÈRES

08000 – Michelin map **306** K4 – pop. 49,975
▶ Paris 233 – Châlons-en-Champagne 130 – Namur 149 – Arlon 120

⚠ Municipal du Mont Olympe

℘ 03 24 33 23 60, *camping-charlevillemezieres@wanadoo.fr*
Address : 174 r. des Paquis (in the town centre)
2.7 ha (120 pitches) flat, grassy
🚐 8 ▣
In a bend of the Meuse river with pedestrian access to the town centre and the Rimbaud museum via a walkway.

Surroundings : ♨ ▭ ♀♀
Leisure activities : ▭ ☀
Facilities : ⅲ ⚬▬ ♨ ☂ ☞ ☝ launderette
Nearby : ☗ ✗ ☃ ☄ hammam, jacuzzi ▭ ⤳ ⚓ marina

GPS
Longitude : 4.72091
Latitude : 49.77914

LE CHESNE

08390 – Michelin map **306** K5 – pop. 986 – alt. 164 – Leisure centre
▶ Paris 232 – Buzancy 20 – Charleville-Mézières 39 – Rethel 32

Homair Vacances Le Lac de Bairon

℘ 03 24 30 11 66, *www.homair.com*
Address : 2.8km northeast along the D 991, follow the signs for Charleville-Mézières and take the turning for Sauville to the right – for caravans, recommended route via the D 977, follow the signs for Sedan and left turn onto D 12
Opening times : from beginning April to end Sept.
6.8 ha (170 pitches) flat, terraced, grassy, fine gravel
Tariff : (2012 price) 19 € 👤👤 🚐 🔲 (½) (10A) – Extra per person 5 € – Reservation fee 5 €
Rental rates : (2012 price) (from beginning April to end Sept.) – 20 🛖.
Per night from 25 to 71 € – Per week from 175 to 497 € – Reservation fee 5 €
🚐 sani-station 3 €
Pleasant location beside the lake.

Surroundings : 🦢 ≤ 🟤 ▲
Leisure activities : 🎮 ⛵ 🚴 🎣
Facilities : ♿ 🚿 ▥ 🍴 launderette
Nearby : ✗ 🏊 ◊

GPS Longitude : 4.77529
Latitude : 49.53198

DIENVILLE

10500 – Michelin map **313** H3 – pop. 828 – alt. 128 – Leisure centre
▶ Paris 209 – Bar-sur-Aube 20 – Bar-sur-Seine 33 – Brienne-le-Château 8

⚠ Le Tertre

℘ 03 25 92 26 50, *www.campingdutertre.fr*
Address : 1 rte de Radonvilliers (take the western exit on the D 11)
Opening times : from mid March to mid Oct.
3.5 ha (155 pitches) flat, grassy, gravelled
Tariff : (2012 price) 👤 4.80 € 🚐 🔲 9.90 € – (½) (10A) 4 € – Reservation fee 12 €
Rental rates : (2012 price) (from mid March to mid Oct.) – 12 🛖. Per week from 180 to 530 €
Reservation fee 12 €
Opposite the leisure centre's sailing centre.

Surroundings : 🗔
Leisure activities : 🍴 ✗ ⛵ 🛶
Facilities : ♿ 🔌 🍴 🚻 🍴 ▦
Nearby : ✗ 🏊 🎣 water skiing, jet skis

GPS Longitude : 4.52737
Latitude : 48.34888

ÉCLARON

52290 – Michelin map **313** J2 – pop. 1,991 – alt. 132
▶ Paris 255 – Châlons-en-Champagne 71 – Chaumont 83 – Bar-le-Duc 37

⛰ Yelloh! Village en Champagne-Les Sources du Lac 👥

℘ 03 25 06 34 24, *www.yellohvillage.com* – limited spaces for one-night stay
Address : RD 384 (situated 2km to the south, follow the signs for Montier-en-Der; beside the Lac du Der)
3 ha (120 pitches) flat, grassy, fine gravel
Rentals : 3 caravans – 50 🛖.
Choose the pitches away from the road in preference.

Surroundings : 🗔 🟤 ▲
Leisure activities : 🍴 🎯 🏃 ⛵ 🚴 🛶 🏊 (beach) 🎣 multi-sports ground
Facilities : ♿ 🔌 🍴 🚻 🍴 launderette 🚿

GPS Longitude : 4.84798
Latitude : 48.57179

ÉPERNAY

51200 – Michelin map **306** F8 – pop. 24,317 – alt. 75
▶ Paris 143 – Amiens 199 – Charleville-Mézières 113 – Meaux 96

⚠ Municipal

℘ 03 26 55 32 14, *www.epernay.fr*
Address : allée de Cumières (located 1.5km north along the D 301; beside the Marne river)
Opening times : from end April to beginning Oct.
2 ha (119 pitches) flat, grassy
Tariff : ♦ 4.40€ ⇌ 2.50€ 🔲 3.40€ – 🔋 (5A) 3.50€
🚐 sani-station 2€

Surroundings : ⌂ ♨♨
Leisure activities : 🏄 ♂♂
Facilities : ♿ ⛗ ⶲ ᵮᵛ launderette
Nearby : ⚓

GPS
Longitude : 3.95026
Latitude : 49.05784

ERVY-LE-CHÂTEL

10130 – Michelin map **313** D5 – pop. 1,224 – alt. 160
▶ Paris 169 – Auxerre 48 – St-Florentin 18 – Sens 62

⚠ Municipal les Mottes

℘ 03 25 70 07 96, *www.ervy-le-chatel.reseaudescommunes.fr/communes/*
Address : chemin des Mottes (1.8km east along the D 374, follow the signs for Auxon, D 92 and take the road to the right after the level crossing)
0.7 ha (53 pitches) flat, grassy
🚐 sani-station – 5 🔲
Beside a small river and a wood.

Surroundings : ♨
Leisure activities : ⌇
Facilities : ♿ ⬚

GPS
Longitude : 3.91827
Latitude : 48.04069

These symbols are used for a campsite that is exceptional in its category:
⚠⚠⚠...⚠ *Particularly pleasant setting, quality and range of services available*
♨♨ *Tranquil, isolated site – quiet site, particularly at night*
≤≤ *Exceptional view – interesting or panoramic view*

FISMES

51170 – Michelin map **306** E7 – pop. 5,377 – alt. 70
▶ Paris 131 – Fère-en-Tardenois 20 – Laon 37 – Reims 29

⚠ Municipal

℘ 03 26 48 10 26, *www.gee-europe.com*
Address : to the northwest along the N 31, near the stadium
0.8 ha (33 pitches) flat, fine gravel

Surroundings : ♀
Leisure activities : ⬓
Facilities : ⚭ ⶲ
Nearby : ⏃

GPS
Longitude : 3.67185
Latitude : 49.30936

GÉRAUDOT

10220 – Michelin map **313** F4 – pop. 294 – alt. 146
▶ Paris 192 – Bar-sur-Aube 36 – Bar-sur-Seine 28 – Brienne-le-Château 26

 ### L'Épine aux Moines

☏ 03 25 41 24 36, www.campinglesrivesdulac.com
Address : 1.3km southeast along the D 43
2.8 ha (186 pitches) flat and relatively flat, grassy
Rentals : 🏠 – 4 ⛺ – 50 gîtes.
🚐 sani-station – 10 ▣
Green setting near the Lac de la Forêt d'Orient.

Surroundings : 🌳
Facilities : 🔥 ⚬🔑 ▥ 👕 🗍
Nearby : 🛒 ✕ 🍴 🏖 (beach) 🐾

GPS Longitude : 4.33751
Latitude : 48.30273

GIFFAUMONT-CHAMPAUBERT

51290 – Michelin map **306** K11 – pop. 261 – alt. 130
▶ Paris 213 – Châlons-en-Champagne 67 – St-Dizier 25 – Bar-le-Duc 52

Village Vacances Marina-Holyder
(rental of small houses only)

☏ 03 26 72 99 90, www.marina-holyder.com
Address : r. de Champaubert (Presqu'Île de Rougemer (peninsula)
Opening times : permanent
2 ha flat
Rental rates : (2012 price) 🅿 – 67 🏠. Per week from 308 to 689 €

Surroundings : 🐟
Leisure activities : 🍽 ✕ 🎮 🏸 🎱 ⛵ hammam, jacuzzi 🏊 🖼 🎣 🐾
Facilities : ⚬🔑 🚿 ☑ ▥ 👕 launderette 🐕
Nearby : 🚴

GPS Longitude : 4.77328
Latitude : 48.54987

The Michelin classification (🏔 ... 🔺) is totally independent of the official star classification system awarded by the local prefecture or other official organisation.

HAULMÉ

08800 – Michelin map **306** K3 – pop. 96 – alt. 175
▶ Paris 248 – Charleville-Mézières 19 – Dinant 64 – Namur 99

Base de Loisirs Départementale

☏ 03 24 32 81 61, campinghaulme@cg08.fr
Address : take the northeastern exit, then continue 800m along the road to the right after the bridge
15 ha (405 pitches) flat, grassy
🚐 sani-station – 5 ▣
Situated beside the Semoy river.

Surroundings : 🐟 ⛰
Leisure activities : 🖼 🏊 🚴 ✕ 🎣
Facilities : 🔥 ⚬🔑 ▥ launderette
Nearby : canoeing, sports trail, sports trail

GPS Longitude : 4.79217
Latitude : 49.85667

LANGRES

52200 – Michelin map **313** L6 – pop. 8,066 – alt. 466
▶ Paris 295 – Châlons-en-Champagne 197 – Chaumont 36 – Dijon 79

Kawan Le Lac de la Liez ▲▴

℘ 03 25 90 27 79, *www.campingliez.com*
Address : at Peigney, at la base nautique (5km east along the D 284)
Opening times : from end March to end Sept.
4.5 ha (160 pitches) terraced, flat, grassy
Tariff : 34€ ♣♣ ⇌ 🔲 (⌁) (10A) – Extra per person 8€ – Reservation fee 6€
Rental rates : (from end March to end Sept.) – 2 🚐 – 24 🏠. Per night from 50 to 114 €
Per week from 350 to 798 € – Reservation fee 30€
🚐 sani-station 6€ – 10 🔲 10€

Surroundings : 🏊 ≤ lake, countryside and the town of Langres ⌁ 🔱
Leisure activities : 🍸 ✗ 🏛 🚴 ⛵ ⛵ ⚔ 🔲 ⛵
Facilities : 👤 ⊶ 🆑 ▥ 🛁 🎣 🚽 🍴 launderette 🔲, 🔧
Nearby : 🚲🛶 (beach) 🎣 🌊 water skiing

| GPS |
| Longitude : 5.3807 |
| Latitude : 47.87146 |

MESNIL-ST-PERE

10140 – Michelin map **313** G4 – pop. 415 – alt. 131
▶ Paris 209 – Châlons-en-Champagne 98 – Troyes 25 – Chaumont 79

Kawan Le Lac d'Orient ▲▴

℘ 03 25 40 61 85, *www.camping-lacdorient .com*
Address : rte du Lac
Opening times : from mid April to end Sept.
4 ha (199 pitches) flat, grassy
Tariff : 34€ ♣♣ ⇌ 🔲 (⌁) (10A) – Extra per person 8€ – Reservation fee 20€
Rental rates : (from mid April to end Sept.) ⛵ – 16 🚐 – 2 🏠. Per night from 55 to 127 €
Per week from 385 to 890 € – Reservation fee 20€
🚐 6 🔲 21€

Surroundings : 🏊 🔱
Leisure activities : 🍸 🏛 🚴 ⚔ 🔲 ⛵ ⚔ multi-sports ground
Facilities : 👤 ⊶ 🆑 ▥ 🛁 🎣 🚽 🍴 launderette 🔲, 🔧
Nearby : 🎣 🌊

| GPS |
| Longitude : 4.34624 |
| Latitude : 48.26297 |

MONTIGNY-LE-ROI

52140 – Michelin map **313** M6 – pop. 2,168 – alt. 404
▶ Paris 296 – Bourbonne-les-Bains 21 – Chaumont 35 – Langres 23

Municipal du Château

℘ 03 25 87 38 93, *www.campingduchateau.com*
Address : r. Hubert Collot (access via the town centre and take the pedestrian path to the village)
Opening times : from mid April to end Sept.
6 ha/2 ha for camping (75 pitches) flat, terraced, grassy
Tariff : ♣ 5.60€ ⇌ 🔲 5.60€ – (⌁) (6A) 4.60€
🚐 sani-station 2€
In a wooded park overlooking the Vallée de la Meuse.

Surroundings : ≤ 🔱
Leisure activities : ⚔ ⛵
Facilities : 👤 ⊶ ▥ 🛁 🍴
Nearby : ✗

| GPS |
| Longitude : 5.4965 |
| Latitude : 48.00068 |

CHAMPAGNE-ARDENNE

RADONVILLIERS

10500 – Michelin map **313** H3 – pop. 384 – alt. 130
▶ Paris 206 – Bar-sur-Aube 22 – Bar-sur-Seine 35 – Brienne-le-Château 6

 Le Garillon

  𝄞 03 25 92 21 46, *http://www.campinglegarillon.fr*
Address : take the southwestern exit along the D 11, follow the signs for Piney and take turning to the right; beside a stream and 250m from the lake, (top of dike via steps)
Opening times : from beginning April to mid Oct.
1 ha (55 pitches) flat, grassy
Tariff : (2012 price) 21€ ♀♀ ⇔ ▤ ⱴ (16A) – Extra per person 4€
Rental rates : (2012 price) (from beginning April to end Oct.) – 11 ▥.
Per night from 32 to 82 € – Per week from 204 to 492 €

Leisure activities : ⤳
Facilities : ६ ⚊ ╢
Nearby : ⤬

GPS Longitude : 4.50206
Latitude : 48.3586

SÉZANNE

51120 – Michelin map **306** E10 – pop. 5,268 – alt. 137
▶ Paris 116 – Châlons-en-Champagne 59 – Meaux 78 – Melun 89

△ Municipal

  𝄞 03 26 80 57 00, *campingdesezanne@wanadoo.fr*
Address : rte de Launat (take the western exit along the D 373, follow the signs for Paris (near N 4) then continue 700m along the road to the left and take turning to the right)
1 ha (79 pitches) terrace, relatively flat, flat, grassy
▥ sani-station
Surroundings : ♀
Leisure activities : ⤼ ⤳ ⤻
Facilities : ६ ⚊ ╢ ▣
Nearby : ⤬

GPS Longitude : 3.70212
Latitude : 48.72154

This guide is not intended as a list of all the camping sites in France; its aim is to provide a selection of the best sites in each category.

SOULAINES-DHUYS

10200 – Michelin map **313** I3 – pop. 311 – alt. 153
▶ Paris 228 – Bar-sur-Aube 18 – Brienne-le-Château 17 – Chaumont 48

△ **La Croix Badeau**

  𝄞 03 25 27 05 43, *www.croix-badeau.com*
Address : 6 r. de La Croix Badeau (to the northeast of the town, near the church)
Opening times : from beginning April to end Sept.
1 ha (39 pitches) relatively flat, grassy, gravelled
Tariff : (2012 price) 16.50€ ♀♀ ⇔ ▤ ⱴ (10A) – Extra per person 3.20€
Rental rates : (2012 price) (from beginning April to end Sept.) – 1 ▥. Per night 50€
Per week 470€
▥ sani-station 2.50€ – 30 ▤ – ⤧9.50€
Surroundings : ▱
Leisure activities : ♟ ⛱
Facilities : ६ ⚊ ▥ ⤴ ⤻ ╢
Nearby : ⤼ ⤬

GPS Longitude : 4.73846
Latitude : 48.37672

300

THONNANCE-LES-MOULINS

52230 – Michelin map **313** L3 – pop. 120 – alt. 282
▶ Paris 254 – Bar-le-Duc 64 – Chaumont 48 – Commercy 55

Les Castels La Forge de Sainte Marie ▲▴

℘ 03 25 94 42 00, *www.laforgedesaintemarie.com*
Address : rte de Joinville (1.7km west along the D 427; beside the Rongeant river)
Opening times : from end April to beginning Sept.
32 ha/3 ha for camping (133 pitches) flat, terraced, relatively flat, grassy, lake
Tariff : 33.50€ ♦♦ ⇌ 🖃 (½) (6A) – Extra per person 8.20€
Rental rates : (2012 price) (from end April to beginning Sept.) – 34 🚐 – 15 gîtes.
Per night from 72 to 163 € – Per week from 240 to 650 €– Reservation fee 12€
🚽 sani-station
Pleasant, green setting based around an old restored forge.

Surroundings : 🦢 🏕 ♀
Leisure activities : ♥ ✗ 🖼 ☺ 🕺 🛶 🚲 🖼 🎣
Facilities : 🔥 ⚡ ⌘🚿 🛁 ♨ 🍴 launderette 🍽 🦮

Longitude : 5.27097
Latitude : 48.40629

TROYES

10000 – Michelin map **313** E4 – pop. 61,188 – alt. 113
▶ Paris 170 – Dijon 185 – Nancy 186

⚠ Municipal

℘ 03 25 81 02 64, *www.troyescamping.net*
Address : at Pont Sainte-Marie, 7 r. Roger Salengro (situated 2km to the northeast, follow the signs for Nancy)
Opening times : from beginning April to mid Oct.
3.8 ha (150 pitches) flat, grassy
Tariff : (2012 price) ♦ 6.20€⇌ 🖃 9.20€ – (½) (10A) 3.20€
🚽 sani-station 3.50€
Close to the bus stop for Troyes town centre and factory outlets at Pont Sainte-Marie.

Surroundings : ♀
Leisure activities : 🖼 🛶 🚲 ♟ 🏊
Facilities : 🔥 ⚡ 🚿 🍴 launderette
Nearby : 🍽 🎣

Longitude : 4.09682
Latitude : 48.31112

© JEUNK / iStockphoto

Maria Gaspar / Michelin

Corsica emerges from the Mediterranean like a glinting jewel. It is indeed the 'Isle of Beauty'. Follow its twisting roads to ancient citadels, perched on the island's rocky flanks in spectacular cliff-top settings, and your efforts will be more than rewarded. Enjoy panoramic views and inhale the fragrance of wild rosemary as you make your way up the rugged hills, clad in *maquis* (Mediterranean shrubs and herbs). The sudden sight of a secluded chapel or timeless village, or indeed an unscheduled encounter with a herd of mountain sheep, are among the many lasting memories that those discovering Corsica on foot, by bike or in their cars take home with them. After exploring the wild interior of the island, plunge into the impossibly clear turquoise waters that surround it and recharge your solar batteries on its warm sandy beaches, dreaming of an *assiette de charcuterie* (pork platter) and traditional cheese. Corsica seduces the eyes and taste buds of every visitor.

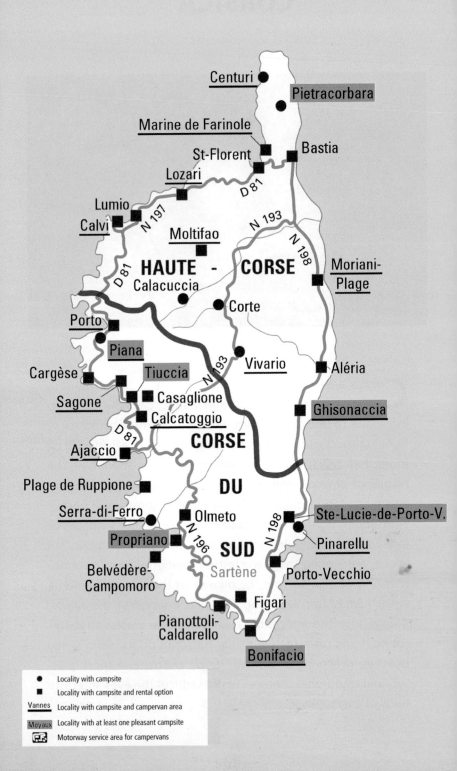

CORSICA

Centuri

Pietracorbara

Marine de Farinole

St-Florent   Bastia

Lozari

D 81

Lumio

N 197

Calvi   Moltifao

N 193

D 81

HAUTE - CORSE

N 198

Calacuccia   Moriani-Plage

Corte

Porto

Cargèse   Vivario   Aléria

N 193

Piana

Tiuccia

Sagone   Casaglione

Calcatoggio   Ghisonaccia

D 81

CORSE

Ajaccio

DU

Plage de Ruppione

Serra-di-Ferro   Olmeto   Ste-Lucie-de-Porto-V.

N 198

Propriano   Pinarellu

N 196   SUD

Belvédère-   Sartène   Porto-Vecchio
Campomoro

Figari

Pianottoli-
Caldarello

Bonifacio

	Locality with campsite
	Locality with campsite and rental option
Vannes	Locality with campsite and campervan area
Moyaux	Locality with at least one pleasant campsite
	Motorway service area for campervans

AJACCIO

20000 – Michelin map **345** B8 – pop. 64,306
▶ Bastia 147 – Bonifacio 131 – Calvi 166 – Corte 80

Les Mimosas

𝒫 04 95 20 99 85, www.camping-lesmimosas.com – ℞ ⌇

Address : rte d'Alata (5km, take the northern exit along the D 61 and take the turning to the left, follow the signs for Les Milelli)

Opening times : from beginning April to beginning Oct.

2.5 ha (70 pitches) terraced, flat, stony

Tariff : ♠ 6€ ⇔ 3€ 🔲 3€ – 🔌 (6A) 2.80€

Rental rates : (from beginning April to beginning Oct.) ⌇ – 12 ⌂ – 4 ⌂ – 1 studio. Per week from 340 to 580 €

🚐 sani-station 8€

Surroundings : 🌿 ♨♨
Facilities : ♿ ⚬ ⌇ ♨ ⚬ launderette, refrigerators

Longitude : 8.73069
Latitude : 41.94066

ALÉRIA

20270 – Michelin map **345** G7 – pop. 1,996 – alt. 20
▶ Bastia 71 – Corte 50 – Vescovato 52

Marina d'Aléria

𝒫 04 95 57 01 42, www.marina-aleria.com

Address : plage de Padulone (3km east of Cateraggio along the N 200; beside the Tavignano river)

Opening times : from end April to beginning Oct.

17 ha/7 ha for camping (252 pitches) flat, sandy, grassy

Tariff : 41€ ♠♠ ⇔ 🔲 🔌 (9A) – Reservation fee 20€

Rental rates : (from end April to beginning Oct.) ⌇ – 135 ⌂ – 31 ⌂. Per night from 45 to 130 € – Per week from 200 to 1,120 € – Reservation fee 20€

Surroundings : 🌿 ⩽ sea and mountain ♨♨ ⚠
Leisure activities : ✕ ⌂ ☺ daytime 🏃 ⚬ 🚲 ⌇ ♣ pedalos ⚬
Facilities : ♿ ⚬ ♨ 🔲 ⚬ ⚬ refrigerated food storage
Nearby : 🐎

Longitude : 9.55
Latitude : 42.11139

BASTIA

20200 – Michelin map **345** F3 – pop. 43,545
▶ Ajaccio 148 – Bonifacio 171 – Calvi 92 – Corte 69

San Damiano

𝒫 04 95 33 68 02, www.campingsandamiano.com

Address : Lido de la Marana (9km southeast along the N 193 and turn left onto D 107)

Opening times : from beginning April to end Oct.

12 ha (280 pitches) flat, sandy

Tariff : (2012 price) 29.40€ ♠♠ ⇔ 🔲 🔌 (6A) – Extra per person 8.20€

Rental rates : (2012 price) (from beginning April to end Oct.) – 8 ⌂ – 48 ⌂. Per night from 364 to 987 € – Per week from 364 to 987 €

Some luxury chalets, some with with a sea view.

Surroundings : 🌿 ⌂ ♨♨ ⚠
Leisure activities : ⚬ ✕ ⌂ ⚬ ⌇ ♣ ⌇
Facilities : ♿ ⚬ ⚬ ♨ launderette ⚬ ⚬
Nearby : ⚬ 🐎

Longitude : 9.46718
Latitude : 42.63114

BELVÉDÈRE-CAMPOMORO

20110 – Michelin map **345** B10 – pop. 135 – alt. 5
▶ Ajaccio 88 – Bonifacio 72 – Porto 82 – Sartène 24

La Vallée

✆ 04 95 74 21 20, *www.campomoro-lavallee.com* – **Ȑ** ✿ (from mid-Jun to end Aug)
Address : at Propriano
Opening times : from beginning May to end Sept.
3.5 ha (199 pitches) flat and relatively flat, stony, grassy, terraced
Tariff : (2012 price) ✦ 8€ ⇌ 5€ 🗉 5€ – ⟨⟩ (12A) 6€
Rental rates : (2012 price) (from beginning May to end Sept.) ✿ **Ⓟ** – 12 ⌂ – 3 apartments.
Per week from 600 to 950 €

Surroundings : ⟍ ♀
Facilities : ⅄ ⊶ ᵀ 🖼
Nearby : ⚓

GPS
Longitude : 8.81625
Latitude : 41.62815

We value your opinion and welcome your feedback.
Do email us at campingfrance@tp.michelin.com

BONIFACIO

20169 – Michelin map **345** D11 – pop. 2,919 – alt. 55
▶ Ajaccio 132 – Corte 150 – Sartène 50

Pertamina Village – U-Farniente ♟♟

✆ 04 95 73 05 47, *www.camping-pertamina.com*
Address : at Canelli (5km northeast along the N 198, follow the signs for Porto-Vecchio – Bastia)
Opening times : from beginning April to mid Oct.
15 ha/3 ha for camping (150 pitches) flat and relatively flat, stony, terrace
Tariff : 41€ ✦✦ ⇌ 🗉 ⟨⟩ (6A) – Extra per person 11€ – Reservation fee 24€
Rental rates : (from beginning April to mid Oct.) – 17 🚐 – 60 ⌂ – 6 apartments – 10 tent
bungalows. Per night from 55 to 160 € – Per week from 360 to 1,180 € – Reservation fee 26€
A pleasant, undulating site with plenty of shade.

Surroundings : ⟍ ⊏⊐ ♀♀
Leisure activities : ✗ 🎠 ⊕ ᵠᵏ 🎿 🛶 ✿ ⽔ ⚓
Facilities : ⅄ ⊶ 🖵 ⏛ ⊗ ᵀ launderette ⚓ ⛟ refrigerated food
storage

GPS
Longitude : 9.17905
Latitude : 41.41825

Rondinara

✆ 04 95 70 43 15, *www.rondinara.fr* – **Ȑ** ✿
Address : at Suartone (18km northeast along the N 198, follow the signs for Porto-Vecchio and take
D 158 to the right, follow the signs for La Pointe de la Rondinara (headland); 400m from the beach)
Opening times : from mid May to end Sept.
5 ha (120 pitches) terraced, relatively flat, flat, stony
Tariff : ✦ 8.40€ ⇌ 4.50€ – ⟨⟩ (6A) 4€
Rental rates : (2012 price) (from mid May to end Sept.) ✿ – 36 🚐.
Per week from 445 to 1,200 € – Reservation fee 16€
🚐 sani-station – 20 🗉

Surroundings : ⟍ ≤ ♀
Leisure activities : ♟ ✗ 🎠 🛶 🏊
Facilities : ⅄ ⊶ 🖼 ⚓ ⛟
Nearby : pedalos

GPS
Longitude : 9.26887
Latitude : 41.47089

Les Îles

⌀ 04 95 73 11 89, *www.camping-desiles.com* ✂

Address : rte de Piantarella (4.5km east, follow the signs for Piantarella, towards the landing stage at Cavallo)

Opening times : from beginning April to end Sept.

8 ha (100 pitches) relatively flat, undulating, stony

Tariff : (2012 price) ⚥ 9.90€ ⟐ 5€ 🅴 7.20€ – (½) (6A) 3.80€

Rental rates : (2012 price) (from beginning April to end Sept.) ✂ – 16 ⟐ – 20 ⌂.
Per week from 360 to 952 €

Panoramic view of Sardinia and the islands from some pitches.

Surroundings : ⩻ ♤♤
Leisure activities : ✗ ⟐ ⚐ ✂ m ⅃
Facilities : ⚹ ⟐ ⟐⟐⟐⟐ ⟐ ⟐ ⟐

GPS Longitude : 9.21034 Latitude : 41.37818

Campo-di-Liccia

⌀ 04 95 73 03 09, *www.campingdiliccia.com*

Address : at Parmentil (5.2km northeast along the N 198, follow the signs for Porto-Vecchio)

Opening times : from beginning April to end Sept.

5 ha (161 pitches) flat, stony, terrace

Tariff : (2012 price) ⚥ 7.90€ ⟐ 3.50€ 🅴 5€ – (½) (4A) 3.20€

Rental rates : (2012 price) (from beginning April to end Sept.) ✂ – 35 ⟐ – 10 ⌂.
Per night from 59 to 90 € – Per week from 369 to 820 €

⟐ sani-station

A pleasant rental park set among trees, shrubs and bushes.

Surroundings : ⟐ ♤♤♤
Leisure activities : ⟐ ✗ ⚐ ⅃
Facilities : ⚹ ⟐ (Jul–Aug) ⟐⟐⟐ ⟐ ⟐ ⟐ refrigerated food storage

GPS Longitude : 9.16882 Latitude : 41.40493

Pian del Fosse

⌀ 04 95 73 16 34, *www.piandelfosse.com*

Address : 3.8 km northeast along the D 58 – or 5km along the N 198 following the signs for Porto-Vecchio and take the D 60 following signs for Santa-Manza

Opening times : from mid April to mid Oct.

5.5 ha (100 pitches) terraced, flat and relatively flat, stony

Tariff : (2012 price) ⚥ 8.20€ ⟐ 4.54€ 🅴 7.60€ – (½) (10A) 4.50€ – Reservation fee 18€

Rental rates : (2012 price) (from mid April to mid Oct.) ✂ – 1 ⟐ – 11 ⌂ – 12 tent bungalows. Per night from 52 to 150€ – Per week from 330 to 1,000 € – Reservation fee 18€

⟐ sani-station

Surroundings : ⟐ ⟐ ♤♤♤
Leisure activities : ✗ ⚐
Facilities : ⚹ ⟐ ℗ ⟐ ⟐ launderette
Nearby : 🐎

GPS Longitude : 9.20083 Latitude : 41.39972

La Trinité

⌀ 04 95 73 10 91, *www.campinglatrinite.com* – ⟐

Opening times : from beginning April to mid Oct.

4 ha (100 pitches) undulating, flat and relatively flat, stony, grassy, rocks

Tariff : (2012 price) ⚥ 8€ ⟐ 3.50€ 🅴 7€ – (½) (6A) 3€

Rental rates : (2012 price) (from beginning April to mid Oct.) – 7 ⟐. Per week 900€

Uninterrupted view of Bonifacio from the top of the site, but choose the pitches away from the road in preference.

Surroundings : ♤
Leisure activities : ⟐ ✗ ⟐ ⅃
Facilities : ⚹ ⟐ ⟐ ⟐ ⟐

GPS Longitude : 9.12688 Latitude : 41.41042

CALACUCCIA

20224 – Michelin map **345** D5 – pop. 316 – alt. 830
▶ Ajaccio 107 – Bastia 76 – Porto-Vecchio 146 – Corte 27

⚠ Acquaviva

🕿 04 95 48 00 08, *http://www.acquaviva-fr.com*
Address : 500m southwest along the D 84 and take road to the left, opposite the service station
Opening times : from mid May to mid Oct.
4 ha (50 pitches) relatively flat, flat, grassy, stony
Tariff : ↟ 6€ ⇌ 3€ 🗉 3€ – ⚡ (16A) 4€

Surroundings : 🐟 ≤ lake and mountains ♀
Leisure activities : 🎬 ⚡
Facilities : ♿ 🛏 ⛺ ⛽ 📷
Nearby : ♟ ✕ ⚓ 🎣

GPS Longitude : 9.01049
Latitude : 42.33341

CALCATOGGIO

20111 – Michelin map **345** B7 – pop. 522 – alt. 250
▶ Ajaccio 23 – Bastia 156

🏔 La Liscia

🕿 04 95 52 20 65, *www.la-liscia.com*
Address : rte de Tiuccia (5km northwest along the D 81; beside the river, in the Golfe de La Liscia (bay)
Opening times : from beginning May to end Sept.
3 ha (100 pitches) flat, terraced, stony, grassy
Tariff : (2012 price) ↟ 8.50€ ⇌ 4.50€ 🗉 4.50€ – ⚡ (6A) 4€ – Reservation fee 17€
Rental rates : (2012 price) (from end April to end Sept.) ⚡ – 11 caravans – 7 ⛺ – 1 🏠 – 3 studios. Per week from 230 to 915€ – Reservation fee 17€
🚐 sani-station

Surroundings : ♀♀
Leisure activities : ♟ ✕ 🎬 🚲
Facilities : ♿ ⛐ ⛺ ⛽ launderette 🧊 refrigerators

GPS Longitude : 8.75526
Latitude : 42.04678

A 'quartier' is a district or area of a town or village.

CALVI

20260 – Michelin map **345** B4 – pop. 5,377
▶ Bastia 92 – Corte 88 – L'Ile-Rousse 25 – Porto 73

🏔 La Pinède

🕿 04 95 65 17 80, *www.camping-calvi.com*
Address : rte de la Pinède
Opening times : from end March to beginning Nov.
5 ha (262 pitches) flat, stony, sandy
Tariff : 36€ ↟↟ ⇌ 🗉 ⚡ (6A) – Extra per person 9.90€ – Reservation fee 15€
Rental rates : (from end March to beginning Nov.) ♿ – 34 ⛺ – 80 🏠.
Per night from 39 to 219€ – Per week from 238 to 1,288 € – Reservation fee 15€
🚐 sani-station – ⚡ 15€
Choose the pitches away from the road in preference.

Surroundings : ♀♀
Leisure activities : ♟ ✕ ⚡ 🎿 🎣 🏊
Facilities : ♿ ⛐ 📼 ⛺ ⛽ launderette 🥘 refrigerated food storage
Nearby : 🛒

GPS Longitude : 8.76795
Latitude : 42.55318

Paduella

📞 04 95 65 06 16, *www.campingpaduella.com* –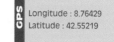

Address : 1.8km southeast along the N 197, follow the signs for l'Ile-Rousse; 400m from the beach

Opening times : from beginning May to beginning Oct.

4.5 ha (160 pitches) flat, stony, sandy

Tariff : (2012 price) ⚹ 8€ 🚐 3.40€ 🔲 3.40€ – 🔌 (10A) 3.75€

Rental rates : (2012 price) (from mid May to beginning Oct.) – 35 tent bungalows.
Per night from 40 to 81 € – Per week from 280 to 567 €

Beautiful pine trees.

Surroundings : 🟢🟢
Leisure activities : 🍸
Facilities : 🚿 ⚡ 🛏️♨️🔥🍴🖼️💦
Nearby : 🛒

GPS
Longitude : 8.76429
Latitude : 42.55219

Bella Vista

📞 04 95 65 11 76, *www.camping-bellavista.com* 🌿

Address : rte de Pietramaggiore (head 1.5km south along the N 197 towards l'Île Rousse and follow the signs for Pietra-Major to the right)

Opening times : from beginning April to end Sept.

6 ha/4 ha for camping (156 pitches) flat and relatively flat, stony, sandy

Tariff : (2012 price) ⚹ 8.20€ 🚐 4.20€ 🔲 4.20€ – 🔌 (10A) 4.70€

Rental rates : (from beginning April to end Sept.) 🌿 – 13 🏠. Per week from 350 to 980 €
🚏 sani-station

Surroundings : 🌊 🟢🟢
Leisure activities : ✗ 🛶
Facilities : 🚿 ⚡ 🅿️ 🖼️♨️🔥🍴🖼️💦

GPS
Longitude : 8.75334
Latitude : 42.55068

Paradella

📞 04 95 65 00 97, *www.camping-paradella.fr* ✉️ 20214 Calenzana

Address : rte de la forêt de Bonifato (9.5km southeast along the N 197, follow the signs for l'Ile-Rousse and take D 81 to the right, follow the signs for the airport and Bonifato)

Opening times : from beginning April to end Sept.

5 ha (150 pitches) flat, stony, sandy

Tariff : (2012 price) ⚹ 7.90€ 🚐 3.20€ 🔲 3.50€ – 🔌 (10A) 3.80€ – Reservation fee 10€

Rental rates : (2012 price) (from beginning April to end Sept.) 🌿 – 2 🚐 – 18 🏠.
Per night from 62 to 118 € – Per week from 300 to 780 € – Reservation fee 10€
🚏 sani-station 5€

Choose the pitches away from the road in preference, sheltered by pines and eucalyptus trees.

Surroundings : 🔲 🟢🟢
Leisure activities : 🛶 🛝
Facilities : 🚿 ⚡ 🍴 🖼️

GPS
Longitude : 8.79166
Latitude : 42.50237

For more information on visiting particular towns or regions, consult the relevant regional MICHELIN Green Guide. We also recommend you use the appropriate Michelin regional map to locate your selected campsite, to calculate distances and to work out the best route.

Les Castors

📞 0495651330, *http://www.camping-castors.fr/*

Address : rte de Piétramaggiore (located 1km south along the N 197 towards L'Île Rousse and follow the signs for Pietra-Major to the right)

Opening times : from beginning April to mid Oct.

2 ha (80 pitches) flat, stony, grassy

Tariff : 🚶 12.50€ 🚗 6€ ▣ 5.50€ – 🔌 (15A) 5.50€

Rental rates : (from beginning April to mid Oct.) – 36 🛖 – 25 studios – 9 apartments. Per night from 84 to 155 € – Per week from 585 to 1,085 € – Reservation fee 10€ 🚐 sani-station 7€ – 20 ▣ 21.50€

Surroundings : ♨♨ Leisure activities : ✕ 🏊 🎣 🛶 Facilities : 🔑 🚿 🚽 🖼	**GPS** Longitude : 8.7561 Latitude : 42.55735

Dolce Vita

📞 0495650599, *www.dolce-vita.fr*

Address : 4.5km southeast along the N 197, follow the signs for l'Ile-Rousse; at the mouth of the Figarella river, 200m from the sea

6 ha (200 pitches) flat, stony, sandy, grassy

On the Calvi-l'Île Rousse train line.

Surroundings : ♨♨♨ Leisure activities : ✕ 🏊 🍴 🎣 Facilities : ♿ 🔑 🚽 🖼 💧 Nearby : ⚓	**GPS** Longitude : 8.78972 Latitude : 42.55582

CARGÈSE

20130 – Michelin map **345** A7 – pop. 1,117 – alt. 75
▶ Ajaccio 51 – Calvi 106 – Corte 119 – Piana 21

Torraccia

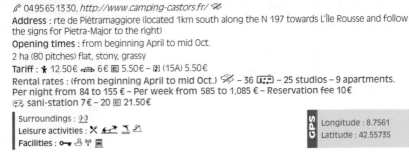

📞 0495264239, *www.camping-torraccia.com*

Address : at Bagghiuccia (4.5km north along the D 81, follow the signs for Porto)

Opening times : from beginning May to end Sept.

3 ha (90 pitches) terraced, flat, stony, grassy

Tariff : (2012 price) 🚶 9€ 🚗 4€ ▣ 4€ – 🔌 (10A) 4.50€ – Reservation fee 18.50€

Rental rates : (2012 price) (from beginning May to end Sept.) – 25 🛖.
Per week from 335 to 880 € – Reservation fee 18.50€

Surroundings : ≤ valley, mountain and sea! ♨♨ Leisure activities : 🏊 Facilities : ♿ 🔑 🚿 🚽 🖼 🛒	**GPS** Longitude : 8.60611 Latitude : 42.15583

CASAGLIONE

20111 – Michelin map **345** B7 – pop. 365 – alt. 150
▶ Ajaccio 33 – Bastia 166

U Sommalu

📞 0495522421, *www.usommalu-camping.fr*

Address : Plaine du Liamone

Opening times : from beginning April to end Sept.

4 ha (123 pitches) terraced, relatively flat, flat, grassy, stony

Tariff : 🚶 8.50€ 🚗 4€ ▣ 5.50€ – 🔌 (10A) 4.50€

Rental rates : (from beginning April to end Sept.) – 15 🛖 – 21 🏠. Per week from 385 to 840 €

Surroundings : 🌿 ♨♨ Leisure activities : 🖼 🏊 🏊 Facilities : 🔑 🚐 🚿 🚽 launderette	**GPS** Longitude : 8.73507 Latitude : 42.07267

CENTURI

20238 – Michelin map **345** F2 – pop. 221 – alt. 228
▶ Ajaccio 202 – Bastia 55

⚠ Isulottu

☎ 04 95 35 62 81, *www.isulottu.fr*

Address : at Marine de Mute (head along the D 35 following the signs for Morsiglia, 200m from the beach)

Opening times : from beginning May to end Sept.

2.3 ha (150 pitches) flat and relatively flat, stony

Tariff : (2012 price) ⚹ 7.50€ ⇔ 3€ 🔲 3.80€ – ⚡ (30A) 3.50€

🚐 sani-station

Surroundings : ⚓ ♨♨
Leisure activities : ▼ ⛵
Facilities : ♿ ☎ ⛺ launderette ⚒
Nearby : scuba diving

Longitude : 9.3515
Latitude : 42.96048

CORTE

20250 – Michelin map **345** D6 – pop. 6,744 – alt. 396
▶ Ajaccio 81 – Bastia 68

⚠ Aire Naturelle St-Pancrace

☎ 04 95 46 09 22, *www.campingsaintpancrace.fr*

Address : Saint-Pancrace quartier (located 1.5km north along the Cours Paoli and take road to the left after the Sous-Préfecture)

Opening times : from mid April to end Oct.

12 ha/1 ha for camping (25 pitches) relatively flat, stony, grassy

Tariff : ⚹ 6€ ⇔ 3€ 🔲 4€ – ⚡ (45A) 4€

Farm campsite.

Surroundings : ⚓ ⩽ ♨♨
Leisure activities : ▭
Facilities : ☎ ⚒ ⊠

Longitude : 9.14994
Latitude : 42.30645

> *The Michelin classification (⚠⚠⚠ … ⚠) is totally independent of the official star classification system awarded by the local prefecture or other official organisation.*

FARINOLE (MARINA DE)

20253 – Michelin map **345** F3 – pop. 224 – alt. 250
▶ Bastia 20 – Rogliano 61 – St-Florent 13

⚠ A Stella

☎ 04 95 37 14 37, *www.campingastella.com*

Address : along the D 80; beside the sea

3 ha (100 pitches) terraced, relatively flat, flat, stony

Rentals : 2 apartments – 1 tent bungalow.

🚐 sani-station

Some sunny pitches with a sea view; close to a pebble beach.

Surroundings : ⚓ ⩽ ♨♨ ⚠
Leisure activities : ▭
Facilities : ⚓ 🔲 ⚒

Longitude : 9.34459
Latitude : 42.7315

FIGARI

20114 – Michelin map **345** D11 – pop. 1,217 – alt. 80
▶ Ajaccio 122 – Bonifacio 18 – Porto-Vecchio 20 – Sartène 39

U Moru

𝄞 0495712340, *www.u-moru.com*
Address : 5km northeast along the D 859
Opening times : from mid June to mid Sept.
6 ha/4 ha for camping (100 pitches) relatively flat, flat, sandy
Tariff : 8€ 3.50€ 4.10€ – (6A) 4€
Rental rates : (from mid June to mid Sept.) – 12. Per week from 560 to 940 €

Surroundings :
Leisure activities : (small swimming pool)
Facilities : refrigerators
Nearby :

Longitude : 9.14131
Latitude : 41.50505

*The classification (1 to 5 tents, black or red) that we award to selected sites
in this guide is our own system. It should not be confused with the
classification (1 to 5 stars) of official organisations.*

GHISONACCIA

20240 – Michelin map **345** F7 – pop. 3,669 – alt. 25
▶ Bastia 85 – Aléria 14 – Ghisoni 27 – Venaco 56

Arinella-Bianca

𝄞 0495560478, *www.arinellabianca.com*
Address : rte de la mer (3.5km east along the D 144 then continue 700m along the road to the right)
Opening times : from mid April to beginning Oct.
10 ha (416 pitches) flat, grassy, sandy
Tariff : 50€ (10A) – Extra per person 13€ – Reservation fee 50€
Rental rates : (from mid April to beginning Oct.) – 176 – 56.
Per night from 45 to 210 € – Per week from 260 to 1,420 € – Reservation fee 50€
sani-station 9€

Surroundings :
Leisure activities : multi-sports ground
Facilities : launderette refrigerated food storage
Nearby :

Longitude : 9.44331
Latitude : 41.9972

Marina d'Erba Rossa

𝄞 0495562514, *www.marina-erbarossa.com*
Address : rte de la Mer (4km east along the D 144; beside the beach)
Opening times : from beginning April to end Oct.
12 ha/8 ha for camping (200 pitches) flat, grassy
Tariff : (2012 price) 9.50€ 25.50€ – (10A) 5.50€ – Reservation fee 25€
Rental rates : (2012 price) (from beginning April to end Sept.) – 350 – 112.
Per night from 30 to 200 € – Per week from 210 to 1,400 € – Reservation fee 25€

Surroundings :
Leisure activities : wildlife park
Facilities : launderette refrigerated food storage
Nearby : disco, scuba diving

Longitude : 9.44339
Latitude : 42.00211

LOZARI

20226 – Michelin map **345** D4
▸ Bastia 61 – Belgodère 10 – Calvi 33 – L'Ile-Rousse 8

Le Clos des Chênes

☎ 0495601513, *http://www.closdeschenes.fr* ✉ 20226 Belgodere
Address : located 1.5km south along the N 197, follow the signs for Belgodère
Opening times : from beginning May to end Sept.
5 ha (235 pitches) flat and relatively flat, stony, grassy
Tariff : (2012 price) ✶ 9.20€ ⇦ 🔲 11€ – (ℑ) (10A) 6.50€
Rental rates : (2012 price) (from beginning July to mid Sept.) ⚡ – 21 🚐 – 24 🏠 – 5 🛏 –
3 apartments. Per night 90€ – Per week 900€ – Reservation fee 24€
🚐 sani-station

Surroundings : 🌳 ♧♧
Leisure activities : ▼ 🏠 🛶 ✕ ⚓
Facilities : ᴿ ⚬━ 🗑 🛁 🖼 🔲 🛁 refrigerated food storage

Longitude : 9.01191
Latitude : 42.62848

Campéole Le Belgodère

☎ 0495602020, *www.campeole.com* – limited spaces for one-night stay
Address : on the N 197, 500m from the beach
Opening times : from beginning May to end Sept.
2.5 ha (112 pitches) flat, grassy, stony
Tariff : 29.60€ ✶✶ ⇦ 🔲 (ℑ) (6A) – Extra per person 9.50€
Rental rates : (from beginning May to end Sept.) – 18 🚐 – 76 tent bungalows.
Per night from 29 to 139 € – Per week from 203 to 973 €

Choose the pitches away from the entrance in preference.

Surroundings : ♧
Facilities : ᴿ ⚬━ ⸙ 🖼

Longitude : 9.01984
Latitude : 42.63658

*There are several different types of sani-station
('borne' in French) – sanitation points providing
fresh water and disposal points for grey water.
See page 12 for further details.*

LUMIO

20260 – Michelin map **345** B4 – pop. 1,250 – alt. 150
▸ Ajaccio 158 – Bastia 83 – Corte 77 – Calvi 10

Le Panoramic

☎ 0495607313, *www.le-panoramic.com*
Address : rte de Lavatoggio (situated 2km northeast on the D 71, follow the signs for Belgodère)
Opening times : from beginning May to end Sept.
6 ha (100 pitches) terraced, stony, sandy, very uneven
Tariff : (2012 price) ✶ 8.20€ ⇦ 3.20€ 🔲 7€ – (ℑ) (6A) 3.80€
Rental rates : (2012 price) (from beginning Sept. to end Sept.) ⚡ – 20 caravans – 7 🚐.
Per week from 300 to 900 €

Panoramic view of the sea from some pitches.

Surroundings : 🌳 ⪇♧♧
Leisure activities : ✕ ⚓
Facilities : ⚬━ ⸙ 🖼 🛁

Longitude : 8.84805
Latitude : 42.58973

MOLTIFAO

20218 – Michelin map **345** D5 – pop. 724 – alt. 420
▶ Ajaccio 113 – Bastia 58

⚠ E Canicce

𝒫 04 95 35 16 75, *http://www.campingecanicce.com*
Address : Vallée de l'Asco (3km south on the D 47; beside the Asco river)
1 ha (25 pitches) flat, stony
Rentals : ⚜ – 7 'gypsy' caravans – 8 ⌂ – 3 gîtes.
⛽ 5 ▣

Surroundings : ⛰ ≼ Monte Cinto and Scala di Santa Régina (gorge) ⚲
Leisure activities : ⚱
Facilities : �o━ 🚿 ▣

GPS
Longitude : 9.11667
Latitude : 42.48849

MORIANI -PLAGE

20230 – Michelin map **345** G5
▶ Bastia 40 – Corte 67 – Vescovato 21

⚠ **Merendella**

𝒫 04 95 38 53 47, *www.merendella.com*
Address : at San Nicolao (1.2km south along the N 198, follow the signs for Porto-Vecchio; beside the beach)
Opening times : permanent
7 ha (206 pitches) flat, grassy, sandy
Tariff : (2012 price) 🚹 8.85€ ⬅ 3.50€ – 🔌 (10A) 5.10€ – Reservation fee 16€
Rental rates : (2012 price) (permanent) – 10 🚐 – 16 ⌂ – 2 apartments.
Per night from 65 to 125 € – Per week from 474 to 872 € – Reservation fee 16€
⛽ sani-station
Some sunny pitches; close to a beach.

Surroundings : ⛺ ♨ ⛰
Leisure activities : ✗ 🏛 ♨ jacuzzi ⚓ ▨ (open-air in season)
Facilities : ♿ o━ 🚿 launderette
Nearby : ⚱ scuba diving

GPS
Longitude : 9.52951
Latitude : 42.36355

The information in the guide may have changed since going to press.

OLMETO

20113 – Michelin map **345** C9 – pop. 1,230 – alt. 320
▶ Ajaccio 64 – Propriano 8 – Sartène 20
to the beach SW : 7 km via D 157

⚠ **L'Esplanade**

𝒫 04 95 76 05 03, *www.camping-esplanade.com*
Address : 1.6km along the D 157, 100m from the beach – direct access
Opening times : from beginning April to end Oct.
4.5 ha (100 pitches) terraced, flat and relatively flat, rocks, extremely uneven
Tariff : 🚹 8.70€ ⬅ 4.50€ ▣ 10€ – 🔌 (6A) 4.50€ – Reservation fee 11€
Rental rates : (from end March to end Oct.) ⚜ – 53 ⌂. Per week from 258 to 958 €
Reservation fee 11€

Surroundings : ⛺ ⚲⚲
Leisure activities : ✗ 🏛 ⚓ ▨
Facilities : ♿ o━ 🚿 ▨ ▣ ⚰

GPS
Longitude : 8.88926
Latitude : 41.69564

PIANA

20115 – Michelin map **345** A6 – pop. 450 – alt. 420
▶ Ajaccio 72 – Calvi 85 – Évisa 33 – Porto 13

Plage d'Arone

℘ 04 95 20 64 54
Address : rte Danièle Casanova (11.5km southwest along the D 824; 500m from the beach – direct access)
Opening times : from end May to end Sept.
3.8 ha (125 pitches) open site, terraced, flat, stony, grassy
Tariff : (2012 price) ♣ 9.20€ ⇔ 🅔 7.20€ – ⚡ (6A) 3.20€
🛒 sani-station

Surroundings : 🌿 ≤ ♧♧
Facilities : ♿ ⚭ ✉ ♨ 🅘 🛁

GPS Longitude : 8.58092
Latitude : 42.20843

To make the best possible use of this guide,
please read pages 2–15 carefully.

PIANOTTOLI-CALDARELLO

20131 – Michelin map **345** D11 – pop. 864 – alt. 60
▶ Ajaccio 113 – Bonifacio 19 – Porto-Vecchio 29 – Sartène 31

Kévano Plage

℘ 04 95 71 83 22, *campingkevano.com*
Address : rte de la plage (3.3km southeast along the D 122 and take right turning; 500m from the beach)
Opening times : from end March to end Oct.
6 ha (100 pitches) terraced, relatively flat, flat, stony, rocks, very uneven
Tariff : 16€ ♣♣ ⇔ 🅔 ⚡ (3A) – Extra per person 9€
Rental rates : (from end March to end Oct.) – 3 🚐 – 5 🏠. Per week from 345 to 815 €
Natural setting in the middle of the maquis (typical Corsican countryside) and granite rocks.

Surroundings : 🌿 ⊡ ♧♧
Leisure activities : ✗
Facilities : ♿ ⚭ ✉ ♟ 🅘 🛁 ⚲

GPS Longitude : 9.04294
Latitude : 41.47111

PIETRACORBARA

20233 – Michelin map **345** F2 – pop. 573 – alt. 150
▶ Paris 967 – Ajaccio 170 – Bastia 21 – Biguglia 31

La Pietra

℘ 04 95 35 27 49, *www.la-pietra.com*
Address : head 4km southeast along the D 232 and take road to the left; 500m from the beach
Opening times : from end March to beginning Nov.
3 ha (66 pitches) flat, grassy, stony
Tariff : (2012 price) ♣ 9.95€ ⇔ 3.80€ 🅔 5€ – ⚡ (6A) 3.50€
Pitches attractively marked out.

Surroundings : 🌿 ≤ ⊡ ♧♧
Leisure activities : ✗ 🎱 ↗ ✎ 🏊
Facilities : ♿ ⚭ ✂ ✉ ♨ ⚘ 🅘 🛁, refrigerated food storage
Nearby : 🐎

GPS Longitude : 9.4739
Latitude : 42.83939

CORSICA

PINARELLU

20124 – Michelin map **345** F9
▶ Ajaccio 146 – Bonifacio 44 – Porto-Vecchio 16

California

℘ 04 95 71 49 24, *www.camping-california.net* ✉ 20144 Ste-Lucie-de-Porto-Vecchio ✕
Address : 800m south along the D 468 and 1.5km along the road to the left; beside the beach
7 ha/5 ha for camping (100 pitches) undulating, sandy, flat, lake
sani-station

Surroundings :
Leisure activities : ✕
Facilities :

Longitude : 9.38084
Latitude : 41.66591

Some information or pricing may have changed since the guide went to press.
We recommend you check the price list online in advance or at the entrance
to the campsite and enquire about possible restrictions.

PORTO

20150 – Michelin map **345** B6 – pop. 544
▶ Ajaccio 84 – Calvi 73 – Corte 93 – Évisa 23

Les Oliviers

℘ 04 95 26 14 49, *www.camping-oliviers-porto.com* ✉ 20150 Ota ✕
Address : near the bridge (follow the D 81 (Pont de Porto road); beside the Porto river and
100m from the village)
Opening times : from end March to beginning Nov.
5.4 ha (216 pitches) terraced, flat, stony, rocks, extremely uneven**Tariff :** (2012 price) ♦ 10€ ⟵ 4€
▣ 3.50€ – 彤 (10A) 4.50€ – Reservation fee 15€
Rental rates : (2012 price) (from end March to beginning Nov.) ✕ – 6 caravans – 46 ⌂.
Per night from 56 to 220 € – Per week from 308 to 1,569 € – Reservation fee 16€
Attractive swimming pool area; spa and camping area in a natural wooded setting.

Surroundings :
Leisure activities : ✕ 🚣 💆 ≋ hammam ⬚ ≌ spa therapy centre
Facilities : ⟵ ℗ 🚿 launderette 🍴 refrigerated food storage
Nearby :

Longitude : 8.71005
Latitude : 42.26242

Sole e Vista

℘ 04 95 26 15 71, *www.camping-sole-e-vista.com* ✉ 20150 Ota
Address : in the village (main access via the supermarket car park – secondary access: head 1km east
along the D 124, follow the signs for Ota, 150m from the Porto river and the village)
Opening times : from beginning March to end Oct.
4 ha (170 pitches) terraced, flat, stony, rocks, extremely uneven
Tariff : (2012 price) ♦ 9€ ⟵ 5€ ▣ 5€ – 彤 (6A) 3.50€
Rental rates : (2012 price) (from beginning March to end Oct.) ✕ – 24 ⟐ – 24 ⌂.
Per night from 55 to 100 € – Per week from 350 to 900 €
sani-station – 70 ▣
Natural wooded setting.

Surroundings :
Leisure activities :
Facilities : ⟵ 🚿 launderette, refrigerators
Nearby :

Longitude : 8.71114
Latitude : 42.26313

Funtana a l'Ora

𝒞 04 95 26 11 65, www.funtanaalora.com
Address : at Ota, rte d'Évisa (1.4km southeast along the D 84, 200m from the Porto river)
Opening times : from beginning April to mid Nov.
2 ha (70 pitches) terraced, flat and relatively flat, stony, rocks, very uneven
Tariff : (2012 price) ⋆ 8.90€ ⇌ 3.50€ 🅴 3.50€ – 🔌 (10A) 4€ – Reservation fee 15€
Rental rates : (2012 price) (from beginning April to mid Nov.) – 7 🏠.
Per night from 44 to 125 € – Per week from 280 to 1,020 € – Reservation fee 15€
🚐 sani-station 7€

Surroundings : 🐾 ⊐ ⏅
Leisure activities : 🏓 🛝 multi-sports ground
Facilities : ♿ ⌐ 🚿 🍴 launderette 🧊 refrigerated food storage

GPS Longitude : 8.71528
Latitude : 42.25887

Le Porto

𝒞 06 85 41 50 74, www.camping-le-porto.com ✉ 20150 Ota –
Address : take the western exit along the D 81, follow the signs for Piana; 200m from the Porto river and 300m from the village
Opening times : from beginning April to end Oct.
2 ha (60 pitches) terraced, stony, extremely uneven
Tariff : (2012 price) ⋆ 7€ ⇌ 3€ 🅴 3.50€ – 🔌 (6A) 4€

Pitches set on lovely terraces with plenty of shade.

Surroundings : ⏅
Facilities : ♿ ⌐ 🚿 🖾 🖼
Nearby : ☲

GPS Longitude : 8.7055
Latitude : 42.26645

Casa del Torrente
(rental of chalets only)

𝒞 04 95 22 45 14, www.casadeltorrente.com
Address : rte Evisa (located 1km southeast along the D 84; beside the Porto river (direct access)
Opening times : from end March to mid Nov.
1.5 ha terraced
Rental rates : 🏘 – 12 🏠 – 1 gîte. Per night from 44 to 224 € – Per week from 280 to 1,420 €
Reservation fee 15€

Free use of the leisure facilities and services at the 'Funtana a l'Ora' campsite 200m opposite, on the other side of the road.

Surroundings : 🐾 ♀
Leisure activities : ☲
Facilities : ⌐ 🚿 🎞 🍴 🖼

GPS Longitude : 8.71797
Latitude : 42.25624

PORTO-VECCHIO

20137 – Michelin map **345** E10 – pop. 11,005 – alt. 40
▶ Ajaccio 141 – Bonifacio 28 – Corte 121 – Sartène 59

Golfo di Sogno

𝒞 04 95 70 08 98, www.golfo-di-sogno.fr
Address : rte de Cala-Rossa (6km northeast along the D 468)
Opening times : from beginning May to end Sept.
22 ha (650 pitches) flat, grassy, sandy
Tariff : (2012 price) 25€ ⋆⋆ ⇌ 🅴 🔌 (10A) – Extra per person 8€
Rental rates : (2012 price) (from beginning May to end Sept.) 🏘 – 12 🚐 – 61 🏠 –
12 teepees – bungalows without sanitary facilities. Per week from 290 to 1,300 €
🚐 sani-station

Some chalets very close to the sea.

Surroundings : ⊐ ♀♀ ⌂
Leisure activities : 🍴 ✗ ⚓ ≋ ⏃ watersports centre
Facilities : ⌐ 🚿 🖾 launderette 🛒 🧊

GPS Longitude : 9.31297
Latitude : 41.62975

La Vetta

℘ 04 95 70 09 86, *www.campinglavetta.com* – ⚑
Address : at La Trinité (5.5km north on N 198, follow the signs for Bastia)
Opening times : from beginning June to end Sept.
8 ha (100 pitches) terraced, sloping, flat, stony, grassy, rocks
Tariff : (2012 price) ✦ 9€ ⇐ 3€ 🅴 5€ – 🄖 (10A) 3.50€
Rental rates : (2012 price) (from mid May to mid Oct.) – 36 🛏 – 6 🏠 .
Per night from 52 to 205 € – Per week from 399 to 1,470 €

Natural setting on the coast, some chalets have a sea view.

Surroundings : 🌳🌳
Leisure activities : ✕ 🛶 🎿
Facilities : ⚡ 🛁 ⛲ 🖼

GPS Longitude : 9.29356
Latitude : 41.63285

Arutoli

℘ 04 95 70 12 73, *www.arutoli.com*
Address : rte de l'Ospédale (situated 2km northwest along the D 368)
Opening times : from beginning April to beginning Nov.
4 ha (150 pitches) flat and relatively flat, stony, rocks
Tariff : ✦ 7.85€ ⇐ 3.40€ 🅴 3.55€ – 🄖 (6A) 3.50€
Rental rates : (from beginning April to beginning Nov.) – 22 🛏 – 5 🏠 .
Per night from 53 to 150 € – Per week from 659 to 1,056 € – Reservation fee 12€

Surroundings : 🌳🌳
Leisure activities : ✕ 🎥 🎿
Facilities : ⚡ ⛲ 🖼 ⛲ 🚿
Nearby : 🐎

GPS Longitude : 9.26641
Latitude : 41.60428

Pitrera

℘ 04 95 70 20 10, *www.pitrera.com*
Address : at La Trinite (head 5.8km north along the N 198, follow the signs for Bastia and take road to the right)
Opening times : from mid April to mid Oct.
3 ha (75 pitches) terraced, stony, relatively flat, rocks, very uneven
Tariff : (2012 price) 25€ ✦✦ ⇐ 🅴 🄖 (12A) – Extra per person 7.30€
Rental rates : (2012 price) (from mid April to mid Oct.) – 1 🛏 – 56 🏠 – 1 yurt.
Per night from 64 to 119 € – Per week from 686 to 1,071 €

Surroundings : 🏔
Leisure activities : ✕ 🎿 ⛷
Facilities : ♿ ⚡ 🛁 ⛲ 🖼 🚿

GPS Longitude : 9.29535
Latitude : 41.63461

U Pirellu

℘ 04 95 70 23 44, *www.u-pirellu.com* – acces to some pitches via steep slope – ⚑ 🦮
Address : rte de Palombaggia (located 9km to the east, at Piccovagia)
Opening times : from mid April to end Sept.
5 ha (150 pitches) terraced, flat and relatively flat, stony, grassy, extremely uneven
Tariff : (2012 price) ✦ 9.80€ ⇐ 4€ 🅴 4.50€ – 🄖 (6A) 3.80€
Rental rates : (2012 price) (from mid April to end Sept.) 🦮 – 12 🏠 .
Per night from 60 to 150 € – Per week from 390 to 1,250 €

Panoramic view of the sea and the headland at La Chiappa from some chalets.

Surroundings : 🌲 🌳🌳
Leisure activities : 🍴 ✕ 🛶 🎿
Facilities : ♿ ⚡ 🅿 🛁 ⛲ 🖼 ⛲ 🚿
Nearby : 🏃

GPS Longitude : 9.34081
Latitude : 41.58228

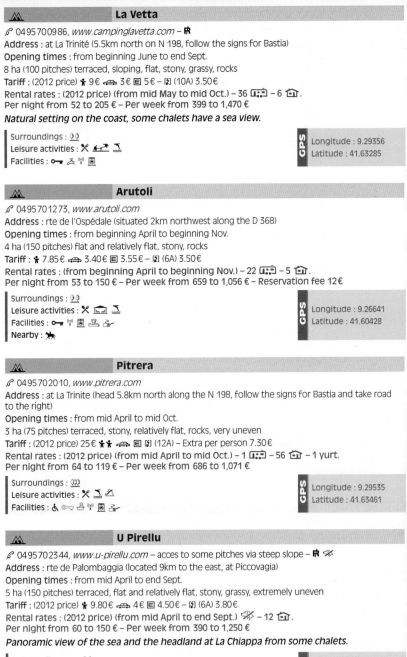

Bella Vista

📞 0495705801, *http://www.bella-vista.cc*
Address : rte de Palombaggia (located 9.3km to the east, at Piccovagia)
Opening times : from beginning June to end Sept.
2.5 ha (100 pitches) terraced, grassy, stony
Tariff : (2012 price) 👤 7 € 🚐 3.50 € 🔲 – 🔌 (6A) 3.50 €
Rental rates : (from beginning April to end Sept.) 🏠 – 8 🏠. Per night from 50 to 110 €
Per week from 450 to 1,400 € – Reservation fee 15 €

Surroundings : ⩽ ♤♤
Leisure activities : ✗ 🛝
Facilities : ♿ ⚷ 🚮 ⛲ 📷

GPS Longitude : 9.3367
Latitude : 41.58672

L'Oso

📞 0495716099
Address : rte de Cala Rossa (located 8km northeast on the D 468; beside the Oso river)
Opening times : from beginning June to end Sept.
3.2 ha (90 pitches) flat, grassy
Tariff : (2012 price) 👤 6 € 🚐 3 € 🔲 3 € – 🔌 (6A) 4 €
Rental rates : (2012 price) – 20 🏠. Per week from 500 to 600 €

Surroundings : ♤♤
Leisure activities : 🛝
Facilities : ♿ ⚷ 🚮 ☑ 📷

GPS Longitude : 9.31793
Latitude : 41.632

Les Ilots d'Or

📞 0495700130, *www.campinglesilotsdor.com*
Address : rte Pezza Cardo (head 6km northeast along the D 568 or the N 198, follow the signs for Bastia and take a right turn along the D 468 b before La Trinité)
Opening times : from beginning May to end Sept.
4 ha (180 pitches) terraced, flat, sandy, grassy, rocks
Tariff : (2012 price) 👤 7 € 🚐 3 € 🔲 3.50 € – 🔌 (6A) 3 €
Rental rates : (2012 price) (from beginning May to end Sept.) 🏠 – 3 🚐 – 23 🏠.
Per night from 50 to 110 € – Per week from 350 to 770 €
Some pitches are very close to the sea.

Surroundings : ♤♤ ⬆
Leisure activities : ✗
Facilities : ♿ ⚷ 🚮 ⛱ ⛲ 📷 🛁
Nearby : 🌊

GPS Longitude : 9.30819
Latitude : 41.6275

Key to rentals symbols:
12 🚐   **Number of mobile homes**
20 🏠   **Number of chalets**
6 🛏   **Number of rooms to rent**
Per night   **Minimum/maximum rate per night**
30–50€
Per week   **Minimum/maximum rate per week**
300–1,000€

PROPRIANO

20110 – Michelin map **345** C9 – pop. 3,292 – alt. 5
▶ Ajaccio 70 – Bastia 202 – Olbia 126 – Sassari 32

Village Vacances U Livanti
(rental of chalets only)

✆ 04 95 76 08 06, *www.ulivanti.com*
Address : at Portigliolo – rte de Campomoro (8km south along the RN 196 and take D 121; in the Gulf of Le Valinco)
Opening times : from mid March to mid Nov.
6 ha terraced
Rental rates : (2012 price) ⚡ ℗ – 92 🏠. Per week from 310 to 1,450 € – Reservation fee 10€
Pleasant restaurant terrace very close to the sea.

Surroundings : 🌳 ⛲ ⛱
Leisure activities : 🍷 ✗ 👫
Facilities : 📞 📮 📶 🖼
Nearby : 🚤 water skiing, scuba diving

GPS
Longitude : 8.86912
Latitude : 41.64491

SAGONE

20118 – Michelin map **345** B7
▶ Ajaccio 38 – Calvi 119 – Corte 106 – Sartène 110

Le Sagone 🏕

✆ 04 95 28 04 15, *www.camping-sagone.com*
Address : rte de Vico (situated 2km north along the D 70)
Opening times : from beginning April to end Sept.
30 ha/9 ha for camping (300 pitches) flat, grassy
Tariff : (2012 price) ⚡ 9.25€ 🚗 5.75€ 🔲 9.80€ – 📶 (6A) 4.50€ – Reservation fee 18.50€
Rental rates : (2012 price) (from beginning Feb. to end Nov.) – 6 🛖 – 30 🏠 – 20 tent bungalows. Per week from 200 to 970 € – Reservation fee 18.50€
🚽 sani-station
On cultivated land with some 2,500 olive, orange, mandarin and lemon trees.

Surroundings : 🌳 📮 ⛲
Leisure activities : ✗ 🎱 🎥 evening 👫 🛶 🏐 🏊 multi-sports ground
Facilities : ♿ 📞 🚿 🧺 launderette 🧊 refrigerated food storage
Nearby : 🛒

GPS
Longitude : 8.70524
Latitude : 42.13097

ST-FLORENT

20217 – Michelin map **345** E3 – pop. 1,636
▶ Bastia 22 – Calvi 70 – Corte 75 – L'Île-Rousse 45

La Pinede

✆ 04 95 37 07 26, *www.camping-la-pinede.com*
Address : at Serriggio (head 1.8km south following signs for l'Ile-Rousse and take road to the left after the bridge; beside the Aliso river)
Opening times : from beginning May to end Sept.
3 ha (100 pitches) terraced, relatively flat, flat, stony, grassy
Tariff : (2012 price) 38€ ⚡⚡ 🚗 🔲 📶 (16A) – Extra per person 6€
Rental rates : (2012 price) ⚡ – 20 🛖 – 10 🏠. Per week from 300 to 820 €

Surroundings : 🌳 ⛲
Leisure activities : 🎱 🏊 🎣
Facilities : ♿ 📞 🔲 launderette 🧊 refrigerators
Nearby : 🐴 ⚓

GPS
Longitude : 9.3004
Latitude : 42.66939

STE-LUCIE-DE-PORTO-VECCHIO

20144 – Michelin map **345** F9
▶ Ajaccio 142 – Porto-Vecchio 16

Homair Vacances Acqua E Sole
(rental of mobile homes and chalets only)

℘ 04 95 50 15 75, *www.homair.com*
Address : at Pianu Di Conca (located 1km northeast along the N 198; follow the signs for Solenzara and take road to the left)
Opening times : from beginning April to end Sept.
5 ha terraced, flat
Rental rates : (2012 price) &. – 117 ⟨⟩ – 28 ⌂ – 7 ⊨. Per night from 38 to 189 €
Per week from 266 to 1,329 € – Reservation fee 25€

Surroundings : ⌇ ♤♤
Leisure activities : ♈ ⤢
Facilities : ⊶ ♨ ⁖ launderette ⤳
Nearby : ⤜

 GPS Longitude : 9.35129
Latitude : 41.70328

Santa-Lucia

℘ 04 95 71 45 28, *www.campingsantalucia.com*
Opening times : from mid April to beginning Oct.
3 ha (160 pitches) flat and relatively flat, sandy, stony, rocks
Tariff : (2012 price) ⟰ 9.50€ ⇔ 3.60€ ▣ 5.65€ – ⚡ (6A) 2.60€ – Reservation fee 10€
Rental rates : (2012 price) (from mid April to beginning Oct.) ⤢ – 20 ⌂ – 1 tent bungalow.
Per week from 195 to 920 € Reservation fee 15€

Surroundings : ♨♨♨
Leisure activities : ✗ ⤜ ⤢ ⌢ ⤢
Facilities : &. ⊶ ⁖ ▣ ⤳
Nearby : ⤟

 GPS Longitude : 9.3434
Latitude : 41.6966

Fautea

℘ 04 95 71 41 51 ⤢
Address : at Fautea, by the sea (5km northeast on the N 198, follow the signs for Solenzara)
Opening times : from beginning May to end Sept.
5 ha (100 pitches) terraced, stony
Tariff : (2012 price) 30€ ⟰⟰ ⇔ ▣ ⚡ (6A)

Choose pitches on the small terraces with a sea view, further away from the road if possible.

Surroundings : ≼♤♤⛰
Leisure activities : ⤢
Facilities : ⊶ ⟐ ⒸⒸ ♨ ▣ ⤢
Nearby : ✗

 **GPS** Longitude : 9.40191
Latitude : 41.71557

Michelin classification:

⋀⋀⋀⋀ *Extremely comfortable, equipped to a very high standard*
⋀⋀⋀ *Very comfortable, equipped to a high standard*
⋀⋀ *Comfortable and well equipped*
⋀ *Reasonably comfortable*
⚠ *Satisfactory*

SERRA-DI-FERRO

20140 – Michelin map **345** B9 – pop. 458 – alt. 140
▶ Ajaccio 47 – Propriano 20 – Sartène 32

△ U Casellu

☎ 0495740180 ✄

Address : at Porto-Pollo (head 5km south along the D 155, follow the signs for Propriano and take D 757 to the right)

3.5 ha (100 pitches) flat, relatively flat, sandy, grassy

⛟ sani-station

Pleasant location beside the sea.

Surroundings : ♀ ⛰
Leisure activities : ♀ ✕
Facilities : ♿ ⟲ 📷

GPS Longitude : 8.80413
Latitude : 41.71234

TIUCCIA

20111 – Michelin map **345** B7
▶ Ajaccio 30 – Cargèse 22 – Vico 22

⋀ **Les Couchants**

☎ 0495522660, *camping-lescouchants.fr* ✉ 20111 Casaglione

Address : rte de Casaglione (4.9km north along the D 81 and turn right onto the D 25)

Opening times : from mid June to mid Sept.

5 ha (120 pitches) terraced, flat, grassy, stony

Tariff : (2012 Price) ♀ 7.50€ ⛌ 4€ 回 5.50€ – (½) (16A) 5€

Rental rates : (2012 price) (from mid June to mid Sept.) ✄ – 8 🏠. Per week from 600 to 770
Reservation fee 20€

Pitches surrounded by multi-coloured olive, eucalyptus and laurel trees.

Surroundings : ⛱ ≤ ♀♀
Leisure activities : ♀ ✕ ⚓ ♏
Facilities : ♿ ⟲ ⊞ ⌀ ⛆ 📷 ⛲

GPS Longitude : 8.74888
Latitude : 42.08126

VIVARIO

20219 – Michelin map **345** E6 – pop. 532 – alt. 850
▶ Bastia 89 – Aléria 49 – Corte 22 – Bocognano 22

△ **Aire Naturelle le Soleil**

☎ 0495472116, *camping-lesoleil@orange.fr* – alt. 800

Address : at Tattone (6 km southwest along the N 193, follow the signs for Ajaccio, near the station)

Opening times : from beginning May to beginning Oct.

1 ha (25 pitches) terraced, flat, grassy, relatively flat

Tariff : ♀ 7€ ⛌ 2€ 回 4€ – (½) (20A) 3€

⛟ 15 回 21€

Surroundings : ⛱ ≤ ♀
Leisure activities : ♀ ✕
Facilities : ⟲ ⌀
Nearby : ⟋

GPS Longitude : 9.15186
Latitude : 42.1532

Hervé Hughes / hemis.fr

Once upon a time in a land called Franche-Comté . . . many of France's tales and legends begin in the secret wilderness of this secluded region on the Swiss border. The high peaks and protected valleys of Jura, cloaked in fragrant conifers, cast a gentle charm over all who explore them. And an irresistible magic spell is woven by its cascading waterfalls, fascinating grottoes and mysterious lakes. The dark blue waters reflect the hills around them while forming a dramatic contrast with the lush green pastures. Nimble-fingered craftsmen transform the local wood into clocks, toys and pipes to the delight of all those who love and appreciate fine craftsmanship. Hungry travellers may want to savour the lovely hazelnut tang of Comté cheese but should beware the region's powerful gastronomic spell. The delicate smoked and salted meats, in which you can almost taste the pine and juniper, along with Franche-Comté's subtle but fruity wines, will have you coming back for more!

BELFORT

90000 – Michelin map **315** F11 – pop. 50,199 – alt. 360
▶ Paris 422 – Lure 33 – Luxeuil-les-Bains 52 – Montbéliard 23

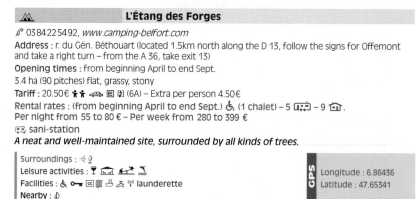

L'Étang des Forges

✆ 03 84 22 54 92, *www.camping-belfort.com*

Address : r. du Gén. Béthouart (located 1.5km north along the D 13, follow the signs for Offemont and take a right turn – from the A 36, take exit 13)

Opening times : from beginning April to end Sept.

3.4 ha (90 pitches) flat, grassy, stony

Tariff : 20.50€ ✯ ✯ ⇌ 🔲 🗲 (6A) – Extra per person 4.50€

Rental rates : (from beginning April to end Sept.) ⅙ (1 chalet) – 5 ⛺ – 9 🏠.
Per night from 55 to 80 € – Per week from 280 to 399 €

🚐 sani-station

A neat and well-maintained site, surrounded by all kinds of trees.

Surroundings : ≤ ♀
Leisure activities : ♈ 🏊 ⛵ ⤢
Facilities : ⅙ ⚡ 🔲 ⚙ 🍴 launderette
Nearby : ♨

GPS
Longitude : 6.86436
Latitude : 47.65341

BONLIEU

39130 – Michelin map **321** F7 – pop. 253 – alt. 785
▶ Paris 439 – Champagnole 23 – Lons-le-Saunier 32 – Morez 24

L'Abbaye

✆ 03 84 25 57 04, *www.camping-abbaye.com*

Address : 2 rte du Lac (located 1.5km east along the N 78, follow the signs for St-Laurent-en-Grandvaux)

Opening times : from beginning May to end Sept.

3 ha (88 pitches) sloping, flat, grassy

Tariff : 18.80€ ✯ ✯ ⇌ 🔲 🗲 (10A) – Extra per person 4.50€

Rental rates : (from beginning May to end Sept.) 🏠 – 4 ⛺ – 3 gîtes. Per night from 45 €
Per week from 270 to 480 €

🚐 sani-station 5€ – 4 🔲 9€

On a pretty site at the base of the cliffs, not far from the Le Hérisson waterfall.

Surroundings : ⛰ ≤ 🏕
Leisure activities : ♈ ✕ ⛵
Facilities : ⅙ ⚡ ⚙ 🍴 launderette 🚿
Nearby : 🐎 canoeing

GPS
Longitude : 5.87562
Latitude : 46.59199

BONNAL

25680 – Michelin map **321** I1 – pop. 21 – alt. 270
▶ Paris 392 – Besançon 47 – Belfort 51 – Épinal 106

Les Castels Le Val de Bonnal ▲

✆ 03 81 86 90 87, *www.camping-valdebonnal.com*

Address : 1 ch. du Moulin

Opening times : from beginning May to beginning Sept.

140 ha/15 ha for camping (280 pitches) flat, grassy

Tariff : (2012 price) 46€ ✯ ✯ ⇌ 🔲 🗲 (10A) – Extra per person 13€ – Reservation fee 20€

Rental rates : (2012 price) (from beginning May to beginning Sept.) 🏠 – 12 ⛺ – 6 🏠 –
2 tent bungalows. Per week from 340 to 1.150€ – Reservation fee 20€

🚐 sani-station

Pleasant location beside l'Ognon river and near a small lake.

Surroundings : ⛰ 🏕 ♀
Leisure activities : ♈ ✕ 🏊 🎮 evening 🏃 ⛵ 🚲 ⤢ △ 🎣
Facilities : ⅙ ⚡ ⚙ 🍴 launderette 🛒 🚿
Nearby : 🥾 forest trail

GPS
Longitude : 6.35619
Latitude : 47.50734

CHALEZEULE

25220 – Michelin map **321** G3 – pop. 1,180 – alt. 252 – ▶ Paris 410 – Dijon 96 – Lyon 229 – Nancy 209

Municipal de la Plage

✆ 0381880426, *www.campingdebesancon.com*
Address : 12 rte de Belfort (4.5km northeast along the N 83; beside the Doubs river)
Opening times : from beginning April to end Sept.
2.5 ha (132 pitches) terrace, flat, grassy
Tariff : (2012 Price) 15€ ✶✶ ⟚ 🔲 ⚡ (16A) – Extra per person 5.15€
Rental rates : (2012 price) (from beginning April to end Sept.) – 4 🛏 – 2 tent bungalows.
Per night from 33 to 85 € – Per week from 225 to 600€
🚐 sani-station 4€ – 10 🔲 17.95€ – 🔋 10.50€
Particular attention has been paid to the landscaping of the site with trees and shrubs etc,
but the sanitary facilities have seen better days.

Surroundings : 🌳🌳
Leisure activities : ✕ ⚓
Facilities : 🚿 ⟜ ▦ 🚻 🏋 launderette
Nearby : 🎿 🚵 🛶 🎣

GPS Longitude : 6.07103
Latitude : 47.26445

CHAMPAGNEY

70290 – Michelin map **314** H6 – pop. 3,728 – alt. 370
▶ Paris 413 – Besançon 115 – Vesoul 48

Domaine Des Ballastières

✆ 0384231122, *www.campinglesballastieres.com*
Address : 20 rue du Pâquis
Opening times : from beginning April to end Oct.
5 ha (110 pitches) relatively flat, flat, grassy
Tariff : (2012 price) 20.60€ ✶✶ ⟚ 🔲 ⚡ (16A) – Extra per person 3.70€
Rental rates : (2012 price) (from beginning April to end Oct.) 🚿 (1 mobile home) – 10 🛏.
Per week from 300 to 500€
🚐 sani-station – 10 🔲
Beside a small lake.

Leisure activities : 🏠 🏃 ⚓ 🚴 🛶
Facilities : 🚿 ⟜ 🆒 launderette
Nearby : 🎿 🎣 🐎 pedalos, forest trail

GPS Longitude : 6.67414
Latitude : 47.70615

CHAMPAGNOLE

39300 – Michelin map **321** F6 – pop. 8,088 – alt. 541
▶ Paris 420 – Besançon 66 – Dole 68 – Genève 86

Municipal de Boyse 🏕

✆ 0384520032, *www.camping.champagnole.com*
Address : 20 r. Georges Vallerey (take the northwestern exit along the D 5, follow the signs for
Lons-le-Saunier and take turning to the left)
Opening times : from beginning June to mid Sept.
9 ha/7 ha for camping (240 pitches) flat, grassy, relatively flat
Tariff : (2012 price) 20.80€ ✶✶ ⟚ 🔲 ⚡ (10A) – Extra per person 5€
Rental rates : (2012 price) (from beginning April to end Sept.) 🚿 (2 chalets) – 25 🏠.
Per night from 65 to 75€ – Per week from 235 to 575 €
🚐 sani-station 3.80€ – 5 🔲 5.50€
Pretty site on a hill looking out over the Ain river from an elevation of 30m. Direct access
along a road to the river.

Surroundings : 🌿 🌳🌳
Leisure activities : ✕ 🔵 🏃 ⚓ 🎣 🛶
Facilities : 🚿 ⟜ 🏋 launderette 🐾
Nearby : 🎿 🧩 🎣 sports trail

GPS Longitude : 5.89741
Latitude : 46.74643

CHÂTILLON

39130 – Michelin map **321** E7 – pop. 131 – alt. 500
▶ Paris 421 – Champagnole 24 – Clairvaux-les-Lacs 15 – Lons-le-Saunier 19

 Domaine de l'Épinette ♣♦

℘ 03 84 25 71 44, *www.domaine-epinette.com*
Address : 15 r. de l'Epinette (1.3km south along the D 151)
7 ha (150 pitches) terraced, relatively flat, flat, grassy, stony
Rentals : 71 ⦿ – 2 ⌂ – 4 tent bungalows.
⊟ sani-station – 12 ▣
Pitches on terraces on the side of a valley overlooking a river.

Surroundings : ⅏ ≼
Leisure activities : ⌨ ⚲ ⚤ ⌗ ⚓ ⚐ ⚒
Facilities : ⅄ ☞ ⚖ launderette ⚒ ⚐

Longitude : 5.72218
Latitude : 46.6513

CHAUX DES CROTENAY

▶ Paris 440 – Besançon 88 – Lons-le-Saunier 48

Municipal du Bois Joli

℘ 03 84 51 50 00, *www.chaletsalesiajura.com*
Address : 8 rte de la piscine
Opening times : from beginning June to end Sept.
1 ha (42 pitches) flat, grassy
Tariff : (2012 price) ♣ 3€ ⇔ ▣ 5.50€ ⚡ (6A)
Rental rates : (2012 price) (permanent) ⅄ (1 chalet) – 5 ⦿ – 8 ⌂. Per night 100€
Per week from 370 to 480 €
Pretty view of the surrounding hills.

Surroundings : ≼ mountains
Leisure activities : ⌨ ⚤
Facilities : ⅄ ☞ ⚞ launderette
Nearby : ⚒ ⚑ ⚙ ⚓ ⌗

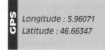
Longitude : 5.96071
Latitude : 46.66347

To visit a town or region, use the MICHELIN Green Guides.

CLAIRVAUX-LES-LACS

39130 – Michelin map **321** E7 – pop. 1,454 – alt. 540
▶ Paris 428 – Bourg-en-Bresse 94 – Champagnole 34 – Lons-le-Saunier 22

Yelloh! Village Le Fayolan ♣♦

℘ 03 84 25 88 52, *www.campinglefayolan.fr*
Address : r. du Langard (1.2km southeast along the D 118)
Opening times : from beginning May to beginning Sept.
17 ha/13 ha for camping (516 pitches) terraced, relatively flat, flat, grassy, pine trees
Tariff : 42€ ♣♣ ⇔ ▣ ⚡ (10A) – Extra per person 8€
Rental rates : (from beginning May to beginning Sept.) – 112 ⦿ – 10 tents.
Per night from 29 to 154 € – Per week from 203 to 1,078 €
⊟ sani-station 19€ – ⛟ ⚡14€
Beside a lake, with numerous services and leisure facilities.

Surroundings : ≼ ⚏ ♀ ⛰
Leisure activities : ⚑ ✗ ⌨ ☺ ⚲ ⛱ hammam ⚤ ▣ ⌗ ⚓ ⚐
entertainment room
Facilities : ⅄ ☞ ⚖ ⚞ ⚙ ⚑ launderette ⚒ ⚐
Nearby : ⚒ fitness trail

Longitude : 5.75
Latitude : 46.56667

Le Grand Lac ♣♣

📞 03 84 25 22 14, *www.odesia-clairvaux.com*
Address : ch. du Langard (800m southeast along the D 118, follow the signs for Châtel-de-Joux and take the road to the right)
2.5 ha (191 pitches) terraced, relatively flat, flat, grassy
Rentals : 33 .
sani-station
Beside the lake with a beautiful beach and an impressive diving board into the lake!

Surroundings : ⩽ ♀ ⚠ Leisure activities : ☺ 🏕 🚣 ⊒ ≅ (beach) 🦢 pedalos Facilities : 🚿 ☎ 🛁 ⚐ launderette Nearby : ♟	**GPS** Longitude : 5.75507 Latitude : 46.56823

CROMARY

70190 – Michelin map **314** E8 – pop. 236 – alt. 219
▶ Paris 419 – Belfort 88 – Besançon 21 – Gray 50

L'Esplanade

📞 03 84 91 82 00, *www.lesplanade.nl*
Address : r.du Pont (south of the town along the D 276)
2.7 ha (65 pitches) flat, grassy
On a rural site with direct access to the river

Surroundings : 🌿 ⩽ 🏞 Leisure activities : ✗ 🦢 Facilities : 🚿 ☎ 🗑	**GPS** Longitude : 6.07865 Latitude : 47.35881

The classification (1 to 5 tents, black or red) that we award to selected sites in this guide is our own system. It should not be confused with the classification (1 to 5 stars) of official organisations.

DOLE

39100 – Michelin map **321** C4 – pop. 24,906 – alt. 220
▶ Paris 363 – Besançon 55 – Chalon-sur-Saône 67 – Dijon 50

Le Pasquier

📞 03 84 72 02 61, *http://www.camping-le-pasquier.com*
Address : 18 ch. Victor et Georges Thévenot (to the southeast along the av. Jean-Jaurès)
Opening times : from mid March to end Oct.
2 ha (120 pitches) flat, grassy, fine gravel
Tariff : (2012 price) 16.40€ ♣♣ ⇌ 🔲 ⚡ (10A) – Extra per person 3.80€ – Reservation fee 10€
Rental rates : (2012 price) (from mid March to end Oct.) – 10 – 4 tent bungalows.
Per night from 30 to 64 € – Per week from 165 to 450 € – Reservation fee 10€
In a lush, green setting near the Doubs river, with a view of the Dole collegiate church.

Surroundings : ♀ Leisure activities : ♟ ✗ ☺ daytime 🚣 ⊒ (small swimming pool) Facilities : 🚿 ☎ 🛁 ⚐ ♨ launderette Nearby : ≅ 🦢	**GPS** Longitude : 5.50357 Latitude : 47.08982

DOUCIER

39130 – Michelin map **321** E7 – pop. 296 – alt. 526
▶ Paris 427 – Champagnole 21 – Lons-le-Saunier 25

Domaine de Chalain ♠♣

📞 03 84 25 78 78, *www.chalain.com*
Address : 3km to the northeast
Opening times : from end April to mid Sept.
30 ha/18 ha for camping (712 pitches) flat, grassy, stony
Tariff : 41€ ♣♣ ⇔ 🔲 🅿 (10A) – Extra per person 7€
Rental rates : (from end April to mid Sept.) 🏕 – 59 🚐 – 35 🏠 – 41 chalets bois (without sanitary facilities). Per night from 42 to 151€ – Per week from 252 to 1,057 €
🚽 sani-station 2€
Attractive location ringed by cliffs, situated by a forest and the Lac de Chalain.

Surroundings : ≤ ♀ ⚠
Leisure activities : 🍴 ✕ 🎦 🛖 ⛹ 🏓 ☔ jacuzzi 🚣 ⛵ ✕ ⛳ 🔲 🏊
⛱ ⛷ ⌖
Facilities : ⚕ ⚷ ▥ ⛺ ⛴ ☂ 🍴 launderette ⚒ ⚒ refrigerated food storage

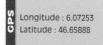
GPS
Longitude : 5.81395
Latitude : 46.66422

FONCINE-LE-HAUT

39460 – Michelin map **321** G7 – pop. 1,027 – alt. 790
▶ Paris 444 – Champagnole 24 – Clairvaux-les-Lacs 34 – Lons-le-Saunier 62

Les Chalets du Val de Saine
(rental of chalets only)

📞 03 84 51 93 11, *www.camping-haut-jura.com* – alt. 900 – chalet rental with some traditional pitches
Address : take the southwestern exit along the D437, follow the signs for St-Laurent-en-Grandvaux and take the turning to the left, by the stadium; beside the Saine river
Opening times : permanent
1.2 ha flat
Rental rates : 🅿 – 14 🏠 . Per night from 60 to 175 € – Per week from 250 to 450 €
🚽 sani-station 3€ – 10 🔲 4€

Surroundings : ⌖
Leisure activities : ⌖
Facilities : 🍴 launderette
Nearby : ⚒ 🍴 ✕ ✕ 🎦

GPS
Longitude : 6.07253
Latitude : 46.65888

FRESSE

70270 – Michelin map **314** H6 – pop. 725 – alt. 472
▶ Paris 405 – Belfort 31 – Épinal 71 – Luxeuil-les-Bains 30

La Broche

📞 03 84 63 31 40, *www.camping-broche.com*
Address : at Le Volvet (take the western exit, follow the signs for Melesey and then take road to the left)
Opening times : from mid April to mid Oct.
2 ha (50 pitches) terrace, relatively flat, flat, grassy
Tariff : 12€ ♣♣ ⇔ 🔲 🅿 (10A) – Extra per person 3€
🚽 sani-station 2€ – 🚐 🅿 12€
A hilly, wooded site beside a lake.

Surroundings : ⌖ ≤ ♀
Leisure activities : ⌖
Facilities : ⚕ ⚷ 🚿 🔲

GPS
Longitude : 6.65269
Latitude : 47.75587

HUANNE-MONTMARTIN

25680 – Michelin map **321** I2 – pop. 83 – alt. 310
▶ Paris 392 – Baume-les-Dames 14 – Besançon 37 – Montbéliard 52

Le Bois de Reveuge

℘ 0381843860, *www.campingduboisdereveuge.com*
Address : rte de Rougemont (1.1km north along the D 113)
Opening times : from end April to beginning Sept.
24 ha/15 ha for camping (320 pitches) terraced, flat, grassy, gravelled, wood
Tariff : (2012 price) 33€ ✦✦ ⇔ 🔲 ⍗ (6A) – Extra per person 8€ – Reservation fee 25€
Rental rates : (2012 price) (from end April to beginning Sept.) – 118 ⬚⬚ – 34 ⌂ .
Per night from 44 to 144 € – Per week from 264 to 1,008 € – Reservation fee 25€
⬚⬚ sani-station 20€ – 50 🔲 20€
Set around two large lakes on the edge of a wood.

Surroundings : ⟰ ⬚ ♤♤
Leisure activities : ⍓ ✕ 🎦 ☷ ⚲ ᷥ ⚡ ᷤ ᷥ 🎦 ⟁ ⟍ 🐴
Facilities : & ⌒ ⟰ ⟿ �"⍟ launderette ⟰

Longitude : 6.3447
Latitude : 47.44346

LABERGEMENT-STE-MARIE

25160 – Michelin map **321** H6 – pop. 1,040 – alt. 859
▶ Paris 454 – Champagnole 41 – Pontarlier 17 – St-Laurent-en-Grandvaux 41

Le Lac

℘ 0381693124, *www.camping-lac-remoray.com*
Address : 10 r. du Lac (take the southwestern exit along the D 437, follow the signs for Mouthe and take turning to the right)
Opening times : from beginning May to end Sept.
1.8 ha (80 pitches) terraced, relatively flat, flat, grassy
Tariff : ✦ 4.80€ ⇔ 🔲 6.60€ – ⍗ (6A) 4.40€ – Reservation fee 5€
Rental rates : (from beginning May to end Sept.) – 4 ⬚⬚ – 4 ⌂ . Per week from 198 to 655 €
Reservation fee 5€
Site is 300m from the Lac de Remoray.

Surroundings : ⟨
Leisure activities : ⍓ ✕ 🎦 ⚲
Facilities : & ⌒ ⟰ launderette ⟰
Nearby : ✕ ⟿ ⟍

Longitude : 6.27563
Latitude : 46.77134

LACHAPELLE-SOUS-ROUGEMONT

90360 – Michelin map **315** G10 – pop. 549 – alt. 400
▶ Paris 442 – Belfort 16 – Basel 66 – Colmar 55

Le Lac de la Seigneurie

℘ 0384230013, *www.camping-lac-seigneurie.com*
Address : 3 r. de la Seigneurie (3.2km north along the D 11, follow the signs for Lauw)
Opening times : from beginning April to end Oct.
4 ha (110 pitches) flat, grassy
Tariff : 17€ ✦✦ ⇔ 🔲 ⍗ (10A) – Extra per person 4€ – Reservation fee 15€
Rental rates : (from beginning April to end Oct.) & (1 chalet) ⟿ – 2 ⬚⬚ – 1 ⌂ .
Per night 120€ – Per week 565€ – Reservation fee 15€
⬚⬚ sani-station 5€ – 9 🔲 17€ – ⟿16.50€
A quiet country location at the edge of a forest and near a lake.

Surroundings : ⟰ ⬚ ♀
Leisure activities : 🎦 ᷤ ⟍
Facilities : & ⌒ launderette
Nearby : ✕ ⟍

Longitude : 7.01498
Latitude : 47.73613

LEVIER

25270 – Michelin map **321** G5 – pop. 1,949 – alt. 719
▶ Paris 443 – Besançon 45 – Champagnole 37 – Pontarlier 22

⚠ La Forêt

℘ 03 81 89 53 46, *www.camping-dela-foret.com*
Address : rte de Septfontaines (located 1km northeast along the D 41)
Opening times : from beginning May to mid Sept.
4 ha/2.5 ha for camping (70 pitches) terrace, relatively flat, flat, grassy
Tariff : 22.40€ ✝✝ ⟵ 🔲 (10A) – Extra per person 4.10€ – Reservation fee 10€
Rental rates : (2012 price) (permanent) – 2 🛏 – 8 🏠. Per night from 53 to 143€
Per week from 258 to 700 € – Reservation fee 10€
🔳 10 🔲 18.80€
Nestling at the edge of a forest in a very beautiful setting of trees and rocky outcrops.

Surroundings : 🌲 ♉♉
Leisure activities : 🎦 ⛵ 🚲 ⛴
Facilities : ⛿ ⊶ 🛁 ⛺ 🚰 launderette
Nearby : sports trail

GPS Longitude : 6.13308
Latitude : 46.95915

LONS-LE-SAUNIER

39000 – Michelin map **321** D6 – pop. 17,907 – alt. 255 – ♨ (beg Apr to end Oct)
▶ Paris 408 – Besançon 84 – Bourg-en-Bresse 73 – Chalon-sur-Saône 61

⚠ La Marjorie

℘ 03 84 24 26 94, *www.camping-marjorie.com*
Address : 640 bd de l'Europe (to the northeast towards Besançon along the bd de Ceinture)
Opening times : from mid March to mid Oct.
9 ha/3 ha for camping (193 pitches) flat, grassy, stony, hard surface areas
Tariff : 21.90€ ✝✝ ⟵ 🔲 (10A) – Extra per person 5.15€ – Reservation fee 15€
Rental rates : (from end March to mid Oct.) ⛿ (1 chalet) – 4 🛏 – 15 🏠.
Per night from 55 to 80 € – Per week from 220 to 650 € – Reservation fee 15€
🔳 sani-station 4.50€ – 38 🔲 15.95€
Attractive trees and shrubs; beside a stream.

Surroundings : 🔲 ♉♉
Leisure activities : 🍸 🎦 🎲 evening 🏃
Facilities : ⛿ ⊶ 🍴 🛁 ⛺ 🚰 launderette 🔲 🔲
Nearby : 🍴 🔲 ⛴

GPS Longitude : 5.56855
Latitude : 46.68422

LUXEUIL-LES-BAINS

70300 – Michelin map **314** G6 – pop. 7,370 – alt. 305
▶ Paris 380 – Besançon 88 – Vesoul 35

⚠ Domaine du Chatigny

℘ 03 84 93 97 97, *www.camping.luxeuil.fr*
Address : 14 r. Grammont
4.5 ha (98 pitches) flat, grassy
Rentals : ⛿ (2 chalets) – 5 🛏 – 15 🏠.
🔳 sani-station – 8 🔲 – 🔋 10€
In the town centre; a pleasant, well-maintained, green setting.

Surroundings : 🌲 ♉
Leisure activities : 🍸 🍴 🎦 ⛵ 🚲 🍴 ⛴ multi-sports ground
Facilities : ⊶ 🍴 🛁 launderette
Nearby : 🛒

GPS Longitude : 6.37876
Latitude : 47.82259

331

MAICHE

25120 – Michelin map **321** K3 – pop. 4,282 – alt. 777
▶ Paris 501 – Baume-les-Dames 69 – Besançon 74 – Montbéliard 43

Municipal St-Michel

0381641256, www.mairie-maiche.fr
Address : 23 r. Saint-Michel (head 1.3km south on the D 422 before joining the D 464, follow the signs for Charquemont and take the D 437 heading for Pontarlier – recommended route via the D 437, follow the signs for Pontarlier)
Opening times : from mid Dec. to mid Nov.
2 ha (70 pitches) terraced, relatively flat, grassy, wood
Tariff : (2012 price) 🚶 3.30€ 🚐 ▣ 4.40€ – (⚡) (10A) 4.40€
Rental rates : (2012 price) (from mid Dec. to mid Nov.) – 5 🏠. Per night 55€ – Per week 275€
🚰 8 ▣ 11€
Near an indoor water park.

Surroundings : ⚲
Leisure activities :
Facilities : ♿ ⌁ ⊞ ▦
Nearby : ⌦ hammam, jacuzzi ▨ ⩘ ⟋

GPS — Longitude : 6.80109 — Latitude : 47.24749

MAISOD

39260 – Michelin map **321** E8 – pop. 316 – alt. 520
▶ Paris 436 – Lons-le-Saunier 30 – Oyonnax 34 – St-Claude 29

Trelachaume

0384420326, www.trelachaume.fr
Address : 50 rte du Mont du Cerf (2.2km south along the D 301 and take turning to the right)
Opening times : from mid April to beginning Sept.
3 ha (180 pitches) relatively flat, flat, grassy, stony
Tariff : (2012 price) 19.70€ 🚶🚶 🚐 ▣ (⚡) (10A) – Extra per person 3.95€
Rental rates : (2012 price) (from beginning April to mid Sept.) ⌘ – 10 ▱ – 6 🏠 –
5 tent bungalows. Per week from 199 to 642 €
Nestling in woods looking down over the Lac de Vouglans.

Surroundings : ⛰ ⚲⚲
Leisure activities : ▭ ◉ ⚡ cinema
Facilities : ♿ ⚷ ⌂ ⚑ launderette

GPS — Longitude : 5.68875 — Latitude : 46.46873

MALBUISSON

25160 – Michelin map **321** H6 – pop. 687 – alt. 900 – Leisure centre
▶ Paris 456 – Besançon 74 – Champagnole 42 – Pontarlier 16

Les Fuvettes 🏕🏕

0381693150, www.camping-fuvettes.com
Address : 24 rte de la Plage et des Perrières (located 1km southwest)
Opening times : from beginning April to end Sept.
6 ha (306 pitches) flat and relatively flat, grassy, stony
Tariff : 25.30€ 🚶🚶 🚐 ▣ (⚡) (6A) – Extra per person 5€ – Reservation fee 10€
Rental rates : (from beginning April to end Sept.) ♿ (1 mobile home) – 35 ▱ – 10 🏠 –
3 tent bungalows. Per night from 70 to 140 € – Per week from 285 to 895 €
Reservation fee 15€
🚰 sani-station 3€
Beside the Lac de St-Point, near a mini water activity park.

Surroundings : ⩻⚲⚠
Leisure activities : ▾ ✗ ▭ ◉ ⚡ ⚡ ⩘ ▨ ⩘ ⟋ mini farm with ponies and alpacas
Facilities : ♿ ⚷ (Jul–Aug) ⌂ ⚑ launderette ⬚ ⤳
Nearby : canoeing, pedalos

GPS — Longitude : 6.29391 — Latitude : 46.79232

MANDEURE

25350 – Michelin map **321** K2 – pop. 4,959 – alt. 336
▶ Paris 473 – Baume-les-Dames 41 – Maîche 34 – Sochaux 15

Municipal les Grands Ansanges

℘ 03 81 35 23 79, *www.ville-mandeure.com*
Address : r. de l'Église (located to the northwest, take exit towards Pont-de-Roide; beside the Doubs)
1.7 ha (96 pitches) flat, grassy

Fairly simple site but perfect for a one-night stay.

Surroundings : 🌳
Leisure activities : 🍺 🏓 🏛 🎣
Facilities : launderette

GPS
Longitude : 6.80556
Latitude : 47.45557

MARIGNY

39130 – Michelin map **321** E6 – pop. 177 – alt. 519
▶ Paris 426 – Arbois 32 – Champagnole 17 – Doucier 5

Les Castels La Pergola ♠♠

℘ 03 84 25 70 03, *www.lapergola.com*
Address : 1 rue des vernois (800m to the south)
Opening times : from beginning May to beginning Sept.
10 ha (350 pitches) terraced, flat, grassy, stony
Tariff : 41€ ♦♦ 🚐 🔲 🔋 (16A) – Extra per person 8€ – Reservation fee 30€
Rental rates : (from beginning May to beginning Sept.) – 154 🚐. Per night from 53 to 165€
Per week from 296 to 1.165€ – Reservation fee 30€
🚐 sani-station – 🔋 🔋 15€

Good swimming pool and sunbathing area overlooking the Lac de Chalain and some luxurious mobile homes.

Surroundings : ≪ 🏕 🌳 ⛰
Leisure activities : 🍺 ✕ 🏓 🎲 🏕 🏊 🚴 🏖 🏊 🎣 💧
Facilities : 🚿 🔌 🔲 🛁 🚐 🚰 ⛲ launderette 🧺 🐕

GPS
Longitude : 5.77984
Latitude : 46.67737

Some campsites benefit from proximity to a municipal leisure centre.

MÉLISEY

70270 – Michelin map **314** H6 – pop. 1,699 – alt. 330
▶ Paris 397 – Belfort 33 – Épinal 63 – Luxeuil-les-Bains 22

La Pierre

℘ 03 84 20 84 38, *http://melisey.cchvo.org/index.php?IdPage=1238083072* – limited spaces for one-night stay – 🏕
Address : at Les Granges Baverey (2.7km north on the D 293, follow the signs for Mélay)
Opening times : from beginning May to end Sept.
1.5 ha (58 pitches) relatively flat, flat, grassy
Tariff : (2012 price) ♦ 3€ 🚐 1.30€ 🔲 3€ – 🔋 (6A) 2.20€
Rental rates : (permanent) – 4 🏠 – 2 gîtes. Per night from 80 to 100€
Per week from 220 to 354 € – Reservation fee 16€
🚐 sani-station 6€ – 8 🔲 4€ – 🔋 10€
Picturesque setting on a wooded site.

Surroundings : 🦌 🏕 🌳
Leisure activities : 🏓 🏊
Facilities : 🚿 🚻 📺

GPS
Longitude : 6.58101
Latitude : 47.77552

MESNOIS

39130 – Michelin map **321** E7 – pop. 202 – alt. 460
▶ Paris 431 – Besançon 90 – Lons 18 – Chalon 77

Beauregard

℘ 03 84 48 32 51, *www.juracampingbeauregard.com*
Address : 2 Grande-Rue (take the southern exit)
Opening times : from beginning April to end Sept.
6 ha/4.5 ha for camping (192 pitches) terraced, relatively flat, grassy
Tariff : (2012 price) 29.50€ ♥♥ ⟵ 回 (♫) (6A) – Extra per person 5.20€ – Reservation fee 10€
Rental rates : (2012 price) (from beginning April to end Sept.) – 38 ⟦⟧ – 5 tent bungalows –
1 gîte. Per night from 35 to 107€ – Per week from 245 to 749 € – Reservation fee 10€

Partially open-air water park.

Surroundings : ⪤ ⟷ ⛲
Leisure activities : ♈ ✗ ⟬ ⪢ hammam, jacuzzi ⟿ ✂ ⟬ ⟬ ⟬ ⟬
Facilities : ⟬ ⟬ ⟬ ⟬ launderette ⟬

GPS Longitude : 5.68878
Latitude : 46.60036

> *We have selected the best campsites in France with our usual care,*
> *listing those with the best facilities in the most pleasant surroundings.*

MONNET-LA-VILLE

39300 – Michelin map **321** E6 – pop. 372 – alt. 550
▶ Paris 421 – Arbois 28 – Champagnole 11 – Doucier 10

Sous Doriat

℘ 03 84 51 21 43, *www.camping-sous-doriat.com*
Address : 34 r. Marcel Hugon (take the northern exit along the D 27e, follow the signs for Ney)
Opening times : from beginning May to end Sept.
3 ha (110 pitches) flat, grassy
Tariff : 19.50€ ♥♥ ⟵ 回 (♫) (10A) – Extra per person 4€ – Reservation fee 10€
Rental rates : (2012 price) (permanent) – 15 ⟦⟧ – 5 ⟬ – 4 tent bungalows.
Per night from 25 to 85 € – Per week from 175 to 600 € – Reservation fee 10€
⟬ sani-station 16€
A fairly simple site with a fine view of the Jura mountains.

Surroundings : ⪤ ⛲
Leisure activities : ⟬ ⟿ ⟬ multi-sports area
Facilities : ⟬ ⟬ ⟬ ⟬ launderette
Nearby : ⟬ ♈ ✗

GPS Longitude : 5.79779
Latitude : 46.72143

Du Gît

℘ 03 84 51 21 17, *http://www.campingdugit.com*
Address : 7 ch. du Gît (located 1km southeast along the D 40, follow the signs for Mont-sur-Monnet
and take the road to the right)
Opening times : from beginning June to end Aug.
6 ha (60 pitches) relatively flat, flat, grassy
Tariff : ♥ 4€ ⟵ 2.50€ 回 2.50€ – (♫) (5A) 3€
Rental rates : (from beginning June to end Aug.) – 2 ⟦⟧. Per night from 40 to 70 €
Per week from 250 to 400 €
⟬ sani-station
A simple site with rather jaded sanitary facilities.

Surroundings : ⟬ ⪤
Leisure activities : ⟬ ⟿
Facilities : ⟬ ⟬ ⟬ ⟬ ⟬

GPS Longitude : 5.79733
Latitude : 46.71234

ORNANS

25290 – Michelin map **321** G4 – pop. 4,152 – alt. 355
▸ Paris 428 – Baume-les-Dames 42 – Besançon 26 – Morteau 48

Domaine Le Chanet ▲▴

℘ 03 81 62 23 44, *www.lechanet.com*
Address : 9 ch. du Chanet (located 1.5km southwest along the D 241, follow the signs for Chassagne-St-Denis and take the road to the right; 100m from the Loue)
Opening times : from beginning April to mid Oct.
1.4 ha (95 pitches) sloping, relatively flat, grassy
Tariff : (2012 price) 27.90€ ✶✶ ⊞ 回 [⚡] (10A) – Extra per person 5€ – Reservation fee 15€
Rental rates : (2012 price) (from beginning April to mid Oct.) – 25 🚐 – 9 tents – 3 gîtes.
Per night from 45 to 90€ – Per week from 220 to 710€ – Reservation fee 15€
🚰 sani-station 3€ – 5 回 15€
In the hills above the town; features an ecological swimming pool.

Surroundings : 🌳 ≤ 👥👥
Leisure activities : ☏ ✗ 🎬 ⚐ 🏊 ⚿ 🛶 🏊
Facilities : 🚿 ⚷ 🗑 🛁 ☂ launderette
Nearby : 🚲 ⚼ 🎣

GPS
Longitude : 6.12779
Latitude : 47.10164

La Roche d'Ully

℘ 03 81 57 17 79, *www.camping-ornans.com*
Address : allée de la Tour de Peilz
Opening times : from beginning April to mid Oct.
2 ha (125 pitches) flat, grassy
Tariff : (2012 price) 33€ ✶✶ ⊞ 回 [⚡] (6A) – Extra per person 5.50€
Rental rates : (2012 price) (from beginning April to mid Oct.) – 7 🏠 – 10 tents.
Per night from 45 to 140 € – Per week from 210 to 880 €
🚰 sani-station

Surroundings : ▭
Leisure activities : ☏ ✗ ⚐ 🛶 🚲
Facilities : 🚿 ⚷ ☂ ⚌ ☂ 🖼 ☂
Nearby : ⚿ hammam, jacuzzi 🏊 🏊 ⚒ 🎣

GPS
Longitude : 6.15807
Latitude : 47.10286

OUNANS

39380 – Michelin map **321** D5 – pop. 371 – alt. 230
▸ Paris 383 – Arbois 16 – Arc-et-Senans 13 – Dole 23

La Plage Blanche ▲▴

℘ 03 84 37 69 63, *www.la-plage-blanche.com*
Address : 3 r. de la Plage (located 1.5km north along the D 71, follow the signs for Montbarey and take road to the left)
Opening times : from beginning April to end Sept.
7 ha (218 pitches) flat, grassy
Tariff : 28€ ✶✶ ⊞ 回 [⚡] (10A) – Extra per person 5.50€
Rental rates : (from beginning April to end Sept.) – 6 🚐 – 4 tent bungalows.
Per night from 40 to 125€ – Per week from 280 to 750 €
🚰 sani-station 5€ – 2 回 10€
Site on the banks of the Loue river.

Surroundings : 🌳 ♨
Leisure activities : ☏ ✗ 🎬 ⚑ evening ⚐ ⚿ jacuzzi 🛶 🏊 🎣 🐎 multi-sports ground
Facilities : 🚿 ⚷ 🗑 ☂ launderette ⚌ ☂
Nearby : 🚲

GPS
Longitude : 5.66333
Latitude : 47.00276

Le Val d'Amour

☎ 03 84 37 61 89, *www.levaldamour.com*

Address : 1 r. du Val d'Amour (take the eastern exit along the D 472, towards Chamblay)
Opening times : from beginning April to mid Oct.
3.7 ha (97 pitches) flat, grassy, fruit trees
Tariff : (2012 price) 20.90€ ✶✶ ⇔ 🅴 🄰 (10A) – Extra per person 5.50€ – Reservation fee 8€
Rental rates : (2012 price) (from beginning April to mid Oct.) – 14 ⬚ – 6 🏠 – 6 tents –
3 mobile homes and 2 huts (without sanitary facilities). Per night from 35 to 90 €
Per week from 220 to 650 € – Reservation fee 8€
🚐 sani-station 3€ – 🚐 17.40€
Attractive floral decoration.

Surroundings : ◔ ♤♤
Leisure activities : ✗ ◈ ⚓ ♧ ⏬ mountain biking
Facilities : ♿ ⚏ ⚐ ⸮ launderette
Nearby : ⚘

Longitude : 5.6733
Latitude : 46.99103

70140 – Michelin map **314** B9 – pop. 1,111 – alt. 205
▶ Paris 387 – Besançon 52 – Vesoul 64 – Dijon 69

La Colombière

☎ 03 84 31 20 15, *mairie-pesmes@wanadoo.fr*

Address : take the southern exit along the D 475, follow the signs for Dole; beside the Ognon river
Opening times : from beginning May to end Oct.
1 ha (70 pitches) flat, grassy
Tariff : (2012 price) 16.20€ ✶✶ ⇔ 🅴 🄰 (16A) – Extra per person 2.40€ – Reservation fee 4.80€
Rental rates : (2012 price) (from beginning May to end Oct.) – 4 ⬚ – 1 gîte.
Per night from 48 € – Per week from 180 to 240€ – Reservation fee 4.80€
🚐 sani-station 2.40€ – 5 🅴 12.60€
Beside the river, not far from the town centre.

Surroundings : ♀
Leisure activities : ⚓ ⬟
Facilities : ♿ ⚏ ⚐ ⊠ ▥ ⛺ ⸮
Nearby : 🍷 ✗ ♧

Longitude : 5.56392
Latitude : 47.27403

The information in the guide may have changed since going to press.

39800 – Michelin map **321** E5 – pop. 4,229 – alt. 373
▶ Paris 397 – Besançon 57 – Dole 45 – Lons-le-Saunier 30

La Croix du Dan

☎ 03 84 73 77 58, *cccg.tv*

Address : rte de Lons-Le-Saunier (located 1km southwest along the N 83 towards Lons-le-Saunier)
Opening times : from beginning June to mid Sept.
1.5 ha (87 pitches) flat, grassy
Tariff : (2012 price) ✶ 2.15€ ⇔ 2.15€ 🅴 2.65€ – 🄰 (10A) 7.50€
🚐 sani-station
On the southern outskirts of the town; ideal for a stopover.

Surroundings : ≤ ♀
Leisure activities : ⚓
Facilities : ♿ ⚏ ⚐ ⸮

Longitude : 5.70078
Latitude : 46.83424

PONTARLIER

25300 – Michelin map **321** I5 – pop. 18,267 – alt. 838
▶ Paris 462 – Basel 180 – Beaune 164 – Belfort 126

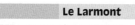

Le Larmont

✆ 03 81 46 23 33, *www.camping-pontarlier.fr* – alt. 880
Address : ch. du Toulombief (to the southeast towards Lausanne, near the riding centre)
Opening times : from mid Dec. to mid Nov.
4 ha (75 pitches) terraced, flat, grassy, gravelled
Tariff : (2012 price) 20.90€ ✖✖ ⇌ ▣ ⒣ (10A) – Extra per person 4€ – Reservation fee 10€
Rental rates : (2012 price) (from mid Dec. to mid Nov.) – 7 ⌂. Per night from 49 to 110€
Per week from 290 to 630 € – Reservation fee 10€
⛽ sani-station 5.50€ – 20 ▣ 9€ – 🛒 9€
On a hillside with well-marked out pitches.

Surroundings : 🦌 ⩽ 🏠
Leisure activities : 🎬 🏊
Facilities : & ⚡ 🏢 ⛺ ⛱ 🚮 🍴 launderette
Nearby : 🏃 sports trail

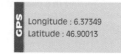
Longitude : 6.37349
Latitude : 46.90013

We value your opinion and welcome your feedback.
Do email us at campingfrance@tp.michelin.com

QUINGEY

25440 – Michelin map **321** F4 – pop. 1,300 – alt. 275
▶ Paris 397 – Baume-les-Dames 40 – Besançon 23 – Morteau 78

Municipal Les Promenades

✆ 03 81 63 74 01, *www.campingquingey.fr*
Address : to the at Les Promenades (take the southern exit, follow the signs for Lons-le-Saunier and take road to the right after the bridge)
Opening times : from beginning May to end Sept.
1.5 ha (75 pitches) flat, grassy, gravelled
Tariff : (2012 price) ✖ 4€ ⇌ 4€ – ⒣ (16A) 3€
Site is on the bank of the Loue river, near the town centre and a water sports leisure and activity park.

Surroundings : 🏠 ♨
Leisure activities : 🏊 ✖ 🎣
Facilities : & ⚡ (Jul–Aug) ⛱ 🚮 launderette
Nearby : 🏊 ✖ 🚲

Longitude : 5.88928
Latitude : 47.10454

RENAUCOURT

70120 – Michelin map **314** C7 – pop. 107 – alt. 209
▶ Paris 338 – Besançon 58 – Bourbonne-les-Bains 49 – Épinal 98

Municipal la Fontaine aux Fées

✆ 03 84 92 06 22
Address : Route de Volon (1.3km southwest, follow the signs for Volon)
2 ha (23 pitches) flat, grassy
On the edge of a wood, near a lake.

Surroundings : 🦌 ♨
Facilities : ⚡ ⛱
Nearby : 🏊 🎣

Longitude : 5.75707
Latitude : 47.63468

ST-CLAUDE

39200 – Michelin map **321** F8 – pop. 11,355 – alt. 450
▶ Paris 465 – Annecy 88 – Bourg-en-Bresse 90 – Genève 60

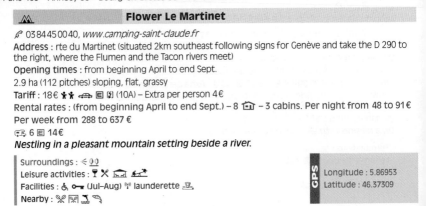

Flower Le Martinet

℘ 03 84 45 00 40, *www.camping-saint-claude.fr*
Address : rte du Martinet (situated 2km southeast following signs for Genève and take the D 290 to the right, where the Flumen and the Tacon rivers meet)
Opening times : from beginning April to end Sept.
2.9 ha (112 pitches) sloping, flat, grassy
Tariff : 18€ �†�†ᕋ ⊡ 闭 (10A) – Extra per person 4€
Rental rates : (from beginning April to end Sept.) – 8 ⌂ – 3 cabins. Per night from 48 to 91€
Per week from 288 to 637 €
ᕋ 6 ⊡ 14€
Nestling in a pleasant mountain setting beside a river.

Surroundings : ⩽ ♋
Leisure activities : ♈ ✕ ⌂ ⸗
Facilities : 𝔤 ⊶ (Jul–Aug) ꜛ launderette ⸽
Nearby : ✕ ⧄ ⤳ ⤳

GPS
Longitude : 5.86953
Latitude : 46.37309

ST-HIPPOLYTE

25190 – Michelin map **321** K3 – pop. 917 – alt. 380
▶ Paris 490 – Basel 93 – Belfort 48 – Besançon 89

Les Grands Champs

℘ 03 81 96 54 53, *www.ville.saint-hippolyte.fr*
Address : located 1km northeast along the D 121, follow the signs for Montécheroux and take the road to the right, near the Doubs (direct access)
2.2 ha (65 pitches) terraced, relatively flat, grassy, stony
ᕋ 5 ⊡
Long, narrow site with pitches set into a slope beside the Doubs river.

Surroundings : ⤳ ⩽ ♀
Leisure activities : ⤳
Facilities : 𝔤 ⊶ ▣

GPS
Longitude : 6.82332
Latitude : 47.32291

ST-LAURENT-EN-GRANDVAUX

39150 – Michelin map **321** F7 – pop. 1,779 – alt. 904
▶ Paris 442 – Champagnole 22 – Lons-le-Saunier 45 – Morez 11

Municipal Champ de Mars

℘ 03 84 60 19 30, *www.st-laurent39.fr*
Address : 8 r. du Camping (take the eastern exit along the N 5)
Opening times : from mid Dec. to end Sept.
3 ha (133 pitches) flat and relatively flat, grassy
Tariff : ☀ 3.30€ᕋ ⊡ 3.10€ – 闭 (10A) 2.40€
Rental rates : (from mid Dec. to end Sept.) 𝔤 (2 chalets) – 10 ⌂. Per week from 304 to 507 €
ᕋ 12 ⊡ 9.70€ – ⸙ 9.20€
Close to the snowshoe hiking trails and cross-country skiing pistes.

Surroundings : ❆ ⩽
Leisure activities : ⌂ ⸗
Facilities : 𝔤 ⊶ ▥ ⸽ ⥻ ꜛ launderette

GPS
Longitude : 5.96294
Latitude : 46.57616

ST-POINT-LAC

25160 – Michelin map **321** H6 – pop. 269 – alt. 860 – Leisure centre
▶ Paris 453 – Champagnole 39 – Pontarlier 13 – St-Laurent-en-Grandvaux 45

Municipal

🎣 0381696164, *www.campingsaintpointlac.com*
Address : 8 r. du Port (in the town)
Opening times : from mid April to mid Oct.
1.8 ha (84 pitches) flat, grassy, fine gravel
Tariff : (2012 price) 16€ ♦♦ ⇔ 🔲 (½) (16A) – Extra per person 3€
🚐 sani-station 7.50€ – 30 🔲 7.50€
The campervan pitches are close to the campsite.

Surroundings : ≤ ⛺
Leisure activities : 🎱 ⚓ 🚲
Facilities : ⚐ ⊶ ▥ ¶ launderette ⚘
Nearby : ⚓ 🎣 watersports centre

Longitude : 6.30336
Latitude : 46.81209

SALINS-LES-BAINS

39110 – Michelin map **321** F5 – pop. 2,987 – alt. 340 – ♣ (beg Mar-end Oct)
▶ Paris 419 – Besançon 41 – Dole 43 – Lons-le-Saunier 52

Municipal

🎣 0384379270, *www.salinscamping.com*
Address : pl. de la Gare (take the northern exit, following signs for Besançon)
Opening times : from beginning April to end Sept.
1 ha (44 pitches) flat, grassy, fine gravel
Tariff : (2012 price) ♦ 3.80€ ⇔ 2.60€ 🔲 5.80€ – (½) (10A) 2.90€ – Reservation fee 5€
Rental rates : (2012 price) (from beginning April to end Sept.) – 2 🏠.
Per night from 40 to 50 € – Per week from 150 to 360 € – Reservation fee 5€
🚐 7 🔲 16.30€
In a valley with a superb view of the citadel and surrounding mountains.

Surroundings : ≤ 🏙
Leisure activities : 🎱 ⚓ 🏊 (small swimming pool)
Facilities : ⚐ ⊶ 🚿 ¶ 🎣

Longitude : 5.87919
Latitude : 46.94625

LA TOUR-DU-MEIX

39270 – Michelin map **321** D7 – pop. 226 – alt. 470
▶ Paris 430 – Champagnole 42 – Lons-le-Saunier 24 – St-Claude 36

Surchauffant

🎣 0384254108, *www.camping-surchauffant.fr*
Address : at the Pont de la Pyle (bridge across Lac de Vouglans) (located 1km southeast along the
D 470 and take road to the left, 150m from the lake – direct access)
Opening times : from end April to mid Sept.
2.5 ha (200 pitches) flat, grassy, stony
Tariff : (2012 price) 23.50€ ♦♦ ⇔ 🔲 (½) (10A) – Extra per person 4.70€
Rental rates : (2012 price) (from end April to mid Sept.) 🏕 – 24 🏠 – 24 🏡.
Per night from 30 to 82€ – Per week from 180 to 574 €
🚐 sani-station 2€ – 15 🔲 9€

Surroundings : 🌳 ≤ ♨
Leisure activities : ✗ 🎱 ⚓ 🚲 🏊
Facilities : ⚐ ⊶ (Jul-Aug) 🚿 🏠 ¶ launderette ⚖ refrigerated food
storage
Nearby : 🍽 ⚓ (beach) 🎣

Longitude : 5.6742
Latitude : 46.52298

UXELLES

39130 – Michelin map **321** I2 – pop. 49 – alt. 598
▶ Paris 440 – Besançon 93 – Genève 86 – Lausanne 102

Village Vacances Odesia Les Crozats
(rental of chalets and rooms only)

𝒞 03 84 25 51 43, *odesia-lacs.com*
Address : r. Principale
Opening times : permanent
2 ha relatively flat, flat, grassy
Rental rates : (2012 price) ✂ 🅿 – 15 🏠 – 28 🛏. Per week from 273 to 804 €
Reservation fee 12€
A small but pretty chalet village in the lake valley with an option for half-board accommodation.

Surroundings : ❄ 🐾
Leisure activities : 🍸 ✕ 🎞 🎱 🕺 🛶 hammam 🚲 🖵 cinema/activity centre
Facilities : ⚊ ⚐ launderette 🐾

GPS — Longitude : 5.78836 / Latitude : 46.60277

VESOUL

70000 – Michelin map **314** E7 – pop. 15,920 – alt. 221 – Leisure centre
▶ Paris 360 – Belfort 68 – Besançon 47 – Épinal 91

International du Lac

𝒞 03 84 76 22 86, *www.camping-vesoul.com*
Address : at Vaivre-et-Montoille, av. des Rives du Lac (2.5km west)
Opening times : permanent
4 ha (183 pitches) flat, grassy
Tariff : 18.40€ ♦♦ ⚌ 🔲 ⚡ (6A) – Extra per person 3€ – Reservation fee 4€
Rental rates : (permanent) ♿ (1 mobile home) ✂ – 7 🚐. Per night from 67 to 90 €
Per week from 285 to 539 €
🚰 sani-station 2.50€ – 30 🔲 18.40€
Beside a large lake.

Surroundings : 🐾 ⌂ ♀
Leisure activities : 🎞 🎱 🏃 🏊 🎣
Facilities : ♿ ⚊ ▥ 🛁 🚿 ⚐ launderette
Nearby : 🍸 ✕ ✂ 🏊 🛶

GPS — Longitude : 6.13084 / Latitude : 47.63121

VILLERSEXEL

70110 – Michelin map **314** G7 – pop. 1,472 – alt. 287
▶ Paris 386 – Belfort 41 – Besançon 59 – Lure 18

Le Chapeau Chinois

𝒞 03 84 63 40 60, *www.camping-villersexel.com*
Address : 92 r. du Quai Militaire (located 1km north along the D 486, follow the signs for Lure and take the road to the right after the bridge)
Opening times : from mid March to beginning Oct.
2 ha (80 pitches) flat, grassy
Tariff : ♦ 3.60€ ⚌ 2€ 🔲 4.30€ – ⚡ (10A) 3.10€
Rental rates : (from end March to beginning Oct.) ✂ – 9 🛏 – 1 gîte.
Per night from 50 to 70 € – Per week from 300 to 600 €
🚰 3 🔲 14€
Beside the Ognon river.

Surroundings : 🐾 ♀
Leisure activities : 🎞 🏃 ✂ 🏊 🎣
Facilities : ♿ ⚊ 🛁 🚿 ⚐ launderette
Nearby : ✕ 🎣

GPS — Longitude : 6.436 / Latitude : 47.55814

Patrick Escudero / hemis.fr

Paris, the 'City of Light' on the River Seine, is at the heart of the Île-de-France. A chic and cosmopolitan capital, it is dominated by the iconic silhouette of the Eiffel Tower. Its former royal palace is now adorned with glass pyramids, a former railway station has been transformed into a magnificent museum and narrow streets lined with bohemian houses branch off from wide, formal, tree-lined boulevards. This is a city of endless contrasts: from busy department stores to elegant cafés, from the *bateaux-mouches* (restaurant boats) that glide along the majestic river at night to the sophisticated glamour of Parisian cabarets. But the region beyond Paris has no intention of staying in the capital's shadow; it is home to secluded châteaux, the magical world of Disneyland and the relaxed ambience of the summer cafés on the banks of the River Marne. And who could forget the magnificent splendour of Versailles, the most beautiful palace in the world?

BAGNEAUX-SUR-LOING

77167 – Michelin map **312** F6 – pop. 1,686 – alt. 45
◪ Paris 84 – Fontainebleau 21 – Melun 39 – Montargis 30

⚠ Municipal de Pierre le Sault

☏ 0164292444, *camping.bagneaux-sur-loing@orange.fr* – limited spaces for one-night stay only
Address : ch. des Grèves (to the northeast of the town, near the sports field, near the canal and the Loing river, 200m from a small lake)
Opening times : from beginning April to end Oct.
3 ha (160 pitches) flat, grassy, wood
Tariff : ✶ 2.80€ ⟵ 回 2.40€ – ฿ (10A) 4.40€
🚲 ⛟ 7.60€
Near a canal and the river, but in an industrial district.

Surroundings : ⊏⊐ ⌀
Leisure activities : 🎦 ⚓ ✗
Facilities : ♿ ⊶ 🖽 🏛 launderette
Nearby : ⌇

GPS Longitude : 2.70376
Latitude : 48.24069

BOULANCOURT

77760 – Michelin map **312** D6 – pop. 357 – alt. 79
◪ Paris 79 – Étampes 33 – Fontainebleau 28 – Melun 44

⚠ Île de Boulancourt

☏ 0164241338, *www.camping-iledeboulancourt.com* – limited spaces for one-night stay only
Address : 6 allée des Marronniers (to the south, follow the signs for Augerville-la-Rivière)
Opening times : permanent
5.5 ha (110 pitches) flat, grassy
Tariff : (2012 price) ✶ 4.40€ ⟵ 回 5.50€ – ฿ (10A) 2.30€
Rental rates : (2012 price) (permanent) ⚶ – 7 ⟦⟧ – 1 ⌂ – 3 chalets (without sanitary facilities). Per week from 180 to 350 €
🚲 sani-station 5€ – 4 回 16.60€ – ⛟ 11.50€
Pleasant, wooded setting at a bend in the Essonne river.

Surroundings : ⌇ ⌀⌀
Leisure activities : 🎦
Facilities : ⊶ 🖽 🏛 ♨ ⚵ 🖼

GPS Longitude : 2.435
Latitude : 48.25583

CHAMPIGNY-SUR-MARNE

Michelin map **312** E3 – pop. 75,090 – alt. 40
◪ Paris 13 – Créteil 10 – Amiens 150 – Bobigny 13

⚠ Homair Vacances Paris Est

☏ 0820201207, *www.campingchampigny.fr* – reserved for residents outside the Île de France
Address : bd des Alliés
Opening times : permanent
(383 pitches) flat, grassy
Tariff : (2012 price) 30.60€ ✶✶ ⟵ 回 ฿ (16A) – Extra per person 7€ – Reservation fee 10€
Rental rates : (2012 price) (permanent) – 125 ⟦⟧ – 40 ⌂. Per night from 49 to 124 €
Per week from 29 to 45 € – Reservation fee 10€
🚲 sani-station 9€ – 40 回 21€
Beside the Marne river with a view of the Pavillon Baltard (elegant 19th-century building hosting shows and exhibitions).

Leisure activities : ⚑ ✗ jacuzzi ⚙
Facilities : ♿ ⊶ 🏛 ♨ ⚶ ♨ launderette ⚊ ⚲
Nearby : ⌇

GPS Longitude : 2.47701
Latitude : 48.82958

CREVECOEUR-EN-BRIE

77610 – Michelin map **312** G3 – pop. 299 – alt. 116
▶ Paris 51 – Melun 36 – Boulogne-Billancourt 59 – Argenteuil 66

Caravaning des 4 Vents

℘ 01 64 07 41 11, *www.caravaning-4vents.fr* – limited spaces for one-night stay only
Address : r. de Beauregard (located 1km west following signs for la Houssaye and take turning to the left)
Opening times : from mid March to beginning Nov.
9 ha (199 pitches) flat, grassy
Tariff : 28€ ♚♚ ⇌ 🅔 🅖 (6A) – Extra per person 6€
Rental rates : (from mid March to beginning Nov.) ⚡ – 5 🏠. Per night from 83 €
Per week from 560 €

In a pleasant, leafy setting with large, well marked-out pitches.

Surroundings : 🐾 ⊏⊐ ♀
Leisure activities : 🎦 🚣 ⚓
Facilities : ♿ ⚊ ✉ 🚿 ⚱ ⅌ launderette
Nearby : ✂ 🐎

GPS Longitude : 2.89722
Latitude : 48.75065

ÉTAMPES

91150 – Michelin map **312** B5 – pop. 22,182 – alt. 80 – Leisure centre
▶ Paris 51 – Chartres 59 – Évry 35 – Fontainebleau 45

Le Vauvert

℘ 01 64 94 21 39, *caravaning.levauvert@orange.fr* – limited spaces for one-night stay only
Address : rte de Saclas (2.3km south along the D 49)
8 ha (230 pitches) flat, grassy

Only 25 to 30 pitches for tents and caravans next to 200 pitches for owner-occupiers.

Surroundings : ⊏⊐ ♀
Leisure activities : ⅌ 🎦 🚣 ✂
Facilities : ♿ ⚊ 🚿 ⚱ ⅌
Leisure/activities centre : ⊠ ⚓ 🐎 climbing

GPS Longitude : 2.14532
Latitude : 48.41215

JABLINES

77450 – Michelin map **312** F2 – pop. 629 – alt. 46 – Leisure centre
▶ Paris 44 – Meaux 14 – Melun 57

L' International

℘ 01 60 26 09 37, *www.camping-jablines.com*
Address : at the base de loisirs (leisure centre) (situated 2km southwest along the D 45, follow the signs for Annet-sur-Marne, 9km from the Disneyland-Paris park)
Opening times : from end March to end Sept.
300 ha/4 ha for camping (154 pitches) flat, grassy
Tariff : 29€ ♚♚ ⇌ 🅔 🅖 (10A) – Extra per person 8€ – Reservation fee 11€
Rental rates : (from mid March to end Sept.) ⚡ – 9 . Per night from 68 to 97 €
Per week from 476 to 680 € – Reservation fee 11€
🚐 sani-station 2.50€ – 145 🅔 29€

Attractive location at a bend in the Marne river, next to a large leisure and activity park.

Surroundings : 🐾 ⊏⊐ ♀♀
Leisure activities : 🚣
Facilities : ♿ ⚊ 🆑 🚿 ⚱ ⅌ launderette 🔌
Leisure/activities centre : ✗ 🍴 🚲 ✂ ≊ (lake) 💧 🐎 cable
wake-boarding

GPS Longitude : 2.73437
Latitude : 48.91367

LOUAN VILLEGRUIS FONTAINE

77560 – Michelin map **312** J4 – pop. 512 – alt. 168
▶ Paris 101 – Melun 77 – Provins 21 – Troyes 68

Yelloh! Paris Ile de France
(exclusive rental of mobile homes, tents and cabins in the trees only)

℘ 0164008014, *www.yellohvillage-paris-iledefrance.com*
Address : at Louan : La Cerclière (D 131)
Opening times : from mid April to mid Nov.
11 ha (200 pitches) undulating, flat, grassy, lake
Rental rates : 140 🏠 – 2 cabins in the trees – 10 tents. Per night from 35 to 199 €
Per week from 210 to 1,194 €

In the heart of the forest, surrounded by green space, 1 hour from Paris and the Disneyland-Paris park.

Surroundings : 🌿 💧
Leisure activities : 🍽 🎱 ⊘ 🏋 🏊 🚴 🎿 🎬 🏊 🏖 🎣 cinema, zip wiring, farm/petting farm, multi-sports ground
Facilities : 🚿 ⚟ 🛗 🚰 launderette 🖨 🔧

GPS Longitude : 3.49077
Latitude : 48.6306

MAISONS-LAFFITTE

78600 – Michelin map **311** I2 – pop. 22,717 – alt. 38
▶ Paris 23 – Versailles 24 – Pontoise 20 – Nanterre 13

Sandaya International

℘ 0139122191, *www.campint.com*
Address : 1 r. Johnson (on the Île de la Commune)
Opening times : from end March to beginning Nov.
6.5 ha (336 pitches) flat, grassy
Tariff : (2012 price) 35.50€ 🧍🧍 🚐 📧 ⚡ (6A) – Extra per person 7,10€ – Reservation fee 15€
Rental rates : (2012 price) (from end March to beginning Nov.) 🚿 (1 mobile home) – 87 🏠 – 2 cabins on stilts. Per night from 69 to 161 € – Per week from 483 to 1,127 €
Reservation fee 15€
🚮 sani-station

On an island in the River Seine.

Surroundings : 🏞 💧
Leisure activities : 🍽 ✕ 🎱 🏊 🎣
Facilities : 🚿 🛗 🚰 🔧 🚰 launderette 🔧
Nearby : 🍽

GPS Longitude : 2.1458
Latitude : 48.94156

MELUN

77000 – Michelin map **312** E4 – pop. 39,400 – alt. 43
▶ Paris 47 – Chartres 105 – Fontainebleau 18 – Meaux 55

La Belle Étoile

℘ 0164394812, *www.campinglabelleetoile.com*
Address : 64bis quai Maréchal Joffre (to the southeast along the N 6, follow the signs for Fontainebleau (left bank)
Opening times : from end March to mid Oct.
3.5 ha (180 pitches) flat, grassy
Tariff : 🧍 7.45€ 🚐 📧 7.20€ – ⚡ (6A) 4€ – Reservation fee 8€
Rental rates : (from end March to mid Oct.) 🚿 – 8 🏠 – 4 🏡 – 3 tent bungalows.
Per night from 32 to 79 € – Per week from 192 to 600 € – Reservation fee 8€
🚮 sani-station 3€

Very green setting, right next to the River Seine in Melun.

Surroundings : 💧
Leisure activities : 🎱 🏊 🛶 (pool)
Facilities : ⚟ 🔲 🛗 🏖 🚰 launderette
Nearby : 🧖 hammam 🍽 🏊 🎣 🏊

GPS Longitude : 2.66765
Latitude : 48.50929

MONTJAY-LA-TOUR

77410 – Michelin map **312** E2
▶ Paris 38 – Melun 50 – Boulogne-Billancourt 45 – Argenteuil 41

Le Parc de Paris

✆ 01 60 26 20 79, *www.campingleparc.fr* – limited spaces for one-night stay only
Address : r. Adèle Claret (take the eastern exit along the D 105 towards the D 104 for Annet)
Opening times : permanent
10 ha (363 pitches) terraced, relatively flat, flat
Tariff : 32€ ♥♥ ⇌ 🔲 ♨ (10A) – Extra per person 8€ – Reservation fee 25€
Rental rates : (permanent) – 150 🛏 – 5 tent bungalows. Per night from 53 to 145 €
Per week from 299 to 870 € – Reservation fee 25€
🚐 sani-station 8€
Well situated between Paris and the Disneyland-Paris park.

Surroundings : 🏕 ♨♨
Leisure activities : 🍷 ✗ 🏛 🏄
Facilities : 🚿 ⚲ 🏧 🛁 🍴 launderette 🚿
Nearby : ✂

GPS Longitude : 2.66724
Latitude : 48.91118

PARIS

75000 – pop. 2,234,105 – alt. 30
Au Bois de Boulogne – 75016

Indigo Paris

✆ 01 45 24 30 00, *www.camping-indigo.com* – reserved for residents outside the Île de France
Address : 2 allée du Bord de l'Eau (between the bridges at Suresnes and Puteaux; beside the Seine)
Opening times : permanent
7 ha (510 pitches) flat, fine gravel
Tariff : (2012 price) 39,10€ ♥♥ ⇌ 🔲 ♨ (10A) – Extra per person 7.50€ – Reservation fee 22€
Rental rates : (2012 price) (permanent) ♿ (1 mobile home) – 17 caravans – 58 🛏.
Per night from 83 to 129 € – Per week from 523 to 833 € – Reservation fee 22€
🚐 sani-station 9€
Choose the pitches beside the River Seine if possible, which are a more peaceful – bus for
La Porte Maillot, Paris (RER-métro).

Surroundings : 🏕 ♨♨
Leisure activities : 🍷 ✗ 🏛
Facilities : 🚿 ⚲ 🏧 🛁 ⚡ launderette 🛁 🚿

GPS Longitude : 2.23464
Latitude : 48.86849

POMMEUSE

77515 – Michelin map **312** H3 – pop. 2,756 – alt. 67
▶ Paris 58 – Château-Thierry 49 – Créteil 54 – Meaux 23

Iris Parc Le Chêne Gris ♣♣

✆ 01 64 04 21 80, *www.lechenegris.com*
Address : 24 pl. de la Gare (situated 2km southwest, behind Faremoutiers-Pommeuse station)
Opening times : from mid March to end Oct.
6 ha (350 pitches) terraced, gravelled, grassy
Tariff : 44€ ♥♥ ⇌ 🔲 ♨ (6A) – Extra per person 5.50€ – Reservation fee 20€
Rental rates : (from mid March to end Oct.) ✳ – 211 🛏 – 80 tents.
Per night from 25 to 142 € – Per week from 200 to 760 € – Reservation fee 20€
A well-equipped indoor children's play area.

Surroundings : 🏕 ♨♨
Leisure activities : ✗ 🏛 🎮 🏃 🏄 🔲 🏊
Facilities : 🚿 ⚲ 🏧 🏛 🛁 🛁 ⚡ 🍴 launderette 🛁 🚿

GPS Longitude : 2.99368
Latitude : 48.80814

RAMBOUILLET

78120 – Michelin map **311** G4 – pop. 26,065 – alt. 160
▶ Paris 53 – Chartres 42 – Étampes 44 – Mantes-la-Jolie 50

Huttopia Rambouillet ♣₁

℘ 01 30 41 07 34, *www.huttopia.com*
Address : rte du Château d'Eau (head 4km south along the N 10, follow the signs for Chartres)
Opening times : from end March to beginning Nov.
8 ha (93 pitches) flat, grassy, gravelled
Tariff : (2012 price) 33.70€ ✱✱ ⇔ 🗐 🕸 (10A) – Extra per person 7.50€ – Reservation fee 20€
Rental rates : (2012 price) (from end March to beginning Nov.) 🄿 – 10 caravans – 10 🏠 –
14 tents. Per night from 62 to 156 € – Per week from 391 to 983 € – Reservation fee 20€
🚽 sani-station 7€
Beside a lake, in the heart of the forest.

Surroundings : 🏔 ⌐ 00
Leisure activities : 🍸 ✕ 🎮 🕴 ⚴ 🛶 🎣
Facilities : 🔥 ⚬➡ 📶 🎍 🛆 ⚡ launderette 🍂
Nearby : 🔲 🏊 wildlife park

GPS
Longitude : 1.84374
Latitude : 48.62634

TOUQUIN

77131 – Michelin map **312** H3 – pop. 1,095 – alt. 112
▶ Paris 57 – Coulommiers 12 – Melun 36 – Montereau-Fault-Yonne 48

Les Étangs Fleuris

℘ 01 64 04 16 36, *www.etangsfleuris.com*
Address : rte de La Couture (3km east)
Opening times : from beginning April to mid Sept.
5.5 ha (195 pitches) relatively flat, flat, grassy
Tariff : 22€ ✱✱ ⇔ 🗐 🕸 (10A) – Extra per person 11€
Rental rates : (from beginning April to mid Sept.) 🏠 – 16 🏠. Per night from 56 to 92 €
Per week from 395 to 645 €
In a green setting, with shade, close to lakes.

Surroundings : 🏔 ⌐ 00
Leisure activities : 🍸 🎮 ⚴ 🏓 🛶 🏊 🎣 multi-sports ground
Facilities : ⚬➡ 📶 🛆 ⚡ ⁑ launderette
Nearby : ✕ 🐎

GPS
Longitude : 3.04728
Latitude : 48.73279

TOURNAN EN BRIE

77220 – Michelin map **312** F3 – pop. 8,116 – alt. 102
▶ Paris 44 – Melun 29 – Amiens 176 – Créteil 38

FranceLoc Fredland – Parc de Combreux

℘ 01 64 07 96 44, *www.campings-franceloc.fr*
Address : 1.5 km at the south by the D 10, rte de Liverdy-en-Brie
Opening times : permanent
26 ha/7 ha for camping (189 pitches) flat, grassy
Tariff : (2012 Price) 29€ ✱✱ ⇔ 🗐 🕸 (6A) – Extra per person 7€ – Reservation fee 27€
Rental rates : (permanent) 🏠 – 43 🏠 – 3 cabins in the trees – 2 tents.
Per night from 39 to 242 € – Per week from 52 to 805 € – Reservation fee 27 €
Situated 800m from the RER station (25min to Paris).

Surroundings : 00
Leisure activities : 🍸 ⚴ 🔲 (small swimming pool) 🏊 🏊 🎣
Facilities : 🔥 ⚬➡ 📶 ⁑ launderette 🔲

GPS
Longitude : 2.76915
Latitude : 48.73517

347

VENEUX-LES-SABLONS

77250 – Michelin map **312** F5 – pop. 4,788 – alt. 76
▶ Paris 72 – Fontainebleau 9 – Melun 26 – Montereau-Fault-Yonne 14

Les Courtilles du Lido

℘ 01 60 70 46 05, *http://www.les-courtilles-du-lido.fr*
Address : ch. du Passeur (located 1.5km to the northeast)
Opening times : from beginning April to end Sept.
5 ha (160 pitches) flat, grassy
Tariff : (2012 price) 🛉 4€ 🚗 2.50€ 🔲 6€ – 🔌 (10A) 3€
Rental rates : (2012 price) (from beginning April to end Sept.) 🏚 – 17 🔲 – 2 tent
bungalows. Per night from 75 to 140 € – Per week from 245 to 680 €
🚽 sani-station 4€ – 17 🔲 19.50€

Surroundings : 🌳 🎢
Leisure activities : 🍸 🚣 🎿
Facilities : 🔌 🚿 🍴 launderette

Longitude : 2.80194
Latitude : 48.38333

VERSAILLES

78000 – Michelin map **311** I3 – pop. 86,477 – alt. 130
▶ Paris 29 – Chartres 80 – Fontainebleau 73 – Rambouillet 35

Huttopia Versailles

℘ 01 39 51 23 61, *www.huttopia.com*
Address : 31 r. Berthelot
Opening times : from end March to beginning Nov.
4.6 ha (180 pitches) terraced, relatively flat, grassy, stony
Tariff : (2012 price) 41,10€ 🛉🛉 🚗 🔲 🔌 (10A) – Extra per person 9.40€ – Reservation fee 20€
Rental rates : (2012 price) (from end March to beginning Nov.) 🏚 (1 chalet) – 15 caravans –
20 🏚 – 14 tents. Per night from 61 to 174 € – Per week from 384 to 1,096 €
Reservation fee 20€
🚽 sani-station 9€
In a wooded setting close to the town.

Surroundings : 🌳 🎢
Leisure activities : ✕ 🚣 🎿
Facilities : 🚿 🔌 🍴 launderette

Longitude : 2.15912
Latitude : 48.79441

VILLIERS-SUR-ORGE

91700 – Michelin map **312** C4 – pop. 3,896 – alt. 75
▶ Paris 25 – Chartres 71 – Dreux 89 – Évry 15

Le Beau Village de Paris

℘ 01 60 16 17 86, *www.campingaparis.com* – limited spaces for one-night stay
Address : 1 voie des Prés (600m southeast via the town centre, 800m from St-Geneviève-des-Bois
station – from A 6, take exit 6)
Opening times : permanent
2.5 ha (124 pitches) flat, grassy
Tariff : 20€ 🛉🛉 🚗 🔲 🔌 (10A) – Extra per person 5€
Rental rates : (permanent) – 11 🔲 – 1 apartment. Per night from 62 to 90 €
Per week from 250 to 540 €
🚽 sani-station 2€ – 33 🔲 20€ – 🚐 🔌 19.20€
In a green setting with some shade beside the Orge river; good pitches for campervans.

Surroundings : 🌳 🌲
Leisure activities : 🍸 🏊 🚣
Facilities : 🚿 🔌 🍴 launderette
Nearby : ✕ 🎿

Longitude : 2.30421
Latitude : 48.65511

LANGUEDOC-ROUSSILLON

René Mattes / hemis.fr

Languedoc-Roussillon is a kaleidoscope of landscapes, cultures and sensations. You will be seduced by the feverish rhythm of its festivals, the dizzying beauty of the Tarn gorges and the Pyrenees, the magical spell of its caves and stone statues, the seclusion of its cliff-top 'Citadels of Vertigo' with their panoramic views and the heady perfumes of its sun-drenched *garrigue*, the local scrubland fragrant with herbs. Admire the nonchalant flamingoes on its long stretches of salt flats, enjoy discovering the splendour of Carcassonne's medieval ramparts or explore the quiet waters of the Midi Canal and the harsh majesty of the Cévennes. Taking in so many different sights may exhaust some visitors, but remedies are close at hand: a plate of *aligot*, made from mashed potato, butter, cream, garlic and cheese, and a simmering *cassoulet*, the famously rich combination of duck, sausage, beans and herbs, followed by a slice of Roquefort cheese and a glass of ruby-red wine.

AGDE

34300 – Michelin map **339** F9 – pop. 24,031 – alt. 5
▶ Paris 754 – Béziers 24 – Lodève 60 – Millau 118

Yelloh! Village Mer et Soleil ♣♠

📞 04 67 94 21 14, *www.camping-mer-soleil.com*
Address : ch. de Notre Dame at Saint Martin, rte de Rochelongue (3km to the south)
Opening times : from mid April to beginning Oct.
8 ha (477 pitches) flat, grassy, sandy
Tariff : 42 € ♥♥ ⇔ 🄴 🄸 (6A) – Extra per person 8 €
Rental rates : (from mid April to beginning Oct.) ♿ ⚡ – 216 🚐 – 9 🏠 – 2 tent bungalows –
42 tents. Per night from 29 to 239 € – Per week from 203 to 1,673 €

Good indoor spa area with some luxury mobile homes.

Surroundings : 🏊 ⛺ 00
Leisure activities : ♟ ✗ 🎦 🌙 evening 🏃 ♨ ⛱ jacuzzi 🚣 🚲 🏓 🎣
🏊 spa therapy centre
Facilities : ♿ ☎ 🚿 🍴 launderette 🔌 🚰
Nearby : 🐎

GPS Longitude : 3.47812
Latitude : 43.28621

Les Champs Blancs

📞 04 67 94 23 42, *www.champs-blancs.fr*
Address : rte de Rochelongue
15 ha/4 ha for camping (336 pitches) flat, grassy, gravelled
Rentals : ⚡ – 80 🚐 – 20 🏠.
🚰 sani-station

Surroundings : ⛺ 00
Leisure activities : ♟ ✗ 🎦 🌙 🏃 🚣 🏓 🎣 🏊 multi-sports ground
Facilities : ♿ ☎ – 120 individual sanitary facilities (🚿🚰🚽 wc) 🍴
launderette 🔌 🚰
Nearby : 🛒

GPS Longitude : 3.47666
Latitude : 43.29644

Village Vacances Les Pescalunes
(rental of chalets only)

📞 04 67 01 37 06, *www.grandbleu.fr*
Address : rte de Luxembourg (follow the signs for Le Cap-d'Agde)
Opening times : from beginning March to beginning Nov.
3 ha very uneven, terraced
Rental rates : ♿ (2 chalets) 🅿 – 78 🏠. Per night from 70 to 110 €
Per week from 266 to 1,001 €

Peaceful chalet village on the side of a hill, with a view of the surrounding area and the
Cévennes mountains.

Surroundings : 🏊 ≤ 00
Leisure activities : 🎦 🏃 🚣 🏊
Facilities : 🔥 launderette

GPS Longitude : 3.50223
Latitude : 43.30109

For more information on visiting particular towns or regions, consult the
relevant regional MICHELIN Green Guide. We also recommend you use
the appropriate Michelin regional map to locate your selected campsite,
to calculate distances and to work out the best route.

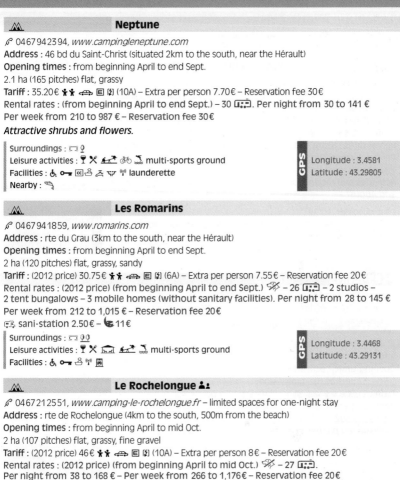

Neptune

℘ 04 67 94 23 94, *www.campingleneptune.com*
Address : 46 bd du Saint-Christ (situated 2km to the south, near the Hérault)
Opening times : from beginning April to end Sept.
2.1 ha (165 pitches) flat, grassy
Tariff : 35.20€ ♦♦ ⇔ 🔲 (10A) – Extra per person 7.70€ – Reservation fee 30€
Rental rates : (from beginning April to end Sept.) – 30 🔲. Per night from 30 to 141 €
Per week from 210 to 987 € – Reservation fee 30€
Attractive shrubs and flowers.

Surroundings : 🔲 ♀
Leisure activities : ♥ ✗ ⚓ ♿ 🌊 multi-sports ground
Facilities : ♿ ⊶ 🔲 ♿ 🔥 ⚓ ⁿⁱ launderette
Nearby : ⚓

GPS Longitude : 3.4581
Latitude : 43.29805

Les Romarins

℘ 04 67 94 18 59, *www.romarins.com*
Address : rte du Grau (3km to the south, near the Hérault)
Opening times : from beginning April to end Sept.
2 ha (120 pitches) flat, grassy, sandy
Tariff : (2012 price) 30.75€ ♦♦ ⇔ 🔲 (6A) – Extra per person 7.55€ – Reservation fee 20€
Rental rates : (2012 price) (from beginning April to end Sept.) ⚡ – 26 🔲 – 2 studios –
2 tent bungalows – 3 mobile homes (without sanitary facilities). Per night from 28 to 145 €
Per week from 212 to 1,015 € – Reservation fee 20€
🔲 sani-station 2.50€ – 🔋 11€

Surroundings : 🔲 ♀♀
Leisure activities : ♥ ✗ 🎣 ⚓ 🌊 multi-sports ground
Facilities : ♿ ⊶ ♿ ⁿⁱ 🔲

GPS Longitude : 3.4468
Latitude : 43.29131

Le Rochelongue ♣♣

℘ 04 67 21 25 51, *www.camping-le-rochelongue.fr* – limited spaces for one-night stay
Address : rte de Rochelongue (4km to the south, 500m from the beach)
Opening times : from beginning April to mid Oct.
2 ha (107 pitches) flat, grassy, fine gravel
Tariff : (2012 price) 46€ ♦♦ ⇔ 🔲 (10A) – Extra per person 8€ – Reservation fee 20€
Rental rates : (2012 price) (from beginning April to mid Oct.) ⚡ – 27 🔲.
Per night from 38 to 168 € – Per week from 266 to 1,176€ – Reservation fee 20€

Surroundings : 🔲 ♀♀
Leisure activities : ♥ ✗ 🎣 ⚓ 🌊
Facilities : ♿ ⊶ ♿ ⁿⁱ launderette ⚓
Nearby : ✗ 🗺 🔥 🐎 watersports centre

GPS Longitude : 3.48139
Latitude : 43.27917

La Pépinière

℘ 04 67 94 10 94, *www.campinglapepiniere.com*
Address : rte du Grau
Opening times : from beginning April to end Sept.
3 ha (100 pitches) flat, grassy
Tariff : 26€ ♦♦ ⇔ 🔲 (10A) – Extra per person 6.50€ – Reservation fee 20€
Rental rates : (from beginning April to end Sept.) – 29 🔲. Per week from 150 to 700 €
Reservation fee 20€
🔲 sani-station
Family-orientated site very near the Hérault river.

Surroundings : 🦌 🔲
Leisure activities : ♥ ✗ 🎣 ⚓ 🌊
Facilities : ♿ ⊶ ⁿⁱ 🔲 ⚓
Nearby : ⚓ ⚓

GPS Longitude : 3.45368
Latitude : 43.29488

LANGUEDOC-ROUSSILLON

AIGUES-MORTES

30220 – Michelin map **339** K7 – pop. 8,116 – alt. 3
▶ Paris 745 – Arles 49 – Montpellier 38 – Nîmes 42

Yelloh! Village La Petite Camargue ♣♣

℘ 0466539898, *www.yellohvillage-petite.camargue.com*
Address : 3.5km west along the D 62, follow the signs for Montpellier .
Opening times : from end April to mid Sept.
42 ha/10 ha for camping (553 pitches) flat, grassy, sandy
Tariff : 49€ ✹ ✹ ⇌ 🔲 🔌 (16A) – Extra per person 9€
Rental rates : (from end April to mid Sept.) ⚡ – 301 🏠. Per night from 39 to 229 €
Per week from 273 to 1,603 €
🚐 sani-station
Activities and facilities suitable for teenagers. Free shuttle service to the beaches July and August.

Surroundings : ⌂ ♤♤
Leisure activities : ♟ ✗ 🎮 ☺ 🏃 ⛵ 🚲 ✗ 🎿 🐎 disco, library, multi-sports ground
Facilities : ♿ ⚡ ☂ ⚐ launderette 🔋 🚿

Longitude : 4.15963
Latitude : 43.56376

ALET-LES-BAINS

11580 – Michelin map **344** E5 – pop. 436 – alt. 186
▶ Paris 786 – Montpellier 187 – Carcassonne 35 – Castelnaudary 49

Val d'Aleth

℘ 0468699040, *www.valdaleth.com*
Address : in the village (D 2118 and take the right turning beside the Aude river)
Opening times : permanent
0.5 ha (37 pitches) flat, grassy, stony
Tariff : 21.50€ ✹ ✹ ⇌ 🔲 🔌 (10A) – Extra per person 4.25€
Rentals : (permanent) ⚡ – 4 🛏.
🚐 8 🔲 17.50€
Well-shaded pitches near the river and a ruined château.

Surroundings : ⌂ ♤♤
Facilities : ♿ ⚡ ⚐

Longitude : 2.25564
Latitude : 42.99486

ALLÈGRE-LES-FUMADES

30500 – Michelin map **339** K3 – pop. 695 – alt. 135
▶ Paris 696 – Alès 16 – Barjac 102 – La Grand-Combe 28

FranceLoc Le Domaine des Fumades ♣♣

℘ 0466248078, *www.domaine-des-fumades.com*
Address : Les Fumades-les-Bains (access via the D 241)
Opening times : from mid April to mid Sept.
15 ha/6 ha for camping (253 pitches) relatively flat, flat, grassy, stony
Tariff : (2012 price) 30€ ✹ ✹ ⇌ 🔲 🔌 (10A) – Extra per person 7€ – Reservation fee 27€
Rental rates : (2012 price) (from mid April to mid Sept.) – 171 🏠 – 27 🏡 – 5 apartments – 8 tents. Per night from 33 to 175€ – Per week from 133 to 1,197 € – Reservation fee 27€
Beside the Alauzène river and close to the spa centre.

Surroundings : 🌊 ⌂ ♤♤
Leisure activities : ♟ ✗ 🎮 ☺ 🏃 ⛵ ✗ 🎯 🖼 🎿 🏊 cinema, multi-sports ground, entertainment room
Facilities : ♿ ⚡ ☂ ⚐ launderette 🔋 🚿
Nearby : 🐎

Longitude : 4.22904
Latitude : 44.18484

ANDUZE

30140 – Michelin map **339** I4 – pop. 3,303 – alt. 135
▶ Paris 718 – Alès 15 – Florac 68 – Lodève 84

L'Arche ♣♨

☎ 04 66 61 74 08, *www.camping-arche.fr*
Address : 1105 chemin de Recoulin (situated 2km to the northwest; beside the Gardon)
Opening times : from end March to end Sept.
5 ha (302 pitches) terraced, flat and relatively flat, grassy, sandy
Tariff : 42€ ♦♦ ⇔ 🔲 🔌 (10A) – Extra per person 8.90€ – Reservation fee 15€
Rental rates : (from end March to end Sept.) ⚡ – 36 🚐. Per week from 390 to 1,180 €
Reservation fee 15€
🚉 sani-station 2€
Pleasant swimming pool and indoor wellness area.

Surroundings : 🐾 ♀ ⛰
Leisure activities : 🍴 ✕ 🎮 🎣 🏃 ≦ hammam ⚓ 🏊 ♨ ⚐ 🐟
multi-sports ground, spa therapy centre
Facilities : 🚿 ⚬ 🏧 🛁 🧊 🚾 🍴 launderette ⚖ ⚒
Nearby : 🛒

GPS — Longitude : 3.97284
Latitude : 44.06873

Cévennes-Provence ♣♨

☎ 04 66 61 73 10, *www.camping-cevennes-provence.fr*
Address : at Corbès-Thoiras; at Le Mas du Pont, beside the Gardon de Mialet river and near the Gardon de St-Jean river
Opening times : from mid March to beginning Oct.
30 ha/15 ha for camping (242 pitches) very uneven, terraced, flat and relatively flat, grassy, stony
Tariff : 28.90€ ♦♦ ⇔ 🔲 🔌 (10A) – Extra per person 7.70€ – Reservation fee 15€
Rental rates : (from mid March to beginning Oct.) – 16 🏠 – 3 studios.
Per week from 330 to 710 €
🚉 sani-station
Choose pitches near the river for swimming or higher up for the view, overlooking the valley.

Surroundings : 🐾 ≼ ⛺ ♀♀ ⛰
Leisure activities : 🍴 ✕ 🎮 🏃 ⚓ ❊ 🎳 ≋ 🐟
Facilities : 🚿 ⚬ 🏧 🛁 🍴 launderette ⚖ ⚒
Nearby : adventure park

GPS — Longitude : 3.96643
Latitude : 44.07711

Les Fauvettes ♣♨

☎ 04 66 61 72 23, *www.lesfauvettes.fr*
Address : rte de St-Jean-du-Gard (1.7km to the northwest)
Opening times : from beginning May to beginning Oct.
7 ha/3 ha for camping (144 pitches) very uneven, terraced, flat and relatively flat, grassy
Tariff : 26€ ♦♦ ⇔ 🔲 🔌 (10A) – Extra per person 5.70€ – Reservation fee 17€
Rental rates : (from beginning April to end Nov.) – 17 🚐 – 24 🏠 – 1 tent bungalow.
Per night 50€ – Per week from 199 to 750 € – Reservation fee 17€
Choose pitches away from the road in preference.

Surroundings : ⛺ ♀
Leisure activities : 🍴 ✕ 🎮 🏃 ⚓ ♨ ⚐ entertainment room
Facilities : 🚿 ⚬ 🛁 🍴 🖥 ⚒
Nearby : 🛒 🚴

GPS — Longitude : 3.9738
Latitude : 44.06027

This guide is updated regularly, so buy your new copy every year!

⋀ Le Bel Eté

☎ 0466617604, *www.camping-bel-ete.com*
Address : 1870 rte de Nîmes (2.5km southeast)
Opening times : from beginning April to end Sept.
2.26 ha (97 pitches) flat, grassy
Tariff : (2012 price) 32€ ♥♥ ⇌ ▣ ⑴ (16A) – Extra per person 7€ – Reservation fee 15€
Rental rates : (2012 price) (from beginning April to end Sept.) – 22 🚐 – 3 mobile homes
(without sanitary facilities). Per night from 50 to 70€ – Per week from 260 to 790 €
Reservation fee 15€
Choose pitches near the Gardon river and away from the road in preference.

Surroundings : ♡♡ **Leisure activities :** ✕ 🏠 ⚤ ☌ ⚓ multi-sports ground **Facilities :** 🚿 ⚬━ ♨ ⚵ ⌁ ☕ ▣ ⚴ **Nearby :** ✂ ☁	

---

*The Michelin classification (⋀⋀⋀ ... ⋀) is totally independent of the
official star classification system awarded by the local prefecture or
other official organisation.*

ARGELÈS-SUR-MER

66700 – Michelin map **344** J7 – pop. 10,033 – alt. 19
▶ Paris 872 – Céret 28 – Perpignan 22 – Port-Vendres 9
Centre

⋀⋀⋀ Le Front de Mer ♣♦

☎ 0468810870, *www.camping-front-mer.com*
Address : av. du Grau (250m from the beach)
Opening times : from beginning April to end Sept.
10 ha (588 pitches) flat, grassy
Tariff : (2012 price) 39.50€ ♥♥ ⇌ ▣ ⑴ (6A) – Extra per person 7€ – Reservation fee 20€
Rental rates : (2012 price) (from beginning April to end Sept.) – 130 🚐.
Per night from 50 to 85 € – Per week from 265 to 1,260€ – Reservation fee 20€
🚐 sani-station
Pretty water park and indoor spa area.

Surroundings : ⊡ ♡♡
Leisure activities : ♟ ✕ ⊛ ⚲ ♫ ⚤ ≋ hammam, jacuzzi ⚤ ☌ ▣ ☌ ⚿
multi-sports ground, spa therapy centre
Facilities : 🚿 ⚬━ ♨ ☕ launderette ▣ ⚴

	Longitude : 3.04687 **Latitude :** 42.54684

⋀⋀⋀ Pujol

☎ 0468810025, *www.campingdepujol.com*
Address : av. de la Rétirada 1939
Opening times : from beginning June to end Sept.
6.2 ha (312 pitches) flat, grassy, sandy
Tariff : 38€ ♥♥ ⇌ ▣ ⑴ (6A) – Extra per person 8€ – Reservation fee 16€
Rental rates : (from beginning April to end Sept.) ♒ – 50 🚐. Per night from 20 to 120 €
Per week from 140 to 840 € – Reservation fee 16€
Numerous pitches for tents or caravans, many with good shade.

Surroundings : ♡♡
Leisure activities : ♟ ✕ ⊛ evening ♫ ⚤ ☌ ☌
Facilities : 🚿 ⚬━ ♨ ☕ launderette ▣ ⚴
Nearby : ✂ ☖

	Longitude : 3.02768 **Latitude :** 42.55532

FranceLoc Paris-Roussillon ♣

⌀ 0468811971, *www.parisroussillon.com*
Address : av. de la Retirada
Opening times : permanent
3.5 ha (206 pitches) flat, grassy
Tariff : (2012 price) 35€ ♦♦ ⇦ 回 ⚡ (10A) – Extra per person 7€ – Reservation fee 27€
Rental rates : (2012 price) (from beginning April to end Sept.) – 126 🛖 – 2 studios –
2 apartments. Per night from 51 to 138 € – Per week from 203 to 959€ – Reservation fee 27€
Plentiful shade. Good choice of mobile homes but pitches for tents and caravans also available.

Surroundings : 🎣 ⏲
Leisure activities : ♟ ✗ ⬚ ⛹ ⛷ ♨ ❑ ⤓ ⛱
Facilities : ♿ ⚿ ♨ ⚑ launderette ⚙
Nearby : 🐎

GPS Longitude : 3.03117
Latitude : 42.55782

Les Ombrages

⌀ 0468812983, *www.les-ombrages.com*
Address : av. du Général de Gaulle (400m from the beach)
Opening times : from beginning May to end Sept.
4.1 ha (270 pitches) flat, grassy, sandy
Tariff : 31€ ♦♦ ⇦ 回 ⚡ (10A) – Extra per person 6.20€ – Reservation fee 20€
Rental rates : (from beginning June to end Sept.) ⚓ – 15 🛖. Per week from 240 to 660 €
Reservation fee 20€
🚐 sani-station
Site is well-shaded, in part beneath plane trees. Note entrance is via the 'Les Peupliers' campsite.

Surroundings : 🏞 ⏲
Leisure activities : 🎱 ⤓ ♩
Facilities : ♿ ⚿ ♨ ⚑ launderette
Nearby : 🚴 ⛷ ♨

GPS Longitude : 3.04214
Latitude : 42.55074

Comangès

⌀ 0468811562, *www.campingcomanges.com*
Address : av. Gal de Gaulle (300m from the beach)
Opening times : from mid April to end Oct.
1.2 ha (90 pitches) flat, grassy
Tariff : (2012 price) 30.99€ ♦♦ ⇦ 回 ⚡ (10A) – Extra per person 6.99€ – Reservation fee 20€
Rental rates : (2012 price) (from mid April to end Sept.) – 19 🛖. Per week from 239 to 799 €
Reservation fee 20€
🚐 sani-station

Surroundings : ⏲
Leisure activities : ⤓
Facilities : ♿ ⚿ ♨ ⚑ ▣
Nearby : 🚴 ⛷ ♩ ♨

GPS Longitude : 3.04423
Latitude : 42.55145

There are several different types of sani-station ('borne' in French) – sanitation points providing fresh water and disposal points for grey water. See page 12 for further details.

Europe

𝒫 0468810810, *www.camping-europe.net*
Address : av. du Gal de Gaulle (500m from the beach)
Opening times : from end March to end Sept.
1.2 ha (91 pitches) flat, grassy
Tariff : 30.10€ ♥♥ ⇔ 🖻 (10A) – Extra per person 7€ – Reservation fee 20€
Rental rates : (from end March to end Sept.) ⅋ – 13 🛏. Per night from 50 to 120 €
Per week from 220 to 700 € – Reservation fee 20€
🚐 sani-station 26€
Good amount of shade, in part provided by plane trees. Good sanitary facilities.

Surroundings : ⑭
Leisure activities : 🏊 �Ⓛ
Facilities : ⅋ ⊶ 🛁 ᵠ launderette 🚿
Nearby : 🏕

GPS Longitude : 3.04185
Latitude : 42.54987

Le Stade

𝒫 0468810440, *www.campingdustade.com*
Address : 87 av. du 8 Mai (known as: rte de la Plage)
Opening times : from beginning April to end Sept.
2.4 ha (185 pitches) flat, grassy
Tariff : 26.50€ ♥♥ ⇔ 🖻 (10A) – Extra per person 5.90€ – Reservation fee 8€
Rental rates : (permanent) ⌗ – 10 🛏. Per night from 40 to 90€
Per week from 300 to 650€ – Reservation fee 10€
🚐 sani-station
Choose pitches away from the road in preference; sanitary facilities rather jaded.

Surroundings : ⑨⑨
Leisure activities : 🏊
Facilities : ⅋ ⊶ 🛁 ᵠ launderette
Nearby : 🍴✗ ⎕ ⌗ 🏕 ⎔

GPS Longitude : 3.03544
Latitude : 42.54774

La Massane

𝒫 0468810685, *www.camping-massane.com*
Address : av. Molière (opposite the 'Espace Jean Carrère')
Opening times : from beginning April to end Sept.
2.7 ha (184 pitches) flat, grassy
Tariff : 34€ ♥♥ ⇔ 🖻 (10A) – Extra per person 6.50€ – Reservation fee 12€
Rental rates : (from beginning April to end Sept.) ⌗ – 23 🛏. Per night from 39 to 86 €
Per week from 270 to 600 € – Reservation fee 12€
Rather old but well maintained sanitary facilities.

Surroundings : ⎕ ⑨⑨
Leisure activities : 🏛 🏊 🏕 ⎔
Facilities : ⅋ ⊶ 🛁 ᵠ launderette
Nearby : ⌗

GPS Longitude : 3.03115
Latitude : 42.55137

*The classification (1 to 5 tents, **black** or **red**) that we award to selected sites in this guide is our own system. It should not be confused with the classification (1 to 5 stars) of official organisations.*

NORTH

La Sirène et l'Hippocampe ♣♣
(rental of mobile homes and chalets only)

📞 0468810461, *www.camping-lasirene.fr*
Address : rte de Taxo
Opening times : from mid April to end Sept.
21 ha (903 pitches) flat, grassy, stony
Rental rates : ♿ (1 mobile home) – 500 �Ⓜ – 20 🏠. Per night from 29 to 256 €
Per week from 203 to 1,792 € – Reservation fee 20€

Site is in 2 distinct sections; 2 water parks; more peaceful and family-orientated on the 'Hippocampe' side.

Surroundings : �︎ 🞌🞌
Leisure activities : 🍸 ✗ (pub) 🎦 🞌 🏃 🤸 ♦🚴 🞌 🞌 🌊 🐎 disco, scuba diving, multi-sports ground
Facilities : ♿ ⚊ 🞌 🞌 🞌 🞌 launderette 🞌 🞌

GPS Longitude : 3.0326
Latitude : 42.57058

Le Soleil ♣♣

📞 0468811448, *www.campmed.com* ✂
Address : rte du Littoral
Opening times : from beginning May to mid Sept.
17 ha (844 pitches) flat, grassy, sandy
Tariff : 46.10€ 🛉🛉 🚐 ▣ (10A) – Extra per person 11.20€ – Reservation fee 20€
Rental rates : (permanent) ✂ – 135 🚐Ⓜ. Per night from 37 to 190 €
Per week from 259 to 1,330 € – Reservation fee 20€

Lush, green setting with good amount of shade, close to the beach.

Surroundings : �︎ 🞌🞌 🞌
Leisure activities : 🍸 ✗ 🎦 🞌 🏃 🞌 🞌 🌊 🐎 disco
Facilities : ♿ ⚊ 🞌 🞌 launderette 🞌 🞌

GPS Longitude : 3.04618
Latitude : 42.5744

Les Marsouins ♣♣

📞 0468811481, *www.campmed.com*
Address : av. de la Retirada
Opening times : from mid April to end Sept.
10 ha (587 pitches) flat, grassy
Tariff : 39.50€ 🛉🛉 🚐 ▣ (6A) – Extra per person 7.50€ – Reservation fee 20€
Rental rates : (from mid April to end Sept.) ♿ (1 mobile home) – 176 🚐Ⓜ.
Per night from 32 to 190 € – Per week from 224 to 1,330 € – Reservation fee 20€
🞌 sani-station – 8 ▣ 39.50€
Attractive pitches for tents and caravans in a leafy environment with flowers..

Surroundings : �︎ 🞌🞌
Leisure activities : 🍸 ✗ 🞌 🏃 🞌 🌊 scuba diving, multi-sports ground
Facilities : ♿ ⚊ 🞌 🞌 🞌 🞌 launderette 🞌 🞌
Nearby : 🐎

GPS Longitude : 3.03471
Latitude : 42.56376

Key to rentals symbols:
12 🚐Ⓜ   **Number of mobile homes**
20 🏠   **Number of chalets**
6 🛏   **Number of rooms to rent**
Per night   **Minimum/maximum rate per night**
30–50€
Per week   **Minimum/maximum rate per week**
300–1,000€

La Marende ♠♣

📞 0468811209, *www.marende.com*
Address : av. du Littoral (400m from the beach)
Opening times : from end April to end Sept.
3 ha (208 pitches) flat, grassy, sandy
Tariff : 38€ ♦♦ ⚡ 回 ⏚ (10A) – Extra per person 7.50€ – Reservation fee 15€
Rental rates : (from end April to end Sept.) – 67 🚐. Per night from 33 to 140 €
Per week from 228 to 980 € – Reservation fee 15€
🚻 sani-station

Good shade from pine and eucalyptus trees but choose pitches away from the road in preference.

Surroundings : 🏕 🌳🌳
Leisure activities : 🍷 ✗ 🎮 evening 🤸 jacuzzi 🚣 🚴 🏊 multi-sports ground
Facilities : ♿ ⚷ 🚿 🍴 launderette 🔌 🚲
Nearby : 🎣 🏇 🚴

GPS Longitude : 3.0422
Latitude : 42.57395

Club Airotel Les Galets ♠♣

📞 0468810812, *http://www.campinglesgalets.fr/* – limited spaces for one-night stay
Address : rte de Taxo at la Mer, Plage Nord (North Beach)
Opening times : from mid April to end Sept.
5 ha (232 pitches) flat, grassy
Tariff : (2012 price) 41€ ♦♦ ⚡ 回 ⏚ (10A) – Extra per person 8.70€ – Reservation fee 45€
Rental rates : (2012 price) (from mid April to end Sept.) ♿ (2 mobile homes) – 170 🚐 –
30 🏠. Per night from 28 to 157 € – Per week from 196 to 1,099 € – Reservation fee 45€
🚻 sani-station 10€ – 2 回 10€ – 🛥 ⏚10€

Family site with a large number of owner-occupier mobile homes, but few places for tents and caravans.

Surroundings : 🏕 🌳🌳
Leisure activities : 🍷 ✗ 🎮 evening 🤸 🚣 🏊 multi-sports ground
Facilities : ♿ ⚷ 🚿 🍴 launderette 🚲
Nearby : 🏇

GPS Longitude : 3.0144
Latitude : 42.57249

Le Roussillonnais ♠♣

📞 0468811042, *www.leroussillonnais.com*
Address : bd de la Mer
Opening times : from beginning April to beginning Nov.
10 ha (690 pitches) flat, grassy, sandy
Tariff : (2012 price) 31€ ♦♦ ⚡ 回 ⏚ (6A) – Extra per person 8€ – Reservation fee 50€
Rental rates : (2012 price) (from beginning April to beginning Nov.) 🏖 – 105 🚐.
Per week from 245 to 900 €– Reservation fee 50€
🚻 sani-station – 18 回 15€

Close to a beach, attractive and shady with plenty of pitches for tents, caravans; groups welcome.

Surroundings : 🌳🌳 ⛰
Leisure activities : 🍷 ✗ 🎮 🤸 🚣 🎣 multi-sports ground
Facilities : ♿ ⚷ (Jul–Aug) 🚿 🍴 launderette 🔌 🚲
Nearby : 🚣 🏇

GPS Longitude : 3.04367
Latitude : 42.56842

Routes nationales are main roads and their identifying numbers begin with N or RN. Routes départementales are generally quieter roads and begin with D or DN.

SOUTH

Les Castels Les Criques de Porteils ♠♣

✆ 0468811273, *www.lescriques.com*
Address : corniche de Collioure, RD 114
Opening times : from end March to end Oct.
4.5 ha (250 pitches) very uneven, terraced, relatively flat, flat, grassy, stony
Tariff : 51€ ♦♦ ⇌ 🖻 ⚡ (10A) – Extra per person 12€ – Reservation fee 26€
Rental rates : (from end March to end Oct.) – 69 🛏 – 10 tent bungalows.
Per week from 218 to 1,317€ – Reservation fee 26€
🚐 sani-station 5.50€ – 5 🖻 37€
Direct access to the beach via steep steps.

Surroundings : 🏖 ≼ Baie d'Argelès-sur-Mer 🏕 ☯☯ ⛰
Leisure activities : 🍷 ✕ 🏓 ⛵ ⛳ 🛝 scuba diving, multi-sports
ground
Facilities : ♿ ⚫ ▦ 🍳 🍴 launderette 🖨 🛒 refrigerated food storage

GPS Longitude : 3.06778
Latitude : 42.53389

La Coste Rouge

✆ 0468810894, *www.lacosterouge.com* – limited spaces for one-night stay
Address : rte de Collioure (3km southeast)
Opening times : from beginning April to end Sept.
3.7 ha (145 pitches) terrace, relatively flat, flat, grassy
Tariff : (2012 price) 32.60€ ♦♦ ⇌ 🖻 ⚡ (6A) – Extra per person 5.50€ – Reservation fee 20€
Rental rates : (2012 price) (from beginning April to end Sept.) – 52 🛏 – 2 🏠 – 6 studios.
Per night 120€ – Per week 825€ – Reservation fee 20€
*Away from the hustle and bustle of Argelès-sur-Mer, but access to the beaches via a free
shuttle.*

Surroundings : 🏕 ☯☯
Leisure activities : 🍷 ✕ 🖼 ⛸ 🛝 🛶 ◿
Facilities : ♿ ⚫ 🍳 🍴 launderette 🖨 🛒
Nearby : 🚲 🐎 water skiing, jet skis

GPS Longitude : 3.05285
Latitude : 42.53301

*We value your opinion and welcome your feedback.
Do email us at campingfrance@tp.michelin.com*

ARLES-SUR-TECH

66150 – Michelin map **344** G8 – pop. 2,757 – alt. 280
▸ Paris 886 – Amélie-les-Bains-Palalda 4 – Perpignan 45 – Prats-de-Mollo-la-Preste 19

Le Vallespir

✆ 0468399000, *http://www.campingvallespir.com/fr/index.html*
Address : situated 2km to the northeast, follow the signs for Amélie-les-Bains-Palalda; beside the
Tech river
Opening times : from beginning April to end Oct.
2.5 ha (141 pitches) relatively flat, flat, grassy
Tariff : (2012 price) 20€ ♦♦ ⇌ 🖻 ⚡ (10A) – Extra per person 5€
Rental rates : (2012 price) (from beginning April to end Oct.) – 50 🛏.
Per night from 31 to 91€ – Per week from 186 to 643€
Attractive and sheltered site that always has plenty of pitches for tents and caravans.

Surroundings : 🏕 ☯☯
Leisure activities : 🍷 ✕ 🖼 🛝 ⛳ 🛶 ◿ ⌇
Facilities : ♿ ⚫ 🍳 🍴 launderette

GPS Longitude : 2.65306
Latitude : 42.46671

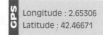

BAGNOLS-SUR-CÈZE

30200 – Michelin map **339** M4 – pop. 18,105 – alt. 51
▶ Paris 653 – Alès 54 – Avignon 34 – Nîmes 56

Les Genêts d'Or

⚲ 0466895867, *www.camping-genets-dor.com* ✖ (Jul–Aug)
Address : ch. de Carmignan (take the northern exit along the N 86 then continue 2km along the D 360 to the right; beside the Cèze river)
Opening times : from mid April to mid Sept.
8 ha/3.5 ha for camping (95 pitches) flat, grassy
Tariff : (2012 price) 29 € ♣♣ ⇔ 🗐 ⚡ (10A) – Extra per person 4.85 € – Reservation fee 10 €
Rental rates : (2012 price) (from mid April to mid Sept.) ✖ (Jul–Aug) – 8 🚐.
Per week from 419 to 611 € – Reservation fee 10 €
🚐 sani-station 29 €
Well-shaded pitches beside the river.

Surroundings : ♤♤ ⚠
Leisure activities : ♈ ✕ ⚓ ⅃ ◟
Facilities : ♿ ⊶ ▥ ♨ ♞ launderette ⚏, ⚗ refrigerators

Longitude : 4.63694
Latitude : 44.17358

We have selected the best campsites in France with our usual care,
listing those with the best facilities in the most pleasant surroundings.

BALARUC-LES-BAINS

34540 – Michelin map **339** H8 – pop. 6,622 – alt. 3 – ♨
▶ Paris 781 – Agde 32 – Béziers 52 – Frontignan 8

Le Mas du Padre ♣♣

⚲ 0467485341, *www.mas-du-padre.com*
Address : 4 ch. du Mas du Padre (situated 2km northeast along the D 2e and take road to the right)
Opening times : from end March to end Oct.
1.8 ha (116 pitches) relatively flat, flat, grassy, fine gravel
Tariff : (2012 price) 29.15 € ♣♣ ⇔ 🗐 ⚡ (10A) – Extra per person 5 € – Reservation fee 10 €
Rental rates : (2012 price) (from end March to end Oct.) ♿ (1 chalet) – 14 🚐 – 1 🏠.
Per night from 39 to 128 € – Per week from 273 to 896 € – Reservation fee 10 €
Site landscaped with attractive shrubs and flowers.

Surroundings : ⚘ ⌂ ♤♤
Leisure activities : 🎱 ⚹ ⚓ ⅃
Facilities : ♿ ⊶ ♨ ♞ 🗖 refrigerators

Longitude : 3.6924
Latitude : 43.4522

Les Vignes

⚲ 0467480493, *www.camping-lesvignes.com* – limited spaces for one-night stay
Address : 1 ch. des Vignes (1.7km northeast along the D 129, D 2e follow the signs for Sète and take road to the left)
Opening times : from beginning April to end Oct.
2 ha (169 pitches) flat, gravelled
Tariff : 25 € ♣♣ ⇔ 🗐 ⚡ (10A) – Extra per person 6 € – Reservation fee 50 €
Rental rates : (from end March to end Oct.) ♿ (1 mobile home) – 20 🚐 – 8 🏠.
Per week from 210 to 590 €
Clearly marked-out pitches on a gravel base, generally for clients visiting the nearby spa town (3 weeks).

Surroundings : ⌂ ♤♤
Leisure activities : ✕ 🎱 ⚓ ⅃
Facilities : ♿ ⊶ ♨ ⚏ ♞ 🗖

Longitude : 3.68806
Latitude : 43.45351

LE BARCARÈS

66420 – Michelin map **344** J6 – pop. 4,018 – alt. 3
▶ Paris 839 – Narbonne 56 – Perpignan 23 – Quillan 84

L'Oasis ▲▲

☏ 04 68 86 12 43, *www.camping-oasis.com*
Address : rte de St-Laurent-de-la-Salanque (1.3km southwest along the D 90)
Opening times : from end April to mid Sept.
10 ha (492 pitches) flat, grassy, sandy
Tariff : 38€ ♥♥ ⇌ 🗐 (10A) – Extra per person 8€ – Reservation fee 28€
Rental rates : (2012 price) (from end April to mid Sept.) – 193 🚐. Per night from 35 to 143 €
Per week from 241 to 1,001 € – Reservation fee 28€

A large number of mobile homes, but pitches for tents and caravans are always available.

Surroundings : ⊂ 🌳
Leisure activities : 🍴 ✕ 🗓 🏃 ⚽ 🎾 🏊 ⛷
Facilities : 🚻 ☛ 🗓🖓 🍴 **launderette** 🔋 🚿

GPS Longitude : 3.02462
Latitude : 42.77619

Sunêlia Le California ▲▲

☏ 04 68 86 16 08, *www.camping-california.fr*
Address : rte de St-Laurent (located 1.5km southwest along the D 90 – on D 83, take exit 9: Canet-en-Roussillon)
Opening times : from beginning April to mid Sept.
5 ha (265 pitches) flat, grassy, stony
Tariff : (2012 price) 36.50€ ♥♥ ⇌ 🗐 (10A) – Extra per person 6€ – Reservation fee 35€
Rental rates : (2012 price) (from beginning April to mid Sept.) 🚻 (2 mobile homes) –
140 🚐 – 20 🏠 – 5 tents. Per night from 34 to 156€ – Per week from 238 to 1,092€
Reservation fee 35€

Large sports area.

Surroundings : ⊂ 🌳🌳
Leisure activities : 🍴 ✕ 🏠 🗓 🏃 ⚽ 🎾 🏊 ⛷
Facilities : 🚻 ☛ 🖓 🍴 **launderette** 🔋 🚿
Nearby : 🛒

GPS Longitude : 3.02346
Latitude : 42.77606

Yelloh! Village Le Pré Catalan ▲▲

☏ 04 68 86 12 60, *www.precatalan.com*
Address : rte de St-Laurent-de-la-Salanque (located 1.5km southwest along the D 90 then continue 600m along the road to the right)
Opening times : from beginning May to mid Sept.
4 ha (250 pitches) flat, grassy, sandy
Tariff : 42€ ♥♥ 🗐 (10A) – Extra per person 8€ – Reservation fee 28€
Rental rates : (from beginning May to mid Sept.) – 90 🚐. Per night from 42 to 215 €
Per week from 294 to 1,505 € – Reservation fee 28€

Pleasant site with activities and facilities suitable for families with young children.

Surroundings : 🏖 ⊂ 🌳🌳
Leisure activities : 🍴 ✕ 🏠 🗓 🏃 ⚽ 🏊 multi-sports ground
Facilities : 🚻 ☛ 🖓 🍴 **launderette** 🚿
Nearby : 🛒

GPS Longitude : 3.02272
Latitude : 42.78086

*Routes nationales are main roads and their identifying numbers
begin with N or RN. Routes départementales are generally quieter
roads and begin with D or DN.*

L'Europe

℘ 04 68 86 15 36, *www.europe-camping.com* – limited spaces for one-night stay
Address : rte de St-Laurent-de-la-Salanque (situated 2km southwest along the D 90, 200m from the Agly river)
Opening times : permanent
6 ha (360 pitches) flat, grassy
Tariff : (2012 price) 50€ ⚤ ⇔ 回 (16A) – Extra per person 8€ – Reservation fee 30€
Rental rates : (permanent) – 50 ⦿ – 25 bungalows. Per night from 40 to 180€
Per week from 240 to 1,200 € – Reservation fee 30€

Choose pitches away from the road in preference. Luxury rental options in mobile homes as well as some very old bungalows.

Surroundings : ⌐ ♀
Leisure activities : ♈ ✗ ⌂ ⊙ ☂ ⚓ ✂ ⊿ ⚐
Facilities : ♿ ⊶ – 339 individual sanitary facilities (⛩⛲ wc) ⚄ ⚒ ⚑ ▣
⚒ ⚒

 Longitude : 3.02064
Latitude : 42.775

La Croix du Sud ♣♦

℘ 04 68 86 16 61, *www.lacroixdusud.fr* – limited spaces for one-night stay
Address : rte de Saint-Laurent-de-la-Salanque (1.4km southwest along the D 90; from D 83, take exit 10)
Opening times : from beginning April to end Sept.
3.5 ha (200 pitches) flat, grassy
Tariff : (2012 price) 41€ ⚤ ⇔ 回 (10A) – Extra per person 9€ – Reservation fee 32€
Rental rates : (2012 price) (from beginning April to end Sept.) ♿ (2 mobile homes) – 110 ⦿ – 22 ⌂. Per night from 36 to 176 € – Per week from 252 to 1,232 €
Reservation fee 32€
⛽ 1 回 15€

Numerous rental options, but pitches for tents and caravans are always available.

Surroundings : ⌐ ♀♀
Leisure activities : ♈ ✗ ⊙ ☂ ⚓ ⊿ multi-sports ground
Facilities : ♿ ⊶ ⚒ ⚑ launderette ⚒ refrigerators

 Longitude : 3.02757
Latitude : 42.77669

Le Soleil Bleu ♣♦
(rental of mobile homes and chalets only)

℘ 04 68 86 15 50, *www.lesoleilbleu.com*
Address : at Mas de la Tourre (1.4km southwest along the D 90 follow the signs for St-Laurent-de-la-Salanque; 100m from the Agly river)
Opening times : from beginning April to end Sept.
3 ha (175 pitches) flat
Rental rates : ♿ (1 mobile home) – 136 ⦿ – 24 ⌂. Per night from 50 to 185 €
Per week from 225 to 1,290 € – Reservation fee 30€

Choose pitches away from the road in preference.

Surroundings : ⌐ ♀♀
Leisure activities : ♈ ✗ ⌂ ⊙ ☂ ⚓ ⚲ ⊿ multi-sports ground
Facilities : ⊶ ⚒ ⚑ launderette ⚒ ⚒

 Longitude : 3.02842
Latitude : 42.77663

These symbols are used for a campsite that is exceptional in its category:
 Particularly pleasant setting, quality and range of services available
Tranquil, isolated site – quiet site, particularly at night
Exceptional view – interesting or panoramic view

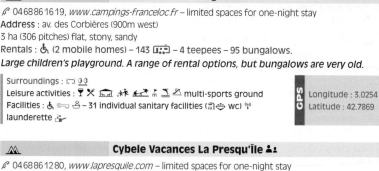

FranceLoc Las Bousigues ♣♣

℘ 04 68 86 16 19, *www.campings-franceloc.fr* – limited spaces for one-night stay
Address : av. des Corbières (900m west)
3 ha (306 pitches) flat, stony, sandy
Rentals : ♿ (2 mobile homes) – 143 🚐 – 4 teepees – 95 bungalows.
Large children's playground. A range of rental options, but bungalows are very old.

Surroundings : 🏕 ⅋⅋
Leisure activities : 🍸 🍴 🎠 🕺 ⚓ 🎣 🏊 ⛷ multi-sports ground
Facilities : ♿ ⊶ 🛁 – 31 individual sanitary facilities (🚿 wc) 🍴
launderette ⚒

GPS Longitude : 3.0254
Latitude : 42.7869

Cybele Vacances La Presqu'Île ♣♣

℘ 04 68 86 12 80, *www.lapresquile.com* – limited spaces for one-night stay
Address : r. de la Presquile (to the north, on the D 83 exit 12)
Opening times : from beginning April to end Sept.
3.5 ha (163 pitches) flat, grassy, sandy
Tariff : (2012 price) 14.50€ ⚭⚭ 🚐 ▣ ⚡ (16A) – Extra per person 3€ – Reservation fee 30€
Rental rates : (2012 price) (from beginning April to end Sept.) – 83 🚐 – 29 🏠 – 8 studios.
Per night from 60 to 90 €– Per week from 210 to 1,020 € – Reservation fee 30€
*Site surrounded by water! Some pitches are not very peaceful and there is a swimming
pool with a snack bar on the other side of the road.*

Surroundings : 🏕 ⅋⅋
Leisure activities : 🍸 🍴 🎠 🕺 jacuzzi ⚓ 🚲 🏓 🏊 ⛷ ⚓
multi-sports ground
Facilities : ♿ ⊶ 🛁 🍴 launderette 🧊 ⚒
Nearby : ⚓

GPS Longitude : 3.02672
Latitude : 42.80528

*Some information or pricing may have changed since the guide went to press.
We recommend you check the price list online in advance or at the entrance
to the campsite and enquire about possible restrictions.*

BARJAC

30430 – Michelin map **339** L3 – pop. 1,546 – alt. 171
▶ Paris 666 – Alès 34 – Aubenas 45 – Pont-St-Esprit 33

La Combe

℘ 04 66 24 51 21, *www.campinglacombe.com*
Address : at Mas de Reboul (3km west along the D 901, follow the signs for Les Vans and turn right
onto the D 384)
Opening times : from beginning May to end Sept.
2.5 ha (100 pitches) relatively flat, flat, grassy
Tariff : (2012 price) 24.20€ ⚭⚭ 🚐 ▣ ⚡ (6A) – Extra per person 8.60€ – Reservation fee 5€
Rental rates : (2012 price) (from beginning May to end Sept.) – 11 🚐 – 4 🏠 – 2 🛏 –
4 tent bungalows – 1 gîte. Per night from 40 to 100€ – Per week from 280 to 650 €
Reservation fee 15€
🚐 sani-station 4€ – ⚡15.20€
Family-orientated site, peaceful with plentiful shade.

Surroundings : 🌲 ⅋⅋
Leisure activities : 🍸 🎠 ⚓ 🏊
Facilities : ♿ ⊶ 🛁 🍴 🖥

GPS Longitude : 4.34784
Latitude : 44.30917

LANGUEDOC-ROUSSILLON

BÉDOUÈS

48400 – Michelin map **330** J8 – pop. 291 – alt. 565
▶ Paris 624 – Alès 69 – Florac 5 – Mende 39

Chon du Tarn

✆ 04 66 45 09 14, http://www.camping-chondutarn.com
Address : chemin du Chon du Tarn (take the northeastern exit, follow the signs for Cocurès)
Opening times : from beginning May to beginning Oct.
2 ha (100 pitches) relatively flat, flat, grassy
Tariff : ✱ 3.90€ ➡ 🔲 3.90€ – (¼) (6A) 2.20€
🚽 sani-station
A pleasant, green setting beside the Tarn river.

Surroundings : 🌿 ≤ 🏞
Leisure activities : 🏊 🎣
Facilities : 🚿 ⚬ 🧺 🔥 ⚑ 🔋
Nearby : 🍷 ✗ climbing

GPS Longitude : 3.60531
Latitude : 44.3446

BELCAIRE

11340 – Michelin map **344** C6 – pop. 440 – alt. 1,002
▶ Paris 810 – Ax-les-Thermes 26 – Axat 32 – Foix 54

Municipal la Mousquière

✆ 04 68 20 39 47, mairie.belcaire@wanadoo.fr
Address : 4 chemin du Lac (take the western exit onto the D 613, follow the signs for Ax-les-Thermes, 150m from a small lake)
Opening times : from beginning June to end Sept.
0.6 ha (37 pitches) relatively flat, grassy
Tariff : (2012 price) ✱ 3€ ➡ 🔲 5€ – (¼) (10A) 3€
Rental rates : (2012 price) (from beginning June to end Sept.) – 2 bungalows (without sanitary facilities). Per night 40€ – Per week 100€
Attractively shaded site, with a small but pretty lake nearby.

Surroundings : 〰
Leisure activities : 🏛
Facilities : 🚿 🔋
Nearby : 🏊 🎿 🎣 🛶 pedalos

GPS Longitude : 1.95022
Latitude : 42.81637

BESSÈGES

30160 – Michelin map **339** J3 – pop. 3,169 – alt. 170
▶ Paris 651 – Alès 32 – La Grand-Combe 20 – Les Vans 18

Les Drouilhèdes

✆ 04 66 25 04 80, www.campingcevennes.com
Address : situated 2km west along the D 17, follow the signs for Génolhac then continue 1km along the D 386 to the right; beside the Cèze river
Opening times : from beginning May to end Sept.
2 ha (90 pitches) flat, grassy, stony
Tariff : 25.50€ ✱✱ ➡ 🔲 (¼) (6A) – Extra per person 5.30€ – Reservation fee 13.75€
Rental rates : (from beginning May to end Sept.) – 6 🏠. Per week from 355 to 665 € Reservation fee 13.75€

Surroundings : 🌿 ≤ 🏞
Leisure activities : 🍷 🏊 ♨ 🛶
Facilities : 🚿 ⚬ 🧺 🔥 ⚑ 🔋 🚿

GPS Longitude : 4.0678
Latitude : 44.29143

BLAJOUX

48320 – Michelin map **330** I8
▶ Paris 638 – Montpellier 180 – Mende 34 – Millau 87

Village Vacances de Blajoux
(rental of maisonettes only)

𝒫 0466494600, *village-gite-blajoux.com*
Address : rte des Gorges du Tarn
0.8 ha terrace, flat
Rentals : 28 ⌂.

Surroundings : ⅋ ≤
Leisure activities : ▱ ⌶
Facilities : ⅋ 🅿 ⊞ ⍦ ▣

GPS Longitude : 3.48578
Latitude : 44.33555

BOISSET-ET-GAUJAC

30140 – Michelin map **339** J4 – pop. 2,302 – alt. 140
▶ Paris 722 – Montpellier 103 – Nîmes 53 – Alès 14

Domaine de Gaujac ♣⚋

𝒫 0466616757, *www.domaine-de-gaujac.com*
Address : 2406 chemin de la Madelaine
Opening times : from beginning April to mid Sept.
10 ha/6.5 ha for camping (293 pitches) terraced, relatively flat, flat, grassy
Tariff : 36€ ⚹⚹ ⇔ ▣ (10A) – Extra per person 6.80€ – Reservation fee 20€
Rental rates : (from beginning April to mid Sept.) – 39 ⟨⟩ – 28 ⌂ – 11 mobile homes
(without sanitary facilities). Per night from 40 to 95 € – Per week from 200 to 819 €
Reservation fee 20€
⟨⟩ sani-station 3.50€ – 8 ▣ 10€
The lower pitches enjoy good shade, while those on the terraces get plenty of sun.

Surroundings : ⌀⌀
Leisure activities : ⍦ ✗ ▱ ⍟ ⸙ jacuzzi ⟐⟐ ※ ↿ ⌶ ⚓
Facilities : ⅋ ⚬⚯ ⊡⊞ ⅋ ⚲ ▽ ⍦ launderette ⚐ ⚲
Nearby : ⚟ ⚲

GPS Longitude : 4.02771
Latitude : 44.03471

BOISSON

30500 – Michelin map **339** K3
▶ Paris 682 – Alès 19 – Barjac 17 – La Grand-Combe 28

Les Castels Le Château de Boisson ♣⚋

𝒫 0466248561, *www.chateaudeboisson.com* ⚋ (Jul-Aug)
Address : Hameau de Boisson (Boissons hamlet), Allegre les Fumades (don't drive through
village itself)
Opening times : from mid April to end Sept.
7.5 ha (165 pitches) very uneven, terraced, flat, grassy
Tariff : 37.50€ ⚹⚹ ⇔ ▣ (6A) – Extra per person 9.50€ – Reservation fee 26€
Rental rates : (from mid April to end Sept.) ⚋ (Jul-Aug) – 57 ⟨⟩ – 11 ⌂ – 15 gîtes.
Per night from 43 to 249€ – Per week from 196 to 1,533€ – Reservation fee 26€
⟨⟩ sani-station 5€ – ⚋ ⌘16€
*Pretty pitches at the base of a restored Cévennes château, with a view over the Cévennes
from some chalets.*

Surroundings : ⅋ ⚋ ⌀⌀
Leisure activities : ⍦ ✗ ▱ ⍟ ⸙ ⟐⟐ ※ ▣ ⌶ ⚓
Facilities : ⅋ ⚬⚯ ⊞ ⅋ – 7 individual sanitary facilities (⊞⚲⚲ wc) ⚲ ▽
⍦ launderette ⚐ ⚲ refrigerators

GPS Longitude : 4.25673
Latitude : 44.20966

LANGUEDOC-ROUSSILLON

LE BOSC

34490 – Michelin map **339** F6 – pop. 1,046 – alt. 90
▶ Paris 706 – Montpellier 51 – Béziers 58 – Sète 68

Relais du Salagou
(rental of chalets only)

☏ 04 67 44 76 44, www.relais-du-salagou.com
Address : at Salelles, 8 r. des Terrasses (4.5km southeast along the D 140 – A 75, take exit 56)
Opening times : from mid March to mid Nov.
12 ha/3 ha for camping flat
Rental rates : ♿ Ⓟ – 27 🏠. Per night from 63 to 152 € – Per week from 304 to 1,005 €
Reservation fee 9€

Surroundings : 🔎
Leisure activities : 🍸 🏠 ➿ hammam, jacuzzi 🏊 ✂ 🎣 🏊 fitness trail, spa therapy centre
Facilities : 🔑 🏢 🍴 launderette

GPS Longitude : 3.41539
Latitude : 43.68268

BRISSAC

34190 – Michelin map **339** H5 – pop. 615 – alt. 145
▶ Paris 732 – Ganges 7 – Montpellier 41 – St-Hippolyte-du-Fort 19

Le Val d'Hérault

☏ 04 67 73 72 29, www.camping-levaldherault.com
Address : av. d'Issensac (4km south along the D 4, follow the signs for Causse-de-la-Selle, 250m from the Hérault river (direct access)
Opening times : from mid March to end Oct.
4 ha (135 pitches) terraced, relatively flat, stony
Tariff : (2012 price) ♦ 6.10€ 🚗 🔌 11.75€ – ⚡ (10A) 4.10€ – Reservation fee 10€
Rental rates : (2012 price) (from mid March to end Oct.) – 20 🛖 – 4 🏠 – 10 tent bungalows.
Per night from 38 to 85€ – Per week from 251 to 865€ – Reservation fee 10€
🚐 sani-station
Well-shaded pitches, some on small terraces.

Surroundings : 🔎 🗑 🔎
Leisure activities : 🍸 ✕ 🏠 ⑨ evening 🏊 🏊 🚣
Facilities : ♿ 🔑 🏕 🚿 🍴 🏢 🏊 🚿
Nearby : 🏖 (beach) climbing

GPS Longitude : 3.70433
Latitude : 43.84677

BROUSSES-ET-VILLARET

11390 – Michelin map **344** E2 – pop. 313 – alt. 412
▶ Paris 768 – Carcassonne 21 – Castelnaudary 36 – Foix 88

Le Martinet-Rouge Birdie

☏ 04 68 26 51 98, www.camping-lemartinetrouge.com
Address : 500m south along the D 203 and take the road to the right, 200m from the Dure river
Opening times : from mid April to end Aug.
2.5 ha (63 pitches) undulating, flat, grassy, stony, rocks
Tariff : 18€ ♦♦ 🚗 🔌 ⚡ (10A) – Extra per person 7.50€ – Reservation fee 6€
Rental rates : (from mid April to end Aug.) – 9 🛖 – 1 🏠. Per night from 37 to 130 €
Per week from 259 to 959 €– Reservation fee 6€
Very pleasant site with pitches near rocks and plenty of shade provided by small Holm oak tees.

Surroundings : 🔎 🗑 🔎
Leisure activities : 🍸 ✕ 🏠 🏊 🏊 🏐 multi-sports ground
Facilities : ♿ 🔑 🏕 🍴 launderette

GPS Longitude : 2.0381
Latitude : 43.33088

CANET

34800 – Michelin map **339** F7 – pop. 3,269 – alt. 42
▶ Paris 717 – Béziers 47 – Clermont-l'Hérault 6 – Gignac 10

Les Rivières

✆ 0467967553, *www.camping-lesrivieres.com*
Address : at la Sablière (1.8km north along the D 131e)
Opening times : from beginning April to mid Sept.
9 ha/5 ha for camping (110 pitches) flat, grassy, stony
Tariff : 29€ ✸✸ ⇔ 🅴 🅗 (10A) – Extra per person 6€ – Reservation fee 10€
Rental rates : (from beginning March to end Oct.) ⚡ – 15 🚐 – 10 🏠 – 3 tent bungalows –
2 gîtes. Per night 49€ – Per week from 190 to 705 € – Reservation fee 10€
🚰 sani-station 10€ – 7 🅴 10€
A spacious site beside the Hérault river, where swimming is always an option.

Surroundings : 🏞 🏕 ♨♨
Leisure activities : 🍴 ✗ 🛋 jacuzzi 🏊 🚲 ⛷ ≋ ⛵ ⚓ climbing wall,
multi-sports ground
Facilities : ♿ ⚡ 🛁 🚻 🖼 🛒
Nearby : 🐎

GPS
Longitude : 3.49229
Latitude : 43.61792

CANET-PLAGE

66140 – Michelin map **344** J6
▶ Paris 849 – Argelès-sur-Mer 20 – Le Boulou 35 – Canet-en-Roussillon 3

Yelloh! Village Le Brasilia ▲▲

✆ 0468802382, *www.brasilia.fr*
Address : av. des Anneaux du Roussillon (beside the Têt river; direct access to the beach)
Opening times : from mid April to beginning Oct.
15 ha (735 pitches) flat, grassy, sandy
Tariff : 56.50€ ✸✸ ⇔ 🅴 🅗 (10A) – Extra per person 9€
Rental rates : (from mid April to beginning Oct.) ♿ (2 mobile homes) ⚡ – 172 🚐 – 2 gîtes.
Per night from 39 to 233 € – Per week from 273 to 1,631 €
🚰 sani-station
Leafy, green pitches and plentiful shade. Small landscaped 'villages' of mobile homes and
a variety of activities make this a real 'village' club.

Surroundings : 🏞 🏕 ♨♨ ⛰
Leisure activities : 🍴 ✗ 🛋 🎱 🏇 🎣 jacuzzi 🏊 🚲 ⛷ disco,
multi-sports ground
Facilities : ♿ ⚡ 🍴 🛁 🚿 🚾 🚻 launderette 🛒 🛍
Nearby : 🎿 🐎

GPS
Longitude : 3.03392
Latitude : 42.69429

Mar Estang ▲▲

✆ 0468803553, *www.marestang.com*
Address : rte de Saint-Cyprien (located 1.5km south along the D 18a, near the lake and the beach)
Opening times : from end April to end Sept.
11 ha (600 pitches) flat, grassy
Tariff : 49€ ✸✸ ⇔ 🅴 🅗 (6A) – Extra per person 15€ – Reservation fee 26€
Rental rates : (from end April to end Sept.) ♿ (1 mobile home) 🅿 – 225 🚐 – 32 tent
bungalows. Per week from 162 to 1,219 € – Reservation fee 26€
Direct access to the beach via a tunnel. Pitches have some shade; activities aimed at
children and teenagers.

Surroundings : 🏕 ♨♨
Leisure activities : ✗ 🛋 🎱 (amphitheatre) 🏇 🎣 🏊 🚲 🎿 ⛷ ≋
disco, multi-sports ground
Facilities : ♿ ⚡ 🛁 🚻 🖼

GPS
Longitude : 3.03256
Latitude : 42.67262

Les Peupliers

📞 0468803587, *www.camping-les-peupliers.fr*
Address : av. des Anneaux-du-Rousssillon (500m from the sea)
Opening times : from end April to mid Sept.
4 ha (237 pitches) flat, grassy, stony
Tariff : 51€ 🏕🏕 🚗 🔲 ⚡ (8A) – Extra per person 8€ – Reservation fee 23€
Rental rates : (from end April to mid Sept.) – 91 🚐 – 9 🏠. Per night from 28 to 115€
Per week from 196 to 805 €– Reservation fee 23€
Plentiful shade for the neat rows of pitches.

Surroundings : 🛣 🞡🞡
Leisure activities : 🍽 ✕ 🎲 ⛵ 🏊 ⛷
Facilities : 🚿 ⊶ 🔄 🚽 launderette 🍴
Nearby : 🛒 🍴 🎣 ♨ 🐎

GPS Longitude : 3.03111 / Latitude : 42.70741

Ma Prairie 🔺🔺

📞 0468732617, *www.maprairie.com*
Address : 1 av. des Côteaux (2.5km west, exit onto D 11, follow the signs for Elne and take the road to the right)
Opening times : from beginning May to end Sept.
4 ha (260 pitches) flat, grassy
Tariff : (2012 price) 43€ 🏕🏕 🚗 🔲 ⚡ (10A) – Extra per person 8.50€ – Reservation fee 20€
Rental rates : (2012 price) (from beginning May to end Sept.) – 50 🚐.
Per night from 35 to 140€ – Per week from 245 to 980 € – Reservation fee 20€
🚽 sani-station
Leisure and recreation area on the other side of the road.

Surroundings : 🛣 🞡🞡
Leisure activities : 🍽 ✕ 📺 🎲 evening 🏃 ⛵ 🏊 multi-sports ground
Facilities : 🚿 ⊶ 🔄🔄 🚽 launderette 🍴
Nearby : 🛒

GPS Longitude : 2.99777 / Latitude : 42.70103

Les Fontaines

📞 0468802257, *www.camping-les-fontaines.com*
Address : 23 av. de St-Nazaire
Opening times : from beginning May to mid Sept.
5.3 ha (160 pitches) flat, grassy, stony
Tariff : 34.50€ 🏕🏕 🚗 🔲 ⚡ (10A) – Extra per person 6.50€ – Reservation fee 15€
Rental rates : (2012 price) (from beginning May to mid Sept.) – 104 🚐.
Per night from 33 to 119 € – Per week from 180 to 830 € – Reservation fee 15€
🚽 sani-station 6€
Natural site with little or no shade; choose pitches near the lake and away from the road in preference.

Surroundings : 🛣
Leisure activities : 🍽 📺 ⛵ 🏊 wildlife park
Facilities : 🚿 ⊶ (Jul–Aug) 🔄 ☂ ♨ 🚽 launderette

GPS Longitude : 2.99892 / Latitude : 42.68909

Do not confuse:
🔺 *to* 🔺🔺🔺 : *MICHELIN classification*
with
★ *to* ★★★★★ : *official classification*

CANILHAC

48500 – Michelin map **330** G8 – pop. 138 – alt. 700
▶ Paris 593 – La Canourgue 8 – Marvejols 26 – Mende 52

⚠ Municipal la Vallée

📞 0466329114, *http://www.la-canourgue.com/tourisme/fetes.htm*
Address : at Miège Rivière (12km north along the N 9, follow the signs for Marvejols, turn left onto D 988, follow the signs for St-Geniez-d'Olt and take the road to the left; beside the Lot river – from A 75, exit 40 towards St-Laurent-d'Olt then continue 5km along the D 988)
Opening times : from mid June to mid Sept.
1 ha (50 pitches) flat, grassy
Tariff : 15€ 🚻 ⇌ 🔲 💧 (32A) – Extra per person 3€
Rental rates : (from mid June to mid Sept.) – 3 🚐. Per night from 36 to 50 €
Per week from 250 to 350 €
🚽 sani-station
In a small but green valley.

Surroundings : 🦎 ⇐ 🏞 ♨	
Leisure activities : 🎣 ⛷ 🎯 ≋ 🎣	
Facilities : ♿ ⊙ 🚿 🚰 🔥	**GPS** Longitude : 3.13992
Nearby : 🎾	Latitude : 44.44047

---

*This guide is not intended as a list of all the camping sites in France;
its aim is to provide a selection of the best sites in each category.*

LA CANOURGUE

48500 – Michelin map **330** H8 – pop. 2,112 – alt. 563
▶ Paris 588 – Marvejols 21 – Mende 40 – Millau 53

⚠ Camping du Golf
(rental of chalets only)

📞 0466328400, *www.lozereleisure.com* – traditional camp. spaces also available
Address : rte des Gorges du Tarn (3.6km southeast along the D 988, follow the signs for Chanac, after the golf course; beside the Urugne river)
8 ha terrace, flat
Rentals : 22 🏠.
🚽 sani-station

Surroundings : 🏞 ♨	
Leisure activities : ⛷ 🎯	**GPS** Longitude : 3.24072
Facilities : ⊙ **launderette**	Latitude : 44.40842
Nearby : 🍸 ✕	

⚠ Village Vacances de la Canourgue
(rental of gîtes only)

📞 0466484848, *www.lozere-resa.com*
Address : at Les Bruguières (located 1.5km west, follow the signs for Banassac, to the right just before the Intermarché supermarket)
3 ha open site, terraced, flat
Rentals : 🅿 – 48 gîtes.

Surroundings : ♨	
Leisure activities : 🎣 🎯	**GPS** Longitude : 3.20391
Facilities : ♿ ⊙ 🏛 🚰 **launderette**	Latitude : 44.43649
Nearby : 🛒	

LANGUEDOC-ROUSSILLON

LE CAP-D'AGDE

34300 – Michelin map **339** G9
▶ Paris 767 – Montpellier 57 – Béziers 29 – Narbonne 59

⋀⋀⋀ La Clape

ℰ 04 67 26 41 32, *www.camping-laclape.com*
Address : 2 r. du Gouverneur (near the beach – direct access)
Opening times : from beginning April to end Sept.
7 ha (450 pitches) flat, grassy, stony
Tariff : (2012 price) 32 € ♟♟ ⇔ 🔲 🗲 (10A) – Extra per person 6.30 € – Reservation fee 27 €
Rental rates : (2012 price) (from beginning April to end Sept.) ♿ (1 chalet) 🛏 – 89 🚐 – 31 🏠 – 9 tent bungalows. Per night from 36 to 105 € – Per week from 252 to 735 €
Reservation fee 27 €
🚐 sani-station 2 € – 22 🔲 10 €
Facilities and parking for campervans off the site.

Surroundings : 🛏 ♤♤
Leisure activities : 🍽 ✗ 🏠 ⚄ ⛷ multi-sports ground
Facilities : ♿ ⊶ 📶 ⌂ ♟ launderette 🔳 ♨ refrigerators

GPS Longitude : 3.5193
Latitude : 43.28534

CARCASSONNE

11000 – Michelin map **344** F3 – pop. 47,854 – alt. 110
▶ Paris 768 – Albi 110 – Béziers 90 – Narbonne 61

⋀⋀⋀ La Cité ♠♠

ℰ 04 68 10 01 00, *www.campingcitecarcassonne.com*
Address : rte de Saint-Hilaire (take the eastern exit along the N 113, follow the signs for Narbonne then continue 1.8km along the D 104, near a branch of the Aude river)
Opening times : from end March to beginning Oct.
7 ha (200 pitches) flat, grassy
Tariff : 24 € ♟♟ ⇔ 🔲 🗲 (10A) – Extra per person 7.70 €
Rental rates : (from end March to beginning Oct.) ♿ (2 mobile homes) – 26 🚐 – 17 tent bungalows – 23 rentals (without sanitary facilities). Per night from 40 to 112 €
Per week from 280 to 784 €
Very close to the old town of Carcassonne.

Surroundings : 🛏 ♤♤
Leisure activities : 🍽 ✗ 🏠 ⊡ ♟♟ ⚄ ⛷ multi-sports ground
Facilities : ♿ ⊶ ⌂ ♟ launderette ♨

GPS Longitude : 2.33716
Latitude : 43.19874

CARNON-PLAGE

34280 – Michelin map **339** I7
▶ Paris 758 – Aigues-Mortes 20 – Montpellier 20 – Nîmes 56

⋀ Les Saladelles

ℰ 04 67 68 23 71, *www.sivom-etang-or.fr*
Address : r. de l'Aigoual (head for Carnon-est, D 59, 100m from the beach)
7.6 ha (340 pitches) flat, sandy
Rentals : 🛏 – 40 🚐.
🚐 sani-station – 18 🔲
Choose pitches away from the road in preference; parking for campervans nearby but off the site.

Surroundings : ♤♤
Leisure activities : ♟♟ multi-sports ground
Facilities : ♿ ⊶ ⌂ ⚲ 🔲

GPS Longitude : 3.99464
Latitude : 43.55079

372

CASTEIL

66820 – Michelin map **344** F7 – pop. 120 – alt. 780
▶ Paris 878 – Montpellier 215 – Perpignan 59 – Carcassonne 126

Domaine St-Martin

 046805 52 09, *www.domainesaintmartin.com* – help moving caravans onto and off pitches avilable on request
Address : 6 bd de la Cascade (take the northern exit along the D 116 and take the road to the right)
Opening times : from beginning April to mid Oct.
4.5 ha (60 pitches) terraced, stony, rocks
Tariff : 26.50€ ♣♣ ⇔ 🔲 🔋 (10A) – Extra per person 4€ – Reservation fee 16.50€
Rental rates : (from beginning April to mid Oct.) – 7 🚐. Per night from 37 to 45 €
Per week from 270 to 635 € – Reservation fee 16.50€
Natural, rural setting at the foot of the Massif du Canigou mountains, near a waterfall.

Surroundings : 🌿 ⊏ 〰〰
Leisure activities : ▾ ✕ 🛶 ⨼
Facilities : ♿ ⍩ 🎽 ⫪ launderette
Nearby : ⅍

Longitude : 2.39464
Latitude : 42.53296

CASTRIES

34160 – Michelin map **339** I6 – pop. 5,671 – alt. 70
▶ Paris 746 – Lunel 15 – Montpellier 19 – Nîmes 44

Le Fondespierre

 046791 20 03, *www.campingfondespierre.com*
Address : 277 rte de Fontmarie (2.5km northeast along the N 110, follow the signs for Sommières and take turning to the left)
Opening times : from mid Jan. to mid Dec.
3 ha (103 pitches) terraced, relatively flat, stony
Tariff : (2012 price) 30.50€ ♣♣ ⇔ 🔲 🔋 (16A) – Extra per person 6€ – Reservation fee 15€
Rental rates : (2012 price) (from mid Jan. to mid Dec.) ⌇ – 20 🚐 – 2 🏠 – 7 tent bungalows. Per night from 56 to 89 € – Per week from 392 to 730 € – Reservation fee 15€
🚐 sani-station 5€

Surroundings : 🌿 ⊏ 〰〰
Leisure activities : 🚴 ⊕ ⨼
Facilities : ♿ ⍩ ☂ ⫪ launderette
Nearby : ⅍

Longitude : 3.99903
Latitude : 43.69125

CELLES

34700 – Michelin map **339** F7 – pop. 22 – alt. 140
▶ Paris 707 – Montpellier 55 – Nîmes 111 – Albi 190

Municipal les Vailhès

 046744 25 98, *www.lodevoisetlarzac.fr*
Address : situated 2km northeast along the D 148E4 follow the signs for Lodève – A75 take exit 54
Opening times : from beginning April to end Sept.
4 ha (246 pitches) terraced, grassy
Tariff : (2012 price) ♣ 3.95€ ⇔ 2€ 🔲 6.80€ – 🔋 (10A) 3.50€
🚐 12 🔲 8€
Attractive location beside the Lac du Salagou.

Surroundings : 🌿 ≤ ⊏ 〰〰 ⛰
Leisure activities : 🚴 ⌇ ◊
Facilities : ♿ ⍩ ⫪ ▦
Nearby : ⌇

Longitude : 3.36012
Latitude : 43.66865

CENDRAS

30480 – Michelin map **339** J4 – pop. 1,930 – alt. 155
▶ Paris 694 – Montpellier 76 – Nîmes 50 – Avignon 76

La Croix Clémentine

🖉 04 66 86 52 69, *www.clementine.fr*
Address : rte de Mende (situated 2km northwest along the D 916 and turn left onto the D 32)
Opening times : from beginning April to mid Sept.
10 ha (250 pitches) terraced, flat, grassy, rocks
Tariff : 28€ ⚥ ⚥ ⇔ 🔲 🔌 (6A) – Extra per person 9€ – Reservation fee 12€
Rental rates : (from beginning April to mid Sept.) – 20 🚐 – 20 🏠 – 10 tent bungalows.
Per night from 32 to 126€ – Per week from 200 to 850 € – Reservation fee 12€
🚽 sani-station 5€
A pleasant, wooded setting.

Surroundings : 🐟 ⊏ 🌲🌲
Leisure activities : 🍴 ✕ 🎦 🔲 evening 🚣 🚲 ✂ ⛵ ⛵ multi-sports ground
Facilities : 🔌 ☕ 🏢 🛁 🧺 🚿 🍽 launderette 🏊 🛒 refrigerators
Nearby : 🎣 🐎

GPS Longitude : 4.04333
Latitude : 44.15167

LE CHAMBON

30450 – Michelin map **339** J3 – pop. 273 – alt. 260
▶ Paris 640 – Alès 31 – Florac 59 – Génolhac 10

Municipal le Luech

🖉 04 66 61 51 32, *mairie-du-chambon@wanadoo.fr*
Address : at Palanquis (600m northwest along the D 29, follow the signs for Chamborigaud)
Opening times : from beginning July to end Aug.
0.5 ha (43 pitches) open site, terraced, relatively flat, stony, grassy
Tariff : (2012 price) ⚥ 2.31€ ⇔ 1.62€ 🔲 1.75€ – 🔌 (4A) 3.40€
Site in 2 sections straddling the road, beside the Luech river.

Surroundings : 🌲🌲
Leisure activities : 🎣
Facilities : 🔌 ☕ 🚽
Nearby : ✂

GPS Longitude : 4.00317
Latitude : 44.30494

CHASTANIER

48300 – Michelin map **330** K6 – pop. 92 – alt. 1,090
▶ Paris 570 – Châteauneuf-de-Randon 17 – Langogne 10 – Marvejols 71

Pont de Braye

🖉 04 66 69 53 04, *www.camping-lozere-naussac.fr*
Address : located 1km west, junction of D 988 and D 34; beside the Chapeauroux river
Opening times : from beginning May to mid Sept.
1.5 ha (35 pitches) terraced, flat, grassy
Tariff : 16€ ⚥ ⚥ ⇔ 🔲 🔌 (6A) – Extra per person 4€ – Reservation fee 7€
Rental rates : (from beginning May to mid Sept.) – 3 yurts – 2 tents – 1 gîte.
Per night from 45 to 60 € – Per week from 219 to 419 € – Reservation fee 7€
🚽 sani-station 2.50€ – 🚐 8€

Leisure activities : 🍴 🎦
Facilities : 🔌 ⚡ 🏢 🧺 🚿 🍽 🔲 🛒
Nearby : ✂ 🐎

GPS Longitude : 3.74755
Latitude : 44.72656

CHIRAC

48100 – Michelin map **330** H7 – pop. 1,161 – alt. 625
▶ Paris 587 – Montpellier 173 – Mende 37 – Marvejols 6

 Village Vacances
(rental of chalets only)

☎ 04 66 48 48 48, *www.lozere-resa.com*
Address : take the northern exit of the town – take exit 39 from the A75 then the D 809 following the signs for Marvejols
1.5 ha flat
Rentals : ♿ 🅿 – 15 🏠.

Surroundings : 🌲 ≤
Leisure activities : 🏖 ⚞ ⛏ multi-sports ground
Facilities : ⚮ ▥ 🗄
Nearby : 🎣

GPS Longitude : 3.26908
Latitude : 44.52684

CLERMONT-L'HÉRAULT

34800 – Michelin map **339** F7 – pop. 7,627 – alt. 92
▶ Paris 718 – Béziers 46 – Lodève 24 – Montpellier 42

 Municipal Campotel Lac du Salagou

☎ 04 67 96 13 13, *www.le-salagou.fr*
Address : at the Lac du Salagou (5km northwest along the D 156e 4, 300m from the lake)
Opening times : from mid Feb. to end Nov.
7.5 ha (388 pitches) terraced, relatively flat, flat, grassy, gravelled
Tariff : (2012 price) 🕴 3€ ⇔ 🅴 9.50€ – (🔌) (10A) 3€ – Reservation fee 15€
Rental rates : (permanent) (from end Feb. to end Nov.) ♿ (1 mobile home) – 10 🚐 – 13 🏠 – 13 gîtes. Per night from 60 to 80 € – Per week from 420 to 560 €
Reservation fee 15€
🚽 sani-station 2€ – 5 🅴 5€
Pleasant location close to the lake and the sailing club.

Surroundings : 🌲 ≤ 🗆 ♨
Leisure activities : 🛶 🏖
Facilities : ♿ ⚮ ▥ 🛁 ⚲ ☂ 🗄 refrigerated food storage
Nearby : 🍴 ✕ 🚴 ⛵ 🎣 ≋

GPS Longitude : 3.38957
Latitude : 43.6455

COLLIAS

30210 – Michelin map **339** L5 – pop. 1,002 – alt. 45
▶ Paris 694 – Alès 45 – Avignon 32 – Bagnols-sur-Cèze 35

 Le Barralet

☎ 04 66 22 84 52, *www.camping-barralet.com*
Address : 6 chemin du Grès (located 1km northeast along the D 3, follow the signs for Uzès and take the road to the right)
Opening times : from beginning April to end Sept.
2 ha (132 pitches) relatively flat, flat, grassy
Tariff : 25.50€ 🕴🕴 ⇔ 🅴 (6A) – Extra per person 5€ – Reservation fee 10€
Rental rates : (permanent) – 36 🚐 – 9 🏠. Per night from 37 to 110€ – Per week from 185 to 770 € – Reservation fee 10€
🚽 sani-station
Superb view of the village and surrounding area from the swimming pool and the terrace of the bar.

Surroundings : 🌲 ≤ ♨
Leisure activities : 🍴 ✕ 🏖 ⛏ multi-sports ground
Facilities : ♿ ⚮ ☂ 🗄 🛁

GPS Longitude : 4.48718
Latitude : 43.95769

CONNAUX

30330 – Michelin map **339** M4 – pop. 1,583 – alt. 86
▶ Paris 661 – Avignon 32 – Alès 52 – Nîmes 48

Le Vieux Verger

✆ 04 66 82 91 62, www.campinglevieuxverger.com
Address : 526 av. des Platanes (south of the town, 200m from the N 86)
Opening times : permanent
3 ha (60 pitches) terraced, grassy, stony
Tariff : 23.90€ ★★ ⇔ 🗉 🗲 (10A) – Extra per person 4.80€ – Reservation fee 10€
Rental rates : (2012 price) (permanent) ⚡ – 11 🚐 – 5 🏠. Per night from 99 to 209 €
Per week from 369 to 720 €– Reservation fee 25€
Additional pitches for tents and caravans at the top of the site, where there is more shade.

Surroundings : ⌂ ♀
Leisure activities : ✕ 🛝
Facilities : 🚻 ⚎ 🚰 🖭
Nearby : ✗

GPS Longitude : 4.59108
Latitude : 44.08478

CRESPIAN

30260 – Michelin map **339** J5 – pop. 325 – alt. 80
▶ Paris 731 – Alès 32 – Anduze 27 – Nîmes 24

Mas de Reilhe ♣♦

✆ 04 66 77 82 12, www.camping-mas-de-reilhe.fr
Address : chemin du Mas de Reilhe (take the southern exit along the N 110)
Opening times : from mid April to mid Sept.
2 ha (95 pitches) very uneven, flat, grassy, stony
Tariff : 29.80€ ★★ ⇔ 🗉 🗲 (10A) – Extra per person 6.50€ – Reservation fee 20€
Rental rates : (from mid April to mid Sept.) – 16 🚐 – 7 🏠 – 4 tent bungalows.
Per night from 30 to 115€ – Per week from 210 to 805€ – Reservation fee 20€
🚻 sani-station

Surroundings : ⌂ ♀♀
Leisure activities : ♟ ✕ 🏛 🎯 ⚡ 🚲 🛝
Facilities : ⚎ 🔟 🗊 ♨ ⛲ 🚰 🚰 launderette 🍴
Nearby : ✗

GPS Longitude : 4.09676
Latitude : 43.88015

Some campsites benefit from proximity to a municipal leisure centre.

EGAT

66120 – Michelin map **344** D7 – pop. 453 – alt. 1,650
▶ Paris 856 – Andorra-la-Vella 70 – Ax-les-Thermes 53 – Bourg-Madame 15

Las Clotes

✆ 04 68 30 26 90
Address : 400m north of the town; beside a little stream
2 ha (80 pitches) terraced, grassy, rocks
🚻 sani-station
Attractive elevated location, on the side of a rocky hill.

Surroundings : 🦌 ⩽ Sierra del Cadi (mountains) and Puigmal (peak)
⌂ ♀♀
Leisure activities : 🏛
Facilities : 🚻 ⚎ 🔟 ♨ 🚰 🖭

GPS Longitude : 2.01765
Latitude : 42.499

ERR

66800 – Michelin map **344** D8 – pop. 640 – alt. 1,350 – Winter sports : 1,850/2,520 m🚡8 🎿
▶ Paris 854 – Andorra-la-Vella 77 – Ax-les-Thermes 52 – Bourg-Madame 10

⚠ Le Puigmal

℘ 0468047183, www.camping-le-puigmal.com
Address : 30 rte du Puigmal (along the D 33b; beside a stream)
Opening times : from beginning Jan. to end Dec.
3.2 ha (125 pitches) relatively flat, flat, grassy
Tariff : 19.20€ ✽✽ ⇔ 🔲 🗗 (6A) – Extra per person 4.35€
Rental rates : (permanent) – 10 🏚. Per night from 118 to 150 € – Per week from 312 to 450 €
Pleasant, green setting, shaded in places. Good sanitary facilities in the centre.

Surroundings : 🏊 ≋
Leisure activities : 🎣 ↙
Facilities : 🚿 ⚬━ 🏢 🍽 launderette
Nearby : ⛷ 🏔

Longitude : 2.03539
Latitude : 42.43751

⚠ Las Closas

℘ 0468047142, www.camping-las-closas.com
Address : 1 pl. Saint-Génis (along the D 33b)
Opening times : permanent
2 ha (114 pitches) relatively flat, flat, grassy
Tariff : 21.40€ ✽✽ ⇔ 🔲 🗗 (10A) – Extra per person 4.25€
Rental rates : (permanent) – 15 🏚 – 1 apartment. Per night from 64 to 76 €
Per week from 360 to 450 €
In the centre of the village, close to the church; pleasant site with good sanitary facilities.

Surroundings : ≋
Leisure activities : 🎣 ↙
Facilities : 🚿 ⚬━ 🏢 ⛲ ❄ 🍽 launderette
Nearby : ✂ ⛷ 🏔

Longitude : 2.03138
Latitude : 42.44014

*The pitches of many campsites are marked out with low hedges
of attractive bushes and shrubs.*

ESTAVAR

▶ Paris 852 – Montpellier 247 – Perpignan 97

⚠⚠ L'Enclave ▲▲

℘ 0468047227, www.camping.lenclave.com
Address : 2 r. Vinyals (take the eastern exit along the D 33; beside the Angoust river)
Opening times : from beginning Jan. to end Sept.
3.5 ha (175 pitches) terrace, flat and relatively flat, grassy, stony
Tariff : 32.50€ ✽✽ ⇔ 🔲 🗗 (10A) – Extra per person 5.60€ – Reservation fee 10€
Rental rates : (from mid Dec. to end Sept.) ⚡ – 28 🏚. Per night from 60 to 150 €
Per week from 200 to 820 € – Reservation fee 10€
🚐 sani-station 6€ – 🚐 10.15€
An attractive, shady site beside a stream with a good playground area.

Surroundings : 🏊 ⛰ ≋
Leisure activities : 🎣 ⛹ 🧖 jacuzzi ↙ ✂ ⛷ 🎱 guided walks,
entertainment room
Facilities : 🚿 ⚬━ 🏢 ⛲ ❄ 🍽 launderette
Nearby : 🏖 🍷 ✗ 🚣 🎣

Longitude : 1.99813
Latitude : 42.4688

Yelloh! Village l'Escapade
(rental of chalets only)

⌀ 0466739739, *www.lescapade.com*
Address : cami del Segre (800m to the south)
Opening times : permanent
5 ha flat, grassy
Rental rates : ⬤ (5 chalets) – 44 🏠. Per night from 39 to 139 € – Per week from 273 to 973€
Pretty village of luxurious real wooden chalets.

Surroundings : ⬤ ♀
Leisure activities : ♀ ✗ 🎣 ⚓ multi-sports ground, entertainment room
Facilities : ⬤ ⚡ ⬛ ⬤ ⁿ launderette ⬤

GPS
Longitude : 1.99921
Latitude : 42.46182

FLORAC

48400 – Michelin map **330** J9 – pop. 1,921 – alt. 542
▶ Paris 622 – Alès 65 – Mende 38 – Millau 84

Municipal le Pont du Tarn

⌀ 0466451826, *www.camping-florac.com*
Address : rte du Pont-de-Montvert (situated 2km north along the N 106, follow the signs for Mende and take D 998 to the right, direct access to the Tarn river)
Opening times : from beginning April to end Oct.
3 ha (181 pitches) terraced, flat, grassy, stony
Tariff : (2012 price) 23.20€ ♀♀ ⬅ ▣ 🗓 (10A) – Extra per person 4.10€ – Reservation fee 12€
Rental rates : (2012 price) (from beginning April to end Oct.) – 22 🏠.
Per week from 219 to 830€ – Reservation fee 12€

Surroundings : ⬤ ♀
Leisure activities : ⚓ m ⬤ ⬤
Facilities : ⬤ ⚡ ⬤ ⬤ ⁿ ▣
Nearby : ✗ ⬤

GPS
Longitude : 3.59013
Latitude : 44.33625

*To make the best possible use of this guide,
please read pages 2–15 carefully.*

FONT-ROMEU

66120 – Michelin map **344** D7 – pop. 2,003 – alt. 1,800 – Winter sports : ⬤ ⬤ ⬤
▶ Paris 860 – Montpellier 245 – Perpignan 90 – Canillo 62

Huttopia Font Romeu ⬤

⌀ 0468300932, *www.huttopia.com* – alt. 1 800
Address : rte de Mont-Louis (RN 618)
Opening times : from mid June to mid Sept.
7 ha (175 pitches) relatively flat, flat, grassy
Tariff : (2012 price) 31.70€ ♀♀ ⬅ ▣ 🗓 (10A) – Extra per person 7€ – Reservation fee 20€
Rental rates : (2012 price) (from mid June to mid Sept.) ⓟ – 34 🏠 – 20 tents.
Per night from 61 to 157€ – Per week from 320 to 1,099€ – Reservation fee 20€
⬤ sani-station 7€
Site is 300m from the cable car station. Good quality rental options.

Surroundings : ⬤ ⬤ Pyrénées ♀
Leisure activities : ♀ ✗ ⬤ ⬤ ⚓
Facilities : ⚡ ⓟ ⬤ ⬤ launderette ⬤

GPS
Longitude : 2.04666
Latitude : 42.50628

FORMIGUERES

66210 – Michelin map **344** D7 – pop. 435 – alt. 1,500
▶ Paris 883 – Montpellier 248 – Perpignan 96

La Devèze

🕿 06 37 59 73 89, *http://www.campingladeveze.com* – alt. 1 600
Address : rte de la Devèze
Opening times : permanent
4 ha (117 pitches) terraced, flat, stony
Tariff : 19.60€ ✹✹ ⇐ 🔲 🕙 (10A) – Extra per person 4€
Rental rates : (permanent) – 1 'gypsy' caravan – 12 🚐 – 4 tents. Per night from 45 to 90€
Per week from 315 to 490 €
🚽 sani-station 3€ – 10 🔲 6€ – 🔋 10.50€
Natural, shaded setting in a pretty mountain location among pine trees.

Surroundings : 🐾 ⌷ 🗐
Leisure activities : ✗ 🔲 ⬈
Facilities : 🚻 ⚊ 🏛 🖰 🐟 ⬭ launderette 🍴

GPS Longitude : 2.0922
Latitude : 42.61035

FRONTIGNAN PLAGE

34110 – Michelin map **339** H8 – pop. 23,068 – alt. 2
▶ Paris 775 – Lodève 59 – Montpellier 26 – Sète 10

Les Tamaris ▲⬩

🕿 04 67 43 44 77, *www.les-tamaris.fr*
Address : 140 av. d'Ingril (to the northeast along the D 60)
Opening times : from beginning April to end Sept.
4 ha (250 pitches) flat, grassy, stony
Tariff : 51€ ✹✹ ⇐ 🔲 🕙 (10A) – Extra per person 9.50€ – Reservation fee 25€
Rental rates : (from beginning April to end Sept.) ⬊ – 70 🚐 – 32 🏠.
Per night from 35 to 170 € – Per week from 220 to 1,180 € – Reservation fee 25€
🚽 sani-station 5€
Pleasant setting close to the beach.

Surroundings : 🐾 ⌷ 🗐 ⬚
Leisure activities : 🍷 ✗ 🔲 🗐 🏊 ⬈ 🏊
Facilities : 🚻 ⚊ 🖰 🐟 ⬭ 🍴 launderette 🖳, 🍴 refrigerated food storage

GPS Longitude : 3.80572
Latitude : 43.44993

FUILLA

66820 – Michelin map **344** F7 – pop. 372 – alt. 547
▶ Paris 902 – Font-Romeu-Odeillo-Via 42 – Perpignan 55 – Prades 9

Le Rotja

🕿 04 68 96 52 75, *www.camping-lerotja.com*
Address : 34 av. de la Rotja (in the village of Fuilla)
Opening times : from beginning April to mid Oct.
1.6 ha (100 pitches) relatively flat, flat, grassy, stony, fruit trees
Tariff : (2012 price) 27.50€ ✹✹ ⇐ 🔲 🕙 (10A) – Extra per person 5€ – Reservation fee 12.50€
Rental rates : (2012 price) (from beginning April to mid Oct.) – 10 🚐. Per night from 42 to 86 € – Per week from 210 to 600 € – Reservation fee 12.50€
🚽 sani-station 15.50€
Pitches arranged on terraces, some with good shade.

Surroundings : 🐾 ⩽ ⌷ 🗐
Leisure activities : ✗ 🏊 (small swimming pool)
Facilities : 🚻 ⚊ 🖰 🍴 🖳
Nearby : 🖳 🍷

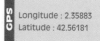

GPS Longitude : 2.35883
Latitude : 42.56181

GALLARGUES-LE-MONTUEUX

30660 – Michelin map **339** K6 – pop. 3,257 – alt. 55
▶ Paris 727 – Aigues-Mortes 21 – Montpellier 39 – Nîmes 25

Les Amandiers ♦♦

℘ 0466352802, *www.camping-lesamandiers.fr*
Address : 20 r. des stades (southwestern exit, follow the signs for Lunel)
Opening times : from beginning April to end Sept.
3 ha (150 pitches) flat, grassy, stony
Tariff : 27€ ♦♦ ⇌ 回 ⚡ (16A) – Extra per person 6€ – Reservation fee 20€
Rental rates : (from beginning April to end Sept.) ⚡ – 44 ▦ – 9 tent bungalows.
Per night from 24 to 140€ – Per week from 168 to 980€ – Reservation fee 20€
Swimming pool is a wellness area with a large jacuzzi, counterflow swimming and a bath with water jets.

Surroundings : ⌑ 00
Leisure activities : ♀ ✕ ⌂ ⊙ ✚ ⌾ ⇌ hammam ⇌ ✕ ⎍
spa therapy centre
Facilities : ⅙ ⚬ ⌂ ⌾ launderette ⤵
Nearby : ⚟

GPS Longitude : 4.16609
Latitude : 43.71612

GIGNAC

34150 – Michelin map **339** G7 – pop. 5,271 – alt. 53
▶ Paris 719 – Béziers 58 – Clermont-l'Hérault 12 – Lodève 25

Municipal la Meuse

℘ 0467579297, *www.campinglameuse.fr*
Address : 1.2km northeast along the D 32, follow the signs for Aniane then take the road to the left, 200m from the Hérault and a water sports centre
Opening times : from beginning April to end Sept.
3.4 ha (100 pitches) flat, grassy
Tariff : (2012 price) ♦ 2.25€⇌ 回 9.30€ – ⚡ (16A) 2.60€ – Reservation fee 7.62€
Rental rates : (2012 price) (from beginning April to end Sept.) ⚡ – 9 ▦.
Per night from 54 to 66 € – Per week from 370 to 460 € – Reservation fee 7.62€
⛽ sani-station 3€
Pleasant, spacious, with pitches that are well marked out and plenty of shade.

Surroundings : ⌑ 00
Leisure activities : ✕ ✕
Facilities : ⅙ ⚬ ⌾ 回
Nearby : ⚟ ⚞ fitness trail

GPS Longitude : 3.55927
Latitude : 43.662

GOUDARGUES

30630 – Michelin map **339** L3 – pop. 1,032 – alt. 77
▶ Paris 667 – Alès 51 – Bagnols-sur-Cèze 17 – Barjac 20

St-Michelet ♦♦

℘ 0466822499, *www.lesaintmichelet.com*
Address : rte de Frigoulet (located 1km northwest along the D 371; beside the Cèze river)
Opening times : from beginning May to mid Sept.
4 ha (160 pitches) terrace, flat and relatively flat, grassy, stony
Tariff : (2012 price) 20.60€ ♦♦ ⇌ 回 ⚡ (10A) – Extra per person 6€
Rental rates : (2012 price) (from beginning May to mid Sept.) ⚡ – 55 ▦.
Per night from 47 to 90 € – Per week from 320 to 610 €
The lower part of the site beside the Cèze river is for tents and caravans; mobile homes occupy the higher part, where the swimming pool is also located.

Surroundings : ⚟ ⌑ 00
Leisure activities : ♀ ✕ ⌂ ✚ ⇌ ⎍ ⚞ ⚞
Facilities : ⅙ ⚬ ⌂ ⌾ 回

GPS Longitude : 4.46271
Latitude : 44.22123

Les Amarines 2

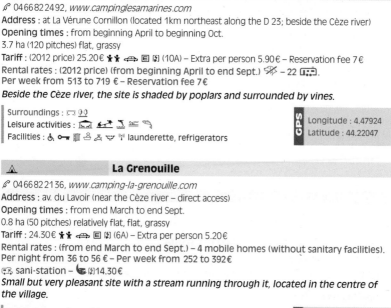

📞 0466822492, www.campinglesamarines.com

Address : at La Vérune Cornillon (located 1km northeast along the D 23; beside the Cèze river)

Opening times : from beginning April to beginning Oct.

3.7 ha (120 pitches) flat, grassy

Tariff : (2012 price) 25.20€ ★★ ⇌ 🔲 🗲 (10A) – Extra per person 5.90€ – Reservation fee 7€

Rental rates : (2012 price) (from beginning April to end Sept.) 🏠 – 22 🚐.
Per week from 513 to 719 € – Reservation fee 7€

Beside the Cèze river, the site is shaded by poplars and surrounded by vines.

Surroundings : 🏕 🛝
Leisure activities : 🎣 🛝 🛶 🚣 🎣
Facilities : ♿ ⚷ 🏛 🚿 🧺 ⚡ 🚰 launderette, refrigerators

GPS Longitude : 4.47924
Latitude : 44.22047

La Grenouille

📞 0466822136, www.camping-la-grenouille.com

Address : av. du Lavoir (near the Cèze river – direct access)

Opening times : from end March to end Sept.

0.8 ha (50 pitches) relatively flat, flat, grassy

Tariff : 24.30€ ★★ ⇌ 🔲 🗲 (6A) – Extra per person 5.20€

Rental rates : (from end March to end Sept.) – 4 mobile homes (without sanitary facilities).
Per night from 36 to 56 € – Per week from 252 to 392€
🚐 sani-station – 🚰 🗲14.30€

Small but very pleasant site with a stream running through it, located in the centre of the village.

Surroundings : 🌿 🏕 🛝
Leisure activities : 🛝 🛶 (small swimming pool) 🎣
Facilities : ♿ ⚷ 🚿 🚰 🔲 refrigerators
Nearby : 🍴

GPS Longitude : 4.46847
Latitude : 44.21468

LA GRANDE-MOTTE

34280 – Michelin map **339** J7 – pop. 8,391 – alt. 1
▶ Paris 747 – Aigues-Mortes 12 – Lunel 16 – Montpellier 28

Le Garden ▲≛

📞 0467565009, www.legarden.fr – ⛺

Address : av. de la Petite Motte (take the western exit along the D 59, 300m from the beach)

Opening times : from beginning April to mid Oct.

3 ha (209 pitches) flat, sandy

Tariff : 44€ ★★ ⇌ 🔲 🗲 (10A) – Extra per person 9.80€

Rental rates : (2012 price) (permanent) – 121 🚐. Per night from 62 to 150€
Per week from 329 to 945 € – Reservation fee 20€

Good sanitary facilities and upmarket rental options.

Surroundings : 🏕 🛝
Leisure activities : 🍴 🍽 🎣 🛝 🛶 🚣
Facilities : ♿ ⚷ 🔲 🚿 🧺 🚰 launderette 🛒 🚿
Nearby : 🏇 🐎

For more information on visiting particular towns or regions, consult the relevant regional MICHELIN Green Guide. We also recommend you use the appropriate Michelin regional map to locate your selected campsite, to calculate distances and to work out the best route.

Les Cigales

⌖ 0467565085, *www.paysdelor.fr*
Address : allée des Pins (take the western exit along the D 59)
Opening times : from beginning April to end Sept.
2.5 ha (180 pitches) flat, sandy
Tariff : 21.50€ ♥ ♥ ⊨ 🔲 🔌 (10A) – Extra per person 6€ – Reservation fee 10€
Rental rates : (from beginning April to end Sept.) – 20 🏠. Per week from 185 to 680€
Reservation fee 10€
🚐 sani-station 16€ – 45 🔲 16€
Large parking area for campervans adjoining the campsite.

Surroundings : ⚲⚲
Leisure activities : ⚓
Facilities : ⚒ ⚳ ⚴ ⚵ ⚶ launderette
Nearby : ⚘

GPS Longitude : 4.07612
Latitude : 43.56722

GRANDRIEU

48600 – Michelin map **330** J6 – pop. 762 – alt. 1,160
▶ Paris 554 – Langogne 28 – Châteauneuf-de-Randon 19 – Marvejols 61

Municipal le Valadio

⌖ 0466463139, *mairie.grandrieu@wanadoo.fr* – alt. 1 200
Address : south of the village, access via the road in front of the post office; 100m from Grandrieu and a lake
Opening times : from mid June to mid Sept.
1 ha (33 pitches) terraced, flat, relatively flat, stony, grassy
Tariff : (2012 price) ♥ 2€ ⊨ 1€ 🔲 2€ – 🔌 (9A) 2€

Surroundings : ≤
Leisure activities : ⚓ ⚲
Facilities : ⚒ ⚴
Nearby : ⚔ ⚵

GPS Longitude : 3.63422
Latitude : 44.78218

This guide is updated regularly, so buy your new copy every year!

LE GRAU-DU-ROI

30240 – Michelin map **339** J7 – pop. 7,995 – alt. 2
▶ Paris 751 – Aigues-Mortes 7 – Arles 55 – Lunel 22

FranceLoc Le Boucanet ♠♠

⌖ 0466514148, *http://campingboucanet.franceloc.fr/* ⚹
Address : rte de Carnon (situated 2km northwest of Le Grau-du-Roi (right bank) following signs for la Grande-Motte; beside beach)
Opening times : from beginning April to end Sept.
7.5 ha (462 pitches) flat, sandy
Tariff : (2012 price) 40€ ♥ ♥ ⊨ 🔲 🔌 (10A) – Extra per person 9€ – Reservation fee 27€
Rental rates : (from beginning April to end Sept.) ⚹ – 2 caravans – 274 🏠.
Per night from 65 to 151€ – Per week from 259 to 1,610 € – Reservation fee 27€
🚐 sani-station 4€ – 5 🔲 40€
Exclusive location beside a beautiful beach.

Surroundings : ⚲ ⚲ ⚠
Leisure activities : ⛾ ✗ ⚲ ⚶ ⚓ ⚵ ⚲ ☒ ⚴ ⚲
Facilities : ⚒ ⚳ ⚴ ⚶ launderette ⚵ ⚴ refrigerated food storage
Nearby : ⚘

GPS Longitude : 4.10753
Latitude : 43.55428

ISPAGNAC

48320 – Michelin map **330** J8 – pop. 851 – alt. 518
▶ Paris 612 – Florac 11 – Mende 28 – Meyrueis 46

Municipal du Pré Morjal

✆ 0466442377, *www.lepremorjal.fr*

Address : chemin du Beldou (take the western exit along the D 907bis, follow the signs for Millau and take road to the left; near the Tarn river)

2 ha (123 pitches) flat, grassy

Rentals : 8.

sani-station

A pleasant, wooded setting at the entrance to the Tarn river gorges.

Surroundings :
Leisure activities :
Facilities : launderette
Nearby :

Longitude : 3.53038
Latitude : 44.37223

Routes nationales are main roads and their identifying numbers begin with N or RN. Routes départementales are generally quieter roads and begin with D or DN.

JUNAS

30250 – Michelin map **339** J6 – pop. 1,085 – alt. 75
▶ Paris 730 – Aigues-Mortes 30 – Aimargues 15 – Montpellier 42

Les Chênes

✆ 0466809907, *www.camping-les-chenes.com*

Address : 95 chemin des Tuileries Basses (1.3km south along the D 140, follow the signs for Sommières and take road to the left)

Opening times : from beginning April to mid Oct.

1.7 ha (90 pitches) terraced, flat and relatively flat, stony

Tariff : 20.80€ ★★ 回 (10A) – Extra per person 4.40€ – Reservation fee 11€

Rental rates : (from beginning April to mid Oct.) – 4 caravans – 9.
Per week from 230 to 580€ – Reservation fee 11€

Site attractively shaded by Holm oaks, with pitches laid out on terraces, some surrounded by low stone walls.

Surroundings :
Leisure activities :
Facilities :

Longitude : 4.123
Latitude : 43.76921

L'Olivier

✆ 0466803952, *www.campinglolivier.fr*

Address : 112 rte de Congenies (take the eastern exit along the D 140 and take the road to the right)

Opening times : from beginning April to end Oct.

1 ha (45 pitches) flat and relatively flat, stony, grassy, rocks

Tariff : (2012 price) 20.90€ ★★ 回 (10A) – Extra per person 4.60€ – Reservation fee 10€

Rental rates : (2012 price) (from beginning April to end Oct.) – 7 – 6 – 3 tent bungalows. Per night from 40 to 60€ – Per week from 180 to 602 € – Reservation fee 10€

Family-friendly site in the shade of Holm oaks and near the village.

Surroundings :
Leisure activities :
Facilities :

Longitude : 4.12489
Latitude : 43.77081

LANUÉJOLS

30750 – Michelin map **339** F4 – pop. 334 – alt. 905
▶ Paris 656 – Alès 109 – Mende 68 – Millau 35

Domaine de Pradines

✆ 04 67 82 73 85, *www.domaine-de-pradines.com* – alt. 800
Address : rte de Millau, D28 (3.5km west along the D 28, follow the signs for Roujarie and take road to the left)
Opening times : from end May to mid Sept.
30 ha (75 pitches) flat, relatively flat, grassy
Tariff : (2012 price) 19€ ✦✦ ⟷ 🔲 🔣 (16A) – Extra per person 8€
Rental rates : (2012 price) (from mid Feb. to end Oct.) – 5 🚐 – 3 🏠 – 4 yurts – 4 gîtes.
Per night from 52 to 90 € – Per week from 364 to 690 €

Surroundings : 🌄 ≤ ♀
Leisure activities : ✗ 🎦 ⛱ ✂ 🎿 🐎
Facilities : ♿ ⊶ 🚰 🅿 ⚱ 🚿

GPS Longitude : 3.34722
Latitude : 44.13306

LAROQUE-DES-ALBÈRES

66740 – Michelin map **344** I7 – pop. 2,028 – alt. 100
▶ Paris 881 – Argelès-sur-Mer 11 – Le Boulou 14 – Collioure 18

Cybele Vacances Les Albères

✆ 04 68 89 23 64, *www.camping-des-alberes.com*
Address : rte du Moulin de Cassagnes (take the northeastern exit along the D 2, follow the signs for Argelès-sur-Mer then continue 0.4km along the road to the right)
Opening times : from beginning April to end Sept.
5 ha (211 pitches) very uneven, terraced, relatively flat, flat, stony, grassy
Tariff : (2012 price) 18€ ✦✦ ⟷ 🔲 🔣 (6A) – Extra per person 6€ – Reservation fee 20€
Rental rates : (2012 price) (from beginning April to end Sept.) – 54 🚐 – 9 🏠 – 3 tents.
Per night from 28 to 70 € – Per week from 195 to 699 € – Reservation fee 30€

Attractively shaded with pitches laid out on terraces.

Surroundings : 🌄 ⟷ ♀♀
Leisure activities : 🍽 ✗ 🎦 🏃 ⛱ ✂ 🎿 multi-sports ground
Facilities : ♿ ⊶ 🚰 🅿 ⚱ 🚿

GPS Longitude : 2.94418
Latitude : 42.52404

To visit a town or region, use the MICHELIN Green Guides.

LATTES

34970 – Michelin map **339** I7 – pop. 15,804 – alt. 3
▶ Paris 766 – Montpellier 7 – Nîmes 54 – Béziers 68

Le Parc

✆ 04 67 65 85 67, *www.leparccamping.com*
Address : rte de Mauguio (situated 2km northeast along the D 172)
Opening times : permanent
1.6 ha (100 pitches) flat, grassy, stony
Tariff : 28€ ✦✦ ⟷ 🔲 🔣 (10A) – Extra per person 6€ – Reservation fee 15€
Rental rates : (permanent) – 28 🚐. Per week from 250 to 720 € – Reservation fee 15€
Close to the tramway (line 3) for Montpellier and Pérols or Lattes.

Surroundings : ⟷ ♀♀
Leisure activities : 🏄 ⛱ 🎿
Facilities : ♿ ⊶ ▥ 🚰 launderette
Nearby : ✂

GPS Longitude : 3.92578
Latitude : 43.57622

AUBERT

48170 – Michelin map **330** J7 – pop. 106 – alt. 1,200 – Winter sports : 1,200/1,264 m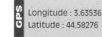
▶ Paris 584 – Langogne 28 – Marvejols 46 – Mende 19

⚠ Municipal la Pontière

✆ 04 66 47 72 09, *mairie.laubert@wanadoo.fr* – limited spaces for one-night stay
Address : rte du Lac de Charpal (500m southwest along the N 88 and D 6, follow the signs for Rieutort-de-Randon to the right)
2 ha (33 pitches) very uneven, relatively flat, rocks, stony, grassy
Rentals : 3 gîtes – Gîtes d'étape.

Surroundings : ⛰⛰
Leisure activities : ♈ ✗ 🏠 ⚓
Facilities : ♿ ⚷ 🚿 📷

GPS Longitude : 3.63536
Latitude : 44.58276

AURENS

34480 – Michelin map **339** E7 – pop. 1,349 – alt. 140
▶ Paris 736 – Bédarieux 14 – Béziers 22 – Clermont-l'Hérault 40

🏔 L'Oliveraie 👥

✆ 04 67 90 24 36, *www.oliveraie.com*
Address : chemin de Bédarieux (situated 2km north and take the road to the right)
7 ha (110 pitches) terraced, relatively flat, flat, grassy, stony
Rentals : 🏚 – 10 🚐 – 2 🏠 – 7 mobile homes (without sanitary facilities).
A shady site with pitches laid out on terraces and a swimming pool surrounded by olive trees.

Surroundings : 🌳 ⛰⛰
Leisure activities : ♈ ✗ ☕ evening 🏃 🎱 ⚓ 🚲 ✂ 🎣 ⛲ 🐎 🪁
Facilities : ♿ ⚷ 🚿 ⛺ 🚾 📷 🧺 🚰

GPS Longitude : 3.18571
Latitude : 43.53631

These symbols are used for a campsite that is exceptional in its category:
🏔🏔...🏔 *Particularly pleasant setting, quality and range of services available*
🦢🦢 *Tranquil, isolated site – quiet site, particularly at night*
≪≪ *Exceptional view – interesting or panoramic view*

E MALZIEU-VILLE

48140 – Michelin map **330** I5 – pop. 868 – alt. 860
▶ Paris 541 – Mende 51 – Le Puy-en-Velay 74 – Saint-Flour 150

🏔 Les Chalets de la Margeride
(rental of chalets only)

✆ 04 66 42 56 00, *www.chalets-margeride.com*
Address : at Chassagnes (4.5km northwest along the D 989, follow the signs for St-Chély-d'Apcher and take the D 4, following signs for La Garde – from A 75: take exit 32)
Opening times : permanent
50 ha/2 ha for camping terraced
Rental rates : ♿ – 21 🏠. Per night from 70 to 147 € – Per week from 281 to 800 €
Attractive panoramic location in the Margeride hills.

Surroundings : 🦢 ≪ Plateau de la Margeride
Leisure activities : ♈ 🏠 ⚓ 🚲 🖼 (open-air in season) 🪁
Facilities : ⚷ 🚿 🍽 launderette 🚰
Nearby : ✂

GPS Longitude : 3.30631
Latitude : 44.87017

La Piscine

✆ 04 66 31 47 63
Address : chemin de la Chazette (located 1.5km north along the D 989, follow the signs for St-Chély-d'Apcher and take road to the left after the bridge; near the swimming pool and a small lake)
1 ha (64 pitches) relatively flat, flat, grassy, stony
Rentals : ♿ – 13 🏠.
sani-station

Surroundings : ⬦ ⟨ 🏠 ♀
Leisure activities : 🚴
Facilities : ♿ o━ ⌂ ⛱ 🖥
Nearby : ♀ ✗ ✗ 🛶 ⬦ pedalos

GPS Longitude : 3.33775
Latitude : 44.85152

Do not confuse:
▲ to ▲▲▲ : MICHELIN classification
with
★ to ★★★★★ : official classification

MARSEILLAN-PLAGE

34340 – Michelin map **339** G8
▶ Paris 765 – Montpellier 51 – Nîmes 100 – Carcassonne 114

Les Méditerranées – Beach Club Nouvelle Floride ♣♦

✆ 04 67 21 94 49, *www.lesmediterranees.com*
Address : 262 av. des Campings
Opening times : from mid March to end Sept.
7 ha (475 pitches) flat, sandy
Tariff : 55€ ♣♣ ⬛ 🔲 (6A) – Extra per person 10€ – Reservation fee 30€
Rental rates : (from mid April to end Sept.) ✗ – 160 🏠. Per night from 35 to 255€
Per week from 245 to 1,785 € – Reservation fee 30€
sani-station
Pleasant location close to a beach.

Surroundings : ⬜ ♀♀ ⬥
Leisure activities : ♀ ✗ 🏠 ⬦ 🏃 ♨ 🚴 🛶 ⬦ multi-sports ground, entertainment room
Facilities : ♿ o━ 🏢 ⬦ ⬦ ⛱ ♀ launderette ⬦ ⬦
Nearby : 🛒 disco

GPS Longitude : 3.54244
Latitude : 43.30923

Les Méditerranées – Beach Garden ♣♦

✆ 04 67 21 92 83, *www.lesmediterranees.com*
Address : av. des Campings
Opening times : from mid April to end Sept.
14 ha (600 pitches) flat, grassy, sandy
Tariff : 51€ ♣♣ ⬛ 🔲 (8A) – Extra per person 10€ – Reservation fee 30€
Rental rates : (from mid April to end Sept.) ✗ – 76 🏠. Per night from 50 to 200 €
Per week from 350 to 1,400 € – Reservation fee 30€
Close to a beach with a panoramic restaurant.

Surroundings : ⬦ ⬜ ♀♀ ⬥
Leisure activities : ♀ ✗ 🏠 ⬦ 🏃 🚴 🛴 🛶
Facilities : ♿ o━ ⬦ ⛱ ♀ launderette ⬦ ⬦
Nearby : 🛒

GPS Longitude : 3.538
Latitude : 43.3058

Les Méditerranées – Beach Club Charlemagne

℘ 04 67 21 92 49, *www.lesmediterranees.com*
Address : av. des Campings (250m from the beach)
Opening times : from mid April to end Sept.
6.7 ha (480 pitches) flat, grassy, sandy
Tariff : 55€ ✷✷ ⇔ 圓 ⚏ (10A) – Extra per person 10€ – Reservation fee 30€
Rental rates : (from mid April to end Sept.) ⌦ – 170 ⟦⟧. Per night from 35 to 255€
Per week from 245 to 1,785 € – Reservation fee 30€
⟦⟧ sani-station
Beside the beach. Free use of the services and leisure facilities at the 'Les Méditerranées – Beach Club Nouvelle Floride' campsite opposite.

Surroundings : ⟦⟧ ◐◐
Leisure activities : ♟ ✗ ⟦⟧ ⚏ ⬳ ⫯ ⊿ disco
Facilities : ⅙ ⊶ ⌂ ⚘ ☞ ♟ launderette ⟦⟧ ⚏ ⚯
Nearby : ⥰ Ƒ⚏

GPS Longitude : 3.54337
Latitude : 43.31052

Le Galet

℘ 04 67 21 95 61, *www.camping-galet.com*
Address : av. des Campings (250m from the beach)
Opening times : from beginning April to end Sept.
3 ha (275 pitches) flat, grassy, sandy
Tariff : 42.50€ ✷✷ ⇔ 圓 ⚏ (10A) – Extra per person 6.70€ – Reservation fee 25€
Rental rates : (from beginning April to end Sept.) – 67 ⟦⟧. Per night from 30 to 140 €
– Per week from 205 to 950 € – Reservation fee 25€
A long, narrow site leading to a pretty water park.

Surroundings : ⟦⟧ ◐
Leisure activities : ✗ ⬳ ⫯ ⊿
Facilities : ⅙ ⊶ ⌂ ♟ launderette
Nearby : ⟦⟧ ♟ ⚯

GPS Longitude : 3.5421
Latitude : 43.31108

La Créole

℘ 04 67 21 92 69, *www.campinglacreole.com*
Address : 74 av. des Campings
Opening times : from beginning April to mid Oct.
1.5 ha (110 pitches) flat, grassy, sandy
Tariff : 34.50€ ✷✷ ⇔ 圓 ⚏ (6A) – Extra per person 6€ – Reservation fee 17€
Rental rates : (from beginning April to mid Oct.) ⌦ – 17 ⟦⟧. Per night from 25 to 90€
Per week from 200 to 645 € – Reservation fee 17€
⟦⟧ sani-station 12€ – 8 圓 12€
Beside a beautiful beach of fine sand.

Surroundings : ⟦⟧ ◐◐ ⚞
Leisure activities : ✗ ⬳
Facilities : ⅙ ⊶ ⌂ ♟ 圓
Nearby : ⚏ ♟ ⚯ ⥰

GPS Longitude : 3.54375
Latitude : 43.31047

*Some information or pricing may have changed since the guide went to press.
We recommend you check the price list online in advance or at the entrance
to the campsite and enquire about possible restrictions.*

MARVEJOLS

48100 – Michelin map **330** H7 – pop. 5,053 – alt. 650
▶ Paris 573 – Espalion 64 – Florac 50 – Mende 28

⚠ VAL V.V.F. Camping et Village

℘ 0466320369, *www.vvf-villages.fr*
Address : at Le Colagnet (1.3km east along the D 999, D 1, follow the signs for Montrodat and take the road to the right; beside the Colagnet – from A 75, take exit 38)
Opening times : from mid May to mid Sept.
3 ha (57 pitches) flat, grassy
Tariff : (2012 price) 17.20€ ✿ ✿ ⇔ 回 (5A) – Extra per person 4.30€ – 30€
Rental rates : (2012 price) (from end April to mid Sept.) – 50 ⌂ – 6 studios – 44 gîtes.
Per night from 35 to 120 € – Per week from 240 to 838 €

Surroundings : ▱ ♨♨
Leisure activities : 🎬
Facilities : 🚿 ⌀ 🅿 🔥 ⚘ ⚑ 🚰
Nearby : 🛒 ⛵ ✗ 🎿 🐎

GPS Longitude : 3.30432 Latitude : 44.55075

MASSILLARGUES-ATTUECH

30140 – Michelin map **339** J4 – pop. 675 – alt. 156
▶ Paris 726 – Montpellier 56 – Nîmes 43 – Avignon 78

⚠ Le Fief ♨♨

℘ 0466618171, *www.campinglefiefdanduze.com*
Address : at Attuech, 195 chemin du Plan d'Eau (located 1.5km to the north along the D 982, near a lake)
Opening times : from beginning April to end Sept.
5.5 ha (80 pitches) flat, grassy
Tariff : 11.50€ ✿ ✿ ⇔ 回 (6A) – Extra per person 2.70€ – Reservation fee 10€
Rental rates : (permanent) – 19 ⌂. Per night from 48 to 109 €– Per week from 285 to 649 €
Reservation fee 10€

Well-shaded pitches but ageing sanitary facilities.

Surroundings : 🌳 ♨♨
Leisure activities : ▾ ✗ 🎬 ⚘ ⛲ hammam, jacuzzi ⛵ 🎿
multi-sports ground
Facilities : 🚿 ⌀ 🔥 ⚑ 🚰 ⛟
Nearby : 🎣

GPS Longitude : 4.02576 Latitude : 44.02946

MATEMALE

66210 – Michelin map **344** D7 – pop. 294 – alt. 1,514
▶ Paris 855 – Font-Romeu-Odeillo-Via 20 – Perpignan 92 – Prades 46

⚠ Le Lac

℘ 0468309449, *www.camping-lac-matemale.com* – alt. 1 540 – limited spaces for one-night stay
Address : 1.7km southwest along the D 52, follow the signs for Les Angles and take the turning to the left, 150m from the lake
Opening times : permanent
3.5 ha (110 pitches) undulating, flat and relatively flat, wood
Tariff : 19.20€ ✿ ✿ ⇔ 回 (6A) – Extra per person 5€
⛽ sani-station 2.50€

Pleasant mountain location in the shade of a pretty pine forest; direct access to the village along a pedestrian path.

Surroundings : 🌳 ♨♨
Leisure activities : 🎬 ⛲ jacuzzi ⛵
Facilities : 🚿 ⌀ 🔥 ⚑ launderette
Nearby : ▾ ✗ 🚲 ✗ 🎿 ≊ 🐎 sports/activities centre (800m)

GPS Longitude : 2.10673 Latitude : 42.58164

MAUREILLAS-LAS-ILLAS

66480 – Michelin map **344** H8 – pop. 2,649 – alt. 130
▶ Paris 873 – Gerona 71 – Perpignan 31 – Port-Vendres 31

⚠ Les Bruyères

☎ 04 68 83 26 64, *www.camping-lesbruyeres.fr*
Address : rte de Céret (1.2km west along the D 618)
Opening times : permanent
4 ha (106 pitches) very uneven, terraced, grassy, stony
Tariff : 25€ ✱✱ 🚐 🗐 🗐 (10A) – Extra per person 5.50€ – Reservation fee 7€
Rental rates : (from mid March to mid Nov.) 🍴 (Jul–Aug) – 18 🚐 – 4 🏠.
Per night from 55 to 120 € – Per week from 320 to 650 € – Reservation fee 10€

Pleasant, wooded setting among cork oaks, but choose pitches away from the road in preference.

Surroundings : 🔲 ⚬⚬
Leisure activities : 🖼 🎣 🏊
Facilities : ᏮᏮ ⚬🔫 ⛺ 🔥 🗑 🗑
Nearby : 🐎

GPS — Longitude : 2.79509
Latitude : 42.49249

MENDE

48000 – Michelin map **330** J7 – pop. 12,285 – alt. 731
▶ Paris 584 – Clermont-Ferrand 174 – Florac 38 – Langogne 46

⚠ Tivoli

☎ 04 66 65 31 10, *www.campingtivoli.com*
Address : situated 2km southwest along the N 88, follow the signs for Rodez and take the road to the right, opposite the sports centre; beside the Lot river
Opening times : permanent
1.8 ha (100 pitches) flat, grassy
Tariff : (2012 price) 23.40€ ✱✱ 🚐 🗐 🗐 (6A) – Extra per person 6.70€ – Reservation fee 25€
Rental rates : (2012 price) (from beginning May to beginning Sept.) 🍴 – 17 🚐.
Per night from 51 to 56€ – Per week from 260 to 620 € – Reservation fee 25€
🚐 sani-station 23.40€

Surroundings : ⚬⚬
Leisure activities : 🏓 🖼 🚣 🏊
Facilities : ᏮᏮ ⚬🔫 🚽 🗑 🗑 🗑 🗑
Nearby : 🍴

GPS — Longitude : 3.45693
Latitude : 44.51268

MEYRUEIS

48150 – Michelin map **330** I9 – pop. 853 – alt. 698
▶ Paris 643 – Florac 36 – Mende 57 – Millau 43

⚠ Capelan

☎ 04 66 45 60 50, *www.campingcapelan.com*
Address : rte de Millau (located 1km northwest along the D 996; beside the Jonte river)
Opening times : from beginning May to mid Sept.
2.8 ha (100 pitches) flat, grassy
Tariff : 29.50€ ✱✱ 🚐 🗐 🗐 (10A) – Extra per person 5.90€ – Reservation fee 16€
Rental rates : (from beginning May to mid Sept.) 🍴 – 44 🚐. Per night from 40 to 111€
Per week from 180 to 775 € – Reservation fee 19€
🚐 sani-station 4.50€ – 🍴 🔥 15€
Pleasant location in the Jonte river gorge with walkway access to the village.

Surroundings : ≤ 🔲 ⚬
Leisure activities : 🏓 🖼 🎲 🚣 🏊 🏊 🎣
Facilities : ᏮᏮ ⚬🔫 🗑⛺ – 3 individual sanitary facilities (🚿 wc) ⛺ 🗑 🗑
launderette 🗑
Nearby : 🍴 🐎 climbing

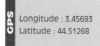

GPS — Longitude : 3.41977
Latitude : 44.18574

Le Champ d'Ayres

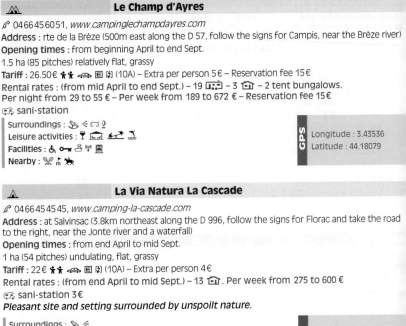

℘ 04 66 45 60 51, *www.campinglechampdayres.com*
Address : rte de la Brèze (500m east along the D 57, follow the signs for Campis, near the Brèze river)
Opening times : from beginning April to end Sept.
1.5 ha (85 pitches) relatively flat, grassy
Tariff : 26.50€ ♦♦ ⇔ 目 ⌀ (10A) – Extra per person 5€ – Reservation fee 15€
Rental rates : (from mid April to end Sept.) – 19 ⌷ – 3 ⌂ – 2 tent bungalows.
Per night from 29 to 55 € – Per week from 189 to 672 € – Reservation fee 15€
⌷ sani-station

Surroundings : ⌁ ≤ ⌷ ⌀
Leisure activities : ⍭ ⌷ ⍩ ⍺
Facilities : ⌖ ⍜ ⌷ ⍢ ⌷
Nearby : ⍯ ⍚ ⍺

Longitude : 3.43536
Latitude : 44.18079

La Via Natura La Cascade

℘ 04 66 45 45 45, *www.camping-la-cascade.com*
Address : at Salvinsac (3.8km northeast along the D 996, follow the signs for Florac and take the road to the right, near the Jonte river and a waterfall)
Opening times : from end April to mid Sept.
1 ha (54 pitches) undulating, flat, grassy
Tariff : 22€ ♦♦ ⇔ 目 ⌀ (10A) – Extra per person 4€
Rental rates : (from end April to mid Sept.) – 13 ⌂. Per week from 275 to 600 €
⌷ sani-station 3€
Pleasant site and setting surrounded by unspoilt nature.

Surroundings : ⌁ ≤
Leisure activities : ⌷ ⍺
Facilities : ⌖ ⍜ ⌷ ⍢ ⌷
Nearby : ⍯ ⍺ ⍺

Longitude : 3.45567
Latitude : 44.19646

Le Pré de Charlet

℘ 04 66 45 63 65, *www.camping-cevennes-meyrueis.com*
Address : rte de Florac (located 1km northeast along the D 996; beside the Jonte)
Opening times : from beginning April to end Oct.
2 ha (70 pitches) terraced, relatively flat, flat, grassy
Tariff : 16.90€ ♦♦ ⇔ 目 ⌀ (16A) – Extra per person 3.50€
Rental rates : (from beginning April to end Oct.) – 6 ⌷. Per night from 40 to 65 €
Per week from 230 to 470€
⌷ sani-station 3.50€

Surroundings : ⌁ ≤ ⍭
Leisure activities : ⌷ ⍺
Facilities : ⌖ ⍜ ⌷ ⍢ ⌷
Nearby : ⍯ ⍚ ⍺ ⍺

Longitude : 3.43831
Latitude : 44.18587

Aire Naturelle le Pré des Amarines

℘ 04 66 45 61 65, *www.camping-amarines.com* – alt. 750
Address : rte de Gatuzières, at Lou Castel (5.7km northeast along the D 996, follow the signs for Florac and take the road to the right; beside the Jonte river)
2 ha (25 pitches) undulating, flat, grassy
Situated in the Vallée de la Jonte.

Surroundings : ⌁ ≤ ⍭
Leisure activities : ⍺
Facilities : ⌖ ⍜ ⌷ ⌷
Nearby : ⍶ ⍯ ⍚ ⍺

Longitude : 3.48341
Latitude : 44.1979

MONTCLAR

11250 – Michelin map **344** E4 – pop. 186 – alt. 210
▶ Paris 766 – Carcassonne 19 – Castelnaudary 41 – Limoux 15

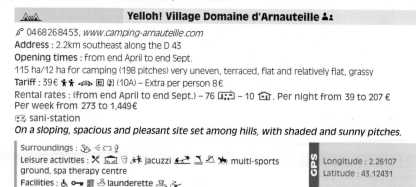

Yelloh! Village Domaine d'Arnauteille ♣♣

☎ 0468268453, *www.camping-arnauteille.com*
Address : 2.2km southeast along the D 43
Opening times : from end April to end Sept.
115 ha/12 ha for camping (198 pitches) very uneven, terraced, flat and relatively flat, grassy
Tariff : 39€ ♦♦ ⇌ ▣ ⚡ (10A) – Extra per person 8€
Rental rates : (from end April to end Sept.) – 76 ⌂ – 10 ⌂. Per night from 39 to 207 €
Per week from 273 to 1,449€
⛽ sani-station
On a sloping, spacious and pleasant site set among hills, with shaded and sunny pitches.

Surroundings : ⅏ ≼ ⌑ ◊
Leisure activities : ✕ ⌂ ⊚ ☚ jacuzzi ☚ ☚ ☚ ☚ multi-sports ground, spa therapy centre
Facilities : ⅊ ⊶ ▥ ⌂ **launderette** ⌂ ⌂

GPS Longitude : 2.26107
Latitude : 43.12431

NARBONNE

11100 – Michelin map **344** J3 – pop. 51,227 – alt. 13
▶ Paris 787 – Béziers 28 – Carcassonne 61 – Montpellier 96

Yelloh! Village Les Mimosas ♣♣

☎ 0468490372, *www.lesmimosas.com*
Address : chaussée de Mandirac (10km to the south, after the suburb La Nautique)
Opening times : from end March to beginning Nov.
9 ha (266 pitches) flat, grassy, sandy, stony
Tariff : (2012 price) 45€ ♦♦ ⇌ ▣ ⚡ (10A) – Extra per person 8€ – Reservation fee 25€
Rental rates : (from end March to beginning Nov.) – 66 ⌂ – 28 ⌂ – 4 studios.
Per night from 39 to 192 € – Per week from 273 to 1,372 €
⛽ sani-station
Pitches surrounded by the vines of the Languedoc and a welcoming wine bar for tastings.

Surroundings : ⅏ ⌑ ◊
Leisure activities : ☿ ✕ ⌂ ⊚ ☚ ☚ ⇌ ☚ ☚ ✄ ☚ ☚ multi-sports ground
Facilities : ⅊ ⊶ ⌂ ⌂ ↻ ☂ **launderette** ⌂
Nearby : ☚

GPS Longitude : 3.02592
Latitude : 43.13658

La Nautique

☎ 0468904819, *www.campinglanautique.com*
Address : ch. de La Nautique (4km to the south; at Port La Nautique)
Opening times : from beginning March to end Oct.
16 ha (390 pitches) flat and relatively flat, fine gravel, grassy
Tariff : 44.50€ ♦♦ ⇌ ▣ ⚡ (10A) – Extra per person 8.25€ – Reservation fee 20€
Rental rates : (from beginning Feb. to end Oct.) ⅊ (1 chalet, 4 mobile homes) – 130 ⌂ –
1 ⌂. Per night from 37 to 137 € – Per week from 259 to 938 € – Reservation fee 20€
⛽ sani-station
Beside the Etang de Bages and Etang de Sigean (lakes).

Surroundings : ≼ ⌑ ◊
Leisure activities : ☿ ✕ ⌂ ⊚ ☚ ☚ ⇌ ✄ ☚ ☚ ⊸ pedalos ☚
Facilities : ⅊ ⊶ – 390 individual sanitary facilities (⌂↻ wc) ⌂ ↻ ☂
launderette ⌂ ⌂
Nearby : ◊

GPS Longitude : 3.00424
Latitude : 43.14703

NASBINALS

48260 – Michelin map **330** G7 – pop. 498 – alt. 1,180
▶ Paris 573 – Aumont-Aubrac 24 – Chaudes-Aigues 27 – Espalion 34

Municipal

℘ 0466325187, *mairie.nasbinals@laposte.net* – alt. 1 100 –
Address : rte de Saint-Urcize (located 1km northwest along the D 12)
Opening times : from mid May to end Sept.
2 ha (75 pitches) relatively flat, flat, grassy
Tariff : (2012 price) 11 € ♣♣ ⬒ 🗉 [♨] (15A) – Extra per person 3 €

Surroundings : ⌇ ≼
Facilities : ⅙ ⊶ (Jul–Aug)
Nearby : 🏇

GPS
Longitude : 3.04016
Latitude : 44.67022

NAUSSAC

48300 – Michelin map **330** L6 – pop. 206 – alt. 920 – Leisure centre
▶ Paris 575 – Grandrieu 26 – Langogne 3 – Mende 46

Les Terrasses du Lac

℘ 0466692962, *www.naussac.com*
Address : at the Lac de Naussac (north of the town along the D 26, follow the signs for Saugues and take the turning to the left; 200m from the lake (direct access)
Opening times : from mid April to mid Oct.
6 ha (180 pitches) terraced, relatively flat to hilly, grassy, stony
Tariff : 19.80 € ♣♣ ⬒ 🗉 [♨] (6A) – Extra per person 4.80 € – Reservation fee 10 €
Rental rates : (from mid April to mid Oct.) – 9 ⌂ – 17 ⊨. Per night from 69 to 71 €
Per week from 299 to 645 € – Reservation fee 10 €
▤ sani-station

Surroundings : ≼ Lac de Naussac
Leisure activities : ▼ ✗ 🎱 ⊝ evening ⚡ ⚲ ⚽ 𝄛 (small swimming pool)
Facilities : ⅙ ⊶ ▥ ⍐ 🗐 ⚱
Nearby : ⚲⁺ ⩯ (beach) ⬧ 🗻 ◊ 🏇 disco

GPS
Longitude : 3.83505
Latitude : 44.73478

A chambre d'hôte is a guesthouse or B & B-style accommodation.

PALAU-DEL-VIDRE

66690 – Michelin map **344** I7 – pop. 2,736 – alt. 26
▶ Paris 867 – Argelès-sur-Mer 8 – Le Boulou 16 – Collioure 15

Le Haras

℘ 0468221450, *www.camping-le-haras.com*
Address : at the Domaine Saint-Galdric (take the northeastern exit along the D 11)
Opening times : from beginning April to end Sept.
2.3 ha (131 pitches) flat, grassy
Tariff : 36.50 € ♣♣ ⬒ 🗉 [♨] (10A) – Extra per person 6.50 € – Reservation fee 20 €
Rental rates : (from beginning April to end Sept.) – 18 ⌂. Per night from 38 to 118 €
Per week from 266 to 826 € – Reservation fee 20 €
▤ sani-station
Plentiful shade and attractive flowers.

Surroundings : ▭ ⌗
Leisure activities : ▼ ✗ 🎱 ⚲⁺ 𝄛
Facilities : ⅙ ⊶ ⒸⒸ ⬧ ⚒ ⍐ launderette ⚱

GPS
Longitude : 2.96474
Latitude : 42.57575

PALAVAS-LES-FLOTS

34250 – Michelin map **339** I7 – pop. 5,996 – alt. 1
▶ Paris 765 – Montpellier 13 – Sète 41 – Lunel 33

Les Roquilles

✆ 04 67 68 03 47, *www.camping-les-roquilles.fr* ⚲
Address : 267 bis av. Saint-Maurice (follow the signs for Carnon-Plage, 100m from the beach)
Opening times : from mid April to mid Sept.
15 ha (792 pitches) flat, grassy, gravelled
Tariff : (2012 price) ♦ 5.20€ ⇜ 2.40€ 回 34.30€ – ⑵ (6A) 4.90€ – Reservation fee 29€
Rental rates : (2012 price) (from mid April to mid Sept.) ♿ (1 mobile home) ⚲ – 60 ⟐ –
41 ⌂. Per week from 265 to 1,200 € – Reservation fee 29€
⟐ sani-station
Some pitches are beside the lake where flamingoes occasionally come to feed.

Surroundings : ⟐ ⚲
Leisure activities : ✕ ⊕ multi-sports ground
Facilities : ♿ ⊶ ⚐

GPS
Longitude : 3.96037
Latitude : 43.53851

Vacances-Directes Palavas

✆ 04 67 68 01 28, *www.palavas-camping.fr* – limited spaces for one-night stay ⚲
Address : rte de Maguelone (right bank)
Opening times : from beginning April to end Sept.
8 ha (430 pitches) flat, fine gravel, sandy
Tariff : (2012 price) 52€ ♦♦ ⇜ 回 ⑵ (6A) – Extra per person 7€ – Reservation fee 20€
Rental rates : (2012 price) (from beginning April to end Sept.) – 386 ⟐.
Per night from 42 to 163 € – Per week from 294 to 1,141 € – Reservation fee 20€
Mobile-home village with some pitches for tents and caravans beside the sea.

Surroundings : ⚲ ⚠
Leisure activities : ✕ 🏄 🚲 kite-surfing, multi-sports ground
Facilities : ♿ ⊶ ⚐ launderette

GPS
Longitude : 3.9095
Latitude : 43.51963

*For more information on visiting particular towns or regions, consult the
relevant regional MICHELIN Green Guide. We also recommend you use
the appropriate Michelin regional map to locate your selected campsite,
to calculate distances and to work out the best route.*

LES PLANTIERS

30122 – Michelin map **339** H4 – pop. 252 – alt. 400
▶ Paris 667 – Alès 48 – Florac 46 – Montpellier 85

Caylou

✆ 04 66 83 92 85, *www.camping-caylou.fr*
Address : at Le Caylou (located 1km northeast along the D 20, follow the signs for Saumane; beside
the Gardon au Borgne river)
4 ha (75 pitches) terraced, relatively flat, grassy, stony
Rentals : 2 ⟐ – 2 gîtes.
Very comfortable gîtes and a lovely bar terrace overlooking the valley.

Surroundings : ⚲ ≤ ⟐ ⚲
Leisure activities : ♦ ✕ 🏓 🏄 ⚲ ⚲ ⚲ entertainment room
Facilities : ♿ ⊶ ⚲

GPS
Longitude : 3.73101
Latitude : 44.12209

LE PONT-DE-MONTVERT

48220 – Michelin map **330** K8 – pop. 278 – alt. 875
▶ Paris 629 – Le Bleymard 22 – Florac 21 – Génolhac 28

△ Aire Naturelle la Barette

℘ 04 66 45 82 16, *www-gites-mont-lozere.com* – alt. 1 200
Address : at Finiels (6km north along the D 20, follow the signs for Bleymard)
1 ha (20 pitches) terraced, relatively flat, stony, grassy, rocks
🚽 15 ▣

Surroundings : ⌖ ≼ Mont Lozère
Leisure activities : 🖼
Facilities : ⊶ 🔳
Nearby : 🚲 ✂

GPS Longitude : 3.74626
Latitude : 44.40398

---

*The prices listed were supplied by the campsite owners in 2012
(if prices were not available, those from the previous year are given).
The fees should be regarded as basic charges and may fluctuate
with inflation.*

PORT-CAMARGUE

30240 – Michelin map **339** J7
▶ Paris 762 – Montpellier 36 – Nîmes 47 – Avignon 93

⋀⋀ Yelloh! Village Secrets de Camargue

℘ 04 66 80 08 00, *www.secretsdecamargue.com* – limited spaces for one-night stay
Address : rte de l'Espiguette
Opening times : from beginning April to beginning Oct.
3.5 ha (177 pitches) flat, sandy
Tariff : 49€ ⋆⋆ ⇔ ▣ ⑭ (16A) – Extra per person 5€
Rental rates : (from mid April to beginning Oct.) ℗ – 155 🚐. Per night from 39 to 145 €
Per week from 273 to 1,015 €
*Campsite reserved for over 18s or parents with children under 3 years, with some pitches
for tents and caravans. Free shuttle service to the beaches.*

Surroundings : ⌖ ⊏⊐ ⚘
Leisure activities : ⍦ ✗ ⌾ daytime 🚲 ⛷
Facilities : ◴ ⊶ ℗ ⌂ ⚲ ⚶ ⍦ launderette ⚡
Nearby : 🛒 🏖 🐎

GPS Longitude : 4.14105
Latitude : 43.5052

⋀⋀ Yelloh! Village Les Petits Camarguais ⚤
(rental of mobile homes only)

℘ 04 66 51 16 16, *www.yellohvillage-petits-camarguais.com*
Address : rte de l'Espiguette
Opening times : from mid April to end Sept.
3.5 ha flat, grassy, sandy
Rental rates : ⍥ – 336 🚐. Per night from 42 to 249 € – Per week from 294 to 1,743 €
Activities and facilities suitable for young children. Free shuttle service to the beaches.

Surroundings : ⊏⊐ ⚘⚘
Leisure activities : ⍦ ✗ ⌾ ⋀ ⎐ 🚲 ⛷ △ multi-sports ground
Facilities : ◴ ⊶ ⌂ ⍦ launderette 🏖 ⚡
Nearby : 🛒 🐎

GPS Longitude : 4.14456
Latitude : 43.50472

◬
Vacances Directes La Marine ♣♣
(rental of mobile homes only)

📞 0466533690, *www.campinglamarine.com*
Address : 2196 rte de l'Espiguette
Opening times : from beginning April to end Sept.
5 ha sandy, flat, grassy
Rental rates : (2012 price) ♿ ✂ – 278 🏠 – 15 tent bungalows. Per night from 29 to 163€
Per week from 203 to 1,141€ – Reservation fee 20€
Choose pitches away from the road in preference – free shuttle service to the beaches.

Surroundings : 〽
Leisure activities : ♟ ✗ 🛖 ⊙ 🕴 ⛵ 🚲 ⛵ ⛱
Facilities : ♿ ⚲ ♨ ♟ launderette ♨ ⚲
Nearby : 🛒 🐎, casino

GPS
Longitude : 4.1457
Latitude : 43.5074

◬
Abri de Camargue

📞 0466515483, *www.abridecamargue.fr* – limited spaces for one-night stay
Address : 320 rte de l'Espiguette (near the Casino (gaming) and opposite the fairground)
Opening times : from beginning April to end Sept.
4 ha (277 pitches) flat, grassy, sandy
Tariff : 28€ ✶✶ ⊕ 目 ⊠ (6A) – Extra per person 12€ – Reservation fee 19€
Rental rates : (from beginning April to end Sept.) – 104 🏠. Per night from 60 to 141€
Per week from 420 to 987 € – Reservation fee 19€
🚐 sani-station 7€ –
Free shuttle service to the beaches.

Surroundings : ▭ 〽
Leisure activities : ♟ ✗ 🛖 ⊙ 🕴 ⛵ ⊠ ⛱ cinema, multi-sports ground
Facilities : ⚲ ♟ launderette ♨ ⚲
Nearby : 🐎, casino

GPS
Longitude : 4.1488
Latitude : 43.52272

PORTIRAGNES-PLAGE

34420 – Michelin map **339** F9
▶ Paris 768 – Montpellier 72 – Carcassonne 99 – Nîmes 121

◬
Les Sablons ♣♣

📞 0467909055, *www.les-sablons.com*
Address : Plage Est (take the northern exit)
Opening times : from end March to end Sept.
15 ha (800 pitches) flat, grassy, sandy, pond
Tariff : 52€ ✶✶ ⊕ 目 ⊠ (10A) – Extra per person 10€ – Reservation fee 25€
Rental rates : (permanent) – 240 🏠 – 85 🏠. Per night from 30 to 122 €
Per week from 180 to 854€ – Reservation fee 25€
🚐 sani-station 3€ – 🛁 ⊠20€
Close to the beach and a lake.

Surroundings : ▭ 〽 ⛰
Leisure activities : ♟ ✗ 🛖 ⊙ 🕴 🎣 ⛵ 🚲 ⚅ ⛵ ⛱ disco
Facilities : ♿ ⚲ ♨ ♟ launderette 🛒 ⚲ refrigerated food storage
Nearby : 🎣 ⚓

GPS
Longitude : 3.36469
Latitude : 43.2788

---

*The classification (1 to 5 tents, **black** or red) that we award to selected sites
in this guide is our own system. It should not be confused with the
classification (1 to 5 stars) of official organisations.*

Les Mimosas ♣♣

📞 0467909292, *www.mimosas.com* – limited spaces for one-night stay
Address : at Port Cassafières
Opening times : from mid May to beginning Sept.
7 ha (400 pitches) flat, grassy
Tariff : 44€ ♠♠ 🚐 🔲 🔌 (6A) – Extra per person 10€ – Reservation fee 36€
Rental rates : (from mid May to beginning Sept.) 🦽 (1 mobile home) – 207 🏠 – 4 🏠 –
12 tent bungalows. Per night from 33 to 260 € – Per week from 231 to 1,820 €
Reservation fee 36€
🚐 sani-station 2€
Large water and play park.

Surroundings : 🏕 ⚬⚬	
Leisure activities : 🍴 ✕ 🎮 🎱 🏓 🎣 🛝 🏄 🚲 🏊 ⛵ multi-sports ground	**GPS** Longitude : 3.37305
Facilities : 🦽 ⚬⛽ ⛺ – 17 individual sanitary facilities (🚿 wc) 🚰 launderette 🧺 🧊 refrigerated food storage	Latitude : 43.2915
Nearby : 🐎 ⚓	

L'Émeraude

📞 0467909376, *www.campinglemeraude.com*
Address : located 1km north, follow the signs for Portiragnes
Opening times : from end May to mid Sept.
4.2 ha (280 pitches) flat, grassy, sandy
Tariff : (2012 price) 34€ ♠♠ 🚐 🔲 🔌 (5A) – Extra per person 7€ – Reservation fee 25€
Rental rates : (2012 price) (from mid May to mid Sept.) 🪁 – 180 🏠 – 11 🏠.
Per night from 36 to 100 € – Per week from 252 to 700 € – Reservation fee 25€
The site has a pleasant water park.

Surroundings : ⚬⚬	
Leisure activities : 🍴 ✕ 🎮 🎱 🏄 🏊 ⛵	**GPS** Longitude : 3.36199
Facilities : 🦽 ⚬⛽ ⛺ 🚰 🔲 🧊 🧊 refrigerated food storage	Latitude : 43.28766
Nearby : 🐎	

11500 – Michelin map **344** E5 – pop. 3,352 – alt. 291
▶ Paris 797 – Andorra-la-Vella 113 – Ax-les-Thermes 55 – Carcassonne 52

Village Vacances l'Espinet
(rental of studios and maisonettes only)

📞 0468208888, *www.lespinet.com*
Address : located 1km north along the D 118
Opening times : permanent
25 ha flat, pond
Rental rates : 🦽 Ⓟ – 158 🏠 – 24 studios. Per night from 40 to 298 €
Per week from 280 to 2,086 €
An upmarket, well-appointed holiday village.

Surroundings : 🏔 ❄ ⚬	
Leisure activities : 🍴 ✕ 🎮 🏓 🛝 🏄 hammam jacuzzi 🎿 🖼 🏊 spa therapy centre	**GPS** Longitude : 2.19776
Facilities : ⚬⛽ 🚰 launderette	Latitude : 42.89268

We welcome your feedback on our listed campsites.
Please email us at: campingfrance@tp.michelin.com
Many thanks in advance!

Municipal la Sapinette

𝒫 0468201352, *www.villedequillan.fr*

Address : 21 av. René Delpech (0.8km west along the D 79, follow the signs for Ginoles)

Opening times : from beginning April to end Oct.

1.8 ha (90 pitches) terrace, flat and relatively flat, grassy

Tariff : (2012 price) 19.97€ ♥♥ ⟵ 🗐 🚾 (16A) – Extra per person 5.80€

Rental rates : (2012 price) (from beginning April to end Oct.) ⤳ – 26 ⌂.
Per week from 305 to 580 €

🚱 sani-station 4€ – 6 🗐 10.50€ – 🔋 🚾 13.80€

Pitches laid out on terraces with a degree of shade.

Surroundings : 🏞 ≤ 🌳
Leisure activities : 🏛 🎿 ⛷
Facilities : ♿ ⚷ 🚿 🚽 🍴 🖼

GPS Longitude : 2.18445
Latitude : 42.87495

---

*Using the traditional Michelin classification method, the guide provides
you with an easy, speedy reference for assessing the category of each site:
1 to 5 tents (see page 10).*

REMOULINS

30210 – Michelin map **339** M5 – pop. 2,405 – alt. 27
▶ Paris 685 – Alès 50 – Arles 37 – Avignon 23

La Sousta ♣♣

𝒫 0466371280, *www.lasousta.com*

Address : av. du Pont du Gard (situated 2km to the northwest, follow the signs for Le Pont du Gard,
right bank)

Opening times : from beginning March to end Oct.

14 ha (300 pitches) undulating, flat and relatively flat, grassy, sandy

Tariff : 27.70€ ♥♥ ⟵ 🗐 🚾 (6A) – Extra per person 8€ – Reservation fee 13€

Rental rates : (permanent) – 60 🚐 – 4 ⌂. Per night from 30 to 65€
Per week from 210 to 750 € – Reservation fee 13€

🚱 sani-station 2€

*Pleasant, wooded setting beside the Gardon river, on the right bank near the Pont
du Gard.*

Surroundings : 🏞 ♨
Leisure activities : 🍸 ✗ 🎮 🏃 🎿 🚲 🎯 🎱 ⛷ 🏊 🚣
Facilities : ♿ ⚷ 🕍 ⛺ 🍴 launderette 🏖 🐾

GPS Longitude : 4.54
Latitude : 43.94

FranceLoc Domaine de La Soubeyranne

𝒫 0466370321, *www.soubeyranne.com*

Address : 1110 rte de Beaucaire (2.5km south along the N 86 and D 986, right bank)

Opening times : from end March to mid Sept.

4 ha (200 pitches) flat, grassy, stony

Tariff : ♥ 14.50€ ⟵ 🗐 29€ – 🚾 (6A) 4€ – Reservation fee 27€

Rental rates : (from end March to mid Sept.) – 150 🚐. Per night from 40 to 166€
Per week from 161 to 1,211 € – Reservation fee 27€

🚱 sani-station

Neat rows of mobile homes and a well-equipped children's playground.

Surroundings : 🏞 ⛺ ♨
Leisure activities : ✗ multi-sports ground
Facilities : ♿ ⚷ ⛺ 🍴

GPS Longitude : 4.56236
Latitude : 43.93031

ROCLES

48300 – Michelin map **330** K6 – pop. 209 – alt. 1 085
▶ Paris 581 – Grandrieu 20 – Langogne 8 – Mende 44

       ### Rondin des Bois

✆ 04 66 69 50 46, *www.camping-rondin.com* – alt. 1 000
Address : at Palhere (3km north following signs for Bessettes and take road for Vaysset to the right)
Opening times : from mid April to end Sept.
2 ha (78 pitches) terraced, relatively flat, flat, stony, rocks
Tariff : 19€ ✶✶ 🚐 🔲 🎔 (10A) – Extra per person 5€ – Reservation fee 10€
Rental rates : (from beginning April to end Oct.) – 6 🚐 – 8 🏠.
Per night from 55 to 90€– Per week from 260 to 630€ – Reservation fee 10€
🚉 sani-station – 5 🔲 9€
On an unspoilt site, close to the Lac de Naussac.

Surroundings : 🏞 ⟨ 🖼
Leisure activities : 🍷 ✗ 🏛 🏃 🚵 🛝 🛶
Facilities : 🚿 🔑 🛎 🔲 🚻
Nearby : 💧 🐎

GPS Longitude : 3.78105
Latitude : 44.73814

ROQUEFEUIL

11340 – pop. 276 – alt. 900
▶ Paris 813 – Montpellier 226 – Carcassonne 78

       ### La Mare aux Fées

✆ 04 68 31 11 37, *www.pyrenees-camping.com*
Address : r. de l'Église (in the village)
Opening times : from beginning Jan. to end Oct.
0.5 ha (23 pitches) terrace, flat, grassy
Tariff : 18€ ✶✶ 🚐 🔲 🎔 (6A) – Extra per person 4€ – Reservation fee 8€
Rental rates : 🚿 (1 chalet) – 3 🚐 – 6 🏠. Per night from 65 to 95 €
Per week from 310 to 700 €– Reservation fee 8€
🚉 sani-station 3€
A well-maintained site near the church.

Surroundings : 🏞 🖼 🍃
Leisure activities : ✗ 🚵 🛶 (small swimming pool)
Facilities : 🚿 🔑 🛏 🚻 🚻 🚽 🔲 🚻
Nearby : 🍴

GPS Longitude : 1.9952
Latitude : 42.8193

ROQUEFORT-DES-CORBIÈRES

11540 – Michelin map **344** I5 – pop. 947 – alt. 50
▶ Paris 813 – Montpellier 118 – Carcassonne 78 – Perpignan 45

▲   ### Gîtes La Capelle
            (rental of gîtes only)

✆ 06 19 50 95 26, *http://giteslacapelle.chez-alice.fr*
Address : 4 r. la Capelle (in the town)
Opening times : from mid March to mid Dec.
0.3 ha flat
Rental rates : 🍴 (Jul to Aug) Ⓟ – 13 gîtes. Per night from 55 to 155 €
Per week from 250 to 1,290 €
Small group of gîtes around a swimming pool.

Surroundings : 🏞 🍃🍃
Leisure activities : 🏛 🛶
Facilities : 🚪 🛏 🛎 🔲

GPS Longitude : 2.95345
Latitude : 42.9897

A ROQUE-SUR-CÈZE

0200 – Michelin map **339** M3 – pop. 173 – alt. 90
Paris 663 – Alès 53 – Bagnols-sur-Cèze 13 – Bourg-St-Andéol 35

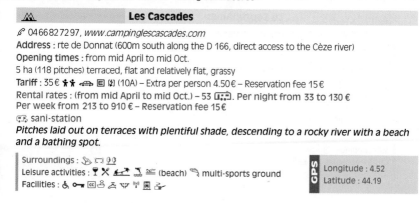

Les Cascades

04 66 82 72 97, *www.campinglescascades.com*
Address : rte de Donnat (600m south along the D 166, direct access to the Cèze river)
Opening times : from mid April to mid Oct.
5 ha (118 pitches) terraced, flat and relatively flat, grassy
Tariff : 35 € ♦♦ ⟳ ▣ ⚡ (10A) – Extra per person 4.50 € – Reservation fee 15 €
Rental rates : (from mid April to mid Oct.) – 53 ⟐. Per night from 33 to 130 €
Per week from 213 to 910 € – Reservation fee 15 €
⟐ sani-station
Pitches laid out on terraces with plentiful shade, descending to a rocky river with a beach and a bathing spot.

Surroundings : ⟲ ⟡ ≋
Leisure activities : ♈ ✗ ⟰ ⟰ ⟰ (beach) ⟲ multi-sports ground
Facilities : ⟐ ⟐ ▣⟐ ⟰ ⟰ ⟐ ▣ ⟐
GPS Longitude : 4.52
Latitude : 44.19

The information in the guide may have changed since going to press.

E ROZIER

3150 – Michelin map **330** H9 – pop. 145 – alt. 400
Paris 632 – Florac 57 – Mende 63 – Millau 23

Les Prades

05 65 62 62 09, *www.campinglesprades.com* ✉ 12720 Peyreleau
Address : at Mostuejouls (right bank) – (head via Peyreleau (left bank), 4km west along the D 187; beside the Tarn river)
Opening times : from beginning May to mid Sept.
3.5 ha (150 pitches) flat, grassy, sandy
Tariff : 31.50 € ♦♦ ⟳ ▣ ⚡ (6A) – Extra per person 6.50 € – Reservation fee 15 €
Rental rates : (from beginning May to mid Sept.) ⟲ – 30 ⟐ – 3 gîtes.
Per night from 56 € – Per week from 245 to 650 € – Reservation fee 15 €

Surroundings : ⟲ ≤ ≋
Leisure activities : ♈ ✗ ⟐ ⟰ ⟰ ⟰ ⟰ ⟰ climbing wall ⟲
Facilities : ⟐ ⟐ ⟰ ⟰ ⟐ ▣ ⟰ ⟐
Nearby : ⟰
GPS Longitude : 3.17332
Latitude : 44.1996

Le St Pal

05 65 62 64 46, *www.campingsaintpal.com* ✉ 12720 Mostuéjouls
Address : rte des Gorges du Tarn (located 1km northwest along the D 907, follow the signs for Millau; beside the Tarn river)
Opening times : from beginning May to mid Sept.
1.5 ha (75 pitches) flat, grassy
Tariff : 28.50 € ♦♦ ⟳ ▣ ⚡ (10A) – Extra per person 5.50 € – Reservation fee 18 €
Rental rates : (from beginning May to mid Sept.) – 17 ⟐. Per night from 50 to 95 €
Per week from 210 to 665 € – Reservation fee 18 €

Surroundings : ≤ ≋ ⟰
Leisure activities : ⟰ ⟰ ⟲
Facilities : ⟐ ⟐ ⟰ ⟰ ▣
Nearby : ⟰ ⟰ ⟰
GPS Longitude : 3.19822
Latitude : 44.19639

ST-ANDRÉ-DE-SANGONIS

34725 – Michelin map **339** G7 – pop. 5,175 – alt. 65
▶ Paris 715 – Béziers 54 – Clermont-l'Hérault 8 – Gignac 5

Le Septimanien

△

☎ 04 67 57 84 23, *www.camping-leseptimanien.com*
Address : rte de Cambous (located 1km southwest along the D 4, follow the signs for Brignac; beside a stream)
Opening times : from beginning May to end Sept.
2.6 ha (86 pitches) terraced, flat, stony
Tariff : (2012 price) 24€ ♣♣ ⇔ 🗐 ⚡ (10A) – Extra per person 4.40€ – Reservation fee 10€
Rental rates : (2012 price) (from beginning May to end Sept.) – 10 🚐 – 9 🏠.
Per week from 340 to 460 € – Reservation fee 10€

Peaceful, family-orientated site.

Surroundings : 🏊 ⊐ 🎣
Leisure activities : ♟ 🛶 ⛱
Facilities : 🚿 ⚡ 🍴 🗄

GPS Longitude : 3.49508
Latitude : 43.64066

ST-BAUZILE

48000 – Michelin map **330** J8 – pop. 579 – alt. 750
▶ Paris 598 – Chanac 19 – Florac 29 – Marvejols 30

Municipal les Berges de Bramont

△

☎ 04 66 47 05 97, *www.saint-bauzile.fr*
Address : at Rouffiac (located 1.5km southwest along the D 41, N 106, follow the signs for Mende, near the Bramont and the sports centre)
Opening times : from beginning July to mid Sept.
1.5 ha (50 pitches) terrace, flat, grassy
Tariff : ♣ 10€ ⇔ 10€ 🗐 10€ – ⚡ (30A) 2.50€
Rental rates : (from beginning July to end Aug.) – 4 🚐. Per week from 350 €
🚽 sani-station 2.50€

Surroundings : ≤
Leisure activities : 🖼 🛶
Facilities : 🚿 ⚡ 📷 🛁 🍴
Nearby : ♟ ✗ 🚴 🍴

GPS Longitude : 3.49428
Latitude : 44.47666

ST-CYPRIEN-PLAGE

66750 – Michelin map **344** J7
▶ Paris 870 – Montpellier 173 – Perpignan 21 – Carcassonne 135

Cala Gogo ♣♣

△△

☎ 04 68 21 07 12, *www.campmed.com*
Address : av. Armand Lanoux – Les Capellans (4km to the south; beside the beach)
Opening times : from beginning May to end Sept.
11 ha (649 pitches) flat, grassy, sandy, stony
Tariff : 43€ ♣♣ ⇔ 🗐 ⚡ (10A) – Extra per person 11€ – Reservation fee 20€
Rental rates : (from beginning May to end Sept.) 🚿 (1 mobile home) – 92 🚐.
Per night from 37 to 190 € – Per week from 259 to 1,330€ – Reservation fee 20€
🚽 sani-station

New, well-appointed rental options; landscaped water park and direct access to the beach

Surroundings : ⊐ 🎣
Leisure activities : ♟ ✗ 🖼 🛶 💆 🍴 🏊 disco
Facilities : 🚿 ⚡ 📷 🛁 🍴 launderette 🐕 🚗

GPS Longitude : 3.03789
Latitude : 42.59998

T-GENIS-DES-FONTAINES

6740 – Michelin map **344** I7 – pop. 2,792 – alt. 63
Paris 878 – Argelès-sur-Mer 10 – Le Boulou 10 – Collioure 17

La Pinède

📞 04 68 89 75 29, *www.campinglapinede66.fr*
Address : av. des Albères (south of the town along the D 2)
1 ha (71 pitches) flat, grassy
Rentals : 📶 – 10 🛖.

Attractively shaded, in places by pine trees. Some of the rental mobile homes are a little old.

Surroundings : 🌳🌳
Leisure activities : 🏊
Facilities : 👤 ⚬🚿 🛁 🖥
Nearby : 🍴

GPS Longitude : 2.9245
Latitude : 42.54093

The pitches of many campsites are marked out with low hedges of attractive bushes and shrubs.

T-GEORGES-DE-LÉVÉJAC

8500 – Michelin map **330** H9 – pop. 259 – alt. 900
Paris 603 – Florac 53 – Mende 45 – Millau 49

Cassaduc

📞 04 66 48 85 80, *www.camping-cassaduc.com*
Address : rte du Point Sublime (1.4km southeast)
Opening times : from beginning July to end Aug.
2.2 ha (75 pitches) terraced, relatively flat, grassy, stony
Tariff : 19.50€ 🚻 🚐 🔲 ⚡ (10A) – Extra per person 6€
Rental rates : (from beginning July to end Aug.) 📶 – 2 🛖. Per week from 430 to 480 €
🚐 5 🔲 19.50€

Site is 500m from the Point Sublime headland.

Surroundings : 🏞 ≤ 🌳🌳
Facilities : 👤 ⚬🚿 🚮 🛁 🚰 🅿 🖥
Nearby : 🍷 🍴

GPS Longitude : 3.24282
Latitude : 44.31532

T-GERMAIN-DU-TEIL

8340 – Michelin map **330** H8 – pop. 810 – alt. 760
Paris 601 – Montpellier 166 – Mende 46 – Millau 58

Les Chalets du Plan d'Eau de Booz
(rental of chalets only)

📞 04 66 48 48 48, *www.lozere-resa.com*
Address : Booz's pond (8km southeast along the D 52, turn onto D 809, after the motorway)
Opening times : from mid April to mid Nov.
5 ha flat, grassy, lake
Rental rates : (2012 price) 👤 (1 chalet) – 43 🏠. Per week from 189 to 609 €
Reservation fee 20€

Surroundings : 🌱
Leisure activities : 🍷 🍴 🎱 🎯 jacuzzi 🚣 🏊 🛶 pedalos 🎣
Facilities : ⚬🚿 🏧 🚰 launderette
Nearby : 🚴 forest trail

GPS Longitude : 3.19764
Latitude : 44.45787

ST-HIPPOLYTE-DU-FORT

30170 – Michelin map **339** I5 – pop. 3,803 – alt. 165
▶ Paris 703 – Alès 35 – Anduze 22 – Nîmes 48

Graniers

✆ 04 66 85 21 44, *camping-graniers.com*
Address : head 4km northeast following signs for Uzès then take D 133, follow the signs for
Monoblet and take the road to the right; beside a stream
Opening times : from mid March to beginning Nov.
2 ha (50 pitches) terraced, relatively flat, grassy, wood
Tariff : 24.10€ ✸✸ 👫 🖃 [½] (6A) – Extra per person 4.10€
Rental rates : (from mid March to beginning Nov.) – 2 🚃 – 3 🏠 – 2 yurts –
3 tent bungalows – 3 mobile homes (without sanitary facilities). Per night from 31 to 80 €
Per week from 205 to 460€
🚐 sani-station 5€ – 5 🖃 12€
A shady site with a range of new and older rental options.

Surroundings : 🌊 ⁰⁰
Leisure activities : 🍹 ✗ 🏊 🚲 🛶
Facilities : 🚿 ⚬━ 🏠 🕯 🖨 🚰

GPS Longitude : 3.88722
Latitude : 43.98084

ST-JEAN-DE-CEYRARGUES

30360 – Michelin map **339** K4 – pop. 158 – alt. 180
▶ Paris 700 – Alès 18 – Nîmes 33 – Uzès 21

Les Vistes

✆ 04 66 83 28 09, *www.lesvistes.com*
Address : rte des Vistes (500m south along the D 7)
Opening times : from beginning April to beginning Nov.
6 ha/3 ha for camping (52 pitches) open site, relatively flat, flat, grassy, stony
Tariff : (2012 price) 26.20€ ✸✸ 👫 🖃 [½] (6A) – Extra per person 6.50€
Rental rates : (2012 price) (from beginning April to beginning Nov.) 🚿 (1 chalet) – 12 🏠.
Per week from 310 to 620€
Attractive, panoramic location.

Surroundings : ⩽ Mt Aigoual ⁰⁰
Leisure activities : 🏠 🏊 🛶
Facilities : 🚿 ⚬━ 🅿 🚰 🕯 🖨 refrigerators

GPS Longitude : 4.23016
Latitude : 44.04734

ST-JEAN-DU-GARD

30270 – Michelin map **339** I4 – pop. 2,687 – alt. 183
▶ Paris 675 – Alès 28 – Florac 54 – Lodève 91

Mas de la Cam 👥

✆ 04 66 85 12 02, *www.masdelacam.fr*
Address : rte de Saint-André-de-Valborgne (3km northwest along the D 907; beside the Gardon de
St-Jean)
Opening times : from end April to end Sept.
6 ha (200 pitches) terraced, grassy, relatively flat
Tariff : 37€ ✸✸ 👫 🖃 [½] (6A) – Extra per person 8.20€ – Reservation fee 17€
Rental rates : (2012 price) (from mid April to mid Sept.) 🚿 – 1 teepee – 7 gîtes.
Per night from 60 to 130 € – Per week from 385 to 850€ – Reservation fee 17€
Attractive children's playground. The site is for tents and caravans exclusively.

Surroundings : 🌊 ⩽ 🏕 ⁰⁰
Leisure activities : 🍹 ✗ 🏠 🎣 ⛹ 🏊 🎿 🛶 🏊 🏓 multi-sports ground
Facilities : 🚿 ⚬━ 🕯 🖨 🚿 🚰

GPS Longitude : 3.85319
Latitude : 44.1123

Les Sources

📞 0466853803, *www.camping-des-sources.fr*
Address : rte de Mialet (located 1km northeast along the D 983 and D 50)
Opening times : from beginning April to end Sept.
3 ha (92 pitches) terraced, relatively flat, grassy
Tariff : 29€ ♦♦ ⇔ 🖳 [½] (10A) – Extra per person 4.50€ – Reservation fee 10€
Rental rates : (from beginning April to end Sept.) – 3 🚐 – 20 🏠 – 3 tent bungalows –
3 mobile homes (without sanitary facilities). Per night from 43 to 90€
Per week from 301 to 630 € – Reservation fee 19€
🚮 sani-station 4€ – 🚿 [½]29€
Family atmosphere and well-shaded pitches.

Surroundings : 🏊 ≤ 🗔 ♨♨
Leisure activities : ♥ ✗ 🔲 ⚓ 🏊
Facilities : 🔥 ⚷ 🔟 🛁 🛋 🚿 ⁱ launderette 🛒

Longitude : 3.89258
Latitude : 44.11393

La Forêt

📞 0466853700, *www.campingalaforet.com*
Address : rte de Falguières (situated 2km north along the D 983, follow the signs for St-Étienne-Vallée-Française then continue 2km along the D 333)
Opening times : from end April to mid Sept.
3 ha (65 pitches) terraced, flat, grassy, stony
Tariff : (2012 price) 33.40€ ♦♦ ⇔ 🖳 [½] (10A) – Extra per person 6.70€ – Reservation fee 5€
Rental rates : (2012 price) (from end April to mid Sept.) ⚞ – 3 🏠 – 5 cabins in the trees.
Per night 70€ – Per week from 154 to 587€ – Reservation fee 5€
At the edge of a vast pine forest.

Surroundings : 🏊 ≤ 🗔 ♨♨
Leisure activities : ⚓ 🏊
Facilities : ⚷ 🖂 🛁 🖳 🛒 refrigerators

Longitude : 3.89072
Latitude : 44.12948

ST-LÉGER-DE-PEYRE

48100 – Michelin map **330** H7 – pop. 174 – alt. 780
Paris 581 – Montpellier 188 – Mende 34 – Marvejols 6

Village Vacances Hameau Ste-Lucie
(rental of gîtes only)

📞 0466484848, *www.lozere-resa.com* – alt. 1 100
Address : at Sainte-Lucie
Opening times : from mid Feb. to beginning Jan.
30 ha/2 ha for camping open site, terraced
Rental rates : (2012 price) – 12 gîtes. Per week from 148 to 648 € – Reservation fee 20€
A 180°-view of the Lozère river, offering absolute peace and quiet, close to the wolf park.

Surroundings : 🏊 ≤ Mont Lozère, Mont Aigoual
Leisure activities : ♥ ✗
Facilities : ⚷ ℗ 🔟 🖳
Nearby : Parc aux loups du Gévaudan (wolf park)

Longitude : 3.28517
Latitude : 44.60649

These symbols are used for a campsite that is exceptional in its category:
🏕🏕...🏕 *Particularly pleasant setting, quality and range of services available*
🏊🏊 *Tranquil, isolated site – quiet site, particularly at night*
≤≤ *Exceptional view – interesting or panoramic view*

LANGUEDOC-ROUSSILLON

ST-PAUL-LE-FROID

48600 – Michelin map **330** J6 – pop. 147 – alt. 1,302 – Winter sports :
▶ Paris 582 – Montpellier 237 – Mende 54 – Le Puy-en-Velay 61

Village Vacances les Baraques des Bouviers
(rental of chalets and 'nordiques' chalets only)

✆ 0466484848, *www.lesbouviers.com* – alt. 1 418
2 ha open site, terraced, flat
Rentals : ♿ – 14 ☎.

Chalets are well spaced-out on the Plateau de La Margeride, close to cross-country ski pistes and snowshoe hiking trails.

Surroundings :
Leisure activities :
Facilities :
Nearby : ♟ ✗ ♿climbing

Longitude : 3.50574
Latitude : 44.76617

ST-VICTOR-DE-MALCAP

30500 – Michelin map **339** K3 – pop. 683 – alt. 140
▶ Paris 680 – Alès 23 – Barjac 15 – La Grand-Combe 25

Domaine de Labeiller

✆ 0466241527, *www.labeiller.fr*
Address : 1701 rte de Barjac (located 1km southeast, access via the D 51, follow the signs for St-Jean-de-Maruéjols and take road to the left)
3 ha (132 pitches) terraced, flat, grassy, stony
Rentals : 20 – 3 gîtes – 5 mobile homes (without sanitary facilities).

An attractive swimming area surrounded by oak trees.

Surroundings :
Leisure activities :
Facilities : ♿ launderette
Nearby :

Longitude : 4.22727
Latitude : 44.24154

This guide is not intended as a list of all the camping sites in France; its aim is to provide a selection of the best sites in each category.

STE-ÉNIMIE

48210 – Michelin map **330** I8 – pop. 525 – alt. 470
▶ Paris 612 – Florac 27 – Mende 28 – Meyrueis 30

Le Couderc

✆ 0466485053, *www.campingcouderc.fr*
Address : rte de Millau (situated 2km southwest along the D 907bis; beside the Tarn river)
Opening times : from beginning April to end Sept.
2.5 ha (113 pitches) terraced, flat, grassy, stony
Tariff : 26€ ♟♟ ⛺ 圓 ⓖ (16A) – Extra per person 4€ – Reservation fee 15€
Rental rates : (from beginning April to end Sept.) – 7 . Per week from 240 to 640 € Reservation fee 15€
⛺ 20 圓 22€
Surroundings :
Leisure activities :
Facilities :

Longitude : 3.39917
Latitude : 44.35194

Les Fayards

0466485736, *www.camping-les-fayards.com*
Address : rte de Millau (3km southwest along the D 907bis; beside the Tarn river)
Opening times : from mid June to beginning Sept.
2 ha (90 pitches) terrace, flat, grassy, stony
Tariff : (2012 price) 29 € ♦♦ ⇌ 🗐 🔌 (16A) – Extra per person 4 €
Rental rates : (2012 price) (from beginning May to beginning Sept.) – 2 caravans –
14 ▦ – 4 ⌂. Per night from 53 to 85 € – Per week from 270 to 695 €

Surroundings :
Leisure activities :
Facilities :

GPS Longitude : 3.39504
Latitude : 44.34583

Le Site de Castelbouc

0466485808, *www.gorges-du-tarn.fr*
Address : 7km southeast along the D 907b, follow the signs for Ispagnac then continue 500m to the right following signs for Castelbouc; beside the Tarn river
Opening times : from mid April to end Sept.
1 ha (60 pitches) open site, relatively flat, flat, grassy
Tariff : 16.50 € ♦♦ ⇌ 🗐 🔌 (5A) – Extra per person 4 €
Rental rates : (from beginning May to end Sept.) – 9 ▦ – 5 ⊨ – 1 gîte.
Per night from 50 to 65 € – Per week from 350 to 540 €

Surroundings :
Leisure activities :
Facilities :

GPS Longitude : 3.46571
Latitude : 44.34423

STE-MARIE

66470 – Michelin map **344** J6 – pop. 4,641 – alt. 4
▸ Paris 845 – Argelès-sur-Mer 24 – Le Boulou 37 – Perpignan 14

Le Palais de la Mer ♣ℓ

0468730794, *www.palaisdelamer.com*
Address : av. de Las Illes (600m north of the resort, 150m from the beach (direct access)
Opening times : from mid May to end Sept.
8 ha/3 ha for camping (181 pitches) flat, sandy
Tariff : 43 € ♦♦ ⇌ 🗐 🔌 (10A) – Extra per person 7 € – Reservation fee 35 €
Rental rates : (from mid May to end Sept.) – 98 ▦ – 2 apartments. Per night from 30 to 145 €
Per week from 210 to 1,020 € – Reservation fee 35 €

Shaded setting with laurel trees lining the paths.

Surroundings :
Leisure activities : ♈ ✗ evening ♣♣ hammam, jacuzzi ✗ wildlife park
Facilities : launderette

GPS Longitude : 3.03307
Latitude : 42.74045

Key to rentals symbols:

12 ▦	*Number of mobile homes*
20 ⌂	*Number of chalets*
6 ⊨	*Number of rooms to rent*
Per night 30–50€	*Minimum/maximum rate per night*
Per week 300–1,000€	*Minimum/maximum rate per week*

La Pergola

𝄡 04 68 73 03 07, www.campinglapergola.com
Address : 500m from the beach
Opening times : from beginning June to end Sept.
3.5 ha (181 pitches) flat, sandy
Tariff : (2012 price) 33€ ✱✱ ⇌ 🔲 ⚡ (10A) – Extra per person 7.50€ – Reservation fee 16€
Rental rates : (2012 price) (from beginning May to end Sept.) ⚓ – 20 🚐 – 9 mobile homes (without sanitary facilities). Per week from 350 to 740€ – Reservation fee 16€
🚐 sani-station 5€

Surroundings : 🌳🌳
Leisure activities : ✗ 🎱 ⚓ 🏊
Facilities : ♿ ⚲ 🚿 ⚷ ♨ ♙ launderette 🧺
Nearby : 🍴

GPS
Longitude : 3.03315
Latitude : 42.72672

There are several different types of sani-station ('borne' in French) – sanitation points providing fresh water and disposal points for grey water. See page 12 for further details.

SÉRIGNAN

34410 – Michelin map **339** E9 – pop. 6,631 – alt. 7
▶ Paris 765 – Agde 22 – Béziers 11 – Narbonne 34

FranceLoc Le Domaine Les Vignes d'Or ♣♣
(rental of mobile homes and chalets only)

𝄡 04 67 32 37 18, www.vignesdor.com
Address : 3.5km to the south, take the side road located behind the Citroën garage
Opening times : from beginning April to end Sept.
4 ha (240 pitches) flat, grassy, stony
Rental rates : (2012 price) ♿ (2 mobile homes) – 173 🚐 – 11 🏠. Per night from 33 to 90€
Per week from 160 to 1,090 € – Reservation fee 27€

Surroundings : 🌿 ⛱ 🌳🌳
Leisure activities : 🍸 ✗ ✵ ⚓ 🎱 🏊 ⚐ multi-sports ground
Facilities : ♿ ⚲ 🚿 ♙ 🔲 🧺
Nearby : 🛒 🍴 🐎

GPS
Longitude : 3.2757
Latitude : 43.2593

Le Paradis

𝄡 04 67 32 24 03, www.camping-leparadis.com ⚓
Address : rte de Valras-Plage (located 1.5km to the south)
Opening times : from beginning April to end Sept.
2.2 ha (129 pitches) flat, grassy
Tariff : 37€ ✱✱ ⇌ 🔲 ⚡ (10A) – Extra per person 6€ – Reservation fee 17€
Rental rates : (2012 price) (from beginning April to end Sept.) ⚓ – 17 🚐 – 5 mobile homes (without sanitary facilities). Per night from 40 to 55 € – Per week from 180 to 600€
Reservation fee 17€
Pleasant setting with spacious pitches and flowers.

Surroundings : ⛱ 🌳🌳
Leisure activities : ✗ 🎱 ⚓ 🏊
Facilities : ♿ ⚲ ▥ 🚿 ⚷ ♨ ♙ launderette 🧺
Nearby : 🛒

GPS
Longitude : 3.28628
Latitude : 43.26829

Le Mas des Lavandes
(rental of mobile homes only)

📞 0467397588, *www.lemasdeslavandes.fr*
Address : chemin de la mer (D 19 follow the signs for Valras-Plage – from the A9 take exit Béziers-est)
Opening times : from beginning April to end Sept.
3.8 ha flat
Rental rates : (2012 price) ♿ (1 mobile home) – 80. Per week from 215 to 944 €
Well-appointed mobile homes, but choose those away from the road in preference.

Surroundings : 🔲 🎯
Leisure activities : 🍴 ✗ 🏠 🛝 🛶 ✂ ⛵ 🏊
Facilities : ♿ 📺 🚿
Nearby : 🛒

 Longitude : 3.2831
Latitude : 43.25732

SÉRIGNAN-PLAGE

34410 – Michelin map **339** E9
▶ Paris 769 – Montpellier 73 – Carcassonne 100

Yelloh! Village Le Sérignan Plage ♣

📞 0467323533, *www.leserignanplage.com*
Address : at L'Orpellière (at the edge of the beach, direct access)
Opening times : from end April to end Sept.
20 ha (1200 pitches) flat, grassy, sandy
Tariff : 53€ 🚻 🚐 🔌 (6A) – Extra per person 10€
Rental rates : (from end April to end Sept.) ✂ – 362 – 53 🏠 – 5 tents.
Per night from 39 to 304€ – Per week from 273 to 2,128€
🚽 sani-station
Natural, sunny pitches, close to the marsh; luxury rental options with plenty of shade close to the beach.

Surroundings : 🏞 🔲 🎯 🌊
Leisure activities : 🍴 ✗ 🏠 🎯 🛝 🛶 🛶 🚴 ✂ 🏊 🏊 spa centre (naturist in mornings), disco , multi-sports ground
Facilities : ♿ 🔑 🚿 🍴 launderette 🛒 🚿
Nearby : 🐎 🏇

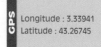 Longitude : 3.3213
Latitude : 43.26401

Yelloh! Village Aloha ♣

📞 0467397130, *www.alohacamping.com*
Address : ch. des Dunes
Opening times : from mid April to mid Sept.
9.5 ha (470 pitches) flat, grassy, sandy
Tariff : 53€ 🚻 🚐 🔌 (10A) – Extra per person 8€
Rental rates : (from mid April to mid Sept.) 🅿 – 187 – 12 🏠. Per night from 39 to 249€
Per week from 273 to 1,743€
🚽 sani-station
Site straddles the path leading to the beach, with rental options in a landscaped setting.

Surroundings : 🏞 🔲 🎯 🌊
Leisure activities : 🍴 ✗ 🏠 🎯 🛝 🛶 jacuzzi 🛶 🚴 ✂ 🏊 multi-sports ground
Facilities : ♿ 🔑 🚿 🍴 launderette 🛒 🚿
Nearby : 🏇 🏇

Longitude : 3.33941
Latitude : 43.26745

In order for the guide to remain wholly objective, the selection of campsites is made on an entirely independent basis.

Domaine de Beauséjour ♠⁑

0467 39 50 93, www.camping-beausejour.com
Address : beside the beach
10 ha/6 ha for camping (380 pitches) flat, grassy, sandy
Rentals : ⚏ – 80 🚐 – 6 🏠.
⛽ sani-station

Surroundings : 🐾 🗐 ⚏ ⛰
Leisure activities : 🍴 ✕ ⓥ evening ✳ 🎣 ☰ hammam, jacuzzi ⛵ 🚲 🏊 disco, watersports centre, mountain biking, spa therapy centre
Facilities : 🚿 🔌 🧺 launderette 🚾 🚮

Longitude : 3.33692
Latitude : 43.26711

Le Clos Virgile ♠⁑

0467 32 20 64, www.leclosvirgile.com
Address : 500m from the beach
Opening times : from beginning May to mid Sept.
5 ha (300 pitches) flat, grassy, sandy
Tariff : (2012 price) 40€ ✶✶ 🚗 ▣ ⚡ (10A) – Extra per person 7€ – Reservation fee 25€
Rental rates : (2012 price) (from beginning May to mid Sept.) – 90 🚐 – 18 🏠.
Per night from 28 to 120€ – Per week from 195 to 840€ – Reservation fee 25€
Shady pitches but the sanitary facilities are rather old.

Surroundings : 🗐 ⚏
Leisure activities : 🍴 ✕ 🏠 ⓥ ✳ jacuzzi ⛵ ▣ 🏊 ⛷ multi-sports ground
Facilities : 🚿 🔌 🧺 🍴 ▣ 🚾 🚮
Nearby : 🏇 🐎

Longitude : 3.33152
Latitude : 43.27204

30250 – Michelin map **339** J6 – pop. 4,496 – alt. 34
▶ Paris 734 – Alès 44 – Montpellier 35 – Nîmes 29

Les Castels Le Domaine de Massereau

0466 53 11 20, www.massereau.com
Address : 1990 rte d'Aubais (Les Hauteurs de Sommières (heights)
Opening times : from beginning April to beginning Nov.
90 ha/7.7 ha for camping (120 pitches) relatively flat, flat, grassy, stony
Tariff : (2012 price) 56.90€ ✶✶ 🚗 ▣ ⚡ (16A) – Extra per person 10€ – Reservation fee 23€
Rental rates : (from beginning April to end Oct.) 🚿 – 35 🚐 – 24 🏠.
Per night from 48 to 178€ – Per week from 340 to 1,246€ – Reservation fee 23€
⛽ sani-station 2€ – 2 ▣ 22.40€
Luxury rental options, in the middle of a wine-growing area crossed by the Sommières-Nîmes cycle trail.

Surroundings : 🐾 🗐 ⚏
Leisure activities : 🍴 ✕ ☰ hammam jacuzzi ⛵ 🚲 🏇 🏊 ⛷ fitness trail, multi-sports ground
Facilities : 🚿 🔌 🧺 ⛲ ☂ 🍴 launderette 🚾 🚮
Nearby : 🎣

Longitude : 4.09735
Latitude : 43.76574

For more information on visiting particular towns or regions, consult the relevant regional MICHELIN Green Guide. We also recommend you use the appropriate Michelin regional map to locate your selected campsite, to calculate distances and to work out the best route.

Municipal de Garanel

📞 0466803349, *campingmunicipal.sommieres@wanadoo.fr*
Address : in the town (near the Vidourle river)
Opening times : from beginning April to end Sept.
7 ha (60 pitches) flat, stony, sandy
Tariff : (2012 price) 14.95€ ✦✦ ⚌ 🔲 🕅 (10A) – Extra per person 3.70€
Very close to the bullring and town centre.

Surroundings : ▱ 🔬🔬
Facilities : ♿ ⚬ 🖼 🛁 🕅 🖼
Nearby : 🏊 🍹✕ ⚒ 🏊

GPS Longitude : 4.08703
Latitude : 43.78738

LA TAMARISSIÈRE

34300 – Michelin map **339** F9
▶ Paris 761 – Montpellier 62 – Béziers 24 – Narbonne 54

La Tamarissière

📞 0467947946, *www.camping-latama.com*
Address : 4 r. du Commandant Malet
Opening times : from beginning April to mid Sept.
10 ha (700 pitches) undulating, flat and relatively flat, sandy, grassy
Tariff : (2012 price) 26.20€ ✦✦ ⚌ 🔲 🕅 (10A) – Extra per person 5€ – Reservation fee 27€
Rental rates : (2012 price) (permanent) ♿ (2 chalets) 🕅 – 60 🏠 – 30 tents.
Per night from 36 to 112 € – Per week from 248 to 784 € – Reservation fee 27€
A pleasant location beside the sea, sheltered by pine trees.

Surroundings : 🔬🔬 ⛰
Leisure activities : 🏀 multi-sports ground
Facilities : ♿ ⚬ 🖼 🛁 🕅 launderette, refrigerated food storage
Nearby : 🏊 🍹✕ ⚒ 🎣

GPS Longitude : 3.44249
Latitude : 43.28821

---

*Routes nationales are main roads and their identifying numbers
begin with N or RN. Routes départementales are generally quieter
roads and begin with D or DN.*

TORREILLES-PLAGE

66440 – Michelin map **344** I6
▶ Paris 853 – Montpellier 157 – Perpignan 20 – Carcassonne 119

Sunêlia Les Tropiques ⚑⚑

📞 0468280509, *www.campinglestropiques.com*
Address : bd de la Plage (500m from the beach)
Opening times : from beginning April to end Sept.
8 ha (450 pitches) flat, stony, sandy
Tariff : 51.50€ ✦✦ ⚌ 🔲 🕅 (10A) – Extra per person 9.60€ – Reservation fee 30€
Rental rates : (from beginning April to end Sept.) ♿ (2 mobile homes) – 260 🚐 – 20 🏠 –
2 tents. Per night from 36 to 201€ – Per week from 250 to 1,407 € – Reservation fee 30€
🚿 sani-station – 🚐 🕅18.50€
Shady pitches and a pleasant spa centre.

Surroundings : ▱ 🔬🔬
Leisure activities : 🍹✕ 🎬 🖼 🏊 🎇 📻 ≋ hammam, jacuzzi 🏀 ⚒ 🏊
🏊 disco, multi-sports ground, spa therapy centre
Facilities : ♿ ⚬ 🛁 🕅 launderette 🏊 ⚒
Nearby : 🏇 🐎

GPS Longitude : 3.02972
Latitude : 42.7675

Mar I Sol ♣♣

📞 0468280407, *www.camping-marisol.com* – limited spaces for one-night stay
Address : bd de la Plage (150m from the beach – direct access)
Opening times : from beginning April to end Sept.
7 ha (377 pitches) flat, grassy, sandy
Tariff : 59€ 👭👭 ⚬ 🔲 ⚡ (10A) – Extra per person 10.70€ – Reservation fee 49.50€
Rental rates : (from beginning April to end Sept.) 🏖 – 170 🚐. Per night from 29 to 184 €
Per week from 203 to 1,288 € – Reservation fee 49.50€

A 'village club' offering lots of activities and a large water park.

Surroundings : 🔲 ♨
Leisure activities : 🍷 ✕ 📺 🎣 🏊 🎿 ⛵ hammam, jacuzzi 🛶 🚲 🎣
🛷 disco, multi-sports ground
Facilities : ♿ ⚬ 🍳 🚰 launderette 🛒 🧺
Nearby : ⛽

GPS Longitude : 3.03327
Latitude : 42.76746

Le Calypso ♣♣

📞 0468280947, *www.camping-calypso.com* – limited spaces for one-night stay
Address : bd de la Plage
6 ha (308 pitches) flat, stony, sandy
Rentals : 78 🚐 – 28 🏠.
🚐, 9 🔲

Pretty play and paddling pool area and indivdual sanitary facilities for some pitches.

Surroundings : 🔲 ♨♨
Leisure activities : 🍷 ✕ 📺 🎣 🏊 🎿 jacuzzi 🛶 🚲 🎣 🛷 multi-sports
ground
Facilities : ♿ ⚬ 🍳 – 9 individual sanitary facilities (🚿🔽🚽 wc) 🚰
launderette 🧺 🧊 refrigerators
Nearby : ⛽ 🏇

GPS Longitude : 3.03043
Latitude : 42.77128

Homair Vacances La Palmeraie ♣♣

📞 0468282064, *www.homair.com* – limited spaces for one-night stay
Address : bd de la Plage
Opening times : from beginning April to mid Sept.
4.5 ha (229 pitches) flat, grassy, sandy
Tariff : (2012 price) 38€ 👭👭 ⚬ 🔲 ⚡ (10A) – Extra per person 8.50€ – Reservation fee 10€
Rental rates : (2012 price) (from beginning April to mid Sept.) – 180 🚐.
Per night from 24 to 170 € – Per week from 168 to 1,190€ – Reservation fee 25€

*A good covering of shade for the mobile homes, but very few places for tents
and caravans.*

Surroundings : 🔲 ♨♨
Leisure activities : 🍷 ✕ 📺 🎣 evening 🏊 🛶 🎣 multi-sports ground
Facilities : ♿ ⚬ 🍳 🚰 launderette 🧺 🧊 refrigerated food storage
Nearby : 🛒 🎿 ⛽ 🏇

GPS Longitude : 3.02806
Latitude : 42.76361

---

*The Michelin classification (ᐃᐃᐃ … ᐃ) is totally independent of the
official star classification system awarded by the local prefecture or
other official organisation.*

TRÈBES

1800 – Michelin map **344** F3 – pop. 5,416 – alt. 84
Paris 776 – Carcassonne 8 – Conques-sur-Orbiel 9 – Lézignan-Corbières 28

▲ A l'Ombre des Micocouliers

 0468786175, *www.campingmicocouliers.com*
Address : chemin de la Lande
Opening times : from beginning April to end Sept.
1.5 ha (70 pitches) flat, grassy, sandy
Tariff : (2012 price) 22€ ♦♦ ⟷ 🔲 🚽 (16A) – Extra per person 5.50€
Rental rates : (2012 price) (from beginning April to end Sept.) – 5 tent bungalows.
Per night from 26 to 40€ – Per week from 130 to 480 €
 sani-station 5€
Situated beside the Aude river in the shade of hackberry trees, but the sanitary facilities are rather old.

Surroundings : ⟐ 00
Leisure activities : ✗ 🖼 ⟷ 🎣 🏊
Facilities : 🚻 ⊶ 🚿 ⊤ 🔲 🚮
Nearby : 🐴 🎿 🖼

Longitude : 2.44237
Latitude : 43.20682

Gîtes range from small maisonettes to old farmhouses with several bedrooms.

UZÈS

0700 – Michelin map **339** L4 – pop. 8,339 – alt. 138
Paris 682 – Alès 34 – Arles 52 – Avignon 38

▲▲▲ Le Moulin Neuf ♠♣

 0466221721, *www.le-moulin-neuf.fr*
Address : at Saint-Quentin-La-Poterie (4.5km northeast along the D 982, follow the signs for Bagnols-sur-Cèze and take the D 5 to the left)
Opening times : from beginning April to mid Sept.
5 ha (140 pitches) terrace, flat, grassy
Tariff : 24€ ♦♦ ⟷ 🔲 🚽 (5A) – Extra per person 6.50€ – Reservation fee 10€
Rental rates : (permanent) – 35 gîtes. Per night from 40 to 100 €– Per week from 245 to 680€
Reservation fee 10€
 sani-station – 🚽 🚽10€
Rectangular site, shaded by poplars; the gîtes are quite old and moderately comfortable.

Surroundings : 🏞 ⟐ 00
Leisure activities : 🍷 ✗ 🖼 ⟷ 🎣 🏓 🏊 multi-sports ground
Facilities : 🚻 ⊶ 🚿 ⊤ 🔲 🚮
Nearby : 🐴

Longitude : 4.45569
Latitude : 44.0321

▲▲ Le Mas de Rey

 0466221827, *www.campingmasderey.com*
Address : rte d'Anduze (3km southwest along the D 982)
Opening times : from end March to mid Oct.
5 ha/2.5 ha for camping (66 pitches) flat, grassy
Tariff : (2012 price) 28.50€ ♦♦ ⟷ 🔲 🚽 (10A) – Extra per person 8€ – Reservation fee 10€
Rental rates : (2012 price) (from end March to mid Oct.) 🚻 (1 chalet) – 6 🏠.
Per night from 70 to 100€ – Per week from 575 to 800€ – Reservation fee 10€
Very peaceful pitches and well-appointed wooden chalets in a pleasant, shady setting.

Surroundings : 🏞 ⟐ 00
Leisure activities : 🖼 ⟷ 🏊
Facilities : 🚻 ⊶ 🚿 ⊤ 🔲 🚮

Longitude : 4.38471
Latitude : 43.99806

LANGUEDOC-ROUSSILLON

VALLABRÈGUES

30300 – Michelin map **339** M5 – pop. 1,318 – alt. 8
▶ Paris 698 – Arles 26 – Avignon 22 – Beaucaire 9

Lou Vincen

✆ 04 66 59 21 29, *www.campinglouvincen.com*
Address : to the west of the town, 100m from the Rhône and a small lake
Opening times : from beginning April to end Oct.
1.4 ha (75 pitches) flat, grassy
Tariff : 24.80€ ✶✶ ⇔ 🗉 🔌 (6A) – Extra per person 7.30€ – Reservation fee 17€
Rental rates : (from mid April to mid Oct.) 🚫 – 10 🛑. Per week from 287 to 636 €
Reservation fee 17€
🚾 sani-station
At the entrance to the town, on the left bank of the Rhône.

Surroundings : 🏞 ⌒ 🌳
Leisure activities : ♨
Facilities : ⌐ ⚄ 🚿 ⛲ 🖥
Nearby : ✗

GPS Longitude : 4.62546
Latitude : 43.85493

VALLERAUGUE

30570 – Michelin map **339** G4 – pop. 1,070 – alt. 346
▶ Paris 684 – Mende 100 – Millau 75 – Nîmes 86

Le Mourétou

✆ 04.67.82.22.30, *www.camping-mouretou.com*
Address : rte de l'Aigoual et chemin at drte (3km west on the D 986)
Opening times : from beginning April to beginning Nov.
1 ha (33 pitches) relatively flat, stony
Tariff : (2012 price) 22€ ✶✶ ⇔ 🗉 🔌 (6A) – Extra per person 6€ – Reservation fee 15€
Rental rates : (2012 price) (from mid Feb. to beginning Nov.) – 4 🛑 – 2 gîtes.
Per night 45€ – Per week from 190 to 490 € – Reservation fee 15€
Well-shaded pitches beside the Hérault river and a small lake.

Surroundings : ⌒ 🌳
Leisure activities : ✗ 🚣
Facilities : 🖥 🍴
Nearby : 🏊 (lake)

GPS Longitude : 3.60785
Latitude : 44.0871

VALRAS-PLAGE

34350 – Michelin map **339** E9 – pop. 4,649 – alt. 1
▶ Paris 767 – Agde 25 – Béziers 16 – Montpellier 76

Domaine de La Yole 👥

✆ 04 67 37 33 87, *www.campinglayole.com*
Address : situated 2km southwest, 500m from the beach
Opening times : from end April to mid Sept.
23 ha (1273 pitches) flat, grassy, sandy
Tariff : 53€ ✶✶ ⇔ 🗉 🔌 (5A) – Extra per person 9.20€ – Reservation fee 30€
Rental rates : (from end April to mid Sept.) Ⓟ – 300 🛑 – 48 🏠 – 10 tents.
Per night from 30 to 212€ – Per week from 210 to 1,484 €– Reservation fee 30€
There's a vineyard nearby, and a farmhouse restaurant.

Surroundings : 💡 🌳
Leisure activities : 🍷 ✗ 🎬 🎱 🚶 🚣 🚴 ✗ 🎪 ♨ 🏊 forest trail, multi-sports ground
Facilities : ♿ ⌐ 🍴 ⚄ 🚿 ⛲ launderette 🍖 🍴
Nearby : 🐎

GPS Longitude : 3.27181
Latitude : 43.23639

Le Méditerranée

℘ 04 67 37 34 29, *www.camping-le-mediterranee.com*
Address : rte de Vendres (located 1.5km southwest, 200m from the beach)
Opening times : from end April to mid Sept.
4.5 ha (367 pitches) flat, grassy, sandy
Tariff : (2012 price) 44.50€ ♦♦ ⇐⇒ 🔲 (6A) – Extra per person 8€ – Reservation fee 25€
Rental rates : (2012 price) (from end April to mid Sept.) – 65 🚐 – 10 🏠 – 5 mobile homes (without sanitary facilities). Per night from 95 to 115 €– Per week from 310 to 920 €
Reservation fee 25€
A shady site with numerous pitches for tents and caravans.

Surroundings : 🔲🔲
Leisure activities : ♈ ✗ ⬜ ⬛⬛ ⬜ ⬜ multi-sports ground
Facilities : ♿ ⛏ ⬜ launderette ⬜ ⬜ refrigerators
Nearby : ⬜⬜⬜⬜⬜⬜

GPS
Longitude : 3.26848
Latitude : 43.23592

La Plage et du Bord de Mer ⬜⬜

℘ 04 67 37 34 38, *www.campinglaplage.net* ⬜
Address : rte de Vendres (located 1.5km southwest; beside the sea)
Opening times : from mid May to mid Sept.
13 ha (655 pitches) flat, grassy, sandy
Tariff : 43€ ♦♦ ⇐⇒ 🔲 (⬜) (10A) – Extra per person 6€ – Reservation fee 30€
Rental rates : (from mid May to mid Sept.) ⬜ – 44 🚐 – 6 tents. Per night from 40 to 180€
Per week from 616 to 1,260 € – Reservation fee 30€
⬜ sani-station
Well-maintained sanitary facilities, though a little old-fashioned.

Surroundings : ⬜ ⬜ ⬜
Leisure activities : ♈ ✗ ⬜ ⬜ ⬛⬛ ⬜ ⬜ ⬜ ⬜ ⬜ multi-sports ground
Facilities : ♿ ⛏ ⬜ ⬜ ⬜ ⬜ launderette ⬜ ⬜
Nearby : ⬜ ⬜

GPS
Longitude : 3.26889
Latitude : 43.23559

Lou Village ⬜⬜

℘ 04 67 37 33 79, *www.louvillage.com* – limited spaces for one-night stay
Address : chemin des Montilles (situated 2km southwest, 100m from the beach)
Opening times : from end April to mid Sept.
8 ha (470 pitches) flat, grassy, sandy, pond
Tariff : (2012 price) 49.70€ ♦♦ ⇐⇒ 🔲 (10A) – Extra per person 8.95€ – Reservation fee 30€
Rental rates : (2012 price) (from end April to mid Sept.) ⬜ – 85 🚐 – 17 🏠.
Per night from 49 to 162€ – Per week from 347 to 1,137 € – Reservation fee 30€
⬜ sani-station
A water park and direct access to the beach.

Surroundings : ⬜ ⬜ ⬜ ⬜
Leisure activities : ♈ ✗ ⬜ ⬜ evening ⬛⬛ ⬛⬛ ⬜ ⬜ ⬜
Facilities : ♿ ⛏ ⬜ ⬜ ⬜ ⬜ ⬜ ⬜ ⬜
Nearby : ⬜ jet skis

GPS
Longitude : 3.26046
Latitude : 43.23386

The prices listed were supplied by the campsite owners in 2012
(if prices were not available, those from the previous year are given).
The fees should be regarded as basic charges and may fluctuate
with inflation.

Les Foulègues ♣♦

📞 04 67 37 33 65, www.campinglesfoulegues.com
Address : at Grau-de-Vendres, av. du Port (5km southwest, 400m from the beach)
Opening times : from mid April to end Sept.
5.3 ha (339 pitches) flat, grassy, sandy
Tariff : (2012 price) 48.50€ ♣♣ ⇔ 回 (∮) (6A) – Extra per person 8.50€ – Reservation fee 33€
Rental rates : (2012 price) (from beginning May to mid Sept.) – 26 🚐 – 7 🏠.
Per week from 290 to 940 € – Reservation fee 33€

A pleasant site with good shade. The chalet rental options are a little old.

Surroundings : 🌊 ♡♡
Leisure activities : 🍷 ✗ 🚣 🎦 evening 🏃 ⛷ ✂ ♪ 🏊
Facilities : ♿ ⚷ 🛁 🗑 🚿 ♨ 回 🛒 🚗
Nearby : 🐎

GPS — Longitude : 3.24222 / Latitude : 43.22575

VERNET-LES-BAINS

66820 – Michelin map **344** F7 – pop. 1,432 – alt. 650 – ♨ (mid-Mar to end Nov)
▶ Paris 904 – Mont-Louis 36 – Perpignan 57 – Prades 11

L'Eau Vive

📞 04 68 05 54 14, www.leauvive-camping.com
Address : chemin St Saturnin (take exit towards Sahorre then continue after the bridge 1.3km along the av. St-Saturnin to the right, near the Cady river)
Opening times : from beginning April to end Oct.
2 ha (90 pitches) relatively flat, flat, grassy
Tariff : (2012 price) 27.50€ ♣♣ ⇔ 回 (∮) (10A) – Extra per person 4€ – Reservation fee 15€
Rental rates : (2012 price) (from beginning April to end Oct.) ♿ (1 chalet) – 5 🚐 – 8 🏠.
Per night from 46 to 68 € – Per week from 235 to 750 € – Reservation fee 15€

In a pleasant location, with an ecological swimming pool.

Surroundings : 🌊 ≤ ♡
Leisure activities : 🍷 ✗ ⛷ ⚤ (pool)
Facilities : ♿ ⚷ 🛁 🗑 🚿 ♨ 回

GPS — Longitude : 2.38342 / Latitude : 42.5527

*Give us your opinion of the camping sites we recommend. Let us know
of your remarks and discoveries: campingfrance@tp.michelin.com.*

VERS PONT DU GARD

30210 – Michelin map **339** M5 – pop. 1,696 – alt. 40
▶ Paris 698 – Montpellier 81 – Nîmes 26 – Avignon 27

FranceLoc Gorges du Gardon ♣♦

📞 04 66 22 81 81, www.franceloc.fr
Address : 762 chemin Barque-Vieille (to the south, D 981 and D 5; beside the Gardon river)
Opening times : from beginning April to end Sept.
4 ha (197 pitches) flat, grassy, stony
Tariff : (2012 price) 20€ ♣♣ ⇔ 回 (∮) (6A) – Extra per person 4.70€ – Reservation fee 11€
Rental rates : (2012 price) (from beginning April to end Sept.) – 100 🚐 – 4 🏠.
Per night from 33 to 88€ – Per week from 133 to 595 € – Reservation fee 27€

Numerous mobile homes and camping pitches descending to the banks of the river.

Surroundings : 🌊 🌊 ♡♡
Leisure activities : 🍷 ✗ 🏃 ⛷ 🏊 ⚤ ♪ ⚲
Facilities : ♿ ⚷ ▥ 🛁 ♨ launderette 🚗 refrigerators

GPS — Longitude : 4.51766 / Latitude : 43.95599

VIAS-PLAGE

34450 – Michelin map **339** F9 – pop. 5,386 – alt. 10
▶ Paris 752 – Agde 5 – Béziers 19 – Narbonne 46

Yelloh! Village Club Farret ⚤

📞 0467216445, *www.camping-farret.com*
Address : chemin des Rosses (Beside the beach)
Opening times : from mid April to beginning Oct.
7 ha (437 pitches) flat, grassy, sandy
Tariff : 54€ ⚤ ⟋ 🔲 (6A) – Extra per person 9€
Rental rates : (from mid April to beginning Oct.) ⟋ – 270 🚐 – 69 🏠.
Per night from 30 to 259 € – Per week from 210 to 1,813€

Pretty landscaped mobile-home villages on different themes: pirates, the Pacific . . . and very good sanitary facilities.

Surroundings : 🌊 ⊏ ♨ ▲
Leisure activities : 🍸 ✕ 🎦 🎲 🏃 🏇 🚣 🚴 ✂ 🏊 ♪
entertainment room
Facilities : ♿ ⚬ ▥ 🚿 🚽 🔩 🍴 launderette 🛒 🚰
Nearby : 🏇 🐎

GPS Longitude : 3.419
Latitude : 43.2911

Sunêlia Domaine de la Dragonnière

📞 0892695926, *www.dragonniere.com* – limited spaces for one-night stay
Address : RD 612 (5km west, follow the signs for Béziers)
Opening times : from end March to mid Sept.
30 ha (980 pitches) flat, stony, grassy
Tariff : 57€ ⚤ ⟋ 🔲 (10A) – Extra per person 10€ – Reservation fee 30€
Rental rates : (from end March to mid Sept.) – 366 🚐 – 373 🏠 – 2 tent bungalows.
Per night from 37 to 298 € – Per week from 259 to 2,086 € – Reservation fee 30€

A wide range of accommodation options offering different levels of comfort, and an upmarket spa centre.

Surroundings : ⊏ ♨
Leisure activities : 🍸 ✕ 🎦 🏃 ♨ hammam, jacuzzi 🚣 🚴 ✂ 🎯
🏊 ⛷ multi-sports ground, spa therapy centre
Facilities : ♿ ⚬ 🚿 🔩 🍴 launderette 🛒 🚰 🚰

GPS Longitude : 3.36335
Latitude : 43.3126

Le Napoléon ⚤

📞 0467010780, *www.camping-napoleon.fr*
Address : 1171 av. de la Méditerranée (250m from the beach)
Opening times : from beginning April to end Sept.
3 ha (239 pitches) flat, grassy, sandy
Tariff : (2012 price) 19€ ⚤ ⟋ 🔲 (10A) – Extra per person 6€ – Reservation fee 28€
Rental rates : (2012 price) (from beginning Nov. to end Sept.) ♿ – 62 🚐 – 2 🛏 –
10 apartments – 5 tent bungalows. Per night from 42 to 135 € – Per week from 294 to 945 €
Reservation fee 28€
🚐 sani-station 18€ – 🚐 19€

Surroundings : ⊏ ♨
Leisure activities : 🍸 ✕ 🎦 🎲 🏃 ♨ hammam 🚣 🚴 🏊
multi-sports ground
Facilities : ♿ ⚬ 🚿 🔩 🍴 launderette 🛒 🚰 refrigerated food
storage
Nearby : disco, sports trail, amusement park

GPS Longitude : 3.41661
Latitude : 43.29179

Méditerranée-Plage

△△△

0467909907, www.mediterranee-plage.com
Address : Côte Ouest (6km southwest along the D 137e2)
Opening times : from beginning April to end Sept.
9.6 ha (490 pitches) flat, grassy, sandy
Tariff : (2012 price) 42.20€ ✚✚ ➡ 🔲 🄷 (6A) – Extra per person 7.70€ – Reservation fee 25€
Rental rates : (2012 price) (permanent) ♿ (1 mobile home) ✂ (Jul–Aug) – 230 🚐.
Per week from 260 to 1,270€ – Reservation fee 25€
🚐 sani-station
Pleasant setting beside the sea with good-quality facilities.

Surroundings : 🐟 ➡ 🎱 ⚠
Leisure activities : 🍴 ✗ 🎬 📶 🏃 🏄 🚲 ✂ 🎣 🏊 🏐 multi-sports
ground
Facilities : ♿ 🔑 🚿 🍴 launderette 🗑 🚰

Longitude : 3.37106
Latitude : 43.28202

Les Flots Bleus ♣♣

△△△

0467216480, www.camping-flotsbleus.com
Address : Côte Ouest (to the southwest; beside the beach)
Opening times : from mid April to end Sept.
5 ha (298 pitches) flat, grassy, sandy
Tariff : (2012 price) 33€ ✚✚ ➡ 🔲 🄷 (6A) – Extra per person 6€ – Reservation fee 22€
Rental rates : (2012 price) (from mid April to end Sept.) ✂ – 105 🚐 – 20 🏠.
Per night from 28 to 128 € – Per week from 190 to 900 € – Reservation fee 22€
🚐 sani-station 5€
Jointly run with the France Floride campsite next door.

Surroundings : ➡ 🎱 ⚠
Leisure activities : 🍴 ✗ 🎬 📶 evening 🏃 🎿 🏊 🏐 multi-sports
ground
Facilities : ♿ 🔑 🚿 🍴 launderette 🗑 🚰

Longitude : 3.4055
Latitude : 43.29

Cap Soleil ♣♣

△△△

0467216477, www.capsoleil.fr – limited spaces for one-night stay
Address : chemin de la Grande Cosse (Côte Ouest, 600m from the beach)
Opening times : from mid April to mid Sept.
4.5 ha (288 pitches) flat, grassy
Tariff : (2012 price) 35€ ✚✚ ➡ 🔲 🄷 (10A) – Extra per person 15€ – Reservation fee 25€
Rental rates : (2012 price) (from mid April to mid Sept.) ♿ (1 mobile home) – 76 🚐.
Per night from 69 to 79 € – Per week from 199 to 1,099 € – Reservation fee 25€
🚐 15 🔲 12€
*The covered swimming pool (uncovered in summer) is reserved for naturists in
July–August.*

Surroundings : ➡ 🎱
Leisure activities : 🍴 ✗ 🎬 📶 🏃 🎿 🚲 ✂ 🖼 (open-air in season)
🏊 🏐 multi-sports ground
Facilities : ♿ 🔑 🚿 – 8 individual sanitary facilities (🚿 wc) 🚰 🧺 🍴
launderette 🗑 🚰 refrigerators
Nearby : 🐎

Longitude : 3.39953
Latitude : 43.29262

Do not confuse:
△ to △△△ : MICHELIN classification
with
★ to ★★★★★ : official classification

Californie Plage ▲▴

📞 04 67 21 64 69, www.californie-plage.fr

Address : chemin du Trou de Ragout (Côte Ouest, to the southwest along the D 137e and take road to the left; beside the sea)

5.8 ha (371 pitches) flat, grassy, sandy

Rentals : ⌇ – 120 ⟦⟧.

Free admission to the water park at the Cap-Soleil campsite (opposite, 100m away).

Surroundings : ⌂ ♨♨ ⌂
Leisure activities : ♈ ✕ ⌷ ⊡ ⋏ ⚡ ⚲ 🔲 multi-sports ground
Facilities : ♿ ⚬ ⌂ ⌂ ⚲ ⚲ launderette ⚟ ⚲ refrigerators
Nearby : ✕ ⚲ ⚲

GPS Longitude : 3.39843
Latitude : 43.29051

L'Air Marin ▲▴

📞 04 67 21 64 90, www.camping-air-marin.fr

Address : Côte Est, behind the football pitch

Opening times : from mid April to mid Sept.

5.5 ha (305 pitches) flat, grassy, sandy

Tariff : 42€ ⚭⚭ ⚬ ▣ ⚡ (6A) – Extra per person 8€ – Reservation fee 25€

Rental rates : (from mid April to mid Sept.) – 130 ⟦⟧ – 15 ⟐. Per night from 40 to 147€
Per week from 280 to 1,030€ – Reservation fee 25€

Squared-off site in the shade of poplars with an attractive swimming area, very close to the Canal du Midi.

Surroundings : ⌂ ♨♨
Leisure activities : ♈ ✕ ⌷ ⊡ evening ⋏ ⚡ ⚲ ✕ 🔲 ⚲ ⚲
boats for hire ⚲ multi-sports ground
Facilities : ♿ ⚬ ⚲ ☑ ⌂ ⚲ launderette ⚟ ⚲
Nearby : ⚲ amusement park

GPS Longitude : 3.42129
Latitude : 43.30076

Vacances Directes Le Petit Mousse ▲▴
(rental of mobile homes only)

📞 04 67 90 99 04, www.vacances-directes.com

Address : rte de la Grande Cosse

Opening times : from end April to mid Sept.

5.2 ha (365 pitches) flat, grassy, sandy

Rental rates : (2012 price) ⌇ – 320 ⟦⟧ – (with/without sanitary facilities).
Per night from 40 to 151 € – Per week from 280 to 1,057€ – Reservation fee 20€

Virtually 'on top of the water' with some rental options facing the sea.

Surroundings : ⚲ ♨♨ ⌂
Leisure activities : ♈ ✕ ⌷ ⊡ ⋏ ⚡ ⚲ ⚲ ⚲
Facilities : ⚬ ⌂ ⚲ launderette ⚟ ⚲

GPS Longitude : 3.40147
Latitude : 43.28994

Hélios ▲

📞 04 67 21 63 66, www.camping-helios.com

Address : av. des Pêcheurs (near the Libron river, 250m from the beach)

Opening times : from beginning May to end Sept.

2.5 ha (215 pitches) flat, grassy, sandy

Tariff : 33.60€ ⚭⚭ ⚬ ▣ ⚡ (6A) – Extra per person 4.40€ – Reservation fee 10€

Rental rates : (from beginning May to end Sept.) – 20 ⟦⟧ – 6 ⟐. Per night from 30 to 90€
Per week from 179 to 578€ – Reservation fee 20€

Beside the Libron river, plenty of shade, with an attractive indoor spa area.

Surroundings : ⚲ ♨♨
Leisure activities : ♈ ✕ ⌷ ⚌ hammam, jacuzzi ⚡ spa therapy centre
Facilities : ♿ ⚬ ⌂ ⚲ ▣ ⚟ ⚲

GPS Longitude : 3.40764
Latitude : 43.29115

LE VIGAN

30120 – Michelin map **339** G5 – pop. 3,959 – alt. 221
▶ Paris 707 – Alès 66 – Lodève 50 – Mende 108

Le Val de l'Arre

⌖ 0467810277, www.valdelarre.com
Address : at Roudoulouse, rte du Pont de la Croix (2.5km east along the D 999, follow the rte de Ganges and take road to the right; beside the Arre)
Opening times : from beginning April to mid Sept.
4 ha (173 pitches) terraced, relatively flat, flat, grassy
Tariff : 24.50€ ♦♦ ⬌ 国 ⟨4⟩ (10A) – Extra per person 6.50€ – Reservation fee 15€
Rental rates : (from beginning April to mid Sept.) ⚡ – 35 ▭ – 1 gîte.
Per night from 29 to 102 € – Per week from 203 to 714 € – Reservation fee 15€
▭ sani-station 3€ – 🔋11€
Divided into 2 separate campsites on either side of the road; pitches for tents and caravans with good shade, near the river.

Surroundings : 〇〇
Leisure activities : 🛖 ⛵ ⛴ ⌖ ⚓
Facilities : ♿ ⊶ ☂ ⚑ launderette ⬜ 🛒

GPS Longitude : 3.63751
Latitude : 43.99128

Michelin classification:

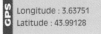

Extremely comfortable, equipped to a very high standard
Very comfortable, equipped to a high standard
Comfortable and well equipped
Reasonably comfortable
Satisfactory

LES VIGNES

48210 – Michelin map **330** H9 – pop. 103 – alt. 410
▶ Paris 615 – Mende 52 – Meyrueis 33 – Le Rozier 12

Village Vacances Castel de la Peyre
(rental of maisonettes only)

⌖ 0466484848, www.lozere-resa.com
Address : located 1km south along the D 16
1 ha open site, terraced
Rentals : 10 ▭.
Small but pretty village of small stone houses.

Surroundings : 🌄 ⌖
Leisure activities : 🛖 ⛴
Facilities : ♿ ⊶ ▥ ⚑ ▦

GPS Longitude : 3.2283
Latitude : 44.27292

La Blaquière

⌖ 0466485493, www.campinggorgesdutarn.fr
Address : 6km northeast along the D 907bis; beside the Tarn river
1 ha (72 pitches) terraced, flat, grassy, stony
Rentals : ⚡ – 10 ▭ – 3 tent bungalows.

Surroundings : ▱ 〇〇 △
Leisure activities : 🛖 ⛵ ⚓
Facilities : ♿ ⊶ ☂ ⚑ ▦ ⬜ 🛒

GPS Longitude : 3.2685
Latitude : 44.3042

VILLEFORT

48800 – Michelin map **330** L8 – pop. 618 – alt. 600
▶ Paris 616 – Alès 52 – Aubenas 61 – Florac 63

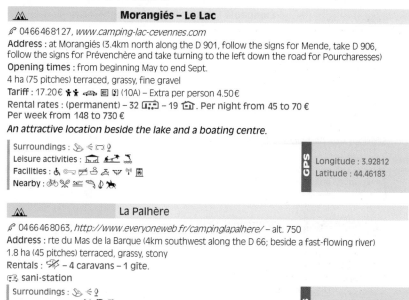 Morangiés – Le Lac

𝒫 0466468127, www.camping-lac-cevennes.com
Address : at Morangiés (3.4km north along the D 901, follow the signs for Mende, take D 906, follow the signs for Prévenchère and take turning to the left down the road for Pourcharesses)
Opening times : from beginning May to end Sept.
4 ha (75 pitches) terraced, grassy, fine gravel
Tariff : 17.20€ ♦♦ ⇔ ▣ (½) (10A) – Extra per person 4.50€
Rental rates : (permanent) – 32 ⏥ – 19 ⛺. Per night from 45 to 70 €
Per week from 148 to 730 €
An attractive location beside the lake and a boating centre.

Surroundings : ⌂ ≤ ⊏ ♀
Leisure activities : ⌂ ⚡ ⟀
Facilities : ♿ ☞ ⊠ △ ⚱ ⚒ ❀ ▣
Nearby : ☊ ⚹ ⊱ ☜ ♪ ♞

Longitude : 3.92812
Latitude : 44.46183

La Palhère

𝒫 0466468063, http://www.everyoneweb.fr/campinglapalhere/ – alt. 750
Address : rte du Mas de la Barque (4km southwest along the D 66; beside a fast-flowing river)
1.8 ha (45 pitches) terraced, grassy, stony
Rentals : ⚟ – 4 caravans – 1 gîte.
⏥ sani-station

Surroundings : ⌂ ≤ ♀
Leisure activities : ✗ ⟀ ⚲
Facilities : ☞ △ △ ⚒ ☞
Nearby : ⚹

Longitude : 3.91026
Latitude : 44.41862

VILLEGLY

11600 – Michelin map **344** F3 – pop. 1,020 – alt. 130
▶ Paris 778 – Lézignan-Corbières 36 – Mazamet 46 – Carcassonne 14

Moulin de Ste-Anne

𝒫 0468722080, www.moulindesainteanne.com
Address : 2 chemin de Sainte-Anne (take the eastern exit along the D 435, follow the signs for Villarzel)
Opening times : from beginning April to end Oct.
1.6 ha (60 pitches) terrace, flat and relatively flat, grassy
Tariff : (2012 price) 26€ ♦♦ ⇔ ▣ (½) (10A) – Extra per person 5.10€ – Reservation fee 17€
Rental rates : (2012 price) (from beginning April to end Oct.) – 15 ⛺ – 2 tent bungalows.
Per week from 295 to 600 € – Reservation fee 17€
⏥ sani-station 8€ – 1 ▣ 27€
Pretty pitches and upmarket rental options on shady terraces.

Surroundings : ⊏ ♀♀
Leisure activities : ♟ ✗ ⌂ ⚡ ⟀
Facilities : ♿ ☞ ⫴ △ △ ⚒ ❀ ▣ ☞
Nearby : ⚹

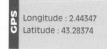
Longitude : 2.44347
Latitude : 43.28374

To make the best possible use of this guide,
please read pages 2–15 carefully.

VILLENEUVE-LÈS-AVIGNON

30400 – Michelin map **339** N5 – pop. 12,463 – alt. 23
▶ Paris 678 – Avignon 8 – Nîmes 46 – Orange 28

Campéole L'Ile des Papes ▲▴

𝒫 04 90 15 15 90, *www.avignon-camping.com*
Address : Barrage de Villeneuve (4.5km northeast along the D 980, follow the signs for Roquemaure and take D 780 to the right, by the River Rhône and the canal)
Opening times : from end March to beginning Nov.
20 ha (210 pitches) flat, grassy, stony, pond
Tariff : (2012 price) 30€ ♟♟ ⇌ 🅴 🔌 (10A) – Extra per person 5€
Rental rates : (2012 price) (from end March to beginning Nov.) – 46 🚐 – 61 tent bungalows. Per night from **31** to **143** € – Per week from **217** to **1,001** €
🚽 sani-station
Spacious site, partially shaded, with a pretty play and paddling pool area.

Surroundings : ⌇ ⪡ ⌑ ⚯
Leisure activities : ♟ ✗ 🎮 🕃 evening 👯 🛶 🚴 ♨ 🏊 🎣
multi-sports ground
Facilities : ♿ �o—ᵣ 🆑 ▦ ☕ ᵗᵗ launderette 🛒 🛁

GPS Longitude : 4.81826
Latitude : 43.99383

Municipal de la Laune

𝒫 04 90 25 76 06, *www.camping-villeneuvelezavignon.com*
Address : chemin Saint Honore (to the northeast, access via the D 980, near the stadium and swimming pools)
Opening times : from beginning April to mid Oct.
2.3 ha (126 pitches) flat, grassy, stony
Tariff : ♟ 5.60€ ⇌ 3.50€ – 🔌 (6A) 3.10€
🚽 sani-station
Situated beside the town's sports facilities. A well-shaded site with only average sanitary facilities.

Surroundings : ⌑ ⚯
Leisure activities : 🎮 🛶
Facilities : ♿ o—ᵣ ᵗᵗ 🖼
Nearby : ✂ 🗔 🏊

GPS Longitude : 4.79711
Latitude : 43.96331

Nicolas Thibaut/Photononstop

L ife in Limousin is led at its own pace: tired Parisians wanting to reconnect with nature come to enjoy the joys of country life, inhale the bracing air of its high plateaus and wander through its woodlands in search of mushrooms and chestnuts. The region boasts hills and gorges and lush green meadows. The sight of cattle grazing happily or lambs frolicking in a spring meadow will rejuvenate the spirits of any jaded city dweller. Limousin is home to ancient village churches and imposing abbey churches and fortresses. In autumn, the forests are swathed in colour, forming a perfect backdrop to the granite and sandstone of the peaceful towns and villages, where ancestral crafts, such as Limoges enamel and porcelain and Aubusson tapestries, still blend the traditional with the best of the new. The food is wholesome – savoury bacon soup, Limousin stew and, as any proud local will tell you, the most tender, succulent beef in the world.

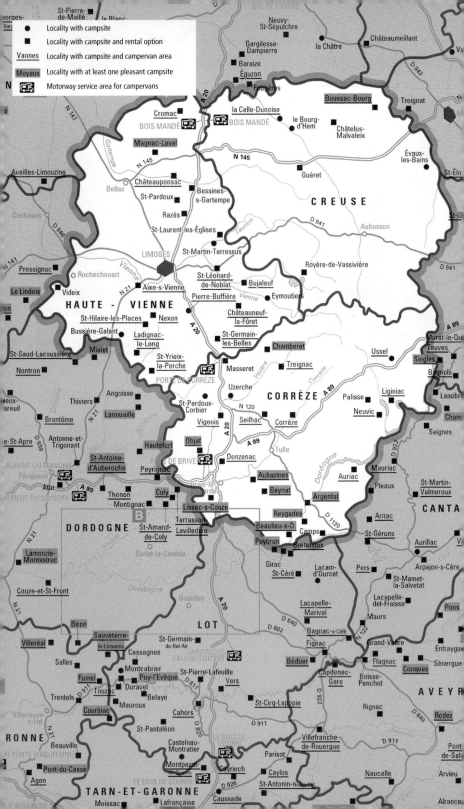

AIXE-SUR-VIENNE

87700 – Michelin map **325** D6 – pop. 5,464 – alt. 204
▶ Paris 400 – Châlus 21 – Confolens 60 – Limoges 14

Municipal les Grèves

✆ 05 55 70 12 98, *www.mairie-aixesurvienne.fr*
Address : r. Jean-Claude Papon (beside the Vienne river)
Opening times : from beginning June to end Sept.
3 ha (80 pitches) flat, grassy
Tariff : 14.60€ ✶✶ ⇔ 🔲 🅷 (10A) – Extra per person 4€
Rental rates : (from beginning April to end Oct.) – 3 🛖. Per night from 50 €
Per week from 400 €
🚐 sani-station 3€
Pleasant site with some pitches beside the Vienne river.

Surroundings : 🌳🌳
Leisure activities : 🍷 🏠 ⚓ ◊
Facilities : ♿ ⚷ ⌇ 🖼
Nearby : 🔳

GPS Longitude : 1.11477
Latitude : 45.8065

*The classification (1 to 5 tents, black or red) that we award to selected sites
in this guide is our own system. It should not be confused with the
classification (1 to 5 stars) of official organisations.*

ARGENTAT

19400 – Michelin map **329** M5 – pop. 3,052 – alt. 183
▶ Paris 503 – Aurillac 54 – Brive-la-Gaillarde 45 – Mauriac 49

Le Gibanel

✆ 05 55 28 10 11, *www.camping-gibanel.com*
Address : 4.5km northeast along the D 18, follow the signs for Égletons then take the road to the right
60 ha/8.5 ha for camping (250 pitches) terrace, flat, grassy
Rentals : ✂ – 10 🛖 – 2 apartments.
In the grounds of a 16th-century château beside a lake.

Surroundings : 🌿 ≤ 🌳🌳 ⛰
Leisure activities : 🍷 ✗ 🏠 🎣 ⚓ 🛶 🎣 ⚑ multi-sports ground
Facilities : ♿ ⚷ 🚿 🔥 ⌇ launderette 🔄 🚰

GPS Longitude : 1.95852
Latitude : 45.1107

Sunêlia Au Soleil d'Oc ♣♣

✆ 05 55 28 84 84, *www.dordogne-soleil.com*
Address : at Monceaux-sur-Dordogne (4.5km southwest along the D 12, follow the signs for Beaulieu then take the D 12e following signs for Vergnolles and take road to the left after the bridge; beside the Dordogne river)
Opening times : from mid April to mid Nov.
4 ha (120 pitches) terrace, flat, grassy
Tariff : 26.80€ ✶✶ ⇔ 🔲 🅷 (6A) – Extra per person 6.80€ – Reservation fee 15€
Rental rates : (from mid April to mid Nov.) – 28 🛖 – 12 🏠 – 5 tent bungalows.
Per night from 28 to 128 € – Per week from 196 to 896 € – Reservation fee 30€
🚐 sani-station 5€ – 5 🔲 10€ – 🔌 🅷10€

Surroundings : 🌿 ≤ 🌳🌳 ⛰
Leisure activities : 🍷 ✗ 🏠 🎣 ⚓ 🎣 🚲 🏓 🔳 🛶 ⚑ 🎣
Facilities : ⚷ 🔳🚿 ⌇ launderette 🚰

GPS Longitude : 1.91836
Latitude : 45.07618

Le Vaurette ▲⚑

℘ 05 55 28 09 67, *www.vaurette.com*

Address : at Vaurette (9km southwest along the D 12, follow the signs for Beaulieu; beside the Dordogne river)

Opening times : from beginning May to mid Sept.

4 ha (120 pitches) terrace, flat, relatively flat, grassy

Tariff : 30.70€ ✶✶ ⇌ 🅿 (6A) – Extra per person 6.20€ – Reservation fee 15€

Rental rates : (from mid May to beginning Sept.) 🛖 – 2 ⬚. Per week from 335 to 720 €
Reservation fee 15€

Surroundings : 🏊 ♨ ⛰
Leisure activities : 🍷 ✗ 🎱 ☺ daytime 🏇 🛶 🎿 ⛷ 🎣 entertainment room
Facilities : ♿ ⚡ 🚿 🍴 launderette 🗑

GPS
Longitude : 1.8825
Latitude : 45.04568

AUBAZINE

19190 – Michelin map **329** L4 – pop. 852 – alt. 345 – Leisure centre
▶ Paris 480 – Aurillac 86 – Brive-la-Gaillarde 14 – St-Céré 50

Campéole Le Coiroux ▲⚑

℘ 05 55 27 21 96, *www.camping-coiroux.com*

Address : Parc touristique du Coiroux (5km east along the D 48, follow the signs for Le Chastang, not far from a small lake and a leisure park)

Opening times : from beginning April to end Sept.

165 ha/6 ha for camping (174 pitches) relatively flat, flat, grassy, wood

Tariff : (2012 price) 25.40€ ✶✶ ⇌ 🅿 (10A) – Extra per person 6.40€ – Reservation fee 25€

Rental rates : (2012 price) (from beginning April to beginning Nov.) ♿ (2 mobile homes) – 41 ⬚ – 10 ⬚ – 27 tent bungalows. Per night from 25 to 57 € – Per week from 233 to 938 €
Reservation fee 25€

🚐 sani-station 3€

Surroundings : 🏊 ☁ ♨
Leisure activities : 🍷 ✗ 🎱 ☺ 🏇 🛶 🎿 ⛷ 🎣 climbing wall
Facilities : ♿ ⚡ 🚿 🍴 launderette 🗑 🚿
Nearby : 🏖 (beach) 🎣 forest trail, paintballing

GPS
Longitude : 1.70739
Latitude : 45.18611

AURIAC

19220 – Michelin map **329** N4 – pop. 226 – alt. 608
▶ Paris 517 – Argentat 27 – Égletons 33 – Mauriac 23

Municipal

℘ 05 55 28 23 02, *www.auriac.fr*

Address : in the village (take the southeastern exit along the D 65, follow the signs for St-Privat, near a lake and a wooded park)

Opening times : from beginning April to mid Nov.

1.7 ha (70 pitches) relatively flat, flat, grassy

Tariff : (2012 price) ✶ 3.61€ ⇌ 1.86€ 🅿 1.86€ – (16A) 3.61€

Rental rates : (2012 price) (from beginning April to beginning Nov.) – 8 ⬚.
Per night from 51 to 62 € – Per week from 217 to 385 €

🚐 sani-station – 1 🅿 6€

A view of the lake from some pitches.

Surroundings : 🏊 ⬚ ♨ ⛰
Leisure activities : 🎱 🛶
Facilities : 🚿 (from mid-Jul to mid-Aug) 🚲 🍴 🖼
Nearby : 🎿 🎣 🏖 (beach) 🎣 pedalos

GPS
Longitude : 2.14772
Latitude : 45.20206

BEAULIEU-SUR-DORDOGNE

19120 – Michelin map **329** M6 – pop. 1,283 – alt. 142
▶ Paris 513 – Aurillac 65 – Brive-la-Gaillarde 44 – Figeac 56

Flower Les Îles

𝒫 05 55 91 02 65, *www.campingdesiles.com*
Address : bd Rodolphe de Turenne (east of the town centre)
Opening times : from end April to end Sept.
4 ha (120 pitches) flat, grassy
Tariff : 28.90€ ✿ ✿ ⇔ 回 ⑭ (10A) – Extra per person 6.90€ – Reservation fee 17€
Rental rates : (from end April to end Sept.) – 24 ⛺ – 16 tent bungalows.
Per night from 28 to 95€ – Per week from 140 to 665€ – Reservation fee 17€
⛽ sani-station – 5 回 10€ – ♨ ⑭10€
A picturesque site and setting on an island in the Dordogne river.

Surroundings : ⌇ ♨♨ ⛰ Leisure activities : ⛵ 🏛 ⚽ ⛴ ⌇ ⛵ Facilities : ♿ ⚬➡ ▥ ⛺ ⚑ launderette ⚘ Nearby : ⚡⚡ ⚔	**GPS** Longitude : 1.84049 Latitude : 44.97968

BESSINES-SUR-GARTEMPE

87250 – Michelin map **325** F4 – pop. 2,847 – alt. 335
▶ Paris 355 – Argenton-sur-Creuse 58 – Bellac 29 – Guéret 55

Le Sagnat

𝒫 05 55 76 17 69
Address : located 1.5km southwest along the D 220, follow the signs for Limoges, take the D 27 following signs for St-Pardoux to the right and take turning to the left; beside the lake
0.8 ha (50 pitches) terraced, flat and relatively flat
Rentals : 3 ⛺.

Surroundings : ⬗ ⛵ ♨♨ Leisure activities : ✗ 🏛 ≈ (beach) ⌇ Facilities : ♿ ⚬➡ 🖼 Nearby : ⛵	**GPS** Longitude : 1.35269 Latitude : 46.10001

We value your opinion and welcome your feedback.
Do email us at campingfrance@tp.michelin.com

BEYNAT

19190 – Michelin map **329** L5 – pop. 1,253 – alt. 420
▶ Paris 496 – Argentat 47 – Beaulieu-sur-Dordogne 23 – Brive-la-Gaillarde 21

Village Vacances Chalets en France Les Hameaux de Miel
(rental of chalets only)

𝒫 05 55 84 34 48, *www.chalets-en-france.com*
Address : at Miel
Opening times : from mid Feb. to mid Nov.
12 ha very uneven, terraced
Rental rates : ♿ (3 chalets) – 98 ⛺. Per week from 190 to 780€ – Reservation fee 13€

Surroundings : ⬗ ⬗ ⚘ Leisure activities : ⛵ 🏛 ⚲ ⚡ ⚽ 🖼 ⛴ multi-sports ground Facilities : ⚬➡ ▥ ⚑ launderette Nearby : ⚔ ⚓ ≈ ⛰ ⌇ pedalos	**GPS** Longitude : 1.76141 Latitude : 45.12932

Airotel Le Lac de Miel

℘ 05 55 85 50 66, *www.camping-miel.com*
Address : 4km east along the N 121, follow the signs for Argentat; beside a small lake
Opening times : from beginning May to end Sept.
50 ha/9 ha for camping (140 pitches) undulating, relatively flat, grassy
Tariff : 27.90€ ✶✶ ⊶ 🗉 ⚄ (10A) – Extra per person 6.80€ – Reservation fee 18€
Rental rates : (from beginning May to end Sept.) – 2 'gypsy' caravans – 50 🔲 – 5 🏠 –
3 tent bungalows – 8 gîtes. Per night from 50 to 110 € – Per week from 50 to 770 €
Reservation fee 18€
🚽 sani-station 13€ – ⛟⚄13€

Surroundings : 🏊 ‹ ⚱ ⛰
Leisure activities : 🍽 ✗ 🎰 ⚓ ⚆ ♫ 🖵 (open-air in season) 🖐
Facilities : ♿ ⚍ (Jul-Aug) ⛺ 🍴 🖼
Nearby : ≝ (beach) pedalos

GPS Longitude : 1.77103
Latitude : 45.13332

LE BOURG-D'HEM

23220 – Michelin map **325** H3 – pop. 225 – alt. 320
▶ Paris 333 – Aigurande 20 – Le Grand-Bourg 28 – Guéret 21

Municipal

℘ 05 55 62 84 36, *www.les3lacs-creuse.com*
Address : to the west along the D 48, follow the signs for Bussière-Dunoise and take the road to the right
0.33 ha (36 pitches) terraced, flat, grassy
A pleasant site and setting beside the Creuse river.

Surroundings : 🏊 ⛺ ⚱⚱ ⛰
Leisure activities : 🖐
Facilities : ♿ ⚘
Nearby : 🍽 ⚓ boats for hire

GPS Longitude : 1.82316
Latitude : 46.29756

For more information on visiting particular towns or regions, consult the relevant regional MICHELIN Green Guide. We also recommend you use the appropriate Michelin regional map to locate your selected campsite, to calculate distances and to work out the best route.

BOUSSAC-BOURG

23600 – Michelin map **325** K2 – pop. 787 – alt. 423
▶ Paris 334 – Aubusson 52 – La Châtre 37 – Guéret 43

Les Castels Le Château de Poinsouze ⚑⚑

℘ 05 55 65 02 21, *www.camping-de-poinsouze.com* ⚘
Address : rte de La Chatre (2.8km north along the D 917)
150 ha/22 ha for camping (144 pitches) flat, grassy, lake
Rentals : ⚘ – 23 🔲 – 2 🏠 – 2 gîtes.
🚽 sani-station
A spacious site in the grounds of a 16th-century château.

Surroundings : 🏊 ‹ ⛺ ⚱⚱
Leisure activities : 🍽 ✗ 🎰 ⚆ ⚓ 🚲 ⚊ ⚄ 🖐 pedalos, windsurfing ⚘
Facilities : ♿ ⚡ ⛺ ⚘ ⚒ 🍴 launderette ⚊ ⚘

GPS Longitude : 2.20472
Latitude : 46.3725

BUJALEUF

87460 – Michelin map **325** G6 – pop. 881 – alt. 380
▶ Paris 423 – Bourganeuf 28 – Eymoutiers 14 – Limoges 35

Municipal du Lac

℘ 05 55 69 54 54, *www.bujaleuf.fr*
Address : located 1km north along the D 16 and take the turning to the left, near the lake
2 ha (110 pitches) very uneven, terraced, flat, grassy
sani-station

Surroundings :
Leisure activities :
Facilities : launderette
Nearby : (beach)

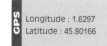
Longitude : 1.6297
Latitude : 45.80166

*Some information or pricing may have changed since the guide went to press.
We recommend you check the price list online in advance or at the entrance
to the campsite and enquire about possible restrictions.*

BUSSIÈRE-GALANT

87230 – Michelin map **325** D7 – pop. 1,394 – alt. 410
▶ Paris 422 – Aixe-sur-Vienne 23 – Châlus 6 – Limoges 36

Municipal les Ribières

℘ 05 55 78 86 12, *www.espace-hermeline.com*
Address : av. du Plan-d'eau (1.7km southwest along the D 20, follow the signs for La Coquille and take
the road to the right, near the stadium and 100m from a small lake)
Opening times : from beginning April to end Sept.
1 ha (25 pitches) terraced, relatively flat, grassy
Tariff : (2012 price) 13 € ★ ★ 🚗 🗐 (6A) – Extra per person 3 €
Rental rates : (2012 price) (permanent). Per night from 60 to 80 € – Per week from 420 to 560 €

Surroundings :
Facilities :
Nearby : (beach) forest trail, draisines (handcars/rail cycling)

Longitude : 1.03086
Latitude : 45.61364

CAMPS

19430 – Michelin map **329** M6 – pop. 246 – alt. 520
▶ Paris 520 – Argentat 17 – Aurillac 45 – Bretenoux 18

Municipal la Châtaigneraie

℘ 05 55 28 53 15, *www.camps.correze.net*
Address : in the village (to the west along the D 13 and take the road to the right)
Opening times : from beginning May to end Sept.
1 ha (23 pitches) relatively flat to hilly, grassy
Tariff : ★ 2.50 € 🚗 🗐 3 € – (2A) 2.50 €
Rental rates : (permanent) – 9 🏠. Per night from 42 to 57 € – Per week from 191 to 467 €
Reservation fee 50 €

Surroundings :
Leisure activities :
Facilities :
Nearby : (beach)

Longitude : 1.98756
Latitude : 44.98368

LA CELLE-DUNOISE

23800 – Michelin map **325** H3 – pop. 607 – alt. 230
▶ Paris 329 – Aigurande 16 – Aubusson 63 – Dun-le-Palestel 11

Municipal de la Baignade

℘ 05 55 51 21 18, www.lacelledunoise.fr
Address : east, along the D 48a, follow the signs for Le Bourg d'Hem, near the Creuse river (direct access)
Opening times : from beginning April to end Oct.
1.4 ha (30 pitches) terrace, flat, grassy
Tariff : (2012 price) ⚥ 2.70 € ⟺ 1.65 € 🔲 1.65 € – 🔌 (10A) 2.70 €
🚐 sani-station 2 €

Surroundings : ♤♤
Leisure activities : 🛶 ✂
Facilities : ♿ 🚱 ♨ launderette
Nearby : ≋ (beach) 🎣 🐎

GPS
Longitude : 1.76928
Latitude : 46.31015

There are several different types of sani-station ('borne' in French) – sanitation points providing fresh water and disposal points for grey water. See page 12 for further details.

CHAMBERET

19370 – Michelin map **329** L2 – pop. 1,318 – alt. 450
▶ Paris 453 – Guéret 84 – Limoges 66 – Tulle 45

Village Vacances Les Roulottes des Monédières
(rental of 'gypsy' caravans only)

℘ 05 55 98 03 03, www.roulottes-monedieres.com
Address : at L'Arboretum
Opening times : from end March to mid Nov.
3 ha relatively flat to hilly, grassy
Rental rates : ♿ ✂ 🅿 – 20 'gypsy' caravans. Per night from 86 to 136 €
Per week from 516 to 816 €
Self-catering or hotel-style accommodation is available.

Surroundings : ♨ ≤♤
Leisure activities : ✕ 🛶 ⚶ 🎣 🚣 🚲 🔲 billiards
Facilities : ⚷ ▥ 🚰 launderette 🔥

GPS
Longitude : 1.71971
Latitude : 45.5926

Village Vacances Les Chalets du Bois Combet
(rental of chalets only)

℘ 05 55 98 30 12, www.chamberet.net – traditional camp. spaces also available
Address : 1.3km southwest along the D 132, follow the signs for Meilhards and take the road to the right, 100m from a small lake and a lake
Opening times : permanent
1 ha flat, grassy
Rental rates : (2012 price) ♿ 🅿 – 10 🏠. Per night from 42 to 57 €
Per week from 191 to 530 €

Surroundings : ♨
Leisure activities : 🚣
Facilities : 🚱 🚰 launderette
Nearby : 🔲 🛶 ♨ 🎣

GPS
Longitude : 1.70994
Latitude : 45.57541

CHÂTEAUNEUF-LA-FORÊT

87130 – Michelin map **325** G6 – pop. 1,641 – alt. 376

▶ Paris 424 – Eymoutiers 14 – Limoges 36 – St-Léonard-de-Noblat 19

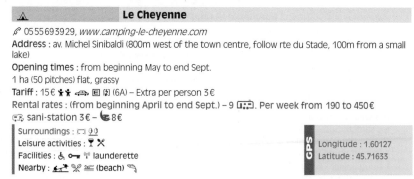

Le Cheyenne

☏ 05 55 69 39 29, *www.camping-le-cheyenne.com*

Address : av. Michel Sinibaldi (800m west of the town centre, follow rte du Stade, 100m from a small lake)

Opening times : from beginning May to end Sept.

1 ha (50 pitches) flat, grassy

Tariff : 15€ ✦✦ ⇔ 🗉 💧 (6A) – Extra per person 3€

Rental rates : (from beginning April to end Sept.) – 9 ⛺. Per week from 190 to 450€

🚰 sani-station 3€ – 🚐 8€

Surroundings : 🏞 🎋

Leisure activities : ▾ ✕

Facilities : ⅙ ⊶ 🚽 launderette

Nearby : 🏊 💥 🏖 (beach) 🎣

Longitude : 1.60127
Latitude : 45.71633

CHÂTEAUPONSAC

87290 – Michelin map **325** E4 – pop. 2,158 – alt. 290

▶ Paris 361 – Bélâbre 55 – Limoges 48 – Bellac 21

Centre Touristique – La Gartempe

☏ 05 55 76 55 33, *www.camping-chateauponsac.com*

Address : av. de Ventenat (take the southwestern exit along the D 711, follow the signs for Nantiat; 200m from the river)

Opening times : permanent

1.5 ha (43 pitches) terraced, relatively flat, flat, grassy

Tariff : 20.40€ ✦✦ ⇔ 🗉 💧 (20A) – Extra per person 4€

Rental rates : (permanent) – 2 ⛺ – 3 🏠 – 11 gîtes. Per night from 41 to 61€

Per week from 280 to 420€ – Reservation fee 5€

🚰 20 🗉 20.40€ – 🚐 💧 20.40€

Surroundings : 🎋

Leisure activities : ▾ ✕ 🎱 🏸 🏊

Facilities : ⅙ ⊶ (Jul–Aug) 🏛 🚽 launderette

Nearby : 🏇 🛶 🎣

Longitude : 1.27046
Latitude : 46.1318

CHÂTELUS-MALVALEIX

23270 – Michelin map **325** J3 – pop. 563 – alt. 410

▶ Paris 333 – Aigurande 25 – Aubusson 46 – Boussac 19

Municipal La Roussille

☏ 05 55 80 70 31, *chatelusmalvaleix.fr*

Address : 10 pl. de la Fontaine (to the west of the village)

Opening times : from beginning June to end Sept.

0.5 ha (33 pitches) relatively flat, flat, grassy

Tariff : (2012 price) ✦ 3€ ⇔ 1.50€ 🗉 2€ – 💧 (16A) 4€

Rental rates : (2012 price) (permanent) ⅙ – 8 🏠. Per night from 50 to 55€

Per week from 180 to 450€

Surroundings : 🐾 🎋 🚡

Leisure activities : 🎱 🚴 (mountain biking) 🎣

Facilities : 🚮 🚾 🚽

Nearby : ▾ 🏊 💥

Longitude : 2.01818
Latitude : 46.3031

CORRÈZE

19800 – Michelin map **329** M3 – pop. 1,168 – alt. 455
▶ Paris 480 – Argentat 47 – Brive-la-Gaillarde 45 – Égletons 22

Municipal la Chapelle

⚲ 05 55 21 25 21, *mairie.correze@wanadoo.fr*
Address : at La Chapelle (take the eastern exit along the D 143, follow the signs for Egletons and take a right turn, follow the signs for Bouysse – divided into two separate parts)
Opening times : from mid June to mid Sept.
3 ha (54 pitches) open site, terrace, relatively flat, flat, grassy, wood
Tariff : (2012 price) ♦ 2.65€ ⇌ 1.40€ 🔲 2.50€ – 🔌 (10A) 2.30€
Rental rates : (2012 price) (from mid April to mid Oct.) ⚡ – 3 🚐 – 1 ⇌ – 1 gîte.
Per week from 200 to 300€– Reservation fee 30€
🚰 sani-station – 10 🔲 8€
Beside the Corrèze river and near a small chapel. A small road runs throught the part of the site containing the camping pitches.

Surroundings : 🌿 ♈
Leisure activities : 🎬 ⚡ 🎣
Facilities : ♿ 🚿 🔳
Nearby : 🏊

GPS Longitude : 1.8798
Latitude : 45.37191

CROMAC

87160 – Michelin map **325** E2 – pop. 266 – alt. 224
▶ Paris 339 – Argenton-sur-Creuse 41 – Limoges 68 – Magnac-Laval 22

Lac de Mondon

⚲ 05 55 76 93 34, *www.campingdemondon.com*
Address : at Les Forges de Mondon (situated 2km south along the D 105, follow the signs for St-Sulpice-les-Feuilles and take the D 60 – recommended route via the D 912)
Opening times : from beginning May to end Sept.
2.8 ha (100 pitches) relatively flat, flat, grassy
Tariff : 13€ ♦♦ ⇌ 🔲 🔌 (10A) – Extra per person 4€
Rental rates : (2012 price) (from end April to mid Sept.) – 7 🏠. Reservation fee 14€
🚰 sani-station 2€

Surroundings : 🌿 ⛺ ♈
Leisure activities : ♈ ✗ 🎬 ⚡ 🚲 ✗ 🏊 ⛵ 🎣 pedalos
Facilities : ♿ 🚿 🔳 ⚓
Nearby : ⛰

GPS Longitude : 1.31153
Latitude : 46.3322

DONZENAC

19270 – Michelin map **329** K4 – pop. 2,492 – alt. 204
▶ Paris 469 – Brive-la-Gaillarde 11 – Limoges 81 – Tulle 27

La Rivière

⚲ 05 55 85 63 95, *www.campingdonzenac.com*
Address : rte d'Ussac (1.6km south of the town, following the signs for Brive; beside the Maumont river)
Opening times : from beginning April to end Oct.
1.2 ha (60 pitches) flat, grassy
Tariff : (2012 price) 15.70€ ♦♦ ⇌ 🔲
Rental rates : (2012 price) (from beginning April to end Oct.) ⚡ – 14 🏠.
Per week from 180 to 560 €
🚰 sani-station – 10 🔲

Surroundings : ⛺ ♈
Leisure activities : 🎣
Facilities : ♿ 🚿 🚽 launderette
Nearby : ✗ ⛰ 🏊

GPS Longitude : 1.52149
Latitude : 45.21761

ÉVAUX-LES-BAINS

23110 – Michelin map **325** L3 – pop. 1,486 – alt. 469 – ♨ (9 Apr-27 Oct)
▣ Paris 353 – Aubusson 44 – Guéret 52 – Marcillat-en-Combraille 16

⚠ Municipal

☏ 05 55 65 55 82, *www.evaux-les-bains.net*
Address : Ouche du Budelle (north of the town, behind the château)
Opening times : from end March to end Oct.
1 ha (49 pitches) relatively flat, flat, grassy
Tariff : (2012 price) ✦ 1.90€ ⇔ 1.39€ ▣ 1.60€ – ⚡ (10A) 3.31€

Surroundings : ⅋ ⊏ ୨୨
Leisure activities : ▭ ♨
Facilities : ৬ ⊐
Nearby : ✗ ♯ ▨

Longitude : 2.48994
Latitude : 46.17851

EYMOUTIERS

87120 – Michelin map **325** H6 – pop. 2,033 – alt. 417
▣ Paris 432 – Aubusson 55 – Guéret 62 – Limoges 44

⚠ Municipal

☏ 05 55 69 10 21, *mairie-eymoutiers@wanadoo.fr*
Address : at St-Pierre (situated 2km southeast along the D 940, follow the signs for Tulle and take road to the left)
Opening times : from beginning June to end Sept.
1 ha (33 pitches) terrace, relatively flat, flat, grassy
Tariff : (2012 price) 6.50€ ✦✦ ⇔ ▣ ⚡ (15A) – Extra per person 1.70€

Surroundings : ⅋ ⊏ ୨୨
Facilities : ৬ ⊐ cc

Longitude : 1.75296
Latitude : 45.73161

We have selected the best campsites in France with our usual care,
listing those with the best facilities in the most pleasant surroundings.

GUÉRET

23000 – Michelin map **325** I3 – pop. 13,844 – alt. 457 – Leisure centre
▣ Paris 351 – Bourges 122 – Châteauroux 90 – Clermont-Ferrand 132

⚠ Municipal du Plan d'Eau de Courtille

☏ 05 55 81 92 24, *www.camping-courtille.com*
Address : rte de Courtille (2.5km southwest along the D 914, follow the signs for Benevent and take road to the left)
Opening times : from beginning April to end Oct.
2.4 ha (70 pitches) relatively flat, flat, grassy
Tariff : (2012 price) ✦ 2.80€ ⇔ 1.80€ ▣ 7.80€ – ⚡ (10A) 2.50€
Rental rates : (2012 price) (from beginning April to end Oct.) – 4 🚐 – 1 🏠.
Per week from 220 to 510€ – Reservation fee 10€

In a pleasant location near a small lake (direct access).

Surroundings : ⅋ ⊏ ୨୨
Leisure activities : ♨
Facilities : ৬ ⚬ ♯ ▣
Nearby : ≋ (beach) ⚲ ♦

Longitude : 1.85824
Latitude : 46.16094

LADIGNAC-LE-LONG

87500 – Michelin map **325** D7 – pop. 1,124 – alt. 334
▶ Paris 426 – Brive-la-Gaillarde 74 – Limoges 35 – Nontron 44

Municipal le Bel Air

℘ 05 55 09 39 82, *www.atouvert.com*
Address : r. Bel'Air (located 1.5km north along the D 11, follow the signs for Nexon and take road to the left)
Opening times : from beginning April to end Oct.
2.5 ha (100 pitches) terraced, flat, grassy
Tariff : (2012 price) 15.20€ ⚹⚹ ⇔ 🄴 (½) (16A) – Extra per person 3€ – Reservation fee 1.45€
Rental rates : (2012 price) (from beginning April to end Oct.) – 5 🚐. Per night from 45 to 55€
Per week from 280 to 340€ – Reservation fee 10€
🚻 sani-station 5€ – 🛒 10.50€
A pleasant location in a wooded setting at the edge of a small lake.

Surroundings : 🏞 🛶 ♨♨
Leisure activities : 🎪
Facilities : ♿ ⚬━ (Jul–Aug) 🔥 🆒 🍴 launderette
Nearby : 🛶 pedalos

Longitude : 1.11185
Latitude : 45.59089

LIGINIAC

19160 – Michelin map **329** P3 – pop. 641 – alt. 665
▶ Paris 464 – Aurillac 83 – Bort-les-Orgues 24 – Clermont-Ferrand 107

Municipal le Maury

℘ 05 55 95 92 28, *www.camping-du-maury.com*
Address : 4.6km southwest following signs for the beach; beside the Lac de Triouzoune –
recommended route via the D 20, follow the signs for Neuvic
Opening times : from mid June to mid Sept.
2 ha (50 pitches) terraced, flat and relatively flat, grassy
Tariff : ⚹ 3€ ⇔ 🄴 3.50€ – (½) (16A) 3.50€
Rental rates : (from mid April to mid Nov.) – 12 🏠 – 9 cabins in the trees – 12 gîtes.
Per night from 36 to 54€ – Per week from 141 to 497€
🚻 sani-station

Surroundings : 🏞 🛶 ♨
Leisure activities : 🎪 🚣 🎯
Facilities : ⚬━ 🔥 launderette
Nearby : 🍷 🍴 ☕ 🏖 (beach) ◊

Longitude : 2.30498
Latitude : 45.39143

LISSAC-SUR-COUZE

19600 – Michelin map **329** J5 – pop. 710 – alt. 170 – Leisure centre
▶ Paris 486 – Brive-la-Gaillarde 11 – Périgueux 68 – Sarlat-la-Canéda 42

Village Vacances Les Hameaux du Perrier
(rental of chalets only)

℘ 05 55 84 34 48, *www.chalets-en-france.com*
Address : at Le Perrier
Opening times : from mid Feb. to mid Nov.
17 ha/10 ha for camping terraced
Rental rates : 94 🏠. Per week from 190 to 747€ – Reservation fee 13€

Surroundings : 🏞 ⩽ ♨♨
Leisure activities : 🍷 🍴 🚣 ♚ 🛝
Facilities : ⚬━ 🎱 🍴 launderette 🐎
Nearby : 🚴 🎯 🏖 🛶 ◊ water skiing, watersports centre

Longitude : 1.43848
Latitude : 45.10029

Village Vacances La Prairie
(rental of chalets only)

℘ 05 55 85 37 97, *www.caussecorrezien.fr* – traditional camp. spaces also available
Address : 1.4km southwest along the D 59 and take road to the left, near the Lac du Causse
5 ha terraced
Rentals : 20 🏠 – 25 gîtes.
🚐 sani-station – 6 ▣

Surroundings : 🕊 ≤ ♀
Leisure activities : 🍴 ✕ 🏊
Facilities : ♿ 🚿 ▥ 🔥 🍴 launderette
Leisure/activities centre : 🚲 🏊 (beach) 🎣 💧 🐴 pedalos

GPS
Longitude : 1.45465
Latitude : 45.10125

MAGNAC-LAVAL

87190 – Michelin map **325** D3 – pop. 1,850 – alt. 231
◼ Paris 366 – Limoges 64 – Poitiers 86 – Guéret 62

Village Vacances Le Hameau de Gîtes des Pouyades
(rental of gîtes only)

℘ 05 55 60 73 45, *www.lelimousinsejoursvacances.com*
Address : at Les Pouyades
Opening times : from beginning Feb. to end Dec.
1.5 ha flat
Rentals : 12 gîtes. – Reservation fee 16€

Surroundings : 🕊 ≤ on the lake ♀
Leisure activities : 🎮 🔥 🎣
Facilities : ♿ ▥ 🍴 launderette

GPS
Longitude : 1.19236
Latitude : 46.20331

Do not confuse:
🔺 *to* 🔺🔺🔺 *: MICHELIN classification*
with
★ *to* ★★★★★ *: official classification*

MASSERET

19510 – Michelin map **329** K2 – pop. 675 – alt. 380
◼ Paris 432 – Guéret 132 – Limoges 45 – Tulle 48

🔺 **Intercommunal Masseret-Lamongerie**

℘ 05 55 73 44 57, *www.domaine-des-forgescampingmasseret*
Address : 3km east along the D 20, follow the signs for Les Meilhards, near the exit from
Masseret-Gare
Opening times : from beginning April to end Sept.
100 ha/2 ha for camping (80 pitches) relatively flat, flat, grassy, fine gravel
Tariff : (2012 price) 👤 2.50€ 🚗 1€ ▣ 2.50€ – 🔌 (70A) 2.30€
Rental rates : (2012 price) (permanent) – 4 🚐. Per night from 45 to 50€
Per week from 210 to 400€

In a pleasant, wooded setting near a small lake.

Surroundings : 🕊 ≤ ♀♀
Leisure activities : 🎮
Facilities : ♿ 🚿 🔥 🔲
Nearby : 🍴 ✕ 🛶 🏊 ⛷ 🏊 (beach) 🎣 sports trail

GPS
Longitude : 1.54908
Latitude : 45.54154

433

MEYSSAC

19500 – Michelin map **329** L5 – pop. 1,245 – alt. 220
▶ Paris 507 – Argentat 62 – Beaulieu-sur-Dordogne 21 – Brive-la-Gaillarde 23

Intercommunal Moulin de Valane

℘ 05 55 25 41 59, *mairie@meyssac.fr*
Address : located 1km to the northwest, follow the signs for Collonges-la-Rouge; beside a stream
Opening times : from beginning May to end Sept.
4 ha (115 pitches) terraced, flat and relatively flat, grassy
Tariff : (2012 price) 18€ ⚬⚬ ⚬⚬ ⚬ ⚬ (10A) – Extra per person 5€
Rental rates : (from mid April to end Sept.) – 11 ⚬⚬⚬. Per night from 50 to 60€
Per week from 190 to 490€

Surroundings : ⚬ ⚬⚬
Leisure activities : ✗ ⚬⚬ ⚬⚬ ⚬⚬ ✗ ⚬ ⚬
Facilities : ⚬ ⚬⚬ (Jul–Aug) ⚬ launderette ⚬

GPS Longitude : 1.66381
Latitude : 45.06102

NEUVIC

19160 – Michelin map **329** O3 – pop. 1,868 – alt. 620 – Leisure centre
▶ Paris 465 – Aurillac 78 – Mauriac 25 – Tulle 56

Municipal du Lac

℘ 05 55 95 85 48, *www.campingdulac-neuvic-correze.com*
Address : rte de la Plage (2.3km east along the D 20, follow the signs for Bort-les-Orgues and turn left onto the beach road; beside the Lac de la Triouzoune)
Opening times : from beginning March to end Nov.
5 ha (100 pitches) terraced, grassy, fine gravel
Tariff : (2012 price) ⚬ 3.10€ ⚬⚬ 1.60€ ⚬ 3.45€ – ⚬ (10A) 2.90€
Rental rates : (2012 price) (from beginning March to end Nov.) ⚬⚬ – 23 ⚬⚬ – 23 gîtes.
Per week from 200 to 468€
⚬⚬ sani-station – 35 ⚬

Surroundings : ⚬ ⚬ ⚬⚬
Leisure activities : ⚬⚬ ⚬⚬ ⚬
Facilities : ⚬⚬ ⚬ ⚬
Nearby : ⚬ ✗ ⚬ ⚬ ⚬⚬ (beach) ⚬ ⚬ pedalos

GPS Longitude : 2.2909
Latitude : 45.38677

NEXON

87800 – Michelin map **325** E6 – pop. 2,457 – alt. 359
▶ Paris 412 – Châlus 20 – Limoges 22 – Nontron 53

Municipal de l'Étang de la Lande

℘ 05 55 58 35 44, *www.camping-nexon.fr*
Address : located 1km south following signs for St-Hilaire, access near the pl. de l'Hôtel-de-Ville
Opening times : from beginning June to end Sept.
2 ha (53 pitches) terrace, relatively flat, grassy
Tariff : 10€ ⚬⚬ ⚬⚬ ⚬ ⚬ (10A) – Extra per person 3.20€
Rental rates : (2012 price) (from mid March to end Oct.) – 6 ⚬⚬. Per night from 42 to 57€
Per week from 191 to 467€ – Reservation fee 24€
⚬⚬ sani-station – 2 ⚬
The site is near a small lake.

Surroundings : ⚬ ⚬⚬
Leisure activities : ⚬⚬ ⚬⚬
Facilities : ⚬ ⚬⚬ ⚬ ⚬ ⚬ ⚬
Nearby : ⚬⚬ (beach) pedalos

GPS Longitude : 1.17997
Latitude : 45.67078

OBJAT

19130 – Michelin map **329** J4 – pop. 3,605 – alt. 131
▶ Paris 495 – Limoges 106 – Tulle 46 – Brive-la-Gaillarde 20

Village Vacances Les Grands Prés
(rental of chalets only)

𝒫 05 55 25 96 73, *www.objat.fr*
Address : at l'espace loisirs (activity centre) : Les Grands Prés
Opening times : permanent
18 ha/4 ha for camping flat
Rental rates : 20 ⌂ – 40 ⊨ – 20 gîtes. Per night 109€ – Per week from 245 to 505€
Reservation fee 16€
⛽ sani-station 5€ – 26 ▣ 5€

Surroundings : ⌔ ≪
Leisure activities : ⛹
Facilities : ⅋ ☴ ▥ launderette
Nearby : ⛵ ⚲ ⛴ ⛷ ⛲

GPS
Longitude : 1.41069
Latitude : 45.26687

---

*This guide is not intended as a list of all the camping sites in France;
its aim is to provide a selection of the best sites in each category.*

PALISSE

19160 – Michelin map **329** O3 – pop. 233 – alt. 650
▶ Paris 460 – Aurillac 87 – Clermont-Ferrand 102 – Mauriac 33

Le Vianon ▲▲

𝒫 05 55 95 87 22, *www.levianon.com*
Address : at Les Plaines (1.1km north along the D 47, follow the signs for Combressol and take
turning to the right; beside a lake)
Opening times : from beginning April to mid Oct.
4 ha (59 pitches) terraced, flat and relatively flat, fine gravel, grassy, lake, wood
Tariff : (2012 price) 18.15€ ⛺ ⛺ ⇌ ▣ – Extra per person 4.50€
Rental rates : (2012 price) (from beginning April to mid Oct.) – 16 ⌂.
Per week from 285 to 735€

Surroundings : ⌔ ⌲
Leisure activities : ▼ ✕ ⛱ ⛹ ⛵ ⚲ ⛳ ⛷ ⛲
Facilities : ⅋ ⚬ ☴ ⌑ ⛲ launderette ⛴

GPS
Longitude : 2.2061
Latitude : 45.42662

PIERRE-BUFFIÈRE

87260 – Michelin map **325** F6 – pop. 1,143 – alt. 330
▶ Paris 408 – Limoges 20 – St-Yriex-la-Perche 29 – Uzerche 38

Intercommunal de Chabanas

𝒫 05 55 00 96 43, *mairie.pierrebuffiere@wanadoo.fr*
Address : 1.8km south along the D 420, follow the signs for Château-Chervix, towards A 20 and take
road to the left, near the stadium – from A 20: take exit 40
1.5 ha (60 pitches) relatively flat, flat, grassy, wood
⛽ sani-station
Pleasant, green site with attractive shrubs and flowers.

Surroundings : ≪ ⌑ ℗
Leisure activities : ⛱ ⛵
Facilities : ⅋ ⛺ ☴ ▣
Nearby : ✕

GPS
Longitude : 1.37108
Latitude : 45.68936

RAZÈS

87640 – Michelin map **325** F4 – pop. 1,107 – alt. 440
▶ Paris 366 – Argenton-sur-Creuse 68 – Bellac 32 – Guéret 65

Aquadis Loisirs Santrop ♣

✆ 0555710808, *www.lac-saint-pardoux.com*
Address : Lac de St-Pardoux (4km west along the D 44; beside the lake)
Opening times : from end April to end Sept.
5.5 ha (152 pitches) relatively flat to hilly, grassy, gravelled
Tariff : (2012 price) 16.50€ ♣♣ ⬚ 🗉 🔲 (6A) – Extra per person 4.30€
Rental rates : (2012 price) (from end April to end Sept.) – 6 🏠 – huts.
Per night from 51 to 92€ – Per week from 143 to 599 €

> **Surroundings** : 🌊 ⬙ 𝄞
> **Leisure activities** : 🍽 ✗ 🏓 🏃 🚣
> **Facilities** : ♿ ⛟ (from mid-Jun to mid-Sept) 🏕 ⊘ ♨ 🗑 🚿
> **Nearby** : ✂ 🏖 (beach) ⛷ water skiing

GPS Longitude : 1.29579
Latitude : 46.03254

REYGADES

19430 – Michelin map **329** M5 – pop. 193 – alt. 460
▶ Paris 516 – Aurillac 56 – Brive-la-Gaillarde 56 – St-Céré 26

La Belle Etoile

✆ 0555285008, *www.camping-belle-etoile.fr*
Address : at Lestrade (located 1km north off the D 41, follow the signs for Beaulieu-sur-Dordogne)
Opening times : from beginning June to end Sept.
5 ha/3 ha for camping (25 pitches) terraced, flat, grassy
Tariff : ♣ 4€ ⬚ 🗉 5.15€ – 🔲 (6A) 3.30€
Rental rates : (permanent) – 6 🚐 – 6 🏠 – 4 tent bungalows. Per night from 30 to 88€
Per week from 185 to 620 €

> **Surroundings** : 🌊 ⬙ 🛏 𝄞
> **Leisure activities** : 🚣 🏊 (small swimming pool), quad biking
> **Facilities** : ♿ ⛟ 🏕 ♨ launderette 🗜

GPS Longitude : 1.90538
Latitude : 45.02405

ROYÈRE-DE-VASSIVIÈRE

23460 – Michelin map **325** I5 – pop. 563 – alt. 735
▶ Paris 412 – Bourganeuf 22 – Eymoutiers 25 – Felletin 29

Les Terrasses du Lac

✆ 0555647677, *campings.lelacdevassiviere.com*
Address : at Vauveix (10km southwest along the D 3 and D 35, follow the signs for Eymoutiers; by the port (direct access)
Opening times : from beginning April to beginning Nov.
4 ha (142 pitches) terraced, relatively flat, flat, grassy, gravelled
Tariff : (2012 price) 19.65€ ♣♣ ⬚ 🗉 🔲 (10A) – Extra per person 4.30€

> **Surroundings** : ⬙ Lac de Vassivière 🛏 𝄞
> **Leisure activities** : 🚣 🏖 (beach) 🎣
> **Facilities** : ⛟ (Jul–Aug) ⊘ ⬚ ♨ launderette
> **Nearby** : 🗜 🍽 ✗ 🚣 ◊ ⛵ water skiing

GPS Longitude : 1.89526
Latitude : 45.78979

The Michelin classification (⋀⋀⋀… ⋀) is totally independent of the official star classification system awarded by the local prefecture or other official organisation.

La Presqui'Île

   ✆ 05 55 64 78 98, *www.presquile.camping.free.fr*

Address : at Broussas (8.5km south along the D 8, D 34, D 3 and take turning to the right, near the Lac de Vassivière)

Opening times : from beginning April to beginning Nov.

7 ha (150 pitches) undulating, flat and relatively flat, grassy

Tariff : (2012 price) 13.70€ ✹✹ ⇌ 🄴 🄰 (10A) – Extra per person 3.55€ – Reservation fee 5€

Rental rates : (2012 price) (from beginning April to beginning Nov.) – 20 🏠 – 3 tents.
Per night from 36 to 86€ – Per week from 168 to 584€ – Reservation fee 15€

In a natural setting beside the lake.

Surroundings : 🌿 ⛺ 🕗🕗 **Facilities :** ⊶ (Jul-Aug) ♨ 🍴 **Nearby :** electric boats	**GPS** Longitude : 1.9223 Latitude : 45.79151

ST-GERMAIN-LES-BELLES

87380 – Michelin map **325** F7 – pop. 1,151 – alt. 432

▶ Paris 422 – Eymoutiers 33 – Limoges 34 – St-Léonard-de-Noblat 31

Le Montréal

   ✆ 05 55 71 86 20, *www.campingdemontreal.com*

Address : r. du Petit Moulin (take the southeastern exit, follow the signs for La Porcherie; beside a small lake)

Opening times : from beginning April to end Oct.

1 ha (60 pitches) terrace, relatively flat, flat, grassy, gravelled

Tariff : 19.70€ ✹✹ ⇌ 🄴 🄰 (10A) – Extra per person 3.80€ – Reservation fee 15€

Rental rates : (from beginning April to end Oct.) – 1 🛏 – 5 🏠 – 6 tent bungalows.
Per night from 34 to 97€ – Per week from 131 to 679€ – Reservation fee 15€

🚐 sani-station 3.80€

Surroundings : 🌿 ⇜ ⛺ 🕗 **Facilities :** ♿ ⊶ 🄲 🎢 🍴 launderette **Nearby :** ✕ 🏊 🎿 ⇌ (beach) 🌊	**GPS** Longitude : 1.5011 Latitude : 45.61143

*The prices listed were supplied by the campsite owners in 2012
(if prices were not available, those from the previous year are given).
The fees should be regarded as basic charges and may fluctuate
with inflation.*

ST-HILAIRE-LES-PLACES

87800 – Michelin map **325** D7 – pop. 870 – alt. 426

▶ Paris 417 – Châlus 18 – Limoges 27 – Nontron 52

Municipal du Lac

   ✆ 05 55 58 12 08, *sainthilairelesplaces.fr*

Address : at the Lac Plaisance (1.2km south of the town along the D 15a and take road to the left; 100m from the lake)

2.5 ha (92 pitches) terraced, grassy

Rentals : 7 🛏 – 12 🏠 – 12 gîtes.

🚐 sani-station – 40 🄴

Surroundings : ⛺ 🕗🕗 **Leisure activities :** 🎬 🛝 🏊 **Facilities :** ♿ ⊶ 🖼 **Nearby :** 🎿 ⛲ ⇌ (beach) 🏔 🌊 🐎 pedalos	**GPS** Longitude : 1.16038 Latitude : 45.63511

ST-LAURENT-LES-ÉGLISES

87240 – Michelin map **325** F5 – pop. 830 – alt. 388
▶ Paris 385 – Bellac 55 – Bourganeuf 31 – Guéret 50

Municipal Pont du Dognon

✆ 05 55 56 57 25, *mairie-st-laurent-les-eglises@wanadoo.fr*

Address : 1.8km southeast along the D 5, follow the signs for St-Léonard-de-Noblat; beside the Taurion river

Opening times : from end March to mid Nov.

3 ha (90 pitches) terraced, stony, grassy

Tariff : (2012 price) 12€ ♣♣ ⇌ 🔲 🖳 (5A) – Extra per person 4€ – Reservation fee 16€

Rental rates : (2012 price) (from end March to mid Nov.) – 3 🛖 – 5 🏠.
Per week from 102 to 455€ – Reservation fee 16€

Surroundings : 🏊 ≤ ⌂ ♀
Leisure activities : 🖼 ⚐ ⚒ ✕ 🏊 🎣 fitness trail
Facilities : & ⚷ 🗑 🖳 launderette
Nearby : ✕ ⛰ ⚓ pedalos

GPS Longitude : 1.5145
Latitude : 45.94293

ST-LÉONARD-DE-NOBLAT

87400 – Michelin map **325** F5 – pop. 4,665 – alt. 347
▶ Paris 407 – Aubusson 68 – Brive-la-Gaillarde 99 – Guéret 62

Municipal de Beaufort

✆ 05 55 56 02 79, *www.campingdebeaufort.fr*

Address : at Beaufort (1.7km along the N 141, following signs for Limoges then continue 1.5km to the left following signs for Masleon; beside the Vienne river)

2 ha (98 pitches) relatively flat, flat, grassy

Rentals : 10 🛖 – 2 🏠.

🚽 sani-station

Surroundings : ⌂ ♀♀
Leisure activities : ⛲ 🖼 ⚒ ♦
Facilities : & ⚷ 🏊 ♈ launderette

GPS Longitude : 1.49211
Latitude : 45.82276

These symbols are used for a campsite that is exceptional in its category:

🔺🔺🔺...🔺 *Particularly pleasant setting, quality and range of services available*

🏊🏊 *Tranquil, isolated site – quiet site, particularly at night*

≤ ≤ *Exceptional view – interesting or panoramic view*

ST-MARTIN-TERRESSUS

87400 – Michelin map **325** F5 – pop. 545 – alt. 280
▶ Paris 383 – Ambazac 7 – Bourganeuf 31 – Limoges 20

🔺 Municipal Soleil Levant

✆ 05 55 39 83 78, *www.st-martin-terressus.fr* – ✜

Address : in the village (continue west along the D 29 and take the road to the right; beside a small lake)

Opening times : from mid June to mid Sept.

0.5 ha (36 pitches) terrace, relatively flat, flat, grassy

Tariff : (2012 price) 8€ ♣♣ ⇌ 🔲 🖳 (18A) – Extra per person 3€

Surroundings : 🏊 ≤ ⌂ ♀ ⚑
Leisure activities : ⛲ 🖼
Facilities : & 🗑 🖳

GPS Longitude : 1.43995
Latitude : 45.91854

ST-PARDOUX

87250 – Michelin map **325** E4 – pop. 536 – alt. 370 – Leisure centre
▶ Paris 366 – Bellac 25 – Limoges 33 – St-Junien 39

         Aquadis Loisirs Le Freaudour

℘ 05 55 76 57 22, *www.aquadis-loisirs.com*
Address : at Base de Loisirs (leisure centre) (1.2km to the south; beside the Lac de St-Pardoux)
Opening times : from beginning March to beginning Nov.
4.5 ha (200 pitches) relatively flat, grassy
Tariff : 18.20€ ✹✹ ⇌ 🔲 🌢 (10A) – Extra per person 3.85€ – Reservation fee 9.90€
Rental rates : (2012 price) (from beginning March to beginning Nov.) – 20 🚐 – 10 🏠.
Per night from 66 to 72€ – Per week from 198 to 559 € – Reservation fee 19.50€

Surroundings : 🌲 ≤ 🛏 ⚲
Leisure activities : 🍷 🎦 🏇 🏊 🛶
Facilities : 🔥 ⚓ (Jul–Aug) 🔄 🏖 🚿 ☕ ⁿ 📷
Nearby : 🏖 (beach)

GPS Longitude : 1.2788
Latitude : 46.04931

ST-PARDOUX-CORBIER

19210 – Michelin map **329** J3 – pop. 360 – alt. 404
▶ Paris 448 – Arnac-Pompadour 8 – Brive-la-Gaillarde 44 – St-Yrieix-la-Perche 27

△   **Le Domaine Bleu**

℘ 05 55 73 59 89, *www.ledomainebleu.eu*
Address : take the eastern exit along the D 50, follow the signs for Vigeois and take the road to the right, near a lake
Opening times : from beginning July to beginning Sept.
1 ha (40 pitches) terraced, flat, grassy, fine gravel
Tariff : 15.50€ ✹✹ ⇌ 🔲 🌢 (16A) – Extra per person 4€

Surroundings : 🌲 🛏 ⚲⚲
Leisure activities : 🛶
Facilities : 🔥 ⚓ 🚿 🔄 🍴 🏖 ☕
Nearby : 🎾

GPS Longitude : 1.45449
Latitude : 45.42973

Fire safety doesn't stop when you leave your accommodation.
Always take care and consider the fire risks.

ST-YRIEIX-LA-PERCHE

87500 – Michelin map **325** E7 – pop. 6,932 – alt. 360
▶ Paris 430 – Brive-la-Gaillarde 63 – Limoges 40 – Périgueux 63

△   **Municipal d'Arfeuille**

℘ 05 55 75 08 75, *camping@saint-yrieix.fr*
Address : rte du Viaduc (2.5km north following signs for Limoges and take the road to the left; beside a small lake)
Opening times : from mid April to mid Sept.
2 ha (100 pitches) terraced, flat, grassy, stony
Tariff : 14.60€ ✹✹ ⇌ 🔲 🌢 (10A) – Extra per person 4.30€
Rental rates : (permanent) 🔥 – 11 🏠. Per week from 214 to 484 €
🚐 sani-station

Surroundings : 🌲 ≤ ⚲⚲
Leisure activities : 🏄 🚲 🎣 🏊 🏖 (beach) pedalos 🎿
Facilities : ☕ ⁿ 📷
Nearby : 🍷 ✕ 🛶

GPS Longitude : 1.20009
Latitude : 45.52791

SEILHAC

19700 – Michelin map **329** L3 – pop. 1,721 – alt. 500
▶ Paris 461 – Aubusson 97 – Brive-la-Gaillarde 33 – Limoges 73

Le Lac de Bournazel

☎ 05 55 27 05 65, *www.camping-lac-bournazel.com*
Address : located 1.5km northwest along the N 120, follow the signs for Uzerche then turn right after 1km
Opening times : from beginning April to end Oct.
6.5 ha (155 pitches) terraced, flat, grassy, stony
Tariff : (2012 price) 14.20€ ✦✦ ⇐ 🗉 (🔌) (10A) – Extra per person 4.40€ – Reservation fee 9€
Rental rates : (2012 price) (from beginning April to end Oct.) – 2 caravans – 10 🏠 – 2 teepees.
Per night from 24 to 88 € – Per week from 168 to 616€ – Reservation fee 9€
🚃 sani-station 4€ – 🔧 (🔌)11.40€

Surroundings : 🐾 ⛱ 🎱	
Leisure activities : 🍽 🏠 ⚓	**GPS** Longitude : 1.7022
Facilities : ♿ ⊶ 🏧 🍴 🖬 ⚖	Latitude : 45.37838
Nearby : 🍴 ⇌ 🎣 🐴 disco, sports trail	

TREIGNAC

19260 – Michelin map **329** L2 – pop. 1,383 – alt. 500 – Leisure centre
▶ Paris 463 – Égletons 32 – Eymoutiers 33 – Limoges 75

Flower La Plage

☎ 05 55 98 08 54, *www.camping-correze.com*
Address : at the Lac des Barriousses (4.5km north along the D 940, follow the signs for Eymoutiers)
Opening times : from beginning April to end Sept.
3.5 ha (130 pitches) terraced, relatively flat, stony, grassy, wood, adjacent wood
Tariff : (2012 price) 13.90€ ✦✦ ⇐ 🗉 (🔌) (6A) – Extra per person 1.50€ – Reservation fee 15€
Rental rates : (2012 price) (from beginning April to end Sept.) – 26 🚐 – 6 tents.
Per night from 35 to 88 € – Per week from 250 to 600 € – Reservation fee 15€
🚃 sani-station 5€ – 10 🗉 9.90€ – 🔧 (🔌)9.90€

Surroundings : ≼ ⛱ 🎱	
Leisure activities : 🖬	**GPS** Longitude : 1.81373
Facilities : ♿ ⊶ 🏧 🍴 launderette	Latitude : 45.55992
Nearby : ✗ ⚖ ⚓ 🚴 ⇌ (beach) 🦢 pedalos	

Gîtes range from small maisonettes to old farmhouses with several bedrooms.

USSEL

19200 – Michelin map **329** O2 – pop. 10,226 – alt. 631
▶ Paris 448 – Limoges 142 – Clermont-Ferrand 82 – Brive-la-Gaillarde 89

Municipal de Ponty

☎ 05 55 72 30 05, *www.ussel19.fr*
Address : r. du Lac (2.7km west following signs for Tulle and take D 157 to the right; near a small lake)
Opening times : from mid May to end Sept.
2 ha (50 pitches) flat and relatively flat, fine gravel, grassy
Tariff : 9€ ✦✦ ⇐ 🗉 (🔌) (12A) – Extra per person 2.70€
🚃 sani-station 2€ – 10 🗉 9€

Surroundings : 🐾 ≼ on the lake ⛱ 🎣	
Leisure activities : 🖬 ⚓	**GPS** Longitude : 2.28603
Facilities : ♿ ⊶ ⛟ 🚿 🍴 🖬	Latitude : 45.54593
Nearby : 🍴 ✗ 🚴 🎱 🎨 ⇌ (beach) 🎣 🐴 mountain biking	

UZERCHE

9140 – Michelin map **329** K3 – pop. 3,226 – alt. 380
Paris 444 – Aubusson 95 – Bourganeuf 76 – Brive-la-Gaillarde 38

Municipal la Minoterie

05 55 73 12 75, *http://camping.uzerche.fr*
Address : at the base de loisirs (leisure centre) of la Minoterie (located to the southwest of the town centre, access via quai Julian-Grimau, between the N 20 and the bridge at Turgot (D 3); beside the Vézère river (left bank)
1.5 ha (65 pitches) terrace, flat, grassy, stony
In a picturesque setting.

Surroundings : ⑀ ≤ ♨♨
Leisure activities : 🎦 ⚓ 🚴 ≊ 🐟 ⚲
Facilities : 🚻 ⌂ 🏠 🚿 launderette
Nearby : climbing wall

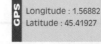

Longitude : 1.56882
Latitude : 45.41927

VIDEIX

7600 – Michelin map **325** B6 – pop. 234 – alt. 260
Paris 443 – Angoulême 53 – Limoges 53 – Nontron 36

Village Vacances Le Hameau de gîtes
(rental of chalets only)

05 55 48 83 39, *www.rochechouart.com*
Address : Plage de La Chassagne (head 1.7km north along the D 87, follow the signs for Pressignac; the area is known as La Chassagne)
3 ha flat, grassy
Rentals : 🅿 – 16 🏠.

Surroundings : ⑀ ≤ lake ⛰
Leisure activities : 🎦 ≊
Facilities : 🚻 🏠 🚽 launderette
Nearby : 🍴 ✕ ⚓ 🐟 ◊ pedalos

Longitude : 0.71585
Latitude : 45.80106

VIGEOIS

9410 – Michelin map **329** K3 – pop. 1,194 – alt. 390
Paris 457 – Limoges 68 – Tulle 32 – Brive-la-Gaillarde 41

Municipal du Lac de Pontcharal

05 55 98 90 86, *www.vigeois.com*
Address : at Pontcharal (situated 2km southeast along the D 7, follow the signs for Brive, near the lake at Pontcharal)
Opening times : from beginning June to mid Sept.
32 ha/1.7 (85 pitches) terrace, flat and relatively flat, grassy
Tariff : 🛉 3.50€ ⇔ 🅴 4.10€ – 🔌 (15A) 3.50€
Rental rates : (from beginning April to end Oct.) – 5 🛏. Per night from 65€
Per week from 250 to 380 €
🚽 sani-station 2€

Surroundings : ⑀ ♨♨ ⛰
Leisure activities : 🍴 ✕ ≊ (beach) 🐟
Facilities : 🚻 ⌂ (Jul–Aug) 🚿 🚽 🏠 🚱
Nearby : pedalos

Longitude : 1.53806
Latitude : 45.36873

In order for the guide to remain wholly objective, the selection of campsites is made on an entirely independent basis.

LORRAINE

Christian Legay / Mairie de Metz

If you want to do justice to the collage of stunning sights of Lorraine, a region that shares borders with Luxembourg, Germany and Belgium, don't forget to pack your walking boots. But before you head for the hills, make sure you leave enough time to discover the artistic heritage of Nancy and admire the lights and contemporary art gallery of historic Metz. Then embark upon the trail of tiny spa resorts and the famous centres of craftsmanship that produce the legendary Baccarat crystal, Longwy enamels and Lunéville porcelain. From there head to historic Domrémy and Colombey. The water, forests and wildlife of the Vosges regional park, nestling in the 'Valley of Lakes', will keep you entranced as you make your way down hillsides dotted with orchards bursting with plums. Stop for a little light refreshment in a *marcairerie* (traditional farmhouse inn) and sample the famous *quiche Lorraine* tarts, a slab of Munster cheese and a delicious kirsch-flavoured dessert.

ANOULD

88650 – Michelin map **314** J3 – pop. 3,336 – alt. 457
■ Paris 430 – Colmar 43 – Épinal 45 – Gérardmer 15

Les Acacias

℘ 03 29 57 11 06, *www.acaciascamp.com*
Address : 191 r. Léonard de Vinci (take the western exit along the N 415, follow the signs for Colmar and take the road to the right)
Opening times : from beginning Dec. to end Sept.
2.5 ha (84 pitches) terraced, flat, grassy
Tariff : (2012 price) 14.90€ ★★ ⇔ 🗉 (9) (10A) – Extra per person 3.90€
Rental rates : (from beginning Dec. to end Sept.) – 2 'gypsy' caravans – 8 📇 – 9 🏠.
Per week from 205 to 550 €
🚽 sani-station – 5 🗉 10€ – 🔋 (9)13.50€

Surroundings : ▭ ⚲
Leisure activities : ♈ 🛖 ⚓ 🏊 (small swimming pool)
Facilities : & ⚲ (Jun–Sept) 🚿 ⚲ 🛁 ♈ launderette
Nearby : walking trails, fitness trail

GPS Longitude : 6.95786
Latitude : 48.18437

LA BRESSE

88250 – Michelin map **314** J4 – pop. 4,732 – alt. 636 – Winter sports : 650/1,350 m 🎿 31 🎿
■ Paris 437 – Colmar 52 – Épinal 52 – Gérardmer 13

Municipal le Haut des Bluches

℘ 03 29 25 64 80, *www.hautdesbluches.com* – alt. 708
Address : 5 rte des Planches (head 3.2km east along the D 34, follow the signs for Le Col de la Schlucht; beside the Moselotte river)
Opening times : from mid Dec. to beginning Nov.
4 ha (140 pitches) terraced, relatively flat, flat, grassy, rocks
Tariff : 19.50€ ★★ ⇔ 🗉 (9) (13A) – Extra per person 3.30€
Rental rates : (from mid Dec. to mid Nov.) & (2 chalets) – 7 🏠 – 13 🛏.
Per night from 38 to 187 € – Per week from 257 to 620 €
🚽 sani-station 3.20€ – 17 🗉 5.90€ – 🔋 (9)11.30€
In a picturesque setting crossed by a stream.

Surroundings : ❄ ≤
Leisure activities : ♈ ✕ 🛖 ⚓ 🐟 adventure park, zip wiring, multi-sports ground
Facilities : & ⚲ ⚲ 🛁 ⚲ ♈ launderette ⚲
Nearby : sports trail

GPS Longitude : 6.91831
Latitude : 47.99878

Belle Hutte

℘ 03 29 25 49 75, *www.camping-belle-hutte.com* – alt. 900
Address : 1bis Vouille de Belle Hutte (head 9km northeast along the D 34, follow the signs for Le Col de la Schlucht; beside the Moselotte river)
Opening times : from mid Dec. to mid Nov.
5 ha (125 pitches) terraced, flat, grassy, stony
Tariff : 34€ ★★ ⇔ 🗉 (9) (10A) – Extra per person 6.50€ – Reservation fee 10€
Rental rates : (from mid Dec. to mid Nov.) & (2 chalets) – 15 🏠. Per night from 75 to 125 €
Per week from 490 to 840 € – Reservation fee 10€
🚽 sani-station 5€
In a pleasant, wooded site.

Surroundings : ❄ ≤ ▭
Leisure activities : ♈ ✕ 🛖 ⚓ 🏊 ⚲
Facilities : & ⚲ ⚲ 🛁 ♈ launderette ⚲
Nearby : ⚲

GPS Longitude : 6.96254
Latitude : 48.0349

BULGNÉVILLE

88140 – Michelin map **314** D3 – pop. 1,400 – alt. 350
▶ Paris 331 – Contrexéville 6 – Épinal 53 – Neufchâteau 22

Porte des Vosges

℘ 03 29 09 12 00, www.Camping-Portedesvosges.com – ℞

Address : at La Grande Tranchée (head 1.3km southeast along the D 164, follow the signs for Contrexéville and take D 14, follow the signs for Suriauville to the right)
Opening times : from mid April to end Sept.
3.2 ha (100 pitches) relatively flat, flat, grassy, gravelled
Tariff : 20€ ✿✿ ⇌ 🅴 ⚡ (6A) – Extra per person 4.50€
🚐 2 🅴 16€
In a rural setting.

Surroundings : ♀
Facilities : ♿ ⊶ ⊠ ⚲ ⚐

GPS Longitude : 5.84514
Latitude : 48.19529

BUSSANG

88540 – Michelin map **314** J5 – pop. 1,604 – alt. 605
▶ Paris 444 – Belfort 44 – Épinal 59 – Gérardmer 38

Sunêlia Domaine de Champé

℘ 03 29 61 61 51, www.domaine-de-champe.com

Address : 14 r. des Champs-Navets (located to the northeast, access via the turning to the left of the church)
Opening times : permanent
3.5 ha (100 pitches) flat, grassy
Tariff : (2012 price) 31€ ✿✿ ⇌ 🅴 ⚡ (10A)
Rental rates : (2012 price) (permanent) – 22 🚐 – 8 🏠. Per night from 75 to 120 €
Per week from 525 to 1,190 €
🚐 sani-station
Beside the Moselle river and a stream.

Surroundings : ⩽
Leisure activities : 🍷 ✕ 🛥 🖫 daytime ⚹ 🎠 ⊜ hammam 🏊 ✂ 🖼 ⛷ ⛱ multi-sports ground
Facilities : ♿ ⊶ 🔳 ⚐ launderette ⚲
Nearby : 🐎

GPS Longitude : 6.85748
Latitude : 47.8889

CELLES-SUR-PLAINE

88110 – Michelin map **314** J2 – pop. 857 – alt. 318 – Leisure centre
▶ Paris 391 – Baccarat 23 – Blâmont 23 – Lunéville 49

Les Lacs ♨♨

℘ 03 29 41 28 00, www.camping-paysdeslacs.com
Address : pl. de la gare (to the southwest of town)
Opening times : from beginning April to end Sept.
15 ha/4 ha for camping (135 pitches) flat, grassy, stony
Tariff : 23€ ✿✿ ⇌ 🅴 ⚡ (10A) – Extra per person 6.50€ – Reservation fee 10€
Rental rates : (permanent) – 20 🏠 – 6 tent bungalows – 10 chalets (without sanitary facilities). Per night from 90 to 200 € – Per week from 300 to 600 € – Reservation fee 16€
🚐 10 🅴 23€
Beside the river and close to the lake.

Surroundings : ⩽ 🖼
Leisure activities : 🍷 🛥 ⚹ 🏊 ✂ ⋔ ⛷ ⚲
Facilities : ♿ ⊶ 🔳 ⚱ ⚲ ⚐ launderette 🐟
At the lake : 🚲 🛶 ⚓

GPS Longitude : 6.94756
Latitude : 48.4557

LA CHAPELLE-DEVANT-BRUYÈRES

88600 – Michelin map **314** I3 – pop. 621 – alt. 457
▶ Paris 416 – Épinal 31 – Gérardmer 22 – Rambervillers 26

⚠ Les Pinasses

✆ 03 29 58 51 10, *www.camping-les-pinasses.com*
Address : 215 rte de Bruyères (located 1.2km to the northwest on the D 60)
Opening times : from mid April to end Sept.
3 ha (139 pitches) flat, grassy, stony, small lake
Tariff : 24.40€ ⚦⚦ ⇔ 🅴 (ℓ) (6A) – Extra per person 5.30€
Rental rates : (from mid April to end Sept.) – 4 🚐 – 88 🏠 – 2 apartments.
Per night from 36 to 81 € – Per week from 230 to 565 €

Surroundings : 🗔 ⚏⚏
Leisure activities : ✗ 🎬 🛶 ⚿ ⚓ 🛝 ⚓
Facilities : ⊶ 🛁 🚿 🗑 ⚑ launderette

GPS Longitude : 6.77411
Latitude : 48.18974

CHARMES

88130 – Michelin map **314** F2 – pop. 4,613 – alt. 282
▶ Paris 381 – Mirecourt 17 – Nancy 43 – Neufchâteau 58

⚠ Les Iles

✆ 03 29 38 87 71, *www.campinglesiles.blogspot.fr*
Address : 20 r. de l'Ecluse (located 1km to the southwest along the D 157 and take the road to the right; near the stadium)
Opening times : from beginning April to end Sept.
3.5 ha (67 pitches) flat, grassy
Tariff : (2012 price) 13.65€ ⚦⚦ ⇔ 🅴 (ℓ) (10A) – Extra per person 3.15€
🚐 sani-station 3€
A pleasant setting near the Canal de l'Est and the Moselle river.

Leisure activities : 🛶 🚲 ⚓
Facilities : ⚿ ⊶ 🗑 ⚑
Nearby : ⚿ ⚓

GPS Longitude : 6.28668
Latitude : 48.37583

The guide is updated each year, so consult the latest edition for the most up-to-date information and pricing.

CONTREXÉVILLE

88140 – Michelin map **314** D3 – pop. 3,440 – alt. 342 – ⚕ (end Mar-mid Oct)
▶ Paris 337 – Épinal 47 – Langres 75 – Luxeuil 73

⚠ Le Tir aux Pigeons

✆ 03 29 08 15 06, *www.camping-letirauxpigeons.fr*
Address : r. du 11 Septembre (located 1km southwest along the D 13, follow the signs for Suriauville)
Opening times : from mid March to end Oct.
1.8 ha (80 pitches) flat, grassy, fine gravel
Tariff : (2012 price) 17.50€ ⚦⚦ ⇔ 🅴 (ℓ) (10A) – Extra per person 5€ – Reservation fee 8€
Rental rates : (2012 price) (from mid March to end Oct.) – 6 🚐 – 4 🏠 – 4 tent bungalows.
Per night from 50 to 70 € – Per week from 240 to 450 € – Reservation fee 8€
🚐 sani-station 17.50€ – 40 🅴 17.50€
At the edge of a wood.

Surroundings : 🌳 ⚏⚏
Leisure activities : 🍷 🎬
Facilities : ⚿ ⊶ 🛁 🚿 🗑 ⚑ 🖥

GPS Longitude : 5.88517
Latitude : 48.18022

CORCIEUX

88430 – Michelin map **314** J3 – pop. 1,668 – alt. 534
▶ Paris 424 – Épinal 39 – Gérardmer 15 – Remiremont 43

Yelloh! Village en Voges Domaine des Bans

℘ 0329516467, *www.domaine-des-bans.fr*
Address : 6 r. James Wiese (near the pl. Notre-Dame)
Opening times : permanent
15.7 ha (634 pitches) flat, grassy, stony
Tariff : 42€ ♥♥ ⇔ ▣ (∮) (6A) – Extra per person 8€
Rental rates : (permanent) – 250 ⟦⟧ – 14 studios – 11 apartments – 44 gîtes.
Per night from 33 to 225 € – Per week from 231 to 1,575 €
⟦⟧ 8 ▣ – ⟦⟧ (∮)12€
Pleasant setting. The campsite is in two parts (Domaine des Bans with 600 pitches, and La Tour with 34 pitches); beside a small lake.

Surroundings : ≤ ⟐ ♀
Leisure activities : ♥ ✕ ⟐ ⟨ ≉ ⬩ ♠ ✕ ▣ ⟐ ⟐ ⟐ disco
Facilities : ♿ ⟐ ▥ ⟐ ⟐ ♈ launderette ⟐ ⟐
Nearby : ⟐

GPS Longitude : 6.87985
Latitude : 48.16867

Au Clos de la Chaume

℘ 0329507676, *www.camping-closdelachaume.com*
Address : 21 r. d'Alsace
Opening times : from beginning April to end Sept.
4 ha (90 pitches) flat, grassy
Tariff : 22.20€ ♥♥ ⇔ ▣ (∮) (10A) – Extra per person 5.70€ – Reservation fee 10€
Rental rates : (from beginning April to end Sept.) – 15 ⟦⟧ – 5 ⟐ – 2 tents.
Per night from 42 to 98 € – Per week from 295 to 688 € – Reservation fee 15€
⟦⟧ sani-station 5.50€ – 10 ▣ 11€ – ⟦⟧ (∮)11€

Surroundings : ♀
Leisure activities : ⟐ ⟐ ⟐ ⟐
Facilities : ♿ ⟐ ⟐ ♈ launderette

GPS Longitude : 6.88383
Latitude : 48.17026

Using the traditional Michelin classification method, the guide provides you with an easy, speedy reference for assessing the category of each site: 1 to 5 tents (see page 10).

DABO

57850 – Michelin map **307** O7 – pop. 2,636 – alt. 500
▶ Paris 453 – Baccarat 63 – Metz 127 – Phalsbourg 18

Le Rocher

℘ 0387074751, *www.ot-dabo.fr*
Address : rte du Rocher (located 1.5km southeast along the D 45, at the junction with the road for Le Rocher)
Opening times : from beginning April to end Sept.
0.5 ha (42 pitches) relatively flat, flat, grassy
Tariff : (2012 price) 13.60€ ♥♥ ⇔ ▣ (∮) (10A) – Extra per person 3.30€
Situated in a pleasant forest of fir trees.

Surroundings : ♀
Leisure activities : ⟐
Facilities : ⟐ ▥

GPS Longitude : 7.25267
Latitude : 48.64844

FRESSE-SUR-MOSELLE

88160 – Michelin map **314** I5 – pop. 1,868 – alt. 515
▶ Paris 447 – Metz 178 – Épinal 54 – Mulhouse 56

⚠ Municipal Bon Accueil

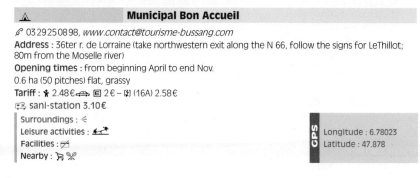

🕿 03 29 25 08 98, *www.contact@tourisme-bussang.com*
Address : 36ter r. de Lorraine (take northwestern exit along the N 66, follow the signs for LeThillot; 80m from the Moselle river)
Opening times : from beginning April to end Nov.
0.6 ha (50 pitches) flat, grassy
Tariff : ☂ 2.48€ 🚗 ▣ 2€ – ⚡ (16A) 2.58€
🚮 sani-station 3.10€

Surroundings : ⬉
Leisure activities : 🏊
Facilities : 🚿
Nearby : 🛒 ✕

GPS Longitude : 6.78023
Latitude : 47.878

Some campsites benefit from proximity to a municipal leisure centre.

GEMAINGOUTTE

88520 – Michelin map **314** K3 – pop. 119 – alt. 446
▶ Paris 411 – Colmar 59 – Ribeauvillé 31 – St-Dié 14

⚠ Municipal le Violu

🕿 03 29 57 70 70, *www.gemaingoutte.fr*
Address : take the western exit along the RD 59, follow the signs for St-Dié; beside a stream
Opening times : from beginning May to end Oct.
1 ha (48 pitches) flat, grassy
Tariff : (2012 price) ☂ 2.50€ 🚗 1.70€ ▣ 1.80€ – ⚡ (30A) 2.20€
Rental rates : (2012 price) (permanent) – 2 🏠. Per night from 55 €
Per week from 220 to 425 €
🚮 sani-station 2€ – 10 ▣ 6.50€

Leisure activities : 🏊
Facilities : 🔥 🚿 🔲

GPS Longitude : 7.08584
Latitude : 48.25361

GÉRARDMER

88400 – Michelin map **314** J4 – pop. 8,757 – alt. 669 – Winter sports : 660/1,350 m ⚡31 ⚡
▶ Paris 425 – Belfort 78 – Colmar 52 – Épinal 40

⚠ Les Sapins

🕿 03 29 63 15 01, *www.camping-gerardmer.com*
Address : 18 chemin de Sapois (located 1.5km southwest, 200m from the lake)
Opening times : from beginning April to mid Oct.
1.3 ha (70 pitches) flat, grassy, gravelled
Tariff : 20.40€ ☂☂ 🚗 ▣ ⚡ (10A) – Extra per person 4.50€ – Reservation fee 8€
Rental rates : (from mid March to end Oct.) – 3 🚐 – 1 apartment.
Per week from 290 to 520 € – Reservation fee 10€
🚮 sani-station 2€

Surroundings : 🛏 ⚲
Leisure activities : ⚑
Facilities : ⊶ 🚿 ⚑
Nearby : 💧 🐎

GPS Longitude : 6.85614
Latitude : 48.0635

Les Granges-Bas

☎ 03 29 63 12 03, *www.lesgrangesbas.fr*
Address : 116 chemin des Granges Bas (4km west along the D 417 then turn left at Costet-Beillard, follow road for 1km)
Opening times : from mid Dec. to mid Oct.
2 ha (100 pitches) relatively flat, flat, grassy
Tariff : 16.55€ ✚ ✚ ⊷ ▣ ⊠ (6A) – Extra per person 3.85€
Rental rates : (from mid Dec. to mid Oct.) – 9 ⟦⟧ – 2 apartments – 1 tent.
Per night from 55 to 130 € – Per week from 270 to 690 € – Reservation fee 10€

Surroundings : ⊰ ⊰ ⊡
Leisure activities : ⊡ ⊷ ⊱
Facilities : ⊶ ⊱ launderette

GPS Longitude : 6.80653
Latitude : 48.06927

HERPELMONT

88600 – Michelin map **314** I3 – pop. 247 – alt. 480
▶ Paris 413 – Épinal 28 – Gérardmer 20 – Remiremont 33

Domaine des Messires

☎ 03 29 58 56 29, *www.domainedesmessires.com*
Address : rue des Messires (located 1.5km to the north)
Opening times : from end April to end Sept.
11 ha/2 ha for camping (100 pitches) flat, grassy
Tariff : ✚ 6.50€ ⊷ ▣ 13.50€ ⊠ (6A) – Reservation fee 12€
Rental rates : (from end April to end Sept.) ⊰ – 22 ⟦⟧. Per night from 45 to 97 €
Per week from 270 to 679 € – Reservation fee 12€

A pleasant site and setting beside a lake.

Surroundings : ⊰ ⊰ lake and mountain ⊡ ⊡ ⊿
Leisure activities : ⊡ ✕ ⊡ ⊷ ⊰ kayaking ⊱
Facilities : ⊱ ⊶ ⊡ ⊱ ⊷ ⊱ launderette ⊡ ⊱

GPS Longitude : 6.74278
Latitude : 48.17854

*Routes nationales are main roads and their identifying numbers
begin with N or RN. Routes départementales are generally quieter
roads and begin with D or DN.*

JAULNY

54470 – Michelin map **307** G5 – pop. 262 – alt. 230
▶ Paris 310 – Commercy 41 – Metz 33 – Nancy 51

La Pelouse

☎ 03 83 81 91 67, *www.campingdelapelouse.com* – limited spaces for one-night stay
Address : chemin de Fey (500m south of the town, access located near the bridge)
Opening times : permanent
2.9 ha (100 pitches) relatively flat, flat, grassy
Tariff : 14.60€ ✚ ✚ ⊷ ▣ ⊠ (6A) – Extra per person 4€
Rental rates : (permanent) ⊱ (2 chalets) – 5 ⊡. Per week from 330 to 550 €
⊡ sani-station – ⊱ ⊠ 11€
On a small wooded hill overlooking the river.

Surroundings : ⊰ ⊡ ⊡
Leisure activities : ✕ ⊡ ⊷ ⊿
Facilities : ⊱ ⊶ ⊡
Nearby : ⊰

GPS Longitude : 5.88658
Latitude : 48.9705

LUNÉVILLE

4300 – Michelin map **307** J7 – pop. 19,937 – alt. 224
Paris 347 – Épinal 69 – Metz 95 – Nancy 36

Les Bosquets

674724973, *www.cc-lunevillois.fr*
Address : chemin de la Ménagerie (head north towards Château-Salins and take a right turn; after the bridge over the Vézouze)
1 ha (36 pitches) terrace, flat, grassy
Rentals : 4.
sani-station
Close to the château park and gardens

Surroundings :
Leisure activities :
Facilities : launderette
Nearby :

GPS Longitude : 6.49886
Latitude : 48.59647

MAGNIÈRES

4129 – Michelin map **307** K8 – pop. 341 – alt. 250
Paris 365 – Baccarat 16 – Épinal 40 – Lunéville 22

Le Pré Fleury

0383738221, *www.campingduprefleury.com*
Address : 18 r. de la Barre (500m west along the D 22, follow the signs for Bayon, 200m from the Mortagne river)
Opening times : from beginning April to end Sept.
1 ha (34 pitches) flat and relatively flat, fine gravel, grassy
Tariff : (2012 price) 13.50€ (10A) – Extra per person 3€
5 10€ – 9.50€
By the old railway station and beside a lake.

Surroundings :
Leisure activities : draisines (handcars/rail cycling)
Facilities :
Nearby :

GPS Longitude : 6.55735
Latitude : 48.44653

We have selected the best campsites in France with our usual care,
listing those with the best facilities in the most pleasant surroundings.

METZ

7000 – Michelin map **307** I4 – pop. 121,841 – alt. 173
Paris 330 – Longuyon 80 – Pont-à-Mousson 31 – St-Avold 44

Municipal Metz-Plage

0387682648, *tourisme.mairie-metz.fr*
Address : allée de Metz-Plage (to the north, near the Les Morts bridge and the bridge at Thionville; beside the Moselle river – from A 31: take the exit for Metz-Nord Pontiffroy)
2.5 ha (150 pitches) flat, grassy, stony
sani-station – 9

Surroundings :
Leisure activities :
Facilities : launderette
Nearby :

GPS Longitude : 6.17058
Latitude : 49.12569

NEUFCHÂTEAU

88300 – Michelin map **314** C2 – pop. 7,040 – alt. 300
▶ Paris 321 – Chaumont 57 – Contrexéville 28 – Épinal 75

⚠ Intercommunal

☎ 03 29 94 19 03, *n.merlin@paysdeneufchateau.com*
Address : r. Georges Joecker (take the western exit, follow the signs for Chaumont and take a right turn, near the sports centre)
Opening times : from mid May to end Sept.
0.8 ha (50 pitches) flat, grassy
Tariff : (2012 price) ✚ 3€ ⟵ 2.80€ ▣ 3€ – ⛽ (16A) 4€
☲ sani-station

> Surroundings : ♀♀
> Facilities : ⅙ ⊶ ⤍ ⊠ ⩙ ⋐
> Nearby : ✗ ▨ ▨ skateboarding

GPS Longitude : 5.68605
Latitude : 48.35725

These symbols are used for a campsite that is exceptional in its category:
AAAA...A *Particularly pleasant setting, quality and range of services available*
✍✍ *Tranquil, isolated site – quiet site, particularly at night*
≤≤ *Exceptional view – interesting or panoramic view*

PLOMBIÈRES-LES-BAINS

88370 – Michelin map **314** G5 – pop. 1,869 – alt. 429 – ⚕ (beg Apr-end Dec)
▶ Paris 378 – Belfort 79 – Épinal 38 – Gérardmer 43

⚠ L'Hermitage

☎ 03 29 30 01 87, *www.hermitage-camping.com*
Address : 54 r. du Boulot (located 1.5km northwest along the D 63, follow the signs for Xertigny then take the D 20, follow the signs for Ruaux)
Opening times : from mid April to mid Oct.
1.4 ha (55 pitches) terraced, relatively flat, flat, grassy, gravelled
Tariff : ✚ 4.70€ ⟵ ▣ 5.10€ – ⛽ (10A) 5.30€ – Reservation fee 10€
Rental rates : (permanent) – 3 ⌂ – 4 ⌂. Per week from 260 to 530 € – Reservation fee 10€
☲ sani-station 4€ – ⛽ ⛽17.82€

> Surroundings : ▭ ♀
> Leisure activities : ▱ ⤢ ⅃
> Facilities : ⅙ ⊶ ❦ ▣ ⤸

GPS Longitude : 6.4431
Latitude : 47.96859

⚠ Le Fraiteux

☎ 03 29 66 00 71, *www.campingdufraiteux.fr*
Address : 81 r. du Camping (4km west along the D 20 and D 20e)
Opening times : from mid March to end Oct.
0.8 ha (35 pitches) relatively flat, flat, grassy, fine gravel
Tariff : ✚ 3.70€ ⟵ ▣ 4.40€ – ⛽ (10A) 4.10€
Rental rates : (permanent) – 1 ⌂ – 3 ⌂. Per night from 40 to 60 €
Per week from 274 to 430 €
☲ sani-station – 6 ▣ 10.50€

> Surroundings : ✍ ▭
> Leisure activities : ⤢
> Facilities : ⊶ ⤍ ⫼ launderette

GPS Longitude : 6.41647
Latitude : 47.96573

REVIGNY-SUR-ORNAIN

55800 – Michelin map **307** A6 – pop. 3,145 – alt. 144
▶ Paris 239 – Bar-le-Duc 18 – St-Dizier 30 – Vitry-le-François 36

⚠ Municipal du Moulin des Gravières

℘ 03 29 78 73 34, *www.ot-revigny-ornain.fr*
Address : 1 r. du Stade (in the town towards southern exit, follow the signs for Vitry-le-François and turn right; 100m from the Ornain)
Opening times : from mid April to end Sept.
1 ha (27 pitches) flat, grassy
Tariff : (2012 price) ⭐ 2.50€ ⇔ 🔲 7.10€ – ⚡ (6A) 3.20€
Rental rates : (2012 price) (permanent) ⚡ – 3 🔳. Per night from 48 to 65 €
Per week from 224 to 308 €
🔳 sani-station – 2 🔳
In a pleasant setting beside a stream.

Surroundings : 🔲 ♀
Leisure activities : 🔲
Facilities : ⛭ 🔲 🔲
Nearby : ✕ 🔲 ⛏

Longitude : 4.98373
Latitude : 48.82669

ST-AVOLD

57500 – Michelin map **307** L4 – pop. 16,298 – alt. 260
▶ Paris 372 – Haguenau 117 – Lunéville 77 – Metz 46

⚠ Le Felsberg

℘ 03 87 92 75 05, *www.mairie-saint-avold.fr*
Address : r. en Verrerie (to the north; near D 603, opposite the Record service station – from A 4: take the exit for St-Avold Carling)
1.2 ha (33 pitches) terraced, relatively flat, flat, grassy, stony
Rentals : ⚡ – 3 🏠 – 11 🔲.
🔳 sani-station
On the wooded slopes near the town.

Surroundings : 🔲 ♀♀
Leisure activities : ♀ ✕ 🔲 🔲 🚲
Facilities : ⛭ ⊶ 🔲 🔲 🔲 🔲

Longitude : 6.71579
Latitude : 49.11102

This guide is not intended as a list of all the camping sites in France; its aim is to provide a selection of the best sites in each category.

ST-DIÉ-DES-VOSGES

88100 – Michelin map **314** J3 – pop. 21,523 – alt. 350
▶ Paris 397 – Belfort 123 – Colmar 53 – Épinal 53

⚠ Vanne de Pierre

℘ 03 29 56 23 56, *www.vannedepierre.com*
Address : 5 r. du Camping (east along the quai du Stade, near the Meurthe river)
3.5 ha (118 pitches) flat, grassy
Rentals : ⚡ – 6 🔳 – 7 🏠.

Surroundings : 🔲 ♀
Leisure activities : ♀ 🔲 🕐 daytime 🔲 ♨ hammam, jacuzzi 🔲 🔲
Facilities : ⛭ ⊶ 🔲 🔲 🔲 🔲 🔲 launderette
Nearby : 🚲 ✕ 🔲

Longitude : 6.96942
Latitude : 48.28584

ST-MAURICE-SUR-MOSELLE

88560 – Michelin map **314** I5 – pop. 1,486 – alt. 560 – Winter sports : 550/1,250 m 8
▶ Paris 441 – Belfort 41 – Bussang 4 – Épinal 56

Les Deux Ballons

03 29 25 17 14, *www.camping-deux-ballons.fr*
Address : 17 r. du Stade (take the southwestern exit along the N 66, follow the signs for Le Thillot; beside a stream)
Opening times : from beginning April to end Sept.
4 ha (160 pitches) terraced, flat, grassy
Tariff : 31.50€ ✶✶ ⇔ 🔲 🄵 (10A) – Extra per person 7€ – Reservation fee 15€
Rental rates : (from beginning April to end Oct.) – 7 🏠. Per week from 470 to 750 €
Reservation fee 15€
sani-station 7.50€

Surroundings :
Leisure activities :
Facilities : launderette
Nearby : walking trails

GPS
Longitude : 6.81124
Latitude : 47.8554

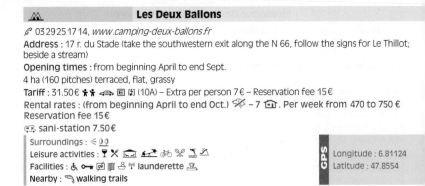

SANCHEY

88390 – Michelin map **314** G3 – pop. 789 – alt. 368
▶ Paris 390 – Metz 129 – Épinal 8 – Nancy 69

Club Lac de Bouzey

03 29 82 49 41, *www.lacdebouzey.com*
Address : 19 r. du Lac (to the south along the D 41)
Opening times : permanent
3 ha (160 pitches) terraced, relatively flat, flat, grassy
Tariff : 35€ ✶✶ ⇔ 🔲 🄵 (10A) – Extra per person 10€ – Reservation fee 25€
Rental rates : (permanent) – 38 🚐. Per night from 70 to 160 €
Per week from 490 to 1,120 € – Reservation fee 25€
sani-station – 21.65€
Opposite the lake; pleasant reception area and good lesiure facillities.

Surroundings :
Leisure activities : ❤ ✗ (cinema/theatre) 🚴 disco
multi-sports ground
Facilities : launderette

GPS
Longitude : 6.3602
Latitude : 48.1667

SAULXURES-SUR-MOSELOTTE

88290 – Michelin map **314** I5 – pop. 2,782 – alt. 464 – Leisure centre
▶ Paris 431 – Épinal 46 – Gérardmer 24 – Luxeuil-les-Bains 53

Lac de la Moselotte

03 29 24 56 56, *www.lac-moselotte.fr*
Address : 336 rte des Amias (located 1.5km west on the old D 43)
23 ha/3 ha for camping (75 pitches) flat, grassy, stony
Rentals : 3 🚐 – 30 🏠.
On a wooded site beside a lake and near a leisure centre.

Surroundings :
Leisure activities : ❤ 🚴 entertainment room
Facilities :
Leisure/activities centre : climbing, walking trails

GPS
Longitude : 6.75236
Latitude : 47.95264

LORRAINE

E THOLY

3530 – Michelin map **314** I4 – pop. 1,589 – alt. 628
Paris 414 – Bruyères 21 – Épinal 30 – Gérardmer 11

Noirrupt

℘ 0329618127, *www.jpvacances.com*
Address : 15 chemin de l'Étang de Noirrupt (1.3km northwest along the D 11, follow the signs for Épinal and take road to the left)
2.9 ha (70 pitches) terraced, flat, grassy, stony
Rentals : ⌂ – 12 ⌂.

Surroundings : ⩽ ♀
Leisure activities : 🍸 ⛳ ⇆s ⚓ ✕ ⊿
Facilities : ⅙ ⊶ ⌂ ⩙ ⇶ 🕯 launderette
Nearby : ⌇

Longitude : 6.72893
Latitude : 48.08881

E VAL-D'AJOL

3340 – Michelin map **314** G5 – pop. 4,069 – alt. 380
Paris 382 – Épinal 41 – Luxeuil-les-Bains 18 – Plombières-les-Bains 10

Municipal

℘ 0329665517, *mairie@valdajol.fr*
Address : r. des Oeuvres (take the northwestern exit along the D 20, follow the signs for Plombières-les-Bains)
Opening times : from mid April to end Sept.
1 ha (46 pitches) flat, grassy
Tariff : 🕯 3.10€ ⇶ 🔲 4€ – [⅌] (6A) 3€
Rental rates : (permanent) ⅙ (1 chalet) – 2 ⌂. Per week from 300 to 400 €

Surroundings : ⩽ ⌗
Leisure activities : ⛳
Facilities : ⅙ ⊶ ⫘ ⩙ ⇶ 🕯 🔲
Nearby : ✕ 🔲 ⋈ ⌇

Longitude : 6.47586
Latitude : 47.92488

To visit a town or region, use the MICHELIN Green Guides.

ERDUN

5100 – Michelin map **307** D4 – pop. 18,557 – alt. 198
Paris 263 – Bar-le-Duc 56 – Châlons-en-Champagne 89 – Metz 78

Les Breuils

℘ 0329861531, *www.camping-lesbreuils.com*
Address : allée des Breuils (take the southwestern exit along the bypass (rocade) D S1 towards Paris and take road to the left)
Opening times : from beginning April to end Sept.
5.5 ha (162 pitches) terraced, relatively flat, flat, grassy, gravelled, wood
Tariff : 21.40€ 🕯🕯 ⇶ 🔲 [⅌] (6A) – Extra per person 5.90€ – Reservation fee 10€
Rental rates : (from beginning April to end Sept.) – 13 ⌂. Per night from 60 to 80 €
Per week from 270 to 650 € – Reservation fee 10€
⇌ sani-station 5€
A rural setting beside a lake.

Surroundings : ⌗ ♀
Leisure activities : 🍸 ⛳ ⚓ 🚲 ⊿ ⋈ ⌇ multi-sports ground
Facilities : ⅙ ⊶ ⫘ ⩙ 🕯 launderette ⬚

Longitude : 5.36598
Latitude : 49.15428

VILLEY-LE-SEC

54840 – Michelin map **307** G7 – pop. 415 – alt. 324
▶ Paris 302 – Lunéville 49 – Nancy 20 – Pont-à-Mousson 51

⋀ Camping de Villey-le-Sec

℘ 03 83 63 64 28, www.campingvilleylesec.com

Address : 34 r. de la Gare (situated 2km south along the D 909, follow the signs for Maron and take turning to the right)

Opening times : from beginning April to end Sept.

2.5 ha (100 pitches) flat, grassy

Tariff : (2012 price) 20.20€ ★★ ⇔ 🅴 🛁 (10A) – Extra per person 3.60€

Rental rates : (2012 price) (from beginning April to end Sept.) 🛶 – 4 🚐.
Per night from 40 to 60 € – Per week from 232 to 462 €

In a pleasant setting beside the Moselle river.

Surroundings : 🏞
Leisure activities : 🍴 ⛵ 🎣 volleyball
Facilities : ♿ ⚗ 🚿 🛁 🚰 launderette 🔌, ♨

GPS | Longitude : 5.98559
Latitude : 48.6526

VITTEL

88800 – Michelin map **314** D3 – pop. 5,434 – alt. 347
▶ Paris 342 – Belfort 129 – Épinal 43 – Chaumont 84

⋀ Aquadis Loisirs de Vittel

℘ 03 29 08 02 71, www.aquadis-loisirs.com

Address : 270 r. Claude Bassot (take the northeastern exit along the D 68, follow the signs for They-sous-Montfort)

Opening times : from end March to mid Oct.

3.5 ha (120 pitches) flat, grassy, fine gravel

Tariff : 16.95€ ★★ ⇔ 🅴 🛁 (10A) – Extra per person 4.85€ – Reservation fee 9.90€

Rental rates : (from end March to mid Oct.) – 12 🚐. Per night from 73 to 83 €
Per week from 196 to 500 € – Reservation fee 19.50€

🚮 sani-station 8.50€ – 12 🅴 16.95€ – 🚐 11€

Surroundings : 🌳 ♨
Leisure activities : 🎱 ⛵
Facilities : ♿ ⚗ 🚿 🚰 launderette

GPS | Longitude : 5.95605
Latitude : 48.2082

XONRUPT-LONGEMER

88400 – Michelin map **314** J4 – pop. 1,580 – alt. 714 – Winter sports : 750/1,300 m 🎿 3 ✦
▶ Paris 429 – Épinal 44 – Gérardmer 4 – Remiremont 32

⋀ La Vologne

℘ 03 29 60 87 23, www.lavologne.com

Address : 3030 rte de Retournemer (4.5km southeast along the D 67a)

Opening times : from mid April to end Sept.

2.5 ha (100 pitches) flat, grassy

Tariff : (2012 price) 11.50€ ★★ ⇔ 🅴 🛁 (6A) – Extra per person 3.40€

Rental rates : (2012 price) (from mid April to end Sept.) – 3 🏠 – 1 yurt – 1 apartment – 2 tent bungalows. Per night from 36 to 85 € – Per week from 216 to 590 – Reservation fee 15€

On a wooded site beside the river.

Surroundings : ⟨
Leisure activities : 🎱 ⛵
Facilities : ♿ ⚗ 🛁 🚰 📷
Nearby : 🏊

GPS | Longitude : 6.96919
Latitude : 48.06245

⚠ Les Jonquilles

℘ 0329633401, *www.camping-jonquilles.com*
Address : 2586 rte du Lac (2.5km southeast)
Opening times : from end April to beginning Oct.
4 ha (247 pitches) relatively flat, grassy
Tariff : 19.20€ ✝✝ ⬅ 回 🗓 (10A) – Extra per person 3.60€
🚽 sani-station
Pleasant location beside the lake.

Surroundings : ≼ Lac de Longemer and wooded mountains ⛰
Leisure activities : 🍷 📺 ⛵ 🎣
Facilities : ♿ ⚡ ♨ ❦ launderette 🔲 🚿

GPS Longitude : 6.94871
Latitude : 48.0677

Giovanni Bertolissio / hemis.fr

ourdes may be famous for its many miracles and is visited by millions of pilgrims every year, but some would say that the whole of the Midi-Pyrénées has been uniquely blessed. France's leading agricultural region – larger in size than Belgium or Switzerland – offers sanctuary to a host of exceptional fauna and flora, including the wild bears that still roam the high peaks of the Pyrenees. At sunset, the towers of medieval cities and fortresses are bathed in the evening light. Forbidding Cathar castles are stained a blood red, Albi is veiled in crimson and Toulouse is tinged a romantic pink. This list of regional marvels would not be complete without a mention of the Garonne Valley's thriving and fertile 'Garden of France', famous for its vegetables, fruit and wine. This land of milk and honey is rich in culinary traditions, and it would be a crime not to taste the delights of *foie gras* or a *confit de canard* (duck confit) before leaving.

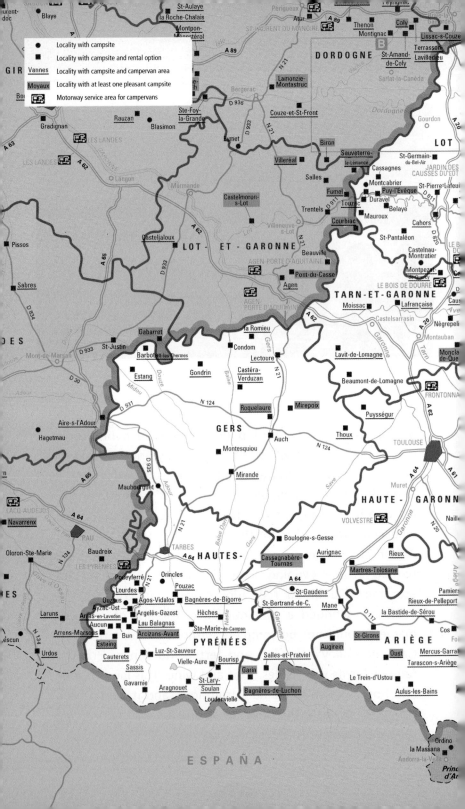

AGOS-VIDALOS

65400 – Michelin map **342** L4 – pop. 380 – alt. 450
▶ Paris 859 – Toulouse 185 – Tarbes 32 – Pau 51

Le Soleil du Pibeste

℘ 05 62 97 53 23, *www.campingpibeste.com*
Address : 16 av. Lavedan (take the southern exit, along the N 21)
Opening times : permanent
1.5 ha (90 pitches) terraced, flat and relatively flat, grassy
Tariff : (2012 price) 36€ ✦✦ ⊕ 国 (4) (10A) – Extra per person 8€
Rental rates : (2012 price) (permanent) – 26 ⛺ – 11 ⌂. Per night from 51 to 136€ –
Per week from 357 to 952€ – Reservation fee 24€
⛽ sani-station

Surroundings : ≤ ♀
Leisure activities : ♼ ✕ ⊡ ⊙ daytime ⛵ ⊿
Facilities : ᴋ ⌾ ⎘ ⊠ ▥ ⊿ ↝ ⌇ launderette ⋞

GPS
Longitude : -0.07081
Latitude : 43.03562

La Châtaigneraie

℘ 05 62 97 07 40, *www.camping-chataigneraie.com*
Address : 46, av. du Lavedan (along the N 21; at Vidalos)
Opening times : from beginning Dec. to mid Oct.
1.5 ha (100 pitches) terraced, relatively flat, flat, grassy
Tariff : (2012 price) 30.50€ ✦✦ ⊕ 国 (4) (10A) – Extra per person 5.10€ – Reservation fee 16.50€
Rental rates : (2012 price) (from beginning Dec. to mid Oct.) – 20 ⛺ – 3 studios –
1 apartment. Per week from 205 to 640€

Surroundings : ≤ ♀♀
Leisure activities : ⊡ ⛵ ⊿ ⟁
Facilities : ᴋ ⌾ ▥ ⊿ ⌇ launderette

GPS
Longitude : -0.07534
Latitude : 43.03201

*Some information or pricing may have changed since the guide went to press.
We recommend you check the price list online in advance or at the entrance
to the campsite and enquire about possible restrictions.*

AIGUES VIVES

09600 – Michelin map **343** J7 – pop. 559 – alt. 425
▶ Paris 776 – Carcassonne 63 – Castelnaudary 46 – Foix 36

La Via Natura La Serre

℘ 05 61 03 06 16, *www.camping-la-serre.com*
Address : 5 chemin de La Serre (to the west of the town)
Opening times : from beginning April to end Sept.
6.5 ha (40 pitches) undulating, terraced, flat, fine gravel
Tariff : 27€ ✦✦ ⊕ 国 (4) (5A) – Extra per person 7€
Rental rates : (from beginning April to end Sept.) – 6 ⛺ – 8 ⌂ – 1 cabin in the trees.
Per night from 80 to 180€ – Per week from 330 to 800€
⛽ sani-station 4€ – 6 国 14€
Spacious, undulating site with tree; some pitches have a view of the Pyrénées.

Surroundings : ⊜ ⊡ ♀♀
Leisure activities : ⊡ ⛵ ⚲ (mountain biking) ⊿
Facilities : ᴋ ⌾ ⎘ ⊿ ⌇ 国

GPS
Longitude : 1.87199
Latitude : 42.99741

ALBI

81000 – Michelin map **338** E7 – pop. 48,858 – alt. 174
▶ Paris 699 – Toulouse 77 – Montpellier 261 – Rodez 71

Albirondack Park

📞 05 63 60 37 06, *www.albirondack.fr*
Address : 1 allée de la Piscine
Opening times : permanent
1.8 ha (84 pitches) terraced, flat, grassy, stony
Tariff : 33.70€ 🌲🌲 ⇦ 🗉 ⚡ (10A) – Extra per person 7€
Rental rates : (permanent) ♿ (1 chalet) 🏠 – 10 🚐 – 27 🏠 – 2 cabins in the trees.
Per night from 90 to 185€ – Per week from 250 to 950€ – Reservation fee 25€
🚽 sani-station

Surroundings : 🗭 ♨♨	
Leisure activities : ⛲ ✗ ♨ hammam, jacuzzi 🛁 spa therapy centre	**GPS** Longitude : 2.16397
Facilities : ♿ 🚰 🚿 🛏 🍴 launderette 🐕	Latitude : 43.93445

ALRANCE

12430 – Michelin map **338** I6 – pop. 404 – alt. 750
▶ Paris 664 – Albi 63 – Millau 52 – Rodez 37

Les Cantarelles

📞 05 65 46 40 35, *www.lescantarelles.com*
Address : at the village, 3km south along the D 25; beside the Lac du Villefranche-de-Panat
Opening times : from beginning May to end Sept.
3.5 ha (165 pitches) relatively flat, flat, grassy
Tariff : 22€ 🌲🌲 ⇦ 🗉 ⚡ (6A) – Extra per person 4.80€
Rental rates : (from beginning April to end Oct.) – 6 🚐 – 2 tent bungalows. Per night 56€
Per week from 295 to 595€

Surroundings : ≤ 🗭 ♨♨ ⛰	
Leisure activities : ⛲ 🖼 🚣 🎣 pedalos 🚵	**GPS** Longitude : 2.68933
Facilities : ♿ 🚰 🚿 🍴 launderette	Latitude : 44.10669

For more information on visiting particular towns or regions, consult the relevant regional MICHELIN Green Guide. We also recommend you use the appropriate Michelin regional map to locate your selected campsite, to calculate distances and to work out the best route.

ARAGNOUET

65170 – Michelin map **342** N8 – pop. 244 – alt. 1,100
▶ Paris 842 – Arreau 24 – Bagnères-de-Luchon 56 – Lannemezan 51

Fouga Pic de Bern

📞 05 62 39 63 37, *fouga.marc@orange.fr*
Address : at Fabian (2.8km northeast along the D 118, follow the signs for St-Lary-Soulan, near the Neste-d'Avre)
3 ha (80 pitches) open site, terraced, relatively flat, flat, grassy
🚽 sani-station – 10 🗉

Surroundings : 🌄 ≤ ♨	
Leisure activities : ⛲ ✗ 🖼	**GPS** Longitude : 0.23608
Facilities : ♿ 🚰 🐕	Latitude : 42.78853

463

ARCIZANS-AVANT

65400 – Michelin map **342** L5 – pop. 360 – alt. 640
▶ Paris 868 – Toulouse 194 – Tarbes 41 – Pau 61

Le Lac

℘ 05 62 97 01 88, *www.camping-du-lac-pyrenees.com*
Address : 29 chemin d'Azun (take the western exit, not far from the lake)
Opening times : from mid May to mid Sept.
2 ha (97 pitches) relatively flat, flat, grassy
Tariff : (2012 price) 31€ ★★ ⇔ 🗐 (2) (10A) – Extra per person 7.90€ – Reservation fee 25€
Rental rates : (2012 price) (permanent) – 11 🏠. Per night from 90€
Per week from 305 to 780 € – Reservation fee 25€
🗐 sani-station 26€ – ⚓ (2)18€
Pretty wooden chalets.

Surroundings : 🐾 ♦♦ **Leisure activities :** 🖼 ⚓ 🚲 ⚓ **Facilities :** & ⊶ 🏖 ¶ launderette ⚓ **Nearby :** 🎣	**GPS** Longitude : -0.10803 Latitude : 42.9857

ARGELÈS-GAZOST

65400 – Michelin map **342** L6 – pop. 3,297 – alt. 462 – ♣
▶ Paris 863 – Lourdes 13 – Pau 58 – Tarbes 32

Sunêlia Les Trois Vallées ♠♦

℘ 05 62 90 35 47, *www.l3v.fr*
Address : av. des Pyrénées (take the northern exit)
Opening times : from end March to mid Oct.
11 ha (438 pitches) flat, grassy
Tariff : 42.50€ ★★ ⇔ 🗐 (2) (10A) – Extra per person 12.50€ – Reservation fee 30€
Rental rates : (from end March to mid Oct.) 🦌 – 250 🖭. Per night from 49 to 99€
Per week from 497 to 1,435€ – Reservation fee 30€
Flowers decorate the swimming and playground areas.

Surroundings : ♦♦ **Leisure activities :** ¶ ✕ 🖼 🏖 🎣 🎿 jacuzzi ⚓ 🖼 🎿 ⚓ disco, multi-sports ground, entertainment room **Facilities :** & ⊶ 🗐 🏖 ¶ launderette ⚓ **Nearby :** 🛒 ✗ 🎣	**GPS** Longitude : -0.09718 Latitude : 43.0121

ARRAS-EN-LAVEDAN

65400 – Michelin map **342** L5 – pop. 527 – alt. 700
▶ Paris 868 – Toulouse 193 – Tarbes 40 – Pau 60

L'Idéal

℘ 05 62 97 03 13, *www.camping-ideal-pyrenees.com* – alt. 600
Address : rte du Val d'Azun (300m northwest along the D 918, follow the signs for Argelès-Gazost)
Opening times : from beginning June to mid Sept.
2 ha (60 pitches) terraced, flat and relatively flat, grassy, stony
Tariff : ★ 4.40€ ⇔ 🗐 4.40€ – (2) (10A) 9.50€
Rental rates : (permanent) 🦌 – 2 🏠. Per night from 70 to 80€ – Per week from 320 to 550€
🗐 sani-station 3€

Surroundings : ◁ ♦♦ **Leisure activities :** 🖼 ⚓ 🎿 **Facilities :** & ⊶ 🗐 🏖 launderette	**GPS** Longitude : -0.11954 Latitude : 42.99483

ARRENS-MARSOUS

65400 – Michelin map **342** K7 – pop. 741 – alt. 885
▶ Paris 875 – Argelès-Gazost 13 – Cauterets 29 – Laruns 37

La Hèche

✆ 05 62 97 02 64, *www.campinglaheche.com* – ⛺

Address : 54 rte d'Azun (800m east along the D 918, follow the signs for Argelès-Gazost and take the road to the right; beside the Gave d'Arrens (river)

Opening times : from beginning June to end Sept.

5 ha (166 pitches) flat, grassy

Tariff : (2012 price) 12.50€ ⚹⚹ ⛺ 回 (4A) – Extra per person 3.60€

Rental rates : (2012 price) (permanent) – 4 . Per week from 220 to 490€
Reservation fee 75€

Surroundings :
Leisure activities :
Facilities : launderette
Nearby :

Longitude : -0.20534
Latitude : 42.95847

Le Moulian

✆ 05 62 97 41 18, *www.le-moulian.com*

Address : 42 r. du Bourg (500m southeast of the village of Marsous)

Opening times : permanent

12 ha/4 ha for camping (100 pitches) flat, grassy

Tariff : ⚹ 4.50€ ⛺ 回 4.50€ – (10A) 8€

Rental rates : (permanent) – 10 – 2 – 2 gîtes. Per night from 50 to 71€
Per week from 350 to 495€

sani-station 5€ – 9€

A pleasant setting in the valley of the Gave d'Azun (river).

Surroundings :
Leisure activities :
Facilities : launderette
Nearby :

Longitude : -0.19638
Latitude : 42.96232

Le Gerrit

✆ 05 62 97 25 85, *www.legerrit.com*

Address : 3 r. du Bourg (east of the village of Marsous)

1 ha (30 pitches) flat, grassy

Rentals : – 4 – 2 gîtes.

Surroundings :
Leisure activities :
Facilities :

Longitude : -0.2008
Latitude : 42.96513

ARVIEU

12120 – Michelin map **338** H5 – pop. 861 – alt. 730
▶ Paris 663 – Albi 66 – Millau 59 – Rodez 31

Le Doumergal

✆ 05 65 74 24 92, *www.camping-doumergal-aveyron.fr*

Address : r. de la Rivière (to the west of the town; beside a stream)

1.5 ha (27 pitches) relatively flat, flat, grassy

Rentals : 3 – 1 .

Surroundings :
Leisure activities :
Facilities :
Nearby :

Longitude : 2.66014
Latitude : 44.19066

ASTON

09310 – Michelin map **343** I8 – pop. 219 – alt. 563
▶ Paris 788 – Andorra-la-Vella 78 – Ax-les-Thermes 20 – Foix 59

Le Pas de l'Ours

☎ 05 61 64 90 33, *www.lepasdelours.fr*
Address : at Les Gesquis (south of the town, near the rapids)
Opening times : from beginning June to mid Sept.
3.5 ha (50 pitches) flat and relatively flat, grassy, rocks
Tariff : 23€ ✱✱ ⬅ 🔲 ⚡ (6A) – Extra per person 5€ – Reservation fee 7€
Rental rates : (permanent) – 11 ▦ – 16 🏠 – 4 gîtes. Per night from 50 to 87€
Per week from 195 to 579€ – Reservation fee 7€
A pleasant site with quality rental options.

Surroundings : 🏊 ⬅ 🏕 ♨
Leisure activities : 🎦 🏃 🚲 ✂ ⚓ entertainment room
Facilities : 🚿 ⊶ (Jul–Aug) 🚰 launderette
Nearby : 🎿 ⛷

GPS Longitude : 1.67181
Latitude : 42.77245

AUCH

32000 – Michelin map **336** F8 – pop. 21,792 – alt. 169
▶ Paris 713 – Agen 74 – Bordeaux 205 – Tarbes 74

Le Castagné

☎ 06 07 97 40 37, *www.domainelecastagne.com*
Address : rte de Toulouse (4km east along the N 21 and take a right turn down the Chemin de Montégut)
Opening times : from end May to beginning Oct.
70 ha/2 ha for camping (24 pitches) relatively flat, grassy
Tariff : 19€ ✱✱ ⬅ 🔲 ⚡ (10A) – Extra per person 5€
Rental rates : (permanent) – 4 ▦ – 6 🏠 – 4 🛏. Per night from 60 to 100€
Per week from 350 to 600€ – Reservation fee 20€
The site also has 4 chambres d'hôte (B & Bs).

Surroundings : 🏊 ⬅ ♨
Leisure activities : 🎦 🏃 ⚓ ⚓ ♨ 🎿 ⚓ pedalos
Facilities : 🚿 ⊶ 🚻 🚰 🖼

GPS Longitude : 0.6337
Latitude : 43.6483

AUCUN

65400 – Michelin map **342** K7 – pop. 261 – alt. 853
▶ Paris 872 – Argelès-Gazost 10 – Cauterets 26 – Lourdes 22

Lascrouts

☎ 05 62 97 42 62, *www.camping-lascrouts.com* – limited spaces for one-night stay
Address : 2 rte de Las Poueyes (700m east along the D 918, follow the signs for Argelès-Gazost and take turning to the right, 300m from the Gave d'Azun (river)
Opening times : permanent
4 ha (72 pitches) terrace, relatively flat, flat, grassy
Tariff : 12€ ✱✱ ⬅ 🔲 ⚡ (10A) – Extra per person 4€
Rental rates : (permanent) – 3 ▦ – 9 🏠 – 2 🛏 – 1 gîte. Per night from 270 to 485€
Per week from 270 to 505€

Surroundings : 🏊 ⬅
Leisure activities : 🎦 ⚓
Facilities : 🚿 ⊶ 🚻 🗄 🚰 🖼
Nearby : paragliding

GPS Longitude : -0.19193
Latitude : 42.97361

Azun Nature

℘ 05 62 97 45 05, *www.camping-azun-nature.com*

Address : 1 rte des Poueyes (700m east along the D 918, follow the signs for Argeles-Gazost and take turning to the right, 300m from the Gave d'Azun (river)

Opening times : from beginning May to end Sept.

1 ha (40 pitches) flat, grassy

Tariff : (2012 price) 17€ ♥♥ ⇔ 🔲 [½] (10A) – Extra per person 4.50€

Rental rates : (permanent) – 10 🏠 – 1 gîte. Per week from 190 to 500€

Surroundings : 🐾
Leisure activities : 🎬 🚣
Facilities : ♿ ⚡ 🏕 🚿 🔥
Nearby : 🚲 (mountain biking) 🚶 walking trails, paragliding

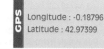

Longitude : -0.18796
Latitude : 42.97399

AUGIREIN

09800 – Michelin map **343** D7 – pop. 63 – alt. 629
▶ Paris 788 – Aspet 22 – Castillon-en-Couserans 12 – St-Béat 30

La Vie en Vert

℘ 05 61 96 82 66, *www.lavieenvert.com*

Address : east of the town; beside the Bouigane river

Opening times : from beginning June to end Aug.

0.3 ha (15 pitches) flat, grassy

Tariff : ♥ 5€ ⇔ 🔲 14€ – [½] (5A) 5€

Rental rates : 1 teepee. Per night from 100€ – Per week from 320€

Based near an old farmhouse made of local stone that has been painstakingly restored.

Surroundings : 🐾 ⛱ ⛰⛰
Leisure activities : 🎬 🚶
Facilities : ♿ ⚡ 📷 ⚡ 🚿 🔥
Nearby : ♟ ✗

Longitude : 0.91978
Latitude : 42.93161

*To make the best possible use of this guide,
please read pages 2–15 carefully.*

AULUS-LES-BAINS

09140 – Michelin map **343** G8 – pop. 221 – alt. 750
▶ Paris 807 – Foix 76 – Oust 17 – St-Girons 34

Le Coulédous

℘ 05 61 66 43 56, *www.camping-aulus-couledous.com*

Address : rte de Saint-Girons (take northwestern exit along the D 32, near the Garbet)

Opening times : permanent

1.6 ha (70 pitches) flat, grassy, stony, fine gravel

Tariff : 21.60€ ♥♥ ⇔ 🔲 [½] (10A) – Extra per person 4.50€

Rental rates : (permanent) – 18 🏠. Per night from 40 to 60€ – Per week from 210 to 450€
🚐 sani-station – 11 🔲 13.10€ – 🔌 [½]13.10€

In the centre of a park boasting some ancient trees, but the chalets and sanitary facilities are also rather old.

Surroundings : ≤ ⛰⛰
Leisure activities : 🎬 🚣
Facilities : ♿ ⚡ 🛗 🚿 launderette
Nearby : ✗ ⛷ 🚶 forest trail

Longitude : 1.33215
Latitude : 42.79394

AURIGNAC

31420 – Michelin map **343** D5 – pop. 1,187 – alt. 430
▶ Paris 750 – Auch 71 – Bagnères-de-Luchon 69 – Pamiers 92

Les Petites Pyrénées

☎ 05 61 87 06 91, *camping.aurignac@live.fr*
Address : rte de Boussens (take the southeastern exit along the D 635, to the right, near the stadium – A64 take exit 21)
Opening times : from beginning April to end Oct.
0.9 ha (48 pitches) flat, grassy
Tariff : ♀ 6€ 🚗 🔲 3€ – 🔌 (16A) 3€
Rental rates : (from beginning April to end Oct.) – 2 🛖. Per night from 50 to 60€
Per week from 250 to 360€ – Reservation fee 50€
🚐 sani-station 4€

Surroundings : 🛶 ⛰⛰
Leisure activities : 🛝
Facilities : ☎ 🚿 ♟ 🖼
Nearby : 🍴 ⛷ 🐎

	GPS
	Longitude : 0.89132
	Latitude : 43.21389

*This guide is not intended as a list of all the camping sites in France;
its aim is to provide a selection of the best sites in each category.*

AX-LES-THERMES

09110 – Michelin map **343** J8 – pop. 1,384 – alt. 720
▶ Paris 805 – Toulouse 129 – Foix 43 – Pamiers 62

Sunêlia Le Malazeou 👥

☎ 05 61 64 69 14, *www.campingmalazeou.com*
Address : RN 20, rte de l'Espagne (situated at Savignac-les-Ormeaux, 1km to the northwest, follow the signs for Foix)
Opening times : permanent
6.5 ha (244 pitches) terraced, flat, grassy, stony
Tariff : 28.50€ ♀♀ 🚗 🔲 🔌 (10A) – Extra per person 7€ – Reservation fee 30€
Rental rates : (permanent) – 7 🛖 – 70 🏠. Per night from 48 to 61€
Per week from 637 to 868€ – Reservation fee 30€
🚐 sani-station 5€
Plenty of shade; beside the Ariège but choose pitches away from the road in preference.

Surroundings : ⛰⛰
Leisure activities : 🍴 ✕ 🛖 🎆 evening 🏃 🎣 ⛵ 🏊 🛶
Facilities : ♿ ☎ 🚿 🖼 ♟ launderette 🚿

	GPS
	Longitude : 1.82538
	Latitude : 42.72852

Village Vacances Résidence et Chalets Isatis
(rental of chalets and apartments only)

☎ 05 34 09 20 05, *www.grandbleu.fr* – alt. 1,000
Address : at Ignaux (head 6km north along the D 613 and take D 52)
Opening times : from beginning June to end Sept.
2 ha terraced
Rental rates : ♿ (2 apartments) 🅿 – 20 🏠 – 20 apartments. Per night from 90€
Per week from 301 to 714€
Panoramic view over the Bonascre ski resort 'Ax 3 Domaines'.

Surroundings : 🏔 ≤ Dent d'Orlu (peak)
Leisure activities : 🛶
Facilities : 🖼 launderette

	GPS
	Longitude : 1.8449
	Latitude : 42.73015

AYZAC-OST

65400 – Michelin map **342** L4 – pop. 399 – alt. 430
▶ Paris 862 – Toulouse 188 – Tarbes 35 – Pau 54

La Bergerie

🅟 05 62 97 59 99, *www.camping-labergerie.com*
Address : 8 chemin de la Bergerie (take the southern exit along the N 21 and take road to the left)
Opening times : permanent
2 ha (105 pitches) flat, grassy
Tariff : (2012 Price) 29€ ✦✦ ⟵ 🗉 ⚡ (6A) – Extra per person 7€ – Reservation fee 15€
Rental rates : (2012 price) (permanent) – 9 ⟐. Per night from 41 to 90€
Per week from 285 to 620€

Surroundings : ⩽ ♤♤
Leisure activities : 🖻 ⚐ ⤒
Facilities : ♿ ⊶ 🛉 ⚑ 🖥
Nearby : 🍴 ✗ ⌁

Longitude : -0.0961
Latitude : 43.01824

BAGNAC-SUR-CÉLÉ

46270 – Michelin map **337** I3 – pop. 1,562 – alt. 234
▶ Paris 593 – Cahors 83 – Decazeville 16 – Figeac 15

Les Berges du Célé

🅟 06 64 99 82 33, *www.camping-sudouest.com*
Address : at La Plaine (to the southeast of the town, behind the station; beside the Célé river)
Opening times : from beginning May to end Sept.
1 ha (44 pitches) flat, grassy
Tariff : 14.80€ ✦✦ ⟵ 🗉 ⚡ (5A) – Extra per person 4.20€
Rental rates : (from beginning May to mid Sept.) – 5 ⟐ – 2 tent bungalows.
Per week from 235 to 570€
🚐 sani-station 4€ – 37 🗉 14.80€

Surroundings : ♤♤
Leisure activities : ⚐ ⤒ ⚓
Facilities : ⊶ ⤙ ⚑ 🖥
Nearby : ⚔

Longitude : 2.16009
Latitude : 44.66461

BAGNÈRES-DE-BIGORRE

65200 – Michelin map **342** M6 – pop. 8,040 – alt. 551 – ♨ (beg Mar-end Nov)
▶ Paris 829 – Lourdes 24 – Pau 66 – St-Gaudens 65

Le Monlôo

🅟 05 62 95 19 65, *www.lemonloo.com*
Address : 5 chemin de Monlôo (take the northeastern exit, along the D 938, follow the signs for Toulouse then take left turn 1.4km along the D 8, follow the signs for Tarbes and take the road to the right)
Opening times : permanent
3 ha (180 pitches) relatively flat, flat, grassy
Tariff : (2012 price) 21.40€ ✦✦ ⟵ 🗉 ⚡ (10A) – Extra per person 5.20€
Rental rates : (2012 price) (permanent) – 22 ⟐ – 5 🏠. Per night from 52 to 91€
Per week from 260 to 665€
🚐 sani-station – 2 🗉 14€

Surroundings : ⧖ ⩽ ♤♤
Leisure activities : 🖻 ⚐ ⚔ ⤒ ⚒
Facilities : ♿ ⊶ ⫘ 🛉 ⚑ launderette

Longitude : 0.15107
Latitude : 43.0817

Les Fruitiers

📞 05 62 95 25 97, *www.camping-les-fruitiers.com*
Address : 9 rte de Toulouse
Opening times : from mid April to end Oct.
1.5 ha (112 pitches) flat, grassy
Tariff : (2012 price) 🏕 4.20€ 🚗 🔲 4.20€ – 🔌 (6A) 5€
Rental rates : (2012 price) (from mid April to end Oct.) 🏠 – 2 🚐 – 3 apartments.
Per night from 50€ – Per week from 250 to 400€
🚐 sani-station 5.50€

Surroundings : ≤ Pic du Midi (peak) 🌲🌲
Leisure activities : 🏛 🏊
Facilities : 🚿 ⬆ 📷
Nearby : 🔳

GPS
Longitude : 0.15746
Latitude : 43.07108

BAGNÈRES-DE-LUCHON

31110 – Michelin map **343** B8 – pop. 2,600 – alt. 630 – Winter sports : Superbagnères : 1,440/2,260 m 🎿
1 🎿 14 🎿
▶ Paris 814 – Bagnères-de-Bigorre 96 – St-Gaudens 48 – Tarbes 98

Pradelongue

📞 05 61 79 86 44, *www.camping-pradelongue.com*
Address : Moustajon (situated 2km north along the D 125, follow the signs for Moustajon, near the Intermarché supermarket)
Opening times : from beginning April to end Sept.
4 ha (135 pitches) flat, grassy, stony
Tariff : 🏕 6.75€ 🚗 🔲 6.95€ – 🔌 (10A) 4€ – Reservation fee 13€
Rental rates : (from beginning April to end Sept.) 🏠 – 18 🚐. Per night from 140 to 265€
Per week from 260 to 640€ – Reservation fee 13€
🚐 sani-station – 7 🔲 18€ – 🛒 11€

Surroundings : ≤ 🏞 🌲🌲
Leisure activities : 🏛 🏊 🏊
Facilities : ♿ 🚿 �🧺 ♨ 🚿 🚽 ⬆ launderette
Nearby : 🛒 🐎

GPS
Longitude : 0.6075
Latitude : 42.81333

Les Myrtilles 🔺

📞 05 61 79 89 89, *www.camping-myrtilles.com* – ℝ
Address : at Pradech (2.5km north along the D 125, towards Moustajon; beside a stream)
Opening times : permanent
2 ha (100 pitches) flat, grassy
Tariff : (2012 price) 18.80€ 🏕🏕 🚗 🔲 🔌 (3A) – Extra per person 4.90€
Rental rates : (2012 price) (permanent) – 19 🚐 – 1 gîte. Per night from 42 to 61€
Per week from 313 to 603€ – Reservation fee 14€

Surroundings : ≤ 🏞 🌲
Leisure activities : 🍽 ✕ 🏛 🚴 🏊 🚲 🏊
Facilities : ♿ 🚿 🚐 ☑ 🧺 ♨ 🚿 🚽 ⬆ launderette 🧺
Nearby : 🐎

GPS
Longitude : 0.59975
Latitude : 42.81663

The prices listed were supplied by the campsite owners in 2012
(if prices were not available, those from the previous year are given).
The fees should be regarded as basic charges and may fluctuate
with inflation.

Domaine Arôme Vanille ♣♣

📞 05 61 79 00 38, *camping-aromevanille.com*
Address : rte de Subercarrère, at Montauban-de-Luchon (located 1.5km east along the D 27)
Opening times : from mid April to mid Oct.
5 ha (250 pitches) flat and relatively flat, grassy
Tariff : 20.50€ ♣♣ ⇔ 🗉 ⚡ (10A) – Extra per person 4.50€
Rental rates : (permanent) – 8 🛏 – 21 🏠. Per night from 60 to 75€
Per week from 319 to 639€ – Reservation fee 10€

Surroundings : 🌲 ⌂ ῼ
Leisure activities : 🏊 ✗ 🎯 🚣
Facilities : ♿ ⊶ 🔥 🚰 🖃 🚿

GPS Longitude : 0.60814
Latitude : 42.79496

BARBOTAN-LES-THERMES

32150 – Michelin map **336** B6
▶ Paris 703 – Aire-sur-l'Adour 37 – Auch 75 – Condom 37

Club Airotel Le Lac de l'Uby ♣♣

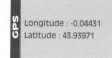

📞 05 62 09 53 91, *www.camping-uby.com*
Address : av. du Lac (located 1.5km southwest, follow the signs for Cazaubon and take the turning to the left, at the leisure and activity park (beside the lake)
Opening times : from beginning April to end Oct.
6 ha (274 pitches) flat, grassy, gravelled
Tariff : (2012 price) 21.50€ ♣♣ ⇔ 🗉 ⚡ (10A) – Extra per person 7€ – Reservation fee 8€
Rental rates : (2012 price) (from beginning April to mid Oct.) – 50 🛏 – 7 🏠.
Per night from 67 to 108€ – Per week from 215 to 720€
🚐 sani-station – 15 🗉 15.50€
There is a pleasant parking spot for campervans 300m away.

Surroundings : 🌲 ≤ ῼῼ ⛰
Leisure activities : ✗ 🏠 🎯 🚣 🚴 🐎 🎣 multi-sports ground, skate park
Facilities : ♿ ⊶ ∭ 🔥 🚰 launderette, refrigerators
Nearby : 🍴 🏊 ≅ (beach) pedalos

GPS Longitude : -0.04431
Latitude : 43.93971

LA BASTIDE DE SÉROU

09240 – Michelin map **343** G6 – pop. 959 – alt. 410
▶ Paris 779 – Foix 18 – Le Mas-d'Azil 17 – Pamiers 38

Club Airotel L'Arize

📞 05 61 65 81 51, *www.camping-arize.com*
Address : take the eastern exit along the D 117, follow the signs for Foix then continue 1.5km along the D 15, follow signs to Nescus to the right; beside the river
Opening times : from beginning March to mid Nov.
7.5 ha/1.5 (90 pitches) flat, grassy
Tariff : 31.60€ ♣♣ ⇔ 🗉 ⚡ (10A) – Extra per person 4.60€ – Reservation fee 19€
Rental rates : (from beginning March to mid Nov.) – 16 🛏 – 4 🏠. Per night from 36 to 127€
Per week from 252 to 889€ – Reservation fee 19€
🚐 sani-station 4.50€ – 9 🗉 17.50€ – 🚐 ⚡14.50€
A small stream runs through the site, separating the shady side from the sunny side!

Surroundings : 🌲 ⌂ ῼῼ
Leisure activities : 🏠 🚣 🚴 🏊 🎣
Facilities : ♿ ⊶ 🔥 🚿 🚽 🚰 launderette
Nearby : ✗ 🐎

GPS Longitude : 1.44509
Latitude : 43.00168

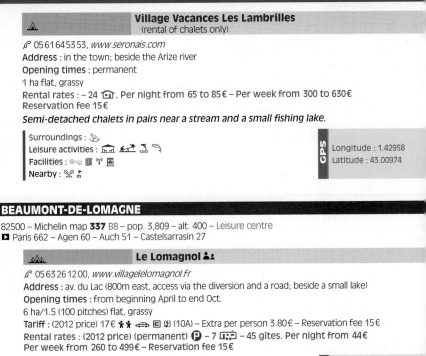

Village Vacances Les Lambrilles
(rental of chalets only)

📞 05 61 64 53 53, *www.seronais.com*

Address : in the town; beside the Arize river
Opening times : permanent
1 ha flat, grassy
Rental rates : – 24 🏠. Per night from 65 to 85€ – Per week from 300 to 630€
Reservation fee 15€

Semi-detached chalets in pairs near a stream and a small fishing lake.

Surroundings : 🐟
Leisure activities : 🎮 ⛵ ♨ 🎣
Facilities : 🔌 🚿 ♨ 🔥
Nearby : 🍴 ⛰

GPS Longitude : 1.42958
Latitude : 43.00974

BEAUMONT-DE-LOMAGNE

82500 – Michelin map **337** B8 – pop. 3,809 – alt. 400 – Leisure centre
▶ Paris 662 – Agen 60 – Auch 51 – Castelsarrasin 27

Le Lomagnol 👥

📞 05 63 26 12 00, *www.villagelelomagnol.fr*

Address : av. du Lac (800m east, access via the diversion and a road; beside a small lake)
Opening times : from beginning April to end Oct.
6 ha/1.5 (100 pitches) flat, grassy
Tariff : (2012 price) 17€ 👥 🚐 🔲 (10A) – Extra per person 3.80€ – Reservation fee 15€
Rental rates : (2012 price) (permanent) 🅿 – 7 🏠 – 45 gîtes. Per night from 44€
Per week from 260 to 499€ – Reservation fee 15€

Surroundings : 🌲 💧
Leisure activities : 🎮 🎬 evening 🏃 ♨ jacuzzi ⛵ 🚴 🍴 ⛰ ♨ 🎣
pedalos 🛶
Facilities : 🔌 🚿 🚽 ♨ 🔥
Nearby : 🍴 🛤 fitness trail

GPS Longitude : 0.99864
Latitude : 43.88295

Some campsites benefit from proximity to a municipal leisure centre.

BÉDUER

46100 – Michelin map **337** H4 – pop. 730 – alt. 260
▶ Paris 572 – Cahors 63 – Figeac 9 – Villefranche-de-Rouergue 36

Pech Ibert

📞 05 65 40 05 85, *www.camping-pech-ibert.com*

Address : at Pech Ibert (located 1km northwest along the D 19, follow the signs for Cajarc and take turning to the right)
Opening times : from mid March to mid Nov.
1 ha (18 pitches) flat, grassy, fine gravel, stony
Tariff : 👤 3.20€ 🚐 1.20€ 🔲 3.20€ – 🔌 (6A) 3.30€
Rental rates : (from mid March to mid Nov.) – 3 🏠 – 4 🏠 – 2 tents. Per night from 10 to 85€
Per week from 290 to 665€ – Reservation fee 10€
🚐 sani-station 6€ – 2 🔲 8.50€ – 🚐 8.50€

Surroundings : 🌲 💧
Leisure activities : 🍴 🎮 ⛵ ♨
Facilities : ♿ 🔌 🚿 ♨ 🔥 refrigerators
Nearby : 🍴

GPS Longitude : 1.9375
Latitude : 44.57833

BELAYE

46140 – Michelin map **337** D5 – pop. 216 – alt. 209
Paris 594 – Cahors 30 – Fumel 21 – Gourdon 46

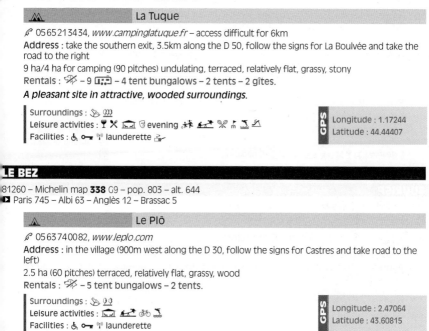

La Tuque

05 65 21 34 34, *www.campinglatuque.fr* – access difficult for 6km
Address : take the southern exit, 3.5km along the D 50, follow the signs for La Boulvée and take the road to the right
9 ha/4 ha for camping (90 pitches) undulating, terraced, relatively flat, grassy, stony
Rentals : 9 – 4 tent bungalows – 2 tents – 2 gîtes.
A pleasant site in attractive, wooded surroundings.

Surroundings :
Leisure activities : evening
Facilities : launderette

Longitude : 1.17244
Latitude : 44.44407

LE BEZ

81260 – Michelin map **338** G9 – pop. 803 – alt. 644
Paris 745 – Albi 63 – Anglès 12 – Brassac 5

Le Plô

05 63 74 00 82, *www.leplo.com*
Address : in the village (900m west along the D 30, follow the signs for Castres and take road to the left)
2.5 ha (60 pitches) terraced, relatively flat, grassy, wood
Rentals : – 5 tent bungalows – 2 tents.

Surroundings :
Leisure activities :
Facilities : launderette

Longitude : 2.47064
Latitude : 43.60815

We welcome your feedback on our listed campsites.
Please email us at: campingfrance@tp.michelin.com
Many thanks in advance!

BOISSE-PENCHOT

12300 – Michelin map **338** F3 – pop. 539 – alt. 169
Paris 594 – Toulouse 193 – Rodez 46 – Aurillac 65

Le Roquelongue

05 65 63 39 67, *www.camping-roquelongue.com*
Address : 4.5km northwest along the D 963, D 21 and take the D 42, follow the signs for Boisse-Penchot, near the Lot river (direct access)
Opening times : permanent
3.5 ha (66 pitches) flat, grassy, stony
Tariff : 4.40€ 8.50€ – (10A) 4.40€
Rental rates : (permanent) – 8 – 7 . Per night from 56 to 96€
Per week from 300 to 620€

Surroundings :
Leisure activities : pedalos
Facilities :

Longitude : 2.22179
Latitude : 44.58224

BOULOGNE-SUR-GESSE

31350 – Michelin map **343** B5 – pop. 1,612 – alt. 320
▶ Paris 735 – Auch 47 – Aurignac 24 – Castelnau-Magnoac 13

 Village Vacances Le Lac
(rental of chalets only)

☏ 05 61 88 20 54, *www.ville-boulogne-sur-gesse.fr*
Address : rte du Lac (1.3km southeast along the D 633, follow the signs for Montréjeau and take turning to the left, 300m from the lake)
Opening times : permanent
2 ha terraced
Rental rates : (2012 price) 🅿 – 24 🏠. Per week from 265 to 560€

Surroundings : ⌕ ⩻ on the lake ♀
Leisure activities : 🖼 🔧
Facilities : ⚯ 🗄 ⯍ 🖼
Nearby : 🛒 🍽 ✕ 🛶 ⤢ ⁒ 🔦 🛶 🏊 pedalos

 Longitude : 0.65712
Latitude : 43.28328

BOURISP

65170 – Michelin map **342** O6 – pop. 147 – alt. 790
▶ Paris 828 – Toulouse 155 – Tarbes 70 – Lourdes 66

 Le Rioumajou

☏ 05 62 39 48 32, *www.camping-le-rioumajou.com*
Address : 1.3km northwest along the D 929, follow the signs for Arreau and take road to the left; beside the Neste d'Aure river
5 ha (240 pitches) flat, grassy, fine gravel, stony
Rentals : – 5 🛖 – 11 tent bungalows.
🚐 sani-station

Surroundings : ❄ ⌕ ▭ ♀
Leisure activities : 🍽 ✕ 🖼 ⊙ daytime ⤢ ⁒ 🛶 🔧
Facilities : 🚻 ⚬ 🖽 🛁 ⩎ ⯔ launderette 🏊 🚿

Longitude : 0.33943
Latitude : 42.83786

> *Do not confuse:*
> 🔺 *to* 🔺🔺🔺 *: MICHELIN classification*
> *with*
> ⋆ *to* ⋆⋆⋆⋆⋆ *: official classification*

BRASSAC

81260 – Michelin map **338** G9 – pop. 1,396 – alt. 487
▶ Paris 747 – Albi 65 – Anglès 14 – Castres 26

 Municipal de la Lande

☏ 05 63 74 09 11, *camping.brassac.fr*
Address : at the stade (take the southwestern exit towards Castres and take a right turn after the bridge; near the Agout river and crossed by a stream)
Opening times : from mid June to end Sept.
1 ha (50 pitches) flat, grassy
Tariff : (2012 Price) ♦ 2€ 🚗 1.30€ 🔲 1.70€ – ⚡ (5A) 1.70€

Surroundings : ⌕ ♀♀
Leisure activities : 🖼
Facilities : 🗄 ▨ 🖼
Nearby : 🚲 ⁒ 🛶 🔧

Longitude : 2.4952
Latitude : 43.63067

BRETENOUX

46130 – Michelin map **337** H2 – pop. 1,342 – alt. 136
◨ Paris 521 – Brive-la-Gaillarde 44 – Cahors 83 – Figeac 48

⚠ La Bourgnatelle

𝒫 05 65 10 89 04, *www.dordogne-vacances.fr*
Address : take the northwestern exit, turn left after the bridge
2.3 ha (135 pitches) flat, grassy
Rentals : 74 ⬛ – 5 tent bungalows.
⬛ sani-station – 3 ▣

| |
Surroundings : ⬳ ♨♨⛰
Leisure activities : 🎬 🏕 ⛷ ⚓
Facilities : ♿ ⚷ launderette ⛵
Nearby : ✂

GPS Longitude : 1.83772
Latitude : 44.91679

BRUSQUE

12360 – Michelin map **338** J8 – pop. 309 – alt. 465
◨ Paris 698 – Albi 91 – Béziers 75 – Lacaune 30

🏔 Village Vacances Val-VVF Le Domaine de Céras

𝒫 05 65 49 50 66, *www.vvfvillages.fr*
Address : 1.6km south along the D 92, follow the signs for Arnac; beside the Dourdou river and a small lake
Opening times : from end April to end Sept.
14 ha (160 pitches) undulating, flat, grassy
Tariff : (2012 Price) 33.60€ ✦✦ ⬅ ▣ ⊠ (10A) – Extra per person 4.30€ – Reservation fee 32€
Rental rates : (2012 price) (from end April to end Sept.) ♿ (3 apartments) – 67 apartments – 20 tent bungalows. Per night from 50 to 71€ – Per week from 350 to 497€ – Reservation fee 32€

In a peaceful and secluded small leafy valley.

Surroundings : ⬳ ≤ ♨♨⛰
Leisure activities : ♟ ✗ 🎬 🎣 🏕 ⛷ ✂ 🏊 (lake) ⚓ fitness trail, multi-sports ground
Facilities : ⚷ ⛏ launderette ⛵

GPS Longitude : 2.95742
Latitude : 43.75666

In order for the guide to remain wholly objective, the selection of campsites is made on an entirely independent basis.

BUN

65400 – Michelin map **342** L5 – pop. 137 – alt. 800
◨ Paris 874 – Toulouse 198 – Tarbes 44 – Pau 64

⚠ Le Bosquet

𝒫 05 62 97 07 81, *info@locations-valdazun.com* – limited spaces for one-night stay
Address : exit west from the town – recommended route for caravans via the D 918, follow the signs for Aucun and then take D 13
1.5 ha (35 pitches) flat, grassy
Rentals : 2 ⬛.

Surroundings : ⬳ ≤ ♨
Leisure activities : 🎬
Facilities : ♿ ⚷ launderette

GPS Longitude : -0.16536
Latitude : 42.97459

LES CABANNES

81170 – Michelin map **338** D6 – pop. 353 – alt. 200
▶ Paris 653 – Albi 27 – Montauban 57 – Rodez 80

Aquadis Loisirs Le Garissou

℘ 05 63 56 27 14, www.aquadis-loisirs.com
Address : 500m to the west along the D 600, follow the signs for Vindrac and take road to the left
Opening times : from beginning April to beginning Nov.
7 ha/4 ha for camping (72 pitches) terraced, flat, grassy, stony
Tariff : 15.90€ ♦♦ ⇔ 🗉 ⚡ (16A) – Extra per person 4€ – Reservation fee 9.90€
Rental rates : (from beginning March to beginning Nov.) Ⓟ – 30 🏠. Per night from 79€
– Per week from 196 to 650€ – Reservation fee 19.50€
🚐 30 🗉 15.90€ – 🗑11€
Attractive elevated location.

Surroundings : 🐾 ≤ Cordes-sur-Ciel and valley 🗆 ♀
Leisure activities : 🏠 🚣 ♪ 🏊 ⛖ multi-sports ground
Facilities : ♿ ⚬ⁱ 🆑 🚿 ♔ launderette

GPS Longitude : 1.94247
Latitude : 44.06767

CAHORS

46000 – Michelin map **337** E5 – pop. 19,948 – alt. 135
▶ Paris 575 – Agen 85 – Albi 110 – Bergerac 108

Rivière de Cabessut

℘ 05 65 30 06 30, www.cabessut.com
Address : r. de la Rivière (3km south along the D 911 towards Rodez then take the road to the left, take quai Ludo-Rolles; beside the Lot river)
Opening times : from beginning April to end Sept.
2 ha (113 pitches) flat, grassy
Tariff : ♦ 5€ ⇔ 🗉 8€ – ⚡ (10A) 2€
Rental rates : (from beginning April to end Sept.) 🚲 – 8 🚐. Per night from 60€
Per week from 310 to 590€
🚐 sani-station 4€ – 9 🗉 – 🗑11€

Surroundings : 🗆 ♀♀
Leisure activities : 🏠 🚣 ♪ 🏊 🚲
Facilities : ♿ ⚬ⁱ 🚽 🏢 🚿 ♔ 🖻
Nearby : ⛖

GPS Longitude : 1.44192
Latitude : 44.46364

LES CAMMAZES

81540 – Michelin map **338** E10 – pop. 309 – alt. 610
▶ Paris 736 – Aurillac 241 – Castres 35 – Figeac 183

La Rigole

℘ 05 63 73 28 99, www.campingdelarigole.com
Address : rte du Barrage (take the southern exit from the D 629 and road to the left)
Opening times : from beginning May to end Sept.
3 ha (66 pitches) terrace, flat and relatively flat, grassy
Tariff : (2012 price) 24€ ♦♦ ⇔ 🗉 ⚡ (13A) – Extra per person 5.30€
Rental rates : (2012 price) (from beginning May to end Sept.) – 10 🚐 – 9 🏠.
Per night from 42 to 49€ – Per week from 252 to 680€
🚐 3 🗉 10.60€

Surroundings : 🐾 🗆 ♀♀
Leisure activities : ♛ ✕ 🚣 🚲 🏊
Facilities : ♿ ⚬ⁱ 🚿 ♔ launderette ⚖

GPS Longitude : 2.08625
Latitude : 43.40787

CANET-DE-SALARS

12290 – Michelin map **338** I5 – pop. 416 – alt. 850
▶ Paris 654 – Pont-de-Salars 9 – Rodez 33 – St-Beauzély 28

Les Castels Le Caussanel ♣♣

℘ 05 65 46 85 19, *www.lecaussanel.com*
Address : at the Lac de Pareloup (2.7km southeast along the D 538 and take a right turn)
Opening times : from beginning May to beginning Sept.
10 ha (235 pitches) terraced, flat and relatively flat, grassy
Tariff : 34.80€ ♣♣ ⇦ 🅴 🄵 (6A) – Extra per person 7.50€ – Reservation fee 30€
Rental rates : (from beginning May to beginning Sept.) – 86 🛖 – 34 🏠.
Per week from 417 to 896€ – Reservation fee 30€

Surroundings : ⌇ ⩽ on the lake ♀ ⌂
Leisure activities : 🍴 ✗ 🎬 ▨ ⵗ 🛝 ⵘ ⛄ 🎱 🏊 ⵏ pedalos, boats for hire, farm/petting farm ⵝ multi-sports ground, entertainment room
Facilities : ♿ ⚷ 🅆♨ ⵓ ⵡ ⵟ launderette ⵥ ⵧ
Nearby : disco

GPS Longitude : 2.76651
Latitude : 44.21426

Soleil Levant

℘ 05 65 46 03 65, *www.camping-soleil-levant.com*
Address : at the Lac de Pareloup (3.7km southeast along the D 538 and D 993, follow the signs for Salles-Curan, to the left, before the bridge)
Opening times : from end May to end Sept.
11 ha (206 pitches) terraced, flat and relatively flat, grassy
Tariff : 27.50€ ♣♣ ⇦ 🅴 🄵 (6A) – Extra per person 7.50€
Rental rates : (from end May to end Sept.) – 15 🛖. Per week from 195 to 695€
A pleasant location beside the Lac de Pareloup.

Surroundings : ⌇ ⩽ ♀♀ ⌂
Leisure activities : 🍴 🎬 🛝 ⵏ ⵝ
Facilities : ♿ ⚷ 🅆♨ ⵓ ⵟ launderette
Nearby : ⵗ ⚓

GPS Longitude : 2.77795
Latitude : 44.21551

*The classification (1 to 5 tents, **black** or **red**) that we award to selected sites in this guide is our own system. It should not be confused with the classification (1 to 5 stars) of official organisations.*

CAPDENAC-GARE

12700 – Michelin map **338** E3 – pop. 4,492 – alt. 175
▶ Paris 587 – Decazeville 20 – Figeac 9 – Maurs 24

Municipal les Rives d'Olt

℘ 05 65 80 88 87, *www.campingcapdenac.fr*
Address : 8 bd Paul Ramadier (take the western exit along the D 994, follow the signs for Figeac and take the turning to the left before the bridge, near the Lot river)
Opening times : from beginning April to end Sept.
1.3 ha (60 pitches) flat, grassy
Tariff : ♣ 3.70€ ⇦ 🅴 4.60€ – 🄵 (16A) 3€
🛢 sani-station 2€
Pleasant setting, lots of green space and a good amount of shade.

Surroundings : ⊏ ⵳⵳
Leisure activities : ⵏ
Facilities : ♿ ⚷ ⵓ ⵟ 🖼
Nearby : ⵥ 🍴 ✗ ⵘ ⵎ ⵣ sports trail

GPS Longitude : 2.07294
Latitude : 44.57209

CARLUCET

46500 – Michelin map **337** F3 – pop. 228 – alt. 322
▶ Paris 542 – Cahors 47 – Gourdon 26 – Labastide-Murat 11

Château de Lacomté

📞 05 65 38 75 46, *www.chateaulacomte.com*
Address : at Lacomté (located 1.8km northwest of the town, by the castle)
Opening times : from mid May to mid Sept.
12 ha/4 ha for camping (100 pitches) terraced, relatively flat, flat, grassy, wood
Tariff : 36€ ♣♣ ⛺ 🅴 💧 (10A) – Extra per person 10€ – Reservation fee 15€
Rental rates : (from mid May to mid Sept.) – 4 🚐 – 5 🏠 – 2 ⛺ – 1 gîte.
Per night from 40 to 99€ – Per week from 250 to 650€ – Reservation fee 15€

Camping reserved for adults (18 yrs and over).

Surroundings : 🏊 ⌂ 🌳
Leisure activities : 🍷 ✕ 🎦 🎯 🚲 ✂ 🛶
Facilities : ♿ ⚡ 🚿 ✈ 🍴 launderette 🐕

GPS Longitude : 1.59692
Latitude : 44.72881

> *There are several different types of sani-station ('borne' in French) – sanitation points providing fresh water and disposal points for grey water. See page 12 for further details.*

CARMAUX

81400 – Michelin map **338** E6 – pop. 10,210 – alt. 241 – Leisure centre
▶ Paris 720 – Toulouse 96 – Albi 18 – Castres 63

Cap' Découverte

📞 05 63 80 15 15, *www.cap-decouverte.net/index.php*
Address : Le Garric
1 ha (105 pitches) flat, grassy, stony
Rentals : 2 yurts – 10 tents.
🚽 sani-station
In the middle of a large leisure centre.

Surroundings : 🏊
Facilities : ♿ 🖥
Nearby : 🍷 ✕ 🎯 🚲 ⛵ 🎣 cable wakeboarding, turf skiing, summer luge, go-carts

GPS Longitude : 2.13641
Latitude : 44.02124

CASSAGNABÈRE-TOURNAS

31420 – Michelin map **343** C5 – pop. 415 – alt. 380
▶ Paris 758 – Auch 78 – Bagnères-de-Luchon 65 – Pamiers 101

Pré Fixe

📞 05 61 98 71 00, *www.instudio4.com/pre-fixe* ✂
Address : rte de St-Gaudens (situated southwest of the town)
1.2 ha (40 pitches) terraced, flat, grassy
Decorative flowers and shrubs.

Surroundings : 🏊 ⌂ 🌳
Leisure activities : 🎦 🛶
Facilities : ♿ ⚡ 🖥
Nearby : ✂

GPS Longitude : 0.79167
Latitude : 43.22889

CASSAGNES

46700 – Michelin map **337** C4 – pop. 209 – alt. 185
▶ Paris 577 – Cahors 34 – Cazals 15 – Fumel 19

Le Carbet

📞 05 65 36 61 79, *www.camping-le-carbet.fr*
Address : at La Barte (located 1.5km northwest along the D 673, follow the signs for Fumel; near a lake)
Opening times : from mid April to mid Sept.
3 ha (29 pitches) open site, terraced, flat, grassy, stony
Tariff : 17€ ★★ ⮑ ▣ ⚡ (6A) – Extra per person 6€ – Reservation fee 10€
Rental rates : (from mid April to mid Sept.) – 10 🚐. Per night from 35 to 49€
Per week from 199 to 500€ – Reservation fee 10€

Surroundings : 🛏 🎋
Leisure activities : 🍸 ✗ 🛶 ⚓
Facilities : 🔑 ⛺ 🚰 ▣ 🚿

GPS Longitude : 1.13102
Latitude : 44.56338

CASTELNAU-DE-MONTMIRAL

81140 – Michelin map **338** C7 – pop. 950 – alt. 287
▶ Paris 645 – Albi 31 – Bruniquel 22 – Cordes-sur-Ciel 22

Le Chêne Vert

📞 05 63 33 16 10, *www.camping-du-chene-vert.com*
Address : at Travers du Rieutort (head 3.5km northwest along the D 964, follow the signs for Caussade, take D 1 and D 87, follow the signs for Penne; on the left)
Opening times : from beginning June to mid Sept.
10 ha/2 ha for camping (130 pitches) undulating, terraced, relatively flat, flat, grassy
Tariff : 22€ ★★ ⮑ ▣ ⚡ (10A) – Extra per person 5.10€ – Reservation fee 15€
Rental rates : (permanent) – 37 🏠 – 5 tent bungalows. Per week from 200 to 680€
Reservation fee 15€
🚐 2 ▣ 9.50€ – 🔋 9.50€

Surroundings : 🏞 ⇇ 🛏 🎋
Leisure activities : 🍸 ✗ 🖼 🛶 ⚓
Facilities : ♿ 🔑 🚰 ▣ 🚿 🚿
Leisure/activities centre (800m) : ⛳ 🎣 ⚓ (beach) ⛷

GPS Longitude : 1.78947
Latitude : 43.97702

The guide covers all 22 regions of France – see the map and list of regions on pages 4–5.

CASTELNAU-MONTRATIER

46170 – Michelin map **337** E6 – pop. 1,837 – alt. 240
▶ Paris 600 – Cahors 30 – Caussade 24 – Lauzerte 23

Municipal des 3 Moulins

📞 05 65 21 94.21, *www.castelnau-montratier.fr* – ⚑
Address : rte de Lauzette (take the northwestern exit along the D 19)
Opening times : from mid June to mid Sept.
1 ha (50 pitches) terraced, flat, grassy
Tariff : (2012 price) ★ 2.50€ ⮑ ▣ 2.60€ – ⚡ (10A) 1.50€

Surroundings : 🎋
Facilities : 🚿
Nearby : ⛳ ⚓ ⛷

GPS Longitude : 1.35119
Latitude : 44.27328

CASTÉRA-VERDUZAN

32410 – Michelin map **336** E7 – pop. 937 – alt. 114 – Leisure centre
▶ Paris 720 – Agen 61 – Auch 40 – Condom 20

La Plage de Verduzan

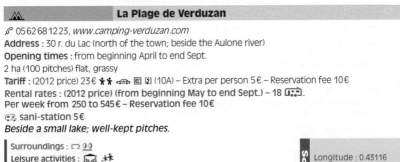

📞 05 62 68 12 23, *www.camping-verduzan.com*
Address : 30 r. du Lac (north of the town; beside the Aulone river)
Opening times : from beginning April to end Sept.
2 ha (100 pitches) flat, grassy
Tariff : (2012 price) 23 € ♦♦ ⇐ 🔲 [ƒ] (10A) – Extra per person 5 € – Reservation fee 10 €
Rental rates : (2012 price) (from beginning May to end Sept.) – 18 🔲.
Per week from 250 to 545 € – Reservation fee 10 €
🚰 sani-station 5 €
Beside a small lake; well-kept pitches.

Surroundings : 🗀 ⓞⓞ
Leisure activities : 🖼 🏃
Facilities : 🚿 ⚷ 🚱 🧺 🍴 🅿
Nearby : 🍴 ⩼ (beach) ⚓ pedalos

GPS
Longitude : 0.43116
Latitude : 43.80817

CAUSSADE

82300 – Michelin map **337** F7 – pop. 6,586 – alt. 109
▶ Paris 606 – Albi 70 – Cahors 38 – Montauban 28

Municipal la Piboulette

📞 05 63 93 09 07, *mairie-caussade.fr*
Address : located 1km northeast along the D 17, follow the signs for Puylaroque and take the turning to the left, by the stadium, 200m from a lake
Opening times : from beginning May to end Sept.
1.5 ha (100 pitches) flat, grassy
Tariff : (2012 price) ♦ 2.70 € ⇐ 🔲 1.90 € – [ƒ] (6A) 1.80 €
🚰 sani-station 4 € – 5 🔲 4 €

Surroundings : 🏊 ⓞⓞ
Facilities : 🚿 ⚷ 🚱 🧺 launderette
Nearby : 🏕 🍴 🍴 ⩧ fitness trail

GPS
Longitude : 1.54624
Latitude : 44.16877

CAUTERETS

65110 – Michelin map **342** L7 – pop. 1,118 – alt. 932 – ⚐ – Winter sports : 1,000/2,350 m ⛷3 ⛷18 ⛷
▶ Paris 880 – Argelès-Gazost 17 – Lourdes 30 – Pau 75

Les Glères

📞 05 62 92 55 34, *www.gleres.com*
Address : 19 rte de Pierrefitte (take the northern exit along the D 920; beside the Gave de Cauterets (river)
Opening times : from beginning Dec. to end Oct.
1.2 ha (80 pitches) flat, grassy, fine gravel
Tariff : 19.10 € ♦♦ ⇐ 🔲 [ƒ] (6A) – Extra per person 4.55 € – Reservation fee 10 €
Rental rates : (from beginning Dec. to end Oct.) 🍴 – 16 🔲 – 5 🏠. Per night 87 €
Per week 599 €
🚰 43 🔲 18.50 €
Near the centre of the village.

Surroundings : ❄ ⩤ 🗀 ⓞⓞ
Leisure activities : 🖼 🏕 ⩧
Facilities : 🚿 ⚷ 🧺 ♨ 🚱 🧺 launderette
Nearby : 🍴 skating rink

GPS
Longitude : -0.11275
Latitude : 42.89625

GR 10

☎ 06 20 30 25 85, *www.gr10camping.com*
Address : at Concé (2.8 km north along the D 920, follow the signs for Lourdes, near the Gave de Pau (river)
Opening times : from end June to beginning Sept.
1.5 ha (61 pitches) relatively flat, flat, grassy, stony
Tariff : 22€ ✱✱ ⇔ 🔲 🔾 (10A) – Extra per person 6.50€
Rental rates : (permanent) – 20 🚐 – 1 🏠 – 2 gîtes. Per week from 450 to 690€
🚏 sani-station – 7 🔲 18€

Surroundings : 🏊 ⇐ 🎣 ♀
Leisure activities : 🏓 🛶 ※ ⏣ forest trail, rafting and canyoning, climbing
Facilities : ♿ ☛ 🚮 [cc] 🏧 ⁱ launderette

| GPS | Longitude : -0.09892 |
| | Latitude : 42.91107 |

Le Cabaliros

☎ 05 62 92 55 36, *www.camping-cabaliros.com*
Address : 93 av. du Mamelon Vert (1.6 km north following signs for Lourdes, across the bridge to left; beside the Gave de Pau (river)
Opening times : from end May to end Sept.
2 ha (100 pitches) relatively flat to hilly, grassy
Tariff : 18.30€ ✱✱ ⇔ 🔲 🔾 (6A) – Extra per person 5.10€
Rental rates : (from beginning Dec. to beginning Oct.) – 6 🚐. Per night from 60 to 65€
Per week from 260 to 550€ – Reservation fee 65€
🚏 sani-station 3€

Surroundings : ⇐ ♀♀
Leisure activities : 🏓 🎣
Facilities : ♿ ☛ 🚿 ⁱ launderette

| GPS | Longitude : -0.10735 |
| | Latitude : 42.90406 |

Le Péguère

☎ 05 62 92 52 91, *www.campingpeguere.com*
Address : 31 rte de Pierrefitte (located 1.5km north following signs for Lourdes; beside the Gave de Pau (river)
Opening times : from beginning April to end Sept.
3.5 ha (160 pitches) relatively flat, flat, grassy
Tariff : 14€ ✱✱ ⇔ 🔲 🔾 (6A) – Extra per person 4.13€
Rental rates : (from beginning April to end Sept.) ⚡ – 3 🚐 – 2 🏠 – 1 gîte.
Per week from 320 to 430€
🚏 sani-station 2€

Surroundings : ⇐ ♀
Leisure activities : 🎣
Facilities : ♿ ☛ 🚿 🚿 ⁱ launderette

| GPS | Longitude : -0.10683 |
| | Latitude : 42.9024 |

Key to rentals symbols:

12 🚐   *Number of mobile homes*
20 🏠   *Number of chalets*
6 🛏   *Number of rooms to rent*
Per night   *Minimum/maximum rate per night*
30–50€
Per week   *Minimum/maximum rate per week*
300–1,000€

CAYLUS

82160 – Michelin map **337** G6 – pop. 1,536 – alt. 228
▶ Paris 628 – Albi 60 – Cahors 59 – Montauban 50

La Bonnette

0563657020, www.campingbonnette.com

Address : at Les Condamines (take the northeastern exit along the D 926, follow the signs for Villefranche-de-Rouergue and turn right onto D 97, follow the signs for St-Antonin-Noble-Val; beside the Bonnette river and not far from a small lake)

Opening times : from end March to mid Oct.

1.5 ha (60 pitches) flat, grassy

Tariff : (2012 price) 22€ ★★ ⌁ ▣ ⚡ (10A) – Extra per person 6€

Rental rates : (2012 price) (from end March to mid Oct.) – 6 ⎚. Per night from 45 to 90€ Per week from 300 to 580€

🚐 sani-station

Surroundings : ⌁ ♦♦
Leisure activities : 🛶 ⅃
Facilities : ᕫ ⚊ ⊠ 🛉 ⚱ ⅋ launderette
Nearby : ⌁

Longitude : 1.77629
Latitude : 44.23375

CAYRIECH

82240 – Michelin map **337** F6 – pop. 264 – alt. 140
▶ Paris 608 – Cahors 39 – Caussade 11 – Caylus 17

Le Clos de la Lère

0563312041, www.camping-leclosdelalere.com

Address : at Clergue (take the southeastern exit along the D 9, follow the signs for Septfonds)

Opening times : from beginning March to mid Nov.

1 ha (49 pitches) flat, grassy

Tariff : 20.50€ ★★ ⌁ ▣ ⚡ (6A) – Extra per person 5.20€

Rental rates : (from beginning March to mid Nov.) ⚡ – 7 ⎚ – 6 🏠.
Per night from 35 to 52€ – Per week from 187 to 668€ – Reservation fee 8€

🚐 sani-station 3€ – 4 ▣ 10€ – ⚡⚡10€

Pretty shrubs and flowers.

Surroundings : 🌿 ⌁ ♦♦
Leisure activities : 🛶 ⅃
Facilities : ᕫ ⚊ ⊞ 🛉 ⅋ launderette ⚘
Nearby : ✂

Longitude : 1.61291
Latitude : 44.21735

CONDOM

32100 – Michelin map **336** E6 – pop. 7,099 – alt. 81
▶ Paris 729 – Agen 41 – Auch 46 – Mont-de-Marsan 80

Municipal

0562281732, www.condom.org/index.php/camping-municipal

Address : chemin de l'Argenté (2 km, southern exit from the D 931, follow the signs for Eauze; near the Baïse river)

2 ha (75 pitches) flat, grassy

Rentals : ᕫ ⚡ – 15 ⎚ – 10 🏠.

Surroundings : ⌁ ♦♦
Leisure activities : 📺
Facilities : ᕫ ⚊ 🛉 ⚱ ⅋ 🔲
Nearby : ⅊ ✕ jacuzzi ✂ ⅃ ⌂ ⌁

Longitude : 0.36436
Latitude : 43.94802

CONQUES

12320 – Michelin map **338** G3 – pop. 280 – alt. 350
▶ Paris 601 – Aurillac 53 – Decazeville 26 – Espalion 42

⚠ Beau Rivage

℘ 05 65 69 82 23, *www.campingconques.com* – ⋔
Address : at Molinols (to the west of the town, along the D 901; beside the Dourdou river)
Opening times : from beginning April to end Sept.
1 ha (60 pitches) flat, grassy
Tariff : 23.50€ ✶✶ ⇔ 回 ฿ (10A) – Extra per person 4.50€
Rental rates : (from beginning April to end Sept.) – 12 ⬜. Per night from 45 to 65€
Per week from 275 to 560€
⬛ sani-station 5€

Surroundings : ⬜ ⵕⵕ
Leisure activities : ✕ 🏖 ⟍ ⟍
Facilities : ♿ ⊶ (season) ⚑ launderette ⬐

GPS Longitude : 2.39285
Latitude : 44.59891

> *The classification (1 to 5 tents, black or red) that we award to selected sites in this guide is our own system. It should not be confused with the classification (1 to 5 stars) of official organisations.*

CORDES-SUR-CIEL

81170 – Michelin map **338** D6 – pop. 1,006 – alt. 279
▶ Paris 655 – Albi 25 – Montauban 59 – Rodez 78

⚠ Moulin de Julien

℘ 05 63 56 11 10, *www.campingmoulindejulien.com*
Address : 1.5 km southeast along the D 922, follow the signs for Gaillac; beside a stream
Opening times : from beginning May to mid Sept.
9 ha (130 pitches) terraced, sloping, flat, grassy, lake
Tariff : 23.80€ ✶✶ ⇔ 回 ฿ (5A) – Extra per person 6€ – Reservation fee 10€
Rental rates : (from beginning May to mid Sept.) ⌁ – 3 ⬜ – 5 ⬜. Per night 150€
Per week 580€ – Reservation fee 10€

Surroundings : ⵕⵕ
Leisure activities : ⛶ 🖼 🏖 ⟍ ⟍
Facilities : ♿ ⊶ ⬒ ⚑ 🖻
Nearby : ⋇

GPS Longitude : 1.97628
Latitude : 44.05036

⚠ Camp Redon

℘ 05 63 56 14 64, *www.campredon.com*
Address : at Livers Cazelles (5km southeast along the D 600, follow the signs for Albi then continue 800m along the D 107, follow the signs for Virac to the left)
Opening times : from end March to mid Oct.
2 ha (40 pitches) relatively flat, flat, grassy
Tariff : 27.35€ ✶✶ ⇔ 回 ฿ (10A) – Extra per person 7.50€
Rental rates : (from end March to mid Oct.) ⌁ – 2 ⬜. Per night from 50€
Per week from 295 to 695€

Surroundings : ⬗ ⟝ ⬜ ⵕ
Leisure activities : 🖼 🏖 ⟍
Facilities : ⊶ ⚑ 🖻

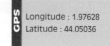

GPS Longitude : 2.01767
Latitude : 44.04318

COS

09000 – Michelin map **343** H7 – pop. 369 – alt. 486
▶ Paris 766 – La Bastide-de-Sérou 14 – Foix 5 – Pamiers 25

Municipal

℘ 0671181038, *www.camping-municipal-cos09.fr*
Address : Le Rieutort (700m southwest on the D 61; beside a stream)
Opening times : permanent
0.7 ha (32 pitches) open site
Tariff : 11.80€ ⚐⚐ ⊞ (6A) – Extra per person 1.50€
Rental rates : (permanent) – 2 🏠. Per week from 200 to 300€
A small, shady site with basic and rather old sanitary facilities.

Surroundings :
Leisure activities :
Facilities :
Nearby :

Longitude : 1.57332
Latitude : 42.97102

CREYSSE

46600 – Michelin map **337** F2 – pop. 296 – alt. 110
▶ Paris 517 – Brive-la-Gaillarde 40 – Cahors 79 – Gourdon 40

Le Port

℘ 0565322082, *www.campingduport.com*
Address : south of the town, near the château; beside the Dordogne river
Opening times : from mid April to end Sept.
3.5 ha (100 pitches) open site, relatively flat, flat, grassy
Tariff : 18.20€ ⚐⚐ ⊞ (10A) – Extra per person 5€ – Reservation fee 10€
Rental rates : (from mid April to end Sept.) – 6 🚐 – 7 tent bungalows.
Per week from 185 to 565€ – Reservation fee 10€
The site has a pleasant beach beside the Dordogne river.

Surroundings :
Leisure activities : 🏓 climbing, caving
Facilities : launderette

Longitude : 0.56537
Latitude : 44.85455

DAMIATTE

81220 – Michelin map **338** D9 – pop. 931 – alt. 148
▶ Paris 698 – Castres 26 – Graulhet 16 – Lautrec 18

Le Plan d'Eau St-Charles

℘ 0563706607, *www.campingplandeau.com*
Address : la Cahuziere (take the exit following signs for Graulhet then continue 1.2km along the turning to the left before the level crossing)
Opening times : from mid May to mid Sept.
7.5 ha/2 ha for camping (82 pitches) flat, grassy, stony
Tariff : (2012 price) 23.80€ ⚐⚐ ⊞ (6A) – Extra per person 6€ – Reservation fee 17€
Rental rates : (2012 price) (from beginning April to end Oct.) – 20 🚐 – 16 🏠 – 9 tent bungalows. Per night 80€ – Per week from 200 to 812€ – Reservation fee 17€
An attractive location set around a small but pretty lake.

Surroundings :
Leisure activities :
Facilities :
Nearby :

Longitude : 1.97011
Latitude : 43.66289

DURAVEL

46700 – Michelin map **337** C4 – pop. 957 – alt. 110
▶ Paris 610 – Toulouse 153 – Cahors 39 – Villeneuve-sur-Lot 37

FranceLoc Le Domaine Duravel

☎ 05 65 24 65 06, *www.franceloc.fr*
Address : rte du Port-de-Vire (2.3km south along the D 58; beside the Lot)
Opening times : from beginning May to end Sept.
9 ha (260 pitches) flat, grassy
Tariff : (2012 Price) 15€ ✚✚ ⇔ 🔲 🅷 (10A) – Extra per person 5€ – Reservation fee 27€
Rental rates : (2012 price) (from beginning May to end Sept.) – 92 🛖 – 33 🏠 – 7 tents.
Per week from 140 to 1,190€ – Reservation fee 27€

Surroundings : 🏞 🏕 00
Leisure activities : ✗ 🛝 🤸
Facilities : ♿ ⚟ 🛁 ⛲
Nearby : climbing

GPS — Longitude : 1.08201
Latitude : 44.49633

*The prices listed were supplied by the campsite owners in 2012
(if prices were not available, those from the previous year are given).
The fees should be regarded as basic charges and may fluctuate
with inflation.*

ENTRAYGUES-SUR-TRUYÈRE

12140 – Michelin map **338** H3 – pop. 1,224 – alt. 236
▶ Paris 600 – Aurillac 45 – Figeac 58 – Mende 128

Le Val de Saures

☎ 05 65 44 56 92, *www.camping-valdesaures.com*
Address : chemin de Saures (1.6km south along the D 904, follow the signs for Espeyrac, on the banks of the Lot river (direct access)
Opening times : from beginning May to end Sept.
4 ha (126 pitches) terrace, flat, grassy
Tariff : (2012 price) 22€ ✚✚ ⇔ 🔲 🅷 (10A) – Extra per person 4€ – Reservation fee 20€
Rental rates : (2012 price) (from beginning April to end Sept.) – 11 🏠 – 5 tents.
Per night from 29 to 97€ – Per week from 203 to 679€ – Reservation fee 30€

Surroundings : 🏞 ← 🏕 00
Leisure activities : 🎱 🚣 🎣
Facilities : ♿ ⚟ 🛁 ⛲ launderette
Nearby : ⛷ 🏊

GPS — Longitude : 2.56352
Latitude : 44.64248

Le Lauradiol

☎ 05 65 44 53 95, *www.camping-lelauradiol.com*
Address : 5km northeast along the D 34, follow the signs for St-Amans-des-Cots; beside the Selves river
1 ha (31 pitches) flat, grassy
Rentals : 2 🛖.
Pleasant location at the bottom of a small valley, on the banks of the river.

Surroundings : 🏞 🏕 00
Leisure activities : 🎱 ⛷ 🏊 🎣
Facilities : ♿ ⚟ 🛁 🚿 📮

GPS — Longitude : 2.58289
Latitude : 44.67768

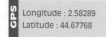

ESPALION

12500 – Michelin map **338** I3 – pop. 4,409 – alt. 342
▶ Paris 592 – Aurillac 72 – Figeac 93 – Mende 101

Le Roc de l'Arche

✆ 05 65 44 06 79, www.rocdelarche.com
Address : Le Foirail (To the east; take r. du Foirail, go along av. de la Gare and take the turning to the left, after the sports field; beside the Lot river)
Opening times : from beginning May to beginning Sept.
2.5 ha (95 pitches) flat, grassy
Tariff : 23.60€ ✶✶ ⇌ 🅴 ⚡ (10A) – Extra per person 5.40€ – Reservation fee 15€
Rental rates : (from beginning May to beginning Sept.) – 20 ⛺. Per night from 54 to 93€
Per week from 322 to 651€ – Reservation fee 15€
⛽ sani-station 3€

Surroundings : ▱ ♡♡
Leisure activities : ⛱ ⚓ ⤳
Facilities : ঊ ⊶ ⌂ ⏚ ⇜ 🚽 🖼
Nearby : ⛺ ✗ ⤳

| GPS | Longitude : 2.76959 |
| --- | Latitude : 44.52244 |

ESTAING

65400 – Michelin map **342** K7 – pop. 77 – alt. 970
▶ Paris 874 – Argelès-Gazost 12 – Arrens 7 – Laruns 43

La Via Natura Pyrénées Natura

✆ 05 62 97 45 44, www.camping-pyrenees-natura.com – alt. 1,000
Address : rte du Lac (north of the town)
Opening times : from end March to mid Oct.
3 ha (65 pitches) terraced, flat, grassy, gravelled
Tariff : 30.90€ ✶✶ ⇌ 🅴 ⚡ (10A) – Extra per person 5.85€ – Reservation fee 75€
Rental rates : (from end March to mid Oct.) – 19 ⛺. Per night from 40 to 91€
Per week from 240 to 730€ – Reservation fee 25€
⛽ sani-station – 3 🅴 17€ – ⚡ 🚽 10€
A beautiful 19th-century barn has been converted into a leisure and recreation space.

Surroundings : ⤳ ⬱ ▱ ♀
Leisure activities : ⛱ ⛱ ◔ daytime (auditorium) ⬱s jacuzzi ⚓ ⤳
Facilities : ঊ ⊶ ⌂ ⏚ ⇜ 🚽 launderette ⬕

| GPS | Longitude : -0.17725 |
| --- | Latitude : 42.94145 |

ESTANG

32240 – Michelin map **336** B6 – pop. 643 – alt. 120
▶ Paris 712 – Aire-sur-l'Adour 25 – Eauze 17 – Mont-de-Marsan 35

Les Lacs de Courtès ♣♣

✆ 05 62 09 61 98, www.lacsdecourtes.com
Address : south of the town along the D 152, behind the church and beside a lake
Opening times : from beginning April to end Oct.
7 ha (136 pitches) terraced, relatively flat, flat, grassy
Tariff : 27.50€ ✶✶ ⇌ 🅴 ⚡ (6A) – Extra per person 5.25€ – Reservation fee 20€
Rental rates : (permanent) – 3 ⛺ – 40 ⌂ – 2 tent bungalows. Per night from 34 to 135€
Per week from 238 to 945€ – Reservation fee 20€
⛽ sani-station 13€ – 4 🅴 13€ – ⚡ 8€

Surroundings : ⤳ ♡♡
Leisure activities : ⛱ ✗ ⛱ ⤟ jacuzzi ⚓ ⛿ ⬱ ⤳ ⇝
Facilities : ঊ ⊶ 🅴 ⌂ 🚽 launderette ⤵

| GPS | Longitude : -0.10254 |
| --- | Latitude : 43.8891 |

FIGEAC

46100 – Michelin map **337** I4 – pop. 9,847 – alt. 214
▶ Paris 578 – Aurillac 64 – Rodez 66 – Villefranche-de-Rouergue 36

 Les Rives du Célé

𝒫 05 61 64 88 54, *www.domainedusurgie.com*

Address : at the Domaine du Surgié (1.2km east along the N 140, follow the signs for Rodez and take the Chemin du Domaine de Surgié; beside the river and a small lake)

Opening times : from beginning April to end Sept.

2 ha (163 pitches) terraced, flat, grassy

Tariff : 26€ ♦♦ ⇌ 🗐 🗐 (10A) – Extra per person 7.50€ – Reservation fee 10€

Rental rates : (from beginning April to end Sept.) 🛋 – 20 🛏 – 30 ⛺ – 6 tent bungalows. Per night 55€ – Per week from 195 to 620€ – Reservation fee 21€

🚐 sani-station 19€ – 103 🗐 26€ – 🔌 ⒣26€

Surroundings : ̲Q̲Q̲
Leisure activities : 🛶 ⚓ 🎣
Facilities : ♿ ⚬ᴛ 🅿 launderette
Nearby : 🍸 ✕ 🐎 🏊 🚴 ♒ 🛶

Longitude : 2.04942
Latitude : 44.61189

FLAGNAC

12300 – Michelin map **338** F3 – pop. 972 – alt. 220
▶ Paris 603 – Conques 19 – Decazeville 5 – Figeac 25

⛺ Flower Le Port de Lacombe

𝒫 05 65 64 10 08, *www.campingleportdelacombe.fr*

Address : located 1km north along the D 963 and take road to the left; near a small lake and the Lot river (direct access)

Opening times : from beginning April to end Sept.

4 ha (97 pitches) flat, grassy

Tariff : 27.90€ ♦♦ ⇌ 🗐 ⒣ (10A) – Extra per person 5.50€ – Reservation fee 20€

Rental rates : (from beginning April to end Sept.) – 38 🛏 – 8 tent bungalows. Per night from 34 to 116 € – Per week from 170 to 812 € – Reservation fee 20€

🚐 sani-station 5€ – 🔌 ⒣10€

Surroundings : 🌊 ⛱ ̲Q̲Q̲
Leisure activities : 🍸 ✕ 🛶 🚴 ♒ ♒ ⛱ 🎣
Facilities : ♿ ⚬ᴛ 🍴 launderette
Nearby : 🎾 🐎 pedalos

Longitude : 2.23533
Latitude : 44.60819

GARIN

31110 – Michelin map **343** B8 – pop. 133 – alt. 1,100
▶ Paris 827 – Toulouse 153 – Tarbes 85 – Lourdes 84

⛺ Les Frênes
(rental of chalets only)

𝒫 05 61 79 88 44, *www.chalets-luchon-peyragudes.com* – traditional camp. spaces also available

Address : east of the town along the D 618, follow the signs for Bagnères-de-Luchon and take the turning to the left, D 76e towards Billière

Opening times : permanent

0.8 ha terraced, relatively flat, grassy, stony

Rental rates : (2012 price) 🅿 – 9 ⛺. Per night from 70 to 86€ – Per week from 437 to 700€

Rental on a nightly basis outside school holidays.

Surroundings : 🌊 ≼ ♀
Leisure activities : 🛶
Facilities : ⚬ᴛ ☲ 🗐 🍴 launderette
Nearby : ♒ ✕

Longitude : 0.51976
Latitude : 42.80933

GAVARNIE

65120 – Michelin map **342** L8 – pop. 140 – alt. 1,350 – Winter sports : 1,350/2,400 m 11
▶ Paris 901 – Lourdes 52 – Luz-St-Sauveur 20 – Pau 96

Le Pain de Sucre

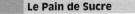

0562924755, *www.camping-gavarnie.com* – alt. 1,273
Address : Couret quartier (3km north along the D 921, follow the signs for Luz-St-Sauveur; beside the Gave de Gavarnie river)
Opening times : from beginning June to end Sept.
1.5 ha (50 pitches) open site, flat, grassy
Tariff : (2012 price) 4.30€ 4.50€ – (10A) 6.25€ – Reservation fee 7€
Rental rates : (2012 price) (from mid Dec. to end Sept.) – 3 – 5 .
Per night from 32 to 40€ – Per week from 190 to 500€

Surroundings :
Leisure activities :
Facilities : launderette

GPS Longitude : NaN
Latitude : 42.75851

GIRAC

46130 – Michelin map **337** G2 – pop. 379 – alt. 123
▶ Paris 522 – Beaulieu-sur-Dordogne 11 – Brive-la-Gaillarde 42 – Gramat 27

Les Chalets sur la Dordogne

0565109333, *www.camping-chalet-sur-dordogne.com*
Address : at the Port (located 1km northwest along the D 703, follow the signs for Vayrac and take road to the left; beside the Dordogne river)
Opening times : from beginning May to end Sept.
2 ha (39 pitches) open site, flat, grassy, sandy
Tariff : 19.20€ (10A) – Extra per person 5.40€ – Reservation fee 12€
Rental rates : (from beginning March to mid Oct.) – 7 – 3 – 1 tent – 1 gîte.
Per night 65€ – Per week from 150 to 599€ – Reservation fee 12€

Surroundings :
Leisure activities :
Facilities : (Jun–Aug) launderette
Nearby :

GPS Longitude : 1.80501
Latitude : 44.91809

GONDRIN

32330 – Michelin map **336** D6 – pop. 1,180 – alt. 174
▶ Paris 745 – Agen 58 – Auch 42 – Condom 17

Le Pardaillan

0562291669, *www.camping-le-pardaillan.com*
Address : 27 r. Pardaillan (situated east of the town)
Opening times : from mid April to beginning Oct.
2.5 ha (115 pitches) terraced, fine gravel, flat, grassy, lake
Tariff : 24€ (10A) – Extra per person 6.20€ – Reservation fee 15€
Rental rates : (from mid April to beginning Oct.) – 23 – 26 – 5 tent bungalows.
Per night 62€ – Per week from 245 to 790€ – Reservation fee 15€
sani-station 3.50€ – 2 – 11€

Surroundings :
Leisure activities :
Facilities : launderette
Nearby :

GPS Longitude : 0.23873
Latitude : 43.88165

GOURDON

46300 – Michelin map **337** E3 – pop. 4,622 – alt. 250
▶ Paris 543 – Bergerac 91 – Brive-la-Gaillarde 66 – Cahors 44

Aire Naturelle le Paradis

✆ 05 65 41 65 01, *www.campingleparadis.com*

Address : at La Peyrugue (situated 2km southwest along the D 673, follow the signs for Fumel and take road to the left, near the Intermarché car park)

Opening times : from beginning April to mid Sept.

1 ha (25 pitches) open site, terraced, flat, grassy

Tariff : 16€ ★★ ⇔ 国 ⟨₺⟩ (10A) – Extra per person 4.75€

Rental rates : (from beginning April to mid Sept.) – 6 ⟨⟩ – 1 ⟨⟩. Per night from 35 to 55€
Per week from 280 to 400€

Surroundings : 🌳 ♨
Leisure activities : 🛶
Facilities : ♿ ⚲ 🚿 ⚐ 🖥
Nearby : 🛒

GPS Longitude : 1.37397
Latitude : 44.72323

GRAND-VABRE

12320 – Michelin map **338** G3 – pop. 406 – alt. 213
▶ Paris 615 – Aurillac 47 – Decazeville 18 – Espalion 50

Village Vacances Grand-Vabre Aventures et Nature
(rental of chalets only)

✆ 05 65 72 85 67, *www.grand-vabre.com*

Address : at Les Passes (located 1km southeast along the D 901, follow the signs for Conques; besides the Dourdou river)

1.5 ha flat, grassy

Rentals : ♿ – 20 ⟨⟩.

Surroundings : ♨
Leisure activities : 🏠 🏃 🚣 🚲 🛶 🎣
Facilities : ⚲ 🏢 ⚐ launderette
Nearby : 🍽 🐎

GPS Longitude : 2.36297
Latitude : 44.62473

The guide covers all 22 regions of France – see the map and list of regions on pages 4–5.

HÈCHES

65250 – Michelin map **342** O6 – pop. 631 – alt. 690
▶ Paris 805 – Arreau 14 – Bagnères-de-Bigorre 35 – Bagnères-de-Luchon 47

La Bourie

✆ 05 62 98 73 19, *www.camping-labourie.com*

Address : situated 2km south along the D 929, follow the signs for Arreau and turn left onto D 26 at Rebouc; beside the Neste d'Aure river

Opening times : permanent

2 ha (120 pitches) terraced, relatively flat, flat, grassy

Tariff : ★ 3.40€ ⇔ 国 3.70€ – ⟨₺⟩ (10A) 5.40€

Rental rates : (from beginning March to end Oct.) – 15 ⟨⟩. Per night from 35 to 58€
Per week from 250 to 589€ – Reservation fee 15€

⚐ sani-station

Surroundings : ≼ ♨
Leisure activities : ✗ 🏠 🛶 🎣
Facilities : ♿ ⚲ 🚿 🏢 ⚐ 🖥

GPS Longitude : 0.37887
Latitude : 43.03815

L'HOSPITALET-PRÈS-L'ANDORRE

09390 – Michelin map **343** I9 – pop. 91 – alt. 1,446
▶ Paris 822 – Andorra-la-Vella 40 – Ax-les-Thermes 19 – Bourg-Madame 26

⚠ Municipal La Porte des Cimes

𝓕 0561052110, www.camping.hospitalet.com – alt. 1,500
Address : 600m north along the N 20, follow the signs for Ax-les-Thermes and take turning to the right.
Opening times : from beginning June to end Sept.
1.5 ha (62 pitches) terraced, flat, grassy, fine gravel
Tariff : (2012 price) 👤 3.50€ 🚗 1€ 🔲 2.50€ – 🔌 (10A) 5€
🚐 sani-station – 8 🔲 – 🚐 🔌 15.40€
Choose pitches further away from the road in preference.

Surroundings : ≤ ⛰
Leisure activities : ✂
Facilities : ♿ 🚿 (Jul–Aug) 🛒 🏪 🛁 ♨ 🍴 launderette
Nearby : 🏊 🎣

GPS Longitude : 1.80343
Latitude : 42.59135

LACAM-D'OURCET

46190 – Michelin map **337** I2 – pop. 129 – alt. 520
▶ Paris 544 – Aurillac 51 – Cahors 92 – Figeac 38

⚠ Les Teuillères

𝓕 0565119055, www.lesteuilleres.com
Address : 4.8km southeast along the D 25, follow the signs for Sousceyrac and then Sénaillac-Latronquière, towards the Lac du Tolerme
3 ha (30 pitches) relatively flat, flat, grassy

Surroundings : 🏞 ≤ 🚐 ⛰
Leisure activities : 🚣
Facilities : ♿ 🔌 🖼

GPS Longitude : 2.04086
Latitude : 44.8342

> *Routes nationales are main roads and their identifying numbers begin with N or RN. Routes départementales are generally quieter roads and begin with D or DN.*

LACAPELLE-MARIVAL

46120 – Michelin map **337** H3 – pop. 1,326 – alt. 375
▶ Paris 555 – Aurillac 66 – Cahors 64 – Figeac 21

⚠ Municipal Bois de Sophie

𝓕 0565408259, http://lacapelle-marival.fr
Address : rte d'Aynac (located 1km northwest along the D 940, follow the signs for St-Céré)
Opening times : from mid April to end Sept.
1 ha (66 pitches) relatively flat, flat, grassy
Tariff : 12.20€ 👤👤 🚗 🔲 🔌 (10A) – Extra per person 2.80€
Rental rates : (from mid April to end Sept.) – 3 🚐 – 6 tent bungalows. Per night 12€
Per week from 202 to 424€
🚐 sani-station

Surroundings : ⛰⛰
Leisure activities : 🖼
Facilities : ♿ 🔌 🛒 🛁 🍴
Nearby : ✂ 🚣

GPS Longitude : 1.91796
Latitude : 44.73314

LACAVE

46200 – Michelin map **337** F2 – pop. 284 – alt. 130
▶ Paris 528 – Brive-la-Gaillarde 51 – Cahors 58 – Gourdon 26

La Rivière

℘ 05 65 37 02 04, *www.campinglariviere.com*
Address : at Le Bougayrou (2.5km northeast along the D 23, follow the signs for Martel and take road to the left; beside the Dordogne river)
Opening times : from mid April to mid Sept.
2.5 ha (110 pitches) flat, grassy, stony
Tariff : ♣ 5.80€ ⇌ 🅴 7.70€ – 🔌 (10A) 4.30€ – Reservation fee 9.50€
Rental rates : (from mid April to end Sept.) – 17 🛏. Per week from 220 to 560€
Reservation fee 9.50€

Surroundings : ⅏ ♋ ▲
Leisure activities : 🍸 ✕ 🚣 ⌂ 🛝 ⤳ ⇜
Facilities : ᵹ ⊶ 🛁 🍴 launderette 🚐

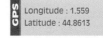

GPS Longitude : 1.559
Latitude : 44.8613

LAFRANÇAISE

82130 – Michelin map **337** D7 – pop. 2,828 – alt. 183 – Leisure centre
▶ Paris 621 – Castelsarrasin 17 – Caussade 41 – Lauzerte 23

Le Lac

℘ 05 63 65 89 69, *www.campings82.fr*
Address : r. Jean Moulin (take the southeastern exit along the D 40, follow the signs for Montastruc and take the turning to the left, 250m from a small lake (direct access)
Opening times : from mid June to mid Sept.
0.9 ha (34 pitches) relatively flat, stony, wood
Tariff : 18.80€ ♣♣ ⇌ 🅴 🔌 (10A) – Extra per person 8€
Rental rates : (permanent) – 19 🛏 – 11 gîtes. Per week from 480 to 565€
🚐 sani-station 9€ – 4 🅴 22€

Surroundings : ⅏ ⊏ ♋
Leisure activities : 🚲
Facilities : ⊶ ⇉ 🍴 🖵
Nearby : 🚣 ⁂ ⤳ 🛝 ⤳ pedalos

GPS Longitude : 1.24675
Latitude : 44.1246

This guide is updated regularly, so buy your new copy every year!

LAGUIOLE

12210 – Michelin map **338** J2 – pop. 1,267 – alt. 1,004 – Winter sports : 1,100/1,400 m ⚡12 ⛷
▶ Paris 571 – Aurillac 79 – Espalion 22 – Mende 83

Municipal les Monts d'Aubrac

℘ 05 65 44 39 72, *www.campinglesmontsdaubraclaguiole.jimdo.com* – alt. 1,050
Address : take the southern exit along the D 921, follow the signs for Rodez then continue 600m along the turning to the left; by the stadium
Opening times : from mid May to mid Sept.
1.2 ha (57 pitches) relatively flat, flat, grassy
Tariff : (2012 price) 9.50€ ♣♣ ⇌ 🅴 🔌 (10A) – Extra per person 2.50€
🚐 sani-station – 🔋 🔌9.50€

Surroundings : ⅏ ≼ ⚲
Facilities : ᵹ ⊶ 🏛 ⩍ 🖵
Nearby : ⁂

GPS Longitude : 2.85501
Latitude : 44.6815

LAMONTÉLARIÉ

81260 – Michelin map **338** H9 – pop. 62 – alt. 847
▶ Paris 736 – Toulouse 116 – Albi 83 – Castres 44

Rouquié

☎ 05 63 70 98 06, *www.campingrouquie.fr*
Address : at the Lac de la Raviège
Opening times : from beginning May to end Oct.
3 ha (97 pitches) very uneven, terraced, flat, grassy
Tariff : (2012 price) 23.35€ ✝✝ ⛺ 🔲 ⚡ (6A) – Extra per person 4.10€ – Reservation fee 15€
Rental rates : (2012 price) (from beginning April to end Oct.) – 10 🛖 – 6 🏠. Per night 65€
Per week 720€ – Reservation fee 15€

Surroundings : 🏞 ≤ ⚌ ⛰
Leisure activities : ⛾ ✗ 🚣 🎣 pedalos, boats for hire ⚬
Facilities : ♿ ⛽ 🍴 🚰 launderette 🚿
Nearby : ⚓

GPS Longitude : 2.60663
Latitude : 43.60038

LAU-BALAGNAS

65400 – Michelin map **342** L5 – pop. 499 – alt. 430
▶ Paris 864 – Toulouse 188 – Tarbes 36 – Pau 70

Le Lavedan

☎ 05 62 97 18 84, *www.lavedan.com*
Address : 44 rte des Vallées (located 1km southeast)
Opening times : permanent
2 ha (137 pitches) flat, grassy
Tariff : 39.70€ ✝✝ ⛺ 🔲 ⚡ (10A) – Extra per person 10€ – Reservation fee 25€
Rental rates : (permanent) – 29 🛖 – 2 🏠 – 2 tent bungalows. Per night from 41 to 78 €
Per week from 250 to 734 € – Reservation fee 25€

Surroundings : ⚌
Leisure activities : ⛾ 🏛 🚣 🏊 (open-air in season)
Facilities : ♿ ⛽ 🆑 🍴 🚰 🚿 launderette 🛒

GPS Longitude : -0.08896
Latitude : 42.98818

Les Frênes

☎ 05 62 97 25 12 – 🏨
Address : 46 rte des Vallées (1.2km southeast)
Opening times : permanent
3 ha (165 pitches) terraced, flat, grassy
Tariff : (2012 price) ✝ 5€ ⛺ 🔲 5.40€ – ⚡ (10A) 11€
Rental rates : (2012 price) (permanent) – 20 🛖. Per week from 310 to 500€

Surroundings : ≤ ⚌
Leisure activities : 🏛 🏊
Facilities : ♿ ⛽ 🍴 🚿 🖼

GPS Longitude : -0.08875
Latitude : 42.98803

La Prairie

☎ 05 62 97 11 87
Address : 6 r. du Sailhet
Opening times : from mid June to mid Sept.
1 ha (60 pitches) flat, grassy
Tariff : (2012 price) ✝ 3.70€ ⛺ 🔲 3.60€ – ⚡ (6A) 6€
🚐 sani-station

Surroundings : ≤ mountains ♀
Facilities : ♿ ⛽ 🖼 🖼

GPS Longitude : -0.09141
Latitude : 42.99774

LAVIT-DE-LOMAGNE

82120 – Michelin map **337** B8 – pop. 1,523 – alt. 217
▶ Paris 668 – Agen 49 – Beaumont-de-Lomagne 12 – Castelsarrasin 23

Municipal de Bertranon

☏ 05 63 94 05 54, *mairie-lavit.de.lomagne@info82.com* – ℝ
Address : rte d'Asques (to the northeast of the town, near the stadium and two lakes)
Opening times : from mid June to end Sept.
0.5 ha (33 pitches) relatively flat, grassy
Tariff : ✦ 2.50€ ⇌ 3€ 回 3€ – ฿ (6A) 2.30€
Rental rates : (permanent) – 2 ⟦⟧. Per night from 30 to 40€ – Per week from 150 to 230€
☞ sani-station 3€

Surroundings : ⚘ ▱ ⚉⚉ Leisure activities : ⚒ ⚲ sports trail Facilities : ᘓ ⤢ ☒	**GPS** Longitude : 0.92311 Latitude : 43.96149

To visit a town or region, use the MICHELIN Green Guides.

LECTOURE

32700 – Michelin map **336** F6 – pop. 3,766 – alt. 155 – Leisure centre
▶ Paris 708 – Agen 39 – Auch 35 – Condom 26

Yelloh! Village Le Lac des 3 Vallées ⚑⚑

☏ 05 62 68 82 33, *www.lacdes3vallees.fr*
Address : 2.4km southeast along the N 21, follow the signs for Auch, then continue 2.3km along the turning to the left beside the lake
Opening times : from beginning June to mid Sept.
40 ha (600 pitches) undulating, terraced, relatively flat, flat, grassy, lake
Tariff : 47€ ✦✦ ⇌ 回 ฿ (10A) – Extra per person 8€
Rental rates : (from beginning June to mid Sept.) – 225 ⟦⟧ – 27 tent bungalows – 19 tents.
Per night from 35 to 149 €– Per week from 245 to 1,043€
☞ sani-station

Surroundings : ⚘ ⟨ ▱ ⚉⚉ Leisure activities : ⚑ ✕ ▦ ⚲ ⚒ ⚡ jacuzzi ⚒ ⚔ ⚲ ⚑ ⚓ (beach) ⟁ ⚲ disco, pedalos ⚐ multi-sports ground, skate park Facilities : ᘓ ⚲ ⚲ ⚲ ⚲ ⚑ launderette ⚲ ⚲ refrigerators	**GPS** Longitude : 0.64533 Latitude : 43.91252

LOUDENVIELLE

65510 – Michelin map **342** O8 – pop. 308 – alt. 987 – Leisure centre
▶ Paris 833 – Arreau 15 – Bagnères-de-Luchon 27 – La Mongie 54

Pène Blanche

☏ 05 62 99 68 85, *www.peneblanche.com*
Address : take the northwestern exit along the D 25, follow the signs for Génos; near the Neste de Louron (stream) and not far from a small lake
Opening times : permanent
4 ha (120 pitches) terraced, relatively flat, grassy
Tariff : 25.90€ ✦✦ ⇌ 回 ฿ (10A) – Extra per person 5€ – Reservation fee 30€
Rental rates : (from beginning Dec. to beginning Nov.) – 19 ⟦⟧ – 2 tents. Per night from 40 to 95€
Per week from 196 to 665€

Surroundings : ⚘ ⟨ ⚉ Facilities : ⚲ (Jul-Aug) ⚑ ⚑ launderette Nearby : ⚑ ✕ hammam, jacuzzi ⚒ ⚲ ⚲ ⟁ ⚲ ⚔ fitness centre, paragliding, windsurfing	**GPS** Longitude : 0.40722 Latitude : 42.79611

LOUPIAC

46350 – Michelin map **337** E3 – pop. 274 – alt. 230
▶ Paris 527 – Brive-la-Gaillarde 51 – Cahors 51 – Gourdon 16

Les Hirondelles ♣♣

🖉 05 65 37 66 25, www.camping-leshirondelles.com
Address : at Al Pech (3km north following signs for Souillac and take road to the left; 200m from the N 20)
Opening times : from mid April to mid Sept.
2.5 ha (70 pitches) relatively flat, flat, grassy, stony
Tariff : 21€ ♣♣ 🚐 🔳 🏕 (6A) – Extra per person 5.50€ – Reservation fee 15€
Rental rates : (2012 price) (from mid April to mid Sept.) ♿ – 25 🛖 – 4 🏠 – 5 tents.
Per night from 37 to 85€ – Per week from 183 to 598€ – Reservation fee 15€

Surroundings : 🏞
Leisure activities : 🍷 ✗ 🏠 🏃 🏊 🏊
Facilities : ♿ ⚡ 🏢 🚿 🍽 launderette 🏧 🐾
Nearby : 🐎

Longitude : 1.46455
Latitude : 44.82934

Some information or pricing may have changed since the guide went to press.
We recommend you check the price list online in advance or at the entrance
to the campsite and enquire about possible restrictions.

LOURDES

65100 – Michelin map **342** L6 – pop. 15,127 – alt. 420
▶ Paris 850 – Bayonne 147 – Pau 45 – St-Gaudens 86

Le Moulin du Monge

🖉 05 62 94 28 15, www.camping-lourdes.com
Address : 28 av. Jean Moulin (1.3km to the north)
Opening times : from beginning April to beginning Oct.
1 ha (67 pitches) terrace, flat and relatively flat, grassy
Tariff : 21.60€ ♣♣ 🚐 🔳 🏕 (6A) – Extra per person 5.60€
Rental rates : (from beginning April to beginning Oct.) – 12 🛖 – 1 🏠 – 2 🛏 – 1 gîte.
Per night 100€ – Per week 700€
🚮 sani-station 4€ – 10 🔳 17.10€

Surroundings : 🌳
Leisure activities : 🏠 ☕ 🏊 🏊
Facilities : ♿ ⚡ 🏢 🍽 launderette 🏧

Longitude : -0.03148
Latitude : 43.11575

Plein Soleil

🖉 05 62 94 40 93, www.camping-pleinsoleil.com
Address : 11 av. du Monge (located 1km to the north)
Opening times : from beginning April to mid Oct.
0.5 ha (35 pitches) terraced, flat, grassy, fine gravel
Tariff : 22€ ♣♣ 🚐 🔳 🏕 (4A) – Extra per person 5€
Rental rates : (from beginning April to end Oct.) – 7 🏠. Per night from 50 to 68€
Per week from 300 to 570€
🚮 sani-station 5€ – 15 🔳 17.50€ – 🚐 🏕17.50€

Surroundings : 🌳
Leisure activities : 🏠 🏊
Facilities : ⚡ 🏢 🚿 🏧 🍽 launderette
Nearby : 🛒

Longitude : -0.03646
Latitude : 43.11438

Sarsan

📞 05 62 94 43 09, *www.lourdes-camping.com*
Address : 4 av. Jean Moulin (located 1.5km east via a diversion)
Opening times : from beginning April to mid Oct.
1.8 ha (66 pitches) relatively flat, flat, grassy
Tariff : 18.70€ � ☖ 🅿 (10A) – Extra per person 4.60€
Rental rates : (from beginning April to mid Oct.) – 8 🛖. Per night from 50 to 80€
Per week from 250 to 550€
🚐 sani-station 3€

Surroundings : ♨♨
Leisure activities : 🎬 ⚓ 🏊 (open-air in season)
Facilities : ♿ ⚓ 🚿 ⚑ 🔥

GPS Longitude : -0.02744
Latitude : 43.10226

Le Ruisseau Blanc

📞 05 62 42 94 83, *cintou.garros@cegetel.net*
Address : at Anclades
1.8 ha (110 pitches) flat, grassy
Rentals : ⚲ – 3 🛖.
🚐 sani-station – 15 🅿

Surroundings : ♒ ⩽ ♨♨
Leisure activities : 🎬 ⚓
Facilities : ⚓ 🔥

GPS Longitude : -0.01816
Latitude : 43.09531

UZ-ST-SAUVEUR

65120 – Michelin map **342** L7 – pop. 1,014 – alt. 710 – ♨ (from beg May to end Oct) – Winter sports :
1,800/2,450 m ⚡14 ☂
▶ Paris 882 – Argelès-Gazost 19 – Cauterets 24 – Lourdes 32

Club Airotel Pyrénées

📞 05 62 92 89 18, *www.airotel-pyrenees.com*
Address : 46 av. du Barège (located 1km northwest along the D 921, follow the signs for Lourdes)
Opening times : from beginning Dec. to end Sept.
2.5 ha (165 pitches) terraced, relatively flat, flat, grassy
Tariff : 35€ ☖☖ ☖ 🅿 (10A) – Extra per person 8€ – Reservation fee 25€
Rental rates : (from beginning Dec. to end Sept.) ⚲ – 48 🛖 – 12 🏠.
Per night from 100 to 190 € – Per week from 199 to 1,095€ – Reservation fee 25€
🚐 sani-station 9€

Surroundings : ❄ ⩽ ⌂ ♀
Leisure activities : 🎬 🛁 ⥮ hammam, jacuzzi ⚓ 🏊 🏊 ⛷
climbing wall, spa therapy centre
Facilities : ♿ ⚓ ▥ 🍴 launderette 🍽 🐾

GPS Longitude : -0.01152
Latitude : 42.88014

International

📞 05 62 92 82 02, *www.international-camping.fr*
Address : 50 av. du Barège (1.3km northwest along the D 921, follow the signs for Lourdes)
Opening times : 15 Dec. to 20 April, 20 May to 30 Sept.
4 ha (133 pitches) terraced, relatively flat, flat, grassy
Rental rates : (from mid Dec. to mid Apr. and mid May to end Sept.) ⚲ – 13 🛖.
Per week from 200 to 750€ Reservation fee 20€

Surroundings : ❄ ⩽ ♨♨
Leisure activities : 🍷 ✗ 🎬 jacuzzi ⚓ 🏊 ⛷ multi-sports ground
Facilities : ♿ ⚓ ▥ 🍴 launderette 🍽 🐾

GPS Longitude : -0.01388
Latitude : 42.88322

Pyrénévasion

📞 0562929154, *www.campingpyrenevasion.com* – alt. 834

Address : rte de Luz-Ardiden (3.4km northwest along the D 921, follow the signs for Gavarnie and take D 12; at Sazos)

Opening times : from end Nov. to mid Oct.

3.5 ha (100 pitches) terraced, relatively flat, grassy, gravelled

Tariff : (2012 price) 22€ ♛ ♛ ⇔ ▤ ⓖ (10A) – Extra per person 6€ – Reservation fee 10€

Rental rates : (from end Nov. to mid Oct.) – 15 🚐 – 8 🏠 – 4 gîtes.
Per week from 210 to 790€ – Reservation fee 12€

🚽 sani-station 6€ – 🛒 ⓖ12€

Surroundings : ≤
Leisure activities : ☉ ✗ jacuzzi ◢◣ ⬓ multi-sports ground
Facilities : ♿ ⊶ ⫘ ♨ ⚏ ⚲ launderette

GPS
Longitude : -0.02417
Latitude : 42.8831

Les Cascades

📞 0562928585, *www.camping-luz.com*

Address : r. Ste-Barbe (south of the town; beside rapids, recommended route via Gavarnie road)

Opening times : from beginning Dec. to end Sept.

1.5 ha (77 pitches) terraced, relatively flat, grassy, stony

Tariff : (2012 price) 27€ ♛ ♛ ⇔ ▤ ⓖ (6A) – Extra per person 6.50€

Rental rates : (2012 price) (from beginning Dec. to end Nov.) – 18 🚐.
Per night from 50 to 70€ – Per week from 250 to 600€

🚽 sani-station 10€

Surroundings : ⬒ ≤ ⬗
Leisure activities : ☉ ✗ ▱ ◢◣ ⬓
Facilities : ♿ ⊶ ⫘ ⚲ launderette ⚏

GPS
Longitude : -0.00145
Latitude : 42.87346

So de Prous

📞 0562928241, *www.sodeprous.com*

Address : Larise quartier (3km northwest along the D 921, follow the signs for Lourdes; 80m from the Gave de Gavarnie river)

2 ha (80 pitches) terraced, flat, relatively flat, grassy

Rentals : 14 🚐 – 2 studios.

Surroundings : ≤ ⬗
Leisure activities : ☉ ▱ ◢◣ ⬓ (small swimming pool)
Facilities : ♿ ⊶ ⫘ ⚲ ▣ ⚏

GPS
Longitude : -0.02919
Latitude : 42.89892

Le Bergons

📞 0562929077, *www.camping-bergons.com*

Address : rte de Barèges (500m east along the D 918)

Opening times : from beginning Dec. to end Oct.

1 ha (78 pitches) terraced, relatively flat, flat, grassy

Tariff : (2012 price) 15€ ♛ ♛ ⇔ ▤ ⓖ (6A) – Extra per person 3.50€ – Reservation fee 10€

Rental rates : (2012 price) (from beginning Dec. to end Oct.) – 5 🚐.
Per week from 235 to 500€

🚽

Surroundings : ❄ ≤ ⬗
Leisure activities : ▱ ◢◣
Facilities : ♿ (Jul–Aug) ⫘ ⚲ launderette

GPS
Longitude : 0.00281
Latitude : 42.87334

Toy

℘ 05 62 92 86 85, www.camping-toy.com
Address : 17 pl. du 8-Mai (town centre; beside the Bastan river)
Opening times : from beginning Dec. to mid April
1.2 ha (83 pitches) terraced, relatively flat, grassy, stony
Tariff : 17.80€ ✹ ✹ ⇌ 🔲 🔌 (6A) – Extra per person 4.20€
🚐 sani-station 12.60€

| Surroundings : 🕸 ≤ 🎋 |
| Leisure activities : 🐟 |
| Facilities : ⚡ 🚿 ⊠ ▥ ❠ launderette |
| Nearby : 🏕 🏊 🍸 ✗ 🎣 |

GPS Longitude : -0.00312
Latitude : 42.87328

Le Bastan

℘ 05 62 92 94 27, www.luz-camping.com – ℞
Address : rte de Barèges, at Esterre (800m east along the D 918; beside the Bastan river)
Opening times : permanent
1 ha (70 pitches) relatively flat, flat, grassy, stony
Tariff : (2012 price) ✹ 3.40€ ⇌ 3€ 🔲 3.50€ – 🔌 (6A) 6€
Rental rates : (2012 price) (permanent) 🛏 – 4 🚐. Per night from 50€
Per week from 250 to 500€
🚐 sani-station 10.30€

| Surroundings : ❄ ≤ 🎋🎋 |
| Leisure activities : 🏛 ⛷ 🎿 🐟 |
| Facilities : 🧑‍🦽 ⚡ ▥ 🛁 ❠ launderette |
| Nearby : ✗ |

GPS Longitude : -0.00594
Latitude : 42.87327

Michelin classification:

🏔🏔🏔🏔🏔	*Extremely comfortable, equipped to a very high standard*
🏔🏔🏔🏔	*Very comfortable, equipped to a high standard*
🏔🏔🏔	*Comfortable and well equipped*
🏔🏔	*Reasonably comfortable*
🏔	*Satisfactory*

MANE

31260 – Michelin map **343** D6 – pop. 998 – alt. 297
▶ Paris 753 – Aspet 19 – St-Gaudens 22 – St-Girons 22

Village Vacances de la Justale

℘ 05 61 90 68 18, www.village-vacances-mane.fr
Address : 2 allée de la Justale (500m southwest of the town along the road near the town hall; beside the Arbas river and a stream)
Opening times : from beginning April to end Oct.
3 ha (23 pitches) flat, grassy
Tariff : ✹ 2.80€ ⇌ 2.50€ – 🔌 (10A) 3.60€ – Reservation fee 25€
Rental rates : (permanent) – 19 🏠 – 19 gîtes. Per week from 210 to 450€
Reservation fee 90€
🚐 sani-station – 26 🔲 7.50€ – 🔋 🔌15.50€
In a pleasant, green setting.

| Surroundings : 🕸 ⌷ 🎋🎋 |
| Leisure activities : 🏛 ⛷ m 🎣 |
| Facilities : 🧑‍🦽 ⚡ 🚿 ❠ launderette |
| Nearby : 🍴 🐎 |

GPS Longitude : 0.94716
Latitude : 43.07621

MARTRES-TOLOSANE

31220 – Michelin map **343** E5 – pop. 2,236 – alt. 268

▶ Paris 735 – Auch 80 – Auterive 48 – Bagnères-de-Luchon 81

Le Moulin 🔺⚏

𝒫 05 61 98 86 40, www.DomaineLeMoulin.com

Address : at Le Moulin (head 1.5km southeast along the rte du Stade, take av. de St-Vidian and then the road to the left after the bridge; beside a stream and a canal, near the Garonne river (direct access)

Opening times : from beginning April to end Sept.

6 ha/3 ha for camping (99 pitches) flat, grassy, stony

Tariff : (2012 price) 29.90€ 🏕🏕 🚐 🔲 🔋 (10A) – Extra per person 6€ – Reservation fee 9€

Rental rates : (2012 price) (permanent) 🔥 (1 chalet) – 2 'gypsy' caravans – 4 🚐 – 17 🏠 – 2 tent bungalows – 2 tents. Per night from 29 to 99€ – Per week from 196 to 910€ Reservation fee 18€

🚽 sani-station 18.90€ – 🚐 13.50€

A pleasant rural site and an old mill.

Surroundings : 🌿 🗺 ⛰

Leisure activities : ✗ 🏛 ⛳ 🏃 🚣 ✂ 🎣 🎣

Facilities : 🔥 ⚏ 🛁 🚿 🚰 🍽 launderette 🧺

GPS
Longitude : 1.0181
Latitude : 43.1905

Do not confuse:

🔺 *to* 🔺🔺🔺 *: MICHELIN classification*

with

★ *to* ★★★★★ *: official classification*

MAUBOURGUET

65700 – Michelin map **342** M2 – pop. 2,449 – alt. 181

▶ Paris 749 – Toulouse 148 – Tarbes 28 – Pau 68

Municipal L'Echez

𝒫 05 62 96 37 44, camping.maubourguet@yahoo.fr

Address : r. Jean Clos Pucheu

0.75 ha (50 pitches) flat, grassy

Surroundings : 🌿 ⛰

Leisure activities : 🏛 🎣

Nearby : ✂ 🎣

GPS
Longitude : 0.03193
Latitude : 43.46656

MAUROUX

46700 – Michelin map **337** C5 – pop. 528 – alt. 213

▶ Paris 622 – Toulouse 152 – Cahors 49 – Agen 50

Village Vacances du Soleil
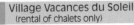
(rental of chalets only)

𝒫 05 65 30 82 59, www.villagedusoleil.fr

Address : at Le Reynou et Clos del Capre

7.5 ha undulating, wood

Rentals : 🔥 – 58 🏠.

Surroundings : 🌿 ⛰

Leisure activities : 🍴 ✗ 🏛 🏃 🚣 🚲 ✂ ⛰ 🎣

Facilities : ⚏ 🍽 launderette 🧺

GPS
Longitude : 1.06093
Latitude : 44.45062

MAZAMET

81200 – Michelin map **338** G10 – pop. 9,975 – alt. 241
🖪 Paris 739 – Albi 64 – Béziers 90 – Carcassonne 50

Municipal la Lauze

℘ 0563612469, *www.camping-mazamet.com*
Address : chemin de la Lauze (take the eastern exit along the N 112, follow the signs for Béziers and take a right turn)
Opening times : from beginning May to end Sept.
1.7 ha (53 pitches) relatively flat, flat, grassy
Tariff : 17.50€ ⋆⋆ ⇔ 🔲 🗓 (16A)
Rental rates : (permanent) 🚫 – 5 �🔲. Per week from 300 to 500€
🔄 sani-station
The Mazamet-Bédarieux Voie Verte (Green Trail, 80km) runs along an old railway track.

Surroundings : 🗐 ΩΩ
Leisure activities : 🔲 ↝↝
Facilities : ⅙ ⌐ ∭ ♨ ♨ ⚐ ⏝ 🖼
Nearby : ⌇ 🔲 ⟋ sports trail

Longitude : 2.39148
Latitude : 43.49692

MERCUS-GARRABET

89400 – Michelin map **343** H7 – pop. 1,153 – alt. 480
🖪 Paris 772 – Ax-les-Thermes 32 – Foix 12 – Lavelanet 25

Le Lac

℘ 0561059061, *www.campinglac.com*
Address : 1 promenade du Camping (800m south along the D 618, follow the signs for Tarascon and take a right turn at the level crossing; beside the Ariège river)
Opening times : from beginning April to end Sept.
1.2 ha (50 pitches) terraced, flat, grassy
Tariff : 27€ ⋆⋆ ⇔ 🔲 🗓 (6A) – Extra per person 7€ – Reservation fee 15€
Rental rates : (from end Oct. to beginning April) – 7 �🔲 – 16 🏠. Per night from 45 to 72€
Per week from 325 to 685€ – Reservation fee 15€
🔄 sani-station 5€
Pitches and rental options with plenty of shade beside the river.

Surroundings : ΩΩ ⛰
Leisure activities : 🔲 ⚊ (small swimming pool) ⟋ ⚲
Facilities : ⅙ ⌐ ♨ ⚐ 🖼

Longitude : 1.62252
Latitude : 42.87154

MÉRENS-LES-VALS

89110 – Michelin map **343** J9 – pop. 185 – alt. 1,055
🖪 Paris 812 – Ax-les-Thermes 10 – Axat 61 – Belcaire 36

Municipal de Ville de Bau

℘ 0561028540, *http://camping.merenslesvals.fr/* – alt. 1,100
Address : at Ville de Bau (located 1.5km southwest along the N 20, follow the signs for Andorra and take the road to the right; beside the Ariège)
Opening times : permanent
2 ha (70 pitches) flat, grassy, stony
Tariff : 16€ ⋆⋆ ⇔ 🔲 🗓 (10A) – Extra per person 3.70€
Rental rates : (permanent) 🚫 – 3 🏠. Per night from 70 to 90€ – Per week from 280 to 600€
Beside the Ariège river. Choose the pitches further away from the road in preference.

Surroundings : ⋖ 🗐 ΩΩ
Leisure activities : 🔲 ⟋
Facilities : ⅙ ⌐ ∭ ♨ ⏝ ⚐ launderette 🔧

Longitude : 1.83104
Latitude : 42.64622

MIERS

46500 – Michelin map **337** G2 – pop. 435 – alt. 302
▶ Paris 526 – Brive-la-Gaillarde 49 – Cahors 69 – Rocamadour 12

Le Pigeonnier

⚲ 05 65 33 71 95, *www.campinglepigeonnier.com*
Address : 700m east along the D 91, follow the signs for Padirac and take the road to the right behind the cemetery
Opening times : from beginning April to beginning Oct.
1 ha (45 pitches) terraced, flat and relatively flat, grassy
Tariff : (2012 price) ⚲ 5.40€ ⚲ 回 5.40€ – ⚡ (16A) 3.50€ – Reservation fee 12€
Rental rates : (2012 price) (from beginning April to beginning Oct.) – 12 ⊞.
Per night from 25 to 65€ – Per week from 170 to 599€ – Reservation fee 12€
⚱ sani-station 5.50€ – 5 回 15€

Surroundings : ⚲ ⊏ ⚲⚲
Leisure activities : ⚲ ⚲ ⚲
Facilities : ⚲ ⚯ ⚲ ⚲ ⚲

GPS Longitude : 1.71028
Latitude : 44.85289

The pitches of many campsites are marked out with low hedges of attractive bushes and shrubs.

MILLAU

12100 – Michelin map **338** K6 – pop. 22,013 – alt. 372
▶ Paris 636 – Albi 106 – Alès 138 – Béziers 122

Club Airotel Les Rivages ⚲⚲

⚲ 05 65 61 01 07, *www.campinglesrivages.com*
Address : 860 av. de l'Aigoual (1.7km east along the D 991, follow the signs for Nant; beside the Dourbie river)
Opening times : from mid April to end Sept.
7 ha (314 pitches) flat, grassy
Tariff : 36€ ⚲⚲ ⚲ 回 ⚡ (10A) – Extra per person 8€ – Reservation fee 17€
Rental rates : (from mid April to end Sept.) – 32 ⊞ – 1 studio – 12 tent bungalows.
Per night from 36 to 110€ – Per week from 216 to 773€ – Reservation fee 17€
⚱ sani-station

Surroundings : ⚲⚲ ⚲
Leisure activities : ⚲ ✕ ⚲ ⚲ ⚲ ⚲ ⚲ ⚲ ⚲ ⚲ ⚲
Facilities : ⚲ ⚯ ⚲ ⚲ ⚲ ⚲ launderette ⚲ ⚲
Nearby : hang-gliding

GPS Longitude : 3.09616
Latitude : 44.10161

Viaduc ⚲⚲

⚲ 05 65 60 15 75, *www.camping-du-viaduc.com*
Address : 121 av. de Millau-Plage (800m northeast along the D 991, follow the signs for Nant and turn left onto D 187 following signs for Paulhe; beside the Tarn river)
Opening times : from end April to mid Sept.
5 ha (237 pitches) flat, grassy
Tariff : 34€ ⚲⚲ ⚲ 回 ⚡ (6A) – Extra per person 7.50€ – Reservation fee 17€
Rental rates : (from end April to mid Sept.) – 39 ⊞ – 6 tent bungalows.
Per night from 35 to 69€ – Per week from 224 to 847€ – Reservation fee 17€
⚱ sani-station

Surroundings : ⊏ ⚲⚲ ⚲
Leisure activities : ⚲ ✕ ⚲ ⚲ ⚲ ⚲ ⚲ ⚲
Facilities : ⚲ ⚯ ⚲ ⚲ ⚲ ⚲ launderette ⚲ ⚲
Nearby : ⚲ ⚲ ⚲ ⚲ paragliding

GPS Longitude : 3.08853
Latitude : 44.10578

Les Érables

𝄞 05 65 59 15 13, *www.campingleserables.fr*

Address : av. de Millau-Plage (900m northeast along the D 991, following signs for Nant and turn left onto D 187, follow the signs for Paulhe; beside the Tarn river)

Opening times : from beginning April to end Sept.

1.4 ha (78 pitches) flat, grassy

Tariff : (2012 Price) 20€ ♟♟ ⇔ ▣ ⁅⁆ (10A) – Extra per person 4.50€ – Reservation fee 16€

Rental rates : (2012 price) (from beginning April to end Sept.) – 6 ⌂⌂.
Per night from 41 to 80€ – Per week from 246 to 560€ – Reservation fee 16€

Surroundings : ≤ ⊏ ♨♨
Leisure activities : 🎬
Facilities : 🚿 ⊶ ⁋ launderette
Nearby : 🛒 ✗ ⌂ ⍭

GPS Longitude : 3.08704
Latitude : 44.11022

32300 – Michelin map **336** E8 – pop. 3,705 – alt. 173
◗ Paris 737 – Auch 25 – Mont-de-Marsan 98 – Tarbes 49

L'Île du Pont

𝄞 05 62 66 64 11, *www.groupevla.fr*

Address : at Le Batardeau (east of the town, on an island in the Grande Baïse river)

10 ha/5 ha for camping (164 pitches) open site, flat, grassy

Rentals : 🚿 (3 mobile homes) – 35 ⌂⌂ – 12 ⌂.
⛽ sani-station – 6 ▣

In a pleasant location on an island.

Surroundings : ⍏ ♨♨
Leisure activities : ▼ ✗ 🎬 ⚷ ⍭⍭ ⍀
Facilities : 🚿 ⊶ ⁋ launderette ⍀
Nearby : ⍭ ⟋ fitness trail

GPS Longitude : 0.40932
Latitude : 43.51376

The Michelin classification (⚟⚟⚟... ⚟) is totally independent of the official star classification system awarded by the local prefecture or other official organisation.

81190 – Michelin map **338** E6 – pop. 1,077 – alt. 393
◗ Paris 653 – Albi 29 – Rodez 51 – St-Affrique 79

Les Clots

𝄞 05 63 76 92 78, *www.domaineclots.com*

Address : at Les Clots (5.5km north along the D 905, follow the signs for Rieupeyroux and take road on the left; 500m from the Viaur river (direct access)

Opening times : from beginning June to mid Sept.

7 ha/4 ha for camping (62 pitches) very uneven, terraced, flat, grassy, stony

Tariff : 33€ ♟♟ ⇔ ▣ ⁅⁆ (6A) – Extra per person 6.20€

Rental rates : (from beginning June to mid Sept.) – 1 ⌂ – 3 tent bungalows – 1 gîte.
Per night from 45 to 90€ – Per week from 300 to 625€

Surroundings : ⍏ ♨♨♨
Leisure activities : 🎬 ⍭⍭ ⌂ ⍭
Facilities : ⊶ ⍰ ⁋ ▣
Nearby : ⍀

GPS Longitude : 2.17881
Latitude : 44.17713

MIREPOIX

32390 – Michelin map **336** G7 – pop. 204 – alt. 150
▶ Paris 696 – Auch 17 – Fleurance 13 – Gimont 25

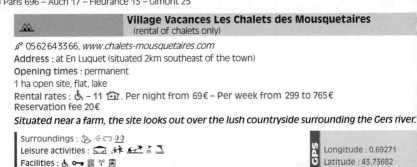

Village Vacances Les Chalets des Mousquetaires
(rental of chalets only)

☎ 05 62 64 33 66, *www.chalets-mousquetaires.com*
Address : at En Luquet (situated 2km southeast of the town)
Opening times : permanent
1 ha open site, flat, lake
Rental rates : ⅙ – 11 🏠. Per night from 69€ – Per week from 299 to 765€
Reservation fee 20€
Situated near a farm, the site looks out over the lush countryside surrounding the Gers river.

Surroundings : 🐾 ≼ ⊏ 𝟬𝟬
Leisure activities : 🔲 ⁂ 🛶 �ⁿ 🏊
Facilities : ⅙ ☛ ⫝̸ ⁿ 🖼
Nearby : 🐾

GPS Longitude : 0.69271
Latitude : 43.73682

MOISSAC

82200 – Michelin map **337** C7 – pop. 12,244 – alt. 76
▶ Paris 632 – Agen 57 – Auch 120 – Cahors 63

L'Île de Bidounet ♣♦

☎ 05 63 32 52 52, *www.camping-moissac.com*
Address : at St-Benoît (located 1km south along the N 113, follow the signs for Castelsarrasin and turn left onto the D 72)
Opening times : from beginning April to end Sept.
4.5 ha/2.5 ha for camping (100 pitches) flat, grassy
Tariff : (2012 price) 20.30€ ⁂ ★★ 🚗 🔲 🚿 (6A) – Extra per person 5.20€ – Reservation fee 7€
Rental rates : (2012 price) (from beginning June to mid Sept.) ⁂ – 12 tent bungalows.
Per night from 40 to 60€ – Per week from 200 to 350€ – Reservation fee 7€
🚐 sani-station – 6 🔲 20.30€
Attractive location on an island in the Tarn river.

Surroundings : 🐾 ⊏ 𝟬𝟬
Leisure activities : 🍴 🔲 ⁂ 🛶 🏊 (small swimming pool) 🐾 ᗪ
Facilities : ⅙ ☛ 🍳 ⁿ 🖼

GPS Longitude : 1.09005
Latitude : 44.09671

MONCLAR-DE-QUERCY

82230 – Michelin map **337** F8 – pop. 1,692 – alt. 178 – Leisure centre
▶ Paris 644 – Toulouse 73 – Montauban 22 – Albi 58

Village Vacances Les Hameaux des Lacs
(rental of chalets only)

☎ 05 55 84 34 48, *www.chalets-en-france.com*
Address : at the base de loisirs des Lacs (leisure centre)
Opening times : from mid Feb. to mid Nov.
5 ha very uneven, terraced, grassy, wood
Rental rates : 113 🏠. Per week from 190 to 780€ – Reservation fee 13€
Situated among trees and near lakes.

Surroundings : 🐾 ≼ 𝟬𝟬
Leisure activities : 🍴 🔲 🛶 🎾 🏊 📺 (open-air in season)
multi-sports ground
Facilities : ☛ ⁿ 🖼
Nearby : 🚣 🎿 ᗪ

GPS Longitude : 1.59544
Latitude : 43.96957

MONTCABRIER

46700 – Michelin map **337** C4 – pop. 367 – alt. 191
▶ Paris 584 – Cahors 39 – Fumel 12 – Tournon-d'Agenais 24

Moulin de Laborde

ℰ 05 65 24 62 06, *www.moulindelaborde.com*
Address : situated 2km northeast along the D 673, follow the signs for Gourdon; beside the Thèze river
Opening times : from beginning May to beginning Sept.
4 ha (90 pitches) flat, grassy, small lake
Tariff : ⚹ 7.30€ 🚗 📱 10.50€ – 🔌 (6A) 3.20€

Near an old mill. Attractive, shaded pitches.

Surroundings : ⚲⚲
Leisure activities : 🍷 ✕ 🎲 🛶 🚲 🏊
Facilities : ♿ ⚬ 🚿 ☒ 🍴 launderette 🔥

Longitude : 1.08247
Latitude : 44.54819

MONTESQUIOU

32320 – Michelin map **336** D8 – pop. 603 – alt. 214
▶ Paris 741 – Auch 32 – Mirande 12 – Mont-de-Marsan 87

Le Haget

ℰ 05 62 70 95 80, *www.lehaget.com*
Address : rte de Miélan (600m west along the D 943, follow the signs for Marciac then take left turn, 1.5km along the D 34 following signs for Miélan)
Opening times : from beginning April to end Sept.
10 ha (70 pitches) relatively flat, grassy
Tariff : 26€ ⚹⚹ 🚗 📱 🔌 (3A) – Extra per person 6.20€ – Reservation fee 14€
Rental rates : (from beginning April to end Oct.) – 4 🛏 – 19 🏠 – 10 🚐.
Per night from 30 to 120€ – Per week from 195 to 875€ – Reservation fee 14€

In the grounds of a château.

Surroundings : 🌿 ⚲⚲
Leisure activities : 🍷 ✕ 🎲 🏊
Facilities : ♿ ⚬ 🍴 🔥

Longitude : 0.32002
Latitude : 43.56579

MONTPEZAT-DE-QUERCY

82270 – Michelin map **337** E6 – pop. 1,461 – alt. 275
▶ Paris 598 – Cahors 28 – Caussade 12 – Castelnau-Montratier 13

Révéa Le Faillal

ℰ 05 63 02 07 08, *www.revea-camping.fr*
Address : at the Parc de Loisirs (leisure park) Le Faillal (take the northern exit along the D 20, follow the signs for Cahors and take the turning to the left)
Opening times : from mid April to beginning Oct.
0.9 ha (47 pitches) terraced, stony, grassy
Tariff : 20.20€ ⚹⚹ 🚗 📱 🔌 (6A) – Extra per person 4€ – Reservation fee 10€
Rental rates : (permanent) 🅿 – 22 🏠. Per night from 55 to 75 € –
Per week from 200 to 665 € – Reservation fee 25€
🛏 2 📱 16.60€

Surroundings : 🌿 🚐 ⚲⚲
Leisure activities : 🤾 🛶 🎵 entertainment room
Facilities : ⚬ ♿ 🚿 🔥 🍴 🔥
Nearby : 🎿 🏊

Longitude : 1.47725
Latitude : 44.24318

NAGES

81320 – Michelin map **338** I8 – pop. 340 – alt. 800 – Leisure centre
▶ Paris 717 – Brassac 36 – Lacaune 14 – Lamalou-les-Bains 45

Village Center Rieu-Montagné ♣⋮

0825005306, www.village-center.fr

Address : at la base de loisirs du Lac de Laouzas (leisure centre) (4.5km south along the D 62 and take turning to the left; 50m from the lake)

Opening times : from end April to end Sept.

8.5 ha (179 pitches) terraced, grassy, stony

Tariff : (2012 price) 25€ ♣♣ ⇔ ▣ ⚡ (10A) – Extra per person 5€ – Reservation fee 10€

Rental rates : (2012 price) (from end April to end Sept.) – 48 🚐 – 13 🏠 – 20 tent bungalows. Per night from 23 to 119€ – Per week from 395 to 831€ – Reservation fee 30€

An attractive elevated location.

Surroundings : 🦢 ≤ Lac du Laouzas and wooded mountains ⌂ ♤♤
Leisure activities : ♟ ✗ 🎪 ☺ daytime ⛷ ⚓ ⤢
Facilities : ⚷ 🔟 ♨ ⟲ ☝ launderette ▨ 🔧
Nearby : 🚲 ✂ ♠ ≊ (beach) ♪ 🐎 pedalos

GPS
Longitude : 2.77806
Latitude : 43.64861

NAILLOUX

31560 – Michelin map **343** H4 – pop. 2,717 – alt. 285 – Leisure centre
▶ Paris 711 – Auterive 15 – Castelnaudary 42 – Foix 50

Le Lac de la Thésauque

0561813467, www.camping-thesauque.com

Address : 3.4km east along the D 622, follow the signs for Villefranche-de-Lauragais, turn left onto D 25 and take road; 100m from the lake

Opening times : permanent

2 ha (60 pitches) terraced, relatively flat, flat, grassy

Tariff : (2012 price) 21.50€ ♣♣ ⇔ ▣ ⚡ (10A) – Extra per person 5.50€ – Reservation fee 10€

Rental rates : (2012 price) (permanent) – 6 🚐 – 4 🏠. Per night from 55 to 75€
Per week from 230 to 490€ – Reservation fee 10€

Surroundings : 🦢 ♤♤
Leisure activities : ♟ ✗ 🎪 ⚓ ✂ ♠ ⤢ 🌿 pedalos ⚽
Facilities : ♿ ⚷ ▥ ☝ 🔟 🔧

GPS
Longitude : 1.64834
Latitude : 43.3554

NANT

12230 – Michelin map **338** L6 – pop. 919 – alt. 490
▶ Paris 669 – Le Caylar 21 – Millau 33 – Montpellier 92

RCN Le Val de Cantobre ♣⋮

0565584300, www.rcn-campings.fr

Address : Domaine de Vellas (4.5km north along the D 991, follow the signs for Millau and take the road to the right; beside the Dourbie river)

Opening times : from end March to end Sept.

6 ha (216 pitches) very uneven, terraced, grassy, rocks, rocky

Tariff : 46.50€ ♣♣ ⇔ ▣ ⚡ (6A) – Extra per person 5.25€ – Reservation fee 19.50€

Rental rates : (from end March to end Sept.) – 37 🚐. Per night from 34 to 167€
Per week from 238 to 1,169€ – Reservation fee 19.50€

🚐 sani-station

Based near an old 15th-century Caussenarde farmhouse.

Surroundings : 🦢 ≤ ⌂ ♤♤
Leisure activities : ♟ ✗ 🎪 ☺ ⛷ ⚓ ♠ ⤢ ⤢ multi-sports ground
Facilities : ♿ ⚷ 🔟 ♨ ⟲ ☝ launderette ▨ 🔧 refrigerated food storage

GPS
Longitude : 3.30177
Latitude : 44.04554

Les Deux Vallées

℘ 05 65 62 26 89, www.lesdeuxvallees.com – **FR**

Address : rte de l'Estrade Basse

Opening times : from beginning April to end Oct.

2 ha (80 pitches) flat, grassy, stony

Tariff : 21€ ✝✝ ⇔ 圁 ⑭ (6A) – Extra per person 4€

Rental rates : (from beginning April to end Oct.) – 12 ⛟. Per night from 30 to 90€
Per week from 210 to 630€

⛟ sani-station 5€ – ⛽11€

Surroundings : 🐟 ⊏ ꗈꗈ
Facilities : 🚿 ⊶ ♨ ♨ ⇝ ♈ launderette
Nearby : 🚴

GPS — Longitude : 3.35457 / Latitude : 44.0241

NAUCELLE

12800 – Michelin map **338** G5 – pop. 2,049 – alt. 490
▶ Paris 652 – Albi 46 – Millau 90 – Rodez 32

Flower Le Lac de Bonnefon

℘ 05 65 69 33 20, www.camping-du-lac-de-bonnefon.com

Address : take the southeastern exit along the D 997, follow the signs for Naucelle-Gare then continue 1.5km following signs for Crespin and turn left towards St-Just; 100m from the lake (direct access)

Opening times : from beginning April to mid Oct.

3 ha (90 pitches) terraced, relatively flat, flat, grassy

Tariff : 26.50€ ✝✝ ⇔ 圁 ⑭ (10A) – Extra per person 5.50€ – Reservation fee 15€

Rental rates : (from beginning April to mid Oct.) – 8 ⛟ – 18 🏠 – 15 tent bungalows – 2 tents. Per night from 36 to 128€ – Per week from 252 to 770€ – Reservation fee 20€

⛟ sani-station 12€ – 4 圁 12€

Surroundings : 🐟 ⊏ ꗈꗈ
Leisure activities : ♈ ✗ ⚓ ₘ ♨ ⚲
Facilities : 🚿 ⊶ ♨ ♈ 圐
Nearby : ✗ 🚴

GPS — Longitude : 2.34867 / Latitude : 44.18902

These symbols are used for a campsite that is exceptional in its category:

🔺🔺🔺...🔺 *Particularly pleasant setting, quality and range of services available*

🐟🐟 *Tranquil, isolated site – quiet site, particularly at night*

≪≪ *Exceptional view – interesting or panoramic view*

NÈGREPELISSE

82800 – Michelin map **337** F7 – pop. 5,056 – alt. 87
▶ Paris 614 – Bruniquel 13 – Caussade 11 – Gaillac 46

Municipal le Colombier

℘ 05 63 64 20 34, www.ville-negrepelisse.fr

Address : to the southwest, near the D 115

Opening times : from mid June to mid Sept.

1 ha (53 pitches) terraced, flat, grassy

Tariff : (2012 price) 10€ ✝✝ ⇔ 圁 ⑭ (10A) – Extra per person 1.90€

Surroundings : ꗈꗈ
Facilities : ⊶ ⇝ ♈ 圐
Nearby : 🛒 ⚓ ♨

GPS — Longitude : 1.51843 / Latitude : 44.07286

ORINCLES

65380 – Michelin map **342** M6 – pop. 315 – alt. 360
▶ Paris 845 – Bagnères-de-Bigorre 16 – Lourdes 13 – Pau 52

▲ Aire Naturelle le Cerf Volant

℘ 09 64 41 50 27, *lecerfvolant1@yahoo.fr*
Address : at Arioune (head 2.2km south along the D 407 and take road opposite, 300m from the D 937; beside a stream)
Opening times : from mid May to mid Oct.
1 ha (23 pitches) open site, flat, grassy
Tariff : ☆ 2.50€ ⇌ 1.50€ ▣ 2€ – ⚡ (15A) 2.50€

Surroundings : ⑂ ♀♀
Leisure activities : 🎮 ⚞
Facilities : ♿ ⊶ 🚾 🖼

GPS Longitude : 0.04931
Latitude : 43.11193

For more information on visiting particular towns or regions, consult the relevant regional MICHELIN Green Guide. We also recommend you use the appropriate Michelin regional map to locate your selected campsite, to calculate distances and to work out the best route.

OUST

09140 – Michelin map **343** F7 – pop. 545 – alt. 500
▶ Paris 792 – Aulus-les-Bains 17 – Castillon-en-Couserans 31 – Foix 61

⛰ Les Quatre Saisons

℘ 05 61 96 55 55, *www.camping4saisons.com*
Address : rte d'Aulus-les-Bains (take southeastern exit along the D 32, near the Garbet)
3 ha (108 pitches) flat, grassy
Rentals : 21 🚐 – 3 🏠 – 6 ⛺ – 3 gîtes.
🚐 sani-station – 20 ▣
Behind the hotel restaurant, very pleasant campsite, with lots of shade and well-kept.

Surroundings : 🌳 ♀♀
Leisure activities : ☕ ✕ 🎮 ⚞ ⏊
Facilities : ♿ ⊶ ▥ ⚑ launderette ⚘
Nearby : ✂ ⚞

GPS Longitude : 1.22103
Latitude : 42.87215

OUZOUS

65400 – Michelin map **342** L4 – pop. 202 – alt. 550
▶ Paris 862 – Toulouse 188 – Tarbes 35 – Pau 55

▲ Aire Naturelle la Ferme du Plantier

℘ 05 62 97 58 01 – ℞
Address : r. de l'Oulet (in the village, D 102)
Opening times : from beginning June to beginning Oct.
0.6 ha (15 pitches) terraced, sloping, flat, grassy
Tariff : 13.50€ ☆☆ ⇌ ▣ ⚡ (6A) – Extra per person 2.50€

Surroundings : ⑂ ≤ mountains ♀
Leisure activities : ⚞
Facilities : ♿ ⊶ 🚾 🖼

GPS Longitude : -0.10663
Latitude : 43.03099

PADIRAC

46500 – Michelin map **337** G2 – pop. 194 – alt. 360
▶ Paris 531 – Brive-la-Gaillarde 50 – Cahors 68 – Figeac 41

FranceLoc Les Chênes ⚑

☎ 05 65 33 65 54, *www.camping.franceloc.fr*
Address : rte du Gouffre (located 1.5km northeast along the D 90)
5 ha (194 pitches) terraced, relatively flat, stony, grassy
Rentals : ♿ ⌗ – 92 🚐 – 19 🏠 – 7 tent bungalows – 2 tents.
🚰 sani-station – 1 回
The site is in 2 sections, one of which is next to the leisure park.

Surroundings : 🏞 🚏 ♈
Leisure activities : ▾ ✕ 🎦 🎲 🏃 ⛵ 🎣 ⛲ cinema, entertainment
room
Facilities : ♿ ⚷ 🛁 🚰 launderette 🏧 🚿
At 500m, leisure/activities park : pedalos

Longitude : 1.74567
Latitude : 44.85125

*In order for the guide to remain wholly objective, the selection is made on an
entirely independent basis. There is no charge for being selected for the guide.*

PAMIERS

09100 – Michelin map **343** H6 – pop. 15,383 – alt. 280
▶ Paris 746 – Toulouse 70 – Carcassonne 77 – Castres 105

Kawan Villages L' Apamée

☎ 05 61 60 06 89, *http://camping-apamee-ariege-pyrenees.fr/*
Address : rte d'Escosse (0.8km northwest along the D119)
Opening times : from beginning April to end Oct.
2 ha (80 pitches) flat, grassy
Tariff : 27€ ♥♥ 🚐 回 ⚡ (10A) – Extra per person 6€ – Reservation fee 25€
Rental rates : (permanent) – 22 🚐 – 10 🏠 – 8 tent bungalows. Per night from 35 to 99€
Per week from 245 to 693€ – Reservation fee 25€
🚰 sani-station 3.50€ – 🚌 ⚡10.50€
*Plentiful shade and a range of rental options, but choose pitches away from the road in
preference.*

Surroundings : ♈
Leisure activities : ▾ ✕ 🏃 🚲 ⛲ 🎣
Facilities : ♿ ⚷ 回🛁 🚰 launderette

Longitude : 1.60205
Latitude : 43.1249

PARISOT

82160 – Michelin map **337** H6 – pop. 549 – alt. 376
▶ Paris 624 – Toulouse 110 – Montauban 59 – Albi 60

Résidence Les Chênes
(rental of chalets only)

☎ 05 63 02 12 50, *www.les-chenes.com*
Address : at Marsarios
Opening times : permanent
1 ha flat
Rental rates : (2012 price) ♿ Ⓟ – 7 🏠. Per week from 300 to 880€

Surroundings : ♈
Leisure activities : 🎦 ⛱ ⛲
Facilities : 🚿 🚽 🍴 📺

Longitude : 1.84095
Latitude : 44.2708

PAYRAC

46350 – Michelin map **337** E3 – pop. 670 – alt. 320
▶ Paris 530 – Bergerac 103 – Brive-la-Gaillarde 53 – Cahors 48

Flower Les Pins ♣♣

℘ 05 65 37 96 32, *www.les-pins-camping.com*
Address : D 820 (take the southern exit)
Opening times : from mid April to beginning Sept.
4 ha (125 pitches) terraced, flat, grassy, stony
Tariff : 31.90€ ♣♣ ⟵ 🗐 🗗 (10A) – Extra per person 6.90€ – Reservation fee 20€
Rental rates : (from mid April to beginning Sept.) – 51 🚐 – 3 🏠 – 5 tent bungalows –
2 tents. Per night from 37 to 130€ – Per week from 185 to 910€ – Reservation fee 20€
🚽 sani-station 6€

Surroundings : 🐾
Leisure activities : 🍽 ✕ 🏠 🏃 🚣 ✂ 🏊 ⛸
Facilities : ♿ ⚡ 🏬 🖨 🏕 🚮 ❄ 🍽 launderette 🐾

Longitude : 1.47214
Latitude : 44.78952

PONS

12140 – Michelin map **338** H2
▶ Paris 588 – Aurillac 34 – Entraygues-sur-Truyère 11 – Montsalvy 12

Municipal de la Rivière

℘ 05 65 66 18 16, *www.sainthippolyte.fr*
Address : located 1km southeast of the town, along the D 526, follow the signs for Entraygues-sur-
Truyère; beside the Goul river
Opening times : from mid June to mid Sept.
0.9 ha (46 pitches) flat, grassy
Tariff : (2012 price) 17.50€ ♣♣ ⟵ 🗐 🗗 (10A) – Extra per person 4€ – Reservation fee 20€
Rental rates : (2012 price) (from beginning April to end Sept.) – 11 🏠.
Per night from 29 to 69€ – Per week from 169 to 413€ – Reservation fee 30€

Surroundings : 🐾 ⌂ 🐾
Leisure activities : 🏠 🚣 ✂ 🏊 🎣
Facilities : ♿ ⚡ 🏕 🍽 🖼

Longitude : 2.56363
Latitude : 44.71119

PONT-DE-SALARS

12290 – Michelin map **338** I5 – pop. 1,606 – alt. 700
▶ Paris 651 – Albi 86 – Millau 47 – Rodez 25

Flower Les Terrasses du Lac ♣♣

℘ 05 65 46 88 18, *www.campinglesterrasses.com*
Address : rte du Vibal (4km north along the D 523)
Opening times : from beginning April to end Sept.
6 ha (180 pitches) very uneven, terraced, flat, grassy
Tariff : 28.90€ ♣♣ ⟵ 🗐 🗗 (6A) – Extra per person 6€ – Reservation fee 20€
Rental rates : (from beginning April to end Sept.) – 45 🚐 – 9 tent bungalows.
Per night from 45 to 102€ – Per week from 230 to 714€ – Reservation fee 20€
🚽 sani-station – 4 🗐 28.90€
An attractive location overlooking the lake.

Surroundings : 🐾 ← ⌂ 🐾
Leisure activities : 🍽 ✕ 🏠 🎯 🏃 🚣 🏊 🎣
Facilities : ♿ ⚡ (Jul-Aug) 🏕 🚮 ❄ 🍽 launderette 🚿
Nearby : ✂ 🎿 🛶 🐎

Longitude : 2.73478
Latitude : 44.30473

Le Lac

📞 0565468486, *www.parc-du-lac.com*
Address : rte du Vibal (located 1.5km north along the D 523)
4.8 ha (200 pitches) very uneven, terraced, relatively flat, flat, grassy
Rentals : 🏠 – 10 🏠 – 3 tent bungalows.
Beside the lake.

Surroundings : ≤ 00 ⛰
Leisure activities : ♈ ✕ 🎱 🕙 evening 🛶 🚲 🏊 🎣
Facilities : ♿ ⛽ 🏕 🚿 ♨ 📷
Nearby : ✗ 🏖 (beach) 🚣

GPS Longitude : 2.72586
Latitude : 44.2921

POUEYFERRÉ

65100 – Michelin map **342** L4 – pop. 826 – alt. 360
◲ Paris 853 – Toulouse 179 – Tarbes 26 – Pau 39

 Relais Océan-Pyrénées

📞 0562945722, *contact@mipycamp.com*
Address : 3 r. des Pyrénées (800m to the south, at the junction of the D 940 and the D 174)
1.2 ha (90 pitches) terraced, relatively flat, flat, grassy
Rental rates : 5 🚐.

Surroundings : ≤ ⊏ 00
Leisure activities : 🎱 🛶 🏊 bowling
Facilities : ♿ ⛽ 🏛 🚿 launderette

GPS Longitude : -0.07542
Latitude : 43.11435

POUZAC

65200 – Michelin map **342** M4 – pop. 1,101 – alt. 505
◲ Paris 823 – Toulouse 149 – Tarbes 19 – Pau 60

 Bigourdan

📞 0562951357, *www.camping-bigourdan.com*
Address : at Pouzac, 79 av. de la Mongie (to the south along the D 935)
1 ha (48 pitches) flat, grassy
Rentals : 🏠 – 8 🚐.
🚐 sani-station

Surroundings : 00
Leisure activities : 🎱 🛶 🏊
Facilities : ♿ ⛽ launderette
Nearby : 🛒

GPS Longitude : 0.13977
Latitude : 43.08036

PUYBRUN

46130 – Michelin map **337** G2 – pop. 906 – alt. 146
◲ Paris 520 – Beaulieu-sur-Dordogne 12 – Brive-la-Gaillarde 39 – Cahors 86

 La Sole

📞 0565385237, *www.la-sole.com*
Address : take the eastern exit, follow the signs for Bretenoux and take the road to the right after the service station
Opening times : from beginning April to end Sept.
2.3 ha (72 pitches) flat, grassy
Tariff : (2012 price) 🧍 5.20€ 🚗 🔲 5.50€ – 🔌 (10A) 3.50€ – Reservation fee 16€
Rental rates : (2012 price) (from beginning April to end Sept.) – 9 🚐 – 5 🏠 – 17 tent bungalows. Per night from 40 to 90€ – Per week from 200 to 500€ – Reservation fee 16€

Surroundings : 🍃 ⊏ 00
Leisure activities : ✕ 🎱 🛶 🏊 multi-sports ground
Facilities : ♿ ⛽ 🏕 🚿 ♨ 📷

GPS Longitude : 1.71431
Latitude : 44.95364

PUY-L'ÉVÊQUE

46700 – Michelin map **337** C4 – pop. 2,159 – alt. 130
▶ Paris 601 – Cahors 31 – Gourdon 41 – Sarlat-la-Canéda 52

L'Évasion

℘ 0565308009, *www.lotevasion.com*
Address : at Martignac (3km northwest along the D 28, follow the signs for Villefranche-du-Périgord and take the road to the right)
Opening times : from beginning April to end Sept.
4 ha/2 ha for camping (50 pitches) undulating, terraced, stony, grassy
Tariff : 26.20€ ♥♥ ⇌ 圓 (6A) – Extra per person 11€ – Reservation fee 10.90€
Rental rates : (from mid March to end Oct.) – 8 – 28 . Per week from 250 to 655€
Reservation fee 10.90€
A pretty water park. Chalets set among tree and shrubs.

Surroundings :
Leisure activities : multi-sports ground
Facilities :
Longitude : 1.12704
Latitude : 44.52546

PUYSSÉGUR

31480 – Michelin map **343** E2 – pop. 119 – alt. 265
▶ Paris 669 – Agen 83 – Auch 51 – Castelsarrasin 48

Namasté

℘ 0561857784, *http://camping.namaste.free.fr* – pitches accessed via steep slope, help moving caravans onto and off pitches avilable on request
Address : take the northern exit along the D 1, follow the signs for Cox and take the road to the right
Opening times : from beginning May to end Sept.
10 ha/2 ha for camping (60 pitches) terraced, relatively flat, flat, grassy, lake, adjacent wood
Tariff : 28.50€ ♥♥ ⇌ 圓 (16A) – Extra per person 8€ – Reservation fee 10€
Rental rates : (from beginning May to end Sept.) – 6 – 15 . Per night from 80 to 120€
Per week from 300 to 720€ – Reservation fee 15€
sani-station 5€
The site organises photographic exhibitions.

Surroundings :
Leisure activities : fitness trail
Facilities :
Longitude : 1.06134
Latitude : 43.75082

REVEL

31250 – Michelin map **343** K4 – pop. 9,253 – alt. 210
▶ Paris 727 – Carcassonne 46 – Castelnaudary 21 – Castres 28

Municipal du Moulin du Roy

℘ 0561833247, *www.mairie-revel.fr*
Address : rte de Soréze (take southeastern exit along the D 1, follow the signs for Dourgne and take a right turn)
Opening times : from beginning June to mid Sept.
1.2 ha (50 pitches) flat, grassy
Tariff : (2012 price) ♥ 3€ ⇌ 2.10€ 圓 2.50€ – (10A) 3.30€
sani-station 3.50€
Pretty shrubs and flowers surround the pitches.

Surroundings :
Facilities :
Nearby :
Longitude : 2.01519
Latitude : 43.45464

RIEUX

31310 – Michelin map **343** F5 – pop. 2,443 – alt. 210 – Leisure centre
▶ Paris 723 – Auterive 35 – Foix 53 – St-Gaudens 54

Les Chalets du Plan d'Eau
(rental of chalets and mobile homes only)

℘ 05 61 87 98 83, *www.camping-rieux.eu* – traditional camp. spaces also available
Address : 11 r. de la Bastide (3km northwest along the D 627, follow the signs for Toulouse and take turning to the left; beside the Garonne river)
Opening times : permanent
3 ha terraced
Rental rates : ♿ – 11 ⌷ – 10 ⌂. Per night from 33 to 60€ – Per week from 198 to 500€
⛺ 3 ▣ 5€

Surroundings : ⌗ ⌂ ♨
Leisure activities : ▦ ⛵ ✗ ⚲
Facilities : ⌁ ⛩ launderette
Nearby : ✗ ⚲ ⛷ ⛴ ◊ pedalos

Longitude : 1.18806
Latitude : 43.27195

The information in the guide may have changed since going to press.

RIEUX-DE-PELLEPORT

09120 – Michelin map **343** H6 – pop. 1,209 – alt. 333
▶ Paris 752 – Foix 13 – Pamiers 8 – St-Girons 47

Les Mijeannes

℘ 05 61 60 82 23, *www.campinglesmijeannes.com*
Address : rte de Ferries (1.4km to the northeast, access via the D 311; beside a canal and near the Ariège river)
Opening times : permanent
10 ha/5 ha for camping (152 pitches) flat, grassy, stony
Tariff : 24.60€ ♣♣ ⇌ ▣ ⚡ (10A) – Extra per person 5.30€
Rental rates : (permanent) – 11 ⌷ – 2 ⌂. Per night from 42 to 51€
Per week from 266 to 665€ – Reservation fee 15€
⛺ sani-station 4€ – ⛟ 11€
Spacious, pleasant site with good shade, near the river.

Surroundings : ⌗ ≤ ⌂ ♨
Leisure activities : ♟ ▦ ⚲ ♒ ⛴ ⚲ ⚲
Facilities : ♿ ⌁ ▥ ♒ launderette

Longitude : 1.62134
Latitude : 43.06293

RIGNAC

12390 – Michelin map **338** F4 – pop. 1,918 – alt. 500
▶ Paris 618 – Aurillac 86 – Figeac 40 – Rodez 27

La Peyrade

℘ 09 51 53 21 13, *www.campinglapeyrade.fr*
Address : south of the town, near a little lake
Opening times : from beginning June to mid Sept.
0.7 ha (36 pitches) terraced, flat and relatively flat, grassy
Tariff : (2012 price) 23€ ♣♣ ⇌ ▣ ⚡ (10A) – Extra per person 5.50€ – Reservation fee 20€
Rental rates : (2012 price) (from beginning May to end Sept.) – 5 ⌷.
Per night from 45 to 70€ – Per week from 196 to 490€ – Reservation fee 20€

Surroundings : ⌗ ⌂ ♨
Facilities : ♿ ⌁ ▥ ⚲ ♒ launderette
Nearby : ⛻ ▦ ⛷ ✗ ⛴

Longitude : 2.28956
Latitude : 44.4058

RIVIÈRE-SUR-TARN

12640 – Michelin map **338** K5 – pop. 1,042 – alt. 380
▶ Paris 627 – Mende 70 – Millau 14 – Rodez 65

Flower Le Peyrelade ▲▲

✆ 05 65 62 62 54, *www.campingpeyrelade.com*

Address : rte des Gorgers du Tarn (situated 2km east along the D 907, follow the signs for Florac; beside the Tarn river)

Opening times : from mid May to mid Sept.

4 ha (190 pitches) terraced, flat, grassy, stony

Tariff : 36€ ✱✱ ⇎ 🔲 (10A) – Extra per person 8€ – Reservation fee 18€

Rental rates : (from mid May to mid Sept.) ⤳ – 43 🚐 – 8 tent bungalows.
Per night from 40 to 133€ – Per week from 196 to 931€ – Reservation fee 18€

🚐 sani-station

Pleasant site and setting at the entrance to the Tarn river gorges.

Surroundings : ≤ 🌳🌳
Leisure activities : 🍴 ✕ 🎬 🛉 🏕 🏊 🎣 🛶 ⚘
Facilities : 🕭 🔑 🛁 🚿 🚽 🚰 🖼 🛒 🚲
Nearby : 🚴 🎿 forest trail

GPS
Longitude : 3.15807
Latitude : 44.18929

Les Peupliers

✆ 05 65 59 85 17, *www.campinglespeupliers.fr*

Address : rte des Gorgers du Tarn (take the southwestern exit follow the signs for Millau and take road to the left; beside the Tarn river)

Opening times : from beginning April to end Sept.

1.5 ha (112 pitches) flat, grassy, stony

Tariff : (2012 price) 35€ ✱✱ ⇎ 🔲 (10A) – Extra per person 7€

Rental rates : (2012 price) (from beginning April to end Sept.) – 16 🚐.
Per week from 310 to 800€

🚐 sani-station 5€ – 11 🔲 32€

Surroundings : ≤ 🏕 🌳🌳
Leisure activities : 🍴 ✕ 🏊 🎣 🛶 ⚘
Facilities : 🕭 🔑 🛁 🚿 🚰 🖼 launderette
Nearby : 🐎

GPS
Longitude : 3.12985
Latitude : 44.18747

*We have selected the best campsites in France with our usual care,
listing those with the best facilities in the most pleasant surroundings.*

ROCAMADOUR

46500 – Michelin map **337** F3 – pop. 689 – alt. 279
▶ Paris 531 – Brive-la-Gaillarde 54 – Cahors 60 – Figeac 47

Les Cigales

✆ 05 65 33 64 44, *www.camping-cigales.com*

Address : rte de Gramat (take the eastern exit along the D 36)

3 ha (100 pitches) relatively flat, flat, grassy, stony

Tariff : 24€ ✱✱ ⇎ 🔲 (10A) – Extra per person 8€ – Reservation fee 15€

Rental rates : (from mid April to end Sept.) – 2 caravans – 42 🚐 – 13 🏠. Per night 50€
Per week from 199 to 725€ – Reservation fee 15€

🚐 sani-station 5€

Surroundings : 🏊 🌳🌳
Leisure activities : 🍴 ✕ 🎬 🏊 🔥 🛶
Facilities : 🕭 🔑 🛁 🚿 🚰 🖼 🚲 refrigerators
Nearby : 🛶

GPS
Longitude : 1.63221
Latitude : 44.80549

Le Roc

☎ 05 65 33 68 50, *www.camping-leroc.com*

Address : at Pech-Alis (3km northeast along the D 673, follow the signs for Alvignac, 200m from the station)

Opening times : from beginning April to beginning Nov.

2 ha/0.5 (49 pitches) flat, grassy, stony

Tariff : 🚶 6€ 🚗 ▣ 6€ – (₰) (10A) 3.50€ – Reservation fee 10€

Rental rates : (from beginning April to beginning Nov.) – 4 🚐 – 8 🏠.
Per week from 270 to 695€ – Reservation fee 14€

🚰 sani-station 13€ – 4 ▣ 13€ – 🔋 13€

Surroundings : 🔲 ⒪⒪
Leisure activities : ✗ 🏊 ☑
Facilities : ⓖ ⚬━ 🛁 ⚐ ♔ ▣ 🚿

GPS
Longitude : 1.65379
Latitude : 44.81947

Le Relais du Campeur

☎ 05 65 33 63 28, *www.lerelaisducampeur.com*

Address : l'Hospitalet (in the town)

Opening times : from beginning April to end Oct.

1.7 ha (100 pitches) relatively flat, stony, grassy

Tariff : (2012 price) 20€ 🚶🚶 🚗 ▣ (₰) (10A) – Extra per person 6€ – Reservation fee 10€

🚰 sani-station 5€

Surroundings : ⒪⒪
Leisure activities : ☑
Facilities : ⚬━ ♔ launderette
Nearby : 🏊 ▼ ✗

GPS
Longitude : 1.62763
Latitude : 44.80442

RODEZ

12000 – Michelin map **338** H4 – pop. 24,358 – alt. 635
▶ Paris 623 – Albi 76 – Alès 187 – Aurillac 87

Village Vacances Campéole Domaine de Combelles ⚑⚑
(rental of mobile homes, chalets and tent bungalows only)

☎ 05 65 78 29 53, *www.camping-rodez.info*

Address : at Le Monastère, at the domaine de Combelles (situated 2km southeast along the D 12, follow the signs for Ste-Radegonde, D 62, turn right towards Flavin and take road to the left)

Opening times : from beginning May to end Oct.

120 ha/20 ha for camping undulating, flat, grassy

Rental rates : (2012 price) ⓖ (2 chalets) – 30 🚐 – 35 🏠 – 27 tent bungalows.
Per night from 30 to 137€ – Per week from 210 to 959€ – Reservation fee 15€

Plenty of activities for both young and old at large riding centre.

Surroundings : 🏊 ≤ 🔲 ⒪⒪
Leisure activities : ▼ ✗ 🎬 ⊙ 🏃 🏊 🚴 ✂ ☑ 🐎
entertainment room
Facilities : ⚬━ Ⓟ 🛁 ♔ launderette 🚿

GPS
Longitude : 2.59147
Latitude : 44.33086

Key to rentals symbols:

12 🚐	**Number of mobile homes**	
20 🏠	**Number of chalets**	
6 🛏	**Number of rooms to rent**	
Per night 30–50€	**Minimum/maximum rate per night**	
Per week 300–1,000€	**Minimum/maximum rate per week**	

Municipal de Layoule

⌕ 05 65 67 09 52, *www.mairie-rodez.fr*

Address : to the northeast of the town

Opening times : from beginning May to end Sept.

2 ha (79 pitches) terraced, flat, grassy, gravelled

Tariff : (2012 price) 10€ ✦✦ ⇌ 🔲 [½] (6A) – Extra per person 4€

🚐 20 🔲 14€

Pleasant, leafy setting with plenty of shade near the Aveyron river.

Surroundings : ≤ ⊏ 🗘🗘
Leisure activities : 🖼 ⚓
Facilities : & ⊶ 🛁 ⏚ ⫯ 🖳
Nearby : ⚲ walking trails

	GPS
	Longitude : 2.58532
	Latitude : 44.35367

Using the traditional Michelin classification method, the guide provides you with an easy, speedy reference for assessing the category of each site: 1 to 5 tents (see page 10).

LA ROMIEU

32480 – Michelin map **336** E6 – pop. 551 – alt. 188
▶ Paris 694 – Agen 32 – Auch 48 – Condom 12

Le Camp de Florence ♣♣

⌕ 05 62 28 15 58, *www.lecampdeflorence.com*

Address : rte Astaffort (take the eastern exit from the town along the D 41)

Opening times : from beginning April to beginning Oct.

10 ha/4 ha for camping (183 pitches) open site, terraced, flat, grassy

Tariff : 33.50€ ✦✦ ⇌ 🔲 [½] (10A) – Extra per person 7.60€

Rental rates : (from beginning April to beginning Oct.) & (3 chalets) – 38 🛖 – 2 🏠 –
6 tents. Per night from 48 to 134€ – Per week from 336 to 938€

🚐 sani-station 4€ – 20 🔲 19.50€

Surroundings : 🏖 ≤ ⊏ 🗘🗘
Leisure activities : 🍷 ✗ 🖼 🄶 🕺 🛝 ⚓ 🚲 🎿 🏊 wildlife park
Facilities : & ⊶ 🔲🛁 🛁 ⏚ ⫯ launderette 🌿

	GPS
	Longitude : 0.50155
	Latitude : 43.98303

ROQUELAURE

32810 – Michelin map **336** F7 – pop. 558 – alt. 206
▶ Paris 711 – Agen 67 – Auch 10 – Condom 39

Yelloh! Village Le Talouch ♣♣

⌕ 05 62 65 52 43, *www.camping-talouch.com*

Address : Au Cassou (3.5km north along the D 272, follow the signs for Mérens then take left turn D 148, follow the signs for Auch)

Opening times : from beginning April to end Sept.

9 ha/5 ha for camping (147 pitches) terrace, flat, grassy

Tariff : 39€ ✦✦ ⇌ 🔲 [½] (10A) – Extra per person 8€

Rental rates : (2012 price) (from beginning April to end Sept.) – 17 🛖 – 35 🏠 – 3 tents.
Per night from 35 to 165€ – Per week from 245 to 1,155€ – Reservation fee 17.50€

🚐 sani-station 10€ – 3 🔲 18€

Surroundings : 🏖 ⊏ 🗘🗘
Leisure activities : ✗ 🖼 🄶 🕺 ⛲ hammam, jacuzzi ⚓ 🚲 🎿 🖻 🏊
Facilities : & ⊶ 🛁 ⫯ launderette 🌿

	GPS
	Longitude : 0.56437
	Latitude : 43.71284

ST-AMANS-DES-COTS

12460 – Michelin map **338** H2 – pop. 775 – alt. 735
▶ Paris 585 – Aurillac 54 – Entraygues-sur-Truyère 16 – Espalion 31

Village Center Les Tours ♣♣
(rental of mobile homes and tents only)

℘ 0825002030, *www.village-center.fr* – alt. 600
Address : at Les Tours (6km southeast along the D 97 and turn left onto D 599; beside the Lac de la Selves)
Opening times : from end April to end Sept.
15 ha (275 pitches) very uneven, terraced, flat, grassy, stony
Rental rates : (2012 price) – 15 ⛺. Per night from 26 to 83€ – Per week from 354 to 675€
🚐 80 ▣ 19€ – 📶15€
A pleasant site overlooking the lake.

Surroundings : ⅗ ≤ ⌂ ♨ ⚠
Leisure activities : ♟ ✗ 🎬 ☺ ⛷ ⚓ ✂ ⚒ ⚐ ⚑ watersports centre
Facilities : ⅄ ⊶ 🅭 ⬙ ♨ ⚘ ♒ launderette ♨ ⚓

GPS
Longitude : 2.68056
Latitude : 44.66803

La Romiguière

℘ 0565444464, *www.laromiguiere.com* – alt. 600
Address : at the Lac de la Selve (8.5km southeast along the D 97 and turn left onto D 599; beside the Lac de la Selves)
Opening times : from beginning April to beginning Nov.
2 ha (62 pitches) terrace, flat, grassy, stony
Tariff : (2012 price) 25.80€ ♣♣ ⚫ ▣ 📶 (10A) – Extra per person 6€ – Reservation fee 16€
Rental rates : (2012 price) (from beginning April to beginning Nov.) – 19 ⛺. Per week from 245 to 651€ – Reservation fee 16€
🚐 sani-station 2€ – 📶11€

Surroundings : ⅗ ≤ ⌂ ♨ ⚠
Leisure activities : ♟ ✗ ⚒ ⚑ pedalos ♒
Facilities : ⅄ ⊶ ♨ ⚘ ♒ launderette ⚓
Nearby : ⚓ water skiing

GPS
Longitude : 2.70639
Latitude : 44.65528

Some campsites benefit from proximity to a municipal leisure centre.

ST-ANTONIN-NOBLE-VAL

82140 – Michelin map **337** G7 – pop. 1,829 – alt. 125
▶ Paris 624 – Cahors 55 – Caussade 18 – Caylus 11

Les Trois Cantons

℘ 0563319857, *www.3cantons.fr*
Address : 7.7km northwest along the D 19, follow the signs for Caylus and take road to the left, after the little bridge over the Bonnette, near an area known as Tarau and the D 926, between Septfonds (6km) and Caylus (9km)
Opening times : from mid April to mid Sept.
20 ha/4 ha for camping (99 pitches) flat and relatively flat, stony, grassy
Tariff : ♣ 6.50€ ⚫ ▣ 9.50€ – 📶 (6A) 4.75€
Rental rates : (from mid April to end Sept.) – 18 ⛺. Per night 100€ – Per week 695€
🚐 sani-station – 2 ▣ 12€ – 📶12€
Natural setting among trees, shrubs and bushes.

Surroundings : ⅗ ⌂ ♨♨
Leisure activities : 🎬 ⚓ ☞ ✂ ⚒
Facilities : ⅄ ⊶ ♒ 🅭
Nearby : farm/petting farm

GPS
Longitude : 1.70698
Latitude : 44.18711

Les Gorges de l'Aveyron ▲▲

℘ 0563306976, www.camping-gorges-aveyron.com

Address : at Marsac bas

Opening times : from beginning April to end Sept.

3.8 ha (80 pitches) flat, grassy

Tariff : 28.90€ ✝✝ ⇔ 🔲 (10A) – Extra per person 5.50€ – Reservation fee 5€

Rental rates : (from beginning April to end Sept.) – 23 — 4 tent bungalows – 4 tents. Per night from 34 to 112 € – Per week from 170 to 784 € – Reservation fee 15€

Surroundings : ⚲ ♒♒

Leisure activities : ♈ 🏠 🏃 ⚓ 🛶 🎣

Facilities : 🚻 ⟲ 🔳 🧺 launderette ⚗ 🐎

Longitude : 1.77256
Latitude : 44.15211

ST-BERTRAND-DE-COMMINGES

31510 – Michelin map **343** B6 – pop. 259 – alt. 581

▶ Paris 783 – Bagnères-de-Luchon 33 – Lannemezan 23 – St-Gaudens 17

Es Pibous

℘ 0561883142, www.es-pibous.fr

Address : chemin de St-Just (800m southeast along the D 26a, follow the signs for St-Béat and take road to the left)

Opening times : from beginning April to end Oct.

2 ha (80 pitches) flat, grassy

Tariff : (2012 price) 17.82€ ✝✝ ⇔ 🔲 (16A) – Extra per person 4.50€

Rental rates : (2012 price) (from beginning May to end Oct.) – 4 — 1 🏠. Per night 55€ Per week 385€ – Reservation fee 99€

🚽 sani-station 4.50€

Surroundings : ⚲ ⋖ Cathédrale de St-Bertrand-de-Comminges ⌐ ♒♒

Leisure activities : 🏠 ⚓ 🛶

Facilities : 🚻 ⟲ 🚿 🧺 🔲

Nearby : 🎣

Longitude : 0.57799
Latitude : 43.02868

The guide is updated each year, so consult the latest edition for the most up-to-date information and pricing.

ST-CÉRÉ

46400 – Michelin map **337** H2 – pop. 3,563 – alt. 152

▶ Paris 531 – Aurillac 62 – Brive-la-Gaillarde 51 – Cahors 80

Le Soulhol

℘ 0565381237, www.campinglesoulhol.com

Address : quai Salesses (take southeastern exit along the D 48; beside the Bave river)

Opening times : from beginning May to mid Sept.

3.5 ha (120 pitches) flat, grassy

Tariff : 19€ ✝✝ ⇔ 🔲 (10A) – Extra per person 4.70€

Rental rates : (from beginning May to mid Sept.) 🏕 – 4 — 10 🏠. Per night from 30 to 50€ – Per week from 230 to 490€

🚽 sani-station – 10 🔲 13.20€

Surroundings : ⚲ ♒♒

Leisure activities : 🏠 🛶 🎣

Facilities : 🚻 ⟲ 🧺 launderette

Nearby : ♈ ✕ ⚒

Longitude : 1.89617
Latitude : 44.85876

ST-CIRQ-LAPOPIE

46330 – Michelin map **337** G5 – pop. 217 – alt. 320
▶ Paris 574 – Cahors 26 – Figeac 44 – Villefranche-de-Rouergue 37

La Truffière ▲▲

✆ 0565302022, www.camping-truffiere.com
Address : at Pradines (3km south along the D 42, follow the signs for Concots)
Opening times : from mid April to mid Sept.
4 ha (96 pitches) terraced, flat, grassy, stony, natural setting among trees and bushes
Tariff : 22€ ✚✚ ⚌ 🗉 (½) (6A) – Extra per person 6€ – Reservation fee 12€
Rental rates : (from mid April to end Sept.) – 11 🏠. Per night from 65 to 80€
Per week from 250 to 710€ – Reservation fee 12€
🚐 sani-station 6€ – 10 🗉 6€
Small but pretty chalet village.

Surroundings : 🌄 ≤ 🞧🞧
Leisure activities : ✗ 🖼 🏃 🛶 🏊
Facilities : ᴋ ⚬ 🔲🕮 🛆 ۳ launderette 🖉

Longitude : 1.6746
Latitude : 44.44842

La Plage ▲▲

✆ 0565302951, www.campingplage.com
Address : at Porte Roques (1.4km northeast along the D 8, follow the signs for Tour-de-Faure, turn left before the bridge)
Opening times : from mid April to end Sept.
3 ha (120 pitches) flat, grassy, stony
Tariff : ✚ 6€ ⚌ 🗉 8€ – (½) (10A) 4€ – Reservation fee 10€
Rental rates : (from mid April to end Sept.) – 12 🛖 – 10 🏠. Per night from 60 to 70€
Per week from 280 to 650€ – Reservation fee 10€
🚐 sani-station 2€ – 15 🗉 7€
On the banks of the Lot river, opposite one of the prettiest villages in France.

Surroundings : 🞧🞧
Leisure activities : ♟ ✗ 🞧 daytime 🏃 🛶 🚲 ⚓ (beach) 🞐 🞐
Facilities : ᴋ ⚬ 🛆 🛆 ۳ launderette 🖉
Nearby : adventure park, climbing, caving, rafting and canyoning

Longitude : 1.6812
Latitude : 44.46914

*The classification (1 to 5 tents, **black** or red) that we award to selected sites in this guide is our own system. It should not be confused with the classification (1 to 5 stars) of official organisations.*

ST-GAUDENS

31800 – Michelin map **343** C6 – pop. 11,225 – alt. 405
▶ Paris 766 – Bagnères-de-Luchon 48 – Tarbes 68 – Toulouse 94

Municipal Belvédère des Pyrénées

✆ 0562001603, www.st-gaudens.com
Address : r. des Chanteurs du Comminges (located 1km west along the N 117, towards Tarbes)
1 ha (83 pitches) flat, grassy
🚐 sani-station – 10 🗉

Surroundings : ≤ Pyrénées 🞧🞧
Facilities : ᴋ ⚬ 🕮
Nearby : 🞐 ♟ ✗

Longitude : 0.70814
Latitude : 43.11

ST-GENIEZ-D'OLT

12130 – Michelin map **338** J4 – pop. 2,068 – alt. 410
▶ Paris 612 – Espalion 28 – Florac 80 – Mende 68

Campéole La Boissière ▲▲

𝄞 05 65 70 40 43, *www.camping-aveyron.info*
Address : rte de la Cascade (1.2km northeast along the D 988, follow the signs for St-Laurent-d'Olt and turn left following signs for Pomayrols; beside the Lot river)
Opening times : from end March to end Sept.
5 ha (250 pitches) terraced, relatively flat, flat, grassy
Tariff : (2012 price) 25.40€ ✶✶ ⇔ ▣ (✱) (8A) – Extra per person 6.40€ – Reservation fee 15€
Rental rates : (2012 price) (from end March to end Sept.) – 23 ▦ – 19 ⌂ – 11 tent bungalows – 8 tents. Per night from 25 to 57€ – Per week from 308 to 805€
Reservation fee 25€
⊟ sani-station 1€
Pleasant, wooded setting beside the Lot river.

Surroundings : ⌂ ⊟ ◖◗	
Leisure activities : ▼ ▦ ⍰ ⋰ ⬳ ✂ ⅃ ⬿	**GPS** Longitude : 2.98366
Facilities : ⅙ ⊶ ⌂ ⍾ launderette, refrigerators	Latitude : 44.47011
Nearby : ⬤⊙ ⚡	

Marmotel ▲▲

𝄞 05 65 70 46 51, *www.marmotel.com*
Address : at La Salle (1.8km west along the D 19, follow the signs for Prades-d'Aubrac and take road to the left, on the outskirts of the craft village; beside the Lot river)
Opening times : from beginning May to mid Sept.
4 ha (173 pitches) flat, grassy
Tariff : (2012 price) 31.60€ ✶✶ ⇔ ▣ (✱) (10A) – Extra per person 6.50€ – Reservation fee 22€
Rental rates : (2012 price) (from beginning May to mid Sept.) – 37 ▦ – 30 ⌂.
Per night from 35 to 75€ – Per week from 210 to 1,000€ – Reservation fee 22€
⊟ sani-station – ⬱ (✱)12€

Surroundings : ⌂ ⊟ ◖◗	
Leisure activities : ▼ ✗ ⍰ ⋰ ⬳ ⅃ ◿ ⬿ multi-sports ground, entertainment room	**GPS** Longitude : 2.9644
Facilities : ⅙ ⊶ ⌂ – 42 individual sanitary facilities (⍾⊹⊡ wc) ⋯ ⬲ ⍾ launderette ⬱	Latitude : 44.462
Nearby : ⬱	

Les Clédelles du Colombier
(rental of maisonettes only)

𝄞 05 65 47 45 72, *www.lesclledelles.com*
Address : r. Rivié (located 1km northeast via D 988, follow the signs for St-Laurent-d'Olt and turn left following signs for Pomayrols; near the Lot)
3 ha flat
Rentals : 42 gîtes.

Surroundings : ⌂	
Leisure activities : ⋰ ⬳ ⅃	**GPS** Longitude : 2.97809
Facilities : ⊶ ⍾ ⍾ ▣	Latitude : 44.46893
Nearby : ⬿	

We welcome your feedback on our listed campsites.
Please email us at: campingfrance@tp.michelin.com
Many thanks in advance!

ST-GERMAIN-DU-BEL-AIR

46310 – Michelin map **337** E4 – pop. 518 – alt. 215
▶ Paris 551 – Cahors 28 – Cazals 20 – Fumel 52

△   Municipal le Moulin Vieux ▲▴

✆ 0565310071, *www-camping-moulin-vieux-lot.com*
Address : to the northwest of the town; beside the Céou river
2 ha (90 pitches) flat, grassy
Rentals : ♿.

Surroundings : ⌇ 🌲🌲
Leisure activities : ⌂ 📽 ♨ ※ ⚲
Facilities : ⚷ ⛺ 🖼
Nearby : ⚊ ⛵

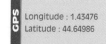

GPS   Longitude : 1.43476
          Latitude : 44.64986

A chambre d'hôte is a guesthouse or B & B-style accommodation.

ST-GIRONS

09200 – Michelin map **343** E7 – pop. 6,608 – alt. 398
▶ Paris 774 – Auch 123 – Foix 45 – St-Gaudens 43

⛰   Audinac ▲▴

✆ 0561664450, *www.audinac.com*
Address : at Audinac-les-Bains, at the lake (head 4.5km northeast along the D 117, follow the signs for Foix and take D 627, follow the signs for Ste-Croix-Volvestre)
Opening times : from beginning April to end Oct.
15 ha/6 ha for camping (115 pitches) terraced, flat and relatively flat, grassy, small lake
Tariff : 17€ ♛♛ ⌕ ▣ ⑤ (16A) – Extra per person 7€ – Reservation fee 7.50€
Rental rates : (from beginning April to end Oct.) ♿ (1 mobile home) – 30 ▥ –
15 ⌂ – 22 tent bungalows. Per night from 35 to 85€ – Per week from 180 to 600€
Reservation fee 10€
⛽ sani-station 5€ – ⛟ ⑤17€
Spacious site with 3 small springs, a lake and a swimming pool beside an old 19th-century spa building.

Surroundings : ⌇ 🌲🌲
Leisure activities : ▟ ✗ 🎦 ▣ evening 📽 ♨ 🚲 ※ ⚊ ⚲
multi-sports ground
Facilities : ♿ ⚷ ⊪ ⛺ ⚑ launderette 🗄 refrigerators

GPS   Longitude : 1.18407
          Latitude : 43.00705

ST-JEAN-DU-BRUEL

12230 – Michelin map **338** M6 – pop. 695 – alt. 520
▶ Paris 687 – Toulouse 295 – Rodez 128 – Millau 41

⛰   La Dourbie

✆ 0565460640, *www.camping-la-dourbie.com*
Address : rte de Nant
Opening times : from mid April to end Sept.
2.5 ha (78 pitches) flat, grassy, stony
Tariff : (2012 price) 21€ ♛♛ ⌕ ▣ ⑤ (16A) – Extra per person 5€
Rental rates : (2012 price) (from mid April to end Sept.) – 6 ▥ – 6 ⌂.
Per night from 40 to 55€ – Per week from 350 to 520€
⛽ sani-station 12€ – 14 ▣ 12€

Surroundings : ⌗ 🌲
Leisure activities : ▟ ✗ ♨ ⚊ ⚲
Facilities : ♿ ⚷ ⊪ ⛺ 🗄 ⚑ ⚑ 🖼 🗄

GPS   Longitude : 3.3466
          Latitude : 44.02004

ST-LARY-SOULAN

65170 – Michelin map **342** N8 – pop. 946 – alt. 820 – Winter sports : 1,680/2,450 m 2 30
▶ Paris 830 – Arreau 12 – Auch 103 – Bagnères-de-Luchon 44

Municipal

 05 62 39 41 58, *www.saintlary-vacances.com*
Address : r. Lalanne (in the town, east of the D 929)
1 ha (76 pitches) relatively flat, flat, grassy, stony
 sani-station – 6
A pleasant, green 'oasis' in the centre of the village.

Surroundings :
Leisure activities :
Facilities :
Nearby :

GPS Longitude : 0.32282
Latitude : 42.81548

There are several different types of sani-station
('borne' in French) – sanitation points providing
fresh water and disposal points for grey water.
See page 12 for further details.

ST-PANTALÉON

46800 – Michelin map **337** D5 – pop. 239 – alt. 269
▶ Paris 597 – Cahors 22 – Castelnau-Montratier 18 – Montaigu-de-Quercy 28

Les Arcades

 09 61 67 74 98, *www.des-arcades.com*
Address : at Le Moulin de St. Martial (4.5km east on the D 653, follow the signs for Cahors; beside the Barguelonnette river)
12 ha/2.6 ha for camping (80 pitches) flat, grassy, stony, small lake
Rentals : – 10 .
The campsite has a club room and small pub in a restored mill.

Surroundings :
Leisure activities :
Facilities :

GPS Longitude : 1.30667
Latitude : 44.36918

ST-PIERRE-LAFEUILLE

46090 – Michelin map **337** E4 – pop. 352 – alt. 350
▶ Paris 566 – Cahors 10 – Catus 14 – Labastide-Murat 23

Quercy-Vacances

 05 65 36 87 15, *www.quercy-vacances.com*
Address : at Mas de la Combe (located 1.5km northeast along the N 20, follow the signs for Brive and take road to the left)
Opening times : from beginning April to end Sept.
3 ha (80 pitches) relatively flat, flat, grassy
Tariff : 5€ 8€ – (10A) 4.50€ – Reservation fee 10€
Rental rates : (from beginning April to end Sept.) – 14 – 8 – 3 tent bungalows.
Per night from 60 to 99€ – Per week from 230 to 595€ – Reservation fee 10€

Surroundings :
Leisure activities :   multi-sports ground
Facilities :

GPS Longitude : 1.45925
Latitude : 44.53165

ST-ROME-DE-TARN

12490 – Michelin map **338** J6 – pop. 853 – alt. 360
▶ Paris 655 – Millau 18 – Pont-de-Salars 42 – Rodez 66

La Cascade

℘ 05 65 62 56 59, *www.camping-cascade-aveyron.com* – pitches accessed via steep slope, help moving caravans onto and off pitches avilable on request
Address : rte du Pont (300m north along the D 993, follow the signs for Rodez; beside the Tarn river)
Opening times : permanent
4 ha (99 pitches) terraced, relatively flat, grassy
Tariff : (2012 price) 29.50€ ★★ ⇔ 圓 ⚡ (6A) – Extra per person 7€ – Reservation fee 15€
Rental rates : (2012 price) (permanent) – 28 📇 – 14 🏠 – 9 tent bungalows.
Per night from 50 to 115€ – Per week from 180 to 810€ – Reservation fee 15€
🚰 sani-station 6€ – 20 圓 19.50€
Pitches on terraces on the side of a hill overlooking the Tarn river.

Surroundings : 🏊 ⇐ 🗗 ⬭⬭ ⚠
Leisure activities : ✗ 🎦 ⑨ ⚗ 🚴 ✂ ⤴ ⬎
Facilities : 🚿 ⚬ 🏕 🚿 🚽 🍴 launderette 🖶 🚰
Nearby : pedalos

GPS
Longitude : 2.89947
Latitude : 44.05336

STE-MARIE-DE-CAMPAN

65710 – Michelin map **342** N7
▶ Paris 841 – Arreau 26 – Bagnères-de-Bigorre 13 – Luz-St-Sauveur 37

L'Orée des Monts

℘ 05 62 91 83 98, *www.camping-oree-des-monts.com* – alt. 950
Address : at La Séoube, at Campan (3km southeast along the D 918, follow the signs for Le Col d'Aspin; beside the Adour de Payolle river)
Opening times : permanent
1.8 ha (101 pitches) relatively flat, flat, grassy
Tariff : 15.90€ ★★ ⇔ 圓 ⚡ (10A) – Extra per person 4.80€
Rental rates : (2012 price) (permanent) – 9 📇. Per week from 270 to 619€
🚰 sani-station 15.90€ – 4 圓 15.90€ – 🚐 11€

Surroundings : ⇐ ⚲
Leisure activities : ⛄ ✗ 🎦 ⑨ ⚗ ⤴ ⬎
Facilities : ⚬ 📖 🏕 🍴 🖶 🖶

GPS
Longitude : 0.24522
Latitude : 42.96664

SALLES-CURAN

12410 – Michelin map **338** I5 – pop. 1,067 – alt. 887
▶ Paris 650 – Albi 77 – Millau 39 – Rodez 40

Les Genêts ⚑⚑

℘ 05 65 46 35 34, *www.camping-les-genets.fr* – alt. 1,000
Address : at the Lac de Pareloup (5km northwest along the D 993 then take left turning along the D 577, follow the signs for Arvieu and continue 2km along the road to the right)
Opening times : from mid May to mid Sept.
3 ha (163 pitches) terraced, flat and relatively flat, grassy
Tariff : 41€ ★★ ⇔ 圓 ⚡ (10A) – Extra per person 8€ – Reservation fee 30€
Rental rates : (from mid May to mid Sept.) – 57 📇 – 11 🏠 – 7 tent bungalows.
Per night from 37 to 79€ – Per week from 416 to 951€ – Reservation fee 30€
Beside the Lac de Pareloup.

Surroundings : 🏊 ⇐ 🗗 ⬭⬭ ⚠
Leisure activities : ⛄ ✗ 🎦 ⚗ 🚴 ⚓ ⤴ ⬎ entertainment room
Facilities : 🚿 ⚬ (from mid-Jun to beg Sept) 🔲 🏕 🚿 🚽 🍴 launderette 🖶

GPS
Longitude : 2.76776
Latitude : 44.18963

Beau Rivage

℘ 05 65 46 33 32, *www.beau-rivage.fr* – alt. 800

Address : rte des Vernhes – Lac de Pareloup (3.5km north along the D 993, follow the signs for Pont-de-Salars and turn left onto D 243)

Opening times : from beginning May to end Sept.

2 ha (80 pitches) terraced, flat, grassy

Tariff : 33.90€ ★ ★ ⇌ ▣ ⒜ (10A) – Extra per person 6.90€ – Reservation fee 20€

Rental rates : (from end March to end Sept.) – 16 ⌷ – 6 ⌂ – 2 tent bungalows. Per night 138€ – Per week from 196 to 966€ – Reservation fee 30€

⌕ sani-station – ⌕ ⒜14€

A pleasant location beside the Lac de Pareloup.

Surroundings : ≤ ⊏ ◌◌ ▲
Leisure activities : ▼ ✗ ⌂ ⚓ ⚲ ⊿ ⍨
Facilities : ╆ ⌒ ⌂ ⌕ launderette ⚟
Nearby : ⌀ forest trail

GPS
Longitude : 2.77585
Latitude : 44.20081

Parc du Charrouzech

℘ 05 65 46 01 11, *www.parcducharouzech.fr*

Address : 5km northwest along the D 993 then take left turning along the D 577, follow the signs for Arvieu and continue 3.4km along the road to the right; near the Lac du Pareloup (direct access)

3 ha (104 pitches) terraced, flat, relatively flat, grassy

Rentals : 20 ⌷ – 35 tent bungalows.

The site looks out over the lake.

Surroundings : ⍟ ≤ ⊏ ◌◌
Leisure activities : ⌂ ⚲ ⚓ ⊿ ⍨ ⍦ ⚞
Facilities : ╆ ⌒ ⌕ ⌕ ⌕ launderette

GPS
Longitude : 2.75659
Latitude : 44.1968

SALLES-ET-PRATVIEL

31110 – Michelin map **343** B8 – pop. 136 – alt. 625

▶ Paris 814 – Toulouse 141 – Tarbes 86 – Lourdes 105

Le Pyrénéen

℘ 05 61 79 59 19, *www.campingdepyreneen-luchon.com*

Address : at Les Sept Molles (600m south along the D 27 and a road; beside the Pique river)

Opening times : permanent

1.1 ha (75 pitches) flat, grassy, stony

Tariff : 18.80€ ★ ★ ⇌ ▣ ⒜ (10A) – Extra per person 4.80€ – Reservation fee 15€

Rental rates : (permanent) – 32 ⌷. Per night from 50 to 75€ – Per week from 399 to 599€ Reservation fee 15€

⌕ sani-station 5€

Surroundings : ❄ ⍟ ≤ ⊏ ◌◌
Leisure activities : ▼ ⌂ ⚓ ⊿
Facilities : ╆ ⌒ ▥ ⌂ ⌕ ⌕ ⌕ launderette
Nearby : ⚘

GPS
Longitude : 0.60637
Latitude : 42.8224

Michelin classification:

⚠⚠⚠⚠ *Extremely comfortable, equipped to a very high standard*
⚠⚠⚠ *Very comfortable, equipped to a high standard*
⚠⚠⚠ *Comfortable and well equipped*
⚠ *Reasonably comfortable*
△ *Satisfactory*

SASSIS

65120 – Michelin map **342** L7 – pop. 92 – alt. 700
▶ Paris 879 – Toulouse 206 – Tarbes 53 – Pau 72

△ Le Hounta

✆ 05 62 92 95 90, *www.campinglehounta.com*
Address : 600m south along the D 12
Opening times : from beginning Jan. to mid Oct.
2 ha (91 pitches) relatively flat, flat, grassy
Tariff : (2012 price) 19.50€ ♥♥ ⇔ 圓 ⒡ (10A) – Extra per person 3.90€ – Reservation fee 4€
Rental rates : (2012 price) (from beginning Jan. to end Dec.) ⚡ – 12 ⊡ – 1 ⌂.
Per night from 44 to 75€ – Per week from 210 to 460€ – Reservation fee 7€
🖳 sani-station 5€ – 🔋 10.80€

Surroundings : ❄ 🐟 ⋜ ⅋
Leisure activities : ⛵
Facilities : ⅋ ⊶ ☷ ⍨ launderette
Nearby : 🎣

GPS Longitude : -0.01491
Latitude : 42.87252

SÉNERGUES

12320 – Michelin map **338** G3 – pop. 481 – alt. 525
▶ Paris 630 – Toulouse 197 – Rodez 50 – Aurillac 62

△ L'Étang du Camp

✆ 05 65 46 01 95, *www.etangducamp.fr*
Address : at Le Camp (6km southwest along the D 242, follow the signs for St-Cyprien-sur-Dourdou; beside a lake)
Opening times : from beginning April to end Sept.
5 ha (60 pitches) flat and relatively flat, stony, rocks
Tariff : 19.50€ ♥♥ ⇔ 圓 ⒡ (6A) – Extra per person 3.50€
Rental rates : (from mid May to end Sept.) ⚡ – 4 teepees. Per night from 36 to 44€
Per week from 210 to 252€
Pretty flowers and shrubs.

Surroundings : 🐟 ⌂ ⅋⅋
Leisure activities : 🎣
Facilities : ⅋ ⊶ (Jul–Aug) ➳ ⛺ ⍨

GPS Longitude : 2.46391
Latitude : 44.55837

SÉNIERGUES

46240 – Michelin map **337** F3 – pop. 136 – alt. 390
▶ Paris 540 – Cahors 45 – Figeac 46 – Fumel 69

⚠ Domaine de la Faurie

✆ 05 65 21 14 36, *www.camping-lafaurie.com*
Address : at La Faurie (6km south along the D 10, follow the signs for Montfaucon then take the D 2, follow the signs for St-Germain-du-Bel-Air and take the road to the right; from the A 20, take exit 56)
Opening times : from mid April to end Sept.
27 ha/5 ha for camping (63 pitches) relatively flat, flat, grassy, stony
Tariff : 29.50€ ♥♥ ⇔ 圓 ⒡ (6A) – Extra per person 7€
Rental rates : (from mid April to end Sept.) ℗ – 8 ⊡ – 17 ⌂ – 5 tent bungalows.
Per night from 30 to 99 €– Per week from 210 to 693€
🖳 sani-station – 7 圓 18€ – 🔋 14€

Surroundings : 🐟 ⋜ ⅋⅋
Leisure activities : ▾ ✗ 🎬 ⛵ 🚲 🏊
Facilities : ⅋ ⊶ 🖸⛺ ⟁ ⍨ launderette

GPS Longitude : 1.53444
Latitude : 44.69175

SÉVÉRAC-L'ÉGLISE

12310 – Michelin map **338** J4 – pop. 412 – alt. 630
▶ Paris 625 – Espalion 26 – Mende 84 – Millau 58

Flower La Grange de Monteillac ♣♣

℘ 05 65 70 21 00, *www.aveyron-location.com*
Address : chemin de Monteillac (take the northeastern exit along the D 28, follow the signs for Laissac, opposite the cemetery)
Opening times : permanent
4.5 ha (70 pitches) terraced, flat and relatively flat, grassy
Tariff : 32.90€ ✶✶ ⇌ 🗉 (10A) – Extra per person 6.50€ – Reservation fee 20€
Rental rates : (from beginning April to mid Oct.) 🅿 – 10 ⤵ – 22 ⌂ – 11 tent bungalows.
Per night from 38 to 132€ – Per week from 190 to 924€ – Reservation fee 20€

Pretty flowers and shrubs.

Surroundings : ▱ ♀
Leisure activities : ♟ ✗ 🎦 🎲 ⚇ 🚴 ♺ ✎ ✑
Facilities : ♿ ⚷ (Jul–Aug) ⚘ ⚐ ¶ launderette ⚏

Longitude : 2.85101
Latitude : 44.36434

SORÈZE

81540 – Michelin map **338** E10 – pop. 2,564 – alt. 272
▶ Paris 732 – Castelnaudary 26 – Castres 27 – Puylaurens 19

St-Martin

℘ 05 63 50 20 19, *www.campingsaintmartin.com*
Address : at Les Vigariés (north of the town, access via the r. de la Mairie; by the stadium)
Opening times : from beginning May to end Sept.
1 ha (54 pitches) flat, grassy, relatively flat
Tariff : (2012 price) 21.60€ ✶✶ ⇌ 🗉 (10A) – Extra per person 5€
Rental rates : (2012 price) (from beginning May to end Sept.) ✎ – 2 'gypsy' caravans – 1 ⤵ – 6 ⌂. Per night from 44 to 49€ – Per week from 264 to 680€
⚑ sani-station – 4 🗉 10.60€

Surroundings : ⚲ ▱ ♀♀
Leisure activities : ⚐ ✑
Facilities : ♿ ⚷ ¶ ▣
Nearby : ✎

Longitude : 2.06594
Latitude : 43.45337

SORGEAT

09110 – Michelin map **343** J8 – pop. 95 – alt. 1,050
▶ Paris 808 – Ax-les-Thermes 6 – Axat 50 – Belcaire 23

Municipal La Prade

℘ 05 61 64 36 34, *www.sorgeat.com* – alt. 1,000 – limited spaces for one-night stay
Address : above the village (800m to the north)
Opening times : permanent
2 ha (40 pitches) open site, terraced, flat, grassy
Tariff : 16.60€ ✶✶ ⇌ 🗉 (10A) – Extra per person 3.30€
Rental rates : (permanent) – 2 ⤵. Per night from 41€ – Per week from 325 to 360€

A pleasant location with a lovely view of the mountains surrounding the Ax valleys.

Surroundings : ⚲ ⬳ Vallée d'Ax-les-Thermes ▱ ♀♀
Leisure activities : 🎦
Facilities : ♿ ⚷ (Jul–Aug) ⧉ ⚘ ⚑ ¶ ▣

Longitude : 1.85378
Latitude : 42.73322

SOUILLAC

46200 – Michelin map **337** E2 – pop. 3,864 – alt. 104
▷ Paris 516 – Brive-la-Gaillarde 39 – Cahors 68 – Figeac 74

Les Castels Le Domaine de la Paille Basse ♣

℘ 05 65 37 85 48, www.lapaillebasse.com
Address : 6.5 km northwest along the D 15, follow the signs for Salignac-Eyvignes then continue 2km along the road to the right
Opening times : from mid May to mid Sept.
80 ha/12 ha for camping (262 pitches) undulating, terraced, flat, grassy, stony
Tariff : 39.90€ ♣♣ ⇔ 🅔 (16A) – Extra per person 9.50€ – Reservation fee 20€
Rental rates : (from mid April to mid Sept.) ⚡ – 82 ▦ – 2 ⌂. Per night from 60 to 200€
Per week from 250 to 1,120€ – Reservation fee 20€
🚐 sani-station
Spacious, undulating site with trees and bushes, based at an old renovated hamlet.

Surroundings : 🌳 ⛆ ♨
Leisure activities : 🍴 ✕ 🎱 🕹 🏃 🎣 🚲 ✂ 🏊 🏓 disco, entertainment room
Facilities : 👤 ⚷ 🔲 🛁 🚿 ‖ launderette 🏊 🛒

GPS
Longitude : 1.44175
Latitude : 44.94482

Municipal les Ondines

℘ 05 65 37 86 44, www.camping-lesondines.com
Address : at Les Ondines (located 1km southwest following signs for Sarlat and take road to the left; near the Dordogne river)
Opening times : from beginning May to end Sept.
4 ha (242 pitches) flat, grassy
Tariff : 24.90€ ♣♣ ⇔ 🅔 (6A) – Extra per person 5€ – Reservation fee 15€
Rental rates : (from beginning May to end Sept.) – 22 ▦ – 25 tent bungalows.
Per night from 36 to 107€ – Per week from 252 to 749€ – Reservation fee 15€
🚐 sani-station 4€

Surroundings : ♨
Leisure activities : 🎣
Facilities : 👤 ⚷ ‖ 🔲
Nearby : 🚲 ✂ 🏃 🏊 🛶 🏓 🐎 forest trail

GPS
Longitude : 1.47604
Latitude : 44.89001

TARASCON-SUR-ARIÈGE

09400 – Michelin map **343** H7 – pop. 3,515 – alt. 474
▷ Paris 777 – Ax-les-Thermes 27 – Foix 18 – Lavelanet 30

Yelloh! Village Le Pré Lombard ♣

℘ 05 61 05 61 94, www.prelombard.com
Address : located 1.5km southeast along the D 23; beside the Ariège
Opening times : from mid March to mid Oct.
4 ha (210 pitches) flat, grassy
Tariff : 36€ ♣♣ ⇔ 🅔 (10A) – Extra per person 8€
Rental rates : (from mid March to mid Oct.) – 91 ▦ – 19 ⌂ – 14 tent bungalows.
Per night from 30 to 107€ – Per week from 210 to 749€
🚐 sani-station 3€
The site is beside the Ariège river, offering plenty of shade and with a range of quality rental options.

Surroundings : 🌳 ♨
Leisure activities : 🍴 ✕ 🎱 🕹 🏃 🎣 🚲 🏊 🏓 multi-sports ground
Facilities : 👤 ⚷ ▦ 🛁 ‖ launderette 🛒
Nearby : 🛒

GPS
Longitude : 1.61227
Latitude : 42.83984

TEILLET

81120 – Michelin map **338** G7 – pop. 462 – alt. 475
▶ Paris 717 – Albi 23 – Castres 43 – Lacaune 49

L'Entre Deux Lacs

☎ 0563557445, *www.campingdutarn.com*
Address : 29 rue du Baron de Solignac (take the southern exit along the D 81, follow the signs for Lacaune)
Opening times : from beginning April to end Sept.
4 ha (65 pitches) terraced, flat, grassy, stony
Tariff : (2012 price) 20.20€ ✦✦ ⇆ 🗐 ⑭ (10A) – Extra per person 4.35€ – Reservation fee 10€
Rental rates : (2012 price) (from beginning April to end Nov.) Ⓟ – 17 🏠 – 2 tent bungalows. Per week from 253 to 618€ – Reservation fee 10€
🚐 sani-station 4€ – 🔌11.50€

Surroundings : 🏊 🚣 ♨
Leisure activities : ▼ ✕ 🎿 🛶
Facilities : 🚿 ☎ 🚻 🖾 🖴

GPS Longitude : 2.34
Latitude : 43.83

The prices listed were supplied by the campsite owners in 2012
(if prices were not available, those from the previous year are given).
The fees should be regarded as basic charges and may fluctuate
with inflation.

THÉGRA

46500 – Michelin map **337** G3 – pop. 492 – alt. 330
▶ Paris 535 – Brive-la-Gaillarde 58 – Cahors 64 – Rocamadour 15

Chalets Dordogne Vacances
(rental of chalets only)

☎ 0565108904, *www.dordogne-vacances.fr*
Address : 500m to the north, behind the new school
2.5 ha sloping
Rentals : 14 🏠.

Surroundings : 🏊 ♀
Leisure activities : 🎬 🎿 🛶
Facilities : 🚿 ☎ Ⓟ ▥ 🖾

GPS Longitude : 1.75607
Latitude : 44.82631

Le Ventoulou ♣♣

☎ 0565336701, *www.camping-leventoulou.com*
Address : 2.8km northeast along the D 14, follow the signs for Loubressac and take D 60, follow the signs for Mayrinhac-Lentour to the right
Opening times : from mid April to end Sept.
2 ha (66 pitches) terrace, flat, grassy
Tariff : 26.90€ ✦✦ ⇆ 🗐 ⑭ (10A) – Extra per person 6.90€ – Reservation fee 15€
Rental rates : (from mid April to end Sept.) – 17 🚐 – 4 🏠 – 6 tent bungalows. Per night from 43 to 123€ – Per week from 240 to 735€ – Reservation fee 15€
🚐 sani-station – 🔌⑭16€

Surroundings : 🏊 ♨
Leisure activities : ▼ 🎬 🏌 🎿 🛶
Facilities : 🚿 ☎ 🍴 🏕 🚿 🚻 🖾 🖴

GPS Longitude : 1.77778
Latitude : 44.82603

THOUX

32430 – Michelin map **336** H7 – pop. 223 – alt. 145 – Leisure centre
▶ Paris 681 – Auch 40 – Cadours 13 – Gimont 14

Lac de Thoux – Saint Cricq

✆ 05 62 65 71 29, *www.camping-lacdethoux.com*
Address : at Lannes (to the northeast along the D 654; beside the lake)
Opening times : from mid April to end Sept.
3.5 ha (130 pitches) flat, relatively flat, grassy
Tariff : (2012 price) 31€ ✝✝ ⟷ ▣ 🔌 (10A) – Extra per person 10€ – Reservation fee 15€
Rental rates : (2012 price) (from beginning March to end Oct.) – 32 ▭.
Per night from 69 to 159€ – Per week from 210 to 889€ – Reservation fee 15€
🚐 sani-station 5€ – 1 ▣ 8€

Surroundings : 🞉🞉 ⛰
Leisure activities : 🏃 🚴 ⛵
Facilities : ♿ ⚷ 🍖 🧺 🚰 ⚐ launderette
Nearby : 🏊 ☕ ✗ 🎣 jacuzzi ⛵ ✗ 🏖 ≃ (beach) 🛶 ⛵ pedalos

GPS
Longitude : 1.00234
Latitude : 43.68587

TOUZAC

46700 – Michelin map **337** C5 – pop. 352 – alt. 75
▶ Paris 603 – Cahors 39 – Gourdon 51 – Sarlat-la-Canéda 63

Le Ch'Timi

✆ 05 65 36 52 36, *www.campinglechtimi.com*
Address : at La Roque (direct access to the Lot river (via steep steps)
Opening times : from beginning April to end Sept.
3.5 ha (79 pitches) relatively flat, flat, grassy
Tariff : ✝ 6€ ⟷ ▣ 9€ – 🔌 (6A) 3.85€ – Reservation fee 10€
Rental rates : (permanent) – 5 ▭ – 2 🏠 – 5 gîtes. Per night from 32 to 90 €
Per week from 230 to 835 € – Reservation fee 10€
🚐 sani-station

Surroundings : 🞉🞉
Leisure activities : ⛵ 🚴 ✗ ⛵ 🛶
Facilities : ⚷ 🍖 ⚐ ▣

GPS
Longitude : 1.06533
Latitude : 44.49889

LE TREIN D'USTOU

09140 – Michelin map **334** F8 – pop. 351 – alt. 739
▶ Paris 804 – Aulus-les-Bains 13 – Foix 73 – St-Girons 31

Le Montagnou

✆ 05 61 66 94 97, *www.lemontagnou.com*
Address : rte de Guzet (take northwestern exit along the D 8, follow the signs for Seix, near the Alet)
Opening times : from beginning Dec. to mid Nov.
1.2 ha (40 pitches) flat, grassy
Tariff : (2012 price) ✝ 8.90€ ⟷ 2€ ▣ 16.50€ – 🔌 (10A) 6€
Rental rates : (2012 price) (permanent) ✂ – 2 ▭ – 2 tents. Per night from 45 to 80 €
Per week from 315 to 550 €
Pleasant pine grove with pitches near the stream.

Surroundings : ♀
Leisure activities : 📺 🛶
Facilities : ♿ ⚷ ▥ 🍖 🚰 ⚐ launderette ⟿
Nearby : ✗

GPS
Longitude : 1.25618
Latitude : 42.81178

LE TRUEL

12430 – Michelin map **338** I6 – pop. 348 – alt. 290
▶ Paris 677 – Millau 40 – Pont-de-Salars 37 – Rodez 52

Municipal la Prade

ℰ 05 65 46 41 46
Address : head east of the town along the D 31, turn left after the bridge; beside the Tarn river
0.6 ha (28 pitches) flat, grassy
Rentals : – 3 – gîte d'étape.

Surroundings :
Leisure activities :
Facilities :
Nearby :

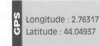
Longitude : 2.76317
Latitude : 44.04937

VAYRAC

46110 – Michelin map **337** G2 – pop. 1,330 – alt. 139 – Leisure centre
▶ Paris 512 – Beaulieu-sur-Dordogne 17 – Brive-la-Gaillarde 32 – Cahors 89

Chalets Mirandol Dordogne
(rental of chalets only)

ℰ 05 65 32 57 12, *www.mirandol-dordogne.com*
Address : at Vormes (2.3km south along the D 116, towards the leisure and activity park)
Opening times : from beginning April to end Sept.
2.6 ha open site, flat, grassy
Rental rates : ℗ – 22 . Per week from 180 to 680 €

Surroundings :
Leisure activities :
Facilities :
Nearby :

Longitude : 1.69771
Latitude : 44.93657

Municipal la Palanquière

ℰ 05 65 32 43 67, *www.vayrac.fr*
Address : at La Palanquière (located 1km south along the D 116, towards the leisure and activity park)
Opening times : from beginning June to mid Sept.
1 ha (33 pitches) flat, grassy
Tariff : (2012 price) ✚ 3.50€ 🚗 ▣ 3.30€ – (½) (6A) 3.60€

Surroundings :
Facilities :

Longitude : 1.70389
Latitude : 44.94464

VERS

46090 – Michelin map **337** F5 – pop. 415 – alt. 132
▶ Paris 565 – Cahors 15 – Villefranche-de-Rouergue 55

La Chêneraie

ℰ 05 65 31 40 29, *www.cheneraie.com* – limited spaces for one-night stay
Address : at Le Cuzoul (2.5km southwest along the D 653, follow the signs for Cahors and take the road to the right after the level crossing)
Opening times : from beginning May to end Sept.
2.6 ha/0.4 (58 pitches) flat, grassy
Tariff : 25€ ✚✚ 🚗 ▣ (½) (16A) – Extra per person 4€ – Reservation fee 9€
Rental rates : (from beginning April to end Sept.) – 28 . Per night from 50 to 85 €
Per week from 290 to 800 € – Reservation fee 9€
sani-station 2€ – 2 ▣ 15€

Surroundings :
Leisure activities :
Facilities :

Longitude : 1.54593
Latitude : 44.47154

VIELLE-AURE

65170 – Michelin map **342** N6 – pop. 355 – alt. 800
▶ Paris 828 – Toulouse 155 – Tarbes 70 – Lourdes 66

Le Lustou

✆ 0562394064, *www.lustou.com*
Address : at Agos (situated 2km northeast along the D 19, near the Neste-d'Aure and a lake)
Opening times : Permanent
2.8 ha (65 pitches) flat, gravelled, grassy
Tariff : (2012 price) ♟ 4.40€ ⟷ 🔲 4.60€ – (½) (10A) 6.80€
Rental rates : (2012 price) (from beginning Dec. to end Sept.) ⤢ – 6 ⏚⏚ – 1 gîte.
Per night from 48 to 50 € – Per week from 310 to 440 €
Beautiful entrance decorated with Pyrenean plants.

Surroundings : ❄ ⟨ 🌳🌳
Leisure activities : 🎦 ⛷ ✗
Facilities : ♿ ⚿ 🏢 🏖 ⛄ ⚐ 🍴 🔲 🚿
Nearby : 🏄 rafting and canyoning

GPS Longitude : 0.33841
Latitude : 42.84492

Fire safety doesn't stop when you leave your accommodation
Always take care and consider the fire risks.

LE VIGAN

46300 – Michelin map **337** E3 – pop. 1,457 – alt. 224
▶ Paris 537 – Cahors 43 – Gourdon 6 – Labastide-Murat 20

Le Rêve

✆ 0565412520, *www.campinglereve.com*
Address : at Revers (3.2km north along the D 673, follow the signs for Souillac then continue 2.8km along the road to the left)
Opening times : from mid May to mid Sept.
8 ha/2.5 ha for camping (60 pitches) relatively flat, flat, grassy, wood
Tariff : 22.80€ ♟♟ ⟷ 🔲 (½) (6A) – Extra per person 5.70€ – Reservation fee 5€
Rental rates : (from mid May to mid Sept.) – 4 ⏚ – 2 tents. Per week from 250 to 560 €
⛽ sani-station
Decorative flowers and shrubs; some pitches surrounded by bushes and shrubs.

Surroundings : 🐟 ⟷ 🌳🌳
Leisure activities : ☂ ⛷ 🏊
Facilities : ♿ ⚿ 🏖 ⛄ 🍴 launderette 🚿

GPS Longitude : 1.44183
Latitude : 44.77274

VILLEFRANCHE-DE-PANAT

12430 – Michelin map **338** I6 – pop. 771 – alt. 710
▶ Paris 676 – Toulouse 177 – Rodez 45 – Millau 46

Le Hameau des Lacs
(rental of chalets only)

✆ 0565658181, *www.les-hameaux.fr*
Address : rte de Rodez
1 ha terraced
Rentals : 🅿 – 22 ⏚.

Surroundings : ⟨ 🌳
Leisure activities : 🎦 🏇 ⛷ 🏊 multi-sports ground
Facilities : ♿ ⚿ 🏢 launderette
Nearby : 🏖 (beach)

GPS Longitude : 2.69457
Latitude : 44.09654

VILLEFRANCHE-DE-ROUERGUE

12200 – Michelin map **338** E4 – pop. 12,213 – alt. 230
▶ Paris 614 – Albi 68 – Cahors 61 – Montauban 80

Le Rouergue

☎ 05 65 45 16 24, *www.campingdurouergue.com*
Address : 35bis av. de Fondies (located 1.5km southwest along the D 47, follow the signs for Monteils)
Opening times : from mid April to end Sept.
1.8 ha (98 pitches) flat, grassy
Tariff : 19.12€ ♥♥ ⇌ 🗉 🅷 (16A) – Extra per person 3€ – Reservation fee 3€
Rental rates : (from mid April to end Sept.) – 7 🚐 – 6 tent bungalows.
Per night from 29 to 80 € – Per week from 130 to 450 € – Reservation fee 3€
🚐 sani-station 3€ – 3 🗉 12€ – 🔋11€

Surroundings : 🗔 ♤♤
Leisure activities : 🎦 🏹
Facilities : ⅋ ⚲ 🛁 🚿 🌱 🖼
Nearby : ♨ jacuzzi ⚲🎿 🖼🏊🏊

GPS Longitude : 2.02615
Latitude : 44.3423

Pierre Cheuve / Photononstop

A local saying claims that the hearts of the men of the north are warm enough to thaw the chilly climate. They certainly throw themselves body and soul into the traditional 'dance of the giants' at local fairs and carnivals. Giants are huge in this part of France as are the street markets: several tonnes of *moules-frites* (mussels and chips) and countless litres of beer sustain around a million visitors to the Braderie, Lille's annual giant street market. The influence of Flanders can be heard in the names of towns and people, seen in the wealth of Gothic architecture and tasted in such delicious regional dishes as beef in amber beer and *potjevleesch*, a terrine made with rabbit, chicken and veal. The sound of bells ringing from tall, slender belfries, neat rows of miners' houses and the distant silhouettes of windmills, all remind visitors that they are on the border with Belgium and within sight of the white cliffs of Dover.

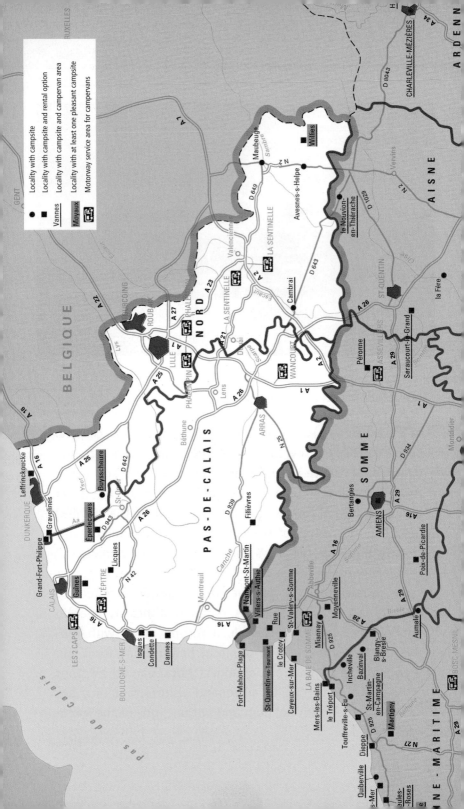

BUYSSCHEURE

59285 – Michelin map **302** B3 – pop. 510 – alt. 25
▶ Paris 269 – Béthune 44 – Calais 47 – Dunkerque 31

⚠ La Chaumière

📞 03 28 43 03 57, *www.campinglachaumiere.com*
Address : 529 Langhemast Straete (in the village)
1 ha (29 pitches) flat, grassy, stony, small lake
🚐 sani-station – 29 ▦

Surroundings : 🌿 ⌁ 🔵🔵
Leisure activities : 🍴 ✕ ⚓ 🎣 ⛵ 🏊
Facilities : ⊶ 🛁 ⚿ ↻ 🚿 🖼

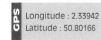

| GPS | Longitude : 2.33942 |
| | Latitude : 50.80166 |

> *These symbols are used for a campsite that is exceptional in its category:*
> ▲▲▲...▲ *Particularly pleasant setting, quality and range of services available*
> 🦢🦢 *Tranquil, isolated site – quiet site, particularly at night*
> ≤≤ *Exceptional view – interesting or panoramic view*

CAMBRAI

59400 – Michelin map **302** H6 – pop. 32,518 – alt. 53
▶ Paris 183 – Lille 67 – Amiens 100 – Namur 139

⚠ Municipal Les 3 Clochers

📞 03 27 70 91 64, *camping@mairie-cambrai.fr*
Address : 77 r. Jean Goude
Opening times : from beginning April to mid Oct.
1 ha (50 pitches) flat, grassy
Tariff : (2012 price) 14.50€ ✳ ✳ ⚓ ▦ (16A) – Extra per person 2€
🚐 sani-station – ♨ 🅿12.50€
Tourist information about Cambrai available.

Surroundings : ⌁ 🔵
Facilities : ♿ ⊶ ⚿ ▥ 🛁 ↻
Nearby : 🏕 🍴 ✕

| GPS | Longitude : 3.21476 |
| | Latitude : 50.17533 |

CONDETTE

62360 – Michelin map **301** C4 – pop. 2,575 – alt. 35
▶ Paris 254 – Boulogne-sur-Mer 10 – Calais 47 – Desvres 19

⚠ Caravaning du Château ♣

📞 03 21 87 59 59, *www.camping-caravaning-du-chateau.com*
Address : 21 r. Nouvelle (take the southern exit along the D 119)
Opening times : from beginning April to end Oct.
1.2 ha (70 pitches) flat, grassy, fine gravel
Tariff : (2012 price) 26.40€ ✳ ✳ ⚓ ▦ (10A) – Extra per person 6€
Rental rates : (2012 price) (from beginning April to end Oct.) – 2 🚐.
Per night from 54 to 69 € – Per week from 445 to 638 €
🚐 sani-station 5€

Surroundings : ⌁ 🔵🔵
Leisure activities : 🏃 ⚓
Facilities : ♿ ⊶ ▥ 🛁 🚿 launderette, refrigerators
Nearby : ✕

| GPS | Longitude : 1.62557 |
| | Latitude : 50.64649 |

DANNES

62187 – Michelin map **301** C4 – pop. 1,303 – alt. 30
▶ Paris 242 – Lille 136 – Arras 133 – Amiens 114

Municipal Le Mont-St-Frieux

☏ 03 21 33 24 76, *www.mairiededannes.fr*
Address : r. de l'Eglise (in the town)
1.5 ha (52 pitches) flat, grassy
Rentals : ⚡ – 3 ⌗.
⛽ sani-station

Surroundings : ⛺ ♀
Leisure activities : 🏊 ⛵ m
Facilities : ♿ ⚓ ♨ launderette

Longitude : 1.60997
Latitude : 50.58924

*The guide covers all 22 regions of France – see the map
and list of regions on pages 4–5.*

ÉPERLECQUES

62910 – Michelin map **301** G3 – pop. 3,162 – alt. 42
▶ Paris 271 – Lille 78 – Arras 86 – St-Omer 14

Château du Gandspette

☏ 03 21 93 43 93, *www.chateau-gandspette.com*
Address : 133 r. du Gandspette
Opening times : from beginning April to end Sept.
11 ha/4 ha for camping (167 pitches) relatively flat, grassy
Tariff : (2012 price) 29 € ★★ ⛟ 🔲 ⚡ (6A) – Extra per person 7 € – Reservation fee 7 €
Rental rates : (2012 price) (from beginning April to end Sept.) ⚡ – 8 ⌗.
Per week from 270 to 605 € – Reservation fee 7 €
⛽ sani-station – 11 🔲
In the wooded grounds of the château.

Surroundings : 🌳 ♀
Leisure activities : 🍷 ✗ 🏊 ⛵ ※ 🎿 multi-sports ground
Facilities : ♿ ⚓ 🚿 🍴 launderette 🐕

Longitude : 2.1789
Latitude : 50.81894

FILLIÈVRES

62770 – Michelin map **301** F6 – pop. 523 – alt. 46
▶ Paris 206 – Arras 52 – Béthune 46 – Hesdin 13

Les Trois Tilleuls

☏ 03 21 47 94 15, *www.camping3tilleuls.com* – limited spaces for one-night stay
Address : 28 r. de Frévent (take the southeastern exit along the D 340)
Opening times : from beginning April to mid Oct.
4.5 ha (120 pitches) open site, relatively flat
Tariff : (2012 price) ★ 4.50 € ⛟ 3 € 🔲 3 € – ⚡ (10A) 3.50 €
Rental rates : (2012 price) (from beginning April to mid Oct.) ♿ (1 mobile home) – 1 caravan –
7 ⌗ – 1 tent. Per night from 24 to 145 € – Per week from 168 to 615 €
In the heart of the Vallée de la Canche.

Surroundings : ⛺ ♀♀
Leisure activities : 🏊 🎣 ⛵ 🎿 multi-sports ground,
entertainment room
Facilities : ♿ ⚓ 🚿 🍴 launderette
Nearby : 🎿

Longitude : 2.15952
Latitude : 50.31417

GRAND-FORT-PHILIPPE

59153 – Michelin map **302** A2 – pop. 5,491 – alt. 5
▶ Paris 289 – Calais 28 – Cassel 40 – Dunkerque 24

⚠ La Plage

☎ 03 28 65 31 95, www.camping-de-la-plage.info
Address : 115 r. du Maréchal Foch (to the northwest)
1.5 ha (84 pitches) flat, grassy
Rental rates : 5 🏚.

Surroundings : 🍃🍃
Leisure activities : 🏄
Facilities : ᶼ ⚬⇥ ▥ ⵀ launderette

Longitude : 2.09746
Latitude : 51.00264

Michelin classification:
🛆🛆🛆🛆 *Extremely comfortable, equipped to a very high standard*
🛆🛆🛆 *Very comfortable, equipped to a high standard*
🛆🛆 *Comfortable and well equipped*
🛆 *Reasonably comfortable*
🛆 *Satisfactory*

GRAVELINES

59820 – Michelin map **302** A2 – pop. 11,499
▶ Paris 309 – Lille 94 – Arras 125 – Brugge 100

⚠ Les Dunes

☎ 03 28 23 09 80, www.camping-des-dunes.com
Address : at Petit-Fort-Philippe, r. Victor-Hugo (beside the beach)
Opening times : from beginning April to end Oct.
8 ha (304 pitches) flat, grassy, sandy
Tariff : 🛉 3.19€ – 🚗 1.45€ 🅿 2.47€ – (₷) (10A) 4.30€
Rental rates : (from beginning April to end Oct.) – 14 🏠 – 10 🏚 – 3 tent bungalows.
Per night from 47 to 124 € – Per week from 155 to 669 €

Surroundings : 🐟 ⌂
Facilities : ᶼ ⚬⇥ ▥ ⵀ launderette

Longitude : 2.11802
Latitude : 51.00754

GUÎNES

62340 – Michelin map **301** E2 – pop. 5,501 – alt. 5
▶ Paris 282 – Arras 102 – Boulogne-sur-Mer 29 – Calais 11

🛆🛆🛆 Les Castels La Bien Assise ♣♣

☎ 03 21 35 20 77, www.camping-bien-assise.fr
Address : D231 (take the southwestern exit along the D 231, follow the signs for Marquise)
20 ha/12 ha for camping (198 pitches) flat, relatively flat, grassy, small lake
Rentals : 6 🏠 – 4 🏚 – 7 🛏.
🖼 sani-station
Hotel and haute cuisine restaurant in the château complex.

Surroundings : 🐟 🍃🍃
Leisure activities : 🍴 ✗ 🎦 ⁂ 🏄 🚲 ※ ♪ 🖼 (open-air in season) ⛳
Facilities : ᶼ ⚬⇥ ▥ 🛁 ⵀ launderette 🏊 🐎

Longitude : 1.85815
Latitude : 50.86631

ISQUES

62360 – Michelin map **301** C3 – pop. 1,173 – alt. 15
▶ Paris 247 – Lille 125 – Arras 122 – Calais 44

▲ Les Cytises

☎ 03 21 31 11 10, *www.lescytises.fr*
Address : chemin Geoges Ducrocq (access via the N 1, near the stadium; from the A 16 take exit 28)
Opening times : permanent
2.5 ha (100 pitches) flat, terrace, grassy
Tariff : (2012 price) 17.70€ ★★ ⇔ 🔲 (4) (10A) – Extra per person 4€
Rental rates : (2012 price) (permanent) – 2 🏠. Per night from 50 € – Per week from 450 €
🚐 sani-station 3€ – 3 🔲 17.70€

Surroundings : 🌾 🌳🌳
Leisure activities : 🏠 🏊
Facilities : 🔥 ⚬ 🚰 launderette
Nearby : 🍴

Longitude : 1.64332
Latitude : 50.67749

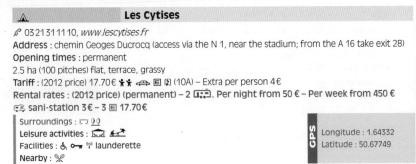

The classification (1 to 5 tents, black or red) that we award to selected sites in this guide is our own system. It should not be confused with the classification (1 to 5 stars) of official organisations.

LEFFRINCKOUCKE

59495 – Michelin map **302** C1 – pop. 4,517 – alt. 5
▶ Paris 292 – Calais 53 – Dunkerque 7 – Hazebrouck 48

▲ Mer et Vacances

☎ 03 28 20 17 32, *www.camping-mer-et-vacances.com* – limited spaces for one-night stay
Address : 216 r. J-B. Charcot (to the northeast)
2 ha (112 pitches) relatively flat, flat, grassy, sandy
Rentals : 10 🏠.
The site is bordered by dunes and near a beach of fine sand.

Surroundings : 🏖 🌾
Leisure activities : 🏠 🍴
Facilities : 🔥 ⚬ 🎱 🖼

Longitude : 2.44051
Latitude : 51.05865

LICQUES

62850 – Michelin map **301** E3 – pop. 1,563 – alt. 81
▶ Paris 276 – Arras 97 – Boulogne-sur-Mer 31 – Calais 25

▲▲ Pommiers des Trois Pays

☎ 03 21 35 02 02, *www.pommiers-3pays.com*
Address : 273 r. du Breuil
Opening times : from mid March to end Oct.
2 ha (58 pitches) flat, grassy
Tariff : (2012 price) 25.50€ ★★ ⇔ 🔲 (4) (16A) – Extra per person 5.90€
Rental rates : (2012 price) (from beginning April to end Oct.) 🔥 (1 chalet) – 7 🏠 – 8 🏡.
Per night from 62 € – Per week from 300 to 610 €
🚐 sani-station 3€ – 6 🔲 15€

Surroundings : 🏖 ⇔ 🌾 🌿
Leisure activities : 🍴 🍴 🏠 🏊 🏊 (covered off season)
Facilities : 🔥 ⚬ 🛁 🚿 ⚬ 🚰 launderette

Longitude : 1.94776
Latitude : 50.77991

MAUBEUGE

59600 – Michelin map **302** L6 – pop. 31,970 – alt. 134
▶ Paris 242 – Charleville-Mézières 95 – Mons 21 – St-Quentin 114

Municipal du Clair de Lune

℘ 03 27 62 25 48, *www.ville-maubeuge.fr*
Address : 212 rte de Mons (located 1.5km north along the N 2)
2 ha (92 pitches) flat, grassy

A pleasant site with decorative flowers and shrubs.

Surroundings : ⌂ ♨
Leisure activities : ≝✦
Facilities : ⴲ ⊶ ▥

Longitude : 3.9766
Latitude : 50.29573

WILLIES

59740 – Michelin map **302** M7 – pop. 165 – alt. 167 – Leisure centre
▶ Paris 225 – Avesnes-sur-Helpe 16 – Cambrai 69 – Charleroi 48

Val Joly

℘ 03 27 61 83 76, *www.valjoly.com*
Address : at Eppé Sauvage, base nautique (sailing centre) du Val Joly (located 1.5km east along the D 133, 300m from the lake)
4 ha (180 pitches) relatively flat, flat, grassy
Rental rates : 30 ⌂.
▦ sani-station

Located 1.5km from the tourist resort and the leisure and activity park.

Surroundings : ⌘ ♨
Leisure activities : ▱ ≝✦ ✂
Facilities : ⊶ ▥ launderette ⊿
Nearby : ⤸ ⬧

Longitude : 4.11518
Latitude : 50.12245

NORMANDY

Bertrand Rieger / hemis.fr

Normandy has inspired many poets and artists, including Baudelaire, Turner and Monet. Today, it also offers rural relaxation and coastal rejuvenation. Take a walk along the coast to fill your lungs with sea air and admire the elegant resorts. You may need to catch your breath when you first see the medieval Benedictine abbey of Mont Saint-Michel rising up from the sands or glimpse the view over Étretat's white cliffs. No visitor could fail to be moved by the memory of the brave men who gave their lives on the Normandy beaches in World War II. Further inland, you will discover acres of neat, hedge-lined fields. Drink in the scent of apple blossom, admire the pretty half-timbered cottages and follow the River Seine as it meanders past medieval cities, impressive castles and venerable abbeys. No experience would be complete without savouring the region's culinary classics, including a plate of boat-fresh seafood, creamy Camembert, cider and Calvados, the famous apple brandy.

Locality with campsite
Locality with campsite and rental option
Vannes — Locality with campsite and campervan area
Moyaux — Locality with at least one pleasant campsite
Motorway service area for campervans

ALDERNEY

Omonville-la-Rogue
CHERBOURG-OCTEVILLE
Maupertus-s-M.

les Pieux

St-Vaast-la-Hougue

le Rozel
Surtainville
Baubigny
Barneville-Carteret
St-Sauveur-le-Vicomte

Ravenoville

Colleville-s-M.
Port-en-Bessin
Arromanches-les-B⁹
Courseulles-s-M.
Bernières-s-M.
St-Aubin-s-M.
Luc-s-M.
Villers-s

St-Jean-de-la-Rivière
Ste-Mère-Église
Ste-Marie-du-Mont
Surrain

Denneville
St-Symphorien-le-Valois
Isigny-s-M.

Houlgate
Dives-s-M.

St-Germain-s-Ay
Carentan
Trévières
Bayeux
Étréham
Creully
Martragny
Merville-Franceville-Pl.
Gonneville-en

N 13
A 13
D 613

Agon-Coutainville
Coutances
St-Lô
MANCHE
CALVADOS
CAEN
N 158

Annoville
LA VALLÉE DE LA VIRE-GOUVET
Thury-Harcourt
le Vey
Falaise

Bréville-s-M.
Donville-les-B.
Bréhal
Pont-Farcy

Granville
St-Pair-s-Mer
Jullouville
D 924
Villedieu-les-Poêles
Vire
Brécey
Flers
Argentan

Genêts
Avranches
Sée

St-Malo
St-Lunaire
St-Briac-s-M.
Cancale
St-Coulomb
Courtils
Ducey
St-Hilaire-du-Harcouët
Domfront
Bagnoles-de-l'O.
ORNE

Roz-sur-Couesnon
St-Jouan-des-Guérets
St-Père
Beauvoir
Pontorson
Les Biards
LA DENTE D'ALENÇ

St-Samson-s-R.
Taden
Dinan
St-Marcan
Dol-de-Bretagne

la Chapelle-aux-Filtzméens
Ambrières-les-Vallées

Tinténiac
Feins
Mayenne

Châtillon-en-Vendelais
Fougères
N 12
Fresnay-s-Sarthe
Sillé-le-Guillaume

RENNES
MAYENNE
Andouillé
Évron
Mézières-s/s-Lavardi

Paimpont
Châteaugiron
St-Berthevin
Laval
Tennie
Loué

ILLE-ET-VILAINE
le Pertre
Meslay-du-Maine

Marcillé-Robert
la Selle-
Villiers-

AGON-COUTAINVILLE

50230 – Michelin map **303** C5 – pop. 2,826 – alt. 36
▶ Paris 348 – Barneville-Carteret 48 – Carenten 43 – Cherbourg 80

Municipal le Marais

☎ 02 33 47 05 20, *http://www.agoncoutainville.fr*
Address : bd Lebel-Jéhenne (take the northeastern exit, near the racecourse)
Opening times : from beginning July to end Aug.
2 ha (104 pitches) flat, grassy
Tariff : (2012 price) ♦ 3.90€ ⟵ 国 5.50€ – [½] (5A) 3.20€
🚐 sani-station 6.10€ – 30 国 6.10€

Surroundings : ▭
Leisure activities : ⚓
Facilities : 🚿 ⚡
Nearby : 🛒 ✗ 🏊 ◊

GPS Longitude : -1.59283
Latitude : 49.04975

Municipal le Martinet

☎ 02 33 47 05 20, *www.agoncoutainville.fr*
Address : Bd. Lebel-Jéhenne (take the northeastern exit, near the racecourse (hippodrome)
Opening times : from beginning April to end Oct.
1.5 ha (122 pitches) flat, grassy
Tariff : (2012 price) ♦ 3.90€ ⟵ 国 5.50€ – [½] (5A) 3.20€
🚐 sani-station 6.10€ – 30 国 6.10€

Surroundings : ▭ ♀
Leisure activities : ⚓
Facilities : 🚿 ⚡ ¶ launderette
Nearby : 🛒 ✗ 🏊 ◊ 🐎

GPS Longitude : -1.59283
Latitude : 49.04958

ALENÇON

61000 – Michelin map **310** J4 – pop. 27,325 – alt. 135
▶ Paris 190 – Chartres 119 – Évreux 119 – Laval 90

Municipal de Guéramé

☎ 02 33 26 34 95, *camping.guerame@orange.fr*
Address : 65 rte de Guéramé (to the southwest along the ring road (périphérique)
1.5 ha (54 pitches) terraced, flat, grassy, fine gravel
🚐 sani-station
A pleasant setting beside the Sarthe river.

Surroundings : ▭ ♀
Leisure activities : 🛶 ⚓ ✗
Facilities : 🚿 ⚡ ▦ ⛱ ❤ launderette
Nearby : 🛒 ⌇ 🏊 ⛱ 🎣 🐎

GPS Longitude : 0.0728
Latitude : 48.4259

ANNOVILLE

50660 – Michelin map **303** C6 – pop. 619 – alt. 28
▶ Paris 348 – Barneville-Carteret 57 – Carenten 48 – Coutances 14

Municipal les Peupliers

☎ 02 33 47 67 73, *camping-annoville.fr*
Address : r. des Peupliers (3km southwest along the D 20 and take the road to the right, 500m from the beach)
2 ha (100 pitches) flat, grassy, sandy
Rentals : ✂ – 5 🚕.

Surroundings : 🏖
Leisure activities : ⚓ 🚲 🏊
Facilities : ⚡ 🔥 🗜

GPS Longitude : -1.55309
Latitude : 48.95767

ARGENTAN

61200 – Michelin map **310** I2 – pop. 14,356 – alt. 160
▶ Paris 191 – Alençon 46 – Caen 59 – Dreux 115

Municipal de la Noë

℘ 02 33 36 05 69, *www.argentan.fr/tourisme*
Address : r. de la Noé
Opening times : from beginning April to end Sept.
0.3 ha (23 pitches) flat, grassy
Tariff : ✦ 2.30€ ⟷ 2€ 回 2.70€ – (⚡) (6A) 2.60€
🚽 sani-station 2.20€
A pleasant location near a park and a small lake.

Surroundings : 🗔
Leisure activities : 🛶
Facilities : ♿ ⟜ ⤵ ⍩ launderette
Nearby : 🏊 ⫙ ⤢ fitness trail

GPS Longitude : -0.01687
Latitude : 48.73995

ARROMANCHES-LES-BAINS

14117 – Michelin map **303** I3 – pop. 608 – alt. 15
▶ Paris 266 – Bayeux 11 – Caen 34 – St-Lô 46

Municipal

℘ 02 31 22 36 78, *arromanches.com*
Address : 9 av. de Verdun
Opening times : from beginning April to beginning Nov.
1.5 ha (126 pitches) terraced, relatively flat, flat, grassy
Tariff : (2012 price) 18€ ✦✦ ⟷ 回 (⚡) (10A) – Extra per person 4.45€
Rental rates : (2012 price) (from beginning April to beginning Nov.) – 6 🚐.
Per night from 75 € – Per week from 355 to 405 €
🚽 sani-station 2€ – 14 回

Surroundings : ♀
Leisure activities : ⤢⤴
Facilities : ♿ ⟜ (from mid-Jun to mid-Sept) ⍩ launderette
Nearby : 🍴 🖼 ♞ ⟆ ⤢

GPS Longitude : -0.62642
Latitude : 49.3381

This guide is updated regularly, so buy your new copy every year!

AUMALE

76390 – Michelin map **304** K3 – pop. 2,405 – alt. 130
▶ Paris 136 – Amiens 48 – Beauvais 49 – Dieppe 69

Municipal le Grand Mail

℘ 02 35 93 40 50, *www.aumale.com* – 🅁
Address : 6 Le Grand Mail
Opening times : from end March to end Sept.
0.6 ha (40 pitches) flat, grassy
Tariff : (2012 price) ✦ 2.70€ ⟷ 2.70€ 回 2.70€ – (⚡) (10A) 2.70€
🚽 sani-station 2€
Situated on the side of a hill above the town.

Surroundings : 🐾 ♀
Facilities : ♿ ⤵ 🛁 ⫼

GPS Longitude : 1.74202
Latitude : 49.76566

BAGNOLES-DE-L'ORNE

61140 – Michelin map **310** G3 – pop. 2,454 – alt. 140 –
▶ Paris 236 – Alençon 48 – Argentan 39 – Domfront 19

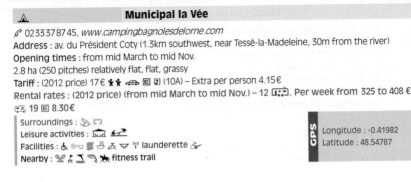

Municipal la Vée

📞 02 33 37 87 45, www.campingbagnolesdelorne.com
Address : av. du Président Coty (1.3km southwest, near Tessé-la-Madeleine, 30m from the river)
Opening times : from mid March to mid Nov.
2.8 ha (250 pitches) relatively flat, flat, grassy
Tariff : (2012 price) 17 € ♣ ♣ ⇦ 🔳 (10A) – Extra per person 4.15 €
Rental rates : (2012 price) (from mid March to mid Nov.) – 12 🛖. Per week from 325 to 408 €
🚐 19 🔳 8.30 €

Surroundings : 〰 🖂
Leisure activities : 🎦 🏇
Facilities : ♿ 🚰 ▥ 🛁 🚿 🗘 🚰 launderette 🖉
Nearby : ✂ 🏓 🏊 🎣 🦌 fitness trail

GPS Longitude : -0.41982
Latitude : 48.54787

In order for the guide to remain wholly objective, the selection is made on an entirely independent basis. There is no charge for being selected for the guide.

BARNEVILLE-CARTERET

50270 – Michelin map **303** B3 – pop. 2,282 – alt. 47
▶ Paris 356 – Caen 123 – Carentan 43 – Cherbourg 39

Les Bosquets

📞 02 33 04 73 62, www.camping-lesbosquets.com
Address : r. du Capitaine Quenault (2.5km southwest following signs for Barneville-Plage and take turning to the left, 450m from the beach)
Opening times : from beginning April to mid Sept.
15 ha/6 ha for camping (331 pitches) very uneven, flat, grassy, sandy
Tariff : ♣ 6.30 € ⇦ 🔳 6.30 € – (10A) 4.30 €
🚐 sani-station
Set in natural surroundings among pine trees and dunes.

Surroundings : 〰 🖂 ♨
Leisure activities : ♟ 🎦 🄸 🏇 🏊
Facilities : 🚰 🛁 launderette
Nearby : ✂ 🐎 🦌 sand yachting

GPS Longitude : -1.76081
Latitude : 49.36587

La Gerfleur

📞 02 33 04 38 41, www.lagerfleur.fr
Address : r. Guillaume-le-Conquérant (800m west along the D 903e, follow the signs for Carteret)
Opening times : from beginning April to end Oct.
2.3 ha (93 pitches) relatively flat, flat, grassy
Tariff : ♣ 5.50 € ⇦ 🔳 6.50 € – (6A) 4.40 €
Rental rates : (2012 price) (permanent) ⛺ – 9 🛖. Per night from 50 €
Per week from 310 to 580 €
Situated beside a small lake.

Surroundings : 🖂 ♨
Leisure activities : ♟ 🎦 🏇 🏊 🎣
Facilities : ♿ 🚰 🛁 launderette
Nearby : 🛒 ✂ 🎋 🏓 🦌

GPS Longitude : -1.76435
Latitude : 49.38346

BAUBIGNY

50270 – Michelin map **303** B3 – pop. 154 – alt. 30
🄳 Paris 361 – Barneville-Carteret 9 – Cherbourg 33 – Valognes 28

Bel Sito

🖉 02 33 04 32 74, *www.bel-sito.com* –
Address : north of the village
Opening times : from mid April to mid Sept.
6 ha/4 ha for camping (85 pitches) relatively flat to hilly, flat, grassy, sandy, dunes
Tariff : ✦ 6.70€ ⤷ 回 9.30€ – ⒃ (6A) 3.90€
Rental rates : (from mid April to end Oct.) – 1 ⛺ – 6 ⌂. Per week from 370 to 850 €
A natural setting among the dunes.

Surroundings : ⛰ ⋖
Leisure activities : 🎦 ⚓
Facilities : ⚲ (Jul–Aug) ⛱ ♨ launderette

Longitude : -1.80513
Latitude : 49.42954

BAYEUX

14400 – Michelin map **303** H4 – pop. 13,348 – alt. 50
🄳 Paris 265 – Caen 31 – Cherbourg 95 – Flers 69

Municipal

🖉 02 31 92 08 43, *www.camping-bayeux.fr*
Address : bd Eindhoven (north of the town)
Opening times : from beginning April to end Oct.
2.5 ha (140 pitches) flat, grassy, hard surface areas
Tariff : (2012 price) ✦ 4.26€ ⤷ 回 4.61€ – ⒃ (5A) 3.76€
Rental rates : (2012 price) (from beginning April to end Oct.) – 5 ⛺. Per night from 96 €
Per week from 410 to 655 €
⛽ sani-station – 38 回 4.61€
Decorative trees and shrubs.

Surroundings : 🌳
Leisure activities : 🎦 ⚓
Facilities : ⚐ ⚲ launderette
Nearby : 🛒 ✗ 🏊 (open-air in season)

Longitude : -0.69774
Latitude : 49.28422

*The pitches of many campsite are marked out with low hedges
of attractive bushes and shrubs.*

BAZINVAL

76340 – Michelin map **304** J2 – pop. 350 – alt. 120
🄳 Paris 165 – Abbeville 33 – Amiens 62 – Blangy-sur-Bresle 9

Municipal de la Forêt

🖉 02 32 97 04 01, *bazinval2@wanadoo.fr*
Address : 10 r. de Saulx (take the southwestern exit along the D 115 and take turning to the left, near the town hall)
0.4 ha (20 pitches) open site, relatively flat, grassy
⛽ sani-station – 2 回
Decorative trees and shrubs surround the pitches.

Surroundings : 🌳
Facilities : 🚿

Longitude : 1.55136
Latitude : 49.95487

BEAUVOIR

50170 – Michelin map **303** C8 – pop. 419
▶ Paris 358 – Caen 125 – St-Lô 91 – Rennes 63

Aux Pommiers

✆ 02 33 60 11 36, *www.camping-auxpommiers.com*
Address : 28 rte du Mont Saint Michel
Opening times : from mid March to mid Nov.
1.79 ha (107 pitches) flat, grassy
Tariff : (2012 price) 24.84 € ★★ ⟴ 🄴 🄷 (10A) – Extra per person 6.62 €
Rental rates : (from mid March to mid Nov.) – 16 🛏 – 5 🏠 – 4 ⊨ – 4 tent bungalows.
Per night from 39 to 86 € – Per week from 223 to 599 €
🚐 sani-station

Surroundings : ♀
Leisure activities : 🍸 ⚓ 🚲 ♨ 🏊 ⛷
Facilities : ⊷ – 2 individual sanitary facilities (🚿⇄ wc) 🚰 launderette
Nearby : ✂ 🔲 🐎

GPS	Longitude : -1.51264
	Latitude : 48.59618

We value your opinion and welcome your feedback.
Do email us at campingfrance@tp.michelin.com

LE BEC-HELLOUIN

27800 – Michelin map **304** E6 – pop. 419 – alt. 101
▶ Paris 153 – Bernay 22 – Évreux 46 – Lisieux 46

Municipal St-Nicolas

✆ 02 32 44 83 55, *campingstnicolas@orange.fr*
Address : 15 r. St-Nicolas (situated 2km east, along the D 39 and D 581, follow the signs for Malleville-sur-le-Bec and take road to the left)
Opening times : permanent
3 ha (90 pitches) flat, grassy
Tariff : (2012 price) 17.40 € ★★ ⟴ 🄴 🄷 (10A) – Extra per person 4 €
Rental rates : (2012 price) (permanent) – 4 🛏. Per night from 48 to 102€
Per week from 170 to 450 €
🚐 sani-station 3 € – 🄷12€
A well-kept site, with flowers.

Surroundings : 🏞 ♀
Leisure activities : ⚓ ✂ library
Facilities : ♿ ⊷ 🇯 🚰 launderette
Nearby : 🐎

GPS	Longitude : 0.72268
	Latitude : 49.23586

BELLÊME

61130 – Michelin map **310** M4 – pop. 1,547 – alt. 241
▶ Paris 168 – Alençon 42 – Chartres 76 – La Ferté-Bernard 23

Municipal

✆ 02 33 85 31 00, *mairie.belleme@wanadoo.fr*
Address : take the western exit along the D 955, follow the signs for Mamers and take road to the left, near the swimming pool
1.5 ha (50 pitches) terraced, relatively flat, flat, grassy

Surroundings : 🏞 ⌁ ♀
Facilities : ♿ ⛷
Nearby : ⊐ ✂ ♨ 🏊

GPS	Longitude : 0.555
	Latitude : 48.3747

BERNAY

27300 – Michelin map **304** D7 – pop. 10,285 – alt. 105
▶ Paris 155 – Argentan 69 – Évreux 49 – Le Havre 72

Municipal

✆ 0232433047, *www.bernay-tourisme.fr*

Address : r. des Canadiens (situated 2km southwest along the N 138, follow the signs for Alençon and take turning to the left – recommended route via the diversion (déviation) and ZI Malouve)
Opening times : from beginning May to end Sept.
1 ha (50 pitches) flat, grassy
Tariff : (2012 price) ★ 3.20€ ⇌ 3.30€ ▣ 5.20€ – ⚡ (8A) 3.65€
Rental rates : (2012 price) (from beginning May to end Sept.) – 2 ⛺. Per night from 46 €
Per week from 290 to 367 € – Reservation fee 99€
⛽ sani-station 2.50€
A well-kept, green campsite.

Surroundings : ▭ ⋒
Leisure activities : ▦ ⚿
Facilities : ♿ ⚷ ▱ ⚲ ↝ ❝ launderette
Nearby : ✗ ▣ ⚊

Longitude : 0.58683
Latitude : 49.07879

BERNIÈRES-SUR-MER

14990 – Michelin map **303** J4 – pop. 2,351
▶ Paris 253 – Caen 20 – Le Havre 114 – Hérouville-Saint-Clair 21

Le Havre de Bernières

✆ 0231966709, *www.camping-normandie.com*

Address : chemin de Quintefeuille
6.5 ha (240 pitches) flat, grassy
Rentals : 38 ⛺.
⛽ sani-station

Surroundings : ⋒⋒
Leisure activities : ▾ ✗ ▦ ⚇ ⛟ ⚿ ⚊
Facilities : ♿ ⚷ ▥ ⚅ launderette ⚶
Nearby : ⛖ ✗ ⚹ ≋ (beach) ⚞ bowling

Longitude : -0.42795
Latitude : 49.33245

LES BIARDS

50540 – Michelin map **303** E8 – alt. 495 – Leisure centre
▶ Paris 358 – Alençon 108 – Avranches 22 – Caen 126

Municipal La Mazure

✆ 0233891950, *www.lamazure.com*

Address : at the base de loisirs (leisure centre) (2.3km southwest along the D 85e, on the banks of the lake at Vezins)
Opening times : from beginning May to end Sept.
3.5 ha/0.4 (28 pitches) terrace, flat, grassy
Tariff : ★ 3.50€ ⇌ ▣ 4.50€ – ⚡ (4A) 3€
Rental rates : (from beginning May to end Sept.) – 12 ⌂ – 4 teepees. Per night 60€
Per week from 300 to 450€

Surroundings : ⚵ ▭
Leisure activities : ▾ ▦ ⚇ ⚿ ⚲ ✗
Facilities : ♿ ⚷ ▱ ⚲ ↝ ❝ launderette ⚶
Leisure/activities centre : ⚓ ⚞ electric boats

Longitude : -1.2047
Latitude : 48.5734

NORMANDY

BLANGY-LE-CHÂTEAU

14130 – Michelin map **303** N4 – pop. 678 – alt. 60
▶ Paris 197 – Caen 56 – Deauville 22 – Lisieux 16

Les Castels Le Brévedent ♣♣

☎ 02 31 64 72 88, *www.campinglebrevedent.com* ⌘
Address : rte du Pin (3km southeast along the D 51, by the château; beside a lake)
6 ha/3.5 ha for camping (140 pitches) sloping, flat, grassy
Rentals : ⌘ – 8 ⬛.
In the grounds of a 14th-century château, with a lake.

Surroundings : ⌘ ⌘ ⌘
Leisure activities : ⌘ ⌘ ⌘ evening ⌘ ⌘ ⌘ ⌘ ⌘ ⌘
Facilities : ⌘ ⌘ ⌘ ⌘ launderette ⌘ ⌘
Nearby : ⌘ ⌘

GPS Longitude : 0.3045
Latitude : 49.2253

To visit a town or region, use the MICHELIN Green Guides.

BLANGY-SUR-BRESLE

76340 – Michelin map **304** J2 – pop. 3,000 – alt. 70
▶ Paris 156 – Abbeville 29 – Amiens 56 – Dieppe 55

Municipal les Etangs

☎ 02 35 94 55 65, *auscygnesdopale.fr*
Address : southeast, near two lakes and 200m from the Bresle river; access via the r. du Maréchal-Leclerc, near the church
Opening times : from beginning April to end Oct.
0.8 ha (57 pitches) flat, grassy
Tariff : (2012 price) 12.50€ ♣♣ ⬛ ⬛ ⬛ (10A) – Extra per person 3€
Rental rates : (2012 price) (from beginning April to end Oct.) – 4 ⬛.
Per night from 80 to 125 € – Per week from 150 to 550 € – Reservation fee 50€

Surroundings : ⌘
Leisure activities : ⌘
Facilities : ⌘ ⌘ ⌘
Nearby : ⌘ ⌘ ⌘

GPS Longitude : 1.63638
Latitude : 49.93096

BOURG-ACHARD

27310 – Michelin map **304** E5 – pop. 2,948 – alt. 124
▶ Paris 141 – Bernay 39 – Évreux 62 – Le Havre 62

Le Clos Normand

☎ 02 32 56 34 84, *www.leclosnormand.eu*
Address : 235 rte de Pont-Audemer (take the western exit)
Opening times : from mid April to end Sept.
1.4 ha (75 pitches) relatively flat, flat, grassy, wood
Tariff : (2012 price) 20.50€ ♣♣ ⬛ ⬛ ⬛ (6A) – Extra per person 5€
Rental rates : (2012 price) (from beginning April to end Sept.) ⌘ – 6 ⬛.
Per night from 65 € – Per week from 250 to 470 €
⬛ sani-station
A green setting with flowers.

Surroundings : ⌘ ⌘
Leisure activities : ⌘ ⌘ ⌘ ⌘
Facilities : ⌘ ⌘ ⌘

GPS Longitude : 0.80765
Latitude : 49.35371

BRÉCEY

50370 – Michelin map **303** F7 – pop. 2,165 – alt. 75
Paris 328 – Avranches 17 – Granville 42 – St-Hilaire-du-Harcouët 20

Intercommunal le Pont Roulland

0233486060, *www.camping-brecey.com*
Address : 1.1km east along the D 911, follow the signs for Cuves
Opening times : from beginning May to beginning Sept.
1 ha (52 pitches) relatively flat, flat, grassy
Tariff : 2.70€ 1.55€ 3.60€ – (6A) 2.80€
Rental rates : (from beginning May to beginning Sept.) – 4. Per night from 120 €
Per week from 300 to 400 €

A rural setting near a small lake.

Surroundings :
Leisure activities :
Facilities :
Nearby :

Longitude : -1.15235
Latitude : 48.72184

The information in the guide may have changed since going to press.

BRÉHAL

50290 – Michelin map **303** C6 – pop. 3,017 – alt. 69
Paris 345 – Caen 113 – St-Lô 48 – St-Malo 101

La Vanlée

0233616380, *www.camping-vanlee.com*
Address : r. des Gabions
Opening times : from beginning May to end Sept.
11 ha (466 pitches) undulating, flat, grassy, sandy
Tariff : (2012 price) 4.95€ 5.60€ – (6A) 4.10€
Rental rates : (2012 price) (permanent) (from beg May to end Sept) – 5 tent bungalows.
Per night from 50 € – Per week from 199 to 389 €
sani-station 4€

A pleasant setting on an unspoilt site beside the sea.

Surroundings :
Leisure activities : multi-sports ground
Facilities : launderette

Longitude : -1.56474
Latitude : 48.90913

BRÉVILLE-SUR-MER

50290 – Michelin map **303** K4 – pop. 803 – alt. 70
Paris 341 – Caen 108 – St-Lô 50 – St-Malo 95

La Route Blanche

0233502331, *www.camping-breville.com*
Address : 6 r. de La Route Blanche (located 1km northwest following signs for the beach, near the golf course)
5.5 ha (273 pitches) flat, grassy, sandy
Rentals : – 25.
sani-station

Surroundings :
Leisure activities : multi-sports ground
Facilities : launderette
Nearby : sports trail

Longitude : -1.56376
Latitude : 48.86966

CANY-BARVILLE

76450 – Michelin map **304** D3 – pop. 3,080 – alt. 25
▶ Paris 187 – Bolbec 34 – Dieppe 45 – Fécamp 21

Municipal

☎ 02 35 97 70 37, *www.cany-barville.fr*
Address : rte de Barville (take the southern exit along the D 268, follow the signs for Yvetot, after the stadium)
Opening times : from beginning April to end Sept.
2.9 ha (100 pitches) flat, grassy, concrete surface areas
Tariff : (2012 price) ⚹ 3.40€ ⛫ 1.70€ ▣ 3.40€ – ⚡ (16A) 10€
sani-station 2.60€ – 38 ▣ 5.10€

Surroundings : ▭
Leisure activities : ⌂ ⚓
Facilities : ♿ ⚲ ▥ ⌁ ☇ ⚐ launderette
Nearby : ☗

Longitude : 0.64231
Latitude : 49.7834

CARENTAN

50500 – Michelin map **303** E4 – pop. 6,056 – alt. 18
▶ Paris 308 – Avranches 89 – Caen 74 – Cherbourg 52

Flower Le Haut Dick

☎ 02 33 42 16 89, *www.camping-lehautdick.com*
Address : 30 chemin du Grand Bas Pays (beside the canal, near the swimming pool)
Opening times : from end March to beginning Oct.
2.5 ha (130 pitches) undulating, flat, grassy, sandy
Tariff : 26.50€ ⚹⚹ ⛫ ▣ ⚡ (6A) – Extra per person 5€
Rental rates : (from end March to beginning Oct.) – 22 ⌂ – 4 tents.
Per night from 50 to 101 € – Per week from 196 to 707 €
sani-station 5€ – 2 ▣ 16€ – 🚐 11€
In a pleasant, leafy setting.

Surroundings : ⚘ ▭ ♨
Leisure activities : ⚐ ✗ ⌂ ⚓ ♜
Facilities : ♿ ⚲ ⚐
Nearby : ✗ ▨ ☇ ⚲

Longitude : -1.23917
Latitude : 49.3087

COLLEVILLE-SUR-MER

14710 – Michelin map **303** G3 – pop. 171 – alt. 42
▶ Paris 281 – Bayeux 18 – Caen 48 – Carentan 36

Le Robinson

☎ 02 31 22 45 19, *www.campinglerobinson.com*
Address : at Hameau de Cabourg (800m northeast along the D 514, follow the signs for Port-en-Bessin)
Opening times : from beginning April to end Sept.
1 ha (67 pitches) flat, grassy
Tariff : ⚹ 5.90€ ⛫ 2.60€ ▣ 5.70€ – ⚡ (6A) 4.50€ – Reservation fee 17€
Rental rates : (from beginning April to end Sept.) ⚒ – 13 ⌂ – 2 ⌂ – 1 tent bungalow.
Per night from 50 to 70 € – Per week from 284 to 663 € – Reservation fee 17€
Direct access to 'Omaha' beach.

sani-station
Surroundings : ▭
Leisure activities : ⚐ ✗ ⚓ ☇ ⚑
Facilities : ♿ ⚲ ⚐ launderette
Nearby : ✗ ⛖

Longitude : -0.83497
Latitude : 49.34968

OURSEULLES-SUR-MER

4470 – Michelin map **303** J4 – pop. 4,185
Paris 252 – Arromanches-les-Bains 14 – Bayeux 24 – Cabourg 41

Municipal le Champ de Course

℘ 02 31 37 99 26, *www.campingcourseulles.com*
Address : av. de la Libération (to the north)
Opening times : from beginning April to end Sept.
7.5 ha (381 pitches) flat, grassy
Tariff : (2012 price) 20.40€ ✝✝ ⇔ 🗐 🗐 (10A) – Extra per person 4.80€
Rental rates : (2012 price) (from beginning April to end Sept.) – 27 🏠 – 7 tent bungalows.
Per night from 65 to 120 € – Per week from 166 to 645 €
🖙 sani-station 2.15€ – 13 🗐 6.20€
Situated near the beach.

Surroundings : ⌑
Leisure activities : 🖼 ⚓
Facilities : ⅙ ⚲ 🛆 ⚲ ⚲ launderette
Nearby : ✕ ⚲ ⌂ ⚊ ⚊ ⚲

Longitude : -0.44606
Latitude : 49.33289

COURTILS

0220 – Michelin map **303** D8 – pop. 245 – alt. 35
Paris 349 – Avranches 13 – Fougères 43 – Pontorson 15

St-Michel

℘ 02 33 70 96 90, *www.campingsaintmichel.com*
Address : 35 rte du Mont Saint Michel (take the western exit along the D 43)
Opening times : from end Feb. to mid Nov.
2.5 ha (100 pitches) flat and relatively flat, grassy
Tariff : ✝ 7€ ⇔ 🗐 7€ – 🗐 (6A) 4€
Rental rates : (from end Feb. to mid Nov.) – 42 🖚. Per night from 45 to 80€
Per week from 252 to 420 €
🖙 sani-station 4.50€ – 🖙 🗐 14.50€

Surroundings : ⌑ ⚲
Leisure activities : ✕ 🖼 ⚓ 🚲 ⚊ wildlife park
Facilities : ⅙ ⚲ 🗐 🛆 ⚲ launderette ⚲
Nearby : ⚲ ⚲

Longitude : -1.41611
Latitude : 48.62829

Gîtes range from small maisonettes to old farmhouses with several bedrooms.

CREULLY

4480 – Michelin map **303** I4 – pop. 1,610 – alt. 27
Paris 253 – Bayeux 14 – Caen 20 – Deauville 62

Intercommunal des 3 Rivières

℘ 02 31 80 90 17, *www.campingdes3rivieres.fr*
Address : rte de Tierceville (800m to the northeast; beside the Seulles river)
2 ha (82 pitches) flat and relatively flat, grassy
Rentals : 5 🖚.
In a peasant, green setting.

Surroundings : 🌄 ⟨ ⌑ ⚲
Leisure activities : 🖼 🚲 ⚲ ⚲
Facilities : ⚲ 🗐 🖾
Nearby : ⚓ fitness trail

Longitude : -0.5295
Latitude : 49.28964

DENNEVILLE

50580 – Michelin map **303** C4 – pop. 539 – alt. 5
▶ Paris 347 – Barneville-Carteret 12 – Carentan 34 – St-Lô 53

⚠ L'Espérance

℘ 02 33 07 12 71, *www.camping-esperance.fr* – limited spaces for one-night stay
Address : 36 r. de la Gamburie (3.5km west along the D 137, 500m from the beach)
Opening times : from beginning April to end Sept.
3 ha (134 pitches) flat, grassy, sandy
Tariff : (2012 price) 28.50€ ★★ ⚎ 🅴 🅹 (6A) – Extra per person 6.20€
Rental rates : (2012 price) (from beginning April to end Sept.) – 12 🛖.
Per night from 62 to 98 € – Per week from 310 to 690€

Surroundings : ⚲ ♀
Leisure activities : ▼ ✕ ⊌ evening 🏊 ✂ ⛱ 🏊
Facilities : ⚲ ⚲ launderette ⚲ ⚲

Longitude : -1.68832
Latitude : 49.30332

To make the best possible use of this guide,
please read pages 2–15 carefully.

DIEPPE

76200 – Michelin map **304** G2 – pop. 32,670 – alt. 6
▶ Paris 197 – Abbeville 68 – Beauvais 107 – Caen 176

⚠ Vitamin'

℘ 02 35 82 11 11, *www.camping-vitamin.com* – limited spaces for one-night stay
Address : 865 chemin des Vertus (3km south along the N 27, follow the signs for Rouen and take
a right turn)
Opening times : from beginning April to mid Oct.
5.3 ha (180 pitches) flat, grassy
Tariff : 23.40€ ★★ ⚎ 🅴 🅹 (10A) – Extra per person 5.40€
Rental rates : (from beginning April to mid Oct.) ♿ – 19 🛖 – 4 🏠.
Per night from 42 to 110 € – Per week from 199 to 640€

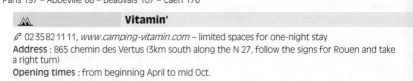

Surroundings : ⊏
Leisure activities : ▼ 🏕 🏊 🏊 🏊 multi-sports ground
Facilities : ♿ ⚲ ⚲ launderette
Nearby : 🛒 ✕ ✂ 🎯 🏊, squash

Longitude : 1.07481
Latitude : 49.90054

⚠ La Source

℘ 02 35 84 27 04, *www.camping-la-source.fr* – limited spaces for one-night stay
Address : 63 r. des Tisserands (3km southwest along the D 925, follow the signs for Le Havre then
turn left onto D 153; at Petit-Appeville)
Opening times : from mid March to mid Oct.
2.5 ha (120 pitches) flat, grassy
Tariff : ★ 6.20€ ⚎ 1.90€ 🅴 8.90€ – 🅹 (10A) 4.20€
Rental rates : (from mid March to mid Oct.) – 4 🛖. Per night from 140 €
Per week from 385 to 555 €
🚐 14 🅴 9.90€
In a picturesque setting beside the Scie river.

Leisure activities : ▼ 🏕 🏊 🚲 🏊 🎣
Facilities : ♿ ⚲ ⚲ ⚲ launderette

Longitude : 1.05526
Latitude : 49.89619

DIVES-SUR-MER

14160 – Michelin map **303** L4 – pop. 5,935 – alt. 3
◧ Paris 219 – Cabourg 2 – Caen 27 – Deauville 22

⚠ Le Golf

✆ 0231247309, *www.campingdugolf.com* – limited spaces for one-night stay
Address : rte de Lisieux (take the eastern exit, D 45 for 3.5km)
Opening times : from beginning April to end Sept.
2.8 ha (155 pitches) flat, grassy
Tariff : (2012 price) 21€ ♦♦ ⚓ 🅴 (10A) – Extra per person 4.50€
Rental rates : (2012 price) (from beginning April to end Sept.) – 15 📟 – 3 🏠 –
1 teepee – 1 tent bungalow. Per night from 39 to 86 € – Per week from 129 to 649 €
Reservation fee 15€
🚰 1 🅴 17.70€

Surroundings : 🗁 ♀
Leisure activities : ♈ ⚔ ⚓
Facilities : ♿ ⚂ ♨ launderette

GPS Longitude : -0.0701
Latitude : 49.2792

*In order for the guide to remain wholly objective, the selection of
campsites is made on an entirely independent basis.*

DOMFRONT

61700 – Michelin map **310** F3 – pop. 3,866 – alt. 185
◧ Paris 250 – Alençon 62 – Argentan 55 – Avranches 65

⚠ Municipal le Champ Passais

✆ 0233373766, *http://camping-municipal-domfront.jimdo.com/*
Address : r. du Champ Passais (head south along the station road and take the turning to the left)
Opening times : from beginning April to end Sept.
1.5 ha (34 pitches) terraced, flat, grassy
Tariff : (2012 price) ♦ 2.65€ ⚓ 🅴 3,05€ – 🅴 (10A) 4€
🚰 sani-station 1.50€

Surroundings : 🗁
Leisure activities : 🎬 ⚔
Facilities : ♿ ⚂ ♨ 🔲
Nearby : 🚵 (mountain biking) ✗ ⚓

GPS Longitude : -0.6505
Latitude : 48.5889

DONVILLE-LES-BAINS

50350 – Michelin map **303** C6 – pop. 3,269 – alt. 40
◧ Paris 341 – Caen 112 – St-Lô 77

⚠ L'Ermitage

✆ 0233500901, *www.camping-ermitage.com*
Address : r. de l'Ermitage (located 1km north along the r. du Champ de Courses)
Opening times : from mid April to mid Oct.
5 ha (298 pitches) relatively flat, flat, grassy, sandy
Tariff : (2012 Price) ♦ 5.10€ ⚓ 2€ 🅴 8.10€ – 🅴 (10A) 8.10€
Situated near a beautiful beach of fine sand.

Surroundings : 🗁
Leisure activities : 🎬 daytime ⚔
Facilities : ♿ ⚂ ♨ launderette
Nearby : ⚓ ♈ ✗ ⚂ 🔲 (open-air in season) ⚘ bowling

GPS Longitude : -1.58075
Latitude : 48.85212

DUCEY

50220 – Michelin map **303** E8 – pop. 2,465 – alt. 15
◨ Paris 348 – Avranches 11 – Fougères 41 – Rennes 80

▲ Municipal la Sélune

℘ 02 33 48 46 49, www.ducey-tourisme.com
Address : r. de Boishue (take the western exit along the N 176 and take the D 178, follow the signs for St-Aubin-de-Terregatte to the left; by the stadium)
Opening times : from beginning April to end Sept.
0.42 ha (40 pitches) flat, grassy
Tariff : (2012 price) ⚹ 2.90€ ⇌ ▣ 2.20€ – ⚡ (5A) 1.90€
🚐 sani-station 2€ – 2 ▣ 8.60€
The pitches well marked out with hedges of thuja.

Surroundings : ⊏⊐
Facilities : ⚹ ⊞ ⚐
Nearby : ✗ ▨ ⤓

GPS Longitude : -1.29452
Latitude : 48.61686

ÉTRÉHAM

14400 – Michelin map **303** H4 – pop. 271 – alt. 30
◨ Paris 276 – Bayeux 11 – Caen 42 – Carentan 40

⋀⋀ Reine Mathilde

℘ 02 31 21 76 55, www.campingreinemathilde.com –
Address : at Le Marais (located 1km west along the D 123 and take the road to the right)
Opening times : from end March to end Sept.
6.5 ha (115 pitches) flat, grassy
Tariff : (2012 price) ⚹ 6.50€ ⇌ ▣ 6.10€ – ⚡ (6A) 4.70€
Rental rates : (2012 price) (from end March to end Sept.) – 6 🛖 – 6 🏠 – 2 tent bungalows.
Per night 72€ – Per week from 423 to 602 €
🚐 sani-station

Surroundings : ⅏ ⊏⊐ 💯
Leisure activities : ⛲ 🎱 ⤓ ⤓
Facilities : ⚹ ⌦ ⌂ ▣ ⤓

GPS Longitude : -0.8025
Latitude : 49.33131

*The guide covers all 22 regions of France – see the map
and list of regions on pages 4–5.*

ÉTRETAT

76790 – Michelin map **304** B3 – pop. 1,502 – alt. 8
◨ Paris 206 – Bolbec 30 – Fécamp 16 – Le Havre 29

▲ Municipal

℘ 02 35 27 07 67
Address : r. Guy de Maupassant (located 1km southeast along the D 39, follow the signs for Criquetot-l'Esneval)
1.2 ha (73 pitches) flat, grassy, gravelled
🚐 sani-station – 30 ▣
The entrance is pretty, with flowers, and the site is very well maintained in general.

Surroundings : ♀
Leisure activities : 🎱 ⤓
Facilities : ⌦ ▥ launderette
Nearby : ✗ ▨

GPS Longitude : 0.21557
Latitude : 49.70063

ALAISE

4700 – Michelin map **303** K6 – pop. 8,333 – alt. 132
Paris 264 – Argentan 23 – Caen 36 – Flers 37

Municipal du Château

⌀ 02 31 90 16 55, *www.falaise-tourisme.com*
Address : r. du Val d'Ante (to the west of the town, in the Val d'Ante)
Opening times : from beginning May to end Sept.
2 ha (66 pitches) terrace, relatively flat, flat, grassy
Tariff : ⚹ 4.50€ ⇔ 🅴 5.30€ – ⚡ (10A) 4.20€
Green setting in the grounds of the château.

Surroundings : ⩽ Château Val de Meuse ♀
Leisure activities : 🖼 🏸 ⚝ library
Facilities : ⚹ ⊶ 🏛 ⚐
Nearby : ⟰ climbing wall

GPS Longitude : -0.2052
Latitude : 48.89563

> *Routes nationales are main roads and their identifying numbers*
> *begin with N or RN. Routes départmentales are generally quieter*
> *roads and begin with D or DN.*

IQUEFLEUR-ÉQUAINVILLE

7210 – Michelin map **304** B5 – pop. 642 – alt. 17
Paris 189 – Deauville 24 – Honfleur 7 – Lisieux 40

Domaine Catinière

⌀ 02 32 57 63 51, *www.camping-catiniere.com*
Address : rte de Honfleur (located 1km south of Fiquefleur along the D 22, near two streams)
Opening times : from mid April to mid Sept.
3.8 ha (130 pitches) flat, grassy
Tariff : 21.50€ ⚹⚹ ⇔ 🅴 ⚡ (13A) – Extra per person 4€
Rental rates : (from mid April to mid Sept.) ⚝ – 19 🛏 – 19 🏠 – 1 ⊨ – 1 gîte.
Per week from 336 to 648 €

Surroundings : ⊡ ♀
Leisure activities : ❢ ✕ 🖼 🏸 ⟰ 🛝 ⚲
Facilities : ⚹ ⊶ 🛉 ⚎ ⚐ launderette

GPS Longitude : 0.30382
Latitude : 49.40161

LERS

1100 – Michelin map **310** F2 – pop. 15,592 – alt. 270
Paris 234 – Alençon 73 – Argentan 42 – Caen 60

Le Pays de Flers

⌀ 02 33 65 35 00, *www.flers-agglomeration.fr/130-camping-de-la-fouquerie.htm*
Address : at La Fouquerie (1.7km east along the D 924, follow the signs for Argentan and take road to the left)
Opening times : from beginning April to end Oct.
1.5 ha (50 pitches) relatively flat, grassy
Tariff : (2012 Price) ⚹ 3€ ⇔ 🅴 3€ – ⚡ (10A) 3€
Rental rates : (2012 price) (permanent) ⚹ – 2 🛏. Per night from 52€
Per week from 258 to 361 €

Surroundings : 🌳 ⊡ ♀
Leisure activities : 🖼 🏸 🎠
Facilities : ⚹ ⊶ 🏛 ⚎ ⚐ ⚍ ⚐
Nearby : ⟰

GPS Longitude : -0.54311
Latitude : 48.75463

GENÊTS

50530 – Michelin map **303** D7 – pop. 427 – alt. 2
▶ Paris 345 – Avranches 11 – Granville 24 – Le Mont-St-Michel 33

△ Les Coques d'Or

℘ 02 33 70 82 57, *www.campinglescoquesdor.com*
Address : 14 Le Bec d'Andaine (700m northwest along the D 35e1, follow the signs for Le Bec d'Andaine)
Opening times : from beginning April to end Sept.
4.7 ha (225 pitches) flat, grassy
Tariff : (2012 price) ♠ 6.50€ ⇌ 2.80€ 🗉 2.80€ – ⑭ (10A) 4.50€
Rental rates : (2012 price) (from beginning April to end Sept.) – 11 ⟨⟩ – 2 ⌂.
Per night from 69 € – Per week from 355 to 585 €
🚰 sani-station 4€ – 20 🗉 3€

Surroundings : ⏚ ⊏ ♀
Leisure activities : ♥ ✕ ⚓ ☗
Facilities : ⅙ ⚬ 占 ⁙ launderette ⚘
Nearby : ⨷ (mountain biking) ♨ walking and horse-riding trail

Longitude : -1.48444
Latitude : 48.68778

GONNEVILLE-EN-AUGE

14810 – Michelin map **303** K4 – pop. 419 – alt. 16
▶ Paris 223 – Caen 20 – Le Havre 84 – Hérouville-St-Clair 16

△ Le Clos Tranquille

℘ 02 31 24 21 36, *www.campingleclostranquille.fr*
Address : 17 rt de Troarn (800m south along the D 95a)
Opening times : from beginning April to end Oct.
1.3 ha (78 pitches) flat, grassy
Tariff : (2012 price) ♠ 5€ ⇌ 🗉 6€ – ⑭ (10A) 5€
Rental rates : (2012 price) (from beginning March to end Nov.) – 4 ⟨⟩ – 2 ⌂ – 3 ⊨.
Per night 100€ – Per week 550€

Surroundings : ⏚ ⊏ ♀
Leisure activities : ⊡ ⚓
Facilities : ⚬ 占 ⁙ launderette
Nearby : ✕ ♨ ⚕

Longitude : -0.17771
Latitude : 49.23853

GRANVILLE

50400 – Michelin map **303** C6 – pop. 12,847 – alt. 10
▶ Paris 342 – Avranches 27 – Caen 109 – Cherbourg 105

⋀⋀⋀ Les Castels Le Château de Lez-Eaux

℘ 02 33 51 66 09, *www.lez-eaux.com*
Address : at St-Aubin-des-Préaux (7km southeast along the D 973, follow the signs for Avranches)
Opening times : from beginning April to mid Sept.
12 ha/8 ha for camping (229 pitches) relatively flat, flat, grassy
Tariff : 28€ ♠♠ ⇌ 🗉 ⑭ (10A) – Extra per person 8€ – Reservation fee 8€
Rental rates : (from beginning April to mid Sept.) ⅙ – 9 ⟨⟩ – 45 ⌂ – 2 cabins in the trees.
Per night from 55 to 222 € – Per week from 385 to 1,554 €– Reservation fee 8€

In the grounds of the château, with an attractive swimming area.

Surroundings : ⏚ ♀
Leisure activities : ♥ ⊡ ⑭ ⚓ ⨷ ✕ 🗺 ☗ ⊿ ⚲
Facilities : ⅙ ⚬ ⦀ 占 ⊿ ⥁ ⁙ launderette ⚘
Nearby : ♨ ◗ ⚕

Longitude : -1.52461
Latitude : 48.79774

La Vague

☎ 0233502997, *www.camping-la-vague.com*
Address : 126 rte de Voudrelin (2.5km southeast along the D 911, follow the signs for St-Pair and take the D 572 to the left; at St Nicolas-Plage)
2 ha (145 pitches) flat, grassy, sandy
Rentals : ⚡ – 7 ⛺.
🚐 sani-station
A green setting that is pleasant and well kept.

Surroundings : 🌳 ♨ Leisure activities : 🎱 🎯 m̂ Facilities : ♿ o━ 🖼 Nearby : 🏊 (open-air in season) 🐎 🏇	**GPS** Longitude : -1.57317 Latitude : 48.82146

LE GROS-THEIL

27370 – Michelin map **304** F6 – pop. 931 – alt. 145
▶ Paris 136 – Bernay 30 – Elbeuf 16 – Évreux 34

Salverte

☎ 0232355134, *www.camping-salverte.com* – limited spaces for one-night stay
Address : 3km southwest along the D 26, follow the signs for Brionne and take road to the left
Opening times : permanent
17 ha/10 ha for camping (300 pitches) flat, grassy
Tariff : 21€ ⚡⚡ 🚐 🔲 ⚡ (6A) – Extra per person 7€
Rental rates : (from beginning May to end Oct.) – 4 ⛺. Per night from 50 €
Per week from 370 to 490 €

A pleasant, wooded site.

Surroundings : 🌊 🌳 ♨♨ Leisure activities : 🍴 🍽 🎱 🎣 ♨ 🎯 👟 m̂ 🏊 🏸 library, entertainment room Facilities : o━ 🔲 🚿 ♨ 🍴 launderette 🏊	**GPS** Longitude : 0.84149 Latitude : 49.22619

This guide is updated regularly, so buy your new copy every year!

HONFLEUR

14600 – Michelin map **303** N3 – pop. 8,163 – alt. 5
▶ Paris 195 – Caen 69 – Le Havre 27 – Lisieux 38

La Briquerie

☎ 0231892832, *www.campinglabriquerie.com* – limited spaces for one-night stay
Address : at Equemauville, follow the signs for Trouville, head 3.5km southwest following signs for Pont-l'Évêque and turn right onto the D 62
Opening times : from beginning April to end Sept.
11 ha (430 pitches) flat, grassy
Tariff : 34.80€ ⚡⚡ 🚐 🔲 ⚡ (10A) – Extra per person 9€
Rental rates : (from beginning April to end Sept.) ⚡ – 8 ⛺ – 3 🏠.
Per week from 350 to 650 €
🚐 sani-station – 🚐 ⚡18€

Surroundings : 🌳 ♨ Leisure activities : 🍴 🍽 🎱 🎣 ♨ jacuzzi 👟 m̂ 🏊 🏊 🏸 multi-sports ground Facilities : ♿ o━ 🔲 🚿 🚿 ♨ 🍴 launderette 🏊 Nearby : 🚴 🏊 🏇	**GPS** Longitude : 0.20826 Latitude : 49.39675

557

HOULGATE

14510 – Michelin map **303** L4 – pop. 1,988 – alt. 11
▶ Paris 214 – Caen 29 – Deauville 14 – Lisieux 33

Yelloh! Village La Vallée ▲⚲

0231244069, www.campinglavallee.com
Address : 88 r. de la Vallée (located 1km south along the D 24a, follow the signs for Lisieux and turn right onto the D 24)
Opening times : from beginning April to beginning Nov.
11 ha (350 pitches) terraced, relatively flat, flat, grassy
Tariff : 45€ ★★ ⇔ 🔲 ⚡ (6A) – Extra per person 8€
Rental rates : (from beginning April to beginning Nov.) – 65 🚐. Per week from 413 to 875 €
🚐 sani-station 2€ – 12 🔲 45€
A pleasant setting based around old Norman-style buildings.

Surroundings : ⩶ ⌂ ⚲
Leisure activities : ♍ ✗ 🛶 ◉ ⛹ 🚣 🚲 ⚒ 🖼 ⌇ ⩟
Facilities : & ⚬━ 🔲⌂ ⚲ ⚓ ⚘ ♍ launderette ⚖ ⚲
Nearby : 🖼 ⚘

GPS
Longitude : -0.06733
Latitude : 49.29422

INCHEVILLE

76117 – Michelin map **304** I1 – pop. 1,357 – alt. 19
▶ Paris 169 – Abbeville 32 – Amiens 65 – Blangy-sur-Bresle 16

Municipal de l'Etang

0235503017, campingdeletang@orange.fr – limited spaces for one-night stay
Address : r. Mozart (take the northeastern exit, follow the signs for Beauchamps and take right turn)
Opening times : from beginning March to end Dec.
2 ha (190 pitches) flat, grassy
Tariff : (2012 Price) ★ 2.65€ ⇔ 🔲 3.55€ – ⚡ (10A) 3.75€
Near a fishing lake.

Surroundings : ⚲
Leisure activities : 🛶 ⚓
Facilities : & ⚬━ ⚲ ⚘ 🖼
Nearby : ⚒ ⚲

GPS
Longitude : 1.50788
Latitude : 50.01238

ISIGNY-SUR-MER

14230 – Michelin map **303** F4 – pop. 2,782 – alt. 4
▶ Paris 298 – Bayeux 35 – Caen 64 – Carentan 14

Le Fanal

0231213320, www.camping-normandie-fanal.fr ⚒
Address : to the west, access via the town centre, near the sports field
6.5 ha/5.5 ha for camping (240 pitches) flat, grassy
Rentals : 90 🚐 – 10 🏠 – 4 tent bungalows.
🚐 sani-station
A pleasant, well-kept setting, set around a small lake.

Surroundings : ⚲ ⚲
Leisure activities : 🛶 ♩ ⚓ ⚒ 🖼
Facilities : & ⚬━ ⫿ ⚲ ⚘ launderette
Nearby : ⚲ ⚲ ⚘ sports trail

GPS
Longitude : -1.10872
Latitude : 49.31923

ULLOUVILLE

0610 – Michelin map **303** C7 – pop. 2,262 – alt. 60
Paris 346 – Avranches 24 – Granville 9 – St-Lô 63

⚠ La Chaussée

℘ 0233618018, *www.camping-lachaussee.com*
Address : 1 av. de la Libération (exit to the north, follow the signs for Granville, 150m from the beach)
Opening times : from beginning April to end Sept.
6 ha/4.7 ha for camping (250 pitches) relatively flat, flat, grassy, sandy
Tariff : (2012 price) 31.80€ 🏕🏕 ⇌ 🅴 (16A) – Extra per person 5.70€
Rental rates : (2012 price) (from beginning April to end Sept.) – 12 ⌂.
Per night from 98 to 159 €= – Per week from 325 to 695 €
🚐 sani-station 5€
A pleasant setting with a small pine wood.

Surroundings : ♀
Leisure activities : 🍷 🛶 ⚓ ⛷ wildlife park, with donkeys
Facilities : ⊶ 🚽 launderette ♨,
Nearby : 🎿 🗼 🐎

Longitude : -1.56709
Latitude : 48.78136

Some campsites benefit from proximity to a municipal leisure centre.

UMIEGES

6480 – Michelin map **304** E5 – pop. 1,719 – alt. 25
Paris 161 – Rouen 29 – Le Havre 82 – Caen 132

⚠ La Forêt

℘ 0235379343, *www.campinglaforet.com*
Address : r. Mainberte
Opening times : from beginning April to end Oct.
2 ha (111 pitches) flat, grassy
Tariff : 25.50€ 🏕🏕 ⇌ 🅴 (10A) – Extra per person 5.50€ – Reservation fee 3€
Rental rates : (from beginning April to mid Oct.) 🐾 – 18 ⌂. Per night from 110 to 160 €
Per week from 240 to 610 € – Reservation fee 4€
🚐 sani-station 6€
In the Brotonne regional park.

Surroundings : 🌿 ⊑ ♀
Leisure activities : 🛶 ⚓ ⛷ ⛷
Facilities : ♿ ⊶ 🛁 🚽 launderette
Nearby : 🎿

Longitude : 0.82883
Latitude : 49.43485

ISIEUX

4100 – Michelin map **303** N5 – pop. 21,826 – alt. 51
Paris 169 – Caen 54 – Le Havre 66 – Hérouville-St-Clair 53

⚠ La Vallée

℘ 0231620040, *www.lisieux-tourisme.com*
Address : 9 r. de la Vallée (take the northern exit along the D 48, follow the signs for Pont-l'Évêque)
1 ha (75 pitches) flat, grassy, fine gravel
Rentals : 5 ⌂.

Surroundings : ♀♀
Facilities : ♿ ⊶ 🛁 launderette
Nearby : 🎿

Longitude : 0.22068
Latitude : 49.16423

LES LOGES

76790 – Michelin map **304** B3 – pop. 1,155 – alt. 92
▶ Paris 205 – Rouen 83 – Le Havre 34 – Fécamp 10

⚠ Club Airotel L'Aiguille Creuse

✆ 02 35 29 52 10, *www.campingaiguillecreuse.com*
Address : 24 res.de l'Aiguille Creuse
Opening times : from beginning April to end Sept.
3 ha (80 pitches) relatively flat, flat, grassy
Tariff : (2012 price) 25.30€ ✶✶ ⇌ 🔲 (10A) – Extra per person 5.60€ – Reservation fee 7 €
Rental rates : (2012 price) (from beginning April to end Sept.) ⚲ – 18 🚐.
Per night from 70 to 85 € – Per week from 320 to 560 € – Reservation fee 15€
🚰 sani-station

Surroundings : ▭
Leisure activities : 🍴 ⛵ 🖼 (open-air in season)
Facilities : ⅋ ⚷ cc ▥ 🚰 🛁
Nearby : ✗

GPS Longitude : 0.27575
Latitude : 49.69884

LOUVIERS

27400 – Michelin map **304** H6 – pop. 17,943 – alt. 15
▶ Paris 104 – Les Andelys 22 – Bernay 52 – Lisieux 75

⚠ Le Bel Air

✆ 02 32 40 10 77, *www.camping-lebelair.fr* – limited spaces for one-night stay
Address : rte de la-Haye-Malherbe (3km west along the D 81)
Opening times : from mid March to mid Oct.
2.5 ha (92 pitches) flat, grassy
Tariff : (2012 price) ✶ 5.50€ ⇌ 🔲 6.70€ – ⚡ (6A) 10€
Rental rates : (2012 price) (from mid March to mid Oct.) ⚲ – 2 🚐 – 3 🏠.
Per night from 63 to 78 € – Per week from 375 to 515 €
🚰 2 🔲 24€
Set among trees offering plenty of shade.

Surroundings : ▭ ◯◯
Leisure activities : 🛖 ⛵ 🏊
Facilities : ⚷ ▥ 🚰 launderette
Nearby : ✗ 🖾

GPS Longitude : 1.1332
Latitude : 49.2152

LUC-SUR-MER

14530 – Michelin map **303** J4 – pop. 3,133
▶ Paris 249 – Arromanches-les-Bains 23 – Bayeux 29 – Cabourg 28

⚠ Municipal la Capricieuse

✆ 02 31 97 34 43, *www.campinglacapricieuse.com*
Address : 2 r. Brummel (to the west, allée Brummel; 200m from the beach)
Opening times : from beginning April to end Sept.
4.6 ha (226 pitches) relatively flat, flat, grassy
Tariff : (2012 price) ✶ 4.90€ ⇌ 🔲 5.85€ – ⚡ (10A) 6.50€
Rental rates : (2012 price) (from beginning April to end Nov.) ⅋ (1 mobile home) ⚲ –
18 🚐 – 10 🏠. Per week from 309 to 709 €
🚰 sani-station 5.20€

Surroundings : ⟨ ▭ ◯
Leisure activities : 🛖 ⛵ ✗ 🌊 (beach), spa therapy centre
Facilities : ⅋ ⚷ 🛁 🚿 🚰 launderette
Nearby : 🛒 🚴 ⛷ 🏊 ♨

GPS Longitude : -0.35781
Latitude : 49.3179

LYONS-LA-FORÊT

7480 – Michelin map **304** I5 – pop. 751 – alt. 88
Paris 104 – Les Andelys 21 – Forges-les-Eaux 30 – Gisors 30

Municipal St-Paul

⌀ 02 32 49 42 02, *www.camping-saint-paul.fr* – limited spaces for one-night stay
Address : 2 rte Saint-Paul (to the northeast along the D 321, by the stadium; beside the Lieure river)
Opening times : from beginning April to end Oct.
3 ha (100 pitches) flat, grassy
Tariff : (2012 price) 20.50€ ♦♦ ⇔ 🔲 🚰 (6A) – Extra per person 5.20€
Rental rates : (2012 price) (from beginning April to end Oct.) – 7 🏠. Per night from 58 to 72€
Per week from 200 to 369 €

Surroundings : ▭ ♀
Leisure activities : 🎦 ⛱
Facilities : & ⚟ ▥ 🛁 ⚱ ⚗ 🍴 🔲
Nearby : ✂ ♨ ⛵ 🐎

GPS Longitude : 1.47657
Latitude : 49.39869

The Michelin classification (△△△… △) is totally independent of the official star classification system awarded by the local prefecture or other official organisation.

MARCHAINVILLE

1290 – Michelin map **310** N3 – pop. 207 – alt. 235
Paris 124 – L'Aigle 28 – Alençon 65 – Mortagne-au-Perche 28

Municipal les Fossés

⌀ 02 33 73 65 80, *mairiemarchainville@wanadoo.fr* – ⊯
Address : to the north along the D 243
Opening times : from beginning April to end Oct.
1 ha (17 pitches) relatively flat, flat, grassy
Tariff : (2012 price) ♦ 2.10€ ⇔ 🔲 – 🚰 (15A) 2.30€

Surroundings : ⌇ ▭
Leisure activities : ✂
Facilities : & ⚟ ⊠ ⚱

GPS Longitude : 0.8135
Latitude : 48.5861

MARTIGNY

6880 – Michelin map **304** G2 – pop. 481 – alt. 24
Paris 196 – Dieppe 10 – Fontaine-le-Dun 29 – Rouen 64

Les Deux Rivières

⌀ 02 35 85 60 82, *www.camping-2-rivieres.com* – limited spaces for one-night stay
Address : D 154 (700m to the northwest, off the rte de Dieppe)
Opening times : from end March to beginning Oct.
3 ha (110 pitches) flat, grassy
Tariff : (2012 price) 15.90€ ♦♦ ⇔ 🔲 🚰 (10A) – Extra per person 3.80€
Rental rates : (2012 price) (from end March to beginning Oct.) – 6 🚐. Per night from 71€
Per week from 520 €

A pleasant location beside river and lakes.

Surroundings : ≤ extensive lakeland and the Château d'Arques ♀
Leisure activities : 🎦 ⛱ 🎠 ⌇
Facilities : & ⚟ launderette ⚱
Nearby : ▧ ◊

GPS Longitude : 1.14417
Latitude : 49.87059

MARTRAGNY

14740 – Michelin map **303** I4 – pop. 367 – alt. 70
▶ Paris 257 – Bayeux 11 – Caen 23 – St-Lô 47

Les Castels Le Château de Martragny

𝒞 02 31 80 21 40, www.chateau-martragny.com
Address : 5 r. de l'Ormelet (on the old N 13, access via the le town centre)
Opening times : from beginning May to beginning Sept.
13 ha/4 ha for camping (160 pitches) flat, grassy
Tariff : ✶ 7.90€ ⇌ 🗉 14.80€ – 🔌 (15A) 4.80€ – Reservation fee 8€
Rental rates : (from end May to end Aug.) ⬮ – 5 ⊨ – 4 tent bungalows – 2 gîtes.
Per night from 130 € – Per week from 370 to 450 € – Reservation fee 8€
🔄 sani-station
Also chambres d'hôte (b&b accommodation) in an 18th-century château.

Surroundings : ⬀ 🎠
Leisure activities : ♟ 🏛 ⚓ ✀ 🎱 ⚲
Facilities : ♿ ⊶ 🅒🛁 ᵑ launderette ⬛ 🔧
Nearby : 🐎

GPS Longitude : -0.60532
Latitude : 49.24406

MAUPERTUS-SUR-MER

50330 – Michelin map **303** D2 – pop. 256 – alt. 119
▶ Paris 359 – Barfleur 21 – Cherbourg 13 – St-Lô 80

Les Castels l'Anse du Brick ⚲⚲

𝒞 02 33 54 33 57, www.anse-du-brick.com
Address : 18 Anse du Brick (to the northwest along the D 116, 200m from the beach, direct access via a walkway)
Opening times : from beginning April to end Sept.
17 ha/7 ha for camping (180 pitches) very uneven, terraced, flat, grassy, stony, wood
Tariff : 40.40€ ✶✶ ⇌ 🗉 🔌 (10A) – Extra per person 8.20€ – Reservation fee 8€
Rental rates : (from beginning April to end Sept.) – 37 ⬚ – 6 ⬚ – 3 gîtes. Per night 140€
Per week 980€ – Reservation fee 8€
🔄 sani-station 6€
In a peasantly leafy setting; an unspoilt site. with plenty of shade.

Surroundings : ⬀ ⊰ ⊡ 🎠
Leisure activities : ♟ 🏛 ⊙ 🏌 ⚓ ⚲ ✀ 🎱 🔲 ⚲ 🏖
Facilities : ♿ ⊶ 🛁 ᵑ launderette ⬛
Nearby : ✗ 🗾 watersports centre

GPS Longitude : -1.49
Latitude : 49.66722

MERVILLE-FRANCEVILLE-PLAGE

14810 – Michelin map **303** K4 – pop. 1,991 – alt. 2
▶ Paris 225 – Arromanches-les-Bains 42 – Cabourg 7 – Caen 20

Seasonova Le Point du Jour

𝒞 02 31 24 23 34, www.camping-lepointdujour.com
Address : rte de Cabourg (take the eastern exit along the D 514)
Opening times : from beginning April to beginning Nov.
2.7 ha (142 pitches) flat, grassy, sandy
Tariff : (2012 price) 34€ ✶✶ ⇌ 🗉 🔌 (10A) – Extra per person 7.80€ – Reservation fee 10€
Rental rates : (2012 price) (from beginning April to beginning Nov.) ⬮ – 28 ⬚.
Per night from 60 to 120 € – Per week from 320 to 960 € – Reservation fee 10€
🔄 sani-station – 🔌 16€
An attractive location close to the beach.

Surroundings : ⊡ ⬖
Leisure activities : ✗ 🏛 jacuzzi ⚓ 🔲 (open-air in season)
Facilities : ♿ ⊶ 🅜 🛁 ᵑ launderette
Nearby : ✗ 🔥ₘ ◊ 🐎

GPS Longitude : -0.19392
Latitude : 49.2833

Les Peupliers

℘ 02 31 24 05 07, www.camping-peupliers.com
Address : allée des Pins (2.5km east, a right turn off the rte de Cabourg; near the entrance to Hôme)
Opening times : from beginning April to end Oct.
3.6 ha (164 pitches) flat, grassy
Tariff : 👤 8.10€ 🚗 🔳 8.80€ – ⚡ (16A) 6.20€
Rental rates : (from beginning April to end Oct.) – 1 'gypsy' caravan – 43 🚐 – 10 🏠.
Per night from 85 to 145 € – Per week from 300 to 960 €
🚽 sani-station

Leisure activities : 🍸 🎦 🕹 (Jul–Aug) 🏊 🏊
Facilities : 👤 🚿 🛁 🚻 launderette
Nearby : 🍴 🚵 🎣 💧 🐴

GPS Longitude : -0.17011
Latitude : 49.2829

MOYAUX

4590 – Michelin map **303** O4 – pop. 1,356 – alt. 160
◀ Paris 173 – Caen 64 – Deauville 31 – Lisieux 13

Le Colombier

℘ 231 636 308, www.camping-lecolombier.com
Address : 3km northeast along the D 143, follow the signs for Lieurey
Opening times : from beginning May to mid Sept.
15 ha/6 ha for camping (180 pitches) flat, grassy
Tariff : 37€ 👤👤 🚗 🔳 ⚡ (6A) – Extra per person 8€
🚽 sani-station
There's a swimming pool in the château's formal garden.

Surroundings : 🏞 💧
Leisure activities : 🍸 ✕ 🎦 🕹 🏊 🚲 🍴 🚵 🏊 library
Facilities : 👤 🚿 🛁 🚿 🚻 launderette 🚽 🚰

GPS Longitude : 0.3897
Latitude : 49.2097

OMONVILLE-LA-ROGUE

0440 – Michelin map **303** A1 – pop. 534 – alt. 25
◀ Paris 377 – Caen 144 – St-Lô 99 – Cherbourg 24

Municipal du Hable

℘ 02 33 52 86 15, www.omonvillelarogue.fr – 🅁
Address : 4 rte de la Hague
1 ha (60 pitches) flat, grassy, fine gravel
🚽 sani-station

Surroundings : 🏞
Facilities : 🚻 launderette
Nearby : 🚊 🍴 💧

GPS Longitude : -1.84087
Latitude : 49.70439

*For more information on visiting particular towns or regions, consult the
relevant regional MICHELIN Green Guide. We also recommend you use
the appropriate Michelin regional map to locate your selected campsite,
to calculate distances and to work out the best route.*

ORBEC

14290 – Michelin map **303** O5 – pop. 2,381 – alt. 110
▶ Paris 173 – L'Aigle 38 – Alençon 80 – Argentan 53

⚠ Les Capucins

℘ 02 31 32 76 22, *camping.sivom@orange.fr*
Address : av. du Bois (located 1.5km northeast along the D 4, follow the signs for Bernay and take road to the left, by the stadium)
Opening times : from mid May to beginning Sept.
0.9 ha (35 pitches) flat, grassy
Tariff : ⚑ 2.50€ ⚗ 1.50€ ▣ 2€ – ⚡ (10A) 2.50€
In a green setting; a very well-kept site.

Surroundings : ♀
Leisure activities : 🎱 ⚷
Facilities : ⚐ ⊡ ⚘ ⊽
Nearby : ⚔ ▧ ⚰

Longitude : 0.40875
Latitude : 49.02982

LES PIEUX

50340 – Michelin map **303** B2 – pop. 3,588 – alt. 104
▶ Paris 366 – Barneville-Carteret 18 – Cherbourg 22 – St-Lô 48

⚠⚠⚠ Le Grand Large

℘ 02 33 52 40 75, *www.legrandlarge.com*
Address : 11 rte du Grand Large (3km southwest along the D 117 and turn right onto the D 517 then continue 1km along the road to the left)
Opening times : from mid April to mid Sept.
3.7 ha (236 pitches) flat and relatively flat, sandy, grassy
Tariff : (2012 price) 37€ ⚑⚑ ⚗ ▣ ⚡ (10A) – Extra per person 8€
Rental rates : (2012 price) (from mid April to mid Sept.) – 51 ⬚. Per night from 70 to 130 €
Per week from 260 to 890 €
⬚ sani-station 8€ – 10 ▣ 37€
An attractive location among the dunes close to the Plage de Sciottot (beach).

Surroundings : ⚲ ← ⊡ ⚑
Leisure activities : ☂ 🎱 ⚙ ⚷ ⚔ ▣ ⚒ paddling pool, spa therapy centre
Facilities : ⚟ ⚏ ▣ ⊞ ⚘ ⚑ launderette

Longitude : -1.8425
Latitude : 49.49361

PONT-AUDEMER

27500 – Michelin map **304** D5 – pop. 8,599 – alt. 15
▶ Paris 165 – Rouen 58 – Évreux 91 – Le Havre 44

⚠ Municipal Risle-Seine – Les Étangs

℘ 02 32 42 46 65, *http://tourisme.ville-pont-audemer.fr*
Address : 19 rte des Étangs at Toutainville (2.5km east, turn left under the motorway bridge, near the water sports centre)
Opening times : permanent
2 ha (61 pitches) flat, grassy
Tariff : (2012 price) 17€ ⚑⚑ ⚗ ▣ ⚡ (10A) – Extra per person 3.20€
Rental rates : (2012 price) (permanent) – 10 ⌂. Per week from 293 to 541€
A small, pretty chalet village on stilts!

Surroundings : ⊡ ♀
Leisure activities : 🎱 ⚷ ⚲
Facilities : ⚟ ⚏ ⚘ ⊽ ⚑ ▣
Nearby : ⚌ (pool) ⚲ ⚲

Longitude : 0.48739
Latitude : 49.3666

ONT-AUTHOU

290 – Michelin map **304** E6 – pop. 711 – alt. 49
Paris 152 – Bernay 22 – Elbeuf 26 – Évreux 45

Municipal les Marronniers

 02 32 42 75 06, *campingmunicipaldesmarronniers@orange.fr* – limited spaces for one-night stay
Address : r. Louise Givon (south of the town, along the D 130, follow the signs for Brionne; beside a stream)
Opening times : permanent
2.5 ha (64 pitches) flat, grassy
Tariff : (2012 price) ♦ 2.70€ ⇔ 1.95€ 🔲 2.70€ – ⚡ (10A) 3.40€
Rental rates : (2012 price) (permanent) – 5 🔲. Per night 42€ – Per week from 210 to 220€
🚐 sani-station 4.55€ – 5 🔲 4.55€

Leisure activities : 🎣
Facilities : ⚐ ⚲ ⌂ 🔓
Nearby : 🚲

GPS Longitude : 0.70332
Latitude : 49.24193

ONT-FARCY

380 – Michelin map **303** F6 – pop. 527 – alt. 72
Paris 296 – Caen 63 – St-Lô 30 – Villedieu-les-Poêles 22

Municipal

 02 31 68 32 06, *www.pont.farcy.fr*
Address : rte de Tessy (take the northern exit along the D 21, follow the signs for Tessy-sur-Vire)
1.5 ha (60 pitches) flat, grassy
Beside the Vire river.

Leisure activities : 🎣 🏊 🎿 ⛳ 🎣
Facilities : ⚐ ⚲

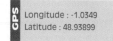
GPS Longitude : -1.0349
Latitude : 48.93899

In order for the guide to remain wholly objective, the selection of campsites is made on an entirely independent basis.

ONTORSON

170 – Michelin map **303** C8 – pop. 4,080 – alt. 15
Paris 359 – Avranches 23 – Dinan 50 – Fougères 39

Haliotis ♦♦

 02 33 68 11 59, *www.camping-haliotis-mont-saint-michel.com*
Address : chemin des Soupirs (situated to the northwest along the D 19, follow the signs for Dol-de-Bretagne; near the Couesnon river)
Opening times : from mid March to mid Nov.
8 ha/3.5 ha for camping (170 pitches) flat, grassy
Tariff : 25.50€ ♦♦ ⇔ 🔲 ⚡ (16A) – Extra per person 6€
Rental rates : (from mid March to mid Nov.) – 33 🔲 – 1 ⌂. Per night from 35 to 85 €
Per week from 220 to 750€
🚐 sani-station

Surroundings : ⛰ 🏞
Leisure activities : 🍴 🎣 ⚲ daytime 🎠 ⛵ jacuzzi 🏊 🚲 ⛳ 🎿
fitness trail, farm/petting farm, multi-sports ground
Facilities : ⚲ 🖥 🔓 ⌂ – 12 individual sanitary facilities (🚿 wc) ♿ ⚑
🕯 launderette
Nearby : 🏊 🎮 🎣 🐎
GPS Longitude : -1.5145
Latitude : 48.55798

PORT-EN-BESSIN

14520 – Michelin map **303** H3 – pop. 2,141 – alt. 10
▶ Paris 277 – Caen 43 – Hérouville-St-Clair 45 – St-Lô 47

Sunêlia Port'Land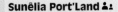

ℰ 02 31 51 07 06, *www.camping-portland.com*
Address : chemin du Castel, 5 km from the beach
Opening times : from beginning April to beginning Nov.
8.5 ha (256 pitches) flat, grassy
Tariff : 42 € ♦♦ ⇔ 🗐 ⚡ (16A) – Extra per person 9 €
Rental rates : (from beginning April to beginning Nov.) – 100 🛖. Per night from 55 to 225 €
Per week from 385 to 1 575 €
🚰 sani-station 5 € – 10 🗐 36 €
Situated near several lakes, with pretty flowers and shrubs.

Surroundings : 🐾 🗔
Leisure activities : 🍷 ✗ 🎱 🗇 🏃 ⚓ 🖾 🛝 ⛷ 🏹 fitness trai, multi-sports ground
Facilities : ᶑ ⚗ 🛁 🚿 ⚟ launderette 🖳 🖘
Nearby : 🍴 🐟

GPS Longitude : -0.77044
Latitude : 49.34716

QUIBERVILLE

76860 – Michelin map **304** F2 – pop. 535 – alt. 50
▶ Paris 199 – Dieppe 18 – Fécamp 50 – Rouen 67

Municipal de la Plage

ℰ 02 35 83 01 04, *www.campingplagequiberville.fr* – limited spaces for one-night stay
Address : 123 r. de la Saane (at Quiberville-Plage, access via the D 127, follow the signs for Ouville-la-Rivière)
Opening times : from beginning April to end Oct.
2.5 ha (202 pitches) flat, grassy
Tariff : (2012 price) ♦ 5.50 € ⇔ 🗐 9.60 € – ⚡ (10A) 5.10 €
🚰 sani-station 3.65 € – 8 🗐 6 €
Situated 100m from the sea.

Surroundings : ≤ 🗔
Leisure activities : 🖾 ⚓
Facilities : ᶑ ⚗ 🛁 ⚟ launderette
Nearby : 🍷 ✗ 🖘 🐟

GPS Longitude : 0.92878
Latitude : 49.90507

RADON

61250 – Michelin map **310** J3 – pop. 1,042 – alt. 175
▶ Paris 200 – Caen 106 – Alençon 11 – Le Mans 67

Ferme des Noyers

ℰ 02 33 28 75 02, *www.ecouves.net*
Address : at Les Noyers (D 1)
Opening times : from beginning April to end Oct.
2 ha (43 pitches) flat, grassy
Tariff : 15.50 € ♦♦ ⇔ 🗐 ⚡ (16A) – Extra per person 3 €
Rental rates : (permanent) – 2 🛖. Per night from 55 to 65 € – Per week from 200 to 280 €
🚰 sani-station 3 € – 5 🗐 11 € – 🔌 ⚡11 €

Surroundings : 🌾
Leisure activities : 🖾 ⚓ 🏹
Facilities : ᶑ ⚗ 🛁 ⚟ 🖳
Nearby : ✗ 🖚 (lake)

GPS Longitude : 0.0684
Latitude : 48.4957

RAVENOVILLE

50480 – Michelin map **303** E3 – pop. 261 – alt. 6
▶ Paris 328 – Barfleur 27 – Carentan 21 – Cherbourg 40

Le Cormoran ▲▲

℘ 02 33 41 33 94, *www.lecormoran.com* – limited spaces for one-night stay
Address : 2 r. du Cormoran (3.5km northeast along the D 421, follow the signs for Utah Beach; near the beach)
Opening times : from beginning April to end Sept.
8 ha (256 pitches) flat, grassy, sandy
Tariff : 42€ ♦♦ ⇐ 目 ⚡ (10A) – Extra per person 8€ – Reservation fee 10€
Rental rates : (from beginning April to end Sept.) ⓟ – 1 'gypsy' caravan – 39 ⛺ – 6 ⌂ – 1 gîte. Per night from 34 to 137 € – Per week from 240 to 959 € – Reservation fee 10€
⛽ sani-station – 10 目 16€ – ⚡16€
Beautiful flowers and shrubs.

Surroundings : ▱
Leisure activities : ♈ ⌂ ⚐ ⚶ ≋ jacuzzi ⤳ ⚲ ✗ ▣ ⊿ farm or petting farm, radio control boats, multi-sports ground
Facilities : ⚹ ⊶ ▣⊿ ☇ ⚲ ⁙ launderette ▨ ⚭
Nearby : ⚞

GPS
Longitude : -1.23527
Latitude : 49.46658

LE ROZEL

50340 – Michelin map **303** B3 – pop. 281 – alt. 21
▶ Paris 369 – Caen 135 – Cherbourg 26 – Rennes 197

Le Ranch

℘ 02 33 10 07 10, *www.camping-leranch.com*
Address : at La Mielle (situated 2km southwest along the D 117 and take the D 62 to the right)
Opening times : from beginning April to end Sept.
4 ha (130 pitches) undulating, terrace, flat, grassy, sandy
Tariff : (2012 price) 36€ ♦♦ ⇐ 目 ⚡ (10A) – Extra per person 7.50€
Rental rates : (2012 price) (from beginning April to end Sept.) – 13 ⛺.
Per night from 90 to 125 € – Per week from 310 to 890 €

Situated close to the beach.

Surroundings : ⚇ ⚠
Leisure activities : ♈ ✗ ⌂ ♪ ≋ ⤳ ▣ ⊿ ⚴
Facilities : ⚹ ⊶ (Jul–Aug) ▥ ⊿ ☇ ⚲ ⁙ launderette
Nearby : ⚞ ⚶ sand yachting

GPS
Longitude : -1.84199
Latitude : 49.48013

ST-ARNOULT

14800 – Michelin map **303** M3 – pop. 1,193 – alt. 4
▶ Paris 198 – Caen 43 – Le Havre 41 – Rouen 90

La Vallée de Deauville ▲▲

℘ 02 31 88 58 17, *www.camping-deauville.com* – limited spaces for one-night stay
Address : av. de la Vallée (located 1km south along the D 27, follow the signs for Varaville and take the D 275 following signs for Beaumont-en-Auge to the left; beside a stream and near a small lake)
Opening times : from beginning April to end Oct.
10 ha (411 pitches) flat, grassy
Tariff : 35.20€ ♦♦ ⇐ 目 ⚡ (10A) – Extra per person 9.41€ – Reservation fee 5€
Rental rates : (2012 price) (from beginning April to end Oct.) – 70 ⛺. Per night from 92 to 127€ – Per week from 330 to 890 € – Reservation fee 23€ ⛽ sani-station 2€

The site is set around a small, pleasant lake.

Surroundings : ▱ ⚐
Leisure activities : ♈ ⌂ ⚐ ⚶ ⤳ ⊿ ⚴ ⚘ multi-sports ground
Facilities : ⚹ ⊶ ▥ ⊿ ⁙ launderette ▨ ⚭
Nearby : ⚑ ✗ ▦ ⚞ ▣ ⚬ ⚞

GPS
Longitude : 0.0862
Latitude : 49.3287

ST-AUBIN-SUR-MER

14750 – Michelin map **303** J4 – pop. 2,048
▶ Paris 252 – Arromanches-les-Bains 19 – Bayeux 29 – Cabourg 32

Yelloh! Village Côte de Nacre ▲▲

℘ 02 31 97 14 45, *www.camping-cote-de-nacre.com* – limited spaces for one-night stay
Address : 17 r. du Gal Moulton (south of the town along the D 7b)
Opening times : from end March to end Sept.
10 ha (350 pitches) flat, grassy
Tariff : 45€ ♦♦ ⇌ ▣ ⅸ (10A) – Extra per person 9€
Rental rates : (from end March to end Sept.) – 260 ⌷⁑. Per night from 39 to 189 €
Per week from 273 to 1,323 €
⇌ sani-station .20€
The site has a partially-covered water park.

Leisure activities : ♈ ⌂ ⑨ ⚊ ⚊ ⚭ ⌧ ⚲ spa facilities,
multi-sports ground
Facilities : ⅙ ⚬ �𝄞 ⌂ ⅙ launderette ⚊ ⚊
Nearby : ✂

Longitude : -0.3946
Latitude : 49.3324

ST-AUBIN-SUR-MER

76740 – Michelin map **304** F2 – pop. 267 – alt. 15
▶ Paris 191 – Dieppe 21 – Fécamp 46 – Rouen 59

Municipal le Mesnil

℘ 02 35 83 02 83, *lemesnil76@orange.fr*
Address : rte de Sotteville (situated 2km west along the D 68, follow the signs for Veules-les-Roses)
2.2 ha (117 pitches) terraced, flat, grassy
Rentals : ⚎ – 2 ⌷⁑.
⇌ sani-station
The site is based around an old Norman farmhouse.

Surroundings : ⚏ ⚊
Leisure activities : ✗ ⌂ ⚊
Facilities : ⅙ ⚬ 𝄞 ⌂ launderette ⚊

Longitude : 0.85204
Latitude : 49.88353

ST-EVROULT-NOTRE-DAME-DU-BOIS

61550 – Michelin map **310** L2 – pop. 452 – alt. 355
▶ Paris 153 – L'Aigle 14 – Alençon 56 – Argentan 42

Municipal des Saints-Pères

℘ 678330494, *catherine-motte@orange.fr*
Address : to the southeast of the village
Opening times : from mid April to end Oct.
0.6 ha (27 pitches) terrace, flat, grassy, fine gravel, wood
Tariff : ♦ 3€ ⇌ 1.50€ ▣ 1.50€ – ⅸ (8A) 2.50€
⇌ sani-station 2€ – ⚊ ⅸ14.50€
In an attractive location beside a small lake.

Surroundings : ♀
Leisure activities : ⚊ ⚊ ⚯ pedalos
Facilities : ⅙ ⚊ ⚆ ⚊
Nearby : ⚊ ✗ ⚊

Longitude : 0.4663
Latitude : 48.7888

ST-GEORGES-DU-VIÈVRE

27450 – Michelin map **304** D6 – pop. 720 – alt. 138
🖸 Paris 161 – Bernay 21 – Évreux 54 – Lisieux 36

Municipal du Vièvre

🖉 0232427679, www.camping-eure-normandie.fr
Address : rte de Noards (take the southwestern exit along the D 38)
Opening times : from beginning April to end Sept.
1.1 ha (50 pitches) flat, grassy
Tariff : (2012 price) ♦ 2.30€ 🚗 1.30€ – ⚡ (5A) 5€
Rental rates : (2012 price) (from beginning April to end Sept.) – 1 🛖. Per week from 300€

Surroundings : 🏞 🗷
Leisure activities : 🚲
Facilities : 🕭 🛱 🌲 🌢
Nearby : 🍴 🏊

GPS Longitude : 0.58064
Latitude : 49.2427

ST-GERMAIN-SUR-AY

50430 – Michelin map **303** C4 – pop. 896 – alt. 5
🖸 Paris 345 – Barneville-Carteret 26 – Carentan 35 – Coutances 27

Aux Grands Espaces

🖉 0233071014, www.auxgrandsespaces.com – limited spaces for one-night stay
Address : 6 r. du Camping (4km west along the D 306; at St-Germain-Plage (beach))
Opening times : from beginning April to end Oct.
16 ha (580 pitches) very uneven, flat, grassy, sandy
Tariff : ♦ 5.50€ 🚗 🗐 6.90€ – ⚡ (10A) 4.50€
Rental rates : (from beginning April to end Sept.) 🏕 – 20 🛖 – 3 tent bungalows.
Per week from 280 to 781€

Surroundings : 🏞 🗷 ♀
Leisure activities : 🍸 🎏 🛶 🍴 ♠ 🏊
Facilities : ☎ (Jul-Aug) 🍴 launderette 🗲
Nearby : 🐎 sand yachting

GPS Longitude : -1.64089
Latitude : 49.23654

---

*This guide is not intended as a list of all the camping sites in France;
its aim is to provide a selection of the best sites in each category*

ST-HILAIRE-DU-HARCOUËT

50600 – Michelin map **303** F8 – pop. 4,036 – alt. 70
🖸 Paris 339 – Alençon 100 – Avranches 27 – Caen 102

Municipal de la Sélune

🖉 0233494374, www.st-hilaire.fr
Address : 700m northwest along the N 176, follow the signs for Avranches and take a right turn,
near the river
Opening times : from beginning April to end Sept.
1.9 ha (70 pitches) flat, grassy
Tariff : (2012 price) 9.65€ ♦♦ 🚗 🗐 ⚡ (10A) – Extra per person 2.35€
Rental rates : (2012 price) (from beginning April to end Sept.) 🏕 – 2 caravans.
Per night from 50 to 75 € – Per week from 250 to 450 €
🛖 sani-station 2€ – 5 🗐 3€ – 🚐 ⚡ 11.35€

Leisure activities : 🎏 🛶
Facilities : 🕭 ☎ 🛱 ⛲ launderette
Nearby : 🍴 🍴 🕸 🗔 ♠

GPS Longitude : -1.09765
Latitude : 48.58127

ST-JEAN-DE-LA-RIVIÈRE

50270 – Michelin map **303** B3 – pop. 355 – alt. 20
▶ Paris 351 – Caen 119 – St-Lô 63 – Cherbourg 40

Yelloh! Village Les Vikings

0233538413, *www.camping-lesvikings.com*
Address : 4 r. des Vikings (along the D 166 and take the road to the right)
Opening times : from end March to end Sept.
6 ha (250 pitches) flat, grassy, sandy
Tariff : 43€ ♦♦ ⇔ 🔲 (10A) – Extra per person 8€
Rental rates : (from end March to end Sept.) ⅋ – 80 ⎕. Per night from 35 to 172 €
Per week from 245 to 1,204 €
sani-station
The entrance is decorated with flowers and palms.

Surroundings :
Leisure activities : ♥ ✗ ⌂ 🔲 ⚡ multi-sports ground, entertainment room
Facilities : ⅋ ⚬ ⚑ launderette
Nearby : ⚡ sand yachting

GPS Longitude : -1.75293
Latitude : 49.36335

ST-MARTIN-EN-CAMPAGNE

76370 – Michelin map **304** H2 – pop. 1,319 – alt. 118
▶ Paris 209 – Dieppe 13 – Rouen 78 – Le Tréport 18

Domaine les Goélands

0235838290, *www.lesdomaines.org* – limited spaces for one-night stay
Address : r. des Grèbes (situated 2km to the northwest, at St-Martin-Plage (beach))
Opening times : from beginning March to mid Nov.
3 ha (140 pitches) terraced, relatively flat, grassy
Tariff : 22.20€ ♦♦ ⇔ 🔲 (16A) – Extra per person 4.10€
Rental rates : (from beginning March to mid Nov.) – 8 ⎕. Per night from 195 €
Per week from 400 to 630 €
4 🔲 13.90€

Surroundings :
Leisure activities : ⌂ ⚡ ⚡ billiards, multi-sports ground
Facilities : ⅋ ⚬ launderette
Nearby : ✗

GPS Longitude : 1.20425
Latitude : 49.96632

ST-PAIR-SUR-MER

50380 – Michelin map **303** C7 – pop. 3,788 – alt. 30
▶ Paris 342 – Avranches 24 – Granville 4 – Villedieu-les-Poêles 29

Angomesnil

0233516433, *www.angomesnil.com*
Address : 891 rte du Guigeois (head 4.9km southeast along the D 21, follow the signs for St-Michel-des-Loups and turn left onto D 154, following signs for St-Aubin-des-Préaux)
Opening times : from mid June to mid Sept.
1.2 ha (45 pitches) flat, grassy
Tariff : ♦ 4.80€ ⇔ 2.60€ 🔲 3.90€ – (6A) 3.60€ – Reservation fee 15€
sani-station 19.70€

Surroundings :
Leisure activities : ⌂ ⚡
Facilities : ⅋ ⚬
Nearby : ⚡ 🔲 (open-air in season) sports trail, roller skating

GPS Longitude : -1.5261
Latitude : 48.79065

ST-SAUVEUR-LE-VICOMTE

50390 – Michelin map **303** C3 – pop. 2,053 – alt. 30
▶ Paris 336 – Barneville-Carteret 20 – Cherbourg 37 – St-Lô 56

Municipal du Vieux Château

☏ 02 33 41 72 04, www.saintsauveurlevicomte.stationverte.com
Address : av. Division Leclerc (in the town; beside the Douve)
1 ha (57 pitches) flat, grassy
In the grounds of the medieval château.

Leisure activities : 🖼
Facilities : ♿ ⛺ launderette
Nearby : 🚣 ✗

Longitude : -1.52779
Latitude : 49.38748

ST-SYMPHORIEN-LE-VALOIS

50250 – Michelin map **303** C4 – pop. 822 – alt. 35
▶ Paris 335 – Barneville-Carteret 19 – Carentan 25 – Cherbourg 47

Club Airotel L'Étang des Haizes ≛≛

☏ 02 33 46 01 16, www.campingetangdeshaizes.com
Address : r. Cauticote (take the northern exit along the D 900, follow the signs for Valognes and turn left onto D 136 towards the town)
Opening times : from beginning April to mid Oct.
4.5 ha (98 pitches) relatively flat, flat, grassy
Tariff : 35€ 🚶🚶 🚐 🔲 🚿 (10A) – Extra per person 8€
Rental rates : (from mid April to end Sept.) ♿ 🚫 (Jul–Aug) – 28 🏠 – 3 🏡 – 1 teepee – 2 tents. Per night from 44 to 126 € – Per week from 264 to 882 €
🚐 sani-station – 8 🔲 15€ – 🛒 🚿15€
A charming, leafy setting around a pretty lake.

Surroundings : ▱
Leisure activities : 🍴 🖼 🎣 🏇 🚣 🚲 🏊 🏓 🎣
Facilities : ♿ ⛽ ▣🚿 🚽 launderette

Longitude : -1.54482
Latitude : 49.29992

ST-VAAST-LA-HOUGUE

50550 – Michelin map **303** E2 – pop. 2,091 – alt. 4
▶ Paris 347 – Carentan 41 – Cherbourg 31 – St-Lô 68

La Gallouette

☏ 02 33 54 20 57, www.lagallouette.com
Address : 10bis r. de la Gallouette (South of the town, 500m from the beach)
Opening times : from beginning April to end Sept.
2.3 ha (183 pitches) flat, grassy
Tariff : 🚶 6.60€ 🚐 🔲 11.15€ – 🚿 (10A) 5€
Rental rates : (from beginning April to end Sept.) – 15 🏠 – 10 🏡. Per night from 73 to 106 € – Per week from 314 to 834 €
🚐 sani-station – 15 🔲 20.30€
Surroundings : ▱
Leisure activities : 🍴 ✗ 🖼 🎣 🚣 🏊 multi-sports ground
Facilities : ♿ ⛽ 🚿 🚽 launderette
Nearby : ✗ 💧 fitness trail

Longitude : -1.26873
Latitude : 49.5846

We have selected the best campsites in France with our usual care, listing those with the best facilities in the most pleasant surroundings.

ST-VALERY-EN-CAUX

76460 – Michelin map **304** E2 – pop. 4,463 – alt. 5
▶ Paris 190 – Bolbec 46 – Dieppe 35 – Fécamp 33

⚠ Municipal Etennemare

℘ 02 35 97 15 79, *servicetourisme@ville-saint-valery-en-caux.fr* – limited spaces for one-night stay
Address : 21 r. du Hameau d'Etennemare (located to the southwest, towards the hamlet of Le Bois d'Entennemare)
4 ha (116 pitches) relatively flat, flat, grassy
Rentals : 10 🏠.

Surroundings : 🐟 ▭
Leisure activities : 🎦
Facilities : 🦽 ⊶ ▥ 🛁 ⬩ launderette

GPS Longitude : 0.70378
Latitude : 49.85878

We welcome your feedback on our listed campsites.
Please email us at: campingfrance@tp.michelin.com
Many thanks in advance!

STE-MARIE-DU-MONT

50480 – Michelin map **303** E3 – pop. 761 – alt. 31
▶ Paris 318 – Barfleur 38 – Carentan 11 – Cherbourg 47

⚠ Flower Utah-Beach

℘ 02 33 71 53 69, *www.camping-utahbeach.com* – limited spaces for one-night stay
Address : 6km northeast along the D 913 and take D 421; 150m from the beach
Opening times : from end March to mid Sept.
5.5 ha (149 pitches) flat and relatively flat, grassy
Tariff : 28.50€ ✦✦ 🚐 🔲 ⚡ (6A) – Extra per person 6€ – Reservation fee 10€
Rental rates : (from end March to mid Sept.) – 10 🛖 – 12 🏠 – 2 tents.
Per night from 44 to 124 € – Per week from 196 to 868 € – Reservation fee 10€
🔄 sani-station 4€ – 🚐 ⚡14€

Surroundings : 🐟 ▭
Leisure activities : 🍴 ✕ 🎦 🏊 jacuzzi 🛝 ⚽ 🎯 🏊 multi-sports ground, entertainment room
Facilities : 🦽 ⊶ 🛁 ⚡ launderette ⬩
Nearby : 🚴 (mountain biking) sand yachting

GPS Longitude : -1.18028
Latitude : 49.42001

STE-MÈRE-ÉGLISE

50480 – Michelin map **303** E3 – pop. 1,643 – alt. 28
▶ Paris 321 – Bayeux 57 – Cherbourg 39 – St-Lô 42

⚠ Municipal

℘ 02 33 41 35 22, *mairie-sme@wanadoo.fr*
Address : 6 r. Airborne (take the eastern exit along the D 17 and take a right turn; near the sports field)
1.3 ha (70 pitches) flat, grassy
🔄 sani-station

Surroundings : 🐟
Leisure activities : 🎦 🛝 🚴 ⚽ 🏞 multi-sports ground
Facilities : ⊶ launderette

GPS Longitude : -1.31018
Latitude : 49.41003

SURRAIN

14710 – Michelin map **303** G4 – pop. 159 – alt. 40
▶ Paris 278 – Cherbourg 83 – Rennes 187 – Rouen 167

⚠ La Roseraie d'Omaha

✆ 0231211771, *www.camping-calvados-normandie.fr*
Address : r. de l'église (take the southern exit along the D 208, follow the signs for Mandeville-en-Bessin)
Opening times : from end March to end Sept.
3 ha (66 pitches) relatively flat, flat, grassy
Tariff : 20.50€ ✝✝ ⇐ 目 ⚡ (10A) – Extra per person 5€
Rental rates : (from end March to end Sept.) – 10 ▦ – 14 ⌂ – 1 gîte.
Per night from 56 to 89 € – Per week from 289 to 730 €
⊕ sani-station – ⊜ ⚡16€

Surroundings : ⊏ ⚲
Leisure activities : ✕ ⊞ ⛵ ⊙ ⊛ ⊓ ⊠ ⊿
Facilities : ⅋ ⊶ ⊼ ⊽ ⚇ launderette
Nearby : ⊰

GPS Longitude : -0.86443
Latitude : 49.32574

SURTAINVILLE

50270 – Michelin map **303** B3 – pop. 1,255 – alt. 12
▶ Paris 367 – Barneville-Carteret 12 – Cherbourg 29 – St-Lô 42

⚠ Municipal les Mielles

✆ 0233043104, *www.surtainville.com.fr*
Address : 80 rte des Laguettes (head 1.5km west along the D 66 and follow the signs for the sea, 80m from the beach, direct access)
25 ha (151 pitches) flat, grassy, sandy, fine gravel
Rentals : ⅋ – 2 ▦.
⊕ sani-station – 5 目

Surroundings : ⊱ ⊏
Leisure activities : ⊞ ⛵
Facilities : ⅋ ⊶ ⊞ ⊼ ⊽ ⚇ launderette
Nearby : ⊛ sand yachting

GPS Longitude : -1.82881
Latitude : 49.46386

THURY-HARCOURT

14220 – Michelin map **303** J6 – pop. 1,968 – alt. 45 – Leisure centre
▶ Paris 257 – Caen 28 – Condé-sur-Noireau 20 – Falaise 27

⚠ Le Traspy

✆ 0231796180, *www.camping-traspy.fr*
Address : r. du Pont Benoît (head east of the town along the bd du 30-Juin-1944 and take road to the left)
Opening times : from beginning April to end Sept.
1.5 ha (78 pitches) terrace, flat, grassy
Tariff : 19.30€ ✝✝ ⇐ 目 ⚡ (10A) – Extra per person 5€ – Reservation fee 12.20€
Rental rates : (from beginning April to end Sept.) – 12 ▦ – 1 ⌂. Per night from 65 to 95 €
Per week from 480 to 600€ – Reservation fee 12.20€
⊕ sani-station 2€ – 6 目 8€ – ⊜ ⚡15€
Beside the Traspy river and near a small lake.

Surroundings : ⊏ ⚲
Leisure activities : ✕ ⊞ ⊜ ⛵
Facilities : ⅋ ⊶ ⊼ ⊽ ⚇ launderette ⊞ ⊱
Nearby : ⊙ ⊛ ⊠ ⊿ ⊸ paragliding

GPS Longitude : -0.46913
Latitude : 48.98896

NORMANDY

TOUFFREVILLE-SUR-EU

76910 – Michelin map **304** H2 – pop. 201 – alt. 45
▶ Paris 171 – Abbeville 46 – Amiens 101 – Blangy-sur-Nesle 35

Municipal Les Acacias

✆ 02 35 50 66 33, *camping-acacias.fr*
Address : at Les Prés du Thil (head 1km to the southeast along the D 226 and take D 454, following the signs for Guilmecourt)
1 ha (50 pitches) flat, grassy

Surroundings :
Facilities :

Longitude : 1.33537
Latitude : 49.99531

TOUSSAINT

76400 – Michelin map **304** C3 – pop. 743 – alt. 105
▶ Paris 196 – Bolbec 24 – Fécamp 5 – Rouen 69

Municipal du Canada

✆ 02 35 29 78 34, *www.commune-de-toussaint.fr* – limited spaces for one-night stay
Address : r. de Rouen (500m northwest along the D 926, follow the signs for Fécamp and take road to the left)
Opening times : from mid March to mid Oct.
2.5 ha (100 pitches) flat and relatively flat, grassy
Tariff : (2012 price) 13 € ♦♦ ⇌ 回 ⓗ (6A) – Extra per person 3.50 €
Rental rates : (2012 price) (from mid March to mid Oct.) – 2 🏠 – 2 🏠.
Per night from 52 to 60 € – Per week from 330 to 435 €

Surroundings :
Facilities :
Nearby :

Longitude : 0.42091
Latitude : 49.73776

LE TRÉPORT

76470 – Michelin map **304** I1 – pop. 5,416 – alt. 12
▶ Paris 180 – Abbeville 37 – Amiens 92 – Blangy-sur-Bresle 26

Municipal les Boucaniers

✆ 02 35 86 35 47, *www.ville-le-treport.fr/camping*
Address : r. Pierre Mendès-France (take the av. des Canadiens; near the stadium)
Opening times : permanent
5.5 ha (166 pitches) flat, grassy
Tariff : (2012 Price) 18 € ♦♦ ⇌ 回 ⓗ (6A) – Extra per person 4.80 €
Rental rates : (2012 price) (permanent) – 50 🏠. Per night from 50 to 80 €
Per week from 280 to 560 € – Reservation fee 5 €
🚐 sani-station – 27 回 11.50 €

Surroundings :
Leisure activities :
Facilities : launderette
Nearby :

Longitude : 1.38882
Latitude : 50.0577

There are several different types of sani-station ('borne' in French) – sanitation points providing fresh water and disposal points for grey water. See page 12 for further details.

TRÉVIÈRES

14710 – Michelin map **303** G4 – pop. 938 – alt. 14
▶ Paris 283 – Bayeux 19 – Caen 49 – Carentan 31

Municipal Sous les Pommiers

⌂ 02 31 92 89 24, *http://www.ville-trevieres.fr/*
Address : take the northern exit along the D 30, follow the signs for Formigny; near a stream
Opening times : from beginning April to end Sept.
1.2 ha (75 pitches) flat, grassy
Tariff : ♦ 3.40€ ⌂ 1.50€ ▣ 2.50€ – ⚡ (16A) 3.50€

Pitches in the shade of apple trees.

Surroundings : ⌂ ♀
Leisure activities : ⚞
Facilities : ⌂ ⌂ ⌂ ▣
Nearby : ⌂ ⌂

GPS
Longitude : -0.90637
Latitude : 49.3132

VEULES-LES-ROSES

76980 – Michelin map **304** E2 – pop. 561 – alt. 15
▶ Paris 188 – Dieppe 27 – Fontaine-le-Dun 8 – Rouen 57

Seasonova Les Mouettes

⌂ 02 35 97 61 98, *www.camping-lesmouettes-normandie.com*
Address : av. Jean-Moulin (take the eastern exit along the D 68, follow the signs for Sotteville-sur-Mer, 500m from the beach)
Opening times : from beginning April to beginning Nov.
3.6 ha (150 pitches) flat, grassy
Tariff : (2012 price) 27€ ♦♦ ⌂ ▣ ⚡ (6A) – Extra per person 5.40€ – Reservation fee 8€
Rental rates : (2012 price) (from beginning April to beginning Nov.) ⌂ – 22 ⌂ – 2 tent bungalows. Per night from 35 to 90 € – Per week from 190 to 840€ – Reservation fee 8€
⌂ sani-station 10€

Surroundings : ⌂ ⌂ ♀
Leisure activities : ⌂ ⌂ ⚞ ⌂ ▣
Facilities : ⌂ ⌂ ⌂ ⌂ ⚞ launderette

GPS
Longitude : 0.80335
Latitude : 49.87579

*To make the best possible use of this guide,
please read pages 2–15 carefully.*

LE VEY

14570 – Michelin map **303** J6 – pop. 87 – alt. 50
▶ Paris 269 – Caen 47 – Hérouville-St-Clair 46 – Flers 23

Les Rochers des Parcs

⌂ 02 31 69 70 36, *www.camping-normandie-clecy.fr*
Address : at La Cour
1.5 ha (90 pitches) relatively flat, flat, grassy
Rentals : 10 ⌂ – 2 ⌂.
⌂ sani-station – 4 ▣

Surroundings : ♀ ⌂
Leisure activities : ⌂ ⚞ ⌂ ⌂ ⌂
Facilities : ⌂ ⌂ launderette
Nearby : ⌂ ⌂ adventure park, paragliding, climbing

GPS
Longitude : -0.47487
Latitude : 48.91391

VILLEDIEU-LES-POÊLES

50800 – Michelin map **303** E6 – pop. 3,882 – alt. 105
▶ Paris 314 – Alençon 122 – Avranches 26 – Caen 82

Flower Les Chevaliers

☎ 02 33 61 02 44, *www.camping-deschevaliers.com*
Address : 2 impasse Pré-de-la-Rose (access via the town centre, take r. des Costils to the left of the post office)
Opening times : from mid March to end Sept.
1.4 ha (82 pitches) flat, grassy, fine gravel
Tariff : 25.90€ ⚥ ⚥ ⟲ 🅴 🅗 (8A) – Extra per person 4.50€
Rental rates : (from mid March to end Sept.) – 21 🛖 – 4 tents. Per night from 40 to 100 €
Per week from 196 to 700 €
🚐 sani-station – 4 🅴 21.90€ – 🚐12€
In a pleasant, well-kept setting, beside the Sienne river.

Surroundings : 🌳 🗠 ♀
Leisure activities : ✗ 🍴 🏊 🚲 ✂ 🎿 multi-sports ground
Facilities : ♿ ⟲ 🔥 🏻 launderette 🛁
Nearby : 🔲 🏕

GPS Longitude : -1.21694
Latitude : 48.83639

VILLERS-SUR-MER

14640 – Michelin map **303** L4 – pop. 2,707 – alt. 10
▶ Paris 208 – Caen 35 – Deauville 8 – Le Havre 52

Bellevue

☎ 02 31 87 05 21, *www.camping-bellevue.com* – limited spaces for one-night stay
Address : rte de Dives (situated 2km southwest along the D 513, follow the signs for Cabourg)
Opening times : from beginning April to end Oct.
5.5 ha (257 pitches) terraced, relatively flat, flat, grassy
Tariff : (2012 price) 22€ ⚥ ⚥ ⟲ 🅴 🅗 (10A) – Extra per person 5.90€ – Reservation fee 16€
Rental rates : (2012 price) (from beginning April to end Oct.) ✂ – 40 🛖.
Per night from 55 to 87€ – Per week from 265 to 710 € – Reservation fee 16€
The site looks out over the Baie de Deauville.

Surroundings : ⟷ 🗠
Leisure activities : 🍴 🍴 ⓘ evening 🎣 🏊 🔲 🎿
Facilities : ♿ ⟲ 🔥 🛁 🐾 🏻 launderette
Nearby : 🛒 🚲 ✂ 🔲 🎿 🐎

GPS Longitude : -0.0195
Latitude : 49.3097

VIMOUTIERS

61120 – Michelin map **310** K1 – pop. 3,828 – alt. 95
▶ Paris 185 – L'Aigle 46 – Alençon 66 – Argentan 31

Municipal la Campière

☎ 02 33 39 18 86, *www.mairie-vimoutiers.fr*
Address : 14 bd Dentu (700m north, in the direction of Lisieux, by the stadium; beside La Vie river)
Opening times : from beginning April to end Oct.
1 ha (40 pitches) flat, grassy
Tariff : (2012 price) ⚥ 3.37€ ⟲ 2.45€ 🅴 2.45€ – 🅗 (10A) 2.45€
Rental rates : (2012 price) (from beginning April to end Oct.) – 4 🛖.
Per night from 56 to 61€ – Per week from 260 to 311€
Norman-style buildings in a lush, green setting surrounded by flowers.

Surroundings : ⟷ ♀
Leisure activities : 🍴 🏊 ✂
Facilities : ♿ ⟲ 🏛
Nearby : 🛒

GPS Longitude : 0.1966
Latitude : 48.9326

Bertrand Rieger / hemis.fr

The 'Garden of France' is renowned for its tranquil atmosphere, glorious châteaux, magnificent floral gardens and acres of orchards and vineyards. Enjoy a glass of light Loire wine with a plate of rillettes (pork pâté), *matelote d'anguilles* (eel stew) or a slice of goat's cheese, perfect partners in the gastronomic experience offered by the region. Continue downriver to Nantes, redolent today of the scent of spices first brought back from the New World. This is the home of the famous dry Muscadet wines. Further south, the Vendée region still echoes with the cries of 18th-century Royalists' before revolutionary fervour took hold. Explore the secrets of its salt marshes, relax in balmy seaside resorts or head for the spectacular attractions of the Puy du Fou amusement park. Simple country fare is the order of the day, so make sure you sample a piping-hot plate of *chaudrée* (fish chowder) or a mouth-watering slice of fresh brioche.

L'AIGUILLON-SUR-MER

85460 – Michelin map **316** I10 – pop. 2,310 – alt. 4
▶ Paris 458 – Luçon 20 – Niort 83 – La Rochelle 51

La Cléroca

℘ 02 51 27 19 92, www.camping-la-cleroca.com
Address : 2.2km northwest along the D 44, follow the signs for Grues
Opening times : from end May to end Aug.
1.5 ha (66 pitches) flat, grassy
Tariff : 30.20€ ♦♦ ⇔ 圓 (∮) (10A) – Extra per person 4.80€
Rental rates : (from mid June to end Aug.) ✣ – 1 yurt. Per week from 250 to 465€
sani-station 11.50€ – 8 圓 11.50€
Leafy green setting offering plenty of shade.

Surroundings : ♀♀
Leisure activities : 🏠 ☎ ⚓ ⅀ multi-sports ground
Facilities : ♿ ⚏ ⊟ ♨ ⴹ launderette

GPS Longitude : -1.31513
Latitude : 46.35003

AIZENAY

85190 – Michelin map **316** G7 – pop. 7,930 – alt. 62
▶ Paris 435 – Challans 26 – Nantes 60 – La Roche-sur-Yon 18

La Forêt

℘ 02 51 34 78 12, www.camping-laforet.com
Address : 1 r. de la Clairière (located 1.5km southeast along the D 948, follow the signs for la Roche-sur-Yon and take road to the left, behind the commercial centre)
Opening times : from beginning April to mid Oct.
2.5 ha (96 pitches) flat, grassy, wood
Tariff : (2012 price) 16.50€ ♦♦ ⇔ 圓 (∮) (6A) – Extra per person 3.20€
Rental rates : (2012 price) (from beginning April to mid Oct.) – 16 🚐.
Per night from 52 to 72€ – Per week from 282 to 443€
sani-station 3€ – 2 圓 16.50€ – ⚓ 12€
A pleasant site with shade.

Surroundings : ♀♀
Leisure activities : ⚓ ✻ ⅀
Facilities : ♿ ⚏ ⴹ ♨ launderette
Nearby : ⏢ ♦ ✕ ⚲ fitness trail, mountain biking

GPS Longitude : -1.58947
Latitude : 46.73427

ALLONNES

49650 – Michelin map **317** J5 – pop. 2,979 – alt. 28
▶ Paris 292 – Angers 64 – Azay-le-Rideau 43 – Chinon 28

Club Airotel Le Pô Doré

℘ 02 41 38 78 80, www.camping-lepodore.com
Address : 51 rte du Pô (3.2km northwest along the D 10, follow the signs for Saumur and take road to the left)
Opening times : from mid March to mid Nov.
2 ha (90 pitches) flat, grassy
Tariff : (2012 price) 27€ ♦♦ ⇔ 圓 (∮) (10A) – Extra per person 6€ – Reservation fee 13€
Rental rates : (2012 price) (from mid March to mid Nov.) – 25 🚐. Per week from 100 to 750€
Reservation fee 13€
25 圓 15.50€ – ⚓ (∮) 13€

Surroundings : ⟋ ⌑
Leisure activities : ♦ ✕ 🏠 ⚓ ⅀
Facilities : ♿ ⚏ ⴹ ⚶ ⴺ ♨ 圓 ⴞ

GPS Longitude : -0.01244
Latitude : 47.29923

AMBRIÈRES-LES-VALLÉES

53300 – Michelin map **310** F4 – pop. 2,778 – alt. 144
▶ Paris 248 – Alençon 60 – Domfront 22 – Fougères 46

⚠ Municipal de Vaux

☏ 02 43 04 90 25, www.parcdevaux.com
Address : situated 2km southeast along the D 23, follow the signs for Mayenne and take the turning to the left; by the swimming pool
Opening times : from beginning April to end Oct.
1.5 ha (61 pitches) terraced, flat, grassy, fine gravel
Tariff : (2012 price) 17.60€ ✶✶ ⇔ 🅴 [½] (10A) – Extra per person 4.60€ – Reservation fee 10€
Rental rates : (2012 price) (permanent) – 10 🛖 – 20 🛖 – 5 tent bungalows.
Per night from 70 to 150€ – Per week from 165 to 695€ – Reservation fee 10€
🚽 sani-station
Pleasant, wooded park beside the Varenne lake.

Surroundings : 🏞 ⌑ 🌳
Leisure activities : 🎯 🚲
Facilities : ♿ ⚬ 🚿 🚽 ⌐ launderette
Nearby : 🚣 ✗ 🎣 🛝 ≌ 🏄 🐎 🐴

GPS Longitude : -0.6171
Latitude : 48.39175

ANCENIS

44150 – Michelin map **316** I3 – pop. 7,543 – alt. 13
▶ Paris 347 – Angers 55 – Châteaubriant 48 – Cholet 49

⚠ L'Île Mouchet

☏ 02 40 83 08 43, www.camping-estivance.com
Address : impasse de l'Île Mouchet (take the western exit along the bd Joubert and take the turning to the left, behind the municipal sports centre)
Opening times : Permanent
3.5 ha (105 pitches) flat, grassy
Tariff : (2012 price) 18€ ✶✶ ⇔ 🅴 [½] (10A) – Extra per person 3.70€
Rental rates : (2012 price) (permanent) – 11 🛖 – 5 tent bungalows. Per night from 35 to 55€
Per week from 175 to 415€
🚽 sani-station 4.50€
Large expanses of grass, with shade, near the municipal stadium and the Loire river.

Surroundings : 🌳
Leisure activities : 🎯 🚣 🛝 ⌂
Facilities : ♿ ⚬ (Jul-Aug) ⌐ launderette
Nearby : ✗ 🎣 🏄 sports trail

GPS Longitude : -1.18707
Latitude : 47.36095

ANDOUILLÉ

53240 – Michelin map **310** E5 – pop. 2,300 – alt. 103
▶ Paris 282 – Fougères 42 – Laval 15 – Mayenne 23

⚠ Municipal le Pont

☏ 02 43 01 18 10, www.ville-andouille.fr
Address : 5 allée des Isles (along the D 104, follow the signs for St-Germain-le-Fouilloux, right next to municipal gardens; beside the Ernée river)
Opening times : from beginning April to end Oct.
0.8 ha (31 pitches) flat, grassy
Tariff : (2012 price) ✶ 1.50€ ⇔ 🅴 – [½] (12A) 2.88€
Rental rates : (2012 price) (permanent) – 4 🛖. Per night from 23 to 49€
Per week from 183 to 364€

Surroundings : ⌑ 🌳
Facilities : ♿ 🏳 🖼
Nearby : 🚣 fitness trail

GPS Longitude : -0.78697
Latitude : 48.17604

PAYS DE LA LOIRE

ANGERS

49000 – Michelin map **317** F4 – pop. 147,305 – alt. 41 – Leisure centre
▶ Paris 294 – Caen 249 – Laval 79 – Le Mans 97

Lac de Maine ♣♨

℘ 02 41 73 05 03, *www.lacdemaine.fr*
Address : av. du Lac de Maine (4km southwest along the D 111, follow the signs for Pruniers, near the lake (direct access) and near the leisure and activity park)
Opening times : from end March to beginning Oct.
4 ha (163 pitches) flat, grassy, fine gravel
Tariff : (2012 price) 25.30€ ♣♣ ⇔ 🏕 🅹 (10A) – Extra per person 3.30€ – Reservation fee 7€
Rental rates : (2012 price) (from end March to beginning Oct.) ♿ (2 mobile homes) – 14 🏠.
Per week from 294 to 627€ – Reservation fee 30€
Public transport links to the centre of Angers are situated 300m from the campsite.

Surroundings : 🔲 ♨
Leisure activities : ♈ ✕ 🏛 🛶 🚣 🚴 🏊 spa facilities
Facilities : ♿ ⊶ 🅲🎏 🍖 🔥 ♨ ‼ 🔲 🍴
Nearby : ✂ 🏊 🎣 🚣 pedalos

GPS Longitude : -0.59654
Latitude : 47.45551

ANGLES

85750 – Michelin map **316** H9 – pop. 2,329 – alt. 10
▶ Paris 450 – Luçon 23 – La Mothe-Achard 38 – Niort 86

L'Atlantique ♣♨

℘ 02 51 27 03 19, *www.camping-atlantique.com*
Address : 5bis r. du Chemin de Fer (in the town, take the exit for la Tranche-sur-Mer and take turning to the left)
Opening times : from beginning April to mid Sept.
6.9 ha (363 pitches) flat, grassy, stony
Tariff : (2012 price) 29€ ♣♣ ⇔ 🏕 🅹 (10A) – Extra per person 6.50€ – Reservation fee 25€
Rental rates : (2012 price) (from beginning April to mid Sept.) – 92 🏠 – 18 🏠.
Per week from 195 to 710€ – Reservation fee 25€
An attractive campsite, although the sanitary facilities and some rental options are a bit old. Free shuttle service to the beaches.

Surroundings : 🔲 ♨♨
Leisure activities : ♈ ✕ 🏛 🎮 🛶 🚣 🚴 ✂ 🔲 🏊 ⬛ entertainment room
Facilities : ♿ ⊶ 🍖 🔥 ♨ ‼ launderette 🍴 free shuttle bus to beaches

GPS Longitude : -1.40552
Latitude : 46.40465

APV Moncalm ♣♨
(rental of mobile homes and chalets only)

℘ 02 51 97 55 50, *www.camping-apv.com*
Address : r. du Chemin de Fer (in the town, take the exit for La Tranche-sur-Mer and take turning to the left)
Opening times : from beginning April to end Sept.
3 ha (200 pitches) flat, grassy, stony
Rental rates : (2012 price) – 85 🏠 – 30 🏠 – 1 tent bungalow – 15 mobile homes (without sanitary facilities). Per night 80€ – Per week from 174 to 880€ – Reservation fee 27€
Mobile home park and chalets with an open-air play and paddling pool area. Free shuttle service to the beaches.

Surroundings : 🔲 ♨♨
Leisure activities : ♈ ✕ 🏛 🎮 🛶 🚣 🚴 🔲 ⬛ multi-sports ground
Facilities : ♿ ⊶ 🍖 ‼ launderette 🍴 free shuttle bus to beaches

GPS Longitude : -1.40548
Latitude : 46.40467

Le Clos Cottet ⚑⚑

🖋 0251289072, *www.camping-clos-cottet.com*
Address : rte de La Tranche-sur-Mer (2.2km to the south, near the D 747)
Opening times : from beginning April to end Sept.
4.5 ha (196 pitches) flat, grassy, small lake
Tariff : (2012 price) 29€ ✝✝ ⇔ 🔲 🗲 (10A) – Extra per person 6.50€
Rental rates : (2012 price) (from beginning April to end Sept.) 🏄 – 100 🚐 – 9 🏠.
Per night from 71 to 156€ – Per week from 99 to 839€ – Reservation fee 25€

Based around a renovated farmhouse with some animals. Free shuttle service to the beaches.

Surroundings : ⌑ 🌳🌳
Leisure activities : 🍹 ✗ ▦ 🏊 ⛹ 🎿 ⛵ hammam ⚓ ♨ 🔲 ⚒ ⛰ 🎣
quad biking, multi-sports ground, entertainment room
Facilities : 🚿 🔑 🛁 🍴 launderette free shuttle bus to beaches

GPS Longitude : -1.40345
Latitude : 46.39248

85220 – Michelin map **316** F7 – pop. 1,546 – alt. 19
▶ Paris 448 – Challans 17 – Nantes 64 – La Roche-sur-Yon 30

Les Charmes

🖋 0251544808, *www.campinglescharmes.com*
Address : at Les Lilas (3.6km north along the D 21, follow the signs for Challans and take turning to the right, towards La Roussière)
Opening times : from mid April to mid Sept.
1 ha (55 pitches) flat, grassy
Tariff : 23.30€ ✝✝ ⇔ 🔲 🗲 (10A) – Extra per person 4.90€ – Reservation fee 15€
Rental rates : (permanent) 🚿 (1 mobile home) – 12 🚐 – 5 🏠. Per night from 36 to 70€
Per week from 230 to 590€ – Reservation fee 15€
🚐 5 🔲 6€
Pleasant site with upmarket rental options and a wellness area.

Surroundings : 🌿 ⌑ 🌳🌳
Leisure activities : 🍹 ▦ ♨ jacuzzi ⚓ ⚒ entertainment room
Facilities : 🚿 🔑 🍴 launderette

GPS Longitude : -1.73397
Latitude : 46.77827

44410 – pop. 1,773 – alt. 12
▶ Paris 454 – Nantes 79 – Rennes 108 – Vannes 48

Moulin de Leclis

🖋 0240017669, *www.camping-moulin-de-leclis.fr*
Address : at Pont Mahé (situated 4km west along the D 82)
Opening times : from end March to mid Nov.
3.8 ha (180 pitches) flat, grassy, sandy
Tariff : (2012 price) ⇔ 🔲 14.10€ – 🗲 (10A) 4.30€ – Reservation fee 20€
Rental rates : (2012 price) (from end March to mid Nov.) 🚿 (1 mobile home) 🏄 – 31 🚐 – 31 🏠 – 1 tent bungalow. Per night 220€ – Per week from 231 to 1,008€ – Reservation fee 20€
🚐 sani-station 4.10€ – ⛽ 6.90€
On the Baie de Pont-Mahé, with a view of La Pointe du Bile headland.

Surroundings : 🌿 ⌑ 🌳🌳⛰
Leisure activities : 🍹 ✗ ⚓ 🔲 (open-air in season) ⚒
Facilities : 🚿 🔑 ▥ 🛁 🍴 launderette ♨
Nearby : skate surfing

GPS Longitude : -2.44795
Latitude : 47.44576

AVOISE

72430 – Michelin map **310** H7 – pop. 539 – alt. 112
▶ Paris 242 – La Flèche 28 – Le Mans 41 – Sablé-sur-Sarthe 11

Municipal des Deux Rivières

🕿 0243927612, *www.tourisme.sablesursarthe.fr*
Address : place des 2 Fonds (in the town, along the D 57)
Opening times : from beginning June to beginning Sept.
1.8 ha (50 pitches) flat, grassy
Tariff : (2012 price) 8.50€ ✚✚ ⬅ 🅔 (16A) – Extra per person 2.10€
Beside the Sarthe river.

Surroundings : ⌐ 🍂🍂
Leisure activities : ⬳⬱
Facilities : ⅆ 🗂 ⬚ ⬟ ⬳ 🕴
Nearby : ⚓

GPS Longitude : -0.20554
Latitude : 47.86545

For more information on visiting particular towns or regions, consult the relevant regional MICHELIN Green Guide. We also recommend you use the appropriate Michelin regional map to locate your selected campsite, to calculate distances and to work out the best route.

AVRILLÉ

85440 – Michelin map **316** H9 – pop. 1,194 – alt. 45
▶ Paris 445 – Luçon 27 – La Rochelle 70 – La Roche-sur-Yon 27

FranceLoc Le Domaine Des Forges ♠♠

🕿 0251223885, *www.campingdomainedesforges.com*
Address : r. des Forges (take the northeastern exit along the D 19, follow the signs for Moutiers-les-Mauxfaits and take the turning to the left, 0.7km along the rue des Forges)
Opening times : from end March to end Sept.
12 ha (295 pitches) flat, grassy, lake
Tariff : (2012 price) 32.50€ ✚✚ ⬅ 🅔 (16A) – Extra per person 6€ – Reservation fee 27€
Rental rates : (2012 price) (from end March to end Sept.) ⅆ (2 mobile homes) –
2 'gypsy' caravans – 80 🛏 – 2 🏠 – 11 tent bungalows. Per night from 48 to 85€
Per week from 150 to 1,009€ – Reservation fee 27€
🚰 sani-station
Based around a small but pretty château and a lake.

Surroundings : 🌊 ⌐ 🍂
Leisure activities : 🍴 🍽 🚗 ⬚ ⬱⬳ 🎣 ⬳⬱ ⛐ 🎿 🎯 ♫ ♨ 🏊 🛶 🚣
Facilities : ⅆ ⟶ ▦ 🧺 ⬚ ⬳ 🕴 launderette 🚿 🍴

GPS Longitude : -1.49467
Latitude : 46.47587

Les Mancellières

🕿 0251903597, *www.lesmancellieres.com*
Address : 1300 rte de Longeville (1.7km south along the D 105)
Opening times : from mid April to end Sept.
2.6 ha (133 pitches) flat and relatively flat, grassy
Tariff : 24.40€ ✚✚ ⬅ 🅔 (6A) – Extra per person 4.40€ – Reservation fee 20€
Rental rates : (from mid April to end Sept.) – 55 🛏 – 4 🏠. Per night from 40 to 105€
Per week from 172 to 740€ – Reservation fee 20€
A pleasant, shady site with plenty of greenery.

Surroundings : ⌐ 🍂🍂
Leisure activities : 🍽 🚗 jacuzzi ⬳⬱ 🎿 🏊 multi-sports ground
Facilities : ⅆ ⟶ 🧺 🕴 launderette

GPS Longitude : -1.48509
Latitude : 46.45608

LA BAULE

44500 – Michelin map **316** B4 – pop. 16,235 – alt. 31
◨ Paris 450 – Nantes 76 – Rennes 120 – St-Nazaire 19

Club Airotel La Roseraie ▲▪

✆ 02 40 60 46 66, *www.laroseraie.com*
Address : 20 av. Jean Sohier (take the northeastern exit for La Baule-Escoublac)
Opening times : from beginning April to end Sept.
5 ha (220 pitches) flat, grassy, sandy
Tariff : (2012 price) 40€ ✝✝ ⇌ 回 (10A) – Extra per person 8€ – Reservation fee 30€
Rental rates : (2012 price) (from beginning April to end Sept.) ৬ (1 mobile home) – 75 🚐 –
3 🏠. Per night from 65 to 110€ – Per week from 299 to 1,216€ – Reservation fee 30€
🚽 sani-station
A pleasant, green setting, but choose pitches away from the road in preference.

Surroundings : 🖵 ♀
Leisure activities : 🍴 ✗ 🎦 🎣 ⚬ jacuzzi ⚓ 🚲 ⚞ 🖽 (open-air
in season) ⚐ multi-sports ground, entertainment room
Facilities : ৬ ⚬ 回◎ ⚶ 🎪 launderette ⚲
GPS Longitude : -2.35776 Latitude : 47.29828

BEAUMONT-SUR-SARTHE

72170 – Michelin map **310** J5 – pop. 2,094 – alt. 76
◨ Paris 223 – Alençon 24 – La Ferté-Bernard 70 – Le Mans 29

Municipal du Val de Sarthe

✆ 02 43 97 01 93, *www.ville-beaumont-sur-sarthe.fr/*
Address : located to the southeast of the town
Opening times : from beginning May to end Sept.
1 ha (73 pitches) flat, grassy
Tariff : ✝ 2.45€ ⇌ 1.95€ 回 1.95€ – (10A) 3.50€
Rental rates : (from beginning June to end Sept.) ⚞ – 2 tent bungalows.
Per week from 165 to 305€
🚽 sani-station 4.70€
Pleasant site and setting beside the Sarthe river.

Surroundings : 🐾 🖵 ♀
Leisure activities : 🎦 ⚓ fitness trail
Facilities : ৬ ⚬ 🖽
Nearby : 🏇 🏊
GPS Longitude : 0.13384 Latitude : 48.2261

LA BERNERIE-EN-RETZ

44760 – Michelin map **316** D5 – pop. 2,541 – alt. 24
◨ Paris 426 – Challans 40 – Nantes 46 – St-Nazaire 36

Les Écureuils ▲▪

✆ 02 40 82 76 95, *www.camping-les-ecureuils.com*
Address : 24 av. Gilbert Burlot (take northeastern exit, follow the signs for Nantes and take the
turning to the left after the level crossing, 350m from the sea)
Opening times : from beginning April to mid Sept.
5.3 ha (312 pitches) flat and relatively flat, grassy
Tariff : 42.50€ ✝✝ ⇌ 回 (10A) – Extra per person 8€ – Reservation fee 20€
Rental rates : (from beginning April to end Sept.) ⚞ – 70 🚐 – 19 🏠.
Per night from 60 to 70€– Per week from 265 to 840€ – Reservation fee 20€
🚽 sani-station

An attractive site with good quality rental options around the swimming and play area.

Surroundings : 🐾 🖵 ♀
Leisure activities : 🍴 🎦 ⚬ evening ⚓ ⚞ 🏊 ⚐ multi-sports ground
Facilities : ৬ ⚬ ⚶ ⚶ ⚲ 🎪 launderette ⚲
Nearby : 🛒 ⚲
GPS Longitude : -2.03558 Latitude : 47.08375

BESSÉ-SUR-BRAYE

72310 – Michelin map **310** N7 – pop. 2,363 – alt. 72
▶ Paris 198 – La Ferté-Bernard 43 – Le Mans 57 – Tours 56

Municipal du Val de Braye

℘ 02 43 35 31 13, *www.campingmunicipal-duvaldebraye.jimdo.com/*
Address : head southeast along the D 303, follow the signs for Pont de Braye
Opening times : from end March to end Oct.
2 ha (120 pitches) flat, grassy
Tariff : 12.50€ ♦♦ ⇔ 回 ⑭ (13A) – Extra per person 2.90€
Rental rates : (from end March to end Oct.) ৬ (1 mobile home) – 6 ⛺ – 4 teepees –
1 tent bungalow. Per night from 23 to 55€ – Per week from 110 to 300€
⊞ sani-station 3€ – ⛟9€
Beautiful trees and shrubs, beside the Braye river.

Surroundings : ⚲
Leisure activities : 🎦 🏇 🎣
Facilities : ৬ ⚬⇥ (Jul–Aug) ⑂ 📷
Nearby : ✗ ✗ 🛶 ⛷

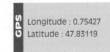
Longitude : 0.75427
Latitude : 47.83119

BLAIN

44130 – Michelin map **316** F3 – pop. 9,284 – alt. 23
▶ Paris 411 – Nantes 41 – Nort-sur-Erdre 22 – Nozay 16

Municipal le Château

℘ 02 40 79 11 00, *www.ville-blain.fr*
Address : r. Henri II de Rohan – Le Gravier – (take the southwestern exit along the N 171, follow the
signs for St-Nazaire and take road to the left, 250m from the Nantes-Brest canal (mooring point)
Opening times : from mid May to end Sept.
1 ha (44 pitches) flat, grassy
Tariff : (2012 Price) 13€ ♦♦ ⇔ 回 ⑭ (10A) – Extra per person 2.50€
⊞ sani-station – 4 回 9€ – ⛟⑭12€
A well-kept, green setting, near a 14th-century château.

Surroundings : ⚲⚲
Leisure activities : 🎦 🏇
Facilities : ৬ (Jul–Aug) ♨ ⛱ ⑂
Nearby : ⛲ ✗ 🏇

Longitude : -1.76763
Latitude : 47.46772

BOUÈRE

53290 – Michelin map **310** G7 – pop. 1,027 – alt. 81
▶ Paris 273 – Nantes 146 – Laval 39 – Angers 70

Village Vacances Nature et Jardin
(rental of chalets only)

℘ 02 43 06 08 56, *www.vacances-nature-jardin.fr*
Address : r. Vierge Vacances (to the south, follow r. des Sencies and take the road to the left)
Opening times : Permanent
3 ha relatively flat, flat, grassy
Rental rates : (2012 price) – 11 🏠. Per night from 75 to 90 – Per week from 190 to 420€
Reservation fee 13€
⊞ sani-station 2€
The 'Nature et Jardin' (Nature and Gardening) workshops are open throughout the year.

Surroundings : 🌿 ⛲
Leisure activities : 🎦 🚴 ⛵ 🎣
Facilities : ⚬⇥ ⑂
Nearby : 🎿

Longitude : -0.47506
Latitude : 47.86306

BRAIN-SUR-L'AUTHION

49800 – Michelin map **317** G4 – pop. 3,330 – alt. 22
◘ Paris 291 – Angers 16 – Baugé 28 – Doué-la-Fontaine 38

Du Port Caroline

✆ 02 41 80 42 18, *www.campingduportcaroline.fr*
Address : r. du Pont Caroline (take the southern exit along the D 113, 100m from L'Authion)
Opening times : from mid March to end Oct.
3.2 ha (121 pitches) flat, grassy
Tariff : 20.50€ ♦♦ ⇔ 🔲 (10A) – Extra per person 4€
Rental rates : (from mid March to end Oct.) – 8 🛏 – 2 🏠 – 2 tent bungalows – 4 tents.
Per night from 35 to 90€ – Per week from 210 to 590€
🚐 sani-station

Surroundings : ▭ ♀
Leisure activities : ✗ 🖼 ⚓ ⌇
Facilities : ⚹ ⊶ 🔲 ▥ ▾ 🔲 ⚗
Nearby : 🏄 skateboarding

GPS
Longitude : -0.40855
Latitude : 47.44386

The guide is updated each year, so consult the latest edition for the
most up-to-date information and pricing.

BREM-SUR-MER

85470 – Michelin map **316** F8 – pop. 2,565 – alt. 13
◘ Paris 454 – Aizenay 26 – Challans 29 – La Roche-sur-Yon 34

Le Chaponnet ▲▴

✆ 02 51 90 55 56, *www.le-chaponnet.com*
Address : 16 r. du Chaponnet (to the west of the town)
Opening times : from beginning April to end Sept.
6 ha (357 pitches) flat, grassy
Tariff : 34.55€ ♦♦ ⇔ 🔲 (6A) – Extra per person 7.10€ – Reservation fee 20€
Rental rates : (from beginning April to end Sept.) ⚹ (1 mobile home) – 55 🛏 – 20 🏠.
Per week from 245 to 1,020€ – Reservation fee 20€

An attractive green setting with flowers; shaded in places. Free shuttle service to
the beaches.

Surroundings : ⌕ ▭ ♀
Leisure activities : ▾ ✗ 🖼 ⚙ ⛹ 🎮 ⚓ ⚓ 🚲 ✗ 🔲 ⌇ 🏊
multi-sports ground
Facilities : ⚹ ⊶ △ ☂ ⚗ ▾ launderette ⚗

GPS
Longitude : -1.83225
Latitude : 46.6043

Cybele Vacances L'Océan ▲▴

✆ 02 51 90 59 16, *www.campingdelocean.fr*
Address : r. des Gabelous (located 1km west, 600 from the beach)
Opening times : from beginning April to end Sept.
13 ha (566 pitches) flat, grassy, sandy
Tariff : 28€ ♦♦ ⇔ 🔲 (10A) – Extra per person 6€ – Reservation fee 25€
Rental rates : (from beginning April to end Sept.) ⚹ (2 mobile homes) – 170 🛏 – 3 tents.
Per night from 21 to 129€ – Per week from 150 to 899€ – Reservation fee 25€

Surroundings : ⌕ ▭
Leisure activities : ▾ ✗ 🖼 ⚙ ⛹ 🎮 ⚓ 🚲 🔲 ⌇ 🏊 multi-sports
ground
Facilities : ⚹ ⊶ △ ▾ launderette 🚿 ⚗
Nearby : ✗

GPS
Longitude : -1.83225
Latitude : 46.6043

Le Brandais ▲▲

0251905587, *www.campinglebrandais.com* – limited spaces for one-night stay
Address : r. du Sablais (take the northwestern exit along the D 38 and take turning to the left)
Opening times : from beginning April to end Sept.
2.3 ha (165 pitches) flat and relatively flat, grassy
Tariff : (2012 price) 27.50€ ★★ ⇔ 🔲 ⚡ (10A) – Extra per person 5.50€ – Reservation fee 15€
Rental rates : (2012 price) (from beginning April to end Sept.) ♿ (1 mobile home) – 60 🚐
– 6 tents. Per night from 45 to 75€ – Per week from 160 to 770€ – Reservation fee 15€

In a residential area, with a range of rental options and some pitches for tents and caravans. Free shuttle service to the beaches.

Surroundings : 🐾 ⌑ ⚘
Leisure activities : 🍸 🏠 🏃 ⛵ 🚲 🖼 🏊
Facilities : ♿ ⌐ 🛁 🚾 launderette 🚌 free shuttle bus to beaches
Nearby : 🍴

Longitude : -1.83949
Latitude : 46.60486

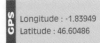

BRÉTIGNOLLES-SUR-MER

85470 – Michelin map **316** E8 – pop. 4,127 – alt. 14
▶ Paris 459 – Challans 30 – La Roche-sur-Yon 36 – Les Sables-d'Olonne 18

Les Vagues ▲▲

0251901948, *www.campinglesvagues.fr* – limited spaces for one-night stay
Address : 20 bd du Nord (to the north along the D 38 towards St-Gilles-Croix-de-Vie)
Opening times : from beginning April to end Sept.
4.5 ha (252 pitches) flat, relatively flat, grassy
Tariff : (2012 price) 30€ ★★ ⇔ 🔲 ⚡ (10A) – Extra per person 6.50€ – Reservation fee 20€
Rental rates : (2012 price) (from mid April to end Sept.) ⚡ – 45 🚐 – 4 🏠.
Per night from 80 to 150€ – Per week from 250 to 700€ – Reservation fee 20€
🚐 1 🔲 15€
Pleasant and shaded; numerous pitches for tents and caravans.

Surroundings : ⌑ ⚘⚘
Leisure activities : 🍸 🍴 🏠 🏃 ⛵ 🖼 🏊 ⛸ multi-sports ground
Facilities : ♿ ⌐ 🛁 🚾 📺

Longitude : -1.85935
Latitude : 46.63012

Chadotel La Trevillière ▲

0251330505, *http://chadotel.com/camping-bretignolles-sur-mer/la-trevilliere/*
Address : r. de Bellevue (take the northern exit along the rte du Stade and take the turning to the left)
Opening times : from beginning April to end Sept.
3 ha (204 pitches) relatively flat, flat, grassy
Tariff : 15.50€ ★★ ⇔ 🔲 ⚡ (10A) – Extra per person 6€ – Reservation fee 25€
Rental rates : (from beginning April to end Sept.) ♿ (1 mobile home) – 29 🚐.
Per night from 50 to 82€ – Per week from 170 to 860€ – Reservation fee 25€

A pleasant, green setting, with shade in places.

Surroundings : 🐾 ⌑ ⚘
Leisure activities : 🍸 🍴 ⛵ 🖼 🏊 ⛸
Facilities : ♿ ⌐ 🛁 🚾 launderette 🚌

Longitude : -1.85822
Latitude : 46.63627

These symbols are used for a campsite that is exceptional in its category:
▲▲▲ ...▲ *Particularly pleasant setting, quality and range of services available*
🐾 🐾 *Tranquil, isolated site – quiet site, particularly at night*
≼ ≼ *Exceptional view – interesting or panoramic view*

Les Cyprès

🌿 02 51 55 38 98, www.campinglescypres.com

Address : 41 r. du Pont Jaunay (2.4km southeast along the D 38 then continue 800m along the road to the right, 60m from Le Jaunay river)

4.6 ha (280 pitches) undulating, flat, sandy

Rentals : 60.

Direct access to the beach across dunes planted with trees.

Surroundings :
Leisure activities : multi-sports ground
Facilities : launderette

Longitude : -1.90919
Latitude : 46.67077

Le Marina

🌿 02 51 33 83 17, www.le-marina.com

Address : r. de La Martinière (take the northwestern exit along the D 38, follow the signs for St-Gilles-Croix-de-Vie then take left turn 1km along the r. de la Martignière)

Opening times : Permanent

2.7 ha (131 pitches) flat, grassy

Tariff : (2012 Price) 22.30€ ★★ (10A) – Extra per person 4.60€ – Reservation fee 15€

Rental rates : (2012 price) (permanent) – 6. Per night from 40 to 80€
Per week from 250 to 580€ – Reservation fee 15€

A green setting in a residential area, but choose pitches away from the road in preference.

Surroundings :
Leisure activities :
Facilities :

Longitude : -1.87185
Latitude : 46.63582

La Motine

🌿 02 51 90 04 42, www.lamotine.com

Address : 4 r. des Morinières (continue along the av. de la Plage and take a right turn)

Opening times : from beginning April to end Sept.

1.8 ha (103 pitches) relatively flat, grassy

Tariff : 27€ ★★ (10A) – Extra per person 5.50€ – Reservation fee 15€

Rental rates : (permanent) – 40. Per night from 96 to 150€ – Per week from 310 to 610€
Reservation fee 15€

sani-station 7€

Decorative trees and shrubs surround the pitches. The site is in a residential area.

Surroundings :
Leisure activities :
Facilities : launderette
Nearby :

Longitude : -1.8644
Latitude : 46.62745

Le Bon Accueil

🌿 02 51 90 15 92

Address : 24 rte de St-Gilles (1.2km northwest along the D 38)

3 ha (146 pitches) relatively flat, flat, grassy

Rentals : 7.

A few rental options and rather old but well-maintained sanitary facilities.

Surroundings :
Leisure activities :
Facilities :

Longitude : -1.86605
Latitude : 46.63625

BRISSAC-QUINCÉ

49320 – Michelin map **317** G4 – pop. 2,898 – alt. 65
▶ Paris 307 – Angers 18 – Cholet 62 – Doué-la-Fontaine 23

L'Étang

& 02 41 91 70 61, *www.campingetang.com*
Address : rte de St-Mathurin (situated 2km northeast along the D 55, and take the road to the right; beside the Aubance river and near a lake)
Opening times : from end April to mid Sept.
3.5 ha (150 pitches) flat, grassy, small lake
Tariff : 34€ ✚✚ ⇔ 国 ⓗ (10A) – Extra per person 6.60€ – Reservation fee 13€
Rental rates : (from end April to mid Sept.) ⌘ – 20 ⟦⟧ – 4 tent bungalows – 4 tents –
3 gîtes. Per night from 33 to 91€ – Per week from 200 to 850€ – Reservation fee 13€
⟦⟧ sani-station – 6 国 8€ – ⟦⟧ ⓗ19€
Spacious and comfortable pitches in the grounds of an old farmhouse.

Surroundings : ✎ ⟦⟧
Leisure activities : ✗ ⟦⟧ ⟦⟧ ⟦⟧ (open-air in season)
Facilities : ⟦⟧ ⟲ ⟦⟧ ⟦⟧ launderette
Nearby : ⟦⟧ ⟦⟧ leisure park

GPS Longitude : -0.43529
Latitude : 47.36082

CHAILLÉ-LES-MARAIS

85450 – Michelin map **316** J9 – pop. 1,902 – alt. 16
▶ Paris 446 – Fontenay-le-Comte 23 – Niort 57 – La Rochelle 34

L'Île Cariot

& 02 51 56 75 27, *www.camping-chaille-les-marais.com*
Address : r. du 8 Mai (south of the town; beside small streams and near the stadium)
Opening times : from beginning April to end Sept.
1.2 ha (50 pitches) flat, grassy
Tariff : (2012 price) 13.35€ ✚✚ ⇔ 国 ⓗ (10A) – Extra per person 4.35€ – Reservation fee 8€
Rental rates : (2012 price) (from beginning April to end Sept.) – 5 ⟦⟧ – 2 tent bungalows.
Per night from 40 to 57€ – Per week from 185 to 483€ – Reservation fee 8€
⟦⟧ sani-station 3€ – ⟦⟧10.50€
A lush, green site beside canals, ideal for canoeing.

Surroundings : ⟦⟧ 9
Leisure activities : ⟦⟧ ⟦⟧ ⟦⟧ ⟦⟧ ⟦⟧
Facilities : ⟦⟧ ⟲ ⟦⟧ launderette
Nearby : ✗

GPS Longitude : -1.0209
Latitude : 46.3927

LA CHAIZE-GIRAUD

85220 – Michelin map **316** F8 – pop. 878 – alt. 15
▶ Paris 453 – Challans 24 – La Roche-sur-Yon 32 – Les Sables-d'Olonne 21

Les Alouettes

& 02 51 22 96 21, *www.lesalouettes.com* – limited spaces for one-night stay
Address : rte de Saint-Gilles (located 1km west along the D 12, follow the signs for St-Gilles-Croix-de-Vie)
Opening times : from beginning April to end Oct.
3 ha (130 pitches) terraced, relatively flat, flat, grassy
Tariff : (2012 price) 29.90€ ✚✚ ⇔ 国 ⓗ (6A) – Extra per person 6.10€ – Reservation fee 25€
Rental rates : (2012 price) (from beginning April to end Oct.) – 66 ⟦⟧ – 19 ⟦⟧ –
5 tent bungalows. Per night 98€ – Per week from 200 to 740€ – Reservation fee 25€
A mobile home and chalet park with some pitches for tents and caravans.

Surroundings : ⟦⟧ 9
Leisure activities : ⟦⟧ ✗ ⟦⟧ ⟦⟧ jacuzzi ⟦⟧ ⟦⟧ ⟦⟧
Facilities : ⟦⟧ ⟲ ⟦⟧ ⟦⟧ launderette

GPS Longitude : -1.83342
Latitude : 46.64832

CHALLAIN-LA-POTHERIE

49440 – Michelin map **317** C3 – pop. 827 – alt. 58

▶ Paris 340 – Ancenis 36 – Angers 47 – Château-Gontier 42

▲ Municipal de l'Argos

℘ 06 77 18 78 60, *mairie.challain@wanadoo.fr*

Address : rte de Loiré (to the northeast of the town along the D 73)

0.8 ha (20 pitches) open site, flat, grassy

An attractive location near a lake and close to a château.

Surroundings : ≤ ⌂ ♀
Leisure activities : ♨⚓ ⚲
Facilities : ♿

GPS Longitude : -1.0455
Latitude : 47.63488

CHALONNES-SUR-LOIRE

49290 – Michelin map **317** E4 – pop. 6,421 – alt. 25

▶ Paris 322 – Nantes 82 – Angers 26 – Cholet 40

▲ Le Candais

℘ 02 41 78 02 27, *www.chalonnes-sur-loire.fr*

Address : rte de Rochefort (located 1km east along the D 751, follow the signs for Les Ponts-de-Cé; beside the Loire river and near a small lake)

Opening times : from mid May to beginning Sept.

3 ha (210 pitches) flat, grassy

Tariff : (2012 price) 11.30€ ☀☀ ⇌ 回 ⑵ (10A) – Extra per person 3.10€

Rental rates : (2012 price) (from mid May to beginning Sept.) – 3 tent bungalows. Per night from 41€ – Per week from 204 to 306€

Surroundings : ♀
Leisure activities : ☲ ⚲
Facilities : ♿ ⊶ ⊐ ⌀ ▣
Nearby : ⛺ ⚲⛐ ✗ ₘ ⌇

GPS Longitude : -0.74813
Latitude : 47.35132

*The classification (1 to 5 tents, **black** or red) that we award to selected sites in this guide is our own system. It should not be confused with the classification (1 to 5 stars) of official organisations.*

CHAMBRETAUD

85500 – Michelin map **316** K6 – pop. 1,460 – alt. 214

▶ Paris 377 – Nantes 83 – La Roche-sur-Yon 56 – Cholet 21

▲▲ Au Bois du Cé

℘ 02 51 91 54 32, *www.camping-auboisduce.com* ✖

Address : rte du Puy-du-Fou (located 1km to the south, on the D 27)

Opening times : from beginning April to end Sept.

5 ha (110 pitches) terraced, flat, grassy

Tariff : (2012 price) 20.30€ ☀☀ ⇌ 回 ⑵ (16A) – Extra per person 4.70€ – Reservation fee 10€

Rental rates : (2012 price) (from beginning April to end Sept.) ✖ – 22 ⎚ – 16 ⌂ – 2 studios. Per night from 50 to 61€ – Per week from 270 to 730€ – Reservation fee 10€

In a green setting; the pitches are laid out around the swimming pool area; a range of upmarket rental options.

Surroundings : ≤ ⌂
Leisure activities : ⛲ ☲ ⊠ ⌇
Facilities : ♿ ⊶ ⫘ ⁿ launderette

GPS Longitude : -0.95
Latitude : 46.915

LA CHAPELLE-HERMIER

85220 – Michelin map **316** F7 – pop. 796 – alt. 58
▶ Paris 447 – Aizenay 13 – Challans 25 – La Roche-sur-Yon 29

 Pin Parasol ▲▴

🕿 02 51 34 64 72, *http://www.campingpinparasol.fr*
Address : at Chateaulong (3.3km southwest along the D 42, follow the signs for L'Aiguillon-sur-Vie then continue 1km along the turning to the left)
Opening times : from mid April to end Sept.
12 ha (379 pitches) terraced, relatively flat, flat, grassy
Tariff : 36.10€ ♚♚ ⇔ 🔲 🕃 (10A) – Extra per person 7.15€ – Reservation fee 20€
Rental rates : (from mid April to end Sept.) ♿ (1 chalet) ⚡ – 81 🚐 – 20 ⌂ – 6 tents.
Per night from 110 to 205€ – Per week from 205 to 1,060€ – Reservation fee 20€
Swimming and paddling pools and a colourful play area. Near the Lac de Jaunay (direct access).

Surroundings : ⚲ ← ⛺ ⚲
Leisure activities : 🍴 ▦ 🎲 daytime ⚶ 🎣 ⛵ hammam 🛶 🚲 ⚿
🔲 ⤓ ⚐ multi-sports ground
Facilities : ♿ ⚡ ▦ 🛁 🍴 launderette ⚲ ⚲
Nearby : ⚲ pedalos

GPS
Longitude : -1.75502
Latitude : 46.66647

 Village Vacances Le Domaine du Pré ▲▴
(rental of of chalets only)

🕿 02 51 08 07 07, *www.domainedupre.com*
Address : at Bellevue (5km southwest along the D 42, follow the signs for L'Aiguillon-sur-Vie then continue along the turning to the left)
Opening times : permanent
11 ha terraced, relatively flat, flat
Rental rates : (2012 price) ♿ (4 chalets) – 83 ⌂. Per night from 65 to 150€
Per week from 294 to 1,106€ – Reservation fee 10€
A chalet village laid out around a large spa and wellness centre.

Surroundings : ⚲ ←
Leisure activities : ▦ ⚶ ⛵ hammam, jacuzzi 🛶 ⤓ 🔲 (small swimming pool) ⤓ multi-sports ground, spa therapy centre
Facilities : ♿ ⚡ 🛁 🍴 launderette ⚲ ⚲
Nearby : ⚲ pedalos

GPS
Longitude : -1.76769
Latitude : 46.66485

A 'quartier' is a district or area of a town or village.

CHÂTEAU-GONTIER

53200 – Michelin map **310** E8 – pop. 11,532 – alt. 33
▶ Paris 288 – Angers 50 – Châteaubriant 56 – Laval 30

 Le Parc

🕿 02 43 07 35 60, *www.campingchateaugontier.fr*
Address : 15 rte de Laval (800m north along the N 162 follow the signs for Laval; near the sports centre)
Opening times : permanent
2 ha (55 pitches) flat and relatively flat, grassy
Tariff : (2012 price) 15€ ♚♚ ⇔ 🔲 🕃 (10A) – Extra per person 4€
Rental rates : (2012 price) (permanent) – 12 ⌂. Per week from 184 to 359€
Pitches are in the shade of a variety of trees, on the banks of the Mayenne river.

Leisure activities : ▦ ⚲
Facilities : ⚲ 🍴
Nearby : climbing wall

GPS
Longitude : -0.6995
Latitude : 47.83866

CHÂTEAUNEUF-SUR-SARTHE

49330 – Michelin map **317** G2 – pop. 2,972 – alt. 20
▶ Paris 278 – Angers 31 – Château-Gontier 25 – La Flèche 33

Municipal du Port

☎ 02 41 69 82 02, *mairie.chateauneufsursarthe@wanadoo.fr*
Address : 14 place R. Le Fort (take the southeastern exit along the D 859, follow the signs for Durtal and take second road to the right after the bridge; beside the Sarthe river (mooring point)
Opening times : from beginning May to end Sept.
1 ha (60 pitches) flat, grassy
Tariff : (2012 price) 10.91€ ♣♣ ⇔ 🗉 🚿 (16A) – Extra per person 2.40€
🚽 sani-station

Surroundings : 🏕 ♀
Facilities : ♿ 🚿 🅿 🚽

GPS   Longitude : -0.48695
      Latitude : 47.67749

CHEMILLÉ

49120 – Michelin map **317** E5 – pop. 6,967 – alt. 84
▶ Paris 331 – Angers 43 – Cholet 22 – Saumur 60

La Via Natura La Coulvée

☎ 02 41 30 39 97, *www.camping-coulvee-chemille.com*
Address : rte de Cholet (take the southern exit along the N 160, follow the signs for Cholet and take the road to the right; near a small lake)
Opening times : permanent
2 ha (42 pitches) flat, grassy
Tariff : 13€ ♣♣ ⇔ 🗉 🚿 (10A) – Extra per person 3.50€
Rental rates : (permanent) – 12 🏠. Per night from 46 to 60€ – Per week from 325 to 420€
🚽 sani-station 3€ – 2 🗉 – 🚿🚿10€

Surroundings : 🏕
Leisure activities : 🚲
Facilities : ♿ 🔌 🆑 🧴 🚿 🚽
Nearby : 🏇 🏊

GPS   Longitude : -0.7359
      Latitude : 47.20308

We value your opinion and welcome your feedback.
Do email us at campingfrance@tp.michelin.com

CHOLET

49300 – Michelin map **317** D6 – pop. 54,121 – alt. 91 – Leisure centre
▶ Paris 353 – Ancenis 49 – Angers 64 – Nantes 60

Centre Touristique Lac de Ribou ♣♣

☎ 02 41 49 74 30, *www.lacderibou.com*
Address : 5km southeast along the D 20, follow the signs for Maulevrier and turn right onto D 600
Opening times : from end April to mid Sept.
5 ha (162 pitches) relatively flat, flat, grassy
Tariff : (2012 price) 26€ ♣♣ ⇔ 🗉 🚿 (10A) – Extra per person 5.50€ – Reservation fee 10€
Rental rates : (2012 price) (permanent) – 14 🏚 – 13 🏠. Per night from 65 to 99€
Per week from 320 to 720€ – Reservation fee 30€€
🚽 sani-station 5.25€ – 🚿🚿18€
The site is situated 100m from the lake (direct access).

Surroundings : 🌲 🏕
Leisure activities : ♈ ✕ 🍴 🎮 evening 🏕 🏊 ⚽ 🎿 🏊
Facilities : ♿ 🔌 🚿 🧴 🧴 🚿 launderette 🚿
Nearby : 🏕 🚣 🏇

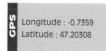

GPS   Longitude : -0.84017
      Latitude : 47.03621

COMMEQUIERS

85220 – Michelin map **316** E7 – pop. 2,910 – alt. 19
▶ Paris 441 – Challans 13 – Nantes 63 – La Roche-sur-Yon 38

La Vie

✆ 02 51 54 90 04, *www.camping-la-vie.com*
Address : at Le Motteau (1.3km southeast along the D 82, follow the signs for Coëx and take road to the left)
Opening times : from beginning April to end Sept.
6 ha (110 pitches) flat, grassy, small lake
Tariff : (2012 price) 23€ ✢✢ ⇔ ▣ ⌀ (6A) – Extra per person 53.50€ – Reservation fee 10€
Rental rates : (2012 price) (from mid April to beginning Sept.) – 15 ⊡.
Per night from 20 to 120€ – Per week from 300 to 590€ – Reservation fee 10€
A peaceful, rural setting. Able to accommodate groups and summer camps.

Surroundings : ⅏ ♀
Leisure activities : ▼ ✗ ⌂ ⋢ ⍋
Facilities : & ⊶ ♨ ♔ launderette

GPS
Longitude : -1.824
Latitude : 46.75902

Le Trèfle à 4 feuilles

✆ 02 51 54 87 54, *www.campingletreflea4feuilles.com*
Address : at La Jouère (3.3km southeast along the D 82, follow the signs for Coëx et 1.4km along the road to the left)
Opening times : from mid April to end Sept.
1.8 ha (50 pitches) terrace, flat, grassy
Tariff : 22.50€ ✢✢ ⇔ ▣ ⌀ (6A) – Extra per person 5.50€ – Reservation fee 7.50€
Rental rates : (from mid April to end Sept.) – 9 ⊡. Per night from 45 to 55€
Per week from 330 to 470 € – Reservation fee 15€
A campsite in the grounds of an arable farm, but with some animals too – sheep, goats, a donkey, chickens . . .

Surroundings : ⅏ ♀♀
Leisure activities : ▼ ⌂ ⋢
Facilities : & ⊶ launderette

GPS
Longitude : -1.78507
Latitude : 46.75935

To visit a town or region, use the MICHELIN Green Guides.

LES CONCHES

85560 – Michelin map **316** H9
▶ Paris 465 – Nantes 109 – La Roche 37 – La Rochelle 63

Le Clos des Pins

✆ 02 51 90 31 69, *www.campingclosdespins.com*
Address : 1336 av. du Dct Joussemet
Opening times : from beginning April to end Sept.
1.6 ha (94 pitches) undulating, flat, sandy
Tariff : 30€ ✢✢ ⇔ ▣ ⌀ (10A) – Extra per person 6.50€
Rental rates : (from beginning April to end Sept.) – 36 ⊡ – 13 ⌂. Per night from 55 to 95€
Per week from 219 to 1,160€ – Reservation fee 15€
⊡ 1 ▣ 19€
Some rental options are a little old, but there are also some luxury mobile homes.

Surroundings : ⌨ ♀♀
Leisure activities : ▼ ⌂ ⋢ ⌂♗ ⋢ ⍋
Facilities : & ⊶ ♨ ♔ launderette
Nearby : ♒

GPS
Longitude : -1.48842
Latitude : 46.38856

Le Sous-Bois

℘ 02 51 33 36 90
Address : at La Haute-Saligotière
1.7 ha (140 pitches) flat, sandy
Rentals : 🚫 – 4 ⛺.

A smple, shady site with well-maintained but rather old facilities.

Surroundings : 🌿 🗔 ⓞⓞ	**GPS** Longitude : -1.48727
Leisure activities : 🎣 ⛴ ✂	Latitude : 46.3956
Facilities : 🔥 ⚬🔞 🚿 🗑 🖼	

Les Ramiers

℘ 02 51 33 32 21, *www.campinglesramiers.com*
Address : 44 r. des Tulipes, chemin des Pins (to the southeast, follow the signs for La Tranche-sur-Mer)
1.4 ha (80 pitches) undulating, terraced, flat, sandy
Rentals : 6 ⛺.

A smple site, with pitches for tents laid out on terraces and among trees.

Surroundings : 🌿 🗔 ⓞⓞ	**GPS** Longitude : -1.46735
Leisure activities : 🍷 ✗	Latitude : 46.3844
Facilities : 🔥 ⚬🔞	

CONCOURSON-SUR-LAYON

49700 – Michelin map **317** G5 – pop. 544 – alt. 55
🗺 Paris 332 – Angers 44 – Cholet 45 – Saumur 25

La Vallée des Vignes

℘ 02 41 59 86 35, *www.campingvdv.com*
Address : at the lieu-it : La Croix Patron (900m west along the D 960, follow the signs for Vihiers and take turning to the right after the bridge; beside the Layon river)
3.5 ha (63 pitches) flat, grassy
Rentals : 🚫 – 5 ⛺.

This campsite has a rural setting.

Surroundings : 🗔	**GPS** Longitude : -0.34766
Leisure activities : 🍷 🎯 ⛴ 🚲 🔥 🛶 ⤣	Latitude : 47.17394
Facilities : 🔥 ⚬🔞 🚿 🗑 🍴 🖼 ⤣	

COUTURES

49320 – Michelin map **317** G4 – pop. 530 – alt. 81
🗺 Paris 303 – Angers 25 – Baugé 35 – Doué-la-Fontaine 23

Yelloh! Village Parc de Montsabert

℘ 02 41 57 91 63, *www.parcdemontsabert.com*
Address : rte de Montsabert (located 1.5km to the northeast, near the château at Montsabert)
Opening times : from mid April to beginning Sept.
5 ha (150 pitches) flat and relatively flat, grassy, stony, wood
Tariff : 34€ 👤👤 🚗 🅴 🄵 (10A) – Extra per person 7 €
Rental rates : (from mid April to beginning Sept.) – 3 'gypsy' caravans – 39 ⛺ – 14 🏠.
Per night from 39 to 142€ – Per week from 273 to 994€
🚐 sani-station 6€ – 🔋 🄵16€
In a pleasant, wooded park.

Surroundings : 🌿 🗔 ⓞⓞ	**GPS** Longitude : -0.34679
Leisure activities : ✗ 🎣 ⛴ ✂ 🔥 🖼 (open-air in season)	Latitude : 47.37448
Facilities : 🔥 ⚬🔞 🍴 🚿 🗑 🍴 launderette	

CRAON

53400 – Michelin map **310** D7 – pop. 4,590 – alt. 75
▶ Paris 309 – Fougères 70 – Laval 29 – Mayenne 60

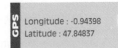 Municipal du Mûrier

☏ 02 43 06 96 33, *www.ville-craon53.fr*
Address : r. Alain Gerbault (800m east, follow the signs for Château-Gontier and take road to the left)
Opening times : from beginning May to end Sept.
1 ha (51 pitches) flat, grassy
Tariff : ☀ 3€⇔ 🔲 3.90€ – 🔋 (10A) 2.40€
Rental rates : (permanent) – 9 🏠. Per night from 50 to 85€ – Per week from 205 to 395€
Reservation fee 32€
⊞ sani-station 2.80€
A pleasant setting near a small lake.

Surroundings : ⊏ ọọ
Leisure activities : 🔲
Facilities : ₺ ⏚
Nearby : 🏪 ✗ ✖ 🔲 🔲 ⚓ ⟍ 🏇

Longitude : -0.94398
Latitude : 47.84837

DAON

53200 – Michelin map **310** F8 – pop. 486 – alt. 42 – Leisure centre
▶ Paris 292 – Angers 46 – Château-Gontier 11 – Châteauneuf-sur-Sarthe 15

⚠ Les Rivières

☏ 02 43 06 94 78, *www.campingdaon.fr*
Address : 1 r. du Port (take the western exit along the D 213, follow the signs for la Ricoullière and take a right turn before the bridge; near the Mayenne river)
Opening times : from beginning April to end Sept.
1.8 ha (98 pitches) flat, grassy
Tariff : (2012 price) 13€ ☀☀ ⇔ 🔲 🔋 (10A) – Extra per person 4€
Rental rates : (2012 price) (permanent) – 10 🏠. Per night from 80 to 175€
Per week from 163 to 349€

Surroundings : 🌿 ⊏ ọ
Leisure activities : 🔲
Facilities : ₺ ⛲ ⏚
Nearby : ✗ 🔲 ⌗ ⚓ ⟍ ⚓ pedalos

Longitude : -0.64059
Latitude : 47.74996

DURTAL

49430 – Michelin map **317** H2 – pop. 3,337 – alt. 39
▶ Paris 261 – Angers 38 – La Flèche 14 – Laval 66

⚠ Les Portes de l'Anjou

☏ 02 41 76 31 80, *www.lesportesdelanjou.com*
Address : 9 r. du Camping (take northeastern exit following signs for la Flèche and take right turn)
Opening times : from beginning April to end Oct.
3.5 ha (127 pitches) flat, grassy
Tariff : (2012 price) 16.10€ ☀☀ ⇔ 🔲 🔋 (10A) – Extra per person 4.50€ – Reservation fee 10€
Rental rates : (2012 price) (from beginning April to end Oct.) – 9 🚐 – 10 tent bungalows – 1 gîte. Per night from 70 to 150€ – Per week from 185 to 670€ – Reservation fee 10€
⊞ 3 🔲 11€
This pleasant site is laid out beside the Loir river.

Surroundings : 🌿 ⊏ ọ
Leisure activities : 🍷 ✗ 🔲 🏃 🛝 ⟍
Facilities : ₺ ⛲ ⏚ 🔲
Nearby : ⚓

Longitude : -0.23518
Latitude : 47.67136

LES EPESSES

85590 – Michelin map **316** K6 – pop. 2,575 – alt. 214
▶ Paris 375 – Bressuire 38 – Chantonnay 29 – Cholet 24

La Bretèche

0251573334, www.campinglabreteche.com

Address : at the base de loisirs (leisure centre) (take the northern exit along the D 752, follow the signs for Cholet and take the road to the right)

Opening times : from beginning April to end Sept.

3 ha (164 pitches) relatively flat, flat, grassy

Tariff : (2012 price) 21.40€ ✝✝ ⊕ ▣ ⑭ (10A) – Extra per person 4.40€ – Reservation fee 10€

Rental rates : (2012 price) (from beginning April to end Sept.) – 24 ⌂ – 12 tent bungalows.
Per night from 32 to 91€ – Per week from 190 to 685€ – Reservation fee 10€

sani-station

An attractive green site, 3km from Le Puy du Fou.

Surroundings : ⌂
Leisure activities : ⚑ ✕ ⌨ ⚓ ⚒
Facilities : ⚷ ⚐ launderette
Nearby : amusement park , Puy du Fou (3km)

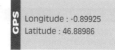
GPS Longitude : -0.89925
Latitude : 46.88986

ÉVRON

53600 – Michelin map **310** G6 – pop. 7,099 – alt. 114
▶ Paris 250 – Alençon 58 – La Ferté-Bernard 98 – La Flèche 69

Municipal de la Zone Verte

0243016536, www.camping-evron.fr

Address : bd du Mal.-Juin (take the western exit)

3 ha (92 pitches) flat and relatively flat, grassy, fine gravel

Rentals : 11 ⌂.

sani-station

Surroundings : ⌂
Leisure activities : ⌨ sports trail
Facilities : ⚐ ⌨ ⚒
Nearby : ⚑ ✕ ⌨ ⚒

GPS Longitude : -0.41321
Latitude : 48.15073

LA FAUTE-SUR-MER

85460 – Michelin map **316** I9 – pop. 916 – alt. 4
▶ Paris 465 – Luçon 37 – Niort 106 – La Rochelle 71

APV Les Flots Bleus

0251271111, www.camping-lesflotsbleus.com – limited spaces for one-night stay

Address : av.des Chardons (located 1km southeast following signs for La Pointe d'Arçay (headland))

Opening times : from beginning April to end Sept.

1.5 ha (104 pitches) flat, grassy, sandy

Tariff : (2012 price) 30.50€ ✝✝ ⊕ ▣ ⑭ (6A) – Extra per person 5.60€ – Reservation fee 25€

Rental rates : (2012 price) (from beginning April to end Sept.) – 58 ⌂ – 2 tents.
Per night from 22 to 121€ – Per week from 154 to 847€ – Reservation fee 25€

In a residential area 200m from the beach.

Surroundings : ⌂
Leisure activities : ✕ ⚓ ⌨ (open-air in season)
Facilities : ⚷ ⚐ ⚒ launderette
Nearby : ⚑

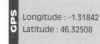
GPS Longitude : -1.31842
Latitude : 46.32508

LA FERTÉ-BERNARD

72400 – Michelin map **310** M5 – pop. 9,278 – alt. 90 – Leisure centre
▶ Paris 164 – Brou 44 – Châteauroux 65 – Le Mans 54

Municipal le Valmer

℘ 02 43 71 70 03, *levalmer@gmail.com*
Address : Espace du lac (located 1.5km southwest along the N 23, at the leisure and activity park; beside the Huisne river)
3 ha (90 pitches) flat, grassy
sani-station – 10

Surroundings :
Leisure activities :
Facilities :
Nearby : (beach)

Longitude : 0.6475
Latitude : 48.17579

LA FLÈCHE

72200 – Michelin map **310** I8 – pop. 15,228 – alt. 33
▶ Paris 244 – Angers 52 – Châteaubriant 106 – Laval 70

Municipal de la Route d'Or

℘ 02 43 94 55 90, *www.camping-laroutedor.com*
Address : allée du Camping (take the southern exit towards Saumur and take a right turn; beside the Loir river)
Opening times : from beginning March to end Oct.
4 ha (250 pitches) flat, grassy
Tariff : 15.20€ ★★ 回 (10A) – Extra per person 3.15€
Rental rates : (from mid April to end Oct.) – 10 . Per night from 72 to 106€
Per week from 303 to 517€
sani-station – 7 15.10€

Surroundings :
Leisure activities :
Facilities :
Nearby :

Longitude : -0.07779
Latitude : 47.69509

The information in the guide may have changed since going to press.

FRESNAY-SUR-SARTHE

72130 – Michelin map **310** J5 – pop. 2,198 – alt. 95
▶ Paris 235 – Alençon 22 – Laval 73 – Mamers 30

Municipal Sans Souci ▲▴

℘ 02 43 97 32 87, *www.camping-fresnaysursarthe.fr*
Address : r. du Haut Ary (located 1km west along the D 310, follow the signs for Sillé-le-Guillaume)
Opening times : from beginning April to end Sept.
2 ha (90 pitches) terraced, flat, grassy
Tariff : (2012 price) 13.16€ ★★ 回 (10A) – Extra per person 2.83€
Rental rates : (2012 price) (permanent) – 5 . Per night from 100 to 246€
Per week from 171 to 491€
sani-station 3.15€
Pretty, clearly marked-out pitches beside the Sarthe river.

Surroundings :
Leisure activities :
Facilities :
Nearby :

Longitude : 0.01589
Latitude : 48.28252

FROMENTINE

85550 – Michelin map **316** D6
▶ Paris 455 – Nantes 69 – La Roche 72 – St-Nazaire 70

Campéole La Grande Côte ▲⁀

☎ 0251685189, *www.campeole.com*
Address : rte de la Grande Côte (situated 2km along the D 38b)
Opening times : from beginning April to end Sept.
21 ha (810 pitches) terraced, flat, sandy
Tariff : (2012 price) 23.70€ ♦♦ ⇦ 回 [¢] (9A) – Extra per person 7.60€ – Reservation fee 25€
Rental rates : (2012 price) (from beginning April to end Sept.) ♿ (1 mobile home) – 95 ▦ – 36 ⌂ – 116 tent bungalows – (with/without sanitary facilities). Per night from 25 to 60€
Per week from 385 to 1,099€ – Reservation fee 25€
⊑ sani-station – ⊜ [¢]12.62€
Situated in the Forêt des Pays de Monts, near the Île de Noirmoutier bridge; close to the beach.

Surroundings : ⚲⚲ ⛰
Leisure activities : ▾ ⛵ ⊙ ⚐⚐ ⚽ ⚲ multi-sports ground
Facilities : ♿ ⚬⛊ ⌂ ⚐ launderette ⚲ ⚲
Nearby : ⚲ ◊

GPS Longitude : -2.14732
Latitude : 46.88553

GIVRAND

▶ Paris 460 – Nantes 79 – La Roche-sur-Yon 39

FranceLoc Domaine Les Dauphins Bleus ▲⁀
(rental of mobile homes and chalets only)

☎ 0251555934, *www.camping-franceloc.fr*
Address : 16 r. du Rocher
Opening times : from beginning April to mid Sept.
7 ha flat
Rental rates : (2012 price) ♿ (2 mobile homes) – 298 ▦ – 13 ⌂. Per night from 37 to 77€
Per week from 147 to 1,155€ – Reservation fee 27€
Chalets and a mobile-home village laid out around a water park.

Surroundings : ⚲ ⚲
Leisure activities : ▾ ✗ ⛵ ⊙ ⚐⚐ ⚽ ⚲⚲ ⚲ ⚲ ⚲ cinema, multi-sports ground
Facilities : ♿ ⚬⛊ ▥ ⌂ ⚐ launderette ⚲ ⚲

GPS Longitude : -1.89497
Latitude : 46.67292

Chadotel Le Domaine de Beaulieu

☎ 0251330505, *http://chadotel.com/camping-sables-olonne/la-dune-des-sables/* – limited spaces for one-night stay
Address : r. du Parc (at Les Temples)
Opening times : from beginning April to end Sept.
8 ha (340 pitches) flat, grassy
Tariff : 15.50€ ♦♦ ⇦ 回 [¢] (10A) – Extra per person 6€ – Reservation fee 25€
Rental rates : (from beginning April to end Sept.) – 36 ▦ – 14 ⌂. Per night from 50 to 82€
Per week from 170 to 860€ – Reservation fee 25€
⊑ 50 回
Some parts of the site are shaded, but the sanitary facilities are rather old.

Surroundings : ⌣ ⚲⚲
Leisure activities : ▾ ✗ ⛵ ⊙ evening jacuzzi ⚐⚐ ⚽ ⚲ ⚲ ⚲ multi-sports ground, entertainment room
Facilities : ♿ ⚬⛊ ⚲ ⚲ ⚐ ⚐ 回 ⚲ ⚲

GPS Longitude : -1.90389
Latitude : 46.67056

LE GIVRE

85540 – Michelin map **316** H9 – pop. 424 – alt. 20
▶ Paris 446 – Luçon 20 – La Mothe-Achard 33 – Niort 88

⚠ La Grisse

✆ 02 51 30 83 03, *www.campinglagrisse.com*
Address : at Le Givre (continue 2.5km south towards La Jonchère along the D 85)
Opening times : permanent
1 ha (79 pitches) flat, grassy
Tariff : ♣ 7.60€ 📷 🔳 8.60€ – ⚡ (16A) 4.10€
Rental rates : (permanent) ⚞ – 6 🚚 – 1 gîte. Per week from 198 to 598€
🚐 sani-station 12€ – 2 🔳 12€ – 🚐 ⚡10€
In the grounds of a farm (visits possible); one part of the site has plentiful shade.

Surroundings : 🌿 ♀
Leisure activities :
Facilities : ♿ ⊶ 🛁 ⁇ launderette

GPS
Longitude : -1.39815
Latitude : 46.44484

GUÉMENÉ-PENFAO

44290 – Michelin map **316** F2 – pop. 4,951 – alt. 37
▶ Paris 408 – Bain-de-Bretagne 35 – Châteaubriant 39 – Nantes 59

⚠ Flower L'Hermitage

✆ 02 40 79 23 48, *www.campinglhermitage.com*
Address : 36 av. du Paradis (1.2km east following signs for Châteaubriant and take the road to the right, near the municipal swimming pool)
Opening times : from beginning April to end Oct.
2.5 ha (83 pitches) flat, relatively flat, grassy
Tariff : 21.50€ ♣♣ 📷 🔳 ⚡ (6A) – Extra per person 5.50€ – Reservation fee 12€
Rental rates : (from beginning May to end Sept.) – 8 🚚 – 5 tent bungalows – 1 gîte.
Per night from 38 to 93€ – Per week from 266 to 651€ – Reservation fee 12€
🚐 sani-station 5€ – 🚐 14€
A pleasant, wooded site.

Surroundings : 🔲 ♀♀
Leisure activities : 📺 🏊 🚴 ⛵ (small swimming pool) ⛷
Facilities : ♿ ⊶ 🛁 ⚗ ⁇ 🔲
Nearby : 🌊 ✂ 🎨 🐟 🐎

GPS
Longitude : -1.81838
Latitude : 47.62572

GUÉRANDE

44350 – Michelin map **316** B4 – pop. 15,446 – alt. 54
▶ Paris 450 – La Baule 6 – Nantes 77 – St-Nazaire 20

⚠ Trémondec

✆ 02 40 60 00 07, *www.camping-tremondec.com* ⚞
Address : at Careil, 48 r. du Château
Opening times : from beginning April to beginning Nov.
2 ha (107 pitches) terraced, relatively flat, grassy
Tariff : 9€ ♣♣ 📷 🔳 ⚡ (10A) – Extra per person 4€ – Reservation fee 5€
Rental rates : (permanent) – 20 🚚 – 23 🏠. Per night from 70 to 105€
Per week from 260 to 855€ – Reservation fee 5€
🚐 sani-station 15€

Surroundings : 🔲 ♀
Leisure activities : 🍴 📺 🏊 🚴 ⛵
Facilities : ♿ ⊶ 🛁 ⁇ launderette 🚿
Nearby : 🛒

GPS
Longitude : -2.40155
Latitude : 47.29792

LA GUYONNIÈRE

85600 – Michelin map **316** I6 – pop. 2,674 – alt. 63
▶ Paris 395 – Nantes 47 – La Roche-sur-Yon 48 – Angers 105

⋀ **La Chausselière**

✆ 02 51 41 98 40, www.chausseliere.fr
Address : rte des Herbiers (1.2km to the south; beside the Lac de La Chausselière)
Opening times : from mid April to end Sept.
1 ha (51 pitches) flat, grassy
Tariff : (2012 price) 17.20€ ♣♣ ⇔ 🗉 🕅 (16A) – Extra per person 3.30€
Rental rates : (2012 price) (permanent) ♿ (1 chalet) ⚡ – 10 🏠. Per night from 62 to 92 €
Per week from 127 to 619€

In a green setting beside the lake.

Surroundings : 🏞 🖵 𝄢
Leisure activities : ⛵ 🏊 multi-sports ground
Facilities : ♿ ⌫ 🛁 ⚲ 🚰 🖼
Nearby : 🎣 🛶

GPS	**Longitude** : -1.2457
	Latitude : 46.95735

This guide is updated regularly, so buy your new copy every year!

ÎLE DE NOIRMOUTIER

85 – Michelin map **316** – alt. 8

Barbâtre 85630 – Michelin map **316** C6 – pop. 1,802 – alt. 5
▶ Paris 453 – Challans 32 – Nantes 70 – Noirmoutier-en-l'Île 11

⋀ **Original Camping Domaine Le Midi** ♣♣

✆ 02 51 39 63 74, www.domaine-le-midi.com
Address : r. du Camping (continue 1km northwest along the D 948 and take road to the left)
Opening times : from beginning April to end Sept.
13 ha (419 pitches) undulating, flat and relatively flat, sandy, grassy
Tariff : (2012 price) 34.50€ ♣♣ ⇔ 🗉 🕅 (16A) – Extra per person 7.20€ – Reservation fee 20€
Rental rates : (2012 price) (from beginning April to end Sept.) – 42 🛏 – 105 🏠 – 8 teepees –
49 tent bungalows. Per week from 249 to 1,499€ – Reservation fee 20€
🚉 sani-station

Close to the beach; a range of rental options in a well laid-out, natural site.

Surroundings : 🏞 🛁 ⛰
Leisure activities : 🎮 🏸 🎿 ⛵ ✂ 🍴 🎱 🏊 🛶 multi-sports
ground, entertainment room
Facilities : ♿ ⌫ 🛁 🚰 launderette
Nearby : 🚣 🚲

GPS	**Longitude** : -2.18447
	Latitude : 46.94531

L'Épine 85740 – Michelin map **316** C6 – pop. 1,727 – alt. 2
▶ Paris 466 – Nantes 79 – La Roche-sur-Yon 81

⋀ **Original Camping La Bosse**

✆ 02 53 46 97 47, www.camping-de-la-bosse.com
Address : r. du Port
Opening times : from beginning April to end Sept.
10 ha (350 pitches) undulating, sandy, grassy
Tariff : (2012 Price) 21.50€ ♣♣ ⇔ 🗉 🕅 (6A) – Extra per person 5€ – Reservation fee 20€

Close to the beach in a natural, hilly setting.

Surroundings : ≼ Port de Morin marina 🛁 ⛰
Leisure activities : ⛵
Facilities : ⌫ 🛁 launderette

GPS	**Longitude** : -2.2833
	Latitude : 46.98523

La Guérinière 85680 – Michelin map **316** C6 – pop. 1,488 – alt. 5
▶ Paris 460 – Challans 39 – Nantes 77 – Noirmoutier-en-l'île 5

Original Camping Domaine Les Moulins ▲▴

☎ 0251395138, *www.domaine-les-moulins.com*
Address : r. des Moulins (take the eastern exit along the D 948 and turn right at the roundabout)
Opening times : from beginning April to end Sept.
5.5 ha (175 pitches) flat and relatively flat, grassy, sandy, dunes
Tariff : (2012 price) 52€ ✦✦ ⇔ 🖬 🗷 (10A) – Extra per person 9€ – Reservation fee 30€
Rental rates : (2012 price) (from beginning April to end Sept.) – 74 🏠 – 19 teepees – 24 tent bungalows. Per week from 329 to 3,790€ – Reservation fee 30€
🚽 sani-station
Close to the beach, with a variety of original rental options – vehicles not permitted.

Surroundings : 🌲 🗆 ⓞⓞ ▲
Leisure activities : ⧧ ✕ 🖼 ⑤ daytime ⋏⋏ ⑮ hammam, jacuzzi ⬳⬱ ⑯
🏊 multi-sports ground, entertainment room
Facilities : ⚲ ⊶ ⑫ ▥ ⑳ ⑪ launderette 🐟
Nearby : ⚲

GPS Longitude : -2.217 Latitude : 46.96675

Le Caravan'île ▲▴

☎ 0251395029, *www.caravanile.com*
Address : 1 r. de la Tresson (take the eastern exit along the D 948 and take a right turn before the roundabout)
Opening times : from mid March to mid Nov.
8.5 ha (385 pitches) relatively flat, flat, grassy, sandy
Tariff : (2012 price) 29.50€ ✦✦ ⇔ 🖬 🗷 (5A) – Extra per person 6.80€ – Reservation fee 20€
Rental rates : (2012 price) (from mid March to mid Nov.) – 95 🏠. Per night from 105 to 195€ Per week from 260 to 855€ – Reservation fee 20€
🚽 sani-station – 🐟 🗷 13€
Close to the beach (direct access via steps down from the dunes).

Surroundings : 🌲 ▲
Leisure activities : ⧧ ✕ 🖼 ⑤ ⋏⋏ ⑮ jacuzzi ⬳⬱ ⑯ ☒ 🏊 ⬱
multi-sports ground
Facilities : ⚲ ⊶ ⑳ ⑪ launderette ⚲ 🐟

GPS Longitude : -2.21674 Latitude : 46.96569

Noirmoutier-en-l'île 85330 – Michelin map **316** C5 – pop. 4,661 – alt. 8
▶ Paris 468 – Nantes 80 – St-Nazaire 82 – Vannes 160

Indigo Noirmoutier

☎ 0251390624, *www.camping-indigo.com*
Address : 23 allée des Sableaux – Bois de la Chaize
Opening times : from mid April to beginning Oct.
12 ha (530 pitches) flat, grassy, sandy
Tariff : (2012 price) 27.10€ ✦✦ ⇔ 🖬 🗷 (10A) – Extra per person 5.20€ – Reservation fee 20€
Rental rates : (2012 price) (from mid April to beginning Oct.) – 100 tents.
Per night from 50 to 105€ – Per week from 245 to 735€ – Reservation fee 20€
🚽 sani-station 7€
An attractive, long, narrow site beside the Plage des Sableaux (beach).

Surroundings : 🌲 ≼ⓞ ▲
Leisure activities : ⧧ ✕ 🖼 ⬳⬱ 🚲
Facilities : ⚲ ⊶ ▣ ⑳ launderette 🐟
Nearby : ⑯

*This guide is not intended as a list of all the camping sites in France;
its aim is to provide a selection of the best sites in each category.*

Municipal le Clair Matin

◭

ℰ 0251390556, *www.noirmoutier-campings.fr*
Address : at Les Sableaux (at Le Bois de la Chaize)
Opening times : from beginning April to end Oct.
6.5 ha (276 pitches) flat, grassy, sandy
Tariff : (2012 price) 22.15€ ✿✿ ⇔ ▣ ⅙ (10A) – Extra per person 4.25€ – Reservation fee 9€
⛽ sani-station
An open site with plenty of natural areas.

Surroundings : ⌇ ᴖᴖ
Leisure activities : ⚓ ⚲
Facilities : ⅙ ☞ (summer) ᵗ ▣
Nearby : ♈ ✕ ⌾

Longitude : -2.2205
Latitude : 46.99567

ILE-D'OLONNE

5340 – Michelin map **316** F8 – pop. 2,668 – alt. 5
Paris 455 – Nantes 100 – La Roche-sur-Yon 35 – Challans 37

Île aux Oiseaux ♠♠

◭

ℰ 0251908996, *www.ile-aux-oiseaux.fr* – limited spaces for one-night stay
Address : r. du Pré Neuf (800m northeast along the D 87)
Opening times : from beginning April to end Oct.
5 ha (215 pitches) flat, grassy
Tariff : (2012 price) 22.50€ ✿✿ ⇔ ▣ ⅙ (10A) – Extra per person 28€
Rental rates : (2012 price) (from beginning April to end Oct.) – 88 ⛺.
Per night from 50 to 60€ – Per week from 193 to 620€ – Reservation fee 16€

A pleasant setting but with very few places for tents or caravans on overnight stays.

Surroundings : ⌇ ⌑ ᵠ
Leisure activities : ▦ ⚔ ⚓ ▨ ⚒ multi-sports ground
Facilities : ⅙ ☞ (Jul–Aug) ⌇ ⚶ ♒ ᵗ launderette

Longitude : -1.77813
Latitude : 46.56624

> *The Michelin classification (◭◭◭... ◭) is totally independent of the official star classification system awarded by the local prefecture or other official organisation.*

ARD-SUR-MER

5520 – Michelin map **316** G9 – pop. 2,497 – alt. 14
Paris 453 – Challans 62 – Luçon 36 – La Roche-sur-Yon 35

Chadotel L'Océano d'Or ♠♠

◭◭◭

ℰ 0251330505, *http://chadotel.com/camping-jard-sur-mer/l-oceano-d-or/*
Address : 58 r. Georges Clemenceau (to the northeast of Jard sur Mer, along the D 21)
Opening times : from beginning April to end Sept.
8 ha (450 pitches) flat, grassy
Tariff : 15.90€ ✿✿ ⇔ ▣ ⅙ (10A) – Extra per person 6€ – Reservation fee 25€
Rental rates : (from beginning April to end Sept.) ⅙ (1 chalet) – 57 ⛺ – 8 ⌂ – 3 ⛺ –
4 gîtes. Per night from 50 to 82€ – Per week from 210 to 1,150€ – Reservation fee 25€

An attractive site with some classic but also luxury mobile-home and gîte rental options

Surroundings : ⌑ ᴖᴖ
Leisure activities : ♈ ▦ ☺ ⚔ Ꝛ ⚓ ⚲ ⚾ ⚒ ♒ multi-sports ground, entertainment room
Facilities : ⅙ ☞ ᵗ ⌇ ⚶ ♒ ᵗ launderette ⚸ ⚷

Longitude : -1.57195
Latitude : 46.42032

Club Airotel Le Curty's ♣♦
(rental of mobile homes and chalets only)

🕾 0251330655, www.campinglecurtys.com
Address : r. de la Perpoise (north of Jard sur Mer)
Opening times : from mid April to mid Sept.
8 ha (360 pitches) flat, grassy
Rental rates : 193 ⬚ – 20 ⬚. Per night from 44 to 135€ – Per week from 310 to 950€
Reservation fee 25€

A mobile-home park for both rentals and residents.

Surroundings : ⬚ ◖
Leisure activities : ♟ ✕ ⬚ ⬚ 🏃 ⬚ 🚲 ✕ ⬚ ⬚ ⬚ multi-sports ground, entertainment room
Facilities : ♿ ⬚ ⬚ ⬚ launderette ⬚
Nearby : ⬚ ⬚

GPS Longitude : -1.57825
Latitude : 46.42032

Chadotel La Pomme de Pin

🕾 0251334385, www.pommedepin.net – limited spaces for one-night stay
Address : r. Vincent Auriol (southeast, 150m from the beach at Boisvinet)
2 ha (150 pitches) flat, sandy
Rental rates : 80 ⬚ – 11 ⬚.

Near the beach, numerous mobile homes around a small (partially covered) water park.

Surroundings : ⬚ ◖
Leisure activities : ♟ ✕ ⬚ ⬚ 🚲 ⬚ ⬚ ⬚
Facilities : ♿ ⬚ ⬚ ⬚ launderette ⬚ ⬚

GPS Longitude : -1.57264
Latitude : 46.41084

La Mouette Cendrée

🕾 0251335904, www.mouettecendree.com
Address : chemin du Faux Prieur (take the northeastern exit along the D 19, follow the signs for St-Hilaire-la-Forêt, at Les Malecots)
Opening times : from beginning April to end Oct.
1.8 ha (101 pitches) flat, grassy
Tariff : 25€ ✝✝ ⬚ ▤ ⬚ (10A) – Extra per person 5€ – Reservation fee 17€
Rental rates : (from beginning April to end Oct.) ♿ (1 mobile home) – 25 ⬚ – 5 tent bungalows. Per night 90€ – Per week from 215 to 720€ – Reservation fee 17€

A leafy, green setting with (mostly modern) mobile homes to rent.

Surroundings : ⬚ ◖◖
Leisure activities : ⬚ ⬚ ⬚
Facilities : ♿ ⬚ ⬚ ▣

GPS Longitude : -1.56702
Latitude : 46.42767

LANDEVIEILLE

85220 – Michelin map **316** F8 – pop. 1,185 – alt. 37
▶ Paris 452 – Challans 25 – Nantes 83 – La Roche-sur-Yon 32

L'Orée de l'Océan ♣♦

🕾 0251229636, www.camping-oreedelocean.com
Address : r. du Capitaine de Mazenod (take the western exit, follow the signs for Brétignolles-sur-Me not far from a lake)
2.8 ha (240 pitches) flat and relatively flat, grassy
Rentals : ♿ (1 mobile home) – 85 ⬚ – 23 tent bungalows.

A pretty, colourful play and paddling pool area.

Surroundings : ⬚ ⬚ ◖◖
Leisure activities : ♟ ✕ ⬚ ⬚ 🏃 ⬚ ⬚ ⬚ ⬚ ⬚ multi-sports ground, entertainment room
Facilities : ♿ ⬚ ⬚ ⬚ launderette
Nearby : ✕

GPS Longitude : -1.80635
Latitude : 46.64087

Pong ⚹⚹

✆ 0251229263, *www.lepong.com* ✖ (Jul–Aug)

Address : r. du Stade (take the northeastern exit)

Opening times : from beginning April to mid Sept.

3 ha (230 pitches) terraced, flat and relatively flat, grassy, small lake

Tariff : 29.90€ ⚹⚹ 🚐 🗐 ⚡ (10A) – Extra per person 5.10€ – Reservation fee 18€

Rental rates : (permanent) – 50 🚐. Per night from 29 to 79€ – Per week from 200 to 550 € Reservation fee 18€

A well-shaded site with a range of rental options, some of which are a little on the old side.

Surroundings : 🏞 🛋 ⛳

Leisure activities : ✗ 🎦 ⛹ 🏊 🎯 🛶 multi-sports ground

Facilities : ♿ ⚓ 🚿 🛁 ⚐ ℗ launderette 📶

GPS Longitude : -1.79937
Latitude : 46.64226

LAVARÉ

72390 – Michelin map **310** M6 – pop. 838 – alt. 122

◪ Paris 173 – Bonnétable 26 – Bouloire 14 – La Ferté-Bernard 19

Le Val de Braye

✆ 0243719644, *www.basedeloisirs-lavare.fr*

Address : rte de Vibraye (take the eastern exit along the D 302, at the leisure and activity park)

Opening times : from end May to mid Oct.

0.3 ha (20 pitches) flat, grassy

Tariff : ⚹ 2€ 🚐 1€ – ⚡ (5A) 2€

Rental rates : (permanent) – 11 🏠. Per night from 45 to 76€ – Per week from 250 to 470€

🚐 16 🗐 2€

An attractive location near a small lake.

Surroundings : ≤ 🛋 ⚑

Leisure activities : 🛶 🎯

Facilities : ⚓ 🚿 🛁

Nearby : ✗ 🛶 🚲 mountain biking

GPS Longitude : 0.64522
Latitude : 48.05326

The pitches of many campsites are marked out with low hedges of attractive bushes and shrubs.

LE LION-D'ANGERS

49220 – Michelin map **317** E3 – pop. 3,638 – alt. 45

◪ Paris 295 – Angers 27 – Candé 27 – Château-Gontier 22

Municipal les Frênes

✆ 0241953156, *www.leliondangers.fr* – 🅡

Address : rte de Chateau Gontier (take the northeastern exit along the N 162, follow the signs for Château-Gontier; beside the Oudon river)

Opening times : from end May to beginning Sept.

2 ha (94 pitches) flat, grassy

Tariff : (2012 price) ⚹ 2€ 🚐 🗐 2.15€ – ⚡ (10A) 2.70€

🚐 sani-station

Set among majestic ash trees; beside the Oudon river.

Surroundings : ⚑

Leisure activities : 🎦 🛶

Facilities : ♿

Nearby : ⚑ racecourse

GPS Longitude : -0.71154
Latitude : 47.63094

LONGEVILLE-SUR-MER

85560 – Michelin map **316** H9 – pop. 2,356 – alt. 10
▶ Paris 448 – Challans 74 – Luçon 29 – La Roche-sur-Yon 31

MS Vacances Les Brunelles ♣♠

𝒞 0251335075, *www.les-brunelles.com* – limited spaces for one-night stay
Address : r. de La Parée (at Le Bouil, 1km to the south)
Opening times : from end April to end Sept.
13 ha (600 pitches) relatively flat, flat, grassy
Tariff : 40€ ♣♣ ⊞ 🗐 🔌 (10A) – Extra per person 9€ – Reservation fee 25€
Rental rates : (from mid April to end Sept.) ♿ (1 mobile home) – 274 🚐 – 10 🏠.
Per night from 50 to 70 € – Per week from 295 to 1,220€ – Reservation fee 25€
🚽 sani-station

Surroundings : 🏞 ☐ ⚲
Leisure activities : ♈ ✗ 🛶 ⊙ ⚶ 🏋 ☯ hammam, jacuzzi 🏊 🚲 ✗
🏊 🏊 △ multi-sports ground
Facilities : ♿ ⚲ cc 🏛 🛁 ⛺ 🚿 🍽 launderette 🗒 🚰
Nearby : 🏇

GPS
Longitude : -1.52191
Latitude : 46.41326

Camp'Atlantique Le Petit Rocher ♣♠

𝒞 0821444153, *www.camp-atlantique.com*
Address : 1250 av. du Dct Mathevet
Opening times : from mid April to end Sept.
5 ha (211 pitches) undulating, terraced, relatively flat, flat, grassy
Tariff : 28€ ♣♣ ⊞ 🗐 🔌 (6A) – Extra per person 7€ – Reservation fee 25€
Rental rates : (from mid April to end Sept.) ♿ (1 mobile home) – 10 'gypsy' caravans –
107 🚐 – 10 tent bungalows – 5 tents. Per week from 129 to 799€ – Reservation fee 25€
A hilly site with lots of shade, 250m from the beach via a pedestrian path.

Surroundings : ☐ ⚲⚲
Leisure activities : ✗ ⊙ ⚶ 🏊 🏊 △ multi-sports ground
Facilities : ♿ ⚲ ⛺ 🍽 launderette
Nearby : 🗒 ♈ 🚰

GPS
Longitude : -1.50727
Latitude : 46.40344

To make the best possible use of this guide,
please read pages 2–15 carefully.

LOUÉ

72540 – Michelin map **310** I7 – pop. 2,129 – alt. 112
▶ Paris 230 – Laval 59 – Le Mans 30

Village Loisirs

𝒞 0243886565, *villageloisirs.com*
Address : pl. Hector Vincent (head towards the northeastern exit along the D 21, rte du Mans;
by the swimming pool)
Opening times : permanent
1 ha (16 pitches) flat, grassy
Tariff : (2012 price) ♣ 8€ ⊞ – 🔌 (10A) 4€
Rental rates : (2012 price) (permanent) – 10 🏠. Per night from 50 to 80€
Per week from 250 to 430€
In a pleasant location beside the Vègre river.

Leisure activities : ♈ ✗ 🛶 🏊 △
Facilities : ♿ ⚲ (Jun–Sept) 🏛 🍽 🔳
Nearby : 🏊 walking trails

GPS
Longitude : -0.14711
Latitude : 47.99734

UCHÉ-PRINGÉ

2800 – Michelin map **310** J8 – pop. 1,658 – alt. 34
Paris 242 – Château-du-Loir 31 – Écommoy 24 – La Flèche 14

Municipal la Chabotière

📞 02 43 45 10 00, *www.lachabotiere.com*
Address : place des Tilleuls (to the west of the town)
Opening times : from beginning April to mid Oct.
3 ha (75 pitches) terraced, flat, grassy
Tariff : 14.70€ ♦♦ 🚐 ▣ (10A) – Extra per person 3.90€ – Reservation fee 30€
Rental rates : (permanent) – 10 🏠 – 10 tent bungalows. Per night from 32 to 89€
Per week from 184 to 525€

In a leisure and activity park; beside the Loir river.

Surroundings :
Leisure activities :
Facilities : (Jul–Aug) 🅿 launderette
Nearby : boats for hire

GPS Longitude : 0.07364
Latitude : 47.70252

A chambre d'hôte is a guesthouse or B & B-style accommodation.

ES LUCS-SUR-BOULOGNE

5170 – Michelin map **316** H6 – pop. 3,251 – alt. 70
Paris 423 – Aizenay 19 – Les Essarts 24 – Nantes 45

Municipal Val de Boulogne

📞 02 51 46 59 00, *www.leslucssurboulogne.fr*
Address : r. Charette (located 1.5km east along the D 18 beside a small lake)
Opening times : from mid June to mid Sept.
0.3 ha (19 pitches) flat and relatively flat, grassy
Tariff : (2012 price) ♦ 2.60€ 🚐 1.75€ ▣ 2.15€ – (6A) 2.70€

A green, sheltered setting near a lake, but with rather old and limited sanitary facilities.

Surroundings :
Facilities :
Nearby :

GPS Longitude : -1.48992
Latitude : 46.84565

E LUDE

2800 – Michelin map **310** J9 – pop. 4,049 – alt. 48
Paris 244 – Angers 63 – Chinon 63 – La Flèche 20

Municipal au Bord du Loir

📞 02 43 94 67 70, *www.campingmunicipallelude.fr*
Address : rte du Mans (0.8km northwest along the D 307, follow the signs for Le Mans)
Opening times : from beginning April to end Sept.
2.5 ha (111 pitches) flat, grassy
Tariff : (2012 price) 12€ ♦♦ 🚐 ▣ (10A) – Extra per person 3.80€
Rental rates : (2012 price) (from beginning April to end Sept.) – 4 – 1 🏠 –
3 tent bungalows. Per night from 25 to 88€ – Per week from 130 to 466€
sani-station 2€ – 14 ▣ 9.88€

A rural setting beside the Loir river.

Surroundings :
Leisure activities :
Facilities :
Nearby : pedalos

GPS Longitude : 0.16247
Latitude : 47.65119

MACHÉ

85190 – Michelin map **316** F7 – pop. 1,337 – alt. 42
▶ Paris 443 – Challans 22 – Nantes 59 – La Roche-sur-Yon 26

⚠ Le Val de Vie

℘ 02 51 60 21 02, www.campingvaldevie.fr
Address : 5 r. du Stade (take the exit for Apremont and take the road to the left; 400m from the lake
Opening times : from beginning April to beginning Oct.
2.5 ha (93 pitches) relatively flat, flat, grassy
Tariff : (2012 price) 23.80€ ✹✹ ⇔ 🗉 🌢 (10A) – Extra per person 4€
Rental rates : (2012 price) (from beginning March to mid Nov.) – 2 🚐 – 2 🏠 .
Per night from 50 to 90€ – Per week from 215 to 600€
🚐 sani-station 10€

Surroundings : 🐾 🖾
Leisure activities : 🏊🏿 🏊 🎣
Facilities : ♿ ⚡ 🖨 🚽 🖼
Nearby : 💥

GPS Longitude : -1.68595
Latitude : 46.75305

MACHECOUL

44270 – Michelin map **316** F6 – pop. 5,872 – alt. 5
▶ Paris 420 – Beauvoir-sur-Mer 23 – Nantes 39 – La Roche-sur-Yon 56

⚠ La Rabine

℘ 02 40 02 30 48, www.camping-la-rabine.com
Address : allée de la Rabine (take the southern exit along the D 95, follow the signs for Challans; beside the Falleron river)
Opening times : from beginning April to end Sept.
2.8 ha (131 pitches) flat, grassy
Tariff : (2012 price) 14.20€ ✹✹ ⇔ 🗉 🌢 (13A) – Extra per person 4€
Rental rates : (2012 price) (from beginning April to end Sept.) – 1 'gypsy' caravan – 3 🏠 .
Per week from 310 to 480€ – Reservation fee 20€
🚐 sani-station – 4 🗉 10.70€
Very near the town centre, encircled by a small river.

Surroundings : ♀
Leisure activities : 🏊🏿 🎣
Facilities : ♿ ⚡ 🚽 launderette
Nearby : 💥 🖾

GPS Longitude : -1.81555
Latitude : 46.9887

MAILLEZAIS

85420 – Michelin map **316** L9 – pop. 962 – alt. 6
▶ Paris 436 – Fontenay-le-Comte 15 – Niort 27 – La Rochelle 49

⚠ Municipal de l'Autize

℘ 06 43 19 14 90, www.maillezais.fr
Address : r. du Champ de foire (take the southern exit, follow the signs for Courçon)
Opening times : from beginning April to end Sept.
1 ha (40 pitches) flat, grassy
Tariff : (2012 price) 9€ ✹✹ ⇔ 🗉 🌢 (13A) – Extra per person 2.50€
🚐 sani-station 2€ – 10 🗉
The site is in a green setting near the exit from town.

Surroundings : 🖾 ♀♀
Leisure activities : 🖳
Facilities : ♿ ⚡ (Jul-Aug) 🍴 🚿 🚽 🖼
Nearby : 🏊🏿 💥

GPS Longitude : -0.73914
Latitude : 46.37133

MALICORNE-SUR-SARTHE

2270 – Michelin map **310** I8 – pop. 1,962 – alt. 39
▸ Paris 236 – Château-Gontier 52 – La Flèche 16 – Le Mans 32

Municipal Port Ste Marie

⌀ 02 43 94 80 14, *www.ville-malicorne.fr*
Address : to the west of the town along the D 41
Opening times : from beginning April to end Sept.
1 ha (80 pitches) flat, grassy
Tariff : (2012 price) 14.75€ ♦♦ ⇌ 🔲 🕭 (12A) – Extra per person 3.25€
Rental rates : (2012 price) (from beginning April to end Sept.) – 4 🛖 – 6 🏠 –
6 tent bungalows. Per night from 48 to 124 €– Per week from 145 to 385€
🚐 sani-station
A pleasant site and setting near the Sarthe river.

Surroundings : ♀
Leisure activities : 🎴 🏇
Facilities : ♿ ⛺ (Jul–Aug) 🌂 ⚑ launderette
Nearby : 🚲 ✎ 🎣 ⚓ 🐎 pedalos

GPS Longitude : -0.0893
Latitude : 47.81763

MAMERS

2600 – Michelin map **310** L4 – pop. 5,545 – alt. 128
▸ Paris 185 – Alençon 25 – Le Mans 51 – Mortagne-au-Perche 25

Municipal du Saosnois

⌀ 02 43 97 68 30, *www.mairie-mamers.fr*
Address : continue 1km north following signs for Mortagne-au-Perche and take D 113 to the left,
following signs for Contilly, near two lakes
Opening times : from beginning March to beginning Nov.
1.5 ha (50 pitches) terraced, relatively flat, grassy
Tariff : 12€ ♦♦ ⇌ 🔲 🕭 (10A) – Extra per person 2€
Rental rates : (from beginning March to beginning Nov.) – 3 🛖 – 5 tent bungalows.
Per night from 25 to 49€ – Per week from 140 to 338€
🚐 sani-station – 9 🔲 5€

Surroundings : 🏞 ♀
Leisure activities : 🍷 🏊 (beach)
Facilities : ⚷ ⛲ 🌂 ⚑ 🖼
Nearby : 🏇 ✎ 🎣 🎣 ⚓ 🐎 fitness trail

GPS Longitude : 0.37303
Latitude : 48.35809

MANSIGNÉ

2510 – Michelin map **310** J8 – pop. 1,579 – alt. 80 – Leisure centre
▸ Paris 235 – Château-du-Loir 28 – La Flèche 21 – Le Lude 17

Municipal de la Plage

⌀ 02 43 46 14 17, *www.atouvert.com*
Address : r. du Plessis (take the northern exit along the D 31, follow the signs for La Suze-sur-Sarthe,
100m from a small lake (with beach)
Opening times : from beginning April to mid Oct.
3 ha (175 pitches) flat, grassy
Tariff : (2012 price) 15.20€ ♦♦ ⇌ 🔲 🕭 (10A) – Extra per person 3€ – Reservation fee 10€
Rental rates : (2012 price) (from beginning April to end Oct.) – 8 🛖 – 20 🏠 – 8 tent
bungalows. Per night from 40 to 120€ – Per week from 150 to 480€ – Reservation fee 10€

Surroundings : ♀
Leisure activities : 🍷 🎴 🚲 ✎ 🎣 🎣
Facilities : ⚷ ⛲ (14 Jul to 16 Aug) ⚑ launderette
Nearby : 🏇 🎣 🏊 ⚓ 🍃 pedalos

GPS Longitude : 0.13284
Latitude : 47.75078

MARÇON

72340 – Michelin map **310** M8 – pop. 1,028 – alt. 59 – Leisure centre
▶ Paris 245 – Château-du-Loir 10 – Le Grand-Lucé 51 – Le Mans 52

Lac des Varennes

📞 02 43 44 13 72, *www.camp-in-ouest.com*
Address : rte de Port Gauthier (located 1km west along the D 61, near the leisure park)
Opening times : from beginning April to end Oct.
5.5 ha (250 pitches) flat, grassy
Tariff : (2012 price) 18.60€ ✦✦ ⬅ 🔳 (6A) – Extra per person 4.90€ – Reservation fee 10€
Rental rates : (2012 price) (from beginning April to end Oct.) – 30 ⬛ – 1 ⬛ – 10 tent
bungalows. Per night from 70 to 170€ – Per week from 165 to 755€ – Reservation fee 10€
🚽 sani-station 3€
In a pleasant location beside a lake with recreational facilities.

Surroundings : ♀
Leisure activities : 🍴 ✕ 🖼 ⚓ 🚲 ☷ (beach) 🎣
Facilities : ♿ ⌕ 🛁 🍴 🔳 🔲 🚿
Nearby : ✂ 🏇 🐎 pedalos

GPS Longitude : 0.4993
Latitude : 47.7125

MAYENNE

53100 – Michelin map **310** F5 – pop. 13,350 – alt. 124
▶ Paris 283 – Alençon 61 – Flers 56 – Fougères 47

Du Gué St-Léonard

📞 02 43 04 57 14, *http://www.paysdemayenne-tourisme.fr*
Address : r. du Gué St-Léonard (north of the town, via av. de Loré and turning to the right)
Opening times : from beginning March to end Sept.
1.8 ha (70 pitches) flat, grassy
Tariff : (2012 price) 12€ ✦✦ ⬅ 🔳 (10A) – Extra per person 2.25€
Rental rates : (2012 price) (from beginning March to end Nov.) – 5 ⬛.
Per night from 22 to 67€ – Per week from 153 to 467€
🚽 sani-station
A pleasant location beside the Mayenne river.

Surroundings : ♀♀
Leisure activities : ✕ 🖼 🌊 🎣
Facilities : ♿ ⌕ ▥ 🛁 🍴 launderette
Nearby : 🛒 ✂

GPS Longitude : -0.61387
Latitude : 48.3142

LE MAZEAU

85420 – Michelin map **316** L9 – pop. 427 – alt. 8
▶ Paris 435 – Fontenay-le-Comte 22 – Niort 21 – La Rochelle 53

Municipal le Relais du Pêcheur

📞 02 51 52 93 23, *www.mairielemazeau@.fr*
Address : rte de la Sèvre (700m south of the town, near canals)
Opening times : from beginning April to end Sept.
1 ha (54 pitches) flat, grassy
Tariff : (2012 price) ✦ 3.30€ ⬅ 🔳 4.10€ – (10A) 3.10€
Rental rates : (2012 price) (from mid May to mid Sept.) 🏚 – 3 tent bungalows.
Per night from 31 to 50€ – Per week from 127 to 284€
Pleasant site and setting near the Venise Verte ('Green Venice' canal).

Surroundings : 🌿 ▱ ♀♀
Leisure activities : 🖼 ⚓
Facilities : ♿ ⌕ (Jul–Aug) 🚽 🔳
Nearby : 🎣

GPS Longitude : -0.67535
Latitude : 46.33052

MÉNIL

3200 – Michelin map **310** E8 – pop. 965 – alt. 32
Paris 297 – Angers 45 – Château-Gontier 7 – Châteauneuf-sur-Sarthe 21

Municipal du Bac

📞 02 43 70 24 54, *campingdubac@orange.fr*
Address : r. du Port (east of the village)
0.5 ha (39 pitches) flat, grassy
Rentals : 5 🏠.
sani-station
A pleasant site and setting near the Mayenne river.

Surroundings : 🐾 🗺 ♀
Leisure activities : ✗ 🚲 🎣
Facilities : 🚿 🍳 ⛲

Longitude : -0.67319
Latitude : 47.77494

MERVENT

5200 – Michelin map **316** L8 – pop. 1,077 – alt. 85
Paris 426 – Bressuire 52 – Fontenay-le-Comte 12 – Parthenay 50

La Joletière

📞 02 51 00 26 87, *www.campinglajoletiere.fr*
Address : 700m west along the D 99
Opening times : from end March to end Oct.
1.3 ha (73 pitches) relatively flat, grassy
Tariff : 20.50€ ✶✶ 🚐 🔲 🔌 (16A) – Extra per person 4.50€ – Reservation fee 5€
Rental rates : (from end March to end Oct.) – 1 'gypsy' caravan – 15 🚐 – 4 🏠 – 3 tent bungalows. Per night from 45 to 75€ – Per week from 260 to 590€ – Reservation fee 10€
A gently sloping green site, with a range of rental options.

Surroundings : 🐾 🗺 ♀♀
Leisure activities : ✗ 🏤 🏊 🚲 🛝 ⚓
Facilities : 🚿 🔧 🏕 ⛲ 📷
Nearby : 🍷

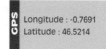
Longitude : -0.7691
Latitude : 46.5214

MESLAY-DU-MAINE

3170 – Michelin map **310** F7 – pop. 2,726 – alt. 90
Paris 268 – Angers 60 – Château-Gontier 21 – Châteauneuf-sur-Sarthe 34

La Chesnaie

📞 02 43 98 48 08, *www.paysmeslaygrez.fr*
Address : at La Chesnaie lake (2.5km northeast along the D 152, follow the signs for St-Denis-du-Maine)
Opening times : from mid April to mid Sept.
7 ha/0.8 (60 pitches) flat, grassy
Tariff : (2012 price) 11.50€ ✶✶ 🚐 🔲 🔌 (8A) – Extra per person 3.20€
Rental rates : (2012 price) (permanent) – 8 🏠. Per night from 75 to 90€
Per week from 165 to 395 €– Reservation fee 13€
sani-station
Beside a small but beautiful lake.

Surroundings : 🐾 ≤ 🗺 ♀
Leisure activities : 🚲
Facilities : 🚿 (Jul–Aug) ⛲
Leisure/activities centre : ✗ 🏤 🏊 🎣 ⚓ fitness trail
Longitude : -0.53002
Latitude : 47.96415

MESQUER

44420 – Michelin map **316** B3 – pop. 1,710 – alt. 6
▶ Paris 460 – La Baule 16 – Muzillac 32 – Pontchâteau 35

Soir d'Été ♣♣

𝒫 02 40 42 57 26, www.camping-soirdete.com
Address : 401 r. de Bel Air (head 2km northwest along the D 352 and take turning to the left)
Opening times : from beginning April to end Sept.
1.5 ha (92 pitches) flat and relatively flat, grassy, sandy
Tariff : (2012 price) 30€ ✿✿ ⬅ 🗐 (4) (6A) – Extra per person 4€
Rental rates : (2012 price) (from end March to end Sept.) – 17 🛏 – 4 🏠.
Per night from 48 to 65€ – Per week from 250 to 740€ – Reservation fee 15€
🚮 sani-station
In a shaded setting besides salt marshes.

Surroundings : 🏞 🔲 ♨
Leisure activities : 🍴 ✕ 🎬 ⛹ ⛵ 🚲 🖼 (open-air in season)
multi-sports ground
Facilities : 🚿 ⚬🛒 🗑 🍴 launderette 🔧
Nearby : ✄ 🎣

GPS Longitude : -2.47575
Latitude : 47.4064

Le Praderoi

𝒫 02 40 42 66 72, http://www.camping-le-praderoi.com
Address : at Quimiac, 14 allée des Barges (2.5km to the northwest, 100m from the beach)
Opening times : from beginning April to end Sept.
0.4 ha (32 pitches) flat, sandy, grassy
Tariff : (2012 price) 21€ ✿✿ ⬅ 🗐 (4) (10A) – Extra per person 4.50€ – Reservation fee 15€
Rental rates : (2012 price) (from beginning April to end Sept.) ✄ – 2 'gypsy' caravans – 2 🛏
Per week from 220 to 620€ – Reservation fee 15€

A small campsite, but very peaceful and good for families.

Surroundings : 🏞 ♀
Leisure activities : ⛵
Facilities : 🚿 ⚬🛒 🗑 🍴 launderette

GPS Longitude : -2.48895
Latitude : 47.40572

*The classification (1 to 5 tents, black or red) that we award to selected sites
in this guide is a system that is our own. It should not be confused with the
classification (1 to 5 stars) of official organisations.*

MÉZIÈRES-SOUS-LAVARDIN

72240 – Michelin map **310** J6 – pop. 634 – alt. 75
▶ Paris 221 – Alençon 38 – La Ferté-Bernard 69 – Le Mans 25

Parc des Braudières

𝒫 02 43 20 81 48, www.campinglesbraudieres.com – limited spaces for one-night stay
Address : 4.5km east along the back road to St-Jean
Opening times : permanent
1.7 ha (52 pitches) flat and relatively flat, grassy
Tariff : (2012 price) 19€ ✿✿ ⬅ 🗐 (4) (10A) – Extra per person 4.20€
Rental rates : (2012 price) (permanent) – 1 🛏. Per night from 50 to 65€
Per week from 350 to 450€
🚮 2 🗐 12€
Beside a small fishing lake.

Surroundings : 🏞 🔲 ♀
Leisure activities : jacuzzi ⛵ 🛝 🎣
Facilities : 🚿 ⚬🛒 🗑 🍴

GPS Longitude : 0.06328
Latitude : 48.15758

MONTREUIL-BELLAY

9260 – Michelin map **317** I6 – pop. 4,041 – alt. 50

Paris 335 – Angers 54 – Châtellerault 70 – Chinon 39

Les Nobis ⚐⚐

℘ 02 41 52 33 66, www.campinglesnobis.com

Address : r. Georges Girouy (take the northwestern exit, follow the signs for Angers and take the road to the left before the bridge)

Opening times : from end March to beginning Oct.

4 ha (165 pitches) terraced, flat, grassy

Tariff : (2012 price) 25€ ⚑⚑ 🚐 🗐 🗓 (10A) – Extra per person 4€ – Reservation fee 8€

Rental rates : (2012 price) (from beginning March to end Nov.) – 18 🚐 – 3 tent bungalows. Per night from 38 to 76€ – Per week from 220 to 570€ – Reservation fee 8€

🚱 sani-station

A pleasant location on the banks of the Thouet river, beside a château.

Surroundings : 🖵 🟢🟢
Leisure activities : 🍽 ✗ 🎦 🟢 daytime 🏃 ⛵ 🚲 ⛴ 🎣
Facilities : 🚿 ⚡ 🗑 🚽 launderette
Nearby : pedalos

Longitude : -0.15897
Latitude : 47.13204

MONTSOREAU

9730 – Michelin map **317** J5 – pop. 485 – alt. 77

Paris 292 – Angers 75 – Châtellerault 65 – Chinon 18

L'Isle Verte

℘ 02 41 51 76 60, www.campingisleverte.com

Address : av. de la Loire (take the northwestern exit along the D 947, follow the signs for Saumur; beside the Loire river)

Opening times : from beginning April to mid Oct.

2.5 ha (105 pitches) flat, grassy

Tariff : 26.50€ ⚑⚑ 🚐 🗐 🗓 (16A) – Extra per person 6€ – Reservation fee 15€

Rental rates : (from beginning April to mid Oct.) – 16 🚐 – 7 tent bungalows. Per night from 45 to 120€ – Per week from 200 to 840€ – Reservation fee 15€

🚱 sani-station 6€

Surroundings : 🟢🟢
Leisure activities : ✗ 🎦 ⛵ 🎿 ⛴
Facilities : 🚿 ⚡ 🔤 🚽 🗑 🚯

Longitude : 0.05165
Latitude : 47.21861

LA MOTHE-ACHARD

5150 – Michelin map **316** G8 – pop. 2,524 – alt. 20

Paris 439 – Aizenay 15 – Challans 40 – La Roche-sur-Yon 19

Le Pavillon

℘ 02 51 05 63 46, www.camping-le-pavillon.com

Address : 175 av. Georges Clemenceau (located 1.5km southwest, follow the signs for Les Sables-d'Olonne)

Opening times : from beginning April to end Sept.

3.6 ha (117 pitches) flat, grassy, lake

Tariff : (2012 price) 28.50€ ⚑⚑ 🚐 🗐 🗓 (10A) – Extra per person 6€ – Reservation fee 68€

Rental rates : (2012 price) (from beginning April to end Sept.) – 20 🚐 – 6 tent bungalows – 6 mobile homes and 5 chalets (without sanitary facilities). Per night from 15 to 22€ Per week from 190 to 711€ – Reservation fee 16€

In a green location with a range of mostly modern rental options.

Surroundings : 🟢🟢
Leisure activities : 🍽 🎦 ⛵ ⛴ 🏂 🎣 multi-sports ground
Facilities : 🚿 ⚡ 🚽 launderette

Longitude : -1.66728
Latitude : 46.60653

MOUCHAMPS

85640 – Michelin map **316** J7 – pop. 2,600 – alt. 81
▶ Paris 394 – Cholet 40 – Fontenay-le-Comte 52 – Nantes 68

Le Hameau du Petit Lay

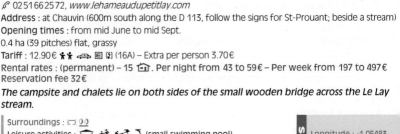

✆ 02 51 66 25 72, *www.lehameaudupetitlay.com*
Address : at Chauvin (600m south along the D 113, follow the signs for St-Prouant; beside a stream)
Opening times : from mid June to mid Sept.
0.4 ha (39 pitches) flat, grassy
Tariff : 12.90€ ★ ★ ⇔ 国 ⑭ (16A) – Extra per person 3.70€
Rental rates : (permanent) – 15 ⌂. Per night from 43 to 59€ – Per week from 197 to 497€
Reservation fee 32€

The campsite and chalets lie on both sides of the small wooden bridge across the Le Lay stream.

Surroundings : ▭ ♡♡
Leisure activities : ⛱ ⚙ ⛵ (small swimming pool)
Facilities : ♿ ⊙ ⚏ 👁
Nearby : ↴

Longitude : -1.05483
Latitude : 46.77585

MOUILLERON-LE-CAPTIF

85000 – Michelin map **316** h7 – pop. 4,511 – alt. 70
▶ Paris 421 – Challans 40 – La Mothe-Achard 22 – Nantes 63

L'Ambois

✆ 02 51 37 29 15, *www.campingambois.com* – limited spaces for one-night stay
Address : take southeastern exit along the D 2, follow the signs for la Roche-sur-Yon, then continue 2.6km along the road to the right
Opening times : permanent
1.75 ha (49 pitches) flat, relatively flat, grassy
Tariff : ★ 4.30€ ⇔ 国 3.80€ – ⑭ (10A) 3.80€
Rental rates : (permanent) – 40 ⛺ – 5 ⌂ – 3 gîtes – 2 guest houses.
Per night from 60 to 85€ – Per week from 265 to 515€

In a rural setting but with very few overnight pitches for tents and caravans.

Surroundings : ⚘ ▭ ♡
Leisure activities : ⛱ ⛵ ♻ ▨ (open-air in season) farm/petting farm
Facilities : ♿ ⊙ ⚏ ⛲ ⚏ launderette ⚏

Longitude : -1.46092
Latitude : 46.69647

NANTES

44000 – Michelin map **316** G4 – pop. 282 047 – alt. 8
▶ Paris 381 – Angers 88 – Bordeaux 325 – Lyon 660

Nantes Camping – Le Petit Port

✆ 02 40 74 47 94, *www.nantes-camping.fr*
Address : 21 bd du Petit Port (situated beside the Cens river)
Opening times : permanent
8 ha (151 pitches) relatively flat, flat, grassy, gravelled
Tariff : (2012 price) 29.90€ ★ ★ ⇔ 国 ⑭ (16A) – Extra per person 6€
Rental rates : (2012 price) (permanent) ♿ (1 chalet) – 58 ⌂. Per night from 37 to 148 €
Per week from 222 to 888€
⛽ sani-station – 15 国 12€

Upmarket rentals, free use of the swimming pool and a tram stop for the town centre.

Surroundings : ⚘ ▭ ♡♡
Leisure activities : ☂ ✗ ⛵ ♻ ⚏
Facilities : ♿ ⊙ ⚏ ⚐ ⚏ ⚏ launderette
Nearby : ▨ ⛸ skating rink

Longitude : -1.5567
Latitude : 47.24346

NOTRE-DAME-DE-MONTS

5690 – Michelin map **316** D6 – pop. 1,866 – alt. 6
Paris 459 – Nantes 74 – La Roche-sur-Yon 72

L'Albizia

02 28 11 28 50, *www.campinglalbizia.com* – limited spaces for one-night stay
Address : 52 r. de la Rive (1.9km to the north)
Opening times : from beginning April to end Sept.
3.6 ha (153 pitches) flat, grassy, sandy
Tariff : 28€ ♣♣ ⇔ 🔲 (16A) – Extra per person 5.60€ – Reservation fee 12€
Rental rates : (from mid Feb. to mid Nov.) – 36 🔲. Per night from 78 to 93€
Per week from 267 to 824 € – Reservation fee 12€

A pleasant campsite. Many of the mobile homes are owner-occupied.

Surroundings : 🖵
Leisure activities : ♈ ✕ 🎦 evening 🕺 🚣 🚲 🎯 🔲 ⛷ multi-sports
ground
Facilities : ♿ ⊶ ↑↑ launderette

GPS Longitude : -2.12755
Latitude : 46.8503

Municipal de l'Orgatte

02 51 58 84 31, *www.notre-dame-de-monts.fr*
Address : av. Abbé Thibaud (à 300m from the beach – 1.2km north along the D 38 and take the
turning to the left (direct access)
Opening times : from beginning April to end Sept.
4.5 ha (315 pitches) undulating, sandy
Tariff : (2012 price) 18.25€ ♣♣ ⇔ 🔲 (10A) – Extra per person 4.90€ – Reservation fee 10€

In a pleasant location surrounded by hills and shaded by a pine wood.

Surroundings : 🦐 🌿
Leisure activities : 🚣 multi-sports ground
Facilities : ⊶ ↑↑ 🖼

GPS Longitude : -2.13882
Latitude : 46.83972

Le Pont d'Yeu

02 51 58 83 76, *www.camping-pontdyeu.com*
Address : r. du Pont d'Yeu (located 1km south along the D 38, follow the signs for St-Jean-de-Monts,
and take turning to the left)
Opening times : from beginning April to end Sept.
1.3 ha (90 pitches) flat, sandy
Tariff : (2012 price) 21.80€ ♣♣ ⇔ 🔲 (10A) – Extra per person 4.90€
Rental rates : (2012 price) (from beginning April to end Sept.) – 27 🔲 – 2 🏠.
Per night from 70 to 95€ – Per week from 215 to 665€

A peaceful, family atmosphere; half the pitches are for owner-occupied mobile homes.

Surroundings : 🖵 🌿
Leisure activities : 🚣 🔲 (open-air in season)
Facilities : ♿ ⊶ 🛁 ↑↑ launderette

GPS Longitude : -2.13585
Latitude : 46.82052

Michelin classification:
🔺🔺🔺🔺 *Extremely comfortable, equipped to a very high standard*
🔺🔺🔺 *Very comfortable, equipped to a high standard*
🔺🔺 *Comfortable and well equipped*
🔺 *Reasonably comfortable*
🔺 *Satisfactory*

NYOISEAU

49500 – Michelin map **317** D2 – pop. 1,305 – alt. 40
▶ Paris 316 – Ancenis 50 – Angers 47 – Châteaubriant 39

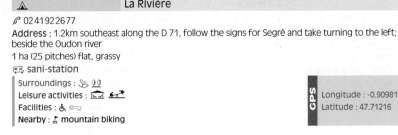

⚠ **La Rivière**

☏ 02 41 92 26 77

Address : 1.2km southeast along the D 71, follow the signs for Segré and take turning to the left; beside the Oudon river

1 ha (25 pitches) flat, grassy

 sani-station

Surroundings : 🌿 ♤♤
Leisure activities : 🖼 🏹
Facilities : ♿ ⛲
Nearby : 🚵 mountain biking

Longitude : -0.90981
Latitude : 47.71216

Some information or pricing may have changed since the guide went to press. We recommend you check the price list online in advance or at the entrance to the campsite and enquire about possible restrictions.

OLONNE-SUR-MER

85340 – Michelin map **316** F8 – pop. 13,279 – alt. 40
▶ Paris 458 – Nantes 102 – La Roche-sur-Yon 36 – La Rochelle 96

Sunêlia La Loubine ♣♣

☏ 02 51 33 12 92, *www.la-loubine.fr* – limited spaces for one-night stay ✖ (Jul–Aug)
Address : 1 rte de la Mer (3km to the west)
Opening times : from beginning April to mid Sept.
8 ha (401 pitches) flat, grassy
Tariff : 38.30€ ✹✹ 🚐 🔲 🅿 (6A) – Extra per person 6.50€ – Reservation fee 22€
Rental rates : (permanent) ♿ (1 mobile home) ✖ (Jul–Aug) – 130 🚐 – 2 🏠.
Per night from 38 to 148€ – Per week from 266 to 1,036€ – Reservation fee 22€
Based around a 16th-century Vendée farm, with a charming landscaped water park and play area.

Surroundings : 🏕 ♤♤
Leisure activities : 🍴 ✖ 🖼 🎦 evening 🏊 🎠 ♨ jacuzzi 🏹 🚲 ✖ 🚵 🔲 🏊 ⛳ multi-sports ground
Facilities : ♿ ⛲ 🚿 🚰 launderette ⛲ 🛒
Nearby : 🐎

Longitude : -1.80647
Latitude : 46.54595

Le Moulin de la Salle ♣♣

☏ 02 51 95 99 10, *www.moulindelasalle.com* – limited spaces for one-night stay
Address : r. du Moulin de la Salle (2.7km to the west)
Opening times : from beginning April to mid Sept.
2.7 ha (216 pitches) flat, grassy
Tariff : (2012 price) 29€ ✹✹ 🚐 🔲 🅿 (10A) – Extra per person 5€ – Reservation fee 25€
Rental rates : (2012 price) (from beginning April to mid Sept.) – 148 🚐 – 6 gîtes.
Per night from 55 to 80€ – Per week from 220 to 810€ – Reservation fee 25€
Numerous mobile homes around a pretty windmill, but very few pitches for tents and caravans on overnight stays only.

Surroundings : 🏕 ♤
Leisure activities : 🍴 ✖ 🖼 🏊 🎠 🏹 🔲 🏊 ⛳ multi-sports ground, entertainment room
Facilities : ♿ ⛲ 🚿 🚰 🚽 🚰 launderette 🛒

Longitude : -1.79217
Latitude : 46.53183

Domaine de l'Orée ▲▲ ♣♣

🕿 02 51 33 10 59, *www.l-oree.com*

Address : 13 rte des Amis de la Nature
Opening times : from mid April to mid Sept.
6 ha (320 pitches) flat, grassy
Tariff : (2012 price) 36.50€ ♣♣ ⇔ 🗐 🗓 (10A) – Extra per person 6€ – Reservation fee 26€
Rental rates : (2012 price) (from mid April to mid Sept.) – 160 🚐 – 10 🏠.
Per night from 52 to 75€ – Per week from 245 to 903€ – Reservation fee 26€
The site is divided into 2 separate sections. Some pitches for tents and caravans benefit from private sanitary facilities.

Surroundings : 🔲 ⚲
Leisure activities : 🍴 ✕ 🎱 🕄 evening 🕺 🏊 jacuzzi 🚣 🚲 🎯 🖼️ 🏑 🏂 multi-sports ground
Facilities : 🚻 🚿 🚮 🗑️ 🅿️ – 10 individual sanitary facilities (🚿⇄🚽 wc) 🛁 🛒 🍴 launderette 🛒 🚯
Nearby : 🐎

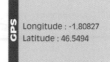

GPS
Longitude : -1.80827
Latitude : 46.5494

Le Puits Rochais ▲▲ ♣♣

🕿 02 51 21 09 69, *info@puitsrochais.com*

Address : 25 r. de Bourdigal (3.5km southeast along the D 559, follow the signs for Bandol)
Opening times : from mid April to end Sept.
3.9 ha (220 pitches) relatively flat, flat, grassy
Tariff : 34.95€ ♣♣ ⇔ 🗐 🗓 (10A) – Extra per person 6.95€ – Reservation fee 25€
Rental rates : (permanent) – 60 🚐 – 2 🏠. Per night 89€ – Per week 620€
Reservation fee 25€
A charming site with a good choice of mobile homes for rental; some have owner-occupiers.

Surroundings : 🔲 ⚲⚲
Leisure activities : 🍴 ✕ 🎱 🕄 daytime 🕺 🚣 🚲 🎯 🏐 🏑 🏂
Facilities : 🚻 🚿 🛁 🛒 🍴 launderette 🚯

GPS
Longitude : -1.73663
Latitude : 46.47978

Nid d'Été ▲

🕿 02 51 95 34 38, *www.leniddete.com*

Address : 2 r. de la Vigne Verte (2.5km to the west)
Opening times : from beginning April to end Sept.
2 ha (119 pitches) flat, grassy
Tariff : (2012 price) 18.60€ ♣♣ ⇔ 🗐 🗓 (10A) – Extra per person 3.60€ – Reservation fee 15€
Rental rates : (2012 price) (from beginning April to end Sept.) – 26 🚐.
Per night from 43 to 110€ – Per week from 193 to 820€ – Reservation fee 15€
The siite divided into 2 separate sections with good sanitary facilities.

Surroundings : 🏞 🔲 ⚲⚲
Leisure activities : 🍴 ✕ 🎱 🚣 🖼️ (open-air in season)
Facilities : 🚻 🔑 🛁 🍴 launderette 🚯

GPS
Longitude : -1.79393
Latitude : 46.53326

Do not confuse:
▲ to ▲▲▲ : MICHELIN classification
with
★ to ★★★★★ : official classification

Le Petit Paris ▲⚲

☎ 02 51 22 04 44, *www.campingpetitparis.com*
Address : 41 r. du Petit-Versailles (located 5.5km southeast)
Opening times : from beginning April to end Oct.
3 ha (154 pitches) flat, grassy
Tariff : (2012 price) 26€ ♥♥ ⇔ 回 ⒤ (10A) – Extra per person 4.50€ – Reservation fee 18€
Rental rates : (2012 price) (from beginning April to end Oct.) – 4 'gypsy' caravans – 25 ⊡ –
2 🏠 – 4 tent bungalows. Per night from 40 to 90€ – Per week from 155 to 800€
Reservation fee 18€

In a geen setting with a range of rental options and one area reserved for tents and caravans.

Surroundings : ⟋ ⊏ ⚲⚲
Leisure activities : ⛲ 🎪 🏕 ⟋ 🏊 (open-air in season) ⟋
multi-sports ground
Facilities : ♿ ⟣ 🔥 ⚐ ⚲ ⚑ launderette 🔧
Nearby : parachuting

GPS Longitude : -1.72041
Latitude : 46.47359

Les Fosses Rouges ▲

☎ 02 51 95 17 95, *www.camping-lesfossesrouges.com*
Address : 8 r. des Fosses Rouges (situated 3km southeast at La Pironnière)
Opening times : from mid April to mid Sept.
3.5 ha (248 pitches) flat, grassy
Tariff : 20.40€ ♥♥ ⇔ 回 ⒤ (10A) – Extra per person 3.70€ – Reservation fee 12€
Rental rates : (from mid April to mid Sept.) – 12 ⊡. Per night from 45 to 55€
Per week from 190 to 560€
⊡ sani-station

In a low-rise residential area. Choose pitches away from the road in preference.

Surroundings : ⊏ ⚲⚲
Leisure activities : ⛲ ⟋ ✂ 🎯 🏊 (open-air in season)
Facilities : ♿ ⟣ 🔥 ⚑ launderette 🔋 🔧

GPS Longitude : -1.74124
Latitude : 46.47956

Sauveterre ▲

☎ 02 51 33 10 58, *www.campingsauveterre.com*
Address : 3 rte des Amis de la Nature (3km to the west)
Opening times : from beginning April to end Sept.
3.2 ha (234 pitches) flat, grassy
Tariff : (2012 price) 20.40€ ♥♥ ⇔ 回 ⒤ (6A) – Extra per person 4.70€ – Reservation fee 20€
Rental rates : (2012 price) (from beginning April to end Sept.) ✂ – 23 ⊡.
Per night from 35 to 65€ – Per week from 140 to 680€ – Reservation fee 20€

Surroundings : ⚲⚲
Leisure activities : ✗ ⟋ ⟋
Facilities : ♿ ⟣ ⚐ ⚑ 🔥 🔋 🔧
Nearby : 🐎

GPS Longitude : -1.80547
Latitude : 46.54697

There are several different types of sani-station ('borne' in French) – sanitation points providing fresh water and disposal points for grey water. See page 12 for further details.

‌IRIAC-SUR-MER

4420 – Michelin map **316** A3 – pop. 2,245 – alt. 7
‌ Paris 462 – La Baule 17 – Nantes 88 – La Roche-Bernard 33

Parc du Guibel ⚑

☎ 02 40 23 52 67, *www.parcduguibel.com*
Address : rte de Kerdrien (3.5km east along the D 52, follow the signs for Mesquer and take turning to the left)
Opening times : from beginning April to end Sept.
14 ha (450 pitches) relatively flat, flat, grassy
Tariff : (2012 price) ⚑ 6€ ⚑ 4€ 🔲 6€ – 🔲 (10A) 4.50€ – Reservation fee 18€
Rental rates : (2012 price) (from beginning April to end Sept.) – 94 🔲 – 34 🔲.
Per night from 48 to 119€ – Per week from 252 to 833€ – Reservation fee 18€
The site is divided is into 2 separate sections; a park in a natural, wooded setting and a partially open-air swimming area.

Surroundings : 🔲 🔲 🔲
Leisure activities : ⚑ ✗ 🔲 🔲 🔲 🔲 🔲 🔲 multi-sports ground
Facilities : 🔲 🔲 🔲 🔲 🔲 🔲 launderette 🔲 🔲
Nearby : 🔲 🔲

Longitude : -2.51024
Latitude : 47.3862

Armor Héol ⚑

☎ 02 40 23 57 80, *www.camping-armor-heol.com*
Address : at Kervin, rte de Guérande (located 1km southeast along the D 333)
Opening times : from beginning April to mid Sept.
4.5 ha (270 pitches) flat, grassy, small lake
Tariff : (2012 price) 36.50€ ⚑⚑ ⚑ 🔲 🔲 (6A) – Extra per person 8€ – Reservation fee 20€
Rental rates : (2012 price) (from beginning April to mid Sept.) – 1 'gypsy' caravan – 58 🔲 – 22 🔲. Per night from 103 to 123€ – Per week from 725 to 860€ – Reservation fee 20€
A partially open-air swimming area; 20 pitches have private sanitary facilities.

Surroundings : 🔲 🔲
Leisure activities : ⚑ ✗ 🔲 🔲 🔲 🔲 🔲 🔲 🔲 🔲 multi-sports ground
Facilities : 🔲 🔲 🔲 – 20 individual sanitary facilities (🔲 🔲 wc) launderette

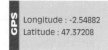

Longitude : -2.53563
Latitude : 47.3748

Mon Calme

☎ 02 40 23 60 77, *www.campingmoncalme.com*
Address : r. de Norvoret (located 1km south following signs for La Turballe and take the turning to the left, 450m from the ocean)
Opening times : from beginning April to end Sept.
1.2 ha (88 pitches) flat, grassy
Tariff : (2012 price) 28.50€ ⚑⚑ ⚑ 🔲 🔲 (10A) – Extra per person 6.80€ – Reservation fee 17€
Rental rates : (2012 price) (from beginning April to end Sept.) – 20 🔲 – 12 apartments.
Per night from 48 to 68 € – Per week from 260 to 640€ – Reservation fee 17€
Good quality apart-hotels, open 11 months of the year.

Surroundings : 🔲
Leisure activities : ✗ 🔲 🔲 🔲
Facilities : 🔲 🔲 🔲 🔲 🔲
Nearby : 🔲 🔲 🔲

Longitude : -2.54882
Latitude : 47.37208

PAYS DE LA LOIRE

LA PLAINE-SUR-MER

44770 – Michelin map **316** C5 – pop. 3,815 – alt. 26
▶ Paris 438 – Nantes 58 – Pornic 9 – St-Michel-Chef-Chef 7

La Tabardière ▲▴

0240215883, www.camping-la-tabardiere.com
Address : 2 rte de la Tabardiere (3.5km east along the D 13, follow the signs for Pornic and take turning to the left)
Opening times : from mid April to mid Sept.
6 ha (270 pitches) terraced, flat, grassy
Tariff : 36.10€ ⚤ ⛺ ▣ ⚡ (8A) – Extra per person 7.70€ – Reservation fee 20€
Rental rates : (from mid April to mid Sept.) 🏕 – 10 ⛺ – 20 🏠. Per night from 34 to 119€
Per week from 236 to 831€ – Reservation fee 20€
⛽ sani-station 14€ – 🚐14€

Surroundings : 🌿 ♤♤
Leisure activities : ♟ 🎯 🏃 ⛹ 🎣 🏊 (open-air in season) ⛵ 🎏
multi-sports ground
Facilities : ♿ ⚬ 🚻 🚿 🍴 launderette 🛢 🚿

GPS Longitude : -2.15313
Latitude : 47.14087

Le Ranch

0240215262, www.camping-le-ranch.com
Address : chemin des Hautes Raillères (3km northeast along the D 96)
Opening times : from beginning April to end Sept.
3 ha (183 pitches) flat, grassy
Tariff : (2012 price) 30.90€ ⚤ ⛺ ▣ ⚡ (10A) – Extra per person 5.90€ – Reservation fee 15€
Rental rates : (2012 price) (from beginning April to end Oct.) 🏕 – 12 ⛺ – 16 🏠.
Per night from 45 to 80 € – Per week from 210 to 745€ – Reservation fee 15€
In a green setting with lots of flowers.

Surroundings : 🌿 ♀
Leisure activities : ♟ ✗ 🎯 🏊 🏖 ⛵ multi-sports ground,
entertainment room
Facilities : ♿ ⚬ 🚿 🍴 launderette 🚿

GPS Longitude : -2.16292
Latitude : 47.15412

We welcome your feedback on our listed campsites.
Please email us at: campingfrance@tp.michelin.com
Many thanks in advance!

LES PONTS-DE-CÉ

49130 – Michelin map **317** F4 – pop. 11,575 – alt. 25
▶ Paris 302 – Nantes 92 – Angers 7 – Cholet 57

Île du Château ▲▴

0241446205, www.camping-ileduchateau.com
Address : av. de la Boire Salée (situated on the Île du Château)
2.3 ha (135 pitches) flat, grassy
Rentals : 5 tent bungalows.
⛽ sani-station – 15 ▣
In a wooded setting near the Loire river and municipal gardens.

Surroundings : ⊏ ♤♤
Leisure activities : ✗ 🎯 🏃 🏖 🚲 🎣
Facilities : ♿ ⚬ 🚿 🛁 ♨ 🖼
Nearby : 🎾 🏊 🚣 ⛵

GPS Longitude : -0.53055
Latitude : 47.4244

PORNIC

4210 – Michelin map **316** D5 – pop. 14,052 – alt. 20
Paris 429 – Nantes 49 – La Roche-sur-Yon 89 – Les Sables-d'Olonne 93

Club Airotel La Boutinardière ♣♣

℘ 02 40 82 05 68, *www.camping-boutinardiere.com*
Address : 23 r. de la Plage de la Boutinardiere (5km southeast along the D 13 and take turning to the right, 200m from the beach)
Opening times : from beginning April to end Sept.
7.5 ha (400 pitches) relatively flat, grassy
Tariff : 49 € 🚹🚹 ⇌ 🔲 🔳 (10A) – Extra per person 8 € – Reservation fee 25 €
Rental rates : (from beginning April to end Sept.) – 220 🛖 – 37 🏠 – 15 apartments.
Per night from 75 € – Per week from 240 to 1,100 € – Reservation fee 25 €
🚐 sani-station 7 € – 🚌 🔳 15 €
A 'village club' with a range of services and good-quality rental apartments.

Surroundings : 🌿 ⊡ 🖉	
Leisure activities : 🍽 ✕ 🎱 🖉 🕴 ≋ hammam 🏊 🚲 🎯 🖾 🎿 🏄 multi-sports ground	**GPS** Longitude : -2.05222 Latitude : 47.09747
Facilities : 🚻 ⚡ 🛁 🚿 🚮 🍴 launderette 🛒 🚲	

Yelloh! Village La Chênaie

℘ 02 40 82 07 31, *www.campinglachenaie.com*
Address : 36 bis r. du Pâtisseau (east along the D 751, follow the signs for Nantes and take turning to the left)
Opening times : from mid April to mid Sept.
8 ha (305 pitches) terraced, relatively flat, flat, grassy
Tariff : 41 € 🚹🚹 ⇌ 🔲 🔳 (10A) – Extra per person 8 €
Rental rates : (from mid April to mid Sept.) 🏕 – 42 🛖 – 3 tent bungalows.
Per night from 35 to 180 € – Per week from 245 to 1,260 €
🚐 sani-station – 5 🔲 14.50 €
Extensive green spaces for relaxation and an enclosure with farm animals for the kids.

Surroundings : 🌿 ⊡ 🖉	
Leisure activities : 🍽 ✕ 🖉 🏊 🚲 🖾 🎿 🏄 multi-sports ground, entertainment room	**GPS** Longitude : -2.07196 Latitude : 47.1187
Facilities : 🚻 ⚡ 🛁 🍴 launderette 🚲	

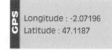

Some campsites benefit from proximity to a municipal leisure centre.

PORNICHET

4380 – Michelin map **316** B4 – pop. 10,466 – alt. 12
Paris 449 – Nantes 74 – Vannes 84 – La Roche-sur-Yon 143

Les Forges

℘ 02 40 61 18 84, *www.campinglesforges.com* – limited spaces for one-night stay
Address : 98 rte de la Villès-Blais, 'Les Forges' quartier
Opening times : from beginning July to end Aug.
2 ha (130 pitches) terraced, flat, grassy
Tariff : 27.50 € 🚹🚹 ⇌ 🔲 🔳 (6A) – Extra per person 7 € – Reservation fee 30 €
Rental rates : (from beginning July to end Aug.) – 23 🛖. Per night from 75 to 85 € Per week from 405 to 730 € – Reservation fee 30 €
Bus stop for the town centre.

Surroundings : ⊡ 🖉	
Leisure activities : 🎱 🏊 🖾 (open-air in season), multi-sports ground	**GPS** Longitude : -2.29379 Latitude : 47.26917
Facilities : 🚻 ⚡ 🔲 🍴 launderette	

LE POULIGUEN

44510 – Michelin map **316** B4 – pop. 4,977 – alt. 4
▶ Paris 453 – Guérande 8 – La Baule 4 – Nantes 80

Municipal les Mouettes

ℰ 02 40 42 43 98, *www.tourisme-lepouliguen.fr* – ℝ
Address : 45 bd de l'Atlantique (to the west of the resort along the D 45, right next to the stadium)
Opening times : from end March to end Oct.
4.7 ha (220 pitches) flat, sandy, grassy, small lake
Tariff : (2012 price) 17.40€ ♣♣ ⇔ ▣ ⓖ (6A) – Extra per person 4.60€
⊑ sani-station 2€
Relatively near the town centre and the shops.

Surroundings : ⊏ 🛝
Leisure activities : 🛶 ⚓
Facilities : ఉ (Jul–Aug) 🎯 ⛺ 🚰 launderette
Nearby : 🛒 ⚓

GPS
Longitude : -2.43942
Latitude : 47.27385

Municipal le Clein

ℰ 02 40 42 43 99, *leclein@mairie-lepouliguen.fr* – ℝ
Address : 22 av. de Kerdun
Opening times : from mid March to end Sept.
1.5 ha (110 pitches) flat, sandy, grassy
Tariff : (2012 price) 17.80€ ♣♣ ⇔ ▣ ⓖ (10A) – Extra per person 4.40€
⊑ sani-station – 26 ▣ 10.20€
Near the town centre and the beach, with a good parking area for campervans.

Surroundings : 🛝
Leisure activities : ⚓
Facilities : ఉ ⚡ 🎯 ⛺ 🚰 launderette
Nearby : 🛒 ⚓

GPS
Longitude : -2.4301
Latitude : 47.27135

For more information on visiting particular towns or regions, consult the relevant regional MICHELIN Green Guide. We also recommend you use the appropriate Michelin regional map to locate your selected campsite, to calculate distances and to work out the best route.

POUZAUGES

85700 – Michelin map **316** K7 – pop. 5,428 – alt. 225
▶ Paris 390 – Bressuire 30 – Chantonnay 22 – Cholet 42

Le Lac

ℰ 02 51 91 37 55, *www.campingpouzauges.com*
Address : at the lake (located 1.5km west along the D 960 bis, follow the signs for Chantonnay and take the road to the right)
Opening times : permanent
1 ha (54 pitches) terrace, relatively flat, flat, grassy
Tariff : (2012 price) 19€ ♣♣ ⇔ ▣ ⓖ (10A) – Extra per person 5€ – Reservation fee 20€
Shade is provided by ash trees. The site is 50m from the lake.

Surroundings : 〰 ⛰
Leisure activities : ✗ ⚓
Facilities : ఉ ⚡ 🚰 launderette
Nearby : 🍴 ⛵ 🎣

GPS
Longitude : -0.8532
Latitude : 46.78183

PRÉFAILLES

44770 – Michelin map **316** C5 – pop. 1,255 – alt. 10
▶ Paris 440 – Challans 56 – Machecoul 38 – Nantes 60

⚑ Éléovic

✆ 02 40 21 61 60, *www.camping-eleovic.com*
Address : rte de la Pointe Saint-Gildas (located 1km west along the D 75)
3 ha (150 pitches) flat, relatively flat, grassy
Rentals : 60 ⌂.
🚐 sani-station
A site overlooking the ocean and picturesque creeks.

Surroundings : ⛰ ⩽ ocean and île de Noirmoutier ⌂ ♀
Leisure activities : ✗ ⌂ ⓖ evening ⫛ ⛷ ⚓ ♋ ☒ (open-air in
season), multi-sports ground
Facilities : ♿ ⛔ 🍴 launderette ⛴

GPS Longitude : -2.23151
Latitude : 47.13292

PRUILLÉ

49220 – Michelin map **317** F3 – pop. 630 – alt. 30
▶ Paris 308 – Angers 22 – Candé 34 – Château-Gontier 33

⚑ **Municipal Le Port**

✆ 02 41 32 67 29, *www.pruille.mairie49.fr*
Address : r. du Bac (north of the town; beside the Mayenne – mooring point)
Opening times : from mid May to mid Sept.
1.2 ha (41 pitches) flat, grassy
Tariff : (2012 price) 10€ ✝✝ ⇔ ▣ ⓕ (6A) – Extra per person 2€
Rental rates : (2012 price) (permanent) – 5 ⌂. Per night from 42 to 49€
Per week from 191 to 419€

Surroundings : ⛰ ♀
Leisure activities : ⚒
Facilities : ⇸

GPS Longitude : -0.66474
Latitude : 47.57897

A 'quartier' is a district or area of a town or village.

LES ROSIERS-SUR-LOIRE

49350 – Michelin map **317** H4 – pop. 2,348 – alt. 22
▶ Paris 304 – Angers 32 – Baugé 27 – Bressuire 66

⚑ **Flower Le Val de Loire**

✆ 02 41 51 94 33, *www.camping-valdeloire.com*
Address : 6 r. Sainte-Baudruche (take the northern exit along the D 59, follow the signs for Beaufort-
en-Vallée, near the junction with the D 79)
Opening times : from beginning April to end Sept.
3.5 ha (110 pitches) flat, grassy
Tariff : 17€ ✝✝ ⇔ ▣ ⓕ (10A) – Extra per person 4€ – Reservation fee 7.50€
Rental rates : (from beginning April to end Sept.) – 2 'gypsy' caravans – 30 ⌂ – 1 ⌂ –
4 tents. Per night from 35 to 111€ – Per week from 49 to 779€ – Reservation fee 10€
🚐 sani-station 12.50€
In a pleasant, leafy setting.

Surroundings : ⌂ ♀
Leisure activities : ✗ ⌂ ⫛ ♋ ☒ ⩚
Facilities : ♿ ⛔ ⊝ ⚶ ⛴ 🍴 ▣
Nearby : ⚒ ♨ ⩘

GPS Longitude : -0.22599
Latitude : 47.35821

LES SABLES-D'OLONNE

85100 – Michelin map **316** F8 – pop. 14,572 – alt. 4
▶ Paris 456 – Cholet 107 – Nantes 102 – Niort 115

Chadotel La Dune des Sables ▲▪

✆ 02 51 33 05 05, *http://chadotel.com/camping-sables-olonne/la-dune-des-sables/* – limited spaces for one-night stay

Address : at Le Paracou – chemin de la Bernardière (4km to the northwest, follow the signs for l'Aubraie)

Opening times : from beginning April to end Sept.

7.5 ha (290 pitches) terraced, undulating, flat, grassy, sandy

Tariff : 20.50€ ☆☆ ⛺ 🔲 🕪 (10A) – Extra per person 6€ – Reservation fee 25€

Rental rates : (from beginning April to end Sept.) – 58 🛏 – 2 tents. Per night from 50 to 73€ Per week from 170 to 875€ – Reservation fee 25€

🚮 sani-station

A mobile-home park near the beach, overlooking the ocean, but with very few pitches for tents or caravans staying overnight only.

Surroundings : 🏞 ⪜ 🗔
Leisure activities : 🍽 ✗ 🎦 ⊡ 🤸 🎯 🚴 🎿 ♨ ⚓ 🏊
Facilities : ♿ ⛲ 🏕 ⛱ 🚱 ⛱ launderette 🔌 🚿

Longitude : -1.81395
Latitude : 46.51207

Chadotel Les Roses

✆ 02 51 33 05 05, *http://chadotel.com/camping-sables-olonne/les-roses/* – ⇄

Address : 61 r. des Roses (400m from the beach)

Opening times : from beginning April to beginning Nov.

3.3 ha (200 pitches) terraced, flat and relatively flat, grassy

Tariff : 20.50€ ☆☆ ⛺ 🔲 🕪 (10A) – Extra per person 6€ – Reservation fee 25€

Rental rates : (from beginning April to beginning Nov.) ♿ (1 mobile home) – 44 🛏 – 9 🏠. Per night from 49 to 82€ – Per week from 190 to 1,150€ – Reservation fee 25€

🚮 sani-station

In a residential area, mobile homes for rental, some very luxurious; pitches for tents and caravans are always available.

Surroundings : 🗔 ⊙⊙
Leisure activities : 🎦 ⚓ 🚴 🏊 ♨ multi-sports ground
Facilities : ♿ ⛲ 🏕 ⛱ launderette
Nearby : 🍽 🚿

Longitude : -1.76482
Latitude : 46.49166

SABLÉ-SUR-SARTHE

72300 – Michelin map **310** G7 – pop. 12,399 – alt. 29
▶ Paris 252 – Angers 64 – La Flèche 27 – Laval 44

Municipal de l'Hippodrome ▲▪

✆ 02 43 95 42 61, *www.tourisme.sablesursarthe.fr*

Address : Allée du Québec (take the southern exit towards Angers and the turning to the left, next to racecourse (hippodrome)

Opening times : from end March to mid Oct.

2 ha (84 pitches) flat, grassy

Tariff : (2012 price) 13€ ☆☆ ⛺ 🔲 🕪 (16A) – Extra per person 2.75€

Rental rates : (2012 price) (from end March to mid Oct.) 🚫 – 4 🛏. Per night from 52 to 72€ Per week from 240 to 365€

🚮 sani-station 2€

Decorative trees and shrubs; located beside the Sarthe river.

Surroundings : 🏞 🗔 ⊙⊙
Leisure activities : 🎦 🤸 ⚓ 🏊 ⟋
Facilities : ♿ ⛲ 🏕 ⛱ launderette
Nearby : ✗ 🗺 ♨ 🐎

Longitude : -0.33193
Latitude : 47.83136

ST-BERTHEVIN

53940 – Michelin map **310** E6 – pop. 7,097 – alt. 108
Paris 289 – Nantes 128 – Laval 10 – Rennes 66

Municipal de Coupeau

02 43 68 30 70, *www.laval-tourisme.com*
Address : at the base de loisirs (leisure centre) (south of the town, 150m from the Vicoin river)
Opening times : from end April to end Sept.
0.4 ha (24 pitches) terraced, flat, grassy
Tariff : (2012 price) 3.40€ 1.90€ 2€ – (10A) 1.80€
Overlooks a green and peaceful valley.

Surroundings :
Leisure activities :
Facilities : (season)
Nearby : fitness trail

Longitude : -0.83235
Latitude : 48.06431

*The guide covers all 22 regions of France – see the map
and list of regions on pages 4–5.*

ST-BREVIN-LES-PINS

44250 – Michelin map **316** C4 – pop. 12,133 – alt. 9
Paris 438 – Challans 62 – Nantes 64 – Noirmoutier-en-l'Ile 70

Sunêlia Le Fief

02 40 27 23 86, *www.lefief.com*
Address : 57 chemin du Fief (2.4km south following signs for Saint-Brévin-l'Océan and take the turning to the left)
Opening times : from end March to end Sept.
7 ha (397 pitches) flat, grassy
Tariff : 47.50€ (6A) – Extra per person 11€ – Reservation fee 35€
Rental rates : (from end March to end Sept.) (1 mobile home) – 205 .
Per night from 53 to 229€ – Per week from 371 to 1,603€ – Reservation fee 35€
sani-station 47.50€
A superb spa centre and truly upmarket VIP rental village within a green garden area.

Surroundings :
Leisure activities : hammam, jacuzzi multi-sports ground, spa therapy centre, entertainment room
Facilities : launderette

Longitude : -2.16768
Latitude : 47.23465

La Courance

02 40 27 22 91, *www.campinglacourance.fr* – limited spaces for one-night stay
Address : 110 av. du Maréchal Foch
Opening times : permanent
2.4 ha (156 pitches) terraced, flat, sandy
Tariff : (2012 price) 25.30€ (10A) – Extra per person 6.60€ – Reservation fee 25€
Rental rates : (2012 price) (permanent) (1 mobile home) – 1 'gypsy' caravan – 40 – 10 – 12 tent bungalows. Per night from 42 to 88€ – Per week from 205 to 770€
Reservation fee 25€
sani-station 3€ – 5 17.50€
Situated beside beach, with view of the St-Nazaire bridge. Swimming spot 500m away.

Surroundings :
Leisure activities : evening
Facilities : launderette
Nearby :

Longitude : -2.1703
Latitude : 47.23786

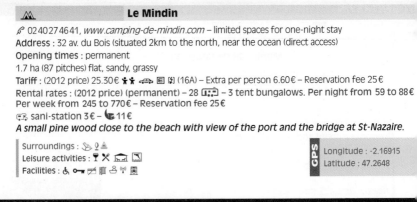

Le Mindin

☏ 02 40 27 46 41, *www.camping-de-mindin.com* – limited spaces for one-night stay
Address : 32 av. du Bois (situated 2km to the north, near the ocean (direct access)
Opening times : permanent
1.7 ha (87 pitches) flat, sandy, grassy
Tariff : (2012 price) 25.30€ ☂☂ ⇔ 🖭 (16A) – Extra per person 6.60€ – Reservation fee 25€
Rental rates : (2012 price) (permanent) – 28 ▦ – 3 tent bungalows. Per night from 59 to 88€
Per week from 245 to 770€ – Reservation fee 25€
🚰 sani-station 3€ – 🛒 11€
A small pine wood close to the beach with view of the port and the bridge at St-Nazaire.

Surroundings : 🌿 ♨ ⛰
Leisure activities : 🍴 ✕ 🏛 🖼
Facilities : & ⊶ 🚿 ▥ 🛁 🍴 🖼

GPS Longitude : -2.16915
Latitude : 47.2648

ST-CALAIS

72120 – Michelin map **310** N7 – pop. 3,482 – alt. 155
▶ Paris 188 – Blois 65 – Chartres 102 – Châteaudun 58

Le Lac

☏ 02 43 35 04 81, *www.saint-calais.fr*
Address : r. du Lac (take the northern exit along the D 249, follow the signs for Montaillé)
Opening times : from beginning April to mid Oct.
2 ha (85 pitches) flat, grassy
Tariff : (2012 price) 13.50€ ☂☂ ⇔ 🖭 (10A) – Extra per person 3.45€
Rental rates : (2012 price) (from beginning April to mid Oct.) – 3 ▦. Per night from 39 to 64€
Per week from 192 to 322€
Near a small lake.

Surroundings : 🔲
Leisure activities : 🖼
Facilities : & ⊶ 🚿 🌦 🖼
Nearby : 🐴 ✕ ⛱ 🎣

GPS Longitude : 0.74426
Latitude : 47.92688

The information in the guide may have changed since going to press.

ST-ÉTIENNE-DU-BOIS

85670 – Michelin map **316** G7 – pop. 1,901 – alt. 38
▶ Paris 427 – Aizenay 13 – Challans 26 – Nantes 49

Municipal la Petite Boulogne

☏ 02 51 34 54 51, *www.stetiennedubois-vendee.fr*
Address : r. du Stade (south of the town along the D 81, follow the signs for Poiré-sur-Vie and take the road to the right; near the river and a lake)
Opening times : from beginning May to end Sept.
1.5 ha (35 pitches) terrace, flat and relatively flat, grassy
Tariff : (2012 price) 17.96€ ☂☂ ⇔ 🖭 (16A) – Extra per person 3.37€
Rental rates : (2012 price) (permanent) – 3 ▦ – 6 🏠. Per night from 59€
Per week from 193 to 373€
A pedestrian path links the campsite to the town. A small chalet village is set among trees and shrubs.

Surroundings : 🌿 🔲 ♨♨
Leisure activities : ⛱ (small swimming pool)
Facilities : & (Jul-Aug) 🚿 ⛱ 🌦 launderette
Nearby : 🚴 ✕ 🎣

GPS Longitude : -1.59293
Latitude : 46.82925

ST-GEORGES-SUR-LAYON

49700 – Michelin map **317** G5 – pop. 769 – alt. 65
▶ Paris 328 – Angers 39 – Cholet 45 – Saumur 27

▲ Les Grésillons

📞 02 41 50 02 32, *www.camping-gresillons.com*
Address : chemin des Grésillons (800m south along the D 178, follow the signs for Concourson-sur-Layon and take the road to the right, near the river)
Opening times : from beginning April to end Sept.
1.5 ha (43 pitches) terraced, relatively flat, grassy
Tariff : 17€ ⚤ ⇔ ▣ (10A) – Extra per person 4€
Rental rates : (2012 price) (from beginning April to end Sept.) – 12 tent bungalows.
Per night from 37 to 60€ – Per week from 143 to 415€ – Reservation fee 20€

Surroundings : ⌇ ≤
Leisure activities : 🚲 ⤓ (small swimming pool) ⌇
Facilities : ⅃ ⌇ (Jul–Aug) ⌂ ▣

GPS Longitude : -0.37032
Latitude : 47.19324

ST-GILDAS-DES-BOIS

44530 – pop. 3,429 – alt. 16
▶ Paris 437 – Nantes 62 – Vannes 64 – Rennes 81

▲ Langâtre

📞 02 40 88 67 19, *www.campinglangatre44.fr*
Address : 7 r. du Clos Roger
Opening times : permanent
0.4 ha (15 pitches) terraced, flat, grassy
Tariff : 15.90€ ⚤ ⇔ ▣ (16A) – Extra per person 3.25€

Surroundings : ⌇ ⊡ ♤♤
Facilities : ⅃ ⌇ ⤳ ▥ ⌇

GPS Longitude : -2.02198
Latitude : 47.50746

In order for the guide to remain wholly objective, the selection is made on an entirely independent basis. There is no charge for being selected for the guide.

ST-HILAIRE-DE-RIEZ

85270 – Michelin map **316** E7 – pop. 10,504 – alt. 8
▶ Paris 453 – Challans 18 – Noirmoutier-en-l'Île 48 – La Roche-sur-Yon 48

Le Pissot (4km to the north)

▲▲▲ Les Biches ♣♦

📞 02 51 54 38 82, *www.campingdesbiches.com* – limited spaces for one-night stay
Address : chemin de Petite Baisse (situated 2km to the north)
Opening times : from mid April to mid Sept.
13 ha/9 ha for camping (434 pitches) flat, grassy, sandy
Tariff : (2012 price) 36.50€ ⚤ ⇔ ▣ (10A) – Extra per person 8.50€ – Reservation fee 20€
Rental rates : (2012 price) (from mid April to mid Sept.) – 240 🚐 – 57 🏠 – 1 ⇔ –
7 studios – 10 mobile homes without sanitary facilities. Per night from 32 to 112€
Per week from 227 to 1,299€ – Reservation fee 20€

A range of rental options in a pleasant pine wood, but with very few pitches for tents and caravans staying overnight only.

Surroundings : ⌇ ⊡ ♤♤
Leisure activities : 🍴 ✕ 🎮 ⌇ ⩍ ⨁ 🚣 🚲 ✂ ⌂ ▣ ⤓ ⟁ disco, multi-sports ground
Facilities : ⅃ ⌇ ▥ ⌂ ⩞ ⤳ ⌇ launderette ▨ ⌇

GPS Longitude : -1.94445
Latitude : 46.74052

Les Demoiselles (10km to the northwest)

Odalys Vitalys Les Demoiselles

✆ 0251581071, *www.odalys-vacances.com* – limited spaces for one-night stay
Address : av. des Becs (9.5km to the northwest, along the D 123 and 300m from the beach)
Opening times : from beginning April to beginning Nov.
13.7 ha (180 pitches) undulating, relatively flat to hilly, sandy, grassy
Tariff : (2012 price) 25€ ♛♛ ⇦ 🗐 🛱 (10A) – Extra per person 5€ – Reservation fee 15€
Rental rates : (2012 price) (from beginning April to beginning Nov.) ♿ (4 mobile homes) –
154 🛏. Per night from 40 to 200€ – Per week from 250 to 1,000€ – Reservation fee 15€

A mobile-home park with good shade and some pitches for tents and caravans staying overnight.

Surroundings : 🌿 🎋
Leisure activities : 🎏 ⛹ 🏊 🚴 ⛷ multi-sports ground
Facilities : ♿ ⚡ 🚿 launderette
Nearby : ✗ 🐴

GPS Longitude : -2.04086
Latitude : 46.76815

La Fradinière (7km to the northwest)

La Puerta del Sol ♛♛

✆ 0251491010, *www.campinglapuertadelsol.com*
Address : 7 chemin des Hommeaux (4.5km to the north)
Opening times : from end March to end Sept.
4 ha (207 pitches) flat, grassy
Tariff : (2012 price) 33€ ♛♛ ⇦ 🗐 🛱 (10A) – Extra per person 6.90€ – Reservation fee 20€
Rental rates : (2012 price) (from end March to end Sept.) ♿ (1 chalet) – 74 🛏 – 40 🏠.
Per night from 80 to 130€ – Per week from 179 to 890€ – Reservation fee 20€

A green setting limited pitches for tents and caravans and a rental park with distinct variations in levels of comfort.

Surroundings : 🌿 🏕 🎋
Leisure activities : 🍽 ✗ 🎦 🎬 evening ⛹ 🏋 ⇋ jacuzzi 🏊 🚴 🎮 ⛷
🏊 multi-sports ground, entertainment room
Facilities : ♿ ⚡ 🚽 🚿 🚰 launderette 🔌 🐴

GPS Longitude : -1.95887
Latitude : 46.76452

La Pège (6km to the northwest)

Les Écureuils ♛♛

✆ 0251543371, *www.camping-aux-ecureuils.com* – limited spaces for one-night stay
Address : 98 av. de la Pège (5.5km to the northwest, 200m from the beach)
Opening times : from end April to beginning Sept.
4 ha (215 pitches) flat, grassy, sandy
Tariff : 38.60€ ♛♛ ⇦ 🗐 🛱 (6A) – Extra per person 6.70€ – Reservation fee 25€
Rental rates : (from end April to beginning Sept.) 🏖 – 19 🛏 – 2 🏠.
Per week from 330 to 982€ – Reservation fee 25€

The site is in 2 distinct sections, in a pleasant setting. Pitches for tents and caravans staying overnight only are limited.

Surroundings : 🌿 🏕 🎋
Leisure activities : 🍽 ✗ 🎦 🎬 evening ⛹ 🏋 ⇋ hammam 🏊 🍽
🎮 ⛷ 🏊
Facilities : ♿ ⚡ 🚽 🚿 🚰 launderette 🐴
Nearby : 🐴 ⛷

GPS Longitude : -2.00897
Latitude : 46.74478

La Ningle

⌀ 02 51 54 07 11, *www.campinglaningle.com*
Address : 66 chemin des Roselières (situated 5.7km to the northwest)
Opening times : from mid May to mid Sept.
3.2 ha (150 pitches) flat, grassy, small lake
Tariff : (2012 price) 34.70€ †† ⇔ 🗐 ½ (10A) – Extra per person 4.80€ – Reservation fee 16€
Rental rates : (2012 price) (from beginning April to mid Sept.) ⅗ – 19 ⊡.
Per night from 45 to 60€ – Per week from 250 to 750€ – Reservation fee 16€
A well-kept site in a pleasant, green setting.

Surroundings : ⸲ ⌐ ♀
Leisure activities : ♈ 🗇 ⅙ ⚡ ⚒ 丄 ⚑
Facilities : 🗘 ⚬ ⚏ 🗘 ⚓ ❞ launderette
Nearby : ⿻ ✗ ⚒ 🕁

GPS
Longitude : -2.00473
Latitude : 46.7446

La Parée Préneau

⌀ 02 51 54 33 84, *www.campinglapareepreneau.com*
Address : 23 av. de La Parée Préneau (3.5km to the northwest)
Opening times : from beginning April to end Sept.
3.6 ha (217 pitches) flat, grassy, sandy
Tariff : 28.90€ †† ⇔ 🗐 ½ (6A) – Extra per person 5.30€ – Reservation fee 18€
Rental rates : (2012 price) (from beginning April to end Sept.) – 38 ⊡ – 7 ⭐ – 5 tent
bungalows. Per night from 70 to 110€ – Per week from 210 to 630€ – Reservation fee 18€
In a pleasant setting, but choose pitches away from the road in preference.

Surroundings : ⌐ ♀♀
Leisure activities : ♈ 🗇 ⚘ evening ⚡ ⚙ 丄 ⚒ multi-sports ground
Facilities : 🗘 ⚬ ⚏ 🗘 ⚓ ❞ launderette

GPS
Longitude : -1.98488
Latitude : 46.74034

Le Bosquet

⌀ 02 51 54 34 61, *www.lebosquet.fr*
Address : 62 av. de la Pège (5km to the northwest)
2 ha (115 pitches) flat, grassy, sandy
Rentals : 38 ⊡ – 3 apartments.
The site is relatively close to the beach (250 m).

Surroundings : ♀♀
Leisure activities : ♈ ✗ 🗇 ⚡ 丄 ⚑
Facilities : 🗘 ⚬ ⚏ launderette ⚒
Nearby : ⿻ 🕁

GPS
Longitude : -2.00326
Latitude : 46.74073

Le Romarin

⌀ 02 51 54 43 82, *www.leromarin.fr*
Address : r. des Martinets (3.8km to the northwest)
Opening times : from beginning April to end Sept.
4 ha/1.5 (97 pitches) undulating, flat, grassy, sandy
Tariff : (2012 price) 28€ †† ⇔ 🗐 ½ (10A) – Extra per person 4.30€ – Reservation fee 19€
Rental rates : (2012 price) (from beginning April to mid Sept.) ⅗ – 6 ⊡.
Per night from 50 to 88€ – Per week from 200 to 620€ – Reservation fee 19€
Mobile homes and some pitches for tents and caravans around a small but pretty
pine wood.

Surroundings : ⌐ ♀♀
Leisure activities : ✗ ⚡ 丄 multi-sports ground
Facilities : 🗘 ⚬ (Jul-Aug) ❞ launderette ⚒

GPS
Longitude : -1.98756
Latitude : 46.74243

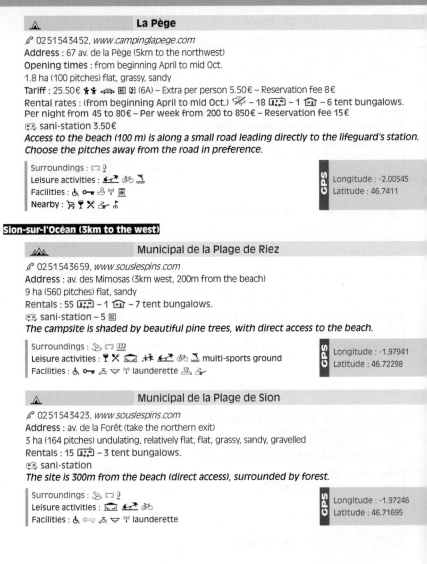

La Pège

📞 0251543452, *www.campinglapege.com*
Address : 67 av. de la Pège (5km to the northwest)
Opening times : from beginning April to mid Oct.
1.8 ha (100 pitches) flat, grassy, sandy
Tariff : 25.50€ ♣ ♣ ⇔ 回 ㉕ (6A) – Extra per person 5.50€ – Reservation fee 8€
Rental rates : (from beginning April to mid Oct.) ⚡ – 18 ⬛ – 1 🏠 – 6 tent bungalows.
Per night from 45 to 80€ – Per week from 200 to 850€ – Reservation fee 15€
🚐 sani-station 3.50€
Access to the beach (100 m) is along a small road leading directly to the lifeguard's station. Choose the pitches away from the road in preference.

Surroundings : ⌐ 𝒬
Leisure activities : 🏊 🚲 ⟱
Facilities : ♿ ⛐ 🛁 ♈ 📷
Nearby : 🛒 🍴 ✗ 🚣 ⛖

GPS Longitude : -2.00545
Latitude : 46.7411

Sion-sur-l'Océan (3km to the west)

Municipal de la Plage de Riez

📞 0251543659, *www.souslespins.com*
Address : av. des Mimosas (3km west, 200m from the beach)
9 ha (560 pitches) flat, sandy
Rentals : 55 ⬛ – 1 🏠 – 7 tent bungalows.
🚐 sani-station – 5 回
The campsite is shaded by beautiful pine trees, with direct access to the beach.

Surroundings : 🌲 ⌐ 𝄞
Leisure activities : 🍴 ✗ 🎞 🏕 🏊 🚲 ⟱ multi-sports ground
Facilities : ♿ ⛐ 🛁 ⟱ ♈ launderette 🔥 🚣

GPS Longitude : -1.97941
Latitude : 46.72298

Municipal de la Plage de Sion

📞 0251543423, *www.souslespins.com*
Address : av. de la Forêt (take the northern exit)
3 ha (164 pitches) undulating, relatively flat, flat, grassy, sandy, gravelled
Rentals : 15 ⬛ – 3 tent bungalows.
🚐 sani-station
The site is 300m from the beach (direct access), surrounded by forest.

Surroundings : 🌲 ⌐ 𝒬
Leisure activities : 🎞 🏊 🚲
Facilities : ♿ ⛐ 🛁 ⟱ ♈ launderette

GPS Longitude : -1.97246
Latitude : 46.71695

Key to rentals symbols:
12 ⬛ *Number of mobile homes*
20 🏠 *Number of chalets*
6 🛏 *Number of rooms to rent*
Per night *Minimum/maximum rate per night*
30–50€
Per week *Minimum/maximum rate per week*
300–1,000€

ST-HILAIRE-LA-FORÊT

85440 – Michelin map **316** G9 – pop. 611 – alt. 23
▶ Paris 449 – Challans 66 – Luçon 31 – La Roche-sur-Yon 31

La Grand' Métairie

✆ 02 51 33 32 38, *www.la-grand-metairie.com* – limited spaces for one-night stay
Address : 8 r. de La Vineuse en Plaine (north of the town along the D 70)
Opening times : from beginning April to end Sept.
3.8 ha (172 pitches) flat, grassy
Tariff : (2012 price) 33 € ♦♦ ⇐ 回 ⑭ (10A) – Extra per person 8 € – Reservation fee 22 €
Rental rates : (2012 price) (from beginning April to end Sept.) – 112 ⟨᠁⟩ – 18 ⟨᠍⟩ .
Per night from 65 to 195 € – Per week from 195 to 1,068 € – Reservation fee 22 €

A good choice of mobile homes in an attractive green setting with flowers.

Surroundings : ⋟ ⊏⊐ ꭫꭫
Leisure activities : ♥ ✗ 🎦 ꭤ evening ᵎ⊡ ᗕ 🚣 ♂⯎ ⅍ ▣ 🗲 ⣤ laundrette ⅋
Facilities : ♿ ᴏ┳ ♨ ♨ ⫯ ⫯ laundrette ⅋
GPS Longitude : -1.52545
Latitude : 46.44776

Les Batardières

✆ 02 51 33 33 85, *www.batardieres.com*
Address : 2 r. des Batardières (continue west along the D 70 and take the turning to the left, following signs for Le Poteau)
1.6 ha (75 pitches) flat, grassy

The pitches are in an attractive setting and well marked out, with good shade.

Surroundings : ⋟ ⊏⊐ ꭫
Leisure activities : 🎦 🚣 ⅍
Facilities : ᴏ┳ ♨ ⫯ 🔲
GPS Longitude : -1.52934
Latitude : 46.44807

*The prices listed were supplied by the campsite owners in 2012
(if prices were not available, those from the previous year are given).
The fees should be regarded as basic charges and may fluctuate
with inflation.*

ST-HILAIRE-ST-FLORENT

49400 – Michelin map **317** I5
▶ Paris 324 – Nantes 131 – Angers 45 – Tours 72

Chantepie ▲▴

✆ 02 41 67 95 34, *www.campingchantepie.com*
Address : rte de Chantepie (5.5km northwest along the D 751, follow the signs for Gennes and take road to the left; at La Mimerolle)
Opening times : from end April to mid Sept.
10 ha/5 ha for camping (150 pitches) flat, grassy
Tariff : 39 € ♦♦ ⇐ 回 ⑭ (16A) – Extra per person 6.60 € – Reservation fee 13 €
Rental rates : (from end April to mid Sept.) – 20 ⟨᠁⟩ – 10 tent bungalows – 2 tents.
Per night from 35 to 143 € – Per week from 210 to 860 € – Reservation fee 13 €
⟨᠍⟩ sani-station – ⟨᠍⟩ ⑭ 13.50 €
Based around an old renovated farmhouse.

Surroundings : ⋟ ⋞ Loire Valley ⊏⊐ ꭫꭫
Leisure activities : ♥ ✗ 🎦 ⅏⧾ 🚣 ♂⯎ ⅍ ▣ 🗲
Facilities : ♿ ᴏ┳ 🅲 ♨ ⫯ laundrette ⅍ ⅋
GPS Longitude : -0.14305
Latitude : 47.2937

PAYS DE LA LOIRE

ST-JEAN-DE-MONTS

85160 – Michelin map **316** D7 – pop. 8,037 – alt. 16
◪ Paris 451 – Cholet 123 – Nantes 73 – Noirmoutier-en-l'Île 34
CENTRE

Aux Coeurs Vendéens ♣:

☎ 02 51 58 84 91, *www.coeursvendeens.com*
Address : 251 rte de Notre-Dame-de-Monts (4km northwest on the D 38)
Opening times : from beginning May to mid Sept.
2 ha (117 pitches) flat, grassy, sandy
Tariff : (2012 price) 29.80€ ♦♦ ⇌ ▣ ⏦ (10A) – Extra per person 5€ – Reservation fee 15€
Rental rates : (2012 price) (from beginning April to end Sept.) ⚡ (Jul–Aug) – 68 ⛺ –
1 🏠 – 3 apartments. Per week from 180 to 880€ – Reservation fee 15€
Choose pitches away from the road in preference.

Surroundings : ⌕ 🌣🌣
Leisure activities : ▼ ✗ 🎲 ☫ ⚓ ⚲ ⚡
Facilities : ♿ ⚟ 🛁 🎏 ↻ ⫶ launderette ⚖
Nearby : ⚘

Longitude : -2.11008
Latitude : 46.80988

Les Pins

☎ 02 51 58 17 42, *ww.camping-despins.fr*
Address : 166 av. Valentine (2.5km southeast on the D 123)
Opening times : from end May to end Sept.
1.2 ha (118 pitches) undulating, terraced, flat, sandy
Tariff : (2012 price) 25.80€ ♦♦ ⇌ ▣ ⏦ (10A) – Extra per person 7.10€ – Reservation fee 20€
Rental rates : (2012 price) (permanent) ⚡ – 15 🏠. Per week from 235 to 609€
Reservation fee 20€
A lovely, undulating pine wood but the rental chalets are a little old.

Surroundings : ⌕ 🌣
Leisure activities : ▼ 🎲 ⚓ ⚲ ⚡
Facilities : ⚟ 🛁 ⫶ ▣
Nearby : ⚘ ⚖

Longitude : -2.03894
Latitude : 46.78081

NORTH

Les Amiaux ♣:

☎ 02 51 58 22 22, *www.amiaux.fr*
Address : 223 rte de Notre-Dame (3.5km to the northwest, on the D 38)
Opening times : from beginning May to end Sept.
17 ha (543 pitches) flat, grassy, sandy
Tariff : ♦ 4.50€ ⇌ 3€ ▣ 20€ ⏦ (10A) – Reservation fee 16€
Rental rates : (from beginning May to end Sept.) ⚡ – 28 ⛺ – 4 apartments.
Per night from 89 to 104€ – Per week from 310 to 910€ – Reservation fee 16€
The site is divided into 2 separate sections connected by a tunnel.

Surroundings : ⌕ 🌣
Leisure activities : ▼ ✗ 🎲 ③ ☫ ⚓ ⚲ ✗ ▦ ⚡ ⚿ multi-sports
ground
Facilities : ♿ ⚟ 🛁 🎏 ↻ ⫶ launderette ⚘ ⚖

Longitude : -2.11517
Latitude : 46.81107

Some information or pricing may have changed since the guide went to press.
We recommend you check the price list online in advance or at the entrance
to the campsite and enquire about possible restrictions.

Le Bois Joly ▲

℘ 02 51 59 11 63, *www.camping-lebois-joly.com*
Address : 46 rte de Notre-Dame-de-Monts (located 1km to the northwest; beside a brook)
Opening times : from beginning April to end Sept.
7.5 ha (356 pitches) flat, grassy, sandy
Tariff : 34€ ✶✶ ⬇ 🔲 (10A) – Extra per person 6€ – Reservation fee 22€
Rental rates : (from beginning April to end Sept.) ♿ (1 mobile home) ⬜ – 2 'gypsy'
caravans – 98 🚐 – 22 🏠. Per night 150€ – Per week from 250 to 930€ – Reservation fee 22€
🚐 sani-station – 5 🔲 18€
An attractive swimming area.

Surroundings : ⬚ ♀
Leisure activities : ♟ ✕ 🎱 ⊙ 🏓 🎿 ⛵ jacuzzi ⛷ 🔲 🏊 ⛷ 🎣
multi-sports ground
Facilities : ♿ ⊶ ▥ 🏕 🚿 ✂ 🍽 launderette 🛒
Nearby : ⛺

GPS
Longitude : -2.07417
Latitude : 46.79918

Club Airotel Les Places Dorées ▲

℘ 02 51 59 02 93, *www.placesdorees.com* – limited spaces for one-night stay
Address : rte de Notre-Dame-de-Monts (4km northwest on the D 38)
Opening times : from mid June to mid Sept.
5 ha (288 pitches) flat, grassy, sandy
Tariff : (2012 price) 37.40€ ✶✶ ⬇ 🔲 (10A) – Extra per person 7€ – Reservation fee 25€
Rental rates : (2012 price) (from mid April to mid Sept.) ⬜ – 75 🚐.
Per night from 41 to 142€ – Per week from 283 to 989€ – Reservation fee 25€
An attractive swimming area.

Surroundings : ⬚ ♀♀
Leisure activities : ♟ ✕ 🏓 🎿 ⛵ hammam jacuzzi ⛷ 🔲 🏊 ⛷
multi-sports ground
Facilities : ♿ ⊶ 🚿 🍽 launderette 🛒
Nearby : 🏊

GPS
Longitude : -2.10997
Latitude : 46.8097

APV Les Aventuriers de la Calypso ▲

℘ 02 51 59 79 66, *www.camping-apv.com* – limited spaces for one-night stay
Address : rte de Notre-Dame-de-Monts, at Les Tonnelles (4.6km to the northwest)
Opening times : from beginning April to end Sept.
4 ha (284 pitches) flat, grassy, sandy
Tariff : (2012 price) 33.30€ ✶✶ ⬇ 🔲 (10A) – Extra per person 8.50€ – Reservation fee 27€
Rental rates : (2012 price) (from beginning April to end Sept.) – 131 🚐 – 42 🏠 – (with/
without sanitary facilities). Per night 82€ – Per week from 182 to 972€ – Reservation fee 27€
*Not many pitches for tents or caravans for overnight stays only, and some rental options
are very old.*

Surroundings : 🦢 ⬚ ♀
Leisure activities : ♟ ✕ 🎱 ⊙ evening 🏓 ⛵ jacuzzi ⛷ 🚲 ✗ 🔲 🏊
⛷ multi-sports ground
Facilities : ♿ ⊶ 🚿 ✂ 🍽 launderette 🛒

GPS
Longitude : -2.11533
Latitude : 46.81232

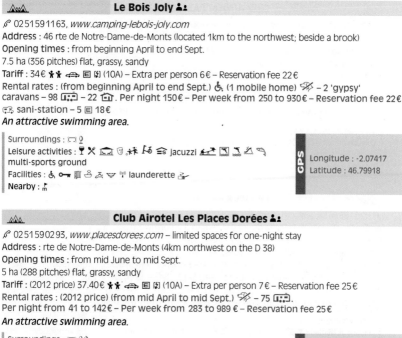

Do not confuse:
▲ *to* ▲▲▲ : *MICHELIN classification*
with
★ *to* ★★★★★ : *official classification*

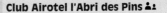

Club Airotel l'Abri des Pins ▲▪

📞 0251588386, *www.abridespins.com* – limited spaces for one-night stay
Address : rte de Notre-Dame-de-Monts (4km northwest on the D 38)
Opening times : from mid June to mid Sept.
3 ha (209 pitches) flat, grassy, sandy
Tariff : (2012 price) 37.40€ ▲▲ ⇔ 🔲 ⚡ (10A) – Extra per person 7€ – Reservation fee 25€
Rental rates : (2012 price) (permanent) 🏠 – 50 🚐 – 23 ⛺. Per night from 41 to 142€
Per week from 283 to 989€ – Reservation fee 25€

A good swimming area. Choose pitches away from the road in preference.

Surroundings : 🛏 ⚯⚯
Leisure activities : ♟ ✗ 🖼 ⚯ 🎿 hammam, jacuzzi 🚣 ✂ 🔳 🏊 ⛷
Facilities : ♿ ⚬⚬ 🏕 🏖 ☔ ⛱ launderette 🛒
Nearby : 🏇

GPS
Longitude : -2.10997
Latitude : 46.8097

Le Vieux Ranch

📞 0251588658, *www.levieuxranch.com*
Address : chemin de la Parée du Jonc (4.3km to the northwest)
Opening times : from beginning April to end Sept.
5 ha (242 pitches) undulating, flat, grassy, sandy
Tariff : (2012 price) 30.60€ ▲▲ ⇔ 🔲 ⚡ (10A) – Extra per person 6.30€ – Reservation fee 15€
Rental rates : (from beginning April to end Sept.) 🏠 – 15 🚐 – 8 ⛺.
Per night from 60 to 128€ – Per week from 279 to 810€ – Reservation fee 15€

In an attractive location among gentle hills, 200m from the beach.

Surroundings : ⚯ 🛏 ⚯⚯
Leisure activities : ♟ 🖼 🎿 🚣 🚴 🏊 ⛷ entertainment room
Facilities : ♿ ⚬⚬ 🏕 🏖 ☔ ⛱ launderette
Nearby : ✗ 🛒

GPS
Longitude : -2.11351
Latitude : 46.80717

Flower Plein Sud ▲▪

📞 0251591040, *www.campingpleinsud.com*
Address : 246 rte de Notre-Dame-de-Monts (4km to the northwest, on the D 38)
Opening times : from mid April to mid Sept.
2 ha (110 pitches) flat, grassy, sandy
Tariff : 29€ ▲▲ ⇔ 🔲 ⚡ (6A) – Extra per person 5€ – Reservation fee 20€
Rental rates : (from mid April to mid Sept.) 🏠 – 35 🚐 – 2 tent bungalows – 2 tents.
Per night from 37 to 102€ – Per week from 185 to 715€ – Reservation fee 20€
🚐 sani-station 25€ – 🚌 ⚡25€

A long, narrow site with well marked-out pitches.

Surroundings : 🛏 ⚯
Leisure activities : ♟ ⚯ 🚣 🚴 🏊 multi-sports ground
Facilities : ♿ ⚬⚬ 🏕 ⛱ ☔ ⛱ launderette

GPS
Longitude : -2.11093
Latitude : 46.8103

Michelin classification:
▲▲▲▲▲ *Extremely comfortable, equipped to a very high standard*
▲▲▲▲ *Very comfortable, equipped to a high standard*
▲▲▲ *Comfortable and well equipped*
▲▲ *Reasonably comfortable*
▲ *Satisfactory*

La Forêt

𝒫 02 51 58 84 63, *www.hpa-laforet.com*
Address : 190 chemin de la Rive (5.5km to the northwest, follow the signs for Notre-Dame-de-Monts and take turning to the left)
Opening times : permanent
1 ha (61 pitches) flat, grassy, sandy
Tariff : 30€ ♥♥ ⊕ 国 〔₤〕 (10A) – Extra per person 5€ – Reservation fee 29€
Rental rates : (permanent) – 16 〔₤〕. Per night from 99 to 105€ – Per week from 229 to 739€
Reservation fee 29€
⊕ sani-station – 15 国 15€ – ⊕〔₤〕16€
Pretty trees and shrubs sourround this eco-friendly campsite.

Surroundings : ⊏⊐ 𝟘𝟘
Leisure activities : 🎮 🚣 🚴 ⛵
Facilities : ⅙ ⊶ 占 🚿 🚽 ⁗ 🖼

GPS Longitude : -2.12993
Latitude : 46.81828

La Davière-Plage

𝒫 02 51 58 27 99, *www.daviereplage.com*
Address : 197 rte de Notre-Dame-de-Monts (3km to the northwest, on the D 38)
Opening times : from beginning May to end Sept.
3 ha (174 pitches) flat, grassy, sandy
Tariff : (2012 price) 25.95€ ♥♥ ⊕ 国 〔₤〕 (10A) – Extra per person 5.60€ – Reservation fee 20€
Rental rates : (2012 price) (from beginning May to end Sept.) – 35 〔₤〕 – 6 tent bungalows – 7 mobile homes (without sanitary facilities). Per night 90€ – Per week from 250 to 700€
Reservation fee 20€
⊕ sani-station 12€ – 15 国 12€
The site is divided into 2 separate sections. Choose pitches away from the road in preference.

Surroundings : ⊏⊐ 𝟘
Leisure activities : ✗ 🎮 🚣 🚴 ⛵
Facilities : ⅙ ⊶ (Jul–Aug) 占 launderette 🚿
Nearby : ⛾

GPS Longitude : -2.10085
Latitude : 46.8054

There are several different types of sani-station
('borne' in French) – sanitation points providing
fresh water and disposal points for grey water.
See page 12 for further details.

SOUTH

La Yole ♣♣

𝒫 02 51 58 67 17, *www.vendee-camping.eu* – limited spaces for one-night stay
Address : chemin des Bosses, at Orouet (7km southeast)
Opening times : from beginning April to end Sept.
5 ha (369 pitches) flat, grassy, sandy
Tariff : 32€ ♥♥ ⊕ 国 〔₤〕 (16A) – Extra per person 7€ – Reservation fee 29€
Rental rates : (from beginning April to end Sept.) ⅙ – 55 〔₤〕. Per night from 36 to 129€
Per week from 250 to 899€ – Reservation fee 29€
In a green, well-kept setting, with flowers and plentiful shade from a nearby pine wood.

Surroundings : 🐾 ⊏⊐ 𝟘𝟘
Leisure activities : ⛾ ✗ 🎮 🎣 🧖 jacuzzi 🚣 🚴 ✂ 📺 ⛵ 🏊
Facilities : ⅙ ⊶ 国占 🚿 🚽 ⁗ launderette 🚿 🛒

GPS Longitude : -2.00728
Latitude : 46.75664

Les Jardins de l'Atlantique

0251580574, *www.camping-jardins-atlantique.com* – limited spaces for one-night stay
Address : 100 r. de la Caillauderie (5.5km to the northeast)
5 ha (318 pitches) undulating, flat and relatively flat, sandy
Rentals : 56.
sani-station
The site is divided into 2 separate sections on either side of the road.

Surroundings :
Leisure activities : jacuzzi multi-sports ground
Facilities : launderette

GPS
Longitude : -2.02751
Latitude : 46.76972

Le Both d'Orouet

0251586037, *http://www.camping-lebothdorouet.com*
Address : 77 av. d'Orouët (6.7km southeast on the D 38, follow the signs for St-Hilaire-de-Riez; at Orouet, beside a stream)
Opening times : from beginning April to end Oct.
4.4 ha (200 pitches) flat, grassy, sandy
Tariff : (2012 price) 26€ (10A) – Extra per person 5€ – Reservation fee 20€
Rental rates : (2012 price) (from beginning April to end Oct.) – 31 – 16.
Per night from 45 to 70€ – Per week from 210 to 680€ – Reservation fee 20€
sani-station
In a leafy, green setting. Games room in an old barn dating back to 1875.

Surroundings :
Leisure activities : jacuzzi multi-sports ground
Facilities : launderette
Nearby :

GPS
Longitude : -1.99759
Latitude : 46.76495

Campéole les Sirènes

0251580131, *http://vendee-camping.info*
Address : av. des Demoiselles (to the southeast, 500m from the beach)
Opening times : from beginning April to mid Sept.
15 ha/5 ha for camping (470 pitches) undulating, flat, sandy
Tariff : (2012 price) 27.90€ (10A) – Extra per person 7.60€ – Reservation fee 25€
Rental rates : (2012 price) (from beginning April to mid Sept.) (2 mobile homes) – 52 – 40 – 40 tent bungalows. Per night from 25 to 47€ – Per week from 140 to 903€
Reservation fee 25€
sani-station
A pleasant, natural setting in Les Pays de Monts (regional pine forest), although the sanitary facilities are rather old.

Surroundings :
Leisure activities : multi-sports ground
Facilities : launderette
Nearby :

GPS
Longitude : -2.0548
Latitude : 46.7799

For more information on visiting particular towns or regions, consult the relevant regional MICHELIN Green Guide. We also recommend you use the appropriate Michelin regional map to locate your selected campsite, to calculate distances and to work out the best route.

Le Logis

📞 0251586067, *www.camping-saintjeandemonts.com* – limited spaces for one-night stay ✕

Address : 4 ch. du Logis (4.3km southeast on the D 38, follow the signs for St-Gilles-Croix-de-Vie)
Opening times : from mid April to beginning Sept.
0.8 ha (44 pitches) terraced, flat, grassy, sandy
Tariff : (2012 price) 23.70€ ✱ ✱ ⬅ 🔲 ⚡ (10A) – Extra per person 5€ – Reservation fee 16€
Rental rates : (2012 price) (from mid April to beginning Sept.) ✕ – 13 🛏 – 2 gîtes.
Per week from 240 to 610€ – Reservation fee 16€
Choose pitches away from the road in preference.

Surroundings : ⌑
Leisure activities : 🎯 ⛵ 🏊 (small swimming pool)
Facilities : ♿ ⚡ 📶 📦
Nearby : 🍷 ✕ 🏇

Longitude : -2.01308
Latitude : 46.77953

ST-JULIEN-DE-CONCELLES

44450 – Michelin map **316** H4 – pop. 6,839 – alt. 24
▶ Paris 384 – Nantes 19 – Angers 89 – La Roche-sur-Yon 80

Le Chêne

📞 0240541200, *www.campingduchene.fr*
Address : 1 rte du Lac (located 1.5km east along the D 37 (diversion), near the small lake)
Opening times : permanent
2 ha (100 pitches) flat, grassy
Tariff : (2012 price) 18.60€ ✱ ✱ ⬅ 🔲 ⚡ (10A) – Extra per person 4.60€
Rental rates : (2012 price) (permanent) – 24 🛏 – 4 tent bungalows. Per night from 37 to 97€
Per week from 190 to 590€
🚐 sani-station – 1 🔲 8.30€
In an attractive, green location, beside a lake.

Surroundings : ⌑ ♨
Leisure activities : 🎯 🏊 (open-air in season)
Facilities : ♿ ⚡ 🛁 launderette
Nearby : 🦆 pedalos

Longitude : -1.37098
Latitude : 47.2492

A chambre d'hôte is a guesthouse or B & B-style accommodation.

ST-JULIEN-DES-LANDES

85150 – Michelin map **316** F8 – pop. 1,331 – alt. 59
▶ Paris 445 – Aizenay 17 – Challans 32 – La Roche-sur-Yon 24

Les Castels La Garangeoire ♟

📞 0251466539, *www.camping-la-garangeoire.com*
Address : head 2.8km north along the D 21
Opening times : from mid April to end Sept.
200 ha/10 ha for camping (356 pitches) undulating, terraced, flat, grassy
Tariff : 38€ ✱ ✱ ⬅ 🔲 ⚡ (16A) – Extra per person 8€ – Reservation fee 25€
Rental rates : (from mid April to mid Sept.) ♿ (1 mobile home) – 25 🛏 – 23 🏠 – 3 gîtes.
Per night from 51 to 168€ – Per week from 248 to 1,170€ – Reservation fee 25€
An extensive, charming site in the grounds of a château, with meadows, lakes and woods.

Surroundings : 🌲 ⌑ ♨
Leisure activities : 🍷 ✕ 🎯 🎮 🏃 ⛲ jacuzzi ⛵ 🚴 ✕ 🏇 🏊 🎿 🎣 🏇
pedalos 🛶 multi-sports ground
Facilities : ♿ ⚡ 🛁 🚿 🔥 🚰 📶 launderette 🧺 🧊 refrigerators

Longitude : -1.71359
Latitude : 46.66229

Sunêlia Village de La Guyonnière ♣♣

℘ 02 51 46 62 59, *www.laguyonniere.com*
Address : head 2.4km northwest along the D 12, follow the signs for Landevieille then continue 1.2km along the road to the right not far from the lake at Le Jaunay
Opening times : from end March to end Sept.
30 ha (294 pitches) relatively flat, flat, grassy, lake
Tariff : 42.90€ ♣♣ ⇔ 回 ⚡ (10A) – Extra per person 10.50€ – Reservation fee 20€
Rental rates : (from end March to end Sept.) ⚡ – 86 🚐 – 25 🏠 – 4 tents.
Per night from 34 to 195 – Per week from 238 to 1,365€ – Reservation fee 20€
🚐 5 回 18.90€
In a leafy, green location, with farm animals nearby.

Surroundings : 🐾 ♀
Leisure activities : ♀ ✕ 🎠 🖼 ⛹ 🏊 hammam, jacuzzi 🏋 🚲 ✕ 🎱
🎿 ⛷ 🐎 multi-sports ground
Facilities : ♿ ⚲ 🏧 ♨ 🚾 launderette 🚮

GPS
Longitude : -1.74963
Latitude : 46.65258

Yelloh! Village Château La Forêt ♣♣

℘ 02 51 46 62 11, *www.chateaulaforet.com*
Address : located 0.5 km northeast along the D 55, follow the signs for Martinet
Opening times : from beginning May to mid Sept.
50 ha/5 ha for camping (209 pitches) flat, grassy, lake, wood
Tariff : 39€ ♣♣ ⇔ 回 ⚡ (6A) – Extra per person 7€
Rental rates : (from beginning May to mid Sept.) – 26 🚐 – 5 🏠 – 1 bubble room.
Per night from 39 to 148€ – Per week from 273 to 1,036€
In a wooded setting in the grounds of the château.

Surroundings : 🐾 🍴 ♀♀
Leisure activities : ♀ ✕ 🎠 🖼 daytime ⛹ 🏋 🚲 ✕ 🎱 🎿 ⛷
disco, zip wiring, forest trail, paintballing
Facilities : ♿ ⚲ ♨ 🚾 🚾 🚾 launderette 🚮 🐕

GPS
Longitude : -1.71135
Latitude : 46.64182

The guide is updated each year, so consult the latest edition for the most up-to-date information and pricing.

ST-LAURENT-SUR-SÈVRE

85290 – Michelin map **316** K6 – pop. 3,442 – alt. 121
▶ Paris 365 – Angers 76 – Bressuire 36 – Cholet 14

Le Rouge Gorge

℘ 02 51 67 86 39, *www.camping-lerougegorge-vendee.com*
Address : rte de La Verrie (located 1km west along the D 111)
Opening times : from mid March to mid Oct.
2 ha (93 pitches) relatively flat, flat, grassy
Tariff : (2012 price) 22.10€ ♣♣ ⇔ 回 ⚡ (13A) – Extra per person 2.80€ – Reservation fee 9.50€
Rental rates : (2012 price) (from mid March to mid Oct.) ⚡ – 7 🚐 – 13 🏠 – 4 tents.
Per night from 45 to 102€ – Per week from 235 to 675€ – Reservation fee 9.50€
🚐 sani-station
A pleasant setting with lots of green space and plenty of shade.

Surroundings : 🍴 ♀♀
Leisure activities : 🎠 🏋 🎿
Facilities : ♿ ⚲ ♨ 🚾 🚾 launderette 🐕
Nearby : 🎣

GPS
Longitude : -0.90307
Latitude : 46.95788

ST-MICHEL-EN-L'HERM

85580 – Michelin map **316** I9 – pop. 2,129 – alt. 9
▶ Paris 453 – Luçon 15 – La Rochelle 46 – La Roche-sur-Yon 47

Les Mizottes

📞 02 51 30 23 63, *www.campinglesmizottes.fr*
Address : 41 r. des Anciens Quais (800m southwest along the D 746, follow the signs for l'Aiguillon-sur-Mer)
Opening times : from beginning April to end Sept.
3 ha (150 pitches) flat, grassy
Tariff : (2012 price) 26.82€ ✝✝ ⚌ 🗉 (6A) – Extra per person 4.50€ – Reservation fee 20€
Rental rates : (2012 price) (from beginning April to end Sept.) ⚐ (1 mobile home) – 40 🚐.
Per night from 55 to 75€ – Per week from 230 to 700€ – Reservation fee 20€
🚐 2 🗉 26.82€
Good-quality services and leisure facillities.

Surroundings : 🐾 ⌓ ♀
Leisure activities : ♈ ✕ 🎱 ✳ 🚲 🏊 ⤴ multi-sports ground, entertainment room
Facilities : ⚐ ⊶ 🏠 ⚑ launderette 🐕

GPS Longitude : -1.25482
Latitude : 46.34943

ST-PÈRE-EN-RETZ

44320 – Michelin map **316** D4 – pop. 4,113 – alt. 14
▶ Paris 425 – Challans 54 – Nantes 45 – Pornic 13

Le Grand Fay

📞 02 40 21 72 89, *www.camping-granfay.com*
Address : r. du Grand Fay (take the eastern exit along the D 78, follow the signs for Frossay then continue 500m down the turning to the right)
Opening times : permanent
1.2 ha (76 pitches) relatively flat, flat, grassy
Tariff : 18.90€ ✝✝ ⚌ 🗉 (6A) – Extra per person 4.50€ – Reservation fee 15€
Rental rates : (permanent) – 6 🚐. Per night from 60 to 120€ – Per week from 220 to 640€
Reservation fee 15€

In a quiet residential area, behind the municipal sports centre and near a lake.

Surroundings : ♀♀
Leisure activities : ⤴ ⤳ 🏊 ⤴
Facilities : ⚐ ⊶ launderette
Nearby : ⚼ ⤙

GPS Longitude : -2.03654
Latitude : 47.20266

ST-PHILBERT-DE-GRAND-LIEU

44310 – pop. 7,806 – alt. 10
▶ Paris 407 – nantes 27 – La Roche-sur-Yon 57 – Angers 112

La Boulogne

📞 02 40 78 88 79, *www.camping-la-boulogne.com*
Address : 1 av. de Nantes
Opening times : from mid April to mid Oct.
4.5 ha (180 pitches) flat, grassy
Tariff : (2012 price) 13.75€ ✝✝ ⚌ 🗉 (6A) – Extra per person 3.70€
Rental rates : (2012 price) (from mid April to end Oct.) – 1 'gypsy' caravan – 8 🚐 – 5 tent bungalows. Per night from 50 to 75€ – Per week from 200 to 515€
🚐 ⚐ 🗉 12€
Beside the Boulogne river and near a small but pleasant lake.

Surroundings : ♀♀
Facilities : ⚐ 🏚 🏠
Nearby : jacuzzi

GPS Longitude : -1.64027
Latitude : 47.0419

ST-RÉVÉREND

85220 – Michelin map **316** F7 – pop. 1,323 – alt. 19
▶ Paris 453 – Aizenay 20 – Challans 19 – La Roche-sur-Yon 36

Le Pont Rouge

℘ 02 51 54 68 50, *www.camping-lepontrouge.com*
Address : r. Georges Clemenceau (take the southwestern exit along the D 94 and take the road to the right; beside a stream)
Opening times : from end March to end Sept.
2.2 ha (73 pitches) relatively flat, flat, grassy
Tariff : (2012 price) 23€ ★★ ⇔ 回 [½] (6A) – Extra per person 5€ – Reservation fee 15€
Rental rates : (2012 price) (from end March to end Sept.) – 13 ⬚ – 1 ⬚ – 7 tent bungalows – (mobile homes with/without sanitary facilities). Per night from 36 to 104€
Per week from 179 to 698€ – Reservation fee 15€
A green, well-kept setting, with a range of rental options.

Surroundings : ⧈ ⊡ ⍟⍟
Leisure activities : ▢ ✕ ⊚ evening ⚐ ⤒
Facilities : ⅋ ⊶ ⌂ ⍏ launderette ⌸

GPS
Longitude : -1.83448
Latitude : 46.69366

ST-VINCENT-SUR-JARD

85520 – Michelin map **316** G9 – pop. 1,205 – alt. 10
▶ Paris 454 – Challans 64 – Luçon 34 – La Rochelle 70

Chadotel La Bolée d'Air

℘ 02 51 33 05 05, *http://chadotel.com/camping-saint-vincent-sur-jard/la-bolee-d-air/*
Address : rte du Bouil (situated 2km east along the D 21 follow the signs for Longeville and take a right turn)
Opening times : from beginning April to end Sept.
5.7 ha (280 pitches) flat, grassy
Tariff : 15.50€ ★★ ⇔ 回 [½] (10A) – Extra per person 6€ – Reservation fee 25€
Rental rates : (from beginning April to end Sept.) – 32 ⬚ – 14 ⬚. Per night from 50 to 82€
Per week from 210 to 910€ – Reservation fee 25€
Choose pitches away from the road in preference.

Surroundings : ⊡ ⍟⍟
Leisure activities : ▢ ⛳ ⊚ ⊜ ⚐ ⛵ ✕ ⌸ ▣ ⤒ ⍄ multi-sports ground
Facilities : ⅋ ⊶ ⌂ ⌢ ⍔ ⍏ launderette ⌸

GPS
Longitude : -1.52622
Latitude : 46.41978

44980 – Michelin map **316** H4 – pop. 11,679 – alt. 9
▶ Paris 378 – Nantes 7 – Angers 82 – Cholet 58

Belle Rivière

℘ 02 40 25 85 81, *www.camping-belleriviere.com*
Address : rte des Perrières (situated 2km northeast along the D 68, follow the signs for Thouaré; at La Gicquelière, take turning to the right for 1km; direct access to a branch of the Loire river)
Opening times : permanent
3 ha (110 pitches) flat, grassy
Tariff : 19.75€ ★★ ⇔ 回 [½] (10A) – Extra per person 4.35€ – Reservation fee 15€
Rental rates : (permanent) ⌲ – 8 ⬚. Per week from 330 to 520€ – Reservation fee 15€
⌸ 2 回 15.85€
A pleasant, leafy setting surrounded by trees and shrubs. Bus stop for town.

Surroundings : ⊡ ⍟⍟
Leisure activities : ⚐ ⍔
Facilities : ⅋ ⊶ (Jun-Aug) ▥ ⌢ ⍏ launderette
Nearby : ⌇ ⚘

GPS
Longitude : -1.45574
Latitude : 47.254

SAUMUR

9400 – Michelin map **317** I5 – pop. 28,070 – alt. 30
◘ Paris 300 – Angers 67 – Châtellerault 76 – Cholet 70

L'Île d'Offard ♣♠

℘ 02 41 40 30 00, *www.cvtloisirs.com*
Address : Bd de Verden (access via the town centre, on an island in the Loire river)
4.5 ha (258 pitches) flat, grassy
Rentals : ⚄ – 44 🚐 – 8 tent bungalows.
🚐 sani-station – 8 ▣
In a pleasant location at the tip of the island with a view of the château.

Surroundings : ⇐ ⌑ ⵠ
Leisure activities : ▾ ✕ 🎬 ☺ daytime ⁂ ⛵ ♏ ⛆ ⟋
Facilities : ⅋ ⊶ 🏛 △ ⌕ ⁝ launderette ⟋
Nearby : ✕

Longitude : -0.0656
Latitude : 47.26022

LA SELLE-CRAONNAISE

3800 – Michelin map **310** C7 – pop. 931 – alt. 71
◘ Paris 316 – Angers 68 – Châteaubriant 32 – Château-Gontier 29

Base de Loisirs de la Rincerie

℘ 02 43 06 17 52, *http://www.la-rincerie.com*
Address : 3.5km northwest along the D 111, D 150, follow the signs for Ballots and take turning to the left
Opening times : from beginning March to end Oct.
120 ha/5 ha for camping (50 pitches) flat, relatively flat, grassy
Tariff : 13.80€ ♣♣ ⇔ ▣ ⑭ (10A) – Extra per person 3.10€
Rental rates : (from beginning March to end Oct.) ⚄ – 1 🚐 – 1 ⌂ – 4 tent bungalows.
Per night from 35 to 100€ – Per week from 200 to 320€
🚐 sani-station 2€
Near a small lake, with plenty of water-based activities.

Surroundings : ⌇ ⇐
Leisure activities : ☺ daytime ♏ ⛆
Facilities : ⅋ ⊶ 🏛 △ ⌕ ▣
Leisure/activities centre : ⛵ ⚲ ⛆ ⟋

Longitude : -1.06528
Latitude : 47.86631

SILLÉ-LE-GUILLAUME

2140 – Michelin map **310** I5 – pop. 2,361 – alt. 161
◘ Paris 230 – Alençon 39 – Laval 55 – Le Mans 35

Indigo Les Molières

℘ 02 43 20 16 12, *www.camping-indigo.com*
Address : at Sillé-Plage (head 2.5km north along the D 5, D 105, D 203 and take the road to the right)
Opening times : from end April to end Sept.
3.5 ha (133 pitches) flat, grassy
Tariff : (2012 price) 25.10€ ♣♣ ⇔ ▣ ⑭ (10A) – Extra per person 4.90€ – Reservation fee 20€
Rental rates : (2012 price) (from end April to end Sept.) – 12 🚐 – 20 tents.
Per night from 42 to 88€ – Per week from 206 to 616€ – Reservation fee 20€
🚐 sani-station 7€
The site is in a forest, near several small lakes.

Surroundings : ⌇ ⵠⵠ
Leisure activities : 🎬
Facilities : ⅋ ⊶
Nearby : ▾ ✕ ✕ ⛆ ⚲ pedalos

Longitude : -0.12917
Latitude : 48.18333

SILLÉ-LE-PHILIPPE

72460 – Michelin map **310** L6 – pop. 1,091 – alt. 35
▶ Paris 195 – Beaumont-sur-Sarthe 25 – Bonnétable 11 – Connerré 15

Les Castels Le Château de Chanteloup

℘ 02 43 27 51 07, www.chateau-de-chanteloup.com
Address : at Chanteloup (situated 2km southwest along the D 301, follow the signs for Le Mans)
Opening times : from beginning May to end Sept.
20 ha (100 pitches) relatively flat, flat, grassy, sandy, lake, natural setting among trees and bushes
Tariff : 35.80€ ✦✦ ⇌ 🗐 🏊 (8A) – Extra per person 8.80€
Rental rates : (permanent) – 3 apartments – 8 tents – 2 gîtes. Per night from 100 to 175€
Per week from 560 to 700€

Surroundings : 🐾 𝄫
Leisure activities : 🍴 ✕ 🎦 🍸 🛶 🚲 🛥
Facilities : ⌾ 🛁 🍴 launderette 🚿

GPS Longitude : 0.34012
Latitude : 48.10461

SOULLANS

85300 – Michelin map **316** E7 – pop. 4,058 – alt. 12
▶ Paris 443 – Challans 7 – Noirmoutier-en-l'Île 46 – La Roche-sur-Yon 48

Municipal le Moulin Neuf

℘ 02 51 68 00 24, camping-soullans@orange.fr
Address : take the northern exit along the D 69, follow the signs for Challans and take the turning to the right
Opening times : from mid June to mid Sept.
1.2 ha (80 pitches) flat, grassy
Tariff : (2012 Price) 9.50€ ✦✦ ⇌ 🗐 🏊 (4A) – Extra per person 2.50€

Near the town, a small and peaceful site with clearly marked-out pitches but only average sanitary facilities.

Surroundings : 🐾 ⊏ ♀
Facilities : ♿ ⌾ 🖥
Nearby : ✕

GPS Longitude : -1.89566
Latitude : 46.79817

TALMONT-ST-HILAIRE

85440 – Michelin map **316** G9 – pop. 6,829 – alt. 35
▶ Paris 448 – Challans 55 – Luçon 38 – La Roche-sur-Yon 30

Yelloh! Village Le Littoral

℘ 02 51 22 04 64, www.campinglelittoral.com
Address : at Le Portea (9.5km southwest along the D 949, D 4a, after Querry-Pigeon, take right turn onto D 129, follow coast road to les Sables-d'Olonne; 100m from the ocean)
Opening times : from mid April to mid Sept.
9 ha (483 pitches) relatively flat, flat, grassy, sandy
Tariff : 44€ ✦✦ ⇌ 🗐 🏊 (10A) – Extra per person 6€
Rental rates : (from mid April to mid Sept.) ♿ (1 mobile home) – 164 🏠 – 15 🏡.
Per night from 39 to 215€ – Per week from 273 to 1,505€
🚮 sani-station
An attractive site with good quality rental options.

Surroundings : ⊏ ♀
Leisure activities : 🍴 ✕ 🎦 🍸 🕺 jacuzzi 🚲 ✕ 🖾 🛥 ♨
multi-sports ground
Facilities : ♿ ⌾ 🖥 🛁 🚿 🍴 launderette 🧺 🚿 free shuttle
bus to beaches

GPS Longitude : -1.70222
Latitude : 46.45195

Odalys Vitalys Les Cottages St-Martin
(rental of mobile homes and gîtes only)

℘ 02 51 21 90 00, *www.odalys-vacances.com*

Address : le porteau (9.5km southwest along the D 949, D 4a, after Querry-Pigeon, take right turn onto D 129, follow coast road to Les Sables-d'Olonne, 200m from the ocean)
Opening times : permanent
3.5 ha flat
Rental rates : (2012 price) – 42 🏠 – 15 apartments. Per night from 60 to 110€
Per week from 220 to 1,145€ – Reservation fee 20€

A mobile-home village for both owner-occupiers and rentals.

Surroundings : 🐚 ☐
Leisure activities : 🖼 ⛹ ⛵ 🚴 ✂ ☒ ☷
Facilities : ♿ ⚷ ♒ launderette
Nearby : ♨ ♟ ✗ ⚓

GPS Longitude : -1.70181
Latitude : 46.45254

Le Paradis

℘ 02 51 22 22 36, *www.camping-leparadis85.com*

Address : r. de la Source (3.7km west along the D 949, follow the signs for Les Sables-d'Olonne, turn left onto D 4a, follow the signs for Querry-Pigeon and take the road to the right)
Opening times : from beginning April to end Sept.
4.9 ha (148 pitches) terraced, flat and relatively flat, grassy, sandy
Tariff : (2012 price) 26€ ⚑⚑ ⇔ 🔲 (10A) – Extra per person 4.50€ – Reservation fee 20€
Rental rates : (2012 price) (from beginning April to end Sept.) – 64 🏠 – 9 🏠 – 8 tent bungalows. Per night 190€ – Per week from 210 to 910€ – Reservation fee 20€

Sloping site, well shaded in places with a range of rental options.

Surroundings : 🐚 ☐ ⛱
Leisure activities : ♟ ✗ 🎮 evening ☷ ☒ (open-air in season)
multi-sports ground
Facilities : ♿ ⚷ (Jul-Aug) ⛺ ♒ launderette ⚓

GPS Longitude : -1.65491
Latitude : 46.46462

THARON-PLAGE

44730 – Michelin map **316** C5
▶ Paris 444 – Nantes 59 – St-Nazaire 25 – Vannes 94

La Riviera

℘ 02 28 53 54 88, *www.campinglariviera.com* – limited spaces for one-night stay
Address : r. des Gâtineaux (east of the resort, along the D 96,follow the signs for St-Michel-Chef-Chef)
Opening times : from beginning March to end Nov.
6 ha (250 pitches) terraced, stony, flat, grassy
Tariff : (2012 price) ⚑ 5€ ⇔ 🔲 24€ – 🔌 (10A) 4€ – Reservation fee 15€
Rental rates : (2012 price) (from beginning March to end Dec.) – 2 🏠 – 5 🏠.
Per night from 42 to 107€ – Per week from 290 to 750€ – Reservation fee 15€

A mobile-home village for owner-occupiers but pitches for tents and caravans also.

Surroundings : ☐
Leisure activities : ♟ 🖼 jacuzzi ☷ ☒
Facilities : ♿ ⚷ ▥ ⛺ ⚶ ♒ ▣

GPS Longitude : -2.15087
Latitude : 47.16492

The Michelin classification (🏕🏕🏕… 🏕) is totally independent of the official star classification system awarded by the local prefecture or other official organisation.

TENNIE

72240 – Michelin map **310** I6 – pop. 1,023 – alt. 100
▶ Paris 224 – Alençon 49 – Laval 69 – Le Mans 26

Municipal de la Vègre

𝒫 0243205944, *camping.tennie.fr* – limited spaces for one-night stay
Address : r. Andrée Le Grou (take the western exit along the D 38, follow the signs for Ste-Suzanne)
Opening times : from beginning April to end Sept.
2 ha (83 pitches) flat, grassy
Tariff : (2012 price) ⚹ 2.20€ ⟵ 1.50€ 🔲 1.80€ – (½) (6A) 3.25€
Rental rates : (2012 price) (permanent) – 5 🏠 – 1 studio – 1 apartment. Per night from 69€
Per week from 279 to 384€
🚽 sani-station 3.30€ – ⛽ (½)11.39€
In a pleasant setting beside a river and a lake.

Surroundings : ⚲ ⊏ ♋♋
Leisure activities : 🎬 ⚓ ✗ ♪ ⛵
Facilities : ♿ o⟶ 🐕 🖽
Nearby : ✗ ⟍

GPS	Longitude : -0.07874 Latitude : 48.10705

*Routes nationales are main roads and their identifying numbers
begin with N or RN. Routes départementales are generally quieter
roads and begin with D or DN.*

LA TRANCHE-SUR-MER

85360 – Michelin map **316** H9 – pop. 2,715 – alt. 4
▶ Paris 459 – Luçon 31 – Niort 100 – La Rochelle 64

Vagues-Océanes Les Blancs Chênes ♣♣

𝒫 0251304170, *www.vagues-oceanes.com* – limited spaces for one-night stay
Address : rte de la Roche-sur-Yon (2.6km northeast along the D 747)
7 ha (375 pitches) flat, grassy
Rentals : 150 🚐 – 60 🏠.
The site offers several landscaped 'quartiers' (areas) of rental options. No vehicles.

Surroundings : ⊏ ♋
Leisure activities : 🍸 ✗ 🎬 ⊙ ⛼ ♬ ⛲ hammam, jacuzzi ⚓ ♧ ✗ ♪
⛑ ⟍ ⚘ multi-sports ground, spa therapy centre, entertainment room
Facilities : ♿ o⟶ 🐕 ⚑ launderette ♨ ⟍

GPS	Longitude : -1.41958 Latitude : 46.36323

Club Airotel Le Jard ♣♣

𝒫 0251274379, *www.campingdujard.fr* ⚸
Address : 123 bd de Lattre de Tassigny (at La Grière-Plage, 3.8km, follow the signs for L'Aiguillon)
Opening times : from beginning May to beginning Sept.
6 ha (350 pitches) flat, grassy
Tariff : (2012 price) 32€ ⚹⚹ ⟵ 🔲 (½) (10A) – Extra per person 6€ – Reservation fee 25€
Rental rates : (2012 price) (from beginning May to beginning Sept.) ⚸ – 60 🚐.
Per night from 55 to 120€ – Per week from 200 to 810€ – Reservation fee 25€
A pleasant site with good sanitary facilities.

Surroundings : ⊏ ♋♋
Leisure activities : 🍸 ✗ 🎬 ⊙ ⛼ ♬ ⛲ ⚓ ♧ ✗ ♪ ⛑ ⟍ ⚘
Facilities : ♿ o⟶ 🐕 ⚐ ⚑ launderette ♨ ⟍

GPS	Longitude : -1.38694 Latitude : 46.34788

Les Préveils ♣♣

☏ 0251303052, *www.lespreveils.pep79.net*

Address : av. Sainte Anne (at La Grière-Plage, follow the signs for L'Aiguillon for 4.2km)

Opening times : from beginning April to end Sept.

4 ha (180 pitches) flat, sandy, grassy, gently undulating

Tariff : (2012 Price) 32€ ♥♥ ⌂ 🖃 🅑 (10A) – Extra per person 7€ – Reservation fee 18€

Rental rates : (2012 price) (from beginning April to end Sept.) ♿ (1 mobile home) – 36 🛏 – 5 🏠 – 6 ⊨ – 17 apartments. Per night from 56 to 66 € – Per week from 462 to 909€ Reservation fee 18€

A pleasant site 200m from the beach.

Surroundings : ⌂ ⚭

Leisure activities : ✗ 🎱 ⚶ 🎿 ≋ jacuzzi ⛵ 🏊 multi-sports ground, entertainment room

Facilities : ♿ ⚬ 🚿 ⚖ 🚮 🍴 launderette 🚱

GPS Longitude : -1.3936
Latitude : 46.34398

Baie d'Aunis

☏ 0251274736, *www.camping-baiedaunis.com* 🐾 (Jul–Aug)

Address : 10 r. du Pertuis Breton (take the eastern exit, follow the signs for l'Aiguillon)

Opening times : from end April to mid Sept.

2.5 ha (149 pitches) flat, sandy

Tariff : (2012 Price) 34.20€ ♥♥ ⌂ 🖃 🅑 (10A) – Extra per person 7.20€ – Reservation fee 30€

Rental rates : (2012 price) (from end April to mid Sept.) 🐾 – 10 🛏 – 9 🏠. Per week from 320 to 850€ – Reservation fee 30€

🚐 sani-station

The site is just 50m from the beach, but choose pitches away from the road in preferences.

Surroundings : ⌂ ⚭

Leisure activities : ▼ ✗ 🎱 ⛵ 🏊

Facilities : ♿ ⚬ 🎱 🚿 🍴 launderette 🚱

Nearby : ✗ 🎣 ⚓

GPS Longitude : -1.4321
Latitude : 46.34602

TRIAIZE

85580 – Michelin map **316** I9 – pop. 1,011 – alt. 3

▶ Paris 446 – Fontenay-le-Comte 38 – Luçon 9 – Niort 71

Municipal

☏ 0251561276, *mairie.triaize@wanadoo.fr*

Address : r. du Stade (in the village)

Opening times : from beginning July to end Aug.

2.7 ha (70 pitches) flat, grassy, stony, lake

Tariff : (2012 price) ♥ 2.55€ ⌂ 1.75€ 🖃 2.15€ – 🅑 (20A) 2.70€

Rental rates : (2012 price) (permanent) 🐾 – 6 🛏. Per week from 210 to 410€

Surroundings : �‚ ⌂

Leisure activities : ⛵ 🎣

Facilities : ♿ 📮 🖼

Nearby : ✗

GPS Longitude : -1.20152
Latitude : 46.39515

Do not confuse:
▲ to ▲▲▲ : MICHELIN classification
with
★ to ★★★★★ : official classification

LA TURBALLE

44420 – Michelin map **316** A3 – pop. 4,515 – alt. 6
▶ Paris 457 – La Baule 13 – Guérande 7 – Nantes 84

Municipal les Chardons Bleus

☏ 02 40 62 80 60, *www.camping-laturballe.fr*
Address : bd de La Grande Falaise (2.5km to the south)
Opening times : from end March to end Sept.
5 ha (300 pitches) flat, grassy, sandy
Tariff : (2012 price) 22.85€ ♣♣ ⇌ 回 ⑭ (10A) – Extra per person 5€ – Reservation fee 10€
Rental rates : (2012 price) (from mid Jan. to mid Dec.) ⅙ (2 chalets) – 10 ⌂.
Per week from 270 to 640€ – Reservation fee 10€
⬭ 29 回 19.80€
For lovers of wide, open spaces; near the beach.

Surroundings : ⌂ ⬭ ⛺
Leisure activities : ▼ ✗ ⬜ ⛴ ⌇
Facilities : ⅙ ⊶ ⌂ ⍦ launderette ⬭ ⅊
Nearby : ⚲ ⅄ **fitness trail**

Longitude : -2.50048
Latitude : 47.32832

Parc Ste-Brigitte

☏ 02 40 24 88 91, *www.campingsaintebrigitte.com*
Address : chemin des Routes (3km southeast, follow the signs for Guérande)
Opening times : from beginning April to end Sept.
10 ha/4 ha for camping (150 pitches) relatively flat, flat, grassy, lake
Tariff : ♣ 6.70€ ⇌ 3.45€ 回 7.65€ – ⑭ (10A) 6.65€ – Reservation fee 16€
Rental rates : (from beginning April to end Sept.) – 15 ⍦. Per night from 55 to 95€
Per week from 380 to 760€ – Reservation fee 16€
⬭ sani-station
Pretty grounds and manor house. The ageing sanitary facilities are fortunately well maintained.

Surroundings : ⌂ ⅏
Leisure activities : ✗ ⬜ ⛴ ⚲ ▣ (open-air in season) ⌇
Facilities : ⅙ ⊶ ⌂ ⍦ ⍦ launderette ⅊

Longitude : -2.4717
Latitude : 47.34254

The information in the guide may have changed since going to press.

VAIRÉ

85150 – Michelin map **316** F8 – pop. 1,474 – alt. 49
▶ Paris 448 – Challans 31 – La Mothe-Achard 9 – La Roche-sur-Yon 27

Le Roc

☏ 02 51 33 71 89, *www.campingleroc.com*
Address : rte de Brem-sur-Mer (located 1.5km northwest along the D 32, follow the signs for Landevieille and turn left towards Brem-sur-Mer)
Opening times : from end Feb. to mid Nov.
1.4 ha (100 pitches) relatively flat, grassy
Tariff : (2012 price) 29€ ♣♣ ⇌ 回 ⑭ (6A) – Extra per person 5€ – Reservation fee 20€
Rental rates : (2012 price) (from end Feb. to mid Nov.) – 28 ⍦ – 3 ⌂ – 2 tent bungalows.
Per night 90€ – Per week from 125 to 815€ – Reservation fee 20€
⬭ sani-station 3€ – 3 回 10€
Shaded setting, but choose pitches away from the road in preference.

Surroundings : ⬭ ♀
Leisure activities : ▼ ✗ ⅃ ⛴ ▣ (small swimming pool) ⌇
Facilities : ⅙ ⊶ (Jul–Aug) ⍦ ⌂ ⍦ launderette

Longitude : -1.76785
Latitude : 46.60815

VARENNES-SUR-LOIRE

49730 – Michelin map **317** J5 – pop. 1,898 – alt. 27
🚗 Paris 292 – Bourgueil 15 – Chinon 22 – Loudun 30

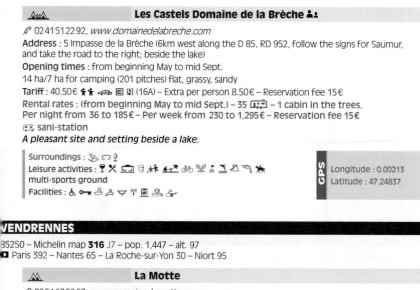

Les Castels Domaine de la Brèche ♣♣

☎ 02 41 51 22 92, *www.domainedelabreche.com*
Address : 5 Impasse de la Brèche (6km west along the D 85, RD 952, follow the signs for Saumur, and take the road to the right; beside the lake)
Opening times : from beginning May to mid Sept.
14 ha/7 ha for camping (201 pitches) flat, grassy, sandy
Tariff : 40.50€ ♥♥ ⇔ 🗐 🗐 (16A) – Extra per person 8.50€ – Reservation fee 15€
Rental rates : (from beginning May to mid Sept.) – 35 🚐 – 1 cabin in the trees.
Per night from 36 to 185€ – Per week from 230 to 1,295€ – Reservation fee 15€
🚽 sani-station
A pleasant site and setting beside a lake.

Surroundings : 🏕 ☐ 🌳
Leisure activities : ♟ ✕ 🏠 🗓 🛝 🏊 🚲 🎯 🎣 🛶 ⛵ 🚣 🐎
multi-sports ground
Facilities : ☕ ☚ 🏖 🧺 🚽 🍴 🗑 🛁 🚿

GPS Longitude : 0.00213
Latitude : 47.24837

VENDRENNES

85250 – Michelin map **316** J7 – pop. 1,447 – alt. 97
🚗 Paris 392 – Nantes 65 – La Roche-sur-Yon 30 – Niort 95

La Motte

☎ 02 51 63 59 67, *www.camping-lamotte.com*
Address : at La Motte (0.4km to the northeast)
Opening times : Permanent
3.5 ha (83 pitches) flat, grassy
Tariff : 19€ ♥♥ ⇔ 🗐 🗐 (16A) – Extra per person 3.50€
Rental rates : (2012 price) (permanent) – 33 🚐 – 3 🏠. Per night from 50 to 180€
Per week from 220 to 1,000€

A green, floral setting around an ornamental lake.

Surroundings : 🏕 ☐
Leisure activities : ♟ ✕ 🏠 🗓 daytime 🛝 🏊 bowling
Facilities : ☕ ☚ 🏖 🧺 🍴 launderette 🚿

GPS Longitude : -1.11854
Latitude : 46.82587

Gîtes range from small maisonettes to old farmhouses with several bedrooms.

VIHIERS

49310 – Michelin map **317** F6 – pop. 4,275 – alt. 100
🚗 Paris 334 – Angers 45 – Cholet 29 – Saumur 40

Municipal de la Vallée du Lys

☎ 02 41 75 00 14, *www.vihiers.fr* – 🅱
Address : rte du Voide (take the western exit along the D 960, follow the signs for Cholet then take the D 54 to the right, following signs for Valanjou; beside the Lys river)
Opening times : from mid June to mid Sept.
0.3 ha (30 pitches) flat, grassy
Tariff : (2012 price) ♥ 2€ ⇔ 🗐 2.55€ – 🗐 (6A) 1.95€

Surroundings : 🏕 🌳
Leisure activities : 🏠 🛝 🎣
Facilities : ☕ 🗑

GPS Longitude : -0.54034
Latitude : 47.1471

VILLIERS-CHARLEMAGNE

53170 – Michelin map **310** E7 – pop. 1,052 – alt. 105
▶ Paris 277 – Angers 61 – Châteaubriant 61 – Château-Gontier 12

Village Vacances Pêche

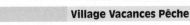

✆ 02 43 07 71 68, *villiers-charlemagne.mairie53.fr*
Address : Village des Haies (take the western exit along the D 4, follow the signs for Cossé-le-Vivien and take road to the left near the stadium)
Opening times : Permanent
9 ha/1 ha for camping (20 pitches) flat, grassy
Tariff : (2012 Price) 16.60€ ♦♦ ⇌ 🗐 🕼 (16A) – Extra per person 5.90€
Rental rates : (permanent) – 12 🏠. Per night from 120 to 260€ – Per week from 200 to 575 €
Reservation fee 13€
🚐 sani-station 7.70€
A pleasant site for fishing, with chalets situated right by the waterfront.

Surroundings : 🐟 ⇐ 🖵 🌳
Leisure activities : 🖵 🎦 daytime 🏌 🚴 🎣
Facilities : ⚐ ⊸ 🛁 – 20 individual sanitary facilities (🚿 ⚲ 🚽 wc) 🛁 🚰
🗊 refrigerators
Nearby : 🎾 🎣

GPS Longitude : -0.68233
Latitude : 47.9208

YVRÉ-L'ÉVÊQUE

72530 – Michelin map **310** K6 – pop. 4,412 – alt. 57
▶ Paris 204 – Nantes 194 – Le Mans 8 – Alençon 66

Le Pont Romain

✆ 02 43 82 25 39, *www.lepontromain.com*
Address : at La Châtaigneraie (leave the village via the the Roman bridge, then take the road to the left, continue for 200m)
Opening times : from mid March to mid Nov.
2.5 ha (80 pitches) flat, grassy
Tariff : (2012 price) 21.75€ ♦♦ ⇌ 🗐 🕼 (16A) – Extra per person 4.19€ – Reservation fee 5€
Rental rates : (2012 price) (from mid March to mid Nov.) 🏕 🅿 – 5 🏚 – 5 🏠 – 3 tent bungalows. Per night from 37 to 76€ – Per week from 215 to 425€ – Reservation fee 15€
🚐 sani-station 3€ – 15 🗐 21.75€

Surroundings : 🌳
Leisure activities : 🖵 🏌 🛝
Facilities : ⊸ 🅿 🎞 🛁 🚰 🚰 launderette
Nearby : 🛥 🍷 ✕

GPS Longitude : 0.27972
Latitude : 48.01944

PICARDY

Philippe Renault / hemis.fr

Are you ready for an action-packed journey through Picardy's fair and historic lands? The region that gave Gaul – now France – her first Christian king, Clovis, is renowned for its wealthy Cistercian abbeys, splendid Gothic cathedrals and flamboyant town halls, along with deeply poignant reminders of two world wars. If you are in the mood to explore the countryside, take a boat trip through the floating gardens of Amiens or explore the botanical reserve of Marais de Cessière. Try a spot of birdwatching on the Somme estuary or at Marquenterre bird sanctuary. Spend time relaxing in unspoilt hills, woods, pastures and vineyards. Picardy has a rich culinary history, so where better to try *soupe aux hortillonages* (vegetable gardener's soup), the famous *agneau pré-salé* (lamb fattened on the salt marshes), a plate of smoked eel or duck pâté, or a dessert laced with Chantilly cream. 'Drink well, eat well and do nothing', to quote Lafleur, the famous 19th-century Amiens puppet.

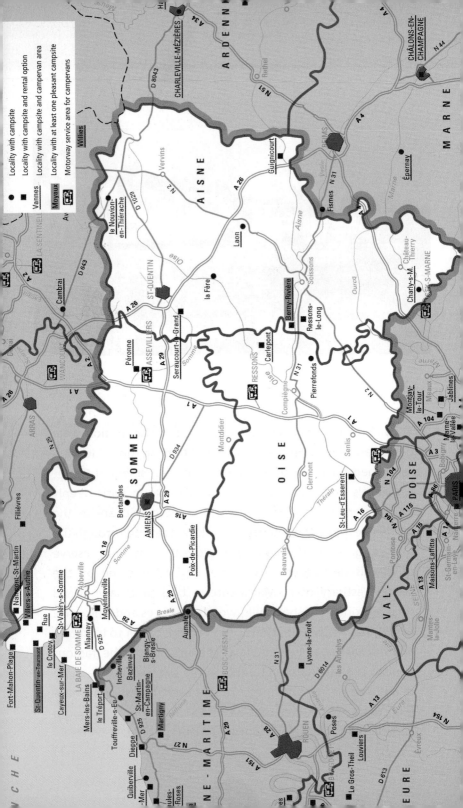

- Locality with campsite
- Locality with campsite and rental option
- Locality with campsite and campervan area
- Locality with at least one pleasant campsite
- Motorway service area for campervans

Vannes

Moyaux

AMIENS

80000 – Michelin map **301** G8 – pop. 133,998 – alt. 34
▶ Paris 135 – Lille 122 – Beauvais 62 – Arras 74

Le Parc des Cygnes

ℰ 03 22 43 29 28, *www.parcdescygnes.com*
Address : 111 av. des Cygnes (ou r. du Grand Marais) (to the northeast, from bypass (rocade), take exit 40 for Amiens Longpré)
Opening times : from beginning April to mid Oct.
3.2 ha (145 pitches) flat, grassy, lake
Tariff : (2012 price) 25.80€ ✝✝ ⇔ 🔲 (4) (10A) – Extra per person 6.20€ – Reservation fee 13€
Rental rates : (2012 price) (permanent) ⚡ – 9 🚐. Per night from 44 to 99 €
Per week from 260 to 614 € – Reservation fee 13€
🚐 sani-station 11.60€ – 🔋 (4)16€
A bus serves the town centre.

Surroundings : 🌳
Leisure activities : 🍽 🏊 ⚽ 🚲 🎣
Facilities : ♿ ⚡ 🧺 🚿 🧴 ♻ 🍴 launderette
Nearby : 🎣

GPS
Longitude : 2.25918
Latitude : 49.92118

BERNY-RIVIÈRE

02290 – Michelin map **306** A6 – pop. 604 – alt. 49
▶ Paris 100 – Compiègne 24 – Laon 55 – Noyon 28

La Croix du Vieux Pont ♣♠

ℰ 03 23 55 50 02, *www.la-croix-du-vieux-pont.com* – limited spaces for one-night stay
Address : r. de la Fabrique (located 1.5km south on the D 91, at the entrance to Vic-sur-Aisne; beside the Aisne river)
Opening times : permanent
34 ha (520 pitches) flat, grassy, lake
Tariff : 28.50€ ✝✝ ⇔ 🔲 (4) (6A) – Extra per person 8.50€
Rental rates : (from beginning April to end Oct.) ♿ (mobile home) ⚡ – 11 🏠.
Per night from 120 € – Per week from 400 to 1,150 €
🚐 sani-station 26€

Surroundings : 🏞 🎣
Leisure activities : 🍽 ✕ 🏊 🍳 🏸 🎣 ♨ jacuzzi ⚽ 🚲 🎾 🏓 🔲 🏊
🏊 (lake) 🛶 🎣 🐴 disco, pedalos, climbing wall, multi-sports ground
Facilities : ♿ ⚡ ✉ 🔲 🧺 🚿 🧴 ♻ 🍴 launderette 🏊 ⛽

GPS
Longitude : 3.1284
Latitude : 49.40495

BERTANGLES

80260 – Michelin map **301** G8 – pop. 591 – alt. 95
▶ Paris 154 – Abbeville 44 – Amiens 11 – Bapaume 49

Le Château

ℰ 03 60 65 68 36, *http://www.chateaubertangles.com*
Address : r. du Château (in the village)
Opening times : from mid April to mid Sept.
0.7 ha (33 pitches) flat, grassy
Tariff : ✝ 4.30€ ⇔ 2.70€ 🔲 4.20€ – (4) (5A) 3.70€
The site is in an orchard, near the château.

Surroundings : 🏞 🌳
Leisure activities : ⚽
Facilities : ♿ 🚿 ✉

GPS
Longitude : 2.30131
Latitude : 49.97167

CARLEPONT

60170 – Michelin map **305** J3 – pop. 1,416 – alt. 59
▶ Paris 103 – Compiègne 19 – Ham 30 – Pierrefonds 21

Les Araucarias

✆ 03 44 75 27 39, *www.camping-les-araucarias.com* – limited spaces for one-night stay
Address : 870 r. du Gén. Leclerc (take the southwestern exit along the D 130, follow the signs for Compiègne)
Opening times : from beginning April to end Oct.
1.2 ha (60 pitches) flat and relatively flat, grassy
Tariff : ✚ 3€ ⇌ 2€ 🅴 3.20€ – (½) (10A) 3€
Rental rates : (permanent) – 6 🚐 – 2 🏠. Per night from 60 to 70 €
Per week from 200 to 400 €
🚽 sani-station 3€ – 3 🅴 14.70€
On the site of a former arboretum, so there's a wide range of trees around the campsite.

Surroundings : 🏞 🛏 ♨♨
Leisure activities : ⛱
Facilities : ♿ ⊙ ▥ ᵞ launderette

GPS
Longitude : 3.01836
Latitude : 49.50728

We welcome your feedback on our listed campsites.
Please email us at: campingfrance@tp.michelin.com
Many thanks in advance!

CAYEUX-SUR-MER

80410 – Michelin map **301** B6 – pop. 2,813 – alt. 2
▶ Paris 217 – Abbeville 29 – Amiens 82 – Le Crotoy 26

Les Galets de la Mollière ♣♦

✆ 03 22 26 61 85, *www.campinglesgaletsdelamolliere.com*
Address : at Mollière, r. Faidherbe (3.3km northeast along the D 102, follow coastal road)
Opening times : from end March to beginning Nov.
6 ha (198 pitches) flat and relatively flat, sandy, grassy
Tariff : 32€ ✚✚ ⇌ 🅴 (½) (10A) – Extra per person 7€ – Reservation fee 10€
Rental rates : (from end March to beginning Nov.) – 39 🚐. Per night from 70 to 95 €
Per week from 220 to 720 € – Reservation fee 10€
🚽 sani-station 3€ – 50 🅴 5€

Surroundings : 🏞 🛏
Leisure activities : ᵞ ✗ 🎦 ⛹ ⛱ ❇ ⛵
Facilities : ♿ ⊙ △ ᵞ launderette

GPS
Longitude : 1.52608
Latitude : 50.20275

Le Bois de Pins

✆ 03 22 26 71 04, *www.campingleboisdepins.com* – limited spaces for one-night stay
Address : at Brighton, av. Guillaume-le-Conquérant (situated 2km northeast along the D 102, coast road, 500m from the sea)
Opening times : from beginning April to beginning Nov.
4 ha (163 pitches) flat, grassy
Tariff : 25€ ✚✚ ⇌ 🅴 (½) (10A) – Extra per person 7€ – Reservation fee 10€

Surroundings : 🏞 🛏 ♨
Leisure activities : 🎦 ⛱
Facilities : ♿ ⊙ ▥ ᵞ launderette
Nearby : ᵞ ✗

GPS
Longitude : 1.51709
Latitude : 50.19725

CHARLY-SUR-MARNE

02310 – Michelin map **306** B9 – pop. 2,741 – alt. 63
▶ Paris 82 – Château-Thierry 14 – Coulommiers 33 – La Ferté-sous-Jouarre 16

Municipal des Illettes

⌖ 03 23 82 12 11, *www.charly-sur-marne.fr*
Address : rte de Pavant (south of the town, 200m from the D 82 (recommended route)
Opening times : from beginning April to end Sept.
1.2 ha (43 pitches) flat, grassy, gravelled
Tariff : (2012 price) 17.50€ � ♦ 🚐 ▣ (10A) – Extra per person 4€
🚰 sani-station 3€

Surroundings : 🗆 ♀♀
Leisure activities : 🔲
Facilities : ♿ 🔌 ⚑ 🅿 ⫿ ☂ ▽ launderette
Nearby : 🛒 ✗ 🎣

GPS Longitude : 3.28209
Latitude : 48.97369

*For more information on visiting particular towns or regions, consult the
relevant regional MICHELIN Green Guide. We also recommend you use
the appropriate Michelin regional map to locate your selected campsite,
to calculate distances and to work out the best route.*

LE CROTOY

80550 – Michelin map **301** C6 – pop. 2,265 – alt. 1
▶ Paris 210 – Abbeville 22 – Amiens 75 – Berck-sur-Mer 29

Le Ridin

⌖ 03 22 27 03 22, *www.campingleridin.com* – limited spaces for one-night stay
Address : at Mayocq (3km north following signs for St-Quentin-en-Tourmont and take the road
to the right)
Opening times : from end March to beginning Nov.
4.5 ha (162 pitches) flat, grassy
Tariff : 30€ ♦ ♦ 🚐 ▣ (10A) – Extra per person 5.80€
Rental rates : (from end March to beginning Nov.) – 28 🏚 – 2 apartments.
Per night from 52 to 105 € – Per week from 260 to 735 € – Reservation fee 15€
🚰 sani-station 15€ – 10 ▣ 15€

Surroundings : 🏞 🗆 ♀
Leisure activities : ♟ ✗ 🔲 ♨ jacuzzi 🏊 🚲 ⚓
Facilities : ♿ 🔌 ▣ ⫿ ⛺ ⫿ launderette ⚘

GPS Longitude : 1.63182
Latitude : 50.23905

Flower Les Aubépines

⌖ 03 22 27 01 34, *www.camping-lesaubepines.com* – limited spaces for one-night stay
Address : at St-Firmin, 800 r. de la Maye (4km to the north, follow the signs for St-Quentin-en-
Tourmont and take road to the left)
Opening times : from end March to beginning Nov.
2.5 ha (196 pitches) flat, grassy, sandy
Tariff : 30€ ♦ ♦ 🚐 ▣ (10A) – Extra per person 5.80€ – Reservation fee 15€
Rental rates : (from end March to beginning Nov.) – 36 🏚 – 5 🏠. Per night from 50 to 143 €
Per week from 250 to 959 € – Reservation fee 15€
🚰 sani-station 16€ – 5 ▣ 16€

Surroundings : 🏞 🗆 ♀
Leisure activities : 🔲 🏊 🚲 ⚓
Facilities : ♿ 🔌 ⫿ ⛺ ☂ ⫿ launderette

GPS Longitude : 1.61139
Latitude : 50.24955

Les Trois Sablières

⌂ 03 22 27 01 33, *www.camping-les-trois-sablieres.com* – limited spaces for one-night stay

Address : 1850 r. de la Maye (4km to the northwest, follow the signs for St-Quentin-en-Tourmont and take the road to the left, 400m from the beach)

Opening times : from end March to beginning Nov.

1.5 ha (97 pitches) flat, grassy, sandy

Tariff : 29.50€ ✝✝ ⇦ 🔲 🔋 (10A) – Extra per person 6.50€

Rental rates : (from end March to beginning Nov.) – 17 🚐 – 2 🏠 – 2 gîtes.
Per night from 55 to 100 € – Per week from 260 to 690 €

🚗 sani-station 6€ – 🔋11.50€

In a green setting with flowers.

Surroundings : 🔧 ⌂ ♀
Leisure activities : 🍽 🎦 🎣 ⛵ ⛱ 🏊
Facilities : ♿ ⊶ 🛁 🚾 launderette

GPS Longitude : 1.59883
Latitude : 50.24825

LA FÈRE

02800 – Michelin map **306** C5 – pop. 3,012 – alt. 54
▶ Paris 137 – Compiègne 59 – Laon 24 – Noyon 31

Municipal du Marais de la Fontaine

⌂ 03 23 56 82 94

Address : r. Vauban (via the town centre towards Tergnier and take a right turn at the sports centre; near a branch of the Oise river)

0.7 ha (26 pitches) flat, grassy

Surroundings : ⌂ ♀
Facilities : ♿ ⊶
Nearby : ✕

GPS Longitude : 3.36353
Latitude : 49.6654

*The prices listed were supplied by the campsite owners in 2012
(if prices were not available, those from the previous year are given).
The fees should be regarded as basic charges and may fluctuate
with inflation.*

FORT-MAHON-PLAGE

80120 – Michelin map **301** C5 – pop. 1,311 – alt. 2
▶ Paris 225 – Abbeville 41 – Amiens 90 – Berck-sur-Mer 19

Club Airotel Le Royon

⌂ 03 22 23 40 30, *www.campingleroyon.com* – limited spaces for one-night stay

Address : 1271 rte de Quend (located 1km to the south)

Opening times : from mid March to end Oct.

4 ha (399 pitches) flat, grassy, sandy

Tariff : 34€ ✝✝ ⇦ 🔲 🔋 (6A) – Extra per person 7€ – Reservation fee 12€

Rental rates : (from mid March to end Oct.) ✕ – 85 🚐. Per night from 70 to 95 €
Per week from 220 to 755 € – Reservation fee 12€

🚗 sani-station 3€ – 10 🔲 19€ – 🔋16€

Surroundings : ⌂ ♀
Leisure activities : 🍽 ⛱ ✕ 🔲 🏊 entertainment room
Facilities : ♿ ⊶ 🏪 🛁 🏊 🚾 launderette
Nearby : 🏇

GPS Longitude : 1.57963
Latitude : 50.33263

Le Vert Gazon

📞 03 22 23 37 69, *www.camping-levertgazon.com* – limited spaces for one-night stay
Address : 741 rte de Quend
Opening times : from beginning April to beginning Oct.
2.5 ha (130 pitches) flat, grassy
Tariff : (2012 price) 25.90€ ✶✶ ⇔ 🔲 🔌 (6A) – Extra per person 7€ – Reservation fee 10€
Rental rates : (2012 price) (permanent) ♿ (1 mobile home) – 1 'gypsy' caravan – 14 🚐 –
4 🏠 – 4 gîtes. Per week from 345 to 609 € – Reservation fee 10€
🚐 sani-station 5€ – 2 🔲 25€
Surroundings : 🔲
Leisure activities : 🍴 🔲 ⚓ 🚴 🏊
Facilities : ♿ 🔲 🚿 👕 launderette

Longitude : 1.57374
Latitude : 50.33438

GUIGNICOURT

02190 – Michelin map **306** F6 – pop. 2,131 – alt. 67
▶ Paris 165 – Laon 40 – Reims 33 – Rethel 39

Municipal du Bord de l'Aisne

📞 03 23 79 74 58, *www.camping-aisne-picardie.fr*
Address : 14 r. des Godins (take the southeastern exit along the D 925 and take right turn)
Opening times : from beginning April to end Oct.
1.5 ha (100 pitches) flat, grassy
Tariff : 27.70€ ✶✶ ⇔ 🔲 🔌 (10A) – Extra per person 8.20€
Rental rates : (from mid March to end Dec.) ✂ – 10 🚐. Per night from 47 to 101 €
Per week from 275 to 627 € – Reservation fee 10€
🚐 sani-station 2€ – 2 🔲 14€
Situated beside the Aisne river.

Surroundings : 🌿
Leisure activities : ✂
Facilities : 🔌 🏛 👕

Longitude : 3.97066
Latitude : 49.43251

There are several different types of sani-station
('borne' in French) – sanitation points providing
fresh water and disposal points for grey water.
See page 12 for further details.

LAON

02000 – Michelin map **306** D5 – pop. 26,094 – alt. 181
▶ Paris 141 – Amiens 122 – Charleville-Mézières 124 – Compiègne 74

Municipal la Chênaie

📞 03 23 20 25 56, *www.ville-laon.fr*
Address : allée de la Chênaie (4km southwest of the station, access via the road near the Foch barracks, at the entrance to the suburb of Semilly; 100m from a small lake)
1 ha (55 pitches) undulating, flat, grassy, stony
🚐 sani-station
Surroundings : 🔲 🌿
Facilities : ♿ 🔌

Longitude : 3.59488
Latitude : 49.56244

MERS-LES-BAINS

80350 – Michelin map **301** B7 – pop. 3,124 – alt. 3
▶ Paris 217 – Amiens 89 – Rouen 99 – Arras 130

Flower Le Domaine du Rompval

✆ 02 35 84 43 21, *www.campinglerompval.com*
Address : at Blengues (situated 2km to the northeast)
3 ha (132 pitches) flat, grassy
Rentals : 13 ⬛ – 5 studios – 2 tent bungalows.
⬛ sani-station
The architecture of the studio accommodation is very unusual.

Surroundings : ♀
Leisure activities : ♈ ⬛ 🛶 🚲 ⬛ (open-air in season)
Facilities : ♿ ⛟ 🛁 ⛺ 🍴 launderette

GPS Longitude : 1.4154
Latitude : 50.0773

MIANNAY

80132 – Michelin map **301** D7 – pop. 568 – alt. 15
▶ Paris 191 – Amiens 63 – Arras 104 – Rouen 109

Le Clos Cacheleux

✆ 03 22 19 17 47, *www.camping-lecloscacheleux.fr*
Address : rte de Bouillancourt-sous-Miannay
Opening times : from mid March to mid Oct.
8 ha (100 pitches) relatively flat, flat, grassy
Tariff : 27.10€ ♈♈ 🚗 ⬛ 💡 (10A) – Extra per person 5.60€ – Reservation fee 12€
⬛ 3 ⬛ 27.10€ – 🔌 11€
In the grounds of a working farm (cattle-rearing).

Surroundings : ⬛ ♀
Leisure activities : 🛶
Facilities : ♿ ⛟ ⛺ 🍴 launderette
Nearby : ♈ ✕ ⬛ 🚴 🛶 ⬛ (open-air in season), activities at the Le Val
de Trie, opposite

GPS Longitude : 1.71536
Latitude : 50.08646

To visit a town or region, use the MICHELIN Green Guides.

MOYENNEVILLE

80870 – Michelin map **301** D7 – pop. 667 – alt. 92
▶ Paris 194 – Abbeville 9 – Amiens 59 – Blangy-sur-Bresle 22

Le Val de Trie ♣⸱

✆ 03 22 31 48 88, *www.camping-levaldetrie.fr*
Address : 1 r. des Sources at Bouillancourt-sous-Miannay (3km northwest along the D 86;
beside a stream)
Opening times : from end March to mid Oct.
2 ha (100 pitches) flat, grassy, small lake
Tariff : 27.10€ ♈♈ 🚗 ⬛ 💡 (10A) – Extra per person 5.60€ – Reservation fee 12€
Rental rates : (from end March to mid Oct.) ♿ (chalet) 🚫 – 19 ⬛ – 5 ⬛.
Per night from 49 to 155 € – Per week from 326 to 1,085 € – Reservation fee 12€
⬛ 15 ⬛ 27.10€

Surroundings : 🌳 ⬛ ♀♀
Leisure activities : ♈ ✕ ⬛ 🚴 🛶 ⬛ (open-air in season)
Facilities : ♿ ⛟ 🆑 ⬛ ⛺ ⛲ 🍴 launderette

GPS Longitude : 1.71508
Latitude : 50.08552

NAMPONT-ST-MARTIN

80120 – Michelin map **301** D5 – pop. 260 – alt. 10

Paris 214 – Abbeville 30 – Amiens 79 – Boulogne-sur-Mer 52

La Ferme des Aulnes

03 22 29 22 69, *www.fermedesaulnes.com* – limited spaces for one-night stay

Address : at Fresne, 1 r. du Marais (3km southwest along the D 85e, follow the signs for Villier-sur-Authie)

4 ha (120 pitches) relatively flat, flat, grassy

Rentals : 19 ⬛ – 19 ⬛.

sani-station – 11 ▣

The site is based around an old Picardy farmhouse.

Surroundings : ⬛ ⬛ ⬛
Leisure activities : ⬛ ✗ ⬛ ⬛ (piano bar) ⬛ ⬛ jacuzzi ⬛ ⬛
(open-air in season), entertainment room
Facilities : ⬛ ⬛ ⬛ ⬛ ⬛ ⬛ launderette ⬛

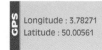

Longitude : 1.71201
Latitude : 50.33631

LE NOUVION-EN-THIÉRACHE

02170 – Michelin map **306** E2 – pop. 2,809 – alt. 185

Paris 198 – Avesnes-sur-Helpe 20 – Le Cateau-Cambrésis 19 – Guise 21

Municipal du Lac de Condé

03 23 98 98 58, www.camping-thierache.com

Address : promenade Henri d'Orléans (situated 2km south along the D 26 and take the road to the left)

Opening times : from beginning April to end Sept.

1.3 ha (56 pitches) flat and relatively flat

Tariff : (2012 price) 12.90€ ⬛ ⬛ ⬛ ▣ ⬛ (8A) – Extra per person 3.40€

sani-station 2€

On the edge of the forest, near a lake and a leisure park.

Surroundings : ⬛ ⬛
Leisure activities : ⬛
Facilities : ⬛ ⬛ ⬛
Nearby : ⬛ ✗ ⬛ ⬛ ⬛ ⬛ bowling, mountain biking

Longitude : 3.78271
Latitude : 50.00561

PÉRONNE

80200 – Michelin map **301** K8 – pop. 7,981 – alt. 52

Paris 141 – Amiens 58 – Arras 48 – Doullens 54

Port de Plaisance

03 22 84 19 31, www.camping-plaisance.com

Address : take the southern exit, following the signs for Paris, near the marina and the commercial port; beside the Canal de la Somme

Opening times : from beginning March to end Oct.

2 ha (90 pitches) flat, grassy, fine gravel

Tariff : (2012 price) 23€ ⬛ ⬛ ⬛ ▣ ⬛ (6A) – Extra per person 4€

Rental rates : (2012 price) (from beginning March to end Oct.) – 4 ⬛. Per night from 78 €
Per week from 287 to 513 €

sani-station 23€

Surroundings : ⬛ ⬛
Leisure activities : ⬛ ⬛ ⬛ ⬛ ⬛
Facilities : ⬛ ⬛ ⬛ ⬛ ⬛ launderette
Nearby : ⬛ ⬛

Longitude : 2.93237
Latitude : 49.91786

PIERREFONDS

60350 – Michelin map **305** I4 – pop. 1,969 – alt. 81
▶ Paris 82 – Beauvais 78 – Compiègne 15 – Crépy-en-Valois 17

⚠ Municipal de Batigny

𝒫 03 44 42 80 83, *mairie@mairie-pierrefonds.fr*
Address : r. de l'Armistice (take northwestern exit along the D 973, follow the signs for Compiègne)
1 ha (60 pitches) terraced, flat, grassy
The site has attractive trees and shrubs.

Surroundings : ⌷ 0 0
Leisure activities : ⚓⛱
Facilities : ⚡ ▥ ⌂ ⌣ ▣
Nearby : ✕

GPS Longitude : 2.97962
Latitude : 49.35194

POIX-DE-PICARDIE

80290 – Michelin map **301** E9 – pop. 2,388 – alt. 106
▶ Paris 133 – Abbeville 45 – Amiens 31 – Beauvais 46

⚠ Municipal le Bois des Pêcheurs

𝒫 03 22 90 11 71, *www.ville-poix-de-picardie.fr*
Address : rte de Verdun (take the western exit along the D 919, follow the signs for Formerie, beside a stream)
Opening times : from beginning April to end Sept.
2 ha (135 pitches) flat, grassy
Tariff : 18€ ✶✶ ⟺ ▣ ⚡ (10A) – Extra per person 2€
Rental rates : (from beginning April to end Sept.) – 2 ⛺. Per night from 100 €
Per week from 250 to 300 €
⛽ sani-station 2€

Surroundings : ⌷ 0
Leisure activities : ▭ ⚓⛱ ⚲
Facilities : ⅊ ⚡ �>⌣ ⍦ launderette
Nearby : ⛒ ✕ ▣

GPS Longitude : 1.9743
Latitude : 49.75

> *Routes nationales are main roads and their identifying numbers*
> *begin with N or RN. Routes départementales are generally quieter*
> *roads and begin with D or DN.*

RESSONS-LE-LONG

02290 – Michelin map **306** A6 – pop. 756 – alt. 72
▶ Paris 97 – Compiègne 26 – Laon 53 – Noyon 31

⛰ La Halte de Mainville

𝒫 03 23 74 26 69, *www.lahaltedemainville.com*
Address : 18 r.du Routy (take the northeastern exit)
Opening times : from mid Jan. to beginning Dec.
5 ha (155 pitches) flat, grassy, small lake
Tariff : (2012 price) 20.50€ ✶✶ ⟺ ▣ ⚡ (8A) – Extra per person 4€
Rental rates : (2012 price) (from beginning April to end Oct.) – 2 ⛺ – 2 ⌂.
Per night 125€ – Per week 455€

Surroundings : ⌷ 0
Leisure activities : ▭ ⚓⛱ ⛴ ⍦
Facilities : ⅊ ⚡ ⌣ ⍰ ▥ ⌂ ⍦ launderette

GPS Longitude : 3.15186
Latitude : 49.39277

RUE

80120 – Michelin map **301** D6 – pop. 3,095 – alt. 9
▶ Paris 212 – Abbeville 28 – Amiens 77 – Berck-Plage 22

⚠ Les Oiseaux

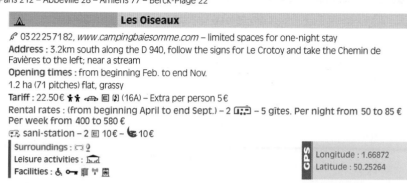

℘ 03 22 25 71 82, *www.campingbaiesomme.com* – limited spaces for one-night stay
Address : 3.2km south along the D 940, follow the signs for Le Crotoy and take the Chemin de Favières to the left; near a stream
Opening times : from beginning Feb. to end Nov.
1.2 ha (71 pitches) flat, grassy
Tariff : 22.50€ ✱ ✱ ⊂⊃ 回 ⸨⸩ (16A) – Extra per person 5€
Rental rates : (from beginning April to end Sept.) – 2 ⸨⸩ – 5 gîtes. Per night from 50 to 85 €
Per week from 400 to 580 €
⚏ sani-station – 2 回 10€ – ⸨ 10€

Surroundings : ⊏⊐ ♀	GPS
Leisure activities : 🖼	Longitude : 1.66872
Facilities : & ⊶ ▥ ⸿ 🖼	Latitude : 50.25264

ST-LEU-D'ESSERENT

60340 – Michelin map **305** F5 – pop. 4,708 – alt. 50 – Leisure centre
▶ Paris 57 – Beauvais 38 – Chantilly 7 – Creil 9

⚠ Campix

℘ 03 44 56 08 48, *www.campingcampix.com*
Address : r. Pasteur (take the northern exit along the D 12, follow the signs for Cramoisy then continue 1.5km along the turning to the right and then a road)
Opening times : from mid March to end Nov.
6 ha (160 pitches) undulating, terraced, flat, grassy, stony
Tariff : ✱ 7€ ⊂⊃ 回 7€ – ⸨⸩ (6A) 4€
Rental rates : (from mid March to end Nov.) – 4 'gypsy' caravans – 7 ⌂.
Per night from 45 to 115 € – Per week from 85 to 525 €
⚏ sani-station 6€
On the site of an old quarry with plentiful shade, overlooking the town and the Oise river.

Surroundings : ⹋ ⊏⊐ ⸿⸿	GPS
Leisure activities : ✗ 🖼 ⸗ ⸜⸝ 🖼	Longitude : 2.42728
Facilities : & ⊶ ⸩⸨ ▥ ⸜ ⸿ launderette ⸗	Latitude : 49.22484

ST-QUENTIN-EN-TOURMONT

80120 – Michelin map **301** C6 – pop. 305
▶ Paris 218 – Abbeville 29 – Amiens 83 – Berck-sur-Mer 24

⚠ Le Champ Neuf

℘ 03 22 25 07 94, *www.camping-lechampneuf.com* – limited spaces for one-night stay
Address : 8 r. du Champ Neuf
Opening times : from beginning April to end Oct.
8 ha/4.5 ha for camping (157 pitches) flat, grassy, wood
Tariff : (2012 price) 30€ ✱ ✱ ⊂⊃ 回 ⸨⸩ (10A) – Extra per person 6.50€
Rental rates : (2012 price) (from beginning April to end Oct.) – 28 ⸨⸩.
Per night from 56 to 92 € – Per week from 240 to 715 €
⚏ sani-station
An indoor water park.

Surroundings : ⹋ ⊏⊐ ♀	GPS
Leisure activities : ⸙ ✗ 🖼 ⸜⸝ ⸗ ⸜⸝ 🖼 ⸜ multi-sports ground, entertainment room	Longitude : 1.60153
Facilities : & ⊶ ▥ ⸜ ⸿ launderette ⸗	Latitude : 50.26978

ST-VALERY-SUR-SOMME

80230 – Michelin map **301** C6 – pop. 2,873 – alt. 27
▶ Paris 206 – Abbeville 18 – Amiens 71 – Blangy-sur-Bresle 45

Club Airotel Le Walric

✆ 0322268197, *www.campinglewalric.com* – limited spaces for one-night stay
Address : rte d'Eu (to the west along the D 3)
Opening times : from beginning April to end Oct.
5.8 ha (286 pitches) flat, grassy, wood
Tariff : 34€ ✶✶ ⚌ 🅴 🔌 (6A) – Extra per person 7€ – Reservation fee 12€
Rental rates : (from beginning April to end Oct.) – 57 🚐. Per night from 70 to 108 €
Per week from 220 to 755€ – Reservation fee 12€
🚰 sani-station
Surroundings : 🔲 ⚲
Leisure activities : 🍸 🏠 🔲 ⚐ 🏊 ✗ 🛝
Facilities : 🔥 ⚬ 🔲 🛁 🚰 launderette
Nearby : 🛶

Longitude : 1.61791
Latitude : 50.1839

SERAUCOURT-LE-GRAND

02790 – Michelin map **306** B4 – pop. 787 – alt. 102
▶ Paris 148 – Chauny 26 – Ham 16 – Péronne 28

Le Vivier aux Carpes

✆ 0323605010, *www.camping-picardie.com*
Address : 10 r. Charles Voyeux (to the north along the D 321, near the post office, 200m from the Somme)
Opening times : from beginning March to end Oct.
2 ha (60 pitches) flat, grassy
Tariff : 20.50€ ✶✶ ⚌ 🅴 🔌 (10A) – Extra per person 4€
Rental rates : (from beginning March to end Oct.) – 1 🚐 – 2 🏠. Per night from 55 to 65 €
Per week from 65 to 75 €
🚰 sani-station 4€ – 7 🅴 20.50€
A pleasant location beside the lakes.

Surroundings : 🌄 🔲 ⚲⚲
Leisure activities : 🔲 🎣
Facilities : 🔥 ⚬ 🔲 🔲 🚰 launderette
Nearby : 🛶

Longitude : 3.21435
Latitude : 49.78272

VILLERS-SUR-AUTHIE

80120 – Michelin map **301** D6 – pop. 411 – alt. 5
▶ Paris 215 – Abbeville 31 – Amiens 80 – Berck-sur-Mer 16

Le Val d'Authie ⚤

✆ 0322299247, *www.valdauthie.fr* – limited spaces for one-night stay
Address : 20 rte de Vercourt (take the southern exit of the town)
Opening times : from end March to beginning Oct.
7 ha/4 ha for camping (170 pitches) flat, grassy, relatively flat
Tariff : 33€ ✶✶ ⚌ 🅴 🔌 (10A) – Extra per person 6€
Rental rates : (from end March to beginning Oct.) – 25 🚐. Per night from 51 to 114 €
Per week from 357 to 798 €
🚰 6 🅴 20€
Attractive shrubs and vegetation.

Surroundings : 🌄 🔲 ⚲⚲
Leisure activities : 🍸 ✗ 🔲 ⚐ 🏋 ♨ ♨ hammam 🏊 🚴 ✗ 🔲
(open-air in season), fitness trail, mountain biking, roller skating,
multi-sports ground, entertainment room
Facilities : 🔥 ⚬ 🔲 🔲 🛁 🚰 🚰 launderette

Longitude : 1.69486
Latitude : 50.31356

Gilles Rigoulet / hemis.fr

Names such as Cognac, Angoulême or La Rochelle all echo through France's history, but there's just as much to appreciate in the Poitou-Charentes region today. Visit a thalassotherapy resort and allow the seawater to revive your spirits and tone aching muscles, or soak up the sun on the sandy beaches, where the scent of pine trees mingles with the fresh sea air. The best way to discover the region's coastal islands is by bike; explore country lanes lined with tiny blue and white cottages and colourful hollyhocks. Back on the mainland, visit the canals of the marshy – and mercifully mosquito-free – Marais Poitevin, or 'Green Venice', with its poplar trees and green duckweed. You will have earned a drop of Cognac or a glass of the local apéritif, a fruity, ice-cold Pineau des Charentes. For a multimedia experience and a trip into the future of the moving image, head to Futuroscope, a hugely popular award-winning theme park located in Poitiers.

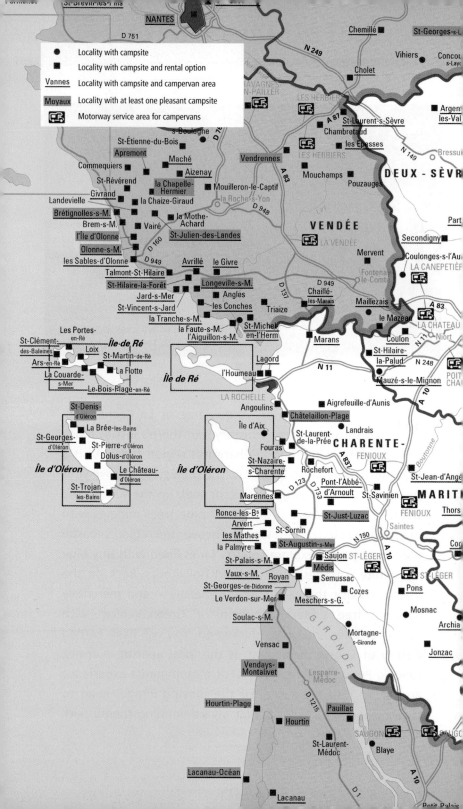

AIGREFEUILLE-D'AUNIS

17290 – Michelin map **324** E3 – pop. 3,682 – alt. 20
▶ Paris 457 – Niort 50 – Rochefort 22 – La Rochelle 25

La Taillée

℘ 05 46 35 55 088, www.lataillee.com ❧
Address : 3 r. du Bois Gaillard (east of the town, near the swimming pool)
Opening times : from mid June to beginning Sept.
2 ha (80 pitches) flat, grassy
Tariff : 17.60€ ✶✶ ⇔ 国 (≴) (6A) – Extra per person 4€
Rental rates : (from beginning May to beginning Sept.) ❧ Ⓟ – 27 ⟨⟩ – 10 tent bungalows
Per night 72€ – Per week from 275 to 585 €

In a pleasant wooded setting among ancient ash and plane trees.

Surroundings : ⊗ ᎧᎧ
Leisure activities : ⌨ ⚔ ⌐
Facilities : 🜨 ⊶ ⫘ ᎙ ⌂ ⌶ ▣
Nearby : ⫛

GPS Longitude : -0.92682
Latitude : 46.11514

ANGOULINS

17690 – Michelin map **324** D3 – pop. 3,720 – alt. 15
▶ Paris 481 – Poitiers 148 – La Rochelle 12 – Niort 73

Les Chirats - La Platère

℘ 05 46 56 94 16, www.campingleschirats.fr
Address : r. du Chay (1.7km west along the r. des Salines and follow the signs for the customs post, 100m from the beach)
Opening times : from beginning April to end Sept.
4 ha (232 pitches) flat and relatively flat, grassy, stony
Tariff : 27.80€ ✶✶ ⇔ 国 (≴) (10A) – Extra per person 5.20€ – Reservation fee 20€
Rental rates : (permanent) – 35 ⟨⟩ – 5 ⟨⟩. Per night from 48 to 85 €
Per week from 450 to 665 € – Reservation fee 20€

Surroundings : ⫏ ᎧᎧ
Leisure activities : ⊺ ⌨ ⊙ ʃⳁ ⇌ jacuzzi ⚔ ⌐ ⟨⟩ (small swimming pool) ⫛ ⬚
Facilities : 🜨 ⊶ ⌂ ⫘ ⫯ ⌶ ▣ ⤸
Nearby : ⬰

GPS Longitude : -1.13076
Latitude : 46.104

ARCHIAC

17520 – Michelin map **324** I6 – pop. 812 – alt. 111
▶ Paris 514 – Angoulême 49 – Barbezieux 15 – Cognac 22

Municipal

℘ 05 46 49 10 46, archiacmairie@free.fr
Address : 7 r. des Voituriers
Opening times : from mid June to mid Sept.
1 ha (44 pitches) terraced, flat, grassy, stony
Tariff : (2012 price) ✶ 2.15€ ⇔ 1.50€ 国 1.50€ – (≴) (5A) 3.80€
⟨⟩ sani-station – 3 国

Close to the municipal sports complex.

Surroundings : ⊗ ⫏ ᎧᎧ
Leisure activities : ⌨
Facilities : ⫘ ▣
Nearby : ✼ ⫛ ⬚

GPS Longitude : -0.30467
Latitude : 45.52322

ARGENTON-LES-VALLEES

79150 – Michelin map **322** D3 – pop. 1,588
▶ Paris 367 – Poitiers 100 – Niort 89 – Nantes 102

Municipal du lac d'Hautibus

℘ 05 49 65 95 08, *campinghautibus@orange.fr* –
Address : r. de la Sablière (to the west of the town (access near the roundabout on D 748 and D 759)
Opening times : from beginning April to end Sept.
1.5 ha (64 pitches) terraced, relatively flat, grassy
Tariff : (2012 price) 🏃 2.25€ 🚗 1.90€ 📧 2.10€ – 🔌 (6A) 2.60€
Rental rates : (2012 price) (permanent) – 6 🏠. Per night from 34 to 46 €
Per week from 230 to 367 €
🛁 sani-station 5€
Situated 150m from the lake, with direct access (a picturesque site).

Surroundings : ≼ ☲ ♀ **Leisure activities** : 🎭 **Facilities** : ⅙ 🗣 launderette **Nearby** : 🍴 🛝 🛶 boats for hire	**GPS** Longitude : -0.45164 Latitude : 46.98764

This guide is not intended as a list of all the camping sites in France;
its aim is to provide a selection of the best sites in each category.

ARVERT

17530 – Michelin map **324** D5 – pop. 3,100 – alt. 20
▶ Paris 513 – Marennes 16 – Rochefort 37 – La Rochelle 74

Le Presqu'île

℘ 05 46 36 81 76, *campinglepresquile.com*
Address : 7 r. des Aigrettes (north of the town, 150m from the D 14)
Opening times : from beginning April to end Sept.
0.8 ha (66 pitches) flat, grassy, sandy
Tariff : (2012 price) 16.50€ 🏃🏃 🚗 📧 🔌 (16A) – Extra per person 3.50€
Rental rates : (2012 price) (permanent) 🚫 (from beg Sept to end Mar) – 3 🏠.
Per night from 17 € – Per week from 290 to 550 €
🛁 sani-station – 12 📧 10€ – 🛁 🔌16.50€

Surroundings : ♀♀ **Leisure activities** : 🎭 ⛵ **Facilities** : ⅙ ⚓ 🍴 📷 **Nearby** : 🍴	**GPS** Longitude : -1.12725 Latitude : 45.74526

Le Petit Pont

℘ 05 46 36 07 20, *www.camping-dupetit.com*
Address : 111 av. de l'Etrade (2.5km northwest on the D 14)
Opening times : from mid April to mid Sept.
1 ha (53 pitches) flat, grassy
Tariff : (2012 price) 25.20€ 🏃🏃 🚗 📧 🔌 (10A) – Extra per person 5.70€ – Reservation fee 11€
Rental rates : (2012 price) (from mid April to mid Sept.) 🚫 – 27 🏠. Per week from
170 to 720 € – Reservation fee 22€

Surroundings : ♀♀ **Leisure activities** : 🎭 ⛵ 🛝 **Facilities** : ⚓ 🗣 🍴 📷	**GPS** Longitude : -1.14085 Latitude : 45.75837

AUNAC

16460 – Michelin map **324** L4 – pop. 353 – alt. 70
▶ Paris 418 – Angoulême 37 – Confolens 43 – Ruffec 15

⚠ Municipal de Magnerit

☏ 05 45 22 24 38, *mairie.aunac@wanadoo.fr*
Address : allée Prairie (1.7km southeast of the village, on the D 27 follow the signs for St-Front and take the road to the left)
1.2 ha (25 pitches) flat, grassy

Surroundings : 🦢 ♨
Leisure activities : 🚣 🎣
Facilities : 🚿

GPS — Longitude : 0.24978
Latitude : 45.91395

AVAILLES-LIMOUZINE

86460 – Michelin map **322** J8 – pop. 1,314 – alt. 142
▶ Paris 410 – Confolens 14 – L'Isle-Jourdain 15 – Niort 100

⚠ Municipal le Parc

☏ 05 49 48 51 22, *camping.leparc@wanadoo.fr*
Address : at Les Places (take the eastern exit along the D 34, to the left after the bridge; beside the Vienne river)
Opening times : from mid April to end Oct.
2.7 ha (100 pitches) flat, grassy
Tariff : 13€ ✳✳ ⛟ 🅴 (⅃) (10A) – Extra per person 2.70€
Rental rates : (2012 price) (from mid April to end Oct.) – 4 🚐 – 3 🏠.
Per night from 42 to 53 € – Per week from 275 to 350 €
🚐 sani-station 2€ – 12 🅴 4€ – 🕭 (⅃)12€

Surroundings : 🦢 ♨♨
Leisure activities : 🎲 🚣 🏕 🛶 🎣 pedalos ✎
Facilities : 🚻 ⊶ 🏛 🚿 ⚲ 🔲
Nearby : 🍴

GPS — Longitude : 0.65829
Latitude : 46.12401

> *The classification (1 to 5 tents, **black** or **red**) that we award to selected sites in this guide is our own system. It should not be confused with the classification (1 to 5 stars) of official organisations.*

AVANTON

86170 – Michelin map **322** H5 – pop. 1,819 – alt. 110
▶ Paris 337 – Poitiers 12 – Niort 84 – Châtellerault 37

⚠⚠ Du Futur

☏ 05 49 54 09 67, *www.camping-du-futur.com*
Address : 9 r. des Bois (1.3km southwest along the D 757, follow the signs for Poitiers and take turning to the right after the level crossing)
Opening times : from beginning April to end Oct.
4 ha/1.5 (68 pitches) flat, grassy
Tariff : (2012 price) 23€ ✳✳ ⛟ 🅴 (⅃) (10A) – Extra per person 3.50€ – Reservation fee 10€
Rental rates : (2012 price) (from beginning April to end Oct.) ✎ – 14 🚐.
Per night from 55 to 90 € – Per week from 252 to 455 € – Reservation fee 15€
🚐 sani-station 4.50€

Surroundings : ⊏⊐ ♡
Leisure activities : 🍸 🚣 🏕 🛶
Facilities : 🚻 ⊶ 🚿 ⚲ launderette

GPS — Longitude : 0.30124
Latitude : 46.65638

BONNES

86300 – Michelin map **322** J5 – pop. 1,688 – alt. 70
▶ Paris 331 – Châtellerault 25 – Chauvigny 7 – Poitiers 25

⚠ Municipal

✆ 05 49 56 44 34, *www.campingbonnes86.fr*
Address : 13 r. de la Varenne (south of the town; beside the Vienne river)
Opening times : from beginning June to mid Sept.
1.2 ha (56 pitches) flat, grassy
Tariff : ♣ 3€ ⇌ 1.30€ 🔲 2.60€ – ⚡ (10A) 2.80€
Rental rates : (permanent) ♿ – 6 🏠. Per night from 37 to 52 € – Per week from 167 to 295 €
🚽 sani-station 3€

Surroundings : ▱ ♀
Leisure activities : 🚣 🚲 ✂
Facilities : ♿ ⚲ 🏕 🚰 launderette
Nearby : 🛶 🏄

Longitude : 0.59856
Latitude : 46.60182

There are several different types of sani-station
('borne' in French) – sanitation points providing
fresh water and disposal points for grey water.
See page 12 for further details.

CHÂTELAILLON-PLAGE

17340 – Michelin map **324** D3 – pop. 6,081 – alt. 3
▶ Paris 482 – Niort 74 – Rochefort 22 – La Rochelle 19

⚠ Club Airotel Village Corsaire des 2 Plages

✆ 05 46 56 27 53, *www.2plages.com*
Address : av. d'Angoulins (follow the signs for La Rochelle; 300 m. from the beach)
Opening times : from beginning May to end Sept.
4.5 ha (265 pitches) flat, grassy, sandy
Tariff : (2012 price) 29.90€ ♣♣ ⇌ 🔲 ⚡ (10A) – Extra per person 6.20€ – Reservation fee 18€
Rental rates : (2012 price) (from mid April to end Sept.) ♿ – 115 🛖.
Per night from 50 to 128 € – Per week from 300 to 896 € – Reservation fee 18€
🚽 sani-station
Choose pitches away from the road in preference.

Surroundings : ▱ ♀♀
Leisure activities : ♟ ✗ 🎮 🚣 🛶 multi-sports ground
Facilities : ♿ ⚲ 🏕 🏕 ⚲ 🚰 launderette 🛁
Nearby : 🚲

Longitude : -1.09344
Latitude : 46.08441

⚠ L'Océan

✆ 05 46 56 87 97, *www.campingocean17.com*
Address : av. d'Angoulins (1.3km north along the D 202, follow the signs for La Rochelle and take a right turn)
Opening times : from mid May to end Sept.
3 ha (94 pitches) flat, grassy
Tariff : (2012 price) 30€ ♣♣ ⇌ 🔲 ⚡ (10A) – Extra per person 6€ – Reservation fee 15€
A small but pretty lake, landscaped but filtered naturally.

Surroundings : ♀♀
Leisure activities : 🎣 🚣 🏊 (lake), entertainment room
Facilities : ♿ ⚲ 🏕 🚰 launderette

Longitude : -1.09412
Latitude : 46.08818

CHÂTELLERAULT

86100 – Michelin map **322** J4 – pop. 32,718 – alt. 52
▶ Paris 304 – Châteauroux 98 – Cholet 134 – Poitiers 36

Le Relais du Miel

🕿 05 49 02 06 27, *www.lerelaisdumiel.com*
Address : at Valette - rte d 'Antran (take the northern exit along the D 910, follow the signs for Paris, then take the bypass (rocade) to the left towards the toll on the A 10, then a right turn along the D 1, near the Vienne river (direct access). From the A 10, take exit 26 Châtellerault-Nord)
7 ha/4 ha for camping (80 pitches) terraced, flat, relatively flat, grassy, stony
Rentals : 1 🏠 – 6 studios – 11 apartments.
In the outbuildings of an 18th-century residence.

Surroundings : 🖼 ♤♤
Leisure activities : ☂ 🖼 🛶 ⚇ 🏊
Facilities : ᵺ ⚬━ 🚿 🌱 ⚑ launderette
Nearby : 🛒

GPS
Longitude : 0.53607
Latitude : 46.84053

CHAUVIGNY

86300 – Michelin map **322** J5 – pop. 6,848 – alt. 65
▶ Paris 333 – Bellac 64 – Le Blanc 36 – Châtellerault 30

Municipal de la Fontaine

🕿 05 49 46 31 94, *www.chauvigny.fr*
Address : r. de la Fontaine (take the northern exit along the D 2, follow the signs for La Puye and take turning to the right; beside a stream)
Opening times : from mid April to end Sept.
2.8 ha (102 pitches) flat, grassy, fine gravel
Tariff : (2012 price) ⚲ 2.45 € 🚗 1.75 € 🅴 1.75 € – 🔌 (16A) 2.85 €
Rental rates : (2012 price) (permanent) – 4 🏠 – 6 studios. Per night from 42 to 75 €
Per week from 210 to 570 €
🚐 sani-station – 10 🅴 6.50 €
Municipal gardens with a water feature.

Surroundings : ≤ Medieval city, several castles ♤♤
Leisure activities : 🖼 🛶
Facilities : ᵺ ⚬━ ▥ 🚿 🌱 ⚑ launderette
Nearby : 🎣

GPS
Longitude : 0.65349
Latitude : 46.57095

COGNAC

16100 – Michelin map **324** I5 – pop. 18,729 – alt. 25
▶ Paris 478 – Angoulême 45 – Bordeaux 120 – Libourne 116

Municipal

🕿 05 45 32 13 32, *www.campingdecognac.com*
Address : Bd de Châtenay (2.3km north along the D 24, follow the signs for Boutiers; near the Charente and the Solençon rivers)
2 ha (160 pitches) flat, grassy
Rental rates : ᵺ – 8 🚐 – 2 tent bungalows.
🚐 sani-station

Surroundings : 🖼 ♤♤
Leisure activities : 🛶 🏊 🎣
Facilities : ᵺ ⚬━ 🚿 ⚑ 🖼
Nearby : ☂ ✗

GPS
Longitude : -0.30726
Latitude : 45.70926

COUHÉ

6700 – Michelin map **322** H7 – pop. 1,885 – alt. 140
Paris 370 – Confolens 58 – Montmorillon 61 – Niort 65

Les Peupliers ▲▲

0549592116, www.lespeupliers.fr
Address : rte de Poitiers (located 1km to the north; at Valence)
Opening times : from beginning May to end Sept.
16 ha/6 ha for camping (160 pitches) flat, grassy, lake
Tariff : ♦ 8€ 回 13.50€ – (½) (10A) 4.50€
Rental rates : (permanent) – 21 – 18 . Per night from 85 to 170 €
Per week from 205 to 1,080 €
sani-station – 14€
A wooded setting crossed by a picturesque river.

Surroundings :
Leisure activities : ▼ ✕ ☒ ⊕ 林 ← ↑ ▲ △ ⤻
Facilities : & ⚬— ♨ ⚲ ▽ ⁙ launderette ▦ ⌂

GPS Longitude : 0.18222
Latitude : 46.31222

COULON

9510 – Michelin map **322** C7 – pop. 2,211 – alt. 6
Paris 418 – Fontenay-le-Comte 25 – Niort 11 – La Rochelle 63

La Venise Verte ▲▲

0549359036, www.camping-laveniseverte.fr
Address : 178 rte des Bords de Sèvre (2.2km southwest along the D 123, follow the signs for Vanneau; beside a canal and near the Sèvre Niortaise river)
Opening times : from beginning April to end Oct.
2.2 ha (140 pitches) flat, grassy
Tariff : 27.50€ ♦♦ ← 回 (½) (10A) – Extra per person 6.50€ – Reservation fee 10€
Rental rates : (permanent) – 8 – 16 . Per night from 46 to 95 €
Per week from 315 to 765 € – Reservation fee 10€
sani-station
A site making great efforts in ecological terms.

Surroundings :
Leisure activities : ▼ ✕ ☒ 林 ← ↺ ▲ ⤻
Facilities : & ⚬— ♨ ⚲ ▽ ⁙ ▦ ⌂
Nearby : ⤻

GPS Longitude : -0.60889
Latitude : 46.31444

COZES

7120 – Michelin map **324** E6 – pop. 1,973 – alt. 43
Paris 494 – Marennes 41 – Mirambeau 35 – Pons 26

Municipal le Sorlut

0546907599, www.villedecozes.fr et www.camping-le-sorlut.com
Address : r. des Chênes (to the north, near the old station, behind the Champion supermarket)
Opening times : from mid April to mid Oct.
1.4 ha (120 pitches) flat, grassy
Tariff : (2012 price) ♦ 2.60€ ← 回 2.75€ – (½) (10A) 2.70€
Rental rates : (2012 price) (permanent) ⚘ – 8 . Per night from 55 to 73 €
Per week from 273 to 515 € – Reservation fee 25€

Surroundings :
Leisure activities : ←
Facilities : ⚬⚬ (Jul-Aug) ⁙ ▦
Nearby : ☰ ✕ ↑ ▲ △

GPS Longitude : -0.83728
Latitude : 45.58649

DIENNE

86410 – Michelin map **322** J6 – pop. 508 – alt. 112
▶ Paris 362 – Poitiers 26 – Niort 107 – Limoges 107

Le Domaine de Dienné

🖉 05 49 45 87 63, *www.domaine-de-dienne.fr*
Address : at La Boquerie (RN 147)
Opening times : from mid Feb. to beginning Jan.
47 ha/1 ha for camping (19 pitches) undulating, flat, grassy, lake, forest
Tariff : 39€ ♣ ♣ ⇔ 🗐 ⚡ (16A) – Extra per person 7.50€
Rental rates : (from mid Feb. to beginning Jan.) ♿ 🅿 – 24 'gypsy' caravans – 7 🏠 –
8 yurts – 24 cabins in the trees – 2 gîtes – 5 'mushroom' houses - 5 'fairy' houses.
Per night from 71 to 179 € – Per week from 355 to 992 €

Spacious site with a range of good quality and unusual facilities, such as a hotel for cats and dogs!

Surroundings : ⚲
Leisure activities : 🍽 ✗ 🖾 📺 ⚶ 🖸 hammam, jacuzzi 🏊 🚲 ♨ 🖾
🏊 🎣 🐎 zip wiring, fitness trail, climbing wall, forest trail, spa therapy
centre
Facilities : ♿ ⟐ 🅿 🏭 🍴 launderette 🛒

GPS
Longitude : 0.56024
Latitude : 46.44614

FOURAS

17450 – Michelin map **324** D4 – pop. 4,092 – alt. 5
▶ Paris 485 – Châtelaillon-Plage 18 – Rochefort 15 – La Rochelle 34

Municipal le Cadoret

🖉 05 46 82 19 19, *www.campings-fouras.com*
Address : bd de Chaterny (North coast; beside the Anse de Fouras, 100m from the beach)
Opening times : permanent
7.5 ha (511 pitches) flat, grassy, sandy
Tariff : (2012 price) 26.40€ ♣ ♣ ⇔ 🗐 ⚡ (10A) – Extra per person 5.60€ – Reservation fee 25€
Rental rates : (2012 price) (from end March to beginning Nov.) ♿ (1 mobile home) – 16 🚐.
Per week from 264 to 610 € – Reservation fee 25€

A well-kept site with plenty of greenery.

Surroundings : 🖾 ⚲⚲
Leisure activities : 🍽 ✗ 🖸 🏊 🏊 ⚓ multi-sports ground
Facilities : ♿ ⟐ 🏭 🖫 🛁 🛒 🍴 launderette 🛒
Nearby : ✗ 🖾

GPS
Longitude : -1.08714
Latitude : 45.99296

L'HOUMEAU

17137 – Michelin map **324** C2 – pop. 2,073 – alt. 19
▶ Paris 478 – Poitiers 145 – La Rochelle 6 – Niort 83

Au Petit Port de l'Houmeau

🖉 05 46 50 90 82, *www.aupetitport.com*
Address : r. des Sartières (take the northeastern exit along the D 106, follow the signs for Nieul-sur-Mer, via the ring road (périphérique) towards Île de Ré and take the exit for Lagord-l'Houmeau)
Opening times : from beginning April to end Sept.
2 ha (132 pitches) relatively flat, flat, grassy
Tariff : (2012 price) ♣ ⇔ 🗐 20€ – ⚡ (10A) 4.60€ – Reservation fee 16€
Rental rates : (2012 price) (permanent) ♿ (1 chalet) – 26 🚐 – 15 🏠.
Per night from 52 to 72 € – Per week from 320 to 740 € – Reservation fee 16€

Surroundings : 🖾 ⚲⚲
Leisure activities : 🍽 🖾 🚲
Facilities : ♿ ⟐ 🛁 🍴 launderette 🛒
Nearby : ✗ 🖾

GPS
Longitude : -1.1883
Latitude : 46.19566

LE-D'AIX

17123 – Michelin map **324** C3 – pop. 227 – alt. 10
◪ Paris 486 – Poitiers 152 – La Rochelle 31 – Niort 78

Le Fort de la Rade

℘ 05 46 84 28 28, *fortdelarade.ifrance.com*
Address : situated at la Pointe Ste-Catherine, 300m from the beach at L'Anse de la Croix
Opening times : from beginning May to end Sept.
3 ha (70 pitches) flat, grassy, terraced
Tariff : (2012 price) 24.50€ ★★ ⬅ 🗉 – Extra per person 4.50€

In the grounds of the Fort de la Rade, surrounded by fortified walls – reserved for tents.

Surroundings : ⬬
Leisure activities : ✗ 🖾 🏊 ◑
Facilities : ⅙ ⚬⚊ ⁇ ⚘ no electrical hook-up
Nearby : ⬓ 🍷 🚲

GPS Longitude : -1.17657
Latitude : 46.00935

LE DE RÉ

17 – Michelin map **324**

Ars-en-Ré 17590 – Michelin map **324** A2 – pop. 1,321 – alt. 4
◪ Paris 506 – Fontenay-le-Comte 85 – Luçon 75 – La Rochelle 34

Club Airotel le Cormoran ♠♣

℘ 05 46 29 46 04, *www.cormoran.com*
Address : rte de Radia (located 1km west)
Opening times : from end March to end Sept.
3 ha (142 pitches) flat, grassy, sandy
Tariff : (2012 price) 51.60€ ★★ ⬅ 🗉 🚿 (10A) – Extra per person 13€ – Reservation fee 25€
Rental rates : (2012 price) (from end March to end Sept.) ⅙ – 93 ⛺ – 2 tents.
Per night from 86 to 263 € – Per week from 225 to 1,401 € – Reservation fee 35€
⛽ sani-station 4€

A leafy, green site with flowers; well kept.

Surroundings : ⬬ 🗔 ◊
Leisure activities : 🍷 ✗ 🖾 ◔ ⚽ ♨ ≋ 🛶 🚲 🎾 🏊 multi-sports ground
Facilities : ⅙ ⚬⚊ ▥ ⚘ ⚶ ⚯ ⁇ launderette ⚘

GPS Longitude : -1.53026
Latitude : 46.21136

Le Bois-Plage-en-Ré 17580 – Michelin map **324** B2 – pop. 2,364 – alt. 5
◪ Paris 494 – Fontenay-le-Comte 74 – Luçon 64 – La Rochelle 23

Sunêlia Interlude ♠♣

℘ 05 46 09 18 22, *www.interlude.fr*
Address : 8 rte de Gros Jonc (2.3km southeast)
Opening times : from mid April to end Sept.
7.5 ha (387 pitches) undulating, flat, grassy, sandy
Tariff : 49€ ★★ ⬅ 🗉 🚿 (10A) – Extra per person 10€ – Reservation fee 30€
Rental rates : (from mid April to end Sept.) ⅙ (1 mobile home) – 196 ⛺.
Per night from 56 to 226 € – Per week from 392 to 1,582 € – Reservation fee 30€
⛽ sani-station 8€

Situated 150m from the beach.

Surroundings : ⬬ 🗔 ◊
Leisure activities : 🍷 ✗ 🖾 ◔ ⚽ ♨ ≋ hammam, jacuzzi 🛶 🚲 ▦
(small swimming pool) 🏊 ◿ multi-sports ground, spa therapy centre
Facilities : ⅙ ⚬⚊ ▥ ⚶ ⚯ ⁇ launderette ⬓ ⚘
Nearby : 🎾 ◑

GPS Longitude : -1.3793
Latitude : 46.17472

Les Varennes

℘ 05 46 09 15 43, www.les-varennes.com

Address : at Raise Maritaise (1.7km southeast)

Opening times : from beginning April to end Sept.

2.5 ha (145 pitches) flat, grassy, sandy

Tariff : (2012 price) 48.70€ ✝✝ ⇔ 🗐 🔌 (10A) – Extra per person 6€ – Reservation fee 20€

Rental rates : (2012 price) (from beginning April to end Sept.) – 85 🛏.

Per night from 56 to 92 € – Per week from 307 to 995 € – Reservation fee 20€

🚐 sani-station 7€

Surroundings : ⅏ ♀♀
Leisure activities : ⊤ ⚓ ⚲ 🔲 (open-air in season)
Facilities : ⅍ ⚮ ⊪ ⌂ ⚐ launderette ⅌
Nearby : ✕

GPS
Longitude : -1.38306
Latitude : 46.17829

APV Antioche

℘ 05 46 09 23 86, www.camping-apv.com

Address : at Clumasses (3km southeast, follow the signs for Ste-Marie)

Opening times : from beginning April to end Sept.

3 ha (134 pitches) terraced, flat and relatively flat, grassy, sandy

Tariff : (2012 price) 33.60€ ✝✝ ⇔ 🗐 🔌 (10A) – Extra per person 8.60€ – Reservation fee 27€

Rental rates : (2012 price) (from beginning April to end Sept.) – 66 🛏.

Per night 82€ – Per week 972€ – Reservation fee 27€

The site is 300m from the beach (direct access).

Surroundings : ⅏ ♀
Leisure activities : ⊤ ✕ 🖼 ⇄ jacuzzi ⚓ ⚲ multi-sports ground
Facilities : ⅍ ⚮ ⌂ ⌂ ⚐ launderette ⅌

GPS
Longitude : -1.36578
Latitude : 46.16937

La Couarde-sur-Mer 17670 – Michelin map **324** B2 – pop. 1,248 – alt. 1
▶ Paris 497 – Fontenay-le-Comte 76 – Luçon 66 – La Rochelle 26

L'Océan

℘ 05 46 29 87 70, www.campingocean.com

Address : 50 r. d'Ars

Opening times : from end April to end Sept.

9 ha (338 pitches) flat, grassy, sandy

Tariff : (2012 price) 49€ ✝✝ ⇔ 🗐 🔌 (10A) – Extra per person 11€ – Reservation fee 32€

Rental rates : (2012 price) (from end April to end Sept.) ⅍ ⚿ – 160 🛏.

Per night from 42 to 198 € – Per week from 294 to 1,386 € – Reservation fee 32€

🚐 sani-station 8€

Surroundings : ▭ ♀
Leisure activities : ⊤ ✕ 🖼 ⚀ ⚓ ⚲ ✕ ♪ ⚘ ⚲ multi-sports ground, entertainment room
Facilities : ⅍ ⚮ 🔲 ⊪ ⌂ ⌂ ⚐ launderette ⚏ ⅌
Nearby : helicopter flights

GPS
Longitude : -1.46737
Latitude : 46.20447

Michelin classification:

⩕⩕⩕⩕ *Extremely comfortable, equipped to a very high standard*
⩕⩕⩕ *Very comfortable, equipped to a high standard*
⩕⩕⩕ *Comfortable and well equipped*
⩕ *Reasonably comfortable*
⩕ *Satisfactory*

La Tour des Prises

🅐 05 46 29 84 82, *www.lesprises.com*
Address : chemin de la Grifforine (1.8km northwest along the D 735 and take the road to the right)
Opening times : from beginning April to end Sept.
2.5 ha (140 pitches) flat, grassy
Tariff : 21.40€ ♦♦ ⇌ 🗐 🕅 (16A) – Extra per person 2€ – Reservation fee 14€
Rental rates : (from beginning April to end Sept.) – 50 🛏. Per night from 50 to 80 €
Per week from 285 to 720 € – Reservation fee 20€
🛱 sani-station 16€ – 🍴 🕅10.50€
On the site of an old orchard and surrounded by vines.

Surroundings : 🐾 ⌂ 🏖
Leisure activities : ✕ 🏛 🏊 🚲 🖵 (open-air in season)
Facilities : 🛁 ⛟ ▥ 🏕 ⇥ 🍴 launderette 🔌

GPS Longitude : -1.4447
Latitude : 46.20473

La Flotte 17630 – Michelin map **324** C2 – pop. 2,918 – alt. 4
▶ Paris 489 – Fontenay-le-Comte 68 – Luçon 58 – La Rochelle 17

Camp'Atlantique Les Peupliers ♦♦

🅐 0821 444 153, *www.camp-atlantique.com* – limited spaces for one-night stay
Address : RD 735 (1.3km southeast)
Opening times :
4.5 ha (239 pitches) flat, grassy, sandy
Rental rates : (from mid April to end Sept.) 🛁 – 143 🛏. Per week from 259 to 989 €
Reservation fee 25€

Surroundings : ⌂ 🏖
Leisure activities : 🍴 ✕ 🏛 🕅 🏓 🛝 hammam, jacuzzi 🏊 🚲 🎱 🏊
multi-sports ground, entertainment room
Facilities : 🛁 ⛟ 🏕 🍴 launderette 🔌

GPS Longitude : -1.308
Latitude : 46.1846

L'Île Blanche
(rental of mobile homes only)

🅐 05 46 09 52 43, *www.ileblanche.com*
Address : ch. des Bardonnières (2.5km west, recommended route via the diversion (déviation))
Opening times : permanent
4 ha flat
Rentals : 100 🛏. Per week from 330 to 780 € – Reservation fee 12€

Surroundings : 🐾 🏖
Leisure activities : ✕ 🏛 🏊 🚲 ⚅ 🖵 (open-air in season)
Facilities : ⛟ 🍴 launderette 🔌

GPS Longitude : -1.34775
Latitude : 46.18988

La Grainetière

🅐 05 46 09 68 86, *www.la-grainetiere.com*
Address : Ch. des Essards rte de Saint-Martin-de-Ré (to the west of the town, follow the signs for Saint-Martin-de-Ré - recommended route via the diversion (déviation))
Opening times : from beginning April to end Sept.
2.3 ha (140 pitches) flat, sandy, grassy
Tariff : 37.50€ ♦♦ ⇌ 🗐 🕅 (10A) – Extra per person 5.50€ – Reservation fee 15€
Rental rates : (from beginning April to end Sept.) – 3 'gypsy' caravans – 70 🛏.
Per night from 60 to 80 € – Per week from 240 to 940 € – Reservation fee 15€

Surroundings : 🏖
Leisure activities : ✕ 🏛 🕅 jacuzzi 🏊 🚲 🖵 (open-air in season)
Facilities : 🛁 ⛟ 🏕 🍴 launderette 🔌

GPS Longitude : -1.34412
Latitude : 46.18747

Loix 17111 – Michelin map **324** B2 – pop. 731 – alt. 4
▶ Paris 505 – Fontenay-le-Comte 84 – Luçon 74 – La Rochelle 33

⩓ Flower Les Ilates ▲▲

𝒞 05 46 29 05 43, www.camping-loix.com
Address : at Le Petit Boucheau - rte du Grouin (take the eastern exit, 500m from the ocean)
4.5 ha (217 pitches) flat, grassy
Rentals : ♿ (2 chalets) – 51 ⬚ – 34 ⌂.
🚮 sani-station

Surroundings : 🦢 🗺
Leisure activities : 🍽 ✗ 🎮 🏃 jacuzzi 🚣 🚲 ⛷ 🏄
Facilities : ♿ ⛢ 🚿 🛁 ⏻ 🍴 launderette 🛒

GPS Longitude : -1.42608
Latitude : 46.22756

Les Portes-en-Ré 17880 – Michelin map **324** B2 – pop. 647 – alt. 4
▶ Paris 514 – Fontenay-le-Comte 93 – Luçon 83 – La Rochelle 43

⩓ La Providence ▲▲

𝒞 05 46 29 56 82, www.campingprovidence.com
Address : rte du Fier et de Trousse-Chemise (east along the D 101, 50m from the beach)
6 ha (298 pitches) flat, grassy, sandy
Rentals : 45 ⬚.
🚮 sani-station

Surroundings : 🦢
Leisure activities : 🎬 🎮 🏃 🚣 🚲 ♨ 🔲 ⛷ entertainment room
Facilities : ♿ ⛢ 🏛 🚿 🍴 launderette 🛒
Nearby : ✗

GPS Longitude : -1.48638
Latitude : 46.24647

St-Clément-des-Baleines 17590 – Michelin map **324** A2 – pop. 721 – alt. 2
▶ Paris 509 – Fontenay-le-Comte 89 – Luçon 79 – La Rochelle 38

⩓ Club Airotel La Plage ▲▲

𝒞 05 46 29 42 62, www.la-plage.com
Address : 408 r. du Chaume
Opening times : from beginning April to end Sept.
2.7 ha (76 pitches) relatively flat, flat, grassy, sandy
Tariff : (2012 price) 51.60€ ✚✚ 🚐 ▣ 💧 (10A) – Extra per person 13€ – Reservation fee 25€
Rental rates : (2012 price) (from beginning April to end Sept.) ℗ – 80 ⬚ – 2 tents.
Per night from 43 to 114 € – Per week from 225 to 1,401 € – Reservation fee 35€
🚮 sani-station
The site is 100m from the beach.

Surroundings : 🗺
Leisure activities : 🍽 ✗ 🎬 🎮 🏃 ⛳ ♨ 🚣 🚲 ⛷ multi-sports ground
Facilities : ♿ ⛢ 🚿 🍴 launderette 🛒
Nearby : ✗ ♨ 🎣

GPS Longitude : -1.55344
Latitude : 46.24112

St-Martin-de-Ré 17410 – Michelin map **324** B2 – pop. 2,585 – alt. 14
▶ Paris 493 – Fontenay-le-Comte 72 – Luçon 62 – La Rochelle 22

⩓ Municipal

𝒞 05 46 09 21 96, www.saint-martin-de-re.fr
Address : r. du Rempart (situated in the town)
3 ha (200 pitches) terraced, flat, relatively flat, grassy
Rentals : 21 ⬚.
🚮 sani-station
Beside the town ramparts.

Surroundings : ♀
Leisure activities : ✗ 🎬 🎮 nocturnal 🚣
Facilities : ♿ ⛢ launderette
Nearby : 🚮

GPS Longitude : -1.36758
Latitude : 46.19921

LE D'OLÉRON

17 – Michelin map **324**

La Brée-les-Bains 17840 – Michelin map **324** B3 – pop. 758 – alt. 5
▷ Paris 531 – Marennes 32 – Rochefort 53 – La Rochelle 90

Antioche d'Oléron

📞 05 46 47 92 00, *www.camping-antiochedoleron.com*
Address : rte de Proires (located 1km northwest along the D 273 follow the signs for St Denis and take a right turn, 150m from the beach)
Opening times : from beginning April to end Sept.
2.5 ha (130 pitches) flat, grassy
Tariff : 39€ ✚✚ ⬅ 🔲 ⚡ (16A) – Extra per person 5.70€ – Reservation fee 22€
Rental rates : (from beginning April to end Sept.) – 43 🚐. Per night from 51 to 96 €
Per week from 233 to 987 € – Reservation fee 22€

Surroundings : ▱ ♨
Leisure activities : 🎬 jacuzzi ⛵ 🏊
Facilities : ♿ ⚲ 🛁 🚿 ♨ ℸ launderette ⊰
Nearby : ✗

Longitude : -1.35773
Latitude : 46.02033

Le Château-d'Oléron 17480 – Michelin map **324** C4 – pop. 3,930 – alt. 9
▷ Paris 507 – Marennes 12 – Rochefort 33 – La Rochelle 70

La Brande ♣♣

📞 05 46 47 62 37, *www.camping-labrande.com*
Address : rte des Huîtres (2.5km to the northwest, 250m from the sea)
Opening times : from end March to mid Nov.
4 ha (199 pitches) flat, grassy, sandy, lake
Tariff : 39€ ✚✚ ⬅ 🔲 ⚡ (10A) – Extra per person 8.10€ – Reservation fee 20€
Rental rates : (from end March to mid Nov.) ♿ (chalet) – 40 🚐 – 40 🏠 – 1 tent.
Per night from 69 to 105 € – Per week from 275 to 1,210 € – Reservation fee 20€
🚽 sani-station 10€

Surroundings : ♨
Leisure activities : 🍴 ✗ 🎬 ⊙ ⚶ ☄ hammam, jacuzzi ⛵ 🚲 ✗ m
🔲 (open-air in season) ⛱ ⊙ multi-sports ground
Facilities : ♿ ⚲ 🔲🛁 – 2 individual sanitary facilities (🚿🚽 wc) 🛁 🚿 ♨
launderette 🔥 ⊰

Longitude : -1.21607
Latitude : 45.90464

Club Airotel Oléron ♣♣

📞 05 46 47 61 82, *www.camping-airotel-oleron.com*
Address : 19 r. de la Libération (1.8km southwest following signs for St-Trojan and turn left onto r. de la Libération)
Opening times : from beginning April to end Sept.
15 ha/4 ha for camping (133 pitches) relatively flat, flat, grassy
Tariff : (2012 price) 29.42€ ✚✚ ⬅ 🔲 ⚡ (10A) – Extra per person 7€ – Reservation fee 16€
Rental rates : (2012 price) (from beginning March to end Oct.) – 55 🚐 – 13 🏠.
Per week from 370 to 860 € – Reservation fee 16€
🚽 sani-station – ⛽10€
Campsite and equestrian centre, near a beautiful coastline. Option for stays on a half-board basis.

Surroundings : 🌿 ▱ ♨
Leisure activities : 🍴 ✗ 🎬 ⊙ ⚶ ⛵ 🚲 ✗ m 🏊 ⛱ 🐎 multi-sports
ground
Facilities : ♿ ⚲ 🛁 ℸ launderette ⊰
Nearby : 🛒

Longitude : -1.20791
Latitude : 45.88444

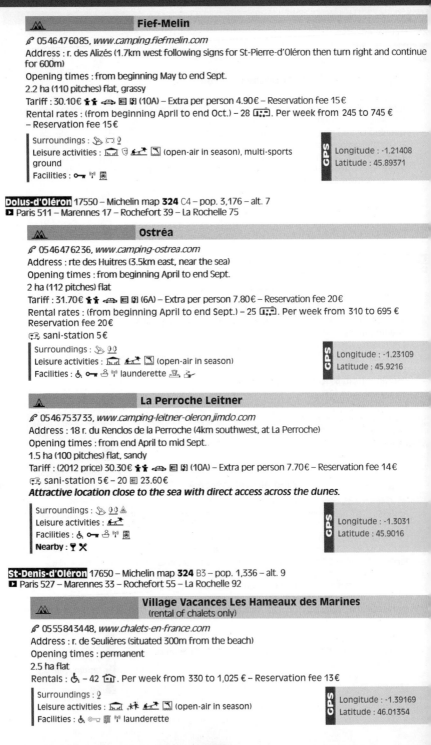

Fief-Melin

℘ 0546476085, www.camping.fiefmelin.com

Address : r. des Alizés (1.7km west following signs for St-Pierre-d'Oléron then turn right and continue for 600m)

Opening times : from beginning May to end Sept.

2.2 ha (110 pitches) flat, grassy

Tariff : 30.10€ ✝✝ ⇆ 圓 ⑨ (10A) – Extra per person 4.90€ – Reservation fee 15€

Rental rates : (from beginning April to end Oct.) – 28 🛏. Per week from 245 to 745 € – Reservation fee 15€

Surroundings : ⅀ ⊡ ℚ
Leisure activities : 🏠 ⑨ ⚓ 🔲 (open-air in season), multi-sports ground
Facilities : ⊶ ⁱᵖ 🔲

GPS
Longitude : -1.21408
Latitude : 45.89371

Dolus-d'Oléron 17550 – Michelin map **324** C4 – pop. 3,176 – alt. 7
◗ Paris 511 – Marennes 17 – Rochefort 39 – La Rochelle 75

Ostréa

℘ 0546476236, www.camping-ostrea.com

Address : rte des Huitres (3.5km east, near the sea)

Opening times : from beginning April to end Sept.

2 ha (112 pitches) flat

Tariff : 31.70€ ✝✝ ⇆ 圓 ⑨ (6A) – Extra per person 7.80€ – Reservation fee 20€

Rental rates : (from beginning April to end Sept.) – 25 🛏. Per week from 310 to 695 € Reservation fee 20€

🛱 sani-station 5€

Surroundings : ⅀ ℚℚ
Leisure activities : 🏠 ⚓ 🔲 (open-air in season)
Facilities : ⅃ ⊶ 🕭 ⁱᵖ launderette ♨ 🐾

GPS
Longitude : -1.23109
Latitude : 45.9216

La Perroche Leitner

℘ 0546753733, www.camping-leitner-oleron.jimdo.com

Address : 18 r. du Renclos de la Perroche (4km southwest, at La Perroche)

Opening times : from end April to mid Sept.

1.5 ha (100 pitches) flat, sandy

Tariff : (2012 price) 30.30€ ✝✝ ⇆ 圓 ⑨ (10A) – Extra per person 7.70€ – Reservation fee 14€

🛱 sani-station 5€ – 20 圓 23.60€

Attractive location close to the sea with direct access across the dunes.

Surroundings : ⅀ ℚℚ ⚠
Leisure activities : ⚓
Facilities : ⅃ ⊶ 🕭 ⁱᵖ 🔲
Nearby : ♀ ✕

GPS
Longitude : -1.3031
Latitude : 45.9016

St-Denis-d'Oléron 17650 – Michelin map **324** B3 – pop. 1,336 – alt. 9
◗ Paris 527 – Marennes 33 – Rochefort 55 – La Rochelle 92

Village Vacances Les Hameaux des Marines
(rental of chalets only)

℘ 0555843448, www.chalets-en-france.com

Address : r. de Seulières (situated 300m from the beach)

Opening times : permanent

2.5 ha flat

Rentals : ⅃ – 42 🏠. Per week from 330 to 1,025 € – Reservation fee 13€

Surroundings : ℚ
Leisure activities : 🏠 ⋇ ⚓ 🔲 (open-air in season)
Facilities : ⅃ ⊶ 🎱 ⁱᵖ launderette

GPS
Longitude : -1.39169
Latitude : 46.01354

Les Seulières

℘ 05 46 47 90 51, www.campinglesseulieres.com

Address : 1371 rte des Seulières - Les Huttes (3.5km southwest, follow the signs for Chaucre; 400m from the beach)

Opening times : from beginning April to end Oct.

2.4 ha (120 pitches) flat, grassy, sandy

Tariff : (2012 price) 22€ ✚✚ ⟵ 🗐 🕭 (10A) – Extra per person 4€ – Reservation fee 15€

Rental rates : (2012 price) (from beginning April to end Oct.) – 5 🚐 – 8 🏠.

Per night from 50 to 60 € – Per week from 300 to 550 € – Reservation fee 15€

Surroundings : ⟿ ♨♨
Leisure activities : ♟ 🖼
Facilities : ὦ ☞ ⬚ ¶ launderette
Nearby : ✕

Longitude : -1.38512
Latitude : 46.0034

St-Georges-d'Oléron 17190 – Michelin map **324** C4 – pop. 3,497 – alt. 10

◪ Paris 527 – Marennes 27 – Rochefort 49 – La Rochelle 85

Camping-Club Verébleu ♣♣

℘ 05 46 76 57 70, www.verebleu.tm.fr ✕

Address : at La Jousselinière (1.7km southeast along the D 273 and turn left, following signs for Sauzelle)

Opening times : from beginning June to mid Sept.

7.5 ha (330 pitches) flat, grassy, sandy

Tariff : (2012 price) 39.50€ ✚✚ ⟵ 🗐 🕭 (8A) – Extra per person 8€ – Reservation fee 25€

Rental rates : (2012 price) (from beginning June to mid Sept.) ✕ – 76 🚐 – 69 🏠.

Per week from 340 to 1,270 € – Reservation fee 25€

🚽 sani-station

Swimming and play area themed around Fort Boyard (film set for French TV adventure show).

Surroundings : ⟿ ⊏ ♨♨
Leisure activities : ⊕ 🏃 🏊 🚲 ✕ ♨ 🏊 🏄 multi-sports ground
Facilities : ὦ ☞ 🗑 🛁 ⬚ ¶ launderette ⤵

Longitude : -1.31759
Latitude : 45.97111

Domaine des 4 Vents

℘ 05 46 76 65 47, www.camping-oleron-4vents.com

Address : at La Jousselinière (2km southeast along the D 273 and turn left, following signs for Sauzelle)

Opening times : from end June to beginning Sept.

7 ha (217 pitches) flat, grassy

Tariff : (2012 price) 30€ ✚✚ ⟵ 🗐 🕭 (10A) – Extra per person 5€ – Reservation fee 10€

Rental rates : (2012 price) (from mid April to mid Sept.) – 80 🚐. Per night from 40 to 65€

Per week from 240 to 830€ – Reservation fee 20€

🚽 sani-station 4€ – 10 🗐 16€ – 🚐 🕭 8€

Surroundings : ⟿ ⊏ ♨
Leisure activities : 🖼 🏃 🏊 🏊 🏄 multi-sports ground
Facilities : ὦ ☞ 🛁 ⬚ ¶ launderette ⤵

Longitude : -1.31995
Latitude : 45.96973

Key to rentals symbols:

12 🚐   *Number of mobile homes*
20 🏠   *Number of chalets*
6 🛏   *Number of rooms to rent*
Per night 30–50€   *Minimum/maximum rate per night*
Per week 300–1,000€   *Minimum/maximum rate per week*

Oléron Loisirs
(rental of mobile homes, chalets and tent bungalows only)

☏ 05 46 76 50 20, *www.oleron-loisirs.com* – traditional pitches also available

Address : at La Jousselinière (1.9km southeast along the D 273 and turn left, following signs for Sauzelle)

Opening times : from beginning April to end Sept.

8 ha (321 pitches) flat, grassy

Rental rates : (1 mobile home) – 200 – 10 – 13 tent bungalows.
Per week from 280 to 730 € – Reservation fee 25€

Surroundings :
Leisure activities : multi-sports ground, entertainment room
Facilities : launderette

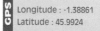

Longitude : -1.31435
Latitude : 45.97062

La Campière

☏ 05 46 76 72 25, *www.la-campiere.com*

Address : chemin de l'Achnau-Chaucre (5.4km southwest following signs for Chaucre and take road to the left)

Opening times : from beginning April to end Sept.

1.7 ha (63 pitches) flat, grassy, sandy

Tariff : 34.80€ (10A) – Extra per person 8€ – Reservation fee 17€

Rental rates : (from beginning April to end Sept.) – 1 – 12 – 3 tent bungalows.
Per week from 200 to 860 € – Reservation fee 17€

sani-station

A pleasantly leafy, green setting and a well-kept site.

Surroundings :
Leisure activities : (small swimming pool)
Facilities : launderette

Longitude : -1.38861
Latitude : 45.9924

WEST COAST

Club Airotel Les Gros Joncs

☏ 05 46 76 52 29, *www.camping-les-gros-joncs.com* – limited spaces for one-night stay

Address : 850 rte de Ponthezière - Les Sables Vignier (5km southwest, 300m from the sea)

Opening times : from beginning April to end Oct.

5 ha (253 pitches) terraced, flat, undulating

Tariff : 49.50€ (10A) – Extra per person 13€ – Reservation fee 18€

Rental rates : (permanent) (5 chalets) – 144 – 60 . Per night from 80 to 140 €
Per week from 354 to 1,399 € – Reservation fee 18€

sani-station – 16€

An attractive swimming area, open-air in part.

Surroundings :
Leisure activities : hammam jacuzzi spa therapy centre, entertainment room
Facilities : launderette

Longitude : -1.379
Latitude : 45.95342

We welcome your feedback on our listed campsites.
Please email us at: campingfrance@tp.michelin.com
Many thanks in advance!

St-Pierre-d'Oléron 17310 – Michelin map **324** C4 – pop. 6,532 – alt. 8
▶ Paris 522 – Marennes 22 – Rochefort 44 – La Rochelle 80

Aqua 3 Masses ♠♠

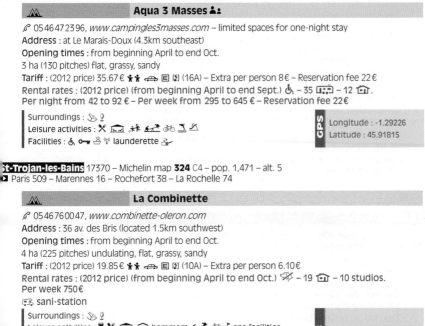

✆ 05 46 47 23 96, *www.campingles3masses.com* – limited spaces for one-night stay
Address : at Le Marais-Doux (4.3km southeast)
Opening times : from beginning April to end Oct.
3 ha (130 pitches) flat, grassy, sandy
Tariff : (2012 price) 35.67€ ♣♣ ⇔ 🔲 🚽 (16A) – Extra per person 8€ – Reservation fee 22€
Rental rates : (2012 price) (from beginning April to end Sept.) ♿ – 35 🚐 – 12 🏠.
Per night from 42 to 92 € – Per week from 295 to 645 € – Reservation fee 22€

Surroundings : 🦌 ♀
Leisure activities : ✗ 🎬 🕴 ⚓ 🎠 ♨ ⛵
Facilities : ♿ ⚓ 🧺 ♨ launderette 🔧

GPS
Longitude : -1.29226
Latitude : 45.91815

St-Trojan-les-Bains 17370 – Michelin map **324** C4 – pop. 1,471 – alt. 5
▶ Paris 509 – Marennes 16 – Rochefort 38 – La Rochelle 74

La Combinette

✆ 05 46 76 00 47, *www.combinette-oleron.com*
Address : 36 av. des Bris (located 1.5km southwest)
Opening times : from beginning April to end Oct.
4 ha (225 pitches) undulating, flat, grassy, sandy
Tariff : (2012 price) 19.85€ ♣♣ ⇔ 🔲 🚽 (10A) – Extra per person 6.10€
Rental rates : (2012 price) (from beginning April to end Oct.) 🏕 – 19 🏠 – 10 studios.
Per week 750€
🚐 sani-station

Surroundings : 🦌 ♀
Leisure activities : ♀ ✗ 🎬 🔲 hammam ⚓ 🎠 ♨ spa facilities
multi-sports ground
Facilities : ♿ ⚓ 🍽 ♨ ⛲ 🚿 ♨ 🔲 ♨ 🔧
Nearby : 🍴

GPS
Longitude : -1.2159
Latitude : 45.82958

86220 – Michelin map **322** J3 – pop. 1,784 – alt. 50
▶ Paris 305 – Châtellerault 7 – Descartes 18 – Poitiers 41

Les Castels Le Petit Trianon de Saint Ustre

✆ 05 49 02 61 47, *www.petit-trianon.com*
Address : 1 r. du Moulin de St-Ustre (3km to the northeast; at St-Ustre)
Opening times : from mid April to mid Sept.
4 ha (95 pitches) flat and relatively flat, grassy
Tariff : 31.60€ ♣♣ ⇔ 🔲 🚽 (10A) – Extra per person 8€ – Reservation fee 10€
Rental rates : (from mid April to mid Sept.) – 24 🚐 – 1 cabin in the trees – 6 teepees – 2 tent
bungalows – 2 gîtes. Per night 150€ – Per week from 205 to 920 € – Reservation fee 10€
🚐 sani-station
Pleasant setting in the grounds of a small château, with a range of rental options.

Surroundings : 🦌 ≤ ♀♀
Leisure activities : 🔲 ⚓ ♨ ⛵
Facilities : ♿ ⚓ ♨ ♨ 🔲 🔧

GPS
Longitude : 0.58653
Latitude : 46.88779

JONZAC

17500 – Michelin map **324** H7 – pop. 3,488 – alt. 40 – ♨ (mid-Feb-beg Dec)
▶ Paris 512 – Angoulême 59 – Bordeaux 84 – Cognac 36

Les Castors

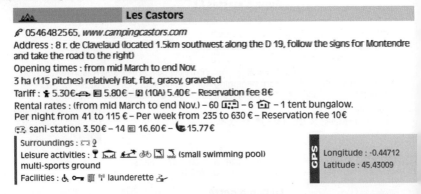

℘ 05 46 48 25 65, *www.campingcastors.com*
Address : 8 r. de Clavelaud (located 1.5km southwest along the D 19, follow the signs for Montendre and take the road to the right)
Opening times : from mid March to end Nov.
3 ha (115 pitches) relatively flat, flat, grassy, gravelled
Tariff : ♦ 5.30€ ⇌ 🗐 5.80€ – (9) (10A) 5.40€ – Reservation fee 8€
Rental rates : (from mid March to end Nov.) – 60 🚐 – 6 🏠 – 1 tent bungalow.
Per night from 41 to 115 € – Per week from 235 to 630 € – Reservation fee 10€
🖙 sani-station 3.50€ – 14 🗐 16.60€ – 🚰 15.77€

Surroundings : 🖙 ♀
Leisure activities : ♀ 🏠 ⚓ 🚲 🖼 ⛴ (small swimming pool) multi-sports ground
Facilities : ♿ ⊶ ▥ 🚽 launderette ⚒

GPS Longitude : -0.44712
Latitude : 45.43009

LAGORD

17140 – Michelin map **324** D2 – pop. 7,243 – alt. 23
▶ Paris 475 – Poitiers 142 – La Rochelle 6 – Niort 75

Municipal le Parc

℘ 05 46 67 61 54, *www.mairie-lagord.fr*
Address : take the western exit, follow r. du Parc, take the ring road (périphérique) towards Île de Ré and take the exit for Lagord
2 ha (120 pitches) flat, grassy
Rentals : 8 🏠.
🖙 sani-station

Surroundings : 🍃 🖙 ♀♀
Leisure activities : 🏠 ⚓ ♠ ⛴
Facilities : ♿ ⊶ ⚒ launderette
Nearby : 🍴 🖼

GPS Longitude : -1.15792
Latitude : 46.19176

In order for the guide to remain wholly objective, the selection of campsites is made on an entirely independent basis.

LANDRAIS

17290 – Michelin map **324** E3 – pop. 680 – alt. 12
▶ Paris 455 – Niort 48 – Rochefort 23 – La Rochelle 32

le Pré Maréchat

℘ 05 46 27 73 69, *www.cc-plaine-aunis.fr*
Address : take northwestern exit along the D 112, follow the signs for Aigrefeuille-d'Aunis and take road to the left, 120m from a lake
Opening times : from mid June to mid Sept.
0.6 ha (37 pitches) flat, grassy, stony
Tariff : (2012 price) 11.50€ ♦♦ ⇌ 🗐 (9) (30A) – Extra per person 2.50€

Surroundings : 🍃 🖙 ♀♀
Leisure activities : ⚓
Facilities : ♿ ⇱
Nearby : 🎣

GPS Longitude : -0.86536
Latitude : 46.06963

LE LINDOIS

16310 – Michelin map **324** N5 – pop. 343 – alt. 270
◘ Paris 453 – Angoulême 41 – Confolens 34 – Montbron 12

L'Étang

✆ 0545650267, www.campingdeletang.com
Address : rte de Rouzède (500m southwest along the D 112)
Opening times : from beginning April to beginning Nov.
10 ha/1.5 (25 pitches) relatively flat, flat, grassy
Tariff : (2012 price) 22€ ✝✝ ⇔ 🉐 (16A) – Extra per person 4.50€
Rental rates : (2012 price) (from beginning April to beginning Nov.) – 4 cabins in the trees.
Per night from 40 to 50 € – Per week from 280 to 350 €

In a pleasantly natural and rural setting, among trees and beside a lake.

Surroundings : ⅍ ⊏ ⑳
Leisure activities : ⛾ ✕ ⚓ (beach) ⏏ boats for hire
Facilities : ⅙ ⊶ ⼞ ⅲ ▣

GPS Longitude : 0.58555
Latitude : 45.73974

> *Routes nationales are main roads and their identifying numbers begin with N or RN. Routes départementales are generally quieter roads and begin with D or DN.*

LOUDUN

86200 – Michelin map **322** G2 – pop. 7,089 – alt. 120
◘ Paris 311 – Angers 79 – Châtellerault 47 – Poitiers 55

Municipal de Beausoleil

✆ 0549981538, http://www.ville-loudun.fr
Address : chemin de l'Étang (2.5km take the northern exit along the D 347, towards Angers and take road to the left after the level crossing; beside a stream and near a lake)
0.6 ha (33 pitches) terrace, flat, grassy

Surroundings : ⊏ ⑨⑨
Leisure activities : ⛾⬈
Facilities : ⅙ ⚲

GPS Longitude : 0.06175
Latitude : 47.00334

MAGNÉ

86160 – Michelin map **322** I6 – pop. 622 – alt. 121
◘ Paris 375 – Poitiers 29 – Niort 82 – Angoulême 94

Les Cabanes du Parc de la Belle
(rental of cabins in the trees only)

✆ 0549878086, www.parcdelabelle.com
Address : r. Anatole de Briey (in town centre, opposite the church)
Opening times : permanent
10 ha flat, wood
Rental rates : ⅍ – 14 cabins among the trees. Per night from 125 to 285 €
Per week from 875 to 1,995 €

Situated in a beautiful park.

Surroundings : ⅍ ⑳
Leisure activities : ⛾⬈
Facilities : ⊶ ⅲ
Nearby : ⛾ ✕

GPS Longitude : 0.39212
Latitude : 46.35716

MANSLE

16230 – Michelin map **324** L4 – pop. 1,543 – alt. 65
▶ Paris 421 – Angoulême 26 – Cognac 53 – Limoges 93

△ **Municipal Le Champion**

𝄞 05 45 20 31 41, *mairie.mansle@wanadoo.fr*
Address : r. de Watlington (take the northeastern exit along the D 18, follow the signs for Ruffec and take a right turn, near the racecourse; beside the Charente river)
2 ha (120 pitches) flat, grassy

Surroundings : ⌷ 0 0
Leisure activities : ⚞
Facilities : ⅙ ⊶ ⚐ ▣
Nearby : ✕ ⚒ ⚔ ↟

GPS Longitude : 0.18178
Latitude : 45.87801

Some information or pricing may have changed since the guide went to press. We recommend you check the price list online in advance or at the entrance to the campsite and enquire about possible restrictions.

MARANS

17230 – Michelin map **324** E2 – pop. 4,623 – alt. 1
▶ Paris 461 – Fontenay-le-Comte 28 – Niort 56 – La Rochelle 24

⚠ **Municipal du Bois Dinot**

𝄞 05 46 01 10 51, *www.ville-marans.fr*
Address : rte de Nantes (500m north along the N 137, 80m from the Marans-La Rochelle canal)
Opening times : from beginning April to end Sept.
7 ha/3 ha for camping (170 pitches) flat, grassy
Tariff : ✶ 3.75 € ⇔ 2.40 € ▣ 3 € – (⨠) (10A) 3 €
Rental rates : (from beginning April to end Sept.) ⅙ (1 chalet) – 12 ☖ .
Per night from 45 to 53 € – Per week from 192 to 546 €
⊞ sani-station 4 € – 10 ▣ 11 € – ⚲ 11 €
In the heart of a wooded park with a former veolodrome for lovers of 2-wheeled transport.

Surroundings : ⌷ 0 0
Leisure activities : ⚔
Facilities : ⅙ ⊶ ⚐ ⚑ launderette
Nearby : ⚌ ⚞ pedalos

GPS Longitude : -0.98945
Latitude : 46.31583

MARENNES

17320 – Michelin map **324** D5 – pop. 5,608 – alt. 10
▶ Paris 494 – Pons 61 – Rochefort 22 – Royan 31

⚠ **Au Bon Air**

𝄞 05 46 85 02 40, *www.aubonair.com*
Address : 9 av. Pierre Voyer (2.5km to the west; at Marennes-Plage)
Opening times : from beginning April to end Sept.
2.4 ha (140 pitches) sandy, flat, grassy
Tariff : 26.70 € ✶✶ ⇔ ▣ (⨠) (16A) – Extra per person 6 € – Reservation fee 17 €
Rental rates : (from beginning April to end Sept.) – 15 ⛺ – 5 ☖ . Per night from 40 to 62 €
Per week from 239 to 789 € – Reservation fee 17 €
⊞ sani-station 2 € – ⚲ 15 €

Surroundings : ⌷ 0 0
Leisure activities : ⚐ ⛱ ⚔ ⚌ ◊
Facilities : ⅙ ⊶ ⚐ ⚑ ⚒ ⚑ launderette

GPS Longitude : -1.13442
Latitude : 45.81882

LES MATHES

7570 – Michelin map **324** D5 – pop. 1,719 – alt. 10
Paris 514 – Marennes 18 – Rochefort 40 – La Rochelle 76

La Pinède

05 46 22 45 13, *www.campinglapinede.com* – limited spaces for one-night stay
Address : 2103 rte de la Fouasse (3km to the northwest)
Opening times : from beginning May to beginning Sept.
8 ha (372 pitches) flat, sandy
Tariff : (2012 price) 56€ ♥♥ ⇔ 回 (5A) – Extra per person 10.15€ – Reservation fee 30.50€
Rental rates : (2012 price) (from beginning April to mid Sept.) 占 – 166 ㎝ – 10 ㎝.
Per week from 279 to 1,308 € – Reservation fee 30.50€
The large swimming area is partially under cover.

Surroundings : ⑤ ⊏ 旦旦
Leisure activities : ♥ ✕ ⌨ ③ 木 ⿱ ⛾ ⛵ ♣ ⛵ ⚽ ⅍ ⅏ ☒ 丄 ⊿ ⚑ ⅀
wildlife park multi-sports ground
Facilities : 占 ⊶ ⍨ ⏚ ⚱ ⅏ launderette ⏛ ⅃
Nearby : amusement park, quad biking

GPS Longitude : -1.17568
Latitude : 45.72784

L'Estanquet

05 46 22 47 32, *www.campinglestanquet.com*
Address : rte de la Fouasse (3.5km to the northwest)
Opening times : from beginning April to end Sept.
6 ha (387 pitches) flat, sandy
Tariff : (2012 price) 30.80€ ♥♥ ⇔ 回 (10A) – Extra per person 6€ – Reservation fee 20€
Rental rates : (2012 price) (from beginning April to end Sept.) – 223 ㎝ – 10 ㎝ – 20 tent
bungalows. Per night from 28 to 140 € – Per week from 159 to 980 € – Reservation fee 20€
Pretty swimming area and free use of the indoor swimming pool at the 'Les Sables de
Cordouan' campsite 200m away.

Surroundings : ⊏ 旦旦
Leisure activities : ♥ ✕ ③ 木 ⛵ ⛵ ⚽ 丄 ⊿ multi-sports ground
Facilities : 占 ⊶ ⍨ ⏚ ⚱ ⅏ launderette ⏛ ⅃
Nearby : ☒ amusement park

GPS Longitude : -1.17661
Latitude : 45.73214

L'Orée du Bois

05 46 22 42 43, *www.camping-oree-du-bois.fr* – limited spaces for one-night stay
Address : 225 rte de la Bouverie (3.5km to the northwest, at La Fouasse)
6 ha (388 pitches) flat, sandy
Rentals : 20 ㎝.

Surroundings : ⊏ 旦旦
Leisure activities : ♥ ✕ ⌨ ③ 木 ⛵ ⛵ ⚽ 丄 ⊿ multi-sports
ground
Facilities : 占 ⊶ – 40 individual sanitary facilities (⍰⍕⍔ wc) ,
launderette ⏛ ⅃

GPS Longitude : -1.17905
Latitude : 45.72998

Monplaisir

05 46 22 50 31, *www.campingmonplaisir.com*
Address : 26 av. de La Palmyre (southwestern exit)
2 ha (114 pitches) flat, grassy
⊞ sani-station
Surroundings : 旦旦
Leisure activities : ⌨ ⛵ ♣ 丄
Facilities : 占 ⊶ ⍨ launderette
Nearby : ⅍ ♥ ✕ amusement park, quad biking

GPS Longitude : -1.15563
Latitude : 45.71541

MAUZÉ-SUR-LE-MIGNON

79210 – Michelin map **322** B7 – pop. 2,758 – alt. 30
▶ Paris 430 – Niort 23 – Rochefort 40 – La Rochelle 43

Municipal le Gué de la Rivière

✆ 0549263035, www.ville-mauze-mignon.fr – ♻
Address : r. du Port (located 1km northwest along the D 101, follow the signs for St-Hilaire-la-Palud and take the turning to the left; near the Mignon river and the canal)
Opening times : from beginning June to beginning Sept.
1.5 ha (75 pitches) flat, grassy
Tariff : (2012 price) ♦ 2.50€ ⇔ 🔲 2.60€ – 🚿 (10A) 3.50€
🚽 sani-station 4€

Surroundings : 🏞 � ♋
Leisure activities : 🏓

GPS Longitude : -0.67959
Latitude : 46.19968

MÉDIS

17600 – Michelin map **324** E6 – pop. 2,698 – alt. 29
▶ Paris 498 – Marennes 28 – Mirambeau 48 – Pons 39

Le Clos Fleuri

✆ 0546056217, www.le-clos-fleuri.com
Address : 8 impasse du Clos Fleuri (situated 2km southeast along the D 117e 3)
Opening times : from beginning June to mid Sept.
3 ha (140 pitches) flat and relatively flat, grassy
Tariff : 36€ ♦♦ ⇔ 🔲 🚿 (10A) – Extra per person 9.50€ – Reservation fee 20€
Rental rates : (from beginning June to mid Sept.) ✂ – 4 🛖 – 10 🏠.
Per week from 270 to 740 € – Reservation fee 20€

In a pleasant rural setting based around an old Charente farmhouse.

Surroundings : 🏞 � ♋
Leisure activities : ♈ ✕ 🏓 📺 ⚽ 🏋 ♒ 🏊
Facilities : ♿ ⚡ 🚿 🚰 launderette 🏪 🚲

GPS Longitude : -0.94633
Latitude : 45.63003

This guide is updated regularly, so buy your new copy every year!

MESCHERS-SUR-GIRONDE

17132 – Michelin map **324** E6 – pop. 2,747 – alt. 5
▶ Paris 511 – Blaye 78 – Jonzac 49 – Pons 37

Le Soleil Levant

✆ 0546027662, www.les-campings.com/camping-soleillevant
Address : 33 allée de la Longée (500m east along the r. Basse)
Opening times : from beginning April to end Sept.
2 ha (238 pitches) flat, grassy
Tariff : 23.50€ ♦♦ ⇔ 🔲 🚿 (10A) – Extra per person 6.50€
Rental rates : (from mid April to end Sept.) ✂ – 25 🛖. Per night from 45 to 60 €
Per week from 280 to 710 €
🚽 sani-station 11€

Surroundings : ♋
Leisure activities : ♈ 🏋 🏊 ⛱
Facilities : ⚡ 🚿 🚰 📷 🚲

GPS Longitude : -0.94639
Latitude : 45.55747

MONTBRON

16220 – Michelin map **324** N5 – pop. 2,161 – alt. 141
◘ Paris 460 – Angoulême 29 – Nontron 25 – Rochechouart 38

Les Castels Les Gorges du Chambon ♟♟

⌖ 05 45 70 71 70, www.camping-gorgesduchambon.com ✇

Address : at Le Chambon (4.4km east along the D 6, follow the signs for Piégut-Pluviers, then take left turn for 3.2km along the D 163, follow the signs for Ecuras and take the road to the right; 80m from the Tardoir river (direct access)

Opening times : from mid April to mid Sept.

28 ha/7 ha for camping (120 pitches) flat, relatively flat, grassy

Tariff : 33.30€ ♟♟ ⇔ 🗐 🖭 (10A) – Extra per person 9.10€ – Reservation fee 10€

Rental rates : (from beginning April to end Oct.) ⚕ (1 mobile home) ✇ – 15 🚐 – 8 🏠 – 1 gîte. Per night from 39 to 89 € – Per week from 196 to 672 € – Reservation fee 20€

🚽 sani-station

Pretty, green setting among trees, based around an old landscaped and renovated farm-house.

Surroundings : 🌫 ⋖ ꕫ
Leisure activities : ♟ ✗ 🖵 🗐 ⚓ ⚓ 🚴 ✇ ♪ 🎣 ⚓ 🎣
Facilities : ⚕ ⌐ ▥ 🛁 🚰 launderette ⚍ ⚏
Nearby : 🐎

GPS Longitude : 0.5593
Latitude : 45.65945

MONTIGNAC-CHARENTE

16330 – Michelin map **324** K5 – pop. 731 – alt. 50
◘ Paris 432 – Angoulême 17 – Cognac 42 – Rochechouart 66

Municipal les Platanes

⌖ 05 45 39 89 16, mairie.montignac-chte@orange.fr

Address : 25 av. de la Boïxe (200m northwest along the D 115, follow the signs for Aigré)

Opening times : from beginning June to end Aug.

1.5 ha (100 pitches) flat, grassy

Tariff : (2012 price) ♟ 5€ ⇔ 🗐 🖭 (12A) 5.80€

Surroundings : ꕫ
Leisure activities : 🖵
Facilities : ⚕ ⚏
Nearby : 🎣

GPS Longitude : 0.11797
Latitude : 45.78189

MONTMORILLON

86500 – Michelin map **322** L6 – pop. 6,410 – alt. 100
◘ Paris 354 – Bellac 43 – Le Blanc 32 – Chauvigny 27

Municipal de l'Allochon

⌖ 05 49 91 02 33, www.ville-montmorillon.fr

Address : 31 av. Fernad-Tribot (take the southeastern exit along the D 54, follow the signs for Le Dorat; 50m from the Gartempe river, beside a stream)

Opening times : from beginning March to end Oct.

2 ha (80 pitches) terraced, flat, grassy

Tariff : (2012 price) ♟ 1.64€ ⇔ 🗐 – 🖭 (10A) 5.27€

Surroundings : ꕫ
Leisure activities : 🖵 ⚓
Facilities : ⚕ ⌐ ⚏ ▥ 🛁 🚰 🖫
Nearby : 🏊 🎣 🎣

GPS Longitude : 0.87526
Latitude : 46.42038

MORTAGNE-SUR-GIRONDE

17120 – Michelin map **324** F7 – pop. 1,027 – alt. 51
▶ Paris 509 – Blaye 59 – Jonzac 30 – Pons 26

 Municipal Bel Air

℘ 05 46 91 48 84, *www.mortagne-sur-gironde*
Address : towards the port
Opening times : from beginning June to end Sept.
1 ha (20 pitches) terraced, relatively flat, flat, grassy
Tariff : (2012 price) 11.30€ ♥ ♥ ⌦ 🏕 🔼 (20A) – Extra per person 3€

Surroundings : 🏞 ≼ estuary and the marina ⌁ 👓
Leisure activities : 🚣
Facilities : ♿ ⌐ 🚿 ☑ 🔥 ☂ ♈ ♈

GPS Longitude : -0.79147
Latitude : 45.47974

MOSNAC

17240 – Michelin map **324** G6 – pop. 476 – alt. 23
▶ Paris 501 – Cognac 34 – Gémozac 20 – Jonzac 11

 Municipal les Bords de la Seugne

℘ 05 46 70 48 45, *mosnac@mairie17.com*
Address : 34 r. de la Seugne (in the village; beside the river)
Opening times : from mid April to mid Oct.
0.9 ha (33 pitches) flat, grassy
Tariff : (2012 price) ♥ 3€ ⌦ 🏕 3€

Surroundings : 🏞 ≼ Église Saint-Saturnin, Mosnac ⌁ 👓
Leisure activities : 🎣
Facilities : 🚿 🏛

GPS Longitude : -0.52293
Latitude : 45.5058

The classification (1 to 5 tents, black or red) that we award to selected sites in this guide is our own system. It should not be confused with the classification (1 to 5 stars) of official organisations.

LA PALMYRE

17570 – Michelin map **324** C5
▶ Paris 524 – Poitiers 191 – La Rochelle 77 – Rochefort 46

 Village Siblu Bonne Anse Plage
(rental of mobile homes only)

℘ 05 46 22 40 90, *www.siblu.fr/bonneanse* – limited spaces for one-night stay
Address : av. de la Coubre (situated 2km west along the D 25, 400m from the beach)
Opening times : from beginning June to end Aug.
18 ha (650 pitches) undulating, flat, grassy, sandy
Rental rates : (2012 price) 🏚 – 100 🚐. Per night from 74 to 196
Per week from 428 to 1,282 € – Reservation fee 15€

A mobile-home park, most of which belong to owner-occupiers.

Surroundings : ⌁ 👓
Leisure activities : 🍷 ✕ 🎲 🏇 🎠 🚵 🚴 🎯 🏊 🏖 climbing wall, multi-sports ground
Facilities : ♿ ⌐ ♈ launderette ▥ 🐾

GPS Longitude : -1.19983
Latitude : 45.69843

Beausoleil

✆ 05 46 22 30 03, *www.campingbeausoleil.com*

Address : 20 av. de la Coubre (take the northwestern exit, 500m from the beach)
Opening times : from beginning June to end Aug.
4 ha (244 pitches) undulating, flat, sandy, grassy
Tariff : (2012 price) 31.28€ ✝✝ ⇔ 回 № (10A) – Extra per person 4.80€ – Reservation fee 17€
Rental rates : (2012 price) (from beginning April to end Sept.) – 18 ⛺ – 2 tent bungalows. Per week from 193 to 750 € – Reservation fee 18€

Surroundings : 🌳🌳
Leisure activities : 🎣 🏖 🏊 (small swimming pool)
Facilities : 🚿 ⚐ 🛁 ⚘ 🏠 🚻 ⚲

GPS
Longitude : -1.18301
Latitude : 45.69242

PARTHENAY

79200 – Michelin map **322** E5 – pop. 10,338 – alt. 175 – Leisure centre
▶ Paris 377 – Bressuire 32 – Châtellerault 79 – Fontenay-le-Comte 69

Le Bois Vert

✆ 05 49 64 78 43, *www.camping-boisvert.com*

Address : 14 r. Boisseau (take the southwestern exit follow the signs for La Roche-sur-Yon and take a right turn after the bridge over the Thouet; near a lake)
Opening times : from beginning April to end Oct.
2 ha (86 pitches) flat, grassy
Tariff : 27.50€ ✝✝ ⇔ 回 № (10A) – Extra per person 6€ – Reservation fee 10€
Rental rates : (from beginning April to end Oct.) 🚿 – 13 ⛺ – 4 🏠. Per night from 56 to 91 € Per week from 336 to 637 € – Reservation fee 10€
🚽 sani-station 8€ – ⚲ № 27.50€

Surroundings : 🌲 🌳
Leisure activities : 🍸 🎣 🏕 🚲 🏊
Facilities : 🚿 ⚐ 🆑 ⚙ ⚘ ⚲ 🏠 launderette
Nearby : 🍴 ⚲ 🏖 🎿 🏇 🚣

GPS
Longitude : -0.2675
Latitude : 46.64194

The pitches of many campsites are marked out with low hedges of attractive bushes and shrubs.

PONS

17800 – Michelin map **324** G6 – pop. 4,446 – alt. 39
▶ Paris 493 – Blaye 64 – Bordeaux 97 – Cognac 24

Les Moulins de la Vergne

✆ 05 46 94 11 49, *www.moulinsdelavergne.nl*

Address : 9 impasse du Moulin de la Vergne (situated 2km north along the D 234, towards Colombiers)
Opening times : permanent
3 ha/1 ha for camping (51 pitches) flat, grassy, wood
Tariff : 23€ ✝✝ ⇔ 回 № (10A) – Extra per person 2€
Rental rates : (from mid Feb. to end Nov.) – 10 🏠. Per night from 80 to 100 € Per week from 550 to 750 €

Surroundings : 🌿 🌳
Leisure activities : 🍸 🍴 🎣 🏊 🚣
Facilities : ⚐ ⚙ ⚲ launderette ⚲

GPS
Longitude : -0.53906
Latitude : 45.59444

Municipal le Paradis

℘ 0546913672, ville.pons@smic17.fr
Address : av. du Paradis (to the west near the swimming pool)
Opening times : from beginning May to end Sept.
1 ha (60 pitches) flat, grassy
Tariff : (2012 price) ♟ 3.50€ ⇌ 圓 7€ – 圓 (10A) 1€
⊂⊟ sani-station 6€ – 5 圓

Surroundings : ΩΩ
Leisure activities : 🎣
Facilities : ᵭ ⟶ 🛁 ⟷ 🍴
Nearby : 🏊 🏞

GPS Longitude : -0.5553
Latitude : 45.57793

PONT-L'ABBÉ-D'ARNOULT

17250 – Michelin map **324** E5 – pop. 1,716 – alt. 20
▶ Paris 474 – Marennes 23 – Rochefort 19 – La Rochelle 59

Parc de la Garenne

℘ 0546970146, www.lagarenne.net
Address : 24 av. Bernard Chambenoit (take the southeastern exit along the D 125, follow the signs for Soulignonne)
Opening times : from beginning April to mid Oct.
2.7 ha (111 pitches) flat, grassy
Tariff : 25.20€ ♟♟ ⇌ 圓 圓 (10A) – Extra per person 4.10€ – Reservation fee 15€
Rental rates : (from beginning April to mid Oct.) – 30 🛖 – 2 tent bungalows.
Per night 130€ – Per week from 199 to 719 € – Reservation fee 15€
⊂⊟ sani-station – 15 圓 14€ – 🚐 10€

Surroundings : 🌳 ▭ Ω
Leisure activities : 🎣 ⛹ 🚲 🏊 multi-sports ground
Facilities : ᵭ ⟶ 🛁 🚿 ⟷ 🍴 launderette ⚡
Nearby : 🏊

GPS Longitude : -0.87096
Latitude : 45.82729

PRAILLES

79370 – Michelin map **322** E7 – pop. 666 – alt. 150 – Leisure centre
▶ Paris 394 – Melle 15 – Niort 23 – St-Maixent-l'École 13

Le Lambon

℘ 0549328511, www.lelambon.com
Address : at Lac du Lambon (Lambon leisure lake) (2.8km southeast)
Opening times : from mid April to end Sept.
1 ha (50 pitches) terraced, sloping, flat, grassy
Tariff : 13.30€ ♟♟ ⇌ 圓 圓 (10A) – Extra per person 4.70€
Rental rates : (permanent) – 7 🛖 – 39 gîtes. Per night 85€ – Per week 408€
⊂⊟ sani-station
Situated 200m from the sailing centre where a number of activities are offered.

Surroundings : 🌳 ΩΩ
Facilities : ᵭ ⤳ 🍴 launderette
Nearby : 🍴 ✕ 🍷 ⛹ 🏊 🛶 ≈ (beach) ⚡ sports trail, forest trail, climbing

GPS Longitude : -0.20753
Latitude : 46.30055

Using the traditional Michelin classification method, the guide provides
you with an easy, speedy reference for assessing the category of each site:
1 to 5 tents (see page 10).

PRESSIGNAC

16150 – Michelin map **324** O5 – pop. 424 – alt. 259
Paris 437 – Angoulême 56 – Nontron 40 – Rochechouart 10

Des Lacs

℘ 0545311780, www.campingdeslacs.fr
Address : at La Guerlie (4.2km southwest along the D 160, follow the signs for Verneuil; by a small lake)
15 ha/6 ha for camping (160 pitches) flat, grassy
Rentals : ⅙ – 60 🛖.
sani-station

Surroundings : ≤ on the lake ⌑
Leisure activities : 🎪 ⊕ daytime ⚹ ⛲ 🏊 ⛲
Facilities : ⅙ ⚬ ⚱ ⚲ launderette
Nearby : ☂ ✗ ⚿ ≋ (beach) ⚓ ⚲ ⚱ pedalos

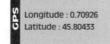

Longitude : 0.70926
Latitude : 45.80433

ROCHEFORT

17300 – Michelin map **324** E4 – pop. 25,317 – alt. 12 – ⚕ (beg Feb-mid-Dec)
Paris 475 – Limoges 221 – Niort 62 – La Rochelle 38

Le Bateau

℘ 0546994100, www.campinglebateau.com
Address : r. des Pécheurs D'Islande (near the Charente river, along the western bypass (bd Bignon) and follow the signs for Port Neuf, near the aquatic centre)
Opening times : from end March to end Oct.
5 ha/1.5 (86 pitches) flat, grassy, stony
Tariff : (2012 price) 14.50€ ⚹⚹ ⇔ 🗐 🗐 (10A) – Extra per person 4.50€
Rental rates : (2012 price) (from end March to end Oct.) – 37 🛖. Per night from 55 to 82 €
Per week from 290 to 520 €

Surroundings : ⚲ ⌑ ⚱
Leisure activities : ☂ ✗ 🎪 jacuzzi ⛲ 🏊 ⛲ ⚓
Facilities : ⅙ ⚬ ⚱ ⚲ ⚲ launderette
Nearby : ⚱

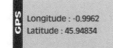

Longitude : -0.9962
Latitude : 45.94834

LA ROCHE-POSAY

86270 – Michelin map **322** K4 – pop. 1,556 – alt. 112 – ⚕ (end Mar-mid Oct)
Paris 325 – Le Blanc 29 – Châteauroux 76 – Châtellerault 23

Club Airotel La Roche-Posay Vacances ⚐

℘ 0549862123, www.larocheposay-vacances.com
Address : rte de Lésigny (located 1.5km north along the D 5, near the racecourse; beside the Creuse river)
Opening times : from mid April to end Sept.
5.5 ha (200 pitches) flat and relatively flat, grassy
Tariff : (2012 price) 28€ ⚹⚹ ⇔ 🗐 🗐 (16A) – Extra per person 6€
Rental rates : (2012 price) (from mid April to end Sept.) – 78 🛖. Per night from 49 to 128 €
Per week from 343 to 896 €
sani-station 6€ – 12 🗐 18€
The pitches are attractively marked out, set around a partially covered water park.

Surroundings : ⚲ ⌑ ⚱⚱
Leisure activities : 🎪 ⊕ ⚹ ⛲ ⚵ 🏊 ⛲ ⚓ boats for hire ⚱
Facilities : ⅙ ⚬ ⚱ ⚲ ⚲ launderette ⚱
Nearby : ⚱

Longitude : 0.80963
Latitude : 46.7991

RONCE-LES-BAINS

17390 – Michelin map **324** D5
▶ Paris 505 – Marennes 9 – Rochefort 31 – La Rochelle 68

Village Siblu La Pignade
(rental of mobile homes only)

🖉 05 46 36 15 35, *www.camping-lapignade.com*
Address : 45 av. du Monard (located 1.5km to the south)
Opening times : from beginning June to beginning Sept.
15 ha (524 pitches) flat, grassy
Rental rates : ⅗ 💱 – 120 ⬛. Per night from 50 to 190 € – Per week from 350 to 1,330 €
Reservation fee 15 €

A mobile-home park; most of the mobile homes belong to owner-occupiers.

Surroundings : 🐾 ▱ ♀
Leisure activities : ▼ ✕ 🕹 ⛹ ⚔ ₘ 🖵 (open-air in season) ⚰
multi-sports ground, entertainment room
Facilities : ⚬━ ☂ launderette 🛢 🔧
Nearby : 🚲 ⚜ quad biking

GPS
Longitude : -1.16204
Latitude : 45.7863

La Clairière ♣

🖉 05 46 36 36 63, *www.camping-la-clairiere.com* – limited spaces for one-night stay
Address : r. des Roseaux (3.6km south along the D 25, follow the signs for Arvert and take turning to the right)
Opening times : from beginning April to mid Sept.
12 ha/4 ha for camping (165 pitches) undulating, flat, grassy, sandy
Tariff : 35 € ♣♣ ⟺ 🗐 (10A) – Extra per person 8 € – Reservation fee 19 €
Rental rates : (from beginning April to mid Sept.) 💱 – 30 ⬛. Per week from 224 to 850 €
Reservation fee 19 €
🚐 sani-station 3 € – 20 🗐 29.50 €

The site has decorative flowers and shrubs.

Surroundings : 🐾 ♀♀
Leisure activities : ▼ ✕ 🖼 🕹 evening ⛹ 🛶 ⚔ ⚜ ₘ 🌊 ⚰
Facilities : ⅗ ⚬━ 🛖 ☂ launderette 🛢 🔧
Nearby : 🐎

GPS
Longitude : -1.16844
Latitude : 45.77502

Les Pins ♣

🖉 05 46 36 07 75, *http://gmic.lespins.com* – limited spaces for one-night stay
Address : 16 av. Côte de Beauté (located 1km to the south)
Opening times : from beginning April to beginning Oct.
1.5 ha (81 pitches) flat, sandy
Tariff : 33.65 € ♣♣ ⟺ 🗐 (16A) – Extra per person 6.49 € – Reservation fee 19 €
Rental rates : (from beginning April to beginning Nov.) – 37 ⬛ – 23 🏠 – 1 gîte.
Per night from 95 to 159 € – Per week from 257 to 889 € – Reservation fee 19 €

Surroundings : ♀♀
Leisure activities : 🖼 ⛹ ⚔ 🚲 🖵 (open-air in season)
Facilities : ⅗ ⚬━ 🛖 ☂ launderette 🔧
Nearby : 🛢 ⚜ activity room

GPS
Longitude : -1.15862
Latitude : 45.78875

ROYAN

17200 – Michelin map **324** D6 – pop. 18,259 – alt. 20
▶ Paris 504 – Bordeaux 121 – Périgueux 183 – Rochefort 40

▲▲▲ Le Royan

✆ 05 46 39 09 06, *www.le-royan.com*

Address : 10 r. des Bleuets (2.5km to the northwest)
Opening times : from beginning April to mid Oct.
3.5 ha (180 pitches) relatively flat, grassy
Tariff : 36 € ♦♦ ⇌ 🅴 🅿 (10A) – Extra per person 8 € – Reservation fee 20 €
Rental rates : (from beginning April to mid Oct.) – 75 🚐 – 13 🏠. Per night from 46 to 98 €
Per week from 285 to 845 € – Reservation fee 20 €

In a green and well-kept setting.

Surroundings : ⌖ 💧💧
Leisure activities : ▼ ✕ ▱ 🛶 🏊 🛶
Facilities : 🚿 ⚲ ♨ 🔥 ♈ ♙ launderette 🟦 🛒

Longitude : -1.04207
Latitude : 45.64456

▲▲ Campéole Clairefontaine

✆ 05 46 39 08 11, *www.campingclairfontaine.com*
Address : allée des Peupliers, at Pontaillac (400m from the beach)
Opening times : from beginning April to end Sept.
5 ha (290 pitches) flat, grassy
Tariff : 20.70 € ♦♦ ⇌ 🅴 🅿 (10A) – Extra per person 4.80 € – Reservation fee 25 €
Rental rates : (from beginning April to end Sept.) – 33 🚐 – 40 🏠 – 50 tent bungalows.
Per night from 31 to 65 € – Per week from 217 to 1,253 € – Reservation fee 25 €
🚐 sani-station

Surroundings : 💧💧
Leisure activities : ▼ ✕ ▱ 🎱 ✕ 🛶
Facilities : 🚿 ⚲ ♨ ♙ launderette 🟦

Longitude : -1.05279
Latitude : 45.63068

▲▲ Le Chant des Oiseaux

✆ 05 46 39 47 47, *www.camping-royan-chantdesoiseaux.com*
Address : 19 r. des Sansonnets (2.3km to the northwest)
Opening times : from beginning April to end Sept.
2.5 ha (150 pitches) flat, grassy, wood
Tariff : (2012 price) 19 € ♦♦ ⇌ 🅴 🅿 (10A) – Extra per person 3.90 € – Reservation fee 16 €
Rental rates : (from beginning April to mid Oct.) – 26 🚐. Per night from 63 to 71 €
Per week from 190 to 860 € – Reservation fee 16 €
🚐 8 🅴 19 €

Rental options of good quality, some offering hotel accommodation.

Surroundings : 🌿 💧
Leisure activities : ✕ ▱ 🎱 evening 🛶 🛶
Facilities : 🚿 ⚲ 🆑 ♨ ♙ 🔳 🟦

Longitude : -1.02872
Latitude : 45.6466

Michelin classification:

▲▲▲▲ *Extremely comfortable, equipped to a very high standard*
▲▲▲ *Very comfortable, equipped to a high standard*
▲▲▲ *Comfortable and well equipped*
▲▲ *Reasonably comfortable*
▲ *Satisfactory*

ST-AUGUSTIN-SUR-MER

17570 – Michelin map **324** D5 – pop. 1,219 – alt. 10
▶ Paris 512 – Marennes 23 – Rochefort 44 – La Rochelle 81

▲▲▲   Le Logis du Breuil

✆ 0546232345, *www.logis-du-breuil.com*
Address : 36 r. du Centre (located to the southeast along the D 145, follow the signs for Royan)
Opening times : from beginning May to end Sept.
30 ha/8.5 ha for camping (390 pitches) undulating, terraced, flat, grassy
Tariff : 29€ ✱✱ ⇆ ▣ 🅟 (6A) – Extra per person 7.50€ – Reservation fee 10€
Rental rates : (from end April to end Sept.) – 7 🕮 – 1 🏠. Per night from 55 €
Per week from 285 to 725 v – Reservation fee 20€
🚰 sani-station
At the edge of the St-Augustin forest.

Surroundings : 🦌 🞅🞅 **Leisure activities** : 🍴 ✕ 🖼 🛶 🚲 ✂ 🏊 multi-sports ground **Facilities** : 🚿 ⚷ 🛠 – 4 individual sanitary facilities (🚿♨ wc) 🚰 launderette 🛒 🐾 **Nearby** : 🐎	**GPS** Longitude : -1.1039 Latitude : 45.68115

These symbols are used for a campsite that is exceptional in its category:
▲▲▲...▲   *Particularly pleasant setting, quality and range of services available*
🦌🦌   *Tranquil, isolated site – quiet site, particularly at night*
≼≼   *Exceptional view – interesting or panoramic view*

ST-CYR

86130 – Michelin map **322** I4 – pop. 1,024 – alt. 62
▶ Paris 321 – Poitiers 18 – Tours 85 – Joué 82

▲▲▲   Flower Lac de St-Cyr

✆ 0549625722, *www.campinglacdesaintcyr.com*
Address : parc de St-Cyr (located 1.5km northeast along the D 4, D 82, follow the signs for
Bonneuil-Matours and take road to the left, near a lake - from N10, access via La Tricherie)
Opening times : from beginning April to end Sept.
5.4 ha (198 pitches) flat, grassy
Tariff : 16€ ✱✱ ⇆ ▣ 🅟 (10A) – Extra per person 3€ – Reservation fee 15€
Rental rates : (from beginning April to end Sept.) – 25 🕮 – 4 yurts – 3 tent bungalows.
Per night from 40 to 101 € – Per week from 280 to 749 € – Reservation fee 15€
🚰 7 ▣ 16€

Surroundings : ≼ ⛺ 🞅🞅 ▲ **Leisure activities** : ✕ 🖼 🎣 🏸 ⛳ 🛶 🚲 ✂ **Facilities** : 🚿 ⚷ 🛠 ♨ 🚰 launderette ♨ 🐾 **Nearby** : 🍴 ⛷ 🎣 🦆 pedalos	**GPS** Longitude : 0.44782 Latitude : 46.72056

ST-GEORGES-DE-DIDONNE

17110 – Michelin map **324** D6 – pop. 5,055 – alt. 7
▶ Paris 505 – Blaye 84 – Bordeaux 117 – Jonzac 56

Bois-Soleil ▲▲

℘ 05 46 05 05 94, *www.bois-soleil.com* ✆ (from beg Apr to end Jun)
Address : 2 av. de Suzac (situated to the south along the D 25, follow the signs for Meschers-sur-Gironde)
Opening times : from beginning April to beginning Oct.
10 ha (453 pitches) undulating, terraced, flat, sandy
Tariff : 15€ ✝✝ ⇔ 🔲 🚰 (10A) – Extra per person 5€ – Reservation fee 30€
Rental rates : (from beginning April to end Sept.) ✆ – 72 🚍 – 15 🏠 – 7 studios.
Per night from 30 to 90 € – Per week from 180 to 1,250 € – Reservation fee 30€
🚐 sani-station 6€

Surroundings : 🔲 🞌🞌 ⛰
Leisure activities : 🍴 ✕ 🖼 🞌 🞌 🕺 🎵 hammam ⛹ 🚲 🎾 🏊
multi-sports ground
Facilities : ♿ 🔌 📷 🏧 🞌 – 6 individual sanitary facilities (🞌🞌 wc) 🞌 🞌
🞌 launderette 🞌 🞌
Nearby : 🐎

GPS
Longitude : -0.98629
Latitude : 45.58371

ST-GEORGES-LÈS-BAILLARGEAUX

86130 – Michelin map **322** I4 – pop. 3,888 – alt. 100
▶ Paris 329 – Poitiers 12 – Joué 89 – Châtellerault 23

Le Futuriste

℘ 05 49 52 47 52, *www.camping-le-futuriste.fr*
Address : south of the town, access via the D 20
Opening times : permanent
2 ha (112 pitches) relatively flat, stony, grassy, small lake
Tariff : 29.10€ ✝✝ ⇔ 🔲 🚰 (6A) – Extra per person 3.50€ – Reservation fee 15€
Rental rates : (permanent) ✆ – 4 🚍 – 6 🏠. Per night from 60 to 121 €
Per week from 418 to 833 € – Reservation fee 15€
🚐 sani-station 6.50€

Surroundings : ≤ Futuroscope 🔲 🞌🞌
Leisure activities : 🍴 ✕ 🖼 ⛹ 🏊 🎵 🞌 multi-sports ground
Facilities : ♿ 🔌 📷 🏧 🞌 🞌 🞌 launderette 🞌

GPS
Longitude : 0.39543
Latitude : 46.66468

ST-HILAIRE-LA-PALUD

79210 – Michelin map **322** B7 – pop. 1,603 – alt. 15
▶ Paris 436 – Poitiers 104 – Niort 24 – La Rochelle 41

Le Lidon

℘ 05 49 35 33 64, *www.le-lidon.com*
Address : at Lidon (3km west along the D 3 follow the signs for Courçon and take road to the left, at the canoeing centre)
Opening times : from mid April to mid Sept.
3 ha (140 pitches) flat, grassy
Tariff : 26.30€ ✝✝ ⇔ 🔲 🚰 (10A) – Extra per person 6.10€ – Reservation fee 13.50€
Rental rates : (permanent) – 1 'gypsy' caravan – 3 🏠 – 4 tent bungalows – 9 tents.
Per night from 42 to 91 € – Per week from 210 to 637 € – Reservation fee 13.50€
🚐 sani-station 4€

Surroundings : 🞌 🞌🞌
Leisure activities : 🍴 ✕ 🖼 🚲 🏊 🎵 boats for hire 🞌
Facilities : ♿ 🔌 📷 🏧 🞌 🞌 launderette 🞌

GPS
Longitude : -0.74324
Latitude : 46.28379

ST-JEAN-D'ANGÉLY

17400 – Michelin map **324** G4 – pop. 7,581 – alt. 25
▶ Paris 444 – Angoulême 70 – Cognac 35 – Niort 48

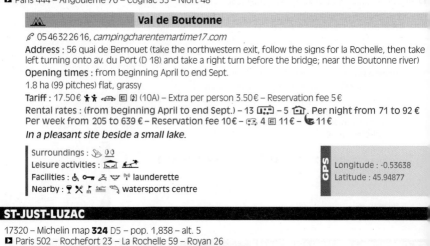

⚠ Val de Boutonne

✆ 05 46 32 26 16, *campingcharentemartime17.com*
Address : 56 quai de Bernouet (take the northwestern exit, follow the signs for la Rochelle, then take left turning onto av. du Port (D 18) and take a right turn before the bridge; near the Boutonne river)
Opening times : from beginning April to end Sept.
1.8 ha (99 pitches) flat, grassy
Tariff : 17.50€ ✶✶ ⟷ 🔲 (10A) – Extra per person 3.50€ – Reservation fee 5€
Rental rates : (from beginning April to end Sept.) – 13 🛏 – 5 🏠. Per night from 71 to 92 €
Per week from 205 to 639 € – Reservation fee 10€ – 🚰 4 🔲 11€ – 🛶 11€
In a pleasant site beside a small lake.

Surroundings : 🌊 ⭕⭕
Leisure activities : 🛖 🚣
Facilities : ♿ ⛽ 🚿 🔧 ⁇ launderette
Nearby : 🍸 🗙 🔥 ⚓ 🎣 watersports centre

GPS
Longitude : -0.53638
Latitude : 45.94877

ST-JUST-LUZAC

17320 – Michelin map **324** D5 – pop. 1,838 – alt. 5
▶ Paris 502 – Rochefort 23 – La Rochelle 59 – Royan 26

⚠ Les Castels Séquoia Parc ⚑

✆ 05 46 85 55 55, *www.sequoiaparc.com*
Address : at La Josephtrie (2.7km northwest along the D 728, follow the signs for Marennes and take the road to the right)
Opening times : from beginning May to beginning Sept.
45 ha/28 ha for camping (426 pitches) flat, grassy, stony, sandy, wood
Tariff : 50€ ✶✶ ⟷ 🔲 (6A) – Extra per person 9€ – Reservation fee 30€
Rental rates : (from beginning May to beginning Sept.) ♿ 🍽 – 321 🛏 – 32 🏠.
Per night from 153 to 232 € – Per week from 1,071 to 1,624 €
🚰 sani-station
A lovely swimming area near a château in a park full of different trees and flowers.

Surroundings : 🌊 ⬚ ⭕⭕
Leisure activities : 🍸 🗙 🛖 🎮 🕹 🚣 🚲 ⁇ ⛳ ⛷ 🏇 wildlife park, multi-sports ground
Facilities : ♿ ⛽ 🛁 🚿 🔧 ⁇ launderette 🛒 🚿

GPS
Longitude : -1.06046
Latitude : 45.81173

ST-LAURENT-DE-LA-PRÉE

17450 – Michelin map **324** D4 – pop. 1,814 – alt. 7
▶ Paris 483 – Rochefort 10 – La Rochelle 31

⚠ Domaine des Charmilles ⚑

✆ 05 46 84 00 05, *www.domainedescharmilles.com*
Address : 1541 rte de l'Océan at Fouras (2.2km northwest along the D 214e 1, follow the signs for Fouras and turn right onto D 937, follow the signs for La Rochelle)
Opening times : from end April to mid Sept.
5 ha (270 pitches) flat, grassy
Tariff : 34€ ✶✶ ⟷ 🔲 (10A) – Extra per person 6€
Rental rates : (from end April to mid Sept.) 🍽 (Jul–Aug) – 100 🛏 – 20 🏠.
Per night from 40 to 170 € – Per week from 279 to 1,199 € – Reservation fee 25€

Surroundings : ⬚ ⭕⭕
Leisure activities : 🍸 🛖 🎮 evening 🎯 🚣 🚲 🔥 🎮 ⛷ ⛳ multi-sports ground
Facilities : ♿ ⛽ 🛁 🚿 🔧 ⁇ launderette 🚿

GPS
Longitude : -1.05034
Latitude : 45.99052

Le Pré Vert

✆ 05 46 84 89 40, *www.camping-prevert.com*

Address : r. du Petit Loir (2.3km northeast along the D 214, follow the signs for la Rochelle; at St-Pierre – take the dual carriageway, Fouras exit)

Opening times : from end March to mid Nov.

3 ha (168 pitches) terraced, flat and relatively flat, grassy

Tariff : (2012 price) 24€ ★★ ⇔ 🔲 🔌 (8A) – Extra per person 5€ – Reservation fee 15€

Rental rates : (2012 price) (from end March to mid Nov.) – 72 🚐 – 8 🏠.

Per night from 60 to 70 € – Per week from 200 to 680 € – Reservation fee 15€

Surroundings : 🗁 ♨♨

Leisure activities : 🖼 ⚓ ≋ (pool)

Facilities : ♿ ⊶ (Jul–Aug) 🛁 ⚐ ♨ ♛ launderette 🐾

GPS Longitude : -1.01917
Latitude : 45.99046

This guide is not intended as a list of all the camping sites in France; its aim is to provide a selection of the best sites in each category.

ST-NAZAIRE-SUR-CHARENTE

7780 – Michelin map **324** D4 – pop. 1,124 – alt. 14

◣ Paris 491 – Fouras 27 – Rochefort 13 – La Rochelle 49

L'Abri-Cotier

✆ 05 46 84 81 65, *www.camping-la-rochelle.net*

Address : 26 La Bernardière (located 1km southwest along the D 125e1)

Opening times : from beginning April to end Sept.

1.8 ha (90 pitches) relatively flat, flat, grassy

Tariff : (2012 price) 24.20€ ★★ ⇔ 🔲 🔌 (6A) – Extra per person 5.10€ – Reservation fee 20€

Rental rates : (2012 price) (from beginning April to end Sept.) – 26 🚐 – 5 🏠.

Per night from 100 to 155 € – Per week from 255 to 635 € – Reservation fee 20€

🚐 sani-station 2€

Surroundings : 🏊 🗁 ♨♨

Leisure activities : ♟ ✗ 🖼 ⚓ 🔲 ⚒

Facilities : ♿ ⊶ 🛁 ♨ launderette 🐾 refrigerators

GPS Longitude : -1.05856
Latitude : 45.93349

ST-PALAIS-SUR-MER

7420 – Michelin map **324** D6 – pop. 3,926 – alt. 5

◣ Paris 512 – La Rochelle 82 – Royan 6

Côte de Beauté

✆ 05 46 23 20 59, *www.camping-cote-de-beaute.com*

Address : 157 av. de la Grande Côte (2.5km to the northwest, 50m from the sea)

Opening times : from mid April to end Sept.

1.7 ha (115 pitches) flat, grassy

Tariff : (2012 price) 28€ ★★ ⇔ 🔲 🔌 (6A) – Extra per person 5€ – Reservation fee 23€

Rental rates : (2012 price) (from mid April to end Sept.) – 14 🚐. Per night from 35 to 80 €

Per week from 245 to 635 € – Reservation fee 23€

🚐 sani-station

In a pleasant setting opposite the ocean.

Surroundings : 🗁 ♀

Leisure activities : 🖼 ⚓

Facilities : ♿ ⊶ 🚿 🛁 🔲

Nearby : 🏊 ♟ ✗ 🐾

GPS Longitude : -1.1191
Latitude : 45.64973

ST-PIERRE-DE-MAILLÉ

86260 – Michelin map **322** L4 – pop. 925 – alt. 79
▶ Paris 333 – Le Blanc 22 – Châtellerault 32 – Chauvigny 21

△   Municipal Le Grand Pré

℘ 05 49 48 64 11, *www.camping-saintpierredemaille.com/*
Address : 16 rte de Vicq (take northwestern exit along the D 11; beside the Gartempe river)
3 ha (93 pitches) relatively flat, flat, grassy
Rentals : 4 tent bungalows – 5 tents.
The site welcomes sports camps and groups.

Surroundings : ⌇ ♀♀
Leisure activities : ⊛ ≅ ⤳ guided walks ✇
Facilities : launderette

Longitude : 0.83897
Latitude : 46.68463

> *The Michelin classification (⋀⋀⋀ … ⋀) is totally independent of the official star classification system awarded by the local prefecture or other official organisation.*

ST-SAVINIEN

17350 – Michelin map **324** F4 – pop. 2,413 – alt. 18
▶ Paris 457 – Rochefort 28 – La Rochelle 62 – St-Jean-d'Angély 15

⋀   L'Île aux Loisirs

℘ 05 46 90 35 11, *www.ilesauxloirs.com*
Address : 102 r. de St-Savinien (500m west along the D 18, follow the signs for Pont-l'Abbé-d'Arnoult; near the Charente river and the canal, 200m from a small lake)
Opening times : from beginning April to end Sept.
1.8 ha (82 pitches) flat, grassy
Tariff : (2012 price) 22.50€ ♥♥ ⇔ 🗉 🕲 (6A) – Extra per person 5.70€ – Reservation fee 16€
Rental rates : (2012 price) (from beginning April to end Sept.) – 16 🛏. Per night 80€
Per week 574€ – Reservation fee 16€
🛏 11€

Surroundings : ⌇ ♀♀
Leisure activities : 🍸 ✗ 🛶 ⊛ ✇
Facilities : 🚿 ⊶ ᗑ ♒ launderette 🔧
Nearby : ✂ 🎣 ⤳ ⋀ ⤳ sports trail

Longitude : -0.68427
Latitude : 45.87786

ST-SORNIN

17600 – Michelin map **324** E5 – pop. 303 – alt. 16
▶ Paris 495 – Marennes 13 – Rochefort 24 – La Rochelle 60

△   Le Valerick

℘ 05 46 85 15 95, *www.camping-le-valerick.fr*
Address : 1 La Mauvinière (1.3km northeast along the D 118, follow the signs for Pont-l'Abbé)
Opening times : from beginning April to end Sept.
1.5 ha (50 pitches) relatively flat, flat, grassy, wood
Tariff : 19.50€ ♥♥ ⇔ 🗉 🕲 (6A) – Extra per person 4.20€ – Reservation fee 30€

Surroundings : ⌇ ♀
Leisure activities : ✗ 🛶
Facilities : 🚿 ⊶ ⇆ ♒ 🔥

Longitude : -0.96521
Latitude : 45.77446

SAUJON

17600 – Michelin map **324** E5 – pop. 6,636 – alt. 7
▶ Paris 499 – Poitiers 165 – La Rochelle 71 – Saintes 28

🏕 Lac de Saujon

📞 05 46 06 82 99, *www.campingloisirsdulac.com*
Address : Aire de la Lande - Voie des Tourterelles
3.7 ha (150 pitches) flat, grassy
Rentals : �
 – 30 🚐 – 4 🏠 – 4 tent bungalows.
🚽 sani-station

Leisure activities : 🍷 ✗ 📺 ⛳ 🎣 🚴
Facilities : ♿ 🚿 ⛺ 🏕 🚰 ⚲ launderette 🔲 🛒
Nearby : 🏞 🏊 🏖 🎿 🛶 🐎 fitness trail

GPS Longitude : -0.94039
Latitude : 45.68258

SECONDIGNY

79130 – Michelin map **322** D5 – pop. 1,773 – alt. 177
▶ Paris 391 – Bressuire 27 – Champdeniers 15 – Coulonges-sur-l'Autize 22

🏕 Le Moulin des Effres

📞 05 49 95 61 97, *www.campinglemoulindeseffres.fr*
Address : take the southern exit along the D 748, follow the signs for Niort and take road to the left, near a lake
Opening times : from beginning April to end Sept.
2 ha (90 pitches) relatively flat, flat, grassy
Tariff : (2012 price) 14.50€ ✹✹ 🚐 🔲 🎔 (10A) – Extra per person 2.90€ – Reservation fee 10€
Rental rates : (2012 price) (from beginning April to end Sept.) – 17 🚐 – 3 teepees – 2 tents.
Per night from 45 to 85 € – Per week from 140 to 590 € – Reservation fee 20€
🚽 sani-station 5€ – 4 🔲 12€ – 🛒 🎔12€

Surroundings : 🌿 ⛺ ♨
Leisure activities : 📺 🚴 🏊 🏖
Facilities : ♿ 🚿 (Jun–Aug) 🏕 🚰 🔲
Nearby : 🍷 ✗ 🚣 🎿 🏕 🛶 pedalos

GPS Longitude : -0.41418
Latitude : 46.60421

We value your opinion and welcome your feedback.
Do email us at campingfrance@tp.michelin.com

SEMUSSAC

17120 – Michelin map **324** E6 – pop. 1,998 – alt. 36
▶ Paris 520 – Poitiers 187 – La Rochelle 85 – Angoulême 111

🏕 Le 2 B

📞 05 46 05 95 16, *www.camping-2b.com*
Address : 9 chemin des Bardonneries (3.8km east along the D 730, follow the signs for St-Georges-de-Didonne)
Opening times : from beginning April to end Sept.
1.8 ha (93 pitches) relatively flat, flat, grassy**Tariff** : 22.80€ ✹✹ 🚐 🔲 🎔 (10A) – Extra per person 4.60€ – Reservation fee 12€
Rental rates : (from beginning April to end Sept.) – 20 🚐. Per night from 35 to 90 €
Per week from 450 to 600 € – Reservation fee 12€

Surroundings : ♨
Leisure activities : 📺 🚣 🏕 🏊
Facilities : ♿ 🚿 ⛺ 🚰

GPS Longitude : -0.94793
Latitude : 45.6041

SIREUIL

16440 – Michelin map **324** K6 – pop. 1,189 – alt. 26
▶ Paris 460 – Angoulême 16 – Barbezieux 24 – Cognac 35

Nizour

𝒫 05 45 90 56 27, *www.campingdunizour.com*
Address : 2 rte de la Charente (located 1.5km southeast along the D 7, follow the signs for Blanzac, turn left before the bridge; 120m from the Charente (direct access)
Opening times : from mid April to mid Oct.
1.6 ha (40 pitches) flat, grassy
Tariff : (2012 price) 20.10€ 🛉🛉 ⏚ 🖿 🛅 (6A) – Extra per person 4.40€ – Reservation fee 8€
Rental rates : (2012 price) (from beginning May to end Sept.) 🏠 – 5 🛏 – 5 🏚.
Per night 76€ – Per week 537€ – Reservation fee 8€

Surroundings : 🖵 00
Leisure activities : 🎣 🚣 🚴 🏊 ⛱ ↝
Facilities : 🖿 ⛟ 🛁 launderette
Nearby : 🎣 ⚓

GPS Longitude : 0.02418
Latitude : 45.60688

THORS

17160 – Michelin map **324** I5 – pop. 418 – alt. 23
▶ Paris 466 – Angoulême 53 – Cognac 84 – Limoges 143

Le Relais de l'Étang

𝒫 05 46 58 26 81, *www.paysdematha.com*
Address : rte de Cognac (take the northern exit along the D 121, follow the signs for Matha; near the lake)
Opening times : from beginning April to end Oct.
0.8 ha (25 pitches) flat, grassy, fine gravel
Tariff : 🛉 2.10€ ⏚ 1.60€ 🖿 1.60€ – 🛅 (10A) 2.60€
Rental rates : (from beginning April to end Oct.) – 3 🛏. Per night from 30 to 50 €
Per week from 250 to 300 €
🛏 4 🖿 1.60€

Surroundings : 🏞 🖵 00
Leisure activities : 🚣
Facilities : 🖿 ⛟ 🛒 🛁 🏻 launderette
Nearby : 🍷 ✕ 🏖 🏊 (beach) 🎣 pedalos

GPS Longitude : -0.30822
Latitude : 45.83662

VAUX-SUR-MER

17640 – Michelin map **324** D6 – pop. 3,835 – alt. 12
▶ Paris 514 – Poitiers 181 – La Rochelle 75 – Rochefort 44

Le Nauzan-Plage

𝒫 05 46 38 29 13, *www.campinglenauzanplage.com*
Address : 39 av. de Nauzan-Plage (500m from the beach)
Opening times : from beginning April to end Sept.
3.9 ha (239 pitches) flat, grassy
Tariff : 38.60€ 🛉🛉 ⏚ 🖿 🛅 (10A) – Extra per person 8.50€ – Reservation fee 20€
Rental rates : (from beginning April to end Sept.) 🏠 – 22 🛏 – (with/without sanitary facilities). Per night from 36 to 81 € – Per week from 150 to 1,130 € – Reservation fee 20€
🛏 sani-station 8€ – 2 🖿 16€ – 🚐 🛅16€
Situated beside a park.

Surroundings : 🖵 0
Leisure activities : 🍷 ✕ 🎣 📺 daytime 🚣 🏊
Facilities : 🖿 ⛟ 🛁 🏻 launderette 🛎 🛒
Nearby : ✂ 🎠 🎣

GPS Longitude : -1.07196
Latitude : 45.64295

Le Val-Vert

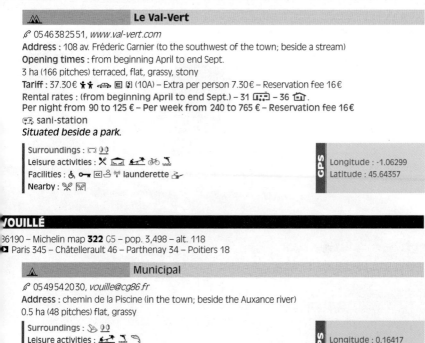

𝒫 05 46 38 25 51, *www.val-vert.com*
Address : 108 av. Fréderic Garnier (to the southwest of the town; beside a stream)
Opening times : from beginning April to end Sept.
3 ha (166 pitches) terraced, flat, grassy, stony
Tariff : 37.30€ ♦♦ ⇔ 回 (10A) – Extra per person 7.30€ – Reservation fee 16€
Rental rates : (from beginning April to end Sept.) – 31 ⟨⟩ – 36 🏠.
Per night from 90 to 125 € – Per week from 240 to 765 € – Reservation fee 16€
⟨⟩ sani-station
Situated beside a park.

Surroundings : ⟨⟩ 00
Leisure activities : ✗ ⟨⟩ ⟨⟩ ⟨⟩ ⟨⟩
Facilities : ⟨⟩ ⟨⟩ ⟨⟩ ⟨⟩ launderette ⟨⟩
Nearby : ⟨⟩ ⟨⟩

GPS Longitude : -1.06299
Latitude : 45.64357

VOUILLÉ

86190 – Michelin map **322** G5 – pop. 3,498 – alt. 118
▶ Paris 345 – Châtellerault 46 – Parthenay 34 – Poitiers 18

Municipal

𝒫 05 49 54 20 30, *vouille@cg86.fr*
Address : chemin de la Piscine (in the town; beside the Auxance river)
0.5 ha (48 pitches) flat, grassy

Surroundings : ⟨⟩ 00
Leisure activities : ⟨⟩ ⟨⟩ ⟨⟩
Facilities : ⟨⟩ ⟨⟩
Nearby : ✗

GPS Longitude : 0.16417
Latitude : 46.64016

VOUNEUIL-SUR-VIENNE

86210 – Michelin map **322** J4 – pop. 1,981 – alt. 58
▶ Paris 316 – Châtellerault 12 – Chauvigny 20 – Poitiers 27

Les Chalets de Moulière
(rental of chalets only)

𝒫 05 49 85 84 40, *www.camping-les-chalets-de-mouliere-vouneuil-sur-vienne* – traditional camp.
spaces also available
Address : r. des Ardentes (take the eastern exit along the D 15, follow the signs for Monthoiron and
take turning to the left, 60m from the Vienne (direct access)
Opening times : from mid March to mid Nov.
1.5 ha flat
Rental rates : ⟨⟩ (1 chalet) – 24 🏠. Per week from 323 to 703 € – Reservation fee 12€
Welcomes summer camps.

Leisure activities : ⟨⟩ ⟨⟩ ⟨⟩
Facilities : ⟨⟩ ⟨⟩ ⟨⟩ ⟨⟩
Nearby : ⟨⟩ ⟨⟩

GPS Longitude : 0.5445
Latitude : 46.71965

Bernard Jaubert / age fotostock

A new day dawns in sun-drenched Provence. As the fishmongers tell jokes, chat and sell their fresh fish under clear blue skies, you cannot help but fall in love with the relaxed, happy-go-lucky spirit of Marseilles. In the countryside beyond, the sun casts its first rays across the ochre walls of a hilltop village and over the fields of lavender in the valley below. The steady chirping of the cicadas is interrupted only by the gentle sound of sheep bells in the hills. Slow down to the gentle pace of the villagers and join them as they gather within the refreshingly cool walls of a café. However, by 2pm you may begin to wonder where everyone is. On hot afternoons, most people exercise their traditional right to a siesta, even those on the chic beaches of St Tropez and in the seaside cabins of the Camargue. Fear not, it will soon be time to wake up and prepare for a serious game of *pétanque* and a chilled glass of pastis.

- ● Locality with campsite
- ■ Locality with campsite and rental option
- Vannes Locality with campsite and campervan area
- Moyaux Locality with at least one pleasant campsite
- Motorway service area for campervans

la Toussuire

Valloire

le Bourg-d'Oisans   la Grave

le Bourg-d'Arud

St-Christophe-
en-Oisans

Névache

Briançon

A 32

ITALIA

A 6

Villar-Loubière

HAUTES-   ALPES

l'Argentière-la-Bessée

la Roche-de-Rame

Pont-du-Fossé

Ceillac

Guillestre

Ancelle   St-Apollinaire

St-Clément-s-Durance

Roche-
-Arnaud

N 94

Embrun

Gap   Chorges   Baratier

Espinasses   Prunières

le Sauzé-du-Lac

Larche

St-Pons

St-Jean

Curbans   Col St-Jean

Méolans-
Revel   Les Thuiles

Seyne

St-Étienne-de-Tinée

Clamensane

le Vernet   Isola

ALPES-DE-HAUTE-

Sisteron

PROVENCE   Colmars

St-Martin-d'Entraunes

St-Sauveur-
s-Tinée

St-Martin-Vésubie

Volonne

Villars-Colmars

Digne-les-Bains   ALPES- MARITIMES

Puimichel   Mézel   Sospel

St-André-les-Alpes

Moustiers-Ste-Marie   Castellane   D 6202

Riez   Loup

Ste-Croix-de-Verdon   la Colle-s-Loup   Vence   A 8   Menton

Montpezat   Monaco

les Salles-s-Verdon   le Bar-s-Loup

St-Laurent-du-Verdon   Grasse   Cagnes-s-Mer

Régusse   Aups   Aunbeau-s-S.   Cros-de-Cagnes
Villeneuve-Loubet

Montmeyan

Callas   Le Cannet

Salernes   Villecroze   St-Paul-   CANNES
en-Forêt

Draguignan   les Adrets-   Mandelieu-la-Napoule
de-l'Esterel

le Muy   A 8   Agay

CAMBARETTE   Argens   Roquebrune-s-Argens   St-Raphaël

Brignoles   Puget-s-A.   Fréjus
St-Aygulf

CAMBARETTE   VAR   Grimaud

Bormes-
les-Mimosas   Ramatuelle

la Croix-Valmer

La Londe-les-Maures   Cavalaire-s-Mer

50   le Lavandou
La Favière

TOULON   Hyères

St-Mandrier-
s-Mer   Giens

ry-s-M.   Îles d'Hyères

LES ADRETS-DE-L'ESTEREL

83600 – Michelin map **340** P4 – pop. 2,063 – alt. 295
▶ Paris 881 – Cannes 26 – Draguignan 44 – Fréjus 17

Les Philippons

℘ 04 94 40 90 67, *www.lesphilippons.com*
Address : head 3km east along the D 237
Opening times : from beginning April to mid Oct.
5 ha (150 pitches) very uneven, terraced, grassy, stony
Tariff : (2012 price) 31 € ♦♦ ⇔ 圓 (5) (10A) – Extra per person 6.10 € – Reservation fee 20 €
Rental rates : (2012 price) (from beginning April to mid Oct.) – 14 ⌂.
Per night from 37 to 128 € – Per week from 259 to 896 € – Reservation fee 30 €
Natural setting shaded by olive trees, eucalyptus and cork oaks.

Surroundings : 🐾 ⇐ ⊏⊐ 🕮
Leisure activities : ♀ ✗ 🛶 ⚓
Facilities : ⚷ ♨ ℉ launderette ⚗ refrigerators

GPS
Longitude : 6.84002
Latitude : 43.52876

> *For more information on visiting particular towns or regions, consult the*
> *relevant regional MICHELIN Green Guide. We also recommend you use*
> *the appropriate Michelin regional map to locate your selected campsite,*
> *to calculate distances and to work out the best route.*

AGAY

83530 – Michelin map **340** Q5 – alt. 20
▶ Paris 880 – Cannes 34 – Draguignan 43 – Fréjus 12

Esterel Caravaning ♠♠

℘ 04 94 82 03 28, *www.esterel-caravaning.fr*
Address : av. des Golfs (situated 4km to the northwest)
Opening times : from end March to end Sept.
15 ha (405 pitches) terraced, relatively flat, stony
Tariff : 52 € ♦♦ ⇔ 圓 (5) (10A) – Extra per person 11 € – Reservation fee 40 €
Rental rates : (from end March to end Sept.) – 218 ⌂. Per night from 30 to 400 €
Per week from 210 to 2,800 € – Reservation fee 30 €
Indoor swimming pool for children, nursery and some pitches with private jacuzzi!

Surroundings : 🐾 ⊏⊐ 🕮
Leisure activities : ♀ ✗ 🖼 ⏱ ⋆⋆ 🎡 🛶 🚲 ⚽ 🎣 ⚓ 🐎 disco,
multi-sports ground, spa therapy centre, skate park
Facilities : ♿ ⚷ ⊠ ▥ ♨ – 18 individual sanitary facilities (🚿⇔ wc) ⚗ ⚏
℉ launderette ⏚ ⚗
Nearby :, squash

GPS
Longitude : 6.83256
Latitude : 43.45419

Campéole Le Dramont ♠♠

℘ 04 94 82 07 68, *www.camping-mer.com*
Address : 986 bd de la 36ème Division du Texas
6.5 ha (374 pitches) undulating, flat, sandy
Rentals : 56 ⌂ – 56 ⌂ – 65 tent bungalows.
⛽ sani-station
Surroundings : 🐾 🕮⚠
Leisure activities : ♀ ✗ 🖼 ⏱ ⋆⋆ 🛶 multi-sports ground
Facilities : ♿ ⚷ ▥ ♨ ℉ launderette ⚗ ⚗
Nearby : scuba diving

GPS
Longitude : 6.84835
Latitude : 43.41782

⚠ Village Vacances Vallée du Paradis ♣♦
(rental of mobile homes only)

℘ 0494821600, www.camping-vallee-du-paradis.fr
Address : av. du Gratadis (located 1km to the northwest; beside the Agay)
3 ha flat
Rentals : 198 ⛺.

Surroundings : ≤ ⌂ ⓠ
Leisure activities : ♈ ✗ ⛱ ☻ 🎯 ⌦ 🎣 ♨ ☂ ⛱ ⌙
Facilities : ♿ ☕ ⛳ ♒ launderette ⛽ ⛲
Nearby : ⚓

GPS — Longitude : 6.85285 / Latitude : 43.43546

⚠ Les Rives de l'Agay

℘ 0494820274, www.lesrivesdelagay.com
Address : 575 av. du Gratadis (700m to the northwest; beside the Agay and 500m from the beach)
Opening times : from mid March to beginning Nov.
2 ha (171 pitches) flat, grassy, sandy
Tariff : (2012 price) 48€ ♦♦ ⟺ ▣ ⒱ (6A) – Extra per person 7€ – Reservation fee 20€
Rental rates : (2012 price) (from mid March to beginning Nov.) – 44 ⛺.
Per night from 38 to 140 € – Per week from 357 to 976 € – Reservation fee 20€

Surroundings : ⌂ ⓠⓠ
Leisure activities : ✗ ⛱ ⛵ scuba diving
Facilities : ♿ ☕ � ⛳ ♒ ☂ ♈ launderette ⛽ ⛲
Nearby : ⚓

GPS — Longitude : 6.85263 / Latitude : 43.43408

⚠ Agay-Soleil

℘ 0494820079, www.agay-soleil.com ☆ (Jul–Aug)
Address : 1152 bd de la Plage (700m east on the D 559, follow the signs for Cannes)
Opening times : from end March to beginning Nov.
0.7 ha (53 pitches) terraced, relatively flat, flat, sandy
Tariff : (2012 price) 33.20€ ♦♦ ⟺ ▣ ⒱ (6A) – Extra per person 5.70€ – Reservation fee 16€
Rental rates : (2012 price) (permanent) ☆ – 5 ⛺ – 2 ☖ – 1 apartment.
Per week from 345 to 759 €
⛽ sani-station 8€

Surroundings : ≤ ⌂ ⓠⓠ ⛰
Leisure activities : ♈ ✗ ⛱
Facilities : ♿ ☕ ⛳ ▣ ⛳ ♒ ♈ ▣ ⛲
Nearby : ☆ watersports centre

GPS — Longitude : 6.86822 / Latitude : 43.43333

⚠ Royal-Camping

℘ 0494820020, www.royalcamping.net
Address : r. Louise Robinson (located 1.5km west along the D 559, follow the signs for St Raphael and take turning to the left)
Opening times : from mid Feb. to mid Nov.
0.6 ha (45 pitches) flat, grassy, gravelled
Tariff : (2012 price) 35€ ♦♦ ⟺ ▣ ⒱ (6A) – Extra per person 7€ – Reservation fee 20€
Rental rates : (2012 price) (from mid March to mid Nov.) – 9 ⛺. Per night from 50 to 65 €
Per week from 325 to 780 € – Reservation fee 20€

Surroundings : ⓠⓠ ⛰
Leisure activities : ⛱
Facilities : ☕ ▣ ♈
Nearby : ▣ ⛽ ♈ ✗ ⛲

GPS — Longitude : 6.85707 / Latitude : 43.42027

AIX-EN-PROVENCE

13100 – Michelin map **340** H4 – pop. 141,895 – alt. 206
▶ Paris 752 – Aubagne 39 – Avignon 82 – Manosque 57

Chantecler ♠♠

℘ 04 42 26 12 98, *www.campingchantecler.com*
Address : 41 av. du Val-Saint-André (2.5km southeast, access via the cours Gambetta – A8 : take exit 31 for Aix – Val-St-André-)
8 ha (240 pitches) undulating, terraced, grassy, stony
Rentals : 32 ⟐ – 13 ⌂ .
🚐 sani-station
A view of Mt Ste-Victoire from some pitches.

Surroundings : 🏕 ⟐
Leisure activities : 🍹 ✕ 🏛 🏃 ⛵ 🏊
Facilities : 🚿 ⚡ 🛒 🚾 🍴 launderette 🪣

GPS Longitude : 5.47416
Latitude : 43.51522

ANCELLE

05260 – Michelin map **334** F5 – pop. 854 – alt. 1,340 – Winter sports : 1,350/1,807 m🎿13 🎿
▶ Paris 665 – Gap 17 – Grenoble 103 – Orcières 18

Les Auches

℘ 04 92 50 80 28, *www.lesauches.com*
Address : at Les Auches (take the northern exit following signs for Pont du Fossé and take turning to the right.)
Opening times : permanent
2 ha (67 pitches) terraced, relatively flat, grassy
Tariff : 23.10€ ✚✚ ⟐ 🔲 ⚡ (6A) – Extra per person 4.60€
Rental rates : (permanent) 🛁 – 8 ⟐ – 11 ⌂ – 4 studios – 1 apartment – 2 tent bungalows. Per week from 250 to 655 € – Reservation fee 15€

Surroundings : 🏔 ⟐
Leisure activities : ✕ 🏛 🏃 jacuzzi ⛵ 🏊
Facilities : 🚿 ⚡ 🛒 🍴 launderette

GPS Longitude : 6.21075
Latitude : 44.62435

Some information or pricing may have changed since the guide went to press.
We recommend you check the price list online in advance or at the entrance
to the campsite and enquire about possible restrictions.

APT

84400 – Michelin map **332** F10 – pop. 11,405 – alt. 250
▶ Paris 728 – Aix-en-Provence 56 – Avignon 54 – Carpentras 49

Le Lubéron

℘ 04 90 04 85 40, *www.campingleluberon.com*
Address : av. de Saignon (situated 2km southeast along the D 48)
Opening times : from beginning April to end Sept.
5 ha (110 pitches) terraced, flat and relatively flat, fine gravel, grassy
Tariff : (2012 price) 30.10€ ✚✚ ⟐ 🔲 ⚡ (6A) – Extra per person 7€ – Reservation fee 18€
Rental rates : (2012 price) (from beginning April to end March) – 16 ⟐ – 15 ⌂ – 6 tent bungalows – 2 gîtes. Per night 150€ – Per week from 250 to 890 € – Reservation fee 18€
🚐 sani-station – 🚐 16.34€

Surroundings : 🏔 ⟐
Leisure activities : 🍹 ✕ ⛵ 🏊
Facilities : 🚿 ⚡ 🛒 🍴 launderette

GPS Longitude : 5.41327
Latitude : 43.86632

Les Cèdres

📞 04 90 74 14 61, *www.camping-les-cedres.fr*
Address : take northwestern exit along the D 22, follow the signs for Rustrel
Opening times : from mid Feb. to mid Nov.
1.8 ha (75 pitches) flat, grassy, stony
Tariff : (2012 price) 🧍 2.70€ 🚐 5.40€ 🔲 – 🔌 (10A) 3.50€
Rental rates : (2012 price) (from mid March to mid Oct.) – 4 tent bungalows. Per night 38€
Per week from 225 to 260 € – Reservation fee 34€
🚐 sani-station 5€

Surroundings : ♀
Leisure activities : 🎱 🧗 climbing wall
Facilities : ♿ ⚡ 🔲 📷 refrigerators
Nearby : 🎿

GPS
Longitude : 5.4013
Latitude : 43.87765

> *The Michelin classification (⚠⚠⚠... ⚠) is totally independent of the official star classification system awarded by the local prefecture or other official organisation.*

L'ARGENTIÈRE-LA-BESSÉE

05120 – Michelin map **334** H4 – pop. 2,328 – alt. 1,024
▶ Paris 696 – Briançon 17 – Embrun 33 – Gap 74

Municipal Les Écrins

📞 04 92 23 03 38, *www.camping-les-ecrins.com*
Address : av. Pierre Sainte (head 2.3km south along the N 94, follow the signs for Gap, and take D 104 to the right)
3 ha (71 pitches) flat, grassy, stony
🚐 sani-station

A natural setting among the mountains. The activities at the whitewater site are well staffed.

Surroundings : ⛰ 🏠 ♀
Leisure activities : 🎱 🧗 ✂ 🎣
Facilities : ♿ ⚡ 🔲 🍽 📷 🚿
Nearby : 🏊 🎿 🛶 (lake), rafting and canyoning

GPS
Longitude : 6.55823
Latitude : 44.77687

ARLES

13200 – Michelin map **340** C3 – pop. 52,979 – alt. 13
▶ Paris 719 – Aix-en-Provence 77 – Avignon 37 – Cavaillon 44
O : 14 km via N 572 rte de St-Gilles and D 37 on the left

Crin Blanc 👫

📞 04 66 87 48 78, *www.camping-crin-blanc.com*
Address : at the Hameau des Saliers (located to the southwest of Saliers along the D 37)
Opening times : from beginning April to end Sept.
4.5 ha (170 pitches) flat, grassy, stony
Tariff : 24€ 🧍🧍 🚐 🔲 🔌 (10A) – Extra per person 5.50€ – Reservation fee 10€
Rental rates : (2012 price) (from beginning March to end Oct.) – 120 .
Per night from 62 to 90 € – Per week from 199 to 850 € – Reservation fee 19€
🚐 sani-station

Surroundings : 🏠
Leisure activities : 🍽 ✕ 🎱 🎮 ⛹ 🧗 🏊 ⛷
Facilities : ♿ ⚡ 🧺 🚿 💧 🍴 launderette 🧺 🚿
Nearby : 🐎

GPS
Longitude : 4.47392
Latitude : 43.66149

AUBIGNAN

84810 – Michelin map **332** D9 – pop. 4,861 – alt. 65
▶ Paris 675 – Avignon 31 – Carpentras 7 – Orange 21

Le Brégoux

℘ 04 90 62 62 50, www.camping-lebregoux.fr
Address : 410 chemin du Vas (800m southeast along the D 55, follow the signs for Caromb and take the road to the right.)
Opening times : from beginning March to end Oct.
3.5 ha (170 pitches) flat, grassy
Tariff : ✦ 3.65€ ⇔ 回 3.55€ – ﴾﴿ (10A) 3.55€
Rental rates : (from beginning March to end Oct.) – 5 ⟨⟩. Per week from 265 to 475 €

Surroundings : 0 0
Leisure activities : 🔲 ♨ ※
Facilities : ☞ ▥ ♨ ♔ launderette

GPS Longitude : 5.03609
Latitude : 44.09808

AUPS

83630 – Michelin map **340** M4 – pop. 2,083 – alt. 496
▶ Paris 818 – Aix-en-Provence 90 – Castellane 71 – Digne-les-Bains 78

International Camping

℘ 04 94 70 06 80, www.internationalcamping-aups.com
Address : 495 rte de Fox-Amphoux (head 500m west along the D 60)
Opening times : from beginning April to end Sept.
4 ha (190 pitches) flat, grassy, stony
Tariff : ✦ 7.80€ ⇔ 回 6.80€ – ﴾﴿ (10A) 6.20€
Rental rates : (2012 price) (permanent) – 25 ⟨⟩. Per week from 300 to 550 €
Picturesque and well-kept setting.

Surroundings : 🔲 ⊡ 0
Leisure activities : ✕ ※ ♨ disco
Facilities : ☞ ♔ 回 ♨

GPS Longitude : 6.21705
Latitude : 43.62465

To visit a town or region, use the MICHELIN Green Guides.

AURIBEAU-SUR-SIAGNE

06810 – Michelin map **341** C6 – pop. 2,945 – alt. 85
▶ Paris 900 – Cannes 15 – Draguignan 62 – Grasse 9

Le Parc des Monges

℘ 04 93 60 91 71, www.parcdesmonges.com
Address : 635 chemin du Gabre (head 1.4km northwest along the D 509, follow the signs for Tanneron)
Opening times : from mid April to end Sept.
1.3 ha (54 pitches) flat, grassy, stony
Tariff : 30.50€ ✦✦ ⇔ 回 ﴾﴿ (10A) – Extra per person 5.80€
Rental rates : (from mid April to end Sept.) ※ – 9 ⟨⟩ – 5 ⌂. Per week from 320 to 850 €
⊡ sani-station 7.50€
Situated beside the Siagne river.

Surroundings : 🔲 ⊡ 0 0
Leisure activities : ♨
Facilities : ♿ ☞ ⊡ ♨ ♔ 回
Nearby : ♼ ✕ ♨ ≌ ♒

GPS Longitude : 6.90252
Latitude : 43.60659

AVIGNON

84000 – Michelin map **332** B10 – pop. 89,592 – alt. 21
▶ Paris 682 – Aix-en-Provence 82 – Arles 37 – Marseille 98

Aquadis Loisirs Le Pont d'Avignon

☎ 04 90 80 63 50, www.aquadis-loisirs.com

Address : 10 chemin de la Barthelasse (take northwestern exit, follow the signs for Villeneuve-lès-Avignon across the Édouard-Daladier bridge and take a right turn, on the Île-de-la-Barthelasse)

Opening times : from beginning March to end Nov.

8 ha (300 pitches) flat, grassy, fine gravel

Tariff : 28.90€ ✚ ✚ ⇔ 圁 ⑭ (10A) – Extra per person 5.35€ – Reservation fee 9.90€

Rental rates : (from beginning March to mid Nov.) – 10 tent bungalows.
Per night from 49 to 84 € – Per week from 200 to 595 € – Reservation fee 19.50€

⛺ 40 圁 28.90€ – 🚐 14€

Surroundings : ⛲ ♤♤
Leisure activities : ⛴ ✗ 🎦 🛝 ✀ 🛶
Facilities : ♿ ⚡ 🍴 launderette 🧺 ⚓

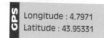

GPS
Longitude : 4.7971
Latitude : 43.95331

Do not confuse:
⛰ *to* ⛰⛰⛰ : *MICHELIN classification*
with
★ *to* ★★★★★ : *official classification*

BARATIER

05200 – Michelin map **334** G4 – pop. 511 – alt. 855
▶ Paris 704 – Marseille 214 – Gap 39 – Digne 90

Les Airelles

☎ 04 92 43 11 57, www.lesairelles.com

Address : rte des Orres (1.2km southeast along the D 40, follow the signs for Les Orres and take turning to the right)

Opening times : from beginning June to mid Sept.

5 ha/4 ha for camping (130 pitches) terraced, relatively flat, flat, grassy, stony

Tariff : ✚ 7€ ⇔ 圁 8€ – ⑭ (10A) 4.80€

Rental rates : (from beginning June to mid Sept.) – 16 ⛺ – 40 🏠.
Per night from 60 to 105 € – Per week from 500 to 760 €

Surroundings : ⛰ ⩽♤♤
Leisure activities : ⛴ ✗ 🎦 ☉ daytime 🛝 🛶 multi-sports ground
Facilities : ♿ ⚡ ⚓ 🍴 launderette

GPS
Longitude : 6.50164
Latitude : 44.5291

Le Verger

☎ 04 92 43 15 87, www.campingleverger.fr – limited spaces for one-night stay

Address : chemin de Jouglar (take the western exit; recommended route for caravans is via the village)

Opening times : permanent

4.3 ha/2.5 ha for camping (110 pitches) terraced, relatively flat, flat, grassy, stony

Tariff : (2012 price) 16.50€ ✚ ✚ ⇔ 圁 ⑭ (10A) – Extra per person 5.50€ – Reservation fee 14€

Rental rates : (2012 price) (permanent) – 14 gîtes. Per week from 425 to 715 €

Surroundings : ⛰ ⛲ ♤♤
Leisure activities : ⛴ ✗ 🎦 🛶
Facilities : ⚡ 🎳 ⚓ 🍴 🚿
Nearby : ✗ 🏇 ↗

Les Deux Bois

℘ 04 92 43 54 14, *www.camping-les2bois.com* – **R**

Address : rte de Pra Fouran (access to the town along the D 204)
Opening times : from mid May to end Sept.
2.5 ha (100 pitches) terraced, sloping, flat, grassy, stony
Tariff : (2012 price) 21.30 € ⚬⚬ ⛺ 🔲 [🚰] (10A) – Extra per person 5.20 €
Rental rates : (2012 price) (from end April to end Nov.) Ⓟ – 4 🚐. Per night from 70 to 90 €
Per week from 560 to 880 €

Luxurious mobile homes available for rental.

Surroundings : 〰 ♨♨
Leisure activities : ▾ ✕ ⚓ ⊿
Facilities : ♿ ⚷ ▥ ♨ 🔳 🚿
Nearby : ✂ 🏇

Longitude : 6.49207
Latitude : 44.53837

Les Grillons

℘ 04 92 43 32 75, *www.lesgrillons.com*

Address : rte de la Madeleine (located 1km north along the D 40, D 340 and take road to the left)
Opening times : from mid May to mid Sept.
1.5 ha (95 pitches) relatively flat, grassy, stony
Tariff : (2012 price) 21.80 € ⚬⚬ ⛺ 🔲 [🚰] (16A) – Extra per person 5 € – Reservation fee 10 €
Rental rates : (2012 price) (from mid May to mid Sept.) – 16 🚐. Per night from 58 to 90 €
Per week from 250 to 670 € – Reservation fee 13 €

Surroundings : 〰 ♨♨♨
Leisure activities : ✂ ⊿
Facilities : ♿ ⚷ ♨ 🍴 launderette

Longitude : 6.49755
Latitude : 44.54689

BARRET-SUR-MÉOUGE

05300 – Michelin map **334** C7 – pop. 220 – alt. 640
▶ Paris 700 – Laragne-Montéglin 14 – Sault 46 – Séderon 21

Les Gorges de la Méouge

℘ 04 92 65 08 47, *www.camping-meouge.com*

Address : at Le Serre (take the eastern exit along the D 942, follow the signs for Laragne-Montéglin and take the road to the right, near the Méouge river)
Opening times : from beginning May to end Sept.
3 ha (115 pitches) flat, grassy
Tariff : 22.10 € ⚬⚬ ⛺ 🔲 [🚰] (10A) – Extra per person 5.40 €
Rental rates : (from beginning May to end Sept.) – 13 🚐. Per night from 60 to 84 €
Per week from 420 to 588 €
🚐 sani-station 2 € – 10 🔲 10 € – 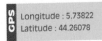 10 €

Surroundings : 〰 ♨♨
Leisure activities : 🚲 ⊿
Facilities : ♿ ⚷ 🍴 ♨ 🚿 〰 🍴 🔳

Longitude : 5.73822
Latitude : 44.26078

Michelin classification:

⚞⚞⚞⚞ *Extremely comfortable, equipped to a very high standard*
⚞⚞⚞ *Very comfortable, equipped to a high standard*
⚞⚞ *Comfortable and well equipped*
⚞ *Reasonably comfortable*
⚞ *Satisfactory*

LE BAR-SUR-LOUP

06620 – Michelin map **341** C5 – pop. 2,805 – alt. 320
▶ Paris 916 – Cannes 22 – Grasse 10 – Nice 31

Les Gorges du Loup

℘ 04 93 42 45 06, *www.lesgorgesduloup.com* – pitches accessed via steep slope, help moving caravans onto and off pitches avilable on request

Address : 965 chemin des Vergers (located 1km northeast along the D 2210, then continue 1km along the Chemin des Vergers)

Opening times : from beginning May to end Sept.

1.6 ha (70 pitches) very uneven, terraced, grassy, stony

Tariff : (2012 price) 28.50€ ♥♥ ⇌ 🔲 🔌 (10A) – Extra per person 5€

Rental rates : (2012 price) (from beginning April to end Sept.) – 9 🚐 – 6 🏠 – 1 apartment. Per week from 290 to 700 € – Reservation fee 15€

Pitches set out on small terraces, many shaded by ancient olive trees.

Surroundings : 🏊 ≤ 🏕 🞈
Leisure activities : 🍴 ⚽ 🏊
Facilities : ⛽ 🅿 🚿 🚰 🚻 🚗

Longitude : 6.99527
Latitude : 43.70183

BEAUMES-DE-VENISE

84190 – Michelin map **332** D9 – pop. 2,283 – alt. 100
▶ Paris 666 – Avignon 34 – Nyons 39 – Orange 23

Municipal de Roquefiguier

℘ 04 90 62 95 07, *www.mairie-de-beaumes-de-venise* – ♯

Address : rte de Lafare (take the northern exit along the D 90, follow the signs for Malaucène and take a right turn; beside the Salette river)

Opening times : from beginning March to end Oct.

1.5 ha (63 pitches) terraced, relatively flat, grassy, stony

Tariff : (2012 price) ♥ 2.75€ ⇌ 1.85€ 🔲 3.30€ – 🔌 (16A) 3€

Surroundings : ≤ 🏕 🞈
Leisure activities : ⚽ 🏛
Facilities : ♿ 🚿 🚻 🚰 � refrigerators
Nearby : 🍴

Longitude : 5.03448
Latitude : 44.12244

To make the best possible use of this guide, please read pages 2–15 carefully.

BEAUMONT-DU-VENTOUX

84340 – Michelin map **332** E8 – pop. 317 – alt. 360
▶ Paris 676 – Avignon 48 – Carpentras 21 – Nyons 28

Mont-Serein

℘ 04 90 60 49 16, *www.camping-ventoux.com* – alt. 1,400

Address : 20km east along the D 974 and take the D 164a, r. du Mont-Ventoux by Malaucène; recommended route via Malaucène

1.2 ha (60 pitches) flat, grassy, stony

Rentals : – 2 🚐 – 5 🏠.
🚽 sani-station
In an attractive elevated location.

Surroundings : 🏊 ≤ Mont Ventoux and the Alps 🏕
Leisure activities : 🍴
Facilities : ⛽ 🏛 🚿 🚻 🚰 🚗

Longitude : 5.25898
Latitude : 44.1811

BÉDOIN

84410 – Michelin map **332** E9 – pop. 3,132 – alt. 295

▶ Paris 692 – Avignon 43 – Carpentras 16 – Vaison-la-Romaine 21

⚠ Municipal la Pinède

℘ 04 90 65 61 03, *la-pinede.camping-municipal@wanadoo.fr*

Address : chemin des Sablières (take the western exit following signs for Crillon-le-Brave and take the road to the right, next to the municipal swimming pool)

Opening times : from mid March to end Oct.

6 ha (121 pitches) terraced, grassy, stony

Tariff : (2012 price) 15€ ✦✦ ⇌ 🗉 (10A) – Extra per person 3.40€

Rental rates : (2012 price) (from mid March to end Oct.) – 3 🏠. Per week from 290 to 470 €

🚐 sani-station 2€

Surroundings : 🞵🞵
Facilities : ♿ ⌦ 🚿 🚰 🖭
Nearby : 🎾 ☌

GPS Longitude : 5.17261
Latitude : 44.12486

BOLLÈNE

84500 – Michelin map **332** B8 – pop. 13,885 – alt. 40

▶ Paris 634 – Avignon 53 – Montélimar 34 – Nyons 35

⚠ La Simioune

℘ 04 90 30 44 62, *www.la-simioune.fr*

Address : Guffiage quartier (5km northeast following signs for Lambisque (access on the D 8 along the old road to Suze-la-Rousse following the Lez) and take road to the left)

Opening times : permanent

2 ha (80 pitches) terraced, flat, sandy

Tariff : (2012 price) 14€ ✦✦ ⇌ 🗉 (6A) – Extra per person 4€ – Reservation fee 10€

Rental rates : (2012 price) (permanent) – 4 🏠. Per night from 40 to 80 €
Per week from 350 to 500 € – Reservation fee 10€

Wooden, ranch-style buildings.

Surroundings : 🞵 🞵🞵
Leisure activities : 🍸 ☌ 🐎
Facilities : ♿ ⌦ 🚐 🞵 🚿 🚰 🖭 🚿

GPS Longitude : 4.74848
Latitude : 44.28203

BONNIEUX

84480 – Michelin map **332** E11 – pop. 1,424 – alt. 400

▶ Paris 721 – Aix-en-Provence 49 – Apt 12 – Cavaillon 27

⚠ Le Vallon

℘ 04 90 75 86 14, *www.campinglevallon.com*

Address : rte de Ménerbes (take the southern exit along the D 3, follow the signs for Ménerbes and take road to the left)

Opening times : from mid March to mid Oct.

1.3 ha (80 pitches) terraced, flat, grassy, stony, wood

Tariff : (2012 price) 22.20€ ✦✦ ⇌ 🗉 (10A) – Extra per person 4€ – Reservation fee 10€

Rental rates : (2012 price) (from mid March to mid Oct.) – 1 🚍 – 3 yurts – 5 tent bungalows.
Per night from 50 to 90 € – Per week from 300 to 595 € – Reservation fee 10€

Surroundings : 🞵 ⇐ 🗔 🞵
Facilities : ⌦ 🚿 🚰 🖭
Nearby : 🚴 🎾

BORMES-LES-MIMOSAS

83230 – Michelin map **340** N7 – pop. 7,321 – alt. 180
▶ Paris 871 – Fréjus 57 – Hyères 21 – Le Lavandou 4

Le Camp du Domaine ♣♣

℘ 04 94 71 03 12, www.campdudomaine.com
Address : at La Favière, 2581 rte de Bénat (situated 2km to the south, near the port)
Opening times : from mid March to end Oct.
38 ha (1200 pitches) very uneven, terraced, flat, stony, rocks
Tariff : 43 € ♥♥ ⇔ 圓 ⑭ (16A) – Extra per person 9 € – Reservation fee 25 €
Rental rates : (from mid March to end Oct.) ⅗ – 50 ⛺ – 100 ⛺.
Per week from 600 to 1,020 € – Reservation fee 25 €
⊡ sani-station – 100 圓
Secluded site on an undulating, wooded peninsula close to the beach. Excursions organised out of season.

Surroundings : ⊡ 00 ⚠
Leisure activities : ▾ ✗ ⛫ ⑤ 🏃 ⚒ ⅗ multi-sports ground
Facilities : ᬽ ⊶ ☑ ⚖ ⚖ ⚡ ⑪ launderette ⚖ ⚖ refrigerated food storage
Nearby : ◊ pedalos

GPS	
Longitude : 6.35129	
Latitude : 43.11788	

Manjastre

℘ 04 94 71 03 28, www.campingmanjastre.com ⅗
Address : 150 chemin des Girolles (5km northwest sur N 98, follow the signs for Cogolin)
Opening times : permanent
3.5 ha (120 pitches) terraced, sloping, flat, stony
Tariff : 28.60 € ♥♥ ⇔ 圓 ⑭ (10A) – Extra per person 6.30 € – Reservation fee 15 €
⊡ sani-station 6 € – 8 圓 15 €
Pitches laid out on attractive terraces among mimosas and cork oaks.

Surroundings : ⚖ ⊡ 00
Leisure activities : ▾ ✗ ⚒ ⚖
Facilities : ᬽ ⊶ ☑ ⊞ ⑪ ⚖ ⚖ ⚡ ⑪ launderette ⚖

GPS	
Longitude : 6.32153	
Latitude : 43.16258	

> *There are several different types of sani-station ('borne' in French) – sanitation points providing fresh water and disposal points for grey water. See page 12 for further details.*

BRIANÇON

05100 – Michelin map **334** H2 – pop. 11,574 – alt. 1,321 – Winter sports :
▶ Paris 681 – Digne-les-Bains 145 – Embrun 48 – Grenoble 89

Les 5 Vallées

℘ 04 92 21 06 27, www.camping5vallees.com
Address : at St-Blaise (situated 2km south along the N 94)
5 ha (180 pitches) flat, grassy, stony
Rentals : ⅗ – 31 ⛺.

Surroundings : 00
Leisure activities : ⛫ ⚒ ⚖
Facilities : ᬽ ⊶ ⚖ ⑪ launderette ⚖ ⚖
Nearby : ⚓

GPS	
Longitude : 6.69323	
Latitude : 45.11898	

CADENET

84160 – Michelin map **332** F11 – pop. 4,061 – alt. 170
▶ Paris 734 – Aix-en-Provence 33 – Apt 23 – Avignon 63

Homair Vacances Val de Durance

℘ 04 90 68 37 75, *www.homair.com*
Address : 570 av. du Club Hippique (2.7km southwest along the D 943, follow the signs for Aix, turn right onto D 59 and take road to the left)
Opening times : from beginning April to end Sept.
10 ha/2.4 ha for camping (232 pitches) flat, grassy, stony
Tariff : (2012 price) 31€ ♣♣ ⛺ ▣ ⚡ (10A) – Extra per person 6.50€ – Reservation fee 10€
Rental rates : (2012 price) (from beginning April to end Sept.) – 220 ⛺.
er night from 36 to 153 € – Per week from 252 to 1,071 € – Reservation fee 25€
Beside a small lake and 300m from the Durance river.

Surroundings : ⛰ ≤ ⌂ ♤♤
Leisure activities : ♟ ✗ ▦ ⛱ daytime (Jul–Aug) ⚬⚬ 🛶 ⚓ ≋ ⚲ multi-sports ground
Facilities : ♿ ⊶ 🚿 ⚐ ⚑ ▣ ⚒ ⛽

GPS
Longitude : 5.35515
Latitude : 43.71957

*The prices listed were supplied by the campsite owners in 2012
(if prices were not available, those from the previous year are given).
The fees should be regarded as basic charges and may fluctuate
with inflation.*

CAGNES-SUR-MER

06800 – Michelin map **341** D6 – pop. 48,024 – alt. 20
▶ Paris 915 – Antibes 11 – Cannes 21 – Grasse 25

La Rivière

℘ 04 93 20 62 27, *www.campinglariviere06.fr* ✖
Address : 168 chemin des Salles (3.5km to the north; beside the Cagne river)
Opening times : from mid March to mid Sept.
1.2 ha (90 pitches) flat, grassy, gravelled
Tariff : 25€ ♣♣ ⛺ ▣ ⚡ (6A) – Extra per person 4€
Rental rates : (from beginning April to end Sept.) ✖ – 4 ⛺. Per week from 240 to 430 €

Surroundings : ⛰ ⌂ ♤♤
Leisure activities : ✗ ▦ 🛶 ⚓
Facilities : ⊶ 🚿 ⚐ ⚑ ▣ ⛽

GPS
Longitude : 7.14283
Latitude : 43.69581

Le Colombier

℘ 04 93 73 12 77, *www.campinglecolombier.com* ✖ (Jul–Aug)
Address : 35 chemin Ste Colombe (head 2km north towards the hills by the road to Vence)
Opening times : from beginning April to end Sept.
0.5 ha (33 pitches) relatively flat, flat, grassy, gravelled
Tariff : (2012 price) 26.60€ ♣♣ ⛺ ▣ ⚡ (16A) – Extra per person 5.50€ – Reservation fee 10€
Rental rates : (from beginning April to end Sept.) ✖ – 2 ⛺ – 1 studio.
Per week from 268 to 570 € – Reservation fee 10€
🚐 sani-station – ⚡ ⚡ 26.60€
The swimming pool is on the other side of the road.

Surroundings : ⛰ ⌂ ♧♧♧
Leisure activities : ▦ ⚓ (small swimming pool)
Facilities : ⊶ ⚑ ⚑ launderette, refrigerators

GPS
Longitude : 7.13893
Latitude : 43.67107

CALLAS

83830 – Michelin map **340** O4 – pop. 1,813 – alt. 398
◨ Paris 872 – Castellane 51 – Draguignan 14 – Toulon 94

Les Blimouses

✆ 04 94 47 83 41, *www.campinglesblimouses.com*
Address : 3km south along the D 25 and take D 225, follow the signs for Draguignan
Opening times : from beginning March to end Dec.
6 ha (170 pitches) terraced, flat and relatively flat, grassy, stony
Tariff : 24€ �%�%�%ⁱ 🚐 ▣ ⍾ (10A) – Extra per person 4€ – Reservation fee 20€
Rental rates : (from beginning March to end Dec.) – 30 🚐 – 7 🏠. Per night from 39 to 65 €
Per week from 250 to 790 € – Reservation fee 20€

Surroundings : 🌄 ⚲⚲
Leisure activities : ✕ 🛶 🏊 ⛷
Facilities : 🚿 ⛽ 🏕 🍴 ▣ 🚮

GPS Longitude : 6.53242
Latitude : 43.57456

CANNES

06400 – Michelin map **341** D6 – pop. 73,372 – alt. 2
◨ Paris 898 – Aix-en-Provence 149 – Marseille 160 – Nice 33

Le Parc Bellevue

✆ 04 93 47 28 97, *www.parcbellevue.com*
Address : at Cannes la Bocca, 67 av. Maurice Chevalier (to the north, behind the municipal stadium)
Opening times : from beginning April to end Sept.
5 ha (250 pitches) very uneven, terraced, gravelled, flat, grassy
Tariff : 29.50€ �%�%�%ⁱ 🚐 ▣ ⍾ (6A) – Extra per person 4.25€
Rental rates : (from beginning April to end Sept.) – 50 🚐. Per week from 270 to 730 €
🚰 sani-station
Choose pitches away from the road in preference.

Surroundings : 🏘 ⚲⚲
Leisure activities : ✕ 🖼 🛶 🏊
Facilities : 🚿 ⛽ 🏕 🍴 ▣ 🚮

GPS Longitude : 6.96042
Latitude : 43.55617

This guide is updated regularly, so buy your new copy every year!

LE CANNET

06110 – Michelin map **341** C6 – pop. 41,725 – alt. 80
◨ Paris 909 – Marseille 180 – Nice 39 – Monaco 54

Le Ranch

✆ 04 93 46 00 11, *www.leranchcamping.fr*
Address : at Aubarède, ch. St. Joseph (located 1.5km northwest along the D 9 then take bd. de l'Esterel to the right)
Opening times : from end April to beginning Oct.
2 ha (130 pitches) terraced, relatively flat, flat, grassy, stony
Tariff : (2012 price) �%ⁱ 7€ 🚐 3€ ▣ 15€ ⍾ (6A) – Reservation fee 10€
Rental rates : (2012 price) (from end April to beginning Oct.) – 14 🚐 – 5 🏠 – 2 🛏. Per week from 260 to 670 € – Reservation fee 10€
🚰 sani-station
Choose pitches away from the road in preference.

Surroundings : 🏘 ⚲⚲
Leisure activities : 🖼 🛶 🏊 (small swimming pool)
Facilities : 🚿 ⛽ 🏕 🚮 🍴 launderette 🚙

GPS Longitude : 6.97698
Latitude : 43.56508

CAROMB

84330 – Michelin map **332** D9 – pop. 3,185 – alt. 95
▶ Paris 683 – Avignon 37 – Carpentras 10 – Malaucène 10

Le Bouquier

℘ 0490623013, *www.lebouquier.com*
Address : av. Charles de Gaulle (located 1.5km north along the D 13)
1.5 ha (50 pitches) terraced, flat, gravelled, stony
Rentals : 3.

Surroundings :
Leisure activities : (small swimming pool)
Facilities :

GPS | Longitude : 5.10994
Latitude : 44.12396

CARPENTRAS

84200 – Michelin map **332** D9 – pop. 29,271 – alt. 102
▶ Paris 679 – Avignon 30 – Cavaillon 28 – Orange 24

Lou Comtadou

℘ 0490670316, *www.campingloucomtadou.com*
Address : 881 av. Pierre de Coubertin (located 1.5km southeast along the D 4, follow the signs for St-Didier and take turning to the right, near the sports centre)
1 ha (99 pitches) flat, grassy, stony, small lake
Rentals : 16 – 2 tent bungalows – 3 tents.
sani-station

Surroundings :
Leisure activities :
Facilities :
Nearby :

GPS | Longitude : 5.05429
Latitude : 44.04417

These symbols are used for a campsite that is exceptional in its category:
▵▵▵...▵ *Particularly pleasant setting, quality and range of services available*
Tranquil, isolated site – quiet site, particularly at night
Exceptional view – interesting or panoramic view

CARRO

13500 – Michelin map **340** F6
▶ Paris 787 – Marseille 44 – Aix-en-Provence 51 – Martigues 13

Yelloh! Village Les Chalets de la Mer
(rental of chalets only)

℘ 0442807346, *www.semovim-martigues.com*
Address : r. de la Tramontane
Opening times : permanent
3 ha flat
Rental rates : (2012 price) (8 chalets) – 68. Per night from 51 to 64 €
Per week from 394 to 1,050 € – Reservation fee 15.50€
Around 20 chalets are rented on a hotel-style basis.

Surroundings :
Leisure activities : evening
Facilities : launderette

GPS | Longitude : 5.04117
Latitude : 43.33291

CASTELLANE

04120 – Michelin map **334** H9 – pop. 1,553 – alt. 730
▶ Paris 797 – Digne-les-Bains 54 – Draguignan 59 – Grasse 64

Les Castels Le Domaine du Verdon ♠♠

☎ 0492836129, *www.camp-du-verdon.com*
Address : at Domaine de la Salaou (Camp du Verdon)
Opening times : from mid May to mid Sept.
9 ha (500 pitches) flat, grassy
Tariff : 27€ ♣♣ ⇌ 🗐 🗐 (16A) – Extra per person 8€ – Reservation fee 20€
Rental rates : (from mid May to mid Sept.) ♿ – 140 🚐 – 3 ⌂. Per night from 49 to 147 €
Per week from 343 to 1,029 € – Reservation fee 20€
🚽 sani-station

Surroundings : 🏊 🗘 ᵠᵠ
Leisure activities : 🍸 ✕ 🎬 🖈 🛶 🚴 🔜 🐾 🛝 🎣
Facilities : ♿ ⚊ 🖎 🖳 🚰 launderette 🗺 🖳 🗲 refrigerated food storage
Nearby : rafting and canyoning

GPS
Longitude : 6.49402
Latitude : 43.83895

RCN Les Collines de Castellane

☎ 0492836896, *www.rcn-campings.fr* – pitches accessed via steep slope, help moving caravans onto and off pitches avilable on request – alt. 1,000
Address : rte de Grasse (7km southeast along the N 85; at La Garde)
Opening times : from end April to end Sept.
7 ha (200 pitches) terraced, relatively flat, grassy, stony, wood
Tariff : 42.75€ ♣♣ ⇌ 🗐 🗐 (12A) – Extra per person 5.20€ – Reservation fee 19.50€
Rental rates : (from end April to end Sept.) – 34 🚐 – 8 ⌂. Per night from 31 to 44 €
Per week from 833 to 1,148 € – Reservation fee 19.50€

Surroundings : 🏊 ≺ 🗘 ᵠᵠ
Leisure activities : ✕ 🎬 ᵠ 🔜 🛝
Facilities : ♿ ⚊ ⚆ 🖳 ⚡ 🚰 🗲

GPS
Longitude : 6.56994
Latitude : 43.8244

International Camping

☎ 0492836667, *www.camping-international.fr*
Address : rte Napoleon
Opening times : from end March to beginning Oct.
6 ha (274 pitches) relatively flat, flat, grassy, stony
Tariff : 32€ ♣♣ ⇌ 🗐 🗐 (10A) – Extra per person 5€ – Reservation fee 10€
Rental rates : (from end March to beginning Oct.) – 30 🚐 – 10 ⌂.
Per night from 50 to 118 € – Per week from 275 to 825 € – Reservation fee 10€
🚽 sani-station – 🚐 🗐 16€

Surroundings : 🗘 ᵠ
Leisure activities : ✕ 🎬 ♯ 🔜
Facilities : ♿ ⚊ 🖎 🖳 ⚡ 🚰 🖳 🗲 refrigerated food storage
Nearby : 🐎

GPS
Longitude : 6.49796
Latitude : 43.85866

Key to rentals symbols:

12 🚐	*Number of mobile homes*	
20 ⌂	*Number of chalets*	
6 🛏	*Number of rooms to rent*	
Per night *30–50€*	*Minimum/maximum rate per night*	
Per week *300–1,000€*	*Minimum/maximum rate per week*	

La Colle

℘ 0492836157, www.camping-lacolle.com

Address : 2.5km southwest along the D 952, follow the signs for Moustiers-Ste-Marie and take GR 4 to the right

Opening times : from beginning April to end Sept.

3.5 ha/1 ha for camping (41 pitches) open site, terraced, relatively flat, flat, grassy, stony

Tariff : 19€ ♣ ♣ ⟵ ▣ ⒜ (10A) – Extra per person 5.70€

Rental rates : (from beginning April to end Sept.) ⚒ – 12 ▦ – 2 ⌂.
Per night from 42 to 80 € – Per week 580€

In a natural setting, beside a stream.

Surroundings : ⛰ ⟨ ⟶ ♡♡
Leisure activities : ▣ ⚙
Facilities : ⚒ ⟶ ⟲ ⟲ ☂ ▣
Nearby : adventure park, rafting and canyoning

Longitude : 6.49312
Latitude : 43.83864

Notre-Dame

℘ 0492836302, www.camping-notredame.com

Address : rte des Gorges du Verdon (500m southwest along the D 952, follow the signs for Moustiers-Ste-Marie; beside a stream)

Opening times : from beginning April to mid Oct.

0.6 ha (44 pitches) flat, grassy

Tariff : (2012 price) 22.50€ ♣ ♣ ⟵ ▣ ⒜ (6A) – Extra per person 6€ – Reservation fee 9€

Rental rates : (2012 price) (from beginning April to mid Oct.) ⚒ – 11 ▦.
Per night from 45 to 99 € – Per week from 225 to 610 € – Reservation fee 9€

▦ sani-station 6€ – ⛽11€

Surroundings : ⟨
Leisure activities : ⟶
Facilities : ⚒ ⟶ ⟲ ☂
Nearby : adventure park, rafting and canyoning

Longitude : 6.50425
Latitude : 43.84545

CAVALAIRE-SUR-MER

83240 – Michelin map **340** O6 – pop. 6,731 – alt. 2
▶ Paris 880 – Draguignan 55 – Fréjus 41 – Le Lavandou 21

Cros de Mouton

℘ 0494641087, www.crosdemouton.com – pitches accessed via steep slope, help moving caravans onto and off pitches avilable on request

Address : chemin du Cros de Mouton (located 1.5km to the northwest)

Opening times : from mid March to beginning Nov.

5 ha (199 pitches) very uneven, terraced, flat, stony

Tariff : (2012 price) ♣ 8.90€ ⟵ ▣ 8.90€ – ⒜ (10A) 4.70€ – Reservation fee 20€

Rental rates : (2012 price) (permanent) – 58 ▦ – 15 ⌂. Per night from 63 to 113 €
Per week from 400 to 975 € – Reservation fee 20€

▦ sani-station

Surroundings : ⛰ ⟨ Baie de Cavalaire ⟶ ♡♡
Leisure activities : ⛱ ✕ ▣ ⚓ ⟲
Facilities : ⚒ ⟶ ▣ ⟲ ⟲ ☂ ▣ ⟲ ⟲

Longitude : 6.51662
Latitude : 43.18243

*Routes nationales are main roads and their identifying numbers
begin with N or RN. Routes départementales are generally quieter
roads and begin with D or DN.*

EILLAC

600 – Michelin map **334** I4 – pop. 307 – alt. 1,640 – Winter sports : 1,700/2,500 m≰6 ⚡
Paris 729 – Briançon 50 – Gap 75 – Guillestre 14

Les Mélèzes

☎ 04 92 45 21 93, *www.campingdeceillac.com*
Address : at La Rua des Reynauds (1.8km southeast)
Opening times : from beginning June to beginning Sept.
3 ha (100 pitches) very uneven, terraced, relatively flat, grassy, stony
Tariff : ✿ 5.50€⇦ ▣ 6.50€ – ⊞ (10A) 3€
A pleasant location and setting beside the Mélezet river.

Surroundings : ⚲ ⋖ ♀
Leisure activities : ⚴⬈
Facilities : �o━ ▥ ♨ ⚎ ♔ ▣

Longitude : 6.78843
Latitude : 44.65389

HÂTEAUNEUF-DE-GADAGNE

1470 – Michelin map **332** C10 – pop. 3,249 – alt. 90
Paris 701 – Marseille 95 – Avignon 14 – Nîmes 58

Le Fontisson

☎ 04 90 22 59 77, *www.campingfontisson.com*
Address : 1125 rte d'Avignon (near the exit from town along the follow the signs for Avignon and take road to the right)
Opening times : from beginning April to mid Oct.
2 ha (55 pitches) relatively flat, grassy, stony
Tariff : (2012 price) 26.20€ ✿✿ ⇦ ▣ ⊞ (10A) – Extra per person 6.60€ – Reservation fee 10€
Rental rates : (2012 price) (from beginning April to mid Oct.) – 19 ⌂ – 4 tent bungalows.
Per night from 75 to 155 € – Per week from 205 to 795 € – Reservation fee 15€

Surroundings : ⚲ ⊏ ♀♀
Leisure activities : ⬚ ⚴⬈ ⚒ ♫ ▨ multi-sports ground
Facilities : ♿ o━ ♨ ♔ ▣

Longitude : 4.93297
Latitude : 43.92846

*We have selected the best campsites in France with our usual care,
listing those with the best facilities in the most pleasant surroundings.*

HÂTEAURENARD

3160 – Michelin map **340** E2 – pop. 14,971 – alt. 37
Paris 692 – Avignon 10 – Carpentras 37 – Cavaillon 23

La Roquette

☎ 04 90 94 46 81, *www.camping-la-roquette.com*
Address : 745 av. Jean-Mermoz (located 1.5km east along the D 28, follow the signs for Noves and take a right turn, near the swimming pool – from A 7 take exit Avignon-Sud)
Opening times : from beginning April to end Oct.
2 ha (74 pitches) flat, grassy
Tariff : (2012 price) 25€ ✿✿ ⇦ ▣ ⊞ (10A) – Extra per person 7€
Rental rates : (2012 price) (from beginning April to end Oct.) ⚲ – 12 ⌂.
Per week from 280 to 790 €

Surroundings : ⊏ ♀
Leisure activities : ♇ ⚒ ⚴⬈ ▨
Facilities : ♿ o━ ⚎ ♔ ▣

Longitude : 4.87017
Latitude : 43.88328

CHORGES

05230 – Michelin map **334** F5 – pop. 2,567 – alt. 864
▶ Paris 676 – Embrun 23 – Gap 18 – Savines-le-Lac 12

Municipal

✆ 04 92 50 67 72, www.baiestmichel.com
Address : Baie St-Michel (4.5km southeast along the N 94, follow the signs for Briançon, 200m from the lake at Serre-Ponçon)
2 ha (110 pitches) terraced, flat, grassy, stony
Rentals : ♿ (1 chalet) – 10 🏠.

Surroundings : ⛰ ≤ ♀
Leisure activities : 🖥 ⛵ ≋ (lake)
Facilities : ♿ ⚬ ♨
Nearby : 🍴 ✕ ⚂ ⚄ ♦ pedalos

GPS Longitude : 6.32379
Latitude : 44.5283

Gites range from small maisonettes to old farmhouses with several bedrooms.

CLAMENSANE

04250 – Michelin map **334** E7 – pop. 166 – alt. 694
▶ Paris 720 – Avignon 180 – Grenoble 158 – Marseille 152

Le Clot du Jay en Provence

✆ 04 92 68 35 32, www.clotdujay.com
Address : rte de Bayons (located 1km east along the D 1, follow the signs for Bayons, near the Sasse river)
Opening times : from beginning May to end Sept.
6 ha/3 ha for camping (50 pitches) very uneven, terraced, flat, grassy, stony, lake
Tariff : (2012 price) 21€ ✦✦ ⇌ ▣ ⚡ (10A) – Extra per person 5€ – Reservation fee 9€
Rental rates : (2012 price) (from beginning May to end Sept.) – 8 🚐 – 11 🏠.
Per week from 260 to 640 € – Reservation fee 9€

Surroundings : ⛰ ⊏ ♀♀
Leisure activities : ✕ ⚄ ⚄
Facilities : ♿ ⚬ ☕ ♨ ⚂
Nearby : ⚄

GPS Longitude : 6.0845
Latitude : 44.3226

LA COLLE-SUR-LOUP

06480 – Michelin map **341** D5 – pop. 7,640 – alt. 90
▶ Paris 919 – Antibes 15 – Cagnes-sur-Mer 7 – Cannes 26

Les Pinèdes ♣♣

✆ 04 93 32 98 94, www.lespinedes.com
Address : rte du Pont de Pierre (located 1.5km west along the D 6, follow the signs for Grasse, 50m from the Loup river)
Opening times : from mid March to end Sept.
3.8 ha (155 pitches) very uneven, terraced, fine gravel, grassy
Tariff : 41.90€ ✦✦ ⇌ ▣ ⚡ (10A) – Extra per person 6€ – Reservation fee 20€
Rental rates : (from mid March to end Sept.) – 32 🚐 – 9 🏠. Per week from 330 to 1,180 €
Reservation fee 20€
🚐 sani-station 6€ – 🔌 12€

Surroundings : ⊏ ♀♀
Leisure activities : 🍴 🖥 ⚄ ⛵ ⚄ multi-sports ground
Facilities : ⚬ ▥ ☕ ⚂ ♨ ♨ launderette ⚄ refrigerated food storage
Nearby : ✕ ≋ 🐴 leisure park

GPS Longitude : 7.08337
Latitude : 43.68177

Le Vallon Rouge

℘ 04 93 32 86 12, *www.auvallonrouge.com* – limited spaces for one-night stay

Address : rte de Gréolières (3.5km west along the D 6, follow the signs for Grasse; beside the Loup river)

Opening times : from beginning April to end Sept.

3 ha (103 pitches) terraced, flat, grassy, sandy, fine gravel

Tariff : (2012 price) 14€ ♠♠ ⬛ 🔲 (10A) – Extra per person 2.60€ – Reservation fee 20€

Rental rates : (2012 price) (from beginning April to end Sept.) – 40 🚐 – 30 🏠.
Per night from 65 to 95 € – Per week from 295 to 780 € – Reservation fee 20€

🚿 sani-station 4€

Surroundings : 🌿 🛏 ♨♨
Leisure activities : ✗ 🎮 🎣 🎿 ☰ multi-sports ground
Facilities : 👤 ⚲ ♨ 🚰 ♉ launderette 🛒

GPS Longitude : 7.07324
Latitude : 43.68452

COLMARS

04370 – Michelin map **334** H7 – pop. 385 – alt. 1,235
▶ Paris 816 – Marseille 206 – Digne-les-Bains 71 – Embrun 94

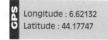 **Aire Naturelle les Pommiers**

℘ 04 92 83 41 56, *www.camping-pommier.com* – alt. 1,250

Address : at Les Buissières (300m to the south)

Opening times : permanent

1 ha (25 pitches) terraced, flat and relatively flat, grassy

Tariff : ♠ 4.50€ ⬛ 🔲 4€ – 🔲 (10A) 2.50€

🚿 sani-station 15.50€ – 2 🔲 15.50€ – 🚐 🔲 15.50€

Surroundings : 🌿 ≤ ♨♨
Facilities : 👤 ⚲ 🚰 📷

GPS Longitude : 6.62132
Latitude : 44.17747

We welcome your feedback on our listed campsites.
Please email us at: campingfrance@tp.michelin.com
Many thanks in advance!

COL-ST-JEAN

04340 – Michelin map **334** G6 – alt. 1,333 – Winter sports : 1,300/2,500 m ⛷ 15 ⛷
▶ Paris 709 – Barcelonnette 34 – Savines-le-Lac 31 – Seyne 10

 Yelloh! Village L'Étoile des Neiges

℘ 04 92 35 01 29, *www.etoile-des-neiges.com* – alt. 1,300

Address : at the Col St-Jean ski resort (station de ski) (800m south along the D 207 and turn right onto the D 307)

Opening times : from mid May to beginning Sept. and from mid-Dec to end Mar

3 ha (150 pitches) terraced, flat, grassy, stony

Tariff : (2012 price) 36€ ♠♠ ⬛ 🔲 (6A) – Extra per person 8€

Rental rates : (2012 price) (from mid May to beginning Sept. and from mid-Dec to end Mar)
🏠 (Jul–Aug) – 60 🚐 – 26 🏠 – 5 apartments – 4 gîtes. Per night from 30 to 115 €
Per week from 210 to 805 €

🚿 sani-station

Surroundings : 🌿 ≤ 🛏
Leisure activities : ✗ 🎮 🎨 evening 💆 🌊 hammam jacuzzi ⛳ 🖼 🎿 multi-sports ground, spa therapy centre
Facilities : 👤 ⚲ 🔲 🍴 ♨ 🚰 🛁 ♉ launderette 🛒
Nearby : 🎿 🚴 🎿 adventure park, paragliding

GPS Longitude : 6.348
Latitude : 44.40927

LA COURONNE

13500 – Michelin map **340** F5
▶ Paris 786 – Marseille 42 – Aix-en-Provence 49 – Martigues 11

Le Mas ♣♣

📞 04 42 80 70 34, *www.camping-le-mas.com* – limited spaces for one-night stay
Address : chemin de Ste Croix (4km southeast along the D 49, follow the signs for Sausset-les-Pins and take a right turn; near the beach at Ste-Croix)
Opening times : from mid March to beginning Nov.
5.5 ha (300 pitches) terraced, flat, stony
Tariff : (2012 price) 41€ ♣♣ ⇔ 🗐 (16A) – Extra per person 8.70€ – Reservation fee 20€
Rental rates : (2012 price) (from mid March to beginning Nov.) ⚡ – 151 🛏 – 45 🏠.
Per week from 224 to 1,225 € – Reservation fee 20€
Some pitches have a sea view.

Surroundings : 🌿 ♨
Leisure activities : ♟ ✗ 🏠 ☺ ♣ ⚓ 🏊 multi-sports ground
Facilities : ♿ ⚬ 🛁 ♻ launderette 🧺
Nearby : 🏖

Longitude : 5.07349
Latitude : 43.33168

Municipal L'Arquet

📞 04 42 42 81 00, *www.semovim-martigues.com*
Address : chemin de la Batterie
6 ha (330 pitches) terraced, flat, sandy, stony
Rentals : 18 🛏.
🚮 sani-station

Surroundings : 🌿 ♨
Leisure activities : 🏠 ♣
Facilities : ♿ ⚬ launderette 🏖 🧺

Longitude : 5.05639
Latitude : 43.33067

Flower Le Marius

📞 04 42 80 70 29, *www.camping-marius.com*
Address : Plage de la Saule (beach) (3km southeast along the D 49)
2 ha (113 pitches) flat, grassy, gravelled
Rentals : ♿ (2 chalets) – 37 🏠 – 15 tent bungalows (with/without sanitary facilities).

Surroundings : 🌿 🖂 ♨
Leisure activities : ♟ ✗ ⚓ 🚲 🏊
Facilities : ♿ ♻ launderette 🧺

Longitude : 5.06744
Latitude : 43.33512

Les Mouettes

📞 04 42 80 70 01, *www.campinglesmouettes.fr* – limited spaces for one-night stay
Address : 16 chemin de la Quiétude (4km southeast along the D 49, follow the signs for Sausset, along the r. du Tamaris, near the beach at Ste-Croix)
Opening times : from beginning April to end Sept.
2 ha (131 pitches) terrace, flat, stony
Tariff : 27€ ♣♣ ⇔ 🗐 (6A) – Extra per person 7€ – Reservation fee 8€
Rental rates : (permanent) – 23 🛏 – 20 🏠 – 10 studios. Per night from 43 to 77 €
Per week from 180 to 800 € – Reservation fee 8€
Some pitches have a sea view.

Surroundings : 🌿 ♨
Leisure activities : ♟ ✗
Facilities : ♿ ⚬ 🏖 ♻ ♻ launderette
Nearby : 🏖

Longitude : 5.07618
Latitude : 43.33024

A CROIX-VALMER

3420 – Michelin map **340** O6 – pop. 3,351 – alt. 120
Paris 873 – Brignoles 70 – Draguignan 48 – Fréjus 35

Sélection Camping ▲ː

℘ 04 94 55 10 30, *www.selectioncamping.com* ⌘ (Jul–Aug)
Address : 12 bd de la Mer (2.5km southwest along the D 559, follow the signs for Cavalaire and take road to the right at the roundabout)
Opening times : from mid March to mid Oct.
4 ha (205 pitches) terraced, flat, grassy, stony
Tariff : (2012 price) 42€ ⚓ ⚓ ⚓ 🅴 🅹 (10A) – Extra per person 11€ – Reservation fee 30€
Rental rates : (2012 price) (from mid March to mid Oct.) ⌘ – 50 🛏 – 15 🏠 – 15 gîtes.
Per night from 52 to 142 € – Per week from 360 to 1,000 € – Reservation fee 30€

Surroundings : 🌳 🚋 ⛰
Leisure activities : 🍴 ✕ ⌨ daytime 🏃 🏊 ⛷ 🏊 multi-sports ground, entertainment room
Facilities : ♿ ⛽ 🏧 ⛺ 🍴 launderette 🏪 🛒

GPS
Longitude : 6.55501
Latitude : 43.19439

The guide covers all 22 regions of France – see the map and list of regions on pages 4–5.

ROS-DE-CAGNES

6800 – Michelin map **341** D6
Paris 923 – Marseille 194 – Nice 12 – Antibes 11

Homair Vacances Green Park ▲ː

℘ 04 93 07 09 96, *www.homair.com* – limited spaces for one-night stay
Address : 159 bis chemin du Vallon des Vaux (3.8km to the north)
Opening times : from beginning April to end Sept.
5 ha (156 pitches) very uneven, terraced, flat, grassy, fine gravel
Tariff : (2012 price) 45€ ⚓ ⚓ ⚓ 🅴 🅹 (10A) – Extra per person 7.50€ – Reservation fee 10€
Rental rates : (2012 price) (from beginning April to end Sept.) ♿ (2 chalets) – 59 🛏 – 59 🏠.
Per night from 44 to 187 € – Per week from 308 to 1,309 € – Reservation fee 25€
Free shuttle service to the beaches in July-August.

Surroundings : 🌳 🚋 ⛰
Leisure activities : 🍴 ✕ 🎱 ⌨ 🏃 🏊 🚲 🏊 multi-sports ground
Facilities : ♿ ⛽ ⛺ 🚿 🍴 launderette 🛒
Nearby : 🏪 ⌘ ⛰

GPS
Longitude : 7.1569
Latitude : 43.68904

Le Val Fleuri

℘ 04 93 31 21 74, *www.campingvalfleuri.fr*
Address : 139 chemin du Vallon des Vaux (3.5km to the north)
Opening times : from beginning April to mid Oct.
1.5 ha (93 pitches) terraced, flat, grassy, stony
Tariff : 30.80€ ⚓ ⚓ ⚓ 🅴 🅹 (10A) – Extra per person 4€
Rental rates : (from beginning April to mid Oct.) – 11 🛏 – 1 studio – 1 apartment.
Per night from 50 to 65 € – Per week from 270 to 630 €
Free shuttle service to the beach in July-August.

Surroundings : 🌳 🚋 ⛰
Leisure activities : 🍴 🏊 🏊
Facilities : ♿ ⛽ 🏧 🍴 🖼
Nearby : ⌘

GPS
Longitude : 7.15577
Latitude : 43.68745

Homair Vacances Le Todos

☎ 04 93 07 09 96, *www.homair.com* – limited spaces for one-night stay
Address : 159 bis chemin du Vallon des Vaux (3.8km to the north)
Opening times : from mid May to mid Sept.
1.6 ha (68 pitches) terrace, flat, grassy, stony
Tariff : (2012 price) 27 € ♣♣ ⇌ 🔲 ⚡ (10A) – Extra per person 7.50 € – Reservation fee 10 €
Rental rates : (2012 price) (from mid May to mid Sept.) – 44 ⬛ – 9 🏠.
Per night from 38 to 160 € – Per week from 266 to 1,120 € – Reservation fee 25 €
Free shuttle service to the beach in July-August.

Surroundings : 🌲 ⌂ 🎡
Leisure activities : 🏊 ⅃
Facilities : ⅄ ⊶ 🍴 launderette ⚏
Nearby : 🍴 ✗ 🛒 🏪 🏕 🚴 ✂ ♠

GPS Longitude : 7.1569
Latitude : 43.68904

CUCURON

84160 – Michelin map **332** F11 – pop. 1,844 – alt. 350
▶ Paris 739 – Aix-en-Provence 34 – Apt 25 – Cadenet 9

Le Moulin à Vent

☎ 04 90 77 25 77, *http://www.le-moulin-a-vent.com*
Address : chemin de Gastoule (located 1.5km south along the D 182; follow the signs for Villelaure then continue 800m along the turning to the left)
Opening times : from end March to beginning Oct.
2.2 ha (80 pitches) terraced, flat and relatively flat, stony
Tariff : 18.60 € ♣♣ ⇌ 🔲 ⚡ (10A) – Extra per person 4.90 €
Rental rates : (from end March to beginning Oct.) ⚿ – 1 ⬛ – 4 🏠.
Per week from 290 to 525 €
🚾 sani-station 5 €
Set among vineyards.

Surroundings : 🌲 ⋖ ⌂ 🎡
Leisure activities : 🏠 ⚏ 🏊
Facilities : ⅄ ⊶ ♨ 🍴 📷 🛒 refrigerators

GPS Longitude : 5.44484
Latitude : 43.75641

To visit a town or region, use the MICHELIN Green Guides.

CURBANS

05110 – Michelin map **334** E6 – pop. 418 – alt. 650
▶ Paris 717 – Marseille 171 – Digne-les-Bains 78 – Gap 20

Le Lac

☎ 04 92 54 23 10, *www.au-camping-du-lac.com* – limited spaces for one-night stay
Address : at Le Fangeas
Opening times : from beginning April to end Oct.
5.2 ha (140 pitches) relatively flat, flat, grassy
Tariff : (2012 price) 26 € ♣♣ ⇌ 🔲 ⚡ (10A) – Extra per person 5.50 € – Reservation fee 12 €
Rental rates : (2012 price) (permanent) – 37 ⬛. Per night from 45 to 58 €
Per week from 270 to 820 € – Reservation fee 12 €
An attractive location near the Lac de Curbans. Although the site has a Hautes-Alpes post code (05), it is located in the Alpes-de-Haute-Provence (04).

Surroundings : ⋖ 🎡
Leisure activities : 🍴 ✗ 🎲 evening ✂ ⅃ ⚏ 🎣 multi-sports ground
Facilities : ⊶ 🍴 launderette 🛒

GPS Longitude : 6.0299
Latitude : 44.42452

DIGNE-LES-BAINS

04000 – Michelin map **334** F8 – pop. 17,172 – alt. 608 – ⊕ (mid-Feb-beg Dec)
▶ Paris 744 – Aix-en-Provence 109 – Antibes 140 – Avignon 167

Les Eaux Chaudes

℘ 04 92 32 31 04, *www.campingleseauxchaudes.com*
Address : 32 av. des Thermes (located 1.5km southeast along the D 20; beside a stream)
Opening times : from mid April to mid Oct.
3.7 ha (90 pitches) flat and relatively flat, grassy
Tariff : 25.50€ ★★ ⇔ 🗐 🗵 (10A) – Extra per person 6.50€ – Reservation fee 15€
Rental rates : (from beginning April to end Oct.) – 51 🛏 – 4 🏠. Per night from 49 to 117 €
Per week from 343 to 819 € – Reservation fee 18€
🚰 sani-station 4€

Surroundings : ≼
Leisure activities : 🖼 ⚡ ⤓
Facilities : 🕭 ⚬ 🔟 🛇 🚰 🚿
Nearby : ✂

GPS Longitude : 6.2507
Latitude : 44.08656

EMBRUN

05200 – Michelin map **334** G5 – pop. 6,188 – alt. 871
▶ Paris 706 – Barcelonnette 55 – Briançon 48 – Digne-les-Bains 97

Municipal de la Clapière

℘ 04 92 43 01 83, *www.camping-embrun-clapiere.com*
Address : av. du Lac (2.5km southwest along the N 94, follow the signs for Gap and take a right turn; at the leisure and activity park)
Opening times : from end March to end Sept.
6.5 ha (291 pitches) terraced, flat, grassy, fine gravel
Tariff : ⇔🗐 17.60€ – 🗵 (16A) 3.90€
Rental rates : (permanent) – 6 🛏 – 14 🏠. Per night from 83 to 97€
Per week from 610 to 710 €
🚰 sani-station
Direct access in season to the leisure and activity park.

Surroundings : 🔆
Leisure activities : 🖼 🕭 evening ⚡
Facilities : 🕭 ⚬ 🏕 🚿 launderette
Nearby : 🛒 ⓨ ✗ 🗗 ✂ 🏓 🖼 🞈 (lake) 🛇 🗗 ⓓ pedalos

GPS Longitude : 6.47875
Latitude : 44.55075

ESPARRON-DE-VERDON

04800 – Michelin map **334** D10 – pop. 433 – alt. 397
▶ Paris 795 – Barjols 31 – Digne-les-Bains 58 – Gréoux-les-Bains 13

Le Soleil

℘ 04 92 77 13 78, *www.camping-le-soleil.com* ✖
Address : 1000 chemin de la Tuillière (take the southern exit along the D 82, follow the signs for Quinson, then continue 1km along the right turn)
Opening times : from beginning April to mid Oct.
2 ha (100 pitches) very uneven, terraced, stony, fine gravel
Tariff : (2012 price) 26€ ★★ ⇔ 🗐 🗵 (6A) – Extra per person 6.75€ – Reservation fee 15€
Rental rates : (2012 price) (from beginning April to mid Oct.) ✖ – 12 🛏.
Per night from 40 to 85 € – Per week from 150 to 620 € – Reservation fee 20€
🚰 sani-station 5€ – 🚐 🗵 26€
In a pleasant setting beside a lake.

Surroundings : 🞈 🗗 🔆 ⛰
Leisure activities : ✗ 🖼 🞈
Facilities : 🕭 ⚬ ⓟ 🚿 🚿 🛇 🗗
Nearby : ⓓ pedalos

GPS Longitude : 5.97062
Latitude : 43.73439

ESPINASSES

05190 – Michelin map **334** F6 – pop. 665 – alt. 630
▶ Paris 689 – Chorges 19 – Gap 25 – Le Lauzet-Ubaye 23

La Viste

📞 04 92 54 43 39, *www.laviste.fr* – alt. 900
Address : Le Belvédère de Serre-Ponçon (head 5.5km northeast along the D 900b, take the D 3 following signs for Chorges and turn left onto D 103)
Opening times : from mid May to mid Sept.
4.5 ha/2.5 ha for camping (170 pitches) terraced, undulating, flat, grassy, stony
Tariff : (2012 price) ♦ 6.80€ ⟺ 回 6.80€ – ⑭ (5A) 3.60€
Rental rates : (2012 price) (from mid May to mid Sept.) – 10 ⟐ – 40 ⟐.
Per night from 46 to 121 € – Per week from 294 to 845 € – Reservation fee 15€
An attractive location overlooking the Lac de Serre-Ponçon.

Surroundings : ⟐ ≤ mountains, lake and Barrage de Serre-Ponçon
(dam) ⟐⟐
Leisure activities : ⟐ ✗ ⟐ daytime ⟐ ⟐
Facilities : ⟐ ⟐ ⟐ launderette ⟐, ⟐
Nearby : ⟐ (lake) ⟐ water skiing, rafting and canyoning

GPS Longitude : 6.26832
Latitude : 44.47613

FAUCON

84110 – Michelin map **332** D8 – pop. 414 – alt. 350
▶ Paris 677 – Marseille 152 – Avignon 59 – Montélimar 68

L'Ayguette

📞 04 90 46 40 35, *www.ayguette.com*
Address : rte de Faucon, take the eastern exit along the D 938, follow the signs for Nyons and continue 4.1 km to the right along the D 71, follow the signs for St-Romains-Viennois then take the D 86
Opening times : from end March to end Sept.
2.8 ha (100 pitches) undulating, flat, grassy, stony
Tariff : 30€ ♦♦ ⟺ 回 ⑭ (10A) – Extra per person 5€ – Reservation fee 6€
Rental rates : (from end March to end Sept.) – 14 ⟐. Per week from 209 to 699 €
Reservation fee 12€
⟐ sani-station
In natural setting at the foot of Mont Ventoux.

Surroundings : ⟐ ⟐ ⟐⟐
Leisure activities : ✗ ⟐ ⟐
Facilities : ⟐ ⟐ ⟐ ⟐ 回 ⟐

GPS Longitude : 5.12933
Latitude : 44.26215

FORCALQUIER

04300 – Michelin map **334** C9 – pop. 4,640 – alt. 550
▶ Paris 747 – Aix-en-Provence 80 – Apt 42 – Digne-les-Bains 50

Indigo Forcalquier

📞 04 92 75 27 94, *www.camping-indigo.com*
Address : rte de Sigonce (take the eastern exit on D 16)
Opening times : from mid April to end Sept.
2.9 ha (115 pitches) terraced, relatively flat, flat, grassy, stony
Tariff : (2012 price) 28.10€ ♦♦ ⟺ 回 ⑭ (10A) – Extra per person 6.20€ – Reservation fee 20€
Rental rates : (2012 price) (from mid April to end Sept.) ⟐ – 33 ⟐ – 4 ⟐ – 17 tents.
Per night from 46 to 112 € – Per week from 225 to 784 € – Reservation fee 20€
⟐ sani-station 7€

Surroundings : ⟐ ⟐⟐
Leisure activities : ✗ ⟐ ⟐ ⟐ ⟐
Facilities : ⟐ ⟐ ⟐ ⟐ ⟐ 回 ⟐
Nearby : ⟐

GPS Longitude : 5.78723
Latitude : 43.96218

FRÉJUS

83600 – Michelin map **340** P5 – pop. 52,203 – alt. 20 – Leisure centre
▶ Paris 868 – Brignoles 64 – Cannes 40 – Draguignan 31

La Baume – la Palmeraie ♣♣

℘ 04 94 19 88 88, *www.labaume-lapalmeraie.com* – limited spaces for one-night stay
Address : 3775 r. des Combattants d'Afrique du Nord (4.5km north along the D 4; follow the signs for Bagnols-en-Forêt)
Opening times : from beginning April to end Sept.
26 ha/20 ha for camping (780 pitches) flat and relatively flat, grassy, stony
Tariff : 51€ ♣♣ ⊂⊃ 🔲 ⅍ (6A) – Extra per person 14€ – Reservation fee 32€
Rental rates : (from end March to end Sept.) ⅙ – 171 ⬜ – 182 apartments.
Per night from 48 to 215 € – Per week from 336 to 1,505 € – Reservation fee 32€
A spacious swimming area with large palm trees.

Surroundings : ▱ ♤♤
Leisure activities : ▼ ✗ ▭ ⑨ (open-air theatre) ⫶ ⌁ hammam,
jacuzzi ⬳ ⬙ ✄ 🔲 ⬙ ⬘ disco, skate park
Facilities : ⅙ ⊶ ⊪ ♤ ⌂ ⌇ ⑪ launderette ⬙ ⬂

GPS Longitude : 6.72319
Latitude : 43.46655

Yelloh! Village Domaine du Colombier ♣♣

℘ 04 94 51 56 01, *www.clubcolombier.com* – limited spaces for one-night stay
Address : 1052 r. des Combattants en Afrique du Nord (situated 2km north along the D 4; follow the signs for Bagnols-en-Forêt)
Opening times : from end March to end Oct.
10 ha (400 pitches) terraced, undulating, flat, grassy
Tariff : 59€ ♣♣ ⊂⊃ 🔲 ⅍ (16A) – Extra per person 9€
Rental rates : (from end March to end Oct.) – 351 ⬜. Per night from 39 to 375 €
Per week from 273 to 2,625 €
Rental options based on different decorative themes (tropical, nautical, Asiatic . . .).

Surroundings : ⪡ ▱
Leisure activities : ▼ ✗ ▭ ⑨ ⫶ ⌁ jacuzzi ⬳ ⬙ 🔲 ⬘ disco
Facilities : ⅙ ⊶ ⊪ ♤ ⌂ ⌇ ⑪ launderette ⬙ ⬂

GPS Longitude : 6.72688
Latitude : 43.44588

Sunêlia Holiday Green

℘ 04 94 19 88 30, *www.holidaygreen.com* – limited spaces for one-night stay
Address : r. des Anciens Combattants d'Afrique du Nord
Opening times : from beginning April to end Sept.
15 ha (680 pitches) very uneven, terraced, stony, flat, grassy
Tariff : 55€ ♣♣ ⊂⊃ 🔲 ⅍ (10A) – Extra per person 10€ – Reservation fee 40€
Rental rates : (from beginning April to end Sept.) ⬢ – 300 ⬜ – 20 ⌂.
Per night from 56 to 236 € – Per week from 385 to 1,652 € – Reservation fee 40€
⬚ 3 🔲 55€

Surroundings : ⬝ ▱ ♤♤
Leisure activities : ▼ ✗ ▭ ⑨ ⫶ ⌁ ✄ 🔲 ⬙ ⬘ disco, multi-sports
ground
Facilities : ⅙ ⊶ ⑪ launderette ⬙ ⬂

GPS Longitude : 6.71683
Latitude : 43.48481

Do not confuse:
△ to △△△ : MICHELIN classification
with
★ to ★★★★★ : official classification

La Pierre Verte ♣♦

℘ 04 94 40 88 30, *www.campinglapierreverte.com*
Address : r. des Anciens Combattants d'Afrique du Nord (6.5km north along the D 4, follow the signs for Bagnols-en-Forêt and take the road to the right)
Opening times : from beginning April to end Sept.
28 ha (440 pitches) very uneven, terraced, stony, rocks
Tariff : 44€ ♣♣ ⇔ ▣ ⑻ (10A) – Extra per person 9€ – Reservation fee 25€
Rental rates : (from beginning April to end Sept.) – 200 ⛺. Per night from 40 to 175 €
Per week from 280 to 1,225 € – Reservation fee 25€

Surroundings : ⟋ ⊏⟍ ♎♎
Leisure activities : ♟ ✕ ⌂ ⃝ ♣ ⛵ ✖ ♫ ⟋ ⟑ multi-sports ground
Facilities : ᵴ ⊶ ♨ ♨ ⇝ ♈ launderette ⛟ ♨

GPS Longitude : 6.72054
Latitude : 43.48382

Le Pont d'Argens

℘ 04 94 51 14 97, *www.camping-caravaning-lepontdargens.com*
Address : 3km south along the N 98, direct access to the beach
7 ha (500 pitches) flat, grassy
Rentals : 50 ⛺.
⛽ sani-station
Beside the Argens river with direct access to the beach. Choose pitches away from the road in preference.

Surroundings : ♎♎
Leisure activities : ♟ ✕ ⌂ ⛵ ⟋
Facilities : ᵴ ⊶ ♨ ♈ launderette ⛟ ♨

GPS Longitude : 6.72489
Latitude : 43.4087

Les Pins Parasols

℘ 04 94 40 88 43, *www.lespinsparasols.com*
Address : 3360 r. des Combattants d'Afrique du Nord (4km north along the D 4, follow the signs for Bagnols-en-Forêt)
Opening times : from beginning April to end Sept.
4.5 ha (189 pitches) terraced, flat, grassy, stony
Tariff : 29.80€ ♣♣ ⇔ ▣ ⑻ (6A) – Extra per person 6.65€
Rental rates : (from beginning April to end Sept.) ⚡ – 9 ⛺. Per week from 215 to 756 €
Attractive pitches laid out on terraces among shady pine trees.

Surroundings : ⊏⟍ ♎♎
Leisure activities : ✕ ⌂ ⛵ ⟋ ⟑
Facilities : ᵴ ⊶ ⇝ ▥ ♨ – 48 individual sanitary facilities (⟲ ♨ ♨ wc)
♈ 回 ⛟ ♨

GPS Longitude : 6.72531
Latitude : 43.464

GAP

05000 – Michelin map **334** E5 – pop. 39,243 – alt. 735
◘ Paris 665 – Avignon 209 – Grenoble 103 – Sisteron 52

Alpes-Dauphiné

℘ 04 92 51 29 95, *www.alpesdauphine.com* – alt. 850
Address : rte Napoleon (3km north along the N 85, follow the signs for Grenoble)
Opening times : from mid April to mid Oct.
10 ha/6 ha for camping (185 pitches) terraced, sloping, grassy
Tariff : ♣ 6.70€ ⇔ ▣ 8.30€ – ⑻ (6A) 3.50€ – Reservation fee 20€
Rental rates : (from mid April to end Sept.) – 40 ⛺ – 17 ⌂ – 2 gîtes.
Per night from 48 to 75 € – Per week from 265 to 595 € – Reservation fee 20€
⛽ sani-station – 17 ▣ 17€

Surroundings : ♎♎
Leisure activities : ♟ ✕ ⌂ jacuzzi ⛵ ⟋
Facilities : ᵴ ⊶ ▥ ♨ ♨ ⇝ ♈ launderette ♨

GPS Longitude : 6.08255
Latitude : 44.58022

GIENS

83400 – Michelin map **340** L7
▶ Paris 869 – Marseille 93 – Toulon 29 – La Seyne-sur-Mer 37

La Presqu'île de Giens ≗≗

📞 0494582286, *www.camping-giens.com* – ⊮
Address : 153 rte de la Madrague
Opening times : from end March to beginning Oct.
7 ha (460 pitches) terraced, flat, grassy, stony
Tariff : (2012 price) 31.50€ ⚬⚬ ⇔ 回 ⚡ (16A) – Extra per person 8€
Rental rates : (2012 price) (from end March to beginning Oct.) – 86 ⟨⟩ – 30 ⌂.
Per night from 259 to 966 € – Per week from 378 to 1,120 € – Reservation fee 15€
⊞ sani-station

Surroundings : ⊏ ꝺꝺ
Leisure activities : �ం ✗ ⊠ ☺ daytime ⚡⚡ ⚡⚡
Facilities : ⊶ 回 ⊞ ⊗ ⚋ launderette ⚐ ⚐
Nearby : bowling, disco

GPS Longitude : 6.14332
Latitude : 43.04084

La Tour Fondue

📞 0494582286, *www.camping-latourfondue.com* – ⊮
Address : av. des Arbanais
Opening times : from end March to mid Nov.
2 ha (140 pitches) flat, grassy
Tariff : (2012 price) 29.20€ ⚬⚬ ⇔ 回 ⚡ (10A) – Extra per person 8€
Rental rates : (2012 price) (from end March to mid Nov.) – 21 ⟨⟩. Per week from 371 to 777 €
Reservation fee 15€
⊞ sani-station

Surroundings : ⊏ ꝺ
Leisure activities : ⊠
Facilities : ⊶ ⚋ launderette
Nearby : ⚐ �ం ✗ ⚓ scuba diving

GPS Longitude : 6.15569
Latitude : 43.02971

*There are several different types of sani-station
('borne' in French) – sanitation points providing
fresh water and disposal points for grey water.
See page 12 for further details.*

LA GRAVE

05320 – Michelin map **334** F2 – pop. 493 – alt. 1,526 – Winter sports : 1,450/3,250 m ⚑2 ⚑2 ⚑
▶ Paris 642 – Briançon 38 – Gap 126 – Grenoble 80

La Meije

📞 0608543084, *www.camping-delameije.com*
Address : head east towards Briançon along the D 1091; beside the Romanche river
Opening times : from mid May to mid Sept.
2.5 ha (50 pitches) terrace, relatively flat, flat, grassy
Tariff : 15€ ⚬⚬ ⇔ 回 ⚡ (6A) – Extra per person 3€
Superb panoramic view of the La Grave glacier.

Surroundings : ⚐ ⚑ ꝺꝺ
Leisure activities : ✗ ⚋ ⚐ ⚑
Facilities : ⚐ ⊶ ⚐ ⚐ ⚋ 回
Nearby : ⚡⚡ rafting and canyoning

GPS Longitude : 6.30911
Latitude : 45.04526

Le Gravelotte

℘ 0476799314, *www.camping-le-gravelotte.com*

Address : 1.2km west along the D 1091, follow the signs for Grenoble and take road to the left; beside the Meije river

Opening times : from mid June to end Sept.

4 ha (75 pitches) flat, grassy

Tariff : 16.10€ ✶✶ ⇔ 🗉 🗵 (10A) – Extra per person 3.70€

Attractive location at the foot of the mountains and beside the Romanche river.

Surroundings : ≤ ♀ Leisure activities : ❢ ⤏ ⤸ Facilities : ⅙ ⍽ ☗ 🖾	**GPS** Longitude : 6.29697 Latitude : 45.04328

GRAVESON

13690 – Michelin map **340** D2 – pop. 3,875 – alt. 14
▶ Paris 696 – Arles 25 – Avignon 14 – Cavaillon 30

Les Micocouliers

℘ 0490958149, *http://www.lesmicocouliers.fr*

Address : 445 rte de Cassoulen (1.2km southeast along the D 28, follow the signs for Châteaurenard and turn right onto D 5, follow the signs for Maillane)

Opening times : from mid March to mid Oct.

3.5 ha (118 pitches) flat, grassy

Tariff : (2012 price) ✶ 7.30€ ⇔ 3€ 🗉 7.40€ – 🗵 (8A) 5.20€ – Reservation fee 10€

Rental rates : (2012 price) (from mid March to mid Oct.) ⅌ – 5 🖿. Per week from 380 to 710 € – Reservation fee 17€

🕮 sani-station 6€

Surroundings : ⌑ ♀ Leisure activities : ⤏ ⤸ Facilities : ⅙ ⍽ 🆒 ☗ 🖾	**GPS** Longitude : 4.78111 Latitude : 43.84389

Some information or pricing may have changed since the guide went to press. We recommend you check the price list online in advance or at the entrance to the campsite and enquire about possible restrictions.

GRÉOUX-LES-BAINS

04800 – Michelin map **334** D10 – pop. 2,510 – alt. 386 – ✢ (beg Mar-end Dec)
▶ Paris 783 – Aix-en-Provence 55 – Brignoles 52 – Digne-les-Bains 69

Yelloh! Village Verdon Parc ♣⅃

℘ 0492780808, *www.campingverdonparc.fr* ⅌

Address : Domaine de la Paludette (600m south along the D 8, follow the signs for St-Pierre and take the turning to the left after the bridge; beside the Verdon river)

Opening times : from beginning April to end Oct.

8 ha (280 pitches) terraced, flat, grassy, stony, gravelled

Tariff : 35€ ✶✶ ⇔ 🗉 🗵 (16A) – Extra per person 7€

Rental rates : (from beginning April to end Oct.) ⅙ (2 mobile homes) ⅌ – 150 🖿. Per night from 39 to 169 € – Per week from 280 to 1,190 €

🕮 sani-station – 100 🗉 18€

Surroundings : ⟰ ⌑ ♀♀ Leisure activities : ❢ ✗ 🎬 🖻 daytime ⅋ ⤏ ⅍ ⤸ multi-sports ground Facilities : ⅙ ⍽ ☗ ☗ launderette ⤻ refrigerators	**GPS** Longitude : 5.884 Latitude : 43.75205

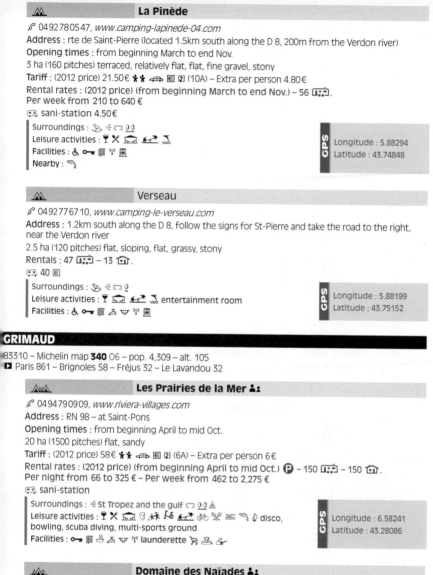

La Pinède

📞 0492780547, *www.camping-lapinede-04.com*

Address : rte de Saint-Pierre (located 1.5km south along the D 8, 200m from the Verdon river)
Opening times : from beginning March to end Nov.
3 ha (160 pitches) terraced, relatively flat, flat, fine gravel, stony
Tariff : (2012 price) 21.50€ ✝✝ ⇔ 🗐 🚻 (10A) – Extra per person 4.80€
Rental rates : (2012 price) (from beginning March to end Nov.) – 56 ⌷.
Per week from 210 to 640 €
sani-station 4.50€

Surroundings :
Leisure activities :
Facilities :
Nearby :

GPS
Longitude : 5.88294
Latitude : 43.74848

Verseau

📞 0492776710, *www.camping-le-verseau.com*

Address : 1.2km south along the D 8, follow the signs for St-Pierre and take the road to the right, near the Verdon river
2.5 ha (120 pitches) flat, sloping, flat, grassy, stony
Rentals : 47 ⌷ – 13 ⌂.
40 🗐

Surroundings :
Leisure activities : entertainment room
Facilities :

GPS
Longitude : 5.88199
Latitude : 43.75152

GRIMAUD

83310 – Michelin map **340** O6 – pop. 4,309 – alt. 105
Paris 861 – Brignoles 58 – Fréjus 32 – Le Lavandou 32

Les Prairies de la Mer ♣♣

📞 0494790909, *www.riviera-villages.com*

Address : RN 98 – at Saint-Pons
Opening times : from beginning April to mid Oct.
20 ha (1500 pitches) flat, sandy
Tariff : (2012 price) 58€ ✝✝ ⇔ 🗐 🚻 (6A) – Extra per person 6€
Rental rates : (2012 price) (from beginning April to mid Oct.) 🅿 – 150 ⌷ – 150 ⌂.
Per night from 66 to 325 € – Per week from 462 to 2,275 €
sani-station

Surroundings : St Tropez and the gulf
Leisure activities : disco, bowling, scuba diving, multi-sports ground
Facilities : launderette

GPS
Longitude : 6.58241
Latitude : 43.28086

Domaine des Naïades ♣♣

📞 0494556780, *www.lesnaiades.com* – limited spaces for one-night stay

Address : at Saint-Pons-les-Mûres
Opening times : from end March to mid Oct.
27 ha/14 ha for camping (492 pitches) terraced, sandy, grassy
Tariff : 58€ ✝✝ ⇔ 🗐 🚻 (10A) – Extra per person 8€
Rental rates : (from end March to mid Oct.) – 224 ⌷. Per night from 49 to 252 €
Per week from 343 to 1,764 €
sani-station 2.50€

Surroundings :
Leisure activities :
Facilities : launderette

GPS
Longitude : 6.57937
Latitude : 43.28517

GUILLESTRE

05600 – Michelin map **334** H5 – pop. 2,308 – alt. 1,000 – Leisure centre
▶ Paris 715 – Barcelonnette 51 – Briançon 36 – Digne-les-Bains 114

Parc Le Villard

℘ 04 92 45 06 54, *www.camping-levillard.com*
Address : rte des campings, at Le Villard (situated 2km west along the D 902a, follow the signs for Gap; beside the Chagne river)
3.2 ha (120 pitches) relatively flat, flat, grassy, stony
Rentals : – 17 – 5 – 2 tent bungalows.
The campsite straddles a small road.

Surroundings : ⩽ ♀
Leisure activities : ✗ 🏠 ⚡ ⚭ ♏ ♒ ♒
Facilities : ♿ ⌐ ♨ 🚿 launderette ☕

GPS Longitude : 6.62687
Latitude : 44.65895

St-James-les-Pins

℘ 04 92 45 08 24, *www.lesaintjames.com*
Address : rte des Campings (head 1.5km west following signs for Risoul and take turning to the right
Opening times : from beginning Jan. to beginning Nov.
2.5 ha (100 pitches) relatively flat, flat, grassy, stony
Tariff : 19.10€ ★★ ⬅ 🅔 🅗 (10A) – Extra per person 3.50€
Rental rates : (permanent) – 10 – 13 – 10 🛏. Per night from 50 to 80 €
Per week from 285 to 650 €
🚮 sani-station 4.60€
The Chagne river flows through the site.

Surroundings : ❄ ♀♀
Leisure activities : 🏠 ⚡ ♒ multi-sports ground
Facilities : ♿ ⌐ ♒ 🚿 🚿 launderette
Nearby : ⚭ ♒

GPS Longitude : 6.63293
Latitude : 44.65685

La Rochette

℘ 04 92 45 02 15, *www.campingguillestre.com*
Address : rte des Campings (head 1km west following signs for Risoul and take turning to the right)
Opening times : from mid May to end Sept.
4 ha (190 pitches) relatively flat, flat, grassy, stony
Tariff : 19€ ★★ ⬅ 🅔 🅗 (10A) – Extra per person 4€ – Reservation fee 9€
Rental rates : (from end May to end Sept.) – 3 tents. Per night from 30 to 60 €
Per week from 200 to 450 € – Reservation fee 9€
🚮 sani-station

Surroundings : ⩽ ♀♀
Leisure activities : 🏠 ⚡ ♒
Facilities : ♿ ⌐ ♒ 🚿 launderette 🚗
Nearby : ✗ ☕ ⚭ ♒

GPS Longitude : 6.63845
Latitude : 44.65895

Michelin classification:
Extremely comfortable, equipped to a very high standard
Very comfortable, equipped to a high standard
Comfortable and well equipped
Reasonably comfortable
Satisfactory

HYÈRES

3400 – Michelin map **340** L7 – pop. 54,686 – alt. 40
Paris 851 – Aix-en-Provence 102 – Cannes 123 – Draguignan 78

Les Palmiers ▲±
(rental of mobile homes only)

℘ 0494663966, *www.camping-les-palmiers.fr*
Address : r. du Ceinturon, L'Ayguade
Opening times : from mid March to mid Oct.
5.5 ha flat, grassy, stony
Rental rates : – 275 . Per night from 45 to 110 € – Per week from 315 to 1,515 €
Reservation fee 30€

Surroundings :
Leisure activities : ♈ ✗ evening hammam
Facilities : launderette

Longitude : 6.16725
Latitude : 43.10344

Le Ceinturon 3

℘ 0494663265, *www.ceinturon3.fr* –
Address : 2 r. des Saraniers (5km southeast, 100m from the sea; at Ayguade-Ceinturon)
Opening times : from mid March to end Sept.
2.5 ha (200 pitches) flat, grassy, sandy
Tariff : 23.95€ ★★ (10A) – Extra per person 6€
Rental rates : (from mid March to end Sept.) – 1 – 40 . Per night from 46 to 115 €
Per week from 320 to 800 € – Reservation fee 15.25€

Surroundings :
Leisure activities : ♈ ✗
Facilities : launderette
Nearby :

Longitude : 6.16962
Latitude : 43.10109

These symbols are used for a campsite that is exceptional in its category:
Particularly pleasant setting, quality and range of services available
Tranquil, isolated site – quiet site, particularly at night
Exceptional view – interesting or panoramic view

L'ISLE-SUR-LA-SORGUE

4800 – Michelin map **332** D10 – pop. 18,936 – alt. 57
Paris 693 – Apt 34 – Avignon 23 – Carpentras 18

Club Airotel La Sorguette

℘ 0490380571, *www.camping-sorguette.com*
Address : 871 rte d'Apt (located 1.5km southeast along the N 100; near the Sorgue)
Opening times : from mid March to mid Oct.
2.5 ha (164 pitches) flat, grassy, stony
Tariff : 27.50€ ★★ (10A) – Extra per person 7.90€ – Reservation fee 20€
Rental rates : (from mid March to mid Oct.) (1 mobile home) – 30 – 3 yurts – 1 teepee –
3 tents. Per night from 36 to 112 € – Per week from 217 to 784 € – Reservation fee 20€
sani-station 5€ – 11€

Surroundings :
Leisure activities : ✗
Facilities : launderette refrigerated food storage

Longitude : 5.07192
Latitude : 43.9146

ISOLA

06420 – Michelin map **341** D2 – pop. 748 – alt. 873
▶ Paris 897 – Marseille 246 – Nice 76 – Cuneo 79

▲ Le Lac des Neiges

℘ 04 93 02 18 16, www.princiland.fr – alt. 875
Address : rte de St-Etienne-de-Tinée (located 1km north of the village along the D 2205)
3 ha (98 pitches) flat, grassy, stony
Rentals : 🦞 – 1 ⬛ – 4 🛏 – 2 studios – 2 gîtes.

Surroundings : 🌳 ♀
Leisure activities : 🍽 ✕ 🖼 🏊 🚴 ⛰ 🎣 pedalos 🏌
Facilities : 🚿 🛒 🧺 🚻 🧹 🍴 🚲
Nearby : 🎿

Longitude : 7.03912
Latitude : 44.18898

LARCHE

04530 – Michelin map **334** J6 – pop. 74 – alt. 1,691
▶ Paris 760 – Barcelonnette 28 – Briançon 81 – Cuneo 70

▲ **Domaine des Marmottes**

℘ 04 92 84 33 64, www.camping-marmottes.fr
Address :at Malboisset (800m southeast down a turning to the right; beside the Ubayette river)
Opening times : from mid May to end Sept.
2 ha (52 pitches) open site, flat, grassy
Tariff : (2012 price) 18.50€ ✝✝ 🚐 ▣ ⚡ (10A) – Extra per person 7.50€
Rental rates : (2012 price) (permanent) – 2 huts. Per night 40€ – Per week from 250 to 350 €
🚏 sani-station 4€

Surroundings : 🦌 🌲 🌳 ♀♀
Leisure activities : ✕
Facilities : 🚿 🛒 🧺 launderette
Nearby : 🍽

Longitude : 6.85257
Latitude : 44.44615

The prices listed were supplied by the campsite owners in 2012
(if prices were not available, those from the previous year are given).
The fees should be regarded as basic charges and may fluctuate
with inflation.

LE LAVANDOU

83980 – Michelin map **340** N7 – pop. 5,747 – alt. 1 – Leisure centre
▶ Paris 873 – Cannes 102 – Draguignan 75 – Fréjus 61

▲ **Beau Séjour**

℘ 04 94 71 25 30, regine.guiol@sfr.fr
Address : at la Grande Bastide (located 1.5km to the southwest)
Opening times : from mid April to end Sept.
1.5 ha (135 pitches) flat, gravelled
Tariff : (2012 price) ✝ 6€ 🚐 ▣ 5€ – ⚡ (10A) 6€
Attractive pitches, well marked-out and shaded.

Surroundings : 🌳 ♀♀
Leisure activities : 🍽 ✕
Facilities : 🚿 🛒 🧺 🚲

Longitude : 6.35165
Latitude : 43.13497

LA LONDE-LES-MAURES

83250 – Michelin map **340** M7 – pop. 9,910 – alt. 24
▶ Paris 861 – Bormes-les-Mimosas 11 – Cuers 31 – Hyères 10

  Les Moulières

𝒞 0494015321, *www.campinglesmoulieres.com* – ৠ
Address : 15 chemin de la Garenne, at Le Puits de Magne (situated 2.5km southeast; follow the signs for Port-de-Miramar and take turning to the right)
Opening times : from beginning June to mid Sept.
3 ha (250 pitches) flat, grassy
Tariff : (2012 price) 36.50€ ✛ ✛ ⇔ ▣ ⑭ (6A) – Extra per person 8€

Surroundings : ⸙ ⚲
Leisure activities : ☂ ✗ ⟿ ⚒
Facilities : ⅋ ⛯ ♨ ⁙ ▣ ⤳

GPS Longitude : 6.23526
Latitude : 43.12236

LOURMARIN

84160 – Michelin map **332** F11 – pop. 1,000 – alt. 224
▶ Paris 732 – Aix-en-Provence 37 – Apt 19 – Cavaillon 73

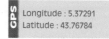 **Les Hautes Prairies**

𝒞 0490680289, *www.campinghautesprairies.com*
Address : rte de Vaugines (700m east along the D 56)
Opening times : from beginning April to end Oct.
3.6 ha (158 pitches) relatively flat, flat, grassy, stony
Tariff : (2012 price) ✛ 4.10€ ⇔ 2.80€ ▣ 4.50€ – ⑭ (10A) 4.10€
Rental rates : (2012 price) (permanent) – 5 ⟦⚏⟧ – 16 ⬡. Per night from 65 €
Per week from 371 to 630 €

Surroundings : ⌁ ⚲
Leisure activities : ☂ ✗ ⟿ ⤲
Facilities : ⅋ ⛯ ⤳ ♨ ⤳ ⁙ ▣ ⤲

GPS Longitude : 5.37291
Latitude : 43.76784

> *The classification (1 to 5 tents, **black** or **red**) that we award to selected sites in this guide is our own system. It should not be confused with the classification (1 to 5 stars) of official organisations.*

MALEMORT-DU-COMTAT

84570 – Michelin map **332** D9 – pop. 1,461 – alt. 208
▶ Paris 688 – Avignon 33 – Carpentras 11 – Malaucène 22

  Font Neuve

𝒞 0490699000, *www.campingfontneuve.com*
Address : Font-Neuve quartier (1.6km southeast along the D 5, follow the signs for Méthanis and take road to the left)
Opening times : permanent
1.5 ha (54 pitches) terraced, relatively flat, flat, grassy, stony
Tariff : ✛ 4.70€ ⇔ 2€ ▣ 5.50€ – ⑭ (10A) 5.10€ – Reservation fee 10€
Rental rates : (permanent) – 5 ⬡. Per night from 63 to 70 € – Per week from 405 to 450 €
Reservation fee 10€

Surroundings : ⸙ ⪕ ⌁ ⚲⚲
Leisure activities : ✗ ⟿ ⚒ ⤲
Facilities : ⅋ ⛯ ⤳ ♨ ⤳ ⁙ ▣ ⤳

GPS Longitude : 5.17098
Latitude : 44.0142

MALLEMORT

13370 – Michelin map **340** G3 – pop. 5,925 – alt. 120
▶ Paris 716 – Aix-en-Provence 34 – Apt 38 – Cavaillon 20

⚠ Durance Luberon

☎ 04 90 59 13 36, *www.campingduranceluberon.com* – for caravans, access via town centre not advised, acces via N 7 and D 561, signs for Charleval
Address : at the Domaine du Vergon (2.8km southeast along the D 23, 200m from the canal, towards the power station – from the A 7 take exits 26 and 7)
Opening times : from beginning April to end Sept.
4 ha (110 pitches) flat, grassy
Tariff : (2012 price) 25.60 € ♥ ♥ ⇔ 🗐 (4) (10A) – Extra per person 5.60 € – Reservation fee 15 €
Rental rates : (2012 price) (from beginning April to end Sept.) – 8 ⬛.
Per night from 70 to 99 € – Per week from 490 to 690 € – Reservation fee 15 €
⬛ sani-station 5 € – ⬛ 13.50 €

Surroundings : 🏞 🗔 ⛰
Leisure activities : ✗ ⛱ 🏊
Facilities : ⅃ ⚬ 🧺 ⬛ 🗐 🚿 ⬛ ⬛ ⬛ 🗐 ⬛
Nearby : 🐎

GPS Longitude : 5.20492 Latitude : 43.72091

Some campsites benefit from proximity to a municipal leisure centre.

MANDELIEU-LA-NAPOULE

06210 – Michelin map **341** C6 – pop. 21,764 – alt. 4
▶ Paris 890 – Brignoles 86 – Cannes 9 – Draguignan 53

⚠ Les Cigales

☎ 04 93 49 23 53, *www.lescigales.com*
Address : 505 av. de la Mer (at Mandelieu)
Opening times : from mid Dec. to mid Nov.
2 ha (115 pitches) flat, grassy, gravelled
Tariff : 45 € ♥ ♥ ⇔ 🗐 (4) (6A) – Extra per person 8 € – Reservation fee 25 €
Rental rates : (from beginning March to beginning Nov.) – 34 ⬛ – 8 studios – 1 apartment.
Per night from 48 to 170 € – Per week from 285 to 980 € – Reservation fee 25 €
⬛ sani-station – 15 🗐 45 €
A green 'oasis' in the town; beside the Siagne river.

Surroundings : 🏞 🗔 ⛰
Leisure activities : ⛱ 🏊
Facilities : ⅃ ⚬ ⬛ ⬛ ⬛ ⬛ 🗐 launderette
Nearby : 🍺 🍷 ✗ 🚿 🚲 ⬛ ⚓

GPS Longitude : 6.9424 Latitude : 43.53883

⚠ Les Pruniers

☎ 04 92 97 00 44, *www.bungalow-camping.com* – limited spaces for one-night stay
Address : 118 r. de la Pinéa (via the av. de la Mer)
Opening times : from beginning April to end Oct.
0.8 ha (64 pitches) flat, grassy, gravelled
Tariff : (2012 price) ♥ 5.20 € ⇔ 4 € 🗐 27 € – (4) (10A) 4 € – Reservation fee 80 €
Rental rates : (2012 price) (from beginning April to end Oct.) – 36 ⬛.
Per night from 40 to 58 € – Per week from 280 to 660 € – Reservation fee 99 €
Beside the Siagne river. Sandy beaches 300m away. Swimming pool.

Surroundings : 🏞 🗔 ⛰
Leisure activities : ⬛ ⛱ 🏊
Facilities : ⚬ ⬛ 🗐 🚿
Nearby : 🍷 ✗ ⬛ ⚓

GPS Longitude : 6.94349 Latitude : 43.53503

MAUBEC

84660 – Michelin map **332** D10 – pop. 1,877 – alt. 120
▶ Paris 706 – Aix-en-Provence 68 – Apt 25 – Avignon 32

Municipal Les Royères du Prieuré

✆ 04 90 76 50 34, www.campingmaubec-luberon.com
Address : 52 chemin de la Combe St-Pierre (south of the town)
Opening times : from beginning April to mid Oct.
1 ha (93 pitches) terraced, flat, grassy, stony
Tariff : (2012 price) 🧍 3.50 € 🚗 2.30 € 🔲 2.30 € – ⚡ (10A) 4.70 € – Reservation fee 10 €
Rental rates : (2012 price) (from beginning April to mid Oct.) 🛖 – 3 🚐 – 1 gîte.
Per night from 140 to 150 € – Per week from 375 to 520 € – Reservation fee 10 €
Pitches are laid out on lovely terraces with plenty of shade.

Surroundings : 🌳 ≤ 🌳🌳
Facilities : 🔌 🚰 🛁

GPS Longitude : 5.1326
Latitude : 43.84032

MAUSSANE-LES-ALPILLES

13520 – Michelin map **340** D3 – pop. 2,076 – alt. 32
▶ Paris 712 – Arles 20 – Avignon 30 – Marseille 81

Municipal les Romarins

✆ 04 90 54 33 60, www.maussane.com
Address : av. des Alpilles (take the northern exit along the D 5, follow the signs for St-Rémy)
3 ha (145 pitches) flat, grassy, stony
Reception is at the Maison du Tourisme (tourist office).

Surroundings : 🏕 🌳🌳
Leisure activities : 🎦 🏓 🍽
Facilities : ♿ 🚰 🛁 🚿 🚰 🍴 launderette
Nearby : 🏊

GPS Longitude : 4.8093
Latitude : 43.72104

We have selected the best campsites in France with our usual care,
listing those with the best facilities in the most pleasant surroundings.

MAZAN

84380 – Michelin map **332** D9 – pop. 5,641 – alt. 100
▶ Paris 684 – Avignon 35 – Carpentras 9 – Cavaillon 30

Le Ventoux

✆ 04 90 69 70 94, www.camping-le-ventoux.com
Address : 1348 chemin de la Combe (3km north along the D 70, follow the signs for Caromb then
take the road to the left, follow the signs for Carpentras, recommended route via D 974)
Opening times : from mid March to end Oct.
0.7 ha (49 pitches) flat, grassy, stony
Tariff : 23.50 € 🧍🧍 🚗 🔲 ⚡ (12A) – Extra per person 5.50 € – Reservation fee 10 €
Rental rates : (from mid March to end Oct.) – 16 🚐. Per night from 70 to 95 €
Per week from 420 to 795 € – Reservation fee 10 €

Surroundings : 🌳 ≤ Mont Ventoux 🌳🌳
Leisure activities : 🍷 🍽 🏓 🏊
Facilities : ♿ 🔌 🚿 🛁 🍴 launderette 🔧

GPS Longitude : 5.11378
Latitude : 44.0805

MENTON

06500 – Michelin map **341** F5 – pop. 28,848
▶ Paris 966 – Marseille 218 – Nice 32 – Antibes 55

Municipal St-Michel

℘ 04 93 35 81 23, *www.menton.fr* – acces difficult for caravans and campervans
Address : chemin du Parc de St-Michel (follow the signs for Les Ciappes de Castellar, Plateau St-Michel)
2 ha (131 pitches) terraced, flat, grassy, fine gravel
Shady pitches under centuries-old olive trees, but the sanitary facilities are pretty dilapidated

Surroundings : ᴏᴏ
Leisure activities : ♀ ✗
Facilities : ◦⌐ 🅸 ⚖ refrigerated food storage

GPS Longitude : 7.498
Latitude : 43.77906

The pitches of many campsites are marked out with low hedges of attractive bushes and shrubs.

MÉOLANS-REVEL

04340 – Michelin map **334** H6 – pop. 333 – alt. 1,080
▶ Paris 787 – Marseille 216 – Digne-les-Bains 74 – Gap 64

Le Rioclar

℘ 04 92 81 10 32, *www.rioclar.com* – alt. 1,073
Address : D 900 (located 1.5km east, follow the signs for Barcelonnette, near the Ubaye river and a small lake)
Opening times : from mid May to beginning Sept.
8 ha (200 pitches) terraced, flat, grassy, stony
Tariff : (2012 price) 26.30€ ♣♣ ⬅ 🅴 ⑨ (10A) – Extra per person 5.80€ – Reservation fee 18€
Rental rates : (2012 price) (from mid May to beginning Sept.) ⌘ – 25 🛏 – 3 🏠.
Per night from 57 to 80 € – Per week from 390 to 690 € – Reservation fee 18€
A pleasant location and setting.

Surroundings : ⬚ ⌐ ᴏᴏ
Leisure activities : ✗ 🎱 ⑨ ᚱ ✂ ᴴ ⌇ rafting and canyoning ⚡ multi-sports ground
Facilities : ⅋ ᴏ⌐ ⌥ ⏲ ⚖ ⚖
Nearby : ≋ (lake)

GPS Longitude : 6.53172
Latitude : 44.39928

Domaine Loisirs de l'Ubaye

℘ 04 92 81 01 96, *www.loisirsubaye.com* – alt. 1,073
Address : D 900 (3km east along the D 900, follow the signs for Barcelonnette; beside the Ubaye river)
Opening times : permanent
9.5 ha (267 pitches) terraced, flat, grassy, stony
Tariff : 27.50€ ♣♣ ⬅ 🅴 ⑨ (6A) – Extra per person 6€ – Reservation fee 15€
Rental rates : (permanent) – 19 🛏 – 19 🏠. Per night from 60 to 90 €
Per week from 310 to 720 € – Reservation fee 15€
🚉 sani-station

Surroundings : ⌐ ᴏᴏ
Leisure activities : ✗ 🎱 ⑨ daytime ⚓ ᚱ ✂ ⌇
Facilities : ⅋ ᴏ⌐ ⦀ ⌥ ⌇ ⚐ ⏲ launderette ⚖ ⚖
Nearby : rafting and canyoning

GPS Longitude : 6.54638
Latitude : 44.39645

MÉZEL

04270 – Michelin map **334** F8 – pop. 680 – alt. 585

▸ Paris 745 – Barrême 22 – Castellane 47 – Digne-les-Bains 15

La Célestine

📞 04 92 35 52 54, *www.camping-lacelestine.fr*

Address : rte de Manosque (3km south along the D 907; beside the Asse river)

Opening times : from beginning May to end Sept.

2.4 ha (100 pitches) flat, grassy

Tariff : 23€ ♥♥ ⇔ 🔲 🔌 (10A) – Extra per person 5€

Rental rates : (from beginning May to end Sept.) – 8 🚐. Per night from 75 to 85 €
Per week from 490 to 590 €

🚐 4 🔲 23€

Surroundings : 🔅🔅
Leisure activities : 🍴 🏠 🏊 🚲 🏖 (pool), quad biking
Facilities : 🚿 ⚡ ⛱

GPS Longitude : 6.19183
Latitude : 43.97002

MONTMEYAN

83670 – Michelin map **340** L4 – pop. 543 – alt. 480

▸ Paris 832 – Marseille 88 – Toulon 87 – Draguignan 46

Château de l'Éouvière

📞 04 94 80 75 54, *www.leouviere.com*

Address : rte de Taverne (500m south along the D 13)

Opening times : from beginning May to mid Sept.

30 ha/5 ha for camping (81 pitches) terraced, stony, grassy

Tariff : (2012 price) 31€ ♥♥ ⇔ 🔲 🔌 (10A) – Extra per person 8€

Rental rates : (2012 price) (from beginning May to mid Sept.) – 10 🚐 – 2 apartments.
Per night from 80 to 110 € – Per week from 450 to 750 €

Surroundings : 🏔 🔅🔅
Leisure activities : 🏠 🏊
Facilities : 🚿 ⚡ 🏪 ⛱ 🔲 ⛲

GPS Longitude : 6.06035
Latitude : 43.63819

The guide is updated each year, so consult the latest edition for the most up-to-date information and pricing.

MONTPEZAT

04500 – Michelin map **334** E10

▸ Paris 806 – Digne-les-Bains 54 – Gréoux-les-Bains 23 – Manosque 37

Village Center Côteau de la Marine

📞 08 25 00 20 30, *www.campings.village-center.fr*

Address : at Vauvert (situated 2km southeast)

Opening times : from beginning April to end Sept.

12 ha (283 pitches) terraced, stony, gravelled

Tariff : (2012 price) 25€ ♥♥ ⇔ 🔲 🔌 (10A) – Extra per person 6€ – Reservation fee 30€

Rental rates : (2012 price) (from beginning April to end Sept.) – 177 🚐 – 36 tents.
Per night from 30 to 95 € – Per week from 415 to 932 € – Reservation fee 30€

Surroundings : 🏔 ⛰ 🗒 🌿
Leisure activities : 🍴 ✖ 🎣 daytime 🏃 🏊 ⛷ 🏊 pedalos, electric boats 🚣
Facilities : ⚡ 🔲 ⛱ 🔲 🏊 ⛲

GPS Longitude : 6.09818
Latitude : 43.74765

MOUSTIERS-STE-MARIE

04360 – Michelin map **334** F9 – pop. 718 – alt. 631
▶ Paris 783 – Aix-en-Provence 90 – Castellane 45 – Digne-les-Bains 47

Le Vieux Colombier

℘ 04 92 74 61 89, *www.lvcm.fr*
Address : St Michel quartier (800m to the south)
Opening times : from mid April to end Sept.
2.7 ha (70 pitches) terraced, relatively flat, stony, grassy
Tariff : 22€ ♣♣ ⇌ 🗉 (6A) – Extra per person 6€ – Reservation fee 9€
Rental rates : (from mid April to mid Sept.) – 13 . Per night from 47 to 56 €
Per week from 260 to 610 € – Reservation fee 9€
sani-station 7€

Surroundings : ≤ ⊡ ⚲
Leisure activities : 🎦
Facilities : & ⊶ ⚄ ♈ 🖼 ⤵
Nearby : ✖

Longitude : 6.22166
Latitude : 43.83956

St-Jean

℘ 04 92 74 66 85, *www.camping-st-jean.fr*
Address : Saint Jean quartier (located 1km southwest along the D 952, follow the signs for Riez; beside the Maïre river)
Opening times : from beginning April to mid Oct.
1.6 ha (125 pitches) relatively flat, flat, grassy
Tariff : (2012 price) 22.20€ ♣♣ ⇌ 🗉 (10A) – Extra per person 5.90€ – Reservation fee 10€
Rental rates : (2012 price) (from beginning April to mid Oct.) – 14 .
Per night from 52 to 60 € – Per week from 290 to 625 € – Reservation fee 10€

Surroundings : 🌿 ≤ ⚲⚲
Leisure activities : 🏖 ♈
Facilities : & ⊶ ⚄ ⇝ ♈ 🖼
Nearby : 🏊

Longitude : 6.21496
Latitude : 43.84366

Manaysse

℘ 04 92 74 66 71, *www.camping-manaysse.com*
Address : Manaysse quartier (900m southwest along the D 952, follow the signs for Riez)
Opening times : from beginning April to end Oct.
1.6 ha (97 pitches) terraced, sloping, flat, grassy, gravelled
Tariff : (2012 price) ♣ 3.70€ ⇌ 🗉 3.50€ – (10A) 3.50€
Rental rates : (from end April to beginning Nov.) – 1 gîte. Per week from 480 to 580 €
sani-station 10.90€ – 70 🗉 10.90€

Surroundings : ⚲⚲
Leisure activities : 🎦 ♈
Facilities : & ⊶ ⤳ ⚑ ♈ 🖼

Longitude : 6.21494
Latitude : 43.84452

Key to rentals symbols:

12		*Number of mobile homes*
20		*Number of chalets*
6		*Number of rooms to rent*
Per night 30–50€		*Minimum/maximum rate per night*
Per week 300–1,000€		*Minimum/maximum rate per week*

MURS

84220 – Michelin map **332** E10 – pop. 428 – alt. 510
▶ Paris 704 – Apt 17 – Avignon 48 – Carpentras 26

Municipal des Chalottes

℘ 0490726084, *www.communedemurs-vaucluse.fr*
Address : take the southern exit along the D 4, follow the signs for Apt then continue 1.8km to the right, after the VVF holiday village
Opening times : from mid April to mid Sept.
4 ha (50 pitches) very uneven, relatively flat to hilly, stony
Tariff : (2012 price) 12.44€ ★★ ⇔ 圓 (10A) – Extra per person 3€

A pleasant site in a wooded setting.

Surroundings : ⏃ ≤ ⁰
Leisure activities : ⚓
Facilities : ⅙ ☞ (Jul–Aug) ⌇

Longitude : 5.22749
Latitude : 43.93864

There are several different types of sani-station
('borne' in French) – sanitation points providing
fresh water and disposal points for grey water.
See page 12 for further details.

LE MUY

83490 – Michelin map **340** O5 – pop. 8,983 – alt. 27
▶ Paris 853 – Les Arcs 9 – Draguignan 14 – Fréjus 17

Les Cigales ♣♣

℘ 0494451208, *www.camping-les-cigales-sud.fr*
Address : 4 chemin de Jas de la Paro (3km southwest, access via the junction with the A 8 and take the road to the right before the toll road)
22 ha (585 pitches) very uneven, terraced, grassy, stony, rocks
Rentals : 187 ⌂ – 41 ⌂.
⌇ sani-station – 10 圓
A pleasant wooded site.

Surroundings : ⛺ ⁰⁰
Leisure activities : ⚑ ✗ ⊙ (Jul–Aug) ⚲ jacuzzi ⚓ ⚽ ⚒ ⚘ forest trail, multi-sports ground
Facilities : ⅙ ☞ ⛺ ⚑ launderette ⚖ ⚒ refrigerators

Longitude : 6.54355
Latitude : 43.46225

RCN Le Domaine de la Noguière

℘ 0494451378, *www.rcn.nl*
Address : 1617 rte de Fréjus
Opening times : from end March to end Oct.
11 ha (350 pitches) very uneven, flat, grassy
Tariff : 46.50€ ★★ ⇔ 圓 (6A) – Extra per person 5.25€ – Reservation fee 19.50€
Rental rates : (from end March to end Oct.) – 37 ⌂. Per night from 34 to 168 €
Per week from 238 to 1,176 € – Reservation fee 19.50€

Surroundings : ⛺
Leisure activities : ⚑ ✗ ⊙ daytime ⚓ ▦ ⚒ ⚘ ⚘ multi-sports ground
Facilities : ☞ ⚃ ⛺ ⚑ launderette ⚖
Nearby : ⚒

Longitude : 6.59222
Latitude : 43.46828

NANS-LES-PINS

83860 – Michelin map **340** J5 – pop. 4,123 – alt. 380
▶ Paris 794 – Aix-en-Provence 44 – Brignoles 26 – Marseille 42

Domaine de La Sainte Baume ▲▲

0494789268, www.saintebaume.com
Address : Delvieux Sud quartier (900m north along the D 80 and take a right turn, from the A 8: take exit St-Maximin-la-Ste-Baume)
Opening times : from beginning April to end Sept.
8 ha (250 pitches) relatively flat, flat, stony, gravelled
Tariff : (2012 price) 35€ ★★ ⟵ 📺 (10A) – Extra per person 9€
Rental rates : (2012 price) (from beginning April to end Sept.) – 150 🚐.
Per night from 30 to 74 € – Per week from 175 to 1,200 €

Surroundings : 🌊 ⌂ 🎲
Leisure activities : ✗ 🎮 🎣 🏊 jacuzzi ⛵ 🎾 🏓 🏖 disco
Facilities : ⚙ ⟲ 🔌 🚿 ⛱ ⚑ launderette 🧺 🚲
Nearby : 🐎

GPS
Longitude : 5.78808
Latitude : 43.37664

NÉVACHE

05100 – Michelin map **334** H2 – pop. 339 – alt. 1,640 – Winter sports : 1,400/2,000 m ⛷2 ⛷
▶ Paris 693 – Bardonècchia 18 – Briançon 21

Fontcouverte

0492213821, m.goiran@orange.fr – access difficult for caravans – alt. 1,860 – 🏠
Address : 1 lot. de l'Aiguille Rouge (6.2km northwest along the D 301t, Vallée de la Clarée)
Opening times : from beginning June to mid Sept.
2 ha (100 pitches) terraced, relatively flat, flat, grassy, stony
Tariff : ★ 2.80€ ⟵ 1.60€ 📺 2.90€ ⚡ (6A)
Pleasant location at the end of the valley and beside a fast-flowing river.

Surroundings : 🌊 ≤ 🎲
Leisure activities : 🎣
Facilities : ⚙ ⟲ 🚿 🔌 🧺
Nearby : ✗

GPS
Longitude : 6.69323
Latitude : 45.11898

The guide is updated each year, so consult the latest edition for the most up-to-date information and pricing.

NIOZELLES

04300 – Michelin map **334** D9 – pop. 237 – alt. 450
▶ Paris 745 – Digne-les-Bains 49 – Forcalquier 7 – Gréoux-les-Bains 33

Moulin de Ventre ▲▲

0492786331, www.moulin-de-ventre.fr
Address : 2.5km east along the N 100, follow the signs for La Brillanne
28 ha/3 ha for camping (124 pitches) terraced, relatively flat, flat, grassy, stony
Rentals : 14 🚐 – 5 🏠 – 3 apartments.
🚐 sani-station
Beside the Lauzon river and a small lake.

Surroundings : 🌊 ⌂ 🎲
Leisure activities : 🍽 ✗ 🎮 🎣 daytime (Jul–Aug) 🏊 ⛵ 🏓 🎣
Facilities : ⚙ ⟲ 🚿 ⛱ ⚑ launderette 🚲
Nearby : pedalos

GPS
Longitude : 5.86798
Latitude : 43.9333

ORANGE

84100 – Michelin map **332** B9 – pop. 28 990 – alt. 97
▶ Paris 655 – Alès 84 – Avignon 31 – Carpentras 24

⚠ Le Jonquier

℘ 04 90 34 49 48, www.campinglejonquier.com
Address : r. Alexis Carrel (to the northwest along the N 7, follow the signs for Montélimar and take turning to the left, passing in front of the swimming pool, in the Le Jonquier quartier – from the A 7 take the northern exit, D 17, follow the signs for Caderousse and take the road to the right)
2.5 ha (75 pitches) flat, grassy
Rentals : 4 🛖 – 2 tent bungalows.
🚐 sani-station

Surroundings : 🦌 🗗 ⚲
Leisure activities : 🛁 jacuzzi ❉ ♒ 🏊 (small swimming pool)
Facilities : ♿ ⌂ launderette

GPS Longitude : 4.7949
Latitude : 44.14659

ORGON

13660 – Michelin map **340** F3 – pop. 3,055 – alt. 90
▶ Paris 709 – Marseille 72 – Avignon 29 – Nîmes 98

⚠ **La Vallée Heureuse**

℘ 04 90 44 17 13, www.camping-lavalleeheureuse.com
Address : Lavau quartier (situated 2km to the south, follow the signs for Sénas then take left turning along the D 73D)
Opening times : from beginning April to mid Sept.
8 ha (80 pitches) terraced, flat, grassy, stony
Tariff : (2012 price) 19.50€ ✹✹ 🚐 🗉 🛭 (16A) – Extra per person 5€ – Reservation fee 17€
In a stunning natural setting.

Surroundings : 🦌 < 🗗 ⚲⚲
Leisure activities : 🛁 🚣
Facilities : ♿ ⚡ ⌂ 🍴 launderette, refrigerated food storage
Nearby : ❌ 🏊 🎣

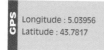
GPS Longitude : 5.03956
Latitude : 43.7817

We value your opinion and welcome your feedback.
Do email us at campingfrance@tp.michelin.com

ORPIERRE

05700 – Michelin map **334** C7 – pop. 326 – alt. 682
▶ Paris 689 – Château-Arnoux 47 – Digne-les-Bains 72 – Gap 55

⚠ **Les Princes d'Orange**

℘ 04 92 66 22 53, www.campingorpierre.com
Address : at Le Flonsaine (300m south of the town, 150m from the Céans river)
Opening times : from beginning April to end Oct.
20 ha/4 ha for camping (120 pitches) very uneven, terraced, flat, grassy, stony
Tariff : (2012 price) 30€ ✹✹ 🚐 🗉 🛭 (10A) – Reservation fee 10€
Rental rates : (2012 price) (from beginning April to end Oct.) – 30 🛖 – 4 🏠.
Per night from 80 to 101 € – Per week from 370 to 710 € – Reservation fee 12€
🚐 sani-station 4€

Surroundings : 🦌 < Orpierre village and mountains ⚲⚲
Leisure activities : 🍸 ❌ 🛁 🚣 🏊 ⚲
Facilities : ♿ ⚡ 🗑 🍴 launderette
Nearby : ♒

GPS Longitude : 5.69652
Latitude : 44.31077

PERNES-LES-FONTAINES

84210 – Michelin map **332** D10 – pop. 10,454 – alt. 75
▶ Paris 685 – Apt 43 – Avignon 23 – Carpentras 6

Municipal de la Coucourelle

⏚ 04 90 66 45 55, *ville-pernes-les-fontaines.fr*
Address : 391 av. René Char (located 1km east along the D 28, follow the signs for St-Didier, at the sports centre)
1 ha (40 pitches) flat, grassy
sani-station
A green site with shrubs and bushes.

Surroundings :
Leisure activities :
Facilities :
Nearby :

Longitude : 5.0677
Latitude : 43.99967

PERTUIS

84120 – Michelin map **332** G11 – pop. 18,706 – alt. 246
▶ Paris 747 – Aix-en-Provence 23 – Apt 36 – Avignon 76

Franceloc les Pinèdes du Luberon ♠♠

⏚ 04 90 79 10 98, *www.campings-franceloc.fr/accueil-camping-les_pinedes_du_luberon*
Address : av. Pierre Augier (situated 2km east along the D 973)
5 ha (180 pitches) terraced, flat, grassy, stony
Rentals : (1 mobile home) – 90 – 6 – 5 tents.
sani-station
Surroundings :
Leisure activities :
Facilities : launderette
Nearby :

Longitude : 5.5253
Latitude : 43.68979

Some information or pricing may have changed since the guide went to press.
We recommend you check the price list online in advance or at the entrance
to the campsite and enquire about possible restrictions.

PEYRUIS

04310 – Michelin map **334** D8 – pop. 2,615 – alt. 402
▶ Paris 727 – Digne-les-Bains 30 – Forcalquier 20 – Manosque 29

Les Cigales
(rental of mobile homes only)

⏚ 04 92 68 16 04, *www.lescigaleshauteprovence.com*
Address : south of the town; near the stadium and a stream
Opening times : permanent
1 ha relatively flat
Rental rates : 10 . Per night from 30 to 99 € – Per week from 210 to 693 €
Reservation fee 30€

Surroundings :
Leisure activities :
Facilities :
Nearby : sports trail

Longitude : 5.93645
Latitude : 44.0228

PONT-DU-FOSSÉ

05260 – Michelin map **334** F4 – pop. 980
▸ Paris 673 – Marseille 204 – Gap 24 – Grenoble 102

Le Diamant

✆ 04 92 55 91 25, *www.campingdiamant.com*
Address : at Pont du Fossé (800m southwest along the D 944, follow the signs for Gap)
Opening times : from beginning May to end Sept.
4 ha (100 pitches) flat, grassy
Tariff : 22.90€ ✶✶ ⇔ 🅴 (½) (20A) – Extra per person 4.60€
Rental rates : (from beginning May to end Sept.) – 15 🚐. Per night from 60 to 75 €
Per week from 200 to 530 €
🚉 sani-station 20.80€ – 10 🅴 20.80€
Situated beside the Drac river.

Surroundings : 🌳🌳
Leisure activities : 🎱 ♨ climbing wall
Facilities : ⚿ ⛗ 🛁 🚿 launderette

Longitude : 6.2197
Latitude : 44.66535

LE PONTET

84130 – Michelin map **332** C10 – pop. 16,891 – alt. 40
▸ Paris 688 – Marseille 100 – Avignon 5 – Aix 83

Le Grand Bois

✆ 04 90 31 37 44, *www.campinglegrandbois.webeasysite.fr*
Address : 1340 chemin du Grand Bois (3km northeast along the D 62, follow the signs for Vedène and take turning to the left, at La Tapy, from A 7: take Avignon-Nord exit)
Opening times : from mid May to mid Sept.
1.5 ha (100 pitches) flat, grassy
Tariff : 25€ ✶✶ ⇔ 🅴 (½) (5A) – Extra per person 6€
🚉 sani-station 4€
A pleasant wooded site.

Surroundings : 🌳🌳
Leisure activities : 🎱 ♨
Facilities : ⚿ ⛗ 🛁 🚿 📷

Longitude : 4.8836
Latitude : 43.97455

A chambre d'hôte is a guesthouse or B & B-style accommodation.

PRUNIÈRES

05230 – Michelin map **334** F5 – pop. 287 – alt. 1,018 – Leisure centre
▸ Paris 681 – Briançon 68 – Gap 23 – Grenoble 119

Le Roustou

✆ 04 92 50 62 63, *www.campingleroustou.com* – ℞
Address : 4km south along the N 94
Opening times : from beginning May to end Sept.
11 ha/6 ha for camping (180 pitches) undulating, terraced, relatively flat, flat, grassy, fine gravel
Tariff : (2012 price) ✶ 7€ ⇔ 🅴 7.40€ – (½) (6A) 3.80€
Rental rates : (2012 price) (from beginning May to end Sept.) – 26 🏠 – 1 apartment.
Per night from 50 to 88 € – Per week from 300 to 769 € – Reservation fee 12€

Surroundings : 🌊 ⇔ 🌳🌳
Leisure activities : 🍴 ✗ 🎱 ♨ ⚔ 🏊
Facilities : ⚿ ⛗ 🛁 📷
Nearby : ⚓

Longitude : 6.34111
Latitude : 44.5225

PUGET-SUR-ARGENS

83480 – Michelin map **340** P5 – pop. 6,722 – alt. 17
▶ Paris 863 – Les Arcs 21 – Cannes 41 – Draguignan 26

La Bastiane ♠♠

 04 94 55 55 94, *www.labastiane.com*
Address : 1056 ch. de Suvière (2.50km to the north)
Opening times : from mid April to end Oct.
4 ha (170 pitches) terraced, flat, grassy, stony
Tariff : 46€ ♣♣ ⊞ (10A) – Extra per person 8€ – Reservation fee 30€
Rental rates : (permanent) – 79 ⌷ – 8 ⌂ – 18 tent bungalows. Per night from 28 to 150 €
Per week from 196 to 1,050 € – Reservation fee 30€

Surroundings : ⌘
Leisure activities : ♈ ✕ ⌂ ⌁ ⌁ ⌁ ✂ ⌁ disco, multi-sports ground
Facilities : ♿ ⊙ ⊞ ☂ launderette
Nearby :

Longitude : 6.67837
Latitude : 43.46975

PUIMICHEL

04700 – Michelin map **334** E9 – pop. 253 – alt. 723
▶ Paris 737 – Avignon 140 – Grenoble 175 – Marseille 112

Les Matherons

04 92 79 60 10, *www.campinglesmatherons.com*
Address : 3km southwest along the D 12, follow the signs for Oraison and take the gravel road to the right
Opening times : from end April to end Sept.
70 ha/4 ha for camping (27 pitches) terraced, relatively flat, flat, grassy, stony
Tariff : (2012 price) ♣ 4.80€ ⊞ 8.80€ – (3A) 2.90€
Rental rates : (2012 price) (permanent) – 2 ⌷. Per night from 39 to 72 €
Per week from 270 to 500 €

A natural, rural setting among trees and the sound of cicadas in the air.

Surroundings : ⌘
Leisure activities : ⌁
Facilities : ⊙ ℗ ⌁ ⌁ ⌁

Longitude : 6.00763
Latitude : 43.96035

PUYLOUBIER

13114 – Michelin map **340** J4 – pop. 1,798 – alt. 380
▶ Paris 775 – Aix-en-Provence 26 – Rians 38 – St-Maximin-la-Ste-Baume 19

Municipal Cézanne

04 42 66 36 33, *www.le-cezanne.com*
Address : chemin Philippe Noclercq (take the eastern exit along the D 57, by the stadium)
Opening times : from mid March to end Oct.
1 ha (50 pitches) terraced, relatively flat, stony, grassy
Tariff : ♣ 6€ ⊞ 2.50€ ⊞ 3€ – (6A) 3€
Rental rates : (from mid March to end Oct.) – 2 caravans – 4 ⌷ – 3 gîtes.
Per night from 50 to 90 € – Per week from 300 to 480 €
⌁ sani-station 2€ – ⌁ 8€
At the foot of Mont Ste-Victoire.

Surroundings : ⌘
Leisure activities : ✂
Facilities : ⊙ ⌁ ⌁

Longitude : 5.68227
Latitude : 43.527

RAMATUELLE

83350 – Michelin map **340** O6 – pop. 2,240 – alt. 136
▶ Paris 873 – Fréjus 35 – Hyères 52 – Le Lavandou 34

Le Kon Tiki ▲▲

✆ 04 94 55 96 96, *www.riviera-villages.com* – limited spaces for one-night stay
Address : Plage de Pampelonne (beach)
Opening times : from mid April to beginning Nov.
flat, grassy, sandy
Tariff : (2012 price) 90 € ♣♣ ⇔ 🅴 🄵 (10A)
Rental rates : (2012 price) (from mid April to beginning Oct.) – 100 🛖 – 200 🏠.
Per night from 55 to 480 € – Per week from 385 to 3,170 €

Attractive Polynesian huts.

Surroundings : ♀ ⚊
Leisure activities : 🍴 ✕ 🎦 ☺ 🚶 🎣 hammam, jacuzzi 🏄 ≋ (beach) ⌒ ♨
Facilities : ⌖ 🎖 ♨ ⚑ 🚾 ⛲ launderette 🐕 🚰
Nearby : 🐎
GPS Longitude : 6.65852 Latitude : 43.23147

Yelloh! Village les Tournels ▲▲

✆ 04 94 55 90 90, *www.tournels.com*
Opening times : from end March to mid Nov.
20 ha (975 pitches) very uneven, terraced, stony, grassy
Tariff : 63 € ♣♣ ⇔ 🅴 – Extra per person 8 €
Rental rates : (from end March to mid Nov.) – 221 🛖 – 119 🏠. Per night from 65 to 218 €
Per week from 455 to 1,913 €
🚽 sani-station

Lovely swimming pool and sunbathing area. Water sports available at the beach.

Surroundings : ⇐ ⛲ ♀♀
Leisure activities : 🍴 ✕ ☺ (amphitheatre) 🚶 🎣 ≋ hammam, jacuzzi 🏄 🚲 ✕ 🏊 ⛲ disco, multi-sports ground
Facilities : ♿ ⌖ 🎖 ♨ ⚑ 🚾 ⛲ launderette 🚰 refrigerated food storage
Nearby : 🚰
GPS Longitude : 6.65112 Latitude : 43.20537

La Toison d'Or ▲▲

✆ 04 94 79 83 54, *www.riviera-villages.com*
Address : rte des Tamaris
5 ha (500 pitches) flat, grassy, sandy
Rentals : 176 🛖 – 50 lodges.

Surroundings : ♀ ⚊
Leisure activities : 🍴 ✕ 🎦 ☺ 🚶 🎣 ≋ hammam, jacuzzi 🏄 ✕ ≋ ♨
Facilities : ⌖ ♨ ⚑ 🚾 ⛲ launderette 🚮 🚰
GPS Longitude : 6.66007 Latitude : 43.23884

Campéole la Croix du Sud ▲▲

✆ 04 94 55 51 23, *www.campeole.com* – limited spaces for one-night stay
Address : rte des Plages
Opening times : from end March to mid Oct.
3 ha (120 pitches) terraced, flat, grassy, stony, sandy
Tariff : (2012 price) 44.50 € ♣♣ ⇔ 🅴 🄵 (12A) – Extra per person 9.70 € – Reservation fee 25 €
Rental rates : (2012 price) (from end March to mid Oct.) – 17 🛖 – 11 🏠.
Per night from 49 to 157 € – Per week from 609 to 1,099 € – Reservation fee 25 €

Surroundings : 🌄 ♀♀
Leisure activities : 🍴 ✕ 🚶 🏄 🚲 🏊
Facilities : ♿ ⌖ ♨ 🚾 🖼
GPS Longitude : 6.64104 Latitude : 43.21426

RÉGUSSE

83630 – Michelin map **340** L4 – pop. 2,067 – alt. 545
▶ Paris 838 – Marseille 113 – Toulon 94 – Digne-les-Bains 75

Homair Vacances Les Lacs du Verdon ▲▴

℘ 04 94 70 17 95, *www.homair.com*
Address : domaine de Roquelande
Opening times : from beginning April to end Sept.
17 ha (400 pitches) flat, grassy, stony
Tariff : (2012 price) 27€ ✦✦ ⇌ 🗐 (10A) – Extra per person 5.50€ – Reservation fee 10€
Rental rates : (2012 price) (from beginning April to end Sept.) – 296 ▥.
Per night from 29 to 155 € – Per week from 203 to 1,085 € – Reservation fee 10€

Surroundings : ▭ ♉♉
Leisure activities : ▮ ✗ 🛏 ☺ ⛹ ⚓ ⛷ ✍ ⛄ ⬥ multi-sports area
Facilities : ⚬┯ ▥ ᗡ ♈ launderette ▨ ⚲
Nearby : 🐎

GPS
Longitude : 6.15073
Latitude : 43.66041

RIEZ

04500 – Michelin map **334** E10 – pop. 1,783 – alt. 520
▶ Paris 792 – Marseille 105 – Digne-les-Bains 41 – Draguignan 64

Rose de Provence

℘ 04 92 77 75 45, *www.rose-de-provence.com*
Address : r. Edouard Dauphin
Opening times : from mid April to beginning Oct.
1 ha (91 pitches) terrace, flat, grassy, gravelled
Tariff : (2012 price) 20.80€ ✦✦ ⇌ 🗐 (6A) – Extra per person 5.40€ – Reservation fee 10€
Rental rates : (2012 price) (from beginning April to end Oct.) – 7 ▥ – 2 🏠 –
2 tent bungalows – 1 gîte. Per night from 30 to 85 € – Per week from 210 to 595 €
Reservation fee 15€

Surroundings : ▭ ♉♉
Leisure activities : jacuzzi ⚓
Facilities : ♿ ⚬┯ ᗡ ♈ 🖥 refrigerated food storage
Nearby : ⛏ ✗

GPS
Longitude : 6.09922
Latitude : 43.81307

Fire safety doesn't stop when you leave your accommodation.
Always take care and consider the fire risks.

LA ROCHE-DE-RAME

05310 – Michelin map **334** H4 – pop. 830 – alt. 1,000
▶ Paris 701 – Briançon 22 – Embrun 27 – Gap 68

Le Verger

℘ 04 92 20 92 23, *www.campingleverger.com*
Address :at Les Gillis (head 1.2km northwest along the N 94, follow the signs for Briançon)
1.6 ha (50 pitches) terraced, relatively flat, grassy
Rentals : 6 ▥ – 1 🏠 – 1 gîte.
▥ sani-station
Pitches enjoy the shade of cherry and apricot trees.

Surroundings : ⛰ ≼♀
Leisure activities : 🛏 ⚓
Facilities : ♿ ⚬┯ ▥ ⚲ ♈ launderette

GPS
Longitude : 6.57951
Latitude : 44.7581

⚠ Municipal du Lac

📞 06 10 03 57 28, *www.campingdulac05.fr*
Address : R.N 94 (take the southern exit)
Opening times : from beginning May to mid Sept.
1 ha (95 pitches) relatively flat, flat, grassy
Tariff : 14.20€ ✝✝ ⇔ 🗉 🔌 (10A) – Extra per person 4.90€
Rental rates : (from beginning May to mid Sept.) – 2 ⨼ – 2 tent bungalows – 1 gîte.
Per night from 50 € – Per week from 380 €
🚐 20 🗉 10.90€ – 💧🔌10.90€

Surroundings : ⩽ ‿
Leisure activities : 🍸
Facilities : ৬ ⌙ ☵ 🚽 🗃
Nearby : ✗ ⤸ ➿ (lake) ⤳ pedalos

GPS | Longitude : 6.58145
Latitude : 44.74673

LA ROCHE DES ARNAUDS

05400 – Michelin map **334** D5 – pop. 1,372 – alt. 945
▶ Paris 672 – Corps 49 – Gap 15 – St-Étienne-en-Dévoluy 33

⚠ Au Blanc Manteau

📞 04 92 57 82 56, *www.campingaublancmanteau.fr* – alt. 900
Address : rte de Ceuze (1.3km southwest along the D 18; beside some rapids)
Opening times : permanent
4 ha (40 pitches) flat, grassy, stony
Tariff : (2012 price) 18€ ✝✝ ⇔ 🗉 🔌 (10A) – Extra per person 4.50€

Surroundings : ❄ ☙ ⩽ ‿‿
Leisure activities : 🍸 🎦 ⚓ 🚲 ✗ 🏊
Facilities : ৬ ⌙ 🚽☒ ▥ 🛁 🗃 ⤸

GPS | Longitude : 5.95085
Latitude : 44.54962

The prices listed were supplied by the campsite owners in 2012
(if prices were not available, those from the previous year are given).
The fees should be regarded as basic charges and may fluctuate
with inflation.

ROQUEBRUNE-SUR-ARGENS

83520 – Michelin map **340** O5 – pop. 12,708 – alt. 13
▶ Paris 862 – Les Arcs 18 – Cannes 49 – Draguignan 23

⋀⋀⋀ Domaine de la Bergerie ♠♠

📞 04 98 11 45 45, *www.domainelabergerie.com* – limited spaces for one-night stay
Address : Vallée du Fournel – rte du Col de Bougnon (head 8km southeast along the D 7, follow the signs for St-Aygulf and turn right onto D 8; beside some lakes)
Opening times : from end April to end Sept.
60 ha (700 pitches) very uneven, terraced, flat, stony
Tariff : 56€ ✝✝ ⇔ 🗉 🔌 (10A) – Extra per person 11.50€ – Reservation fee 25€
Rental rates : (from beginning March to mid Nov.) – 300 ⟐. Per night from 63 to 214 €
Per week from 441 to 1,498 €

Surroundings : ‿‿
Leisure activities : 🍸 ✗ 🎦 🍸 (open-air theatre) 🏸 ≋ hammam, jacuzzi ⚓ 🚲 ✗ ▥ 🏊 ⟋ ⤳ disco, multi-sports ground, entertainment room
Facilities : ৬ ⌙ 🛁 🏖 ⛟ 🚽 launderette ⛲ ⤸

GPS | Longitude : 6.67535
Latitude : 43.39879

Les Pêcheurs ♣♣

0494457125, www.camping-les-pecheurs.com
Address : 700m northwest along the D 7
Opening times : from beginning April to end Sept.
3.3 ha (220 pitches) flat, grassy
Tariff : (2012 price) 46.50€ ♛♛ ⇔ 国 ☼ (10A) – Extra per person 8.80€ – Reservation fee 22€
Rental rates : (2012 price) (from beginning April to end Sept.) – 31 ⛺ – 20 ☖.
Per night from 52 to 157 € – Per week from 350 to 1,095 € – Reservation fee 22€
⛽ sani-station
Pleasant wooded setting with flowers beside the Argens river and near a small lake.

> Surroundings : ⌒ ♨♨
> Leisure activities : ✗ 🎞 ☺ daytime ⚱ ≋ hammam, jacuzzi ⚓ ♒ ⛵
>   ⌇ pedalos ⚘
> Facilities : ⚙ ⟲ ▥ ⛲ ⛄ launderette ⚖ ⛲
> Nearby : ≝
> **Longitude :** 6.63354
> **Latitude :** 43.45094

Lei Suves

0494454395, www.lei-suves.com – limited spaces for one-night stay
Address : Blavet quartier (head 4km north along the D 7 and take underpass under A 8)
Opening times : from beginning April to mid Oct.
7 ha (310 pitches) terraced, flat, grassy, stony
Tariff : 48€ ♛♛ ⇔ 国 ☼ (6A) – Extra per person 10.30€ – Reservation fee 25€
Rental rates : (from beginning April to mid Oct.) ⚒ – 30 ⛺. Per night from 53 to 143 €
Per week from 370 to 1,000 € – Reservation fee 25€
A pleasant wooded setting and a well-kept site.

> Surroundings : ⌇ ⌒ ♨♨
> Leisure activities : ♟ ✗ ☺ (open-air theatre) ⚱ ⚓ ⚒ ⛵ multi-sports ground
> Facilities : ⚙ ⟲ ⚱ ⚘ launderette ⚖ ⛲
> **Longitude :** 6.63882
> **Latitude :** 43.47821

Moulin des Iscles

0494457074, www.campingdesiscles.com
Address : chemin du Moulin des Iscles (head 1.8km east along the D 7, follow the signs for St-Aygulf and take road to the left)
Opening times : from beginning April to end Sept.
1.5 ha (90 pitches) flat, grassy
Tariff : 25.50€ ♛♛ ⇔ 国 ☼ (6A) – Extra per person 3.40€ – Reservation fee 15€
Rental rates : (from beginning April to end Sept.) – 5 ⛺ – 1 ⊨ – 3 studios – 2 apartments.
Per night 110€ – Per week 750€ – Reservation fee 15€
Situated beside the Argens river.

> Surroundings : ⌇ ♨♨
> Leisure activities : ✗ 🎞 ⌇ ⌇ ⚘
> Facilities : ⚙ ⟲ 🆑 ▥ ⛄ ⚱ ⚘ ⚖ ⛲
> **Longitude :** 6.65784
> **Latitude :** 43.44497

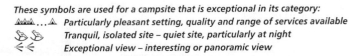

These symbols are used for a campsite that is exceptional in its category:
▲▲▲…▲ *Particularly pleasant setting, quality and range of services available*
⌇⌇ *Tranquil, isolated site – quiet site, particularly at night*
≤≤ *Exceptional view – interesting or panoramic view*

LA ROQUE-D'ANTHÉRON

3640 – Michelin map **340** G3 – pop. 5,143 – alt. 183
◪ Paris 726 – Aix-en-Provence 29 – Cavaillon 34 – Manosque 60

Village Center Les Iscles
(rental of mobile homes only)

𝄐 0825002030, *www.village-center.com*
Address : at la Durance (head 3km south along the D 23)
Opening times : from mid April to end Sept.
10 ha (269 pitches) flat, grassy, stony
Rental rates : (2012 price) – 264 . Per night from 30 to 135 € – Per week from 210 to 950 €
Reservation fee 15€

Surroundings : 🌿 ♨♨
Leisure activities : 🍴 ✕ ⊗ 🏹 ⚓ 💈 ⅃ ≊ (lake) ⛷ 🏊 🏄
Facilities : ⊶ 🚻 ⚏ 🎵 launderette 🚿 🚰

GPS Longitude : 5.32099
Latitude : 43.72819

ST-ANDRÉ-LES-ALPES

4170 – Michelin map **334** H9 – pop. 930 – alt. 914
◪ Paris 786 – Castellane 20 – Colmars 28 – Digne-les-Bains 43

Municipal les Iscles

𝄐 0492890229, *camping-les-iscles.com* – alt. 894
Address : chemin des Iscles (located 1km south along the N 202, follow the signs for Annot and take the turning to the left, 300m from the Verdon river)
Opening times : from beginning April to beginning Nov.
2.5 ha (200 pitches) flat, grassy, stony
Tariff : (2012 price) 🧍 4€ ⬅ 1.50€ 🅔 – 🔌 (10A) 3€
Rental rates : (2012 price) (from beginning April to beginning Nov.) ♿ (1 mobile home) 🛏 –
16 . Per night from 30 to 75 € – Per week from 210 to 630 € – Reservation fee 10€

A pleasant site among pine trees.

Surroundings : 🌿 ♨♨
Leisure activities : 🎮 ⚓
Facilities : ♿ ⊶ 🎵 🎵 🖥
Nearby : 🛒 💈 ⛰ sports trail, paragliding

GPS Longitude : 6.50844
Latitude : 43.9612

ST-APOLLINAIRE

5160 – Michelin map **334** G5 – pop. 117 – alt. 1,285
◪ Paris 684 – Embrun 19 – Gap 27 – Mont-Dauphin 37

Campéole Le Clos du Lac

𝄐 0492442743, *www.camping-closdulac.com* – access difficult for caravans and campervans –
alt. 1,450
Address : rte des Lacs (2.3km northwest along the D 509; 50m from the small lake at St-Apollinaire)
Opening times : from mid May to mid Sept.
2 ha (68 pitches) terraced, relatively flat, grassy
Tariff : (2012 price) 19.30€ 🧍🧍 ⬅ 🅔 🔌 (7A) – Extra per person 5.40€
Rental rates : (2012 price) (from mid May to mid Sept.) – 18 . Per night from 37 to 100 €
Per week from 259 to 700 € – Reservation fee 15€

In an attractive elevated location.

Surroundings : 🌿 ≼ Lac de Serre-Ponçon and mountains ♀
Leisure activities : ⚓
Facilities : ⊶ 🎵 🎵 🖥
Nearby : 🍴 ✕ 🚰 ⛰ ≊ (lake) 💈

GPS Longitude : 6.34642
Latitude : 44.56127

ST-AYGULF

83370 – Michelin map **340** P5
▶ Paris 872 – Brignoles 69 – Draguignan 35 – Fréjus 6

L'Étoile d'Argens ♣♣

℘ 0494810141, *www.etoiledargens.com*
Address : chemin des Étangs (5km northwest along the D 7, follow the signs for Roquebrune-sur-Argens and turn right onto the D 8; beside the Argens river)
Opening times : from mid April to mid Oct.
11 ha (493 pitches) flat, grassy
Tariff : (2012 price) 55 € ♣♣ ⇌ 🔲 [6] (10A) – Extra per person 10 € – Reservation fee 30 €
Rental rates : (2012 price) (permanent) ⚡ – 74 🚐. Per night from 48 to 220 €
Per week from 336 to 1,540 € – Reservation fee 30 €

Pretty, spacious pitches with shade. River shuttle service to the beaches (duration: 30 min).

Surroundings : 🐾 ⊑ 🎠
Leisure activities : ♈ ✗ ☺ ☘ jacuzzi 🚣 🚲 ⚽ ♨ ⛲ disco, multi-sports ground
Facilities : ♿ ☛ ⧈ 🍴 🚿 ☂ 🍳 launderette 🧺 🛒
Nearby : ⚓

GPS Longitude : 6.70562
Latitude : 43.41596

Au Paradis des Campeurs

℘ 0494969355, *www.paradis-des-campeurs.com*
Address : at La Gaillarde-Plage (2.5km south along the N 98, follow the signs for Ste-Maxime)
Opening times : from beginning April to beginning Oct.
6 ha/3.5 ha for camping (180 pitches) terrace, flat, grassy
Tariff : 30 € ♣♣ ⇌ 🔲 [6] (6A) – Extra per person 6 € – Reservation fee 30 €
Rental rates : (from beginning April to beginning Oct.) – 15 🚐. Per week from 280 to 730 €
Reservation fee 30 €

Some pitches have a sea view and direct access to the beach.

Surroundings : ⊑ ⚲
Leisure activities : ♈ ✗ 🎦 🚣
Facilities : ♿ ☛ ⧈ 🚿 ☂ 🍳 launderette 🧺 🛒
Nearby : disco

GPS Longitude : 6.71235
Latitude : 43.366

Résidence du Campeur

℘ 0494810159, *www.sandaya.fr* – limited spaces for one-night stay
Address : 3km northwest along the D 7, follow the signs for Roquebrune-sur-Argens
Opening times : from beginning April to mid Oct.
10 ha (451 pitches) flat, gravelled
Tariff : 62 € ♣♣ ⇌ 🔲 [6] (10A) – Extra per person 7 € – Reservation fee 30 €
Rental rates : (from beginning April to mid Oct.) – 215 🚐 – 2 apartments –
20 tent bungalows. Per night from 35 to 130 € – Per week from 245 to 1,533 €
Reservation fee 30 €
🚐 177 🔲 62 €

Surroundings : ⊑ 🎠
Leisure activities : ♈ ✗ 🎦 ☺ ☘ 🚣 🚲 ⚽ ♨ ⛲ multi-sports ground
Facilities : ☛ – 451 individual sanitary facilities (🚿🚽🛁 wc) ☂ 🍳 launderette 🧺 🛒
Nearby : open-air cinema

GPS Longitude : 6.70875
Latitude : 43.40867

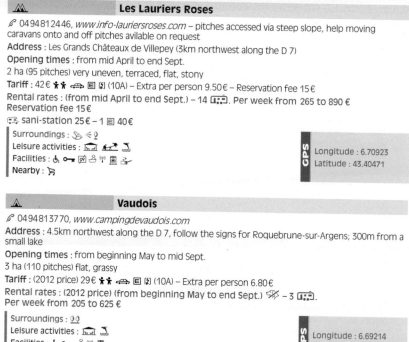

Les Lauriers Roses

☎ 04 94 81 24 46, *www.info-lauriersroses.com* – pitches accessed via steep slope, help moving caravans onto and off pitches avilable on request

Address : Les Grands Châteaux de Villepey (3km northwest along the D 7)

Opening times : from mid April to end Sept.

2 ha (95 pitches) very uneven, terraced, flat, stony

Tariff : 42€ ★★ ⊕ 🗐 (10A) – Extra per person 9.50€ – Reservation fee 15€

Rental rates : (from mid April to end Sept.) – 14 ⨳. Per week from 265 to 890 € Reservation fee 15€

🚾 sani-station 25€ – 1 🗐 40€

Surroundings : 🌳 ⩗ 👤
Leisure activities : 🎯 🏊
Facilities : ♿ ⛖ 🚻 🍴 🔥 🚿
Nearby : 🛒

GPS
Longitude : 6.70923
Latitude : 43.40471

Vaudois

☎ 04 94 81 37 70, *www.campingdevaudois.com*

Address : 4.5km northwest along the D 7, follow the signs for Roquebrune-sur-Argens; 300m from a small lake

Opening times : from beginning May to mid Sept.

3 ha (110 pitches) flat, grassy

Tariff : (2012 price) 29€ ★★ ⊕ 🗐 (10A) – Extra per person 6.80€

Rental rates : (2012 price) (from beginning May to end Sept.) ⌀ – 3 ⨳. Per week from 205 to 625 €

Surroundings : 👤👤
Leisure activities : 🎯 🏊
Facilities : ♿ ⛖ 🚻 🍴 🔥
Nearby : 🎣

GPS
Longitude : 6.69214
Latitude : 43.41084

ST-CLÉMENT-SUR-DURANCE

05600 – Michelin map **334** H5 – pop. 285 – alt. 872
▶ Paris 715 – L'Argentière-la-Bessée 21 – Embrun 13 – Gap 54

Les Mille Vents

☎ 04 92 45 10 90

Address : located 1km east along the N 94, follow the signs for Briançon and take D 994d to the right after the bridge and the white water sports centre

3.5 ha (100 pitches) terrace, flat, grassy, grassy

Rentals : 3 ⌂.

🚾 sani-station

Situated beside the river.

Surroundings : ⩗ 👤
Leisure activities : 🏊 🏊
Facilities : ♿ ⛖ 🔥 ⛱ 🔥
Nearby : ✕ rafting and canyoning

GPS
Longitude : 6.6618
Latitude : 44.66362

In order for the guide to remain wholly objective, the selection of campsites is made on an entirely independent basis.

ST-CYR-SUR-MER

83270 – Michelin map **340** J6 – pop. 11,865 – alt. 10
▶ Paris 810 – Bandol 8 – Brignoles 70 – La Ciotat 10

Le Clos Ste-Thérèse

℘ 04 94 32 12 21, *www.clos-therese.com* – pitches accessed via steep slope, help moving caravans
onto and off pitches avilable on request – limited spaces for one-night stay
Address : 3.5km southeast along the D 559
Opening times : from beginning April to end Sept.
4 ha (123 pitches) very uneven, terraced, flat, grassy, stony
Tariff : 34€ ♣♣ ⇔ 🔲 🕖 (10A) – Extra per person 6.20€ – Reservation fee 23€
Rental rates : (2012 price) (from beginning April to end Sept.) – 6 🚐 – 25 🏠.
Per night from 55 to 107 € – Per week from 339 to 749 € – Reservation fee 23€

Surroundings : 🏕 ♤♤
Leisure activities : ⛑ 🏓 🎣 🏊 spa facilities
Facilities : ♿ ⚬ 🛏 🎿 🚿 🔲 🚻
Nearby : 🍴

GPS
Longitude : 5.72951
Latitude : 43.15955

ST-ÉTIENNE-DE-TINÉE

06660 – Michelin map **341** C2 – pop. 1,311 – alt. 1,147
▶ Paris 788 – Grenoble 226 – Marseille 262 – Nice 90

Municipal du Plan d'Eau

℘ 04 93 02 41 57, *mairie@saintetiennedetinee.fr*
Address : rte du col de la Bonette (500m north of the town)
0.5 ha (23 pitches) terraced, stony, flat
🚐 sani-station – 6 🔲
*Situated beside the Tinée river, overlooking a small but pretty small lake – reserved
for tents.*

Surroundings : 🏞 ≤ 🏕
Leisure activities : 🏓 🏖 (beach) 🎣
Facilities : ⚬ 🅿 no electrical hook-up
Nearby : fitness trail

GPS
Longitude : 6.92299
Latitude : 44.25858

To visit a town or region, use the MICHELIN Green Guides.

ST-ÉTIENNE-DU-GRÈS

13103 – Michelin map **340** D3 – pop. 2,202 – alt. 7
▶ Paris 706 – Arles 16 – Avignon 24 – Les Baux-de-Provence 15

Municipal du Grès

℘ 04 90 49 00 03, *campingalpilles.com*
Address : av. du Dr-Barberin (take the northwestern exit along the D 99, follow the signs for Tarascon;
near the stadium, 50m from the Vigueira)
Opening times : permanent
0.6 ha (40 pitches) flat, grassy, stony
Tariff : 17€ ♣♣ ⇔ 🔲 🕖 (16A) – Extra per person 3.50€
Rental rates : (permanent) – 2 🚐. Per night from 65 to 75 € – Per week from 450 to 500 €
Reservation fee 15€

Surroundings : 🏕 ♤♤
Facilities : ⚬ 🎿 🛏 🎿 🚻 🍴 launderette

GPS
Longitude : 4.71772
Latitude : 43.78628

ST-LAURENT-DU-VERDON

04500 – Michelin map **334** E10 – pop. 92 – alt. 468
◪ Paris 797 – Marseille 118 – Digne-les-Bains 59 – Avignon 166

La Farigoulette

☎ 04 92 74 41 62, www.camping-la-farigoulette.com
Address : Lac de St Laurent (located 1km north follow signs along the C 1 for Montpezat)
Opening times : from mid May to mid Sept.
14 ha (200 pitches) relatively flat, stony, grassy
Tariff : (2012 price) 31.60€ ✹✹ ⊕ 目 ⑭ (5A) – Extra per person 5.10€ – Reservation fee 15€
Rental rates : (2012 price) (from mid May to mid Sept.) – 25 ⬛ – 25 ⬛.
Per night from 40 to 128 € – Per week from 280 to 896 € – Reservation fee 20€
⬛ sani-station

Surroundings : ⬛ ⬛ ⬚⬚
Leisure activities : ✗ ⬛ daytime ⬛ ⬚ ⬚ ⬛ pedalos ⬛ multi-sports ground
Facilities : ⬛ ⬛ ⬛ launderette ⬛ ⬛ ⬛

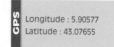

GPS
Longitude : 6.0777
Latitude : 43.73407

ST-MANDRIER-SUR-MER

83430 – Michelin map **340** K7 – pop. 5,773 – alt. 1
◪ Paris 836 – Bandol 20 – Le Beausset 22 – Hyères 30

Homair Vacances La Presqu'île
(rental of mobile homes only)

☎ 04 94 30 74 70, www.homair.com
Address : Pin Rolland quartier (2.5km west, carr. D 18 and follow the signs for La Pointe de Marégau (headland), near the marina)
Opening times : from beginning April to end Sept.
2.5 ha very uneven, terraced, flat, stony
Rental rates : (2012 price) – 125 ⬛. Per night from 33 to 179 € – Per week from 231 to 1,253 €
Reservation fee 10€

Surroundings : ⬚⬚
Leisure activities : ⬛ ✗ ⬛ ⬛ ⬛ ⬚
Facilities : ⬛ ⬛ ⬛ ⬛ ⬛
Nearby : ⬛ ⬛

GPS
Longitude : 5.90577
Latitude : 43.07655

This guide is updated regularly, so buy your new copy every year!

ST-MARTIN-D'ENTRAUNES

06470 – Michelin map **341** B3 – pop. 83 – alt. 1,050
◪ Paris 778 – Annot 39 – Barcelonnette 50 – Puget-Théniers 44

Le Prieuré

☎ 04 93 05 54 99, http://www.le-prieure.com – alt. 1,070 ⬛
Address : rte des Blancs (located 1km east along the D 2202, follow the signs for Guillaumes then continue 1.8km along the road to the left, after the bridge over the Var)
Opening times : from beginning May to end Sept.
12 ha/1.5 (35 pitches) terraced, relatively flat, flat, grassy
Tariff : ✹ 4.80€ ⊕ 目 7.80€ – ⑭ (10A) 3.50€ – Reservation fee 10€
Rental rates : (permanent) ⬛ – 8 ⬛ – 5 tent bungalows – 10 gîtes. Per night from 45 to 70 €
Per week from 315 to 540 € – Reservation fee 10€

Surroundings : ⬛ ⬛ ⬚⬚
Leisure activities : ✗ ⬛ ⬛ ⬛ ⬛ ⬛ (small swimming pool)
Facilities : ⬛ ⬛ ⬛ ⬛ ⬛

GPS
Longitude : 6.76283
Latitude : 44.14895

06450 – Michelin map **341** E3 – pop. 1,325 – alt. 1,000
▶ Paris 899 – Marseille 235 – Nice 65 – Cuneo 140

À la Ferme St-Joseph

℘ 06 70 51 90 14, www.camping-alafermestjoseph.com
Address : to the southeast of the town along the D 2565 follow the signs for Roquebillière, near Saint-Martin-Vésubie
Opening times : from end April to end Sept.
0.6 ha (50 pitches) sloping, flat, grassy
Tariff : (2012 price) 24.50€ ✶✶ ⬅ 🅴 🅷 (6A) – Extra per person 4.80€ – Reservation fee 10€
Rental rates : (2012 price) (from end April to end Sept.) 🚲 – 3 🛏. Per night from 49 to 52 €
Per week from 343 to 364 €
🚉 sani-station
Surroundings : 🌿 ≤ ♀
Facilities : ☐ (Jul–Aug) 🚿 ☑ 🚽 🖼
Nearby : 🍴 🚶

Longitude : 7.25711
Latitude : 44.06469

83440 – Michelin map **340** P4 – pop. 1,616 – alt. 310
▶ Paris 884 – Cannes 46 – Draguignan 27 – Fayence 10

Le Parc ♟

℘ 04 94 76 15 35, campingleparc.com
Address : 408 quartier Trestaure (3km north along the D 4, follow the signs for Fayence then take the road to the right)
Opening times : from beginning April to end Sept.
3 ha (100 pitches) terraced, flat, grassy, stony
Tariff : 40.80€ ✶✶ ⬅ 🅴 🅷 (10A) – Extra per person 6.80€ – Reservation fee 26€
Rental rates : (from beginning April to end Sept.) – 11 🚐 – 4 🏠 – 1 🛏 – 2 tents – 1 gîte.
Per night from 42 to 61 € – Per week from 160 to 980 € – Reservation fee 26€
🚉 4 🅴 24€
Surroundings : 🌿 ♒
Leisure activities : 🍴 ☒ ☀ daytime 🎯 🏊 🍴 🐴 🚶
Facilities : ♿ ☐ ▥ 🚿 🚽 launderette 🚿
Nearby : 🐎

Longitude : 6.68979
Latitude : 43.58445

04400 – Michelin map **334** H6 – pop. 742 – alt. 1,157
▶ Paris 797 – Marseille 227 – Digne-les-Bains 84 – Gap 74

Village Vacances Le Loup Blanc du Riou
(rental of chalets only)

℘ 04 92 81 44 97, www.leloupblanc.com
Address : located 1km southwest, behind Ubaye aerodrome
Opening times : permanent
2 ha terraced, flat
Rental rates : 8 🏠 – 8 apartments. Per night from 80 to 90 € – Per week from 295 to 745 €
Pleasant small chalet village, in the shade of pine trees.

Surroundings : 🌿 ≤ ♀♀
Leisure activities : ☒ 🏊 🚶
Facilities : 🅿 ▥ 🚽 🖼
Nearby : 🚴 🍴 🐎 adventure park, leisure park, gliding

Longitude : 6.6122
Latitude : 44.39107

ST-RAPHAËL

83700 – Michelin map **340** P5 – pop. 34,269
▶ Paris 870 – Aix-en-Provence 121 – Cannes 42 – Fréjus 4

Les Castels Douce Quiétude ⚐⚐

℘ 04 94 44 30 00, www.douce-quietude.com – limited spaces for one-night stay
Address : 3435 bd Jacques Baudino (take northeastern exit towards Valescure then continue 3km – from A8, take exit 38)
Opening times : from end March to mid Oct.
10 ha (400 pitches) undulating, terraced, flat, grassy, stony
Tariff : (2012 price) 58€ ✹✹ ⛺ ▣ ⚡ (16A) – Extra per person 10.60€ – Reservation fee 30€
Rental rates : (from end March to mid Oct.) – 255 ⛺. Per night from 41 to 252 €
Per week from 287 to 1,764 € – Reservation fee 30€

Surroundings :
Leisure activities : ♈ ✗ ⚐ ☇ ☶ ⚐ hammam, jacuzzi ☇ ☇ ✗ ☶ ☶ ☇ disco
Facilities : ⚐ ⚐ ⚐ ☇ ☇ ☇ ☇ launderette ☇ ☇

GPS
Longitude : 6.80587
Latitude : 43.44734

The information in the guide may have changed since going to press.

ST-RÉMY-DE-PROVENCE

13210 – Michelin map **340** D3 – pop. 10,458 – alt. 59
▶ Paris 702 – Arles 25 – Avignon 20 – Marseille 89

Monplaisir

℘ 04 90 92 22 70, www.camping-monplaisir.fr
Address : chemin de Monplaisir (800m northwest along the D 5, follow the signs for Maillane and take road to the left)
Opening times : from mid March to mid Oct.
2.8 ha (140 pitches) flat, grassy, stony
Tariff : (2012 price) 31.80€ ✹✹ ⛺ ▣ ⚡ (10A) – Extra per person 8€ – Reservation fee 17€
Rental rates : (2012 price) (from mid March to mid Oct.) ☇ – 12 ⛺.
Per week from 350 to 730 €
⛐ sani-station
A pleasant site with flowers, based around a Provençal 'mas' (traditional farmhouse).

Surroundings :
Leisure activities : ♈ ✗ ☇ ☇ ☇
Facilities : ⚐ ⚐ ☇ ☇ launderette ☇ ☇
Nearby : ☇

GPS
Longitude : 4.8729
Latitude : 43.78417

Mas de Nicolas ⚐⚐

℘ 04 90 92 27 05, www.camping-masdenicolas.com
Address : av. Plaisance du Touch (take the northern exit, follow the signs for Avignon then continue 1km along the D 99, follow the signs for Cavaillon, then take the r. Théodore-Aubanel; behind the stadium and Glanum college)
Opening times : from mid March to end Oct.
4 ha (167 pitches) relatively flat, flat, grassy, stony
Tariff : (2012 price) 28.50€ ✹✹ ⛺ ▣ ⚡ (6A) – Extra per person 8€ – Reservation fee 17€
Rental rates : (2012 price) (from mid March to end Oct.) ⚐ (1 mobile home) – 21 ⛺ – 13 ☷.
Per night from 55 to 100 € – Per week from 300 to 730 € – Reservation fee 17€
⛐ sani-station – ☇ 14€

Surroundings :
Leisure activities : ☇ ☇ ☶ ⚐ hammam, jacuzzi ☇ ☇ ☇
Facilities : ⚐ ⚐ ☇ ☇ ☇ ☇ ▣ refrigerated food storage

GPS
Longitude : 4.83913
Latitude : 43.79594

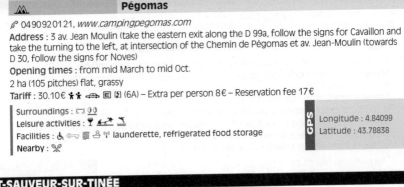

Pégomas

✆ 04 90 92 01 21, *www.campingpegomas.com*

Address : 3 av. Jean Moulin (take the eastern exit along the D 99a, follow the signs for Cavaillon and take the turning to the left, at intersection of the Chemin de Pégomas et av. Jean-Moulin (towards D 30, follow the signs for Noves)

Opening times : from mid March to mid Oct.

2 ha (105 pitches) flat, grassy

Tariff : 30.10€ ♣♣ ⇔ 🔲 (A) (6A) – Extra per person 8€ – Reservation fee 17€

Surroundings : 🗔 🟡🟡
Leisure activities : 🍸 🛶 🏊
Facilities : ᵬ ⚬🚽 🏦 🛁 🚰 launderette, refrigerated food storage
Nearby : 🍴

GPS Longitude : 4.84099
Latitude : 43.78838

ST-SAUVEUR-SUR-TINÉE

06420 – Michelin map **341** D3 – pop. 336 – alt. 500
▶ Paris 816 – Auron 31 – Guillaumes 42 – Isola 2000 28

Municipal

✆ 04 93 02 03 20, *mairie.st-sauveur-sur-tinee@wanadoo.fr* – ♯

Address : Les Plans quartier (800m north on the D 30, follow the signs for Roubion, before the bridge; beside the Tinée river, direct pedestrian path to the village)

Opening times : from mid June to mid Sept.

0.37 ha (20 pitches) terraced, flat, stony, fine gravel

Tariff : (2012 price) 16.50€ ♣♣ ⇔ 🔲 (A) (3A) – Extra per person 4.50€

Surroundings : 🏞 ⩽ 🗔 🟡🟡
Facilities : ᵬ 🅿 🚽 🔐 🖼
Nearby : 🛶 🍴 🎣 fitness trail

GPS Longitude : 7.10611
Latitude : 44.08722

There are several different types of sani-station ('borne' in French) – sanitation points providing fresh water and disposal points for grey water. See page 12 for further details.

STE-CROIX-DE-VERDON

04500 – Michelin map **334** E10 – pop. 124 – alt. 530 – Leisure centre
▶ Paris 780 – Brignoles 59 – Castellane 59 – Digne-les-Bains 51

Municipal les Roches

✆ 04 92 77 78 99, *www.blog4ever.com*

Address : rte du Lac (located 1km northeast of the village, 50m from the lake at Ste-Croix – caravans are not permitted through village)

Opening times : from beginning April to end Sept.

6 ha (233 pitches) undulating, terraced, flat, grassy, fine gravel

Tariff : (2012 price) 17€ ♣♣ ⇔ 🔲 (A) (6A) – Extra per person 3.30€ – Reservation fee 30€

Relax in the shade of olive and almond trees.

Surroundings : ⩽ 🟡🟡
Facilities : ᵬ ⚬🚽 🖼 refrigerated food storage
Nearby : 🍴 ≈ 🚣 pedalos

GPS Longitude : 6.15381
Latitude : 43.76043

STES-MARIES-DE-LA-MER

13460 – Michelin map **340** B5 – pop. 2,308 – alt. 1
▶ Paris 761 – Aigues-Mortes 31 – Arles 40 – Marseille 131

Sunêlia Le Clos du Rhône

℘ 04 90 97 85 99, www.camping-leclos.fr
Address : rte d'Aigues-Mortes (head 2km west along the D 38 and take the turning to the left)
Opening times : from end March to beginning Nov.
7 ha (420 pitches) flat, stony, sandy
Tariff : (2012 price) 32.40€ ♥♥ ⇌ 🗐 🗓 (16A)
Rental rates : (2012 price) (from end March to beginning Nov.) ♿ (1 mobile home) – 83 🏠 –
12 tent bungalows. Per week from 273 to 1,185 € – Reservation fee 23€
Near the Petit Rhône river and the beach.

Surroundings : ♀ ≜
Leisure activities : ✗ 🖼 ⛹ ⛴ 🎣
Facilities : ♿ ⊶ 🚿 🖾 🖵 🗓 🍴 💈 laverette 🛆 🔧 refrigerated
food storage
Nearby : 🐎 boat trips on the Rhône

GPS
Longitude : 4.40231
Latitude : 43.44996

SALERNES

83690 – Michelin map **340** M4 – pop. 3,574 – alt. 209
▶ Paris 830 – Aix-en-Provence 81 – Brignoles 33 – Draguignan 23

Municipal les Arnauds

℘ 04 94 67 51 95, www.village-vacances-lesarnauds.com
Address : Les Arnauds quartier (take the northwestern exit along the D 560, follow the signs for
Sillans-la-Cascade and take the turning to the left – access to the village along the pedestrian path
beside the river)
Opening times : from beginning May to end Sept.
2 ha (52 pitches) flat, grassy
Tariff : 27.50€ ♥♥ ⇌ 🗐 🗓 (10A) – Extra per person 7.50€
Rental rates : (from beginning May to end Sept.) – 4 🏠 – 4 studios – 16 apartments.
Per week from 288 to 526 €
Pretty shrubs and flowers, near the Bresque river.

Surroundings : 🏞 🚐 ♀♀
Leisure activities : 🖼 🏊 🎣 🛶 (lake)
Facilities : ♿ ⊶ 💈 🛆 🍴 launderette, refrigerated food storage

GPS
Longitude : 6.2257
Latitude : 43.56623

LES SALLES-SUR-VERDON

83630 – Michelin map **340** M3 – pop. 231 – alt. 440
▶ Paris 790 – Brignoles 57 – Digne-les-Bains 60 – Draguignan 49

Les Pins

℘ 04 98 10 23 80, www.campinglespins.com
Address : take the southern exit along the D 71 then continue 1.2km along the road to the right,
100m from the Lac de Ste-Croix – direct access to the town
Opening times : from beginning April to mid Oct.
3 ha/2 ha for camping (104 pitches) terraced, flat, grassy, stony
Tariff : (2012 price) ♥ 5.80€ ⇌ 🗐 5.90€ – 🗓 (6A) 6€ – Reservation fee 25€
🚾 sani-station
Pleasant, shaded surroundings, with pine trees nearby.

Surroundings : 🏞 🚐 ♀♀
Leisure activities : 🖼 🏊
Facilities : ♿ ⊶ 💈 🛆 🍴 launderette, refrigerated food storage
Nearby : 🛶 🎣 ⌀ fitness trail

GPS
Longitude : 6.2084
Latitude : 43.77603

SALON-DE-PROVENCE

13300 – Michelin map **340** F4 – pop. 42 440 – alt. 80
▸ Paris 720 – Aix-en-Provence 37 – Arles 46 – Avignon 50

⌂ Nostradamus

☎ 04 90 56 08 36, www.camping-nostradamus.com
Address : rte d'Eyguières (5.8km northwest along the D 17 and turn left onto D 72D)
Opening times : from beginning March to end Oct.
2.7 ha (83 pitches) flat, grassy
Tariff : 25.45€ ✝✝ ⇌ 🔳 ⚡ (6A) – Extra per person 6.20€ – Reservation fee 20€
Rental rates : (from beginning March to end Oct.) – 17 ⬚. Per night from 85 to 150 €
Per week from 410 to 770 € – Reservation fee 20€
🚰 sani-station
Situated beside a canal.

Surroundings : 🏞 ⌑ ♒
Leisure activities : 🏛 ⚓ ☇
Facilities : & ⊶ 🆑 ▥ ⚖ ☞ ⚐ launderette

GPS — Longitude : 5.06229
Latitude : 43.68401

---

*Using the traditional Michelin classification method, the guide provides
you with an easy, speedy reference for assessing the category of each site:
1 to 5 tents (see page 10).*

SANARY-SUR-MER

83110 – Michelin map **340** J7 – pop. 16,806 – alt. 1
▸ Paris 824 – Aix-en-Provence 75 – La Ciotat 23 – Marseille 55

⌂⌂⌂ Campasun Mas de Pierredon ▲▴

☎ 04 94 74 25 02, www.campasun.eu
Address : 652 chemin Raoul Coletta (3km to the north, follow the signs for Ollioules and take the
turning to the left after the motorway bridge)
Opening times : from mid April to end Sept.
6 ha/2.5 ha for camping (122 pitches) terraced, flat, grassy, stony
Tariff : 47€ ✝✝ ⇌ 🔳 ⚡ (10A) – Extra per person 9.70€ – Reservation fee 25€
Rental rates : (from mid April to end Sept.) – 41 ⬚ – 15 ⌂. Per night from 60 to 180 €
Per week from 210 to 1,000 € – Reservation fee 25€
🚰 sani-station 5€ – 🔌 ⚡16€

Surroundings : ⌑ ♒
Leisure activities : ▾ ✕ 🏛 ⚓ ☇ ※ ☞ ⚒ ☇
Facilities : & ⊶ ⚖ ⚐ ☞ ⚐ 🔳 ⚐

GPS — Longitude : 5.81452
Latitude : 43.13159

⌂⌂⌂ Campasun Parc Mogador ▲▴

☎ 04 94 74 53 16, www.campasun.eu ⚡ (Jul–Aug)
Address : 167 chemin de Beaucours
Opening times : from end March to beginning Nov.
3 ha (180 pitches) terrace, flat, grassy, stony
Tariff : 43€ ✝✝ ⇌ 🔳 ⚡ (10A) – Extra per person 9.70€ – Reservation fee 25€
Rental rates : (from beginning April to beginning Nov.) ⚡ (Jul–Aug) – 72 ⬚ – 8 ⌂.
Per night from 60 to 160 € – Per week from 210 to 990 € – Reservation fee 25€
🚰 sani-station 5€ – 🔌 ⚡16€

Surroundings : 🏞 ⌑ ♒
Leisure activities : ✕ 🏛 ⚓ ☇ ☇ bowling
Facilities : & ⊶ ⚖ ⚐ ☞ ⚐ launderette ⚐

GPS — Longitude : 5.78777
Latitude : 43.12367

LE SAUZÉ-DU-LAC

05160 – Michelin map **334** F6 – pop. 129 – alt. 1,052
▶ Paris 697 – Barcelonette 35 – Digne-les-Bains 74 – Gap 40

La Palatrière

✆ 0492442098, *www.lapalatriere.com*
Address : site des Demoiselles Coiffées (4.6km south along the D 954, follow the signs for Savines-Lac)
Opening times : from beginning May to end Sept.
3 ha (30 pitches) terraced, flat, grassy, stony
Tariff : 24.50€ ✶✶ 🚐 🗐 🗓 (16A) – Extra per person 7€
Rental rates : (from beginning April to end Oct.) – 4 🛏 – 10 🏠. Per night from 49 to 100 €
Per week from 220 to 710 €
An attractive location overlooking the Lac de Serre-Ponçon.

Surroundings : 🏊 ≤ Lac de Serre-Ponçon and mountains ♋♋
Leisure activities : 🍷 ✗ 🖼 jacuzzi 🛶 ⅃
Facilities : ᕕ ⊶ ⑪ 🖾

Longitude : 6.34543
Latitude : 44.49909

SERRES

05700 – Michelin map **334** C6 – pop. 1,308 – alt. 670
▶ Paris 670 – Die 68 – Gap 41 – Manosque 89

Domaine des Deux Soleils ♛♜

✆ 0492670133, *www.domaine-2soleils.com* – alt. 800
Address : av. Des Pins – La Flamenche (800m southeast along the N 75, follow the signs for Sisteron then continue 1km along the turning to the left; at Super-Serres)
26 ha/12 ha for camping (72 pitches) terraced, flat, grassy, stony
Rentals : 8 🛏 – 19 🏠.
Many of the pitches are among trees, shrubs and bushes, in a natural setting.

Surroundings : 🏊 ⊏ ♀
Leisure activities : ✗ 🏕 🛶 ⅃ multi-sports ground
Facilities : ᕕ ⊶ 🛋 ⑪ 🖾 🚿

Longitude : 5.72767
Latitude : 44.4203

SEYNE

04140 – Michelin map **334** G6 – pop. 1,434 – alt. 1,200
▶ Paris 719 – Barcelonnette 43 – Digne-les-Bains 43 – Gap 54

Les Prairies

✆ 0492351021, *www.campinglesprairies.com*
Address : at Haute Gréyère, chemin Charcherie (located 1km south along the D 7, follow the signs for Auzet and take road to the left; beside the Blanche river)
Opening times : from end April to beginning Sept.
3.6 ha (100 pitches) open site, flat, grassy, stony
Tariff : (2012 price) 19.90€ ✶✶ 🚐 🗐 🗓 (10A) – Extra per person 5.60€ – Reservation fee 16€
Rental rates : (from end April to beginning Sept.) – 8 🛏 – 8 🏠. Per night from 47 to 85 €
Per week from 260 to 630 € – Reservation fee 16€
🚽 sani-station

Surroundings : 🏊 ≤ ⊏ ♋♋
Leisure activities : 🍷 ✗ 🖼 🛶 ⅃
Facilities : ᕕ ⊶ ▥ 🛋 launderette 🚿
Nearby : 🎿 🔲

Longitude : 6.35972
Latitude : 44.34262

SISTERON

04200 – Michelin map **334** D7 – pop. 7,427 – alt. 490
▶ Paris 704 – Barcelonnette 100 – Digne-les-Bains 40 – Gap 52

Municipal des Prés-Hauts

📞 04 92 61 19 69, *www.sisteron.fr*

Address : 44 chemin des Prés Hauts (3km north following signs for Gap and take D 951 to the right, follow the signs for La Motte-du-Caire, near the Durance river)

Opening times : from beginning April to end Sept.

4 ha (141 pitches) flat and relatively flat, grassy

Tariff : 25.70€ ✳✳ ⇐ 🗉 🕼 (10A) – Extra per person 4€ – Reservation fee 10€

Rental rates : (from beginning May to mid Sept.) 🕸 – 10 🚐. Per night from 90 to 135 €
Per week from 280 to 590 €

🚐 16 🗉 25.70€

The pitches well marked out in a green setting.

Surroundings : 🏊 ⇐ 🗔 ♭
Leisure activities : 🖾 ⚓ ✂ 🛝
Facilities : 🚻 ⛽ 🏛 ♨ 🚮 🚽 🛁

Longitude : 5.93645
Latitude : 44.21432

SOSPEL

06380 – Michelin map **341** F4 – pop. 3,523 – alt. 360
▶ Paris 967 – Breil-sur-Roya 21 – L'Escarène 22 – Lantosque 42

Domaine Ste-Madeleine

📞 04 93 04 10 48, *www.camping-sainte-madeleine.com*

Address : rte de Moulinet (4.5km northwest along the D 2566, follow the signs for Le Col de Turini)

Opening times : from beginning April to end Sept.

3 ha (90 pitches) terraced, grassy, stony

Tariff : 25€ ✳✳ ⇐ 🗉 🕼 (10A) – Extra per person 4.80€

Rental rates : (from beginning April to end Sept.) 🕸 (From beg Jul to end Aug) – 3 🚐 – 10 🏠. Per night from 55 to 80 € – Per week from 320 to 620 €

🚐 sani-station 3€

Surroundings : 🏊 ⇐ ♭♭
Leisure activities : 🛝
Facilities : 🚻 ⛽ 🚽 🚽 🛁

Longitude : 7.41575
Latitude : 43.8967

LE THOR

84250 – Michelin map **332** C10 – pop. 8,099 – alt. 50
▶ Paris 688 – Avignon 18 – Carpentras 16 – Cavaillon 14

FranceLoc Domaine Le Jantou

📞 04 90 33 90 07, *www.campings-franceloc.fr*

Address : 535 chemin des Coudelières (head 1.2km west via the northern exit towards Bédarrides; direct access to the Sorgue, recommended route via the D 1 (bypass))

Opening times : from beginning April to end Sept.

6 ha/4 ha for camping (195 pitches) flat, grassy

Tariff : (2012 price) 37€ ✳✳ ⇐ 🗉 🕼 (10A) – Extra per person 7€ – Reservation fee 11€

Rental rates : (2012 price) (from beginning April to end Sept.) – 9 caravans – 6 tents.
Per night from 61 to 107 € – Per week from 161 to 728 € – Reservation fee 27€

Surroundings : 🏊 ♭♭
Leisure activities : 🖾 ⚓ 🖂 🛝 ♨ 🎣
Facilities : 🚻 ⛽ 🏛 ♨ 🚽 🚽 🛁 launderette 🧊 refrigerators
Nearby : 🍴

Longitude : 4.98282
Latitude : 43.92969

LES THUILES

04400 – Michelin map **334** H6 – pop. 374 – alt. 1,130

Paris 752 – Marseille 221 – Digne-les-Bains 82 – Gap 62

Le Fontarache

𝄞 0492819042, www.camping-fontarache.com – alt. 1,108

Address : at Les Thuiles Basses (take the eastern exit of the town, D 900 follow the signs for Barcelonnette, near the Ubaye river)

Opening times : from beginning June to mid Sept.

6 ha (150 pitches) flat, stony, gravelled

Tariff : 23.20€ ✱✱ ⇌ ▣ ⒱ (6A) – Extra per person 5€ – Reservation fee 12€

Rental rates : (from beginning June to mid Sept.) ⚡ – 13 ⟐ – 2 ⟐.
Per night from 40 to 115 € – Per week from 250 to 650 € – Reservation fee 12€

🚐 sani-station 5€ – 📮 10€

Surroundings : ≤ ⊏ 🛈🛈

Leisure activities : 🍴 ✗ ⚒ multi-sports ground

Facilities : & ⚊ 🍴 launderette

Nearby : 🏊 ✗ 🚣 ≌ (lake), rafting and canyoning

GPS
Longitude : 6.57537
Latitude : 44.3924

Some campsites benefit from proximity to a municipal leisure centre.

VAISON-LA-ROMAINE

84110 – Michelin map **332** D8 – pop. 6,153 – alt. 193

Paris 664 – Avignon 51 – Carpentras 27 – Montélimar 64

FranceLoc Le Carpe Diem ♣♣

𝄞 0490360202, www.camping-carpe-diem.com

Address : rte de St-Marcellin (situated 2km southeast at the intersection of the D 938 (rte de Malaucène) and the D 151)

Opening times : from beginning April to beginning Nov.

10 ha/6.5 ha for camping (232 pitches) terraced, relatively flat, flat, grassy

Tariff : (2012 price) 39€ ✱✱ ⇌ ▣ ⒱ (10A) – Extra per person 7€ – Reservation fee 27€

Rental rates : (2012 price) (from beginning April to beginning Nov.) – 185 ⟐ – 14 ⟐ – 1 cabin in the trees – 8 tents. Per night from 33 to 168 € – Per week from 133 to 1,141 € Reservation fee 27€

🚐 sani-station

Reconstruction of a Roman amphitheatre by the swimming pool.

Surroundings : 🏊 ⊏ 🛈🛈

Leisure activities : 🍴 ✗ 🎱 ⊙ 🎣 🚣 🎰 🏊 ⚒

Facilities : & ⚊ 🏠 🍴 🖼 🏊 🚣 refrigerated food storage

GPS
Longitude : 5.08945
Latitude : 44.23424

Le Soleil de Provence

𝄞 0490464600, www.camping-soleil-de-provence.fr

Address : Trameiller quartier (3.5km northeast along the D 938, follow the signs for Nyons)

Opening times : from mid March to end Oct.

4 ha (153 pitches) terraced, relatively flat, flat, grassy, stony

Tariff : (2012 price) ✱ 7.50€ ⇌ 6€ ▣ 6€ – ⒱ (10A) 4€ – Reservation fee 10€

Rental rates : (2012 price) (from mid May to end Oct.) ⚡ – 26 ⟐.
Per week from 280 to 690 € – Reservation fee 10€

🚐 sani-station 2€ – 4 ▣

Surroundings : ≤ Ventoux and mountains of Nyons ⊏ 🛈

Leisure activities : 🎱 🎣 🏊 ⚒

Facilities : & ⚊ 🚿 🕮 🏠 🍴 🖼

GPS
Longitude : 5.10616
Latitude : 44.26838

Théâtre Romain

📞 0490287866, www.camping-theatre.com

Address : Les Arts quartier – Chemin du Brusquet (to the northeast of the town, recommended route via the bypass (rocade)

Opening times : from mid March to mid Nov.

1.2 ha (75 pitches) flat, grassy, fine gravel

Tariff : ♦ 8€ ⇦ 🅴 9€ – [⨏] (10A) 4.50€ – Reservation fee 11€

Rental rates : (from mid March to mid Nov.) – 9 ⟦⟧. Per night from 35 to 95 €
Per week from 220 to 650 € – Reservation fee 11€

🚻 sani-station 5€ – 🚐14€

Surroundings : ⌖ ♧♧
Leisure activities : 🎮 ⚓ ⅃ (small swimming pool)
Facilities : ♿ ⟲ 🛉 ⚴ ⬚ ♈ 🔲
Nearby : ✗

GPS — Longitude : 5.07843 / Latitude : 44.24505

A 'quartier' is a district or area of a town or village.

VENCE

06140 – Michelin map **341** D5 – pop. 19,183 – alt. 325
▶ Paris 923 – Antibes 20 – Cannes 30 – Grasse 24

Domaine de la Bergerie

📞 0493580936, www.camping-domainedelabergerie.com

Address : 1330 chemin de la Sine (4km west along the D 2210, follow the signs for Grasse and take road to the left)

Opening times : from end March to mid Oct.

30 ha/13 ha for camping (450 pitches) terraced, flat, grassy, stony

Tariff : (2012 price) 30.50€ ♦♦ ⇦ 🅴 [⨏] (5A) – Extra per person 5.10€ – Reservation fee 15€

🚻 sani-station 4€

In a very pleasant natural setting on the site of an old sheep farm that has been attractively restored.

Surroundings : ⟿ ⌖ ♧♧♧
Leisure activities : ♈ ✗ ⚓ ✗ ⅃
Facilities : ♿ ⟲ 🔲🛉 ⚴ ♈ launderette ⚏ ⬚
Nearby : sports trail

GPS — Longitude : 7.08981 / Latitude : 43.71253

LE VERNET

04140 – Michelin map **334** G7 – pop. 123 – alt. 1,200
▶ Paris 729 – Digne-les-Bains 32 – La Javie 16 – Gap 68

Lou Passavous

📞 0492351467, www.loupassavous.com

Address : rte Roussimal (800m north following signs for Roussimat; beside the Bès river)

Opening times : from beginning May to mid Sept.

1.5 ha (60 pitches) open site, relatively flat, flat, grassy, stony

Tariff : (2012 price) 25.25€ ♦♦ ⇦ 🅴 [⨏] (6A) – Extra per person 3.50€ – Reservation fee 12.50€

Rental rates : (2012 price) (from beginning May to mid Sept.) ⚿ – 2 ⟦⟧ – 2 tent bungalows.
Per week from 450 to 700 € – Reservation fee 12.50€

Surroundings : ⟿ ⚘♀
Leisure activities : ♈ ✗ ⚓
Facilities : ♿ ⟲ 🔲 🛉 ♈ 🔲 ⬚
Nearby : ✗ ⅃ ↝ ⚞

GPS — Longitude : 6.39139 / Latitude : 44.28194

VEYNES

05400 – Michelin map **334** C5 – pop. 3,166 – alt. 827
▶ Paris 660 – Aspres-sur-Buëch 9 – Gap 25 – Sisteron 51

⚠ Les Prés

℘ 04 92 57 26 22, *www.camping-les-pres.com* – alt. 960 – ⛺

Address : at le Petit Vaux (3.4km northeast along the D 994 follow the signs for Gap, then continue 5.5km along the D 937 following signs for Superdevoluy and take road to the left via the bridge over the Béoux)

Opening times : from beginning May to end Sept.

0.35 ha (25 pitches) flat and relatively flat, grassy

Tariff : (2012 price) 17.95 € ✸✸ ⛟ 🅴 🕻 (6A) – Extra per person 3.65 € – Reservation fee 30 €

Rental rates : (2012 price) (from beginning May to end Sept.) – 1 caravan – 3 tent bungalows. Per night from 42 to 63 € – Per week from 280 to 435 €

🚉 sani-station

> Surroundings : 🌲 ⩽ ♀
> Facilities : ⴆ ⊶ 🚿 🍴 🖼

GPS	Longitude : 5.84995 Latitude : 44.58842

VILLAR-LOUBIÈRE

05800 – Michelin map **334** E4 – pop. 48 – alt. 1,026
▶ Paris 648 – La Chapelle-en-Valgaudémar 5 – Corps 22 – Gap 43

⚠ Municipal Les Gravières

℘ 04 92 55 35 35, *http://www.sudrafting.fr/camping-villar-loubiere.html*

Address : 700m east following signs for La Chapelle-en-Valgaudémar and take the road to the right

Opening times : from mid June to mid Sept.

2 ha (50 pitches) flat, grassy, stony, wood

Tariff : 14 € ✸✸ ⛟ 🅴 🕻 (2A) – Extra per person 2.60 € – Reservation fee 3.60 €

🚉 5 🅴 15 €

A good choice for fans of whitewater sports.

> Surroundings : 🌲 ⩽ ♀♀
> Leisure activities : 🎣 ⚲ 🪁 rafting and canyoning
> Facilities : ⴆ (Jul–Aug) 🖼

GPS	Longitude : 6.1464 Latitude : 44.82373

Gîtes range from small maisonettes to old farmhouses with several bedrooms.

VILLARS-COLMARS

04370 – Michelin map **334** H7 – pop. 246 – alt. 1,225
▶ Paris 774 – Annot 37 – Barcelonnette 46 – Colmars 3

⚠ Le Haut-Verdon

℘ 04 92 83 40 09, *www.lehautverdon.com* – access via Col d'Allos strictly not advised

Address : 0.6km south along the D 908, follow the signs for Castellane; beside the Verdon river

Opening times : from beginning May to end Sept.

3.5 ha (109 pitches) flat, stony

Tariff : 28 € ✸✸ ⛟ 🅴 🕻 (10A) – Extra per person 5 € – Reservation fee 15 €

Rental rates : (permanent) – 7 🚐 – 4 🏠. Per week from 270 to 700 € – Reservation fee 15 €

🚉 sani-station 3 €

> Surroundings : ⩽ 🌳 ♀♀
> Leisure activities : 🍽 ✗ 🎣 🚣 ⚲ 🏊 🪁
> Facilities : ⊶ 🚿 🍴 🖼 ⚿

GPS	Longitude : 6.60573 Latitude : 44.1604

VILLECROZE

83690 – Michelin map **340** M4 – pop. 1,128 – alt. 300
▶ Paris 835 – Aups 8 – Brignoles 38 – Draguignan 21

Le Ruou ♠♨

℘ 04 94 70 67 70, *www.leruou.com* – limited spaces for one-night stay
Address : 309 RD 560 (5.4km southeast along the D 251, follow the signs for Barbebelle and take D 560, follow the signs for Flayosc, recommended route via the D 560)
Opening times : from mid April to mid Oct.
4.3 ha (134 pitches) very uneven, terraced, flat, grassy
Tariff : (2012 price) ♦ 5.50€ ⇆ 2.50€ ▣ 19.50€ – ⚡ (10A) 5€ – Reservation fee 25€
Rental rates : (2012 price) (from mid April to mid Oct.) – 39 ⛺ – 19 ⌂ – 26 tent bungalows.
Per night from 23 to 140 € – Per week from 161 to 980 € – Reservation fee 25€
🚻 sani-station 5€
The pretty pitches are set out on terraces.

Surroundings : ≤ 🌳🌳
Leisure activities : ♈ ✕ 🎬 🛶 🏊 🎿
Facilities : ⚐ ⛟ ▣ 🚿 ⚑ launderette 🛒

GPS Longitude : 6.29796
Latitude : 43.55343

A chambre d'hôte is a guesthouse or B & B-style accommodation.

VILLENEUVE-LOUBET-PLAGE

06270 – Michelin map **341**
▶ Paris 919 – Marseille 191 – Nice 24 – Monaco 38

La Vieille Ferme

℘ 04 93 33 41 44, *www.vieilleferme.com*
Address : 296 bd des Groules (2.8km south along the N 7, follow the signs for Antibes and take a right turn)
Opening times : Permanent
2.9 ha (153 pitches) terraced, flat, grassy, fine gravel
Tariff : 42.94€ ♦♦ ⇆ ▣ ⚡ (10A) – Extra per person 6€ – Reservation fee 28€
Rental rates : (permanent) – 32 ⛺ – 32 ⌂. Per night from 55 to 120 €
Per week from 350 to 850 € – Reservation fee 28€

Surroundings : ⛱ 🌳🌳
Leisure activities : ✕ 🎬 🌀 daytime, jacuzzi 🏊 🖼 (open-air in season)
Facilities : ⚐ ⛟ ▥ 🚿 🛁 ⚑ launderette 🛒 refrigerated food storage

GPS Longitude : 7.12579
Latitude : 43.61967

Parc des Maurettes

℘ 04 93 20 91 91, *www.parcdesmaurettes.com*
Address : 730 av. du Dr Lefèbvre (along the N 7)
Opening times : from beginning Jan. to mid Nov.
2 ha (140 pitches) terraced, stony, gravelled
Tariff : (2012 price) 37.35€ ♦♦ ⇆ ▣ ⚡ (16A) – Extra per person 5.40€ – Reservation fee 25€
Rental rates : (2012 price) (from beginning Jan. to mid Nov.) – 14 ⌂ – 2 ⇚ – 3 studios.
Per night from 59 to 123 € – Per week from 372 to 736 € – Reservation fee 25€
🚻 sani-station 6€ – 5 ▣ 15.75€
A pleasant spa and relaxation area.

Surroundings : ⛱ 🌳🌳
Leisure activities : 🎬 ⇄ jacuzzi 🏊
Facilities : ⚐ ⛟ 🅿 ▥ 🛁 ⚑ launderette 🛒
Nearby : 🍴

GPS Longitude : 7.12964
Latitude : 43.63111

L'Hippodrome

📞 04 93 20 02 00, *www.camping-hippodrome.com*
Address : 5 av. des Rives (400m from the beach, behind the Géant Casino commercial centre)
Opening times : permanent
0.8 ha (46 pitches) flat, fine gravel
Tariff : 34 € ♦♦ 🚐 🗐 🚿 (10A) – Extra per person 5.55 € – Reservation fee 16 €
Rental rates : (permanent) 🏠 – 15 🏠 – 15 studios. Per night from 46 to 70 €
Per week from 320 to 490 € – Reservation fee 16 €
🚰 sani-station

Surroundings : 🏕 🎣
Leisure activities : 🎯 ⛵ 🏊 (open-air in season)
Facilities : ♿ 🚿 🚽 🚻 🔥 launderette, refrigerators
Nearby : 🛒 ✕

GPS
Longitude : 7.13771
Latitude : 43.64199

VILLES-SUR-AUZON

84570 – Michelin map **332** E9 – pop. 1,296 – alt. 255
🔃 Paris 694 – Avignon 45 – Carpentras 19 – Malaucène 24

Les Verguettes

📞 04 90 61 88 18, *www.provence-camping.com*
Address : rte de Carpentras (take the western exit along the D 942)
2 ha (88 pitches) terraced, relatively flat, flat, grassy, stony
Rentals : 6 🏠.
🚰 sani-station

Surroundings : 🌿 ≤ Mont Ventoux 🏕 🎣
Leisure activities : 🎯 🏓 🏊
Facilities : ♿ 🚿 🚽 🚻 🔥 🗄 refrigerators

GPS
Longitude : 5.22834
Latitude : 44.05686

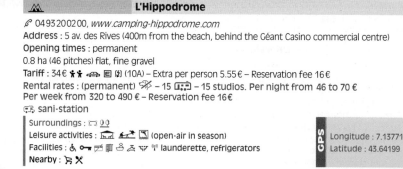

Key to rentals symbols :

12 🏠	*Number of mobile homes*	
20 🏡	*Number of chalets*	
6 🛏	*Number of rooms to rent*	
Per night 30–50€	*Minimum/maximum rate per night*	
Per week 300–1,000€	*Minimum/maximum rate per week*	

VIOLÈS

84150 – Michelin map **332** C9 – pop. 1,546 – alt. 94
🔃 Paris 659 – Avignon 34 – Carpentras 21 – Nyons 33

Les Favards

📞 04 90 70 90 93, *www.favards.com*
Address : rte d'Orange (1.2km west along the D 67)
20 ha/1.5 (49 pitches) flat, grassy
Rentals : 1 tent bungalow – 1 gîte.
Situated in the heart of a vineyard

Surroundings : 🌿 ≤ 🏕 🎣
Leisure activities : 🍷 🏊
Facilities : ♿ 🚿 🚻 🗄 refrigerated food storage

GPS
Longitude : 4.93528
Latitude : 44.16229

VISAN

84820 – Michelin map **332** C8 – pop. 1,956 – alt. 218
▶ Paris 652 – Avignon 57 – Bollène 19 – Nyons 20

⚠ L'Hérein

🕿 04 90 41 95 99, www.campingvisan.com
Address : rte de Bouchet (located 1km west along the D 161, follow the signs for Bouchet; near a stream)
Opening times : from end March to mid Oct.
3.3 ha (75 pitches) flat, grassy, stony
Tariff : (2012 price) 16 € ✶ ✶ ⇌ 🔲 ⚡ (10A) – Extra per person 4.50 € – Reservation fee 10 €
Rental rates : (2012 price) (from end March to mid Oct.) – 4 🚐. Per night from 45 to 65 €
Per week from 285 to 360 € – Reservation fee 10 €
🚐 sani-station – 120 🔲 11 €

Surroundings : 🌳 ⌂ 🎲🎲
Leisure activities : ✕ 🛶 🔥 m ⛷
Facilities : ♿ ⚬⟞ ⬚ 🚿 🗑 ⁙ 🔲 🛒

GPS Longitude : 4.93601
Latitude : 44.31236

VOLONNE

04290 – Michelin map **334** E8 – pop. 1,658 – alt. 450
▶ Paris 718 – Château-Arnoux-St-Aubin 4 – Digne-les-Bains 29 – Forcalquier 33

⛰ Sunêlia L'Hippocampe ♣↓

🕿 04 92 33 50 00, www.l-hippocampe.com
Address : rte Napoléon (500m southeast along the D 4)
Opening times : from beginning May to end Sept.
8 ha (447 pitches) flat, grassy, fruit trees
Tariff : 40 € ✶ ✶ ⇌ 🔲 ⚡ (10A) – Extra per person 7 € – Reservation fee 30 €
Rental rates : (from beginning May to end Sept.) – 203 🚐 – 42 🏠 – 16 tent bungalows.
Per night from 35 to 214 € – Per week from 245 to 1,498 € – Reservation fee 30 €
🚐 sani-station 5 € – 🔌 ⚡ 11 €
In a pleasant setting, beside the Durance river.

Surroundings : ⬳ ⌂ 🎲🎲
Leisure activities : 🍸 ✕ 🎲 🏊 🔥 🎱 ⛷ 🏊 disco, pedalos ⛷
entertainment room
Facilities : ♿ ⚬⟞ 🔲🚿 🚿 ⁙ ⁙ launderette 🏊 🛒

GPS Longitude : 6.0173
Latitude : 44.1054

VOLX

04130 – Michelin map **334** D9 – pop. 2,953 – alt. 350
▶ Paris 748 – Digne-les-Bains 51 – Forcalquier 15 – Gréoux-les-Bains 22

⚠ Flower La Vandelle

🕿 04 92 79 35 85, www.camping-lavandelle.com
Address : av. de la Vandelle (1.3km southwest of the town)
2 ha (50 pitches) flat, grassy, wood
Rentals : 2 tent bungalows – 1 tent.

Surroundings : 🌳 🎲🎲
Leisure activities : ⛷
Facilities : ♿ ⚬⟞ ⁙ 🔲

GPS Longitude : 5.83162
Latitude : 43.869

RHÔNE-ALPES

Gérard Labriet / Photononstop

Rhône-Alpes is a region of contrasts and a cultural crossroads. Its lofty peaks are a snow-covered paradise for skiers, climbers and hikers, drawn by the beauty of its shimmering glaciers and tranquil lakes; stylish Chamonix and Courchevel set the tone and the pace in cool Alpine chic. Descend from the roof of Europe, past herds of cattle on the mountain pastures and into the bustle of the Rhône valley. From Roman roads to speedy TGVs, playing host to the main arteries between north and south has forged the region's reputation for economic drive. Holidaymakers may rush through Rhône-Alpes in summer but those in the know linger to enjoy its culinary specialities. The region boasts a host of Michelin-starred restaurants: three-starred trendsetters and the legendary neighbourhood *bouchons* (small, family-run bistros) of Lyon, capital of this gastronomic paradise, make it a compulsory stop. Enjoy a Bresse chicken, cheese and sausages from Lyon and a glass of Côtes du Rhône.

LAUSANNE

● Locality with campsite
■ Locality with campsite and rental option
Vannes Locality with campsite and campervan area
Moyaux Locality with at least one pleasant campsite
Motorway service area for campervans

St-Laurent-en-Grandvaux
nlieu
x-les-Lacs
Divonne-les-Bains
Excenevex
Evian-les-B.
Lugrin
Thonon-les-Bains
Claude
Gex
Sciez
Châtel
Morzine
les Gets
Taninges
Verchaix
Samoëns
Vallorcine
Argentière
les Bossons
les Praz-de-Chamonix
Chamonix-Mont-Blanc
St-Gervais-les-Bains
HAUTE-
SAVOIE
Neydens
Groisy
Bonneville
SAVOIE
le Grand-Bornand
la Clusaz
Sallanches
Seyssel
La Balme-de-S.
Alex
Vallières
ANNECY
Menthon-St-Bernard
Mégève
Rumilly
Sévrier
Duingt
Praz-s-Arly
Ruffieux
St-Jorioz
Bout-du-Lac
Chanaz
Lathuile
ssignieu-de-Rives
Doussard
Beaufort
Aix-les-Bains
Lescheraines
Albertville
Le Bourget-du-Lac
le Châtelard
Bourg-St-Maurice
Séez
la Rosière 1850
L'ARCLUSAZ
CHAMBÉRY
Aigueblanche
Montchavin
aise-Lac
Lépin-le-lac
Challes-les-Eaux
VAL-GELON
Brides-les-Bains
lban-
ontbel
les Marches
SAVOIE
Pralognan-la-Vanoise
la Rochette
Termignon
Lanslevillard
St-Laurent-du-Pont
Allevard
St-Jean-de-Maurienne
St-Pierre-
a-Chartreuse
la Ferrière
Aussois
St-Colomban-des-Villards
Villarembert
Bramans
GRENOBLE
la Toussuire
Valloire
TORINO
Vizille
le Bourg-d'Oisans
la Grave
N 85
Petichet
le Bourg-d'Arud
Névache
héoffroy
St-Laurent-en-Beaumont
St-Christophe-en-Oisans
Salle-
Beaumont
Villar-Loubière
HAUTE-
alley
Pont-du-Fossé
la-
aute
la Roche-des-Arnaud
Ancelle
Gap
Chorges
Veynes
Espinasses
Curbans
Col St-Jean
Seyne
Clamensane
ALPES-
Sisteron
PRO
Volonne
Digne-le-
Peyruis
St-André-les-Alpes

C

St-Cirgues-en-Montagne
Privas
St-Julien-en-St-Alban
Meyras
N 102
Ucel
Darbres
Cruas
Jaujac
St-Privat
ARDÈCHE
Aubenas
St-Jean-le-Centenier
Montélimar
St-Laurent-les-Bains
Joannas
Chassiers
Vogüé
Montréal
Laurac-en-V.
Largentière
St-Maurice-d'A.
Sablières
Ribes
Chauzon
Pradons
St-Maurice-d'Ibie
Viviers
Joyeuse
Rosières
Ruoms
Larnas
DRÔME
Malarce-s-la-Thines
Chassagnes
Auriolles
St-Alban
les Mazes
Gravières
les Vans
Sampzon
St-Remèze
Le Chambon
Casteljau
Vallon-Pont-d'Arc
St-Martin-d'Ardèche
Berrias et Casteljau
Maison-Neuve
Salavas
St-Just
Malbosc
Vagnas
Orgnac-l'Aven
St-Sauveur-de-Cruzières
Barjac
Bollène
Bessèges
Cèze
GARD
84
St-Victor-de-Malcap
Boisson
Goudargues

48

N 94

A 57

A 51

D 104

N 102

RHÔNE

A 7

LES ABRETS

38490 – Michelin map **333** G4 – pop. 3,186 – alt. 398
▶ Paris 514 – Aix-les-Bains 45 – Belley 31 – Chambéry 38

Le Coin Tranquille ♨

🕿 04 76 32 13 48, *www.coin-tranquille.com*

Address : 6 chemin des Vignes (head 2.3km east along the N 6, follow the signs for Le Pont-de-Beauvoisin and take turning to the left)

Opening times : from end March to end Oct.

4 ha (180 pitches) relatively flat, flat, grassy

Tariff : 34.50€ ✦✦ 🚐 🔲 ⚡ (6A) – Extra per person 7.50€ – Reservation fee 16€

Rental rates : (from end March to beginning Nov.) 🅿 – 15 🏠. Per night from 80 to 120€
Per week from 315 to 840€ – Reservation fee 31€

🚰 sani-station

Surroundings : ⅍ ⌑ 🎿
Leisure activities : 🍴 ✕ 🎦 🎇 daytime 🎠 🚣 🚴 🏊
Facilities : ♿ ⚲ 🔲 🗄 ⛺ 🍴 launderette 🪣 🚿

Longitude : 5.6084
Latitude : 45.54139

AIGUEBLANCHE

73260 – Michelin map **333** M4 – pop. 3,129 – alt. 461
▶ Paris 641 – Lyon 174 – Chambéry 74 – Albertville 25

Marie-France

🕿 04 79 24 22 21, *www.camping-studios-savoie.com*

Address : 453 av. de Savoie

0.5 ha (30 pitches) terraced, flat, grassy

Rentals : 15 🏠 – 15 studios – 5 apartments.

🚰 sani-station – 10 🔲

Surroundings : ⋖ ⌑ 🎿
Leisure activities : 🎣
Facilities : ♿ ⚲ 🍴 🖼
Leisure/activities centre : 🍴 ✕ 🏤 🚣 ✂ 🎳 🏂 🏊 ⛷ 🦆 🐎
sports trail, rafting and canyoning

Longitude : 6.48946
Latitude : 45.50924

AIX-LES-BAINS

73100 – Michelin map **333** I3 – pop. 26,819 – alt. 200 – ♨
▶ Paris 539 – Annecy 34 – Bourg-en-Bresse 115 – Chambéry 18

International du Sierroz

🕿 04 79 61 21 43, *www.camping-sierroz.com*

Address : bd Robert Barrier (2.5km to the northwest)

Opening times : from mid March to mid Nov.

5 ha (290 pitches) flat, grassy, gravelled

Tariff : 23.70€ ✦✦ 🚐 🔲 ⚡ (10A) – Extra per person 4.50€ – Reservation fee 12€

Rental rates : (from mid March to mid Nov.) – 34 🚐. Per night from 44 to 97€
Per week from 266 to 644€ – Reservation fee 12€

🚰 sani-station 5€

A wooded site, near a lake.

Surroundings : ⌑ 🎿
Leisure activities : 🍴 🎦
Facilities : ♿ ⚲ 🔲 🗄 🪣 ⛺ 🍴 launderette 🪣 🚿
Nearby : 🏖 🦆 💧

Longitude : 5.88628
Latitude : 45.70104

ALEX

4290 – Michelin map **328** K5 – pop. 980 – alt. 589
▶ Paris 545 – Albertville 42 – Annecy 12 – La Clusaz 20

▲ La Ferme des Ferrières

℘ 0450028709, www.camping-des-ferrieres.com
Address : located 1.5km west along the D 909, follow the signs for Annecy and take the road to the right
Opening times : from beginning June to end Sept.
5 ha (200 pitches) relatively flat, grassy
Tariff : (2012 price) 15.30€ ♦♦ ⇔ 回 ⁅⁆ (6A) – Extra per person 2.70€

Surroundings : ⊗ ≤ ⓞ
Leisure activities : ⚑ ⛱ ⛵
Facilities : ♿ ⊶ ⤱ ⏚ ▨

Longitude : 6.22346
Latitude : 45.89015

ALLEVARD

8580 – Michelin map **333** J5 – pop. 3,768 – alt. 470 – ⚕
▶ Paris 593 – Albertville 50 – Chambéry 33 – Grenoble 40

▲▲ Clair Matin

℘ 0476975519, www.camping-clair-matin.com
Address : 20 r. des Pommiers (take the southwestern exit along the D 525, follow the signs for Grenoble to the right)
Opening times : from mid April to mid Oct.
5.5 ha (200 pitches) terraced, relatively flat, flat, grassy
Tariff : 27.25€ ♦♦ ⇔ 回 ⁅⁆ (10A) – Extra per person 4.15€ – Reservation fee 8€
Rental rates : (from end April to beginning Oct.) – 29 ⛺ – 2 ⌂. Per night from 30 to 128€
Per week from 207 to 916€ – Reservation fee 13€
⛽ sani-station – 5 回 13.45€ – ⛟ 11€

Surroundings : ⊗ ≤ ⓞⓞ
Leisure activities : ✗ ⛱ ▨
Facilities : ♿ ⊶ ⏚ ⏛ ⤲ ⁌ launderette
Nearby : ⏛

Longitude : 6.06591
Latitude : 45.38869

ANSE

69480 – Michelin map **327** H4 – pop. 5,604 – alt. 170
▶ Paris 436 – L'Arbresle 17 – Bourg-en-Bresse 57 – Lyon 27

▲▲▲ Les Portes du Beaujolais

℘ 0474671287, www.camping-beaujolais.com
Address : 495 av. Jean Vacher (take the southeastern exit, follow the signs for Lyon and 600m along the road to the left before the bridge, where the Azergues and the Saône rivers meet)
Opening times : from beginning March to end Oct.
7.5 ha (198 pitches) flat, grassy
Tariff : 27.50€ ♦♦ ⇔ 回 ⁅⁆ (16A) – Extra per person 4.80€ – Reservation fee 2€
Rental rates : (permanent) – 25 ⛺ – 40 ⌂ – 1 teepee – 1 tent. Per night from 40 to 190€
Per week from 315 to 1,149€ – Reservation fee 5€
⛽ sani-station

Surroundings : ⊡ ⓞ
Leisure activities : ⚑ ✗ ⛱ ⛵ ⚲ ⁁ ▨ ⟁
Facilities : ♿ ⊶ ⌨ ⊪ ⏛ ⤲ ⁌ ▨ ⏛
Nearby : ⊼

Longitude : 4.72616
Latitude : 45.94106

ARGENTIÈRE

74400 – Michelin map **328** O5 – alt. 1,252 – Winter sports : Chamonix
▶ Paris 619 – Annecy 106 – Chamonix-Mont-Blanc 10 – Vallorcine 10

Le Glacier d'Argentière

☎ 04 50 54 17 36, *www.campingchamonix.com*
Address : 161 chemin des Chosalets (located 1km south following signs for Chamonix, 200m from the Arve river)
1 ha (80 pitches) sloping, grassy

Surroundings : ⩽ ⊉
Leisure activities : 🎦
Facilities : 🔥 ⊶ launderette

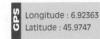
Longitude : 6.92363
Latitude : 45.9747

ARTEMARE

01510 – Michelin map **328** H5 – pop. 1,112 – alt. 245
▶ Paris 506 – Aix-les-Bains 33 – Ambérieu-en-Bugey 47 – Belley 18

Le Vaugrais

☎ 04 79 87 37 34, *www.camping-le-vaugrais.fr*
Address : 2 chemin le Vaugrais (700m west along the D 69d, follow the signs for Belmont; beside the Séran at Cerveyrieu)
Opening times : from beginning Feb. to mid Nov.
1 ha (33 pitches) flat, grassy
Tariff : (2012 price) 14.50€ ✦✦ ⇔ 🗉 [⚡] (6A) – Extra per person 3.50€ – Reservation fee 7€
Rental rates : (2012 price) (from beginning Feb. to mid Nov.) – 6 🛏 – 1 🏠.
Per night from 65 to 110€ – Per week from 185 to 620€ – Reservation fee 7€

Surroundings : ⩽ ▭ ⊉
Leisure activities : 🍽 🎦 🚣 🚲 🛶 🎣
Facilities : 🔥 ⊶ 🏭 🚿 ♨ 🍴 🖼

Longitude : 5.68383
Latitude : 45.87465

*Using the traditional Michelin classification method, the guide provides
you with an easy, speedy reference for assessing the category of each site:
1 to 5 tents (see page 10).*

AUSSOIS

73500 – Michelin map **333** N6 – pop. 677 – alt. 1,489
▶ Paris 670 – Albertville 97 – Chambéry 110 – Lanslebourg-Mont-Cenis 17

Municipal la Buidonnière

☎ 04 79 20 35 58, *www.camping-aussois.com*
Address : rte de Cottériat (take the southern exit along the D 215, follow the signs for Modane and take road to the left)
Opening times : permanent
4 ha (160 pitches) terraced, relatively flat, stony, grassy
Tariff : 18.50€ ✦✦ ⇔ 🗉 [⚡] (10A) – Extra per person 6.40€
🚐 sani-station 2€
Free shuttle service to the ski lifts.

Surroundings : ❄ 🌄 ⩽ Parc de la Vanoise ▭
Leisure activities : 🎦 🚣 ⚔ ♨ 🎿 (pool), sports trail
Facilities : 🔥 ⊶ 🏭 🍴 launderette

Longitude : 6.74586
Latitude : 45.22432

AUTRANS

38880 – Michelin map **333** G6 – pop. 1,676 – alt. 1,050 – Winter sports : 1,050/1,650 m 13
▶ Paris 586 – Grenoble 36 – Romans-sur-Isère 58 – St-Marcellin 47

Yelloh! Village au Joyeux Réveil

04 76 95 33 44, *www.camping-au-joyeux-reveil.fr*
Address : at le Château (take the northeastern exit following signs for Montaud and take a right turn)
Opening times : from beginning May to end Sept.
1.5 ha (100 pitches) flat, grassy
Tariff : 43 € (6A) – Extra per person 8 € – Reservation fee 10 €
Rental rates : (from beginning May to end Sept.) – 30 . Per night from 45 to 162 €
Per week from 315 to 1,134 €– Reservation fee 15 €
sani-station 5 €
Some luxury rental options are available.

Surroundings :
Leisure activities : hammam, jacuzzi
spa therapy centre
Facilities :

GPS Longitude : 5.54844
Latitude : 45.17555

BALAZUC

07120 – Michelin map **331** I6 – pop. 336 – alt. 170
▶ Paris 651 – Lyon 188 – Privas 45 – Montpellier 133

Le Chamadou

08 20 36 61 97, *www.camping-le-chamadou.com*
Address : at Mas de Chaussy (3.2km southeast along the D 579, follow the signs for Ruoms and take road to the left, 500m from a lake)
Opening times : from beginning April to end Oct.
1 ha (86 pitches) relatively flat, flat, grassy
Tariff : (2012 price) 25 € (10A) – Extra per person 6 € – Reservation fee 14 €
Rental rates : (from beginning April to end Oct.) – 24 . Per night from 32 to 120 €
Per week from 250 to 1,200 € – Reservation fee 14 €

Surroundings :
Leisure activities :
Facilities :
Nearby :

GPS Longitude : 4.40384
Latitude : 44.50826

BALBIGNY

42510 – Michelin map **327** E5 – pop. 2,809 – alt. 331
▶ Paris 423 – Feurs 10 – Noirétable 44 – Roanne 29

La Route Bleue

04 77 27 24 97, *Http://camping-de-la-route-bleue.fr* –
Address : at Pralery (2.8km northwest along the N 82 and turn left onto D 56, follow the signs for St-Georges-de-Baroille)
Opening times : from mid March to end Oct.
2 ha (100 pitches) relatively flat, flat, grassy
Tariff : (2012 price) 20 € (10A) – Extra per person 5 €
In a pleasant location beside the Loire river.

Surroundings :
Leisure activities :
Facilities : launderette

GPS Longitude : 4.15725
Latitude : 45.82719

LA BALME-DE-SILLINGY

74330 – Michelin map **328** J5 – pop. 4,891 – alt. 480
▶ Paris 524 – Dijon 250 – Grenoble 111 – Lons-le-Saunier 136

△ La Caille

✆ 0450688521, *www.domainedelacaille.com*
Address : 18 ch. de la Caille (4km north on N 508 towards Frangy and take the road to the right)
4 ha/1 ha for camping (30 pitches) relatively flat, flat, grassy
Rentals : Ⓟ – 13 🚐 – 13 🏠 – 7 ⛺ – 2 gîtes.

Surroundings : 🏞 ▭ ♨
Leisure activities : ♈ ✗ 🛶 🚴 ⚞ 🏊
Facilities : ♿ ⛱ 🅰 🔧

GPS Longitude : 6.03609 / Latitude : 45.97828

BARBIÈRES

26300 – Michelin map **332** D4 – pop. 771 – alt. 426
▶ Paris 586 – Lyon 124 – Valence 23 – Grenoble 79

△ Le Gallo-Romain

✆ 0475474407, *www.legalloromain.net*
Address : rte du Col de Tourniol (1.2km southeast along the D 101; beside the Barberolle river)
3 ha (62 pitches) terrace, flat and relatively flat, stony, grassy
Rentals : 13 🚐.

Surroundings : 🏞 ⩻ ▭ ♨♨
Leisure activities : ♈ ✗ 🛶 🏊 ⚓
Facilities : ♿ ⛱ 🗄 ⛺ launderette 🔧 refrigerators

GPS Longitude : 5.15092 / Latitude : 44.94456

BEAUFORT

73270 – Michelin map **333** M3 – pop. 2,206 – alt. 750
▶ Paris 601 – Albertville 21 – Chambéry 72 – Megève 37

△ **Municipal Domelin**

✆ 0479383388, *camping-beaufort@orange.fr*
Address : in the town (RD 925)
Opening times : from beginning June to end Sept.
2 ha (100 pitches) relatively flat, flat, grassy
Tariff : (2012 price) ♦ 3.67 € 🚗 2.25 € 🔲 3 € – 🔌 (10A) 3 €

Surroundings : 🏞 ⩻ ♨
Facilities : ♿ ⛱ (Jul–Aug) ⛱ launderette
Nearby : ⚞ 🏊 ⛷ ⚓ sports trail, leisure and activity park/centre

GPS Longitude : 6.56403 / Latitude : 45.7218

BELMONT-DE-LA-LOIRE

42670 – Michelin map **327** F3 – pop. 1,515 – alt. 525
▶ Paris 405 – Chauffailles 6 – Roanne 35 – St-Étienne 108

△ Municipal les Écureuils

✆ 0477637225, *www.belmontdelaloire.fr*
Address : at the base de loisirs du plan d'eau (leisure centre by the lake) (1.4km west along the D 4,
follow the signs for Charlieu and take road to the left, 300m from a lake)
0.6 ha (28 pitches) terraced, relatively flat to hilly, gravelled, grassy
Rentals : 8 🏠.
🚐 sani-station – 2 🔲
Situated beside a leisure and activity park.

Surroundings : 🏞 ▭
Leisure activities : 🚣
Facilities : 🅰
Nearby : ✗ ⚓

GPS Longitude : 4.33819 / Latitude : 46.1662

ENIVAY-OLLON

5170 – Michelin map **332** E8 – pop. 66 – alt. 450
Paris 689 – Lyon 227 – Valence 126 – Avignon 71

L'Écluse

☎ 0475280732, *www.campecluse.com*
Address : at Barastrage (located 1km south on the D 347; beside a stream)
Opening times : from mid April to end Sept.
4 ha (75 pitches) undulating, terraced, flat, fine gravel, stony, grassy
Tariff : 24€ ✦✦ 🚐 🗐 ⚡ (6A) – Extra per person 6€ – Reservation fee 20€
Rental rates : (from mid April to end Sept.) ⚹ 🐾 (Jul–Aug) – 12 🚐 – 12 🏠 – 2 gîtes.
Per night from 60 to 120€ – Per week from 300 to 770€ – Reservation fee 20€
The site is shaded by cherry trees and surrounded by vineyards.

Surroundings : 🏊 ⇐ 🌳
Leisure activities : ♈ ✕ 🎱 🚣 ⤢ ⛷ 🎣
Facilities : ⚹ 🚿 🚽 ♨ 🚰
GPS
Longitude : 5.18545
Latitude : 44.30298

---

*For more information on visiting particular towns or regions, consult the
relevant regional MICHELIN Green Guide. We also recommend you use
the appropriate Michelin regional map to locate your selected campsite,
to calculate distances and to work out the best route.*

ERRIAS ET CASTELJAU

7460 – Michelin map **331** H7 – pop. 643 – alt. 126
Paris 668 – Aubenas 40 – Largentière 29 – St-Ambroix 18

Les Cigales

☎ 0475393033, *www.camping-cigales-ardeche.com*
Address : at La Rouvière (located 1km to the northeast)
Opening times : from beginning April to end Sept.
3 ha (110 pitches) terrace, flat and relatively flat, grassy
Tariff : 26€ ✦✦ 🚐 🗐 ⚡ (10A) – Extra per person 5€
Rental rates : (from beginning April to end Sept.) – 23 🚐 – 7 🏠 – 5 gîtes.
Per week from 240 to 590€

Surroundings : 🏊 🌳
Leisure activities : ♈ ✕ 🎱 🚣 🎯 ⛷
Facilities : ⚹ 🚿 🚽 ♨ 🚰 🛒
GPS
Longitude : 4.21133
Latitude : 44.37829

La Source

☎ 0475393913, *www.camping-source-ardeche.com*
Address : chemin de la Rouvière (take the northeastern exit, follow the signs for Casteljau)
Opening times : from end April to mid Sept.
2.5 ha (93 pitches) flat, stony, grassy
Tariff : (2012 price) 25.60€ ✦✦ 🚐 🗐 ⚡ (6A) – Extra per person 6€
Rental rates : (2012 price) (from end April to mid Sept.) – 22 🚐 – 4 🏠.
Per night from 95 to 110€ – Per week from 255 to 650€

Surroundings : 🏊 🌳
Leisure activities : ✕ 🎱 🚣 ⛷ 🎣
Facilities : ⚹ 🚿 🚽 ♨ 🚰 🛁 🛒
GPS
Longitude : 4.20646
Latitude : 44.37725

BILIEU

38850 – Michelin map **333** C5 – pop. 1,232 – alt. 580
▶ Paris 526 – Belley 44 – Chambéry 47 – Grenoble 38

Municipal Bord du Lac

⌀ 04 76 06 67 00, *http://campingleborddulac.fr* – limited spaces for one-night stay – ⛺
Address : Le Petit Bilieu – rte de Charavines (1.9km west – recommended route via the D 50d and D 90)
1.3 ha (81 pitches) terraced, flat, grassy, fine gravel

Surroundings : 🏞 ≤ ⚲⚲ ⛰
Leisure activities : 🎣
Facilities : ♿ ⌁ ▥ ♈ 🖼
Nearby : ⚓

GPS
Longitude : 5.5312
Latitude : 45.44615

LES BOSSONS

74400 – Michelin map **328** O5 – alt. 1,005
▶ Paris 614 – Lyon 222 – Annecy 89 – Thonon 99

Les Deux Glaciers

⌀ 04 50 53 15 84, *www.les2glaciers.com*
Address : 80 rte des Tissières-les-Bossons (follow the signs for Le Tremplin-Olympique)
Opening times : permanent
1.6 ha (130 pitches) terraced, flat, grassy
Tariff : (2012 price) 20.70€ ✸✸ ⇌ 🅴 ⓗ (10A) – Extra per person 5.90€
Rental rates: (2012 price) (permanent) 🏚 – 2 ▦ – 4 🏠. Per night from 40 to 90€
Per week from 250 to 610€

In a pleasant setting not far from the glaciers.

Surroundings : ❄ ≤ ⚲⚲
Leisure activities : ✗
Facilities : ♿ ⌁ ▥ ♒ ♈ launderette ⚗

GPS
Longitude : 6.83684
Latitude : 45.90228

We have selected the best campsites in France with our usual care,
listing those with the best facilities in the most pleasant surroundings.

BOURDEAUX

26460 – Michelin map **332** D6 – pop. 621 – alt. 426
▶ Paris 608 – Crest 24 – Montélimar 42 – Nyons 40

Yelloh! Village Les Bois du Châtelas

⌀ 04 75 00 60 80, *www.chatelas.com*
Address : rte de Bourdeaux (1.4km southwest along the D 538)
Opening times : from mid April to mid Sept.
17 ha/7 ha for camping (80 pitches) terraced, relatively flat, stony, grassy
Tariff : 24€ ✸✸ ⇌ 🅴 ⓗ (10A) – Extra per person 6€ – Reservation fee 23€
Rental rates : (from mid April to mid Sept.) – 47 ▦ – 25 🏠 – 3 teepees – 8 tent bungalows
Per night from 33 to 90€ – Per week from 231 to 1,414€ – Reservation fee 23€
⛽ sani-station 1€ – 🚐 ⓗ 16€
Panoramic views from the chalets and restaurant.

Surroundings : 🏞 ≤ 🏘
Leisure activities : ♈ ✗ 🎦 ♨ hammam, jacuzzi ⚽ 🚲 🏊 ⛷ ♨
multi-sports ground
Facilities : ♿ ⌁ ▥ ♒ ♓ ☡ ♈ 🖼 🛒 ⚗
Nearby : ⚽ 🐎

GPS
Longitude : 5.12783
Latitude : 44.57832

LE BOURG-D'ARUD

8520 – Michelin map **333** J8 – Leisure centre
Paris 628 – L'Alpe-d'Huez 25 – Le Bourg-d'Oisans 15 – Les Deux-Alpes 29

Le Champ du Moulin

0476800738, *www.champ-du-moulin.com*
Address : take the western exit along the D 530
Opening times : from beginning Jan. to mid Sept.
1.5 ha (80 pitches) open site, flat, grassy, stony
Tariff : 27.30€ ✶✶ ⇔ 🔲 💧 (10A) – Extra per person 5.90€ – Reservation fee 17€
Rental rates : (from beginning Jan. to mid Sept.) – 4 🚐 – 9 🏠 – 4 apartments – 2 tent bungalows. Per night from 42 to 96€ – Per week from 294 to 672€ – Reservation fee 17€
sani-station – 11€
Surrounded by the Oisans mountains and beside the Vénéon river.

Surroundings : ❄ 🦌 🎋
Leisure activities : 🍸 ✗ 🎱 ⛵ 🎣
Facilities : ♿ ⊶ ▥ 🍳 🚿 🔥 🐾
Leisure/activities centre : 🛶 🎿 ⛷ 🏊 rafting and canyoning, adventure park

GPS Longitude : 6.11986
Latitude : 44.98596

We value your opinion and welcome your feedback.
Do email us at campingfrance@tp.michelin.com

LE BOURG-D'OISANS

8520 – Michelin map **333** J7 – pop. 3,381 – alt. 720 – Winter sports :
Paris 614 – Briançon 66 – Gap 95 – Grenoble 52

À la Rencontre du Soleil

0476791222, *www.alarencontredusoleil.com*
Address : rte de l'Alpe d'Huez (1.7km to the northeast)
Opening times : from beginning May to end Sept.
1.6 ha (73 pitches) flat, grassy
Tariff : 37.90€ ✶✶ ⇔ 🔲 💧 (10A) – Extra per person 7.80€ – Reservation fee 16€
Rental rates : (permanent) 🅿 – 4 'gypsy' caravans – 12 🚐 – 11 🏠.
Per night from 46 to 115€ – Per week from 320 to 1,045€ – Reservation fee 13€
2 🔲 26.50€

Surroundings : ⇜ ▭ 🎋
Leisure activities : ✗ 🎱 🛶 🏊 multi-sports ground
Facilities : ⊶ 🍳 🍸 launderette 🐾
Nearby : 🛒

GPS Longitude : 6.03716
Latitude : 45.06296

Les Castels Le Château de Rochetaillée 👤

0476110440, *www.camping-le-chateau.fr*
Address : at Rochetaillée, ch. de Bouthéon
Opening times : from mid May to mid Sept.
2.6 ha (135 pitches) flat, grassy
Tariff : 40.20€ ✶✶ ⇔ 🔲 💧 (10A) – Extra per person 9€ – Reservation fee 19€
Rental rates : (from mid May to mid Sept.) – 48 🚐 – 3 ⊨ – 6 tents.
Per night from 30 to 120€ – Per week from 200 to 850€ – Reservation fee 19€
5 🔲 35€ – 16€

Surroundings : ⇜ ▭ 🎋
Leisure activities : 🍸 ✗ 🎱 🌳 🏃 💆 ⛵ hammam, jacuzzi 🛶 🏊 climbing wall
Facilities : ♿ ⊶ 🍳 🚿 ⊙ 🍸 launderette 🔥 🐾

GPS Longitude : 6.00512
Latitude : 45.11543

RCN Belledonne

ℰ 0476800718, *www.rcn-belledonne.fr*
Address : at Rochetaillée
3.5 ha (180 pitches) flat, grassy
Rentals : 24 🚐.
A very green site with flowers.

Surroundings : ≤ 🄌🄌
Leisure activities : 🍽 ✗ 🎦 🄶 ⛲ hammam ⚓ 🚴 ⚔ 🏊 sports trail
Facilities : 🕭 ⛽ 🏢 🗳 🍴 launderette 🄋 🄍

Longitude : 6.01095
Latitude : 45.11331

Le Colporteur ♣

ℰ 0476791144, *www.camping-colporteur.com*
Address : Le Mas du Plan (south of the town, access via r. de la Piscine)
Opening times : from mid April to end Sept.
3.3 ha (135 pitches) flat, grassy
Tariff : (2012 price) 27€ ✶✶ ⇔ 🄴 🄸 (16A) – Extra per person 8€ – Reservation fee 17€
Rental rates : (2012 price) (from mid April to end Sept.) – 4 'gypsy' caravans – 4 🚐 – 35 🏠.
Per night 32€ – Per week from 315 to 800€ – Reservation fee 17€ – 🄬 8 🄴 19€
Situated beside a small river.

Surroundings : 🄴 ≤ 🄌 🄌🄌
Leisure activities : 🍽 ✗ 🎦 ⚡ ⚓
Facilities : 🕭 ⛽ (season) 🗳 🍴 🄶 🄍
Nearby : 🛒 🏊 🏄

Longitude : 6.03546
Latitude : 45.0527

La Cascade

ℰ 0476800242, *www.lacascadesarenne.com*
Address : located 1.5km to the northeast, follow the signs for L'Alpe-d'Huez, near the Sarennes river
Opening times : from mid Dec. to end Sept.
2.4 ha (140 pitches) flat, grassy, stony
Tariff : (2012 price) 33.30€ ✶✶ ⇔ 🄴 🄸 (16A) – Extra per person 8€ – Reservation fee 17€
Rental rates : (2012 price) (from mid Dec. to end Sept.) – 18 🏠. Per night from 54 to 84€
Per week from 340 to 756€ – Reservation fee 17€

Surroundings : ❄ ≤ 🄌 🄌🄌
Leisure activities : 🎦 ⚓ 🏊
Facilities : ⛽ 🏢 🗳 🍴 🄶
Nearby : 🛒

Longitude : 6.03988
Latitude : 45.06446

BOURG-EN-BRESSE

01000 – Michelin map **328** E3 – pop. 39,586 – alt. 251
▶ Paris 424 – Annecy 113 – Besançon 152 – Chambéry 120

Municipal de Challes

ℰ 0474453721, *www.bourgenbresse.fr* – 🅟
Address : 5 allée du Centre Nautique (take northeastern exit following signs for Lons-le-Saunier; by the swimming pool)
Opening times : from beginning April to mid Oct.
1.3 ha (120 pitches) flat, relatively flat, grassy
Tariff : (2012 price) ✶ 4€ ⇔ 🄴 7.70€ – 🄸 (16A) 2.60€
🄬 25 🄴 16.55€ – 🄬🄸 15.70€
The pitches are pleasantly shaded.

Surroundings : 🄌🄌
Leisure activities : ✗
Facilities : ⛽ 🏢 🄶 🗳 🍴 🄶
Nearby : 🏊

Longitude : 5.2403
Latitude : 46.20905

OURGET-DU-LAC

3370 – Michelin map **333** I4 – pop. 4,277 – alt. 240
Paris 531 – Aix-les-Bains 10 – Annecy 44 – Chambéry 13

International l'Île aux Cygnes

0479250176, *www.lebougetdulac.com*
Address : 501 bd E.Coudurier (located 1km to the north; beside the lake)
Opening times : from end April to end Sept.
2.5 ha (267 pitches) flat, grassy, fine gravel
Tariff : (2012 price) 23.60€ ★★ ⇔ 圓 🄵 (6A) – Extra per person 5.50€ – Reservation fee 15€
Rental rates : (2012 price) (from end April to end Sept.) – 4 🛏 – 4 🏠.
Per night from 92 to 112€ – Per week from 376 to 589€ – Reservation fee 15€
🗑 sani-station 10.65€ – 🚲🄵13€
The campervan pitches are at the entrance to the campsite.

Surroundings : ⩽ ♤♤ ⌂
Leisure activities : ✗ ▭ ◷ daytime 🏄 🚲 ☝ ⌇
Facilities : ⊶ 🖤 ⟂ ⚡ ⚐ launderette 🏊 🐾
Nearby : 🎨 ✗ 🍴 🏊 🛶 🎣 ⚓

Longitude : 5.86308
Latitude : 45.65307

OURG-ST-MAURICE

3700 – Michelin map **333** N4 – pop. 7,650 – alt. 850 – Winter sports : Les Arcs : 1,600/3,226 m 🎿6 ⚡54 ⚡
Paris 635 – Albertville 54 – Aosta 79 – Chambéry 103

Le Versoyen

0479070345, *www.leversoyen.com*
Address : rte des Arcs RD 119 (take the northeastern exit along the N 90, follow the signs for Séez then continue 500m along the turning to the right, near some rapids)
Opening times : from end May to end Oct. and mid-Dec to mid-Apr
3.5 ha (200 pitches) flat, grassy, stony, wood
Tariff : 21.30€ ★★ ⇔ 圓 🄵 (10A) – Extra per person 5.60€ – Reservation fee 10€
Rental rates : (from end May to end Oct. and mid-Dec to mid-Apr) ⚡ – 2 'gypsy' caravans – 11 🛏. Per week from 200 to 540€ – Reservation fee 10€
🗑 sani-station 3€ – 25 圓 14.50€
Free shuttle service to the funicular railway.

Surroundings : ❄ ⚶ ⩽ ♤
Leisure activities : ▭ 🏄
Facilities : ⊶ ▦ ⚐ launderette
Leisure/activities park : 🎯 ✗ 🍴 🏊 🛶 🐎 sports trail

Longitude : 6.78373
Latitude : 45.6221

OUT-DU-LAC

4210 – Michelin map **328** K6
Paris 553 – Albertville 29 – Annecy 17 – Megève 43

International du Lac Bleu

0450443018, *www.camping-lac-bleu.com*
Address : rte de la Plage (follow the signs for Albertville)
3.3 ha (221 pitches) flat, grassy, stony
Rentals : ⚡ – 32 🛏.
In a pleasant location beside the lake (with a beach).

Surroundings : ⩽ ⌂ ♤♤ ⌂
Leisure activities : 🍴 ✗ ◷ 🏄 🚲 🛶
Facilities : 🖤 ⊶ 🖤 ⚐ launderette 🐾
Nearby : 🏊 ✗ 🍴 🎣 ⚓ 🪂 paragliding, tandem paragliding

Longitude : 6.21648
Latitude : 45.79103

BRAMANS

73500 – Michelin map **333** N6 – pop. 388 – alt. 1,200
▶ Paris 673 – Albertville 100 – Briançon 71 – Chambéry 113

Municipal Le Val d'Ambin

☎ 0479050305, *www.camping-bramansvanoise.com*
Address : 700m northeast of Bramans, near the church and 200m from some rapids – recommended route via Le Verney, on the N6
Opening times : from beginning May to end Oct.
4 ha (166 pitches) open site, terraced, undulating, flat, grassy, lake
Tariff : � 3.30€ **⇔** 1.90€ 🗉 3.30€ – 🔌 (8A) 3.90€
Rental rates : (permanent) – 10 🏠 – 5 tents. Per night from 26 to 112€
Per week from 175 to 650€
🚉 sani-station 2€
In an attractive panoramic location.

Surroundings : 🐾 ≼
Leisure activities : 🎰 🛶 ✂ 🎣
Facilities : & ⚡ (Jul–Aug) 📶 ⚗ ↝ 🍴 launderette

GPS Longitude : 6.78144
Latitude : 45.22787

BRIDES-LES-BAINS

73570 – Michelin map **333** M5 – pop. 560 – alt. 580
▶ Paris 612 – Albertville 32 – Annecy 77 – Chambéry 81

▲ La Piat

☎ 0479552274, *www.camping-brideslesbains.com*
Address : av. du Comte Greyfié de Bellecombe
Opening times : from mid April to mid Oct.
2 ha (60 pitches) terraced, flat, grassy
Tariff : (2012 price) 15.64€ **☗☗ ⇔** 🗉 🔌 (10A) – Extra per person 3.40€
Rental rates : (2012 price) (from mid April to mid Oct.) – 7 🚐. Per week from 222 to 320€
🚉 sani-station 3€

Surroundings : ≼ ♀
Facilities : & ⚡ 📶 ⚗ 🍴 launderette

GPS Longitude : 6.56172
Latitude : 45.453

*The Michelin classification (▲▲▲… ▲) is totally independent of the
official star classification system awarded by the local prefecture or
other official organisation.*

BUIS-LES-BARONNIES

26170 – Michelin map **332** E8 – pop. 2,291 – alt. 365
▶ Paris 685 – Carpentras 39 – Nyons 29 – Orange 50

La Fontaine d'Annibal

☎ 0475280312, *directeur.fontaine.annibal@orange.fr*
Address : rte de Séderon (located 1km to the north, road to the left just after the bridge over the Ouvèze river)
(50 pitches) terraced, relatively flat, grassy, stony
Rentals : & – 2 🚐 – 8 🏠.

Surroundings : ⌑ ♀
Leisure activities : 🎰 ⚒
Facilities : & ⚡ 📶 ⚗ ⚗ ↝ 🍴 launderette
Nearby : 🛒 🍽 🎣

GPS Longitude : 5.28187
Latitude : 44.28438

Les Éphélides

℘ 0475281015, *www.ephelides.com*

Address : in the Tuves quaartier (1.4km southwest along av. de Rieuchaud)

Opening times : from mid May to mid Sept.

2 ha (40 pitches) flat, grassy, stony

Tariff : (2012 price) 24.20€ ♣♣ ⇌ 🅴 🕏 (16A) – Extra per person 4.50€ – Reservation fee 12€

Rental rates : (2012 price) (from beginning April to mid Oct.) – 1 'gypsy' caravan – 6 ⛺ –
5 🏠. Per night from 30 to 68€ – Per week from 200 to 650€ – Reservation fee 12€

Shaded by cherry trees, near the Ouvèze. The site welcomes dogs.

Surroundings : 🌿 ⩽ ♀
Leisure activities : ✗ ⚓ 🏊
Facilities : ♿ ⚍ 🏕 🔥
Nearby : 🎾 🐎 skateboarding

GPS Longitude : 5.26793
Latitude : 44.21875

Domaine de la Gautière

℘ 0475280268, *www.camping-lagautiere.com*

Address : at La Gautière (5km southwest along the D 5, then take a right turn)

Opening times : from beginning April to end Oct.

6 ha/3 ha for camping (40 pitches) terraced, relatively flat, stony, grassy

Tariff : ♣ 5.60€⇌ 🅴 6.30€ – 🕏 (10A) 4.90€ – Reservation fee 10€

Rental rates : (from beginning April to mid Nov.) – 9 ⛺ – 3 🏠. Per week from 280 to 750€
Reservation fee 15€

🚽 sani-station 4€ – 💧10€

Much of the site is beneath the shade of olive trees.

Surroundings : 🌿 ⩽ ♀
Leisure activities : 🏓 ⚓ 🏊
Facilities : ♿ ⚍ 🏕 🍴 🔥

GPS Longitude : 5.24258
Latitude : 44.2517

⊠7460 – Michelin map **331** H7
◼ Paris 665 – Aubenas 38 – Largentière 28 – Privas 69

La Rouveyrolle

℘ 0475390067, *www.campingrouveyrolle.fr*

Address : Hameau La Rouveyrolle (east of the town, 100m from the Chassezac)

Opening times : from beginning April to mid Sept.

3 ha (100 pitches) flat, grassy, stony

Tariff : 33.90€ ♣♣ ⇌ 🅴 🕏 (6A) – Extra per person 9€ – Reservation fee 25€

Rental rates : (from beginning April to mid Sept.) – 64 ⛺. Per night from 90 to 157€
Per week from 245 to 1 05€ – Reservation fee 25€

Surroundings : 🌿 ⊏ ♀♀
Leisure activities : ♟ ✗ 🏓 🏋 🔆 jacuzzi ⚓ 🏊
Facilities : ♿ ⚍ 🍴 launderette 🧺 🚰
Nearby : 🏊 🎣

GPS Longitude : 4.22222
Latitude : 44.39583

*There are several different types of sani-station
('borne' in French) – sanitation points providing
fresh water and disposal points for grey water.
See page 12 for further details.*

Les Tournayres

℘ 0475393639, www.lestournayes.ea26.com

Address : at Les Tournaires (500m to the north, follow the signs for Chaulet-Plage)

1.3 ha (30 pitches) flat and relatively flat, grassy

Rentals : 22 – 3 mobile homes (without sanitary facilities).

Surroundings : ⌐ ♀
Leisure activities : ♉ ✕ 🏠 ⚤ ⛵
Facilities : ☰ ☞ 🜂 ⚲ ▣ ☜
Nearby : ⌐

GPS Longitude : 4.21574
Latitude : 44.4006

Chaulet Plage

℘ 0475393027, www.chaulet-plage.com

Address : Terres du Moulin (600m to the north, follow the signs for Chaulet-Plage)

1.5 ha (62 pitches) terraced, flat, grassy, stony

Rental rates : – 6 🏠 – 6 gîtes.

A pleasant location, with direct access to the Chassezac river.

Surroundings : ⌐ ♀♀ ⛰
Leisure activities : ♉ ✕ ⌐ ⚲
Facilities : ☰ ☞ 🜂 ⚲ ▣ ☲ ☜

GPS Longitude : 4.21528
Latitude : 44.40453

CHABEUIL

26120 – Michelin map **332** D4 – pop. 6,568 – alt. 212
▶ Paris 569 – Crest 21 – Die 59 – Romans-sur-Isère 18

FranceLoc Le Grand Lierne

℘ 0475598314, www.grandlierne.com ⚡ (Jul–Aug)

Address : 5km northeast along the D 68, follow the signs for Peyrus, turn left onto D 125 and turn right onto D 143 – from A 7, Valence-Sud exit towards Grenoble

Opening times : from mid April to mid Sept.

3.6 ha (160 pitches) flat, stony, grassy

Tariff : (2012 price) 39€ ✚✚ ⇔ ▣ ⚡ (10A) – Extra per person 7€ – Reservation fee 27€

Rental rates : (2012 price) (from mid April to mid Sept.) ⚡ – 163 – 6 🏠 – 8 tents.
Per night from 37 to 168€ – Per week from 245 to 1,141€ – Reservation fee 27€

🚏 sani-station

Surroundings : ⌐ ♀♀
Leisure activities : ♉ ✕ 🏠 ⚤ 🚲 🜂 🏊 (small swimming pool) 🛝 ⛷
Facilities : ☰ ☞ 🜂 ⚲ ▣ ☲ ☜ refrigerated food storage

GPS Longitude : 5.065
Latitude : 44.91572

Key to rentals symbols:

12	*Number of mobile homes*	
20 🏠	*Number of chalets*	
6 🛏	*Number of rooms to rent*	
Per night *30–50€*	*Minimum/maximum rate per night*	
Per week *300–1,000€*	*Minimum/maximum rate per week*	

CHALLES-LES-EAUX

73190 – Michelin map **333** I4 – pop. 5,073 – alt. 310 – ♨ (beg Apr to end Oct)
🔼 Paris 566 – Albertville 48 – Chambéry 6 – Grenoble 52

le Savoy

📞 04 79 72 97 31, www.ville-challesleseaux.com
Address : av. du Parc (take the r. Denarié, 100m from the N 6)
Opening times : from end March to end Oct.
2.8 ha (88 pitches) flat, grassy, fine gravel
Tariff : (2012 price) ♦ 3.40€ ⇌ 1.45€ 🔲 5.30€ – ⚡ (10A) 3€ – Reservation fee 11€
Rental rates : (2012 price) (from end March to end Oct.) – 1 ▥ – 6 🏚 – 3 tents.
Per night from 30 to 66€ – Per week from 187 to 380€ – Reservation fee 11€
🚐 15 🔲 14.55€
Pretty pitches lined with hedges, near a small lake.

Surroundings : 🌳 ♀
Leisure activities : 🎱 ⛵ 🚲
Facilities : ♿ 🚿 ☂ 🚰 ⛲ 📶
Nearby : 🍴 🏊
GPS Longitude : 5.98418
Latitude : 45.55152

CHAMONIX-MONT-BLANC

74400 – Michelin map **328** O5 – pop. 9,054 – alt. 1,040 – Winter sports : 1,035/3,840 m ⛷ 14 🚡 36 ⛄
🔼 Paris 610 – Albertville 65 – Annecy 97 – Aosta 57

L'Île des Barrats

📞 04 50 53 51 44, www.campingdesbarrats.com – ♨
Address : 185 chemin de l'Île des Barrats (to the southwest of the town, 150m from the Arve river)
Opening times : from mid June to mid Sept.
0.8 ha (56 pitches) flat and relatively flat, grassy
Tariff : 29.20€ ♦♦ ⇌ 🔲 ⚡ (10A) – Extra per person 6.70€
Rental rates : (from beginning June to end Sept.) 🛏 – 4 🏚. Per week from 700 to 1,000€

Surroundings : ≤ Mont Blanc mountain range and glaciers 🌳 ♀
Leisure activities : 🎱
Facilities : ♿ 🚿 ☂ 🚰 ⛲ launderette
GPS Longitude : 6.86135
Latitude : 45.91463

The information in the guide may have changed since going to press.

CHAMPDOR

01110 – Michelin map **328** G4 – pop. 462 – alt. 833
🔼 Paris 486 – Ambérieu-en-Bugey 38 – Bourg-en-Bresse 51 – Hauteville-Lompnes 6

Municipal le Vieux Moulin

📞 650542898, http://www.champdor.jimdo.com
Address : rte de Corcelles (800m northwest along the D 57a)
Opening times : permanent
1.6 ha (62 pitches) flat, grassy
Tariff : (2012 price) ♦ 3.30€ ⇌ 1.10€ 🔲 1.70€ – ⚡ (10A) 3.50€
Rental rates : (2012 price) (permanent) – 2 yurts – 3 cabins. Per night 90€ – Per week 250€
In the hills of Le Bugey hills and close to natural lakes – one for swimming, one for fishing.

Surroundings : 🏊 ≤
Leisure activities : 🎱 ⛵
Facilities : ♿ 🚿 (Jul-Aug) ☂ ⛲ ⛲
Nearby : 🍴 🏊 (pool) 🎣
GPS Longitude : 5.59138
Latitude : 46.023

CHANAZ

73310 – Michelin map **333** H3 – pop. 510 – alt. 232
▶ Paris 521 – Aix-les-Bains 21 – Annecy 53 – Bellegarde-sur-Valserine 44

Municipal des Îles

℘ 0479545851, *www.campingdechanaz.fr* – limited spaces for one-night stay
Address : at the base de loisirs (leisure centre) (located 1km west along the D 921, follow the signs for Culoz and take road to the left after the bridge, 300m from the Rhône (small lake and marina)
Opening times : permanent
1.5 ha (103 pitches) flat, gravelled, grassy
Tariff : (2012 price) 16€ ★★ ⇌ ▣ ⚡ (10A) – Extra per person 2€
Rental rates : (2012 price) (permanent) – 18 🏠. Per night from 45 to 95€
Per week from 210 to 695€
🚽 sani-station 2€ – 10 ▣ 12€ – 🚰 ⚡10€
Near a picturesque village and the Canal de Savière.

Surroundings : ≤ 🞉🞉
Leisure activities : 🖵
Facilities : ⅙ �o━ 🗑 🏛 ⚲ 🗘 🍴 🖼
Nearby : 🍷 ✗ 🏊 🎾 🏊 (small swimming pool) 🎣 ⚓

Longitude : 5.79378
Latitude : 45.8091

CHANCIA

01590 – Michelin map **321** D8 – pop. 237 – alt. 320
▶ Paris 452 – Bourg-en-Bresse 48 – Lons-le-Saunier 46 – Nantua 30

Municipal les Cyclamens

℘ 0474758214, *www.camping-chancia.com* – limited spaces for one-night stay
Address : La Presqu'île (located 1.5km southwest along the D 60e and take road to the left, where the Ain and the Bienne rivers meet)
2 ha (155 pitches) flat, grassy

Beside the Lac de Coiselet; a lovely rural site surrounded by cliffs.

Surroundings : 🞈 ≤ 🞉
Leisure activities : 🖵 🏊
Facilities : ⅙ �o━ ⚲ 🍴 launderette
Nearby : 🏊 🎣 ⚓

Longitude : 5.6311
Latitude : 46.34203

CHARAVINES

38850 – Michelin map **333** G5 – pop. 1,758 – alt. 500
▶ Paris 534 – Belley 47 – Chambéry 49 – Grenoble 40

Les Platanes

℘ 0476066470, *www.camping-lesplatanes.com*
Address : 85 r. du Camping (take the northern exit along the D 50d, 150m from the lake)
Opening times : from beginning April to end Sept.
1 ha (67 pitches) flat, grassy
Tariff : (2012 price) 17.50€ ★★ ⇌ ▣ ⚡ (10A) – Extra per person 4.30€ – Reservation fee 12€
Rental rates : (2012 price) (from beginning April to end Sept.) 🍽 – 10 🚐.
Per night from 48 to 112€ – Per week from 495 to 535€ – Reservation fee 12€
🚽 sani-station 2.50€ – 9 ▣ 13€

Surroundings : 🞉🞉
Leisure activities : ✗ 🖵
Facilities : ⅙ �o━ 🏛 🍴 🖼
Nearby : 🛒 🍷 🎾 🏊 (beach) 🎣 ⚓ pedalos

Longitude : 5.51545
Latitude : 45.43096

CHASSAGNES

07140 – Michelin map **331** H7
▶ Paris 644 – Lyon 209 – Privas 67 – Nîmes 85

Les Chênes

℘ 04 75 37 34 35, *www.domaine-des-chenes.fr* – limited spaces for one-night stay
Address : at Chassagnes Haut
Opening times : from beginning April to end Sept.
2.5 ha (122 pitches) terraced, flat, grassy, stony
Tariff : 31 € ♦♦ ⇔ 🄴 [2] (10A) – Extra per person 6 € – Reservation fee 25 €
Rental rates : (from beginning April to end Sept.) – 4 'gypsy' caravans – 21 ⊡ – 14 ⌂ –
4 tents. Per night from 36 to 80 € – Per week from 252 to 1,225 € – Reservation fee 25 €
🚱 sani-station 18 € – 4 🄴 18 €

Surroundings : 🏞 ≤ ♀
Leisure activities : ♀ ✗ 🎱 ᚠᵟ ≋ hammam, jacuzzi ⠼
Facilities : 🚻 ⊶ 🍴 🛠 🄰
Nearby : 🎣

GPS Longitude : 4.13218
Latitude : 44.39899

Lou Rouchétou

℘ 04 75 37 33 13, *www.lou-rouchetou.com*
Address : at Chassagnes (follow the signs for Les Vans along the D 104)
1.5 ha (100 pitches) flat and relatively flat, grassy, stony
Rentals : 20 ⊡ – 1 gîte.
🚱 sani-station – 10 🄴
Situated beside the Chassezac river.

Surroundings : 🏞 ≤ ♀♀ ⛰
Leisure activities : ♀ ✗ 🛶 ⠼ 🎣
Facilities : 🚻 ⊶ 🍴 🛠 🄰 ⛲ 🚿

GPS Longitude : 4.16823
Latitude : 44.4065

*For more information on visiting particular towns or regions, consult the
relevant regional MICHELIN Green Guide. We also recommend you use
the appropriate Michelin regional map to locate your selected campsite,
to calculate distances and to work out the best route.*

CHASSIERS

07110 – Michelin map **331** H6 – pop. 1,008 – alt. 340
▶ Paris 643 – Aubenas 16 – Largentière 4 – Privas 48

Sunêlia Domaine Les Ranchisses ▲▲

℘ 04 75 88 31 97, *www.lesranchisses.fr*
Address : rte de Rocher (1.6km to the northwest, access via the D 5, follow the signs for Valgorge)
Opening times : from mid April to end Sept.
6 ha (226 pitches) terraced, relatively flat, flat, grassy
Tariff : 47 € ♦♦ ⇔ 🄴 [2] (10A) – Extra per person 10 € – Reservation fee 15 €
Rental rates : (from mid April to end Sept.) – 101 ⊡ – 2 gîtes. Per night from 35 to 179 €
Per week from 220 to 1,253 € – Reservation fee 30 €
Based around an old farmhouse dating from 1824; beside the Ligne river.

Surroundings : 🖼 ♀♀ ⛰
Leisure activities : ♀ ✗ 🎮 🏕 ≋ hammam, jacuzzi 🛶 ✗ 🎿 🄻 ⠼ ⠼ 🎣
🏊 multi-sports ground, spa therapy centre, skate park
Facilities : 🚻 ⊶ 🄺 🍴 🚿 🏧 🛠 🄰 ⛲ 🚿

GPS Longitude : 4.28536
Latitude : 44.56137

RHÔNE-ALPES

CHÂTEAUNEUF-DE-GALAURE

26330 – Michelin map **332** C2 – pop. 1,557 – alt. 253
▶ Paris 531 – Annonay 29 – Beaurepaire 19 – Romans-sur-Isère 27

Iris Parc Château de Galaure

✆ 0475686522, *www.chateaudegalaure.com* ✇
Address : rte de St-Vallier (800m southwest along the D 51)
Opening times : from end April to end Sept.
12 ha (400 pitches) flat, grassy
Tariff : 39€ ✱✱ ⇦ ▣ ⑭ (6A) – Extra per person 7.50€ – Reservation fee 20€
Rental rates : (from mid April to end Sept.) ✇ – 144 ⌷⌷ – 80 tents.
Per night from 25 to 139€ – Per week from 200 to 1,112€ – Reservation fee 20€
Pleasant, green site with good shade.

Surroundings : ⚏
Leisure activities : ♈ ✕ ⌂ ⑤ ⚤ ⍼ ⚐ skateboarding
Facilities : ♿ ⊶ ⊡⚏ ⑪ ▣ ⚐ ⚌
Nearby : ⚞ ☒ ⚒ fitness trail, zip wiring

GPS
Longitude : 4.95644
Latitude : 45.23029

CHÂTEAUNEUF-SUR-ISÈRE

26300 – Michelin map **332** C3 – pop. 3,707 – alt. 118
▶ Paris 561 – Lyon 98 – Valence 13 – Privas 55

Sunêlia Le Soleil Fruité ♠♣

✆ 0475841970, *www.lesoleilfruite.com*
Address : 4km, take exit 14 Valence Nord towards Châteauneuf sur Isére, continue along the D 877;
near the 'Les Folies du Lac' cabaret
4 ha (138 pitches) flat, grassy
Rentals : 34 ⌷⌷.
⌷⌷ sani-station
Surroundings : ⚐ ⌕ ⚏
Leisure activities : ♈ ✕ ⌂ ⑤ ☆ ⚤ ⍼ ⚐
Facilities : ⊶ ⚏ ⑪ launderette ⚞ ⚌

GPS
Longitude : 4.89372
Latitude : 44.99707

This guide is updated regularly, so buy your new copy every year!

CHÂTEL

74390 – Michelin map **328** O3 – pop. 1,213 – alt. 1,180 – Winter sports : 1,200/2,100 m ⚐2 ⚐52 ⚐
▶ Paris 578 – Annecy 113 – Évian-les-Bains 34 – Morzine 38

L'Oustalet ♠♣

✆ 0450732197, *www.oustalet.com* – alt. 1,110
Address : 1428 rte des Freinets (head 2km southwest following the signs for Le Col de Bassachaux;
beside the Dranse river)
Opening times : from mid June to beginning Sept. and from mid-Dec to mid-Apr
3 ha (100 pitches) flat and relatively flat, stony, grassy, fine gravel
Tariff : 34.80€ ✱✱ ⇦ ▣ ⑭ (10A) – Extra per person 6.20€ – Reservation fee 10€
Rental rates : (from mid June to beginning Sept. and from mid-Dec to mid-Apr) ✇ – 16 ⌷⌷.
Per night from 60 to 110€ – Per week from 380 to 730€ – Reservation fee 10€
⌷⌷ sani-station 6€ – 14 ▣ 6€
A pleasant location in the Vallée d'Abondance.

Surroundings : ❄ ≼
Leisure activities : ♈ ⌂ ⑤ daytime ☆ ⊜ ⚤ ⚞ ☒ ⚒
Facilities : ♿ ⊶ ⑪ ⚏ ⑪ launderette
Nearby : ⚞ ✕ ⚌ ⚲ ⚐

GPS
Longitude : 6.82981
Latitude : 46.25755

LE CHÂTELARD

73630 – Michelin map **333** J3 – pop. 645 – alt. 750
▶ Paris 562 – Aix-les-Bains 30 – Annecy 30 – Chambéry 35

⚠ Les Cyclamens

✆ 0479548019, *www.camping-cyclamens.com*
Address : head towards the northwestern exit and take road to the left, follow the signs for Le Champet
Opening times : from beginning April to end Oct.
0.7 ha (34 pitches) flat, grassy
Tariff : (2012 price) ⚲ 3.70€ ⇌ 🅴 4.70€ – (⚡) (10A) 3.10€ – Reservation fee 4€
Rental rates : (from beginning April to end Oct.) – 1 cabin in the trees. Per night from 95 €
Per week from 525€
🚿 sani-station 4€ – 2 🅴 12.10€

Surroundings : 🗻 ≤ ♨
Leisure activities : 🎱 ⚔
Facilities : ⅏ ⊶ 🛏 🛁 ☂ 🖼

GPS Longitude : 6.13263
Latitude : 45.68782

CHÂTILLON-EN-DIOIS

26410 – Michelin map **332** F5 – pop. 561 – alt. 570
▶ Paris 637 – Die 14 – Gap 79 – Grenoble 97

⚠⚠ Le Lac Bleu

✆ 0475218530, *www.lacbleu-diois.com*
Address : in the La Touche quartier (4km southwest along the D 539, follow the signs for Die and take D 140, follow the signs for Menglon, take road to the left before the bridge)
Opening times : from beginning April to end Sept.
9 ha/3 ha for camping (90 pitches) flat, grassy, stony
Tariff : (2012 price) 32.80€ ⚲⚲ ⇌ 🅴 (⚡) (6A) – Extra per person 7.30€ – Reservation fee 13€
Rental rates : (2012 price) (from beginning April to end Sept.) – 77 🛏 – 77 🏠 – 9 tent bungalows. Per night from 32 to 112€ – Per week from 214 to 784€ – Reservation fee 18€

Surroundings : ≤ ♨ ⛰
Leisure activities : 🍽 ✕ 🎱 🖥 🏸 jacuzzi ⚔ 🖼 🗻 🚣
Facilities : ⅏ ⊶ 🛁 ☂ 🖼 🚿 🚰

GPS Longitude : 5.45332
Latitude : 44.68457

CHÂTILLON-SUR-CHALARONNE

01400 – Michelin map **328** C4 – pop. 4,899 – alt. 177
▶ Paris 418 – Bourg-en-Bresse 28 – Lyon 55 – Mâcon 28

⚠ Municipal du Vieux Moulin

✆ 0474550479, *www.camping-vieuxmoulin.com* – limited spaces for one-night stay
Address : r. Jean Jaurès (take southeastern exit along the D 7, follow the signs for Chalamont; beside the Chalaronne, 150m from a lake – direct access)
Opening times : from beginning May to end Sept.
3 ha (140 pitches) flat, grassy
Tariff : (2012 price) 20.60€ ⚲⚲ ⇌ 🅴 (⚡) (10A) – Extra per person 4.80€ – Reservation fee 10€
Rental rates : (2012 price) (from beginning April to end Sept.) – 5 🏠.
Per week from 306 to 418€ – Reservation fee 10€
🚿 sani-station 20.60€ – 17 🅴 20.60€
In a shaded, green setting beside river.

Surroundings : 🗻 ♨
Leisure activities : 🎱 ⚔ 🚣 multi-sports ground
Facilities : ⅏ ⊶ ☂ ☂ 🖼
Nearby : 🛒 🍽 ✕ 🏊 🛶 ⛷

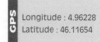
GPS Longitude : 4.96228
Latitude : 46.11654

CHAUZON

07120 – Michelin map **331** I7 – pop. 341 – alt. 128
▶ Paris 649 – Aubenas 20 – Largentière 14 – Privas 51

La Digue

𝄞 0475396357, *www.camping-la-digue.fr* – access difficult for caravans
Address : at Les Aires (located 1km east of the town, 100m from the Ardèche river (direct access)
Opening times : from mid March to end Oct.
2 ha (106 pitches) terraced, flat, grassy
Tariff : (2012 price) 34.80€ ♦♦ ⇔ 🔲 🛁 (10A) – Extra per person 6.50€ – Reservation fee 10€
Rental rates : (2012 price) (from end March to mid Oct.) – 34 🔲 – 8 🏠.
Per night from 32 to 130€ – Per week from 224 to 910€ – Reservation fee 10€

Surroundings : 🌊 🏖
Leisure activities : 🍸 ✗ 🚣 ✂ 🏊
Facilities : 👤 🔑 ▥ 🚿 🍴 🔲 🔃
Nearby : 🏊

GPS Longitude : 4.37337
Latitude : 44.48437

CHAVANNES-SUR-SURAN

01250 – Michelin map **328** F3 – pop. 650 – alt. 312
▶ Paris 442 – Bourg-en-Bresse 20 – Lons-le-Saunier 51 – Mâcon 57

Municipal

𝄞 0474517052, *http://campingchavannes.over-blog.com/*
Address : rte des Orchidées (take the eastern exit along the D 3, follow the signs for Arnans)
1 ha (25 pitches) flat, grassy
A green location beside the Suran river.

Surroundings : 🌊 ⩽ ▱
Leisure activities : 🎣

GPS Longitude : 5.42851
Latitude : 46.26473

*Routes nationales are main roads and their identifying numbers
begin with N or RN. Routes départementales are generally quieter
roads and begin with D or DN.*

LE CHEYLARD

07160 – Michelin map **331** I4 – pop. 3,289 – alt. 450
▶ Paris 598 – Aubenas 50 – Lamastre 21 – Privas 47

Municipal la Chèze

𝄞 0475290953, *www.camping-lecheylard.fr*
Address : rte de St-Christol (take the northeastern exit along the D 120, follow the signs for la Voulte
then take right turn, 1km along the D 204 and take D 264; by the château)
Opening times : from mid May to end Sept.
3 ha (96 pitches) terraced, flat, grassy
Tariff : (2012 price) 14.50€ ♦♦ ⇔ 🔲 🛁 (10A) – Extra per person 3€
Rental rates : (2012 price) (from mid June to mid Sept.) – 4 tent bungalows – 1 gîte.
Per night from 30 to 45€ – Per week from 170 to 280€
🔃 sani-station – 5 🔲 6€
In an attractive elevated location in the grounds of a château.

Surroundings : 🌊 ⩽ small town of Le Cheylard and mountains 🏖
Leisure activities : 📺 🚣 fitness trail
Facilities : 👤 🔑 🍴 🔲

GPS Longitude : 4.43052
Latitude : 44.90691

CHORANCHE

38680 – Michelin map **333** F7 – pop. 132 – alt. 280
▶ Paris 588 – La Chapelle-en-Vercors 24 – Grenoble 52 – Romans-sur-Isère 32

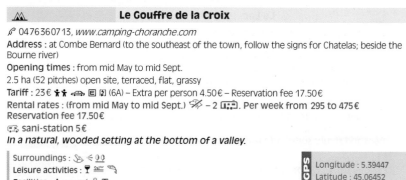

Le Gouffre de la Croix

℘ 0476360713, www.camping-choranche.com
Address : at Combe Bernard (to the southeast of the town, follow the signs for Chatelas; beside the Bourne river)
Opening times : from mid May to mid Sept.
2.5 ha (52 pitches) open site, terraced, flat, grassy
Tariff : 23€ ✝✝ ⇔ 🗉 🗓 (6A) – Extra per person 4.50€ – Reservation fee 17.50€
Rental rates : (from mid May to mid Sept.) ⅌ – 2 🛏. Per week from 295 to 475€
Reservation fee 17.50€
🚽 sani-station 5€
In a natural, wooded setting at the bottom of a valley.

Surroundings : 🌳 ≤ 🏔
Leisure activities : 🍷 ≊ 🎣
Facilities : 🕭 ⊶ 🚿 🖫 🖼

GPS Longitude : 5.39447
Latitude : 45.06452

LA CLUSAZ

74220 – Michelin map **328** L5 – pop. 1,876 – alt. 1,040 – Winter sports : 1,100/2,600 m ≰6 ⅘49 ⚡
▶ Paris 564 – Albertville 40 – Annecy 32 – Bonneville 26

FranceLoc Le Plan du Fernuy

℘ 0450024475, www.franceloc.fr
Address : rte des Confins (located 1.5km to the east)
Opening times : from mid Dec. to end April
1.3 ha (60 pitches) terraced, relatively flat, gravelled, grassy
Tariff : 28€ ✝✝ ⇔ 🗉 🗓 (13A) – Extra per person 6€ – Reservation fee 27€
Rental rates : (from mid Dec. to end April) ⅌ – 18 🛏 – 12 🏠 – 1 studio – 3 apartments.
Per night 126€ – Per week 1,099€ – Reservation fee 27€
🚽 sani-station
Attractive indoor swimming pool and a pleasant location at the foot of Les Aravis mountains.

Surroundings : ❄ 🌳 ≤ 🗆 🌿
Leisure activities : 🍷 🎬 ⚽ 🔲
Facilities : 🕭 ⊶ 🏬 🚿 🖫 ⇆ 🚻 launderette

GPS Longitude : 6.45174
Latitude : 45.90948

CORDELLE

42123 – Michelin map **327** D4 – pop. 896 – alt. 450
▶ Paris 409 – Feurs 35 – Roanne 14 – St-Just-en-Chevalet 27

De Mars

℘ 0477649442, www.camping-de-mars.com
Address : 4.5km south along the D 56 and take the road to the right
1.2 ha (63 pitches) terraced, flat, relatively flat, grassy
Rental rates : 🕭 (1 mobile home) – 13 🛏 – 2 🏠 – 2 tent bungalows.
In an attractive location overlooking the Loire river gorges.

Surroundings : 🌳 ≤ 🗆 🌿
Leisure activities : 🍷 ✕ 🎬 ⚽ 🚲 🌊
Facilities : 🕭 ⊶ 🚿 🖫 ⇆ launderette 🛒
Nearby : 🎣

GPS Longitude : 4.06101
Latitude : 45.91668

CORMORANCHE-SUR-SAÔNE

01290 – Michelin map **328** B3 – pop. 1,051 – alt. 172 – Leisure centre
▶ Paris 399 – Bourg-en-Bresse 44 – Châtillon-sur-Chalaronne 23 – Mâcon 10

⚠ Le Lac

℘ 03 85 23 97 10, *www.lac-cormoranche.com*

Address : at Les Luizants (take the western exit along the D 51a and continue 1.2km along the turning to the right; Leisure and activity park)

Opening times : from beginning May to end Sept.

48 ha/4.5 ha for camping (117 pitches) flat, grassy, sandy, wood

Tariff : (2012 price) 20.20€ ✚ ✚ ⇔ 国 ⚡ (10A) – Extra per person 5.20€ – Reservation fee 6€

Rental rates : (2012 price) (from beginning May to end Sept.) ⚡ – 9 ⚏ – 12 ⌂ – 3 teepees. Per night from 41 to 92€ – Per week from 153 to 549€ – Reservation fee 6€

🚰 sani-station

Trees and shrubs surround the pitches; near a small but pretty lake.

Surroundings : ⌑ ♀
Leisure activities : 🍴 ✗ 🚣 🚲 🎣 ≈ (beach) 🎿 ♪ entertainment room
Facilities : ♿ ⚮ ☕ 🚿 ❖ ♈ launderette 🔥

Longitude : 4.82573
Latitude : 46.25105

CREST

26400 – Michelin map **332** D5 – pop. 7,857 – alt. 196
▶ Paris 585 – Die 37 – Gap 129 – Grenoble 114

⚠ Les Clorinthes ♣♣

℘ 04 75 25 05 28, *www.lesclorinthes.com*

Address : quai Soubeyran (take the southern exit along the D 538 then take the road to the left after the bridge, near the Drôme river and the sports centre)

Opening times : from mid April to mid Sept.

4 ha (160 pitches) relatively flat, flat, grassy

Tariff : (2012 price) 26.40€ ✚ ✚ ⇔ 国 ⚡ (6A) – Extra per person 6.50€ – Reservation fee 21€

Rental rates : (2012 price) (from mid April to mid Sept.) – 10 ⚏ – 4 ⌂. Per night from 67€
Per week from 322 to 658€ – Reservation fee 21€

Surroundings : ≤ ♀
Leisure activities : 🍴 ✗ 📺 daytime 🏃 🚣 🚲 🏊
Facilities : ♿ ⚮ ☕ ♈ launderette
Nearby : ✗ 🐎

Longitude : 5.0277
Latitude : 44.724

CRUAS

07350 – Michelin map **331** K6 – pop. 2,669 – alt. 83
▶ Paris 594 – Aubenas 49 – Montélimar 16 – Privas 24

△ Les Ilons

℘ 04 75 49 55 43, *www.campinglesilons.fr* ⚡

Address : chemin du Camping (1.4km east, follow the signs for Le Port, near a lake; 300m from the Rhône)

Opening times : permanent

2.5 ha (80 pitches) flat, grassy, fine gravel

Tariff : (2012 price) ✚ 4.50€ ⇔ 2.50€ 国 16€ – ⚡ (10A) 4.50€ – Reservation fee 20€

Rental rates : (2012 price) (permanent) ⚡ – 12 ⚏ – 2 ⌂. Per week from 350 to 600€
Reservation fee 20€

🚰 sani-station 3.50€ – 1 国 17€

Surroundings : ⛰ ♀
Leisure activities : 📺 🚣 🎣 🏊 🎿
Facilities : ♿ ⚮ 🚿 ♈ 🔥
Nearby : ✗

Longitude : 4.77699
Latitude : 44.65815

CUBLIZE

69550 – Michelin map **327** F3 – pop. 1,242 – alt. 452
▶ Paris 422 – Amplepuis 7 – Chauffailles 29 – Roanne 30

Intercommunal du Lac des Sapins

☎ 0474895283, *www.lac-des-sapins.fr* – limited spaces for one-night stay
Address : r. du Lac (800m to the south; beside the Reins stream and 300m from the lake (direct access)
4 ha (155 pitches) flat, grassy, stony, fine gravel
Rentals : 4 🚐 – 22 🏠.
🚽 sani-station

Surroundings : ⌇ ⪕ 🏕
Leisure activities : ⚞ multi-sports ground
Facilities : ⅙ ⊶ 🏕 ⚡ ⍾ 🗒
Leisure/activities centre : 🏊 ⍾ ⚓ ⚮ ⚲

Longitude : 4.37849
Latitude : 46.0132

CULOZ

01350 – Michelin map **328** H5 – pop. 2,920 – alt. 248
▶ Paris 512 – Aix-les-Bains 24 – Annecy 55 – Bourg-en-Bresse 88

Le Colombier

☎ 0479871900, *http://camping.colombier.free.fr*
Address : Ile de Verbaou (1.3km east, at junction of D 904 and D 992; beside a stream)
Opening times : from end April to end Sept.
1.5 ha (81 pitches) flat, fine gravel, grassy
Tariff : 19.50€ ⚦⚦ 🚐 🗒 ⚡ (10A) – Extra per person 5.50€ – Reservation fee 10€
Rental rates : (from end April to end Sept.) – 5 🚐. Per night from 25 to 50€ –
Per week from 250 to 510€ – Reservation fee 10€
🚽 40 🗒 19.50€
Situated near a leisure centre.

Surroundings : ⪕ 🏕 ⚲
Leisure activities : ⛷ 🏊 🚲
Facilities : ⅙ ⊶ 🏕 ⚡ ⍾ 🏕 launderette ⚮
Nearby : ⚞ 🗒 ⍾ ⚓

Longitude : 5.79346
Latitude : 45.85158

Some campsites benefit from proximity to a municipal leisure centre.

DARBRES

07170 – Michelin map **331** J6 – pop. 252 – alt. 450
▶ Paris 618 – Aubenas 18 – Montélimar 34 – Privas 21

Les Lavandes

☎ 0475942065, *www.les-lavandes-darbres.com*
Address : in the town
Opening times : from mid April to end Sept.
1.5 ha (70 pitches) terraced, flat, stony, grassy
Tariff : 25.60€ ⚦⚦ 🚐 🗒 ⚡ (6A) – Extra per person 3.90€ – Reservation fee 15€
Rental rates : (from mid April to end Sept.) – 12 🏠 – 1 🚐. Per night from 53 to 59€ –
Per week from 260 to 640€ – Reservation fee 15€

Surroundings : ⪕ ⚲
Leisure activities : ⛷ ✕ 🏊 ⚮
Facilities : ⊶ 🏕 ⍾ 🗒 ⚓

Longitude : 4.50402
Latitude : 44.64701

DARDILLY

69570 – Michelin map **327** H5 – pop. 8,384 – alt. 338
▶ Paris 457 – Lyon 13 – Villeurbanne 21 – Vénissieux 26

Indigo International Lyon

☎ 04 78 35 64 55, *www.camping-indigo.com*
Address : Porte de Lyon (10km northwest along the N 6, follow the signs for Mâcon – from the A 6, take the exit at Dardilly for Limonest)
Opening times : permanent
6 ha (150 pitches) flat, grassy, fine gravel
Tariff : (2012 price) 27.30€ ✦✦ ⇌ 🗐 🚾 (10A) – Extra per person 4.75€ – Reservation fee 20€
Rental rates : (2012 price) (permanent) – 6 'gypsy' caravans – 41 🚐 – 5 🏠 – 6 tents.
Per night from 38 to 106€ – Per week from 186 to 594€ – Reservation fee 20€
🚮 sani-station 7€

Surroundings : ♀ Leisure activities : 🍸 ✕ 🖻 🏊 🛶 Facilities : 🚻 ⚬ₘ 🖂 🛉 🖙 launderette	**GPS** Longitude : 4.76125 Latitude : 45.81817

The prices listed were supplied by the campsite owners in 2012
(if prices were not available, those from the previous year are given).
The fees should be regarded as basic charges and may fluctuate
with inflation.

DIE

26150 – Michelin map **332** F5 – pop. 4,357 – alt. 415
▶ Paris 623 – Gap 92 – Grenoble 110 – Montélimar 73

Le Glandasse

☎ 04 75 22 02 50, *www.camping-glandasse.com* – max height 2.80m
Address : in the La Maldrerie quartier (located 1km southeast along the D 93, follow the signs for Gap then take the road to the right)
Opening times : from mid April to end Sept.
3.5 ha (120 pitches) relatively flat, flat, grassy, stony
Tariff : (2012 price) 17.50€ ✦✦ ⇌ 🗐 🚾 (10A) – Extra per person 5.50€ – Reservation fee 10€
Rental rates : (2012 price) (from mid April to end Sept.) – 2 🚐 – 15 🏠.
Per night from 40 to 81€ – Per week from 280 to 567€ – Reservation fee 10€
Situated beside the Drôme river.

Surroundings : 🏞 ⟨ 🛏 ♀♀ Leisure activities : ✕ 🖻 🎣 jacuzzi 🏊 🚲 🛝 🛶 ⛵ 🛶 Facilities : 🚻 ⚬ₘ 🛁 🚽 launderette 🛒	**GPS** Longitude : 5.38403 Latitude : 44.73993

Le Riou Merle

☎ 04 75 22 21 31, *www.camping-rerioumerle.com*
Address : rte de Romeyer (head north along the D 742)
2.5 ha (97 pitches) flat, grassy
Rentals : 9 🚐 – 3 🏠.
🚮 sani-station

Surroundings : 🛏 ♀ Leisure activities : 🍸 ✕ 🖻 🛶 Facilities : ⚬ₘ 🚽 launderette 🛒	**GPS** Longitude : 5.37776 Latitude : 44.75441

DIEULEFIT

26220 – Michelin map **332** D6 – pop. 3,028 – alt. 366
▶ Paris 614 – Crest 30 – Montélimar 29 – Nyons 30

Huttopia Dieulefit

✆ 0475546394, *www.huttopia.com*

Address : in the Espeluche quartier (3km north along the D 540 follow the signs for Bourdeaux then take the road to the left)

Opening times : from beginning April to mid Oct.

17 ha (140 pitches) undulating, flat, grassy

Tariff : (2012 price) 42.80€ ✸✸ ⇌ 🔲 🕃 (10A) – Extra per person 7€ – Reservation fee 20€

Rental rates : (2012 price) – 14 🏠 – 40 tents. Per night from 62 to 161 €
Per week from 434 to 1,127€ – Reservation fee 20€

🚐 sani-station 7€

Surroundings : 🦌
Leisure activities : ✗ 🖼 🛶 🏊
Facilities : ⛲ 🛁 🚰 launderette 🔌

GPS Longitude : 5.05826
Latitude : 44.53987

Le Domaine des Grands Prés

✆ 0475499436, *www.lesgrandspres-dromeprovencale.com*

Address : in the Grands Prés quartier (take the western exit along the D 540, follow the signs for Montélimar, near the Jabron – direct access to the town along the pedestrian path)

Opening times : from end March to beginning Nov.

1.8 ha (91 pitches) flat, grassy

Tariff : (2012 price) 21.90€ ✸✸ ⇌ 🔲 🕃 (10A) – Extra per person 7€

Rental rates : (2012 price) (from end March to beginning Nov.) – 9 caravans – 5 🏠 – 6 yurts – 3 🛏 – 1 cabin in the trees – 2 teepees – 7 tent bungalows – 2 tents – 1 gîte.
Per night from 40 to 140€ – Per week from 240 to 770€

Surroundings : 🦌 ♨
Leisure activities : 🖼 🎣
Facilities : ♿ ⛲ 🏛 🛁 🚰 launderette
Nearby : 🛒 🍴 🏊

GPS Longitude : 5.06149
Latitude : 44.52141

Fire safety doesn't stop when you leave your accommodation.
Always take care and consider the fire risks.

DIVONNE-LES-BAINS

01220 – Michelin map **328** J2 – pop. 7,926 – alt. 486 – ♨ (mid-Mar-end Nov)
▶ Paris 488 – Bourg-en-Bresse 129 – Genève 18 – Gex 9

Homair Vacances Le Fleutron

✆ 0450200195, *www.homair.com*

Address : 2465 Vie de L'Etraz (3km to the north, after Villard)

Opening times : from beginning April to mid Oct.

8 ha (253 pitches) terraced, sloping, stony, grassy

Tariff : (2012 price) 27€ ✸✸ ⇌ 🔲 🕃 (6A) – Extra per person 5.50€ – Reservation fee 10€

Rental rates : (2012 price) (from beginning April to mid Oct.) – 92 🛖.
Per night from 33 to 142€ – Per week from 231 to 994€ – Reservation fee 10€

🚐 sani-station 5€

In a wooded setting at the foot of a mountain.

Surroundings : 🦌 ♨
Leisure activities : 🍴 ✗ 🖼 🛝 🛶 🎠 🏊 🏊
Facilities : ♿ ⛲ 🏛 🛁 🚰 🚰 launderette 🔌 🔌

GPS Longitude : 6.1178
Latitude : 46.37137

DOUSSARD

74210 – Michelin map **328** K6 – pop. 3,473 – alt. 456
▶ Paris 555 – Albertville 27 – Annecy 20 – La Clusaz 36

Campéole la Nublière ♣♣

☎ 04 50 44 33 44, *www.campeole.com*
Address : 30 allée de la Nublière (located 1.8km to the north)
Opening times : from beginning May to mid Sept.
9.2 ha (467 pitches) flat, grassy, stony
Tariff : (2012 price) 27.90 € ♦♦ ⊞ ▤ ⚡ (6A) – Extra per person 7.30 € – Reservation fee 25 €
Rental rates : (2012 price) (from beginning May to mid Sept.) – 56 ⬛ – 10 ⬛ – 40 tent bungalows – 10 tents. Per night from 30 to 139 €– Per week from 343 to 987 €
Reservation fee 25 €
▤ sani-station
In a pleasant location beside a lake (with a beach).

Surroundings : ⟨⟨⟨ ▲
Leisure activities : ♈ ✕ ♠♠ ⚤ ≊ ⬍ entertainment room
Facilities : ⅋ ⊶ ♨ ♈ ▥ ⚬
Nearby : ▨ ✕ ♠ ♦ ♣ paragliding, tandem paragliding

GPS Longitude : 6.21763
Latitude : 45.79014

La Ferme de Serraz

☎ 04 50 44 30 68, *www.campinglaserraz.com*
Address : r. de la Poste (in the town, take the eastern exit near the post office)
3.5 ha (197 pitches) flat, grassy
Rentals : 40 ⬛.
▤ sani-station
Surroundings : ⩽ ⧠⧠
Leisure activities : ♈ ✕ ⬛ ⚤ ♻ ⬍
Facilities : ⅋ ⊶ ♨ ♠ ⚘ ♈ launderette

GPS Longitude : 6.22588
Latitude : 45.77508

> **Michelin classification:**
> ⩕⩕⩕⩕ *Extremely comfortable, equipped to a very high standard*
> ⩕⩕⩕ *Very comfortable, equipped to a high standard*
> ⩕⩕ *Comfortable and well equipped*
> ⩕ *Reasonably comfortable*
> ▲ *Satisfactory*

DUINGT

74410 – Michelin map **328** K6 – pop. 891 – alt. 450
▶ Paris 548 – Albertville 34 – Annecy 12 – Megève 48

▲ Municipal les Champs Fleuris

☎ 04 50 68 57 31, *www.camping-duingt.com*
Address : 631 voie Romaine – Les Perris (located 1km west)
1.3 ha (112 pitches) terraced, flat and relatively flat, grassy
Rentals : 4 ⬛ – 2 tent bungalows.
▤ sani-station – 10 ▤
Surroundings : ⩽
Leisure activities : ⚤
Facilities : ⅋ ⊶ ♈ launderette

GPS Longitude : 6.18882
Latitude : 45.82658

ECLASSAN

07370 – Michelin map **331** K3 – pop. 910 – alt. 420
▶ Paris 534 – Annonay 21 – Beaurepaire 46 – Condrieu 42

La Via Natura L'Oasis

📞 04 75 34 56 23, *www.oasisardeche.com* – pitches accessed via steep slope, help moving caravans onto and off pitches avilable on request
Address :at Le Petit Chaléat (4.5km northwest, follow the signs for Fourany and take road to the left)
Opening times : from end April to beginning Sept.
4 ha (59 pitches) terraced, stony, grassy
Tariff : (2012 price) 28€ ✦✦ 🚐 📧 🏠 (6A) – Extra per person 5€ – Reservation fee 6€
Rental rates : (2012 price) (from end April to beginning Sept.) – 4 🚐 – 12 🏠 – 4 tent bungalows – 4 tents. Per night from 36 to 134€ – Per week from 250 to 714€
Reservation fee 6€

In an attractive location with pitches set out on terraces, near the Ay river.

Surroundings : 🏞 ≤ 🏕 ♨
Leisure activities : ♈ ✗ 🎰 🏊 🎣 🛶 🎿
Facilities : ♿ ⚡ 🏖 🚿 🗑 🍴 🅿 🖼

Longitude : 4.73944
Latitude : 45.17889

EXCENEVEX

74140 – Michelin map **328** L2 – pop. 988 – alt. 375
▶ Paris 564 – Annecy 71 – Bonneville 42 – Douvaine 9

Campéole La Pinède

📞 04 50 72 85 05, *www.camping-lac-leman.info* – limited spaces for one-night stay
Address : 10 av. de la plage (located 1km southeast along the D 25)
Opening times : from mid April to mid Sept.
12 ha (619 pitches) relatively flat, flat, grassy
Tariff : (2012 price) 27.90€ ✦✦ 🚐 📧 🏠 (12A) – Extra per person 7.30€ – Reservation fee 15€
Rental rates : (2012 price) (from end March to mid Sept.) – 82 🚐 – 20 🏠 – 57 tent bungalows. Per night from 20 to 79€ – Per week from 343 to 966€ – Reservation fee 25€

A pleasant, wooded site close to a beach on Lake Geneva.

Surroundings : 🏕 ♨♨
Leisure activities : 🎰 🎠 🏃 ≘ jacuzzi 🏊 🚲 🖼 (open-air in season), multi-sports ground
Facilities : ♿ ⚡ 🏖 🍴 launderette 🔧
Nearby : ♈ ✗ 🏖 ✂ 🏊 🎿 ⚓ pedalos

Longitude : 6.35799
Latitude : 46.34543

FARAMANS

38260 – Michelin map **333** D5 – pop. 906 – alt. 375
▶ Paris 518 – Beaurepaire 12 – Bourgoin-Jallieu 35 – Grenoble 60

Municipal des Eydoches

📞 04 74 54 21 78, *mairie.faramans@wanadoo.fr* – limited spaces for one-night stay
Address : 515 av. des Marais (take the eastern exit along the D 37, follow the signs for La Côte-St-André)
Opening times : permanent
1 ha (60 pitches) flat, grassy
Tariff : ✦ 4.80€ 🚐 📧 5.60€ – 🏠 (5A) 3.80€
Rental rates : (permanent) – 2 🏠. Per night from 82 to 88€ – Per week from 270 to 380€
🚐 sani-station 12€

Surroundings : ♨
Facilities : ♿ 🏖 🍴 🚿 🖼
Nearby : ✂ 🎿

Longitude : 5.17563
Latitude : 45.39348

FÉLINES

07340 – Michelin map **331** K2 – pop. 1,475 – alt. 380
▶ Paris 520 – Annonay 13 – Beaurepaire 31 – Condrieu 24

Bas-Larin

⌂ 04 75 34 87 93, *www.camping-bas-larin.com*
Address : 88 rte de Larin-le-Bas (situated 2km southeast, along the N 82, follow the signs for Serrières and take the road to the right)
Opening times : from beginning April to end Sept.
1.5 ha (67 pitches) terraced, relatively flat to hilly, grassy
Tariff : 21.30€ ✦✦ ⇐ 🔲 💧 (10A) – Extra per person 3.50€
Rental rates : (from beginning April to end Sept.) – 7 🚐 – 1 🏠 – 3 tent bungalows. Per night from 40 to 80€ – Per week from 220 to 590€
🚐 sani-station 17.50€

Surroundings : 〰 ♀
Leisure activities : 🍷 ✕ 🎦 🏇 🔥 🏊
Facilities : & ⊶ 🛁 🎇 🚽 🍴 🖼 🎣

GPS Longitude : 4.75284
Latitude : 45.30671

LA FERRIÈRE

38580 – Michelin map **333** J6 – pop. 226 – alt. 926
▶ Paris 613 – Lyon 146 – Grenoble 52 – Chambéry 47

Neige et Nature

⌂ 04 76 45 19 84, *www.neige-nature.fr* – alt. 900
Address : chemin de Montarmand (to the west of the village; beside the Bréda river)
Opening times : from mid May to mid Sept.
1.2 ha (45 pitches) terraced, relatively flat, flat, grassy
Tariff : 22.10€ ✦✦ ⇐ 🔲 💧 (10A) – Extra per person 5.70€
Rental rates : (permanent) – 2 🚐 – 2 🏠. Per night from 70 to 90€
Per week from 315 to 630€ – Reservation fee 10€
🚐 15 🔲 17.80€
A green and well-kept campsite.

Surroundings : 🌿 ≤ 〰 ♀
Leisure activities : 🎦
Facilities : & ⊶ 🎇 🍴 🛁 🍴 🖼 🎣
Nearby : 🏊 (pool)

GPS Longitude : 6.08331
Latitude : 45.3184

To visit a town or region, use the MICHELIN Green Guides.

FEURS

42110 – Michelin map **327** E5 – pop. 7,741 – alt. 343
▶ Paris 433 – Lyon 69 – Montbrison 24 – Roanne 38

Municipal du Palais

⌂ 04 77 26 43 41, *mairie.camping@feurs.fr*
Address : rte de Civens (take the northern exit along the N 82, follow the signs for Roanne and take a right turn)
5 ha (385 pitches) flat, grassy, lake
🚐 sani-station – 25 🔲
In a peaceful location, not far from the town centre.

Surroundings : ♀♀
Leisure activities : 🏇
Facilities : & ⊶ 🍴 🛁 🎇 🚽 🍴 🎣
Nearby : ✕ 🏊

GPS Longitude : 4.22572
Latitude : 45.75429

FLEURIE

69820 – Michelin map **327** H2 – pop. 1,250 – alt. 320
▶ Paris 410 – Bourg-en-Bresse 46 – Chauffailles 44 – Lyon 58

Municipal la Grappe Fleurie

✆ 0474698007, *www.camping-beaujolais.fr*
Address : r. de la Grappe Fleurie (600m south of the town along the D 119e and take a right turn)
2.5 ha (96 pitches) flat, grassy
Rentals : 4 🏠.
sani-station
In the heart of a vineyard.

Surroundings :
Leisure activities :
Facilities : launderette
Nearby :

Longitude : 4.7001
Latitude : 46.18854

LES GETS

74260 – Michelin map **328** N4 – pop. 1,254 – alt. 1,170 – Winter sports : 1,170/2,000 m 5 47
▶ Paris 579 – Annecy 77 – Bonneville 33 – Chamonix-Mont-Blanc 60

Le Frêne

✆ 0450758060, *www.alpensport-hotel.com* – alt. 1,315 – ℞
Address : at Les Cornus (take the southwestern exit along the D 902 then continue 2.3km, following signs for Les Platons to the right)
Opening times : from end June to beginning Sept.
0.3 ha (32 pitches) terraced, open site, relatively flat, grassy
Tariff : (2012 price) 20.50€ ✱✱ 🚐 🗉 (10A) – Extra per person 7€

Surroundings : Aiguille du Midi, Mt Blanc mountain range
Leisure activities :
Facilities :

Longitude : 6.64296
Latitude : 46.15065

*This guide is not intended as a list of all the camping sites in France;
its aim is to provide a selection of the best sites in each category.*

GEX

01170 – Michelin map **328** J3 – pop. 9,882 – alt. 626
▶ Paris 490 – Genève 19 – Lons-le-Saunier 93 – Pontarlier 110

Municipal les Genêts

✆ 0450428457, *www.pays-de-gex.org*
Address : rte de Divonne-les-Bains (located 1km east along the D 984 and take the road to the right)
Opening times : from beginning May to end Sept.
3.3 ha (140 pitches) flat and relatively flat, grassy, fine gravel
Tariff : (2012 price) ✱ 4.20€ 🚐 🗉 6.10€ – (16A) 3.30€
Rental rates : (2012 price) (from beginning May to end Sept.) – 4 🛏.
Per week from 253 to 493€
sani-station 3€
A pretty situation between Lake Geneva and the Jura mountains.

Surroundings :
Leisure activities :
Facilities : launderette
Nearby :

Longitude : 6.06841
Latitude : 46.33564

LE GRAND-BORNAND

74450 – Michelin map **328** L5 – pop. 2,195 – alt. 934 – Winter sports : 1,000/2,100 m 2 37
▶ Paris 564 – Albertville 47 – Annecy 31 – Bonneville 23

L'Escale

 0450022069, *www.campinglescale.com*
Address : rte de la Patinoire (east of the town, near the church, near the Borne river)
Opening times : from mid May to end Sept.
2.8 ha (149 pitches) terraced, flat and relatively flat, grassy, stony
Tariff : (2012 price) 29.90€ ✝✝ (10A) – Extra per person 580€ – Reservation fee 12€
Rental rates : (2012 price) (permanent) – 26 – 26 – 2 – 6 studios – 24 apartments.
Per night from 45 to 65€ – Per week from 290 to 695€ – Reservation fee 12€
Pleasant water park and play area.

Surroundings :
Leisure activities : ✗ jacuzzi
Facilities : launderette
Nearby : sports trail

Longitude : 6.42817
Latitude : 45.94044

Le Clos du Pin

 0450027057, *www.le-clos-du-pin.com* – alt. 1,015 – limited spaces for one-night stay
Address : 1.3km east along the follow the signs for Le Bouchet; beside the Borne river
Opening times : from mid June to mid Sept. and from beg Dec to mid-May
1.3 ha (61 pitches) relatively flat, grassy
Tariff : (2012 price) 21.40€ ✝✝ (10A) – Extra per person 4.40€ – Reservation fee 8€
Rental rates : (2012 price) (from mid June to mid Sept. and from beg Dec to mid-May) – 1
Per night from 40 to 66€ – Per week from 280 to 460€ – Reservation fee 8€
 sani-station 16€

Surroundings : Chaîne des Aravis mountains
Leisure activities :
Facilities : launderette

Longitude : 6.44281
Latitude : 45.93971

*Using the traditional Michelin classification method, the guide provides
you with an easy, speedy reference for assessing the category of each site:
1 to 5 tents (see page 10).*

GRANE

26400 – Michelin map **332** C5 – pop. 1,730 – alt. 175
▶ Paris 583 – Crest 10 – Montélimar 34 – Privas 29

Les Quatre Saisons

 0475626417, *www.camping-4saisons.com*
Address : take the southeastern exit, 900m along the D 113, follow the signs for la Roche-sur-Grâne
Opening times : from beginning April to end Sept.
2 ha (80 pitches) terraced, relatively flat, flat, grassy, sandy
Tariff : 31€ ✝✝ (6A) – Extra per person 5€ – Reservation fee 10€
Rental rates : (from beginning April to end Sept.) – 4 – 11 – 4 tents.
Per night from 42 to 110€ – Per week from 210 to 770€ – Reservation fee 15€
 sani-station

Surroundings :
Leisure activities :
Facilities : launderette
Nearby :

Longitude : 4.92671
Latitude : 44.72684

GRAVIÈRES

07140 – Michelin map **331** G7 – pop. 391 – alt. 220
▶ Paris 636 – Lyon 213 – Privas 71 – Nîmes 92

⚠ Le Mas du Serre

𝒫 0475373384, *www.campinglemasduserre.com*
Address : at Le Serre (1.3km southeast along the D 113 and take the road to the left, 300m from the Chassezac)
Opening times : from beginning April to end Sept.
1.5 ha (75 pitches) terraced, relatively flat, flat, grassy
Tariff : 24.50€ ✚✚ ⇔ 🔲 🗓 (5A) – Extra per person 6€
Rental rates : (permanent) – 6 🚐. Per night from 52 to 94€ – Per week from 370 to 660€
🚽 sani-station 15€
In an attractive location based around a 'mas' (old regional house).

Surroundings : 🏞 ≤ 🌳🌳
Leisure activities : 🏊 🖊 🏊
Facilities : ⅙ ⚊⚊ 🖊 🕯 🖥
Nearby : ≋

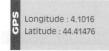
Longitude : 4.1016
Latitude : 44.41476

GRESSE-EN-VERCORS

38650 – Michelin map **333** G8 – pop. 394 – alt. 1,205 – Winter sports : 1,300/1,700 m ⚡16 ⚡
▶ Paris 610 – Clelles 22 – Grenoble 48 – Monestier-de-Clermont 14

⚠ Les 4 Saisons

𝒫 0476343027, *www.camping-les4saisons.com*
Address : 1.3km southwest, at La Ville
Opening times : from beginning May to mid Oct.
2.2 ha (90 pitches) terraced, flat, stony, fine gravel, grassy
Tariff : 23.60€ ✚✚ ⇔ 🔲 🗓 (10A) – Extra per person 5€ – Reservation fee 6€
Rental rates : (from beginning May to mid Oct.) 🍴 – 9 🚐 – 3 🏠.
Per week from 383 to 670€ – Reservation fee 16€
🚽 sani-station 5€
A pleasant location at the foot of the Massif du Vercors mountains.

Surroundings : ❄ 🏞 ≤ Massif du Vercors mountains
Leisure activities : ▼ ✗ 🖼 🖊 🏊
Facilities : ⅙ ⚊⚊ ▥ 🕯 launderette
Nearby : 🛶 ✗

Longitude : 5.55559
Latitude : 44.8965

GRIGNAN

26230 – Michelin map **332** C7 – pop. 1,564 – alt. 198
▶ Paris 629 – Crest 46 – Montélimar 25 – Nyons 25

⚠ Les Truffières

𝒫 0475469362, *www.lestruffieres.com* 🚭
Address : 1100 chemin Belle-Vue-d'Air, in the Nachony quartier (situated 2km southwest along the D 541, follow the signs for Donzère and take the D 71, follow the signs for Chamaret)
Opening times : from end April to mid Sept.
1 ha (85 pitches) flat, grassy, stony, wood
Tariff : 24.20€ ✚✚ ⇔ 🔲 🗓 (10A) – Extra per person 5€ – Reservation fee 12€
Rental rates : (from end April to mid Sept.) 🚭 – 12 🚐 – 12 🏠. Per night from 50 to 95€
Per week from 230 to 760€ – Reservation fee 12€
The site is wooded and shady.

Surroundings : 🏞 ⌂ 🌳🌳
Leisure activities : ✗ 🖼 🖊 🏊
Facilities : ⅙ ⚊⚊ 🖊 🕯 🖥

Longitude : 4.89121
Latitude : 44.41163

GROISY

74570 – Michelin map **328** K4 – pop. 2,976 – alt. 690
▶ Paris 534 – Dijon 228 – Grenoble 120 – Lons-le-Saunier 146

Le Moulin Dollay

℘ 0450680031, *www.moulindollay.fr*
Address : 206 r. du Moulin Dollay (situated 2km southeast, junction of D 2 and N 203; beside a stream at Le Plot)
Opening times : from beginning May to beginning Oct.
3 ha (30 pitches) flat, grassy, stony, wood
Tariff : 22€ ⚹⚹ ⇔ 🄴 (6A) – Extra per person 5€
🚗 sani-station 5€ – 6 🄴 15€ – 🔋15€

Surroundings : 🛏 ♀
Leisure activities : 🎣 ⚘
Facilities : ⚹ ⚯ 🚿 ⫝̸ ⛱ ♨ ⚐ ⚑ launderette

GPS Longitude : 6.19076
Latitude : 46.00224

HAUTECOURT

01250 – Michelin map **328** F4 – pop. 760 – alt. 370
▶ Paris 442 – Bourg-en-Bresse 20 – Nantua 24 – Oyonnax 33

L'Île de Chambod

℘ 0474372541, *www.campingilechambod.com*
Address : 3232 rte du Port (4.5km southeast along the D 59, follow the signs for Poncin then take the turning to the left, 300m from the Ain (small lake)
Opening times : from mid April to end Sept.
2.4 ha (110 pitches) flat, grassy
Tariff : (2012 price) ⚹ 4.90€ ⇔ 2.90€ 🄴 3.50€ – 🄱 (10A) 3.90€
Rental rates : (2012 price) (from mid April to end Sept.) – 8 🛏 – 4 tents.
Per night from 23 to 95€ – Per week from 161 to 665€ – Reservation fee 18.50€
🚗 sani-station 2.50€

Surroundings : ⟨ 🛏 ♀
Leisure activities : ⚑ ✗ ♨ ⚓
Facilities : ⚹ ⚯ ⛱ ♨ 🄿
Nearby : ⚓ ⚒ sports trail

GPS Longitude : 5.42819
Latitude : 46.12761

We welcome your feedback on our listed campsites.
Please email us at: campingfrance@tp.michelin.com
Many thanks in advance!

ISSARLÈS

07470 – Michelin map **331** G4 – pop. 165 – alt. 946
▶ Paris 574 – Coucouron 16 – Langogne 36 – Le Monastier-sur-Gazeille 18

La Plaine de la Loire

℘ 0466462577, *www.campinglaplainedelaloire.fr* – alt. 900
Address : Le Moulin du Lac – Pont de Laborie (3km west along the D 16, follow the signs for Coucouron and take the road to the left before the bridge)
1 ha (55 pitches) flat, grassy
Situated beside the Loire river.

Surroundings : ⛰ ⟨ ♀
Leisure activities : ✗ ⚘ ⚓ ⚒
Facilities : ⚯ ♨

GPS Longitude : 4.05191
Latitude : 44.818

JAUJAC

07380 – Michelin map **331** H6 – pop. 1,212 – alt. 450
▶ Paris 612 – Privas 44 – Le Puy-en-Velay 81

⚠ **Bonneval**

𝒫 04 75 93 27 09, *www.campingbonneval.com* ✉ 07380 Fabras
Address : at Les Plots at Fabras (situated 2km northeast along the D 19 and take D 5, follow the signs for Pont-de-Labeaume, 100m from the Lignon river and basaltic lava flow)
Opening times : from beginning April to end Sept.
3 ha (60 pitches) terraced, relatively flat, flat, grassy
Tariff : (2012 price) 24.50€ ✤✤ ⇔ 🖩 🔌 (6A) – Extra per person 5.50€
Rental rates : (2012 price) (from beginning April to end Sept.) – 4 🛏 – 4 🏠.
Per week from 270 to 640€

Surroundings : ⌇ ≼ Chaine du Tanargue mountains 🌿🌿
Leisure activities : 🍴 ⚐🏊 ♿ 🎾
Facilities : 🚿 ⚡ (season) 📮🏕 ⛽ 🎦
Nearby : 🏊

GPS Longitude : 4.25825
Latitude : 44.64168

JEANSAGNIÈRE

42920 – Michelin map **327** C5 – pop. 84 – alt. 1,050
▶ Paris 440 – Lyon 111 – St-Étienne 84 – Clermont-Ferrand 88

⚠ **Village de la Droséra**
(rental of chalets only)

𝒫 04 77 24 81 44, *www.ladrosera.fr*
Address : at La Droséra
Opening times : permanent
16 ha terraced, grassy, stony, rocks
Rentals : 7 🏠. Per night from 115€ – Per week from 580€
Pretty wooden chalets in a mountain park.

Surroundings : ⌇ ≼ of the Monts du Forez 🌿🌿
Leisure activities : 🎮 ⚐🏊 🎿 walking trails
Facilities : ⚡ 📮

GPS Longitude : 3.83592
Latitude : 45.73828

To make the best possible use of this guide,
please read pages 2–15 carefully.

JOANNAS

07110 – Michelin map **331** H6 – pop. 342 – alt. 430
▶ Paris 650 – Aubenas 23 – Largentière 8 – Privas 55

⚠ **La Marette**

𝒫 04 75 88 38 88, *www.lamarette.com*
Address : rte de Valgorge (2.4km west along the D 24, after La Prade)
Opening times : from beginning May to mid Sept.
4 ha (91 pitches) undulating, terraced, grassy, wood
Tariff : 27.50€ ✤✤ ⇔ 🖩 🔌 (10A) – Extra per person 5.40€
Rental rates : (from beginning May to mid Sept.) – 2 'gypsy' caravans – 24 🛏 – 19 🏠.
Per night from 30 to 112€ – Per week from 206 to 785€

Surroundings : ⌇ ≼ ▱ 🌿🌿
Leisure activities : 🍴 🎮 ⚐🏊 🎣 🛶
Facilities : 🚿 ⚡ 🎦 ⛽

GPS Longitude : 4.22913
Latitude : 44.56662

Le Roubreau

0475883207, www.leroubreau.com

Address : rte de Valgorge (1.4km west along the D 24 and take road to the left)
Opening times : from mid April to mid Sept.
3 ha (100 pitches) relatively flat, flat, grassy, stony
Tariff : 26€ ⚭ ⚭ ⟶ 回 ⚡ (4A) – Extra per person 6.50€ – Reservation fee 7.50€
Rental rates : (from mid April to mid Sept.) – 14 ⟐ – 15 ⌂ – 2 tent bungalows.
Per night from 29 to 85€ – Per week from 200 to 620€ – Reservation fee 7.50€
sani-station 5€
Situated beside the Roubreau river.

Surroundings : ⛰ ⟨ ⊏ 🏕
Leisure activities : ⛲ ✕ 🎦 🚣 🎿 🛶
Facilities : ♿ ⟶ (Jul–Aug) 🏕 ⛺ 🔳 ⛽

GPS Longitude : 4.23865
Latitude : 44.55964

JOYEUSE

07260 – Michelin map **331** H7 – pop. 1,640 – alt. 180
▶ Paris 650 – Alès 54 – Mende 97 – Privas 55

La Nouzarède

0475399201, www.camping-nouzarede.fr

Address : north of the town along the rte du Stade, 150m from the Beaume river (direct access)
Opening times : from beginning April to end Sept.
2 ha (103 pitches) flat, grassy, stony
Tariff : (2012 price) 29.60€ ⚭ ⚭ ⟶ 回 ⚡ (10A) – Extra per person 6.50€
Rental rates : (2012 price) (from beginning April to end Sept.) – 42 ⟐ – 1 ⌂.
Per night from 45 to 63€ – Per week from 245 to 765€ – Reservation fee 14€

Surroundings : ⊏ 🏕
Leisure activities : ⛲ ✕ 🎦 🚣 🎿 🐴
Facilities : ♿ ⟶ 🏕 ⛺ ⟲ ⛽ 🔳 🏊 ⛽
Nearby : 🎿 ⛷ 🛶

GPS Longitude : 4.23526
Latitude : 44.48368

A 'quartier' is a district or area of a town or village.

LALLEY

38930 – Michelin map **333** H9 – pop. 205 – alt. 850
▶ Paris 626 – Grenoble 63 – La Mure 30 – Sisteron 80

Belle Roche

0476347533, www.camping-belleroche.com – alt. 860

Address : chemin de Combe Morée (head south of the town following signs for Mens and take the road to the right)
Opening times : from end March to mid Oct.
2.4 ha (60 pitches) flat, terrace, stony, grassy
Tariff : (2012 price) 20€ ⚭ ⚭ ⟶ 回 ⚡ (10A) – Extra per person 6€
Rental rates : (2012 price) (from end March to mid Oct.) – 6 ⟐ – 1 tent – 1 cabin.
Per night from 45 to 60€ – Per week from 250 to 610€
sani-station
A pleasant location opposite the village.

Surroundings : ⛰ ⟨ ⊏ 🏕
Leisure activities : ⛲ ✕ 🏓 🚣 🎿 multi-sports ground
Facilities : ♿ ⟶ ⟲ ⛽ 🏊 launderette ⛽
Nearby : 🎿

GPS Longitude : 5.67889
Latitude : 44.75472

LALOUVESC

07520 – Michelin map **331** J3 – pop. 496 – alt. 1,050
▶ Paris 553 – Annonay 24 – Lamastre 25 – Privas 80

▲ Municipal le Pré du Moulin

✆ 0475678486, *www.lalouvesc.com*
Address : chemin de l'Hermuzière (north of the village)
2.5 ha (70 pitches) terraced, relatively flat, grassy
Rentals : 5 🏠.
sani-station

Surroundings : ⚲
Leisure activities : 🎦 ⚓ ⚒ 🏊
Facilities : ⚹ ⚬ 🛁 ☕ 🍴 🧺

GPS Longitude : 4.53392
Latitude : 45.12388

LAMASTRE

07270 – Michelin map **331** J4 – pop. 2,501 – alt. 375
▶ Paris 577 – Privas 55 – Le Puy-en-Velay 72 – Valence 38

▲ Le Retourtour

✆ 0475064071, *www.camping-de-retourtour.com*
Address : 1 r. de Retourtour
Opening times : from mid April to end Sept.
2.9 ha (130 pitches) flat and relatively flat, grassy, fine gravel
Tariff : 23.96€ ✶✶ ⚐ 🅴 🄴 (13A) – Extra per person 4.98€ – Reservation fee 10€
Rental rates : (from mid April to end Sept.) – 13 🏠 – 3 tent bungalows – 2 tents – 2 gîtes.
Per night from 39 to 89€ – Per week from 182 to 595€ – Reservation fee 10€
sani-station – ⚡10.56€
Situated near a small lake.

Surroundings : ⚲ ♨
Leisure activities : 🍷 ✗ 🎦 🅖 evening 🎵 ⚓ 🏊
Facilities : ⚹ ⚬ 🛁 🛀 ☕ 🍴 🚿
Nearby : ≋ (beach)

GPS Longitude : 4.56483
Latitude : 44.99164

Do not confuse:
▲ to ▲▲▲ : MICHELIN classification
with
★ to ★★★★★ : official classification

LANSLEVILLARD

73480 – Michelin map **333** O6 – pop. 457 – alt. 1,500 – Winter sports : 1,400/2,800 m ⚞1 ⚟21 ⚡
▶ Paris 689 – Albertville 116 – Briançon 87 – Chambéry 129

▲ Caravaneige Municipal

✆ 0479059052, *www.camping-valcenis.com/*
Address : r. sous l'Eglise (southwestern exit, follow the signs for Lanslebourg; beside rapids)
3 ha (100 pitches) flat, grassy, stony
sani-station

Surroundings : ❄ ≋
Leisure activities : 🍷 ✗ 🎦 🖼 ⚓
Facilities : ⚹ ⚬ 🧺 launderette 🚿
Nearby : ⚒ 🏊

GPS Longitude : 6.90928
Latitude : 45.29057

LARNAS

07220 – Michelin map **331** J7 – pop. 97 – alt. 300
▶ Paris 631 – Aubenas 41 – Bourg-St-Andéol 12 – Montélimar 24

FranceLoc Le Domaine d'Imbours 🏕

☏ 0475543950, *www.domaine-imbours.com*
Address : 2.5km southwest along the D 262 – for caravans, from Bourg-St-Andéol, go via St-Remèze and Mas du Gras (D 4, D 362 and D 262)
Opening times : from beginning April to end Sept.
270 ha/10 ha for camping (694 pitches) relatively flat, flat, stony, grassy
Tariff : (2012 price) 31€ ♣♣ 🚐 🗉 (6A) – Extra per person 7€ – Reservation fee 27€
Rental rates : (2012 price) (from beginning April to end Sept.) – 2 'gypsy' caravans – 324 🚐 – 46 🏠 – 12 studios – 21 tents – 88 gîtes – hotel (96 rooms). Per night from 33 to 61€ – Per week from 133 to 1,169€ – Reservation fee 27€

> **Surroundings :** 🌿 ♨
> **Leisure activities :** ♈ ✗ 🎱 🎳 🏃 ⛹ 🚴 ✂ ⛳ 🏐 🏊 ⛵ multi-sports ground
> **Facilities :** ♿ ⚟ 🛁 ♨ 🍴 🛒 🚮 🚿
> **Nearby :** 🐎

GPS Longitude : 4.5764
        Latitude : 44.4368

The guide is updated each year, so consult the latest edition for the most up-to-date information and pricing.

LATHUILE

74210 – Michelin map **328** K6 – pop. 960 – alt. 510
▶ Paris 554 – Albertville 30 – Annecy 18 – La Clusaz 38

Les Fontaines

☏ 0450443122, *www.campinglesfontaines.com*
Address : 1295 rte de Chaparon (situated 2km to the north at Chaparon)
Opening times : from mid May to mid Sept.
3 ha (170 pitches) terraced, relatively flat, flat, grassy
Tariff : (2012 price) 30.30€ ♣♣ 🚐 🗉 (6A) – Extra per person 7€ – Reservation fee 16€
Rental rates : (2012 price) (from mid April to end Sept.) ✂ (from mid-Apr to end Jun) – 55 🚐 – 3 🏠 – 8 teepees. Per night from 45 to 117€ – Per week from 278 to 820€ – Reservation fee 16€

> **Surroundings :** 🌿 ≤ ♨
> **Leisure activities :** ♈ ✗ 🎱 🎳 🏃 🏊 ⛵ multi-sports ground
> **Facilities :** ♿ ⚟ 🛁 ♨ launderette 🚮 🚿

GPS Longitude : 6.20444
        Latitude : 45.80037

L'Idéal

☏ 0450443297, *www.camping-ideal.com*
Address : 715 rte de Chaparon (located 1.5km to the north)
Opening times : from beginning May to mid Sept.
3.2 ha (300 pitches) flat and relatively flat, grassy
Tariff : (2012 price) 30.30€ ♣♣ 🚐 🗉 (10A) – Extra per person 7€ – Reservation fee 16€
Rental rates : (2012 price) (from end April to mid Sept.) ♿ (1 mobile home) ✂ – 69 🚐 – 8 apartments. Per week from 250 to 790€ – Reservation fee 16€
Close to lakes and mountains, with an attractive swimming area.

> **Surroundings :** 🌿 ≤ ♀
> **Leisure activities :** ♈ ✗ 🎱 🎳 jacuzzi ⛵ 🏐 🏊 ⛵ multi-sports ground
> **Facilities :** ♿ ⚟ 🛁 ♨ launderette 🚮 🚿

GPS Longitude : 6.20582
        Latitude : 45.79537

La Ravoire

ℰ 04 50 44 37 80, *www.camping-la-ravoire.fr*
Address : rte de la Ravoire (2.5km to the north)
Opening times : from beginning May to mid Sept.
2 ha (110 pitches) flat, grassy
Tariff : 34.10€ ✝✝ ⇔ 🅴 🅸 (15A) – Extra per person 6.50€ – Reservation fee 16€
Rental rates : (2012 price) (from end April to mid Sept.) ⟡ – 16 🛖 – 4 🏠.
Per night from 50 to 80€ – Per week from 250 to 798€ – Reservation fee 16€
In a beautiful green setting near the lake.

Surroundings : ≤ 🌳🌳
Leisure activities : 🍽 ✗ 🎱 🚣 🏊 ⛵ multi-sports ground
Facilities : 🚾 ⚡ 🔌🛁 🚿 🚰 🚻 launderette
Nearby : 🎣

Longitude : 6.20975
Latitude : 45.80244

Le Taillefer

ℰ 04 50 44 30 30, *www.campingletaillefer.com*
Address : 1530 rte de Chaparon (situated 2km to the north, at Chaparon)
Opening times : from beginning May to end Sept.
1 ha (32 pitches) terraced, sloping, flat, grassy
Tariff : 22€ ✝✝ ⇔ 🅴 🅸 (6A) – Extra per person 5€

Surroundings : ≤ 🌳
Leisure activities : 🍽 🎱 🚣 🚲
Facilities : 🚾 ⚡ 🚿 🚻 launderette

Longitude : 6.20565
Latitude : 45.80231

AURAC-EN-VIVARAIS

7110 – Michelin map **331** H6 – pop. 885 – alt. 182
Paris 646 – Alès 60 – Mende 102 – Privas 50

Les Châtaigniers

ℰ 04 75 36 86 26, *www.chataigniers-laurac.com*
Address : at Peyrot (to the southeast of the town, recommended route via the D 104)
1.2 ha (71 pitches) relatively flat, flat, grassy
Rentals : ⟡ – 10 🛖.
🚐 3 🅴
Surroundings : 🌳🌳
Leisure activities : 🎱 🚣 🏊
Facilities : 🚾 ⚡ 🛁 🖼

Longitude : 4.29497
Latitude : 44.50429

ÉPIN-LE-LAC

3610 – Michelin map **333** H4 – pop. 407 – alt. 400
Paris 555 – Belley 36 – Chambéry 24 – Les Échelles 17

Le Curtelet

ℰ 04 79 44 11 22, *www.camping-le-curtelet.com*
Address : 1.4km to the northwest
Opening times : from mid May to end Sept.
1.3 ha (94 pitches) relatively flat, grassy
Tariff : (2012 price) 19.20€ ✝✝ ⇔ 🅴 🅸 (10A) – Extra per person 4.10€ – Reservation fee 10€

Surroundings : ≤ 🌳⛰
Leisure activities : 🍽 🚣 🏊 🎣
Facilities : 🚾 ⚡ (Jul-Sept) 🚿🛁 🚻 launderette
Nearby : ✂ 🔭

Longitude : 5.77916
Latitude : 45.54002

RHÔNE-ALPES

LESCHERAINES

73340 – Michelin map **333** J3 – pop. 731 – alt. 649 – Leisure centre
▶ Paris 557 – Aix-les-Bains 26 – Annecy 26 – Chambéry 29

Municipal l'Île

℘ 0479638000, www.savoie-camping.com
Address : at the base de loisirs (leisure centre) : Les Îles du Chéran (2.5km southeast along the D 912, follow the signs for Annecy and take the turning to the right, 200m from the Chéran)
Opening times : from mid April to end Sept.
7.5 ha (250 pitches) open site, terraced, flat, grassy
Tariff : 18.25€ ✸✸ ⇔ ▣ [ᵷ] (10A) – Extra per person 4.30€ – Reservation fee 10€
Rental rates : (from mid April to end Sept.) – 14 ▥ – 5 ⌂ – 3 gîtes. Per night from 36 to 83€ – Per week from 250 to 580€
▥ sani-station 1€ – 10 ▣ 5€
Beside a small lake, surrounded by woods and mountains.

Surroundings : ▨ ⩽ ⌕ ⚠
Leisure activities : ▭
Facilities : ♿ ⌾ ♨ ⚘ ⇲ ⁇ launderette
Leisure/activities centre : ☗ ✕ ⚲ ⚒ ⚲ ≋ ⚶ ⚑ pedalos

GPS Longitude : 6.11207 Latitude : 45.70352

LUGRIN

74500 – Michelin map **328** N2 – pop. 2,260 – alt. 413
▶ Paris 584 – Annecy 91 – Évian-les-Bains 8 – St-Gingolph 12

Vieille Église

℘ 0450760195, www.campingvieilleeglise.com
Address : 53 rte des Préparraux (situated 2km west, at Vieille-Église)
Opening times : from beginning April to end Oct.
1.6 ha (100 pitches) terraced, flat and relatively flat, grassy
Tariff : (2012 price) 23.30€ ✸✸ ⇔ ▣ [ᵷ] (10A) – Extra per person 6.80€ – Reservation fee 5€
Rental rates : (2012 price) (from beginning April to end Oct.) – 27 ▥ – 1 ⌂ – 2 studios – 1 apartment. Per night from 45 to 75€ – Per week from 250 to 690€ – Reservation fee 5€
▥ sani-station 7€

Surroundings : ⩽ ⌂ ⌕
Leisure activities : ⚲ ⚲
Facilities : ♿ ⌾ ⓒ ▥ ⚘ ⁇ launderette

GPS Longitude : 6.64655 Latitude : 46.40052

LUS-LA-CROIX-HAUTE

26620 – Michelin map **332** H6 – pop. 507 – alt. 1,050
▶ Paris 638 – Alès 207 – Die 45 – Gap 49

Champ la Chèvre

℘ 0492585014, www.campingchamplachevre.com
Address : to the southeast of the town, near the swimming pool
Opening times : from end April to mid Sept.
3.6 ha (100 pitches) terraced, relatively flat, flat, grassy
Tariff : (2012 price) 21.80€ ✸✸ ⇔ ▣ [ᵷ] (6A) – Extra per person 6.50€ – Reservation fee 15€
Rental rates : (2012 price) (permanent) – 4 ▥ – 8 ⌂. Per night from 50 to 98 € – Per week from 255 to 725 € – Reservation fee 15€
▥ sani-station – 2 ▣ 21.80€

Surroundings : ▨ ⩽ ⌕
Leisure activities : ▭ ▨ (open-air in season)
Facilities : ♿ ⌾ ▥ ⁇ ▣
Nearby : ⚑

GPS Longitude : 5.70998 Latitude : 44.6629

MAISON-NEUVE

07230 – Michelin map **331** H7

Paris 662 – Aubenas 35 – Largentière 25 – Privas 67

Pont de Maisonneuve

0475393925, *www.camping-pontdemaisonneuve.com* 07460 Beaulieu

Address : take the southern exit along the D 104, follow the signs for Alès and take a right turn, follow the signs for Casteljau, after the bridge

Opening times : from beginning April to end Sept.

3 ha (100 pitches) flat, grassy

Tariff : (2012 price) 18€ ✝✝ (6A) – Extra per person 4.20€

Rental rates : (2012 price) (from beginning April to end Sept.) – 12 .
Per night from 40 to 70€ – Per week from 260 to 540€

sani-station 5€

Situated beside the Chassezac river.

Surroundings :
Leisure activities :
Facilities :

Longitude : 4.21881
Latitude : 44.39051

MALARCE-SUR-LA-THINES

07140 – Michelin map **331** G7 – pop. 231 – alt. 340

Paris 626 – Aubenas 48 – Largentière 38 – Privas 79

Les Gorges du Chassezac

0475394512, *www.campinggorgeschassezac.com*

Address : at Champ d'Eynes (4km southeast along the D 113, follow the signs for Les Vans)

Opening times : from beginning May to mid Sept.

2.5 ha (80 pitches) terraced, relatively flat, flat, stony, grassy

Tariff : (2012 price) 18€ ✝✝ (6A) – Extra per person 3€

Rental rates : (2012 price) (from beginning May to mid Sept.) – 9 .
Per night from 40 to 50€ – Per week from 300 to 450€

Situated beside the Chassezac river (direct access).

Surroundings :
Leisure activities :
Facilities : (Jul-Aug)

Longitude : 4.07
Latitude : 44.44

MALBOSC

07140 – Michelin map **331** G7 – pop. 152 – alt. 450

Paris 644 – Alès 45 – La Grand-Combe 29 – Les Vans 19

Le Moulin de Gournier

0475373550, *www.camping-moulin-de-gournier.com*

Address : le Gournier (7km northeast along the D 216, follow the signs for Les Vans)

Opening times : from beginning May to end Sept.

4 ha/1 ha for camping (29 pitches) terraced, stony, grassy

Tariff : (2012 price) 18€ ✝✝ (3A) – Extra per person 6€ – Reservation fee 8€

Rental rates : (2012 price) (from mid June to mid Sept.) – 1 . Per week from 500 to 600€ – Reservation fee 8€

3 18€

In a pleasant setting beside the Ganière river.

Surroundings :
Leisure activities :
Facilities :

Longitude : 4.07302
Latitude : 44.34524

LES MARCHES

73800 – Michelin map **333** I5 – pop. 2,453 – alt. 328
▶ Paris 572 – Albertville 43 – Chambéry 12 – Grenoble 44

La Ferme du Lac

📞 0479281348, *www.campinglafermedulac.fr*
Address : located 1km southwest along the N 90, follow the signs for Pontcharra and take the D 12 to the right
2.6 ha (100 pitches) flat, grassy
Rentals : 🏕 – 9 🚐 – 1 🏠.
sani-station – 8 ▣

Surroundings : 🌲 🟢🟢
Leisure activities : 🛖 🏊
Facilities : 🚻 ⚬━ 🍽 🍴 🚿

GPS Longitude : 5.99327
Latitude : 45.49595

MARS

07320 – Michelin map **331** H3 – pop. 279 – alt. 1,060
▶ Paris 579 – Annonay 49 – Le Puy-en-Velay 44 – Privas 71

La Prairie

📞 0475302447, *www.camping-laprairie.com*
Address : at Laillier (to the northeast of the town along the D 15, follow the signs for St-Agrève and take road to the left)
Opening times : from mid May to mid Sept.
0.6 ha (30 pitches) flat, grassy, sandy
Tariff : (2012 price) 🧍 3.30€ 🚗 1.50€ ▣ 2.90€ – 🔌 (6A) 3€
sani-station 4€

Surroundings : 🌿 ≤
Leisure activities : ✕ 🎣 🚴
Facilities : 🚻 ⚬━ 🚽 🚿
Nearby : 🐴 ✗ 🏊 (lake)

GPS Longitude : 4.32632
Latitude : 45.02393

These symbols are used for a campsite that is exceptional in its category:
🏔🏔...🏔 *Particularly pleasant setting, quality and range of services available*
🌿🌿 *Tranquil, isolated site – quiet site, particularly at night*
≤≤ *Exceptional view – interesting or panoramic view*

MASSIGNIEU-DE-RIVES

01300 – Michelin map **328** H6 – pop. 591 – alt. 295
▶ Paris 516 – Aix-les-Bains 26 – Belley 10 – Morestel 37

Le Lac du Lit du Roi

📞 0479421203, *www.camping-savoie.com*
Address : at La Tuillère (2.5km north following signs for Belley and take the road to the right)
4 ha (120 pitches) terraced, flat, grassy
Rentals : 23 🚐 – 5 🏠.
sani-station
In a pleasant location beside a small lake formed by the Rhône river.

Surroundings : 🌿 ≤ lake and hills 🌲 🟢 ⛰
Leisure activities : 🍴 ✕ 🎣 🚴 ✗ 🏊 🎣 pedalos 🦆
Facilities : 🚻 ⚬━ 🚿 🚰 🍴 🚿

GPS Longitude : 5.77001
Latitude : 45.76861

MATAFELON-GRANGES

01580 – Michelin map **328** G3 – pop. 653 – alt. 453
D Paris 460 – Bourg-en-Bresse 37 – Lons-le-Saunier 56 – Mâcon 75

Les Gorges de l'Oignin

℘ 0474768097, *www.gorges-de-loignin.com*
Address : r. du Lac (900m south of the village, near the Oignin river)
Opening times : from mid April to mid Sept.
2.6 ha (128 pitches) terraced, flat, grassy, gravelled
Tariff : 24.30€ ✱✱ ⬅ 🔲 (1) (10A) – Extra per person 6.20€ – Reservation fee 16€
Rental rates : (from mid April to mid Sept.) ⍟ (Jul–Aug) – 2 🏚 – 10 🏠.
Per night from 50 to 95€ – Per week from 240 to 630€ – Reservation fee 16€
🔄 15 🔲 23.60€
Situated near a lake.

Surroundings : ≤
Leisure activities : 🍴 ✕ 🏊 🎣
Facilities : 🔧 ⊶ ⛲ 🔥 🚿 🏴 🍴 📷
Nearby : 🏊 🎣

GPS Longitude : 5.55723
Latitude : 46.25534

> The classification (1 to 5 tents, **black** or red) that we award to selected sites
> in this guide is our own system. It should not be confused with the
> classification (1 to 5 stars) of official organisations.

LES MAZES

07150 – Michelin map **331** I7
D Paris 669 – Lyon 207 – Privas 58 – Nîmes 83

La Plage Fleurie

℘ 0475880115, *www.laplagefleurie.com* ⍟
Address : 3.5km west
Opening times : from beginning May to beginning Sept.
12 ha/6 ha for camping (300 pitches) terraced, flat and relatively flat, grassy
Tariff : 45.90€ ✱✱ ⬅ 🔲 (1) (10A) – Extra per person 9.35€ – Reservation fee 20€
Rental rates : (from beginning May to beginning Sept.) ⍟ – 145 🏚 – 32 tent bungalows.
Per night from 54 to 183€ – Per week from 378 to 1,281€ – Reservation fee 25€
🔄 sani-station
Beside the Ardèche river.

Surroundings : ≤ 🌳🌳 ⛰
Leisure activities : 🍴 ✕ 🎯 🏊 🎣 🦆
Facilities : 🔧 ⊶ 🍴 📷 🏊 🛁

GPS Longitude : 4.3546
Latitude : 44.40837

Beau Rivage

℘ 0475880354, *www.beaurivage-camping.com*
Address : at Les Mazes
Opening times : from end April to beginning Sept.
2 ha (100 pitches) terraced, flat, grassy
Tariff : 32€ ✱✱ ⬅ 🔲 (1) (10A) – Extra per person 5.90€ – Reservation fee 16€
Rental rates : (from end April to beginning Sept.) ⍟ – 14 🏚. Per night from 55 to 70€
Per week from 350 to 770€ – Reservation fee 23€

Surroundings : 🌊 🌳🌳 ⛰
Leisure activities : ✕ 🏊 🎣 🦆
Facilities : 🔧 ⊶ 🔥 🍴 📷 🏊

GPS Longitude : 4.36903
Latitude : 44.40519

Arc-en-Ciel

☎ 0475880465, *www.arcenciel-camping.com*
Address : at Les Mazes
Opening times : from end April to mid Sept.
5 ha (218 pitches) flat and relatively flat, grassy, stony
Tariff : (2012 price) 34€ ✚✚ ⟵ 🔲 [🚿] (10A) – Extra per person 7€ – Reservation fee 15€
Rental rates : (2012 price) (from end April to mid Sept.) – 62 [🚐] – 2 gîtes.
Per week from 550 to 860€ – Reservation fee 20€
Beside the Ardèche river (with a small lake).

Surroundings : ⛱ ♨♨ ⛰
Leisure activities : 🍹 ✕ 🎦 🏄 🏊 🎣
Facilities : & ⟼ 🛖 🍴 🔲 🚿 ⛲

Longitude : 4.39485
Latitude : 44.40695

MÉAUDRE

38112 – Michelin map **333** G7 – pop. 1,321 – alt. 1,012 – Winter sports : 1,000/1,600 m✖10 ⛷
▶ Paris 588 – Grenoble 38 – Pont-en-Royans 26 – Tullins 53

Les Buissonnets

☎ 0476952104, *www.camping-les-buissonnets.com* – limited spaces for one-night stay
Address : at Les Grangeons (500m northeast along the D 106 and take turning to the right,
200m from the Méaudret river)
Opening times : from mid Dec. to beginning Nov.
2.8 ha (100 pitches) relatively flat, flat, grassy
Tariff : 24.30€ ✚✚ ⟵ 🔲 [🚿] (10A) – Extra per person 5€
Rental rates : (from mid Dec. to beginning Nov.) 🅿 – 10 [🚐] – 3 🏠. Per night from 55 to 75€
Per week from 290 to 466€
🚐 sani-station 5€ – 9 🔲 15.80€ – 🚐15€

Surroundings : ❄ ⛱ ≤♨
Leisure activities : 🎦 🏄
Facilities : & ⟼ ▥ 🛖 🍴 🔲
Nearby : ✗ 🏊

Longitude : 5.53243
Latitude : 45.12955

⛺ Les Eymes

☎ 0476952485, *www.camping-les-eymes.com*
Address : 3.8km north along the D 106c, follow the signs for Autrans and take turning to the left
Opening times : permanent
1.3 ha (40 pitches) terraced, relatively flat, grassy, stony, wood
Tariff : (2012 price) 19.50€ ✚✚ ⟵ 🔲 [🚿] (10A) – Extra per person 7€
Rental rates : (2012 price) (permanent) – 8 [🚐] – 3 🏠. Per night from 47 to 96€
Per week from 282 to 576€
🚐 sani-station 5€ – 3 🔲 16.50€ – 🚐11€

Surroundings : ⛱ ≤
Leisure activities : ✕ 🏊
Facilities : & ⟼ ▥ 🛖 🌬 🍴 🔲 🚿 ⛲

Longitude : 5.51574
Latitude : 45.14468

*Routes nationales are main roads and their identifying numbers
begin with N or RN. Routes départementales are generally quieter
roads and begin with D or DN.*

MEGÈVE

74120 – Michelin map **328** M5 – pop. 3,907 – alt. 1,113 – Winter sports : 1,113/2,350 m 9 70
▶ Paris 598 – Albertville 32 – Annecy 60 – Chamonix-Mont-Blanc 33

Bornand

0450930086, *www.camping-megeve.com* – alt. 1,060
Address : 57 rte du Grand Bois – Demi quartier (3km northeast along the N 212, follow the signs for Sallanches and the Rte de la télécabine (cable car) to the right)
Opening times : from mid June to end Aug.
1.5 ha (80 pitches) open site, terraced, sloping, grassy
Tariff : (2012 price) ★ 3.90€ 4.30€ – (6A) 3.50€
Rental rates : (2012 price) (permanent) – 4 . Per week from 305 to 554€
sani-station

Surroundings :
Leisure activities :
Facilities : launderette
Nearby : ✕

GPS Longitude : 6.64161
Latitude : 45.87909

MENGLON

26410 – Michelin map **332** F6 – pop. 406 – alt. 550
▶ Paris 645 – Lyon 183 – Valence 80 – Grenoble 90

L'Hirondelle

0475218208, *www.campinghirondelle.com*
Address : bois de Saint Ferréol (head 2.8km northwest along the D 214 and D 140, follow the signs for Die; near the D 539 (recommended route))
Opening times : from beginning May to mid Sept.
7.5 ha (180 pitches) open site, undulating, flat, grassy, slightly hilly/uneven
Tariff : (2012 price) 32.40€ ★★ (6A) – Extra per person 9.75€ – Reservation fee 18€
Rental rates : (2012 price) (from beginning April to end Sept.) – 20 – 20 – 13 tent bungalows. Per night from 42 to 129€ – Per week from 292 to 899€ – Reservation fee 18.50€
3 18€

A pleasant site and setting beside the Bez river.

Surroundings :
Leisure activities : ✕ evening (lake) multi-sports ground
Facilities : launderette

GPS Longitude : 5.44746
Latitude : 44.68143

MENTHON-ST-BERNARD

74290 – Michelin map **328** K5 – pop. 1,876 – alt. 482
▶ Paris 552 – Lyon 148 – Annecy 9 – Genève 51

Le Clos Don Jean

0450601866, *www.clos-don-jean.com*
Address : 435 rte du Clos-Don-Jean
Opening times : from beginning June to beginning Sept.
1 ha (60 pitches) relatively flat, flat, grassy
Tariff : (2012 price) 18.50€ ★★ (6A) – Extra per person 4.30€
Rental rates : (2012 price) (from beginning June to beginning Sept.) – 9 .
Per night from 50 to 80€ – Per week from 250 to 500€

Surroundings :
Leisure activities :
Facilities :

GPS Longitude : 6.19699
Latitude : 45.86298

MEYRAS

07380 – Michelin map **331** H5 – pop. 842 – alt. 450
▶ Paris 609 – Aubenas 17 – Le Cheylard 54 – Langogne 49

Domaine de La Plage

℘ 0475364059, *www.lecampingdelaplage.com* – limited spaces for one-night stay
Address : at Neyrac-les-Bains (3km southwest along the N 102, follow the signs for Le Puy-en-Velay)
Opening times : from beginning April to end Oct.
0.8 ha (45 pitches) terraced, flat, grassy, stony
Tariff : 35€ ♦♦ ⇔ 圁 ⚡ (10A) – Extra per person 5€
Rental rates : (permanent) – 27 🛖 – 12 🏚 – 7 gîtes. Per night from 45 to 100€
Per week from 250 to 710€

An attractive location beside the Ardèche river.

Surroundings : 🌄 ⪕ 🖙 ◊◊
Leisure activities : ♈ ✗ 🎦 ☺ daytime 🛶 ♨ ≋ ✎ entertainment room
Facilities : ♿ ⚿ 𝄞 ♨ 🚿 ⚱ ⚐ launderette 🚿

Longitude : 4.26067
Latitude : 44.67315

Le Ventadour

℘ 0475941815, *www.leventadour.com*
Address : at the Pont de Rolandy (3.5km southeast, along the N 102, follow the signs for Aubenas; beside the Ardèche river)
Opening times : from mid April to beginning Oct.
3 ha (142 pitches) flat and relatively flat, grassy
Tariff : 23€ ♦♦ ⇔ 圁 ⚡ (10A) – Extra per person 6€ – Reservation fee 15€
Rental rates : (permanent) – 15 🛖. Per week from 199 to 780€ – Reservation fee 15€

Surroundings : ⪕ 🖙 ⚱ ⛰
Leisure activities : ♈ ✗ 🛶 🚲 ≋ ✎
Facilities : ♿ ⚿ 𝄞 ♨ ⚐ 🖥 🚿

Longitude : 4.28291
Latitude : 44.66757

The Michelin classification (⚠⚠⚠ ... ⚠) is totally independent of the official star classification system awarded by the local prefecture or other official organisation.

MEYRIEU-LES-ÉTANGS

38440 – Michelin map **333** E4 – pop. 839 – alt. 430 – Leisure centre
▶ Paris 515 – Beaurepaire 31 – Bourgoin-Jallieu 14 – Grenoble 78

Base de Loisirs du Moulin

℘ 0474593034, *www.camping-meyrieu.com*
Address : rte de Saint-Anne (800m southeast along the D 56b, follow the signs for Châtonnoy and turn left towards Ste-Anne; near a small lake)
1 ha (58 pitches) terraced, relatively flat, flat, grassyRental rates : Ⓟ – 3 🛖 – 11 🏚.
🚐 sani-station
The pitches are set out on terraces looking out over the lake.

Surroundings : 🌄 🖙 ◊◊
Leisure activities : 🎦 ⚸ ✎
Facilities : ♿ ⚱ 🚿 🖥
Nearby : ♈ ✗ 🚿 🛶 ♨ ≋ pedalos

Longitude : 5.20175
Latitude : 45.5152

MIRABEL-ET-BLACONS

26400 – Michelin map **332** D5 – pop. 904 – alt. 225
▶ Paris 595 – Crest 7 – Die 30 – Dieulefit 33

 ### Gervanne

℘ 0475400020, *www.gervanne-camping.com*

Address : in the Bellevue quartier (situated where the Drôme and the Gervanne rivers meet, at Blacons)

Opening times : from beginning April to end Sept.

3.7 ha (150 pitches) flat and relatively flat, grassy

Tariff : (2012 price) 27€ ✝✝ ⇌ 目 ⁄ (6A) – Extra per person 6.70€ – Reservation fee 15€

Rental rates : (2012 price) (from beginning April to end Sept.) ৬ (1 chalet) ⅍ – 3 'gypsy' caravans – 3 ⬛ – 18 ⬛. Per night from 63 to 86€ – Per week from 294 to 826€ Reservation fee 15€

⬛ sani-station 4€

In a green setting beside the Gervanne and Drôme rivers.

> Surroundings : ⬛ ♒ ⬛
> Leisure activities : ☂ ✗ ⬛ ⬛ ⬛ ⬛ ⬛
> Facilities : ৬ ⬛ ⬛ ⬛ launderette ⬛ ⬛
> Nearby : fitness trail

GPS Longitude : 5.08917
Latitude : 44.71083

MONTALIEU-VERCIEU

38390 – Michelin map **333** F3 – pop. 3,021 – alt. 213 – Leisure centre
▶ Paris 478 – Belley 36 – Bourg-en-Bresse 54 – Crémieu 25

⬛ ### Vallée Bleue

℘ 0474886367, *www.camping-valleebleue.com*

Address : at the base de loisirs (leisure centre), port Bigara (take the northern exit along the N 75, follow the signs for Bourg-en-Bresse then continue 1.3km along the D 52f to the right)

120 ha/1.8 (119 pitches) flat, relatively flat, grassy, gravelled

Rentals : 7 ⬛.

⬛ sani-station

Beside the left bank of the River Rhône (with a small lake).

> Surroundings : ⬛ ⩻ ♒
> Leisure activities : ☂ ✗ ⬛ ⬛ ⬛
> Facilities : ৬ ⬛ ⬛ ⬛ ⬛
> Nearby : ⬛ ⬛ ⬛ ⬛ ⬛ ⬛ ⬛ jet skis

GPS Longitude : 5.4207
Latitude : 45.82745

MONTCHAVIN

73210 – Michelin map **333** N4
▶ Paris 672 – Lyon 206 – Chambéry 106 – Albertville 57

⬛ ### Caravaneige de Montchavin

℘ 0479078323, *www.montchavin-lescoches.com* – alt. 1,250

Address : at Montchavin

Opening times : permanent

1.33 ha (90 pitches) terraced, flat, grassy

Tariff : 23.80€ ✝✝ ⇌ 目 ⁄ (10A) – Extra per person 5.10€

Rental rates : (permanent) ⅍ – 2 ⬛. Per night from 92€ – Per week from 276 to 644€

⬛ sani-station 5€

The location and view are superb.

> Surroundings : ⬛ ⬛ ⩻ Vallée de la Tarentaise and mountains ♒
> Leisure activities : ⬛
> Facilities : ৬ ⬛ ⬛ ⬛ launderette
> Nearby : ⬛ ☂ ✗ ⬛ ⬛ skating rink

GPS Longitude : 6.73933
Latitude : 45.56058

MONTRÉAL

07320 – Michelin map **331** H6 – pop. 462 – alt. 180
▶ Paris 649 – Aubenas 22 – Largentière 5 – Privas 53

 Le Moulinage (rental of chalets, mobile homes, 'gypsy' caravans and tent bungalows only)

✆ 04 42 54 29 25, *www.ardeche-camping.com*
Address : rte des Défilés de Ruoms (5.5km southeast along the D 5, D 104 and take D 4, follow the signs for Ruoms)
4 ha terraced, relatively flat, grassy, stony
Rentals : ♿ – 1 'gypsy' caravan – 14 ▦ – 10 ⌂ – 3 tent bungalows.
Situated beside the Ligne river.

Surroundings : ≤ 🏞️
Leisure activities : 🍸 ✕ 🖥️ ♪ 🎿 🏊 ⚓
Facilities : ⚷ 🛁 🚰 🗑️ 🚿

GPS Longitude : 4.31831
Latitude : 44.50099

MONTREVEL-EN-BRESSE

01340 – Michelin map **328** D2 – pop. 2,363 – alt. 215 – Leisure centre
▶ Paris 395 – Bourg-en-Bresse 18 – Mâcon 25 – Pont-de-Vaux 22

La Plaine Tonique ♣♣

✆ 04 74 30 80 52, *www.laplainetonique.com*
Address : at the base de loisirs (leisure centre) (500m east along the D 28; open-air leisure park)
Opening times : from mid April to mid Sept.
27 ha/15 ha for camping (548 pitches) relatively flat, flat, grassy
Tariff : 🧍 7€ 🚗 ▦ 15.30€ ⚡ (10A)
Rental rates : (from mid April to mid Sept.) 🏠 – 5 ▦ – 57 ⌂ – 3 teepees.
Per night from 105 to 136€ – Per week from 281 to 748€
🚐 sani-station 3€ – 3 ▦ 15.30€
Beside a lake, with an attractive swimming area.

Surroundings : 🌳 ♀ ⛰️
Leisure activities : 🍸 ✕ 🖥️ ⊙ 🛝 🛶 🚤 🎿 ♪ 🖼️ 🏊 🏄 ⚓ ◊ sports trail
Facilities : ♿ ⚷ 🛁 🚿 🚰 🗑️ 🚿

GPS Longitude : 5.136
Latitude : 46.33902

*We have selected the best campsites in France with our usual care,
listing those with the best facilities in the most pleasant surroundings.*

MONTRIGAUD

26350 – Michelin map **332** D2 – pop. 496 – alt. 462
▶ Paris 560 – Lyon 97 – Valence 51 – Grenoble 75

La Grivelière

✆ 04 75 71 70 71, *www.lagriveliere.com*
Address : rte de Roybon
2.6 ha (59 pitches) flat, grassy
Rentals : 2 'gypsy' caravans – 4 ▦ – 2 ⌂ – 2 tent bungalows.

Surroundings : 🌿 🌳 ♀
Leisure activities : 🍸 ✕ 🖥️ 🚤 🎿
Facilities : 🛁 🚰 launderette 🚿

GPS Longitude : 5.16711
Latitude : 45.22176

MORNANT

69440 – Michelin map **327** H6 – pop. 5,438 – alt. 380
▶ Paris 478 – Givors 12 – Lyon 26 – Rive-de-Gier 13

⚠ Municipal de la Trillonière

℘ 0478441647, *www.ville-mornant.fr*
Address : bd Gal de Gaulle (southern exit, junction of D 30 and D 34, near a stream)
Opening times : from mid April to end Sept.
1.5 ha (60 pitches) relatively flat, flat, grassy
Tariff : (2012 price) 16.40€ ♟♟ ⏛ ▣ ⌧ (10A) – Extra per person 4€
🚐 sani-station – 30 ▣ 16.40€ – 🔋⌧15.58€
At the foot of the medieval old town. Bus stop for Lyon.

Facilities : ⅍ ⌛☞ ⌗ ⌦
Nearby : ✀ ⅍ₘ ⌇

GPS Longitude : 4.67073
Latitude : 45.61532

MORZINE

74110 – Michelin map **328** N3 – pop. 2,930 – alt. 960 – Winter sports : 1,000/2,100 m ⚞6 ⚡61 ⚘
▶ Paris 586 – Annecy 84 – Chamonix-Mont-Blanc 67 – Cluses 26

⚠ Les Marmottes

℘ 0450757444, *www.campinglesmarmottes.com* – alt. 938
Address : at Essert-Romand (3.7km northwest along the D 902, follow the signs for Thonon-les-Bains and take D 329 to the left)
Opening times : from mid June to beginning Sept. and from mid-Dec to end Mar
0.5 ha (26 pitches) flat, grassy, gravelled
Tariff : 25€ ♟♟ ⏛ ▣ ⌧ (6A) – Extra per person 7.80€ – Reservation fee 5€
Rental rates : (from mid June to mid Sept. and from mid-Dec to end Mar) ✂ – 2 ⊞ – 1 ⊨ – 1 studio. Per week from 383 to 585€ – Reservation fee 10€
A shuttle service serves the centre of Morzine.

Surroundings : ✿ ≼
Leisure activities : ▭
Facilities : ⅍ ⌛☞ ⌗ ▥ ⌂ ⌲ ↴ launderette

GPS Longitude : 6.67725
Latitude : 46.19487

MURS-ET-GELIGNIEUX

01300 – Michelin map **328** G7 – pop. 236 – alt. 232
▶ Paris 509 – Aix-les-Bains 37 – Belley 17 – Chambéry 42

⚠ Île de la Comtesse

℘ 0479872333, *www.ile-de-la-comtesse.com*
Address : located 1km southwest on the D 992
Opening times : from end April to beginning Sept.
3 ha (100 pitches) stony, flat, grassyTariff : 30€ ♟♟ ⏛ ▣ ⌧ (6A) – Extra per person 7.50€ – Reservation fee 14€
Rental rates : (from end April to beginning Sept.) – 30 ⊞ – 15 ⌂. Per night from 98 to 118€ Per week from 686 to 826€ – Reservation fee 28€
🚐 sani-station 5.50€
Near the River Rhône (with a small lake).

Surroundings : ≼
Leisure activities : ⌇ ✗ ▭ ⌲ ⚲ ⌇ ⊿
Facilities : ⅍ ⌛ ⌂ ⌨ launderette ⌸ ⌾
Nearby : ⌇

GPS Longitude : 5.64876
Latitude : 45.63993

NEYDENS

74160 – Michelin map **328** J4 – pop. 1,486 – alt. 560
▶ Paris 525 – Annecy 36 – Bellegarde-sur-Valserine 33 – Bonneville 34

La Colombière

📞 04 50 35 13 14, *www.camping-la-colombiere.com*
Address : 166 chemin Neuf (east of the town)
Opening times : from end March to mid Nov.
2.5 ha (156 pitches) flat, grassy, gravelled
Tariff : 35€ ✿✿ ⇌ 🄴 🄶 (10A) – Extra per person 6€ – Reservation fee 12€
Rental rates : (permanent) – 20 ⛺ – 8 🏠. Per night from 80 to 120€
Per week from 340 to 840€ – Reservation fee 12€
🚐 sani-station 5€ – 2 🄴 14€ – 🛥 14€

> **Surroundings :** ≤ 🛋 ⚲
> **Leisure activities :** ♈ ✕ 🛶 🌣 daytime 🏊 🚲 🎬 (small swimming pool) 🏊
> **Facilities :** 🔥 ⚡ 🏕 🛁 🛱 🚰 🍴 launderette 🌱

GPS
Longitude : 6.10578
Latitude : 46.11997

LES NOËS

42370 – Michelin map **327** C3 – pop. 182 – alt. 610
▶ Paris 401 – Lyon 109 – Saint-Étienne 100 – Clermont-Ferrand 101

Parc Résidentiel de Loisirs
(rental of chalets only)

📞 04 77 64 21 13, *www.gite-des-noes.fr*
Address : in the village
Opening times : permanent
1 ha terraced, grassy
Rental rates : (2012 price) 🔥 🅿 – 8 🏠. Per night from 65€ – Per week from 210 to 430€

At the gateway to the Monts de la Madeleine mountains, on a green, sloping site at the edge of the forest.

> **Leisure activities :** 🚲 🏊 🎣
> **Facilities :** 🛱
> **Nearby :** launderette ♈ ✕ quad biking

GPS
Longitude : 3.85624
Latitude : 46.02772

Some campsites benefit from proximity to a municipal leisure centre.

NOVALAISE-LAC

73470 – pop. 1,712 – alt. 427
▶ Paris 524 – Belley 24 – Chambéry 21 – Les Échelles 24

Le Grand Verney

📞 04 79 36 02 54, *www.camping-legrandverney.info* – limited spaces for one-night stay
Address : Le Neyret (1.2km southwest along the C 6)
Opening times : from beginning April to end Oct.
2.5 ha (112 pitches) terraced, relatively flat, flat, grassy
Tariff : 18.50€ ✿✿ ⇌ 🄴 🄶 (10A) – Extra per person 4.50€
Rental rates : (from beginning April to end Oct.) – 24 ⛺. Per night from 65 to 80€
Per week from 310 to 610€

> **Surroundings :** ≤ 🛋 ⚲
> **Leisure activities :** 🏊
> **Facilities :** 🔥 ⚡ 🛱 🚰 🍴 🖼

GPS
Longitude : 5.78371
Latitude : 45.5683

NYONS

26110 – Michelin map **332** D7 – pop. 7,104 – alt. 271
▶ Paris 653 – Alès 109 – Gap 106 – Orange 43

⚠ L'Or Vert

☎ 04 75 26 24 85, www.camping-or-vert.com ⚑ (Jul–Aug)
Address : at Aubres, quai de la Charité (3km northeast along the D 94, follow the signs for Serres; beside the Eygues)
Opening times : from beginning April to end Sept.
1 ha (79 pitches) terraced, flat, stony, fine gravel, grassy, small orchard
Tariff : (2012 price) 24.50€ ✶✶ ⇔ 回 ⚡ (6A) – Extra per person 6€ – Reservation fee 10€
Rental rates : (2012 price) (from beginning April to end Sept.) ⚑ – 1 🚐 – 7 🏠.
Per night from 42 to 85€ – Per week from 290 to 760€ – Reservation fee 10€

Surroundings : ⟨ 🔲 ⚲⚲
Leisure activities : ✗ 🖼 ⚓ ≈ ⚒
Facilities : ⚷ 🚿 ♨ ⚐ 🅿 refrigerators

GPS Longitude : 5.16272
Latitude : 44.37273

⚠ Les Terrasses Provençales

☎ 04 75 27 92 36, www.lesterrassesprovencales.com
Address : Les Barroux – Novezan (7km northwest along the D 538, then take the D 232 to the right)
2.5 ha (70 pitches) terraced, flat, grassy, fine gravel, stony
Rentals : ⚑ – 10 🚐.
🚉 sani-station

Surroundings : ⚲ ⟨ ♀
Leisure activities : 🍽 ✗ 🖼 ⚲⚲ ⚒
Facilities : ⚒ 🚿 ♨ ♨ ♨ launderette

GPS Longitude : 5.08047
Latitude : 44.40949

*The prices listed were supplied by the campsite owners in 2012
(if prices were not available, those from the previous year are given).
The fees should be regarded as basic charges and may fluctuate
with inflation.*

LES OLLIÈRES-SUR-EYRIEUX

07360 – Michelin map **331** J5 – pop. 927 – alt. 200
▶ Paris 593 – Le Cheylard 28 – Lamastre 33 – Montélimar 53

⚠ Le Mas de Champel

☎ 04 75 66 23 23, www.masdechampel.com
Address : at the Domaine de Champel (north of the town along the D 120, follow the signs for La Voulte-sur-Rhône and take the road to the left, near L'Eyrieux)
Opening times : from end April to mid Sept.
4 ha (95 pitches) terraced, flat, grassy
Tariff : 29.10€ ✶✶ ⇔ 回 ⚡ (6A) – Extra per person 6.90€ – Reservation fee 25€
Rental rates : (from end April to mid Sept.) – 50 🚐 – 1 teepee – 8 tent bungalows.
Per night from 48 to 79€ – Per week from 155 to 553€ – Reservation fee 25€
🚉 sani-station

Surroundings : ⟨ ♀
Leisure activities : 🍽 ✗ 🖼 ⚲⚲ jacuzzi ⚓ ⚲⚲ ⚒ ≈ ⚒
Facilities : ⚒ ⚷ ♨ 🅿 ⚒

GPS Longitude : 4.6146
Latitude : 44.80603

FranceLoc Domaine des Plantas ♣♀

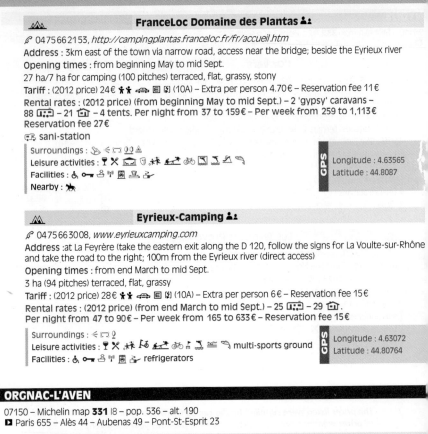

✆ 0475662153, *http://campingplantas.franceloc.fr/fr/accueil.htm*
Address : 3km east of the town via narrow road, access near the bridge; beside the Eyrieux river
Opening times : from beginning May to mid Sept.
27 ha/7 ha for camping (100 pitches) terraced, flat, grassy, stony
Tariff : (2012 price) 24€ ♥♥ ⇔ 🖹 ⚡ (10A) – Extra per person 4.70€ – Reservation fee 11€
Rental rates : (2012 price) (from beginning May to mid Sept.) – 2 'gypsy' caravans –
88 🚐 – 21 🏠 – 4 tents. Per night from 37 to 159€ – Per week from 259 to 1,113€
Reservation fee 27€
🚽 sani-station

Surroundings : 🖾 ⟨ 🗠 ♤♤ 🛆
Leisure activities : 🍴 ✕ 🖭 🖎 🏕 🏊 🚲 🖾 🏊 🛆 🏐   Longitude : 4.63565
Facilities : ♿ ⚬☞ 🏕 🚽 🖻 🚿 🛒   Latitude : 44.8087
Nearby : 🐎

Eyrieux-Camping ♣♀

✆ 0475663008, *www.eyrieuxcamping.com*
Address :at La Feyrère (take the eastern exit along the D 120, follow the signs for La Voulte-sur-Rhône
and take the road to the right; 100m from the Eyrieux river (direct access)
Opening times : from end March to mid Sept.
3 ha (94 pitches) terraced, flat, grassy
Tariff : (2012 price) 28€ ♥♥ ⇔ 🖹 ⚡ (10A) – Extra per person 6€ – Reservation fee 15€
Rental rates : (2012 price) (from end March to mid Sept.) – 25 🚐 – 29 🏠.
Per night from 47 to 90€ – Per week from 165 to 633€ – Reservation fee 15€

Surroundings : ⟨ 🗠 ♀
Leisure activities : 🍴 ✕ 🏕 🖎 🏊 🚲 🏊 🏊 🏊 🏐 multi-sports ground   Longitude : 4.63072
Facilities : ♿ ⚬☞ 🏕 🚽 🖻 🛒 refrigerators   Latitude : 44.80764

ORGNAC-L'AVEN

07150 – Michelin map **331** I8 – pop. 536 – alt. 190
▶ Paris 655 – Alès 44 – Aubenas 49 – Pont-St-Esprit 23

Municipal

✆ 0475386368, *www.orgnacvillage.com*
Address : north of the town along the D 217
2.6 ha (150 pitches) flat, stony

Surroundings : ♤♤
Leisure activities : 🖾 ✕ 🏊   Longitude : 4.4317
Facilities : ♿ ⚬☞ 🖻   Latitude : 44.31282
Nearby : 🏊

Michelin classification:
🏔🏔🏔🏔 *Extremely comfortable, equipped to a very high standard*
🏔🏔🏔 *Very comfortable, equipped to a high standard*
🏔🏔 *Comfortable and well equipped*
🏔 *Reasonably comfortable*
🏔 *Satisfactory*

LA PACAUDIÈRE

42310 – Michelin map **327** C2 – pop. 1,078 – alt. 363
▶ Paris 370 – Lapalisse 24 – Marcigny 21 – Roanne 25

Municipal Beausoleil

℘ 04 77 64 11 50, *lapacaudiere@wanadoo.fr*
Address : at Beausoleil (700m east along the D 35, follow the signs for Vivans and take a right turn, near the sports field and the college)
Opening times : from beginning May to end Sept.
1 ha (35 pitches) relatively flat, grassy
Tariff : ✦ 3.70€ ⇌ 1.70€ 🔲 2€ – ⚡ (6A) 3€
Rental rates : (from beginning May to end Sept.) – 5 🏠 – 1 apartment. Per night 63€
Per week 345€
🚰 sani-station 12.50€ – 30 🔲 12.50€
On the outskirts of the town; lovely swimming pool and a pretty chalet village.

Surroundings : ▱
Leisure activities : 🎦 🏇 ⚒ 🎣 ☰ 🏊
Facilities : ♿ ⊶ 🚽 ♨ 🗑 ☂ 🔅

Longitude : 3.87236
Latitude : 46.17562

PALADRU

38850 – Michelin map **333** G5 – pop. 1,044 – alt. 503
▶ Paris 523 – Annecy 84 – Chambéry 47 – Grenoble 43

Le Calatrin

℘ 04 76 32 37 48, *www.camping-paladru.fr*
Address : 799 r. de la Morgerie (near the exit from town, towards Charavines)
2 ha (60 pitches) terraced, flat, grassy
Rentals : 3 🏠.
🚰 sani-station

Surroundings : ⧖ ≼
Leisure activities : 🎦 ⬞
Facilities : ♿ ⊶ 🗑 🔅
Nearby : 🍷 ✕ ≅ (beach)

Longitude : 5.54673
Latitude : 45.47077

Some information or pricing may have changed since the guide went to press.
We recommend you check the price list online in advance or at the entrance
to the campsite and enquire about possible restrictions.

PETICHET

38119 – Michelin map **333** H7
▶ Paris 592 – Le Bourg-d'Oisans 41 – Grenoble 30 – La Mure 11

Ser-Sirant

℘ 04 76 83 91 97, *www.sersirant.com*
Address : at the Lac de Laffrey Petichet (take the eastern exit and take road to the left)
2 ha (100 pitches) terraced, flat, grassy, stony, wood
Rentals : 6 🏠.
🚰 sani-station – 5 🔲

Surroundings : ⧖ ♨♨ ⛰
Leisure activities : 🍷 🎦 🏇 ⬞ boats for hire
Facilities : ⊶ launderette
Nearby : ♦

Longitude : 5.77759
Latitude : 45.00038

LE POËT-LAVAL

26160 – Michelin map **332** D6 – pop. 922 – alt. 311
▶ Paris 619 – Crest 35 – Montélimar 25 – Nyons 35

Municipal Lorette

📞 0475910062, www.campinglorette.fr
Address : in the Lorette quartier (located 1km east along the D 540, follow the signs for Dieulefit)
Opening times : from beginning May to end Sept.
2 ha (60 pitches) relatively flat to hilly, grassy
Tariff : (2012 price) 14.40€ ✝✝ ⟵ 🄴 (6A) – Extra per person 3.20€
🚽 sani-station
Beside the Jabron river.

Surroundings : ≤ ♀
Leisure activities : 🏊 🛶 🎣
Facilities : 🚿 🧺 🚰 🔥
Nearby : ✂

GPS Longitude : 5.02277
Latitude : 44.52922

PONCIN

01450 – Michelin map **328** F4 – pop. 1,618 – alt. 255
▶ Paris 456 – Ambérieu-en-Bugey 20 – Bourg-en-Bresse 28 – Nantua 25

Vallée de l'Ain

📞 0474357211, www.campingvalleedelain.com – limited spaces for one-night stay –
Address : rte d'Allement (500m northwest along the D 91 and D 81, follow the signs for Meyriat, near the Ain river)
Opening times : from beginning April to end Sept.
1.5 ha (89 pitches) flat, grassy
Tariff : (2012 price) 21.70€ ✝✝ ⟵ 🄴 (16A) – Extra per person 4.90€ – Reservation fee 10€
Rental rates : (2012 price) (from beginning April to end Sept.) – 4 🛏 – 3 🏠.
Per night from 35 to 85€ – Per week from 230 to 600€ – Reservation fee 10€
🚽 sani-station 5€ – 12 🄴 21.70€

Surroundings : ♀
Leisure activities : 🍴 ✗ 🛶 🚣
Facilities : 🔑 🧺 🚰
Nearby : ✂ 🚣 🎣

GPS Longitude : 5.40407
Latitude : 46.08996

PONCINS

42110 – Michelin map **327** D5 – pop. 869 – alt. 339
▶ Paris 446 – Lyon 77 – St-Étienne 50 – Clermont-Ferrand 109

Village Vacances Le Nid Douillet
(rental of chalets only)

📞 0477278036, www.le-nid-douillet.com
Address : at Les-Baraques-des-Rotis, rte de Montbrison-es-Baraques-des-Rotis
Opening times : permanent
2 ha flat, grassy
Rental rates : 6 🏠. Per night from 37 to 125€ – Per week from 325 to 500€
The chalets are set in a lovely, green landscape.

Surroundings : 🌳
Leisure activities : ✗ 🖼 🛶
Facilities : 🔑 🧺
Nearby : 🐎

GPS Longitude : 4.1615
Latitude : 45.7123

PONT-DE-VAUX

01190 – Michelin map **328** C2 – pop. 2,187 – alt. 177
▶ Paris 380 – Bourg-en-Bresse 40 – Lons-le-Saunier 69 – Mâcon 24

Champ d'Été

☎ 03 85 23 96 10, *www.camping-champ-dete.com*
Address : 800m northwest along the D 933, towards Mâcon and take the road to the right, near a small lake
Opening times : from beginning May to mid Oct.
3.5 ha (150 pitches) flat, grassy
Tariff : ★ 4€ ⇔ 13€ – (10A) 10€
Rental rates : (from beginning March to end Nov.) – 30 ⌂ – 1 gîte.
Per week from 220 to 570€
sani-station 2€
Leisure activities :
Facilities :
Nearby :

Longitude : 4.93301
Latitude : 46.42966

Aux Rives du Soleil ♣♣

☎ 03 85 30 33 65, *www.rivesdusoleil.com*
Address : at le Port
8 ha (160 pitches) flat, grassy
Rentals : 10 – 10 tent bungalows.
At the confluence of the Saône and Reyssouze rivers.

Surroundings :
Leisure activities :
Facilities : launderette

Longitude : 4.89892
Latitude : 46.44701

Les Ripettes

☎ 03 85 30 66 58, *www.camping-les-ripettes.com*
Address : at Les Tourtes
Opening times : from beginning April to end Sept.
2.5 ha (54 pitches) flat, grassy
Tariff : 19€ ★★ ⇔ (10A) – Extra per person 4€
Rental rates : (from mid April to end Sept.) – 1 . Per night from 40 to 60€
Per week from 280 to 420€
3 19€
A very well-kept, green camping area.

Surroundings :
Leisure activities :
Facilities : launderette

Longitude : 4.98073
Latitude : 46.44449

These symbols are used for a campsite that is exceptional in its category:
Particularly pleasant setting, quality and range of services available
Tranquil, isolated site – quiet site, particularly at night
Exceptional view – interesting or panoramic view

POUILLY-SOUS-CHARLIEU

42720 – Michelin map **327** D3 – pop. 2,582 – alt. 264
▶ Paris 393 – Charlieu 5 – Digoin 43 – Roanne 15

Municipal les Ilots

☎ 0477 60 80 67, *www.pouillysouscharlieu.fr* – **R**
Address : rte de Marcigny (take the northern exit along the D 482, follow the signs for Digoin and take right turn; beside the Sornin river)
Opening times : from mid May to mid Sept.
1 ha (50 pitches) flat, grassy
Tariff : (2012 price) 🏕 2.40€ 🚗 🅿 2.30€ – 🔌 (16A) 3.20€
The site has a family atmosphere, situated a little distance from the town.

Surroundings : 🌳 ♨
Leisure activities : 🏛 🚴
Facilities : ♿ ⚡ 🚿 🏢 🍴 🔲
Nearby : ✂ 🎣

GPS Longitude : 4.11135
Latitude : 46.15101

POULE-LES-ÉCHARMEAUX

69870 – Michelin map **327** F3 – pop. 1,045 – alt. 570
▶ Paris 446 – Chauffailles 17 – La Clayette 25 – Roanne 47

Municipal les Écharmeaux

☎ 06 48 03 21 04
Address : to the west of the village
0.5 ha (21 pitches) terraced, fine gravel, grassy
The pitches are laid out on individual terraces looking out over a lake.

Surroundings : 🌳 ← 🏞
Leisure activities : ✂
Facilities : ⚡ 🔲

GPS Longitude : 4.4598
Latitude : 46.14871

> *Using the traditional Michelin classification method, the guide provides*
> *you with an easy, speedy reference for assessing the category of each site:*
> *1 to 5 tents (see page 10).*

POËT-CÉLARD

26460 – Michelin map **332** D6 – pop. 133 – alt. 590
▶ Paris 618 – Lyon 156 – Valence 53 – Avignon 114

Le Couspeau

☎ 0475 53 30 14, *www.couspeau.com* – alt. 600
Address : in the Bellevue quartier (1.3km southeast along the D 328A)
Opening times : from beginning April to mid Sept.
6 ha (133 pitches) terraced, relatively flat, flat, grassy
Tariff : (2012 price) 36€ 🏕🏕 🚗 🅿 🔌 (6A) – Extra per person 7€
Rental rates : (2012 price) (from mid April to mid Sept.) – 20 🚐 – 20 🏠 – 6 tents.
Per night from 39 to 121€ – Per week from 273 to 847€
An elevated, panoramic location.

Surroundings : 🌳 ← 🏞 ♨
Leisure activities : 🍴 ✕ ⛵ 🚴 ✂ 🔲 (small swimming pool) 🏊
Facilities : ♿ ⚡ 🚿 🚽 🏢 🔥 💧 🍴 launderette 🔲 🔧

GPS Longitude : 5.11152
Latitude : 44.59641

PRADONS

07120 – Michelin map **331** I7 – pop. 421 – alt. 124
Paris 647 – Aubenas 20 – Largentière 16 – Privas 52

Les Coudoulets

04 75 93 94 95, *www.coudoulets.com*
Address : chemin de l'Ardèche (to the northwest of the town)
Opening times : from mid April to mid Sept.
3.5 ha/2.5 ha for camping (123 pitches) flat and relatively flat, stony, grassy
Tariff : 33.70€ ♦♦ ⇔ 🗉 (½) (16A) – Extra per person 7€ – Reservation fee 10€
Rental rates : (from mid April to mid Sept.) – 25 – 4 gîtes. Per night from 40 to 103€
Per week from 270 to 720€ – Reservation fee 10€
sani-station

Surroundings : ⌇ ⌂ ♀ ⚠
Leisure activities : ♈ ✕ ⚓ ⌇
Facilities : ⚹ ⌂ ⌂ ⌶ 🖼
Nearby : launderette ✖

GPS Longitude : 4.3572
Latitude : 44.47729

Laborie

04 75 39 72 26, *www.campingdelaborie.com*
Address : rte de Ruoms (1.8km northeast along the follow the signs for Aubenas)
Opening times : from mid April to end Sept.
3 ha (100 pitches) flat, grassy
Tariff : 28.50€ ♦♦ ⇔ 🗉 (½) (6A) – Extra per person 4.80€ – Reservation fee 10€
Rental rates : (from mid April to mid Sept.) ✖ (from mid-Apr to beg Jul) – 12 .
Per night from 40 to 95€ – Per week from 220 to 665€ – Reservation fee 10€

Surroundings : ∿
Leisure activities : ♈ ⌂ ⚓ ⌇ ≈ ⌇
Facilities : ⚹ ⌂ ⌂ ⌶ 🖼

GPS Longitude : 4.3783
Latitude : 44.48161

Le Pont

04 75 93 93 98, *www.campingdupontardeche.com*
Address : chemin du Cirque de Gens (300m west along the D 308, follow the signs for Chauzon)
Opening times : from mid March to end Sept.
1.2 ha (65 pitches) flat, grassy, stony
Tariff : (2012 price) 28.50€ ♦♦ ⇔ 🗉 (½) (10A) – Extra per person 6.50€ – Reservation fee 10€
Rental rates : (2012 price) (from mid March to end Sept.) – 16 . Per night from 30 to 70€
Per week from 273 to 833€ – Reservation fee 10€
Direct access to the Ardèche river via steps.

Surroundings : ⌂ ♀♀
Leisure activities : ♈ ⌂ ⚓ ⌇ ≈ ⌇
Facilities : ⚹ ⌂ ⌶ 🖼

GPS Longitude : 4.35337
Latitude : 44.47392

Key to rentals symbols:
12 **Number of mobile homes**
20 ⌂ **Number of chalets**
6 ⌂ **Number of rooms to rent**
Per night **Minimum/maximum rate per night**
30–50€
Per week **Minimum/maximum rate per week**
300–1,000€

PRALOGNAN-LA-VANOISE

73710 – Michelin map **333** N5 – pop. 754 – alt. 1,425 – Winter sports : 1,410/2,360 m 1 13

▶ Paris 634 – Albertville 53 – Chambéry 103 – Moûtiers 28

Le Parc Isertan

✆ 0479087524, *www.camping-isertan.com*
Address : in the Isertan quartier (south of the town)
Opening times : from mid May to end Sept. and from mid-dec to mid-Apr
4.5 ha (180 pitches) open site, terraced, grassy, stony
Tariff : 36€ ✦✦ 🚐 🅴 (10A) – Extra per person 6.50€ – Reservation fee 5€
Rental rates : (from mid May to end Sept. and from mid-Dec to mid-Apr) – 3 🏠 – 4 tents – 1 gîte. Per week from 300 to 1,050€ – Reservation fee 15€
🚐 sani-station 3€ – 10 🅴 9€ – 9€
A pleasant location beside a fast-flowing river.

Surroundings : ❄ 🐾 ≼
Leisure activities : ☂ ✕ 🎮 🎯
Facilities : 🚿 ⚡ 📶 🔥 ♨
Nearby : 🎿 ⛷ 🛷 🎿 climbing, skating rink

Longitude : 6.72883
Latitude : 45.37189

LES PRAZ-DE-CHAMONIX

74400 – Michelin map **328** O5 – alt. 1,060
▶ Paris 620 – Lyon 237 – Annecy 104 – Aosta / Aoste 61

La Mer de Glace

✆ 0450534403, *www.chamonix-camping.com* – ℞
Address : 200 chemin de la Bagna (at Les Bois, 80m from the Arveyron (direct access)
Opening times : from end April to end Sept.
2 ha (150 pitches) flat, grassy, stony
Tariff : ✦ 7.80€ 🚐 🅴 8.60€ – (10A) 3€

Surroundings : 🐾 ≼ valley and Mont Blanc mountain range 🏕 ♨
Leisure activities : 🎮
Facilities : 🚿 ⚡ 📶 🏠 📶 🔥 launderette

Longitude : 6.89142
Latitude : 45.93846

To visit a town or region, use the MICHELIN Green Guides.

PRAZ-SUR-ARLY

74120 – Michelin map **328** M5 – pop. 1,353 – alt. 1,036
▶ Paris 609 – Lyon 179 – Annecy 55 – Genève 75

Les Prés de l'Arly

✆ 0610440233, *www.campinglespresdelarly.com* – limited spaces for one-night stay
Address : at Les Thouvassieres
Opening times : permanent
1 ha (81 pitches) open site, flat, grassy, stony
Tariff : 13.70€ ✦✦ 🚐 🅴 (10A) – Extra per person 3.60€
Rental rates : (permanent) – 2 🛏 – 1 🏠 – 1 studio – 3 apartments – 1 teepee.
Per night from 20 to 50€ – Per week from 150 to 450€
🚐 sani-station 6€ – 3 🅴 10€ – 10€

Surroundings : ❄ 🐾 ≼
Leisure activities : 🎮 🎿
Facilities : ⚡ 📶 📶 🔥 🗄
Nearby : ⛷ 🛷 🧗 climbing wall

Longitude : 6.57047
Latitude : 45.83762

PRIVAS

07000 – Michelin map **331** J5 – pop. 8,461 – alt. 300
▶ Paris 596 – Alès 107 – Mende 140 – Montélimar 34

Ardèche Camping ♣♣

✆ 0475640580, *www.ardechecamping.fr*
Address : bd de Paste (located 1.5km south along the D 2, follow the signs for Montélimar; beside the Ouvèze river)
Opening times : from mid April to end Sept.
5 ha (166 pitches) terraced, relatively flat, flat, grassy
Tariff : 31€ ♣♣ ⇔ 🔲 🔋 (10A) – Extra per person 6€ – Reservation fee 20€
Rental rates : (from mid April to end Sept.) – 2 'gypsy' caravans – 27 🛏 – 20 🏠 – 4 tent bungalows. Per night from 50 to 115€ – Per week from 350 to 800€ – Reservation fee 20€

Surroundings : ≤ ♨
Leisure activities : ▼ ✕ ⚓ 🎣 ⚽ 🎯 🏊 ⌢
Facilities : ♿ ⚬ 🔲🛁 🍴 📷 ⛽
Nearby : 🛒 ✕

GPS Longitude : 4.59698
Latitude : 44.72597

RECOUBEAU-JANSAC

26310 – Michelin map **332** F6 – pop. 240 – alt. 500
▶ Paris 637 – La Chapelle-en-Vercors 55 – Crest 51 – Die 14

Le Couriou

✆ 0475213323, *www.lecouriou.fr*
Address : at Combe Lambert (head 700m northwest along the D 93, follow the signs for Dié)
7 ha/4.5 ha for camping (138 pitches) open site, terraced, relatively flat, grassy, stony, gravelled, wood
Rentals : 22 🛏 – 15 🏠.

A pleasant swimming area and a small but pretty chalet village.

Surroundings : ≤ ⌑ ♨
Leisure activities : ▼ ✕ 🏠 ❂ hammam, jacuzzi ⚽ 🏊 ⛷ multi-sports ground, spa therapy centre
Facilities : ♿ ⚬ 🛁 🍴 launderette ⛽

GPS Longitude : 5.41098
Latitude : 44.65689

*The pitches of many campsites are marked out with low hedges
of attractive bushes and shrubs.*

RIBES

07260 – Michelin map **331** H7 – pop. 266 – alt. 380
▶ Paris 656 – Aubenas 30 – Largentière 19 – Privas 61

Les Cruses

✆ 0475395469, *www.campinglescruses.com*
Address : at Le Champcros (located 1km southeast of the town, along the D 450)
0.7 ha (37 pitches) terraced, flat, stony
Rentals : 2 'gypsy' caravans – 8 🛏 – 17 🏠 – 2 gîtes.
🚰 sani-station – 2 🔲

Surroundings : ❧ ♒
Leisure activities : 🏠 ⚽ 🎠 🏊 (small swimming pool)
Facilities : ⚬ 🛁 ⚞ ✉ 🍴 📷
Nearby : ✕

GPS Longitude : 4.20972
Latitude : 44.49722

LA ROCHETTE

73110 – Michelin map **333** J5 – pop. 3,431 – alt. 360
▶ Paris 588 – Albertville 41 – Allevard 9 – Chambéry 28

Municipal le Lac St-Clair

℘ 0479257355, *www.larochette.com*
Address : chemin des Plaines Lac Saint-Clair (1.4km southwest along the D 202 and follow the signs for Détrier to the left)
2.2 ha (65 pitches) flat and relatively flat, grassy
Rentals : 8 🏠.

Surroundings : ⩽ ♀
Facilities : ♿ ⊶ ⚗ 🗘 🖼
Nearby : ✗ ♒ ⦚

Longitude : 6.10308
Latitude : 45.4499

LA ROSIÈRE 1850

73700 – Michelin map **333** O4 – alt. 1,850 – Winter sports : 1,100/2,600 m ⚡20 ⚹
▶ Paris 657 – Albertville 76 – Bourg-St-Maurice 22 – Chambéry 125

La Forêt

℘ 0479068621, *www.camping-larosiere.com* – alt. 1,730
Address : situated 2km south along the N 90, follow the signs for Bourg-St-Maurice – direct access to the village
1.5 ha (67 pitches) open site, terraced, relatively flat, stony
Rentals : 3 🚐 – 1 🏠 – 3 huts.
An attractive location looking out over a valley.

Surroundings : ❄ ⚘ ⩽ ♀♀
Leisure activities : ♟ ⚓ ⊿ (small swimming pool)
Facilities : ♿ ⊶ ▥ ⚑ 🖼
Nearby : ✗

Longitude : 6.85425
Latitude : 45.62341

In order for the guide to remain wholly objective, the selection is made on an entirely independent basis. There is no charge for being selected for the guide.

ROSIÈRES

07260 – Michelin map **331** H7 – pop. 1,121 – alt. 175
▶ Paris 649 – Aubenas 22 – Largentière 12 – Privas 54

Arleblanc

℘ 0475395311, *www.arleblanc.com*
Address : take the northeastern exit, follow the signs for Aubenas and proceed 2.8km along the road to the right, beside the Intermarché commercial centre
Opening times : from end March to end Oct.
7 ha (167 pitches) flat, grassy
Tariff : 32€ ⛺⛺ ⇌ ▤ ⚡ (4A) – Extra per person 7€ – Reservation fee 16€
Rental rates : (from end March to end Oct.) – 34 🚐 – 6 🏠 – 4 apartments.
Per night from 50 to 100€ – Per week from 315 to 690€ – Reservation fee 16€
In a pleasant location beside the Beaume river.

Surroundings : ♀♀
Leisure activities : ♟ ✗ ⚓ ⚘ ♒ ⊿ ⩵ ⦚
Facilities : ♿ ⊶ ▥ ⛲ ⚗ 🗘 ⚑ 🖼 ⚏ ⚒
Nearby : 🐎

Longitude : 4.27221
Latitude : 44.46552

La Plaine

℘ 0475395135, www.campinglaplaine.com
Address :at Les Plaines (700m northeast along the D 104)
Opening times : from beginning April to mid Sept.
4.5 ha/3.5 ha for camping (128 pitches) flat, relatively flat, grassy
Tariff : 31€ ⚤ ⚤ ⊷ 🔲 🔋 (10A) – Extra per person 6€ – Reservation fee 18€
Rental rates : (from beginning April to mid Sept.) – 54 🚐 – 2 🏠. Per week from 200 to 740€
Reservation fee 18€

Surroundings : ▭ ⚏
Leisure activities : 🍴 🖼 ⚓ 🎾 ⛷ 🏊
Facilities : 🚿 🛒 🚮 ⚒ 🔲
Nearby : 🍴

GPS Longitude : 4.26677
Latitude : 44.48608

Les Platanes

℘ 0475395231, www.campinglesplatanesardeche.com
Address :at La Charve (take the northeastern exit, follow the signs for Aubenas and proceed 3.7km along the road to the right, beside the Intermarché commercial centre)
Opening times : from beginning April to mid Oct.
2 ha (90 pitches) flat, grassy
Tariff : (2012 price) 28€ ⚤ ⚤ ⊷ 🔲 🔋 (16A) – Extra per person 5€
Rental rates : (2012 price) (from beginning April to mid Oct.) 🍖 – 20 🚐.
Per night from 45 to 50€ – Per week from 235 to 740€
🚐 sani-station

Surroundings : 🌿 ⚏ ⛰
Leisure activities : 🍴 ✗ 🖼 ⚓ 🏊 🎣
Facilities : 🚿 🛒 ⚒ 🔲 🚿 🍴
Nearby : 🐎

GPS Longitude : 4.27766
Latitude : 44.45702

Les Hortensias

℘ 0475399138, www.camping-leshortensias.com
Address : in the Ribeyre-Bouchet quartier (1.8km northwest along the D 104, follow the signs for Joyeuse, D 303, follow the signs for Vernon to the right, and take road to the left)
Opening times : from beginning May to end Sept.
1 ha (43 pitches) flat, grassy, sandy
Tariff : 26.50€ ⚤ ⚤ ⊷ 🔲 🔋 (10A) – Extra per person 4.50€
Rental rates : (from beginning May to end Sept.) – 20 🚐 – 5 tent bungalows – 1 gîte.
Per night 55€ – Per week from 300 to 660€

Surroundings : 🌿 ▭ ⚏
Leisure activities : 🏊
Facilities : 🚿 🛒 (Jul–Aug) 🚮 🏖 ⚒ 🔲
Nearby : ≃ (lake) 🎣

GPS Longitude : 4.23976
Latitude : 44.48755

There are several different types of sani-station ('borne' in French) – sanitation points providing fresh water and disposal points for grey water. See page 12 for further details.

RUFFIEUX

73310 – Michelin map **333** I2 – pop. 800 – alt. 282
▶ Paris 517 – Aix-les-Bains 20 – Ambérieu-en-Bugey 58 – Annecy 51

⚠ Saumont

🕿 0479542626, *www.campingsaumont.com*
Address : at Saumont (1.2km west, access on the D 991, near the carr. du Saumont, towards Aix-les-Bains and take the road to the right; beside a stream)
Opening times : from beginning April to mid Oct.
1.6 ha (66 pitches) open site, flat, grassy, gravelled
Tariff : (2012 price) 24€ ✹ ✹ ⇔ 🗉 🙌 (10A) – Extra per person 4.80€ – Reservation fee 10€
Rental rates : (2012 price) (from beginning April to mid Oct.) – 14 🚐.
Per night from 82 to 97€ – Per week from 574 to 684€ – Reservation fee 10€

Surroundings : 🛏 ♨
Leisure activities : 🍷 🚣 ✗ 🛝 ⛵
Facilities : 🕭 ⊶ 🎪 🛁 🚿 ⇆ 🚰 launderette

Longitude : 5.88483
Latitude : 45.8491

RUMILLY

74150 – Michelin map **328** I5 – pop. 13,197 – alt. 334 – Leisure centre
▶ Paris 530 – Aix-les-Bains 21 – Annecy 19 – Bellegarde-sur-Valserine 37

⚠ Le Madrid

🕿 0450011257, *www.camping-le-madrid.com*
Address : rte de Saint-Félix (3km southeast along the D 910, follow the signs for Aix-les-Bains then turn left onto D 3 and take D 53 to the right; 500m from a small lake)
Opening times : permanent
3.2 ha (109 pitches) flat, grassy, stony
Tariff : (2012 price) 25€ ✹ ✹ ⇔ 🗉 🙌 (16A) – Extra per person 4€ – Reservation fee 15€
Rental rates : (2012 price) (permanent) – 4 🚐 – 23 🏠. Per night from 84 to 88€
Per week from 470 to 650€ – Reservation fee 15€
🚽 sani-station 3€ – 4 🗉 19€

Surroundings : 🛏 ♨
Leisure activities : 🍷 ✗ 🎬 🚣 🛝
Facilities : 🕭 ⊶ 🆑 🎪 🛁 🚿 ⇆ 🚰 launderette 🗜 refrigerated food storage
Nearby : 🚤 🎣

Longitude : 5.96239
Latitude : 45.84084

RUOMS

07120 – Michelin map **331** I7 – pop. 2,249 – alt. 121
▶ Paris 651 – Alès 54 – Aubenas 24 – Pont-St-Esprit 49

⚠ Domaine de Chaussy ▲±

🕿 0475939966, *www.domainedechaussy.com*
Address : in the Petit Chaussy quartier (2.3km east along the D 559, follow the signs for Lagorce)
Opening times : from mid April to mid Sept.
18 ha/5.5 ha for camping (250 pitches) undulating, flat, grassy, stony, sandy
Tariff : 42€ ✹ ✹ ⇔ 🗉 🙌 (16A) – Extra per person 7€ – Reservation fee 20€
Rental rates : (from beginning April to end Sept.) – 120 🚐 – 40 🛏 – 17 gîtes – Hotel.
Per night from 49 to 64 € – Per week from 280 to 1,004€ – Reservation fee 20€

Surroundings : 🦌 ♨
Leisure activities : 🍷 ✗ 🎬 🏖 🚸 🛝 hammam, jacuzzi 🚣 🚲 ✗ 🎿 🛝 ⛷ fitness trail
Facilities : 🕭 ⊶ 🛁 🚰 launderette 🗜 🗜

Longitude : 4.36913
Latitude : 44.4472

RCN Domaine de la Bastide ▲:

📞 0475396472, *www.rcn.fr*
Address : rte d'Alès – D111 (4km southwest, at Labastide)
7 ha (300 pitches) flat, grassy, stony
Rental rates : – 38 ▭.

Surroundings : ≤ 🏠🏔
Leisure activities : 🍴 ✕ ⛹ 🛶 ✵ 🎣
Facilities : 🚿 ⊶ ⬛ 🚻 ♨ ⚙ 🐟 🔴 🚮 🚐

GPS
Longitude : 4.32524
Latitude : 44.42326

Yelloh! Village La Plaine

📞 0475396583, *www.yellohvillage-la-plaine.com*
Address : in the Grand Terre quartier (3.5km to the south)
Opening times : from mid April to mid Sept.
4.5 ha (217 pitches) flat, relatively flat, sandy, grassy
Tariff : 45€ 🏕🏕 🚐 🔲 🕎 (6A) – Extra per person 8€
Rental rates : (from mid April to mid Sept.) 🏕 – 77 ▭. Per night from 49 to 152€
Per week from 343 to 1,064€
🚐 sani-station
Situated beside the Ardèche river.

Surroundings : 🏞 ≤ 🏠🏔
Leisure activities : 🍴 ✕ 🛶 🚴 🎣 🎣 🏊 ✵ 🦢 multi-sports ground
Facilities : 🚿 ⊶ ⬛ ♨ ⚙ 🐟 🔴 🚮

GPS
Longitude : 4.33596
Latitude : 44.42666

Sunêlia Aluna Vacances ▲:

📞 0475939315, *www.alunavacances.fr*
Address : rte de Lagorce (situated 2km east along the D 559, follow the signs for Lagorce)
Opening times : from mid April to mid Sept.
7 ha (200 pitches) terraced, relatively flat, stony
Tariff : (2012 price) 44€ 🏕🏕 🚐 🔲 🕎 (16A) – Extra per person 10.60€ – Reservation fee 30€
Rental rates : (2012 price) (from mid April to mid Sept.) ♿ (1 mobile home) – 350 ▭ –
2 tents. Per night from 35 to 206 € – Per week from 245 to 1,442€ – Reservation fee 30€

Surroundings : 🗭 🏠
Leisure activities : 🍴 ✕ 🎬 🎲 ⛹ 🛶 🚴 ✵ 🏊 ✵ 🐎
Facilities : ⊶ ♨ 🕎 launderette 🏪 🚮 🚐
Nearby : walking trails

GPS
Longitude : 4.3526
Latitude : 44.44962

Les Paillotes

📞 0475396205, *www.campinglespaillotes.com* – limited spaces for one-night stay
Address : chemin de l'Espédès (600m north along the D 579, follow the signs for Pradons and take road to the left)
1 ha (45 pitches) flat, grassy
Rentals : 30 ▭ – 5 tent bungalows – 2 gîtes.

Surroundings : 🗭
Leisure activities : 🍴 ✕ 🛶 🏊
Facilities : 🚿 ⊶ ♨ 🕎 🕎 🔴

GPS
Longitude : 4.34184
Latitude : 44.45938

Do not confuse:
▲ to 🔺🔺🔺 : MICHELIN classification
with
★ to ★★★★★ : official classification

La Grand'Terre ▲▲

✆ 0475396494, *www.camping-lagrandterre.com*
Address : 3.5km to the south
Opening times : from beginning April to mid Sept.
10 ha (300 pitches) flat, sandy, stony
Tariff : 37€ ✝✝ ⟷ 回 (✱) (16A) – Extra per person 8.60€
Rental rates : (from beginning April to mid Sept.) ⤧ – 66 ⟐. Per night from 40 to 141€
Per week from 280 to 987€
⟐ sani-station 2€ – 6 回 15€
Beside the Ardèche river (direct access).

Surroundings : ⟰
Leisure activities : ♟ ✗ ⌂ ☺ evening ⋈ ⛵ ☂ ⚅ multi-sports ground
Facilities : ⚹ ⟞ ⌂ ⚏ launderette ⟲

GPS Longitude : 4.33892
Latitude : 44.43831

La Chapoulière

✆ 0475396498, *www.lachapouliere.com*
Address : 3.5km to the south
Opening times : from end March to mid Oct.
2.5 ha (100 pitches) flat and relatively flat, grassy
Tariff : (2012 price) 36€ ✝✝ ⟷ 回 (✱) (10A) – Extra per person 8.50€
Rental rates : (2012 price) (from end March to mid Oct.) ⤧ – 21 ⟐. Per night from 43€
Per week from 298 to 875€
⟐ sani-station – 3 回 31.50€
Beside the Ardèche river.

Surroundings : ⟰ ⟰
Leisure activities : ♟ ✗ ⌂ ⛵ ⚅ ⟿ ⟲
Facilities : ⚹ ⟞ ⌂ ⚏ 回 ⟲
Nearby : ✂ ⛢

GPS Longitude : 4.32972
Latitude : 44.43139

Le Petit Bois

✆ 0475396072, *www.campinglepetitbois.fr*
Address : 87 rue du petit bois (800m north of the town, 80m from the Ardèche river)
Opening times : from beginning April to end Sept.
2.5 ha (84 pitches) terraced, terraced, flat and relatively flat, stony, grassy, rocks
Tariff : 35€ ✝✝ ⟷ 回 (✱) (10A) – Extra per person 7.50€ – Reservation fee 15€
Rental rates : (from beginning April to mid Sept.) ⤧ – 25 ⟐ – 15 ⌂ – 2 studios – 2 gîtes.
Per night from 36 to 118€ – Per week from 252 to 826€ – Reservation fee 15€

Surroundings : ⟰ ⟐
Leisure activities : ♟ ✗ ⌂ ⟐ hammam ⛵ ⟐ (open-air in season) ⟲ multi-sports ground
Facilities : ⚹ ⟞ ⌂ ⚏ 回
Nearby : ⟲

GPS Longitude : 4.33789
Latitude : 44.45882

Le Carpenty

✆ 0475397429, *www.campinglecarpenty.com*
Address : 3.6km south along the D 111
0.7 ha (45 pitches) flat, stony, grassy
Beside the Ardèche river (direct access).

Surroundings : ⟰ ⟰
Leisure activities : ⛵ ⟿
Facilities : ⚹ ⟞ 回

GPS Longitude : 4.32866
Latitude : 44.42548

SABLIÈRES

07260 – Michelin map **331** G6 – pop. 144 – alt. 450
▶ Paris 629 – Aubenas 48 – Langogne 58 – Largentière 38

La Drobie

℘ 04 75 36 95 22, www.ladrobie.com
Address : at Le Chambon (3km west along the D 220 and take turning to the right; beside the river, for caravans recommended route is via Lablachère along the D 4)
Opening times : from mid May to end Sept.
1.5 ha (80 pitches) terraced, sloping, grassy, stony
Tariff : (2012 price) 16.50€ ✶✶ ⇌ 🗐 🕭 (10A) – Extra per person 5.30€ – Reservation fee 5€
Rental rates : (2012 price) (from beginning April to end Oct.) – 3 ⛺ – 10 🏠 – 1 gîte.
Per night from 45 to 60€ – Per week from 340 to 545€ – Reservation fee 5€

Surroundings : 🌳 ≼
Leisure activities : 🍸 ✗ ⚤ 🎽 🏊 ⛵ 🎣
Facilities : ঌ ᎐ 🕯 🗐 🛁 🚰

GPS Longitude : 4.07425
Latitude : 44.53144

SAHUNE

26510 – Michelin map **332** E7 – pop. 322 – alt. 330
▶ Paris 647 – Buis-les-Baronnies 27 – La Motte-Chalancon 22 – Nyons 16

Vallée Bleue

℘ 04 75 27 44 42, www.lavalleebleue.com
Address : take the southwestern exit along the D 94, follow the signs for Nyons; beside the Eygues
Opening times : from end April to beginning Sept.
3 ha (45 pitches) flat, grassy, stony
Tariff : 15€ ✶✶ ⇌ 🗐 🕭 (6A) – Extra per person 4€
Rental rates : (from beginning April to end Sept.) ⚤ – 2 🏠. Per night from 60 to 70€
Per week from 400 to 850€
⛽ sani-station 5€

Surroundings : ≼ ⌖
Leisure activities : ✗ ⚤ ⛰ 🏊
Facilities : ঌ ᎐ ⟃ 🗺 🛁 🕯 🗐

GPS Longitude : 5.26139
Latitude : 44.41148

We welcome your feedback on our listed campsites.
Please email us at: campingfrance@tp.michelin.com
Many thanks in advance!

ST-AGRÈVE

07320 – Michelin map **331** I3 – pop. 2,522 – alt. 1,050
▶ Paris 582 – Aubenas 68 – Lamastre 21 – Privas 64

Le Riou la Selle

℘ 04 75 30 29 28, www.campinglerioulaselle.fr
Address : 2.8km southeast along the D 120, follow the signs for Cheylard, take the D 21, follow the signs for Nonières to the left and take the Chemin de la Roche to the right
Opening times : from beginning May to end Sept.
1 ha (29 pitches) terraced, flat and relatively flat, grassy
Tariff : 22.50€ ✶✶ ⇌ 🗐 🕭 (16A) – Extra per person 6€
Rental rates : (permanent) – 2 ⛺ – 2 🏠. Per night from 85 to 110€
Per week from 300 to 590€

Surroundings : 🌳 ⌂ ⌖
Leisure activities : 🍸 🎱 🏊
Facilities : ঌ ᎐ (Jul-Aug) ⏚ 🛁 🕯 🗐 🚰

GPS Longitude : 4.41111
Latitude : 44.99546

ST-ALBAN-AURIOLLES

07120 – Michelin map **331** H7 – pop. 994 – alt. 108
▶ Paris 656 – Alès 49 – Aubenas 28 – Pont-St-Esprit 55

Sunêlia Le Ranc Davaine ♣♣

℘ 0475396055, *www.camping-ranc-davaine.fr*
Address : rte de Chandolas (2.3km southwest along the D 208, follow the signs for Chandolas)
Opening times : from mid April to mid Sept.
13 ha (435 pitches) flat and relatively flat, stony, grassy
Tariff : 46€ ✶✶ ⇌ ▣ ⚡ (10A) – Extra per person 11€ – Reservation fee 30€
Rental rates : (from mid April to mid Sept.) ⤮ – 200 ⬚. Per night from 49 to 219€
Per week from 343 to 1,533€ – Reservation fee 30€
⊞ sani-station
Situated near the Chassezac river.

Surroundings : ⌂ ♀
Leisure activities : ♟ ✗ ⛴ ☺ ⋔ ⅃◠ ⇌ hammam, jacuzzi ⚓ ⅋ ▣
⤓ ⇌ △ ⬙ disco ⤸
Facilities : ₺ ⊶ ☖ ⚶ ⇝ ⅋ ▣ ⬚ ⤻

GPS Longitude : 4.27296
Latitude : 44.41447

Le Mas du Sartre

℘ 0475397174, *www.masdusartre.com*
Address : at Auriolles, chemin de la Vignasse (1.8km to the northwest)
Opening times : from mid April to mid Sept.
1.6 ha (49 pitches) terraced, flat and relatively flat, stony, grassy
Tariff : (2012 price) 27€ ✶✶ ⇌ ▣ ⚡ (10A) – Extra per person 6.50€ – Reservation fee 5€
Rental rates : (2012 price) (from mid April to mid Sept.) – 10 ⬚ – 4 ⬚. Per night
from 77 to 82€ – Per week from 540 to 580€ – Reservation fee 5€
⊞ sani-station 10€ – 5 ▣ 10€ – ⬚ 10€

Surroundings : ♀♀
Leisure activities : ✗ ⛴ ⚓ ⤓
Facilities : ₺ ⊶ ☖ ⅋ ▣ ⤻ refrigerators

GPS Longitude : 4.31514
Latitude : 44.43956

Some information or pricing may have changed since the guide went to press.
We recommend you check the price list online in advance or at the entrance
to the campsite and enquire about possible restrictions.

ST-ALBAN-DE-MONTBEL

73610 – Michelin map **333** H4 – pop. 605 – alt. 400
▶ Paris 551 – Belley 32 – Chambery 21 – Grenoble 74

Base de Loisirs du Sougey ♣♣

℘ 0479360144, *www.camping-sougey.com*
Address : at Le Sougey (1.2km to the northeast, 300m from the lake)
Opening times : from beginning May to mid Sept.
4 ha (159 pitches) terraced, relatively flat, flat, grassy, fine gravel
Tariff : (2012 price) 26.70€ ✶✶ ⇌ ▣ ⚡ (10A) – Extra per person 4€
Rental rates : (from beginning May to mid Sept.) ⤮ – 7 ⬚ – 8 ⬚.
Per night from 60 to 100 € – Per week from 290 to 640€

Surroundings : ⌂ ♀
Leisure activities : ♟ ⛴ ⋔ ⚓
Facilities : ₺ ⊶ ☖ ⚶ ⇝ ⅋ launderette ⤻
Nearby : ⤓ ✗ ⅋ ⇌ ⬙ ⚑ pedalos

GPS Longitude : 5.79069
Latitude : 45.55562

ST-AVIT

6330 – Michelin map **332** C2 – pop. 326 – alt. 348
Paris 536 – Annonay 33 – Lyon 81 – Romans-sur-Isère 22

Domaine la Garenne

📞 0475686226, *www.domaine-la-garenne.com*
Address : 156 ch. de Chablezin
Opening times : permanent
14 ha/6 ha for camping (112 pitches) terraced, relatively flat to hilly, flat, grassy
Tariff : 29€ ♦♦ ⟵ 🔲 (2) (6A) – Extra per person 6.50€ – Reservation fee 10€
Rental rates : (permanent) ⟋ – 30 🔲 – 6 🏠 – 3 tent bungalows. Per night from 50 to 124€
Per week from 350 to 868€ – Reservation fee 10€
sani-station

Surroundings : ⟋ < ⛲⛲
Leisure activities : ✗ 🔲 ⟋ ⟋
Facilities : & ⟋ ⟋ 🏠
Nearby : ⟋

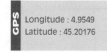

Longitude : 4.9549
Latitude : 45.20176

ST-CHRISTOPHE-EN-OISANS

8520 – Michelin map **333** K8 – pop. 123 – alt. 1,470
Paris 635 – L'Alpe-d'Huez 31 – La Bérarde 12 – Le Bourg-d'Oisans 21

Municipal la Bérarde

📞 0476792045– access narrow, sometimes only possible using passing places – alt. 1,738
Address : at La Bérarde (10.5km southeast along the D 530; difficult access for caravans (steep slope)
2 ha (165 pitches) open site, terraced, relatively flat, flat, stony, grassy, rocks
Very pleasant rural site beside the Vénéon river.

Surroundings : ⟋ < Parc National des Écrins ⚲
Leisure activities : 🔲 ⟋
Facilities : ⟋ 🏠 🏠
Nearby : ⟋ ♦ ✗

Longitude : 6.29205
Latitude : 44.93309

To make the best possible use of this guide,
please read pages 2–15 carefully.

ST-CIRGUES-EN-MONTAGNE

7510 – Michelin map **331** G5 – pop. 248 – alt. 1,044
Paris 586 – Aubenas 40 – Langogne 31 – Privas 68

Les Airelles

📞 0475389249, *www.camping-les-airelles.fr*
Address : rte de Lapalisse (take the northern exit along the D 160, follow the signs for the Lac-d'Issarlès, right bank of the Vernason river)
Opening times : from beginning April to end Oct.
0.7 ha (50 pitches) terraced, relatively flat, stony, grassy
Tariff : 16€ ♦♦ ⟵ 🔲 (2) (6A) – Extra per person 4.50€
Rental rates : (from beginning April to end Oct.) – 9 🔲 – 9 ⟋. Per week from 230 to 450€
sani-station 4€

Surroundings : ⟋ < ⚲
Leisure activities : ♦ ✗ 🔲 ⟋ ⟋
Facilities : ⟋ (season) ⟋ launderette
Nearby : ⟋ ⟋ ♦

Longitude : 4.0949
Latitude : 44.75648

835

RHÔNE-ALPES

ST-CLAIR-DU-RHÔNE

38370 – Michelin map **333** B5 – pop. 3,886 – alt. 160
▶ Paris 501 – Annonay 35 – Givors 26 – Le Péage-de-Roussillon 10

Le Daxia

⌀ 0474563920, www.campingledaxia.com
Address : rte du Péage – av. du Plateau des Frères (2.7km south along the D 4 and take road to the left, recommended route via the N 7 and D 37)
Opening times : from beginning April to end Sept.
7.5 ha (120 pitches) flat, grassy
Tariff : (2012 price) 22.30€ ✚✚ ⌂ 回 ⚡ (6A) – Extra per person 4.60€ – Reservation fee 15€
Rental rates : (2012 price) (from beginning April to end Sept.) – 2 ⌂.
Per night from 55 to 70€ – Per week from 270 to 495€ – Reservation fee 20€
⌿ sani-station – 6 回 18.30€
Pretty, marked-out pitches; beside the Varèze river.

Surroundings :
Leisure activities :
Facilities :

Longitude : 4.78129
Latitude : 45.42128

ST-COLOMBAN-DES-VILLARDS

73130 – Michelin map **333** K6 – pop. 187 – alt. 1,100
▶ Paris 643 – Lyon 176 – Chambéry 76 – Grenoble 106

FranceLoc La Perrière

⌀ 0479052860, www.campings-franceloc.fr
Opening times : from mid Dec. to mid April
2 ha (46 pitches) terraced, flat, grassy, wood
Tariff : (2012 price) 21€ ✚✚ ⌂ 回 ⚡ (10A) – Extra per person 5€ – Reservation fee 11€
Rental rates : (2012 price) (permanent) – 10 ⌂ – 6 ⌂. Per night from 45 to 110€
Per week from 175 to 441€ – Reservation fee 25€
⌿ sani-station – 10 回 21€

Surroundings : ≤ Mountains and Pic du Puy Gris (2.950m)
Leisure activities :
Facilities :
Nearby : climbing , (via ferrata and climbing wall)

Longitude : 6.22667
Latitude : 45.29417

ST-DONAT-SUR-L'HERBASSE

26260 – Michelin map **332** C3 – pop. 3,825 – alt. 202
▶ Paris 545 – Grenoble 92 – Hauterives 20 – Romans-sur-Isère 13

Domaine du Lac de Champos

⌀ 0475451781, www.lacdechampos.com
Address : situated 2km northeast along the D 67
Opening times : from end April to beginning Sept.
43 ha/6 ha for camping (60 pitches) terraced, flat, grassy
Tariff : 19€ ✚✚ ⌂ 回 ⚡ (10A) – Extra per person 4€
Rental rates : (from beginning April to end Oct.) – 21 ⌂ – 2 tent bungalows – 2 tents.
Per night from 79 to 135€ – Per week from 185 to 549€ – Reservation fee 15€
⌿ sani-station – 5 回 16€ – 11€
In a peasant setting beside the Lac de Champos.

Surroundings :
Leisure activities : pedal go-carts
Facilities : launderette

Longitude : 5.00543
Latitude : 45.13615

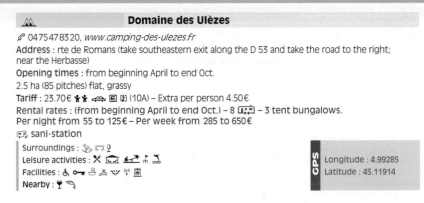

Domaine des Ulèzes

℘ 04 75 47 83 20, *www.camping-des-ulezes.fr*
Address : rte de Romans (take southeastern exit along the D 53 and take the road to the right; near the Herbasse)
Opening times : from beginning April to end Oct.
2.5 ha (85 pitches) flat, grassy
Tariff : 23.70€ ♣♣ ⇔ ▣ ⚡ (10A) – Extra per person 4.50€
Rental rates : (from beginning April to end Oct.) – 8 ⏚ – 3 tent bungalows.
Per night from 55 to 125€ – Per week from 285 to 650€
⏚ sani-station

Surroundings : ⌁ ⌁ ⚲
Leisure activities : ✗ ⛵ ⚓ m ⛴
Facilities : ♿ ⚷ ♨ ⚶ ⚑ ⚏ ▣
Nearby : ⚐ ⚘

GPS Longitude : 4.99285
Latitude : 45.11914

ST-FERRÉOL-TRENTE-PAS

26110 – Michelin map **332** E7 – pop. 228 – alt. 417
▣ Paris 634 – Buis-les-Baronnies 30 – La Motte-Chalancon 34 – Nyons 14

Le Pilat

℘ 04 75 27 72 09, *www.campinglepilat.com*
Address : rte de Bourdeau (located 1km north along the D 70; beside a stream)
Opening times : from beginning April to end Sept.
1 ha (90 pitches) flat, stony, grassy
Tariff : 27.60€ ♣♣ ⇔ ▣ ⚡ (6A) – Extra per person 6.80€
Rental rates : (from beginning April to end Sept.) ⚶ – 19 ⏚ – 2 gîtes.
Per night from 50 to 96€ – Per week from 250 to 795€
⏚ sani-station – 3 ▣ 27.60€

Surroundings : ⌁ ◁ ⌁ ⚲
Leisure activities : ✗ ⛵ ⚓ ⛴ ≃ ⚏ ⚘
Facilities : ♿ ⚷ ♨ ⚑ ▣ ⚏

GPS Longitude : 5.21195
Latitude : 44.43406

ST-GALMIER

42330 – Michelin map **327** E6 – pop. 5,596 – alt. 400
▣ Paris 457 – Lyon 82 – Montbrison 25 – Montrond-les-Bains 11

Campéole Val de Coise ♣♣

℘ 04 77 54 14 82, *www.camping-valdecoise.com* – limited spaces for one-night stay
Address : rte de la Thiery (situated 2km east along the D 6 and take the road to the left; beside the Coise river)
Opening times : from mid April to mid Oct.
3.5 ha (92 pitches) terraced, relatively flat, flat, grassy
Tariff : 20.30€ ♣♣ ⇔ ▣ ⚡ (16A) – Extra per person 5.70€
Rental rates : (2012 price) (from mid April to mid Oct.) – 11 ⏚ – 5 ⛺ – 4 tent bungalows.
Per night from 26 to 95€ – Per week from 182 to 665€ – Reservation fee 25€
⏚ sani-station 1€
Neare the Badoit spring and the river.

Surroundings : ⚲
Leisure activities : ⛵ ⚐ ⚵ ⚓ m ⛴
Facilities : ♿ ⚷ ▥ ♨ ⚑ launderette
Nearby : ⚘

GPS Longitude : 4.33552
Latitude : 45.59308

RHÔNE-ALPES

ST-GENEST-MALIFAUX

42660 – Michelin map **327** F7 – pop. 2,916 – alt. 980
▶ Paris 528 – Annonay 33 – St-Étienne 16 – Yssingeaux 46

Municipal de la Croix de Garry

℘ 04 77 51 25 84, *st-genest-malifaux.fr* – alt. 928 – limited spaces for one-night stay
Address : at La Croix de Garry (Take the southern exit along the D 501, follow the signs for Montfaucon-en-Velay; near a lake and 150m from the Semène river)
Opening times : from mid April to mid Oct.
2 ha (85 pitches) terraced, relatively flat, flat, grassy
Tariff : (2012 price) 15€ ♣♣ ⟺ 🗉 🗓 (6A) – Extra per person 3.90€
Rental rates : (2012 price) (permanent) ♿ (1 chalet) ⌗ – 8 🏠 – 1 gîte. Per night from 90€
Per week from 250 to 390€
Situated a llittle distance from the town, beside a small lake that is ideal for fishing.

Surroundings : ⩽
Leisure activities : ♞⟋
Facilities : ♿ ⌿ ▥ 🗒
Nearby : ※ ⌇

GPS Longitude : 4.42258
Latitude : 45.33357

ST-GERVAIS-LES-BAINS

74170 – Michelin map **328** N5 – pop. 5,673 – alt. 820 – ⚓ – Winter sports :
▶ Paris 597 – Annecy 84 – Bonneville 42 – Chamonix-Mont-Blanc 25

Les Dômes de Miage

℘ 04 50 93 45 96, *http://www.natureandlodge.fr/* – alt. 890
Address : 197 rte des Contamines (situated 2km south along the D 902, at les Bernards)
Opening times : from beginning May to mid Sept.
3 ha (150 pitches) flat, grassy
Tariff : 28.50€ ♣♣ ⟺ 🗉 🗓 (12A) – Extra per person 5.50€ – Reservation fee 10€
Rental rates : (permanent) ⌗ – 1 🏠. Per night from 134 to 264€
Per week from 630 to 1,850€
🚐 sani-station – 30 🗉 24.80€ – ⌁ 11€

Surroundings : ⩜ ⩽
Leisure activities : ♞⟋
Facilities : ♿ ⊶ ⌂ ❞ launderette ⚖
Nearby : ⌇ ※ ⌇

GPS Longitude : 6.72022
Latitude : 45.87355

ST-JEAN-DE-MAURIENNE

73300 – Michelin map **333** L6 – pop. 8,374 – alt. 556
▶ Paris 641 – Lyon 174 – Chambéry 75 – St-Martin-d'Hères 105

Municipal les Grands Cols

℘ 04 79 64 28 02, *www.campingdesgrandscols.com*
Address : 422 av. du Mont Cenis
Opening times : from mid May to mid Sept.
2.5 ha (80 pitches) terraced, flat, grassy
Tariff : (2012 price) 19€ ♣♣ ⟺ 🗉 🗓 (16A) – Extra per person 5€ – Reservation fee 7€
Rental rates : (from mid May to mid Sept.) – 7 🚐. Per night from 45 to 90€
Per week from 250 to 550€ – Reservation fee 7€
🚐 sani-station 4€

Surroundings : ⩽ mountains
Leisure activities : ✕ 🖵 ♞⟋ multi-sports ground
Facilities : ⊶ ⌂ ⌿ ❞ 🗒

GPS Longitude : 6.3515
Latitude : 45.2716

ST-JEAN-DE-MUZOLS

07300 – Michelin map **331** K3 – pop. 2,444 – alt. 123
◨ Paris 541 – Annonay 34 – Beaurepaire 53 – Privas 62

⚠ Le Castelet

℘ 04 75 08 09 48, www.camping-lecastelet.com
Address : 113 rte du Grand Pont (2.8km southwest along the D 238, follow the signs for Lamastre; beside the Doux river)
Opening times : from beginning April to beginning Sept.
3 ha (66 pitches) terraced, flat, grassy, stony
Tariff : 25.50€ ✿✿ ⬅ 🗉 🖟 (10A) – Extra per person 6€ – Reservation fee 5€
Rental rates : (from beginning April to beginning Sept.) – 3 🛏 – 4 🏠. Per night from 75€
Per week from 389 to 611€ – Reservation fee 10€

Surroundings : ⬙ ≤ ⌂ ♀
Leisure activities : ♟ 🎏 🚣 🏊 🌊 🎣
Facilities : ⊶ 🚮 🛁 🚿 🔋

GPS Longitude : 4.78564
Latitude : 45.0681

ST-JEAN-LE-CENTENIER

07580 – Michelin map **331** J6 – pop. 668 – alt. 350
◨ Paris 623 – Alès 83 – Aubenas 20 – Privas 24

⚠ Les Arches

℘ 04 75 36 75 45, www.camping-les-arches.com
Address : at Le Cluzel (1.2km west along the D 458a and take D 258, follow the signs for Mirabel then take the road to the right)
Opening times : from end April to mid Sept.
1.5 ha (97 pitches) terraced, relatively flat, flat, grassy
Tariff : 29.70€ ✿✿ ⬅ 🗉 🖟 (10A) – Extra per person 6€
Rental rates : (permanent) – 25 🏠 – 2 gîtes. Per week from 250 to 745€ – Reservation fee 10€

Surroundings : ⬙
Leisure activities : 🚣 🚲 🌊 (lake)
Facilities : ♿ ⊶ 🛁 🚿 🔋

GPS Longitude : 4.52576
Latitude : 44.58759

This guide is not intended as a list of all the camping sites in France;
its aim is to provide a selection of the best sites in each category.

ST-JORIOZ

74410 – Michelin map **328** J5 – pop. 5,716 – alt. 452
◨ Paris 545 – Albertville 37 – Annecy 9 – Megève 51

⛰ International du Lac d'Annecy

℘ 04 50 68 67 93, www.camping-lac-annecy.com ⚲
Address : 1184 rte d'Albertville (located 1km southeast)
Opening times : from end April to mid Sept.
2.5 ha (163 pitches) flat, grassy
Tariff : (2012 price) 34€ ✿✿ ⬅ 🗉 🖟 (6A) – Extra per person 5.90€ – Reservation fee 2?
Rental rates : (2012 price) (from end April to mid Sept.) ⚲ – 24 🛏 – 3 🏠
Per week from 294 to 903€ – Reservation fee 22€

Surroundings : ♀
Leisure activities : ♟ ✗ 🎏 jacuzzi 🚣 🚲 🌊 🏄 multi-sports ground
Facilities : ♿ ⊶ 🛁 🚿 🚻 🖟 launderette

Europa ♣♣

ℰ 0450685101, *www.camping-europa.com*
Address : 1444 rte d'Albertville (1.4km southeast)
Opening times : from end April to mid Sept.
3 ha (210 pitches) flat, grassy, stony
Tariff : (2012 price) 41.80€ ♦♦ ⇦ 🗐 ⋬ (10A) – Extra per person 7.90€ – Reservation fee 25€
Rental rates : (2012 price) (from end April to mid Sept.) ⅏ – 55 🛏 – 4 🏠 .
Per week from 300 to 996€ – Reservation fee 25€
The site has an attractive swimming area.

Surroundings : ⩽ ♀
Leisure activities : ♟ ✗ 🎯 🚴 ⚓ 🚲 ⅃ ⌁ multi-sports ground
Facilities : 🚻 ⚬━ 🛁 🗮 ☂ ⁙ launderette ⛽

GPS Longitude : 6.18185
     Latitude : 45.83

Le Solitaire du Lac

ℰ 0450685930, *www.campinglesolitaire.com* – access difficult
Address : 615 rte de Sales (located 1km to the north)
Opening times : from beginning April to mid Sept.
3.5 ha (200 pitches) flat, grassy
Tariff : (2012 price) 25.60€ ♦♦ ⇦ 🗐 ⋬ (6A) – Extra per person 5€ – Reservation fee 8€
Rental rates : (2012 price) (from beginning April to mid Sept.) ⅏ (from beg Apr to beg Jul) –
15 🛏. Per night from 48 to 115€ – Per week from 287 to 742€ – Reservation fee 8€
🛢 sani-station
In a pleasant location near a lake (direct access).

Surroundings : ⌑ ♀♀ ⛰
Leisure activities : 🛶 ⚓ 🚲 ♪
Facilities : 🚻 ⚬━ 🛁 ⁙ launderette ⛽

GPS Longitude : 6.14492
     Latitude : 45.8407

07000 – Michelin map **331** K5 – pop. 1,311 – alt. 131
▶ Paris 587 – Aubenas 41 – Crest 29 – Montélimar 35

L'Albanou

ℰ 0475660097, *www.camping-albanou.com*
Address : chemin de Pampelonne (head 1.4km east along the N 304, follow the signs for Pouzin and take the Celliers road to the right; near the Ouvèze river)
Opening times : from end April to end Sept.
1.5 ha (60 pitches) flat, grassy
Tariff : 26€ ♦♦ ⇦ 🗐 ⋬ (10A) – Extra per person 5€ – Reservation fee 5€
Rental rates : (from end April to end Sept.) – 3 🛏. Per night from 50 to 70€
Per week from 360 to 640€ – Reservation fee 5€
🛢 sani-station

Surroundings : ⌑ ⩽ ⌑ ♀
Leisure activities : jacuzzi ⚓ ⅃ ⌁ spa facilities
Facilities : 🚻 ⚬━ ⁙ 🖼 ⛽

GPS Longitude : 4.71369
     Latitude : 44.75651

These symbols are used for a campsite that is exceptional in its category:
ᴀᴀᴀ...ᴀ *Particularly pleasant setting, quality and range of services available*
⌑ ⌑ *Tranquil, isolated site – quiet site, particularly at night*
⩽⩽ *Exceptional view – interesting or panoramic view*

ST-JUST

07700 – Michelin map **331** J8 – pop. 1,558 – alt. 64

Paris 637 – Montélimar 36 – Nyons 51 – Pont-St-Esprit 6

La Plage

℘ 04 75 04 69 46, *www.campingdelaplage.com*

Address : head 2.5km south along the N 86, follow the signs for Pont-St-Esprit and take a right turn before the bridge, 100m from the Ardèche

Opening times : from beginning April to end Sept.

2.5 ha (117 pitches) flat, grassy

Tariff : 19.60€ ★★ ⇔ 回 ⒥ (10A) – Extra per person 5.20€ – Reservation fee 9€

Rental rates : (from beginning April to end Sept.) ⌘ – 10 ⬚⬚. Per week from 578 to 665€
Reservation fee 16€

Surroundings : ⌁ ⍬⍬
Leisure activities : ⌅ ⌇
Facilities : o━ ⅌ 圖
Nearby : ⚎

Longitude : 4.61516
Latitude : 44.2815

ST-LAURENT-DU-PAPE

07800 – Michelin map **331** K5 – pop. 1,549 – alt. 100

Paris 578 – Aubenas 56 – Le Cheylard 43 – Crest 29

La Garenne

℘ 04 75 62 24 62, *www.lagarenne-ardeche.fr*

Address : in the La Garenne quartier (north of the town, access near the post office)

Opening times : from beginning March to end Oct.

6 ha/4 ha for camping (116 pitches) flat, grassy

Tariff : (2012 price) 32.50€ ★★ ⇔ 回 ⒥ (6A) – Extra per person 6€ – Reservation fee 20€

Rental rates : (2012 price) (from beginning March to end Oct.) ⌘ – 2 ⬚⬚.
Per week from 210 to 775€ – Reservation fee 20€

Surroundings : ⍬
Leisure activities : ✕ ⌂ ⌅ ⌇ ⌇
Facilities : ⅋ o━ ⍁ ⌇ ⌇ ⅌ 圖 ⍁ ⍁

Longitude : 4.76221
Latitude : 44.82627

*Routes nationales are main roads and their identifying numbers
begin with N or RN. Routes départementales are generally quieter
roads and begin with D or DN.*

ST-LAURENT-DU-PONT

38380 – Michelin map **333** H5 – pop. 4,496 – alt. 410

Paris 560 – Chambéry 29 – Grenoble 34 – La Tour-du-Pin 42

Municipal les Berges du Guiers

℘ 04 76 55 20 63, *www.camping-chartreuse.com*

Address : av. de la gare (take the northern exit along the D 520, follow the signs for Chambéry and take the turning to the left; beside the Guiers Mort – pedestrian walkway to village)

Opening times : from mid June to mid Sept.

1 ha (45 pitches) flat, grassy

Tariff : (2012 price) 13.50€ ★★ ⇔ 回 ⒥ (5A) – Extra per person 4.50€ – Reservation fee 10€

Surroundings : ⩽ ⍬
Facilities : ⅋ o━ ⍁ ⅌ 圖
Nearby : ⌅ ⌇ ⌇

Longitude : 5.73615
Latitude : 45.39068

RHÔNE-ALPES

ST-LAURENT-EN-BEAUMONT

38350 – Michelin map **333** I8 – pop. 436 – alt. 900
▶ Paris 613 – Le Bourg-d'Oisans 43 – Corps 16 – Grenoble 51

Belvédère de l'Obiou

℘ 0476304080, www.camping-obiou.com
Address : at Les Égats (1.3km southwest along the N 85)
Opening times : from mid April to mid Oct.
1 ha (45 pitches) terraced, relatively flat, flat, grassy
Tariff : 26.50€ ✚✚ ⟅⟆ 🔲 (10A) – Extra per person 5.70€ – Reservation fee 15€
Rental rates : (2012 price) (from beginning May to end Sept.) – 5 🛏 – 2 🛏.
Per week from 294 to 630€ – Reservation fee 15€
🚱 sani-station 5€ – 2 🔲 20.50€ – 🚐11€

Surroundings : ≤ ♀
Leisure activities : ✗ ⟦⟧ ⟅⟆ 🖼
Facilities : ♿ ⟶ 🅒 ⟦⟧ ⟅⟆
Nearby : 🍸

GPS Longitude : 5.83779 Latitude : 44.87597

ST-LAURENT-LES-BAINS

07590 – Michelin map **331** F6 – pop. 156 – alt. 840
▶ Paris 603 – Aubenas 64 – Langogne 30 – Largentière 52

Le Ceytrou

℘ 0466460203, campingleceytrou.free.fr
Address : situated 2.1km to the southeast along the D 4
Opening times : from beginning April to mid Nov.
2.5 ha (60 pitches) terraced, flat and relatively flat, stony, grassy
Tariff : 13€ ✚✚ ⟅⟆ 🔲 (10A) – Extra per person 3.40€
Rental rates : (2012 price) (from beginning April to mid Nov.) – 12 🏠.
Per week from 150 to 420€

A charming location in the heart of the Vivarais Cévenol mountains.

Surroundings : ⟦⟧ ≤ ♀
Leisure activities : ⟦⟧ ⟅⟆ ♒ ⟅⟆
Facilities : ♿ ⟶ ⟦⟧ ⟅⟆ 🅒

GPS Longitude : 3.97962 Latitude : 44.59922

ST-MARTIN-D'ARDÈCHE

07700 – Michelin map **331** I6 – pop. 886 – alt. 46
▶ Paris 641 – Bagnols-sur-Cèze 21 – Barjac 27 – Bourg-St-Andéol 13

Le Pontet

℘ 0475046307, www.campinglepontet.com
Address : at Le Pontet (located 1.5km east along the D 290, follow the signs for St-Just and take road to the left)
Opening times : from beginning April to end Sept.
1.8 ha (100 pitches) terraced, flat, grassy
Tariff : (2012 price) 23.60€ ✚✚ ⟅⟆ 🔲 (6A) – Extra per person 5.40€ – Reservation fee 9€
Rental rates : (2012 price) (from beginning April to end Sept.) – 17 🏠.
Per night from 75 to 145€ – Per week from 210 to 660€ – Reservation fee 26€
🚱 sani-station 3€ – 4 🔲 8€ – 🚐8€

Surroundings : ⟦⟧ ♀♀
Leisure activities : 🍸 ✗ ⟦⟧ ⟅⟆ 🚲 ⟅⟆
Facilities : ♿ ⟶ 🅒 ⟦⟧ 🅒

GPS Longitude : 4.58453 Latitude : 44.30409

△ Les Gorges

☏ 0475046109, *www.camping-des-gorges.com*
Address : chemin de Sauze (located 1.5km to the northwest)
Opening times : from beginning May to mid Sept.
1.2 ha (92 pitches) terraced, flat, grassy, stony
Tariff : (2012 price) 33.50€ ♥♥ ⊶ 🗉 🗷 (10A) – Extra per person 7.50€ – Reservation fee 30€
Rental rates : (2012 price) (from beginning May to mid Sept.) – 24 🛏 – 1 gîte.
Per night from 45 to 142€ – Per week from 315 to 994€ – Reservation fee 30€
🗺 sani-station

Surroundings : ≤ 00
Leisure activities : 🍷 ✕ 🖾 🛶 🏊 ⚓ 🎣
Facilities : 🚿 ⊶ 🎖 🛖 ⛲ 🖾 🛒 🛗

GPS Longitude : 4.55547
Latitude : 44.31155

△ Indigo le Moulin

☏ 0475046620, *www.camping-indigo.com*
Address : take southeastern exit along the D 290, follow the signs for St-Just and take a right turn
(D 200); beside the Ardèche river
Opening times : from mid April to end Sept.
6.5 ha (200 pitches) relatively flat, flat, grassy, sandy
Tariff : (2012 price) 31€ ♥♥ ⊶ 🗉 🗷 (10A) – Extra per person 6.30€ – Reservation fee 20€
Rental rates : (2012 price) (from mid April to end Sept.) – 16 'gypsy' caravans – 42 tents.
Per night from 44 to 105€ – Per week from 216 to 735€ – Reservation fee 20€
🗺 sani-station 7€

Surroundings : 0
Leisure activities : ✕ 🖾 🛶 🏊 ⚓ 🎣
Facilities : 🚿 ⊶ 🛒 🖾 🛗

GPS Longitude : 4.5695
Latitude : 44.3004

T-MARTIN-DE-CLELLES

8930 – Michelin map **333** G8 – pop. 157 – alt. 750
◀ Paris 616 – Lyon 149 – Grenoble 48 – St-Martin-d'Hères 49

△ La Chabannerie

☏ 0476340038, *www.camping-isere.net*
Address : Lotissement La Chabannerie
Opening times : from mid May to mid Sept.
2.5 ha (49 pitches) terraced, flat and relatively flat, stony, grassy
Tariff : 19€ ♥♥ ⊶ 🗉 🗷 (10A) – Extra per person 5€
🗺 sani-station 8€ – 5 🗉 19€

Surroundings : 🏔 ≤ 🗠 00
Leisure activities : 🖾 🏊
Facilities : ⊶ 🗷 🎖 ⛲ 🖾 🛗

GPS Longitude : 5.61624
Latitude : 44.82574

Michelin classification:
△△△△ *Extremely comfortable, equipped to a very high standard*
△△△ *Very comfortable, equipped to a high standard*
△△△ *Comfortable and well equipped*
△△ *Reasonably comfortable*
△ *Satisfactory*

ST-MARTIN-EN-VERCORS

26420 – Michelin map **332** F3 – pop. 378 – alt. 780
▶ Paris 601 – La Chapelle-en-Vercors 9 – Grenoble 51 – Romans-sur-Isère 46

⚠ La Porte St-Martin

ℰ 04 75 45 51 10, *www.camping-laportestmartin.com*
Address : take the northern exit along the D 103
Opening times : from beginning May to end Sept.
1.5 ha (66 pitches) terraced, sloping, flat, grassy, gravelled, stony
Tariff : (2012 price) 17.80€ ✹ ✹ ⇌ 🅴 ⓖ (12A) – Extra per person 6.50€
Rental rates : (2012 price) (permanent) ⌲ – 3 🏠 – 4 tent bungalows – 1 gîte.
Per night from 60 to 100€ – Per week from 230 to 630€
🚽 sani-station 8€

Surroundings : ⟨ ♀
Leisure activities : 🖼 🚲 🏊 (small swimming pool)
Facilities : & ⊶ ⚑ 🖼

GPS Longitude : 5.44336
Latitude : 45.02456

ST-MAURICE-D'IBIE

07170 – Michelin map **331** I6 – pop. 206 – alt. 220
▶ Paris 636 – Alès 64 – Aubenas 23 – Pont-St-Esprit 63

⚠ Le Sous-Bois

ℰ 04 75 94 86 95, *www.le-sous-bois.fr*
Address : at Les Plots (situated 2km south along the D 558, follow the signs for Vallon-Pont-d'Arc, then take the gravel road to the right.)
Opening times : from end April to mid Sept.
2 ha (50 pitches) open site, stony, flat, grassy
Tariff : 24.50€ ✹ ✹ ⇌ 🅴 ⓖ (10A) – Extra per person 7.50€ – Reservation fee 10€
Rental rates : (from end April to mid Sept.) – 13 🚐 – 2 studios – 3 tent bungalows.
Per night from 35 to 60€ – Per week from 250 to 610€ – Reservation fee 10€
Beside the Ibie river, in a pleasant, natural setting.

Surroundings : 🞱 ♀♀
Leisure activities : ♟ ✗ 🛶 🏊 multi-sports ground
Facilities : & ⊶ (Jul–Aug) 🛁 ⚑ 🖼 🚿

GPS Longitude : 4.47487
Latitude : 44.49038

In order for the guide to remain wholly objective, the selection is made on an entirely independent basis. There is no charge for being selected for the guide.

ST-NAZAIRE-EN-ROYANS

26190 – Michelin map **332** E3 – pop. 716 – alt. 172
▶ Paris 576 – Grenoble 69 – Pont-en-Royans 9 – Romans-sur-Isère 19

⚠ Municipal du Lac

ℰ 04 75 48 41 18, *jm.combier@hotmail.fr*
Address : 100B r. des Condamines (700m southeast, follow the signs for St-Jean-en-Royans)
1.5 ha (75 pitches) flat and relatively flat, grassy
Rentals : 2 tents – 2 'gypsy' caravans.
Situated beside the Bourne river (with a small lake).

Surroundings : 🞱 ♀♀
Leisure activities : 🖼 🎣
Facilities : & ⊶ ⚑ 🖼

GPS Longitude : 5.25368
Latitude : 45.05912

T-PAUL-DE-VÉZELIN

2590 – Michelin map **327** D4 – pop. 303 – alt. 431
Paris 415 – Boën 19 – Feurs 30 – Roanne 26

Arpheuilles

𝒫 04 77 63 43 43, *www.camping-arpheuilles.com* – access difficult for caravans
Address : 4km to the north, at Port Piset, near the river (and lake)
3.5 ha (80 pitches) terraced, relatively flat, grassy
An attractive location in a valley of the Loire river, on a secluded and unspoilt site.

Surroundings : ⛰ ≤ 🏞 ⛲
Leisure activities : 🍴 ✗ 🎬 🎯 🏊 🎣 🚣 🛶
Facilities : 🚻 🔌 🚿 🗑 launderette 🧺
Nearby : 🏖

GPS Longitude : 4.06314
     Latitude : 45.91178

The guide is updated each year, so consult the latest edition for the most up-to-date information and pricing.

T-PIERRE-DE-CHARTREUSE

8380 – Michelin map **333** H5 – pop. 999 – alt. 885 – Winter sports : 900/1,800 m ⛷ 1 ⛷ 13 ⛷
Paris 571 – Belley 62 – Chambéry 39 – Grenoble 28

De Martinière

𝒫 04 76 88 60 36, *www.campingdemartiniere.com*
Address : rte du Col de Porte (3km southwest along the D 512, follow the signs for Grenoble)
Opening times : from beginning May to mid Sept.
1.5 ha (100 pitches) open site, relatively flat, flat, grassy
Tariff : 26.40€ ✶✶ �car 🔲 🔌 (10A) – Extra per person 6€ – Reservation fee 8€
Rental rates : (from beginning May to mid Sept.) 🏠 – 4 🚐 – 1 🏚.
Per week from 245 to 700€ – Reservation fee 8€
🚱 sani-station – 2 🔲 20.40€ – 🚐 11€
A pleasant location in the heart of the Chartreuse mountains.

Surroundings : ≤ 🌳
Leisure activities : 🎬 ⛷ 🏊
Facilities : 🔌 🍴 🚿 🗑
Nearby : ✗

GPS Longitude : 5.79717
     Latitude : 45.32583

T-PRIVAT

7200 – Michelin map **331** I6 – pop. 1,588 – alt. 304
Paris 631 – Lyon 169 – Privas 26 – Valence 65

Le Plan d'Eau

𝒫 04 75 35 44 98, *www.campingleplandeau.fr*
Address : rte de Lussas (situated 2km southeast along the D 259)
Opening times : from end April to beginning Sept.
3 ha (100 pitches) flat, stony, grassy
Tariff : 28.50€ ✶✶ 🚗 🔲 🔌 (8A) – Extra per person 6.70€ – Reservation fee 20€
Rental rates : (from end April to beginning Sept.) 🏠 – 7 🚐 – 16 🏚.
Per night from 40 to 120€ – Per week from 220 to 820€ – Reservation fee 20€

Surroundings : ⛰ 🌳
Leisure activities : 🍴 ✗ ⛷ 🏊 🏖 🎣
Facilities : 🚻 🔌 🚿 🍴 launderette

GPS Longitude : 4.43296
     Latitude : 44.61872

ST-REMÈZE

07700 – Michelin map **331** J7 – pop. 863 – alt. 365
▶ Paris 645 – Barjac 30 – Bourg-St-Andéol 16 – Pont-St-Esprit 27

Carrefour de l'Ardèche

℘ 0475041575, www.ardechecamping.net
Address : in the Gourdaud quartier (take the eastern exit, along the D 4)
Opening times : from beginning April to mid Oct.
1.7 ha (90 pitches) relatively flat, flat, grassy, stony
Tariff : 24€ ♦♦ ⇌ 🗉 (₤) (10A) – Extra per person 8.50€ – Reservation fee 24€
Rental rates : (from beginning April to mid Oct.) – 20 🖭 – 9 🏠. Per night from 39 to 72€
Per week from 180 to 730€ – Reservation fee 24€

Surroundings : ⩽ 🗂
Leisure activities : ♈ ✗ 🖼 🛥 ᴣ
Facilities : ᕦ ⊶ ᵞ 🗉 ᴂ

GPS
Longitude : 4.51629
Latitude : 44.38755

La Résidence d'Été

℘ 0475042687, www.campinglaresidence.com
Address : r. de la Bateuse
Opening times : from beginning April to end Oct.
1.6 ha (60 pitches) terraced, relatively flat to hilly, grassy, stony, fruit trees
Tariff : 25€ ♦♦ ⇌ 🗉 (₤) (12A) – Extra per person 8€ – Reservation fee 10€
Rental rates : (from beginning April to end Oct.) – 19 🖭. Per night from 38 to 98€
Per week from 260 to 650€ – Reservation fee 10€

Surroundings : ⩽ ⵚ
Leisure activities : ✗ 🛥 ᴣ
Facilities : ᕦ ⊶ ᵞ 🗉 ᴂ

GPS
Longitude : 4.50711
Latitude : 44.39417

Domaine de Briange

℘ 0475041443, www.campingdebriange.com
Address : rte de Gras (situated 2km north along the D 362)
Opening times : from beginning May to mid Sept.
4 ha (80 pitches) relatively flat, flat, grassy, sandy, stony
Tariff : 33€ ♦♦ ⇌ 🗉 (₤) (6A) – Extra per person 8€
Rental rates : (from beginning May to mid Sept.) – 1 'gypsy' caravan – 18 🏠 –
1 cabin in the trees – 6 tent bungalows – 6 gîtes. Per night from 56 to 169€
Per week from 280 to 1,014€

Surroundings : 🌄 ⵚ
Leisure activities : ✗ 🛥 ✂ ᴣ
Facilities : ᕦ ⊶ ᵞ 🗉

GPS
Longitude : 4.49364
Latitude : 44.39008

Key to rentals symbols:

12 🖭	**Number of mobile homes**
20 🏠	**Number of chalets**
6 ᗐ	**Number of rooms to rent**
Per night 30–50€	**Minimum/maximum rate per night**
Per week 300–1,000€	**Minimum/maximum rate per week**

ST-SAUVEUR-DE-CRUZIÈRES

07460 – Michelin map **331** H8 – pop. 535 – alt. 150
▣ Paris 674 – Alès 28 – Barjac 9 – Privas 81

△ La Claysse

℘ 0475354065, *www.campingdelaclaysse.com* – For caravans and campervans, access via the top of the village.

Address : at La Digue (To the northwest of the town; beside the river)
Opening times : from beginning April to end Sept.
5 ha/1 ha for camping (60 pitches) terraced, flat, grassy
Tariff : 26€ ★★ ⇦ 国 ⎙ (10A) – Extra per person 4.50€ – Reservation fee 15€
Rental rates : (from beginning April to end Sept.) ⌇ – 13 ⤶. Per night from 50 to 70€
Per week from 220 to 680€ – Reservation fee 15€

Surroundings : ῼ
Leisure activities : ✕ ▦ ♨ ⬧ ⚲ ≃ ⌇
Facilities : ⟳ ☷ ⚘ ▣
Nearby : climbing

Longitude : 4.25085
Latitude : 44.29984

ST-SAUVEUR-DE-MONTAGUT

07190 – Michelin map **331** J5 – pop. 1,144 – alt. 218
▣ Paris 597 – Le Cheylard 24 – Lamastre 29 – Privas 24

⋀⋀ L'Ardéchois

℘ 0475666187, *www.ardechois-camping.fr*
Address : situated 8.5km west along the D 102, follow the signs for Albon
Opening times : from mid May to mid Sept.
37 ha/5 ha for camping (107 pitches) terraced, flat, grassy
Tariff : (2012 price) 30.50€ ★★ ⇦ 国 ⎙ (10A) – Extra per person 6.85€ – Reservation fee 23€
Rental rates : (2012 price) (from mid May to mid Sept.) – 18 ⤶ – 8 ⌂.
Per week from 325 to 860€ – Reservation fee 23€

Situated beside the Glueyre river.

Surroundings : ⬩ ⩽ ῼ
Leisure activities : ♀ ✕ ▦ ♨ ⬧ ⚲ ≃ ⌇
Facilities : ⟁ ⟳ ⌷ ⚘ ⚘ ▣ ⚖

Longitude : 4.52294
Latitude : 44.82893

Fire safety doesn't stop when you leave your accommodation.
Always take care and consider the fire risks.

ST-SYMPHORIEN-SUR-COISE

69590 – Michelin map **327** F6 – pop. 3,438 – alt. 558
▣ Paris 489 – Andrézieux-Bouthéon 26 – L'Arbresle 36 – Feurs 30

⋀ Intercommunal Centre de Loisirs de Hurongues

℘ 0478484429, *www.camping-hurongues.com*
Address : 3.5km west along the D 2, follow the signs for Chazelles-sur-Lyon, 400m from a small lake
3.6 ha (120 pitches) terraced, relatively flat, stony
⤶ sani-station
In a pleasant wooded setting based around a leisure park.

Surroundings : ⬩ ▱ ῼ
Leisure activities : ▦
Facilities : ⟳ ⦀ ⚘ ▣
Nearby : ♨ ⌇ ▥ ⌇

Longitude : 4.4282
Latitude : 45.63481

ST-THÉOFFREY

38119 – Michelin map **333** H8 – pop. 444 – alt. 936
▶ Paris 595 – Le Bourg-d'Oisans 44 – Grenoble 33 – La Mure 10

Au Pré du Lac

☏ 04 76 83 91 34, *www.aupredulac.eu*
Address : at the Hameau Pétichet
3 ha (96 pitches) flat, grassy
Rentals : 4 ▭ – 3 ▭ – 1 gîte.

Surroundings : ♀ ▲
Leisure activities : ♈ ✗ ▭ ▰ ▱ ⟋ ◊
Facilities : ♿ ⚲ ▥ ☶ ⸋ launderette ⤴
Nearby : ⇝ ⚓

GPS Longitude : 5.77224
Latitude : 45.00454

*The prices listed were supplied by the campsite owners in 2012
(if prices were not available, those from the previous year are given).
The fees should be regarded as basic charges and may fluctuate
with inflation.*

ST-VALLIER

26240 – Michelin map **332** B2 – pop. 4,000 – alt. 135
▶ Paris 526 – Annonay 21 – St-Étienne 61 – Tournon-sur-Rhône 16

Municipal les Îsles de Silon

☏ 04 75 23 22 17, *www.saintvallier.com*
Address : at Les Îles (situated to the north, near the Rhône river)
Opening times : from mid March to mid Nov.
1.35 ha (92 pitches) flat, grassy, stony
Tariff : (2012 price) ♣ 2.70€ ⇌ 4€ ▣ 2.80€ – ฿ (10A) 2.50€
Rental rates : (2012 price) (from mid March to mid Nov.) – 4 ▭. Per night from 55 to 70€
Per week from 260 to 400€

Surroundings : ⇐ ⊏ ♀♀
Leisure activities : ▰
Facilities : ⚲ ▥ ⸋ ▣
Nearby : ✗ ⤒

GPS Longitude : 4.81237
Latitude : 45.1879

STE-CATHERINE

69440 – Michelin map **327** G6 – pop. 911 – alt. 700
▶ Paris 488 – Andrézieux-Bouthéon 38 – L'Arbresle 37 – Feurs 43

Municipal du Châtelard

☏ 04 78 81 80 60, *http://mairie-saintecatherine.fr* – alt. 800 – limited spaces for one-night stay
Address : at le Châtelard (situated 2km to the south)
Opening times : from beginning March to end Nov.
4 ha (61 pitches) terraced, grassy, gravelled
Tariff : ♣ 2.25€ ⇌ ▣ 2.55€ – ฿ (6A) 2.80€

Surroundings : ▨ ⇐ Mont Pilat and Monts du Lyonnais ⊏
Leisure activities : ▱
Facilities : ⸋ ▣

GPS Longitude : 4.57344
Latitude : 45.58817

SALAVAS

07150 – Michelin map **331** I7 – pop. 530 – alt. 96
▶ Paris 668 – Lyon 206 – Privas 58 – Nîmes 77

Le Péquelet

𝒫 04 75 88 04 49, *lepequelet.com*
Address : at Le Cros (take the southern exit along the D 579, follow the signs for Barjac and continue along the turning to the left for 2km)
Opening times : from beginning April to end Sept.
2 ha (60 pitches) flat, grassy
Tariff : 28.50€ ✶✶ ⬌ 🔲 ⚡ (10A) – Extra per person 7.50€ – Reservation fee 10€
Rental rates : (from beginning April to end Sept.) – 10 🚐 – 7 🏠 – 2 apartments – 2 tent bungalows. Per night from 35 to 90€ – Per week from 250 to 720€ – Reservation fee 10€
🚽 sani-station 5€
Beside the Ardèche river (direct access).

Surroundings : 🏞 ⊐ ♨ ⛰
Leisure activities : 🛶 ✗ 🏊 🎣 ⛵
Facilities : ⅔ ⊶ 🛁 🚾 🏪

GPS Longitude : 4.39806
Latitude : 44.39075

SALLANCHES

74700 – Michelin map **328** M5 – pop. 15,619 – alt. 550
▶ Paris 585 – Annecy 72 – Bonneville 29 – Chamonix-Mont-Blanc 28

Village Center Les Îles

𝒫 08 25 00 53 18, *http://campings.village-center.fr/rhones-alpes/camping-montagne-iles.php*
Address : 245 chemin de la Cavettaz (situated 2km to the southeast; beside a stream and 250m from a lake)
Opening times : permanent
4.6 ha (260 pitches) flat, grassy, stony
Tariff : (2012 price) 19€ ✶✶ ⬌ 🔲 ⚡ (10A) – Extra per person 4€
Rental rates : (2012 price) (from beginning April to end Sept.) – 8 🚐.
Per night from 25 to 30€ – Per week from 506 to 689€ – Reservation fee 30€
🚽 sani-station 4€ – 🚐 ⚡11€

Surroundings : ⟨ ⊐ ♨
Leisure activities : 🍸 🎨 daytime
Facilities : ⅔ ⊶ 🚾🛁 🛀 🌿 🏪
Nearby : 🏊 🎣 🏊 🐎

GPS Longitude : 6.65103
Latitude : 45.92404

LA SALLE-EN-BEAUMONT

38350 – Michelin map **333** I8 – pop. 297 – alt. 756
▶ Paris 614 – Le Bourg-d'Oisans 44 – Gap 51 – Grenoble 52

Le Champ Long

𝒫 04 76 30 41 81, *www.camping-champlong.com* – help moving caravans onto and off pitches available on request
Address :at Le Champ-Long (2.7km southwest along the N 85, follow the signs for la Mure and take road to the left)
Opening times : permanent
5 ha (97 pitches) open site, very uneven, terraced, flat, grassy
Tariff : 23€ ✶✶ ⬌ 🔲 ⚡ (10A) – Extra per person 5€ – Reservation fee 15€
Rental rates : (permanent) – 5 🚐 – 9 🏠 – 3 🛏. Per night from 90 to 100€
Per week from 550 to 650€ – Reservation fee 15€
🚽 sani-station 5€ – 10 🔲 18€ – 🚐13€

Surroundings : 🏞 ⟨ Lac du Sautet and valley ⊐ ♨
Leisure activities : 🍸 ✗ 🛶 🚴 🏊
Facilities : ⅔ ⊶ 🌿 launderette 🍴

GPS Longitude : 5.84416
Latitude : 44.85725

SAMOËNS

74340 – Michelin map **328** N4 – pop. 2,311 – alt. 710
▶ Paris 598 – Lyon 214 – Annecy 82 – Genève 63

Club Airotel Le Giffre

℘ 04 50 34 41 92, *www.camping-samoens.com*
Address : at La Glière
Opening times : permanent
7 ha (312 pitches) flat, grassy, stony
Tariff : 22.45€ ✚✚ ⇌ ▣ ⛽ (10A) – Extra per person 4.10€
Rental rates : (permanent) – 1 ⬛ – 6 ⌂ – 5 tents. Per night from 40 to 66€
Per week from 199 to 599€
🚮 sani-station 5€ – 14 ▣ 19.20€ – 🚐11€
In a pleasant location, near a lake and a leisure park.

Surroundings : ❄ ⩽ ♀
Leisure activities : 🎮 🎣
Facilities : ♿ ⊶ ▣ ⬚ △ ☂ ⛱ ❝ ▣
Nearby : ♈ ✗ 🏌 ⛳ ☈ ⛷ ♨ sports trail, rafting and canyoning, skating rink

GPS Longitude : 6.71917
Latitude : 46.07695

We welcome your feedback on our listed campsites.
Please email us at: campingfrance@tp.michelin.com
Many thanks in advance!

SAMPZON

07120 – pop. 224 – alt. 120
▶ Paris 660 – Lyon 198 – Privas 56 – Nîmes 85

Yelloh! Village Soleil Vivarais ♟♟

℘ 04 75 39 67 56, *www.soleil-vivarais.com*
Address : follow the signs for Vallon Pont d'Arc
12 ha (350 pitches) flat, grassy, stony
Rental rates : 250 ⬛ – 5 ⌂ .
🚮 sani-station
On the Sampzon peninsula (an elongated bend in the Ardèche river), with a lovely swimming area.

Surroundings : ⩽ ♀♀ ⛰
Leisure activities : ♈ ✗ 🎮 ⛹ 🏌 🚴 ⛳ ☈ ⛱ 🎣
Facilities : ♿ ⊶ ▦ ⬚ △ ☂ ❝ launderette ⬛ ♒

GPS Longitude : 4.35528
Latitude : 44.42916

Sun Camping

℘ 6 72 71 42 68, *www.suncamping.com*
Address : 10 chemin des Piboux (200m from the Ardèche river)
Opening times : from mid April to mid Sept.
1.2 ha (70 pitches) terraced, flat, grassy
Tariff : 31.70€ ✚✚ ⇌ ▣ ⛽ (10A) – Extra per person 6€ – Reservation fee 8€
Rental rates : (from mid April to mid Sept.) – 12 ⬛ – 2 tent bungalows.
Per night from 25 to 93€ – Per week from 175 to 651€ – Reservation fee 13€
On the Sampzon peninsula (an elongated bend in the river).

Surroundings : ♀♀
Leisure activities : ♈ ✗ 🏌 ☈
Facilities : ♿ ⊶ (Jul–Aug) ⬚ ❝ ▣
Nearby : ⬛ ♒ ⛱

GPS Longitude : 4.35515
Latitude : 44.4288

Le Mas de la Source

0475396798, *www.campingmasdelasource.com*
Address : La Tuillière
Opening times : from beginning April to end Sept.
1.2 ha (30 pitches) terraced, flat, grassy
Tariff : (2012 price) 31.50€ (6A) – Extra per person 6.60€ – Reservation fee 15€
Rental rates : (2012 price) (from beginning April to end Sept.) – 4.
Per week from 650 to 720€ – Reservation fee 15.50€

On the Sampzon peninsula, an elongated bend in the Ardèche river (direct access).

Surroundings :
Leisure activities :
Facilities :

GPS Longitude : 4.3466
Latitude : 44.42242

SATILLIEU

07290 – Michelin map **331** J3 – pop. 1,616 – alt. 485
Paris 542 – Annonay 13 – Lamastre 36 – Privas 87

Municipal le Grangeon

0475349641, *www.mairie-satillieu.fr et www.ideoguide.com*
Address : rte de Lalouvesc (head 1.1km southwest along the D 578a; follow the signs for Lalouvesc and take the turning to the left)
Opening times : from end March to end Oct.
1 ha (52 pitches) terraced, grassy
Tariff : (2012 price) 2.60€ 2€ 2.60€ – (5A) 3.55€
Rental rates : (2012 price) (permanent) – 5. Per night from 80 to 160€
Per week from 235 to 385€

Siituated beside the Ay river.

Surroundings :
Leisure activities :
Facilities :
Nearby : (lake with recreational facilities)

GPS Longitude : 4.60389
Latitude : 45.14438

The guide covers all 22 regions of France – see the map and list of regions on pages 4–5.

SCIEZ

74140 – Michelin map **328** L3 – pop. 5,269 – alt. 406
Paris 561 – Abondance 37 – Annecy 69 – Annemasse 24

Le Chatelet

0450725260, *www.camping-chatelet.com* – limited spaces for one-night stay
Address : 658 chemin des Hutins Vieux (3km northeast along the N 5, follow the signs for Thonon-les-Bains and turn left onto the rte du Port at Sciez-Plage, 300m from the beach)
Opening times : from beginning April to end Oct.
2.5 ha (121 pitches) flat, grassy, stony
Tariff : (2012 price) 18€ (10A) – Extra per person 5.50€ – Reservation fee 8€
Rental rates : (2012 price) (from beginning March to end Nov.) (1 chalet) – 12.
Per night from 47 to 119€ – Per week from 309 to 833€ – Reservation fee 12€
sani-station 4€

Surroundings :
Leisure activities :
Facilities : launderette
Nearby : pedalos

GPS Longitude : 6.39705
Latitude : 46.34079

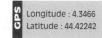

SÉEZ

73700 – Michelin map **333** N4 – pop. 2,332 – alt. 904
▶ Paris 638 – Albertville 57 – Bourg-St-Maurice 4 – Moûtiers 31

Le Reclus

✆ 04 79 41 01 05, *www.campinglereclus.com*
Address : rte de Tignes (take northwestern exit along the N 90, follow the signs for Bourg-St-Maurice, beside the Reclus river)
Opening times : permanent
1.5 ha (108 pitches) terraced, relatively flat, grassy, stony
Tariff : (2012 price) 19.20€ ✝✝ ⇌ 🅴 (🖋) (10A) – Extra per person 4.80€ – Reservation fee 10€
Rental rates : (permanent) – 4 'gypsy' caravans – 5 🚐 – 4 🏠 – 5 yurts – 3 🛏 – 1 apartment.
Per night from 50 to 85€ – Per week from 50 to 590€ – Reservation fee 10€
🚿 sani-station 4€ – 6 🅴 11€ – 🛢11€

Surroundings : ✿ ᵔᵔ
Leisure activities : ✗ 🏛
Facilities : ᕫ ☞ ▥ ᵞᵞ launderette

GPS
Longitude : 6.78529
Latitude : 45.62577

SERRIÈRES-DE-BRIORD

01470 – Michelin map **328** F6 – pop. 1,143 – alt. 218 – Leisure centre
▶ Paris 481 – Belley 29 – Bourg-en-Bresse 57 – Crémieu 24

Le Point Vert

✆ 04 74 36 13 45, *www.camping-ain-bugey.com* – limited spaces for one-night stay
Address : rte du Point Vert (2.5km west, Leisure and activity park)
Opening times : permanent
1.9 ha (137 pitches) flat, grassy
Tariff : 20€ ✝✝ ⇌ 🅴 (🖋) (10A) – Extra per person 50€
Rental rates : (permanent) – 6 🚐. Per night from 140 to 170€ – Per week from 400 to 550€
🚿 sani-station
Beside a small lake near the River Rhône.

Surroundings : ≤ ᵔ ⛰
Leisure activities : 🏛 🕐 daytime 🛶 🚣 🚲 🏊 🎣
Facilities : ᕫ ☞ 🗖 🗠 ᵞᵞ launderette 🏬
Nearby : 🍽 ✗ 🚣 🍴 🏖 (beach) 🦆 pedalos

GPS
Longitude : 5.42731
Latitude : 45.81633

SÉVRIER

74320 – Michelin map **328** J5 – pop. 3,835 – alt. 456
▶ Paris 541 – Albertville 41 – Annecy 6 – Megève 55

Le Panoramic

✆ 04 50 52 43 09, *www.camping-le-panoramic.com*
Address : 22 chemin des Bernets (located 3.5km to the south)
Opening times : from beginning May to end Sept.
3 ha (209 pitches) flat, sloping, grassy
Tariff : 24€ ✝✝ ⇌ 🅴 (🖋) (10A) – Extra per person 5€ – Reservation fee 10€
Rental rates : (from end April to end Sept.) – 18 🚐 – 17 🏠 – 4 studios – 3 apartments.
Per night from 45 to 85€ – Per week from 260 to 720€ – Reservation fee 10€
🚿 sani-station 5€
The site looks out over a lake.

Surroundings : ≤ ᵔ
Leisure activities : 🍽 ✗ 🏛 🕐 daytime 🚣 🚲 🏊
Facilities : ᕫ ☞ 🗖 ᵞᵞ launderette 🏬 🚣
Nearby : 🐎

GPS
Longitude : 6.1417
Latitude : 45.84308

⚠ Au Coeur du Lac

℘ 0450524645, *www.campingaucoeurdulac.com*
Address : 3233 rte d'Albertville (located 1km to the south)
1.7 ha (100 pitches) terraced, relatively flat, grassy, fine gravel
Rentals : ⚡ – 10 🚐.
🚉 sani-station – 10 🅴
In a pleasant location near the lake (direct access).

Surroundings : ≤ ⌑ ♀
Leisure activities : 🖵 🖑 daytime 🏊 🚲 🛶
Facilities : ♿ ⚐ ▥ ♨ ♈ launderette 🛒
Nearby : 🛒 ✗ 🎣 🐎

GPS
Longitude : 6.14399
Latitude : 45.85487

SEYSSEL

01420 – Michelin map **328** H5 – pop. 948 – alt. 258
▶ Paris 517 – Aix-les-Bains 33 – Annecy 41 – Genève 52

⚠ L' International

℘ 0450592847, *www.camp-inter.fr*
Address : chemin de la Barotte (2.4km southwest along the D 992, follow the signs for Culoz and take the road to the right)
Opening times : from beginning May to end Sept.
1.5 ha (45 pitches) terraced, flat, grassy
Tariff : 27 € ✸✸ 🚐 🅴 🔌 (10A) – Extra per person 5 € – Reservation fee 12 €
Rental rates : (from beginning May to end Sept.) – 15 🚐. Per night from 71 to 87 €
Per week from 280 to 620 € – Reservation fee 17 €
The site enjoys a peaceful setting in the hills.

Surroundings : 🌄 ≤ ⌑ ♀
Leisure activities : ✗ 🖵 🏊 🚲 🛶
Facilities : ⚐ ♈ launderette 🛒

GPS
Longitude : 5.82349
Latitude : 45.94957

The classification (1 to 5 tents, black or red) that we award to selected sites in this guide is our own system. It should not be confused with the classification (1 to 5 stars) of official organisations.

SEYSSEL

74910 – Michelin map **328** I5 – pop. 2,262 – alt. 252
▶ Paris 517 – Aix-les-Bains 32 – Annecy 40

⚠ Le Nant-Matraz

℘ 0450590368, *campinglenantmatraz@bbox.fr*
Address : take the northern exit along the D 992
Opening times : from beginning April to end Sept.
1 ha (74 pitches) flat and relatively flat, grassy
Tariff : (2012 price) 17 € ✸✸ 🚐 🅴 🔌 (6A) – Extra per person 5 €

Surroundings : ≤ ⌑ ♀♀
Leisure activities : ♈
Facilities : ⚐ 🖼
Nearby : 🛒

GPS
Longitude : 5.83574
Latitude : 45.96339

TAIN-L'HERMITAGE

26600 – Michelin map **332** C3 – pop. 5,883 – alt. 124

▶ Paris 545 – Grenoble 97 – Le Puy-en-Velay 105 – St-Étienne 76

Municipal les Lucs

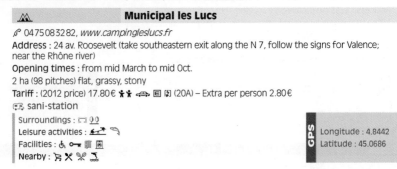

✆ 04 75 08 32 82, *www.campingleslucs.fr*

Address : 24 av. Roosevelt (take southeastern exit along the N 7, follow the signs for Valence; near the Rhône river)

Opening times : from mid March to mid Oct.

2 ha (98 pitches) flat, grassy, stony

Tariff : (2012 price) 17.80€ ✝✝ ⇌ ▣ ⚡ (20A) – Extra per person 2.80€

🚉 sani-station

Surroundings : ▱ 〇〇	
Leisure activities : 🏊 ✎	**GPS** Longitude : 4.8442
Facilities : ✆ ⊶ ▥ ▣	Latitude : 45.0686
Nearby : 🛒 ✗ ✗ 🛶	

Some information or pricing may have changed since the guide went to press. We recommend you check the price list online in advance or at the entrance to the campsite and enquire about possible restrictions.

TANINGES

74440 – Michelin map **328** M4 – pop. 3,414 – alt. 640

▶ Paris 570 – Annecy 68 – Bonneville 24 – Chamonix-Mont-Blanc 51

Municipal des Thézières

✆ 04 50 34 25 59, *www.taninges.com*

Address : les Vernays-sous-la-Ville (take the southern exit, follow the signs for Cluses river; beside the Foron river and 150m from the Giffre river)

Opening times : permanent

2 ha (113 pitches) flat, grassy, stony

Tariff : (2012 price) 14.40€ ✝✝ ⇌ ▣ ⚡ (10A) – Extra per person 2.75€

🚉 sani-station 4.70€ – 3 ▣ 9.70€

Surroundings : ⬡ ≤ 〇〇	
Leisure activities : ✎	**GPS** Longitude : 6.58837
Facilities : ✆ ▥ �🚻 launderette	Latitude : 46.09866
Nearby : ▱ 🏊 ✗	

TERMIGNON

73500 – Michelin map **333** N6 – pop. 423 – alt. 1,290

▶ Paris 680 – Bessans 18 – Chambéry 120 – Lanslebourg-Mont-Cenis 6

Les Mélèzes

✆ 04 79 20 51 41, *www.camping-termignon-lavanoise.com*

Address : rte du Doron (in the village; beside a fast-flowing river)

Opening times : from mid Dec. to mid Oct.

0.7 ha (66 pitches) flat, grassy

Tariff : 18.50€ ✝✝ ⇌ ▣ ⚡ (10A) – Extra per person 3.10€

Rental rates : (from mid Dec. to mid Oct.) ⚏ – 3 ▦. Per night 70€ – Per week 460€

Surroundings : ⬡ ≤ 〇〇	
Leisure activities : ▱ ✎	**GPS** Longitude : 6.81535
Facilities : ✆ ⊶ (from mid-Jun to mid-Sept) ⚏ ▥ ⚡ ▣	Latitude : 45.27815

TOURNON-SUR-RHÔNE

07300 – Michelin map **331** L3 – pop. 10,674 – alt. 125
▶ Paris 545 – Grenoble 98 – Le Puy-en-Velay 104 – St-Étienne 77

⚠ Les Acacias

℘ 04 75 08 83 90, www.acacias-camping.com
Address : 190 rte de Lamastre (2.6km west along the D 532, direct access to the Doux river)
Opening times : from beginning April to end Sept.
2.7 ha (80 pitches) flat, grassy
Tariff : (2012 price) 23.26€ ⚿⚿ ⟵⟶ 🅴 🄵 (10A) – Extra per person 4.98€ – Reservation fee 10€
Rental rates : (2012 price) (from beginning April to end Sept.) – 12 🚐 – 4 🏠.
Per night from 80 to 130€ – Per week from 280 to 790€ – Reservation fee 20€
🚰 sani-station
Surroundings : ♧♧
Leisure activities : ✗ 🔲 🛶 🎣 ⚓ 🏊 ⤳
Facilities : ♿ ⊶ 🍴 🔲 ⚓

Longitude : 4.80805
Latitude : 45.06687

LA TOUSSUIRE

73300 – Michelin map **333** K6 – alt. 1,690
▶ Paris 651 – Albertville 78 – Chambéry 91 – St-Jean-de-Maurienne 16

⚠ Caravaneige du Col

℘ 04 79 83 00 80, www.camping-du-col.com – alt. 1,640
Address : 1 km east of La Toussuire, on rte de St-Jean-de-Maurienne
Opening times : from mid June to beginning Sept. and from mid-Dec to end Apr
0.8 ha (40 pitches) flat, grassy
Tariff : 21€ ⚿⚿ ⟵⟶ 🅴 🄵 (10A) – Extra per person 4.60€ – Reservation fee 10€
Rental rates : (permanent) – 7 🚐 – 3 🏠 – 2 apartments. Per week from 330 to 560€
Reservation fee 10€
🚰 sani-station 6€
A free shuttle service to the resort.

Surroundings : ❄ ⛷ ≤ Les Aiguilles d'Arves (peaks)
Leisure activities : 🍴 ✗ 🔲 ⊙ daytime ⤢ 🛶 🏊
Facilities : ♿ ⊶ ⊞ ⚓ 🍴 launderette

Longitude : 6.2739
Latitude : 45.25727

This guide is updated regularly, so buy your new copy every year!

TREPT

38460 – Michelin map **333** E3 – pop. 1,741 – alt. 275 – Leisure centre
▶ Paris 495 – Belley 41 – Bourgoin-Jallieu 13 – Lyon 52

⚠ Les 3 Lacs du Soleil

℘ 04 74 92 92 06, www.camping-les3lacsdusoleil.com
Address : at La Plaine Serrière (2.7km east along the D 517, follow the signs for Morestel and take the road to the right, near two lakes)
Opening times : from end April to mid Sept.
25 ha/3 ha for camping (160 pitches) flat, grassy
Tariff : 34.50€ ⚿⚿ ⟵⟶ 🅴 🄵 (6A) – Extra per person 7€
Rental rates : (from end May to mid Sept.) ❄ – 26 🚐 – 7 🏠 – 18 tent bungalows.
Per night from 44 to 127€ – Per week from 308 to 889€
Surroundings : ⛰ ♧ ⚘
Leisure activities : 🍴 ✗ 🔲 ⊙ daytime ⤢ 🛶 🎾 🎣 🏊 ⚓ (beach) ⛷ ⤳
Facilities : ♿ ⊶ 🍴 launderette

Longitude : 5.33447
Latitude : 45.69039

RHÔNE-ALPES

TULETTE

26790 – Michelin map **332** C8 – pop. 1,915 – alt. 147
▶ Paris 648 – Avignon 53 – Bollène 15 – Nyons 20

⚠ Les Rives de l'Aygues

☎ 04 75 98 37 50, *www.lesrivesdelaygues.com*
Address : rte de Cairanne (head 3km south along the D 193 and take road to the left)
Opening times : from beginning May to end Sept.
3.6 ha (100 pitches) flat, stony, grassy
Tariff : 22€ ⚹⚹ ⇦ 🔲 🔋 (6A) – Extra per person 5.80€ – Reservation fee 10€
Rental rates : (from beginning May to end Sept.) 🏠 – 2 ▦ – 6 🏠.
Per week from 279 to 650€ – Reservation fee 10€

In a natural setting surrounded by vines.

Surroundings : ⛰ ▱ ♉
Leisure activities : 🍹 ✕ 🎮 ⚓ 🛶
Facilities : 🚿 ⚡ 🗑 🏺 🔥

GPS Longitude : 4.933 Latitude : 44.2648

UCEL

07200 – Michelin map **331** I6 – pop. 1,929 – alt. 270
▶ Paris 626 – Aubenas 6 – Montélimar 44 – Privas 31

⛰ Domaine de Gil

☎ 04 75 94 63 63, *www.domaine-de-gil.com*
Address : rte de Vals (take northwestern exit along the D 578b)
Opening times : from end April to mid Sept.
4.8 ha/2 ha for camping (80 pitches) flat, grassy, stony
Tariff : 38€ ⚹⚹ ⇦ 🔲 🔋 (10A) – Extra per person 6.50€ – Reservation fee 20€
Rental rates : (from end April to mid Sept.) 🏠 (Jul–Aug) – 52 ▦. Per week from 245 to 895€
Reservation fee 20€
▦ sani-station – 🚐 14€

Situated beside the Ardèche river.

Surroundings : ⟨ ▱ ♉ ⛰
Leisure activities : 🍹 ✕ 🎮 evening ⚓ 🍴 🎣 🛶 🦢
multi-sports ground
Facilities : 🚿 ⚡ 🏺 💧 🚽 launderette 🔥

GPS Longitude : 4.37959 Latitude : 44.64308

VAGNAS

07150 – Michelin map **331** I7 – pop. 521 – alt. 200
▶ Paris 670 – Aubenas 40 – Barjac 5 – St-Ambroix 20

⛰ La Rouvière-Les Pins

☎ 04 75 38 61 41, *www.rouviere07.com*
Address : at La Rouviere (take the southern exit following signs for Barjac then continue 1.5km along the road to the right)
Opening times : from beginning April to mid Sept.
2 ha (100 pitches) terraced, flat and relatively flat, grassy
Tariff : (2012 price) ⇦ 🔲 21.60€ – 🔋 (6A) 4.60€ – Reservation fee 15€
Rental rates : (2012 price) (from mid April to mid Sept.) – 2 ▦ – 3 tent bungalows.
Per week from 240 to 710€ – Reservation fee 15€
▦ sani-station

Surroundings : ⛰ ♀
Leisure activities : 🍹 ✕ 🎮 ⚓ 🛶
Facilities : ⚡ 🏺 🚽 💧 🗑

GPS Longitude : 4.34194 Latitude : 44.3419

VALLIÈRES

74150 – Michelin map **328** I5 – pop. 1,393 – alt. 347
▶ Paris 533 – Lyon 132 – Annecy 30 – Genève 59

Les Charmilles

℘ 0450621060, www.campinglescharmilles.com
Address : 625 rte de Val de Fier
Opening times : from beginning April to end Oct.
3 ha (81 pitches) flat, grassy
Tariff : 17€ ♦♦ ⇦ 🔲 🔌 (10A) – Extra per person 4€ – Reservation fee 10€
Rental rates : (from beginning April to end Oct.) – 10 🚐 – 13 🏠. Per night from 50€
Per week from 190 to 650€ – Reservation fee 10€
🚰 sani-station 12€ – 4 🔲 12€ – 🛒 10€

Surroundings : ≤ ♨♨
Leisure activities : 🍽 ✗ 🛶 🏊 ⚽ 🛝
Facilities : ♿ ⚲ 🏕 🍴 launderette

Longitude : 5.9285
Latitude : 45.90286

The information in the guide may have changed since going to press.

VALLOIRE

73450 – Michelin map **333** L7 – pop. 1,299 – alt. 1,430 – Winter sports : 1,430/2,600 m 🚡2 🎿31 🎿
▶ Paris 664 – Albertville 91 – Briançon 52 – Chambéry 104

Ste Thècle

℘ 0479833011, www.valloire.net
Address : rte des Villards (north of the town, at the confluence of two sets of rapids)
1.5 ha (81 pitches) terraced, relatively flat, flat, grassy, stony
🚰 sani-station – 11 🔲

Surroundings : ❄ 🦢 ≤
Leisure activities : 🛶 🏊
Facilities : ♿ ⚲ 🎰 📺
Nearby : ⚽ 🛝 ⛸ skating rink, bowling

Longitude : 6.42872
Latitude : 45.16587

VALLON-PONT-D'ARC

07150 – Michelin map **331** I7 – pop. 2,337 – alt. 117
▶ Paris 658 – Alès 47 – Aubenas 32 – Avignon 81

Les Castels L'Ardéchois ⚑⚑

℘ 0475880663, www.ardechois-camping.com
Address : rte Touristique des Gorges de l'Ardèche (located 1.5km southeast along the D 290)
Opening times : permanent
5 ha (244 pitches) flat, grassy
Tariff : 51€ ♦♦ ⇦ 🔲 🔌 (6A) – Extra per person 10.30€ – Reservation fee 40€
Rental rates : (from end March to end Sept.) – 25 🚐. Per night from 66 to 165€
Per week from 825 to 1,480€ – Reservation fee 40€
🚰 sani-station
Direct access to the Ardèche river.

Surroundings : ≤ 🏕 ♨♨ 🏔
Leisure activities : 🍽 ✗ 🛶 🎣 🚣 🏊 ⚽ 🛝 🤿 🎯 multi-sports
ground, spa therapy centre
Facilities : ♿ ⚲ ✉ 🏕 🚿 🚰 🍴 launderette 🍽 🛥
Nearby :

Longitude : 4.39673
Latitude : 44.39672

Mondial-Camping ▲▲

0475880044, *www.mondial-camping.com*
Address : rte des Gorges de l'Ardèche (located 1.5km southeast)
Opening times : from end March to mid Sept.
4 ha (240 pitches) flat, grassy
Tariff : (2012 price) 44€ ✝✝ 🚐 ▣ (½) (10A) – Extra per person 9.20€ – Reservation fee 30€
Rental rates : (2012 price) (from end March to mid Sept.) – 24 – 5 tent bungalows.
Per night from 60 to 110€ – Per week from 300 to 1,100 €– Reservation fee 30€
sani-station
Direct access to the Ardèche river.

Surroundings :
Leisure activities : 🍴 ✕ launderette
Facilities : launderette
Nearby :

Longitude : 4.40139
Latitude : 44.39695

La Roubine ▲▲

0475880456, *www.camping-roubine.com*
Address : rte de Ruoms (located 1.5km west)
Opening times : from end April to mid Sept.
7 ha/4 ha for camping (135 pitches) flat, grassy, sandy
Tariff : (2012 price) 46.50€ ✝✝ 🚐 ▣ (½) (10A) – Extra per person 9.40€ – Reservation fee 30€
Rental rates : (2012 price) (from end April to mid Sept.) – 32 .
Per night from 43 to 184€ – Per week from 301 to 1,288€ – Reservation fee 30€
Beside the Ardèche river (with a small lake).

Surroundings :
Leisure activities : 🍴 ✕ multi-sports ground
Facilities : launderette

Longitude : 4.37835
Latitude : 44.40636

International

0475880099, *www.internationalcamping07.com*
Address : La Plaine Salavas (located 1km southwest)
2.7 ha (130 pitches) flat, relatively flat, grassy, sandy
Rental rates : – 11 – 2 .
Situated beside the Ardèche river.

Surroundings :
Leisure activities : 🍴 ✕
Facilities :

Longitude : 4.38203
Latitude : 44.39925

La Rouvière ▲▲

0475371007, *www.campinglarouviere.com*
Address : rte des Gorges Chames (6.6km southeast along the D 290; at Chames)
Opening times : from beginning March to mid Oct.
3 ha (152 pitches) terraced, relatively flat, sandy
Tariff : 29.50€ ✝✝ 🚐 ▣ (½) (10A) – Extra per person 8€ – Reservation fee 10€
Rental rates : (from beginning March to mid Oct.) – 39 – 3 tent bungalows.
Per night from 43 to 116€ – Per week from 240 to 810€ – Reservation fee 15€
Direct access to the Ardèche river.

Surroundings :
Leisure activities : ✕ multi-sports ground
Facilities :

Longitude : 4.42649
Latitude : 44.37796

Le Midi

⚠

℘ 0475880678, *www.camping-midi.com*

Address : rte des Gorges de l'Ardèche (6.5km southeast along the D 290; at Chames)
Opening times : from beginning April to end Sept.
1.6 ha (52 pitches) terraced, relatively flat, grassy, sandy
Tariff : 28.50€ ♣♣ ⇔ 🔲 🔌 (10A) – Extra per person 8€ – Reservation fee 15€
Rental rates : (2012 price) (from beginning April to mid Oct.) – 4 🚐 – 5 tents.
Per night from 60 to 200€ – Per week from 380 to 1,400 €– Reservation fee 15€

Direct access to the Ardèche river.

Surroundings : 🏞 ⩽ ⌂ ♨ ⛰
Leisure activities : 🚣 🎣
Facilities : ♿ ⚷ 🗡 🚿 🔳 🧺

GPS	Longitude : 4.41196
	Latitude : 44.38271

L'Esquiras

⚠

℘ 0475880416, *www.camping-esquiras.com*

Address : chemin du Fez (2.8km northwest along the D 579, follow the signs for Ruoms and take the road to the right after the Intermarché service station)
Opening times : from beginning April to end Sept.
2 ha (105 pitches) relatively flat, flat, grassy, stony
Tariff : 32€ ♣♣ ⇔ 🔲 🔌 (10A) – Extra per person 7€ – Reservation fee 12€
Rental rates : (2012 price) (from beginning April to end Sept.) 🏊 – 40 🚐.
Per night from 52 to 65€ – Per week from 260 to 800€ – Reservation fee 12€
🚐 sani-station 5€ – 6 🔲 8€

Surroundings : 🏞 ⩽
Leisure activities : ✗ 🏓 🚣 ⛷
Facilities : ♿ ⚷ 🚿 🚿 🔳
Nearby : forest trail

GPS	Longitude : 4.37913
	Latitude : 44.41536

VALLORCINE

74660 – Michelin map **328** O4 – pop. 419 – alt. 1,260 – Winter sports : 1,260/1,400 m🚡2 🎿
▶ Paris 628 – Annecy 115 – Chamonix-Mont-Blanc 19 – Thonon-les-Bains 96

Les Montets

⚠

℘ 0546756154, *www.campinglemontet.fr* – alt. 1,300

Address : at Le Montet (2.8km southwest along the N 506, access via Chemin de la Gare, at Le Buet)
Opening times : from mid April to end Sept.
1.7 ha (75 pitches) terraced, open site, relatively flat, flat, grassy, stony
Tariff : (2012 price) 16.34€ ♣♣ ⇔ 🔲 🔌 (6A) – Extra per person 4.25€
Rental rates : (2012 price) (from mid April to end Sept.) – 5 🚐. Per week from 168 to 511€
🚐 sani-station 10€

A pleasant location beside a stream and near the Eau Noire river.

Surroundings : 🏞 ⩽ ♨
Leisure activities : ✗
Facilities : ♿ ⚷ 🅿 🚿 🔳
Nearby : 🎾 🎣

GPS	Longitude : 6.92376
	Latitude : 46.02344

For more information on visiting particular towns or regions, consult the relevant regional MICHELIN Green Guide. We also recommend you use the appropriate Michelin regional map to locate your selected campsite, to calculate distances and to work out the best route.

LES VANS

07140 – Michelin map **331** G7 – pop. 2,805 – alt. 170
▶ Paris 663 – Alès 44 – Aubenas 37 – Pont-St-Esprit 66

△ **Le Pradal**

℘ 04 75 37 25 16, *www.camping-lepradal.com*
Address : 1.5km west along the D 901
Opening times : from beginning April to end Oct.
1 ha (36 pitches) terraced, relatively flat, grassy, stony
Tariff : ♦ 6€ ▣ 18€ – (½) (6A) 3.80€
Rental rates : (from beginning April to end Oct.) – 2 ⬛ – 1 ⬛. Per night from 50 to 80€
Per week from 200 to 700€
🚽 sani-station 7€

Surroundings : ⌂ ♀
Leisure activities : ♈ ⌂ ⫯
Facilities : ﯼ ⚷ ⊐

GPS Longitude : 4.11023
Latitude : 44.40809

Gîtes range from small maisonettes to old farmhouses with several bedrooms.

VERCHAIX

74440 – Michelin map **328** N4 – pop. 661 – alt. 800
▶ Paris 580 – Annecy 74 – Chamonix-Mont-Blanc 59 – Genève 52

△ **Municipal Lac et Montagne**

℘ 04 50 90 10 12, *www.mairie-verchaix.fr* – alt. 660 – ⚑
Address : 1.8km south along the D 907; beside the Giffre river
Opening times : permanent
2 ha (107 pitches) open site, flat, grassy, stony
Tariff : ♦ 2.50€ ▱ 1.50€ ▣ 3.50€ – (½) (10A) 4.10€

Surroundings : ⩽ ♀
Leisure activities : ⫯ ⚬ ⟍
Facilities : ﯼ ⚷ ⫿ launderette
Nearby : ♈ ✕ ⌄

GPS Longitude : 6.67527
Latitude : 46.09001

VERNIOZ

38150 – Michelin map **333** C5 – pop. 1,182 – alt. 250
▶ Paris 500 – Annonay 38 – Givors 25 – Le Péage-de-Roussillon 12

⋀⋀⋀ **Le Bontemps**

℘ 04 74 57 83 52, *www.camping-lebontemps.com*
Address : 5 imp.du Bontemps (4.5km east along the D 37 and take the road to the right; beside the Varèze river, at St-Alban-de-Varèze)
Opening times : from beginning April to end Sept.
6 ha (175 pitches) flat, grassy, lake
Tariff : 31€ ♦♦ ▱ ▣ (½) (10A) – Extra per person 7€ – Reservation fee 20€
Rental rates : (from beginning April to end Sept.) ⫿ – 8 ⬛ – 2 ⬛.
Per night from 45 to 113€ – Per week from 315 to 795€ – Reservation fee 20€
🚽 sani-station – 10 ▣ 25€

Surroundings : ⌂ ▱ ♀♀
Leisure activities : ♈ ✕ ⌂ ⚬ ⌄ ⫯ ⚲ ⌄ ⟍ ⟍
entertainment room
Facilities : ﯼ ⚷ ⊡ ⚲ ⚯ ⫿ launderette ⚯

GPS Longitude : 4.92836
Latitude : 45.42798

VILLARD-DE-LANS

38250 – Michelin map **333** G7 – pop. 4,031 – alt. 1,040 – Winter sports : 1,160/2,170 m ⚡2 🚠27 🎿
▶ Paris 584 – Die 67 – Grenoble 34 – Lyon 123

🏕 **FranceLoc Domaine de L'Oursière**

𝒫 0476951477, www.camping-oursiere.fr

Address : av. du Gal de Gaulle (take the northern exit along the D 531, follow the signs for Grenoble; pedestrian path to village)

Opening times : from mid Dec. to end Sept.

4 ha (186 pitches) relatively flat, flat, grassy, stony, gravelled

Tariff : 19€ 🚻 🚐 🔳 🔌 (10A) – Extra per person 5€ – Reservation fee 15€

Rental rates : (permanent) – 40 🚐 – 40 🏠. Per night from 39 to 82€

Per week from 159 to 630€ – Reservation fee 25€

🚽 sani-station 5€ – 30 🔳 16€

Surroundings : ❄ ≼

Leisure activities : 🛶 🏇 🎯 🏊 ⛷ 🎣 spa facilities

Facilities : ♿ ⛟ 🏛 🚿 🚰 🔱 🛒

Nearby : 🎿 bowling, skating rink

GPS Longitude : 5.55639 / Latitude : 45.0775

VILLAREMBERT

73300 – Michelin map **333** K6 – pop. 253 – alt. 1,296
▶ Paris 647 – Aiguebelle 49 – Chambéry 87 – St-Jean-de-Maurienne 12

🏕 **Municipal la Tigny**

𝒫 0479567465, mairie.villarembert@wanadoo.fr

Address : take the southern exit along the D 78 and take road to the left

Opening times :

0.3 ha (27 pitches) open site, terraced, relatively flat, flat, grassy, gravelled

Tariff : (2012 price) 🚶 3.50€ 🚐 2.30€ 🔳 2.90€ – 🔌 (32A) 2.90€

🚽 10 🔳 2.90€

In a green setting near a stream.

Surroundings : ≼ ♨

Leisure activities : 🏇

Facilities : 🚽 🔲 🚿 🚰

GPS Longitude : 6.28033 / Latitude : 45.24581

VILLARS-LES-DOMBES

01330 – Michelin map **328** D4 – pop. 4,328 – alt. 281
▶ Paris 433 – Bourg-en-Bresse 29 – Lyon 37 – Villefranche-sur-Saône 29

🏕 **Indigo Parc des Oiseaux**

𝒫 0474980021, http://www.camping-indigo.com/fr/camping-indigo-parc-des-oiseaux-d – limited spaces for one-night stay

Address : av. des Nations (southwestern exit, follow the signs for Lyon and take the turning to the left; near the swimming pool)

Opening times : from end March to beginning Nov.

5 ha (238 pitches) relatively flat, flat, grassy

Tariff : (2012 price) 🚶 4.50€ 🚐 4€ 🔳 18.50€ – 🔌 (10A) 4.50€ – Reservation fee 20€

Rental rates : (2012 price) (from end March to beginning Nov.) – 4 'gypsy' caravans – 35 tents.

Per night from 45 to 95€ – Per week from 252 to 532€ – Reservation fee 20€

🚽 sani-station 4€

In a pleasant setting beside the Chalaronne river.

Surroundings : ▭ ♨

Leisure activities : 🍽 ✗ 🏠 🚶 🏇

Facilities : ♿ ⛟ 🆒 🔱 🖼

Nearby : 🎿 🖼 🛶 ⛷

GPS Longitude : 5.03039 / Latitude : 45.99749

VINSOBRES

26110 – Michelin map **332** D7 – pop. 1,109 – alt. 247
▶ Paris 662 – Bollène 29 – Grignan 24 – Nyons 9

Franceloc Le Sagittaire ▲▲

℘ 04 75 27 00 00, www.campings-franceloc.fr
Address : at le Pont de Mirabel (Junction of D 94 and D 4, near the Eygues (direct access)
Opening times : permanent
14 ha/8 ha for camping (274 pitches) flat, grassy, fine gravel
Tariff : (2012 price) 32€ ★★ ⟵ ▤ ⑭ (8A) – Extra per person 8€ – Reservation fee 27€
Rental rates : (2012 price) (permanent) – 6 'gypsy' caravans – 84 ▦ – 64 ⌂ – 4 teepees –
2 gîtes. Per night from 31 to 94€ – Per week from 182 to 1,477€ – Reservation fee 27€
▦ sani-station
A pretty swimming and play area.

Surroundings : ◁ ▭ ♉♉
Leisure activities : ♈ ✗ ▱ ▯ ⚘ ◮ ⚓ ✗ ▥ ☇ ≋ (lake)◭ ⚒
multi-sports ground
Facilities : ₺ ⊶ ▦ ♨ ⚘ ⛟ ♛ launderette ♨ ⚗

GPS Longitude : 5.08002
Latitude : 44.22661

Municipal Chez Antoinette

℘ 04 75 27 61 65, camping-municipal@club-internet.fr
Address : in the Champessier quartier (located south of the town along the D 190; by the stadium)
Opening times : from mid March to end Oct.
1.9 ha (70 pitches) flat, grassy, stony
Tariff : (2012 price) 14.36€ ★★ ⟵ ▤ ⑭ (8A) – Extra per person 3.15€
Rental rates : (2012 price) (from mid March to end Oct.) – 1 ▦. Per night from 50€
Per week from 360 to 460€

Surroundings : ◁ ♉♉
Leisure activities : ⚓
Facilities : ₺ ⊶ (May-Oct) ▨ ♛ ▥ refrigerators

GPS Longitude : 5.06594
Latitude : 44.32912

VION

07610 – Michelin map **331** K3 – pop. 905 – alt. 128
▶ Paris 537 – Annonay 30 – Lamastre 34 – Tournon-sur-Rhône 7

L'Iserand

℘ 04 75 08 01 73, www.iserandcampingardeche.com
Address : 1307 r. Royale (located 1km north along the N 86, follow the signs for Lyon)
Opening times : from mid April to mid Sept.
1.3 ha (60 pitches) terraced, grassy, stony
Tariff : 22€ ★★ ⟵ ▤ ⑭ (10A) – Extra per person 6€
Rental rates : (from mid April to mid Sept.) ⚏ – 8 ⌂. Per night 65€ – Per week 620€
▦ sani-station – 10 ▤ 22€

Surroundings : ◁ ♉
Leisure activities : ✗ ⚓ ◴ ♛ ☇
Facilities : ₺ ⊶ ▨ ♛ ▥ ⚗

GPS Longitude : 4.80027
Latitude : 45.12117

*The prices listed were supplied by the campsite owners in 2012
(if prices were not available, those from the previous year are given).
The fees should be regarded as basic charges and may fluctuate
with inflation.*

VIVIERS

07220 – Michelin map **331** K7 – pop. 3,864 – alt. 65
▶ Paris 618 – Montélimar 12 – Nyons 50 – Pont-St-Esprit 30

Rochecondrie Loisirs

℘ 04 75 52 74 66, *www.campingrochecondrie.com*
Address : in the Rochecondrie quartier (located 1.5km northwest along the N 86, follow the signs for Lyon, direct access to the Escoutay river)
Opening times : from mid April to mid Oct.
1.5 ha (80 pitches) flat, grassy
Tariff : 24.50€ ★★ ⇔ 🔲 🕸 (6A) – Extra per person 6€
Rental rates : (from mid April to mid Oct.) ⚡ – 9 🛖. Per week from 230 to 510

Surroundings : 🗔 ⴲ
Leisure activities : 🍺 🖼 🐎 🏊 walks with lamas
Facilities : 🔌 🏕 🚿
Nearby : 🎣

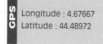

Longitude : 4.67667
Latitude : 44.48972

VIZILLE

38220 – Michelin map **333** H7 – pop. 7,592 – alt. 270
▶ Paris 582 – Le Bourg-d'Oisans 32 – Grenoble 20 – La Mure 22

Le Bois de Cornage

℘ 06 83 18 17 87, *www.campingvizille.com*
Address : chemin du Camping (take the northern exit towards the N 85, follow the signs for Grenoble and turn right onto av. de Venaria)
Opening times : from end March to end Oct.
2.5 ha (128 pitches) terraced, relatively flat, grassy
Tariff : 15.90€ ★★ ⇔ 🔲 🕸 (16A) – Extra per person 5€ – Reservation fee 10€
Rental rates : (permanent) – 14 🛖. Per night from 46 to 61€ – Per week from 320 to 570€
🚽 sani-station 3€
Partially shaded by centuries-old trees.

Surroundings : 🖼 ⩽ ⴲ
Leisure activities : ✖ 🏊
Facilities : 🔌 ⧉ 🏕 🚿 🧺

Longitude : 5.76948
Latitude : 45.08706

VOGÜÉ

07200 – Michelin map **331** I6 – pop. 917 – alt. 150
▶ Paris 638 – Aubenas 9 – Largentière 16 – Privas 40

Domaine du Cros d'Auzon

℘ 04 75 37 04 14, *www.domaine-cros-auzon.com*
Address : 2.5km south along the D 579 and take the road to the right
Opening times : from beginning April to mid Sept.
18 ha/6 ha for camping (170 pitches) flat, grassy, stony, sandy
Tariff : 32€ ★★ ⇔ 🔲 🕸 (6A) – Extra per person 8€ – Reservation fee 30€
Rental rates : (from beginning April to mid Sept.) ♿ (4 mobile homes) – 37 🛖 – 3 🏠 –
37 🛏. Per night from 29 to 142€ – Per week from 203 to 994€ – Reservation fee 30€
🚽 sani-station 2€ – 🚐 🕸 9€
Pleasant location and setting beside the Ardèche river.

Surroundings : 🖼 🗔 ⴲ
Leisure activities : 🍺 ✖ 🖼 ⵛ 🏃 🐎 🚴 ✂ 🎿 🏊 ≈ 🏄 🎣
sports trail
Facilities : ♿ 🔌 🚿 🚰 🏕 launderette 🧺

Longitude : 4.40678
Latitude : 44.53178

Les Peupliers

📞 04 75 37 71 47, *www.campingpeupliers.com*

Address : at Gourgouran (head 2km south along the D 579 and take the road to the right; at Vogüe-Gare)

Opening times : from end March to end Sept.

3 ha (100 pitches) flat, grassy, sandy, stony

Tariff : 29.45€ ♦♦ ⇔ 🔲 ⚡ (6A) – Extra per person 5.95€ – Reservation fee 19€

Rental rates : (from beginning April to end Sept.) – 10 🚐 – 9 🏠. Per night from 35 to 112€
Per week from 230 to 780€ – Reservation fee 19€

🚐 sani-station 4€

Beside the Ardèche river.

Surroundings : 🌿 ♨
Leisure activities : 🍴 ✗ 🏄 m 🎣 🏊 🛶
Facilities : 🚿 🛒 🛁 🍴 🖼 🏊

GPS
Longitude : 4.40996
Latitude : 44.53714

L'Oasis des Garrigues

📞 04 75 37 03 27, *www.oasisdesgarrigues.com*

Address : in the Brugière quartier (situated 2km south along the D 579, take a right turn at the roundabout)

1.2 ha (61 pitches) flat, grassy, stony

Rentals : 🏠 – 8 🚐 – 6 🏠.

🚐 sani-station

Leisure activities : 🍴 🎣
Facilities : ♿ 🛒 🛁 🍴 🖼
Nearby : 🏊 🛶

GPS
Longitude : 4.41094
Latitude : 44.53841

Les Roches

📞 04 75 37 70 45, *www.campinglesroches.fr*

Address : in the Bausson quartier (located 1.5km south along the D 579; at Vogüe-Gare, 200m from the Auzon and the Ardèche rivers)

2.5 ha (120 pitches) undulating, flat, grassy, rocks

Rentals : 🏠 – 8 🚐.

🚐 sani-station

In a natural setting.

Surroundings : 🌿 ♨
Leisure activities : 🍴 🏡 🏄 ✗ 🎣
Facilities : ♿ 🛒 🛁 🍴 launderette, refrigerators
Nearby : 🏊

GPS
Longitude : 4.41406
Latitude : 44.542

Les Chênes Verts

📞 04 75 37 71 54, *www.camping-chenesverts.com* – pitches accessed via steep slope, help moving caravans onto and off pitches avilable on request

Address : Champ Redon (1.7km southeast along the D 103)

Opening times : from mid June to mid Sept.

2.5 ha (42 pitches) terraced, flat, stony, grassy

Tariff : (2012 price) 20€ ♦♦ ⇔ 🔲 ⚡ (16A) – Extra per person 4€

Rental rates : (2012 price) (from beginning April to end Oct.) – 26 🏠.
Per night from 55 to 85€ – Per week from 270 to 710€ – Reservation fee 30€

Surroundings : ♨
Leisure activities : ✗ 🏄 🎣
Facilities : ♿ 🛒 🔌 🍴 🖼 🏊
Nearby : ✗

GPS
Longitude : 4.42038
Latitude : 44.54547

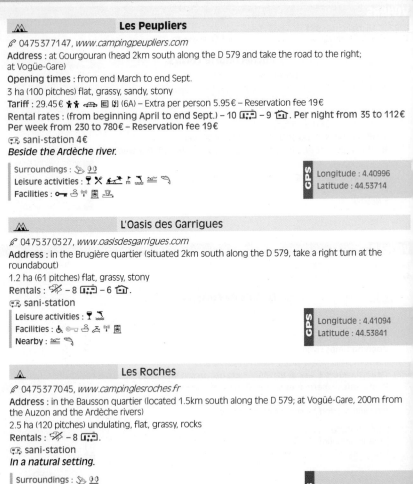

CANILLO

AD100 – Michelin map **343** H9 – pop. 4,826 – alt. 1,531
▶ Andorra-la-Vella 13

⚠ Santa-Creu

𝒫 (00-376)851462, *www.elsmeners.com*
Address : in the town (beside the Valira-del-Orient (left bank)
Opening times : from beginning June to mid Sept.
0.5 ha terraced, relatively flat, grassy
Tariff : ♀ 4.10€ ⇌ 4.10€ 🔲 4.10€ ⚡ (5A)

The campsite is in a shady field near the town centre.

Surroundings : ≤ ♀
Leisure activities : ⵏ
Facilities : ♿ ⚡ 🗷 ☑ ⫯ 🗃

Longitude : 1.59978
Latitude : 42.56579

⚠ Jan-Ramon

𝒫 (00-376)751454, *www.elsmeners.com*
Address : ctra. General (400m northeast following signs for Port d'Envalira; beside the Valira del Orient (left bank)
Opening times : from mid June to mid Sept.
0.6 ha flat, grassy
Tariff : ♀ 4,10€ ⇌ 4.10€ 🔲 4.10€ ⚡ (5A)
Rental rates : (from beginning June to mid Oct.) 🏖 – 5 🏠. Per week from 490 to 1,105€
Reservation fee 99€

Pleasant and partially shaded green site, but there is noise from the nearby road.

Surroundings : ≤ ♀
Leisure activities : ⵏ ✗
Facilities : ⚡ ☑ ⫯ 🗃 🍴

Longitude : 1.59975
Latitude : 42.56594

LA MASSANA

AD400 – Michelin map **343** H9 – pop. 9,744 – alt. 1,241
▶ Andorra-la-Vella 6

⚠⚠⚠ Xixerella

𝒫 (00-376)738613, *www.campingxixerella.com* – alt. 1,450
Address : at Xixerella (3.5km northeast along the CG 4 then continue to Erts, taking turning to the left)
5 ha terraced, relatively flat, stony, grassy
Rentals : 14 🏠 – 28 apartments.

A shaded field for tents and caravans; a range of good-quality rental options.

Surroundings : ≤ ♀♀
Leisure activities : ⵏ ✗ 🛋 ♨ hammam, jacuzzi 🏊 ₘ 🖼
Facilities : ♿ ⚡ 🏛 ☺ ⫯ launderette 🏷 🍴

Longitude : 1.48882
Latitude : 42.55327

Michelin classification:

⚠⚠⚠⚠ *Extremely comfortable, equipped to a very high standard*
⚠⚠⚠ *Very comfortable, equipped to a high standard*
⚠⚠⚠ *Comfortable and well equipped*
⚠⚠ *Reasonably comfortable*
⚠ *Satisfactory*

MALAHIDE LIBRARY
PH: 8704430

ORDINO

AD300 – Michelin map **343** H9 – pop. 4,322 – alt. 1,304
▶ Andorra-la-Vella 8

Borda d'Ansalonga

✆ (00-376) 85 03 74, *www.campingansalonga.com*

Address : carretera Gal del Serrat (2.3km northwest along the follow the signs for Le Circuit de Tristaina; beside the Valira del Nord river)

Opening times : from mid June to mid Sept.

3 ha flat, grassy

Tariff : 2.90€ ♦♦ ⇔ 回 [½] (10A) – Extra per person 3.90€

A shaded field; choose pitches near the stream and away from the road in preference.

Surroundings : ≤ ♀♀
Leisure activities : ♀ ✕ ⌂ ⇎ ⅃
Facilities : ⅙ ⊙ ☒ ▥ ⓣ launderette ⅍

GPS
Longitude : 1.52162
Latitude : 42.56855

The following pages feature an index of all the localities listed in the book, divided by region and showing various facilities and services.

Key

BRITTANY	Name of the region
Carnac	(Name of the locality printed in red) Locality with at least one pleasant campsite (⚑ ... ⚑⚑⚑)
👥	Locality with at least one campsite suitable for families
🐿	Locality with at least one quiet and peaceful campsite
Permanent	Open all year
P	Locality with at least one campsite open all year round
L	Locality with a campsite offering rental of mobile homes, chalets and other holiday accommodation only
M	Locality with at least one campsite offering rental of traditional camping pitches alongside mobile homes, chalets, caravans and other holiday accommodation
🚐	Locality with at least one campsite with a service bay for campervans or areas reserved for campervans
🎭	Locality with at least one campsite offering entertainment/organised activities

● **For more details on specific sites refer to the individual campsite entries**

Locality	Page	👥	✦	Permanent	Rental	🚐	◔
Maisons-Laffitte	345	—	—	—	M	🚐	—
Melun	345	—	—	—	M	🚐	—
Montjay-la-Tour	346	—	—	P	M	🚐	—
Paris	346	—	—	P	M	🚐	—
Pommeuse	346	👥	—	—	M	—	◔
Rambouillet	347	👥	—	—	M	🚐	—
Touquin	347	—	✦	—	M	—	—
Tournan-en-Brie	347	—	—	P	M	—	—
Veneux-les-Sablons	348	—	—	—	M	🚐	—
Versailles	348	—	✦	—	M	—	—
Villiers-sur-Orge	348	—	—	P	M	🚐	—

LANGUEDOC-ROUSSILLON

Locality	Page	👥	✦	Permanent	Rental	🚐	◔
Agde	352	👥	✦	—	M	🚐	◔
Aigues-Mortes	354	👥	—	—	M	🚐	◔
Alet-les-Bains	354	—	—	P	M	🚐	—
Allègre-les-Fumades	354	👥	—	—	M	—	◔
Anduze	355	👥	✦	—	M	🚐	◔
Argelès-sur-Mer	356	👥	—	P	M	🚐	◔
Arles-sur-Tech	361	—	—	—	M	—	—
Bagnols-sur-Cèze	362	—	—	—	M	🚐	—
Balaruc-les-Bains	362	👥	—	—	M	—	—
Le Barcarès	363	👥	—	P	M	🚐	◔
Barjac	365	—	✦	—	M	🚐	—
Bédouès	366	—	—	—	—	🚐	—
Belcaire	366	—	—	—	M	—	—
Bessèges	366	—	—	—	M	—	—
Blajoux	367	—	✦	—	L	—	—
Boisset-et-Gaujac	367	👥	—	—	M	🚐	◔
Boisson	367	👥	—	—	M	🚐	◔
Le Bosc	368	—	—	—	L	—	—
Brissac	368	—	—	—	M	🚐	◔
Brousses-et-Villaret	368	—	—	—	M	—	—
Canet	369	—	—	—	M	🚐	—
Canet-Plage	369	👥	—	—	M	🚐	◔
Canilhac	371	—	—	—	M	—	—
La Canourgue	371	—	—	—	L	🚐	—
Le-Cap-d'Agde	372	—	—	—	M	🚐	—
Carcassonne	372	👥	—	—	M	—	◔
Carnon-Plage	372	—	—	—	M	🚐	—
Casteil	373	—	✦	—	M	—	—
Castries	373	—	✦	—	M	🚐	—
Celles	373	—	✦	—	—	🚐	—
Cendras	374	—	—	—	M	🚐	◔
Le Chambon	374	—	—	—	M	—	—
Chastanier	374	—	—	—	M	🚐	—
Chirac	375	—	—	—	L	—	—
Clermont-l'Hérault	375	—	—	—	M	🚐	—
Collias	375	—	—	—	M	🚐	—
Connaux	376	—	—	P	M	—	—
Crespian	376	👥	—	—	M	🚐	—
Égat	376	—	✦	—	—	🚐	—
Err	377	—	✦	P	M	—	—
Estavar	377	👥	✦	—	M	🚐	—
Florac	378	—	—	—	M	—	—
Font-Romeu	378	👥	—	—	M	🚐	◔
Formiguères	379	—	✦	P	M	🚐	—
Frontignan-Plage	379	👥	—	—	M	🚐	◔
Fuilla	379	—	—	—	M	🚐	—
Gallargues-le-Montueux	380	👥	—	—	—	—	◔
Gignac	380	—	—	—	M	🚐	—
Goudargues	380	👥	—	—	M	🚐	—
La Grande-Motte	381	👥	—	—	M	🚐	◔
Grandrieu	382	—	—	—	M	—	—
Le Grau-du-Roi	382	👥	—	—	M	🚐	◔
Ispagnac	383	—	—	—	M	🚐	—
Junas	383	—	—	—	M	—	—
Lanuéjols	384	—	✦	—	M	—	—
Laroque-des-Albères	384	—	✦	—	M	🚐	—
Lattes	384	—	—	P	M	—	—
Laubert	385	—	—	—	M	—	—
Laurens	385	👥	—	—	M	—	◔
Le Malzieu-Ville	385	—	✦	—	M	🚐	—
Marseillan-Plage	386	👥	✦	—	M	🚐	◔
Marvejols	388	—	—	—	M	—	—
Massillargues-Attuech	388	👥	—	—	M	—	—
Matemale	388	—	✦	P	—	🚐	—
Maureillas-Las-Illas	389	—	—	P	M	—	—
Mende	389	—	—	P	M	🚐	—
Meyrueis	389	—	✦	—	M	🚐	◔
Montclar	391	👥	✦	—	M	🚐	◔
Narbonne	391	👥	—	—	M	🚐	◔
Nasbinals	392	—	—	—	M	—	—
Naussac	392	—	—	—	M	🚐	◔
Palau-Del-Vidre	392	—	—	—	M	🚐	—
Palavas-les-Flots	393	👥	—	—	M	🚐	◔
Les Plantiers	393	—	—	—	M	—	—
Le-Pont-de-Montvert	394	—	—	—	—	🚐	—
Port-Camargue	394	👥	✦	—	M	🚐	◔
Portiragnes-Plage	395	👥	—	—	M	🚐	◔
Quillan	396	—	—	—	M	🚐	—
Remoulins	397	👥	—	—	M	🚐	◔
Rocles	398	—	—	—	M	🚐	—
Roquefeuil	398	—	—	—	M	🚐	—
Roquefort-des-Corbières	398	—	—	—	L	—	—
La Roque-sur-Cèze	399	—	—	—	M	🚐	—
Le Rozier	399	—	—	—	M	—	—
Saint-André-de-Sangonis	400	—	—	—	M	—	—
Saint-Bauzile	400	—	—	—	M	🚐	—
Saint-Cyprien-Plage	400	👥	—	—	M	🚐	◔
Saint-Génis-des-Fontaines	401	—	—	—	M	—	—
Saint-Georges-de-Lévéjac	401	—	✦	—	M	🚐	—
Saint-Germain-du-Teil	401	—	—	—	L	—	—
Saint-Hippolyte-du-Fort	402	—	✦	—	M	🚐	—

Michelin Travel Partner

Société par actions simplifiées au capital de 11 629 590 EUR
27 cours de l'Ile Seguin - 92100 Boulogne Billancourt (France)
R.C.S. Nanterre 433 677 721

No part of this publication may be reproduced in any form
without the prior permission of the publisher.

© Michelin Travel Partner
ISBN 978-2-067186-61-3

Although the information in this guide was believed by the
authors and publisher to be accurate and current at the time
of publication, they cannot accept responsibility for any
inconvenience, loss or injury sustained by any person relying
on information or advice contained in this guide. Things
change over time and travellers should take steps to verify
and confirm information, especially time-sensitive information
related to prices, hours of operation and availability.

Layout: Jean-Luc Carnet
Translation: JMS Books llp (www.jmswords.com)
Layout of English edition: Chris Bell, cbdesign
Printed: March 2013
Printed and bound by Printer Trento, Italy
Printed on paper from sustainable forests